The fourth edition of Malcolm Shaw's bestselling textbook on international law represents a major revision of its predecessor. Alongside substantial new chapters dealing with human rights and the United Nations, Professor Shaw has incorporated new material on international environmental law, state succession, recognition, the settlement of disputes by peaceful means and international institutions. Above all the book remains a comprehensive and highly readable work on international law. It sets the subject firmly in the context of world political events, and brings out the importance of the many economic, political and cultural influences that affect it. *International Law* remains an excellent and wide-ranging work on the subject for students of law, international relations and the political sciences and for practitioners.

INTERNATIONAL LAW

Malcolm N. Shaw

INTERNATIONAL
L A W

FOURTH EDITION

Malcolm N. Shaw

*Sir Robert Jennings Professor of International Law,
University of Leicester*

A GROTIUS PUBLICATION

CAMBRIDGE
UNIVERSITY PRESS

PUBLISHED BY THE PRESS SYNDICATE OF THE UNIVERSITY OF CAMBRIDGE
The Pitt Building, Trumpington Street, Cambridge CB2 1RP, United Kingdom

CAMBRIDGE UNIVERSITY PRESS
The Edinburgh Building, Cambridge CB2 2RU, United Kingdom
40 West 20th Street, New York, NY 10011-4211, USA
10 Stamford Road, Oakleigh, Melbourne 3166, Australia

Third Edition first published by Grotius Publishers 1991
Fourth Edition first published by Cambridge University Press 1997

Printed in the United Kingdom at the University Press, Cambridge

Typeset in 10/13pt Plantin   [SE]

A catalogue record for this book is available from the British Library

Library of Congress Cataloguing in Publication data

Shaw, Malcolm N. (Malcolm Nathan). 1947–
International law / Malcolm Shaw. – 4th ed.
p.   cm.
Includes index.
ISBN 0 521 59384 0. – ISBN 0 521 57667 9 (pbk.)
1. International law.   I. Title.
JX3275.S4I57   1997
341–dc21 97-1587 CIP

ISBN 0 521 59384 0 hardback
ISBN 0 521 57667 9 paperback

To my wife, Judith
and to my mother, Paulette
and in memory of my father, Ben Shaw CBE
and of my mother-in-law, Denise Axelrod

CONTENTS

PREFACE

I have been able to revise this edition extensively since the last edition appeared in 1991. In view of the rapidly growing practice, and importance, of international human rights, the previous single chapter has been divided into two, one covering international protection of human rights and the other covering regional protection. In addition, the material on the United Nations has been gathered into a new chapter and extensive additions incorporated to include the wide-ranging practice of the organisation during the critical early and mid-1990s.

Certain chapters have been completely rewritten. These are primarily the chapters on International Environmental Law and on State Succession, while other chapters, such as those on Recognition, the Settlement of Disputes by Peaceful Means and International Institutions have had considerable additional material incorporated. Most of the remaining chapters have benefited from the insertion of further material. I have also been able to correct some errors and to attempt to improve the style.

I would like to thank Cambridge University Press for permitting me the indulgence of thoroughly revising this work and for their encouragement and assistance. Particular gratitude is owed to Robin Pirrie and to Christopher Hart. In so thanking Cambridge University Press, I would like to reiterate my deep appreciation to Grotius Publications, now part of the Press but happily retaining their distinctive imprint. A particular word of thanks is due to Professor Eli Lauterpacht CBE, QC for his help and advice in the publication and development of this work. I remain grateful to my many colleagues for their advice and encouragement, while reassuring them that all responsibility for the end product rests squarely with me.

As ever, the real and deepest thanks are due to my wife Judith and my children, Talia, Ilan and Daniella. They have borne the brunt of my travails over the years and endured the inevitable pressures and have done so in a caring and loving manner. Their support remains the indispensable foundation of this work.

MALCOLM N. SHAW
Faculty of Law
University of Leicester
Autumn 1996

TABLE OF CASES

TABLE OF TREATIES AND AGREEMENTS

ABBREVIATIONS

AC	Law Reports, Appeal Cases
AFDI	Annuaire Français de Droit International
AJIL	American Journal of International Law
All ER	All England Law Reports
ALR	Argus Law Reports
Annuaire	Annuaire de l'Institut de Droit International
Australian YIL	Australian Yearbook of International Law
BFSP	British and Foreign State Papers
Burr.	Burrow's Reports
BYIL	British Year Book of International Law
Cal	California Reports
Canadian YIL	Canadian Yearbook of International Law
Cd., Cmd. or Cmnd.	UK Command Papers
CERD	Committee on the Elimination of Racial Discrimination
Ch.	Law Reports, Chancery Division
Cl. Ct.	US Court of Claims Reports
CLR	Commonwealth Law Reports
CMLR	Common Market Law Reports
COMECON	Council for Mutual Economic Assistance
Cranch	Cranch Reports, United States Supreme Court
C.Rob.	C. Robinson's Admiralty Reports
Dall.	Dallas, Pennsylvania and United States Reports
DLR	Dominion Law Reports
Dod.	Dodson's Admiralty Reports
DR	Decisions and Reports of the European Commission of Human Rights
DUSPIL	Digest of US Practice in International Law
EC	European Communities
ECHR	European Convention on Human Rights
ECOSOC	Economic and Social Council
ECR	European Court Reports

ECSC	European Coal and Steel Community
EEC	European Economic Community
EJIL	European Journal of International Law
Encyclopedia	Encyclopedia of Public International Law
ER	English Reports
Euratom	European Atomic Energy Community
Ex.D.	Law Reports, Exchequer Division
Fam.	Law Reports, Family Division
FAO	Food and Agriculture Organisation
FCO	Foreign and Commonwealth Office
F.(J.)	Faculty of Advocates
F.Supp.	Federal Supplement
F.2d	Federal Reporter (Second Series)
Finnish YIL	Finnish Yearbook of International Law
GAOR	General Assembly Official Records
GDR	German Democratic Republic
German YIL	German Yearbook of International Law
HC Deb.	House of Commons Debates
HLC	House of Lords Reports (Clark)
HL Deb.	House of Lords Debates
HMSO	Her Majesty's Stationery Office
HR	Hague Academy of International Law, Recueil des Cours
HRJ	Human Rights Journal
HRLJ	Human Rights Law Journal
HRQ	Human Rights Quarterly
ICAO	International Civil Aviation Organisation
ICJ	International Court of Justice
ICLQ	International and Comparative Law Quarterly
ICRC	International Committee of the Red Cross
ILA	International Law Association
ILC	International Law Commission
ILM	International Legal Materials
ILO	International Labour Organisation
ILR	International Law Reports (incorporating the Annual Digest and Reports of Public International Law Cases)
IR	Irish Reports
Iran–US CTR	Iran–United States Claims Tribunal Reports
ITU	International Telecommunications Union
KB	Law Reports, King's Bench Division

LL. R	Lloyd's Law Reports
LNOJ	League of Nations Official Journal
LNTS	League of Nations Treaty Series
LQR	Law Quarterly Review
MLR	Modern Law Review
NATO	North Atlantic Treaty Organisation
NE	Northeastern Reporter
Netherlands YIL	Netherlands Yearbook of International Law
NILR	Netherlands International Law Review
NLM	National Liberation Movement
NQHR	Netherlands Quarterly of Human Rights
NY	New York Reports
NYS	New York Supplement
NZLR	New Zealand Law Reports
OAS	Organisation of American States
OAU	Organisation of African Unity
OECD	Organisation for Economic Co-operation and Development
OECS	Organisation of Eastern Caribbean States
P	Law Reports, Probate, Divorce and Admiralty Division, 1891–
PAIGC	Partido Africano da Independencia da Guine e Cabo Verde
PASIL	Proceedings of the American Society of International Law
PCA	Permanent Court of Arbitration
PCIJ	Permanent Court of International Justice
PD	Law Reports, Probate, Divorce and Admiralty Division, 1875–90
Pet.	Peter's United States Supreme Court Reports
PLO	Palestine Liberation Organisation
QB	Law Reports, Queen's Bench Division
RGDIP	Revue Génèrale de Droit International Public
RIAA	United Nations Reports of International Arbitral Awards
SADR	Saharan Arab Democratic Republic
SC	Supreme Court
SCOR	Security Council Official Records
S. Ct.	Supreme Court Reporter
Stat.	United States Statutes at Large
TFSC	Turkish Federated State of Cyprus

TRNC	Turkish Republic of Northern Cyprus
UKMIL	United Kingdom Materials in International Law
UNCIO	United Nations Conference on International Organisation
UNESCO	United Nations Educational, Scientific and Cultural Organisation
UNJYB	United Nations Juridical Yearbook
UNTS	United Nations Treaty Series
US	United States Reports (Supreme Court)
USC	United States Code
USLW	United States Law Weekly
Va JIL	Virginia Journal of International Law
Ves. Jun.	Vesey Junior's Chancery Reports
Wheat	Wheaton, United States Supreme Court Reports
WHO	World Health Organisation
WLR	Weekly Law Reports
YBWA	Yearbook of World Affairs
ZaöRV	Zeitschrift für ausländisches öffentliches Recht und Völkerrecht

CHAPTER 1

THE NATURE AND DEVELOPMENT OF
INTERNATIONAL LAW

In the long march of mankind from the cave to the computer a central role
has always been played by the idea of law – the idea that order is necessary
and chaos inimical to a just and stable existence. Every society, whether it
be large or small, powerful or weak, has created for itself a framework of
principles within which to develop. What can be done, what cannot be done,
permissible acts, forbidden acts, have all been spelt out within the
consciousness of that community. Progress, with its inexplicable leaps and
bounds, has always been based upon the group as men and women combine
to pursue commonly accepted goals, whether these be hunting animals,
growing food or simply making money.

Law is that element which binds the members of the community together
in their adherence to recognised values and standards. It is both permissive,
in allowing individuals to establish their own legal relations with rights and
duties, as in the creation of contracts, and coercive, as it punishes those who
infringe its regulations. Law consists of a series of rules regulating behaviour, and reflecting, to some extent, the ideas and preoccupations of the
society within which it functions.

And so it is with what is termed international law, with the important
difference that the principal subjects of international law are nation-states,
not individual citizens. There are many contrasts between the law within a
country (municipal law) and the law that operates outside and between
states, international organisations and, in certain cases, individuals.

International law itself is divided into conflict of laws (or private international law as it is sometimes called) and public international law (usually just
termed international law).[1] The former deals with those cases, *within* particular legal systems, in which foreign elements obtrude, raising questions
as to the application of foreign law or the role of foreign courts.[2] For
example, if two Englishmen make a contract in France to sell goods situated
in Paris, an English court would apply French law as regards the validity of

---

[1] This term was first used by J. Bentham, see *Introduction to the Principles of Morals and Legislation*, London, 1780.
[2] See e.g. C. Cheshire and P. North, *Private International Law*, 12th edn, London, 1992.

that contract. By contrast, public international law is not simply an adjunct of a legal order, but a separate system altogether, [3] and it is this field that will be considered in this book.

It may be universal or general, in which case the stipulated rules bind all the states (or practically all depending upon the nature of the rule) or regional, whereby a group of states linked geographically or ideologically may recognise special rules applying only to them, for example, the practice of diplomatic asylum that has developed to its greatest extent in Latin America.[4] The rules of international law must be distinguished from what is called international comity, or practices such as saluting the flags of foreign warships at sea, which are implemented solely through courtesy and are not regarded as legally binding.[5] Similarly, the mistake of confusing international law with international morality must be avoided. While they may meet at certain points, the former discipline is a legal one both as regards its content and its form, while the concept of international morality is a branch of ethics. This does not mean, however, that international law can be divorced from its values.

In this chapter and the next, the characteristics of the international legal system and the historical and theoretical background necessary to a proper appreciation of the part to be played by the law in international law will be examined.

Law and politics in the world community

Probably the first reaction upon an introduction to international law is to question its legal quality. It is recalled that in practically every international dispute both sides proclaim their adherence to the principles of the system and declare that they are acting in accordance with its provisions. It is alleged, for example, that the other side has committed unprovoked aggression and the only suitable reaction is to follow the dictates of the rules governing self-defence or perhaps the principles of self-determination have been ignored and the values of international law must be upheld.

Again a state may have taken over certain foreign owned enterprises and counter criticism by pleading national sovereignty and non-intervention in domestic affairs. The tendency is to become cynical because above all there is no independent institution able to determine the issue and give a final decision.

Virtually everybody who starts reading about international law does so having learned or absorbed something about the principal characteristics of

---

[3] See the *Serbian Loans* case, PCIJ, Series A, No. 14, pp. 41–2.   [4] See further *infra*, p. 72.
[5] *North Sea Continental Shelf* cases, ICJ Reports, 1969, p. 44; 41 ILR, p. 29. See also M. Akehurst, 'Custom as a Source of International Law', 47 BYIL, 1974–5, p. 1.

ordinary or domestic law. What are those identifying marks? A recognised body to legislate or create laws, a hierarchy of courts with compulsory jurisdiction to settle disputes over such laws and an accepted system of enforcing those laws. Without a legislature, judiciary and executive, one cannot talk about a legal order.[6] How can one accept a universal system of international law therefore if this is the case?

International law has no legislature. True there is the General Assembly of the United Nations comprising delegates from all the member states, but its resolutions are not legally binding on anybody save for certain of the organs of the United Nations for certain purposes.[7] There is no system of courts. The International Court of Justice does exist at The Hague but it can only decide cases when both sides agree[8] and it cannot ensure that its decisions are complied with. It is important but it is only peripheral to the international community. Above all there is no executive or governing entity. The Security Council of the United Nations, which was intended to have such a role in a sense, has at times been effectively constrained by the veto power of the five permanent members (USA; USSR, now the Russian Federation; China; France and the United Kingdom).[9] Thus, if there is no identifiable institution either to establish rules, or clarify them or see that those who break them are punished, how can what is called international law be law?

It will, of course, be realised that the basis for this line of argument is the comparison of domestic law with international law, and the assumption of an analogy between the national system and the international order. And this is at the heart of all discussions about the nature of international law.

The English philosopher John Austin elaborated at the turn of the nineteenth century a theory of law based upon the notion of a sovereign issuing a command backed by a sanction or punishment. Since international law did not fit within that definition it was relegated to the category of 'positive morality'.[10] This concept has been criticised for oversimplifying and even confusing the true nature of law within a society and for overemphasising the role of the sanction within the system by linking it to every rule.[11] This is not the place for a comprehensive summary of Austin's theory but the idea

---

[6] See generally, R. Dias, *Jurisprudence*, 5th edn, London, 1985 and H. L. Hart, *The Concept of Law*, Oxford, 1961.

[7] See article 17(1) of the United Nations Charter. See also D. Johnson, 'The Effect of Resolutions of the General Assembly of the United Nations', 32 BYIL, 1955–6, p. 97 and *infra*, Chapter 20.

[8] See article 36 of the Statute of the International Court of Justice and *infra*, Chapter 18.

[9] See D. W. Bowett, *The Law of International Institutions*, 4th edn, London, 1982 and *infra*, Chapter 21.

[10] See J. Austin, *The Province of Jurisprudence Determined* (ed. H. L. A. Hart), London, 1954, pp. 134–42.   [11] See e.g. Hart, *Concept of Law*, Chapter X.

of coercion as an integral part of any legal order is a vital one that needs looking at in the context of international law.

The role of force

There is no unified system of sanctions[12] in international law in the sense that there is in municipal law, but there are circumstances in which the use of force is regarded as justified and legal. Within the United Nations system, sanctions may be imposed by the Security Council upon the determination of a threat to the peace, breach of the peace or act of aggression.[13] Such sanctions may be economic, for example those proclaimed in 1966 against Rhodesia,[14] or even military as in the Korean war in 1950,[15] or indeed both, as in 1990 against Iraq.[16]

Coercive action within the framework of the UN is rare because it requires co-ordination amongst the five permanent members of the Security Council and this obviously needs an issue not regarded by any of the great powers as a threat to their vital interests.

Korea was an exception and joint action could only be undertaken because of the fortuitous absence of the USSR from the Council as a protest at the seating of the Nationalist Chinese representatives.[17]

Apart from such institutional sanctions, one may note the bundle of rights to take violent action known as self-help.[18] This procedure to resort to force to defend certain rights is characteristic of primitive systems of law with blood-feuds, but in the domestic legal order such procedures and methods are now within the exclusive control of the established authority. States may use force in self-defence, if the object of aggression, and may take action in response to the illegal acts of other states. In such cases the states themselves decide whether to take action, and if so, the extent of their measures, and

---

[12] See e.g. W. M. Reisman, 'Sanctions and Enforcement' in *The Future of the International Legal Order* (eds. C. Black and R. A. Falk), New York, 1971, p. 273; J. Brierly, 'Sanctions', 17 *Transactions of the Grotius Society*, 1932, p. 68; Hart, *Concept of Law*, pp. 211–21; A. D'Amato, 'The Neo-Positivist Concept of International Law', 59 AJIL, 1965, p. 321; G. Fitzmaurice, 'The Foundations of the Authority of International Law and the Problem of Enforcement', 19 MLR, 1956, p. 1 and *The Effectiveness of International Decisions* (ed. S. Schwebel), 1971.   [13] Chapter VII of the United Nations Charter. See *infra* Chapter 20.
[14] Security Council resolution 221 (1966). Note also Security Council resolution 418 (1977) imposing a mandatory arms embargo on South Africa.
[15] Security Council resolutions of June 25, June 27 and July 7, 1950. See D. W. Bowett, *United Nations Forces*, London, 1964.
[16] Security Council resolutions 661 and 678 (1990). See *The Kuwait Crisis: Basic Documents* (eds. E. Lauterpacht, C. Greenwood, M. Weller and D. Bethlehem), Cambridge, 1991, pp. 88 and 98. See also *infra*, Chapter 20.
[17] See E. Luard, *A History of the United Nations*, London, vol. I, *The Years of Western Domination 1945–55*, London, 1982, pp. 229–74 and *infra*, Chapter 20.
[18] See D. W. Bowett, *Self-Defence in International Law*, Manchester, 1958 and I. Brownlie, *International Law and the Use of Force by States*, Oxford, 1963.

there is no supreme body to rule on their legality or otherwise, in the absence of an examination by the International Court of Justice, acceptable to both parties, although international law does lay down relevant rules.[19]

Accordingly those writers who put the element of force to the forefront of their theories face many difficulties in describing the nature, or rather the legal nature of international law, with its lack of a coherent, recognised and comprehensive framework of sanctions. To see the sanctions of international law in the states' rights of self-defence and reprisals,[20] is to misunderstand the role of sanctions within a system because they are at the disposal of the states, not the system itself. Neither must it be forgotten that the current trend in international law is to restrict the use of force as far as possible, thus leading to the absurd result that the more force is controlled in international society, the less legal international law becomes.

Since one cannot discover the nature of international law by reference to a definition of law predicated upon sanctions, the character of the international legal order has to be examined in order to seek to discover whether in fact states feel obliged to obey the rules of international law and if so, why. If, indeed, the answer to the first question is negative, that states do not feel the necessity to act in accordance with such rules, then there does not exist any system of international law worthy of the name.

The international system[21]

It has already been hinted that the key to the search lies within the unique attributes of the international system. While the legal structure within all but the most primitive societies is hierarchical and authority is vertical, rather like a pyramid with the sovereign person or unit in a position of supremacy on top, the international system is horizontal consisting of over 180 independent states, all equal in legal theory (in that they all possess the characteristics of sovereignty) and recognising no one in authority over them. The law is above individuals in domestic systems, but international law only exists as between the states. Individuals only have the choice as to whether to obey the law or not. They do not create the law. That is done by

[19] *Infra*, Chapter 19. See also M. Barkin, *Law Without Sanctions*, New Haven, 1967.
[20] See e.g. H. Kelsen, *General Theory of Law and State*, London, 1946, pp. 328 *et seq.*
[21] See L. Henkin, *How Nations Behave*, 2nd ed., New York, 1979 and *Henkin, International Law: Politics and Values*, Dordrecht, 1995; M. A. Kaplan and N. Katzenbach, *The Political Foundations of International Law*, New York, 1961; C. W. Jenks, *The Common Law of Mankind*, London, 1958; W. Friedmann, *The Changing Structure of International Law*, New York, 1964; A. Sheikh, *International Law and National Behaviour*, New York, 1974; O. Schachter, *International Law in Theory and Practice*, Dordrecht, 1991; T. M. Franck, *The Power of Legitimacy Among Nations*, Oxford, 1990; R. Higgins, *Problems and Process*, Oxford, 1994 and *Oppenheim's International Law* (eds. R. Y. Jennings and A. D. Watts), 9th edn, London, 1992, vol. I, Chapter 1.

specific institutions. In international law, on the other hand, it is the states themselves that create the law and obey or disobey it.[22] This, of course, has profound repercussions as regards the sources of law as well as the means for enforcing accepted legal rules.

International law, as will be shown in succeeding chapters, is primarily formulated by international agreements, which create rules binding upon the signatories, and customary rules, which are basically state practices recognised by the community at large as laying down patterns of conduct that have to be complied with.

However, it may be argued that since states themselves sign treaties and indulge in courses of action that they may or may not regard as legally obligatory, international law would appear to consist of a series of rules displayed as if on a market stall for states to pick and choose from. And if this is so, how can one identify international law with domestic law? Is it not merely an illusion behind which lurks the real regulator of world affairs – brute force?

Contrary to popular belief, states do observe international law, and violations are comparatively rare. However, such violations (like armed attacks and racial oppression) are well publicised and strike at the heart of the system, the creation and preservation of international peace and justice. But just as incidents of murder, robbery and rape do occur within national legal orders without bringing down the whole edifice or stimulating citizens to deny that law exists, so analogously assaults upon international legal rules point up the weaknesses of the system without denigrating their validity or their necessity. Thus, despite the occasional gross violation, the vast majority of the provisions of international law are followed.[23]

In the daily routine of international life, tens of thousands of agreements are observed and many customs are adhered to. The need is felt in the hectic interplay of world affairs for some kind of regulatory framework, for some kind of rules network within which the game can be played, and international law fulfils that requirement. States feel this necessity because it imports an element of stability and predictability into the situation.

Where countries are involved in a disagreement or a dispute, it is handy to have recourse to the rules of international law even if there are conflicting interpretations, since at least there is a common frame of reference and one state will be aware of how the other state will develop its argument. They will both be talking a common language and this factor of communication

---

[22] This leads Rosenne to refer to international law as a law of co-ordination, rather than, as in internal law, a law of subordination; *Practice and Methods of International Law*, Dordrecht, 1984, p. 2.

[23] See H. Morgenthau, *Politics Among Nations*, 5th edn, New York, 1973, pp. 290–1; Henkin, *How Nations Behave*, pp. 46–9; J. Brierly, *The Outlook for International Law*, Oxford, 1944, p. 5 and P. Jessup, *A Modern Law of Nations*, 1948, pp. 6–8.

is vital since misunderstandings occur so easily and often with tragic consequences. Where the antagonists dispute the understanding of a particular rule and adopt opposing stands as regards its implementation they are at least on the same wavelength and communicate by means of the same phrases. That is something. It is not everything, for it is a mistake as well as inaccurate to claim for international law more than it can possibly deliver. It can constitute a mutually understandable vocabulary book and suggest possible solutions which follow from a study of its principles. What it cannot do is solve every problem no matter how dangerous or complex merely by being there. International law has not yet been developed, if it ever will, to that particular stage, and one should not exaggerate its capabilities while pointing to its positive features.

But what is to stop a state from simply ignoring international law when proceeding upon its chosen policy? Can a legal rule against aggression, for example, of itself prevail over political temptations? There is no international police force to prevent such an action, but there are a series of other considerations closely bound up with the character of international law which might well cause a potential aggressor to forbear.

There is the element of reciprocity at work and a powerful weapon it can be. States quite often do not pursue one particular course of action which might bring them short-term gains, because it could disrupt the mesh of reciprocal tolerance which could very well bring long-term disadvantages. For example, states everywhere protect the immunity of foreign diplomats for not to do so would place their own officials abroad at risk.[24] Thus, usually it is, though of course it need not be, an inducement to states to act reasonably and moderate demands in the expectation that this will similarly encourage other states to act reasonably and so avoid confrontations. Because the rules can ultimately be changed by states altering their patterns of behaviour and causing one custom to supersede another, or by mutual agreement, a certain definite reference to political life is retained. But the point must be made that a state, after weighing up all possible alternatives, might very well feel that the only method to protect its vital interests would involve a violation of international law and that responsibility would just have to be taken. Where survival is involved international law may take second place.

Another significant factor is the advantages, or 'rewards', that may occur in certain situations from an observance of international law. It may encourage friendly or neutral states to side with one country involved in a conflict rather than its opponent, and even take a more active role than might

---

[24] See *Case Concerning United States Diplomatic and Consular Staff in Teheran*, ICJ Reports, 1980, p. 3; 61 ILR, p. 502.

otherwise have been the case. In many ways, it is an appeal to public opinion for support and all states employ this tactic.

In many ways, it reflects the esteem that law is held in. The Soviet Union made considerable use of legal arguments in its effort to establish its non-liability to contribute towards the peace-keeping operations of the United Nations[25] and the Americans too, justified their activities with regard to Cuba[26] and Vietnam[27] by reference to international law. In some cases it may work and bring considerable support in its wake, in many cases it will not, but in any event the very fact that all states do it is a constructive sign.

A further element worth mentioning in this context is the constant formulation of international business in characteristically legal terms. Points of view and disputes, in particular, are framed legally with references to precedent, international agreements and even the opinions of juristic authors. Claims are pursued with regard to the rules of international law and not in terms of, for example, morality or ethics.[28] This has brought into being a class of officials throughout governmental departments, in addition to those working in international institutions, versed in international law and carrying on the everyday functions of government in a law-orientated way. Many writers have, in fact, emphasised the role of officials in the actual functioning of law and the influence they have upon the legal process.[29]

Having come to the conclusion that states do observe international law and will usually only violate it on an issue regarded as vital to their interests, the question arises as to the basis of this sense of obligation.[30] The nineteenth century with its business-orientated philosophy stressed the importance of the contract, as the legal basis of an agreement freely entered into by both (or all) sides, and this influenced the theory of consent in international law.[31] States were independent, and free agents, and accordingly they could only be bound with their own consent. There was no authority in existence able theoretically or practically to impose rules upon the various nation-states. This approach found its extreme expression in the theory of auto-limitation, or self-limitation, which declared that states could only be

[25] See *Certain Expenses of the United Nations*, ICJ Reports, 1962, p. 151; 34 ILR, p. 281 and R. Higgins, *United Nations Peace-Keeping; Documents and Commentary*, 4 vols., Oxford, 1969–81.
[26] See e.g. A. Chayes, *The Cuban Missile Crisis*, Oxford, 1974, and Henkin, *How Nations Behave*, pp. 279–302.
[27] See e.g. *The Vietnam War and International Law* (ed. R. A. Falk), 4 vols., Princeton, 1968–76; J. N. Moore, *Law and the Indo-China War*, Charlottesville, 1972 and Henkin, *How Nations Behave*, pp. 303–12.   [28] See Hart, *Concept of Law*, p. 223.
[29] See e.g. M. S. McDougal, H. Lasswell and W. M. Reisman, 'The World Constitutive Process of Authoritative Decision' in *International Law Essays* (eds. M. S. McDougal and W. M. Reisman), New York, 1981, p. 191.
[30] See e.g. J. Brierly, *The Basis of Obligation in International Law*, Oxford, 1958.
[31] See W. Friedmann, *Legal Theory*, 5th edn, London, 1967, pp. 573–6. See also the *Lotus* case, PCIJ, Series A, No. 10, p. 18.

obliged to comply with international legal rules if they had first agreed to be so obliged.[32]

Nevertheless, this theory is most unsatisfactory as an account of why international law is regarded as binding or even as an explanation of the international legal system.[33] To give one example, there are about 100 states that have come into existence since the end of the Second World War and by no stretch of the imagination can it be said that such states have consented to all the rules of international law formed prior to their establishment. It could be argued that by 'accepting independence', states consent to all existing rules, but to take this view relegates consent to the role of a mere fiction.[34]

This theory also fails as an adequate explanation of the international legal system, because it does not take into account the tremendous growth in international institutions and the network of rules and regulations that have emerged from them within the last generation.

To accept consent as the basis for obligation in international law[35] begs the question as to what happens when consent is withdrawn. The state's reversal of its agreement to a rule does not render that rule optional or remove from it its aura of legality. It merely places that state in breach of its obligations under international law if that state proceeds to act upon its decision. Indeed, the principle that agreements are binding (*pacta sunt servanda*) upon which all treaty law must be based cannot itself be based upon consent.[36]

One current approach to this problem is to refer to the doctrine of consensus.[37] This reflects the influence of the majority in creating new norms of international law and the acceptance by other states of such new rules. It attempts to put into focus the change of emphasis that is beginning to take place from exclusive concentration upon the nation-state to a consideration of the developing forms of international co-operation where such concepts as consent and sanction are inadequate to explain what is happening.

Of course, one cannot ignore the role of consent in international law. To recognise its limitations is not to neglect its significance. Much of

---

[32] E.g. G. Jellinek, *Allgemeine Rechtslehre*, Berlin, 1905.
[33] See also Hart, *Concept of Law*, pp. 219–20. But see P. Weil, 'Towards Relative Normativity in International Law ?', 77 AJIL, 1983, p. 413 and responses thereto, e.g. R. A. Falk, 'To What Extent are International Law and International Lawyers Ideologically Neutral?' in *Change and Stability in International Law-Making* (eds. A. Cassese and J. Weiler), Berlin, 1989, p. 137 and A. Pellet, 'The Normative Dilemma: Will and Consent in International Law-Making', 12 Australian YIL, 1992, p. 22.   [34] See further *infra*, p. 72.
[35] See e.g. J. S. Watson, 'State Consent and the Sources of International Obligation', PASIL, 1992, p. 108.   [36] See *infra*, Chapter 3.
[37] See e.g. A. D'Amato, 'On Consensus', 8 Canadian YIL, 1970, p. 104. Note also the 'gentleman's agreement on consensus' in the Third UN Conference on the Law of the Sea: see Sohn, 'Voting Procedures in United Nations Conferences for the Codification of International Law', 69 AJIL, 1975, p. 318 and UN Doc.A/Conf.62/WP.2.

international law is constituted by states expressly agreeing to specific normative standards, most obviously by entering into treaties. This cannot be minimised. Nevertheless, it is preferable to consider consent as important not only with regard to specific rules specifically accepted (which is not the sum total of international law, of course) but in the light of the approach of states generally to the totality of rules, understandings, patterns of behaviour and structures underpinning and constituting the international system.[38] In a broad sense, states accept or consent to the general system of international law, for in reality without that no such system could possibly operate. It is this approach which may be characterised as consensus or the essential framework within which the demand for individual state consent is transmuted into community acceptance.

It is important to note that while states from time to time object to particular rules of international law and seek to change them, no state has sought to maintain that it is free to object to the system as a whole. Each individual state, of course, has the right to seek to influence by word or deed the development of specific rules of international law but the creation of new customary rules is not dependent upon the express consent of each particular state.

The function of politics

It is clear that there can never be a complete separation between law and policy. No matter what theory of law or political philosophy is professed, the inextricable bonds linking law and politics must be recognised.

Within developed societies a distinction is made between the formulation of policy and the method of its enforcement. In the United Kingdom, Parliament legislates while the courts adjudicate and a similar division is maintained in the United States between the Congress and the courts system. The purpose of such divisions, of course, is to prevent a concentration of too much power within one branch of government. Nevertheless, it is the political branch which makes laws and in the first place creates the legal system. Even within the hierarchy of courts, the judges have leeway in interpreting the law and in the last resort make decisions from amongst a number of alternatives.[39] This position, however, should not be exaggerated because a number of factors operate to conceal and lessen the impact of politics upon the legal process. Foremost amongst these is the psychological element of tradition and the development of the so-called 'law-habit'.[40] A

---

[38] See e.g. J. Charney, 'Universal International Law', 87 AJIL, 1993, p. 529.
[39] See e.g. R. Dworkin, *Taking Rights Seriously*, London, 1977.
[40] See e.g. K. Llewellyn, *The Common Law Tradition*, Boston, 1960, and generally D. Lloyd, *Introduction to Jurisprudence*, 4th edn, London, 1979.

particular legal atmosphere has been created, which is buttressed by the political system and recognises the independent existence of law institutions and methods of operation characterised as 'just' or 'legal'. In most countries overt interference with the juridical process would be regarded as an attack upon basic principles and hotly contested. The use of legal language and accepted procedures together with the pride of the legal profession, reinforce the system and emphasise the degree of distance maintained between the legislative-executive organs and the judicial structure.[41]

However, when one looks at the international legal scene the situation changes. The arbiters of the world order are, in the last resort, the states, and they both make the rules (ignoring for the moment the secondary, if growing, field of international organisations) and interpret and enforce them.

While it is possible to discern an 'international legal habit' amongst governmental and international officials, the machinery necessary to enshrine this does not exist.

Politics is much closer to the heart of the system than is perceived within national legal orders, and power much more in evidence.[42] The interplay of law and politics in world affairs is much more complex and difficult to unravel, and signals a return to the earlier discussion as to why states comply with international rules. Power politics stresses competition, conflict and supremacy and adopts as its core the struggle for survival and influence.[43] International law aims for harmony and the regulation of disputes. It attempts to create a framework, no matter how rudimentary, which can act as a kind of shock-absorber clarifying and moderating claims and endeavouring to balance interests. In addition, it sets out a series of principles declaring how states should behave. Just as any domestic community must have a background of ideas and hopes to aim at even if few can be or are ever attained, so the international community, too, must bear in mind its ultimate values.

Although, these ultimate values are in a formal sense kept at arms-length from the legal process. As the International Court noted in the South West Africa case,[44] 'It is a court of law, and can take account of moral principles only in so far as these are given a sufficient expression in legal form. Law exists, it is said, to serve a social need; but precisely for that reason it can do so only through and within the limits of its own discipline. Otherwise, it is not a legal service that would be rendered.'[45]

---

[41] See A. W. H. Dias, *Jurisprudence*, 5th edn, London, 1985, Chapter 3.
[42] See generally Henkin, *How Nations Behave*, and Schachter, *International Law*, pp. 5–9.
[43] See G. Schwarzenberger, *Power Politics*, 3rd edn, London, 1964 and Schwarzenberger, *International Law*, 3rd edn, London,1957, vol. I; H. Morgenthau, *Politics Among Nations*.
[44] ICJ Reports, 1966, pp. 6, 34.
[45] But see Higgins' criticism that such a formulation may be question-begging with regard to the identity of such 'limits of its own discipline', *Problems*, 1994, p. 5.

International law cannot be a source of instant solutions to problems of conflict and confrontation because of its own inherent weaknesses in structure and content. To fail to recognise this encourages a utopian approach which when faced with reality will fail.[46] On the other hand, the cynical attitude with its obsession with brute power is equally inaccurate, if more depressing.

It is the medium road, recognising the strength and weakness of international law and pointing out what it can achieve and what it cannot, which offers the best hope. Man seeks order, welfare and justice not only within the state in which he lives, but also within the international system in which he lives.

Historical development[47]

The foundations of international law (or the law of nations) as it is understood today lie firmly in the development of Western culture and political organisation.

The growth of European notions of sovereignty and the independent nation-state required an acceptable method whereby inter-state relations could be conducted in accordance with commonly accepted standards of behaviour, and international law filled the gap. But although the law of nations took root and flowered with the sophistication of Renaissance Europe, the seeds of this particular hybrid plant are of far older lineage. They reach far back into history.

Early origins

While the modern international system can be traced back some four hundred years, certain of the basic concepts of international law can be discerned in political relationships thousands of years ago. Around 2100 BC, for instance, a solemn treaty was signed between the rulers of Lagash and Umma, the city-states situated in the area known to historians as

---

[46] Note, of course, the important distinction between the existence of an obligation under international law and the question of the enforcement of that obligation. Problems with regard to enforcing a duty cannot affect the legal validity of that duty, see e.g. Judge Weeramantry's Separate Opinion in the Order of 13 September 1993, in the *Bosnia* case, ICJ Reports, 1993, pp. 325, 374; 95 ILR, pp. 43, 92.

[47] See in particular A. Nussbaum, *A Concise History of the Law of Nations*, New York, 1962; *Encyclopedia of Public International Law* (ed. R. Bernardt), Amsterdam, vol. VII, 1984, pp. 127–273 and J. W. Verzijl, *International Law in Historical Perspective*, Leiden, 10 vols., 1968–79. See also A. Cassese, *International Law in a Divided World*, Oxford, 1986; Nguyen Quoc Dinh, P. Daillier and A. Pellet, *Droit International Public*, 5th edn, Paris, 1994, p. 39; H. Thierry, 'L'Évolution du Droit International', 222 HR, 1990 III, p. 9; D. Korff, 'Introduction à l'histoire de droit international public', 1 HR, 1923 I, p. 1 and P. Le Fur, 'Le développement historique de droit international', 41 HR, 1932 III, p. 501.

Mesopotamia. It was inscribed on a stone block and concerned the establishment of a defined boundary to be respected by both sides under pain of alienating a number of Sumerian gods.[48] The next major instance known of an important, binding, international treaty is that concluded over a thousand years later between Rameses II of Egypt and the king of the Hittites for the establishment of eternal peace and brotherhood.[49] Other points covered in that agreement signed, it would seem, at Kadesh, north of Damascus, included respect for each other's territorial integrity, the termination of a state of aggression and the setting up of a form of defensive alliance.

Since that date many agreements between the rival Middle Eastern powers were concluded, usually aimed at embodying in a ritual form a state of subservience between the parties or attempting to create a political alliance to contain the influence of an over-powerful empire.[50]

The role of ancient Israel must also be noted. A universal ethical stance coupled with rules relating to warfare were handed down to other peoples and religions and the demand for justice and a fair system of law founded upon strict morality permeated the thought and conduct of subsequent generations.[51]

For example, the Prophet Isaiah declared that sworn agreements, even where made with the enemy, must be performed.[52] Peace and social justice were the keys to man's existence, not power.

After much neglect, there is now more consideration of the cultures and standards evolved, before the birth of Christ, in the Far East, in the Indian[53] and Chinese[54] civilisations. Many of the Hindu rules displayed a growing sense of morality and generosity and the Chinese Empire devoted much

[48] Nussbaum, *Law of Nations*, pp. 1–2. Note the recent discovery in the excavated city of Ebla, the capital of a civilisation at least 4,500 years old, of a copy of a political treaty between Ebla and the city of Abarsal, see *Times Higher Education Supplement*, 19 May 1995, p. 20. See also R. Cohen, *On Diplomacy in the Ancient Near East: The Amarna Letters*, Discussion Paper of the Centre for the Study of Diplomacy, University of Leicester, 1995.
[49] Nussbaum, *Law of Nations*, pp. 1–2.
[50] Preiser emphasises that the era between the seventeenth and fifteenth centuries BC witnessed something of a competing state system involving five independent (at various times) states: *Encyclopedia*, pp. 133–4.
[51] See P. Weil, 'Le Judaisme et le Développement du Droit International', 151 HR, p. 253 and S. Rosenne, 'The Influence of Judaism on International Law', *Nederlands Tijdschrift voor Internationaal Recht*, 1958, p. 119. [52] See Nussbaum, *Law of Nations*, p. 3.
[53] *Ibid.* See also C. H. Alexandrowicz, *An Introduction to the History of the Law of Nations in the East Indies*, Leiden, 1967 and Alexandrowicz, 'The Afro-Asian World and the Law of Nations (Historical Aspects)', 123 HR, p. 117; L. Chatterjee, *International Law and Inter-State Relations in Ancient India*, 1958 and Nagendra Singh, 'The Distinguishing Characteristics of the Concept of the Law of Nations as it Developed in Ancient India', *Liber Amicorum for Lord Wilberforce* (eds. A. Bos and I. Brownlie), Oxford, 1987, p. 91.
[54] Nussbaum, *Law of Nations*, p. 4. See also P. Gong, *The Standard of 'Civilisation' in International Society*, 1984, pp. 130–63; pp. 164–200 with regard to Japan; pp. 201–37 with regard to Siam; Hsu, *China's Entrance into the Family of Nations*, 1960, and H. Iriye, 'The Principles of International law in the Light of Confucian Doctrine', 120 HR, p. 1.

thought to harmonious relations between its constituent parts. Regulations controlling violence and the behaviour of varying factions with regard to innocent civilians were introduced and ethical values instilled in the education of the ruling classes. In times of Chinese dominance, a regional tributary-states system operated which fragmented somewhat in times of weakness, but this remained culturally alive for many centuries.

However, the predominant approach of ancient civilisations was geographically and culturally restricted. There was no conception of an international community of states co-existing within a defined framework. The scope for any 'international law' of states was extremely limited and all that one can point to is the existence of certain ideals, such as the sanctity of treaties, which have continued to this day as important elements in society. But the notion of a universal community with its ideal of world order was not in evidence.

The era of classical Greece, from about the sixth-century BC and onwards for a couple of hundred years, has, one must note, been of overwhelming significance for European thought. Its critical and rational turn of mind, its constant questioning and analysis of man and nature and its love of argument and debate were spread throughout Europe and the Mediterranean world by the Roman Empire which adopted Hellenic culture wholesale, and penetrated Western consciousness with the Renaissance. However, Greek awareness was limited to their own competitive city-states and colonies. Those of different origin were barbarians not deemed worthy of association. The value of Greece in a study of international law lies partly in the philosophical, scientific and political analyses bequeathed to mankind and partly in the fascinating state of inter-relationship built up within the Hellenistic world.[55] Numerous treaties linked the city-states together in a network of commercial and political associations.

Rights were often granted to the citizens of the states in each other's territories and rules regarding the sanctity and protection of diplomatic envoys developed. Certain practices were essential before the declaration of war and the horrors of war were somewhat ameliorated by the exercise, for example, of religious customs regarding sanctuaries. But no overall moral approach similar to those emerging from Jewish and Hindu thought, particularly, evolved. No sense of a world community can be traced to Greek ideology in spite of the growth of Greek colonies throughout the Mediterranean area. This was left to the able administrators of the Roman Empire.[56]

The Romans had a profound respect for organisation and the law.[57] The

[55] Nussbaum, *Law of Nations*, pp. 5–9. See also Ténékidès, 'Droit International et Communautés Fédérales dans la Grèce des Cités', 90 HR, p. 469, and *Encyclopaedia of Public International Law*, vol. VII, pp. 154–6.
[56] *Encyclopedia*, pp. 136–9 and Nussbaum, *Law of Nations*, pp. 10–16.
[57] See e.g. A. Jolowicz, *Historical Introduction to Roman Law*, 3rd edn, London, 1972.

law knitted together their empire and constituted a vital source of reference for every inhabitant of the far flung domain. The early Roman law (the *jus civile*) applied only to Roman citizens. It was formalistic and hard and reflected the status of a small, unsophisticated society rooted in the soil.

It was totally unable to provide a relevant background for an expanding, developing nation. This need was served by the creation and progressive augmentation of the *jus gentium*. This provided simplified rules to govern the relations between foreigners, and between foreigners and citizens. The instrument through which this particular system evolved was the official known as the Praetor Peregrinus, whose function it was to oversee all legal relationships, including bureaucratic and commercial matters, within the empire.

The progressive rules of the *jus gentium* gradually overrode the narrow *jus civile* until the latter system ceased to exist. Thus, the *jus gentium* became the common law of the Roman Empire and was deemed to be of universal application.

It is this all-embracing factor which so strongly distinguishes the Roman from the Greek experience, although, of course, there was no question of the acceptance of other nations on a basis of equality and the *jus gentium* remained a 'national law' for the Roman Empire.

One of the most influential of Greek concepts taken up by the Romans was the idea of Natural Law.[58] This was formulated by the Stoic philosophers of the third century BC and their theory was that it constituted a body of rules of universal relevance. Such rules were rational and logical and because the ideas and precepts of the 'law of nature' were rooted in human intelligence, it followed that such rules could not be restricted to any nation or any group but were of world-wide relevance. This element of universality is basic to modern doctrines of international law and the Stoic elevation of human powers of logical deduction to the supreme pinnacle of 'discovering' the law foreshadows the rational philosophies of the West. As well as being a fundamental concept in legal theory, Natural Law is vital to an understanding of international law, as well as being an indispensible precursor to contemporary concern with human rights.

Certain Roman philosophers incorporated those Greek ideas of Natural Law into their own legal theories, often as a kind of ultimate justification of the *jus gentium*, which was deemed to enshrine rational principles common to all civilised nations.

However, the law of nature was held to have an existence over and above that of the *jus gentium*.

This led to much confusion over the exact relationship between the two

---

[58] See e.g. Lloyd, *Introduction to Jurisprudence*, pp. 79–169.

ideas and different Roman lawyers came to different conclusions as to their identity and characteristics. The important factors though that need to be noted are the theories of the universality of law and the rational origins of legal rules that were founded, theoretically at least, not on superior force but on superior reason.

The classical rules of Roman law were collated in the *Corpus Juris Civilis*, a compilation of legal material by a series of Byzantine philosophers completed in 534 AD.[59] Such a collection was to be invaluable when the darkness of the early Middle Ages, following the Roman collapse, began gradually to evaporate. For here was a body of developed laws ready made and awaiting transference to an awakening Europe.

At this stage reference must be made to the growth of Islam.[60] Its approach to international relations and law was predicated upon a state of hostility towards the non-Moslem world and the concept of unity, Dar al-Islam, as between Moslem countries. Generally speaking, humane rules of warfare were developed and the 'peoples of the book' (Jews and Christians) were treated better than non- believers, although in an inferior position to Moslems. Once the period of conquest was over and power was consolidated, norms governing conduct with non-Moslem states began to develop. The law dealing with diplomats was founded upon notions of hospitality and safety (*aman*), while rules governing international agreements grew out of the concept of respecting promises made.[61]

The Middle Ages and the Renaissance

The Middle Ages were characterised by the authority of the organised Church and the comprehensive structure of power that it commanded.[62] All Europe was of one religion, and the ecclesiastical law applied to all, notwithstanding tribal or regional affiliations. For much of the period, there were struggles between the religious authorities and the rulers of the Holy Roman Empire.

These conflicts were eventually resolved in favour of the Papacy, but the victory over secularism proved of relatively short duration. Religion and a common legacy derived from the Roman Empire were strongly unifying influences, while political and regional rivalries were not. But before a recog-

[59] See generally with regard to Byzantium, H. De Taube, 'L'Apport de Byzance au Développement du Droit International Occidental', 67 HR, p. 233 and A. Verosta, 'International Law in Europe & Western Asia between 100–650 AD', 113 HR, p. 489.

[60] See e.g. A. Draz, 'Le Droit International Public et l'Islam', 5 *Revue Egyptienne de Droit International*, p. 17; H. Khadduri, 'Islam and the Modern Law of Nations', 50 AJIL, p. 358 and *War and Peace in the Law of Islam*, 2nd edn, 1962; and L. Mahmassani, 'The Principles of International Law in the Light of Islamic Doctrine', 117 HR, p. 205.

[61] See *Encyclopedia*, pp. 141–2, and Nussbaum, *Law of Nations*, pp. 51–4.

[62] *Ibid.*, pp. 17–23 and *Encyclopedia*, pp. 143–9.

nised system of international law could be created, social changes were essential.

Of particular importance during this era was the authority of the Holy Roman Empire and the supranational character of canon law.[63] Nevertheless, commercial and maritime law developed apace. English law established the *Law Merchant*, a code of rules covering foreign traders, and this was declared to be of universal application.[64]

Throughout Europe, mercantile courts were set up to settle disputes between tradesmen at the various fairs, and while it is not possible to state that a Continental *Law Merchant* came into being, a network of common regulations and practices wove its way across the commercial fabric of Europe and constituted an embryonic international trade law.[65]

Similarly, maritime customs began to be accepted throughout the Continent. Founded upon the Rhodian Sea Law, a Byzantine work, many of whose rules were enshrined in the Rolls of Oleron in the twelfth century, and other maritime textbooks, a series of commonly applied customs relating to the sea permeated the naval powers of the Atlantic and Mediterranean coasts.[66]

Such commercial and maritime codes while at this stage merely expressions of national legal systems were amongst the forerunners of international law because they were created and nurtured upon a backcloth of cross-national contacts and reflected the need for rules that would cover international situations.

Such rules, growing out of the early Middle Ages, constituted the seeds of international law, but before they could flourish, European thought had first to be developed by that intellectual explosion known as the Renaissance.

This complex of ideas changed the face of European society and ushered in the modern era of scientific humanistic and individualistic thought.[67]

The collapse of the Byzantine Empire centred on Constantinople before the Turkish armies in 1453 drove many Greek scholars to seek sanctuary in Italy and enliven Europe's cultural life. The introduction of printing during the fifteenth century provided the means to disseminate knowledge, and the undermining of feudalism in the wake of economic growth and the rise of the merchant classes provided the background to the new inquiring attitudes taking shape.

---

[63] Note in particular the influence of the Church on the rules governing warfare and the binding nature of agreements: see Nussbaum, *Law of Nations*, pp. 17–18 and *Encyclopedia*, pp. 146–7.   [64] See G. Holdsworth, *A History of English Law*, vol. 5, 1924, pp. 60–3.
[65] *Ibid.*, pp. 63–129.
[66] Nussbaum, *Law of Nations*, pp. 29–31. Note also the influence of the Consolato del Mare, composed in Barcelona in the mid fourteenth century and the Maritime Code of Wisby (approx. 1407) followed by the Hanseatic League.
[67] See e.g. Friedmann, *Changing Structure*, pp. 114–16.

Europe's developing self-confidence manifested itself in a sustained drive overseas for wealth and luxury items. By the end of the fifteenth century, the Arabs had been ousted from the Iberian peninsula and the Americas reached.

The rise of the nation-states of England, France and Spain, in particular, characterised the process of the creation of territorially consolidated independent units, in theory and doctrine, as well as in fact. This led to a higher degree of interaction between sovereign entities and thus the need to regulate such activities in a generally acceptable fashion. The pursuit of political power and supremacy became overt and recognised, as Machiavelli's *The Prince* (1513) demonstrated.

The city-states of Italy struggled for supremacy and the Papacy too became a secular power. From these hectic struggles emerged many of the staples of modern international life; diplomacy, statesmanship, the theory of the balance of power and the idea of a community of states.[68]

Notions such as these are immediately appreciable and one can identify with the various manoeuvres for political supremacy. Alliances, betrayals, manipulations of state institutions and the drive for power are not unknown to us. We recognise the roots of our society.

It was the evolution of the concept of an international community of separate, sovereign, if competing, states, that marks the beginning of what is understood by international law. The Renaissance bequeathed the prerequisites of independent, critical thought and a humanistic, secular approach to life as well as the political framework for the future. But it is the latter factor which is vital to the subsequent growth of international law. The Reformation and the European religious wars that followed emphasised this, as did the growing power of the nations. In many ways these wars marked the decline of a continental system founded on religion and the birth of a continental system founded on the supremacy of the state.

Throughout these countries the necessity was felt for a new conception of human as well as state relationships. This search was precipitated, as has been intimated, by the decline of the Church and the rise of what might be termed 'free-thinking'. The theory of international law was naturally deeply involved in this reappraisal of political life and it was tremendously influenced by the rediscovery of Greco-Roman ideas. The Renaissance stimulated a rebirth of Hellenic studies and ideas of Natural Law, in particular, became popular.

Thus, a distinct value-system to underpin international relations was brought into being and the law of nations was heralded as part of the universal law of nature.

---

[68] See e.g. G. Mattingley, *Renaissance Diplomacy*, London, 1955.

With the rise of the modern state and the emancipation of international relations, the doctrine of sovereignty emerged. This concept, first analysed systematically in 1576 in the *Six Livres de la République* by Jean Bodin, was intended to deal with the structure of authority within the modern state. Bodin, who based his study upon his perception of the politics of Europe rather than on a theoretical discussion of absolute principles, emphasised the necessity for a sovereign power within the state that would make the laws. While such a sovereign could not be bound by the laws he himself instituted, he was subject to the laws of God and of nature.[69]

The idea of the sovereign as supreme legislator was in the course of time transmuted into the principle which gave the state supreme power *vis-à-vis* other states. The state was regarded as being above the law. Such notions as these formed the intellectual basis of the line of thought known as positivism which will be discussed later.[70]

The early theorists of international law were deeply involved with the ideas of Natural Law and used them as the basis of their philosophies. Included within that complex of Natural Law principles from which they constructed their theories was the significant merging of Christian and Natural Law ideas that occurred in the philosophy of St Thomas Aquinas.[71] He maintained that Natural Law formed part of the law of God, and was the participation by rational creatures in the Eternal Law. It complemented that part of the Eternal Law which had been divinely revealed. Reason, declared Aquinas, was the essence of man and thus must be involved in the ordering of life according to the divine will. Natural Law was the fount of moral behaviour as well as of social and political institutions and it led to a theory of conditional acceptance of authority with unjust laws being unacceptable. Aquinas' views of the late thirteenth century can be regarded as basic to an understanding of present Catholic attitudes, but should not be confused with the later interpretation of Natural Law which stressed the concepts of natural rights.

It is with such an intellectual background that Renaissance scholars approached the question of the basis and justification of a system of international law. Maine, a British historical lawyer, wrote that the birth of modern international law was the grandest function of the law of nature and while that is arguable, the point must be taken.[72] International law began to emerge as a separate topic to be studied within itself, although derived from the principles of Natural Law.

---

[69] See Gardot, 'Jean Bodin – sa place parmi les fondateurs du droit international', 50 HR, p. 549. See also for a discussion of sovereignty and the treaty-making power in the late middle ages, T. Meron, 'The Authority to Make Treaties in the Late Middle Ages', 89 AJIL, 1995, p. 1.   [70] *Infra*, p. 21.   [71] *Summa Theologia*, English edn, 1927.
[72] H. Maine, *Ancient Law*, London, 1861, pp. 56 and 64–6.

The founders of modern international law

The essence of the new approach to international law can be traced back to the Spanish philosophers of that country's Golden Age.[73] The leading figure of this school was Francisco Vitoria, Professor of Theology at the University of Salamanca (1480–1546). His lectures were preserved by his students and published posthumously. He demonstrated a remarkably progressive attitude for his time towards the Spanish conquest of the South American Indians and contrary to the views prevalent until then, maintained that the Indian peoples should be regarded as nations with their own legitimate interests. War against them could only be justified on the grounds of a just cause. International law was founded on the universal law of nature and this meant that non-Europeans must be included within its ambit.

However, Vitoria by no means advocated the recognition of the Indian nations as equal to the Christian states of Europe. For him, opposing the work of the missionaries in the territories was a just reason for war, and he adopted a rather extensive view as to the rights of the Spaniards in South America. Vitoria was no liberal and indeed acted on behalf of the Spanish Inquisition, but his lectures did mark a step forward in the right direction.[74]

Suarez (1548–1617), was a Jesuit and Professor of Theology and deeply immersed in medieval culture. He noted that the obligatory character of international law was based upon Natural Law, while its substance derived from the Natural Law rule of carrying out agreements entered into.[75]

From a totally different background but equally, if not more, influential was Alberico Gentili (1552–1608). He was born in Northern Italy and fled to England to avoid persecution, having converted to Protestantism. In 1598 his *De Jure Belli* was published.[76] It is a comprehensive discussion of the law of war and contains a valuable section on the law of treaties. Gentili, who became a professor at Oxford, has been called the originator of the secular school of thought in international law and he minimised the hitherto significant theological theses.

It is, however, Hugo Grotius, a Dutch scholar, who towers over this period and has been celebrated, if a little exaggeratedly, as the father of inter-

---

[73] Note Preiser's view that '[t]here was hardly a single important problem of international law until the middle of the 17th century which was not principally a problem of Spain and the allied Habsburg countries': *Encyclopedia, Law of Nations*, p. 150. See also Nussbaum, *Law of Nations*, pp. 79–93.

[74] Nussbaum, *Law of Nations*, pp. 79–84 and *Encyclopedia*, pp. 151–2. See also Vitoria, *De Indis et de Jure Belli Relectiones*, Classics of International Law, 1917 and J. B. Scott, *The Spanish Origin of International Law, Francisco de Vitoria and his Law of Nations*, 1934.

[75] Nussbaum, *Law of Nations*, pp. 84–91. See also *ibid.*, pp. 92–3 regarding the work of Ayala (1548–84).

[76] *Ibid.*, pp. 94–101. See also A. Van der Molen, *Alberico Gentili and the Development of International Law*, 2nd edn, London, 1968.

national law. He was born in 1583 and was the supreme Renaissance man. A scholar of tremendous learning, he mastered history, theology, mathematics and the law.[77] His primary work was the *De Jure Belli ac Pacis*, written during 1623 and 1624. It is an extensive work and includes rather more devotion to the exposition of private law notions than would seem appropriate today. He refers both to Vitoria and Gentili and the latter was of special influence with regard to many matters, particularly organisation of material.

Grotius finally excised theology from international law and emphasised the irrelevance in such a study of any conception of a divine law. He remarked that the law of nature would be valid even if there were no God. A statement which, although suitably clothed in religious protestation, was extremely daring. The law of nature now reverted to being founded exclusively on reason. Justice was part of man's social make-up and thus not only useful but essential. Grotius conceived of a comprehensive system of international law and his work rapidly became a university textbook. However, in many spheres he followed well-trodden paths. He retained the theological distinction between a just and an unjust war, a notion that was soon to disappear from treatises on international law, but which in some way underpins modern approaches to aggression, self-defence and liberation.

One of his most enduring opinions consists in his proclamation of the freedom of the seas. The Dutch scholar opposed the 'closed seas' concept of the Portuguese that was later elucidated by the English writer John Selden[78] and emphasised instead the principle that the nations could not appropriate to themselves the high seas. They belonged to all. It must, of course, be mentioned, parenthetically, that this theory happened to accord rather nicely with prevailing Dutch ideas as to free trade and the needs of an expanding commercial empire.

However, this merely points up what must not be disregarded, namely that concepts of law as of politics and other disciplines are firmly rooted in the world of reality, and reflect contemporary preoccupations. No theory develops in a vacuum, but is conceived and brought to fruition in a definite cultural and social environment. To ignore this is to distort the theory itself.

Positivism and naturalism

Following Grotius, but by no means divorced from the thought of previous scholars, a split can be detected and two different schools identified. On the one hand the 'naturalist' school, exemplified by Samuel Pufendorf

---

[77] Nussbaum, *Law of Nations*, pp. 102–14. See also B. Knight, *The Life and Works of Hugo Grotius*, 1925 and *Commemoration of the Fourth Century of the Birth of Grotius* (various articles), 182 HR, pp. 371–470.   [78] In *Mare Clausum Sive de Dominio Maris*, 1635.

(1632–94)[79] who attempted to identify international law completely with the law of nature and on the other hand the exponents of 'positivism', who distinguished between international law and Natural Law and emphasised practical problems and current state practices. Pufendorf regarded Natural Law as a moralistic system, and misunderstood the direction of modern international law by denying the validity of the rules about custom. He also refused to acknowledge treaties as in any way relevant to a discussion of the basis of international law. Other 'naturalists' echoed those sentiments in minimising or ignoring the actual practices of states in favour of a theoretical construction of absolute values that seemed slowly to drift away from the complexities of political reality.

One of the principal initiators of the positivist school was Richard Zouche (1590–1660), who lived at the same time as Pufendorf, but in England.[80] While completely dismissing Natural Law he paid scant regard to the traditional doctrines. His concern was with specific situations and his book contains many examples from the recent past. He elevated the law of peace above a systematic consideration of the law of war and eschewed theoretical expositions.

In similar style Bynkershoek (1673–1743), stressed the importance of modern practice, and virtually ignored Natural Law. He made great contributions to the developing theories of the rights and duties of neutrals in war, and after careful studies of the relevant facts decided in favour of the freedom of the seas.[81]

The positivist approach, like much of modern thought, was derived from the empirical method adopted by the Renaissance. It was concerned not with an edifice of theory structured upon deductions from absolute principles, but rather with viewing events as they occurred and discussing actual problems that had arisen. Empiricism as formulated by Locke and Hume[82] denied the existence of innate principles and postulated that ideas were derived from experience. The scientific method of experiment and verification of hypotheses emphasised this approach.

From this philosophical attitude, it was a short step to reinterpreting international law in terms not of concepts derived from reason but rather in terms of what actually happened between the competing states. What states actually do was the key, not what states ought to do given basic rules of the law of nature. Agreements and customs recognised by the states were the essence of the law of nations.

Positivism developed as the modern nation-state system emerged, after the Peace of Westphalia in 1648, from the religious wars. It coincided, too,

---

[79] *On the Law of Nature and of Nations*, 1672. See also Nussbaum, *Law of Nations*, pp. 147–50.
[80] *Ibid.*, pp. 165–7.   [81] *Ibid.*, pp. 167–72.   [82] See Friedmann, *Legal Theory*, pp. 253–5.

with theories of sovereignty such as those propounded by Bodin and Hobbes,[83] which underlined the supreme power of the sovereign and led to notions of the sovereignty of states.

Elements of both positivism and naturalism appear in the works of Vattel (1714–67), a Swiss lawyer of the eighteenth century. His *Droit des Gens* was based on Natural Law principles yet practically orientated. He introduced the doctrine of the equality of states into international law, declaring that a small republic was no less of a sovereign than the most powerful kingdom, just as a dwarf was as much a man as a giant. By distinguishing between laws of conscience and laws of action and stating that only the latter were of practical concern, he minimised the importance of Natural Law.[84]

Ironically, at the same time that positivist thought appeared to demolish the philosophical basis of the law of nature and relegate that theory to history, it re-emerged in a modern guise replete with significance for the future. Natural Law gave way to the concept of natural rights.[85]

It was an individualistic assertion of political supremacy. The idea of the social contract, that an agreement between individuals pre-dated and justified civil society, emphasised the central role of the individual, and whether such a theory was interpreted pessimistically to demand an absolute sovereign as Hobbes declared, or optimistically to mean a conditional acceptance of authority as Locke maintained, it could not fail to be a revolutionary doctrine. The rights of man constitute the heart of the American[86] and French Revolutions and the essence of modern democratic society.

Yet, on the other hand, the doctrine of Natural Law has been employed to preserve the absoluteness of sovereignty and the sanctity of private possessions. The theory has a reactionary aspect because it could be argued that what was, ought to be, since it evolved from the social contract or was divinely ordained, depending upon how secular one construed the law of nature to be.

The nineteenth century

The eighteenth century was a ferment of intellectual ideas and rationalist philosophies that contributed to the evolution of the doctrine of international law. The nineteenth century by contrast was a practical, expansionist and positivist era. The Congress of Vienna, which marked the conclusion of

---

[83] *Leviathan*, 1651.

[84] See Nussbaum, *Law of Nations*, pp. 156–64. See also N. Onuf, '*Civitas Maxima*: Wolff, Vattel and the Fate of Republicanism', 88 AJIL, 1994, p. 280.

[85] See e.g. J. Finnis, *Natural Law and Natural Rights*, Oxford, 1980 and R. Tuck, *Natural Rights Theories*, Cambridge, 1979.

[86] See e.g. N. Onuf and O. Onuf, *Federal Unions, Modern World*, 1994.

the Napoleonic wars, enshrined the new international order which was to be based upon the European balance of power. International law became Eurocentric, the preserve of the civilised, Christian states, into which overseas and foreign nations could enter only with the consent of and on the conditions laid down by the Western powers. Paradoxically, whilst international law became geographically internationalised through the expansion of the European empires, it became less universalist in conception and more, theoretically as well as practically, a reflection of European values.[87]

There are many other features that mark the nineteenth century. Democracy and nationalism, both spurred on by the wars of the French revolution and empire, spread throughout the Continent and changed the essence of international relations.[88] No longer the exclusive concern of aristocratic élites, foreign policy characterised both the positive and negative faces of nationalism. Self-determination emerged to threaten the multinational empires of Central and Eastern Europe, while nationalism reached its peak in the unifications of Germany and Italy and began to exhibit features such as expansionism and doctrines of racial superiority. Democracy brought to the individual political influence and a say in government. It also brought home the realities of responsibility, for wars became the concern of all.

Conscription was introduced throughout the Continent and large national armies replaced the small professional forces.[89] The Industrial Revolution mechanised Europe, created the economic dichotomy of capital and labour and propelled Western influence throughout the world. All these factors created an enormous increase in the number and variety of both public and private international institutions, and international law grew rapidly to accommodate them.[90]

European conferences proliferated and contributed greatly to the development of rules governing the waging of war. The International Committee of the Red Cross, founded in 1863, helped promote the series of Geneva Conventions beginning in 1864 dealing with the 'humanisation' of conflict, and the Hague Conferences of 1899 and 1907 established the Permanent Court of Arbitration and dealt with the treatment of prisoners and the control of warfare.[91] Numerous other conferences, conventions and congresses emphasised the expansion of the rules of international law and the close network of international relations.

Positivist theories dominate this century. The proliferation of the powers

[87] See Nussbaum, *Law of Nations*, pp. 186–250 and, e.g. C. H. Alexandrowicz, *The European-African Confrontation*, Leiden, 1973.
[88] See especially A. Cobban, *The Nation State and National Self-Determination*, London, 1969.
[89] G. Best, *Humanity in Warfare*, London, 1980 and Best, *War and Law Since 1945*, Oxford, 1994, and S. Bailey, *Prohibitions and Restraints in War*, Oxford, 1972.
[90] See e.g. D. W. Bowett, *Law of International Institutions*, and *The Evolution of International Organisations* (ed. E. Luard), Oxford, 1966.   [91] See further *infra*, Chapter 19, p. 806.

of states and the increasing sophistication of municipal legislation gave force to the idea that laws were basically commands issuing from a sovereign person or body. Any question of ethics or morality was irrelevant to a discussion of the validity of man-made laws. The approach was transferred onto the international scene and immediately came face to face with the reality of a lack of supreme authority.

Since law was ultimately dependent upon the will of the sovereign in national systems, it seemed to follow that international law depended upon the will of the sovereign states.

This implied a confusion of the supreme legislator within a state with the state itself and thus positivism had to accept the metaphysical identity of the state. The state had a life and will of its own and so was able to dominate international law. This stress on the abstract nature of the state did not appear in all positivist theories and was a late development.[92]

It was the German thinker Hegel who first analysed and proposed the doctrine of the will of the state. The individual was subordinate to the state, because the latter enshrined the 'wills' of all citizens and had evolved into a higher will, and on the external scene the state was sovereign and supreme.[93] Such philosophies led to disturbing results in the twentieth century and provoked a reawakening of the law of nature, dormant throughout the nineteenth century.

The growth of international agreements, customs and regulations induced positivist theorists to tackle this problem of international law and the state; and as a result two schools of thought emerged.

The monists claimed that there was one fundamental principle which underlay both national and international law. This was variously posited as 'right' or social solidarity or the rule that agreements must be carried out (*pacta sunt servanda*). The dualists, more numerous and in a more truly positivist frame of mind, emphasised the element of consent.

For Triepel, another German theorist, international law and domestic (or municipal) law existed on separate planes, the former governing international relations, the latter relations between individuals and between the individual and the state. International law was based upon agreements between states (and such agreements included, according to Triepel, both treaties and customs) and because it was dictated by the 'common will' of the states it could not be unilaterally altered.[94]

This led to a paradox. Could this common will bind individual states and, if so, why? It would appear to lead to the conclusion that the will of the sovereign state could give birth to a rule over which it had no control.

[92] See *infra*, Chapter 2.
[93] See e.g. S. Avineri, *Hegel's Theory of the Modern State*, London, 1972, and Friedmann, *Legal Theory*, pp. 164–76.   [94] *Ibid.*, pp. 576–7. See also *infra*, Chapter 4.

The state will was not, therefore, supreme but inferior to a collection of states' wills. Triepel did not discuss these points, but left them open as depending upon legal matters. Thus did positivist theories weaken their own positivist outlook by regarding the essence of law as beyond juridical description. The nineteenth century also saw the publication of numerous works on international law, which emphasised state practice and the importance of the behaviour of countries to the development of rules of international law.[95]

The twentieth century

The First World War marked the close of a dynamic and optimistic century. European empires ruled the world and European ideologies reigned supreme, but the 1914–18 Great War undermined the foundations of European civilisation. Self-confidence faded, if slowly, the edifice weakened and the universally accepted assumptions of progress were increasingly doubted. Self-questioning was the order of the day and law as well as art reflected this.

The most important legacy of the 1919 Peace Treaty from the point of view of international relations was the creation of the League of Nations.[96] The old anarchic system had failed and it was felt that new institutions to preserve and secure peace were necessary. The League consisted of an Assembly and an executive Council, but was crippled from the start by the absence of the United States and the Soviet Union for most of its life and remained a basically European organisation.

While it did have certain minor successes with regard to the maintenance of international order, it failed when confronted with determined aggressors. Japan invaded China in 1931 and two years later withdrew from the League. Italy attacked Ethiopia and Germany embarked unhindered upon a series of internal and external aggressions. The Soviet Union, in a final forlorn gesture, was expelled from the organisation in 1939 following its invasion of Finland.

Nevertheless, much useful groundwork was achieved by the League in its short existence and this helped to consolidate the United Nations later on.[97]

The Permanent Court of International Justice was set up in 1921 at The Hague to be succeeded in 1946 by the International Court of Justice; the International Labour Organisation was established soon after the end of the

---

[95] See e.g. H. Wheaton, *Elements of International Law*, New York, 1836; W. E. Hall, *A Treatise on International Law*, Oxford, 1880; Von Martens, *Völkerrecht*, 2 vols., 1883–6; Pradier-Fodéré, *Traité de Droit International Public*, 8 vols., 1855–1906; and Fiore, *Il Diritto Internazionale Codificato e la Sua Sanzione Giuridica*, 1890.
[96] See Nussbaum, *Law of Nations*, pp. 251–90 and *infra*, Chapter 21.
[97] See also G. Scott, *The Rise and Fall of the League of Nations*, London, 1973.

First World War and it still exists today, and many other international institutions were inaugurated or increased their work during this period.

Other ideas of international law that first appeared between the wars included the system of mandates, by which colonies of the defeated powers were administered by the Allies for the benefit of their inhabitants rather than being annexed outright, and an attempt made to provide a form of minority protection guaranteed by the League. This latter creation was not a great success but it paved the way for later concern to secure human rights.[98]

After the trauma of the Second World War the League was succeeded in 1946 by the United Nations Organisation, which tried to remedy many of the defects of its predecessor. It established its site at New York, reflecting the realities of the shift of power away from Europe, and determined to become a truly universal institution. The advent of decolonisation fulfilled this expectation and the General Assembly of the United Nations today has 160 member states.

Many of the trends which first came into prominence in the nineteenth century have continued to this day. The vast increase in the number of international agreements and customs, the strengthening of the system of arbitration and the development of international organisations have established the essence of international law as it exists today.

Communist approaches to international law

Classic Marxist theory described law and politics as the means whereby the ruling classes maintained their domination of society. The essence of economic life was the ownership of the means of production, and all power flowed from this control. Capital and labour were the opposing theses and their mutual antagonism would eventually lead to a revolution out of which a new, nonexploitive form of society would emerge.[99] National states were dominated by the capitalist class and would have to disappear in the reorganising process. Indeed, the theory was that law and the state would wither away once a new basis for society had been established[100] and because classical international law was founded upon the state, it followed that it too would go.

However, the reality of power and the existence of the USSR surrounded by capitalist nations led to a modification in this approach. The international system of states could not be changed overnight into a socialist order, so a period of transition was inevitable. Nevertheless, basic changes were seen as having been wrought.

---

[98] *Infra*, Chapter 6.
[99] See Lloyd, *Jurisprudence*, Chapter 10 and Friedmann, *Legal Theory*, Chapter 29.
[100] Engels, *Anti-Duhring*, quoted in Lloyd, *Jurisprudence*, pp. 773–4.

Professor Tunkin, for example, emphasised that the Russian October revolution produced a new series of international legal ideas. These, it is noted, can be divided into three basic, interconnected groups: (a) principles of socialist internationalism in relations between socialist states; (b) principles of equality and self-determination of nations and peoples, primarily aimed against colonialism; and (c) principles of peaceful co-existence aimed at relations between states with different social systems.[101]

We shall briefly look at these concepts in this section, but first an historical overview is necessary.

During the immediate post-revolution period, it was postulated that a transitional phase had commenced. During this time, international law as a method of exploitation would be criticised by the socialist state, but it would still be recognised as a valid system. The two Soviet theorists Korovin and Pashukanis were the dominant influences in this phase. The transitional period demanded compromises, in that until the universal victory of the revolution some forms of economic and technical co-operation would be required since they were fundamental for the existence of the international social order.[102] Pashukanis expressed the view that international law was an interclass law within which two antagonistic class systems would seek accommodation until the victory of the socialist system. Socialism and the Soviet Union could still use the legal institutions developed by and reflective of the capitalist system.[103] However, with the rise of Stalinism and the 'socialism in one country' call, the position hardened. Pashukanis altered his line and recanted. International law was not a form of temporary compromise between capitalist states and the USSR but rather a means of conducting the class war. The Soviet Union was bound only by those rules of international law which accorded with its purposes.[104]

The new approach in the late 1930s was reflected politically in Russia's successful attempt to join the League of Nations and its policy of wooing the Western powers, and legally by the ideas of Vyshinski. He adopted a more legalistic view of international law and emphasised the Soviet acceptance of such principles as national self-determination, state sovereignty and the equality of states, but not others. The role of international law did not constitute a single international legal system binding all states. The Soviet Union would act in pursuance of Leninist–Stalinist foreign policy ideals and

[101] *Theory of International Law*, London, 1974, p. 4 and *International Law* (ed. G. I. Tunkin), Moscow, 1986, Chapter 3 . See also B. S. Chimni, *International Law and World Order*, New Delhi, 1993, Chapter 5; K. Grzybowski, *Soviet Public International Law*, Leyden, 1970, especially Chapter 1, and generally H. Baade, *The Soviet Impact on International Law*, Leyden, 1964 and Friedmann, *Legal Theory*, pp. 327–40.

[102] Tunkin, *International Law*, p. 5.

[103] *Ibid.*, pp. 5–6. See also H. Babb and J. Hazard, *Soviet Legal Philosophy*, Cambridge, MA, 1951.   [104] Grzybowski, *Soviet Public International Law*, pp. 6–9.

would not be bound by the rules to which it had not given express consent.[105]

The years that followed the Second World War saw a tightening up of Soviet doctrine as the Cold War gathered pace, but with the death of Stalin and the succession of Khrushchev a thaw set in. In theoretical terms the law of the transitional stage was replaced by the international law of peaceful co-existence. War was no longer regarded as inevitable between capitalist and socialist countries and a period of mutual tolerance and co-operation was inaugurated.[106]

Tunkin recognised that there was a single system of international law of universal scope rather than different branches covering socialist and capitalist countries, and that international law was founded upon agreements between states which are binding upon them. He defined contemporary general international law as:

> the aggregate of norms which are created by agreement between states of different social systems, reflect the concordant wills of states and have a generally democratic character, regulate relations between them in the process of struggle and co-operation in the direction of ensuring peace and peaceful co-existence and freedom and independence of peoples, and are secured when necessary by coercion effectuated by states individually or collectively.[107]

It is interesting to note the basic elements here, such as the stress on state sovereignty, the recognition of different social systems and the aim of peaceful co-existence. The role of sanctions in law is emphasised and reflects much of the positivist influence upon Soviet thought. Such preoccupations were also reflected in the definition of international law contained in the leading Soviet textbook by Professor Kozhevnikov where it was stated that:

> international law can be defined as the aggregate of rules governing relations between states in the process of their conflict and co-operation, designed to safeguard their peaceful co-existence, expressing the will of the ruling classes of these states and defended in case of need by coercion applied by states individually or collectively.[108]

Originally, treaties alone were regarded as proper sources of international law but custom became accepted as a kind of tacit or implied agreement with great stress laid upon *opinio juris* or the legally binding element of custom. While state practice need not be general to create a custom, its recognition as a legal form must be.[109]

---

[105] *Ibid.*, p. 9.

[106] *Ibid.*, pp. 16–22. See also R. Higgins, *Conflict of Interests*, London, 1964, Part III.

[107] *Theory of International Law*, p. 251. See also G. I. Tunkin, 'Co-existence and International Law', 95 HR, pp. 1, 51 *et seq.* and E. McWhinney, 'Contemporary Soviet General Theory of International Law: Reflections on the Tunkin Era', 25 Canadian YIL, 1989, p. 187.

[108] *International Law*, 1961.

[109] *Theory of International Law*, p. 118. See also G. I. Tunkin, 'The Contemporary Soviet Theory of International Law', *Current Legal Problems*, London, 1978, p. 177.

Peaceful co-existence itself rested upon certain basic concepts, for example, non-intervention in the internal affairs of other states and the sovereignty of states. Any idea of a world authority was condemned as a violation of the latter principle. The doctrine of peaceful co-existence was also held to include such ideas as good neighbourliness, international co-operation and the observance in good faith of international obligations.

The concept was regarded as based on specific trends of laws of societal development and as a specific form of class struggle between socialism and capitalism, one in which armed conflict is precluded.[110] It was an attempt, in essence, to reiterate the basic concepts of international law in a way that was taken to reflect an ideological trend. But it must be emphasised that the principles themselves have long been accepted by the international community.

While Tunkin at first attacked the development of regional systems of international law, he later came around to accepting a socialist law which reflected the special relationship between communist countries. The Soviet interventions in Eastern Europe, particularly in Czechoslovakia in 1968, played a large part in augmenting such views.[111] In the Soviet view relations between socialist (communist) states represented a new, higher type of international relations and a socialist international law. Common socio-economic factors and a political community created an objective basis for lasting friendly relations, whereas, by contrast, international capitalism involved the exploitation of the weak by the strong. The principles of socialist or proletarian internationalism constituted a unified system of international legal principles between countries of the socialist bloc arising by way of custom and treaty. Although the basic principles of respect for state sovereignty, non-interference in internal affairs and equality of states and peoples existed in general international law, the same principles in socialist international law were made more positive by the lack of economic rivalry and exploitation and by increased co-operation. Accordingly, these principles incorporated not only material obligations not to violate each other's rights, but also the duty to assist each other in enjoying and defending such rights against capitalist threats.[112]

The Soviet emphasis on territorial integrity and sovereignty, while designed in practice to protect the socialist states in a predominantly capitalist environment, proved of great attraction to the developing nations of the Third World, anxious too to establish their own national identities and counteract Western financial and cultural influences.

---

[110] Tunkin, 'Soviet Theory', pp. 35–48. See also F. Vallat, 'International Law – A Forward Look', 18 YBWA, 1964, p. 251; J. Hazard, 'Codifying Peaceful Co-existence', 55 AJIL, 1961, pp. 111–12; E. McWhinney, *Peaceful Co-existence and Soviet-Western International Law*, 1964 and K. Grzybowski, 'Soviet Theory of International Law for the Seventies', 77 AJIL, 1983, p. 862. [111] See Grzybowski, *Soviet Public International Law*, pp. 16–22.
[112] Tunkin, *Theory*, pp. 431–43.

With the decline of the Cold War and the onset of *perestroika* (restructuring) in the Soviet Union, a process of re-evaluation in the field of international legal theory took place.[113] The concept of peaceful co-existence was modified and the notion of class warfare eliminated from the Soviet political lexicon. Global interdependence and the necessity for international co-operation were emphasised, as it was accepted that the tension between capitalism and socialism no longer constituted the major conflict in the contemporary world and that beneath the former dogmas lay many common interests.[114] The essence of new Soviet thinking was stated to lie in the priority of universal human values and the resolution of global problems, which is directly linked to the growing importance of international law in the world community. It was also pointed out that international law had to be universal and not artificially divided into capitalist, socialist and Third World 'international law' systems.[115]

Soviet writers and political leaders accepted that activities such as the interventions in Czechoslovakia in 1968 and Afghanistan in 1979 were contrary to international law, while the attempt to create a state based on the rule of law was seen as requiring the strengthening of the international legal system and the rule of law in international relations. In particular, a renewed emphasis upon the role of the United Nations became evident in Soviet policy.[116]

The dissolution of the Soviet Union in 1991 marked the end of the Cold War and the re-emergence of a system of international relations based upon multiple sources of power untrammelled by ideological determinacy. From that point,[117] Russia as the continuation of the former Soviet Union (albeit in different political and territorial terms) entered into the Western political system and defined its actions in terms of its own national interests free from principled hostility. The return to statehood of the Baltic states and the independence of the other former republics of the Soviet Union, coupled with the collapse of Yugoslavia, has constituted a political upheaval of major significance. The Cold War had imposed a dualistic superstructure upon international relations that had had implications for virtually all serious international political disputes and had fettered the operations of the United Nations in particular. Although the Soviet regime had been changing its

---

[113] See, e.g. *Perestroika and International Law* (eds. A. Carty and G. Danilenko), 1990; R. Mullerson, 'Sources of International Law: New Tendencies in Soviet Thinking', 83 *AJIL*, 1989, p. 494; V. Vereshchetin and R. Mullerson, 'International Law in an Interdependent World', 28 *Columbia Journal of Transnational Law*, 1990, p. 291 and R. Quigley, '*Perestroika* and International Law', 82 AJIL, 1988, p. 788.

[114] Vereschetin and Mullerson, *International Law*, p. 292.   [115] *Ibid.*

[116] See Quigley, '*Perestroika*', p. 794.

[117] See e.g. R. Mullerson, *International Law, Rights and Politics*, London, 1994. See also *The End of the Cold War* (eds. P. Allan and K. Goldmann), Dordrecht, 1992 and W. M. Reisman, 'International Law after the Cold War', 84 *AJIL*, 1990, p. 859.

approach quite significantly, the formal demise both of the communist system and of the state itself altered the nature of the international system and this inevitably has had consequences for international law.[118] The ending of inexorable superpower confrontation has led to an increase in instability in Europe and emphasised paradoxically both the revitalisation and the limitations of the United Nations.

While relatively little has been known previously of Chinese attitudes a few points can be made. Western concepts are regarded primarily as aimed at preserving the dominance of the bourgeois class on the international scene. Soviet views were partially accepted but since the late 1950s and the growing estrangement between the two major communist powers, the Chinese concluded that the Russians were interested chiefly in maintaining the *status quo* and Soviet–American superpower supremacy. The Soviet concept of peaceful co-existence as the mainstay of contemporary international law was treated with particular suspicion and disdain.[119]

The Chinese conception of law was, for historical and cultural reasons, very different from that developed in the West. 'Law' never attained the important place in Chinese society that it did in European civilisation.[120] A sophisticated bureaucracy laboured to attain harmony and equilibrium and a system of legal rights to protect the individual in the Western sense did not really develop. It was believed that society would be best served by example and established morality, rather than by rules and sanctions. This Confucian philosophy, however, was swept aside after the successful communist revolution, to be replaced by strict Marxism–Leninism, with its emphasis on class warfare.[121]

The Chinese seem to have recognised several systems of international law, for example, Western, socialist, and revisionist (Soviet Union) and to have implied that only with the ultimate spread of socialism would a universal system be possible.[122] International agreements are regarded as the primary source of international law and China has entered into many treaties and conventions and carried them out as well as other nations.[123] One exception,

---

[118] See e.g. R. Bilder, 'International Law in the "New World Order": Some Preliminary Reflections', 1 *Florida State University Journal of Transnational Law and Policy*, 1992, p. 1.

[119] See H. Chiu, 'Communist China's Attitude towards International Law', 60 AJIL, 1966, p. 245; J. K. Fairbank, *The Chinese World Order*, Cambridge, 1968; J. Cohen, *China's Practice of International Law*, Princeton, 1972; Anglo-Chinese Educational Trust, *China's World View*, 1979; J. Cohen and H. Chiu, *People's China and International Law*, 2 vols., Princeton, 1974, and C. Kim, 'The People's Republic of China and the Charter-based International Legal Order' 72 AJIL, 1978, p. 317.

[120] See Lloyd, *Jurisprudence*, pp. 760–3; S. Van der Sprenkel, *Legal Institutions in Northern China*, New York, 1962 and R. Unger, *Law in Modern Society*, New York, 1976, pp. 86–109.

[121] Lloyd, *Jurisprudence*, and H. Li, 'The Role of Law in Communist China', *China Quarterly*, 1970, p. 66 cited in Lloyd, *Jurisprudence*, pp. 801–8.

[122] See e.g. Cohen and Chiu, *People's China*, pp. 62–64.

[123] *Ibid.*, pp. 77–82, and Part VIII generally.

of course, is China's disavowal of the so-called 'unequal treaties' whereby Chinese territory was annexed by other powers, in particular the Tsarist Empire, in the nineteenth century.[124]

On the whole, international law has been treated as part of international politics and subject to considerations of power and expediency, as well as ideology. Where international rules conform with Chinese policies and interests, then they will be observed. Where they do not, they will be ignored.

However, now that the isolationist phase of its history appears to be over, relations with other nations established and its entry into the United Nations secured, communist China appears to be adopting a more cautious approach in international relations. This appears to have led to a legalisation of its view of international law as occurred with the Soviet Union, and as China seeks in a multipower world to increase its influence and power.

The Third World

In the evolution of international affairs since the Second World War one of the most decisive events has been the disintegration of the colonial empires and the birth of scores of new states in the so-called Third World. This has thrust onto the scene states which carry with them a legacy of bitterness over their past status as well as a host of problems relating to their social, economic and political development.[125] In such circumstances it was only natural that the structure and doctrines of international law would come under attack. The nineteenth-century development of the law of nations founded upon Eurocentrism and imbued with the values of Christian, urbanised and expanding Europe[126] did not, understandably enough, reflect the needs and interests of the newly independent states of the mid and late twentieth century. It was felt that such rules had encouraged and then reflected their subjugation, and that changes were required.[127]

It is basically those ideas of international law that came to fruition in the

---

[124] See e.g. I. Detter, 'The Problem of Unequal Treaties', 15 ICLQ 1966, p. 1069; Nozari, *Unequal Treaties in International Law*, 1971; Chiu, 'Communist China's Attitude', pp. 239–67 and Chen, *State Succession Relating to Unequal Treaties*, 1974.

[125] See e.g. R. P. Anand, 'Attitude of the Afro-Asian States Towards Certain Problems of International Law', 15 ICLQ, 1966, p. 35; T. O. Elias, *New Horizons in International Law*, Leiden, 1980 and Higgins, *Conflict of Interests*, Part II. See also Hague Academy of International Law, Colloque, *The Future of International Law in a Multicultural World*, especially pp. 117–42 and Henkin, *How Nations Behave*, pp. 121–7.

[126] See e.g. Verzijl, *International Law in Historical Perspective*, vol. I, pp. 435–6. See also B. Roling, *International Law in an Expanded World*, Leiden, 1960, p. 10.

[127] The converse of this has been the view of some writers that the universalisation of international law has led to a dilution of its content, see e.g. Friedmann, p. 6; J. Stone, *Quest for Survival: The Role of Law and Foreign Policy*, 1961, p. 88 and J. Brierly, *The Law of Nations*, 6th edn, Oxford, p. 43.

last century that have been so clearly rejected, that is, those principles that enshrined the power and domination of the West.[128] The underlying concepts of international law have not been discarded. On the contrary; the new nations have eagerly embraced the ideas of the sovereignty and equality of states and the principles of non-aggression and non-intervention, in their search for security within the bounds of a commonly accepted legal framework.

While this new internationalisation of international law that has occurred in the last twenty years has destroyed its European-based homogeneity, it has emphasised its universalist scope.[129] The composition of, for example, both the International Court of Justice and the Security Council of the United Nations mirrors such developments. Article 9 of the Statute of the International Court of Justice points out that the main forms of civilisation and the principal legal systems of the world must be represented within the Court, and there is an arrangement that of the ten non-permanent seats in the Security Council five should go to Afro-Asian states and two to Latin American states (the others going to Europe and other states). The composition of the International Law Commission has also recently been increased and structured upon geographic lines.[130]

The influence of the new states has been felt most of all within the General Assembly, where they constitute a majority of the 185 member states.[131] The content and scope of the various resolutions and declarations emanating from the Assembly are proof of their impact and contain a record of their fears, hopes and concerns.

The Declaration on the Granting of Independence to Colonial Countries and Peoples of 1960, for example, enshrined the right of colonies to obtain their sovereignty with the least possible delay and called for the recognition of the principle of self-determination. This principle, which is discussed elsewhere in this book,[132] is regarded by most authorities as a settled rule of international law although with undetermined borders. Nevertheless, it symbolises the rise of the post-colonial states and the effect they are having upon the development of international law.

Their concern for the recognition of the sovereignty of states is complemented by their support of the United Nations and its Charter and supplemented by their desire for 'economic self-determination' or the right of permanent sovereignty over natural resources.[133] This expansion of international law into the field of economics is a major development of this century

---

[128] See e.g. Alexandrowicz, *European-African Confrontation*.

[129] See F. C. Okoye, *International Law and the New African States*, London, 1972; T. O. Elias, *Africa and the Development of International Law*, Leiden, 1972 and *Encyclopedia of Public International Law*, vol. VII, 1984, pp. 205–51.

[130] By General Assembly resolution 36/39, twenty-one of the thirty-four members are to be nationals of Afro-Asian-Latin American states.   [131] As of autumn 1996.

[132] See *infra*, Chapter 5, p. 177.   [133] See *infra*, Chapter 14, p. 577.

and is evidenced in myriad ways, for example, by the creation of the General Agreement on Tariffs and Trade, the United Nations Conferences on Trade and Development, and the establishment of the International Monetary Fund and World Bank.

The interests of the new states of the non-Western, non-communist Third World are often in conflict with those of the industrialised nations, witness disputes over nationalisations. But it has to be emphasised that, contrary to many fears expressed in the early years of the decolonisation saga, international law has not been discarded nor altered beyond recognition. Its framework has been retained as the new states, too, wish to obtain the benefits of rules such as those governing diplomatic relations and the controlled use of force, while campaigning against rules which run counter to their perceived interests.

While the new countries share a common history of foreign dominance and underdevelopment, compounded by an awakening of national identity, it has to be recognised that they are not a homogenous group. Widely differing cultural, social and economic attitudes and stages of development characterise them and the rubric of the 'Third World' masks diverse political affiliations. On many issues the interests of the new states conflict with each other and this is reflected in the different positions adopted. The states possessing oil and other valuable natural resources are separated from those with few or none and the states bordering on oceans are to be distinguished from land-locked states. The list of diversity is endless and variety governs the make-up of the southern hemisphere to a far greater degree than in the north.

It is possible that in legal terms tangible differences in approach may emerge in the future as the passions of decolonisation die down and the Western supremacy over international law is further eroded. This trend will also permit a greater understanding of, and greater recourse to, historical traditions and conceptions that pre-date colonisation and an increasing awareness of their validity for the future development of international law.[134]

In the medium term, however, it has to be recognised that with the end of the Cold War and the rapid development of Soviet (then Russian)–American co-operation, the axis of dispute is turning from East–West to North–South. This is beginning to manifest itself in a variety of issues ranging from economic law to the law of the sea and human rights, while the impact of modern technology has hardly yet been appreciated.[135]

---

[134] See e.g. H. Sarin, 'The Asian-African States and the Development of International Law', in Hague Academy Colloque, p. 117; *Encyclopedia*, vol. VII, pp. 205–51 and R. Westbrook, 'Islamic International Law and Public International Law: Separate Expressions of World Order', 33 Va JIL, 1993, p. 819. See also C. W. Jenks, *The Common Law of Mankind*, Oxford, 1958, p. 169 and Cassese, *International Law*, pp. 64 *et seq.*

[135] See e.g. M. Lachs, 'Thoughts on Science, Technology and World Law', 86 *AJIL*, 1992, p. 673.

CHAPTER 2

INTERNATIONAL LAW TODAY

The expanding legal scope of international concern

International law in the second half of the twentieth century has been developing in many directions, as the complexities of life in the modern era have multiplied. For, as already emphasised, law reflects the conditions and cultural traditions of the society within which it operates. The community evolves a certain specific set of values, social, economic and political, and this stamps its mark on the legal framework which orders life in that environment. Similarly, international law is a product of its environment. It has developed in accordance with the prevailing notions of international relations and to survive it must be in harmony with the realities of the age.

Nevertheless, there is a continuing tension between those rules already established and the constantly evolving forces that seek changes within the system. One of the major problems of international law is to determine when and how to incorporate new standards of behaviour and new realities of life into the already existing framework, so that, on the one hand the law remains relevant and on the other, the system itself is not too vigorously disrupted.

Changes that occur within the international community can be momentous and reverberate throughout the system. For example, the advent of nuclear arms created a status quo in Europe and a balance of terror throughout the world. It currently constitutes a factor of unease as certain states seek to acquire nuclear technology. Another example is the technological capacity to mine the oceans and the consequent questions as to the nature and beneficiaries of exploitation.[1] There are several instances of how modern developments demand a constant reappraisal of the structure of international law and its rules.

The scope of international law today is immense. From the regulation of space expeditions to the question of the division of the ocean floor, and from the protection of human rights to the management of the international financial system, its involvement has spread out from the primary concern

---

[1] See *infra*, Chapter 11.

with the preservation of peace, to embrace all the interests of contemporary international life.

But the *raison d'être* of international law and the determining factor in its composition remains the needs and characteristics of the international political system. Where more than one entity exists within a system, there has to be some conception as to how to deal with other such entities, whether it be on the basis of co-existence or hostility. International law as it has developed since the seventeenth century has adopted the same approach and has in general (though with notable exceptions) eschewed the idea of permanent hostility and enmity. Because the state, while internally supreme, wishes to maintain its sovereignty externally and needs to cultivate other states in an increasingly interdependent world, so it must acknowledge the rights of others. This acceptance of rights possessed by all states, something unavoidable in a world where none can stand alone, leads inevitably on to a system to regulate and define such rights and, of course, obligations.

And so one arrives at some form of international legal order, no matter how unsophisticated and how occasionally positively disorderly.[2] The current system developed in the context of European civilisation as it progressed, but this is changing. The rise of the United States and the Soviet Union mirrored the decline of Europe, while the process of decolonisation is also making a considerable impact.

This means that international law, faced with radical changes in the world structure of power, has had to come to terms with new ideas that could no longer be ignored.

The Eurocentric character of international law has been gravely weakened in the last sixty years or so and the opinions, hopes and needs of other cultures and civilisations are beginning to play an increasing role in the evolution of world juridical thought.[3]

International law reflects first and foremost the basic state-oriented character of world politics. Units of formal independence benefiting from equal sovereignty in law and equal possession of the basic attributes of statehood[4] have succeeded in creating a system enshrining such values. Examples that could be noted here include non-intervention in internal affairs, territorial integrity, non-use of force and equality of voting in the United Nations General Assembly. In addition to this, many factors cut across state borders and create tension in world politics, such as inadequate economic relationships, international concern for human rights and the rise in new

---

[2] For views as to the precise definition and characteristics of the international order or system or community, see G. Schwarzenberger and E. D. Brown, *A Manual of International Law*, 6th edn, London, 1976, pp. 9–12; H. Yalem, 'The Concept of World Order', 29 YBWA, 1975 and I. Pogany, 'The Legal Foundations of World Order', *ibid.*, 1983, p. 277.

[3] See e.g. L. C. Green, 'Is There a Universal International Law Today?', 23 Canadian YIL, 1985, p. 3.   [4] See *infra*, Chapter 5, p. 152.

technological forces.[5] State policies and balances of power, both international and regional, are a necessary framework within which international law operates, as indeed are domestic political conditions and tensions. Law mirrors the concern of forces within states and between states.

It is also important to realise that states need law in order to seek and attain certain goals, whether these be economic well-being, survival and security or ideological advancement. The system therefore has to be certain enough for such goals to be ascertainable, and flexible enough to permit change when this becomes necessary due to the confluence of forces demanding it.[6]

International law, however, has not just expanded horizontally to embrace the new states which have been established relatively recently; it has extended itself to include individuals, groups and international organisations within its scope. It has also moved into new fields covering such issues as international trade, problems of environmental protection and outer space exploration.

The growth of positivism in the nineteenth century had the effect of focusing the concerns of international law upon sovereign states. They alone were the 'subjects' of international law and were to be contrasted with the status of non-independent states and individuals as 'objects' of international law. But the gradual sophistication of positivist doctrine, combined with the advent of new approaches to the whole system of international relations, has broken down this exclusive emphasis and extended the roles played by non-state entities, such as individuals, multinational firms and international institutions.[7] It was, of course, long recognised that individuals were entitled to the benefits of international law, but it is only recently that they have been able to act directly rather than rely upon their national states.

The Nuremberg and Tokyo Tribunals set up by the victorious Allies after the close of the Second World War were a vital part of this process. Many of those accused were found guilty of crimes against humanity and against peace and were punished accordingly. It was a recognition of individual responsibility under international law without the usual interposition of the state. Similarly the 1948 Genocide Convention provided for the punishment of offenders after conviction by national courts or by an international criminal tribunal.[8] The developing concern with human rights is another aspect of this move towards increasing the role of the individual in international law. The Universal Declaration of Human Rights adopted by the United Nations in 1948 lists a series of political and social rights, although it is only a guideline and not legally binding as such. The European Convention for

---

[5] For examples of this in the context of the law relating to territory, see M. N. Shaw, *Title to Territory in Africa: International Legal Issues*, Oxford, 1986, pp. 1–11.
[6] See S. Hoffman, 'International Systems and International Law', 14 *World Politics*, 1961–2, p. 205.   [7] See further *infra*, Chapter 5, p. 182.   [8] *Ibid.*

the Protection of Human Rights and Fundamental Freedoms signed in 1950 and the International Covenants on Human Rights of 1966 are of a different nature and binding upon the signatories. In an effort to function satisfactorily various bodies of a supervisory and implementational nature were established. Within the European Union, individuals and corporations have certain rights of direct appeal to the European Court of Justice against decisions of the various Union institutions. In addition, individuals may appear before certain international tribunals. Nevertheless, the whole subject has been highly controversial, with some writers (for example, Soviet theorists prior to *perestroika*) denying that individuals may have rights as distinct from duties under international law, but it is indicative of the trend away from the exclusivity of the state.[9]

International organisations have now been accepted as possessing rights and duties of their own and a distinctive legal personality. The International Court of Justice in 1949 delivered an Advisory Opinion[10] in which it stated that the United Nations was a subject of international law and could enforce its rights by bringing international claims, in this case against Israel following the assassination of Count Bernadotte, a United Nations official. Such a ruling can be applied to embrace other international institutions, like the International Labour Organisation and the Food and Agriculture Organisation, which all have a judicial character of their own. Thus, while states remain the primary subjects of international law, they are now joined by other non-state entities, whose importance is likely to grow in the future. The growth of regional organisations should also be noted at this stage. Many of those were created for reasons of military security, for example NATO and the opposing Warsaw Pact organisations, others as an expression of regional and cultural identity such as the Organisation of African Unity and the Organisation of American States. In a class of its own is the European Union which has gone far down the road of economic co-ordination and standardisation and has a range of common institutions serviced by a growing bureaucracy stationed primarily at Brussels.

Such regional organisations have added to the developing sophistication of international law by the insertion of 'regional-international law subsystems' within the universal framework and the consequent evolution of rules that bind only member states.[11]

The range of topics covered by international law has expanded hand in hand with the upsurge in difficulties faced and the proliferation in the number of participants within the system. It is no longer exclusively concerned with issues relating to the territory or jurisdiction of states

---

[9] See further *infra*, Chapter 6.
[10] *Reparation for Injuries Suffered in the Service of the United Nations*, ICJ Reports, 1949, p. 174; 16 ILR, p. 318.   [11] See generally *infra*, Chapter 21.

narrowly understood, but is beginning to take into account the specialised problems of contemporary society. Many of these have already been referred to, such as the vital field of human rights, the growth of an international economic law covering financial and development matters, concern with environmental despoliation, the space exploration effort and the exploitation of the resources of the oceans and deep sea-bed. One can mention also provisions relating to the bureaucracy of international institutions (international administrative law), international labour standards, health regulations and communications controls.

Modern theories and interpretations

At this point some modern theories as to the nature and role of international law will be briefly noted.

Positive Law and Natural Law

Throughout the history of thought there has been a complex relationship between idealism and realism, between the way things ought to be and the way things are, and the debate as to whether legal philosophy should incorporate ethical standards or confine itself to an analysis of the law as it stands is a vital one that continues today.[12]

The positivist school, which developed so rapidly in the pragmatic, optimistic world of the nineteenth century, declared that law as it exists should be analysed empirically shorn of all ethical elements. Moral aspirations were all well and good but had no part in legal science. Man-made law must be examined as such and the metaphysical speculations of Natural Law rejected because what counted were the practical realities, not general principles which were imprecise and vague, not to say ambiguous.[13]

This kind of approach to law in society reached its climax with Kelsen's 'Pure Theory of Law'. Kelsen defined law solely in terms of itself and eschewed any element of justice, which was rather to be considered within the discipline of political science. Politics, sociology and history were all excised from the pure theory which sought to construct a logical unified structure based on a formal appraisal.[14]

---

[12] See e.g. Lyons, *Ethics and the Rule of Law*, London, 1984; R. Dworkin, *Taking Rights Seriously*, 1977; H. L. Hart, *The Concept of Law*, London, 1961 and P. Stein and Shand, *Legal Values in Western Society*, 1974. See also Lloyd, and R. Dias, *Jurisprudence*, 5th edn, London, 1985.

[13] See Hart, *Concept of Law*, and Hart, 'Positivism and the Separation of Law and Morals', 71 *Harvard Law Review*, 1958, p. 593. Cf. L. Fuller, 'Positivism and Fidelity to Law – A Reply to Professor Hart', *ibid.*, p. 630. See also Anzilotti, *Cours de Droit International*, 1929.

[14] 'The Pure Theory of Law', 50 LQR, 1934, pp. 474, 477–85 and 51 LQR, 1935, pp. 517–22.

Law was to be regarded as a normative science, that is, consisting of rules which lay down patterns of behaviour. Such rules, or norms, depend for their legal validity on a prior norm and this process continues until one reaches what is termed the basic norm of the whole system. This basic norm is the foundation of the legal edifice, because rules which can be related back to it therefore become *legal* rules. To give a simple example, a court order empowering an official to enforce a fine is valid if the court had that power which depends upon an Act of Parliament establishing the court. A rule becomes a legal rule if it is in accordance with a previous (and higher) legal rule and so on. Layer builds upon layer and the foundation of it all is the basic norm.[15]

The weakness of Kelsen's 'pure' system lies primarily in the concept of the basic norm for it relies for its existence upon non-legal issues. In fact, it is a political concept, and in the United Kingdom it would probably be the principle of the supremacy of Parliament.[16]

This logical, structured system of validity founded upon an extra-legal concept encounters difficulties when related to international law. For Kelsen, international law is a primitive legal order because of its lack of strong legislative, judicial and enforcement organs and its consequent resemblance to a pre-state society. It is accordingly characterised by the use of self-help. [17] The principles of international law are valid if they can be traced back to the basic norm of the system, which is hierarchical in the same sense as a national legal system. For Kelsen, the basic norm is the rule that identifies custom as the source of law, or stipulates that, as he wrote, 'the states ought to behave as they customarily behaved'.[18] One of the prime rules of this category is *pacta sunt servanda* declaring that agreements must be carried out in good faith and upon that rule is founded the second stage within the international legal order. This second stage consists of the network of norms created by international treaties and conventions and leads on to the third stage which includes those rules established by organs which have been set up by international treaties, for instance, decisions of the International Court of Justice.[19]

The problem with Kelsen's formulation of the basic norm of international law is that it appears to be tautological: it merely repeats that states which obey rules ought to obey those rules.[20] It seems to leave no room for the progressive development of international law by new practices accepted as law

[15] *Ibid.* See also Lloyd, Chapter 5.
[16] *Ibid.*, pp. 291–6. See also J. Stone, 'Mystery and Mystique in the Basic Norm', 26 MLR, 1963, p. 34 and J. Raz, *Practical Reason and Norms*, Oxford, 1975, pp. 129–31.
[17] *General Theory of Law and State*, 1946, pp. 328 *et seq.* See also J. Lador-Lederer, 'Some Observations on the "Vienna School" in International Law', 17 NILR, 1970, p. 126.
[18] Kelsen, *General Theory of Law and State*, pp. 369–70.   [19] *Ibid.*
[20] Hart terms this 'mere useless reduplication': *The Concept of Law*, Oxford, 1961, p. 230.

for that involves states behaving differently from the way they have been behaving. Above all, it fails to answer the question as to why custom is binding.

Nevertheless, it is a model of great logical consistency which helps explain, particularly with regard to national legal systems, the proliferation of rules and the importance of validity which gives as it were a mystical seal of approval to the whole structured process. It helps illustrate how rule leads to rule as stage succeeds stage in a progression of norms forming a legal order.

Another important element in Kelsen's interpretation of law is his extreme 'monist' stance. International law and municipal law are not two separate systems but one interlocking structure and the former is supreme. Municipal law finds its ultimate justification in the rules of international law by a process of delegation within one universal normative system.[21]

Kelsen's pure theory seemed to mark the end of that particular road, and positivism was analysed in more sociological terms by Hart in his book *The Concept of Law*, 1961.

Hart comprehends law as a system of rules, based upon the interaction of primary and secondary rules. The former, basically, specify standards of behaviour while the latter provide the means for identifying and developing them and thus specify the constitutional procedures for change. Primitive societies would possess only the primary rules and so would be characterised by uncertainty, inefficiency and stagnation, but with increasing sophistication the secondary rules would develop and identify authority and enable the rules to be adapted to changing circumstances in a regular and accepted manner.[22]

The international legal order is a prime example of a simple form of social structure which consists only of the primary rules, because of its lack of a centralised legislature, network of recognised courts with compulsory jurisdiction and organised means of enforcement. Accordingly, it has no need of, or rather has not yet evolved, a basic norm or in Hart's terminology a rule of recognition, by reference to which the validity of all the rules may be tested. Following this train of thought, Hart concludes that the rules of international law do not as yet constitute a 'system' but are merely a 'set of rules'. Of course, future developments may see one particular principle, such as *pacta sunt servanda*, elevated to the state of a validating norm, but in the present situation this has not yet occurred.[23]

This approach can be criticised for its overconcentration upon rules to the

---

[21] *General Theory of Law and State*, pp. 366–8. See further *infra*, Chapter 4.

[22] *The Concept of Law*, Chapter 5. See also e.g. Dworkin, *Taking Rights Seriously;* Raz, *Practical Reason*, and N. MacCormick, *Legal Reasoning and Legal Theory*, Oxford, 1978.

[23] *The Concept of Law, op. cit.*, pp. 228–31.

exclusion of other important elements in a legal system such as principles and policies,[24] and more especially as regards international law, for failing to recognise the sophistication or vitality of the system. In particular, the distinction between a system and a set of rules in the context of international law is a complex issue and one difficult to delineate.

The strength of the positivist movement has waned this century as the old certainties disintegrated and social unrest grew. Law, as always, began to reflect the dominant pressures of the age, and new theories as to the role of law in society developed. Writers started examining the effects of sociological phenomena upon the legal order and the nature of the legal process itself, with analyses of judicial behaviour and the means whereby rules were applied in actual practice. This was typified by Roscoe Pound's view of the law as a form of social engineering, balancing the various interests within the society in the most efficacious way.[25] Law was regarded as a method of social control and conceptual approaches were rejected in favour of functional analyses. What actually happened within the legal system, what claims were being brought and how they were satisfied: these were the watchwords of the sociological school.[26]

It was in one sense a move away from the ivory tower and into the court room. Empirical investigations proliferated, particularly in the United States, and the sciences of psychology and anthropology as well as sociology became allied to jurisprudence. Such concern with the wider social context led on to the theories of Realism, which treated law as an institution functioning within a particular community with a series of jobs to do. A study of legal norms within a closed logical system in the Kelsenite vein was regarded as unable to reveal very much of the actual operation of law in society. For this an understanding of the behaviour of courts and the various legal officials was required. Historical and ethical factors were relegated to a minor role within the realist-sociological tradition, with its concentration upon field studies and 'technical' dissections. Legal rules were no longer to be accepted as the heart of the legal system.[27]

Before one looks at contemporary developments of this approach and how they have affected interpretations of international law, the revival of Natural Law this century has first to be considered.

In the search for meaning in life and an ethical basis to law, Natural Law has adopted a variety of different approaches. One of them has been a refurbishment of the principles enumerated by Aquinas and adopted by the Catholic Church, emphasising the dignity of man and the supremacy of

---

[24] See Dworkin, *Taking Rights Seriously.*
[25] See e.g. *Philosophy of Law*, 1954, pp. 42–7. See also Freeman, *The Legal Structure*, 1974, Chapter 4.   [26] *Outlines of Jurisprudence*, 5th edn, 1943, pp. 116–19.
[27] See e.g. K. Llewellyn, *The Common Law Tradition*, Boston, 1960 and *Jurisprudence*, 1962. See also W. Twining, *Karl Llewellyn and the Realist Movement*, London, 1973 and L. Loevinger, 'Jurimetrics – The Next Step Forward', 33 *Minnesota Law Review*, 1949, p. 455.

reason together with an affirmation of the immorality (though not necessarily the invalidity) of law contrary to right reason and the eternal law of
God.[28] A more formalistic and logic-orientated trend has been exemplified
by writers such as Stammler, who tried to erect a logical structure of law
with an inbuilt concept of 'Natural Law with a changing content'.

This involved contrasting the *concept* of law, which was intended to be an
abstract, formal definition universally applicable, with the *idea* of law, which
embodies the purposes and direction of the system. This latter precept
varied, of necessity, in different social and cultural contexts.[29]

As distinct from this formal idealist school, there has arisen a sociologically inspired approach to the theme of Natural Law represented by Gény
and Duguit. This particular trend rejected the emphasis upon form, and
concentrated instead upon the definition of Natural Law in terms of universal factors, physical, psychological, social and historical, which dominate
the framework of society within which the law operated.[30]

The discussion of Natural Law increased and gained in importance following the Nazi experience. It stimulated a German philosopher, Radbruch,
to formulate a theory whereby unjust laws had to be opposed by virtue of a
higher, Natural Law.[31]

As far as international law is concerned, the revival of Natural Law came
at a time of increasing concern with international justice and the formation
of international institutions. Many of the ideas and principles of international law today are rooted in the notion of Natural Law and the relevance
of ethical standards to the legal order, such as the principles of non-aggression and human rights.[32]

New approaches[33]

Traditionally, international law has been understood in a historical manner
and studied chronologically. This approach was especially marked in the

[28] See e.g. J. Maritain, *Man and the State*, Paris, 1951 and J. Dabin, *General Theory of Law*, 2nd edn, 1950.
[29] See e.g. Stammler, *Theory of Justice* and Del Vecchio, *Formal Bases of Law*, 1921.
[30] See e.g. Gény, *Méthode d'Interprétation et Sources en Droit Privé Positif*, 1899 and Duguit, *Law in the Modern State*, 1919 and 'Objective Law', 20 *Columbia Law Review*, 1920, p. 817.
[31] *Introduction to Legal Philosophy*, 1947. See also Hart, 'Positivism', and Fuller, 'Positivism', and Fuller, 'The Legal Philosophy of Gustav Radbruch', 6 *Journal of Legal Education*, 1954, p. 481.
[32] See H. Lauterpacht, *International Law and Human Rights*, London, 1950. Note more gener-ally the approach of J. Rawls, *A Theory of Justice*, Oxford, 1971, and A. D'Amato, 'International Law and Rawls' Theory of Justice', 5 *Denver Journal of International Law and Policy*, 1975, p. 525. See also J. Boyle, 'Ideals and Things: International Legal Scholarship and the Prison-house of Language', 26 *Harvard International Law Journal*, 1985, p. 327; A. D'Amato, 'Is International Law Part of Natural Law ?', 9 *Vera Lex*, 1989; E. Midgley, *The Natural Law Tradition and the Theory of International Relations*, London, 1975 and C. Dominicé, 'Le Grand Retour du Droit Naturel en Droit des Gens', *Mélanges Grossen*, 1992, p. 399.
[33] See e.g. B. S. Chimni, *International Law and World Order*, New Delhi, 1993.

nineteenth century as international relations multiplied and international conferences and agreements came with an increasing profusion. Between the world wars, the opening of government archives released a wealth of material and further stimulated a study of diplomatic history, while the creation of such international institutions as the League of Nations and the Permanent Court of International Justice encouraged an appreciation of institutional processes.

However, after the Second World War a growing trend appeared intent upon the analysis of power politics and the comprehension of international relations in terms of the capacity to influence and dominate. The approach was a little more sophisticated than might appear at first glance for it involved a consideration of social and economic as well as political data that had a bearing upon a state's ability to withstand as well as direct pressures.[34]

Nevertheless, it was a pessimistic interpretation because of its centring upon power and its uses as the motive force of interstate activity.

The next 'wave of advance', as it has been called, witnessed the successes of the behaviouralist movement. This particular train of thought introduced elements of psychology, anthropology and sociology into the study of international relations and paralleled similar developments within the realist school. It reflected the altering emphasis from analyses in terms of idealistic or cynical ('realistic') conceptions of the world political order, to a mechanistic discussion of the system as it operates today, by means of field studies and other tools of the social sciences. Indeed, it is more a method of approach to law and society than a theory in the traditional sense.[35]

One can trace the roots of this school of thought to the changing conceptions of the role of government in society. The nineteenth-century ethic of individualism and the restriction of state intervention to the very minimum has changed radically in the last three generations. The emphasis is now more upon the responsibility of the government towards its citizens and the phenomenal growth in welfare legislation illustrates this. Rules and regulations controlling wide fields of human activity, something that would have been unheard of in the mid-nineteenth century, have proliferated throughout the nations of the developed world and theory has had to try and keep up with such reorientations.

Since the law now plays a much deeper role in society with the increase in

---

[34] See e.g. H. Morgenthau, Politics Among Nations, 4th edn, New York, 1967 and K. Thompson, *Political Realism and the Crisis of World Politics: An American Approach to Foreign Policy*, Princeton, 1960. See also A. Slaughter Burley, 'International Law and International Relations Theory: A Dual Agenda', 87 AJIL, 1993, p. 205 and R. Aron, *Paix et Guerre Entre des Nations*, Paris, 1984.

[35] See e.g. *Contending Approaches to International Politics* (eds. K. Knorr and J. Rosenau), Princeton, 1969, and W. Gould and M. Barkun, *International Law and the Social Sciences*, Princeton, 1970.

governmental intervention, impetus has been given to legal theories that reflect this growing involvement. Law, particularly in the United States, is seen as a tool to effect changes in society and realist doctrine underlines this. It emphasises that it is community values and policy decisions that determine the nature of the law and accordingly the role of the judge is that much more important. He is no longer an interpreter of a body of formal legal rules, but should be seen more as an active element in making decisions of public policy.

This means that to understand the operation of law, one has to consider the character of the particular society, its needs and values. Law thus becomes a dynamic process and has to be studied in the context of society and not merely as a collection of legal rules capable of being comprehended on their own. The social sciences have led the way in this reinterpretation of society and their influence has been very marked on the behavioural method of looking at the law, not only in terms of general outlook but also in providing the necessary tools to dissect society and discover the way it operates and the direction in which it is heading. The interdisciplinary nature of the studies in question was emphasised, utilising all the social sciences, including politics, economics and philosophy.[36] In particular, the use of the scientific method, such as obtaining data and quantitative analysis, has been very much in evidence.

Behaviouralism has divided the field of international relations into basically two studies, the first being a consideration of foreign policy techniques and the reasons whereby one particular course of action is preferred to another, and the second constituting the international systems analysis approach.[37] This emphasises the interaction of the various players on the international stage and the effects of such mutual pressures upon both the system and the participants. More than that, it examines the various international orders that have existed throughout history in an attempt to show how the dynamics of each particular system have created their own rules and how they can be used as an explanation of both political activity and the nature of international law. In other words, the nature of the international system can be examined by the use of particular variables in order to explain and to predict the role of international law.

[36] Note Barkun's comment that 'the past theoretical approaches of the legal profession have involved logical manipulations of a legal corpus more often than the empirical study of patterns of human behaviour', *Law Without Sanctions*, New Haven, 1968, p. 3. See also R. A. Falk, 'New Approaches to the Study of International Law', in *New Approaches to International Relations* (ed. M. A. Kaplan), New York, 1968, pp. 357–80, and J. Frankel, *Contemporary International Theory and the Behaviour of States*, London, 1973, pp. 21–2.

[37] See e.g. C. A. McClelland, *Theory and International Systems*, 1966; M. A. Kaplan, *System and Process in International Politics*, New York, 1964; M. A. Kaplan and N. Katzenbach, *The Political Foundations of International Law*, New York, 1961, and R. A. Falk and C. Black, The Future of International Legal Order, 1969. See also A. Kiss and D. Shelton, 'Systems Analysis of International Law: A Methodological Inquiry', 17 Netherlands YIL, 1986, p. 45.

For example, the period between 1848 and 1914 can be treated as the era of the 'balance of power' system. This system depended upon a number of factors, such as a minimum number of participants (accepted as five), who would engage in a series of temporary alliances in an attempt to bolster the weak and restrict the strong, for example, the coalitions Britain entered into to overawe France. It was basic to this system that no nation wished totally to destroy any other state, but merely to humble and weaken, and this contributed to the stability of the order.[38]

This system nurtured its own concepts of international law, especially that of sovereignty which was basic to the idea of free-floating alliances and the ability of states to leave the side of the strong to strengthen the weak. The balance of power collapsed with the First World War and after a period of confusion a discernible, loose 'bipolar' system emerged in the years following the Second World War.

This was predicated upon the polarisation of capitalism and communism and the consequent rigid alliances that were created. It included the existence of a Third World of basically non-aligned states, the objects of rivalry and of competition while not in themselves powerful enough to upset the bipolar system. This kind of order facilitated 'frontier' conflicts where the two powers collided, such as Korea, Berlin and Vietnam, as well as modifying the nature of sovereignty within the two alliances thus allowing such organisations as NATO and the European Community (subsequently European Union) on the one hand, and the Warsaw Pact and COMECON on the other, to develop. The dark side of this coin has been the freedom felt by the superpowers to control wavering states within their respective spheres of influence, for example, the Soviet actions in Poland, Hungary and Czechoslovakia and those of the USA particularly within Latin America.[39]

Behaviouralism has been enriched by the use of such techniques as games theory.[40] This is a mathematical method of studying decision-making in conflict situations where the parties react rationally in the struggle for benefits. It can be contrasted with the fight situation where the essence is the actual defeat of the opponent (for example, the Israel–Arab conflict) and with the debate situation, which is an effort to convince the participants of the rightness of one's cause. Other factors which are taken into account

---

[38] See J. Frankel, *International Relations in a Changing World*, London, 1979, pp. 152–57, and Kaplan and Katzenbach, *Political Foundations*, pp. 62–70.

[39] Kaplan and Katzenbach, *Political Foundations*, pp. 50–5. As far as the systems approach is concerned see also S. Hoffman, 'International Systems and International Law' in *The International System* (eds. K. Knorr and S. Verba), Westport, 1961, p. 205; G. Clark and L. Sohn, *World Peace Through World Law*, 3rd edn, Boston, 1966, and *The Strategy of World Order* (eds. R. A. Falk and S. Mendlovitz), 4 vols., New York, 1966.

[40] See e.g. R. Lieber, *Theory and World Politics*, London, 1972, Chapter 2; *Game Theory and Related Approaches to Social Behaviour* (ed. H. Shubik), London, 1964, and W. J. M. Mackenzie, Politics and Social Sciences, London, 1967.

include communications, integration, environment and capabilities. Thus the range and complexity of this approach far exceeds that of prior theories.

All this highlights the switch in emphasis that has taken place in the consideration of law in the world community. The traditional view was generally that international law constituted a series of rules restricting the actions of independent states and forming exceptions to state sovereignty. The new theories tend to look at the situation differently, more from the perspective of the international order expanding its horizons than the nation-state agreeing to accept certain defined limitations upon its behaviour.

The rise of quantitative research has facilitated the collation and ordering of vast quantities of data. It is primarily a methodological approach utilising political, economic and social data and statistics, and converting facts and information into a form suitable for scientific investigation. Such methods with their behavioural and quantitative aspects are beginning to impinge upon the field of international law. They enable a greater depth of knowledge and comprehension to be achieved and a wider appreciation of all the various processes at work.[41]

The behavioural approach to international relations has been translated into international law theory by a number of writers, in particular Professor McDougal, with some important modifications. This 'policy-orientated' movement regards law as a comprehensive process of decision-making rather than as a defined set of rules and obligations. It is an active all-embracing approach seeing international law as a dynamic system operating within a particular type of world order.[42] It therefore minimises the role played by rules, for such a traditional conception of international law 'quite obviously offers but the faintest glimpse of the structures, procedures and types of decision that take place in the contemporary world community'.[43] It has been emphasised that the law is a constantly evolving process of decision-making and the way that it evolves will depend on the knowledge and

---

[41] Note also the functionalist approach to international law. This orientation emphasises the practical benefits to states of co-operation in matters of mutual interest: see e.g. W. Friedmann, *An Introduction to World Politics*, 5th edn, London, 1965, p. 57; F. Haas, *Beyond the Nation State*, 1964; D. Mitrany, *A Working Peace System*, London, 1946; C. W. Jenks, *Law, Freedom and Welfare*, London, 1964 and J. Stone, *Legal Controls of International Conflict*, London, 1959. See also D. Johnston, 'Functionalism in the Theory of International Law', 25 Canadian YIL, 1988, p. 3.

[42] See e.g. M. S. McDougal, 'International Law, Power and Policy', 82 HR, p. 133; M. S. McDougal, H. Lasswell and W. M. Reisman, 'Theories about International Law: Prologue to a Configurative Jurisprudence', 8 Va JIL, 1968, p. 188; M. S. McDougal, 'International Law and the Future', 50 *Mississippi Law Journal*, 1979, p. 259 and H. Lasswell and M. S. McDougal, *Jurisprudence for a Free Society*, Yale, 1992. See also G. Scelle, Manuel de Droit International, Paris, 1948 and Chimni, *International Law*, Chapter 3.

[43] M. S.McDougal and W. M. Reisman, *International Law in Contemporary Perspective*, New Haven, 1980, p. 5.

insight of the decision-maker.[44] In other words, it is the social process of constant human interaction that is seen as critical and, in this process, claims are continually being made in an attempt to maximise values at the disposal of the participants. Eight value-institution categories have been developed to analyse this process: power, wealth, enlightenment, skill, well-being, affection, respect and rectitude. This list may be further developed. It is not exhaustive. Law is to be regarded as a product of such social processes.[45] International law is the whole process of authoritative decision-making involving crucially the concepts of authority and control. The former is defined in terms of the structure of expectation concerning the identity and competence of the decision-maker, whilst the latter refers to the actual effectiveness of a decision, whether or not authorised.[46]

McDougal's work and that of his followers emphasises the long list of values, interests and considerations that have to be taken into account within the international system by the persons actually faced with the decisions to make. This stress upon the so-called 'authoritative decision-maker', whether he be in the United States Department of State, in the British Foreign Office or 'anyone whose choice about an event can have some international significance',[47] as the person who in effect has to choose between different options respecting international legal principles, emphasises the practical world of power and authority. Such a decision-maker is subject to a whole series of pressures and influences, such as the values of the community in which he operates, and the interests of the particular nation-state he serves. He will also have to consider the basic values of the world order, for instance human dignity.

This approach involves a complex dissection of a wide-ranging series of factors and firmly fixes international law within the ambit of the social sciences, both with respect to the procedures adopted and the tools of analysis. International law is seen in the following terms, as,

> a comprehensive process of authoritative decision in which rules are continuously made and remade; that the function of the rules of international law is to communicate the perspectives (demands, identifications and expectations) of the peoples of the world about this comprehensive process of decision; and that the national application of these rules in particular instances requires their interpretation, like that of any other communication, in terms of who is using

---

[44] 'The Policy-Oriented Approach to Law', 40 *Virginia Quarterly Review*, 1964, p. 626. See also Suzuki, 'The New Haven School of International Law: An Invitation to a Policy-Oriented Jurisprudence', 1 *Yale Studies in World Public Order*, 1974, p. 1.

[45] Suzuki, 'Policy-Oriented Jurisprudence', pp. 22–3. See also M. S. McDougal, 'Some Basic Theoretical Concepts about International Law: A Policy-Oriented Framework of Inquiry', 4 *Journal of Conflict Resolution*, 1960, pp. 337–54.

[46] M. S. McDougal and H. Lasswell, 'The Identification and Appraisal of Diverse Systems of Public Order', 53 AJIL, 1959, pp. 1, 9.

[47] McDougal and Reisman, *International Law*, p. 2.

them, with respect to whom, for what purposes (major and minor), and in what context.[48]

Legal rules articulate and seek to achieve certain goals and this value factor must not be ignored. The values emphasised by this school are basically those of human dignity, familiar from the concepts of Western democratic society.[49] Indeed, Reisman has emphasised the natural law origins of this approach as well as the need to clarify a jurisprudence for those persons whose activities have led to innovations in such fields of international law as human rights and the protection of the environment.[50]

The policy-oriented movement has been greatly criticised by traditional international lawyers as unduly minimising the legal content of the subject and for ignoring the fact that nations generally accept international law as it is and obey its dictates.[51] States rarely indulge in a vast behavioural analysis, studiously considering every relevant element in a particular case and having regard to fundamental objectives like human dignity and welfare. Indeed, so to do may weaken international law, it has been argued.[52] In addition, the insertion of such value-concepts as 'human dignity' raises difficulties of subjectivity that ill fit within a supposedly objective analytical structure.

Other writers, such as Professor Falk, accept the basic comprehensive approach of the McDougal school, but point to its inconsistencies and overfulsome cataloguing of innumerable interests. They tend to adopt a global outlook based upon a deep concern for human welfare and morality, but with an emphasis upon the importance of legal rules and structure.[53]

Professor Franck, however, has sought to refocus the essential question of the existence and operation of the system of international law in terms of inquiring into why states obey international law despite the undeveloped condition of the international legal system's structures, processes and

---

[48] M. S. McDougal, 'A Footnote', 57 AJIL, 1963, p. 383.
[49] See M. S. McDougal, H. Lasswell and L. C. Chen, *Human Rights and World Public Order*, New Haven, 1980. For a discussion of the tasks required for a realistic inquiry in the light of defined goals, see McDougal, 'International Law and the Future', pp. 259, 267.
[50] 'The View from the New Haven School of International Law', PASIL, 1992, p. 118.
[51] See in particular P. Allott, 'Language, Method and the Nature of International Law' , 45 BYIL, p. 79. R. Higgins has vividly drawn attention to the differences in approach to international law adopted by American and British writers: 'Policy Considerations and the International Judicial Process', 17 ICLQ, 1968, p. 58. See also T. Farer, 'Human Rights in Law's Empire: The Jurisprudence War', 85 *AJIL*, 1991, p. 117,
[52] Allott, 'Language', p. 128 *et seq.*
[53] See e.g. R. A. Falk, *Human Rights and State Sovereignty*, New York, 1981 and Falk, *On Human Governance*, Cambridge, 1995. See also *The United Nations and a Just World Order* (eds. R. Falk, S. Kim and S. Mendlovitz), Boulder, 1991, and Chimni, *International Law*, Chapter 4. But note the approach of, e.g., J. S. Watson, 'A Realistic Jurisprudence of International Law', 34 YBWA, 1980, p. 265 and M. Lane, 'Demanding Human Rights: A Change in the World Legal Order', 6 *Hofstra Law Review*, 1978, p. 269. See also Boyle, 'Ideals and Things'.

enforcement mechanisms.[54] The answer is seen to lie in the concept of legitimacy. States will obey the rules because they see such rules and their institutional framework as possessing a high degree of legitimacy. Legitimacy itself is defined as 'a property of a rule or rule-making institution which itself exerts a pull towards compliance on those addressed normatively because those addressed believe that the rule or institution has come into being and operates in accordance with generally accepted principles of right process'.[55] Legitimacy may be empirically demonstrated but compliance may be measured not only by observing states acting in accordance with the principle in question, but also by observing the degree to which a violator actually exhibits deference to that principle even while violating it.

Legitimacy will depend upon four specific properties, it is suggested, determinacy (or readily ascertainable normative content or 'transparency'); symbolic validation (or authority approval); coherence (or consistency or general application) and adherence (or falling within an organised hierarchy of rules). In other words, it is proposed that there exist objectively verifiable criteria which help us to ascertain why international rules are obeyed and thus why the system works. This approach is supplemented by the view that legitimacy and justice as morality are two aspects of the concept of fairness, which is seen by Franck as the most important question for international law.[56]

The recurring themes of the relationship between sovereign states and international society and the search for a convincing explanation for the binding quality of international law in a state-dominated world appear also in very recent approaches to international law theory which fall within the general critical legal studies framework.[57] Such approaches have drawn attention to the many inconsistencies and incoherences that persist within the international legal system. The search for an all-embracing general theory of international law has been abandoned in mainstream thought as being founded upon unverifiable propositions, whether religiously or

---

[54] T. M. Franck, *The Power of Legitimacy Among Nations*, Oxford, 1990. See also T. M. Franck, 'Fairness in the International Legal and Institutional System', 240 HR, 1993 III, p. 13, Chapter II and Franck, *Fairness in International Law and Institutions*, Oxford, 1995, Chapter 2.   [55] Franck, *Legitimacy*, p. 24.   [56] Franck, 'Fairness'. p, 26.

[57] See e.g. *The Structure and Processes of International Law* (eds. R. St. J. Macdonald and D. Johnston), Dordrecht, 1983; Boyle, 'Ideals and Things'; A. Carty, *The Decay of International Law ? A Reappraisal of the Limits of Legal Imagination in International Affairs*, Manchester, 1986; D. Kennedy, *International Legal Structure*, Boston, 1987; M. Koskenniemi, *From Apology to Utopia*, Helsinki, 1989; F. V. Kratochwil, *Rules, Norms and Decisions: On the Conditions of Practical and Legal Reasoning in International Relations and Domestic Affairs*, Cambridge, 1989; P. Allott, *Eunomia*, Oxford, 1990; *Theory and International Law; An Introduction* (ed. P. Allott), London, 1991 and *International Law* (ed. M. Koskenniemi), Aldershot, 1992. See also I. Scobbie, 'Towards the Elimination of International Law: Some Radical Scepticism about Sceptical Radicalism', 61 BYIL, 1990, p. 339.

sociologically based, and attention has switched to the analysis of particular areas of international law and in particular procedures for the settlement of disputes. The critical legal studies movement notes that the traditional approach to international law has in essence involved the transposition of 'liberal' principles of domestic systems onto the international scene, but that this has led to further problems.[58] Specifically, liberalism tries constantly to balance individual freedom and social order and, it is argued, inevitably ends up siding with either one or other of those propositions.[59] Additionally, there are only two possibilities with regard to justice itself: it is either simply subjective or it is imposed. In either case, liberalism is compromised as a system.

The critical legal studies approach notes the close relationship that exists between law and society, but emphasises that conceptual analysis is also crucial since such concepts are not in themselves independent entities but reflect particular power relationships. The point is made that the nexus between state power and international legal concepts needs to be taken into consideration as well as the way in which such concepts in themselves reflect political factors. As Koskenniemi writes, 'a post-realist theory . . . aims to answer questions regarding the relationship of law and society and the legitimacy of constraint in a world of sovereigns as aspects of one single problem: the problem of power in concepts'.[60] The problem posed by the growth in the world community and the need to consider the range of different cultures and traditions within that community leads, it is suggested, to the decline of universality as such and the need to focus upon the specific contexts of particular problems.

It is the typical lawyer's answer in any event to declare that all depends upon the particular circumstances of the case, and this approach is generalised in order to deal with the question of which of several relevant international rules is to predominate. It is in fact a way of noting that superior operating principles are difficult to find or justify and thus concluding that the search for universal concepts or principles is of little value. In effect, it is proposed that no coherent international system as such actually exists and that one should rather concentrate upon *ad hoc* legal concepts as reflecting power considerations and within the confines of the specific contexts in which the particular questions or issues have arisen. Like the policy-oriented approach, the critical legal studies view is to accept that international law is more than a set of rules, but it then proceeds to emphasise the indeterminacy as such of law rather than seeing law as a collection of competing norms between which choices must be made.[61]

---

[58] See e.g. M. Koskenniemi in *International Law* (ed. M. Koskenniemi) at p. xvi.
[59] M. Koskenniemi, *From Apology to Utopia*, p. 52.   [60] *Ibid.*, p. xxi.
[61] See Higgins, *Problems and Process*, p. 9.

The range of theories and approaches to international law[62] testifies both to the importance of the subject and the inherent difficulties it faces. International law is clearly much more that a simple set of rules. It is a culture in the broadest sense in that it constitutes a method of communicating claims, counter-claims, expectations and anticipations as well as providing a framework for assessing and prioritising such demands.

International law functions in a particular, concrete world system, involving a range of actors from states to international organisations, companies and individuals, and as such needs to be responsive to the needs and aspirations of such participants. Law is not the only way in which issues transcending borders are negotiated and settled or indeed fought over. It is one of a number of methods for dealing with an existing complex and shifting system, but it is a way of some prestige and influence for it is of its very nature in the form of mutually accepted obligations. Law and politics cannot be divorced. They are not identical, but they do interact on several levels. They are engaged in a crucial symbiotic relationship. It does neither discipline a service to minimise the significance of the other.

[62] See also e.g. H. Charlesworth, C. M. Chinkin and Wright, 'Feminist Approaches to International Law', 85 AJIL, 1991, p. 613 and F. Tesón, 'Feminism and International Law: A Reply', 33 Va JIL, 1993, p. 647.

CHAPTER 3

SOURCES

The operation of ascertainment of the law on any given point in domestic legal orders is not usually too difficult a process.[1] In the English legal system, for example, one looks to see whether the matter is covered by an Act of Parliament and, if it is, the law reports are consulted as to how it has been interpreted by the courts. If the particular point is not specifically referred to in a statute, court cases will be examined to elicit the required information. In other words, there is a definite method of discovering what the law is. In addition to verifying the contents of the rules, this method also demonstrates how the law is created, namely, by parliamentary legislation or judicial case law. This gives a degree of certainty to the legal process because one is able to tell when a proposition has become law, and the necessary mechanism to resolve any disputes about the law is evident. It reflects the hierarchical character of a national legal order with its gradations of authority imparting to the law a large measure of stability and predictability.

The contrast is very striking when one considers the situation in international law. The lack of a legislature, executive and structure of courts within international law has been noted and the effects of this will become clearer as one proceeds. There is no single body able to create laws internationally binding upon everyone, nor a proper system of courts with compulsory jurisdiction to interpret and extend the law. One is therefore faced with the problem of discovering where the law is to be found and how one can tell

---

[1] See generally C. Parry, *The Sources and Evidences of International Law*, Cambridge, 1965; M. Sørensen, *Les Sources de Droit International*, Paris, 1946; *Oppenheim's International Law* (eds. R. Y. Jennings and A. D. Watts), 9th edn, London, 1992, p. 22; I. Brownlie, *Principles of Public International Law*, 4th edn, Oxford, 1990, Chapter 1; Nguyen Quoc Dinh, P. Daillier and A. Pellet, *Droit International Public*, 5th edn, Paris, 1994, p. 111; G. M. Danilenko, *Law-Making in the International Community*, 1993; G. I. Tunkin, *Theory of International Law*, London, 1974, pp. 89–203; J. W. Verzijl, *International Law in Historical Perspective*, 1968, vol. I, p. 1; H. Lauterpacht, *International Law: Collected Papers*, Cambridge, 1970, vol. I, p. 58; *Change and Stability in International Law-Making* (eds. A. Cassese and J. Weiler), 1988 ; A. Bos, *A Methodology of International Law*, 1984; M. Virally, 'The Sources of International Law' in *Manual of Public International Law* (ed. M. Sørensen), London 1968, p. 116; C. Tomuschat, 'Obligations Arising for States Without or Against Their Will', 241 HR, 1993, p. 195 and O. Schachter, 'Recent Trends in International Law-Making', 12 Australian YIL, 1992.

whether a particular proposition amounts to a legal rule. This perplexity is reinforced because of the anarchic nature of world affairs and the clash of competing sovereignties. Nevertheless, international law does exist and is ascertainable. There are 'sources' available from which the rules may be extracted and analysed.

By 'sources' one means those provisions operating within the legal system on a technical level, and such ultimate sources as reason or morality are excluded, as are more functional sources such as libraries and journals. What is intended is a survey of the process whereby rules of international law emerge.[2]

Article 38(1) of the Statute of the International Court of Justice is widely recognised as the most authoritative statement as to the sources of international law.[3] It provides that:

> the Court, whose function is to decide in accordance with international law such disputes as are submitted to it, shall apply:
> (a) international conventions, whether general or particular, establishing rules expressly recognised by the contesting states; (b) international custom, as evidence of a general practice accepted as law; (c) the general principles of law recognised by civilised nations; (d) subject to the provisions of Article 59, judicial decisions and the teachings of the most highly qualified publicists of the various nations, as subsidiary means for the determination of rules of law.

Although this formulation is technically limited to the sources of international law which the International Court must apply, in fact since the function of the Court is to decide disputes submitted to it 'in accordance with international law' and since all member states of the United Nations are *ipso facto* parties to the Statute by virtue of article 93 of the United Nations Charter (states that are non-members of the UN can specifically become parties to the Statute of the court, Switzerland is the most obvious example of this), there is no serious contention that the provision expresses the universal perception as to the enumeration of sources of international law.

Some writers have sought to categorise the distinctions in this provision, so that international conventions, custom and the general principles of law are described as the three exclusive law-creating processes while judicial decisions and academic writings are regarded as law-determining agencies, dealing with the verification of alleged rules.[4] But in reality it is not always possible to make hard and fast divisions. The different functions overlap to a great extent so that in many cases treaties (or conventions) merely reiterate accepted rules of customary law, and judgments of the International

---

[2] See also, e.g., M. S. McDougal and W. M. Reisman, 'The Prescribing Function: How International Law is Made', 6 *Yale Studies in World Public Order*, 1980, p. 249.
[3] See e.g. Brownlie, *Principles*, p. 3; *Oppenheim's International Law*, p. 24 and M. O. Hudson, *The Permanent Court of International Justice*, 1934, pp. 601 *et seq.*
[4] See e.g. G. Schwarzenberger, *International Law*, 3rd edn, London, 1957, vol. I, pp. 26–7.

Court of Justice may actually create law in the same way that municipal judges formulate new law in the process of interpreting existing law.[5]

A distinction has sometimes been made between formal and material sources.[6] The former, it is claimed, confer upon the rules an obligatory character, while the latter comprise the actual content of the rules. Thus the formal sources appear to embody the constitutional mechanism for identifying law while the material sources incorporate the essence or subject-matter of the regulations. This division has been criticised particularly in view of the peculiar constitutional set-up of international law, and it tends to distract attention from some of the more important problems by its attempt to establish a clear separation of substantive and procedural elements, something difficult to maintain in international law.

Custom[7]

Introduction

In any primitive society certain rules of behaviour emerge and prescribe what is permitted and what is not. Such rules develop almost subconsciously within the group and are maintained by the members of the group by social pressures and with the aid of various other more tangible implements. They are not, at least in the early stages, written down or codified, and survive

---

[5] There are a number of examples of this: see *infra*, Chapter 4, p. 104.

[6] See e.g. Brownlie, *Principles*, p. 1. See also Nguyen Quoc Dinh et al., *Droit International Public*, p. 111, where it is noted that 'les sources *formelles* du droit sont les *procédés* d'élaboration du droit, les diverses techniques qui autorisent à considérer qu'une règle appartient au droit positif. Les sources *materielles* constituent les fondements sociologiques des normes internationales, leur base politique, morale ou économique plus ou moins explicitée par la doctrine ou les sujets du droit.'

[7] See generally, A. D'Amato, *The Concept of Custom in International Law*, Cornell, 1971; M. Akehurst, 'Custom as a Source of International Law', 47 BYIL, 1974–5, p. 1; B. Cheng, 'Custom: The Future of General State Practice in a Divided World' in *The Structure and Process of International Law* (eds. R. St. J. Macdonald and D. Johnston), Dordrecht, 1983, p. 513; H. Thirlway, *International Customary Law and Codification*, 1972; K. Wolfke, *Custom in Present International Law*, 2nd edn, 1993 and Wolfke, 'Some Persistent Controversies Regarding Customary International Law', Netherlands YIL, 1993, p. 1; Kopelmanas, 'Custom as a Means of the Creation of International Law', 18 BYIL, 1937, p. 127; H. Lauterpacht, *The Development of International Law by the International Court*, Cambridge, 1958, pp. 368–93; Kunz, 'The Nature of Customary International Law', 47 AJIL, 1953, p. 662; R. J. Dupuy, 'Coutume Sage et Coutume Sauvage', *Mélanges Rousseau*, 1974, p. 75; Stern, 'La Coutume au Coeur du Droit International', *Mélanges Reuter*, 1981, p. 479; R. Y. Jennings, 'Law-Making and Package Deal', *ibid.*, p. 347; G. Danilenko, 'The Theory of International Customary Law', German YIL, 1988, p. 9; Barberis, 'Réfléxions sur la Coutume Internationale', AFDI, 1990, p. 9; L. Condorelli, 'Custom', *International Law: Achievements and Perspectives* (ed. Bedjaoui), 1991, p. 206; M. Byers, 'Custom, Power and the Power of Rules', 17 *Michigan Journal of International Law*, 1995, p. 109; H. Thirlway, 'The Law and Procedure of the International Court of Justice: 1960–89', 61 BYIL, 1990, pp. 3, 31 and A. Carty, *The Decay of International Law?*, Manchester, 1986, Chapter 3.

ultimately because of what can be called an aura of historical legitimacy.[8] As the community develops it will modernise its code of behaviour by the creation of legal machinery, such as courts and legislature. Custom, for this is how the original process can be described, remains and may also continue to evolve.[9] It is regarded as an authentic expression of the needs and values of the community at any given time.

Custom within contemporary legal systems, particularly in the developed world, is relatively cumbersome and unimportant and often of only nostalgic value.[10] In international law on the other hand it is a dynamic source of law in the light of the nature of the international system, and its lack of centralised government organs.

The existence of customary rules can be deduced from the practice and behaviour of states and this is where the problems begin. How can one tell when a particular line of action adopted by a state reflects a legal rule or is merely prompted by, for example, courtesy? Indeed, how can one discover what precisely a state is doing or why, since there is no living 'state' but rather thousands of officials in scores of departments exercising governmental functions? Other issues concern the speed of creation of new rules and the effect of protests.

There are disagreements as to the value of a customary system in international law. Some writers deny that custom can be significant today as a source of law, noting that it is too clumsy and slow-moving to accommodate the evolution of international law any more, [11] while others declare that it is a dynamic process of law creation and more important than treaties since it is of universal application.[12] Another view recognises that custom is of value since it is activated by spontaneous behaviour and thus mirrors the contemporary concerns of society. However, since international law now has to contend with a massive increase in the pace and variety of state activities as well as having to come to terms with many different cultural and political traditions, the role of custom is perceived to be much diminished.[13]

There are elements of truth in each of these approaches. Amidst a wide variety of conflicting behaviour, it is not easy to isolate the emergence of a

---

[8] See e.g. R. Unger, *Law in Modern Society*, London, 1976, who notes that customary law can be regarded as 'any recurring mode of interaction among individuals and groups, together with the more or less explicit acknowledgement by these groups and individuals that such patterns of interaction produce reciprocal expectations of conduct that ought to be satisfied', p. 49. See also R. Dias, *Jurisprudence*, 5th edn, London, 1985, Chapter 9 and H. L. A. Hart, *The Concept of Law*, Oxford, 1961.

[9] See e.g. D. Lloyd, *Introduction to Jurisprudence*, 4th edn, London, 1979, p. 649 and H. Maine, *Ancient Law*, 1861.   [10] See e.g. Dias, *Jurisprudence*.

[11] See e.g. W. Friedmann, *The Changing Structure of International Law*, 1964, pp. 121-3. See also I. De Lupis, *The Concept of International Law*, 1987, pp. 112-16.

[12] E.g. D'Amato, *Concept of Custom*, p. 12.

[13] C. De Visscher, *Theory and Reality in Public International Law*, 3rd edn, 1960, pp. 161-2.

new rule of customary law and there are immense problems involved in collating all the necessary information. It is not always the best instrument available for the regulation of complex issues that arise in world affairs, but in particular situations it may meet the contingencies of modern life. As will be seen, it is possible to point to something called 'instant' customary law in certain circumstances that can prescribe valid rules without having to undergo a long period of gestation, and custom can and often does dovetail neatly within the complicated mechanisms now operating for the identification and progressive development of the principles of international law.

More than that, custom does mirror the characteristics of the decentralised international system. It is democratic in that all states may share in the formulation of new rules, though the precept that some are more equal than others in this process is not without its grain of truth. If the international community is unhappy with a particular law it can be changed relatively quickly without the necessity of convening and successfully completing a world conference. It reflects the consensus approach to decision-making with the ability of the majority to create new law binding upon all, while the very participation of states encourages their compliance with customary rules. Its imprecision means flexibility as well as ambiguity. Indeed, the creation of the concept of the exclusive economic zone in the law of the sea may be cited as an example of this process. This is discussed further in Chapter 11. The essence of custom according to article 38 is that it should constitute 'evidence of a general practice accepted as law'. Thus, it is possible to detect two basic elements in the make-up of a custom. These are the material facts, that is, the actual behaviour of states, and the psychological or subjective belief that such behaviour is 'law'.

It is understandable why the first requirement is mentioned, since customary law is founded upon the performance of state activities and the convergence of practices, in other words, what states actually do. It is the psychological factor that needs some explanation. If one left the definition of custom as state practice then one would be faced with the problem of how to separate international law from principles of morality or social usage. This is because states do not restrict their behaviour to what is legally required. They may pursue a line of conduct purely through a feeling of goodwill and in the hope of reciprocal benefits. States do not have to allow tourists in or launch satellites. There is no law imposing upon them the strict duty to distribute economic aid to developing nations. The bare fact that such things are done does not mean that they have to be done.

The issue therefore is how to distinguish behaviour undertaken because of a law from behaviour undertaken because of a whole series of other reasons ranging from goodwill to pique, and from ideological support to political bribery. And if customary law is restricted to the overt acts of states, one cannot solve this problem.

Accordingly, the second element in the definition of custom has been elaborated. This is the psychological factor, the belief by a state that behaved in a certain way that it was under a legal obligation to act that way. It is known in legal terminology as *opinio juris* and was first formulated by the French writer François Gény as an attempt to differentiate legal custom from mere social usage.[14]

However, the relative importance of the two factors, the overt action and the subjective conviction, is disputed by various writers. Positivists, with their emphasis upon state sovereignty, stress the paramount importance of the psychological element. States are only bound by what they have consented to, so therefore the material element is minimised to the greater value of *opinio juris*. If states believe that a course of action is legal and perform it, even if only once, then it is to be inferred that they have tacitly consented to the rule involved. Following on from this line of analysis, various positivist thinkers have tended to minimise many of the requirements of the overt manifestation, for example, with regard to repetition and duration.[15] Other writers have taken precisely the opposite line and maintain that *opinio juris* is impossible to prove and therefore of no tremendous consequence. Kelsen, for one, has written that it is the courts that have the discretion to decide whether any set of usages is such as to create a custom and that the subjective perception of the particular state or states is not called upon to give the final verdict as to its legality or not.[16]

The material fact

The actual practice indulged in by states constitutes the initial factor. There are a number of points to be considered concerning its nature, including the duration, consistency, repetition and generality of a particular practice by states. As far as the duration is concerned, most countries specify a recognised time-scale for the acceptance of a practice as a customary rule within

---

[14] *Méthode d'Interprétation et Sources en Droit Privé Positif*, 1899, para. 110.

[15] See e.g. Anzilotti, *Corso di Diritto Internazionale*, 3rd edn, 1928, pp. 73–6; Strupp, 'Les Règles Générales du Droit de la Paix', 47 HR, p. 263; Tunkin, *Theory of International Law*, pp. 113–33 and 'Remarks on the Juridical Nature of Customary Norms of International Law', 49 *California Law Review*, 1961, pp. 419–21, and B. Cheng, 'United Nations Resolutions on Outer Space: "Instant" International Customary Law?', 5 *Indian Journal of International Law*, 1965, p. 23.

[16] 'Théorie du Droit International Coutumier', 1 *Revue International de la Théorie du Droit*, 1939, pp. 253, 264–6. See also P. Guggenheim, *Traité de Droit International Public*, Paris, 1953, pp. 46–8; T. Gihl, 'The Legal Character of Sources of International Law', 1 *Scandinavian Studies in Law*, 1957, pp. 53, 84, and *Oppenheim's International Law*, pp. 27–31.

their municipal systems. This can vary from 'time immemorial' in the English Common Law dating back to 1189, to figures from thirty or forty years on the Continent.

In international law there is no rigid time element and it will depend upon the circumstances of the case and the nature of the usage in question. In certain fields, such as air and space law, the rules have developed quickly; in others, the process is much slower. Duration is thus not the most important of the components of state practice.[17] The essence of custom is to be sought elsewhere.

The basic rule as regards continuity and repetition was laid down in the *Asylum* case by the International Court of Justice (ICJ), decided in 1950.[18] The Court declared that a customary rule must be 'in accordance with a constant and uniform usage practised by the States in question'.[19] The case concerned Haya de la Torre, a Peruvian, who was sought by his government after an unsuccessful revolt. He was granted asylum by Colombia in its embassy in Lima, but Peru refused to issue a safe conduct to permit Torre to leave the country. Colombia brought the matter before the International Court of Justice and requested a decision recognising that it (Colombia) was competent to define Torre's offence, as to whether it was criminal as Peru maintained, or political, in which case asylum and a safe conduct could be allowed.

The Court, in characterising the nature of a customary rule, held that it had to constitute the expression of a right appertaining to one state (Colombia) and a duty incumbent upon another (Peru). However, the Court felt that in the *Asylum* litigation, state practices had been so uncertain and contradictory as not to amount to a 'constant and uniform usage' regarding the unilateral qualification of the offence in question.[20] The issue involved here dealt with a regional custom pertaining only to Latin America and it may be argued that the same approach need not necessarily be followed where a general custom is alleged and that in the latter instance a lower standard of proof would be upheld.[21]

The ICJ emphasised its view that some degree of uniformity amongst state practices was essential before a custom could come into existence in the *Anglo-Norwegian Fisheries* case.[22] The United Kingdom, in its arguments against the Norwegian method of measuring the breadth of the territorial sea, referred to an alleged rule of custom whereby a straight line may be

---

[17] See D'Amato, *Concept of Custom*, pp. 56–8 and Akehurst, '*Custom as a Source*', pp. 15–16. Judge Negulesco in an unfortunate phrase emphasised that custom required immemorial usage: *European Commission of the Danube*, PCIJ, Series B, No. 14, 1927, p. 105. See also Brownlie, *Principles*, p. 5 and the *North Sea Continental Shelf* cases, ICJ Reports, 1969, pp. 3, 43; 41 ILR, pp. 29, 72.   [18] ICJ Reports, 1950, p. 266; 17 ILR, p. 280.
[19] *Ibid.*, pp. 276–7; 17 ILR, p. 284.   [20] *Ibid.*   [21] See further, *infra*, p. 72.
[22] ICJ Reports, 1951, pp. 116, 131, 138; 18 ILR, p. 86.

drawn across bays of less than 10 miles from one projection to the other, which could then be regarded as the baseline for the measurement of the territorial sea. The Court dismissed this by pointing out that the actual practice of states did not justify the creation of any such custom. In other words, there had been insufficient uniformity of behaviour.

⯈ In the *North Sea Continental Shelf* cases,[23] which involved a dispute between Germany on the one hand and Holland and Denmark on the other over the delimitation of the continental shelf, the ICJ remarked that state practice had to be 'both extensive and virtually uniform in the sense of the provision invoked'. This was held to be indispensable to the formation of a new rule of customary international law.[24] However, the Court emphasised in the *Nicaragua* v. *United States* case[25] that it was not necessary that the practice in question had to be 'in absolutely rigorous conformity' with the purported customary rule. The Court continued:

> In order to deduce the existence of customary rules, the Court deems it sufficient that the conduct of states should, in general, be consistent with such rules, and that instances of state conduct inconsistent with a given rule should generally have been treated as breaches of that rule, not as indications of the recognition of a new rule.[26]

The threshold that needs to be attained before a legally binding custom can be created will depend both upon the nature of the alleged rule and the opposition it arouses. This partly relates to the problem of ambiguity where it is not possible to point to the alleged custom with any degree of clarity, as in the *Asylum* case where a variety of conflicting and contradictory evidence had been brought forward.

On the other hand, an unsubstantiated claim by a state cannot be accepted because it would amount to unilateral law-making and compromise a reasonably impartial system of international law. If a proposition meets with a great deal of opposition then it would be an undesirable fiction to ignore this and talk of an established rule. Another relevant factor is the strength of the prior rule which is purportedly overthrown.[27] For example, the customary law relating to a state's sovereignty over its airspace developed very quickly in the years immediately before and during the First World War. Similarly, the principle of non-sovereignty over the space route followed by

---

[23] ICJ Reports, 1969, p. 3; 41 ILR, p. 29.

[24] *Ibid.*, p. 43; 41 ILR, p. 72. Note that the Court was dealing with the creation of a custom on the basis of what had been purely a treaty rule. See Akehurst, 'Custom as a Source', p. 21, especially footnote 5. See also the *Paquete Habana* case, 175 US 677 (1900) and the *Lotus* case, PCIJ, Series A, No. 10, 1927, p. 18; 4 ILR, p. 153.

[25] ICJ Reports, 1986, p. 14; 76 ILR, p. 349.   [26] *Ibid.*, p. 98; 76 ILR, p. 432.

[27] See D'Amato, *Concept of Custom*, pp. 60–61 and Akehurst, 'Custom as a Source', p. 19. See also Judge Alvarez, the *Anglo-Norwegian Fisheries* case, ICJ Reports, 1951, pp. 116, 152; 18 ILR, pp. 86, 105 and Judge Loder, the *Lotus* case, PCIJ, Series A, No. 10, 1927, pp. 18, 34.

artificial satellites came into being soon after the launching of the first Sputniks. Bin Cheng has argued that in such circumstances repetition is not at all necessary provided the *opinio juris* could be clearly established. Thus, 'instant' customary law is possible.[28]

This contention that single acts may create custom has been criticised, particularly in view of the difficulties of proving customary rules any other way but through a series of usages. Nevertheless, the conclusion must be that it is the international context which plays the vital part in the creation of custom. In a society constantly faced with new situations because of the dynamics of progress, there is a clear need for a reasonably speedy method of responding to such changes by a system of prompt rule formation. In new areas of law, customs can be quickly established by state practices by virtue of the newness of the situations involved, the lack of contrary rules to be surmounted and the overwhelming necessity to preserve a sense of regulation in international relations.

One particular analogy that has been used to illustrate the general nature of customary law was considered by de Visscher. He likened the growth of custom to the gradual formation of a road across vacant land. After an initial uncertainty as to direction, the majority of users begin to follow the same line which becomes a single path. Not long elapses before that path is transformed into a road accepted as the only regular way, even though it is not possible to state at which precise moment this latter change occurs. And so it is with the formation of a custom. De Visscher develops this idea by reflecting that just as some make heavier footprints than others due to their greater weight, the more influential states of the world mark the way with more vigour and tend to become the guarantors and defenders of the way forward.[29]

The reasons why a particular state acts in a certain way are varied but are closely allied to how it perceives its interests. This in turn depends upon the power and role of the state and its international standing. Accordingly, custom should to some extent mirror the perceptions of the majority of states, since it is based upon usages which are practised by nations as they express their power and their hopes and fears. But it is inescapable that some states are more influential and powerful than others and that their activities should be regarded as of greater significance. This is reflected in international law so that custom may be created by a few states, provided those states are intimately connected with the issue at hand, whether because of their wealth and power or because of their special relationship with the

---

[28] Cheng, 'United Nations Resolutions'.
[29] De Visscher, *Theory and Reality*, p. 149. See also Lauterpacht, *Development of International Law*, p. 368; P. Cobbett, *Leading Cases on International Law*, 4th edn, 1922, p. 5 and Akehurst, 'Custom as a Source', pp. 22–3.

subject-matter of the practice, as for example maritime nations and sea law. Law cannot be divorced from politics or power and this is one instance of that proposition.[30]

The influence of the United Kingdom, for example, on the development of the law of the sea and prize law in the nineteenth century when it was at the height of its power, was predominant. A number of propositions later accepted as part of international customary law appeared this way. Among many instances of this, one can point to navigation procedures. Similarly, the impact of the Soviet Union (now Russia) and the United States on space law has been paramount.[31]

One can conclude by stating that for a custom to be accepted and recognised it must have the concurrence of the major powers in that particular field. A regulation regarding the breadth of the territorial sea is unlikely to be treated as law if the great maritime nations do not agree to or acquiesce in it, no matter how many land-locked states demand it. Other countries may propose ideas and institute pressure, but without the concurrence of those most interested, it cannot amount to a rule of customary law. This follows from the nature of the international system where all may participate but the views of those with greater power carry greater weight.

Accordingly, the duration and generality of a practice may take second place to the relative importance of the states precipitating the formation of a new customary rule in any given field. Universality is not required, but some correlation with power is. Some degree of continuity must be maintained but this again depends upon the context of operation and the nature of the usage.

Those elements reflect the external manifestations of a practice and establish that it is in existence and exhibited as such. That does not mean that it is law and this factor will be considered in the next subsection. But it does mean that all states who take the trouble can discover its existence. This factor of conspicuousness emphasises both the importance of the context within which the usage operates and the more significant elements of the overt act which affirms the existence of a custom.

The question is raised at this stage of how significant a failure to act is. Just how important is it when a state, or, more particularly, a major state, does not participate in a practice? Can it be construed as acquiescence in the performance of the usage? Or, on the other hand, does it denote indifference implying the inability of the practice to become a custom until a decision one way or the other has been made? Failures to act are in

[30] See e.g. the *North Sea Continental Shelf* cases, ICJ Reports, 1969, pp. 3, 42–3; 41 ILR, pp. 29, 71–3.
[31] See e.g. Cheng, 'United Nations Resolutions'; C. Christol, *The Modern International Law of Outer Space*, New York, 1982, and Christol, *Space Law: Past, Present and Future*, 1991.

themselves just as much evidence of a state's attitudes as are actions. They similarly reflect the way in which a nation approaches its environment. Britain consistently fails to attack France, while Chad consistently fails to send a man to the moon. But does this mean that Britain recognises a rule not to attack its neighbour and that Chad accepts a custom not to launch rockets to the moon? Of course, the answer is in the first instance yes, and in the second example no. Thus, a failure to act can arise from either a legal obligation not to act, or an incapacity or unwillingness in the particular circumstances to act. Indeed, it has been maintained that the continued habit of not taking actions in certain situations may lead to the formation of a legal rule.[32]

The danger of saying that a failure to act over a long period creates a negative custom, that is, a rule actually not to do it, can be shown by remarking the absurdity of the proposition that a continual failure to act until the late 1950s is evidence of a legal rule not to send artificial satellites or rockets into space. On the other hand, where a particular rule of behaviour is established it can be argued that abstention from protest by states may amount to agreement with that rule.

In the particular circumstances of the *Lotus* case[33] the Permanent Court of International Justice, the predecessor of the International Court of Justice, laid down a high standard by declaring that abstention could only give rise to the recognition of a custom if it was based on a conscious duty to abstain. In other words, states had actually to be aware that they were not acting a particular way because they were under a definite obligation not to act that way. The decision has been criticised and would appear to cover categories of non-acts based on legal obligations, but not to refer to instances where, by simply not acting as against a particular rule in existence, they are tacitly accepting the legality and relevance of that rule.

It should be mentioned, however, that acquiescence must be based upon full knowledge of the rule invoked. Where a failure to take a course of action is in some way connected or influenced or accompanied by a lack of knowledge of all the relevant circumstances, then it cannot be interpreted as acquiescence.

What is state practice?

Some of the ingredients of state activities have been surveyed and attempts made to place them in some kind of relevant context. But what is state practice? Does it cover every kind of behaviour initiated by the state, or is it

---

[32] See e.g. Tunkin, *Theory of International Law*, footnote 1, pp. 116–17. But cf. D'Amato, *Concept of Custom*, pp. 61–3 and 88–9.
[33] PCIJ, Series A, No. 10, 1927, p. 18; 4 ILR, p. 153.

limited to actual, positive actions? To put it more simply, does it include such things as speeches, informal documents and governmental statements or is it restricted to what states actually do?

It is how states behave in practice that forms the basis of customary law, but evidence of what a state does can be obtained from numerous sources. A state is not a living entity, but consists of governmental departments and thousands of officials, and state activity is spread throughout a whole range of national organs. There are the state's legal officers, legislative institutions, courts, diplomatic agents and political leaders. Each of these engages in activity which relates to the international field and therefore one has to examine all such material sources and more in order to discover evidence of what states do.[34]

The obvious way to find out how countries are behaving is to read the newspapers, consult historical records, listen to what governmental authorities are saying and peruse the many official publications. There are also memoirs of various past leaders, official manuals on legal questions, diplomatic interchanges and the opinions of national legal advisors. All these methods are valuable in seeking to determine actual state practice.

In addition, one may note resolutions in the General Assembly, comments made by governments on drafts produced by the International Law Commission, decisions of the international judicial institutions, decisions of national courts, treaties and the general practice of international organisations.[35]

International organisations in fact may be instrumental in the creation of customary law. For example, the Advisory Opinion of the International Court of Justice declaring that the United Nations possessed international personality was partly based on the actual behaviour of the UN.[36] The International Law Commission has pointed out that 'records of the cumulative practice of international organisations may be regarded as evidence of customary international law with reference to states' relations to the organisations'.[37]

---

[34] See e.g. *Yearbook of the ILC*, 1950, vol. II, pp. 368–72 and the *Interhandel* case, ICJ Reports, 1959, p. 27. Note also Brierly's comment that not all contentions put forward on behalf of a state represent that state's settled or impartial opinion, *The Law of Nations*, 6th edn, Oxford, 1963, p. 60. See also Brownlie, *Principles*, p. 5 and Akehurst, 'Custom as a Source', p. 2.

[35] The United States has produced an extensive series of publications covering its practice in international law. See the Digests of International Law produced by Wharton (1887), Moore (1906) and Whiteman (1963–70). From 1973–80, an annual *Digest of US Practice in International Law* has been produced, while three composite volumes covering the years 1981–8 have appeared. See also H. A. Smith, *Great Britain and the Law of Nations*, 2 vols., 1932–5; A. D. McNair, *International Law Opinions*, 3 vols., 1956; C. Parry, *British Digest of International Law*, 1965, and E. Lauterpacht, *British Practice in International Law*, 1963–7. Several yearbooks now produce sections devoted to national practice, e.g. *British Yearbook of International Law* and *Annuaire Français de Droit International*.

[36] The *Reparation* case, ICJ Reports, 1949, p. 174; 16 ILR, p. 318. See also the *Reservations to the Genocide Convention* case, ICJ Reports, 1951, pp. 15, 25; 18 ILR, p. 364.

[37] *Yearbook of the ILC*, 1950, vol. II, pp. 368–72. See also Akehurst, 'Custom as a Source', p. 12.

States' municipal laws may in certain circumstances form the basis of customary rules. In the *Scotia* case decided by the US Supreme Court in 1871,[38] a British ship had sunk an American vessel on the high seas. The Court held that British navigational procedures established by an Act of Parliament formed the basis of the relevant international custom since other states had legislated in virtually identical terms. Accordingly, the American vessel, in not displaying the correct lights, was at fault. The view has also been expressed that mere claims as distinct from actual physical acts cannot constitute state practice. This is based on the precept that 'until it [a state] takes enforcement action, the claim has little value as a prediction of what the state will actually do'.[39] But as has been demonstrated this is decidedly a minority view.[40] Claims and conventions of states in various contexts have been adduced as evidence of state practice and it is logical that this should be so,[41] though the weight to be attached to such claims, may, of course, vary according to the circumstances. This approach is clearly the correct one since the process of claims and counterclaims is one recognised method by which states communicate to each other their perceptions of the status of international rules and norms. In this sense they operate in the same way as physical acts. Whether *in abstracto* or with regard to a particular situation, they constitute the raw material out of which may be fashioned rules of international law.[42] It is suggested that the formulation that 'state practice covers any act or statements by a state from which views about customary law may be inferred',[43] is substantially correct.

Opinio juris[44]

Once one has established the existence of a specified usage, it becomes necessary to consider how the state views its own behaviour. Is it to be regarded

---

[38] 14 Wallace 170 (1871). See also the *Nottebohm* case, ICJ Reports, 1955, pp. 4, 22; 22 ILR, p. 349 and the *Paquete Habana* case, 175 US 677 (1900).

[39] D'Amato, *Concept of Custom*, p. 88 and pp. 50–1. See also Judge Read (dissenting), the *Anglo-Norwegian Fisheries* case, ICJ Reports, 1951, pp. 116, 191; 18 ILR, pp. 86, 132.

[40] Akehurst, 'Custom as a Source', pp. 2–3. See also Thirlway, *International Customary Law*, p. 58.

[41] E.g. the *Asylum* case, ICJ Reports, 1950, pp. 266, 277; 17 ILR, p. 280; the *Rights of US Nationals in Morocco* case, ICJ Reports, 1952, pp. 176, 200, 209; 19 ILR, p. 255, and the *North Sea Continental Shelf* cases, ICJ Reports, 1969, pp. 3, 32–3, 47 and 53; 41 ILR, p. 29. See also the *Fisheries Jurisdiction* cases, ICJ Reports, 1974, pp. 3, 47, 56–8, 81–8, 119–20, 135 and 161; 55 ILR, p. 238.   [42] But see Thirlway, *International Customary Law*, pp. 58–9.

[43] Akehurst, 'Custom as a Source', p. 10. This would also include omissions and silence by states: *ibid.*

[44] *Ibid.*, pp. 31–42 and D'Amato, *Concept of Custom*, pp. 66–72. See also Bos, *Methodology*, pp. 236 *et seq.*; Haggenmacher, 'Des Deux Éléments du Droit Coutumier dans la Pratique de la Cour Internationale', *Revue Générale de Droit International Public*, 1985, p. 5; O. Elias, 'The Nature of the Subjective Element in Customary International Law', 44 ICLQ, 1995, p. 501 and I. M. Lobo de Souza, 'The Role of State Consent in the Customary Process', *ibid.*, p. 521.

as a moral or political or legal act or statement? The *opinio juris*, or belief that a state activity is legally obligatory, is the factor which turns the usage into a custom and renders it part of the rules of international law. To put it slightly differently, states will behave a certain way because they are convinced it is binding upon them to do so.

The Permanent Court of International Justice expressed this point of view when it dealt with the *Lotus* case.[45] The issue at hand concerned a collision on the high seas (where international law applies) between the *Lotus*, a French ship, and the *Boz-Kourt*, a Turkish ship. Several people aboard the latter ship were drowned and Turkey alleged negligence by the French officer of the watch. When the *Lotus* reached Istanbul, the French officer was arrested on a charge of manslaughter and the case turned on whether Turkey had jurisdiction to try him. Among the various arguments adduced, the French maintained that there existed a rule of customary law to the effect that the flag state of the accused (France) had exclusive jurisdiction in such cases and that accordingly the national state of the victim (Turkey) was barred from trying him. To justify this, France referred to the absence of previous criminal prosecutions by such states in similar situations and from this deduced tacit consent in the practice which therefore became a legal custom.

The Court rejected this and declared that even if such a practice of abstention from instituting criminal proceedings could be proved in fact, it would not amount to a custom. It held that 'only if such abstention were based on their [the states] being conscious of a duty to abstain would it be possible to speak of an international custom'.[46] Thus the essential ingredient of obligation was lacking and the practice remained a practice, nothing more.

A similar approach occurred in the *North Sea Continental Shelf* cases.[47] In the general process of delimiting the continental shelf of the North Sea in pursuance of oil and gas exploration, lines were drawn dividing the whole area into national spheres. However, West Germany could not agree with either Holland or Denmark over the respective boundary lines and the matter came before the International Court of Justice.

✴Article 6 of the Geneva Convention on the Continental Shelf of 1958 provided that where agreement could not be reached, and unless special circumstances justified a different approach, the boundary line was to be determined in accordance with the principle of equidistance from the nearest points of the baselines from which the breadth of the territorial sea of each state is measured. This would mean a series of lines drawn at the point where Germany met Holland on the one side and Denmark on the

---

[45] PCIJ, Series A, No. 10, 1927, p. 18; 4 ILR, p. 153.   [46] *Ibid.*, p. 28; 4 ILR, p. 159.
[47] ICJ Reports, 1969, p. 3; 41 ILR, p. 29.

other and projected outwards into the North Sea. However, because Germany's coastline is concave, such equidistant lines would converge and enclose a relatively small triangle of the North Sea. The Federal Republic had signed but not ratified the 1958 Geneva Convention and was therefore not bound by its terms. The question thus was whether a case could be made out that the 'equidistance – special circumstances principle' had been absorbed into customary law and was accordingly binding upon Germany.

The Court concluded in the negative and held that the provision in the Geneva Convention did not reflect an already existing custom. It was emphasised that when the International Law Commission had considered this point in the draft treaty which formed the basis of discussion at Geneva, the principle of equidistance had been proposed with considerable hesitation, somewhat on an experimental basis and not at all as an emerging rule of customary international law.[48] The issue then turned on whether practice subsequent to the Convention had created a customary rule. The Court answered in the negative and declared that although time was not of itself a decisive factor (only three years had elapsed before the proceedings were brought):

> an indispensable requirement would be that within the period in question, short though it might be, state practice, including that of states whose interests are specially affected, should have been both extensive and virtually uniform in the sense of the provision invoked, and should moreover have occurred in such a way as to show a general recognition that a rule of law or legal obligation is involved.[49]

This approach was maintained by the Court in the *Nicaragua* case[50] and express reference made to the *North Sea Continental Shelf* cases. The Court noted that:

> for a new customary rule to be formed, not only must the acts concerned 'amount to a settled practice', but they must be accompanied by the *opinio juris sive necessitatis*. Either the States taking such action or other States in a position to react to it, must have behaved so that their conduct is 'evidence of a belief that this practice is rendered obligatory by the existence of a rule of law requiring it. The need for such a belief, i.e. the existence of a subjective element, is implicit in the very notion of the *opinio juris sive necessitatis*.'[51]

It is thus clear that the Court has adopted and maintained a high threshold with regard to the overt proving of the subjective constituent of customary law formation.

---

[48] *Ibid.*, pp. 32–41.
[49] *Ibid.*, p. 43. See also e.g. the *Asylum* case, ICJ Reports, 1950, pp. 266, 277; 17 ILR, p. 280 and the *Right of Passage* case, ICJ Reports, 1960, pp. 6, 42–3; 31 ILR, pp. 23, 55.
[50] ICJ Reports, 1986, p. 14; 76 ILR, p. 349.
[51] *Ibid.*, pp. 108–9; 76 ILR, pp. 442–3, citing ICJ Reports, 1969, p. 44; 41 ILR, p. 73.

The great problem connected with the *opinio juris* is that if it calls for behaviour in accordance with law, how can new customary rules be created since that obviously requires action different from or contrary to what until then is regarded as law? If a country claims a 3 mile territorial sea in the belief that this is legal, how can the rule be changed in customary law to allow claims of, for example, 12 miles since that cannot also be in accordance with prevailing law?[52] Obviously if one takes a restricted view of the psychological aspects, then logically the law will become stultified and this demonstrably has not happened.

Thus, one has to treat the matter in terms of a process whereby states behave in a certain way in the belief that such behaviour is law or is becoming law. It will then depend upon how other states react as to whether this process of legislation is accepted or rejected. It follows that rigid definitions as to legality have to be modified to see whether the legitimating stamp of state activity can be provided or not. If a state proclaims a 12 mile limit to its territorial sea in the belief that although the 3 mile limit has been accepted law, the circumstances are so altering that a 12 mile limit might now be treated as becoming law, it is vindicated if other states follow suit and a new rule of customary law is established. If other states reject the proposition, then the projected rule withers away and the original rule stands, reinforced by state practice and commonly accepted. As the Court itself noted in the *Nicaragua* case,[53] '[r]eliance by a State on a novel right or an unprecedented exception to the principle might, if shared in principle by other States, tend towards a modification of customary international law'. The difficulty in this kind of approach is that it is sometimes hard to pinpoint exactly when one rule supersedes another, but that is a complication inherent in the nature of custom. Change is rarely smooth but rather spasmodic.

This means taking a more flexible view of the *opinio juris* and tying it more firmly with the overt manifestations of a custom into the context of national and international behaviour. This should be done to accommodate the idea of an action which, while contrary to law, contains the germ of a new law and relates to the difficulty of actually proving that a state, in behaving a certain way, does so in the belief that it is in accordance with the law. An extreme expression of this approach is to infer or deduce the *opinio juris* from the material acts. Judge Tanaka, in his dissenting opinion in the *North Sea Continental Shelf* cases, remarked that there was:

> no other way than to ascertain the existence of *opinio juris* from the fact of the external existence of a certain custom and its necessity felt in the international

---

[52] See Akehurst, 'Custom as a Source', pp. 32–4 for attempts made to deny or minimise the need for *opinio juris*.   [53] ICJ Reports, 1986, pp. 14, 109; 76 ILR, pp. 349, 443.

community, rather than to seek evidence as to the subjective motives for each example of State practice.[54]

However, states must be made aware that when one state takes a course of action, it does so because it regards it as within the confines of international law, and not as, for example, purely a political or moral gesture. There has to be an aspect of legality about the behaviour and the acting state will have to confirm that this is so, so that the international community can easily distinguish legal from non-legal practices. This is essential to the development and presentation of a legal framework amongst the states.[55]

Protest, acquiescence and change in customary law[56]

Customary law is thus established by virtue of a pattern of claim, absence of protest by states particularly interested in the matter at hand and acquiescence by other states.[57]

Generally, where states are seen to acquiesce in the behaviour of other states without protesting against them, the assumption must be that such behaviour is accepted as legitimate.[58]

Some writers have maintained that acquiescence can amount to consent to a customary rule and that the absence of protest implies agreement. In other words where a state or states take action which they declare to be legal, the silence of other states can be used as an expression of *opinio juris* or concurrence in the new legal rule. This means that actual protests are called for to break the legitimising process.[59]

---

[54] ICJ Reports, 1969, pp. 3, 176; 41 ILR, pp. 29, 171. Lauterpacht wrote that one should regard all uniform conduct of governments as evidencing the *opinio juris*, except where the conduct in question was not accompanied by such intention. *Development of International Law*, p. 580; but cf. Cheng, 'Custom; The Future', p. 36 and Cheng, 'United Nations Resolutions', pp. 530–2.

[55] Note D'Amato's view that to become a custom, a practice has to be preceded or accompanied by the 'articulation' of a rule, which will put states on notice that an action etc. will have legal implications, 'Concept of Custom', p. 75. Cf. Akehurst, 'Custom as a Source', pp. 35–6, who also puts forward his view that 'the practice of states needs to be accompanied by *statements* that something is already law before it can become law': such statements need not be beliefs as to the truths of the given situation, *ibid.*, p. 37. Akehurst also draws a distinction between permissive rules, which do not require express statements as to *opinio juris* and duty-imposing rules, which do; *ibid.*, pp. 37–8.

[56] See H. Lauterpacht, 'Sovereignty over Submarine Areas', 27 BYIL, 1950, p. 376; I. MacGibbon, 'Some Observations on the Part of Protest in International Law', 29 BYIL, 1953, p. 293 and MacGibbon, 'Customary International Law and Acquiescence', 33 BYIL, 1957, p. 115 and Wolfke, *Custom*, pp. 157–65.

[57] See for a good example the decision of the International Court in the *El Salvador/Honduras* case, ICJ Reports, 1992, pp. 351, 601; 97 ILR, pp. 266, 517, with regard to the joint sovereignty over the historic waters of the Gulf of Fonseca beyond the territorial sea of the three coastal states.

[58] See e.g. *Grand-Duchy of Luxembourg v. Cie. Luxembourgeoise de Télédiffusion*, 91 ILR, pp. 281, 286.

[59] See e.g. MacGibbon, 'Customary International Law', p. 131 and H. S. McDougal *et al.*, *Studies in World Public Order*, New Haven, 1960, pp. 763–72.

In the *Lotus* case, the Court held that 'only if such abstention were based on their [the states] being conscious of having a duty to abstain would it be possible to speak of an international custom'.[60] Thus, one cannot infer a rule prohibiting certain action merely because states do not indulge in that activity. But the question of not reacting when a state behaves in a certain way is a slightly different one. It would seem that where a new rule is created in new fields of international law, for example space law, acquiescence by other states is to be regarded as reinforcing the rule whether it stems from actual agreement or lack of interest, depending always upon the particular circumstances of the case. Acquiescence in a new rule which deviates from an established custom is more problematic.

The decision in the *Anglo-Norwegian Fisheries* case[61] may appear to suggest that where a state acts contrary to an established customary rule and other states acquiesce in this, then that state is to be treated as not bound by the original rule. The Court noted that 'in any event the . . . rule would appear to be inapplicable as against Norway inasmuch as she had always opposed any attempt to apply it to the Norwegian coast'.[62] In other words, a state opposing the existence of a custom from its inception would not be bound by it, but the problem of one or more states seeking to dissent from recognised customs by adverse behaviour coupled with the acquiescence or non-reaction of other states remains unsettled.

States fail to protest for very many reasons. A state might not wish to give offence gratuitously or it might wish to reinforce political ties or other diplomatic and political considerations may be relevant. It could be that to protest over every single act with which a state does not agree would be an excessive requirement. It is, therefore, unrealistic to expect every state to react to every single act of every other state. If one accepted that a failure to protest validated a derogation from an established custom in every case then scores of special relationships would emerge between different states depending upon acquiescence and protest. In many cases a protest might be purely formal or part of diplomatic manoeuvring designed to exert pressure in a totally different field and thus not intended to alter legal relationships.

Where a new rule which contradicts a prior rule is maintained by a large number of states, the protests of a few states would not overrule it, and the abstention from reaction by other countries would merely reinforce it. Constant protest on the part of a particular state when reinforced by the acquiescence of other states might create a recognised exception to the rule, but it will depend to a great extent on the facts of the situation and the views

---

[60] *Supra*, footnote 46. [61] ICJ Reports, 1951, p. 116; 18 ILR, p. 86.
[62] *Ibid.*, p. 131; 18 ILR, p. 93. See also the *North Sea Continental Shelf* cases, ICJ Reports, 1969, pp. 3, 26–7; 41 ILR, pp. 29, 55–6 and the *Asylum* case, ICJ Reports, 1950, pp. 266, 277–8; 17 ILR, pp. 280, 285.

of the international community. Behaviour contrary to a custom contains within itself the seeds of a new rule and if it is endorsed by other nations, the previous law will disappear and be replaced, or alternatively there could be a period of time during which the two customs co-exist until one of them is generally accepted,[63] as was the position for many years with regard to the limits of the territorial sea.[64] It follows from the above, therefore, that customary rules are binding upon all states except for such states as have dissented from the start of that custom.[65] This raises the question of new states and custom, for the logic of the traditional approach would be for such states to be bound by all existing customs as at the date of independence. The opposite view, based upon the consent theory of law, would permit such states to choose which customs to adhere to at that stage, irrespective of the attitude of other states.[66] However, since such an approach could prove highly disruptive, the proviso is often made that by entering into relations without reservation with other states, new states signify their acceptance of the totality of international law.[67]

Local custom[68]

It is possible for rules to develop which will bind only a set group of states, or indeed just two states.[69]

In the *Asylum* case,[70] the International Court of Justice discussed the Colombian claim of a regional or local custom peculiar to the Latin American states, which would validate its position over the granting of asylum. The Court declared that the 'party which relies on a custom of this kind must prove that this custom is established in such a manner that it has become binding on the other party'.[71] It found that such a custom could not be proved because of uncertain and contradictory evidence.

In such cases, the standard of proof required, especially as regards the obligation accepted by the party against whom the local custom is main-

---

[63] See also protests generally: Akehurst, 'Custom as a Source', pp. 38–42.

[64] See *infra*, Chapter 11, p. 401.

[65] See e.g. the *North Sea Continental Shelf* cases, ICJ Reports, 1969, pp. 3, 38, 130; 41 ILR, pp. 29, 67, 137 and *The Third Restatement of US Foreign Relations Law*, St Paul, 1987, vol. I, pp. 25–6. See also T. Stein, 'The Approach of the Different Drummer: The Principle of the Persistent Objector in International Law', 26 *Harvard International Law Journal*, 1985, p. 457 and J. Charney, 'The Persistent Objector Rule and the Development of Customary International Law', 56 BYIL, 1985, p. 1.

[66] See e.g. Tunkin, *Theory of International Law*, p. 129.   [67] *Ibid.*

[68] See Akehurst, 'Custom as a Source', pp. 29–31; D'Amato, *Concept of Custom*, Chapter 8; G. Cohen-Jonathan, 'La Coutume Locale', AFDI, 1961, p. 133 and Wolfke, *Custom*, pp. 88–90. Sometimes referred to as regional or special custom.

[69] Note the claim by Honduras in the *El Salvador/Honduras* case, ICJ Reports, 1992, pp. 351, 597: 97 ILR, pp. 266, 513 that a 'trilateral local custom of the nature of a convention' could establish a condominium arrangement.   [70] ICJ Reports, 1950, p. 266; 17 ILR, p. 280.

[71] *Ibid.*, p. 276; 17 ILR, p. 284.

tained, is higher than in cases where an ordinary or general custom is alleged.

In the *Right of Passage over Indian Territory* case,[72] Portugal claimed that there existed a right of passage over Indian territory as between the Portuguese enclaves, and this was upheld by the International Court of Justice over India's objections that no local custom could be established between only two states. The Court declared that it was satisfied that there had in the past existed a constant and uniform practice allowing free passage and that the 'practice was accepted as law by the parties and has given rise to a right and a correlative obligation'.[73]

Such local customs therefore depend upon a particular activity by one state being accepted by the other state (or states) as an expression of a legal obligation or right. While in the case of a general customary rule the process of consensus is at work so that a majority or a substantial minority of interested states can be sufficient to create a new custom, a local custom needs the positive acceptance of both (or all) parties to the rule.[74] This is because local customs are an exception to the general nature of customary law, which involves a fairly flexible approach to law-making by all states, and instead constitutes a reminder of the former theory of consent whereby states are bound only by what they assent to. Exceptions may prove the rule, but they need greater proof than the rule to establish themselves.

Treaties[75]

In contrast with the process of creating law through custom, treaties (or international conventions) are a more modern and more deliberate method.[76] Article 38 refers to 'international conventions, whether general or particular, establishing rules expressly recognised by the contracting states'. Treaties will be considered in more detail in Chapter 16 but in this survey of the sources of international law reference must be made to the role of international conventions.

Treaties are known by a variety of differing names, ranging from Conventions, International Agreements, Pacts, General Acts, Charters, through to Statutes, Declarations and Covenants. All these terms refer to a similar transaction, the creation of written agreements whereby the states

---

[72] ICJ Reports, 1960, p. 6; 31 ILR, p. 23.
[73] *Ibid.*, p. 40; 31 ILR, p. 53. See Wolfke, *Custom*, p. 90.
[74] See Cohen-Jonathan, 'La Coutume Locale'.
[75] See generally A. D. McNair, *The Law of Treaties*, Oxford, 1961. See further *infra*, Chapter 16.
[76] *Oppenheim's International Law* emphasises that 'not only is custom the original source of international law, but treaties are a source the validity and modalities of which themselves derive from custom', p. 31.

participating bind themselves legally to act in a particular way or to set up particular relations between themselves. A series of conditions and arrangements are laid out which the parties oblige themselves to carry out.[77]

It is possible to divide treaties into 'law-making' treaties, which are intended to have universal or general relevance, and 'treaty-contracts', which apply only as between two, or a small number of states. Such a distinction is intended to reflect the general or local applicability of a particular treaty and the range of obligations imposed. It cannot be regarded as hard and fast and there are many grey areas of overlap and uncertainty.[78]

Treaties are express agreements and are a form of substitute legislation undertaken by states. They bear a close resemblance to contracts in a superficial sense in that the parties create binding obligations for themselves, but they have a nature of their own which reflects the character of the international system. The number of treaties entered into has expanded over the last century, witness the growing number of volumes of the United Nations Treaty Series or the United Kingdom Treaty Series. They fulfil a vital role in international relations.

As governmental controls increase and the technological and communications revolutions affect international life, the number of issues which require some form of interstate regulation multiplies.

For many writers, treaties constitute the most important sources of international law as they require the express consent of the contracting parties. Treaties are thus seen as superior to custom, which is regarded in any event as a form of tacit agreement.[79] As examples of important treaties one may mention the Charter of the United Nations, the Geneva Conventions on the treatment of prisoners and the protection of civilians and the Vienna Conventions on Diplomatic Relations. All kinds of agreements exist ranging from the regulation of outer space exploration to the control of drugs and the creation of international financial and development institutions. It would be impossible to telephone abroad or post a letter overseas or take an aeroplane to other countries without the various international agreements that have laid down the necessary, recognised conditions of operation.

---

[77] See the Vienna Convention on the Law of Treaties 1969. Article 2(1) a defines a treaty for the purposes of the Convention as 'an international agreement concluded between states in written form and governed by international law, whether embodied in a single instrument or in two or more related instruments and whatever its particular designation'. See further *infra* p. 92 with regard to non-binding international agreements.

[78] See Virally, 'The Sources', p. 126; Sørensen, *Les Sources*, p. 58 *et seq.* and Tunkin, *Theory of International Law*, pp. 93–5.

[79] Tunkin, *Theory of International Law*, pp. 91–113. See also R. Mullerson, 'Sources of International Law: New Tendencies in Soviet Thinking', 83 AJIL, 1989, pp. 494, 501–9 and G. Danilenko, 'The Theory of International Customary Law', 31 German YIL, 1988, p. 9.

It follows from the essence of an international treaty that, like a contract, it sets down a series of propositions which are then regarded as binding upon the parties. How then is it possible to treat conventions as sources of international law, over and above the obligations imposed upon the contracting parties? It is in this context that one can understand the term 'law-making treaties'. They are intended to have an effect *generally*, not restrictively, and they are to be contrasted with those treaties which merely regulate limited issues between a few states. ₁Law-making treaties are those agreements whereby states elaborate their perception of international law upon any given topic or establish new rules which are to guide them for the future in their international conduct. Such law-making treaties, of necessity, require the participation of a large number of states to emphasise this effect, and may produce rules that will bind all.[80] They constitute normative treaties, agreements that prescribe rules of conduct to be followed. Examples of such treaties may include the Antarctica Treaty and the Genocide Convention. There are also many agreements which declare the existing law or codify existing customary rules, such as the Vienna Convention on Diplomatic Relations of 1961.[81]

Parties that do not sign and ratify the particular treaty in question are not bound by its terms. This is a general rule and was illustrated in the *North Sea Continental Shelf* cases[82] where West Germany had not ratified the relevant Convention and was therefore under no obligation to heed its terms. However, where treaties reflect customary law then non-parties are bound, not because it is a treaty provision but because it reaffirms a rule or rules of customary international law. Similarly, non-parties may come to accept that provisions in a particular treaty can generate customary law, depending always upon the nature of the agreement, the number of participants and other relevant factors.

The possibility that a provision in a treaty may constitute the basis of a rule which, when coupled with the *opinio juris*, can lead to the creation of a binding custom governing all states, not just those party to the original treaty, was considered by the International Court of Justice in the *North Sea Continental Shelf* cases[83] and regarded as one of the recognised methods of formulating new rules of customary international law. The Court, however, declared that the particular provision had to be 'of a fundamentally

[80] But this may depend upon the attitude of other states. This does not consitute a form of international legislation, see e.g. *Oppenheim's International Law*, p. 32; the *Reparations* case, ICJ Reports, 1949, p. 185, 16 ILR, p. 318, and the *Namibia* case, ICJ Reports, 1971, p. 56, 49 ILR, p. 2. See also Brownlie, *Principles*, pp. 12–13 and R. Baxter, 'Treaties and Custom', 129 HR, p. 27. See also O. Schachter, 'Entangled Treaty and Custom' in *International Law at a Time of Perplexity* (ed. Y. Dinstein), Dordrecht, 1989, p. 717.
[81] Brownlie, *Principles*, p. 12.   [82] ICJ Reports, 1969, pp. 3, 25; 41 ILR, pp. 29, 54.
[83] *Ibid.*, p. 41; 41 ILR, p. 71. The Court stressed that this method of creating new customs was not to be lightly regarded as having been attained, *ibid.*

norm-creating character',[84] that is, capable of forming the basis of a general rule of law. What exactly this amounts to will probably vary according to the time and place, but it does confirm that treaty provisions may lead to custom providing other states, parties and non-parties to the treaty fulfil the necessary conditions of compatible behaviour and *opinio juris*. It has been argued that this possibility may be extended so that generalisable treaty provisions may of themselves, without the requirement to demonstrate the *opinio juris* and with little passage of time, generate *ipso facto* customary rules.[85] This, while recognising the importance of treaties, particularly in the human rights field, containing potential norm-creating provisions, is clearly going too far. The danger would be of a small number of states legislating for all, unless dissenting states actually entered into contrary treaties.[86] This would constitute too radical a departure for the current process of law-formation within the international community.

It is now established that even where a treaty rule comes into being covering the same ground as a customary rule, the latter will not be simply absorbed within the former but will maintain its separate existence. The Court in the *Nicaragua* case[87] did not accept the argument of the US that the norms of customary international law concerned with self-defence had been 'subsumed' and 'supervened' by article 51 of the United Nations Charter. It was emphasised that 'even if a treaty norm and a customary norm relevant to the present dispute were to have exactly the same content, this would not be a reason for the Court to hold that the incorporation of the customary norm into treaty law must deprive the customary norm of its applicability as distinct from the treaty norm'.[88] The Court concluded that 'it will therefore be clear that customary international law continues to exist and to apply separately from international treaty law, even where the two categories of law have an identical content'.[89] The effect of this in the instant case was that the Court was able to examine the rule as established under customary law, whereas due to an American reservation, it was unable to analyse the treaty-based obligation.

Of course, two rules with the same content may be subject to different principles with regard to their interpretation and application; thus the approach of the Court as well as being theoretically correct is of practical

---

[84] But see the minority opinions, *ibid.*, pp. 56, 156–8, 163, 169, 172–80, 197–200, 221–32 and 241–7; 41 ILR, p. 85. See also the *Gulf of Maine* case, ICJ Reports, 1984, pp. 246, 295; 71 ILR, pp. 74, 122 and the *Libya–Malta Continental Shelf* case, ICJ Reports, 1985, pp. 13, 29–34; 81 ILR, pp. 239, 261–6.

[85] See D'Amato, *Concept of Custom*, p. 104 and D'Amato, 'The Concept of Human Rights in International Law', 82 *Columbia Law Review*, 1982, pp. 1110, 1129–47. See also Akehurst, 'Custom as a Source', pp. 42–52.   [86] D'Amato, 'Concept of Human Rights', p. 1146.

[87] ICJ Reports, 1986, p. 14; 76 ILR, p. 349.

[88] *Ibid.*, pp. 94–5; 76 ILR, pp. 428–9. See also W. Czaplinski, 'Sources of International Law in the *Nicaragua* case', 38 ICLQ, 1989, p. 151.   [89] *Ibid.*, p. 96; ILR, *ibid.*, p. 430.

value also. In many cases, such dual source of existence of a rule may well
suggest that the two versions are not in fact identical, as in the case of self-
defence under customary law and article 51 of the Charter, but it will always
depend upon the particular circumstances.[90]

Certain treaties attempt to establish a 'regime' which will, of necessity,
also extend to non-parties.[91] The United Nations Charter, for example, in
its creation of a definitive framework for the preservation of international
peace and security, declares in article 2(6) that 'the organisation shall ensure
that states which are not members of the United Nations act in accordance
with these Principles [listed in article 2] so far as may be necessary for the
maintenance of international peace and security'. One can also point to the
1947 General Agreement on Tariffs and Trade (GATT) which set up a
common code of conduct in international trade and has had an important
effect on non-party states as well.

On the same theme, treaties may be constitutive in that they create international institutions and act as constitutions for them, outlining their proposed powers and duties.

'Treaty-contracts' on the other hand are not law-making instruments in
themselves since they are between only small numbers of states and on a
limited topic, but may provide evidence of customary rules. For example, a
series of bilateral treaties containing a similar rule may be evidence of the
existence of that rule in customary law, although this proposition needs to
be approached with some caution in view of the fact that bilateral treaties by
their very nature often reflect discrete circumstances.[92]

General principles of law[93]

In any system of law, a situation may very well arise where the court is considering a case before it realises that there is no law covering exactly that
point, neither parliamentary statute nor judicial precedent. In such
instances the judge will proceed to deduce a rule that will be relevant, by
analogy from already existing rules or directly from the general principles

---

[90] See further Chapter 19, *infra* p. 787.   [91] See further *infra*, Chapter 16, p. 652.
[92] See further *infra* p. 482 with regard to extradition treaties and *infra* p. 580 with regard to
bilateral investment treaties.
[93] See e.g. B. Cheng, *General Principles of Law as Applied by International Courts and Tribunals*,
London, 1953; A. D. McNair, 'The General Principles of Law Recognised by Civilised
Nations', 33 BYIL, 1957, p. 1; H. Lauterpacht, *Private Law Sources and Analogies of
International Law*, 1927; G. Hercegh, *General Principles of Law and the International Legal
Order*, Budapest, 1969; O. Schachter, *International Law in Theory and Practice*, Dordrecht,
1991, pp. 50–5; Vikanyi, 'Les Positions Doctrinales Concernant le Sens de la Notion de
"Principes Généraux de Droit Reconnus par les Nations Civilisées"', *Revue Générale de Droit
International Public*, 1982, p. 48; H. Waldock, 'General Course on Public International
Law', 106 HR, p. 54; M. Sørensen, 'Principes de Droit International', 101 HR, 1960, p. 16
and V. Degan, 'General Principles of Law', 3 Finnish YIL, 1992, p. 1.

that guide the legal system, whether they be referred to as emanating from justice, equity or considerations of public policy. Such a situation is perhaps even more likely to arise in international law because of the relative under-development of the system in relation to the needs with which it is faced.

There are fewer decided cases in international law than in a municipal system and no method of legislating to provide rules to govern new situations. It is for such a reason that the provision of 'the general principles of law recognised by civilised nations' was inserted into article 38 as a source of law, to close the gap that might be uncovered in international law and solve this problem which is known legally as *non liquet*.[94] The question of gaps in the system is an important one. It is important to appreciate that while there may not always be an immediate and obvious rule applicable to every international situation, 'every international situation is capable of being determined *as a matter of law*'.[95]

There are various opinions as to what the general principles of law concept is intended to refer. Some writers regard it as an affirmation of Natural Law concepts, which are deemed to underlie the system of international law and constitute the method for testing the validity of the positive (i.e. man-made) rules.[96] Other writers, particularly positivists, treat it as a subheading under treaty and customary law and incapable of adding anything new to international law unless it reflects the consent of states. Soviet writers like Tunkin subscribed to this approach and regarded the 'general principles of law' as reiterating the fundamental precepts of international law, for example, the law of peaceful co-existence, which have already been set out in treaty and custom law.[97]

Between these two approaches, most writers are prepared to accept that the general principles do constitute a separate source of law but of fairly limited scope, and this is reflected in the decisions of the Permanent Court of International Justice and the International Court of Justice. It is not clear, however, in all cases, whether what is involved is a general principle of law

---

[94] See e.g. J. Stone, *Of Law and Nations*, London, 1974, Chapter 3; H. Lauterpacht, 'Some Observations on the Prohibition of Non Liquet and the Completeness of the Legal Order', *Symbolae Verzijl*, 1958, p. 196, and H. Thirlway, 'The Law and Procedure of the International Court of Justice', BYIL, 1988, p. 76. See also the *North Sea Continental Shelf* cases, ICJ Reports, 1969, p. 46; 41 ILR, p. 29, and the *Nicaragua* case, ICJ Reports, 1986, p. 135; 76 ILR, p. 349.

[95] *Oppenheim's International Law*, p. 13. See, however, the conclusion of the International Court that it was unable to state whether there was a rule of international law prohibiting or permitting the threat or use of nuclear weapons by a state in self-defence where its very survival was at stake, the *Legality of the Threat or Use of Nuclear Weapons* case, ICJ Reports, 1996, paras. 36–40; 35 ILM, 1996, pp. 809, 830 and 831. Cf. the Dissenting Opinion of Judge Higgins, *ibid.*; 35 ILM, pp. 934 *et seq.*

[96] See e.g. Lauterpacht, *Private Law Sources*. See also Waldock, 'General Course', p. 54; C. W. Jenks, *The Common Law of Mankind*, London, 1958, p. 169 and Judge Tanaka (dissenting), *South West Africa* case (Second Phase), ICJ Reports, 1966, pp. 6, 294–9; 37 ILR, pp. 243, 455–9.   [97] Chapter 7.

appearing in municipal systems or a general principle of international law. But perhaps this is not a terribly serious problem since both municipal legal concepts and those derived from existing international practice can be defined as falling within the recognised catchment area.[98]

While the reservoir from which one can draw contains the legal operations of 190 or so states, it does not follow that judges have to be experts in every legal system. There are certain common themes that run through the many different orders. Anglo-American Common Law has influenced a number of states throughout the world, as have the French and Germanic systems. There are many common elements in the law in Latin America, and most Afro-Asian states have borrowed heavily from the European experience in their efforts to modernise the structure administering the state and westernise economic and other enterprises.[99]

Reference will now be made to some of the leading cases in this field to illustrate how this problem has been addressed.

In the *Chorzów Factory* case in 1928,[100] which followed the seizure of a nitrate factory in Upper Silesia by Poland, the Permanent Court of International Justice declared that 'it is a general conception of law that every violation of an engagement involves an obligation to make reparation'. The Court also regarded it as:

> a principle of international law that the reparation of a wrong may consist in an indemnity corresponding to the damage which the nationals of the injured state have suffered as a result of the act which is contrary to international law.

The most fertile fields, however, for the implementation of municipal law analogies have been those of procedure, evidence and the machinery of the judicial process. In the *German Settlers in Poland* case,[101] the Court, approaching the matter from the negative point of view,[102] declared that 'private rights acquired under existing law do not cease on a change of sovereignty . . . It can hardly be maintained that, although the law survived, private rights acquired under it perished. Such a contention is based on no principle and would be contrary to an almost universal opinion and

---

[98] See Brownlie, *Principles*, pp. 15–17 and Virally, 'The Sources', pp. 144–8.

[99] See generally, R. David and J. Brierley, *Major Legal Systems in the World Today*, 2nd edn, London, 1978. Note that the Tribunal in *AMCO v. Republic of Indonesia* stated that while a practice or legal provisions common to a number of nations would be an important source of international law, the French concepts of administrative unilateral acts or administrative contracts were not such practices or legal provisions, 89 ILR, pp. 366, 461.

[100] PCIJ, Series A, No. 17, 1928, p. 29; 4 ILR, p. 258. See also the Chile–United States Commission decision with regard to the deaths of Letelier and Moffitt, 31 ILM, 1982, pp. 1, 9.   [101] PCIJ, Series B, No. 6, p. 36.

[102] See also the *South West Africa* cases, ICJ Reports, 1966, pp. 3, 47; 37 ILR, pp. 243, 280–1, for a statement that the notion of *actio popularis* was not part of international law as such nor able to be regarded as imported by the concept of general principles of law.

practice.'[103] The International Court of Justice in the *Corfu Channel* case,[104] when referring to circumstantial evidence, pointed out that 'this indirect evidence is admitted in all systems of law and its use is recognised by international decisions'. Five years later, in the *Administrative Tribunal* case,[105] the Court dealt with the problem of the dismissal of members of the United Nations Secretariat staff and whether the General Assembly had the right to refuse to give effect to awards made to them by the relevant Tribunal.

In giving its negative reply, the Court emphasised that:

> according to a well-established and generally recognised principle of law, a judgment rendered by such a judicial body is *res judicata* and has binding force between the parties to the dispute.[106]
>
> The Court in the preliminary objections phase of the *Rights of Passage* case,[107] stated that 'it is a rule of law generally accepted, as well as one acted upon in the past by the Court, that, once the Court has been validly seized of a dispute, unilateral action by the respondent state in terminating its Declaration [i.e. accepting the jurisdiction of the Court], in whole or in part, cannot divest the Court of jurisdiction'.

The Court has also considered the principle of estoppel which provides that a party that has acquiesced in a particular situation cannot then proceed to challenge it. In the *Temple* case[108] the International Court of Justice applied the doctrine, but in the *Serbian Loans* case[109] in 1929, in which French bondholders were demanding payment in gold francs as against paper money upon a series of Serbian loans, the Court declared the principle inapplicable.

As the International Court noted in the *ELSI* case,[110] there were limitations upon the process of inferring an estoppel in all circumstances, since 'although it cannot be excluded that an estoppel could in certain circumstances arise from a silence when something ought to have been said, there are obvious difficulties in constructing an estoppel from a mere failure to mention a matter at a particular point in somewhat desultory diplomatic exchanges'.[111]

---

[103] See also the *Certain German Interests in Polish Upper Silesia* case, PCIJ, Series A, No. 7, p. 42 and the *Free Zones of Upper Savoy and the District of Gex* case, PCIJ, Series A/B, No. 46, p. 167.   [104] ICJ Reports, 1949, pp. 4, 18; 16 ILR, pp. 155, 157.

[105] ICJ Reports, 1954, p. 47; 21 ILR, p. 310.

[106] Ibid., p. 53; 21 ILR, p. 314. See also *AMCO* v. *Republic of Indonesia*, 89 ILR, pp. 366, 558; Cheng, *General Principles*, Chapter 17 and S. Rosenne, *The Law and Practice of the International Court*, Leiden, 1965, vol. II, pp. 623 *et seq.*

[107] ICJ Reports, 1957, pp. 125, 141–2: 24 ILR, pp. 840, 842–3.

[108] ICJ Reports, 1962, pp. 6, 23, 31 and 32; 33 ILR, pp. 48, 62, 69–70.

[109] PCIJ, Series A, No. 20; 5 ILR, p. 466.

[110] ICJ Reports, 1989, pp. 15, 44; 84 ILR, pp. 311, 350.

[111] See also the *Eastern Greenland* case, PCIJ, Series A/B, No. 53, pp. 52 *et seq.*; 6 ILR, pp. 95, 100–2 and H. Thirlway, 'The Law and Procedure of the International Court of Justice, 1960–89, Part One', 60 BYIL, 1989, pp. 4, 29.

Another example of a general principle was provided by the Arbitration Tribunal in the *AMCO* v. *Republic of Indonesia* case,[112] where it was stated that 'the full compensation of prejudice, by awarding to the injured party the *damnum emergens* and *lucrum cessans* is a principle common to the main systems of municipal law, and therefore, a general principle of law which may be considered as a source of international law'. Another principle would be that of respect for acquired rights.[113] One crucial general principle of international law is that of *pacta sunt servanda*, or the idea that international agreements are binding. The law of treaties rests inexorably upon this principle since the whole concept of binding international agreements can only rest upon the presupposition that such instruments are commonly accepted as possessing that quality.[114]

Perhaps the most important general principle, underpinning many international legal rules is that of good faith.[115] This principle is enshrined in the United Charter, which provides in article 2(2) that 'all Members, in order to ensure to all of them the rights and benefits resulting from membership, shall fulfil in good faith the obligations assumed by them in accordance with the present Charter' and the elaboration of this provision in the Declaration on Principles Concerning Friendly Relations and Co-operation among States adopted by the General Assembly in resolution 2625(XXV), 1970, referred to the obligations upon states to fulfil in good faith their obligations resulting from international law generally, including treaties. It therefore constitutes an indispensable part of the rules of international law generally.

The International Court declared in the *Nuclear Tests* cases[116] that:

> One of the basic principles governing the creation and performance of legal obligations, whatever their source, is the principle of good faith. Trust and confidence are inherent in international co-operation, in particular in an age when this co-operation in many fields is becoming increasingly essential. Just as the very rule of *pacta sunt servanda* in the law of treaties is based on good faith, so also is the binding character of an international obligation assumed by unilateral obligation.

---

[112] 89 ILR, pp. 366, 504.
[113] See e.g.the *German Interests in Polish Upper Silesia* case, PCIJ, Series A, No. 7, 1926, p. 22; *Starrett Housing Corporation* v. *Iran*, 85 ILR, p. 34; the *Shufeld* claim, 5 *AD*, p. 179 and *AMCO* v. *Republic of Indonesia* 89 ILR, pp. 366, 496. See further *infra* p. 573.
[114] See Brownlie, *Principles*, p. 616 and McNair, *The Law of Treaties*, vol. I, Chapter 30. See also article 26 of the Vienna Convention on the Law of Treaties 1969 and *AMCO* v. *Republic of Indonesia*, 89 ILR, pp. 366, 495–7.
[115] *Oppenheim's International Law* notes that this is 'of overriding importance', p. 38. See E. Zoller, *Bonne Foi en Droit International Public*, Paris, 1977; H. Thirlway, 'The Law and Procedure of the International Court of Justice', 60 BYIL, 1989, pp. 3, 7 et seq. and G. Fitzmaurice, *The Law and Procedure of the International Court of Justice*, Cambridge, 1986, vol. I, p. 183 and vol. II, p. 609.
[116] ICJ Reports, 1974, pp. 253, 267; 57 ILR, pp. 398, 412.

Nevertheless, the Court has made the point that good faith as a concept is 'not in itself a source of obligation where none would otherwise exist'.[117] The principle of good faith, therefore, is a background principle informing and shaping the observance of existing rules of international law and in addition constraining the manner in which those rules may legitimately be exercised.[118]

Thus it follows that it is the Court which has the discretion as to which principles of law to apply in the circumstances of the particular case under consideration, and it will do this upon the basis of the inability of customary and treaty law to provide the required solution. In this context, one must consider the *Barcelona Traction* case[119] between Belgium and Spain. The International Court of Justice relied heavily upon the municipal law concept of the limited liability company and emphasised that if the Court were to decide the case in disregard of the relevant institutions of municipal law it would, without justification, invite serious legal difficulties. It would lose touch with reality, for there are no corresponding institutions of international law to which the Court could resort.[120]

However, international law did not refer to the municipal law of a particular state, but rather to the rules generally accepted by municipal legal systems which, in this case, recognise the idea of the limited company.

Equity and international law[121]

Apart from the recourse to the procedures and institutions of municipal legal systems to reinforce international law, it is also possible to see in a number of

---

[117] The *Border and Transborder Armed Actions* case (Nicaragua v. Honduras), ICJ Reports, 1988, p. 105; 84 ILR, p. 218. See also Judge Ajibolo's Separate Opinion in the *Libya/Chad* case, ICJ Reports, 1994, pp. 6, 71–4. See also the statement by the Inter-American Court of Human Rights in the *Re-introduction of the Death Penalty in Peru* case, 16 *Human Rights Law Journal*, 1995, pp. 9, 13.

[118] See also the *Fisheries Jurisdiction* cases, ICJ Reports, 1974, pp. 3, 33: 55 ILR, pp. 238, 268; the *North Sea Continental Shelf* cases, ICJ Reports, 1969, pp. 3, 46–7: 41 ILR, pp. 29, 76; the *Lac Lannoux* case, 24 ILR, p. 119 and the *Legality of the Threat or Use of Nuclear Weapons* case, ICJ Reports, paras. 102 *et seq.;* 35 ILM, pp. 809, 830–1. Note also Principles 19 and 27 of the Rio Declaration on Environment and Development 1992, 31 ILM, 1992, p. 876.

[119] ICJ Reports, 1970, p. 3; 46 ILR, p. 178.

[120] *Ibid.*, p. 37; 46 ILR, p. 211. See also generally the *Abu Dhabi* arbitration, 1 ICLQ, 1952, p. 247; 18 ILR, p. 44 and *Texaco v. Libya*, 53 ILR, p. 389.

[121] See M. Akehurst, 'Equity and General Principles of Law', 25 ICLQ, 1976, p. 801; B. Cheng, 'Justice and Equity in International Law', 8 *Current Legal Problems*, 1955, p. 185; V. Degan, *L'Équité et le Droit International*, Paris, 1970; C. de Visscher, *De L'Équité dans le Réglement Arbitral ou Judiciaire des Litiges de Droit International Public*, Paris, 1972; E. Lauterpacht, 'Equity, Evasion, Equivocation and Evolution in International Law', *Proceedings of the American Branch of the ILA*, 1977–8, p. 33 and Lauterpacht, *Aspects of the Administration of International Justice*, 1991, pp. 117–52; R. Y. Jennings, 'Equity and Equitable Principles', *Annuaire Suisse de Droit International*, 1986, p. 38; *Oppenheim's International Law*, p. 43; R. Higgins, *Problems and Process*, Oxford, 1994, Chapter 13; Miyoshi, *Considerations of Equity in the Settlement of Territorial and Boundary Disputes*, 1993;

cases references to equity[122] as a set of principles constituting the values of the system. The most famous decision on these lines was that of Judge Hudson in the *Diversion of Water from the Meuse* case[123] in 1937 regarding a dispute between Holland and Belgium. Hudson pointed out that what are regarded as principles of equity have long been treated as part of international law and applied by the courts. 'Under article 38 of the Statute', he declared, 'if not independently of that article, the Court has some freedom to consider principles of equity as part of the international law which it must apply.' However, one must be very cautious in interpreting this, although, on the broadest level, it is possible to see equity (in an analogy with domestic law) as constituting a creative charge in legal development, producing the dynamic changes in the system rendered inflexible by the strict application of rules.[124]

The concept of equity[125] has been referred to in several cases. In the *Rann of Kutch Arbitration* between India and Pakistan in 1968[126] the Tribunal agreed that equity formed part of international law and that accordingly the parties could rely on such principles in the presentation of their cases.[127] The International Court of Justice in the *North Sea Continental Shelf* cases directed a final delimitation between the parties, West Germany, Holland and Denmark, 'in accordance with equitable principles'[128] and

---

S. Rosenne, 'Equitable Principles and the Compulsory Jurisdiction of International Tribunals', *Festschrift für Rudolf Binbdschedler*, 1980, p. 410 and Rosenne, 'The Position of the International Court of Justice on the Foundations of the Principle of Equity in International Law', *Forty Years International Court of Justice: Jurisdiction, Equality and Equity* (eds. A. Bloed and P. Van Dijk), Dordrecht, 1988, p. 108; Pirotte, 'La Notion d'Equité dans la Jurisprudence Récente de la CIJ', 77 *Revue Générale de Droit International Public*, 1973, p. 131; Chattopadhyay, 'Equity in International Law: Its Growth and Development', 5 *Georgia Journal of International and Comparative Law*, 1975, p. 381; R. Lapidoth, 'Equity in International Law', 22 *Israel Law Review*, 1987, p. 161; O. Schachter, *International Law in Theory and Practice*, 1991, p. 49: A. V. Lowe, 'The Role of Equity in International Law', 12 Australian YIL, 1992, p. 54 and Thirlway, 'Law and Procedure', p. 49. Note especially Judge Weeramantry's study of equity in the *Jan Mayern (Denmark* v. *Norway)* case, ICJ Reports, 1993, pp. 38, 211; 99 ILR, pp. 395, 579.

[122] Equity generally may be understood in the contexts of adapting law to particular areas or choosing between several different interpretations of the law (equity *infra legem*); filling gaps in the law (equity *praetor legem*) and as a reason for not applying unjust laws (equity *contra legem*): see Akehurst, 'Equity' and Judge Weeramantry, the *Jan Mayern* case, ICJ Reports, 1993, pp. 38, 226–34; 99 ILR, pp. 395, 594–602. See also *infra*, Chapter 17 for the extensive use of equity in the context of state succession.

[123] PCIJ, Series A/B, No. 70, pp. 73, 77; 8 ILR, pp. 444, 450.

[124] See e.g. Judge Weeramantry, the *Jan Mayern (Denmark* v. *Norway)* case, ICJ Reports, 1993, pp. 38, 217; 99 ILR, pp, 395, 585. Cf. Judge Schwebel's Separate Opinion, *ibid.*, p. 118; ILR, *ibid.*, p. 486.

[125] Note that the International Court in the *Tunisia /Libya Continental Shelf* case, ICJ Reports, 1982, pp. 18, 60; 67 ILR, pp. 4, 53 noted that 'equity as a legal concept is a direct emanation of the idea of justice'. [126] 50 ILR, p. 2.

[127] *Ibid.*, p. 18. In deciding the course of the boundary in two deep inlets, the Tribunal had recourse to the concept of equity: *ibid.*, p. 520.

[128] ICJ Reports, 1969, pp. 3, 53; 41 ILR, pp. 29, 83. Equity was used in the case in order to exclude the use of the equidistance method in the particular circumstances: *ibid.*, pp. 48–50; 41 ILR, pp. 78–80.

discussed the relevance to equity in its consideration of the *Barcelona Traction* case.[129] Judge Tanaka, however, has argued for a wider interpretation in his dissenting opinion in the Second Phase of the *South West Africa* cases[130] and has treated the broad concept as a source of human rights ideas.[131]

However, what is really in question here is the use of equitable principles in the context of a rule requiring such an approach. The relevant courts are not applying principles of abstract justice to the cases,[132] but rather deriving equitable principles and solutions from the applicable law.[133] The Court declared in the *Libya/Malta* case[134] that 'the justice of which equity is an emanation, is not an abstract justice but justice according to the rule of law; which is to say that its application should display consistency and a degree of predictability; even though it also looks beyond it to principles of more general application'.

Equity has been used by the courts as a way of mitigating certain inequities, not as a method of refashioning nature to the detriment of legal rules.[135] Its existence, therefore, as a separate and distinct source of law is at best highly controversial. As the International Court noted in the *Tunisia/Libya Continental Shelf* case,[136]

> it is bound to apply equitable principles as part of international law, and to balance up the various considerations which it regards as relevant in order to produce an equitable result. While it is clear that no rigid rules exist as to the exact weight to be attached to each element in the case, this is very far from being an exercise of discretion or conciliation; nor is it an operation of distributive justice.[137]

The use of equitable principles, however, has been particularly marked in the 1982 Law of the Sea Convention. Article 59, for example, provides that

---

[129] ICJ Reports, 1970, p. 3; 46 ILR, p. 178. See also the *Burkina Faso* v. *Mali* case, ICJ Reports, 1986, pp. 554, 631–3; 80 ILR, pp. 459, 532–5.

[130] ICJ Reports, 1966, pp. 6, 294–9; 37 ILR, pp. 243, 455–9. See also the *Corfu Channel* case, ICJ Reports, 1949, pp. 4, 22; 16 ILR, p. 155.

[131] See also *AMCO* v. *Republic of Indonesia* 89 ILR, pp. 366, 522–3.

[132] The International Court of Justice may under article 38(2) of its Statute decide a case '*ex aequo et bono*' if the parties agree, but it has never done so.

[133] See the *North Sea Continental Shelf* cases, ICJ Reports, 1969, pp. 3, 47; 41 ILR, pp. 29, 76, and the *Fisheries Jurisdiction* cases, ICJ Reports, 1974, pp. 3, 33; 55 ILR, pp. 238, 268. The Court reaffirmed in the *Libya/Malta* case, ICJ Reports, 1985, pp. 13, 40; 81 ILR, pp. 238, 272, 'the principle that there can be no question of distributive justice'.

[134] ICJ Reports, 1985, pp. 13, 39; 81 ILR, pp. 238, 271.

[135] See the *North Sea Continental Shelf* cases, ICJ Reports, 1969, pp. 3, 49–50; 41 ILR, pp. 29, 78–80, and the *Anglo-French Continental Shelf* case, Cmnd. 7438, 1978, pp. 116–17; 54 ILR, pp. 6, 123–4. See also the *Tunisia/Libya Continental Shelf* case, ICJ Reports, 1982, pp. 18, 60; 67 ILR, pp. 4, 53, and the *Gulf of Maine* case, ICJ Reports, 1984, pp. 246, 313–14 and 325–30; 71 ILR, pp. 74, 140–1 and 152–7.

[136] ICJ Reports, 1982, pp. 18, 60; 67 ILR, pp. 4, 53.

[137] See generally R. Y. Jennings, 'The Principles Governing Marine Boundaries', in *Festschrift für Karl Doehring*, 1989, p. 408 and M. Bedjaoui, 'L'énigme' des "principes équitables" dans le Droit des Délimitations Maritimes', *Revista Español de Derecho Internacional*, 1990, p. 376.

conflicts between coastal and other states regarding the exclusive economic zone are to be resolved 'on the basis of equity', while by article 74 delimitation of the zone between states with opposite or adjacent coasts is to be effected by agreement on the basis of international law in order to achieve an equitable solution. A similar provision applies by article 83 to the delimitation of the continental shelf.[138] These provisions possess flexibility, which is important, but are also somewhat uncertain. Precisely how any particular dispute may be resolved, and the way in which that is likely to happen and the principles to be used are far from clear and an element of unpredictability may have been introduced. The Draft Articles produced by the International Law Commission in 1994 on the Non-Navigational Uses of International Watercourses[139] also lays great emphasis upon the concept of equity. Article 5, for example, provides that watercourse states shall utilise an international watercourse in an equitable and reasonable manner both in their own territories and in participating generally in the use, development and protection of such a watercourse.

Equity may also be used in certain situations in the delimitation of non-maritime boundaries. Where there is no evidence as to where a boundary line lies, an international tribunal may resort to equity. In the case of *Burkina Faso/Republic of Mali*,[140] for example, the Court noted with regard to the pool of Soum, that 'it must recognise that Soum is a frontier pool; and that in the absence of any precise indication in the texts of the position of the frontier line, the line should divide the pool of Soum in an equitable manner'. This would be done by dividing the pool equally. Although equity did not always mean equality, where there are no special circumstances the latter is generally the best expression of the former.[141] The Court also emphasised that 'to resort to the concept of equity in order to modify an established frontier would be quite unjustified'.[142]

Although generalised principles or concepts that may be termed community value-judgments inform and pervade the political and therefore the legal orders in the broadest sense, they do not themselves constitute as such binding legal norms. This can only happen if they have been accepted as legal norms by the international community through the mechanisms and techniques of international law creation. Nevertheless, 'elementary principles of humanity' may lie at the base of such norms and help justify their existence in the broadest sense, and may indeed perform a valuable role in endowing such norms with an additional force within the system. The

---

[138] See also article 140 providing for the equitable sharing of financial and other benefits derived from activities in the deep-sea-bed area.
[139] Report of the International Law Commission on the Work of its Forty-Sixth Session, A/49/10, 1994, pp. 197, 218 *et seq.*   [140] ICJ Reports, 1986, pp. 554, 633.
[141] Ibid.   [142] Ibid. See also the *El Salvador/Honduras* case, ICJ Reports, 1992, pp. 351, 514–5.

International Court has, for example, emphasised in the *Legality of the Threat or Use of Nuclear Weapons* advisory opinion[143] that at the heart of the rules and principles concerning international humanitarian law lies the 'overriding consideration of humanity'.

Judicial decisions[144]

Although these are, in the words of article 38, to be utilised as a subsidiary means for the determination of rules of law rather than as an actual source of law, judicial decisions can be of immense importance. While by virtue of article 59 of the Statute of the International Court of Justice the decisions of the Court have no binding force except as between the parties and in respect of the case under consideration, the Court has striven to follow its previous judgments and insert a measure of certainty within the process: so that while the doctrine of precedent as it is known in the Common Law, whereby the rulings of certain courts must be followed by other courts, does not exist in international law, one still finds that states in disputes and text-book writers quote judgments of the Permanent Court and the International Court of Justice as authoritative decisions.

The International Court of Justice itself will closely examine its previous decisions and will carefully distinguish those cases which it feels should not be applied to the problem being studied. But just as English judges, for example, create law in the process of interpreting it, so the judges of the International Court of Justice sometimes do a little more than merely 'determine' it. One of the most outstanding instances of this occurred in the *Anglo-Norwegian Fisheries* case,[145] with its statement of the criteria for the recognition of baselines from which to measure the territorial sea, which was later enshrined in the 1958 Geneva Convention on the Territorial Sea and Contiguous Zone.

Other examples include the *Reparation* case,[146] which recognised the legal personality of international institutions in certain cases, the *Genocide* case,[147] which dealt with reservations to treaties and the *Nottebohm* case,[148] which considered the role and characteristics of nationality.

Of course, it does not follow that a decision of the Court invariably will

---

[143] ICJ Reports, 1996, paras. 79 and 95; 35 ILM, 1996, pp. 809, 827 and 829. See also the *Corfu Channel* case, ICJ Reports, 1949, pp. 4, 22; 16 ILR, p. 155. See further *infra*, Chapter 19, p. 806.
[144] See e.g. Lauterpacht, *Development of International Law*; Waldock, 'General Course', and Schwarzenberger, *International Law*, pp. 30 *et seq*. See also H. Thirlway, 'The Law and Procedure of the International Court of Justice 1960–1989 (Part Two)', 61 BYIL, 1990, pp. 3, 127.
[145] ICJ Reports, 1951, p. 116; 18 ILR, p. 86. See further *infra*, Chapter 11, p. 395.
[146] ICJ Reports, 1949, p. 174; 16 ILR, p. 318. See further *infra*, Chapter 21, p. 909.
[147] ICJ Reports, 1951, p. 15; 18 ILR, p. 364.   [148] ICJ Reports, 1955, p. 4; 22 ILR, p. 349.

be accepted in later discussions and formulations of the law. One example of this is part of the decision in the *Lotus* case,[149] which was criticised and later abandoned in the Geneva Conventions on the Law of the Sea. But this is comparatively rare and the degree of respect accorded to the Court and its decisions renders its opinions vital to the growth and exposition of international law.

In addition to the Permanent Court and the International Court of Justice, the phrase 'judicial decisions' also encompasses international arbitral awards and the rulings of national courts. There have been many international arbitral tribunals such as the Permanent Court of Arbitration created by the Hague Conferences of 1899 and 1907 and the various mixed-claims tribunals, including the Iran–US Claims Tribunal, and, although they differ from the international courts in some ways, many of their decisions have been extremely significant in the development of international law.

This can be seen in the existence and number of the Reports of International Arbitral Awards published since 1948 by the United Nations.

One case that should be mentioned is the *Alabama Claims* arbitration,[150] which marked the opening of a new era in the peaceful settlement of international disputes, in which increasing use was made of judicial and arbitration methods in resolving conflicts. This case involved a vessel built in Liverpool to the specifications of the Confederate States, which succeeded in capturing some seventy Federal ships during the American Civil War. The United States sought compensation after the war for the depredations of the *Alabama* and other ships and this was accepted by the Tribunal. Britain had infringed the rules of neutrality and was accordingly obliged to pay damages to the United States.

Another illustration of the impact of such arbitral awards is the *Island of Palmas* case[151] which has proved of immense significance in the subject of territorial sovereignty and will be discussed later.

As has already been seen, the decisions of municipal courts[152] may provide evidence of the existence of a customary rule. They may also constitute evidence of the actual practice of states which, while not a description of the law as it has been held to apply, nevertheless affords examples of how states actually behave, in other words the essence of the material act

[149] PCIJ, Series A, No. 10, 1927, p. 18; 4 ILR, p. 5. See *infra*, p. 425.
[150] J. B. Moore, *International Arbitrations*, New York, 1898, vol. I, p. 653.
[151] 2 RIAA, p. 829; 4 ILR, p. 3. See also the *Beagle Channel* award, HMSO, 1977; 52 ILR, p. 93 and the *Anglo-French Continental Shelf* case, Cmnd. 7438, 1978; 54 ILR, p. 6.
[152] See e.g. *Thirty Hogsheads of Sugar, Bentzon* v. *Boyle*, 9 Cranch 191 (1815); the *Paquete Habana*, 175 US 677 (1900) and the *Scotia*, 14 Wallace 170 (1871). See also the *Lotus* case, PCIJ, Series A, No. 10, 1927, p. 18; 4 ILR, p. 153. For further examples in the fields of state and diplomatic immunities particularly, see *infra*, Chapter 13.

INTERNATIONAL LAW

which is so necessary in establishing a rule of customary law. British and American writers, in particular, tend to refer fairly extensively to decisions of national courts.

One may, finally, also point to decisions by the highest courts of federal states, like Switzerland and the United States, in their resolution of conflicts between the component units of such countries, as relevant to the development of international law rules in such fields as boundary disputes. A boundary disagreement between two US states which is settled by the Supreme Court is in many ways analogous to the International Court of Justice considering a frontier dispute between two independent states, and as such provides valuable material for international law.[153]

Writers[154]

Article 38 includes as a subsidiary means for the determination of rules of law, 'the teachings of the most highly qualified publicists of the various nations'.

Historically, of course, the influence of academic writers on the development of international law has been marked. In the heyday of Natural Law it was analyses and juristic opinions that were crucial, while the role of state practice and court decisions was of less value. Writers such as Gentilis, Grotius, Pufendorf, Bynkershoek and Vattel were the supreme authorities of the sixteenth to eighteenth centuries and determined the scope, form and content of international law.[155]

With the rise of positivism and the consequent emphasis upon state sovereignty, treaties and custom assumed the dominant position in the exposition of the rules of the international system, and the importance of legalistic writings began to decline. Thus, one finds that textbooks are used as a method of discovering what the law is on any particular point rather than as the fount or source of actual rules. There are still some writers who have had a formative impact upon the evolution of particular laws, for example Gidel on the law of the sea,[156] and others whose general works on international law tend to be referred to virtually as classics, for example Oppenheim and Rousseau, but the general influence of textbook writers has somewhat declined this century.

Nevertheless, books are important as a way of arranging and putting into focus the structure and form of international law and of elucidating the

---

[153] See e.g. *Vermont* v. *New Hampshire*, 289 US 593 (1933) and *Iowa* v. *Illinois*, 147 US 1 (1893).

[154] See e.g. Parry, *British Digest*, pp. 103–5 and Lauterpacht, *Development of International Law by the International Court*, pp. 23–5.   [155] See *supra*, Chapter 1.

[156] *Droit International Public de la Mer*, 3 vols., 1932–4.

nature, history and practice of the rules of law. Academic writings also have a useful role to play in stimulating thought about the values and aims of international law as well as pointing out the defects that exist within the system, and making suggestions as to the future.

Because of the lack of supreme authorities and institutions in the international legal order, the responsibility is all the greater upon the publicists of the various nations to inject an element of coherence and order into the subject as well as to question the direction and purposes of the rules.

States in their presentation of claims, national law officials in their opinions to their governments, the various international judicial and arbitral bodies in considering their decisions, and the judges of municipal courts when the need arises, all consult and quote the writings of the leading juristic authorities.[157]

Of course, the claim can be made, and often is, that textbook writers merely reflect and reinforce national prejudices,[158] but it is an allegation which has been exaggerated. It should not lead us to dismiss the value of writers, but rather to assess correctly the writer within his particular environment.

Other possible sources of international law

In the discussion of the various sources of law prescribed by the Statute of the International Court of Justice, it might have been noted that there is a distinction between, on the one hand, actual sources of rules, that is those devices capable of instituting new rules such as law-making treaties, customary law, and many decisions of the International Court of Justice, since they cannot be confined to the category of merely determining or elucidating the law, and, on the other hand, those practices and devices which afford evidence of the existence of rules, such as juristic writings, many treaty-contracts and some judicial decisions both at the international and municipal level. In fact, each source is capable, to some extent, of both developing new law and identifying existing law. This results partly from the disorganised state of international law and partly from the terms of article 38 itself.

A similar confusion between law-making, law-determining and law-evidencing can be discerned in the discussion of the various other methods of developing law that have emerged since the conclusion of the Second World War. Foremost among the issues that have arisen and one that reflects the growth in the importance of the Third World states and the gradual de-Europeanisation of the world order is the question of the standing of the

---

[157] See Brownlie, *Principles*, pp. 25–6.
[158] See e.g. Huber in the *Spanish Zone of Morocco* case, 2 RIAA, pp. 615, 640; 2 ILR, pp. 157, 164 (note). See also Carty, *Decay of International Law?*, pp. 128–31.

resolutions and declarations of the General Assembly of the United Nations.[159]

Certain resolutions of the Assembly[160] are binding upon the organs and member states of the United Nations. Other resolutions, however, are not legally binding and are merely recommendatory, putting forward opinions on various issues with varying degrees of majority support. This is the classic position and reflects the intention that the Assembly was to be basically a parliamentary advisory body with the binding decisions to be taken by the Security Council.

Nowadays, the situation is somewhat more complex. The Assembly has produced a great number of highly important resolutions and declarations and it was inevitable that these should have some impact upon the direction adopted by modern international law. The way states vote in the General Assembly and the explanations given upon such occasions constitute evidence of state practice and state understanding as to the law. Where a particular country has consistently voted in favour of, for example, the abolition of apartheid, it could not afterwards deny the existence of a usage condemning racial discrimination and it may even be that that usage is for that state converted into a binding custom.

The Court in the *Nicaragua* case tentatively expressed the view that the *opinio juris* requirement could be derived from the circumstances surrounding the adoption and application of a General Assembly resolution. It noted that the relevant

> *opinio juris* may, though with all due caution, be deduced from, *inter alia*, the attitude of the Parties [i.e. the US and Nicaragua] and the attitude of States towards certain General Assembly resolutions, and particularly resolution 2625(XXV) entitled 'Declaration on Principles of International Law concerning Friendly Relations and Co-operation among States in accordance with the Charter of the United Nations'.[161]

The effect of consent to resolutions such as this one 'may be understood as acceptance of the validity of the rule or set of rules declared by the resolution by themselves'.[162] This comment, however, may well have referred

---

[159] See e.g. Asamoah, *The Legal Significance of the Declarations of the General Assembly of the United Nations*, 1966; D. Johnson, 'The Effect of Resolutions of the General Assembly of the United Nations', 32 BYIL, 1955–6, p. 97; J. Castañeda, *Legal Effects of United Nations Resolutions*, 1969 and R. A. Falk, 'On the Quasi-Legislative Competence of the General Assembly', 60 AJIL, 1966, p. 782. See also A. Cassese, *International Law in a Divided World*, London, 1986, pp. 192–5; B. Sloan, 'General Assembly Resolutions Revisited (40 Years After)', 58 BYIL, 1987, p. 39; Thirlway, 'Law and Procedure', p. 6 and S. Schwebel, 'United Nations Resolutions, Recent Arbitral Awards and Customary International Law' in *Realism in Law-Making* (eds. M. Bos and Siblesz), 1986, p. 203. See also Judge Weeramantry's Dissenting Opinion in the *East Timor* case, ICJ Reports, 1995, pp. 90, 185.

[160] See e.g. article 17 of the UN Charter.

[161] ICJ Reports, 1986, pp. 14, 99–100; 76 ILR, pp. 349, 433–4.

[162] *Ibid.*, p. 100; 76 ILR, p. 434.

solely to the situation where the resolution in question defines or elucidates an existing treaty (i.e. Charter) commitment.

Where the vast majority of states consistently vote for resolutions and declarations on a topic, that amounts to a state practice and a binding rule may very well emerge provided that the requisite *opinio juris* can be proved. For example, the 1960 Declaration on the Granting of Independence to Colonial Countries and Peoples, which was adopted with no opposition and only nine abstentions and followed a series of resolutions in general and specific terms attacking colonialism and calling for the self-determination of the remaining colonies, has, it would seem, marked the transmutation of the concept of self-determination from a political and moral principle to a legal right and consequent obligation, particularly taken in conjunction with the 1970 Declaration on Principles of International Law.[163]

Declarations such as that on the Legal Principles Governing Activities of States in the Exploration and Use of Outer Space (1963) can also be regarded as examples of state practices which are leading to, or have led to, a binding rule of customary law. As well as constituting state practice, it may be possible to use such resolutions as evidence of the existence of or evolution towards an *opinio juris* without which a custom cannot arise. Apart from that, resolutions can be understood as authoritative interpretations by the Assembly of the various principles of the United Nations Charter depending on the circumstances.[164]

Accordingly, such resolutions are able to speed up the process of the legalisation of a state practice and thus enable a speedier adaptation of customary law to the conditions of modern life. The presence of representatives of virtually all of the states of the world in the General Assembly enormously enhances the value of that organ in general political terms and in terms of the generation of state practice that may or may not lead to binding custom. As the International Court noted, for example, in the *Nicaragua* case,[165] 'the wording of certain General Assembly declarations adopted by states demonstrates their recognition of the principle of the prohibition of force as definitely a matter of customary international law'. The Court put the issue the following way in the *Legality of the Threat or Use of Nuclear Weapons* advisory opinion:[166]

> The Court notes that General Assembly resolutions, even if they are not binding, may sometimes have normative value. They can, in certain circumstances,

---

[163] See further *infra*, Chapter 5, p. 179.

[164] See e.g. O. Schachter, 'Interpretation of the Charter in the Political Organs of the United Nations' in *Law, States and International Order*, 1964, p. 269; R. Higgins, *The Development of International Law Through the Political Organs of the United Nations*, Oxford, 1963 and M. N. Shaw, *Title to Territory in Africa: International Legal Issues*, Oxford, 1986, Chapter 2.

[165] ICJ Reports, 1986, pp. 14, 102; 76 ILR, pp. 349, 436.

[166] ICJ Reports, 1996, para. 70; 35 ILM, 1996, pp. 809, 826.

provide evidence important for establishing the existence of a rule or the emergence of an *opinio juris*. To establish whether this is true of a General Assembly resolution, it is necessary to look at its content and the conditions of its adoption; it is also necessary to see whether an *opinio juris* exists as to its normative character. Or a series of resolutions may show the gradual evolution of the *opinio juris* required for the establishment of a new rule.

The Court in this case examined a series of General Assembly resolutions concerning the legality of nuclear weapons and noted that several of them had been adopted with substantial numbers of negative votes and abstentions. It was also pointed out that the focus of such resolutions had not always been constant. The Court therefore concluded that these resolutions fell short of establishing the existence of an *opinio juris* on the illegality of nuclear weapons.[167]

Nevertheless, one must be alive to the dangers in ascribing legal value to everything that emanates from the Assembly. Resolutions are often the results of political compromises and arrangements and comprehended in that sense, never intended to constitute binding norms. Great care must be taken in moving from a plethora of practice to the identification of legal norms.

As far as the practice of other international organisations is concerned,[168] the same approach, but necessarily tempered with a little more caution, may be adopted. Resolutions may evidence an existing custom or constitute usage that may lead to the creation of a custom and the *opinio juris* requirement may similarly emerge from the surrounding circumstances, although care must be exercised here.[169]

It is sometimes argued more generally that particular non-binding instruments or documents or non-binding provisions in treaties form a special category that may be termed 'soft law'. This terminology is meant to indicate that the instrument or provision in question is not of itself 'law', but its importance within the general framework of international legal development is such that particular attention requires to be paid to it.[170] 'Soft law' is not

---

[167] *Ibid.*, para. 71; 35 ILM, 1996, p. 826.

[168] See generally as to other international organisations in this context, Tammes, 'Decisions of International Organs as a Source of International Law', 94 HR, p. 265; M. Virally, 'La Valeur Juridique des Recommandations des Organisations Internationales', AFDI, 1956, p. 66 and Thierry, 'Les Résolutions des Organes Internationaux dans la Jurisprudence de la Cour Internationale de Justice', 167 HR, p. 385.

[169] See the *Nicaragua* case, ICJ Reports, 1986, pp. 14, 100–2; 76 ILR, pp. 349, 434–6.

[170] See e.g. M. Bothe, 'Legal and Non-Legal Norms – A Meaningful Distinction in International Relations', 11 Netherlands YIL, 1980, p. 65; I. Seidl-Hohenveldern 'International Economic Soft Law', 163 HR, 1980, p. 164 and Seidl-Hohenveldern, *International Economic Law*, 1992, p. 42; J. Gold, 'Strengthening the Soft International Law of Exchange Arrangements', 77 AJIL, 1983, p. 443; PASIL, 1988, p. 371; Van Hoof, *Rethinking the Sources of International Law*, 1983, p. 187; C. M. Chinkin, 'The Challenge of Soft Law: Development and Change in International Law', 38 ICLQ, 1989, p. 850; L. Henkin, *International Law, Politics and Values*, Dordrecht, 1995, pp. 94 and 192; Thierry, 'Les Resolutions', pp. 70–1 and W. M. Reisman, 'The Concept and Functions of Soft Law in International Politics', *Essays in Honour of Judge Taslim Olawale Elias* (eds. Bello and San), 1992, vol. I, p. 135.

law. That needs to be emphasised, but a document, for example, does not need to constitute a binding treaty before it can exercise an influence in international politics. The Helsinki Accord of 1975 is a prime example of this. This Accord was not a binding agreement, but its influence in Central and Eastern Europe in emphasising the role and importance of international human rights proved incalculable.[171] Certain areas of international law have generated more 'soft law', in the sense of the production of important but non-binding instruments, than others. Here one may cite particularly international economic law[172] and international environmental law.[173] The use of such documents, whether termed, for example, recommendations, guidelines, codes of practice or standards, are significant in signalling the evolution and establishment of guidelines, which ultimately may be converted into legally binding rules. They are important and influential, but do not in themselves constitute legal norms.

A recent study by the US State Department concerning non-binding international agreements between states[174] noted that

> it has long been recognised in international practice that governments may agree on joint statements of policy or intention that do not establish legal obligations. In recent decades, this has become a common means of announcing the results of diplomatic exchanges, stating common positions on policy issues, recording their intended course of action on matters of mutual concern, or making political commitments to one another. These documents are sometimes referred to as non-binding agreements, gentlemen's agreements, joint statements or declarations.

What is determinative as to status in such situations is not the title given to the document in question, but the intention of the parties as inferred from all the relevant circumstances as to whether they intended to create binding legal relationships between themselves on the matter in question.

The International Law Commission

The International Law Commission was established by the General Assembly in 1947 with the declared object of promoting the progressive development of international law and its codification.[175] It consists of thirty-

[171] See e.g. the reference to it in the *Nicaragua* case, ICJ Reports, 1986, pp. 3, 100; 76 ILR, pp. 349, 434.
[172] See e.g. I. Seidl-Hohenveldern, *International Economic Law*, 2nd edn, Dordrecht, 1992, pp. 42 *et seq.*
[173] See e.g. P. Birnie and A. Boyle, *International Law and the Environment*, Oxford, 1992, p. 26 *et seq.*
[174] Memorandum of the Assistant Legal Adviser for Treaty Affairs, US State Department, quoted in 88 AJIL, 1994, pp. 515 *et seq.*
[175] See as to the relationship between codification and progressive development, Judge ad hoc Sorensen's Dissenting Opinion in the *North Sea Continental Shelf* cases, ICJ Reports, 1969, pp. 3, 242–3; ILR, pp. 29, 217–19.

four members from Africa, Asia, America and Europe, who remain in office for five years each and who are appointed from lists submitted by national governments. The Commission is aided in its deliberations by consultations with various outside bodies including the Asian-African Legal Consultative Committee, the European Commission on Legal Co-operation and the Inter-American Council of Jurists.[176]

Many of the most important international conventions have grown out of the Commission's work. Having decided upon a topic, the International Law Commission will prepare a draft. This is submitted to the various states for their comments and is usually followed by an international conference convened by the United Nations. Eventually a treaty will emerge. This procedure was followed in such international conventions as those on the Law of the Sea in 1958, Diplomatic Relations in 1961, Consular Relations in 1963, Special Missions in 1969 and the Law of Treaties in 1969. Of course, this smooth operation does not invariably occur, witness the many conferences at Caracas in 1974, and Geneva and New York from 1975 to 1982, necessary to produce a new Convention on the Law of the Sea.

Apart from preparing such drafts, the International Law Commission also issues reports and studies, and has formulated such documents as the Draft Declaration on Rights and Duties of States of 1949 and the Principles of International Law recognised in the Charter of the Nuremberg Tribunal and in the Judgment of the Tribunal of 1950. The Commission produced a set of draft articles on the problems of jurisdictional immunities in 1991 and a draft statute for an international criminal court in 1994 and is at present considering the question of state responsibility, amongst other matters.

Thus, one can see that the International Law Commission is involved in at least two of the major sources of law. Its drafts may form the bases of international treaties which bind those states which have signed and ratified them and which may continue to form part of general international law, and its work is part of the whole range of state practice which can lead to new rules of customary law. Its drafts, indeed, may constitute evidence of custom as well as contribute to the corpus of usages which may create new law. In addition, it is not to be overlooked that the International Law Commission is a body composed of eminently qualified publicists including many governmental legal advisers whose reports and studies may be

---

[176] See articles 2, 3 and 8 of the Statute of the ILC. See also e.g. B. Ramcharan, *The International Law Commission*, Leiden, 1977; *The Work of the International Law Commission*, 4th edn, 1988; I. Sinclair, *The International Law Commission*, Cambridge, 1987; S. Rosenne, 'The International Law Commission 1949–59', 36 BYIL, 1960, p. 104 and Rosenne, 'Relations Between Governments and the International Law Commission', 19 YBWA, 1965, p. 183; B. Graefrath, 'The International Law Commission Tomorrow: Improving Its Organisation and Methods of Work', 85 AJIL, 1991, p. 597 and R. P. Dhokalia, *The Codification of Public International Law*, Manchester, 1970.

used as a method of determining what the law actually is, in much the same way as books.

Other bodies

Although the International Law Commission is by far the most important of the organs for the study and development of the law, there do exist certain other bodies which are involved in the same mission. The United Nations Commission on International Trade Law (UNCITRAL) and the United Nations Conference on Trade and Development (UNCTAD), for example, are actively increasing the range of international law in the fields of economic, financial and development activities, while temporary organs such as the Committee on the Principles of International Law have been engaged in producing various declarations and statements. Nor can one overlook the tremendous work of the many specialised agencies like the International Labour Organisation and the United Nations Educational, Scientific and Cultural Organisation (UNESCO), which are constantly developing international law in their respective spheres.

There are also some independent bodies which are actively involved in the field. The International Law Association and the Institut de Droit International are the best known of such organisations which study and stimulate the law of the world community, while the various Harvard Research drafts produced before the Second World War are still of value today.

Unilateral acts

In certain situations, the unilateral acts of states may give rise to international legal obligations.[177] For this to happen, the intention of the state making the declaration in question to be bound is crucial as will be the element of publicity or notoriety.[178] Such intention may be ascertained by way of interpretation of the act, and the principle of good faith plays a crucial role. The International Court has stressed that where states make statements by which their freedom of action is limited, a restrictive interpretation is required.[179] Recognition will be important here in so far as third states

---

[177] See Virally, 'The Sources', pp. 154–6; Brownlie, *Principles*, pp. 637–40; E. Suy, *Les Actes Unilateraux en Droit International Public*, Paris, 1962, and J. Garner, 'The International Binding Force of Unilateral Oral Declarations', 27 AJIL, 1933, p. 493.

[178] The *Nuclear Tests* cases, ICJ Reports, 1974, pp. 253, 267; 57 ILR, pp. 398, 412. See also the *Request for an Examination of the Situation in Accordance with Paragraph 63 of the Court's Judgment of 20 December 1974 in the Nuclear Tests (New Zealand v. France) Case*, ICJ Reports, 1995, pp. 288, 305.

[179] *Nuclear Tests* cases, ICJ Reports, 1974. See also the *Nicaragua case*, ICJ Reports, 1986, pp. 14, 132; 76 ILR, pp. 349, 466 and the *Burkina Faso v. Mali case*, ICJ Reports, 1986, pp. 554, 573–4; 80 ILR, pp. 459, 477–8.

are concerned, in order for such an act or statement to be opposable to them. Beyond this, such unilateral statements may be used as evidence of a particular view taken by the state in question.[180]

Hierarchy of sources and *jus cogens*[181]

Judicial decisions and writings clearly have a subordinate function within the hierarchy in view of article 38(1), while the role of general principles of law as a way of complementing custom and treaty law places that category fairly firmly in third place. The question of priority as between custom and treaty law is more complex.[182] As a general rule, the later in time will have priority. Treaties are usually formulated to replace or codify existing custom,[183] while treaties in turn may themselves fall out of use and be replaced by new customary rules. There is a principle to the effect that a special rule prevails over a general rule (*lex specialis derogat legi generali*), so that, for example, treaty rules between states as *lex specialis* would have priority as against general rules of customary law between the same states.[184]

The International Court stated in the *Barcelona Traction* case,[185] that there existed an essential distinction between the obligations of a state towards the international community as a whole and those arising *vis-à-vis* another state in the field of diplomatic protection. By their very nature the former concerned all states and 'all states can be held to have a legal interest in their protection; they are obligations *erga omnes*'. Examples of such obligations included the outlawing of aggression and of genocide and the protection from slavery and racial discrimination.[186] This easing of the traditional rules concerning *locus standi* in certain circumstances with regard to the pursuing of a legal remedy against the alleged offender state may be linked to the separate question of superior principles in international law.

[180] See e.g. the references to a press release issued by the Ministry of Foreign Affairs of Norway and the wording of a communication of the text of an agreement to Parliament by the Norwegian Government in the *Jan Mayern* case, ICJ Reports, 1993, pp. 38, 51. See also Judge Ajibola's Separate Opinion in the *Libya/Chad* case, ICJ Reports, 1994, pp. 6, 58.
[181] See M. Akehurst, 'The Hierarchy of the Sources of International Law', 47 BYIL, 1974–5, p. 273, and Virally, 'The Sources', pp. 165–6. See also to this effect the *Third Restatement of US Foreign Relations Law*, pp. 27–8. See T. Dalton, 'International Agreements in the Revised Restatement', 25 *Va JIL*, 1984, pp. 153, 157–8, cf. H. Mosler, *The International Society as a Legal Community*, Leiden, 1980, pp. 84–6. See also Thirlway, 'Law and Procedure', p. 143.
[182] See H. Villager, *Customary International Law and Treaties*, Dordrecht, 1985.
[183] See R. Baxter, 'Multilateral Treaties as Evidence of Customary International Law', BYIL, 1965–6, p. 275.
[184] See the *Tunisia/Libya Continental Shelf* case, ICJ Reports, 1982, pp. 18, 38; 67 ILR, pp. 4, 31 and the *Nicaragua* case, ICJ Reports, 1986, pp. 3, 137; 76 ILR, pp. 349, 471.
[185] ICJ Reports, 1970, pp. 3, 32; 46 ILR, pp. 178, 206.
[186] See also the *Nicaragua* case, ICJ Reports, 1986, pp. 3, 134; 76 ILR, pp. 349, 468 and Judge Weeramantry's Dissenting Opinion in the *East Timor* case, ICJ Reports, 1995, pp. 90, 172 and 204.

Article 53 of the Convention on the Law of Treaties, 1969, provides that a treaty will be void 'if, at the time of its conclusion, it conflicts with a peremptory norm of general international law'. This rule (*jus cogens*) will also apply in the context of customary rules so that no derogation would be permitted to such norms by way of local or special custom.

Such a peremptory norm is defined by the Convention as one 'accepted and recognised by the international community of states as a whole as a norm from which no derogation is permitted and which can be modified only by a subsequent norm of general international law having the same character'. The concept of *jus cogens* is based upon an acceptance of fundamental and superior values within the system and in some respects is akin to the notion of public order or public policy in domestic legal orders.[187] It also reflects the influence of natural law thinking. Various examples of the content of *jus cogens* have been provided, particularly during the discussions on the topic in the International Law Commission, such as an unlawful use of force, genocide, slave trading and piracy.[188] However, no clear agreement has been manifested regarding other areas, and even the examples given are by no means uncontroverted. More important, perhaps, is the identification of the mechanism by which rules of *jus cogens* may be created, since once created no derogation is permitted.

A two stage approach is here involved in the light of article 53: first, the establishment of the proposition as a rule of general international law and secondly the acceptance of that rule as a peremptory norm by the international law community of states as a whole. It will be seen therefore that a stringent process is involved, and rightly so, for the establishment of a higher level of binding rules has serious implications for the international law community. The situation to be avoided is that of foisting peremptory norms upon a political or ideological minority, for that in the long run would devalue the concept. The appropriate test would thus require universal acceptance of the proposition as a legal rule by states and recognition of it as a rule of *jus cogens* by an overwhelming majority of states, crossing ideological and political divides.[189] It is also clear that only rules based on custom or treaties may form the foundation of *jus cogens* norms. This is particularly so in view of the hostile attitude of many states to general principles as an independent source of international law and the universality requirement of

---

[187] See e.g. J. Sztucki, *Jus Cogens and the Vienna Convention on the Law of Treaties*, 1974; I. Sinclair, *The Vienna Convention on the Law of Treaties*, 2nd edn, Manchester, 1984, p. 203; M. Virally, 'Réflexions sur le *jus cogens*', 12 AFDI, 1966, p. 1; Rozakis, *The Concept of Jus Cogens in the Law of Treaties*, 1976; Gomez Robledo, 'Le *jus cogens* international', 172 HR, p. 17; Gaja, '*Jus Cogens* beyond the Vienna Conventions', *ibid.*, p. 279 and L. Hannikainen, *Peremptory Norms (Jus Cogens) in International Law*, Helsinki, 1988. See also *infra*, Chapter 16, p. 665. [188] *Yearbook of the ILC*, 1966, vol. II, p. 248.

[189] See e.g. Sinclair, *Vienna Convention*, pp. 218–24 and Akehurst, 'Hierarchy'.

jus cogens formation. The dangers of not being sufficiently stringent are visible in the ILC's draft on State Responsibility, article 18(2) of which provides that an unlawful act may be rendered lawful if such an act has subsequently become compulsory as a result of a rule of *jus cogens*. This apparently retroactive provision may be the cause of problems in the future.[190]

As article 53 of the Vienna Convention notes, a treaty that is contrary to an existing rule of *jus cogens* is void *ab initio*,[191] whereas by virtue of article 64 an existing treaty that conflicts with an emergent rule of *jus cogens* terminates from the date of the emergence of the rule. It is not void *ab initio*, nor by article 71 is any right, obligation or legal situation created by the treaty prior to its termination affected, provided that its maintenance is not in itself contrary to the new peremptory norm.

The relationship between the rules of *jus cogens* and article 103 of the United Nations Charter, which states that obligations under the Charter have precedence as against obligations under other international agreements, was discussed by Judge Lauterpacht in his Separate Opinion in the *Bosnia* case.[192] He noted in particular that 'the relief which article 103 of the Charter may give the Security Council in case of conflict between one of its decisions and an operative treaty obligation cannot – as a matter of simple hierarchy of norms – extend to a conflict between a Security Council resolution and *jus cogens*'.

---

[190] See *Yearbook of the ILC*, vol. II, pp. 91–2.   [191] Ibid.
[192] ICJ Reports, 1993, pp. 325, 440; 95 ILR, pp. 43, 158.

CHAPTER 4

INTERNATIONAL LAW AND MUNICIPAL LAW

The role of the state in the modern world is a complex one. According to legal theory, each state is sovereign and equal.[1] In reality, with the phenomenal growth in communications and consciousness, and with the constant reminder of global rivalries, not even the most powerful of states can be entirely sovereign. Interdependence and the close-knit character of contemporary international commercial and political society ensures that virtually any action of a state could well have profound repercussions upon the system as a whole and the decisions under consideration by other states.

Thus, reality circumscribes the concept of sovereignty in operation and increases the necessity for world-wide coordination of matters as different as the policies adopted to combat economic problems, environmental dangers and terrorist threats.

With the rise and extension of international law, questions begin to arise paralleling the role played by the state within the international system and concerned with the relationship between the internal legal order of a particular country and the rules and principles governing the international

---

[1] See generally, *Oppenheim's International Law* (eds. R. Y. Jennings and A. D. Watts), 9th edn, London, 1992, vol. I, p. 52; J. W. Verzijl, *International Law in Historical Perspective*, 1968, vol. 1, p. 90; R. A. Falk, *The Role of Domestic Courts in the International Legal Order*, Princeton, 1964; H. Kelsen, *Principles of International Law*, 2nd edn, 1966, pp. 290–4 and 551–88; I. Brownlie, *Principles of Public International Law*, 4th edn, Oxford, 1990, Chapter 2; H. Lauterpacht, *International Law: Collected Papers*, Cambridge, vol. I, 1970, pp. 151–77; A. Cassese, 'Modern Constitutions and International Law', 192 HR, 1985 III, p. 335; Nguyen Quoc Dinh, P. Daillier and A. Pellet, *Droit International Public*, 5th edn, Paris, 1994, p. 92; R. Higgins, *Problems and Process*, Oxford, 1994, Chapter 12; K. Marek, 'Les Rapports entre le Droit International et le Droit Interne à la Lumière de la Jurisprudence de la CIJ', *Revue Générale de Droit International Public*, 1962, p. 260; L. Ferrari-Bravo, 'International Law and Municipal Law: The Complementarity of Legal Systems', *The Structure and Process of International Law* (eds. R. St J. Macdonald and D. Johnston), Dordrecht, 1983, p. 715; F. Morgenstern, 'Judicial Practice and the Supremacy of International Law', 27 BYIL, 1950, p. 42; B. Conforti, *International Law and the Role of Domestic Legal Systems*, 1993; J. G. Starke, 'Monism and Dualism in the Theory of International Law considered from the standpoint of the Rule of Law', 92 HR, pp. 5, 70–80; H. Thirlway, 'The Law and Procedure of the International Court of Justice 1960–1989', 60 BYIL, 1989, pp. 4, 114; Report of the Committee on International Law and Municipal Law, *International Law Association: Report of the Sixty-Sixth Conference*, 1994, p. 326; V. Erades, *Interactions Between International and Municipal Law – A Comparative Case Law Study*, Leiden, 1993, and V. Heiskanen, *International Legal Topics*, Helsinki, 1992, Chapter 1.

community as a whole. Municipal law governs the domestic aspects of government and deals with issues between individuals, and between individuals and the administrative apparatus, while international law focuses primarily upon the relations between states. Nevertheless, there are many instances where problems can emerge and lead to difficulties between the two systems. In a case before a municipal court a rule of international law may be brought forward as a defence to a charge. For example, a vessel may be prosecuted for being in what, in domestic terms, is regarded as territorial waters but in international law would be treated as part of the high seas.

There may also be questions as to the precise status of a municipal legal rule before an international tribunal. It is questions such as these that will be looked at in this chapter. But first some of the various ideas put forward as to the required frames of reference will be briefly considered.

The theories[2]

Positivism stresses the overwhelming importance of the state and tends to regard international law as founded upon the consent of states. It is actual practice, illustrated by custom and by treaty, that formulates the role of international law, and not formalistic structures, theoretical deductions or moral stipulations. Accordingly, when positivists such as Triepel[3] and Strupp[4] consider the relationship of international law to municipal law, they do so upon the basis of the supremacy of the state, and the existence of wide differences between the two functioning orders. This theory is known as *dualism* (or sometimes as *pluralism*) and stresses that the rules of the systems of international law and municipal law exist separately and cannot purport to have an effect on, or overrule, the other.

This is because of the fundamentally different nature of inter-state and intra-state relations and the different legal structure employed on the one hand by the state and on the other hand as between states. Where municipal legislation permits the exercise of international law rules, this is on sufferance as it were and is an example of the supreme authority of the state within its own domestic jurisdiction, rather than of any influence maintained by international law within the internal sphere.[5]

Those writers who disagree with this theory and who adopt the *monist* approach tend to fall into two distinct categories: those who, like Lauterpacht, uphold a strong ethical position with a deep concern for

---

[2] See *supra*, Chapters 1 and 2. See also J. H. Jackson, 'Status of Treaties in Domestic Legal Systems: A Policy Analysis', 86 AJIL, 1992, p. 310.

[3] H. Triepel, *Völkerrecht und Landesrecht*, Berlin, 1899.

[4] R. Strupp, 47 HR, p. 389. See also D. Anzilotti, *Corso di Diritto Internazionale*, 3rd edn, Rome, 1928, vol. I, pp. 43 *et seq.*   [5] See *Oppenheim's International Law*, p. 53.

human rights, and others, like Kelsen, who maintain a monist position on formalistic logical grounds. The monists are united in accepting a unitary view of law as a whole and are opposed to the strict division posited by the positivists.

The 'naturalist' strand represented in England by Lauterpacht's works sees the primary function of all law as concerned with the well-being of individuals, and advocates the supremacy of international law as the best method available of attaining this. It is an approach characterised by deep suspicion of an international system based upon the sovereignty and absolute independence of states, and illuminated by faith in the capacity of the rules of international law to imbue the international order with a sense of moral purpose and justice founded upon respect for human rights and the welfare of individuals.[6]

The method by which Kelsen elucidates his theory of monism is markedly different and utilises the philosophy of Kant as its basis. Law is regarded as constituting an order which lays down patterns of behaviour that ought to be followed, coupled with provision for sanctions which are employed once an illegal act or course of conduct has occurred or been embarked upon. Since the same definition appertains both within the internal sphere and the international sphere, a logical unity is forged, and because states owe their legal relationship to one another to the rules of international law, such as the one positing equality, since states cannot be equal before the law without a rule to that effect, it follows that international law is superior to or more basic than municipal law.[7]

Reference has already been made to Kelsen's hierarchical system whereby the legality of a particular rule is affirmed once it conforms to an anterior rule. This process of referring back to previous or higher rules ends with the so-called basic norm of the legal order. However, this basic norm is basic only in a relative sense, since the legal character of states, such as their jurisdiction, sovereignty and equality, is fixed by international law. Thus, Kelsen emphasises the unity of the entire legal order upon the basis of the predominance of international law by declaring that it is the basic norm of the international legal order which is the ultimate reason of validity of the national legal orders too.[8]

A third approach, being somewhat a modification of the dualist position and formulated by Fitzmaurice and Rousseau amongst others, attempts to establish a recognised theoretical framework tied to reality. This approach

---

[6] Lauterpacht, *International Law,* see also *International Law and Human Rights,* London, 1950.
[7] Kelsen, *Principles,* pp. 557–9. See also Kelsen, *General Theory of Law and State,* 1945, pp. 363–80. Note that Scelle, for example, founds international legal monism upon an inter-social monism, essentially a sociological explanation, see Nguyen Quoc Dinh *et al., Droit International Public,* p. 96.   [8] See further, *supra,* Chapter 2, p. 41.

begins by denying that any common field of operation exists as between international law and municipal law by which one system is superior or inferior to the other. Each order is supreme in its own sphere, much as French law and English law are in France and England. And just as one cannot talk in terms of the supremacy of French law over English law, but only of two distinct legal systems each operating within its own field, so it is possible to treat international law and municipal law in the same way. They are both the legal element contained within the domestic and international systems respectively, and they exist within different juridical orders.

What may, and often does, happen is what is termed a conflict of obligations, that is the state within its own domestic sphere does not act in accordance with its obligations as laid down by international law. In such a case, the domestic position is unaffected (and is not overruled by the contrary rule of international law) but rather the state as it operates internationally has broken a rule of international law and the remedy will lie in the international field, whether by means of diplomatic protest or judicial action.

This method of solving the problem does not delve deeply into theoretical considerations, but aims at being practical and in accord with the majority of state practice and international judicial decisions.[9]

The role of municipal rules in international law[10]

The general rule with regard to the position of municipal law within the international sphere is that a state which has broken a stipulation of international law cannot justify itself by referring to its domestic legal situation. It is no defence to a breach of an international obligation to argue that the state acted in such a manner because it was following the dictates of its own municipal laws. The reasons for this inability to put forward internal rules as an excuse to evade international responsibility are obvious. Any other situation would permit international law to be evaded by the simple method of domestic legislation.

Accordingly, state practice and decided cases have established this provision and thereby prevented countries involved in international litigation

[9] G. Fitzmaurice, 'The General Principles of International Law Considered from the Standpoint of the Rule of Law', 92 HR, 1957 II, pp. 5, 70–80. See also C. Rousseau, *Droit International Public*, Paris, 1979, pp. 4–16; Borchard, 'The Relations between International Law and Municipal Law', 27 *Virginia Law Review*, 1940, p. 137; M. S. McDougal, 'The Impact of International Law upon National Law: A Policy-Orientated Perspective' in McDougal *et al.*, *Studies in World Public Order*, New Haven, 1960, p. 157.

[10] See e.g. C. W. Jenks, *The Prospects of International Adjudication*, London, 1964, Chapter 9; H. Lauterpacht, *The Development of International Law by the International Court*, London, 1958 and Morgenstern, 'Judicial Practice', pp. 43 *et seq.*

from pleading municipal law as a method of circumventing international law. Article 27 of the Vienna Convention on the Law of Treaties 1969 lays down that in so far as treaties are concerned, a party may not invoke the provisions of its internal law as justification for its failure to carry out an international agreement.[11] And this provision is reflected in the rules governing international litigation.

In the *Alabama Claims* arbitration of 1872, the United States objected strenuously when Britain allowed a Confederate ship to sail from Liverpool to prey upon American shipping. It was held that the absence of British legislation necessary to prevent the construction or departure of the vessel could not be brought forward as a defence, and Britain was accordingly liable to pay damages for the depredations caused by the warship in question.[12]

The International Court, in the *Applicability of the Obligation to Arbitrate* case,[13] has underlined 'the fundamental principle of international law that international law prevails over domestic law', while Judge Shahabuddeen emphasised in the *Lockerbie* case[14] that inability under domestic law to act was no defence to non-compliance with an international obligation. By way of contrast, the International Court pointed out in the *Elettronica Sicula SpA (ELSI)* case[15] that the fact that an act of a public authority may have been unlawful in municipal law did not necessarily mean that the act in question was unlawful in international law.

However, such expressions of the supremacy of international law over municipal law in international tribunals do not mean that the provisions of domestic legislation are either irrelevant or unnecessary.[16] On the contrary, the role of internal legal rules is vital to the workings of the international legal machine. One of the ways that it is possible to understand and discover a state's legal position on a variety of topics important to international law is by examining municipal laws.[17] A country will express its opinion on such vital international matters as the extent of its territorial sea, or the

---

[11] Note also article 13 of the Draft Declaration on the Rights and Duties of States, 1949, which provides that every state 'has the duty to carry out in good faith its obligations arising from treaties and other sources of international law, and it may not invoke provisions in its constitution or its laws as an excuse for failure to perform this duty', *Yearbook of the ILC*, 1949, pp. 286, 289.

[12] J. B. Moore, *International Arbitrations*, New York, 1898, vol. I, pp. 495, 653. See also e.g. the *Free Zones* case, PCIJ, Series A/B, No. 46, 1932, p. 167; 6 ILR, p. 362; the *Greco-Bulgarian Communities* case, PCIJ, Series B, No. 17, 1930, p. 32; 5 ILR, p. 4 and the *Nottebohm* case, ICJ Reports, 1955, pp. 4, 20–1; 22 ILR, pp. 349, 357–8.

[13] ICJ Reports, 1988, pp. 12, 34; 82 ILR, pp. 225, 252.

[14] ICJ Reports, 1992, pp. 3, 32; 94 ILR, pp. 478, 515. See also *Westland Helicopters Ltd and AOI*, 80 ILR, pp. 595, 616.   [15] ICJ Reports, 1989, pp. 15, 73–4; 84 ILR, pp. 311, 379–80.

[16] See e.g. Jenks, *Prospects*, pp. 547–603 and K. Marek, *Droit International et Droit Interne*, Paris, 1961. See also Brownlie, *Principles*, pp. 39–43.

[17] See e.g. the *Anglo-Iranian Oil Co.* case, ICJ Reports, 1952, p. 93; 19 ILR, p. 507.

jurisdiction it claims or the conditions for the acquisition of nationality through the medium of its domestic law-making. Thus, it is quite often that in the course of deciding a case before it, an international court will feel the necessity to make a study of relevant pieces of municipal legislation. Indeed, there have been instances, such as the *Serbian Loans* case of 1929,[18] when the crucial issues turned upon the interpretation of internal law, and the rules of international law in a strict sense were not at issue.

In addition to the role of municipal law as revealing the legal position of the state on topics of international importance, the rules of municipal law can be utilised as evidence of compliance or non-compliance with international obligations. This was emphasised in the *Certain German Interests in Polish Upper Silesia* case,[19] where the Permanent Court of International Justice declared that:

> the Court is certainly not called upon to interpret the Polish law as such; but there is nothing to prevent the Court's giving judgment on the question whether or not, in applying that law, Poland is acting in conformity with its obligations towards Germany under the Geneva Convention.[20]

Nevertheless, and despite the many functions that municipal law rules perform within the sphere of international law, the point must be emphasised that the presence or absence of a particular provision within the internal legal structure of a state, including its constitution if there is one, cannot be applied to evade an international obligation. Any other solution would render the operations of international law rather precarious.

International law before municipal courts[21]

The problem of the role of international law within the municipal law system is, however, rather more complicated than the position discussed above, and there have been a number of different approaches to it. We shall look first at the attitudes adopted by the British courts, and then proceed to note the views taken by the United States and other countries.[22]

---

[18] PCIJ, Series A, No. 20; 5 ILR, p. 466. See also the *Brazilian Loans* case, *ibid.*, No. 21.

[19] PCIJ, Series A, No. 7, p. 19.

[20] It was noted that municipal laws are merely facts in international law, *ibid.*, at 12. For criticism, see e.g. Brownlie, *Principles*, pp. 42–3.

[21] See e.g. Morgenstern, 'Judicial Practice', pp. 48–66 and Conforti, *International Law*, See also E. Benveniste, 'Judges and Foreign Affairs: A Comment on the Institut de Droit International's Resolution on "The Activities of National Courts and the International Relations of their State"', 5 EJIL, 1994, p. 423.

[22] Note the view expressed in *Oppenheim's International Law*, p. 54, that 'states show considerable flexibility in the procedures whereby they give effect within their territories to the rules of international law ... while the procedures vary, the result that effect is given within states to the requirements of international law is by and large achieved by all states'.

The United Kingdom[23]

As regards the applicability of international law rules to the domestic scene, various theories have been put forward. These attempt to explain the precise nature of the relationship and provide a guide for the courts faced with an international element in a case before it.

One expression of the positivist-dualist position has been the doctrine of *transformation*. This is based upon the perception of two quite distinct systems of law, operating separately, and maintains that before any rule or principle of international law can have any effect within the domestic jurisdiction, it must be expressly and specifically 'transformed' into municipal law by the use of the appropriate constitutional machinery, such as an Act of Parliament. This doctrine grew from the procedure whereby international agreements are rendered operative in municipal law by the device of ratification by the sovereign and the idea has developed from this that any rule of international law must be transformed, or specifically adopted, to be valid within the internal legal order.

Another approach, known as the doctrine of *incorporation*, holds that international law is part of the municipal law automatically without the necessity for the interposition of a constitutional ratification procedure. The best known exponent of this theory is the eighteenth-century lawyer Blackstone, who declared in his Commentaries that:

> the law of nations, wherever any question arises which is properly the object of its jurisdiction, is here adopted in its full extent by the common law, and it is held to be a part of the law of the land.[24]

This doctrine refers to customary international law and different rules apply to treaties.

(a) Customary international law

It is in this sphere that the doctrine of incorporation has become the main British approach. It is an old established theory dating back to the eighteenth century, owing its prominence at that stage to the considerable discussion then taking place as to the precise extent of diplomatic immunity. In the case of *Buvot* v. *Barbuit*,[25] Lord Talbot declared unambiguously that 'the law of nations in its full extent was part of the law of England', so that

---

[23] See e.g. Morgenstern, 'Judicial Practice'; H. Lauterpacht, 'Is International Law A Part of the Law of England?', 25 *Transactions of the Grotius Society*, 1939, p. 51; J. E. S. Fawcett, *The British Commonwealth in International Law*, London, 1963, Chapter 2; *Oppenheim's International Law*, pp. 56–63 and W. Holdsworth, *Essays in Law and History*, 1946, p. 260. See also J. Collier, 'Is International Law Really Part of the Law of England?', 38 ICLQ, 1989, p. 924 and Higgins, *Problems and Process*, Chapter 12.

[24] *Commentaries*, IV, Chapter 5.   [25] (1737) Cases t. Talbot 281.

a Prussian commercial agent could not be rendered liable for failing to perform a decree. This was followed twenty-seven years later by *Triquet* v. *Bath*,[26] where Lord Mansfield, discussing the issue as to whether a domestic servant of the Bavarian Minister to Britain could claim diplomatic immunity, upheld the earlier case and specifically referred to Talbot's statement.

This acceptance of customary international rules as part and parcel of the common law of England so vigorously stated in a series of eighteenth-century cases, was subject to the priority granted to Acts of Parliament and tempered by the principle of *stare decisis* or precedent, maintained by the British courts and ensuring that the judgments of the higher courts are binding upon the lower courts of the hierarchical system. Accordingly, a rule of international law would not be implemented if it ran counter to a statute or decision by a higher court.[27]

In the nineteenth century, a series of cases occurred which led many writers to dispute the validity of the hitherto accepted incorporation doctrine and replace it with the theory of transformation, according to which the rules of customary international law only form part of English law if they have been specifically adopted, either by legislation or case law. The turning point in this saga is marked by the case of *R* v. *Keyn*[28] which concerned a German ship, the *Franconia*, which collided with and sank a British vessel in the English Channel within 3 miles of the English coast. The German captain was indicted for manslaughter following the death of a passenger from the British ship, and the question that came before the Court for Crown Cases Reserved was whether an English court did indeed have jurisdiction to try the offence in such circumstances.

The Court came to the conclusion that no British legislation existed which provided for jurisdiction over the 3 mile territorial sea around the coasts. It was true that such a rule might be said to exist in international law, but it was one thing to say that the state had the right to legislate over a part of what had previously been the high seas, and quite another to conclude that the state's laws operate at once there, independently of any legislation. One thing did not follow from another, and it was imperative to keep distinct on the one hand the power of Parliament to make laws, and on the other the authority of the courts, without appropriate legislation, to apply the criminal law where it could not have been applied before. The question, as Lord Cockburn emphasised, was whether, acting judicially, the Court could treat the power of Parliament to legislate as making up for the absence of actual legislation. The answer came in the negative and the German captain was released.

---

[26] (1764) 3 Burr. 1478.
[27] But see now *Trendtex Trading Corporation* v. *Central Bank of Nigeria* [1977] 2 WLR 356; 64 ILR, p. 111, *infra*, p. 108.   [28] (1876) 2 Ex.D. 63

This case was seen by some as marking a change to a transformation approach,[29] but the judgment was in many respects ambiguous, dealing primarily with the existence or not of any right of jurisdiction over the territorial sea.[30] It must also be pointed out that in many respects the differences between the incorporation and transformation theories as interpreted in modern times lie more in a shift in presumption than any comprehensive theoretical revolution.[31] In any event, any doubts as to the outcome of any further *Franconia* situations were put to rest by the Territorial Waters Jurisdiction Act, 1878, which expressed British jurisdiction rights in similar circumstances.

The opinions put forward in the *West Rand Gold Mining Co.* case[32] showed a further blurring of the distinction between the incorporation and transformation theories. Lord Alverstone declared that whatever had received the common consent of civilised nations, must also have received the assent of Great Britain and as such would be applied by the municipal tribunals. However, he went on to modify the impact of this by noting that any proposed rule of international law would have to be proved by satisfactory evidence to have been 'recognised and acted upon by our own country' or else be of such a nature that it could hardly be supposed any civilised state would repudiate it. Lord Mansfield's view in *Triquet's* case could not be so interpreted as to include within the common law rules of international law which appear in the opinions of textbook writers and as to which there is no evidence that Britain ever assented.[33] This emphasis on assent, it must be noted, bears a close resemblance to the views put forward by the Court in *R* v. *Keyn* as to the necessity for conclusive evidence regarding the existence and scope of any particular rule of customary law. Indeed, the problem is often one of the uncertainty of existence and scope of customary law.

Not long after the *West Rand* case, another important dispute came before the courts. In *Mortensen* v. *Peters*,[34] a Danish captain was convicted by a Scottish court for contravening a fishing by-law regarding the Moray Firth. His ship had been operating within the Moray Firth and was within the area covered by the relevant by-law, but it was beyond the 3 mile limit recognised by international law. The issue came to the Scottish Court of Justiciary, where Lord Dunedin, in discussing the captain's appeal, concentrated upon the correct construction to be made of the relevant legislation. He noted that an Act of Parliament duly passed and assented to was supreme and the

---

[29] See e.g. Holdsworth, *Essays*, pp. 263–66 and W. Halsbury, *Laws of England*, 3rd edn, vol. London, 1968, VII, p. 264.
[30] See e.g. Lauterpacht, 'Is International Law a Part . . .', pp. 60–1.
[31] See e.g. Brownlie, *Public International law*, p. 47.   [32] [1905] 2 KB 391.
[33] *Ibid.*, pp. 407–8.   [34] (1906) 8 F.(J.) 93.

Court had no option but to give effect to its provisions. In other words, statutes had predominance over customary law, and a British court would have to heed the terms of an Act of Parliament even if it involved the breach of a rule of international law. This is so even though there is a presumption in British law that the legislation is to be so construed as to avoid a conflict with international law. Where such a conflict does occur, the Statute has priority and the state itself will have to deal with the problem of the breach of a customary rule.[35]

This modified incorporation doctrine was clearly defined by Lord Atkin in *Chung Chi Cheung* v. *R.*[36] He noted that:

> international law has no validity except in so far as its principles are accepted and adopted by our own domestic law . . . The courts acknowledge the existence of a body of rules which nations accept among themselves. On any judicial issue they seek to ascertain what the relevant rule is, and having found it they will treat it as incorporated into the domestic law, so far as it is not inconsistent with rules enacted by statutes or finally declared by their tribunals.

It goes without saying, of course, that any alleged rule of customary law must be proved to be a valid rule of international law, and not merely an unsupported proposition.

One effect of the doctrines as enunciated by the courts in practice is that international law is not treated as a foreign law but in an evidential manner as part of the law of the land. This means that whereas any rule of foreign law has to be proved as a fact by evidence, as occurs with other facts, the courts take judicial notice of any rule of international law and may refer, for example, to textbooks rather than require the presence and testimony of expert opinion.

In ascertaining the existence and nature of any particular rule, the courts may have recourse to a wider range of authoritative material than would normally be the case, such as 'international treaties and conventions, authoritative textbooks, practice and judicial decisions' of the courts of other countries.[37]

The case of *Trendtex Trading Corporation* v. *Central Bank of Nigeria*[38] raised anew many of these issues. The case concerned a claim for sovereign or state immunity by the Central Bank of Nigeria.[39] In *Trendtex* all three judges of the Court of Appeal accepted the incorporation doctrine as the correct one.

---

[35] See also 170 HC Deb., col. 472, 4 March 1907 and the Trawling in Prohibited Areas Prevention Act, 1909.

[36] [1939] AC 160; 9 ILR, p. 264. See also *Commercial and Estates Co. of Egypt* v. *Board of Trade* [1925] 1 KB 271, 295; 2 ILR, p. 423.

[37] Per Lord MacMillan, *The Cristina* [1938] AC 485, 497; 9 ILR, p. 250. See *Re Piracy Jure Gentium* [1934] AC 586, 588; 7 ILR, p. 213 and Stephenson LJ, *Trendtex Trading Corporation* v. *Central Bank of Nigeria* [1977] 2 WLR 356, 379; 64 ILR, pp. 111, 135. But see also Lauterpacht, 'Is International Law a Part', p. 87, note m.

[38] [1977] 2 WLR 356; 64 ILR, p. 111.   [39] See further *infra*, Chapter 13.

Lord Denning, reversing his opinion in an earlier case,[40] stressed that otherwise the courts could not recognise changes in the norms of international law.[41] Stephenson LJ emphasised in an important statement that:

> it is the nature of international law and the specific problems of ascertaining it which create the difficulty in the way of adopting or incorporating or recognising as already incorporated a new rule of international law.[42]

The issue of *stare decisis*, or precedent, and customary international law was also discussed in this case. It had previously been accepted that the doctrine of *stare decisis* would apply in cases involving customary international law principles as in all other cases before the courts, irrespective of any changes in the meantime in such law.[43] This approach was reaffirmed in *Thai-Europe Tapioca Service Ltd* v. *Government of Pakistan*.[44] However, in *Trendtex*, Lord Denning and Shaw LJ emphasised that international law did not know a rule of *stare decisis*.[45] Where international law had changed, the court could implement that change 'without waiting for the House of Lords to do it'.[46] The true principle, noted Shaw LJ, was that 'the English courts must at any given time discover what the prevailing international rule is and apply that rule'.[47] This marked a significant approach and one that in the future may have some interesting consequences, for example, in the human rights field.

The dominant incorporationist approach was clearly reaffirmed by the Court of Appeal in *Maclaine Watson* v. *Department of Trade and Industry*.[48] This case concerned the consequences of the demise of the International Tin Council and the attempts *inter alia* to render states that were members of the ITC liable for the debts incurred by that unfortunate organisation. Nourse LJ emphasised that the *Trendtex* case had resolved the rivalry between the incorporation and transformation doctrines in favour of the former.[49] One of the major points at issue in the *Tin Council* litigation was whether a rule existed in international law stipulating that the states members of an international organisation with separate personality could be rendered liable for the latter's debts.

If such a rule did exist, the question would then arise as to how that would be accepted or manifested in the context of municipal law. This, of course,

---

[40] *R* v. *Secretary of State for the Home Department, ex p. Thakrar* [1974] 2 WLR 593, 597; 59 ILR, p. 450.

[41] [1977] 2 WLR 356, 365; 64 ILR, pp. 111, 128. See also Shaw LJ, *ibid.*, 386 and Stephenson LJ, *ibid.*, 378–81.   [42] *Ibid.*, p. 379.

[43] See e.g. Brownlie, *Principles*, pp. 45–6 and *Chung Chi Cheung* v. *R* [1939] AC 160, 169; 9 ILR, p. 214. But see Morgenstern, 'Judicial Practice', pp. 80–2.

[44] [1975] 3 All ER 961, 967, 969–70; 64 ILR, p. 81.

[45] [1977] 2 WLR 356, 365; 64 ILR, pp. 111, 128.   [46] Per Lord Denning, *ibid.*, 366.

[47] *Ibid.*, 388; 64 ILR, p. 152. But cf. Stephenson LJ, *ibid.*, 381. See also e.g. Goff J., *I° Congreso del Partido* [1977] 3 WLR 778, 795; 64 ILR, p. 154.

[48] [1988] 3 WLR 1033; 80 ILR, p. 49.   [49] *Ibid.*, p. 1116; 80 ILR, p. 132.

would depend upon the precise content of such a claimed international rule and, as Kerr LJ noted, no such rule did exist in international law permitting action against member states 'in any national court'.[50] It was also not possible for an English court to remedy the gap in international law by itself creating such a rule.[51] Nourse LJ, however, took a different position on this point, stating that 'where it is necessary for an English court to decide such a question [i.e. an uncertain question of international law], and whatever the doubts and difficulties, it can and must do so'.[52] This, with respect, is not and cannot be the case, not least because it strikes at the heart of the community-based system of international law creation.

Lord Oliver in the House of Lords judgment[53] clearly and correctly emphasised that

> It is certainly not for a domestic tribunal in effect to legislate a rule into existence for the purposes of domestic law and on the basis of material that is wholly indeterminate.[54]

(b) Treaties[55]

As far as treaties are concerned, different rules apply as to their application within the domestic jurisdiction for very good historical and political reasons. While customary law develops through the evolution of state practice, international conventions are in the form of contracts binding upon the signatories. For a custom to emerge it is usual, though not always necessary, for several states to act in a certain manner believing it to be in conformity with the law. Therefore, in normal circumstances the influence of one particular state is not usually decisive. In the case of treaties, the states involved may create new law that would be binding upon them irrespective of previous practice or contemporary practice. In other words, the influence of the executive is generally of greater impact where treaty law is concerned than is the case with customary law.

It follows from this that were treaties to be rendered applicable directly within the state without any intermediate stage after signature and ratification and before domestic operation, the executive would be able to

---

[50] *Ibid.*, p. 1095; 80 ILR, p. 109.   [51] *Ibid.*   [52] *Ibid.*, p. 1118; 80 ILR, p. 135.
[53] [1989] 3 All ER 523; 81 ILR, p. 671.   [54] *Ibid.*, at 554; 81 ILR, p. 715.
[55] See generally A. D. McNair, *The Law of Treaties*, Oxford, 1961, pp. 81–97; F. A. Mann, 'The Enforcement of Treaties by English Courts', 44 *Transactions of the Grotius Society*, 1958–9, p. 29; R. Higgins in *The Effect of Treaties in Domestic Law* (eds. F. Jacobs and S. Roberts), London, 1987, p. 123; D. Lasok, 'Les Traités Internationaux dans la Système Juridique Anglaise', 70 *Revue Générale de Droit International Public*, 1966, p. 961; I. Sinclair, 'The Principles of Treaty Interpretation and their Application by the English Courts' 12 ICLQ, 1963, p. 508 and I. Sinclair and S. J. Dickson, 'National Treaty Law and Practice: United Kingdom' in *National Treaty Law and Practice* (eds. M. Leigh and M. R. Blakeslee), Washington, 1995, p. 223.

legislate without the legislature. Because of this, any incorporation theory approach to treaty law has been rejected. Indeed, as far as this topic is concerned, it seems to turn more upon the particular relationship between the executive and legislative branches of government than upon any pre-conceived notions of international law.

One of the principal cases in English law illustrating this situation is the case of the *Parlement Belge*.[56] This involved a collision between this ship and a British tug, and the claim for damages brought by the latter vessel before the Probate, Divorce and Admiralty division of the High Court. The *Parlement Belge* belonged to the King of the Belgians and was used as a cargo boat. During the case, the Attorney-General intervened to state that the Court had no jurisdiction over the vessel as it was the property of the Belgian monarch and that further, by a political agreement of 1876 between Britain and Belgium, the same immunity from foreign legal process as applied to warships should apply also to this packet boat. In discussing the case, the Court concluded that only public ships of war were entitled to such immunity and that such immunity could not be extended to other categories by a treaty without parliamentary consent. Indeed, it was stated that this would be 'a use of the treaty-making prerogative of the Crown . . . without precedent, and in principle contrary to the law of the constitution'.[57]

It is the Crown which in the UK possesses the constitutional authority to enter into treaties and this prerogative power cannot be impugned by the courts.[58] However, this power may be affected by legislation. Section 6 of the European Parliamentary Elections Act 1978 provided, for example, that no treaty providing for any increase in the powers of the European Parliament would be ratified by the UK without being first approved by Parliament.[59]

Thus it is that treaties cannot operate of themselves within the state, but require the passing of an enabling statute. The Crown in Britain retains the right to sign and ratify international agreements, but is unable to legislate directly. Before a treaty can become part of English law, an Act of Parliament is essential. This fundamental proposition was clearly spelt out by Lord Oliver in the House of Lords decision in *Maclaine Watson* v. *Department of Trade and Industry*.[60] He noted that:

> as a matter of the constitutional law of the United Kingdom, the royal prerogative, whilst it embraces the making of treaties, does not extend to altering the law or conferring rights on individuals or depriving individuals of rights which they enjoy in domestic law without the intervention of Parliament.

---

[56] (1879) 4 PD 129.   [57] *Ibid.*, p. 154.
[58] See e.g. *Council of Civil Service Unions* v. *Minister for the Civil Service* [1985] AC 374, 418.
[59] See *R* v. *Secretary of State for Foreign and Commonwealth Affairs, ex parte Rees-Mogg* [1994] 2 WLR 115.   [60] [1989] 3 All ER 523, 531; 81 ILR, pp. 671, 684.

Treaties, as it is sometimes expressed, are not self-executing. Quite simply, a treaty is not part of English law unless and until it has been incorporated into the law by legislation.[61]

It therefore followed that as far as individuals were concerned such treaties were *res inter alia acta* from which they cannot derive rights and by which they cannot be deprived of rights or subjected to obligations.[62] Such sentiments were also expressed by Lord Templeman[63] and thus constitute a major restatement of the English law position.

However, this rule does not apply to all treaties. Those relating to the conduct of war or cession of territory do not need an intervening act of legislation before they can be made binding upon the citizens of the country.[64] A similar situation exists also with regard to relatively unimportant administrative agreements which do not require ratification, providing of course they do not purport to alter municipal law. Such exceptions occur because it is felt that, having in mind the historical compromises upon which the British constitutional structure is founded, no significant legislative powers are being lost by Parliament. In all other cases where the rights and duties of British subjects are affected, an Act of Parliament is necessary to render the provisions of the particular treaty operative within Britain.

It is the practice in the UK to lay before both Houses of Parliament all treaties which the UK has either signed or to which it intends to accede.[65] The text of any agreement requiring ratification, acceptance, approval or accession has to be laid before Parliament at least twenty-one sitting days before any of these actions is taken. This is termed the 'Ponsonby Rule'.[66]

---

[61] *Ibid.*, at pp. 544–5; 81 ILR, p. 701. See also *Littrell* v. *USA (No. 2)* [1995] 1 WLR 82. But see R. Y. Jennings, 'An International Lawyer Takes Stock', 39 ICLQ, 1990, pp. 513, 523–6.

[62] *Ibid.*   [63] *Ibid.*, at p. 526; 81 ILR, p. 676.

[64] See e.g. Brownlie, *Principles*, p. 48; S. de Smith and R. Brazier, *Constitutional and Administrative Law*, London, 6th edn, 1989, pp. 140–2 and W. Wade and O. H. Phillips, *Constitutional and Administrative Law*, 9th edn, London, 1977, pp. 303–6. See also *Attorney-General for Canada* v. *Attorney-General for Ontario* [1937] AC 326, 347; 8 ILR, p. 41; *Walker* v. *Baird* [1892] AC 491; *Republic of Italy* v. *Hambro's Bank* [1950] 1 All ER 430; *Cheney* v. *Conn* [1968] 1 WLR 242; 41 ILR, p. 421; *Porter* v. *Freudenberg* [1915] 1 KB 857, 874–80 and McNair, *Law of Treaties*, pp. 89–91.

[65] It is also the practice to put before Parliament Orders in Council made under the United Nations Act 1946 in order to, for example, implement United Nations sanctions internally, see s. 1(4) of the Act and H. Fox and C. Wickremasinghe, 'UK Implementation of UN Economic Sanctions', 42 ICLQ, 1993, pp. 945, 959. See also *R* v. *HM Treasury and the Bank of England, ex parte Centro-Com*, Times Law Report, 7 October 1993.

[66] See 171 HC Deb., col. 2001, 1 April 1924. This is regarded not as a binding rule, but as a constitutional usage: see Wade and Phillips, *Constitutional and Administrative Law*, p. 304. See also the Foreign and Commonwealth Office Nationality, Treaty and Claims Department's handbook entitled *International Agreements: Practice and Procedure – Guidance Notes*, 1992, quoted in UKMIL, 63 BYIL, 1992, p. 705. If primary or secondary legislation is required in order to ensure compliance with obligations arising under a treaty, the Government will not ratify a treaty until such legislation has been implemented, see Parliamentary Under-Secretary of State, HC Debs., vol. 220, WA, cols. 483–4, 9 March 1993, quoted in UKMIL, 64 BYIL, 1993, p. 629.

There is in English law a presumption that legislation is to be so construed as to avoid a conflict with international law. This operates particularly where the Act of Parliament which is intended to bring the treaty into effect is itself ambiguous. Accordingly, where the provisions of a statute implementing a treaty are capable of more than one meaning, and one interpretation is compatible with the terms of the treaty while others are not, it is the former approach that will be adopted. For, as Lord Diplock pointed out: 'Parliament does not intend to act in breach of international law, including therein specific treaty obligations.'[67]

However, where the words of a statute are unambiguous the courts have no choice but to apply them irrespective of any conflict with international agreements.[68] Attempts have been made to consider treaties in the context of domestic legislation not directly enacting them, or as indications of public policy, particularly with regard to human rights treaties,[69] and it seems that account may be taken of them in seeking to interpret ambiguous provisions.[70] However, ministers are under no obligation to do this in reaching decisions.[71]

In the interpretation of international treaties incorporated by statute, the English courts have adopted a broader approach than is customary in statutory interpretation. In particular, recourse to the relevant *travaux préparatoires* may be possible.[72]

---

[67] *Salomon* v. *Commissioners of Customs and Excise* [1967] 2 QB 116, 143; *Post Office* v. *Estuary Radio Ltd* [1968] 2 QB 740 and *Brown* v. *Whimster* [1976] QB 297. See also *National Smokeless Fuels Ltd* v. *IRC, The Times*, 23 April 1986, p. 36 and Lord Oliver in *Maclaine Watson* v. *Department of Trade and Industry* [1989] 3 All ER 523, 545; 81 ILR, pp. 671, 702.

[68] *Ellerman Lines* v. *Murray* [1931] AC 126 and *IRC* v. *Collco Dealings Ltd* [1962] AC 1. See Sinclair, 'Principles of Treaty Interpretation', and C. Schreuer, 'The Interpretation of Treaties by Domestic Courts', 45 BYIL, 1971, p. 255. See also F. A. Mann, *Foreign Affairs in English Courts*, Oxford, 1986, pp. 97–114 and R. Gardiner, 'Treaty Interpretation in the English Courts since *Fothergill* v. *Monarch Airlines* (1980)', 44 ICLQ, 1995, p. 620.

[69] See e.g. *Blathwayt* v. *Baron Cawley* [1976] AC 397.

[70] See e.g. in the context of the European Convention on Human Rights, *R* v. *Secretary of State for the Home Department, ex p. Bhajan Singh* [1975] 2 All ER 1081; 61 ILR, p. 260; *R* v. *Chief Immigration Officer, Heathrow Airport, ex p. Salamat Bibi* [1976] 3 All ER 843; 61 ILR, p. 267; *R* v. *Secretary of State for the Home Department, ex p. Phansopkar* [1976] QB 606; 61 ILR, p. 390; *Waddington* v. *Miah* [1974] 1 WLR 683; 57 ILR, p. 175; *Cassell* v. *Broome* [1972] AC 1027; *Malone* v. *MPC* [1979] Ch.344; 74 ILR, p. 304; *R* v. *Secretary of State for the Home Department, ex p. Anderson* [1984] 1 All ER 920 and *Trawnik* v. *Ministry of Defence* [1984] 2 All ER 791. In *R* v. *Secretary of State for the Home Department, ex p. Brind* [1990] 1 All ER, it was held that subordinate legislation and executive discretion did not fall into this category. See also *Derbyshire County Council* v. *Times Newspapers Ltd* [1993] AC 534 HL; *Rantzen v Mirror Group Newspapers (1986) Ltd* [1993] 4 WLR 953 CA; *Attorney-General v. Associated Newspapers Ltd* [1993] 3 WLR 74; *R* v. *Secretary of State for the Home Department, ex parte Wynne* [1993] 1 WLR 115 and *R* v. *Brown* [1993] 2 WLR 556. See also A. Cunningham, 'The European Convention on Human Rights, Customary International Law and the Constitution', 43 ICLQ, 1994, p. 537.

[71] See e.g. *R* v. *Secretary of State for the Home Department, ex p. Fernandes* [1984] 2 All ER 390.

[72] See *Buchanan* v. *Babco* [1978] AC 141 and *Fothergill* v. *Monarch Airlines* [1981] AC 251; 74 ILR, p. 648. Compare in the latter case the restrictive approach of Lord Wilberforce, *ibid.*, p. 278; 74 ILR, p. 656 with that of Lord Diplock, *ibid.*, p. 283; 74 ILR, pp. 661–2. See also

Lord Oliver in *Maclaine Watson* v. *Department of Trade and Industry*[73] has also emphasised that the conclusion of an international treaty is a question of fact and that while a treaty may be referred to as part of the factual background against which a particular issue arises, the legal results that flow from such a treaty in international law are not such questions of fact and are thus not justiciable before the English courts.

There are many reasons why certain issues may be non-justiciable before the English courts,[74] ranging from judicial propriety to act of state and state immunity situations, but whether the doctrine can or should be expressed quite so baldly may be questioned. There may indeed be situations where legal consequences will be deemed to flow from the existence and nature of particular unincorporated treaties.[75]

In conclusion, it may be stated that parliamentary legislation will be required where a treaty for its application in the UK requires a modification of or addition to existing common law or statute, affects private rights, creates financial obligations for the UK, provides for an increase in the powers of the European Parliament, involves the cession of British territory or increases the powers of the Crown.[76]

Reference should also be made to the growing importance of entry into the European Communities in this context. The case law of the Communities demonstrates that fundamental rights are an integral part of the general principles of law, the observance of which the European Court of Justice seeks to ensure. The system provides that Community law prevails over national law and that the decisions of the European Court are to be applied by the domestic courts of the member states. The potential for change through this route is, therefore, significant.[77]

The United States[78]

As far as the American position on the relationship between municipal law and customary international law is concerned, it appears to be very

Goldman v. *Thai Airways International Ltd* [1983] 3 All ER 693. Note also that in *Wahda Bank* v. *Arab Bank plc*, Times Law Reports, 16 December 1992, Phillips J referred to UN sanctions resolutions in examining the question of the applicability of the Order in Council implementing the sanctions internally to the case in question.

[73] [1989] 3 All ER 523, 545; 81 ILR, pp. 671, 702.   [74] See further *infra*, p. 129.
[75] See Kerr LJ, *Maclaine Watson* v. *Department of Trade and Industry* [1988] 3 WLR 1033, 1075–6; 80 ILR, pp. 49, 86–8.
[76] Sinclair and Dickson, *National Treaty Law and Practice*, p. 230.
[77] See e.g. *Nold* v. *EC Commission* [1974] ECR 491, 508 and *Rutili* v. *Ministry of Interior of French Republic* [1975] ECR 1219.
[78] See e.g. J. J. Paust, *International Law as Law of the United States*, Durham, NC, 1996; Morgenstern, 'Judicial Practice'; I. Seidl-Hohenveldern, 'Transformation or Adoption of International Law into Municipal Law', 12 ICLQ, 1963, p. 88; *Oppenheim's International Law*, pp. 74 *et seq.*; C. Dickinson, 'The Law of Nations as part of the National Law of the

similar to the English practice, apart from the need to take the Constitution into account. An early acceptance of the incorporation doctrine was later modified as in the UK. It was stated in the *Paquete Habana* case[79] that:

> international law is part of our law and must be ascertained and administered by the courts of justice of appropriate jurisdiction as often as questions of right depending upon it are duly presented for their determination.[80]

Similarly, the early pure incorporation cases gave way to a more cautious approach.[81] The current accepted position is that customary international law in the US is federal law and that its determination by the federal courts is binding on the state courts.[82]

The similarity of approach with the UK is not surprising in view of common historical and cultural traditions, and parallel restraints upon the theories are visible. American courts are bound by the doctrine of precedent and the necessity to proceed according to previously decided cases, and they too must apply statute as against any rules of customary international law that do not accord with it.[83] The Court of Appeals recently reaffirmed this position in the *Committee of United States Citizens Living in Nicaragua v. Reagan*[84] case, where it was noted that 'no enactment of Congress can be challenged on the ground that it violates customary international law'.[85] It has been noted that the political and judicial organs of the United States have the power to ignore international law, where this occurs pursuant to a statute or 'controlling executive act'. This has occasioned much controversy,[86] as has the general relationship between custom and inconsistent

United States', 101 *University of Pennsylvania Law Review*, 1953, p. 793; R. A. Falk, *The Role of Domestic Courts in the International Legal Order*, Princeton, 1964; R. B. Lillich, 'Domestic Institutions' in *The Future of the International Legal Order* (eds. C. Black and R. A. Falk), New York, 1972, vol. IV, p. 384; L. Henkin, *Foreign Affairs and the Constitution*, New York, 1972; L. Henkin, 'International Law as Law in the United States', 82 *Michigan Law Review*, 1984, p. 1555; J. J. Paust, 'Customary International Law: Its Nature, Sources and Status as Law in the United States', 12 *Michigan Journal of International Law*, 1990, p. 59 and L. Henkin, R. C. Pugh, O. Schachter and H. Smit, *International Law Cases and Materials*, 3rd edn, St Paul, 1993, Chapter 3.

[79] 175 US 677 (1900). See also *Respublica v. De Longchamps*, 1 Dall. 111.

[80] *Ibid.*, p. 700. See *Hilton v. Guyot*, 159 US 113 and *United States v. Melekh*, 190 F.Supp. 67 (1960), cf. *Pauling v. McElroy*, 164 F.Supp. 390 (1958).

[81] See e.g. *Cook v. United States*, 288 US 102 (1933); 6 ILR, p. 3 and *United States v. Claus*, 63 F.Supp. 433 (1944).

[82] See *US v. Belmont*, 301 US 324, 331, 57 S. Ct. 758, 761 (1937); 8 ILR, p. 34 and *Third Restatement of US Foreign Relations Law*, St Paul, 1987, Vol. I, pp. 48–52.

[83] See e.g. *Schroeder v. Bissell*, 5 F.2d 838, 842 (1925).   [84] 859 F.2d 929 (1988).

[85] *Ibid.*, at 939. See also *Tag v. Rogers*, 267 F.2d 664, 666 (1959); 28 ILR, p. 467 and *US v. Yunis (no. 3)*, 724 F 2d. 1086, 1091 (1991); 88 ILR, pp. 176, 181.

[86] See *Brown v. United States*, 12 US (8 Cranch) 110, 128 (1814) and *Whitney v. Robertson*, 124 US 190, 194 (1888). See also Henkin, 'International Law', p. 1555. See also *Rodriguez-Fernandez v. Wilkinson*, 654 F.Supp. 1382 (1981); 505 F.Supp. 787 (1980); *US v. PLO*, 695 F.Supp. 1456 (1988) and *Klinghoffer v. SNC Achille Lauro*, 739 F.Supp. 854 (1990).

pre-existing statutes.[87] However, it is now accepted that statutes supersede earlier treaties or customary rules of international law.[88] There does exist, as in English law, a presumption that legislation is not assumed to run counter to international law and as it was stated by the Court in *Schroeder* v. *Bissell*:[89]

> unless it unmistakably appears that a congressional act was intended to be in disregard of a principle of international comity, the presumption is that it was intended to be in conformity with it.[90]

The relationship between US law and customary law has been the subject of recent re-examination in the context of certain human rights situations. In *Filartiga* v. *Pena-Irala*,[91] the US Court of Appeals for the Second Circuit dealt with an action brought by Paraguayans against a Paraguayan for the torture and death of the son of the plaintiff. The claim was based on the Alien Tort Claims Act of 1789[92] which provides that '[t]he district courts shall have original jurisdiction of any civil action by an alien for a tort only, committed in violation of the law of nations'. The Court of Appeals held that torture constituted a violation of international customary law and was thus actionable. The Court accordingly held against the defendant despite the fact that both parties were alien and all the operative acts occurred in Paraguay. The Court also noted that in ascertaining the content of international law, the contemporary rules and principles of international law were to be interpreted and not those as of the date of the prescribing statute.[93]

Other cases came before the courts in which the incorporation of international customary law provisions concerning human rights issues was argued with mixed success.[94] An attempt to obtain a judgment in the US against the Republic of Argentina for torturing its own citizens, however, ultimately foundered upon the doctrine of sovereign immunity,[95] while it has recently been held that acts of 'international terrorism' are not actionable under the

---

[87] See *Third Restatement of US Foreign Relations Law*, pp. 63–9 (§115); the *Reagan* case, 859 F.2d 929 and L. Goldklang, 'Back on Board the *Paquete Habana*', 25 *Va JIL*, 1984, p. 143.
[88] See previous footnote.   [89] 5 F.2d 838 (1925).
[90] *Ibid.*, p. 842. See also *Macleod* v. *United States*, 229 US 416 (1913) and *Littlejohn & Co.* v. *United States*, 270 US 215 (1926); 3 ILR, p. 483.
[91] 630 F.2d 876 (1980); 77 ILR, p. 169. See e.g. R. B. Lillich, *Invoking Human Rights Law in Domestic Courts*, Charlottesville, 1985 and Comment, 'Torture as a Tort in Violation of International Law', 33 *Stanford Law Review*, 1981, p. 353.   [92] 28 USC 1350 (1988).
[93] 630 F.2d 876, 881 (1980); 77 ILR, pp. 169, 175. See also *Amerada Hess* v. *Argentine Republic*, 830 F.2d 421; 79 ILR, p. 1. The norms of international law were to be found by 'consulting the works of jurists, writing professedly on public law; or by the general usage and practice of nations; or by judicial decisions recognising and enforcing that law', 630 F.2d 876 at 880; 77 ILR, p. 174, quoting *United States* v. *Smith*, 18 US (5 Wheat.), 153, 160–1. See also *Kadic* v. *Karadzic*, 34 ILM, 1995, p. 1592.
[94] See e.g. *Fernandez* v. *Wilkinson*, 505 F.Supp. 787 (1980) and *In re Alien Children Education Litigation*, 501 F.Supp. 544 (1980).
[95] *Siderman* v. *Republic of Argentina*, No. CV 82–1772–RMT (MCx) and *International Practitioner's Notebook*, July 1985, p. 1. See also *infra*, Chapter 13.

Alien Tort Claims Act.[96] However, in *Kadic* v. *Karadzic*,[97] US Court of Appeals for the Second Circuit held that claims based on official torture and summary executions did not exhaust the list of actions that may be covered by the Alien Tort Act and that allegations of genocide, war crimes and other violations of international humanitarian law would also be covered.[98]

The relative convergence of practice between Britain and the United States with respect to the assimilation of customary law is not reflected as regards the treatment of international treaties.[99] In the United Kingdom, it is the executive branch which negotiates, signs and ratifies international agreements, with the proviso that parliamentary action is required prior to the provisions of the agreement being accepted as part of English Law. In the United States, on the other hand, Article VI Section 2 of the Constitution provides that:

> all Treaties made or which shall be made with the authority of the United States, shall be the supreme law of the land and the Judges in every state shall be bound thereby, anything in the Constitution or Laws of any state to the contrary notwithstanding.[100]

There is also a difference in the method of approval of treaties, for Article II of the Constitution notes that while the President has the power to make international agreements, he may only ratify them if at least two-thirds of the Senate approve.

There is an exception and this is the institution of the executive agreements. These are usually made by the President on his own authority, but still constitute valid treaties within the framework of international law. As distinct from ordinary treaties, the creation of executive agreements is not expressly covered by the Constitution, but rather implied from its terms and subsequent practice, and they have been extensively used. The Supreme Court, in cases following the 1933 Litvinov Agreement, which established American recognition of the Soviet government and provided

---

[96] *Tel-Oren* v. *Libyan Arab Republic*, 517 F.Supp. 542 (1981), *aff'd per curiam*, 726 F.2d 774 (1984), *cert. denied* 53 USLW. 3612 (1985); 77 ILR, p. 192. See e.g. A. D'Amato, 'What Does Tel-Oren Tell Lawyers?', 79 AJIL, 1985, p. 92. See also *De Sanchez* v. *Banco Central de Nicaragua*, 770 F.2d 1385, 1398 (1985); 88 ILR, pp. 75, 90 and *Linder* v. *Portocarrero*, 747 F.Supp 1452; 99 ILR, p. 55.   [97] 34 ILM, 1995, p. 1592.

[98] Note that the US Torture Victim Protection Act 1992 provides a cause of action for official torture and extrajudicial killing where an individual, under actual or apparent authority or colour of law of any foreign law subjects engages in such activities. This is not a jurisdictional statute, so that claims of official torture will be pursued under the jurisdiction conferred by the Alien Tort Act or under the general federal question jurisdiction of section 1331, see e.g. *Xuncax* v. *Gramajo*, 886 F.Supp. 162 (1995).

[99] See e.g. Jackson, 'Status of Treaties in Domestic Legal Systems', p. 310.

[100] See e.g. *Ware* v. *Hylton*, 3 US (3 Dall.) 199 (1796) and *Foster* v. *Nielson*, 27 US (2 Pet.) 253 (1829). See also on treaty powers and the 'reserved powers' of the states the tenth amendment, *Missouri* v. *Holland*, 252 US 416 (1920); 1 ILR, p. 4 and *United States* v. *Curtiss-Wright Export Corporation*, 299 US 304 (1936); 8 ILR, p. 48.

for the assignment to the US of particular debts owing to the USSR, emphasised that such executive agreements possessed the same status and dignity
as treaties made by the President with the advice and consent of the Senate
under Article II of the Constitution.[101]

American doctrines as to the understanding of treaty law are founded
upon the distinction between 'self-executing' and 'non-self-executing'
treaties.[102] The former are able to operate automatically within the domestic sphere, without the need for any municipal legislation, while the latter
require enabling acts before they can function inside the country and bind
the American courts. Self-executing treaties apply directly within the United
States as part of the supreme law of the land, whereas those conventions
deemed not self-executing are obliged to undergo a legislative transformation and until they do so they cannot be regarded as legally enforceable
against American citizens or institutions.[103]

But how does one know when an international agreement falls into one
category or the other? This matter has absorbed the courts of the United
States for many years, and the distinction appears to have been made upon
the basis of political content. In other words, where a treaty involves political questions of definition or exposition, then the issue should be left to the
legislative organs of the nation, rather than automatic operation.[104]
Examples of this would include the acquisition or loss of territory and
financial arrangements. The Supreme Court in *Edye* v. *Robertson*[105] declared
that treaties which

> contain provisions which are capable of enforcement as between private
> parties in the courts of the country . . . [are] in the same category as other laws
> of Congress.

This would seem to mean that an international convention would become
a law of the land, where its terms determine the rights and duties of private
citizens, and contrasts with the position where a political issue is involved
and the treaty thereby treated as non-self-executing.

Of course such generalisations as these are bound to lead to considerable

---

[101] See e.g. *United States* v. *Pink*, 315 US 203 (1942); 10 ILR, p. 48. See, as regards the
President's power to settle claims and create new rules of law applicable to pending legislation, *Dames & Moore* v. *Regan*, 101 SC 2972 (1981); 72 ILR, p. 270.
[102] See e.g. Y. Iwasawa, 'The Doctrine of Self-Executing Treaties in the United States: A
Critical Analysis', 26 Va JIL, 1986, p. 635; J. Paust, 'Self-Executing Treaties', 82 AJIL,
1986, p. 760; T. Buergenthal, 'Self-Executing and Non-Self-Executing Treaties in National
and International Law', 235 HR, 1992 IV, p. 303 and C. M. Vázquez, 'The Four Doctrines
of Self-Executing Treaties', 89 AJIL, 1995, p. 695.
[103] See e.g. *Foster* v. *Neilson*, 27 U.S. (2 Pet.) 253, 311, 7 L.Ed. 415 (1829); *United States* v.
Percheman, 32 US (7 Pet.) 51 (1833); *United States* v. *Postal*, 589 F.2d. 862, 875 (5th Cir.
1979), *cert. denied*, 444 U.S. 832 and *Linder* v. *Portocarrero*, 747 F.Supp 1452, 1463; 99
ILR, pp. 55, 67–8.
[104] See Chief Justice Marshall, *Foster* v. *Neilson*, 27 US (2 Pet.) 253, 314 (1829).
[105] 112 US 580 (1884).

ambiguity and doubt in the case of very many treaties; and the whole matter was examined again in 1952 before the Supreme Court of California in *Sei Fujii* v. *California*.[106] The plaintiff was a Japanese citizen who had purchased some land in 1948 in California. By legislation enacted in that state, aliens had no right to acquire land. To prevent the property from going to the state, the plaintiff argued that, amongst other things, such legislation was not consistent with the Charter of the United Nations, an international treaty which called for the promotion of human rights without racial distinction.

The issue raised was whether the UN Charter was a self-executing treaty and, by virtue of such, part of the law of the land, which would supersede inconsistent local statutes. The Court declared that in making a decision as to whether a treaty was self-executing or not, it would have to consult the treaty itself to try to deduce the intentions of the signatories and examine all relevant circumstances. Following *Edye's* case it would have to see whether the provisions of the treaty laid down rules that were to be enforceable of themselves in the municipal courts.

The Court concluded after a comprehensive survey that the relevant provisions of the UN Charter were not intended to be self-executing. They laid down various principles and objectives of the United Nations Organisation, but 'do not purport to impose legal obligations on the individual member nations or to create rights in private persons'. The Court held that it was obvious that further legislative action by the signatories would be called for to turn the principles of the UN into domestic laws binding upon the individual citizens of states.[107] Accordingly, they could not be regarded as part of the law of the land and could not operate to deflect the Californian legislation in question. The case was decided in favour of the plaintiff, but on other grounds altogether.[108]

As is the case with the UK system, it is possible for the American legislature to take action which not only takes no account of international law rules but may be positively contrary to them, and in such an instance the legislation would be supreme within the American jurisdiction.

In *Diggs* v. *Schultz*,[109] for example, the Court had to consider the effect of the Byrd Amendment which legalised the importation into the USA of strategic materials, such as chrome from Rhodesia, a course of action which was expressly forbidden by a United Nations Security Council resolution which in the circumstances was binding. The Court noted that the Byrd Amendment was 'in blatant disregard of our treaty undertakings' but

---

[106] 38 Cal (2d) 718 (1952).   [107] *Ibid.*, p. 721.
[108] See e.g. *People of Saipan ex rel. Guerrero* v. *United States Department of Interior*, 502 F.2d 90 (1974); 61 ILR, p. 113. See also *Camacho* v. *Rogers*, 199 F.Supp. 155 (1961) and *Diggs* v. *Dent*, 14 ILM, 1975, p. 797. Note also O. Schachter, 'The Charter and the Constitution', 4 *Vanderbilt Law Review*, 1951, p. 643.
[109] 470 F.2d 461, 466–7 (1972); 60 ILR, pp. 393, 397.

concluded that: 'under our constitutional scheme, Congress can denounce treaties if it sees fit to do so, and there is nothing the other branches of government can do about it'.

Although in municipal terms the Amendment was unchallengeable, the United States was, of course, internationally liable for the breach of an international legal rule.[110]

However, there is a presumption that Congress will not legislate contrary to the international obligations of the state[111] and a principle of interpretation that where an act and a treaty deal with the same subject, the courts will seek to construe them so as to give effect to both of them without acting contrary to the wording of either. Where the two are inconsistent, the general rule has been posited that the later in time will prevail, provided the treaty is self-executing.[112] The question of a possible conflict between treaty obligations and domestic legislation was raised in *United States* v. *Palestine Liberation Organisation*.[113] The Anti-Terrorism Act of the previous year[114] provided for the closure of all PLO offices in the United States and this was construed by the Attorney-General to include the PLO mission to the United Nations, an action which would have breached the obligations of the US under the United Nations Headquarters Agreement. However, the District Court found that it could not be established that the legislation clearly and unequivocally intended that an obligation arising out of the Headquarters Agreement, a valid treaty, was to be violated.[115]

Other countries

In other countries where the English common law was adopted, such as the majority of Commonwealth states and, for example, Israel,[116] it is possible

---

[110] This, of course, reflects the general rule. See e.g. G. Hackworth, *Digest of International Law*, Washington, 1940–4, vol. V, pp. 185–6 and 324–5. See also *Third US Restatement of Foreign Relations Law*, 1987, para. 115(1)b.

[111] See e.g. Marshall CJ, *Murray* v. *Schooner Charming Betsy*, 6 US (2 Cranch) 64; *Weinberger* v. *Rossi*, 456 US 25 (1982) and *Cook* v. *United States*, 288 US 102 (1933). See also R. Steinhardt, 'The Role of International Law as a Canon of Domestic Statutory Construction', 43 *Vanderbilt Law Review*, 1990, p. 1103.

[112] See the decision of the Supreme Court in *Whitney* v. *Robertson*, 124 US 190 (1888). The *Third US Restatement of Foreign Relations Law*, pp. 63 *et seq.* suggests that an act of Congress will supersede an earlier rule of international law or a provision in an international agreement 'if the purpose of the act to supersede the earlier rule or provision is clear or if the act and the earlier rule or provision cannot be fairly reconciled'.

[113] 695 F.Supp. 1456 (1988).   [114] 22 USCA, paras. 5201–3.

[115] *Ibid.* See the Advisory Opinion of the International Court in the *Applicability of the Obligation to Arbitrate* case, ICJ Reports, 1988, p. 12; 82 ILR, p. 225. See also DUSPIL, 1981–8, Part I, pp. 8 *et seq.*

[116] See the *Eichmann* case, 36 ILR, p. 5, and R. Lapidoth, *Les Rapports entre le Droit International Public et le Droit Interne en Israel*, Paris, 1959. See also the *Affo* case before the Israeli Supreme Court, 29 ILM, 1990, pp. 139, 156–7; 83 ILR, p. 121, and R. Lapidoth, 'International Law Within the Israel Legal System', 24 *Israel Law Review*, 1990, p, 251.

to say that in general the same principles apply. Customary law is regarded on the whole as part of the law of the land.[117] Municipal laws are presumed not to be inconsistent with rules of international law, but in cases of conflict the former have precedence.

As far as treaties are concerned, Lord Atkin expressed the general position in *Attorney-General for Canada* v. *Attorney-General for Ontario*,[118] which was a case dealing with the respective legislative competences of the Dominion parliament and the Provincial legislatures. He noted that within the then British Empire it was well enshrined that the making of a treaty was an executive act, while the performance of its obligations, if they involved alteration of the existing domestic law, required legislative action. 'The question', remarked Lord Atkin,

> is not how is the obligation formed, that is the function of the executive, but how is the obligation to be performed, and that depends upon the authority of the competent legislature or legislatures.[119]

The relationship between treaties and domestic law was recently examined by the High Court of Australia in *Minister of State for Immigration and Ethnic Affairs* v. *Ah Hin Teoh FC*.[120] The Court upheld the traditional doctrine to the effect that the provisions of an international treaty to which Australia is a party do not form part of Australian law unless those provisions had been validly incorporated into municipal law by statute.[121] It was noted that this was because of the constitutional separation of functions whereby the executive made and ratified treaties, while the legislature made and altered laws.[122] The majority of the Court, however, went on to hold that the fact that a treaty had not been incorporated did not mean that its ratification by the executive held no significance for Australian law. Where a statute or subordinate legislation was ambiguous, the courts should favour that construction which accorded with Australia's obligations under the particular treaty,[123] while a statute generally had to be interpreted as far as its language permitted so that it was in conformity and not in conflict with the established rules of international law. Indeed, the

---

[117] But see as to doubts concerning the application of the automatic incorporation of customary international law into Australia, I. Shearer, 'The Internationalisation of Australian Law', 17 *Sydney Law Review*, 1995, pp. 121, 124. See also G. Triggs, 'Customary International Law and Australian Law' in *The Emergence of Australian Law* (eds. M. P. Ellinghaus, A. J. Bradbrook and A. J. Duggan), 1989, p. 376. Note that Brennan J. in *Mabo* v. *Queensland* (1992) 175 CLR 1, 41–2, stated that 'international law is a legitimate and important influence on the development of the common law'.

[118] [1937] AC 326; 8 ILR, p. 41.   [119] *Ibid.*, pp. 347–8; 8 ILR, pp. 43–4.

[120] No. 95/013, 7 April1995. Lexis transcript.

[121] See e.g. judgment by Mason CJ and Deane J. See also *Dietrich* v. *The Queen* (1992) 177 CLR 292, 305.   [122] See e.g. *Simsek* v. *Macphee* (1982) 148 CLR 636, 641–2.

[123] Judgment of Mason CJ and Deane J, paragraph 26. See also *Chung Kheng Lin* v. *Minister for Immigration* (1992) 176 CLR 1, 38.

Court felt that a narrow conception of ambiguity in this context should be rejected.[124] Moving beyond this approach which is generally consistent with common law doctrines, the majority of the Court took the view that ratification of a convention itself would constitute an adequate foundation for a legitimate expectation (unless there were statutory or executive indications to the contrary) that administrative decision-makers would act in conformity with the unincorporated but ratified convention.[125] This particular proposition is controversial in legal doctrine, but is an interesting example of the fact that internal decision-makers may not always be expected to be immune from the influence of obligations undertaken by the state.[126]

Although the basic approach adopted by the majority of common law states is clear, complications have arisen where the country in question has a written constitution, whether or not specific reference is made therein to the treatment of international agreements. An example of the latter is India, whose constitution refers only in the vaguest of terms to the provisions of international law,[127] whereas by contrast the Irish Constitution clearly states that the country will not be bound by any treaty involving a charge upon public funds unless the terms of the agreement have been approved by the Dáil.[128] Under article 169 (3) of the Cyprus Constitution, treaties concluded in accordance with that provision have as from publication in the Official Gazette of the Republic 'superior force to any municipal law on condition that such treaties, conventions and agreements are applied by the other party thereto'.[129] In such cases where there is a written constitution, serious questions of constitutional law may be involved, and one would have to consider the situation as it arises and within its own political

---

[124] *Ibid.* See also *Polites* v. *The Commonwealth* (1945) 70 CLR 60, 68–9, 77, 80–1.

[125] *Ibid.*, para. 34. See also para. 32 of the judgment of Toohey J., and para. 6 of the judgment of Gaudron J. Cf. para. 33 of the judgment of McHugh J.

[126] Note that after the decision in *Teoh*, the Minister for Foreign Affairs and the Attorney-General issued a Joint Statement (10 May 1995) denying the existence of any such legitimate expectation upon the ratification of a treaty, see M. Allars, 'One Small Step for Legal Doctrine, One Giant Leap Towards Integrity in Government: *Teoh's* Case and the Internationalisation of Administrative Law', 17 *Sydney Law Review*, 1995, pp. 204, 237–41. The government also introduced the Administrative Decisions (Effect of International Instruments) Bill 1995 into the Parliament with the specific purpose of denying that treaties or conventions give rise to a legitimate expectation of how a decision-maker will make a decision in an area affected by such international instruments. See also *Trick or Treaty? Commonwealth Power to Make and Implement Treaties*, a Report by the Senate Legal and Constitutional References Committee, November 1995.

[127] See e.g. Basu, *Commentaries on the Constitution of India*, vol. II, 1962, and *Constitutions of the World* (ed. R. Peaslee), 3rd edn, New York, 1968, vol. II, p. 308. See also K. Thakore, 'National Treaty Law and Practice: India' in *National Treaty Law and Practice*, p. 79.

[128] Peaslee, *Constitutions*, vol. III, p. 463 (article 29(5)2). Article 29 also states that Ireland accepts the generally recognised principles of international law as its rule of conduct in its relations with other states. See e.g. *Re O'Laighléis*, 24 ILR, p. 420 and *Re Woods*, 53 ILR, p. 552. See also *Crotty* v. *An Taoiseach*, 93 ILR, p. 480 and *McGimpsey* v. *Ireland* [1988] IR 567.   [129] See e.g. *Malachtou* v. *Armefti and Armefti*, 88 ILR, p. 199.

context.[130] But in general common law states tend to adopt the British approach.

The practice of those states which possess the civil law system, based originally on Roman law, manifests certain differences.[131]

The Basic Law of the Federal Republic of Germany,[132] for example, specifically states in article 25 that 'the general rules of public international law are an integral part of federal law. They shall take precedence over the laws and shall directly create rights and duties for the inhabitants of the federal territory.'[133] This provision, which not only treats international law as part of municipal law but regards it as superior to municipal legislation, has been the subject of a great deal of controversy as writers and lawyers have tried to establish whether international legal rules would invalidate any inconsistent municipal legislation and, indeed, whether international rules could override the Constitution. Similarly, the phrase 'general rules of public international law' has led to problems over interpretation as it may refer to all aspects of international law, including customary and treaty rules, or merely general principles common to all, or perhaps only certain nations.[134]

As far as treaties are concerned, the German federal courts will regard these as superior to domestic legislation, though they will not be allowed to operate so as to affect the constitution. Article 59 of the Basic Law declares that treaties which regulate the political relations of the federation or relate to matters of federal legislation shall require the consent or participation, in the form of a federal law, of the bodies competent in any specific case for such federal legislation. Thereafter such treaties will be treated as incorporated into German law, but with the status (no higher) of a federal law. Such

---

[130] See e.g. *International Law in Australia* (ed. Ryan), 1984; A. Byrnes and H. Charlesworth, 'Federalism and the International Legal Order: Recent Developments in Australia, 79 AJIL, 1985, p. 622 and *Koowarta* v. *Bjelke-Petersen*, High Court of Australia, 39 ALR 417 (11 May 1982); 68 ILR, p. 181; *Tabag* v. *Minister for Immigration and Ethnic Affairs*, Federal Court of Australia, 45 ALR 705 (23 December 1982); *Commonwealth of Australia* v. *State of Tasmania*, High Court of Australia, 46 ALR 625 (1 July 1983); 68 ILR, p. 266; *Polyukhovich* v. *Commonwealth* (1991) 172 CLR 501 and *Minister for Foreign Affairs* v. *Magno* (1992) 37 FCR 298 . See also *International Law Chiefly as Interpreted and Applied in Canada* (ed. Kindred), 4th edn, 1987, Chapter 4 and *Re Newfoundland Continental Shelf* [1984] 1 SCR 86, and C. Okeke, *The Theory and Practice of International Law in Nigeria*, London, 1986.

[131] See e.g. L. Wildhaber and Breitenmoser, 'The Relationship Between Customary International Law and Municipal Law in Western European Countries', 48 ZaöRV, 1988, p. 163; *Oppenheim's International Law*, pp. 63 *et seq.* and Henkin *et al.*, *International Law Cases and Materials*, pp. 154 *et seq.*

[132] See H. D. Treviranus and H. Beemelmans, 'National Treaty Law and Practice: Federal Republic of Germany', *National Treaty Law and Practice*, p. 43.

[133] See e.g. the *Parking Privileges for Diplomats* case, 70 ILR, p. 396.

[134] See e.g. D. P. O'Connell, *International Law*, 2nd edn, London, 1970, vol. I, pp. 71–6, and sources therein cited. See also generally A. Drzemczewski, *The European Human Rights Convention in Domestic Law*, Oxford, 1983, and Peaslee, *Constitutions*, vol. III, p. 361.

laws may indeed be challenged before the German courts by means of a constitutional complaint if the treaty in question contains provisions directly encroaching upon the legal sphere of the individual.[135]

The Netherlands has approached the whole topic in much more of a monist frame of mind. Articles 93 and 94 of the 1983 revised constitution provide that treaties have precedence over domestic laws and that any municipal legislation, whether enacted prior to or subsequent to an international agreement, is invalid if its provisions prove incompatible with those of the agreement.[136] Customary international law is deemed to apply internally, although it seems that statute will prevail in cases of conflict.[137]

The French Constitution of 1958 declares that treaties duly ratified and published shall operate as laws within the domestic system. However, the constitution provides that on an extensive range of international agreements, ratification can only take place by means of legislation. Examples include commercial treaties which entail some form of financial outlay, treaties modifying legislation and treaties affecting personal status. Once the relevant legislation has been passed, the agreement is promulgated and becomes binding upon the courts. Article 55 of the constitution provides that the provisions of the particular treaty will be superior to those of domestic laws, but only if this situation applies also as regards the other party or parties to the treaty.[138] It is also now accepted that the French courts may declare a statute inapplicable for conflicting with an earlier treaty.[139]

In 1993, South Africa adopted a new (interim) constitution.[140] Whereas

---

[135] See the *Unification Treaty Constitutionality* case, 94 ILR, pp. 42, 54. See also the *East Treaties Constitutionality* case, 73 ILR, p. 691.

[136] See e.g. E. A. Alkema, 'Fundamental Human Rights and the Legal Order of the Netherlands', in *International Law in the Netherlands* (ed. H. Van Panhuys *et al.*), Dordrecht, vol. III, 1980, p. 109; Peaslee, vol. III, p. 652; *Oppenheim's International Law*, p. 69 and H. Schermers, *The Effect of Treaties in Domestic Law* (eds., F. Jacobs and S. Roberts), Leiden, 1987, p. 109. See also e.g. *Nordstern Allgemeine Versicherungs AG* v. *Vereinigte Stinees Rheinreedereien*, 74 ILR, p. 2 and *Public Prosecutor* v. *JO*, 74 ILR, p. 130. Note also J. Klabbers, 'The New Dutch Law on the Approval of Treaties', 44 ICLQ, 1995, p. 629.

[137] See e.g. *Handelskwekerij GJ Bier BV* v. *Mines de Potasse d'Alsace SA*, 11 Netherlands YIL, 1980, p. 326.

[138] See e.g. O'Connell, *International Law*, pp. 65–8; Rousseau, *Droit International Public*, and Peaslee, vol. III, p. 312. See also *SA Rothmans International France and SA Philip Morris France*, 93 ILR, p. 308.

[139] See the *Cafés Jacques Vabre* case, 16 *Common Market Law Review*, 1975, p. 336 and *In re Nicolo*, 84 AJIL, 1990, p. 765; 93 ILR, p. 286. Under article 54 of the constitution, the Constitutional Council may declare a treaty to be contrary to the constitution, so that the constitution must first be amended before the treaty may be ratified or approved. See e.g. *Re Treaty on European Union*, 93 ILR, p. 337. See also *Ligue Internationale Contre le Racisme et l'antisémitisme*, AFDI, 1993, p. 963 and AFDI, 1994, pp. 963 *et seq.*

[140] See 33 ILM, 1994, p. 1043. This interim constitution came into force on 27 April 1994 and was intended to remain in force for five years to be replaced by a constitution adopted by a Constitutional Assembly consisting of the National Assembly and Senate of Parliament, see *infra*. See also J. Dugard, *International Law: A South African Perspective*, Kerwyn, 1994, Chapter 4 and Postscript.

the previous constitution of 1910, 1961 and 1983 had been silent on the question of international law, the 1993 Constitution contained several relevant provisions. Section 231(4) states that 'the rules of customary international law binding on the Republic, shall, unless inconsistent with this Constitution or an Act of Parliament, form part of the law of the Republic'. This formulation confirms essentially the common law position and would also suggest that the principle of *stare decisis* is not applicable to customary international law. As far as treaties are concerned, the previous position whereby an Act of Parliament was required in order to incorporate an international agreement, has been modified. While the negotiation and signature of treaties is a function of the President (section 82(1) i), ratification is now a function of the Parliament (section 231(2)),[141] section 231(3) provides that 'such international agreement shall be binding on the Republic and shall form part of the law of the Republic, provided Parliament expressly so provides and such agreement is not inconsistent with this constitution'. Thus South Africa has moved from the British system to a position akin to the civil law tradition. It should also be noted that this interim constitution expressly provides that the National Defence Force shall 'not breach international customary law binding on the Republic relating to aggression', while in armed conflict, it would 'comply with its obligations under international customary law and treaties binding on the Republic' (section 227(2)).[142]

These provisions were considered and refined by the Constitutional Assembly, which on 8 May 1996 adopted a new constitution.[143] Section 231(1) of this constitution provides that the negotiating and signing of all international agreements is the responsibility of the national executive, while such an agreement would only bind the Republic after approval by resolution in both the National Assembly and the National Council of Provinces.[144] Any international agreement becomes domestic law when enacted into law by national legislation, although a self-executing provision of an agreement that has been approved by Parliament is law in the Republic unless it is inconsistent with the Constitution or an Act of

---

[141] See Dugard, *International Law*, pp. 266–7 and 342–3. Note that this change means that treaties entered into before the constitution came into force do not form part of municipal law unless expressly incorporated by legislation, while those treaties that postdate the new constitution may, *ibid.*, p. 343.

[142] Note that article 144 of the Namibian Constitution provides that 'unless otherwise provided by this Constitution or Act of Parliament, the general rules of public international law and international agreements binding upon Namibia under this Constitution shall form part of the law of Namibia', see B. Erasmus, 'The Namibian Constitution and the Application of International Law', 15 *South African Yearbook of International Law*, 1989–9, p. 81. [143] See *supra* note 140.

[144] Section 231(2). This is unless either such an agreement is of a 'technical, administrative or executive nature' or it is one not requiring ratification (or accession), in which case tabling in the Assembly and the Council within a reasonable time is required, section 231(3).

Parliament.[145] Section 232 provides that customary international law is law in the Republic unless it is inconsistent with the Constitution or an Act of Parliament, while section 233 stipulates that when interpreting any legislation, every court must prefer any reasonable interpretation of the legislation which is consistent with international law over any alternative interpretation that is inconsistent with international law. It is also to be particularly noted that section 200(2) of the Constitution states that the primary object of the defence force is to defend and protect the Republic, its territorial integrity and its people, 'in accordance with the Constitution and the principles of international law regulating the use of force'.

The Russian Federation adopted a new constitution in 1993.[146] Under article 86, the President negotiates and signs treaties and signs the ratification documents, while under article 106 the Federal Council (the upper chamber of the federal parliament) must consider those federal laws adopted by the State Duma (the lower chamber) that concern the ratification and denunciation of international agreements. The Constitutional Court may review the constitutionality of treaties not yet in force (article 125(2)) and treaties that conflict with the constitution are not to be given effect (article 125(6)). Article 15(4) of the new constitution provides that 'the generally recognised principles and norms of international law and the international treaties of the Russian Federation shall constitute part of its legal system. If an international treaty of the Russian Federation establishes other rules than those stipulated by the law, the rules of the international treaty shall apply.' Thus both treaty law and customary law are incorporated into Russian law, while treaty rules have a higher status than domestic laws.[147]

Under article 73(3) of the Japanese Constitution of 1946,[148] the Cabinet has authority to conclude treaties with the prior or subsequent approval of the Diet, although executive agreements may be entered into without such approval, usually by simple exchange of notes. Promulgation of a treaty takes place by publication in the Official Gazette under the name of the Emperor once the Diet has approved and the Cabinet ratified the agreement

---

[145] Section 231(4).

[146] See G. M. Danilenko, 'The New Russian Constitution and International Law', 88 AJIL, 1994, p. 451. See as regards the practice of the Soviet Union, K. Grzybowski, *Soviet Public International Law*, Leiden, 1970, pp. 30–2.

[147] See also article 5 of the Russian Federal Law on International Treaties adopted on 16 June 1995, 34 ILM, 1995, p. 1370. This also provides that 'the provisions of officially published international treaties of the Russian Federation which do not require the publication of intra-state acts for application shall operate in the Russian Federation directly. Respective legal acts shall be adopted in order to effectuate other provisions of international treaties of the Russian Federation'.

[148] See generally S. Oda, *The Practice of Japan in International Law 1961–1970*, Leiden, 1982 and Y. Iwasawa, 'The Relationship Between International Law and National Law: Japanese Experiences', 64 BYIL, 1993, p. 333.

(article 7). Article 98(2) provides that 'treaties concluded by Japan and established laws of nations shall be faithfully observed' and this provision is taken as incorporating international law, both relevant treaty and customary law, into Japan's legal system.[149] Japan has also experienced some difficulty[150] in the context of the relative definition of self-governing and non-self-governing treaties.[151]

This survey of the attitudes adopted by various countries of the common law and civil law traditions leads to a few concluding remarks. The first of these is that a strict adherence to either the monist or dualist position will not enable one to get to grips with the situation as it actually exists. Most countries accept the operation of customary rules within their own jurisdictions, providing there is no conflict with existing laws, and some even will allow international law to prevail over municipal provisions. One can regard this as a significant element in extending the principles and protection of international law, whether or not it is held that the particular provision permitting this, whether by constitutional enactment or by case law, illustrates the superiority of municipal law in so acting.

The situation as regards treaties is much more complex, as different attitudes are maintained by different states. In some countries, certain treaties will operate internally by themselves (self-executing) while others must undergo a process of domestic legalisation. There are countries where legislation is needed for virtually all international agreements, for example, Belgium.[152] It is by no means settled as a general principle whether treaties prevail over domestic rules. Some countries allow treaties to supersede all municipal laws, whether made earlier or later than the agreement. Others, such as Norway, adopt the opposite stance. Where there are written constitutions, an additional complicating factor is introduced and some reasonably stable hierarchy incorporating ordinary laws, constitutional provisions and international law has to be maintained. This is particularly so where a federal system is in operation. It will be up to the individual country to adopt its own list of preferences.[153]

Of course, such diverse attitudes can lead to confusion and by no means assist in explaining what international law is and how it operates. But in the light of the present state of international law, it is inevitable that its

---

[149] Iwasawa, 'Relationship', p. 345.   [150] *Ibid.*, pp. 349 *et seq.*
[151] See generally with regard to China, T. Wang, 'International Law in China', 221 HR, 1990, p. 195.
[152] See article 68 of the Constitution, which deals basically with treaties of commerce and treaties which impose obligations on the state or on individuals.
[153] See generally Drzemczewski, *Domestic Law*, and Peaslee, *Constitutions*, vol. III, pp. 76 and 689. See also as regards the Philippines, the decision of the Supreme Court (en banc) in *The Holy See v. Starbright Sales Enterprises Inc.*, 102 ILR, p. 163 and as regards Poland, W. Czaplinski, 'International Law and Polish Municipal Law – A Case Study', 8 *Hague Yearbook of International Law*, 1995, p. 31.

enforcement and sphere of activity will become entangled with the ideas and practices of municipal law. Indeed, it is precisely because of the inadequate enforcement facilities that lie at the disposal of international law that one must consider the relationship with municipal law as of more than marginal importance. This is because the extent to which domestic courts apply the rules of international law may well determine the effectiveness of international legislation and judicial decision-making.

However, to declare that international legal rules therefore prevail over all relevant domestic legislation at all times is incorrect in the vast majority of cases and would be to overlook the real in the face of the ideal. States jealously guard their prerogatives, and few are more meaningful than the ability to legislate free from outside control; and, of course, there are democratic implications. The consequent supremacy of municipal legal systems over international law in the domestic sphere is not exclusive, but it does exist as an undeniable general principle.

It is pertinent to refer here briefly to the effect of the European Communities upon their member states.[154] In addition to the treaties creating the EC, there is a great deal of secondary legislation issuing forth from its institutions, which can apply to the member states. This takes the form of regulations, decisions or directives. Of these, the first two are directly applicable and enforceable within each of the countries concerned without the need for enabling legislation. While it is true that the legislation for this type of activity has been passed by, for example section 2(1) of the European Communities Act, 1972, in the UK, which permits in advance this form of indirect law-making, and is thus assimilated into municipal law, the fact remains that the member states have accepted an extraterritorial source of law, binding in certain circumstances upon them. In this context, it is worth noting the acceptance by the House of Lords in *Factortame Ltd* v. *Secretary of State for Transport*[155] that one of the consequences of UK entry into the European Communities and the European Communities Act 1972 was that an interim injunction could be granted, the effect of which would be to suspend the operation of a statute on the grounds that the legislation in question allegedly infringed Community law. This is one illustration of the major effect joining the Community has had in terms of the English legal system and previously accepted legal principles. The mistake, however, should not be made of generalising from this specific relationship to the sphere of international law as a whole.

---

[154] See e.g. S. Weatherill and P. Beaumont, *EC Law*, 2nd edn, London, 1995; L. Collins, *European Community Law in the United Kingdom*, 4th edn, London, 1990 and H. Kovar, 'The Relationship between Community Law and National Law' in *Thirty Years of Community Law* (Commission of the European Communities), 1981, p. 109. See also *supra*, p. 114.

[155] See *The Times*, 12 October 1990, p. 31. See also *R* v. *Secretary of State for Transport, ex parte Factortame*, European Court of Justice case C-213/89, *The Times*, 20 June 1990, p. 31.

Justiciability, act of state and related doctrines

An issue is justiciable basically if it can be tried according to law.[156] It would, therefore, follow that matters that fall within the competence of the executive branch of government are not justiciable before the courts. Accordingly, the test as to whether a matter is or is not justiciable involves an illumination of that grey area where the spheres of executive and judiciary merge and overlap. One important aspect of justiciability is the doctrine of act of state. An act of state generally relates to the activities of the executive in relations with other states,[157] but in the context of international law and municipal courts it refers particularly to the doctrine that no state can exercise jurisdiction over another state.[158] As such it is based upon the principles of the sovereignty and equality of states.[159]

The concept of non-justiciability applies with regard to both domestic and foreign executive acts. In the former case,[160] the courts will refuse to adjudicate upon an exercise of sovereign power, such as making war and peace, making international treaties or ceding territory.[161] As far as the latter instance is concerned, Lord Wilberforce declared in *Buttes Gas and Oil Co. v. Hammer (No. 3)*[162]

> there exists in English law a general principle that the courts will not adjudicate upon the transactions of foreign sovereign states . . . it seems desirable to consider this principle . . . not as a variety of 'act of state' but one for judicial restraint or abstention.[163]

Such a principle was not one of discretion, but inherent in the nature of the judicial process. Although that case concerned litigation in the areas of libel and conspiracy, the House of Lords felt that a determination of the issue would have involved the court in reviewing the transactions of four sovereign states and having to find that part of those transactions was contrary to international law. Quite apart from the possibility of embarrassment to the foreign relations of the executive, there were no judicial or manageable standards by which to judge such issues.[164]

---

[156] See Mann, 'Enforcement', Chapter 4.
[157] See e.g. Wade and Phillips, *Constitutional and Administrative Law*, pp. 299–303; J. B. Moore, *Acts of State in English Law*, New York, 1906; Mann, 'Enforcement', Chapter 9: M. Singer, 'The Act of State Doctrine of the UK', 75 AJIL, 1981, p. 283; M. Akehurst, 'Jurisdiction in International Law', 46 BYIL, 1972–3, pp. 145, 240 and M. Zander, 'The Act of State Doctrine', 53 AJIL, 1959, p. 826.
[158] See Lord Pearson, *Nissan* v. *Attorney-General* [1970] AC 179, 239; 44 ILR, pp. 359, 390.
[159] See *Oppenheim's International Law*, p. 365.
[160] See *Nissan* v. *Attorney-General* [1970] AC 179 and *Buron* v. *Denman* (1848) 145 ER 450. See also S. de Smith and R. Brazier, *Constitutional and Administrative Law*, 6th edn, London, 1989, pp. 145–51 and Mann, 'Enforcement', Chapter 10.
[161] See also *Council for Civil Service Unions* v. *Minister for the Civil Service* [1984] 3 All ER 935, 956.   [162] [1982] AC 888; 64 ILR, p. 331.
[163] *Ibid.*, p. 931; 64 ILR, p. 344. See also *Duke of Brunswick* v. *King of Hanover* (1848) 1 HLC 1.
[164] *Ibid.*, p. 938; 64 ILR, p. 351.

It has been held, for example, that judicial review would not be appropriate in a matter which would have serious international repercussions and which was more properly the sphere of diplomacy,[165] although the Court of Appeal has noted that the keeping and disposal of foreign bank notes for commercial purposes in the UK could not be treated as sovereign acts so as to bring the activity within the protection of the *Buttes* non-justiciability doctrine.[166]

Legislation can, of course, impinge upon the question as to whether an issue is or is not justiciable, and sovereign, or state, immunity is particularly relevant here, especially as it too is founded upon the principles of the sovereignty and equality of states. The UK State Immunity Act 1978, for example, removed sovereign immunity for commercial transactions.[167] One of the questions that the Court of Appeal addressed in *Maclaine Watson* v. *International Tin Council*[168] was whether in such circumstances the doctrine of non-justiciability survived. It was emphasised that the two concepts of immunity and non-justiciability had to be kept separate and concern was expressed that the *Buttes* non-justiciability principle could be used to prevent proceedings being brought against states in commercial matters, contrary to the Act.[169]

This warning should be heeded. Non-justiciability acts, in essence, as an evidential bar, since an issue cannot be raised or proved, whereas the immunity doctrine provides that the courts cannot exercise jurisdiction with regard to the matter in question, although it is open to the state concerned to waive its immunity and thus remove the jurisdictional bar. Indeed, whereas non-justiciability in the above sense relates to a clear inter-state relationship or situation which is impleaded in a seemingly private action, immunity issues will invariably arise out of a state–private party relationship that will not relate to inter-state activities as such.[170] Nevertheless, in practice, it is often difficult to disentangle the different conceptual threads, although the end result in terms of the inability of the plaintiff to surmount the sovereign hurdle may often be the same.

The issue of justiciability was discussed in *Maclaine Watson* v. *Department of Trade and Industry* both by the Court of Appeal[171] and the House of Lords[172] in the context of the creation of the collapsed International Tin Council by a group of states by a treaty which was unincorporated into English law. Kerr LJ emphasised that the doctrine in this context rested

[165] See e.g. *R* v. *Secretary of State for Foreign and Commonwealth Affairs, ex parte Pirbai, The Times,* 17 October, 1985, p. 4 (Court of Appeal).
[166] *A Ltd* v. *B Bank, The Times,* 15 August 1996, p. 37.
[167] See *Empresa Exportadora de Azucar* v. *Industria Azucarera Nacional S.A.* [1983] 2 Ll.R 171, 194–5; 64 ILR, p. 368. See further Chapter 13.
[168] [1988] 3 WLR 1169; 80 ILR, p. 191   [169] *Ibid.,* p. 1188 *per* Kerr LJ; 80 ILR, p. 209.
[170] See e.g. *Amalgamated Metal Trading* v. *Department of Trade and Industry, The Times,* 21 March 1989, p. 40.   [171] [1988] 3 WLR 1033; 80 ILR, p. 49.
[172] [1989] 3 All ER 523; 81 ILR, p. 671.

upon the principles that unincorporated treaties do not form part of the law of England and that such international agreements were not contracts which the courts could enforce.[173] However, this did not prevent reference to an unincorporated treaty where it was necessary or convenient, for example in order to assess the legal nature of the International Tin Council.[174]

Lord Oliver in the House of Lords decision reaffirmed the essence of the doctrine of non-justiciability. He noted that it was

> axiomatic that municipal courts have not and cannot have the competence to adjudicate upon or to enforce the rights arising out of transactions entered into by independent sovereign states between themselves on the plane of international law.[175]

However, this did not mean that the court must never look at or construe a treaty. A treaty could be examined as a part of the factual background against which a particular issue has arisen.[176] It was pointed out that the creation of the Council by a group of states was a sovereign act and that the adjudication of the rights and obligations between the member states of the Council and the Council itself could only be undertaken on the international plane.[177] In other words, the situation appeared to involve not only the *Buttes* form of act of state non-justiciability, but also non-justiciability on the basis of an unincorporated treaty.

Hoffmann LJ in *Littrell* v. *USA (No. 2)*[178] pointed out in the context of a status of forces agreement (providing for the placement of NATO troops in the UK) that the courts could look at such agreement to ensure that the foreign troops were here by invitation since the conclusion of a treaty was as much a fact as any other,[179] but this could not be taken to mean that the courts would actually enforce the terms of an unincorporated treaty. Additionally, it would not be open to the courts to determine whether a foreign sovereign state had broken a treaty.[180]

---

[173] [1988] 3 WLR 1033, 1075; 80 ILR, pp. 49, 86.
[174] *Ibid.*, 1075–6. See also Nourse LJ, *ibid.*, p. 1130; 80 ILR, p. 148.
[175] [1989] 3 All ER 523, 544; 81 ILR, pp. 671, 700.   [176] *Ibid.*, p. 545; 81 ILR, p. 701.
[177] *Ibid.*, p. 559; 81 ILR, p. 722. See also Ralph Gibson LJ in the Court of Appeal judgment [1988] 3 WLR 1033, 1143–4; 80 ILR, pp. 49, 163.   [178] [1995] 1 WLR 82, 93.
[179] Similarly, Colman J. in *Westland Helicopters Ltd* v. *Arab Organisation for Industrialisation* [1995] 2 WLR 126, 149, held that reference to the terms of the treaty establishing an international organisation and to the terms of the basic statute of that organisation in order to ascertain the governing law of that organisation and its precise nature did not transgress the boundary between what was justiciable and what was non-justiciable.
[180] See *British Airways Board* v. *Laker Airways Ltd* [1985] AC 58, 85–6; *Ex parte Moyneaux* [1986] 1 WLR 331; 87 ILR, p. 329 and *Westland Helicopters Ltd* v. *Arab Organisation for Industrialisation* [1995] 2 WLR 126. 136. See also *Minister for Arts Heritage and Environment* v. *Peko-Wallsend Ltd* (1987) 75 ALR 218, 250–4; 90 ILR, pp. 32, 51–5, where the Australian Federal Court held that a Cabinet decision involving Australia's international relations in implementing a treaty was not a justiciable matter and *Arab Republic of Syria* v. *Arab Republic of Egypt*, 91 ILR, pp. 288, 305–6, where the Supreme Court of Brazil held that the courts of a third state could not exercise jurisdiction in a matter essentially of state succession between two other states even where the property was within the jurisdiction.

The principle of non-justiciability, which includes but goes beyond the concept of act of state, must exist in an international system founded upon sovereign and formally equal states. Having said that, there is no doubt that the extent of the doctrine is open to question. While the courts would not inquire into the validity of acts done in a sovereign capacity, such as the constitutionality of foreign laws as such,[181] they may not feel constrained from investigating in a dispute involving private rights the legal validity of an act done by a citizen purporting to act on behalf of the sovereign or sovereign state.[182]

The US courts have similarly recognised the existence of areas of non-justiciability for sensitive political reasons. This is usually referred to as the political question doctrine and operates to prevent the courts from considering issues of political delicacy in the field of foreign affairs.[183] In the *Greenham Women against Cruise Missiles* v. *Reagan case*,[184] for example, the Court held that a suit to prevent the US deployment of cruise missiles at an air force base in the UK constituted a non-justiciable political question, not appropriate for judicial resolution.[185] Much will depend upon the particular circumstances of the case. In *Linder* v. *Portocarrero*,[186] for instance, concerning the murder of a US citizen working for the Nicaraguan government by rebel forces (the Contras), the US Court of Appeals for the Eleventh Circuit held that the political question doctrine was not implicated since the complaint neither challenged the legitimacy of US policy on Nicaragua nor sought to require the Court to decide who was right and who was wrong in the civil war in that country. The complaint was rather narrowly focused on the lawfulness of the conduct of the defendants in a single incident. In *Koohi* v. *United States*,[187] the US Court of Appeals for the Ninth Circuit held that the courts were not precluded from reviewing military decisions, whether taken during war or peacetime, which caused injury to US or enemy civilians. As the Court noted in *Baker* v. *Carr*,[188] not every case touching foreign relations is non-justiciable and as the Court of Appeals underlined in *Kadic* v. *Karadzic*,[189] 'judges should not reflexively invoke these doctrines [political question and act of state doctrines] to avoid difficult and somewhat

---

[181] See *Buck* v. *Attorney-General* [1965] I Ch. 745; 42 ILR, p. 11.
[182] See e.g. *Dubai Bank* v. *Galadari*, *The Times*, 14 July 1990.
[183] See e.g. *Underhill* v. *Hernandez*, 168 US 250 (1897) and *Baker* v. *Carr*, 369 US 181 (1962). See also *International Law Cases and Materials*, p. 178; L. Henkin, 'Is There a "Political Question" Doctrine?', 85 *Yale Law Journal*, 1976, p. 597; J. Charney, 'Judicial Deference in Foreign Relations', 83 AJIL, 1989, p. 805, and T. M. Franck, *Political Questions/Judicial Answers: Does the Rule of Law Apply to Foreign Affairs?*, 1992.
[184] 591 F.Supp. 1332 (1984); 99 ILR, p. 44.
[185] But see *Japan Whaling Association* v. *American Cetacean Society*, 478 US. 221 (1986), where the Supreme Court held that the judicial interpretation of a US statute, even if it involved foreign relations, was not a political question precluding justiciability. See also *Dellums* v. *Bush*, 752 F.Supp. 1141 (1990).   [186] 963 F.2d 332, 337 (1992); 99 ILR, pp. 54, 79.
[187] 976 F.2d 1328, 1331–2 (1992); 99 ILR, pp. 80, 84–5.   [188] 369 US 186, 211 (1962).
[189] 1995 US App. LEXIS 28826.

sensitive decisions in the context of human rights'. The fact that judicially discoverable and manageable standards exist would indicate that the issues involved were indeed justiciable.[190]

Also relevant in the context of non-justiciability, is the doctrine of act of state. The *Third US Restatement of Foreign Relations Law*[191] provides that 'in the absence of a treaty or other unambiguous agreements regarding controlling legal principles, courts in the United States will generally refrain from examining the validity of a taking by a foreign state of property within its own territory, or from sitting in judgment on other acts of a governmental character done by a foreign state within its own territory and applicable there'.[192]

In *Banco Nacional de Cuba* v. *Sabbatino*,[193] the US Supreme Court held that the act of state concept was not a rule of public international law, but related instead to internal constitutional balances.[194] It was a rule of judicial self-restraint. The Court declared that the judicial branch would not examine the validity of a taking of property within its own territory by a foreign sovereign government,[195] irrespective of the legality in international law of that action.[196] This basic approach was supported in a subsequent case,[197] whereas in *Alfred Dunhill of London Inc.* v. *Republic of Cuba*[198] the Supreme Court employed sovereign immunity concepts as the reason for not recognising the repudiation of the commercial obligations of a state instrumentality as an act of state. However, it now appears that there is an exception to the strict act of state doctrine where a relevant treaty provision between the parties specifies the standard of compensation to be payable and thus provides 'controlling legal principles'.[199]

---

[190] See e.g. *Klinghoffer* v. *SNC Achille Lauro*, 937 F.2d 44 (1991); *Nixon* v. *United States*, 122 L.Ed.2d 1 (1993) and *Can* v. *United States*, 12 F.3d 160.

[191] 1987, para. 443, pp. 366–7.

[192] This doctrine is subject to modification by act of Congress, *ibid.*, para. 444.

[193] 376 US 398 (1964); 35 ILR, p. 2.

[194] *Ibid.*, pp. 427–8; 35 ILR, p. 37. In *United States* v. *Noriega*, 746 F.Supp. 1506, 1521–3 (1990); 99 ILR, pp. 143, 163–5, the US District Court noted that the act of state doctrine was a function of the separation of powers, since it precluded judicial examination of the acts of foreign governments which might otherwise hinder the Executive's conduct of foreign relations.   [195] 376 US 398 (1964), pp. 427–8.

[196] This approach was reversed by Congress in the Hickenlooper Amendment to the Foreign Assistance Act of 1964, Pub L No 86–663, para. 301(d)(4), 78 Stat. 1013 (1964), 79 Stat. 653, 659, as amended 22 USC, para. 23470(e)(2), (1982). Note that in *Williams & Humbert Ltd* v. *W & H Trade Marks (Jersey) Ltd*, [1986] 1 All ER 129; 75 ILR, p. 312, the House of Lords held that an English court would recognise a foreign law effecting compulsory acquisition and any change of title to property which came under the control of the foreign state as a result and would accept and enforce the consequences of that compulsory acquisition without considering its merits.

[197] *First National City Bank* v. *Banco Nacional de Cuba*, 406 US 759 (1972); 66 ILR, p. 102.

[198] 96 Sup. Ct. 1854 (1976); 66 ILR, p. 212. See also M. Halberstam, 'Sabbatino Resurrected', 79 AJIL, 1985, p. 68.

[199] See *Kalamazoo Spice Extraction Co* v. *Provisional Military Government of Socialist Ethiopia*, 729 F.2d 422 (1984). See also *AIG* v. *Iran*, 493 F.Supp. 522 (1980) and Justice Harlan in the *Sabbatino* case, 376 US 398, 428 (1964); 35 ILR, pp. 25, 37.

In an important recent case, the Supreme Court examined anew the extent of the act of state doctrine. *Kirkpatrick* v. *Environmental Tectonics*[200] concerned a claim brought by an unsuccessful bidder on a Nigerian government contract in circumstances where the successful rival had bribed Nigerian officials. The Court unanimously held that the act of state doctrine did not apply since the validity of no foreign sovereign act was at issue. While the doctrine clearly meant that a US court had to accept that the acts of foreign sovereigns taken within their jurisdictions were to be deemed valid, this did not extend to cases and controversies that may embarrass foreign governments in situations falling outside this. Act of state was not to be extended.[201]

Executive certificates

There is an established practice adopted by the British courts of applying to the executive branch of government for the conclusive ascertainment of certain facts. Examples include the status of a foreign state or government, questions as to whether a state of war is in operation as regards a particular country or as between two foreign states and whether or not a particular person is entitled to diplomatic status. This means that in such matters of state the courts will consult the government and regard the executive certificate (or Foreign Office certificate as it is sometimes called), which is issued following the request, as conclusive, irrespective of any relevant rules of international law.[202] This was firmly acknowledged in *Duff Development Co Ltd* v. *Kelantan*,[203] which concerned the status of the State of Kelantan in the Malay Peninsula and whether it was able to claim immunity in the English courts. The government declared it was regarded as an independent state and the House of Lords noted that 'where such a statement is forthcoming, no other evidence is admissible or needed', and that:

> it was not the business of the Court to inquire whether the Colonial Office rightly concluded that the Sultan [of Kelantin] was entitled to be recognised as a sovereign by international law.[204]

---

[200] 29 ILM, 1990, p. 182; 88 ILR, p. 93.

[201] See also *Third Restatement of US Foreign Relations Law*, pp. 366–89, and *Bandes* v. *Harlow & Jones*, 82 AJIL, 1988, p. 820, where the Court of Appeals held that the act of state doctrine was inapplicable to takings by a foreign state of property located outside its territory.

[202] See e.g. *Oppenheim's International Law*, pp. 1046 *et seq.*

[203] [1924] AC 797; 2 ILR, p. 124. See also *The Fagernes* [1927] P.311; 3 ILR, p. 126 and *Post Office* v. *Estuary Radio Ltd* [1968] 2 QB 740; 43 ILR, p. 114. But cf. *Hesperides Hotels* v. *Aegean Turkish Holidays* [1978] 1 All ER 277; 73 ILR, p. 9.

[204] Note that under s.7, Diplomatic Privileges Act, 1964 and s. 21, State Immunity Act, 1978, such certificates are 'conclusive evidence' as to issues of diplomatic and state immunity. See further *infra*, Chapter 13.

This basic position was reaffirmed in *R* v. *Secretary of State for Foreign and Commonwealth Affairs, ex p. Trawnik*,[205] in which it was held that certificates under section 40(3) of the Crown Proceedings Act, 1947 and section 21 of the State Immunity Act, 1978 were reviewable in the courts only if they constituted a nullity in that they were not genuine certificates or if on their face they had been issued outside the scope of the relevant statutory power. The contents of such certificates were conclusive of the matters contained therein and in so far as they related to recognition of foreign states were matters within the realm of the royal prerogative and not subject to judicial review.

Problems may very well arise in the context of the decision of the UK announced in 1980 not to accord recognition to governments, but rather to treat the question of an unconstitutional change of regimes as one relating to diplomatic relations.[206] It is unclear whether the courts will continue to request certificates from the executive in such cases and if so what the nature of the response will be. The executive may not wish to issue certificates or may not provide a conclusive statement as to the status of the new regime. If certificates are provided which include no 'recognition' element, it will be interesting to see whether generally and to what extent the courts will take it upon themselves to determine the status of the new government and what facts will be considered in the process.

In *Republic of Somalia* v. *Woodhouse Drake and Carey (Suisse) SA*,[207] the court was faced with a confused situation concerning whether the interim government of Somalia was actually in effective control and the extent to which other factions controlled different areas of the country. The court noted that in reaching its decision as to whether the interim government was or was not the valid successor to the former legitimate government in the light of the degree of actual control exercised over the country, letters from the Foreign and Commonwealth Office became part of the evidence in the case. In so far as the three letters concerned statements as to what was happening in the country 'such letters may not be the best evidence' but in so far as they dealt with the question as to whether and to what extent the UK government had dealings with the foreign government such letters 'will almost certainly be the best and only conclusive evidence of that fact'.[208]

---

[205] *The Times*, 18 April, 1985, p. 4. See also C. Warbrick, 'Executive Certificates in Foreign Affairs: Prospects for Review and Control', 35 ICLQ, 1986, p. 138 and E. Wilmshurst, 'Executive Certificates in Foreign Affairs:The United Kingdom', *ibid.*, p. 157.
[206] See further *infra*, Chapter 8, p. 307.   [207] [1993] QB 54, 64–8; 94 ILR, pp. 608, 618–23.
[208] [1993] QB 54, 65; 94 ILR, pp. 608, 619.

The United States State Department similarly offers 'suggestions' on such matters, although they tend to be more extensive than their British counterparts, and include comments upon the issues and occasionally the views of the executive.[209]

---

[209] O'Connell, pp. 119–22. See *The Pisaro*, 255 US 216 (1921); *Anderson v. N.V. Transandine Handelmaatschappij*, 289 NY 9 (1942); 10 ILR, p. 10; *Mexico v. Hoffman*, 324 US 30 (1945); 12 ILR, p. 143 and the *Navemar*, 303 US 68 (1938); 9 ILR, p. 176.

THE SUBJECTS OF INTERNATIONAL LAW

Legal personality – introduction

In any legal system, certain entities, whether they be individuals or companies, will be regarded as possessing rights and duties enforceable at law.[1]
Thus an individual may prosecute or be prosecuted for assault and a
company can sue for breach of contract. They are able to do this because
the law recognises them as 'legal persons' possessing the capacity to have
and to maintain certain rights, and being subject to perform specific duties.
Just which persons will be entitled to what rights in what circumstances will
depend upon the scope and character of the law. But it is the function of
the law to apportion such rights and duties to such entities as it sees fit.
Legal personality is crucial. Without it institutions and groups cannot
operate, for they need to be able to maintain and enforce claims. In municipal law individuals, limited companies and public corporations are recognised as each possessing a distinct legal personality, the terms of which are
circumscribed by the relevant legislation.[2] It is the law which is the foundation of legal personality for it will determine the scope and nature of personality. There are things that an individual can do which an organisation
cannot do, for example commit an act of physical assault, and vice versa.
So that being accepted as a subject of the law does not mean the same thing

---

[1] See e.g. I. Brownlie, *Principles of Public International Law*, Oxford, 4th edn, 1990, Part II; J.
Crawford, *The Creation of Statehood in International Law*, Oxford, 1979; D. P. O'Connell,
International Law, London, 2nd edn, 1970, vol. I; J. W. Verzijl, *International Law in Historical
Perspective*, Leyden, 1969, vol. II; O. Lissitzyn, 'Territorial Entities other than Independent
States in the Law of Treaties', 125 HR, p. 5; Berezowski, *Mélanges Offerts à Juraj Andrassy*
(ed. Ibler), 1968, p. 31; H. Lauterpacht, *International Law: Collected Papers*, Cambridge, vol.
II, 1975, p. 487; C. Rousseau, *Droit International Public*, Paris, vol. II, 1974; N. Mugerwa,
'Subjects of International Law', *Manual of Public International Law* (ed. M. Sørensen),
London, 1968, p. 247; G. Schwarzenberger, *International Law*, 3rd edn, London, 1957, vol.
I, p. 89; A. Cassese, *International Law in a Divided World*, Oxford, 1986, Chapter 4;
International Law: Achievements and Prospects (ed. M. Bedjaoui), Paris, 1991, Part 1, Title
1; *Oppenheim's International Law* (R. Y. Jennings and A. D. Watts), 9th edn, London, 1992,
Chapter 2; R. Higgins, *Problems and Process*, Oxford, 1994, Chapter 3 and L. Henkin, R.
Pugh, O. Schachter and H. Smit, *International Law Cases and Materials*, 3rd edn, St Paul,
1993, Chapters 4 and 5.
[2] R. Dias, *Jurisprudence*, 5th edn, London, 1985, Chapter 12.

in all cases. Different subjects will have different rights and duties in different ways.

Personality involves the examination of certain concepts within the law such as status, capacity, competence as well as the nature and extent of particular rights and duties. The status of a particular entity may well be determinative of certain powers and obligations, while capacity will link together the status of a person with particular rights and duties. The whole process operates within the confines of the relevant legal system, which circumscribes personality, its nature and definition. This is especially true in international law. A particular view adopted of the system will invariably reflect upon the question of the identity and nature of international legal persons.[3]

Personality in international law necessitates the consideration of the interrelationship between rights and duties afforded under the international system and capacity to enforce claims. One needs to have close regard to the rules of international law in order to determine the precise nature of the capacity of the entity in question. Certain preliminary issues need to be faced. Does the personality of a particular claimant, for instance, depend upon its possession of the capacity to enforce rights? Indeed, is there any test of the nature of enforcement, or can even the most restrictive form of operation on the international scene be sufficient? One view suggests, for example, that while the quality of responsibility for violation of a rule usually co-exists with the quality of being able to enforce a complaint against a breach in any legal person, it would be useful to consider those possessing one of these qualities as indeed having juridical personality.[4] Some writers, on the other hand, emphasise the crucial role played by the element of enforceability of rights within the international system.[5]

However, a range of factors needs to be carefully examined before it can be determined whether an entity has international personality and, if so, what rights, duties and competences apply in the particular case. Personality is a relative phenomenon varying with the circumstances. It will always involve a test of judgment and perception of the situation at hand and the overall context of the current nature and requirements of the international community at large.

One of the distinguishing characteristics of contemporary international law has been the wide range of participants performing on the international scene. These include states, international organisations, regional organisations, non-government organisations, public companies, private companies and individuals. Not all such entities will constitute legal persons, although

[3] See, for example, the Soviet view, G. I. Tunkin, *Theory of International Law*, London, 1974.
[4] See e.g. M. Sørensen, 'Principes de Droit International Public', 101 HR, pp. 5, 127. For a wider definition, see H. Mosler, *The International Society As a Legal Community*, Dordrecht, 1980, p. 32.   [5] See e.g. Verzijl, *International Law*, p. 3.

they may act with some degree of influence upon the international plane. International personality is participation plus some form of community acceptance. The latter element will be dependent upon many different factors, including the type of personality under question. It may be manifested in many forms and may in certain cases be inferred from practice. It will also reflect a need. Particular branches of international law here are playing a crucial role. Human rights law, the law relating to armed conflicts and international economic law are specially important in generating and reflecting increased participation and personality in international law.

States

As Lauterpacht observes: 'the orthodox positivist doctrine has been explicit in the affirmation that only states are subjects of international law'.[6] However, it is less clear that in practice this position was maintained. The Holy See (particularly from 1871 to 1929), insurgents and belligerents, international organisations, chartered companies and various territorial entities such as the League of Cities were all at one time or another treated as possessing the capacity to become international persons.[7]

Creation of statehood[8]

The relationship in this area between factual and legal criteria is a crucial shifting one. Whether the birth of a new state is primarily a question of fact or law and how the interaction between the criteria of effectiveness and other relevant legal principles may be reconciled are questions of considerable complexity and significance. Since *terrae nullius* are no longer apparent,[9] the creation of new states in the future, once the decolonisation process is at an end, can only be accomplished as a result of the diminution or disappearance of existing states, and the need for careful regulation thus arises. Recent events such as the break-up of the Sovet Union, the Socialist Federal

---

[6] Lauterpacht, *International Law*, p. 489.
[7] See e.g. Verzijl, *International Law*, pp. 17–43 and Lauterpacht, *International Law*, pp. 494–500. See also the *Western Sahara* case, ICJ Reports, 1975 pp. 12, 39; 59 ILR, pp. 30, 56 and *Survey of International Law in Relation to the work of Codification of the International Law Commission*, Memorandum of the Secretary General, 1949, A/CN.4/1/Rev.1 p. 24.
[8] See in particular Crawford, *Creation of Statehood*; R. Higgins, *The Development of International Law through the Political Organs of the United Nations*, Oxford, 1963, pp. 11–57; K. Marek, *Identity and Continuity of States in Public International Law*, 2nd edn, Leyden, 1968; M. Whiteman, *Digest of International Law*, Washington, 1963, vol. I, pp. 221–33, 283–476 and Nguyen Quoc Dinh, P. Daillier and A. Pellet, *Droit International Public*, 5th edn, Paris, 1994, p. 397. See also Société Française pour le Droit International, *L'État Souverain*, Paris, 1994 and L. Henkin, *International Law: Politics and Values*, Dordrecht, 1995, Chapter 1.
[9] See as regards Antarctica, O'Connell, *International Law*, p. 451. See also *infra*, p. 364.

Republic of Yugoslavia and Czechoslovakia underline this. In addition, the decolonisation movement has stimulated a re-examination of the traditional criteria. Article 1 of the Montevideo Convention on Rights and Duties of States 1933[10] lays down the most widely accepted formulation of the criteria of statehood in international law. It notes that the state as an international person should possess the following qualifications: '(a) a permanent population; (b) a defined territory; (c) government; and (d) capacity to enter into relations with other states'.

The Arbitration Commission of the European Conference on Yugoslavia[11] in Opinion No. 1 declared that 'the state is commonly defined as a community which consists of a territory and a population subject to an organised political authority' and that 'such a state is characterised by sovereignty'. It was also noted that the form of internal political organisation and constitutional provisions constituted 'mere facts', although it was necessary to take them into account in order to determine the government's sway over the population and the territory.[12]

Such provisions are neither exhaustive nor immutable. As will be seen below, other factors may be relevant, including self-determination and recognition, while the relative weight given to such criteria in particular situations may very well vary. What is clear, however, is that relevant framework revolves essentially around territorial effectiveness.

The existence of a permanent population[13] is naturally required and there is no specification of a minimum number of inhabitants, as examples such as Nauru and Tuvalu demonstrate. However, one of the issues raised by the Falkland Islands conflict does relate to the question of an acceptable minimum with regard to self-determination issues,[14] and it may be that the matter needs further clarification as there exists a number of small islands awaiting decolonisation.[15]

The need for a defined territory focuses upon the requirement for a particular territorial base upon which to operate. However, there is no neces-

---

[10] 165 LNTS 19. International law does not require the structure of a state to follow any particular pattern: *Western Sahara* case, ICJ Reports, 1975, pp. 12, 43–4; 59 ILR, pp. 30, 60–1.

[11] Established pursuant to the Declaration of 27 August 1991 of the European Community, see Bull. EC, 7/8 (1991). See generally, M. Craven, 'The EC Arbitration Commission on Yugoslavia', 66 BYIL, 1995, p. 333 and *infra* p. 142.

[12] 92 ILR, pp. 162, 165. Note that *Oppenheim's International Law*, p. 120, provides that 'a state proper is in existence when a people is settled in a territory under its own sovereign government'.

[13] A nomadic population might not thus count for the purposes of territorial sovereignty, although the International Court in the *Western Sahara* case, ICJ Reports, 1975, pp. 12, 63–5; 59 ILR, pp. 30, 80–2, held that nomadic peoples did have certain rights with regard to the land they traversed.   [14] *Infra*, p. 177.

[15] But see as regards artificial islands, *United States* v. *Ray*, 51 ILR, p. 225; *Chierici and Rosa* v. *Ministry of the Merchant Navy and Harbour Office of Rimini*, 71 ILR, p. 283 and *Re Duchy of Sealand*, 80 ILR, p. 683.

sity in international law for defined and settled boundaries. A state may be recognised as a legal person even though it is involved in a dispute with its neighbours as to the precise demarcation of its frontiers, so long as there is a consistent band of territory which is undeniably controlled by the government of the alleged state. For this reason at least, therefore, the 'State of Palestine' declared in November 1988 at a conference in Algiers cannot be regarded as a valid state. The Palestinian organisations did not control any part of the territory they claim.[16]

Albania prior to the First World War was recognised by many countries even though its borders were in dispute. More recently, Israel has been accepted by the majority of nations as well as by the United Nations as a valid state despite the fact that its frontiers have not to this day been finally settled and despite its involvement in hostilities with its Arab neighbours over its existence and territorial delineation.[17] What matters is the presence of a stable community within a certain area, even though its frontiers may be uncertain. Indeed it is possible for the territory of the state to be split into distinct parts, for example Pakistan, prior to the Bangladesh secession of 1971.

For a political society to function reasonably effectively it needs some form of government or central control. However, this is not a pre-condition for recognition as an independent country.[18] It should be regarded more as an indication of some sort of coherent political structure and society, than as the necessity for a sophisticated apparatus of executive and legislative organs.[19] The requirement relates to the nineteenth-century concern with 'civilisation' as an essential of independent statehood and ignores the modern tendency to regard sovereignty for non-independent peoples as the paramount consideration, irrespective of administrative conditions.[20]

As an example of the former tendency one may note the *Aaland Islands*

---

[16] See *Keesing's Record of World Events*, p. 36438 (1989). See also General Assembly resolution 43/77. See *infra* p. 174, with regard to the evolution of Palestinian autonomy in the light of the Israel–Palestine Liberation Organisation (PLO) Declaration on Principles.

[17] Brownlie, *Principles*, p. 73. In fact most of the new states emerging after the First World War were recognised *de facto* or *de jure* before their frontiers were determined by treaty: H. Lauterpacht, *Recognition in International Law*, 1948, p. 30. See *Deutsche Continental Gas-Gesellschaft v. Polish State* (1929), 5 ILR, pp. 11, 15 and the *Mosul Boundary* case, PCIJ, Series B, No. 12, p. 21. The general rule is reaffirmed in the *North Sea Continental Shelf* cases, ICJ Reports 1969, pp. 3, 32; 41 ILR, pp. 29, 62. See also Jessup speaking on behalf of the US regarding Israel's admission to the UN, SCOR, 3rd year, 383rd meeting, p. 41. The Minister of State of the Foreign and Commonwealth Office in a statement on 5 February 1991, UKMIL, 62 BYIL, 1991, p. 557, noted that the UK 'recognises many states whose borders are not fully agreed with their neighbours'.

[18] See e.g. The Congo Case, Higgins, *Development*, pp. 162–4 and C. Hoskyns, *The Congo Since Independence*, Oxford, 1965. See also Higgins, *Problems and Process, op. cit.* p. 40 and Nguyen Quoc Dinh *et al.*, *Droit International Public*, p. 407.

[19] See the *Western Sahara* case, ICJ Reports, 1975, pp. 12, 43–4; 59 ILR, pp. 30, 60–61.

[20] See *infra* p. 177 on the right to self-determination.

case of 1920. The report of the International Committee of Jurists appointed to investigate the status of the islands remarked with regard to the establishment of the Finnish Republic in the disordered days following the Russian revolution that it was extremely difficult to name the date that Finland became a sovereign state. It was noted that:

> [t]his certainly did not take place until a stable political organisation had been created, and until the public authorities had become strong enough to assert themselves throughout the territories of the state without the assistance of the foreign troops.[21]

Recent practice with regard to the new states of Croatia and Bosnia-Herzegovina emerging out of the former Yugoslavia suggests the modification of the criterion of effective exercise of control by a government throughout its territory. Both Croatia and Bosnia-Herzegovina were recognised as independent states by European Community member states[22] and admitted to membership of the United Nations (which is limited to 'states' by article 4 of the UN Charter[23])[24] at a time when both states were faced with a situation where non-governmental forces controlled substantial areas of the territories in question in civil war conditions.

The capacity to enter into relations with other states is an aspect of the existence of the entity in question as well as an indication of the importance attached to recognition by other countries. It is a capacity not limited to sovereign nations, since both international organisations and non-independent states can enter into legal relations with other entities under the rules of international law. But it is essential for a sovereign state to be able to create such legal relations with other units as it sees fit. Where this is not present, the entity cannot be an independent state. One is not talking here of political pressure by one country over another which may cause it to adopt, or reject, a particular course of action, something which is constantly occurring throughout the spectrum of the international community, but rather the lack of competence to enter into legal relations. The difference is the pres-

---

[21] LNOJ Sp. Supp. No. 4 (1920), pp. 8–9. But cf. the view of the Commission of Rapporteurs in this case, LN Council Doc. B7 21/68/106 (1921), p. 22.

[22] On 15 January 1992 and 6 April 1992 respectively, see *Keesing's*, 1992, pp. 38703, 38704 and 38833. But see the Yugoslav Arbitration Commission's Opinion No. 5 of 11 January 1992 noting that Croatia had not met the requirements laid down in the Draft Convention on Yugoslavia of 4 November 1991 and in the Declaration on Yugoslavia and Guidelines on the Recognition of New States in Eastern Europe and in the Soviet Union of 16 December 1991, see 92 ILR, p. 178. Opinion No. 4 expressed reservations concerning the independence of Bosnia-Herzegovina pending the holding of a referendum. A referendum showing a majority for independence, however, was held prior to recognition by the EC member states and admission by the UN, *ibid.*, p. 173. See also *infra* p. 309.

[23] See e.g. V. Gowlland-Debbas, 'Collective Responses to the Unilateral Declarations of Independence of Southern Rhodesia and Palestine', 61 BYIL, 1990, p. 135.

[24] On 22 May 1992, See M. Weller, 'The International Response to the Dissolution of the Socialist Federal Republic of Yugoslavia', 86 AJIL, 1992, p. 569.

ence or absence of legal capacity, not the degree of persuasion or influence that may affect decisions.

The essence of such capacity is independence. This is crucial to statehood and amounts to a conclusion of law in the light of particular circumstances. It is a formal statement that the state is subject to no other sovereignty and is unaffected either by factual dependence upon other states or submission to the rules of international law.[25] It is arguable that a degree of actual as well as formal independence may also be necessary. This question was raised in relation to the grant of independence by South Africa to its Bantustans. In the case of the Transkei, for example, a considerable proportion, perhaps 90 per cent, of its budget at one time was contributed by South Africa, while Bophuthatswana was split into a series of areas divided by South African territory.[26] Both the Organisation of African Unity and the United Nations declared such 'independence' invalid and called upon all states not to recognise the new entities. These entities were, apart from South Africa, totally unrecognised.[27] However, many states are as dependent upon aid from other states and economic success would not have altered the attitude of the international community. Since South Africa as a sovereign state is able to alienate parts of its own territory under international law, these entities would appear in the light of the formal criteria of statehood to have been formally independent. However, it is suggested that the answer as to their status lay elsewhere than in an elucidation of this category of the criteria of statehood. It lay rather in understanding that actions taken in order to pursue an illegal policy, such as apartheid, cannot be sustained.[28]

An example of the complexities that may attend such a process is provided by the unilateral declaration of independence by Lithuania, one of the Baltic states unlawfully annexed by the Soviet Union in 1940, on 11 March 1990.[29] The 1940 annexation was never recognised *de jure* by the Western states and thus the control exercised by the USSR was accepted only upon a *de facto*

---

[25] See *Austro-German Customs Union* case (1931) PCIJ, Series A/B, No. 41, pp. 41 (Court's Opinion) and 57–8 (Separate Opinion of Judge Anzilotti); 6 ILR, pp. 26, 28, and *infra*, p. 132. See also Marek, *Identity*, pp. 166–80; Crawford, *Creation of Statehood*, pp. 48–52 and Rousseau, *Droit International Public*, pp. 53, 93.

[26] This was cited as one of the reasons for UK non-recognition, by the Minister of State, FCO, see UKMIL, 57 BYIL, 1986, pp. 507–8.

[27] The 1993 South African Constitution provided for the repeal of all laws concerning apartheid, including the four Status Acts which purported to create the 'independent states' of the four Bantustans, thus effectively re-incorporating these areas into South Africa, see J. Dugard, *International Law – A South African Perspective*, Kenwyn, 1994, p. 346.

[28] See M. N. Shaw, *Title to Territory in Africa: International Legal Issues*, Oxford, 1986, pp. 161–2. See also OAU Resolution, CM. Res. 493(XXVII), General Assembly resolution, 31/61A and Security Council statements on 21 September 1979 and 15 December 1981. Note that the Minister of State at the Foreign and Commonwealth Office declared that 'the very existence of Bophuthatswana is a consequence of apartheid and I think that that is the principal reason why recognition has not been forthcoming', HC Deb., vol. 126, cols. 760–1, 3 February 1988.   [29] See *Keesing's Record of World Events*, p. 37299 (1990).

basis. The 1990 declaration of independence was politically very sensitive, coming at a time of increasing disintegration within the Soviet Union, but went unrecognised by any state. In view of the continuing constitutional crisis within the USSR and the possibility of a new confederal association freely accepted by the fifteen Soviet republics, it was at that time premature to talk of Lithuania as an independent state, not least because the Soviet authorities maintained substantial control within that territory.[30] The independence of Lithuania and the other Baltic states was recognised during 1991 by a wide variety of states, including, crucially, the Soviet Union.[31]

Self-determination and the criteria of statehood

It is the criterion of government which, as suggested above, has been most affected by the development of the legal right to self-determination. The traditional exposition of the criterion concentrated upon the stability and effectiveness needed for this factor to be satisfied,[32] while the representative and democratic nature of the government has also been put forward as a requirement. The evolution of self-determination has affected the standard necessary as far as the actual exercise of authority is concerned, so it appears that a lower level of effectiveness, at least in decolonisation situations, has been accepted. This can be illustrated by reference to a couple of cases.

The former Belgian Congo became independent on 30 June 1960 in the midst of widespread tribal fighting which had spread to the capital. Within a few weeks the Force Publique had mutinied, Belgian troops had intervened and the province of Katanga announced its secession. Notwithstanding the virtual breakdown of government, the Congo was recognised by a large number of states after independence and was admitted to the UN as a member state without opposition. Indeed, at the time of the relevant General Assembly resolution in September 1960, two different factions of the Congo government sought to be accepted by the UN as the legitimate representatives of the state. In the event, the delegation authorised by the Head of State was accepted and that of the Prime Minister rejected.[33] A rather different episode occurred with regard to the Portuguese colony of Guinea-Bissau. In 1972, a UN Special Mission was dispatched to the 'liberated areas' of the territory and concluded that the colonial power had lost effective administrative control of large areas of the territory. Foreign observers appeared to accept the claim of the PAIGC, the local

---

[30] See e.g. the view of the UK government, 166 HC Deb., col. 697, Written Answers, 5 February 1990.

[31] See e.g. R. Müllerson, *International Law, Rights and Politics*, London, 1994, pp. 119 *et seq.*

[32] See Lauterpacht, *Recognition*, p. 28.

[33] *Keesings Contemporary Archives*, pp. 17594–5 and 17639–40 and Hoskyns, *Congo*, pp. 96–9.

liberation movement, to control between two-thirds and three-quarters of the area. The inhabitants of these areas, reported the Mission, supported the PAIGC which was exercising effective *de facto* administrative control. [34] On 24 September 1973, the PAIGC proclaimed the Republic of Guinea-Bissau an independent state. The issue of the 'illegal occupation by Portuguese military forces of certain sections of the Republic of Guinea-Bissau' came before the General Assembly and a number of states affirmed the validity of the independence of the new state in international law. Western states denied that the criteria of statehood had been fulfilled. However, ninety-three states voted in favour of Assembly resolution 3061(XXVIII) which mentioned 'the recent accession to independence of the people of Guinea-Bissau thereby creating the sovereign state of the Republic of Guinea-Bissau'. Many states argued in favour of this approach on the basis that a large proportion of the territory was being effectively controlled by the PAIGC, though neither a majority of the population nor the major towns. [35]

In addition to modifying the traditional principle with regard to the effectiveness of government in certain circumstances, the principle of self-determination may also be relevant as an additional criterion of statehood. In the case of Rhodesia, UN resolutions denied the legal validity of the unilateral declaration of independence on 11 November 1965 and called upon member states not to recognise it. [36] No state did recognise Rhodesia and a civil war ultimately resulted in its transformation into the recognised state of Zimbabwe. Rhodesia might have been regarded as a state by virtue of its satisfaction of the factual requirements of statehood but this is a dubious proposition. The evidence of complete non-recognition, the strenuous denunciations of its purported independence by the international community and the developing civil war militate strongly against this. It could be argued on the other hand that, in the absence of recognition, no entity could become a state but this constitutive theory of recognition is not acceptable. [37] The best approach is to accept the development of self-determination as an additional criterion of statehood, denial of which would obviate statehood. This can only be acknowledged in relation to self-determination situations and would not operate in cases, for example, of secessions from existing

---

[34] *Yearbook of the UN*, 1971, pp. 566–7 and A/AC.109/L 804, p. 19. See also A/8723/Rev. 1 and Assembly resolution 2918(XXVII).

[35] See GAOR, 28th Session, General Committee, 213rd meeting, pp. 25–6, 28, 30 and 31, GAOR, 28th session, plenary, 2156th meeting, pp. 8, 12 and 16 and 2157th meeting, pp. 22–5 and 65–7. See also *Yearbook of the UN*, 1973, pp. 143–7 and CDDH/SR.4., pp. 33–7. See also the Western Sahara situation, *infra*, p. 167.

[36] E.g. General Assembly resolutions 2024(XX) and 2151(XXI) and Security Council resolutions 216 (1965) and 217 (1966). See R. Higgins, *The World Today*, 1967, p. 94 and Crawford, *Creation of Statehood*, pp. 103–6. See also Shaw, *Title*.

[37] *Infra*, Chapter 8, p. 296.

states. In other words, in the case of an entity seeking to become a state and accepted by the international community as being entitled to exercise the right of self-determination, it may well be necessary to demonstrate that the internal requirements of the principle have not been offended. One cannot define this condition too rigorously in view of state practice to date, but it would appear to be a sound proposition that systematic and institutionalised discrimination might invalidate a claim to statehood.

In particular, one may point to the practice of the international community concerning the successor states to the former Yugoslavia. The European Community adopted Guidelines on Recognition of New States in Eastern Europe and the Soviet Union on 16 December 1991,[38] which constituted a common position on the process of recognition of such new states and referred specifically to the principle of self-determination. The Guidelines underlined the need to respect the rule of law, democracy and human rights and mentioned specifically the requirement for guarantees for the rights of minorities. Although these Guidelines deal with the issue of recognition and not as such the criteria for statehood, the two are interlinked and conditions required for recognition may in the circumstances, especially where expressed in general and not specific terms, often in practice be interpreted as additions to the criteria for statehood.

Recognition

Recognition is a method of accepting certain factual situations and endowing them with legal significance, but this relationship is a complicated one. In the context of the creation of statehood, recognition may be viewed as constitutive or declaratory, as will be noted in more detail in Chapter 8. The former theory maintains that it is only through recognition that a state comes into being under international law, whereas the latter approach maintains that once the factual criteria of statehood have been satisfied, a new state exists as an international person, recognition becoming merely a political and not a legal act in this context. Various modifications have been made to these theories, but the role of recognition, at the least in providing strong evidential demonstration of satisfaction of the relevant criteria, must be acknowledged. In many situations, expressed requirements for recognition may be seen as impacting upon the question of statehood as the comments in the previous section on the EC Guidelines indicate. There is also an integral relationship between recognition and the criteria for statehood in the sense that the more overwhelming the scale of international recognition is in any given situation, the less may be demanded in terms of the objective

---

[38] For the text see 31 ILM, 1992, pp. 1486–7.

demonstration of adherence to the criteria. Conversely, the more sparse international recognition is, the more attention will be focused upon proof of actual adherence to the criteria concerned.

Extinction of statehood[39]

Extinction of statehood may take place as a consequence of merger, absorption or, historically, annexation. It may also occur as a result of the dismemberment of an existing state.[40] In general, caution needs to be exercised before the dissolution of a state is internationally accepted.[41] While the disappearance, like the existence, of a state is a matter of fact,[42] it is a matter of fact that is legally conditioned in that it is international law that will apportion particular legal consequences to particular factual situations and the appreciation of these facts will take place within a certain legal framework.

While it is not unusual for governments to disappear, it is rather rarer for states to become extinct. This will not happen in international law as a result of the illegal use of force, as the Kuwait crisis of August 1990 and the consequent United Nations response clearly demonstrates,[43] nor as a consequence of internal upheavals within a state,[44] but it may occur by consent. Three recent examples may be noted. On 22 May 1990, North and South Yemen united, or merged, to form one state, the Republic of Yemen,[45] while on 3 October 1990, the two German states reunified as a result of the constitutional accession of the *Länder* of the German Democratic Republic to the Federal Republic of Germany.[46] The dissolution of Czechoslovakia[47] on 1 January 1993 and the establishment of the two new states of the Czech Republic and Slovakia constitutes a further example of a relatively amicable dismemberment, or disappearance of a state.[48]

During 1991, the process of disintegration of the Soviet Union gathered force as the Baltic states reasserted their independence[49] and the other

---

[39] See e.g. Crawford, *Creation of Statehood*, pp. 417 *et seq.* and *Oppenheim's International Law*, p. 206. See also H. Ruiz-Fabri, 'Genèse et Disparition de l'État à l'Époque Contemporaine', AFDI, 1992, p. 153.   [40] *Oppenheim's International Law*, pp. 206–7.

[41] See e.g. Yugoslav Arbitration Commission, Opinion No. 8, 92 ILR, pp. 199, 201.

[42] *Ibid.*   [43] See further Chapter 20, *infra*, p. 867.

[44] Such as Somalia in the early 1990s, see e.g. Security Council resolutions 751 (1992); 767 (1992); 794 (1992); 814 (1993); 837 (1993); 865 (1993); 885 (1993) and 886 (1993). See also Crawford, *Creation of Statehood*, p. 417.

[45] See *Keesing's Record of World Events*, p. 37470 (1990). See also 91 ILM, 1991, p. 820 and R. Goy, 'La Réunification du Yémen', AFDI, 1990, p. 249.

[46] See *infra* p. 163. See also C. Schrike, 'L'Unification Allemande', AFDI, 1990, p. 47 and W. Czaplinski, 'Quelques Aspects sur la Réunification de l'Allemagne', *ibid.*, p. 89.

[47] Termed at that stage the Czech and Slovak Federal Republic.

[48] See e.g. J. Malenovsky, 'Problèmes Juridiques Liés à la Partition de la Tchécoslovaquie', AFDI, 1993, p. 305.

[49] See L. Kherad, 'La Reconnaissance Internationale des États Baltes', RGDIP, 1992, p. 843.

Republics of the USSR stated their intention to become sovereign. In December of that year, the Commonwealth of Independent States (CIS) was proclaimed, and it was stated in the Alma Ata Declaration[50] that with the establishment of the CIS, 'the Union of Soviet Socialist Republics ceases to exist'. The states of the CIS agreed to support 'Russia's continuance of the membership of the Union of Soviet Socialist Republics in the United Nations, including permanent membership of the Security Council, and other international organisations'.[51] It has been commonly accepted that Russia constitutes a continuation of the USSR, with consequential adjustments to take account of the independence of the other former Republics of the Soviet Union.[52] It is therefore a case of dismemberment basically consisting of the transformation of an existing state. The disappearance of the USSR was accompanied by the claim, internationally accepted, of the Russian Federation to be the continuation of that state. While the element of continuity is crucial in the framework of the rules of state succession,[53] it does constitute a complication in the context of extinction of states.

By way of contrast, not all the relevant parties have accepted that the process of dissolution of the former Socialist Federal Republic of Yugoslavia during 1991–2 has resulted in the dissolution of that state.[54] The Federal Republic of Yugoslavia, which comprises the former Republics of Serbia and Montenegro, sees itself as the continuation of the former state within reduced boundaries, while the other former Republics have disputed this and have maintained rather that the Federal Republic of Yugoslavia (Serbia and Montenegro) is a successor to the former Yugoslavia precisely on the same basis as the other former Republics such as Croatia, Slovenia and Bosnia-Herzegovina. The matter was discussed by the Yugoslav Arbitration Commission. In Opinion No. 1 on 29 November 1991, it was noted that at that stage the Socialist Federal Republic of Yugoslavia was 'in the process of dissolution'.[55] However, in Opinion No. 8 adopted on 4 July 1992, the Arbitration Commission stated that the process of dissolution had been completed and that the Socialist Federal Republic of Yugoslavia (SFRY) no longer existed. This conclusion was reached on the basis of the fact that Slovenia, Croatia and Bosnia-Herzegovina had been recognised as new states, the republics of Serbia and Montenegro had adopted a new constitution for the 'Federal Republic of Yugoslavia' and UN resolutions had been

---

[50] See 31 ILM, 1992, pp. 148–9.   [51] *Ibid.*, p. 151.   [52] See further *infra* p. 677.
[53] See *infra*, Chapter 17.
[54] See also A. Pellet, 'La Commission d'Arbitrage de la Conférence Européenne pour la Paix en Yougaslavie', AFDI, 1991, p. 329; *ibid.*, 1992, p. 220 and *ibid.*, 1993, p. 286.
[55] 92 ILR, pp. 164–5. One should note the importance of the federal structure of the state in determining the factual situation regarding dissolution. The Arbitration Commission pointed out that in such cases 'the existence of the state implies that the federal organs represent the components of the Federation and wield effective power', *ibid.*, p. 165.

adopted referring to 'the former SFRY'.[56] The Commission also emphasised that the existence of federal states was seriously compromised when a majority of the constituent entities, embracing a majority of the territory and population of the federal state, constitute themselves as sovereign states with the result that federal authority could no longer be effectively exercised.[57] The UN Security Council in resolution 777 (1992) stated that 'the state formerly known as the Socialist Federal Republic of Yugoslavia has ceased to exist'. This was reiterated in resolution 1022 (1995) in which the Security Council, in welcoming the Dayton Peace Agreement (the General Framework Agreement for Peace in Bosnia and Herzegovina) between the states of the former Yugoslavia and suspending the application of sanctions, stated that the Socialist Federal Republic of Yugoslavia 'has ceased to exist'.

The fundamental rights of states

The fundamental rights of states exist by virtue of the international legal order, which is able, as in the case of other legal orders, to define the characteristics of its subjects.

(a) Independence[58]

Perhaps the outstanding characteristic of a state is its independence. This was defined in the Draft Declaration on the Rights and Duties of States prepared in 1949 by the International Law Commission, as the capacity of a state to provide for its own well-being and development free from the domination of other states, providing it does not impair or violate their legitimate rights.[59] By independence, one is referring to a legal concept and it is no deviation from independence to be subject to the rules of international law. Any political or economic dependence that may in reality exist does not affect the legal independence of the state, unless that state is formally compelled to submit to the demands of a superior state, in which case dependent status is concerned.

A discussion on the meaning and nature of independence took place in

---

[56] See e.g. Security Council resolutions 752 and 757 (1992). See also the resolution adopted by the European Community at the Lisbon Council on 27 June 1992, quoted in part in Opinion No. 9, 92 ILR, p. 204–5.

[57] Opinion No, 9, 92 ILR, p. 201. In Opinions Nos. 9 and 10, the Arbitration Commission noted that the Federal Republic of Yugoslavia (Serbia and Montenegro) could not consider itself as the continuation of the SFRY, but was instead one of the successors to that state on the same basis as the recognised new states, *ibid.*, pp. 205 and 208.

[58] *Oppenheim's International Law*, p. 382.

[59] *Yearbook of the ILC*, 1949, p. 286. Judge Huber noted in the *Island of Palmas* case that 'independence in regard to a portion of the globe is the right to exercise therein, to the exclusion of any other state, the functions of a state' (1928) 2 RIAA, pp. 829, 838; 4 ILR, p. 3.

the *Austro-German Customs Union* case before the Permanent Court of International Justice in 1931.[60] It concerned a proposal to create a free trade customs union between the two German-speaking states and whether this was incompatible with the 1919 Peace Treaties (coupled with a subsequent protocol of 1922) pledging Austria to take no action to compromise its independence. In the event, and in the circumstances of the case, the Court held that the proposed union would adversely affect Austria's sovereignty. Speaking generally, however, Judge Anzilotti noted that restrictions upon a state's liberty, whether arising out of customary law or treaty obligations, do not as such affect its independence. As long as such restrictions do not place the state under the legal authority of another state, the former maintains its status as an independent country. As it was declared in this important but dissenting opinion:

> restrictions on its liberty of action which a state may agree to do not affect its independence, provided that the state does not thereby deprive itself of its organic powers.[61]

The Permanent Court emphasised in the *Lotus* case[62] in a seminal pronouncement that '[r]estrictions upon the independence of states cannot therefore be presumed'. A similar point in different circumstances was made by the Court in the *Nicaragua* case,[63] where it was stated that 'in international law there are no rules, other than such rules as may be accepted by the state concerned, by treaty or otherwise, whereby the level of armaments of a sovereign state can be limited, and this principle is valid for all states without exception'. The Court also underlined in the *Legality of the Threat or Use of Nuclear Weapons*[64] that '[s]tate practice shows that the illegality of the use of certain weapons as such does not result from an absence of authorisation but, on the contrary, is formulated in terms of prohibition'. The basic proposition is still operative in the sense that the starting point for the consideration of the rights and obligations of states within the international legal system is that international law permits freedom of action for states, unless there is a rule constraining this. However, it must be emphasised that such freedom exists within and not outside the international legal system and it is therefore international law which dictates the scope and content of the independence of states and not the states themselves individually and unilaterally.

---

[60] PCIJ Series A/B, no. 41, 1931; 6 ILR, p. 26.
[61] PCIJ Series A/B, no. 41, p. 77; 6 ILR, p. 30. See also the *North Atlantic Coast Fisheries* case, (1910), Scott, *Hague Court Reports*, p. 141 at p. 170 and the *Wimbledon* case, PCIJ, Series A, No. 1, 1923, p. 25; 2 ILR, p. 99.
[62] PCIJ, Series A, No. 10, p. 18; 4 ILR, pp. 153, 155.
[63] ICJ Reports, 1986, pp. 3, 135; 76 ILR, pp. 349, 469. See also the *Legality of the Threat or Use of Nuclear Weapons*, ICJ Reports, 1996, paras. 21–2; 35 ILM, 1996, pp. 809, 819–20.
[64] ICJ Reports, 1996, para. 52; 35 ILM, 1996, pp. 809, 823.

The notion of independence in international law implies a number of rights and duties: for example, the right of a state to exercise jurisdiction over its territory and permanent population, or the right to engage upon an act of self-defence in certain situations. It implies also the duty not to intervene in the internal affairs of other sovereign states. Precisely what constitutes the internal affairs of a state is open to dispute and is in any event a constantly changing standard. It was maintained by the Western powers for many years that any discussion or action by the United Nations[65] with regard to their colonial possessions was contrary to international law.

However, this argument by the European colonial powers did not succeed and the United Nations examined many colonial situations.[66] In addition, issues related to human rights and racial oppression would not now appear to fall within the closed category of domestic jurisdiction, or internal affairs, so that international law permits outside scrutiny. It was stated on behalf of the European Community, for example, that the 'protection of human rights and fundamental freedoms can in no way be considered an interference in a state's internal affairs'. Reference was also made to 'the moral right to intervene whenever human rights are violated'.[67]

This duty not to intervene in matters within the domestic jurisdiction of any state was included in the Declaration on Principles of International Law Concerning Friendly Relations and Co-operation among States adopted in October 1970 by the United Nations General Assembly. It was emphasised that:

> [n]o state or group of states has the right to intervene, directly or indirectly, for any reason whatever, in the internal or external affairs of any other state. Consequently, armed intervention and all other forms of interference or attempted threats against the personality of the state or against its political, economic and cultural elements, are in violation of international law.

The prohibition also covers any assistance or aid to subversive elements aiming at the violent overthrow of the government of a state. In particular,

---

[65] Article 2(7) of the UN Charter provides that 'nothing in the present Charter shall authorise the United Nations to intervene in matters which are essentially within the domestic jurisdiction of any state'. On the relationship between this article and the general international law provision, see Brownlie, *Principles*, p. 293.

[66] See Higgins, *Development*, pp. 58–130; Brownlie, *Principles*, pp. 291–2; M. Rajan, *United Nations and Domestic Jurisdiction*, 2nd edn, London, 1961 and H. Kelsen, *Principles of International Law*, 2nd edn, London, 1966.

[67] E/CN.4/1991/SR. 43, p. 8, quoted in UKMIL, 62 BYIL, 1991, p. 556. See also statement of the European Community in 1992 to the same effect, UKMIL, 63 BYIL, pp. 635–6. By way of contrast, the Iranian *fatwa* condemning the British writer Salman Rushdie to death was criticised by the UK government as calling into question Iran's commitment to honour its obligations not to interfere in the internal affairs of the UK, *ibid.*, p. 635. See also W. M. Reisman, 'Sovereignty and Human Rights in Contemporary International Law', 84 AJIL, 1990, p. 866.

the use of force to deprive peoples of their national identity amounts to a violation of this principle of non-intervention.[68]

The principles surrounding sovereignty, such as non-intervention, are essential in the maintenance of a reasonably stable system of competing states. By setting limits on the powers of states *vis-à-vis* other states, it contributes to some extent to a degree of stability within the legal order. As the International Court of Justice pointed out in the *Corfu Channel* case in 1949, 'between independent states, respect for territorial sovereignty is an essential foundation of international relations'.[69]

By a similar token a state cannot purport to enforce its laws in the territory of another state, nor may it dispatch policemen or other governmental officials to arrest alleged criminals residing abroad without the consent of the state concerned. However, international law would seem to permit the state to continue to exercise its jurisdiction, notwithstanding the illegality of the apprehension.[70] It also follows that the presence of foreign troops on the territory of a sovereign state requires the consent of that state.[71]

(b) Equality[72]

One other crucial principle is the legal equality of states. It is a concept of law and should not be confused with political equality. What is referred to here is equality of legal rights and duties. Malta is a sovereign state as is the United States. It has the same juridical capacities and functions, and is likewise entitled to one vote in the United Nations General Assembly. In many ways, the doctrine of the legal equality of states is an umbrella category, for it includes within its scope the recognised rights and obligations which fall upon all states. This was recognised in the 1970 Declaration on Principles of International Law. This provides that:

> All states enjoy sovereign equality. They have equal rights and duties and are equal members of the international community, notwithstanding differences of an economic, social, political or other nature.
>
> In particular, sovereign equality includes the following elements:
>
> (a) States are juridically equal;
> (b) Each state enjoys the rights inherent in full sovereignty;
> (c) Each state has the duty to respect the personality of other states;
> (d) The territorial integrity and political independence of the state are inviolable;

---

[68] See also the use of force, *infra*, Chapter 19.
[69] ICJ Reports, 1949, pp. 4, 35; 16 ILR, pp. 155, 167. See *infra*, p. 408.
[70] See e.g. the *Eichmann* case, 36 ILR, p. 5. But see further *infra*, p. 478.
[71] See the statement made on behalf of the European Community on 25 November 1992 with regard to the presence of Russian troops in the Baltic states, UKMIL, 63 BYIL, 1992, p. 724.   [72] *Oppenheim's International Law*, p. 339.

(e) Each state has the right freely to choose and develop its political, social, economic and cultural systems;

(f) Each state has the duty to comply fully and in good faith with its international obligations and to live in peace with other states.[73]

In many respects this doctrine owes its origins to Natural Law thinking. Just as equality was regarded as the essence of man and thus contributed philosophically to the foundation of the state, so naturalist scholars treated equality as the natural condition of states. With the rise in positivism, the emphasis altered and rather than postulating a general rule applicable to all and from which a series of rights and duties may be deduced, international lawyers concentrated upon the sovereignty of each and every state, and the necessity that international law be founded upon the consent of states.

The notion of equality before the law is accepted by states in the sense of equality of legal personality and capacity. However, it would not be strictly accurate to talk in terms of the equality of states in creating law. The major powers will always have an influence commensurate with their status, if only because their concerns are much wider and their interests much deeper, not ignoring the unassailable truth that their capacity to uphold their views is far greater than that of smaller nations.

Within the General Assembly of the United Nations, the doctrine is maintained by the rule of one state, one vote, irrespective of the realities of power. It is a situation that has elicited much criticism, especially from the West as the preponderance of the Third World Afro-Asian–Arab bloc has become clearer as the universality of membership is extended.[74] However, one should not overlook the existence of the veto possessed by the USA, Russia, China, France and the United Kingdom in the Security Council.[75]

(c) Peaceful co-existence

One concept falling within the province of the basic rights and obligations of states that has been developing over the last twenty or so years is the idea of peaceful co-existence. It has been formulated in different ways and with different views as to its legal nature by the USSR, China and the Third World. The theory was elaborated in 1954 as the Five Principles of Peaceful Co-existence by India and China, which concerned the mutual respect for

---

[73] See also Final Act of the Conference on Security and Co-operation in Europe, Helsinki, 1975, Cmnd. 6198, pp. 2–3. See also O'Connell, *International Law*, pp. 322–4; P. Kooijmans, *The Doctrine of the Legal Equality of States*, Leiden, 1964 and Marshall CJ, *The Antelope*, 10 Wheat, pp. 66, 122.

[74] See e.g. L. Sohn, *Cases on UN Law*, 2nd edn, New York, 1967, pp. 232–90 and Clark and L. Sohn, *World Peace Through World Law*, 3rd edn, New York, 1966, pp. 399–402.

[75] The doctrine of equality of states is also influential in areas of international law such as jurisdictional immunities, *infra* Chapter 13, p. 491, and act of state, *supra* Chapter 3, p. 129.

each other's territorial integrity and sovereignty, mutual non-aggression, non-interference in each other's affairs and the principle of equality.[76] The idea was expanded in a number of international documents such as the final communiqué of the Bandung Conference in 1955 and in various resolutions of the United Nations.[77] Its recognised constituents also appear in the list of Principles of the Charter of the Organisation of African Unity. Among the points enumerated are the concepts of sovereign equality, non-interference in the internal affairs of states, respect for the sovereignty and territorial integrity of states as well as a condemnation of subversive activities carried out from one state and aimed against another. Other concepts that have been included in this category comprise such principles as non-aggression and the execution of international obligations in good faith. The Soviet Union had also expressed the view that peaceful co-existence constituted the guiding principle in contemporary international law.[78]

The exposition of such a theory involves in effect the elaboration of the basic rights and duties of states. Peaceful co-existence in its fundamental form merely connotes an alternate classification of principles already known and accepted as rules of international law. Its existence and evident popularity as a separate category relate to political developments and the recognition of a world system emerging gradually from a bipolar Soviet–American shape into a rather less secure multipolar situation with a number of power centres.[79]

Protectorates and protected states[80]

A distinction is sometimes made between a protectorate and a protected state. In the former case, in general, the entity concerned enters into an arrangement with a state under which, while separate legal personality may be involved, separate statehood is not. In the case of a protected state, the entity concerned retains its status as a separate state but enters into a valid treaty relationship with another state affording the latter certain extensive functions possibly internally and externally. However, precisely which type of arrangement is made and the nature of the status, rights and duties in

---

[76] See e.g. Tunkin, *Theory*, pp. 69–75. See also L. Ramondo, *Peaceful Co-existence*, 1967 and R. Higgins, *Conflict of Interests*, London, 1965, pp. 99–170.

[77] See e.g. General Assembly resolutions 1236(XII) and 1301(XIII). See also *Yearbook of the UN*, 1957, pp. 105–9; *ibid.* 1961, p. 524 and *ibid.* 1962, p. 488.

[78] Tunkin, *Theory*, pp. 35–48.

[79] See also as regards the fundamental rights of states, A. Kiss, *Répertoire de la Pratique Française en Matière de Droit International Public*, Paris, vol. II, 1966, pp. 21–50 and *Survey of International Law*, prepared by the UN Secretary-General, A/CN.4/245.

[80] See *Oppenheim's International Law*, p. 266; Crawford, *Creation of Statehood*, pp. 187–208; O'Connell, *International Law*, pp. 341–4, and Verzijl, *International Law*, pp. 412–27. Note also the special institution of the colonial protectorate, Shaw, *Title*, Chapter 1.

question will depend upon the circumstances and in particular the terms of the relevant agreement and third party attitudes.[81] In the case of Morocco, the Treaty of Fez of 1912 with France gave the latter the power to exercise certain sovereign powers on behalf of the former, including all of its international relations. Nevertheless, the ICJ emphasised that Morocco had in the circumstances of the case remained a sovereign state.[82]

The extent of powers delegated to the protecting state in such circumstances may vary, as may the manner of the termination of the arrangement. In these cases, formal sovereignty remains unaffected and the entity in question retains its status as a state, and may act as such in the various international fora, regard being had of course to the terms of the arrangement. The obligation may be merely to take note of the advice of the protecting state, or it may extend to a form of diplomatic delegation subject to instruction, as in the case of Liechtenstein. Liechtenstein was refused admission to the League of Nations since it was held unable to discharge all the international obligations imposed by the Covenant in the light of its delegation of sovereign powers such as diplomatic representation, administration of Post, Telegraph and Telephone services and final decisions in certain judicial cases.[83] Liechtenstein, however, has been a party to the Statute of the International Court of Justice and was a party to the *Nottebohm*[84] case before the Court, a facility only open to states. In autumn 1990, Liechtenstein joined the United Nations.

Federal states[85]

There are various forms of federation or confederation, according to the relative distribution of power between the central and local organs. In some states, the residue of power lies with the central government, in others with the local or provincial bodies. A confederation implies a more flexible arrangement, leaving a considerable degree of authority and competence with the component units to the detriment of the central organ.[86]

The Yugoslav Arbitration Commission noted in Opinion No. 1 that in the

---

[81] See the *Tunis and Morocco Nationality Decrees* case (1923) PCIJ, Series B, No. 4, p. 27; 2 ILR, p. 349. See also the question of the Ionian Islands, M. F. Lindley, *The Acquisition and Government of Backward Territory in International Law*, London, 1926, pp. 181–2.

[82] *Rights of Nationals of the United States of America in Morocco*, ICJ Reports, 1952, pp. 176, 188; 19 ILR, pp. 255, 263. See also to the same effect, *Benaïm c./ Procureur de la République de Bordeaux*, AFDI, 1993, p. 971.

[83] See Crawford, *Creation of Statehood*, p. 190; Report of the 5th Committee of the League, 6 December 1920, G. Hackworth, *Digest of International Law*, Washington, 1940, vol. I, pp. 48–9; Higgins, *International Law*, p. 34, note 30.

[84] ICJ Reports, 1955, p. 4; 22 ILR, p. 349.

[85] See *Oppenheim's International Law*, p. 245. See also I. Bernier, *International Legal Aspects of Federalism*, London, 1973; and 17 *Revue Belge de Droit International*, 1983, p. 1.

[86] See also *infra* p. 157.

case of a federal state embracing communities possessing a degree of autonomy where such communities participate in the exercise of political power
within the framework of institutions common to the federation, the 'existence of the state implies that the federal organs represent the components
of the federation and wield effective power'.[87] In addition, the existence of
such a federal state would be seriously compromised 'when a majority of
these entities, embracing the greater part of the territory and population,
constitute themselves as sovereign states with the result that federal authority may no longer be effectively exercised'.[88]

The division of powers inherent in such arrangements often raises important questions for international law, particularly in the areas of personality,
responsibility and immunity. Whether the federation dissolves into two or
more states also brings into focus the doctrine of self-determination in the
form of secession. Such a dissolution may be the result of an amicable and
constitutional agreement or may occur pursuant to a forceful exercise of
secession. In the latter case, international legal rules may be pleaded in aid,
but the position would seem to be that (apart from recognised colonial situations) there is no right of self-determination applicable to independent states
that would justify the resort to secession. There is, of course, no international legal duty to refrain from secession attempts: the situation remains
subject to the domestic law. However, should such a secession prove
successful in fact, then the concepts of recognition and the appropriate criteria of statehood would prove relevant and determinative as to the new
situation.[89]

The federal state will itself, of course, have personality, but the question
of the personality and capability of the component units of the federation on
the international plane can really only be determined in the light of the
constitution of the state concerned and state practice. For instance, the
Soviet Republics of Byelorussia and the Ukraine were admitted as members
of the United Nations in 1945 and to that extent possessed international
personality.[90] Component states of a federation that have been provided
with a certain restricted international competence may thus be accepted as
having a degree of international personality. The issue has arisen especially
with regard to treaties. Lauterpacht, in his Report on the Law of Treaties,
for example, noted that treaties concluded by component units of federal
states 'are treaties in the meaning of international law',[91] although
Fitzmaurice adopted a different approach in his Report on the Law of
Treaties by stating that such units act as agents for the federation which

---

[87] 92 ILR, p. 165.   [88] Opinion No. 8, *ibid.*, p. 201.   [89] *Infra*, p. 354.
[90] See e.g. Bernier, *Federalism*, pp. 64–6. These entities were also members of a number of
international organisations and signed treaties.
[91] *Yearbook of the ILC*, 1953, vol. II, p. 139.

alone possesses international personality and which is the entity bound by the treaty and responsible for its implementation.[92] Article 5(2) of the International Law Commission's Draft Articles on the Law of Treaties provided that

[s]tates members of a federal union may possess a capacity to conclude treaties if such capacity is admitted by the federal constitution and within the limits there laid down

but this was ultimately rejected at the Vienna Conference on the Law of Treaties,[93] partly on the grounds that the rule was beyond the scope of the convention itself. The major reasons for the rejection, however, were that the provision would enable third states to intervene in the internal affairs of federal states by seeking to interpret the constitutions of the latter and that, from another perspective, it would unduly enhance the power of domestic law to determine questions of international personality to the detriment of international law. This perhaps would indeed have swung the balance too far away from the international sphere of operation.

Different federations have evolved different systems with regard to the allocation of treaty-making powers. In some cases, component units may enter into such arrangements subject to varying conditions. The constitution of Switzerland, for example, enables the cantons to conclude treaties with foreign states on issues concerning public economy, frontier relations and the police, subject to the provision that the Federal Council acts as the intermediary.[94] In the case of the United States, responsibility for the conduct of foreign relations rests exclusively with the Federal Government,[95] although American states have entered into certain compacts with foreign states or component units (such as Manitoba and Quebec provinces of Canada) dealing with the construction and maintenance of highways and international bridges, following upon consultations with the foreign state conducted by the federal authorities. In any event, it is clear that the internal constitutional structure is crucial in endowing the unit concerned with capacity. However, what turns this into international capacity is recognition.

An issue recently the subject of concern and discussion has been the question of the domestic implementation of treaty obligations in the case of federations, especially in the light of the fact that component units may

---

[92] *Yearbook of the ILC*, 1958, vol. II, p. 24. Cf. Waldock, *ibid.*, 1962, vol. II, p. 36.

[93] A/CONF.39/SR.8, 28 April 1969.

[94] See e.g. A. Looper, 'The Treaty Power in Switzerland', 7 *American Journal of Comparative Law*, 1958, p. 178.

[95] See e.g. Article I, Section 10 of the US Constitution; *US* v. *Curtiss-Wright Export Corp.*, 299 US 304 (1936); 8 ILR, p. 48 and *Zachevning* v. *Miller*, 389 US 429 (1968). See also generally, Brownlie, *Public International Law*, pp. 62–3; Whiteman, *Digest*, vol. 14, pp. 13–17 and Rousseau, *Droit International Public*, pp. 138–213 and 264–8.

possess legislative power relating to the subject-matter of the treaty concerned. Although this issue lies primarily within the field of domestic constitutional law, there are important implications for international law. In the US, for example, the approach adopted has been to insert 'federal' reservations to treaties in cases where the states of the Union have exercised jurisdiction over the subject-matter in question, providing that the Federal Government would take appropriate steps to enable the competent authorities of the component units to take appropriate measures to fulfil the obligations concerned.[96] In general, however, there have been few restrictions on entry into international agreements.[97]

The question as to divided competence in federations and international treaties has arisen in the past particularly with regard to conventions of the International Labour Organisation, which typically encompass areas subject to the law-making competence of federal component units. In Canada, for example, early attempts by the central government to ratify ILO conventions were defeated by the decisions of the courts on constitutional grounds, supporting the views of the provinces,[98] while the US has a poor record of ratification of ILO conventions on similar grounds of local competence and federal treaty-making.[99] The issue that arises therefore is the position of a state that either refuses to ratify or sign a treaty on grounds of component unit competence in the area in question or alternatively the problem of implementation and thus responsibility where ratification does take place. In Australia, for instance, the issue has turned on the interpretation of the constitutional grant of federal power to make laws 'with respect to . . . external affairs'.[100] Two recent cases have analysed this, in the light particularly of the established principle that the Federal Government could under this provision legislate on matters, not otherwise explicitly assigned to it, which possessed an intrinsic international aspect.[101] In *Koowarta v. Bjelke-Petersen*[102] in 1982, the Australian High Court in dealing with an action against the Premier of Queensland for breach of the Racial Discrimination Act 1975 (which incorporated parts of the International Convention on the Elimination of All Forms of Racial Discrimination adopted in 1965) held that the relevant legislation was valid with respect to

---

[96] See e.g. the proposed reservations to four human rights treaties in 1978, *US Ratification of the Human Rights Treaties* (ed. R. B. Lillich), Charlottesville, 1981, pp. 83–103.

[97] See e.g. *Missouri v. Holland*, 252 US 416 (1920); 1 ILR, p. 4.

[98] See especially, *Attorney-General for Canada v. Attorney-General for Ontario* [1937] AC 326; 8 ILR, p. 41.

[99] Bernier, *Federalism*, pp. 162–3, and B. Looper, 'Federal State Clauses in Multilateral Instruments', 32 BYIL, 1955–6, p. 162.

[100] See e.g. Zines, *The High Court and the Constitution*, 1981 and A. Byrnes and H. Charlesworth, 'Federalism and the International Legal Order: Recent Developments in Australia', 79 AJIL, 1985, p. 622.

[101] *R v. Burgess, ex p. Henry*, 55 CLR 608 (1936); 8 ILR, p. 54.   [102] 68 ILR, p. 181.

the 'external affairs' provision under section 51(29) of the Constitution. In other words, the 'external affairs' power extended to permit the implementation of an international agreement, despite the fact that the subject-matter concerned was otherwise outside federal power. It was felt that if Australia accepted a treaty obligation with respect to an aspect of its own internal legal order, the subject of the obligation thus became an 'external affair' and legislation dealing with this fell within section 51(29), and was thereby valid constitutionally.[103] It was not necessary that a treaty obligation be assumed: the fact that the norm of non-discrimination was established in customary international law was itself sufficient in the view of Stephen J. to treat the issue of racial discrimination as part of external affairs.[104]

In *Commonwealth of Australia* v. *Tasmania*,[105] the issue concerned the construction of a dam in an area placed on the World Heritage List established under the 1972 UNESCO Convention for the Protection of the World Cultural and Natural Heritage, to which Australia was a party. The Federal Government in 1983 wished to stop the scheme by reference *inter alia* to the 'external affairs' power as interpreted in *Koowarta*, since it possessed no specific legislative power over the environment. The majority of the Court held that the 'external affairs' power extended to the implementation of treaty obligations. It was now necessary that the subject-matter of the treaty be inherently international.

The effect of these cases seen, of course, in the context of the Australian Constitution, is to reduce the problems faced by federal states of implementing international obligations in the face of local jurisdiction. From the point of view of international law it is a heartening trend in that it minimises the power of component units to prevent the implementation of international duties. It remains to be seen how far other federal states will manifest this trend.

Federal practice in regulating disputes between component units is often of considerable value in international law. This operates particularly in cases of boundary problems, where similar issues arise.[106] Conversely, international practice may often be relevant in the resolution of conflicts between component units. Questions relating to responsibility and immunities also arise in respect of federal states and these are referred to in the appropriate chapters.[107]

---

[103] *Ibid.*, pp. 223–4 (Stephen J); p. 235 (Mason J) and p. 255 (Brennan J).
[104] *Ibid.*, pp. 223–4.   [105] *Ibid.*, p. 266. The case similarly came before the High Court.
[106] See e.g. E. Lauterpacht, 'River Boundaries: Legal Aspects of the Shatt-Al-Arab Frontier', 9 ICLQ, 1960, pp. 208, 216 and A. O. Cukwurah, *The Settlement of Boundary Disputes in International Law*, Manchester, 1967.   [107] See *infra*, Chapters 13 and 14.

Sui generis territorial entities

Mandated and trust territories[108]

After the end of the First World War and the collapse of the Axis and Russian empires, the Allies established a system for dealing with the colonies of the defeated powers that did not involve annexation. These territories would be governed according to the principle that 'the well-being and development of such peoples form a sacred trust of civilisation'. The way in which this principle would be put into effect would be to entrust the tutelage of such people to 'advanced nations who by reason of their resources, their experience or their geographical position' could undertake the responsibility. The arrangement would be exercised by them as mandatories on behalf of the League.[109]

Upon the conclusion of the Second World War and the demise of the League, the mandate system was transmuted into the United Nations trusteeship system under Chapters XII and XIII of the UN Charter.[110] The strategic trust territory of the Pacific, taken from Japan, the mandatory power, was placed in a special category subject to Security Council rather than Trusteeship Council supervision for security reasons,[111] while South Africa refused to place its mandated territory under the system. Quite who held sovereignty in such territories was the subject of extensive debates over many decades.[112]

As far as the trust territory of the Pacific was concerned, the US signed a Covenant with the Commonwealth of the Northern Mariana Islands and Compacts of Free Association with the Federated States of Micronesia and

---

[108] See generally Duncan Hall, *Mandates, Dependencies and Trusteeships*, London, 1948; Whiteman, *Digest*, vol. I, pp. 598–911 and vol. XIII, pp. 679 *et seq.*; L. Toussaint, *The Trusteeship System of the United Nations*; Verzijl, *International Law*, vol. II, pp. 545–73; Q. Wright, *Mandates Under the League of Nations*, New York, 1930; J. Dugard, *The South West Africa/Namibia Dispute*, 1973 and S. Slonim, *South West Africa and the United Nations*, Leiden, 1973. See also *Oppenheim's International Law*, pp. 295 and 308.

[109] See article 22 of the Covenant of the League of Nations. See also the *International Status of South West Africa*, ICJ Reports, 1950, pp. 128, 132; 17 ILR, p. 47; the *Namibia* case, ICJ Reports, 1971, pp. 16, 28–9; 49 ILR, pp. 2, 18–19 and *Certain Phosphate Lands in Nauru*, ICJ Reports, 1992, pp. 240, 256; 97 ILR, pp. 1, 23.

[110] See e.g. *Certain Phosphate Lands in Nauru*, ICJ Reports, 1992, pp. 240, 257; 97 ILR, pp. 1, 24. See also the discussion by Judge Shahabuddeen in his Separate Opinion, ICJ Reports, pp. 276 *et seq.*, 97 ILR, p. 43. Note that the Court in this case stated that the arrangements whereby Nauru was to be administered under the trusteeship agreement by the governments of the UK, Australia and New Zealand together as 'the administering authority' did not constitute that authority an international legal person separate from the three states so designated, ICJ Report, p. 258, 97 ILR, p. 25.

[111] See O. McHenry, *Micronesia: Trust Betrayed*, 1975; Whiteman, *Digest*, vol. I, pp. 769–839; de Smith, *Micro-States and Micronesia*, 1970; DUSPIL, 1973, pp. 59–67; *ibid.*, 1974, pp. 54–64; *ibid.*, 1975, pp. 94–104; *ibid.*, 1976, pp. 56–61; *ibid.*, 1977, pp. 71–98 and *ibid.*, 1978, pp. 204–31.

[112] See in particular Judge McNair, *International Status of South West Africa*, ICJ Reports, 1950, pp. 128, 150 and the Court's view, *ibid.*, p. 132; 17 ILR, pp. 47, 49.

with the Republic of the Marshall Islands. Upon their entry into force in autumn 1986, it was determined that the trusteeship had been terminated. This procedure providing for political union with the US was accepted by the Trusteeship Council as a legitimate exercise of self-determination.[113] However, the proposed Compact of Free Association with the Republic of Palau (the final part of the former trust territory) did not enter into force as a result of disagreement over the transit of nuclear-powered or armed vessels and aircraft through Palauan waters and airspace and, therefore, the US continued to act as administering authority under the trusteeship agreement.[114] These difficulties were eventually resolved.[115]

South West Africa was administered after the end of the First World War as a mandate by South Africa, which refused after the Second World War to place the territory under the trusteeship system. Following this, the International Court of Justice in 1950 in its Advisory Opinion on the *International Status of South West Africa*[116] stated that while there was no legal obligation imposed by the United Nations Charter to transfer a mandated territory into a trust territory, South Africa was still bound by the terms of the mandate agreement and the Covenant of the League of Nations, and the obligations that it had assumed at that time. The Court emphasised that South Africa alone did not have the capacity to modify the international status of the territory. This competence rested with South Africa acting with the consent of the United Nations, as successor to the League of Nations. Logically flowing from this decision was the ability of the United Nations to hear petitioners from the territory in consequence of South Africa's refusal to heed United Nations decisions and in pursuance of League of Nations practices.[117]

In 1962 the ICJ heard the case brought by Ethiopia and Liberia, the two African members of the League, that South Africa was in breach of the terms of the mandate and had thus violated international law. The Court initially affirmed that it had jurisdiction to hear the merits of the dispute.[118] However, by the Second Phase of the case, the Court (its composition having slightly altered in the meanwhile) decided that Ethiopia and Liberia did not have any legal interest in the subject-matter of the claim (the existence and supervision of the mandate over South West Africa) and accordingly their contentions were rejected.[119] Having thus declared on the lack of standing of the two African appellants, the Court did not discuss any of the substantive questions which stood before it.

[113] See Security Council resolution 683 (1990).
[114] See *Contemporary Practice of the United States Relating to International Law*, 81 AJIL, 1987, pp. 405–8. See also *Bank of Hawaii* v. *Balos*, 701 F.Supp. 744 (1988).
[115] See Security Council resolution 956 (1994).
[116] ICJ Reports, 1950, pp. 128, 143–4; 17 ILR, pp. 47, 57–60.
[117] ICJ Reports, 1955, p. 68; 22 ILR, p. 651 and *ibid.*, 1956, p. 23; 23 ILR, p. 38.
[118] ICJ Reports, pp. 141 and 143.   [119] ICJ Reports, 1966, p. 6; 37 ILR, p. 243.

This judgment aroused a great deal of feeling particularly in the Third World and occasioned a shift in emphasis in dealing with the problem of the territory in question.[120]

The General Assembly began to take a more active part and in October 1966 resolved that since South Africa had failed to fulfil its obligations, the mandate was therefore terminated. South West Africa (or Namibia as it was to be called) was to come under the direct responsibility of the United Nations.[121] The Security Council in a number of resolutions upheld the action of the Assembly and called upon South Africa to withdraw its administration from the territory. It also requested other states to refrain from dealing with the South African government in so far as Namibia was concerned.[122]

The Security Council ultimately turned to the International Court and requested an Advisory Opinion as to the *Legal Consequences for States of the Continued Presence of South Africa in Namibia*.[123] The Court concluded that South Africa's presence in Namibia was indeed illegal in view of the series of events culminating in the United Nations resolutions on the grounds of a material breach of a treaty (the mandate agreement) by South Africa, and further that 'a binding determination made by a competent organ of the United Nations to the effect that a situation is illegal cannot remain without consequence'. South Africa was obligated to withdraw its administration from the territory, and other states members of the United Nations were obliged to recognise the illegality and the invalidity of its acts with regard to that territory and aid the United Nations in its efforts concerning the problem.[124]

The opinion was approved by the Security Council in resolution 301 (1971), which also reaffirmed the national unity and territorial integrity of Namibia. In 1978 South Africa announced its acceptance of proposals negotiated by the five Western contact powers (UK, USA, France, Canada and West Germany) for Namibian independence involving a UN supervised electing and peace-keeping force.[125] However, negotiations continued with a variety of problems arising, including, for example, the issue of linkage with the withdrawal of Cuban forces from Angola. In April 1981, the Security Council failed to adopt four draft resolutions which would have imposed comprehensive and mandatory sanctions against South Africa

---

[120] See e.g. Dugard, *Southwest Africa/Namibia*, p. 378.

[121] Resolution 2145(XXI). A Council was established to oversee the territory, see General Assembly resolutions 2145(XXI) and 2248(XXII).

[122] See e.g. Security Council resolutions 263 (1969), 269 (1969) and 276 (1970).

[123] ICJ Reports, 1971, p. 16; 49 ILR, p. 3.   [124] *Ibid.*, pp. 52–8.

[125] 17 ILM, May 1978, pp. 762–9 and DUSPIL, 1978, pp. 38–54. See Security Council resolution 435 (1978). See also *Africa Research Bulletin*, April 1978, p. 4829 and July 1978, p. 4935.

because of the Namibian situation as a result of the negative votes cast by the UK, USA and France.[126] However, Namibia finally obtained its independence on 23 April 1990.[127]

Germany 1945

With the defeat of Germany on 5 June 1945, the Allied Powers assumed 'supreme authority' with respect to that country, while expressly disclaiming any intention of annexation.[128] Germany was divided into four occupation zones with four-power control over Berlin. The Control Council established by the Allies acted on behalf of Germany and in such capacity entered into binding legal arrangements. The state of Germany continued, however, and the situation, as has been observed, was akin to legal representation or agency of necessity.[129] Under the 1952 Treaty between the three Western powers and the Federal Republic of Germany, full sovereign powers were granted to the latter subject to retained powers concerning the making of a peace treaty and in 1972 the Federal Republic of Germany and the German Democratic Republic, established in 1954 by the Soviet Union in its zone, recognised each other as sovereign states.[130]

However, following a series of dramatic events during 1989 in Central and Eastern Europe, deriving in essence from the withdrawal of Soviet control, the drive for a reunified Germany in 1990 became unstoppable.[131] A State Treaty on German Economic, Monetary and Social Union was signed by the Finance Ministers of the two German states on 18 May and this took effect on 1 July.[132] A State Treaty on Unification was signed on 31 August, providing for unification on 3 October by the accession to the Federal Republic of Germany of the Länder of the German Democratic Republic under article 23 of the Basic Law of the Federal Republic, with Berlin as the capital.[133] The external obstacle to unity was removed by the signing on 12 September of the Treaty on the Final Settlement with Respect to Germany, between the two German states and the four wartime allies (UK, USA, USSR and France).[134] Under this treaty, a reunified Germany agreed to

---

[126] See S/14459; S/14460/Rev. 1; S/14461 and S/14462.
[127] See 28 ILM, 1989, p. 944.   [128] See Whiteman, *Digest*, vol. I, pp. 325–26.
[129] Brownlie, *Public International Law*, p. 109. See also Whiteman, *Digest*, vol. I, p. 333.
[130] 12 ILR, p. 16. Note also *Kunstsammlungen Zu Weiner v. Elicofon*, 94 ILR, p. 135. Both states became members of the UN the following year. See Crawford, *Creation of Statehood*, pp. 273–81 and F. A. Mann, *Studies in International Law*, Oxford, 1973, pp. 634–59 and 660–706.
[131] See e.g. J. Frowein, 'The Reunification of Germany', 86 AJIL, 1992, p. 152; C. Schrike, 'L'Unification Allemande', AFDI, 1990, p. 47 and W. Czaplinski, 'Quelques Aspets sur la Réunification de l'Allemagne', *ibid.*, p. 89.
[132] See *Keesing's Record of World Events*, p. 37466 (1990). See also 29 ILM, 1990, p. 1108.
[133] *Ibid.*, p. 37661. See also 30 ILM, 1991, pp. 457 and 498.
[134] See 29 ILM, 1990, p. 1186.

accept the current Oder–Neisse border with Poland and to limit its armed forces to 370, 000 persons, while pledging not to acquire atomic, chemical or biological weapons. The Agreement on the Settlement of Certain Matters Relating to Berlin between the Federal Republic and the three Western powers on 25 September 1990 provided for the relinquishment of Allied rights with regard to Berlin.[135]

Condominium

In this instance two or more states equally exercise sovereignty with respect to a territory and its inhabitants. There are arguments as to the relationship between the states concerned, the identity of the sovereign for the purposes of the territory and the nature of the competences involved.[136] In the case of the New Hebrides, a series of Anglo-French agreements established a region of joint influence with each power retaining sovereignty over its nationals and neither exercising separate authority over the area.[137] A Protocol listed the functions of the condominial government and vested the power to issue joint regulations respecting them in a British and French High Commissioner. This power was delegated to resident commissioners who dealt with their respective nationals. Three governmental systems accordingly co-existed with something of a legal vacuum with regard to land tenure and the civil transactions of the indigenous population.[138] The process leading to the independence of the territory also reflected its unique status as a condominium.[139] It was noted that the usual independence Bill would not have been appropriate, since the New Hebrides was not a British colony. Its legal status as an Anglo-French condominium had been established by international agreement and could only be terminated in the same fashion. The nature of the condominium was such that it assumed that the two metropolitan powers would always act together and unilateral action was not provided for in the basic constitutional documents.[140] The territory became independent on 30 July 1980 as the state of Vanuatu. The entity involved prior to independence grew out of an international treaty and established an administrative entity arguably distinct from its metropolitan

---

[135] See 30 ILM, 1991, p. 445. See also the Exchange of Notes of the same date concerning the presence of allied troops in Berlin, *ibid.*, p. 450.

[136] Brownlie, *Public International Law*, pp. 116–17; see also O'Connell, *International Law*, pp. 327–8; Coret, *Le Condominium*, 1960, and *Oppenheim's International Law*, p. 565.

[137] See e.g., 99 BFSP, p. 229 and 114 BFSP, p. 212.

[138] O'Connell, *International Law*, p. 328.

[139] Lord Trefgarne, the government spokesman, moving the second reading of the New Hebrides Bill in the House of Lords, 404 HL Deb., cols. 1091–92, 4 February 1980.

[140] See Mr Luce, Foreign Office Minister, 980 HC Deb., col. 682, 8 March 1980 and 985 HC Deb., col. 1250, 3 June 1980. See also D. P. O'Connell, 'The Condominium of the New Hebrides', 43 BYIL, p. 71.

governments but more likely operating on the basis of a form of joint agency with a range of delegated powers.[141]

The Central American Court of Justice in 1917[142] held that a condominium existed with respect to the Gulf of Fonseca providing for rights of co-ownership of the three coastal states of Nicaragua, El Salvador and Honduras. The issue was raised in the *El Salvador/Honduras* case before the International Court of Justice.[143] The Court noted that a condominium arrangement being 'a structured system for the joint exercise of sovereign governmental powers over a territory' was normally created by agreement between the states concerned, although it could be created as a juridical consequence of a succession of states (as in the Gulf of Fonseca situation itself), being one of the ways in which territorial sovereignty could pass from one state to another. The Court concluded that the waters of the Gulf of Fonseca beyond the 3 mile territorial sea were historic waters and subject to a joint sovereignty of the three coastal states. It based its decision, apart from the 1917 judgment, upon the historic character of the Gulf waters, the consistent claims of the three coastal states and the absence of protest from other states.[144]

International territories

In such cases a particular territory is placed under a form of international regime, but the conditions under which this has been done have varied widely, from autonomous areas within states to relatively independent entities.[145] Attempts were made to create such a regime for Jerusalem under the General Assembly partition resolution for Palestine in 1947 as a '*corpus separatum* under a special international regime . . . administered by the United Nations', but this never materialised for a number of reasons.[146] The term 'international territory' has no legal meaning as such and the nature and

---

[141] See also the joint Saudi Arabian–Kuwaiti administered Neutral Zone based on the treaty of 2 December 1922, 133 BFSP, 1930 Part II, pp. 726–7. See e.g. *The Middle East* (ed. P. Mansfield), 4th edn, London, 1973, p. 187. Both states enjoyed an equal right of undivided sovereignty over the whole area. However, on 7 July 1965, both states signed an agreement to partition the neutral zone, although the territory apparently retained its condominium status for exploration of resources purposes; see 4 ILM, 1965, p. 1134 and Albaharna, *The Legal Status of the Arabian Gulf States*, 2nd revised edn, 1975, pp. 264–77.

[142] 11 AJIL, 1917, p. 674.

[143] ICJ Reports, 1992, pp. 351, 597 *et seq.*; 97 ILR, pp. 266, 513 *et seq.* El Salvador and Nicaragua were parties to the 1917 decision but differed over the condominium solution, Nicaragua was not a party to that case and opposed the condominium idea.

[144] *Ibid.*, p. 601; ILR, *ibid.*, p. 517.

[145] See Ydit, *International Territories*, 1961; Crawford, *Creation of Statehood*, pp. 160–9; Brownlie, *Public International Law*, pp. 62–3 and Rousseau, *Droit International Public*, vol. II, pp. 413–48.

[146] Resolution 18(II). See e.g. E. Lauterpacht, *Jerusalem and the Holy Places*, 1968 and Ydit, *International Territories*, pp. 273–314.

capacity of the entity created will depend upon all the relevant circumstances. In some instances a separate legal person will here be established, in others not. In any event, such institutions have not on the whole worked successfully and the device is unlikely to be used frequently in the future.

Taiwan[147]

This territory was ceded by China to Japan in 1895 and remained in the latter's hands until 1945. Japan undertook on surrender not to retain sovereignty over Taiwan and this was reaffirmed under the Peace Treaty between the Allied Powers (but not the USSR and China) and Japan, under which all rights to the island were renounced without specifying any recipient. After the Chinese Civil War, the communist forces took over the mainland while the nationalist regime installed itself on Taiwan (Formosa) and the Pescadores. The key point affecting status has been that both governments have claimed to represent the whole of China. No claim of separate statehood for Taiwan has been made and in such a case it is difficult to maintain that such an unsought status exists.[148] Total lack of recognition merely reinforces this point. Accordingly, Taiwan would appear to be a non-state territorial entity which is *de jure* part of China but under separate administration. It is interesting to note that when in early 1990 Taiwan sought accession to the General Agreement on Tariffs and Trade (GATT), it did so by requesting entry for the 'customs territory' of 'Taiwan, Penghu, Kinmen and Matsu', thus avoiding an assertion of statehood.[149]

The Turkish Federated State of Cyprus[150]

In 1974, following a coup in Cyprus backed by the military regime in Greece, Turkish forces invaded the island. The Security Council in resolution 353 (1974) called upon all states to respect the sovereignty, inde-

---

[147] See e.g. *China and the Question of Taiwan* (ed. L. Chen); W. M. Reisman, 'Who Owns Taiwan?', 81 *Yale Law Journal*, p. 599; Morello, *The International Legal Status of Formosa*, 1966; Li, *De-Recognising Taiwan*, 1977 and L. C. Chiu, 'The International Legal Status of The Republic of China', 8 *Chinese Yearbook of International Law and Affairs*, 1990, p. 1.

[148] See Crawford, *Creation of Statehood*, p. 145. Note that the 1972 USA–China communiqué accepted that Taiwan was part of China, 11 ILM, pp. 443, 445. In 1979 the USA withdrew its recognition of Taiwan as the government of China; see 73 AJIL, p. 227. See also 833 HC Deb., col. 32, 13 March 1972, and *Reel v. Holder* [1981] 1 WLR 1226.

[149] See *Keesing's Record of World Events*, p. 37671 (1990). This failed, however, to prevent a vigorous protest by China; *ibid.* Note also the Agreements Concerning Cross-Straits Activities between unofficial organisations established in China and Taiwan in order to reach functional, non-political agreements, 32 ILM, 1993, p. 1217. As to Rhodesia (1965–79) and the Bantustans, see *supra*, pp. 145, and 143.

[150] See Z. M. Nadjatigil, *The Cyprus Conflict: A Lawyer's View*, 3rd edn, 1983; G. White, *The World Today*, April 1981, p. 135 and Crawford, *Creation of Statehood*, p. 118.

pendence and territorial integrity of Cyprus and demanded an immediate end to foreign military intervention in the island that was contrary to such respect. On 13 February 1975 the Turkish Federated State of Cyprus was proclaimed in the area occupied by Turkish forces. A resolution adopted at the same meeting of the Council of Ministers and the Legislative Assembly of the Autonomous Turkish Cypriot Administration, at which the proclamation was made, emphasised the determination 'to oppose resolutely all attempts against the independence of Cyprus and its partition or union with any other state' and resolved to establish a separate administration until such time as the 1960 Cyprus Constitution was amended to provide for a federal republic.[151]

On 15 November 1983, the Turkish "Republic of Northern Cyprus" proclaimed its independence.[152] This was declared illegal by the Security Council in resolution 541 (1983) and its withdrawal called for. All states were requested not to recognise the 'purported state' or assist it in any way. This was reiterated in Security Council resolution 550 (1984). In the light of this and the very heavy dependence of the territory upon Turkey, it cannot be regarded as a sovereign state, but remains as a *de facto* administered entity within the recognised confines of the Republic of Cyprus and dependent upon Turkish assistance.[153]

The Saharan Arab Democratic Republic[154]

In February 1976, the Polisario liberation movement conducting a war to free the Western Saharan territory from Moroccan control declared the independent sovereign Saharan Arab Democratic Republic.[155] Over the succeeding years, many states recognised the new entity, including a majority of OAU members. In February 1982, the OAU Secretary-General sought to seat a delegation from SADR on that basis, but this provoked a boycott by some nineteen states and a major crisis. However, in November 1984, the Assembly of Heads of State and Government of the OAU did agree to seat a delegation from SADR, despite Morocco's threat of withdrawal from the organisation.[156] This, therefore, can be taken as OAU recognition of statehood and as such of major evidential significance. Indeed, in view of the reduced importance of the effectiveness of control criterion in such self-determination situations, a strong argument can now be made regarding

---

[151] Resolution no. 2 in Supplement IV, Official Gazette of the TFSC, cited in Nadjatigil, *Cyprus Conflict*, p. 123.
[152] See *The Times*, 16 November 1983, p. 12 and 21(4) *UN Chronicle*, 1984, p. 17.
[153] See also Foreign Affairs Committee, Third Report, Session 1986–7, Cyprus: HCP 23 (1986–7).   [154] See Shaw, *Title*, Chapter 3.
[155] *Africa Research Bulletin*, June 1976, p. 4047 and July 1976, pp. 4078 and 4081.
[156] See *Keesings Contemporary Archives*, pp. 33324–45.

SADR's statehood, although the issue is still controversial, particularly in view of the continuing hostilities.

Associations of states

There are a number of ways in which states have become formally associated with one another. Such associations do not constitute states but have a certain effect upon international law. Confederations, for example, are probably the closest form of co-operation and they generally involve several countries acting together by virtue of an international agreement, with some kind of central institutions with limited functions.[157] This is to be contrasted with the situation as it exists with regard to federations. A federal unit is a state with strong centralised organs and usually a fairly widespread bureaucracy with extensive powers over the citizens of the state, even though the powers of the state are divided between the different units.[158]

There are in addition certain 'associated states' which by virtue of their smallness and lack of development have a close relationship with another state. One instance is the connection between the Cook Islands and New Zealand, where internal self-government is allied to external dependence.[159] Another example was the group of islands which constituted the Associated States of the West Indies. These were tied to the United Kingdom by the terms of the West Indies Act, 1967, which provided for the latter to exercise control with regard to foreign and defence issues. Nevertheless, such states were able to and did attain their independence.[160]

The status of such entities in an association relationship with a state will depend upon the constitutional nature of the arrangement and may in certain circumstances involve international personality distinct from the metropolitan state depending also upon international acceptance. It must, however, be noted that such status is one of the methods accepted by the UN of exercising the right to self-determination.[161] Provided that an acceptable level of powers, including those dealing with domestic affairs, remain

---

[157] Note, for example, the Preliminary Agreement Concerning the Establishment of a Confederation between the Federation of Bosnia and Herzegovina and the Republic of Croatia, 1994, 33 ILM, 1994, p. 605. This Agreement 'anticipated' the creation of a Confederation, but provides that its 'establishment shall not change the international identity or legal personality of Croatia or of the Federation'. The Agreement provided for co-operation between the parties in a variety of areas and for Croatia to grant the Federation of Bosnia and Herzegovina free access to the Adriatic through its territory.

[158] See Crawford, *Creation of Statehood*, p. 291 and *supra*, p. 155. See also with regard to the proposed arrangement between Gambia and Senegal, 21 ILM, 1982, pp. 44–7.

[159] Crawford, *Creation of Statehood*, pp. 372–4. See also as regards Puerto Rico and Niue, *ibid.*

[160] See e.g. J. E. S. Fawcett, *Annual Survey of Commonwealth Law*, London, 1967, pp. 709–11.

[161] See with regard to the successors of the trust territory of the Pacific, *supra*, p. 160.

with the associated state, and that the latter may without undue difficulty revoke the arrangement, some degree of personality would appear desirable and acceptable.

The Commonwealth of Nations (the former British Commonwealth) is perhaps the best known of the loose associations which group together sovereign states on the basis usually of common interests and historical ties. Its members are all fully independent states who co-operate through the assistance of the Commonwealth Secretariat and periodic conferences of heads of government. Regular meetings of particular ministers also take place. The Commonwealth does not constitute a legally binding relationship, but operates as a useful forum for discussions. Relations between Commonwealth members display certain special characteristics, for example, ambassadors are usually referred to as High Commissioners. It would appear unlikely in the circumstances that it possesses separate international personality.[162] However, the more that the Commonwealth develops distinctive institutions and establishes common policies with the capacity to take binding decisions, the more the argument may be made for international legal personality.

Following the dissolution of the Soviet Union and the coming to independence of the constituent republics, with the Russian Federation being deemed the continuation of the Soviet Union, it was decided to establish the Commonwealth of Independent States. Originally formed by Russia, Belarus and Ukraine on 8 December 1991, it was enlarged on 21 December 1991 to include eleven former republics of the USSR. Georgia joined the CIS on 8 October 1993. Thus all the former Soviet republics, excluding the three Baltic states, are now members of that organisation.[163] The agreement establishing the CIS provided for respect for human rights and other principles and called for co-ordination between the member states. The Charter of the CIS was adopted on 22 June 1993 as a binding international treaty[164] and laid down a series of principles ranging from respect for the sovereignty and territorial integrity of states, self-determination of peoples, prohibition of the use or threat of force and settlement of disputes by peaceful means. It was noted that the CIS was neither a state nor 'supranational' (article 1) and a number of common co-ordinating institutions were established. In particular, the Council of Heads of State is the 'highest body of the Commonwealth' and it may 'take decisions on the principal issues

---

[162] See J. E. S. Fawcett, *The British Commonwealth in International Law*, London, 1963; *Oppenheim's International Law*, p. 256; O'Connell, *International Law*, pp. 346–56; Whiteman, *Digest*, vol. I, pp. 476–544; Rousseau, *Droit International Public*, vol. II, pp. 214–64 and Sale, *The Modern Commonwealth*, 1983. See also as regards the French Community, Whiteman, *Digest*, pp. 544–82 and O'Connell, *International Law*, pp. 356–9.

[163] See 31 ILM, 1992, pp. 138 and 147 and 34 ILM, 1995, p. 1298.

[164] See 34 ILM, 1995, p. 1279.

relating to the activity of the member states in the field of their mutual interests' (article 21), while the Council of the Heads of Government has the
function of co-ordinating co-operation among executive organs of member
states (article 22). Both Councils may take decisions on the basis of consensus (article 23). A Council of Foreign Ministers was also established
together with a Co-ordination and Consultative Committee, as a permanent
executive and co-ordinating body of the Commonwealth.[165] The CIS has
adopted in addition a Treaty on Economic Union[166] and a Convention on
Human Rights and Fundamental Freedoms.[167] The increasing development
of the CIS as a directing international institution suggests its possession of
international legal personality.

The European Union[168] is an association, of currently fifteen states, which
has established a variety of common institutions and which has the competence to adopt not only legal acts binding upon member states but also acts
having direct effect within domestic legal systems. The Union consists
essentially of the European Community (itself an amalgam of the European
Coal and Steel Community, EURATOM and the European Economic
Community) and two additional pillars, viz. the Common Foreign and
Security Policy, and Justice and Home Affairs. Only the European Coal and
Steel Community Treaty provided explicitly for international legal personality (article 6), but the case law of the European Court of Justice demonstrates its belief that the other two communities also possess such
personality.[169] It is also established that Community Law has superiority
over domestic law. The European Court of Justice early in the history of the
Community declared that the Community constituted 'a new legal order of
international law'.[170] In the circumstances, it seems hard to deny that the
Community possesses international legal personality, but unlikely that the
co-operative processes involved in the additional two pillars are so
endowed.[171]

[165] Note also the creation of the Council of Defence Ministers, the Council of Frontier Troops
Chief Commanders, an Economic Court, a Commission on Human Rights, an Organ of
Branch Co-operation and an Interparliamentary Assembly (articles 30–35).
[166] 24 September 1993, 34 ILM, 1995, p. 1298.
[167] 26 May 1995, see Council of Europe Information Sheet No. 36, 1995, p. 195.
[168] Established as such by article A, Title I of the Treaty on European Union signed in
February 1992 and in force as from 1 January 1993,
[169] See e.g. *Costa* [1964] ECR 585, 593; *Commission* v. *Council* [1971] ECR 263, 274; *Kramer*
[1976] ECR 1279, 1308 and *Protection of Nuclear Materials* [1978] ECR 2151, 2179. See
also *The Oxford Encyclopaedia of European Community Law* (ed. A. Toth), 1991, p. 351 and
D. Lasok and J. Bridge, *Law and Institutions of the European Union* (ed. P. Lasok), 6th edn,
London, 1994, Chapter 2.
[170] *Van Gend en Loos* v. *Nederlandse Asministratie des Belastingen* [1963] ECR 1.
[171] See e.g. the Second Legal Adviser of the Foreign and Commonwealth Office, UKMIL, 63
BYIL, 1992, p. 660. But see also *Oppenheim's International Law*, p. 20. Note also the
European Court of Justice's *Opinion No. 1/94, Community Competence to Conclude Certain
International Agreements*, 1994 ECR I 5276.

Conclusions

Whether or not the entities discussed above constitute international persons or indeed states or merely part of some other international person is a matter for careful consideration in the light of the circumstances of the case, in particular the claims made by the entity in question, the facts on the ground especially with regard to third party control and the degree of administrative effectiveness manifested and the reaction of other international persons. The importance here of recognition, acquiescence and estoppel is self-evident. Acceptance of some international personality need not be objective so as to bind non-consenting states nor unlimited as to time and content factors. These elements will be considered below. It should, however, be noted here that the international community itself also has needs and interests that bear upon this question as to international status. This is particularly so with regard to matters of responsibility and the protection of persons via the rules governing the recourse to and conduct of armed conflicts.[172]

Special cases

The Sovereign Order of Malta

This Order, established during the Crusades as a military and medical association, ruled Rhodes from 1309 to 1522 and was given Malta by treaty with Charles V in 1530 as a fief of the Kingdom of Sicily. This sovereignty was lost in 1798 and in 1834 the Order established its headquarters in Rome as a humanitarian organisation.[173] The Order already had international personality at the time of its taking control of Malta and even when it had to leave the island it continued to exchange diplomatic legations with most European countries. The Italian Court of Cassation in 1935 recognised the international personality of the Order, noting that 'the modern theory of the subjects of international law recognises a number of collective units whose composition is independent of the nationality of their constituent members and whose scope transcends by virtue of their universal character the territorial confines of any single state'.[174] This is predicated upon the functional needs of the entity as accepted by third parties. It is to be noted, for example, that the Order maintains diplomatic relations with over forty states.

---

[172] As to the specific regime established in the Antarctica Treaty 1959, see *infra*, p. 364. See also *infra*, p. 444, with regard to the International Seabed Authority under the Law of the Sea Convention, 1982.

[173] *Oppenheim's International Law*, p. 329, note 7; O'Connell, *International Law*, pp. 85–6 and Whiteman, *Digest*, vol. I, pp. 584–7.

[174] *Nanni v. Pace and the Sovereign Order of Malta*, 8 ILR, p. 2. See also *Scarfo v. Sovereign Order of Malta*, 24 ILR, p. 1 and *Sovereign Order of Malta v. Soc. An. Commerciale*, 22 ILR, p. 1.

The Holy See and the Vatican City[175]

In 1870, the conquest of the Papal states by Italian forces ended their existence as sovereign states. The question therefore arose as to the status in international law of the Holy See, deprived, as it then was, of normal territorial sovereignty. In 1929 the Lateran Treaty was signed with Italy which recognised the state of the Vatican City and 'the sovereignty of the Holy See in the field of international relations as an attribute that pertains to the very nature of the Holy See, in conformity with its traditions and with the demands of its mission in the world'.[176] The question thus interrelates with the problem of the status today of the Vatican City. The latter has no permanent population apart from Church functionaries and exists only to support the work of the Holy See. Italy carries out a substantial number of administrative functions with regard to the City. Some writers accordingly have concluded that it cannot be regarded as a state.[177] Nevertheless, it is a party to many international treaties and is a member of the Universal Postal Union and the International Telecommunications Union. It would appear that by virtue of recognition and acquiescence in the context of its claims, it does exist as a state. The Vatican City is closely linked with the Holy See and they are essentially part of the same construct.

The Holy See continued after 1870 to engage in diplomatic relations and enter into international agreements and concordats.[178] Accordingly its status as an international person was accepted by such partners. In its joint eleventh and twelfth report submitted to the UN Committee on the Elimination of Racial Discrimination in 1993,[179] the Holy See reminded the Committee of its 'exceptional nature within the community of nations; as a sovereign subject of international law, it has a mission of an essentially religious and moral order, universal in scope, which is based on minimal territorial dimensions guaranteeing a basis of autonomy for the pastoral ministry of the Sovereign Pontiff'.[180]

---

[175] See *Oppenheim's International Law*, p. 325; Crawford, *Creation of Statehood*, pp. 152–60; Rousseau, *Droit International Public*, vol. II, pp. 353–77; *Le Saint-Siège dans les Relations Internationales* (ed. Ororio), 1989 and Graham, *Vatican Diplomacy: A Study of Church and State on the International Plane*, 1959.

[176] 130 BFSP, p. 791. See also O'Connell, *International Law*, p. 289 and *Re Marcinkus, Mennini and De Strobel*, 87 ILR, p. 48.

[177] See Crawford, *Creation of Statehood*, p. 154 and M. Mendelson, 'The Diminutive States in the United Nations', 21 ICLQ, 1972, p. 609. See also Brownlie, *Principles*, p. 65.

[178] See e.g. the Fundamental Agreement between the Holy See and the State of Israel of 30 December 1993, 33 ILM, 1994, p. 153.

[179] CERD/C/226/Add. 6 (15 February 1993).

[180] See also the decision of the Philippines Supreme Court (en banc) in *The Holy See v Starbright Sales Enterprises Inc.*, 102 ILR, p. 163.

Insurgents and belligerents

International law has recognised that such entities may in certain circumstances, primarily dependent upon the *de facto* administration of specific territory, enter into valid arrangements.[181] In addition they will be bound by the rules of international law with respect to the conduct of hostilities and may in due course be recognised as governments. The traditional law is in process of modification as a result of the right to self-determination, and other legal principles such as territorial integrity, sovereign equality and non-intervention in addition to recognition will need to be taken into account.[182]

National liberation movements (NLMs)

The question of whether or not NLMs constitute subjects of international law and if so, to what extent, is bound up with the development of the law relating to non-self-governing territories and the principle of self-determination. The trusteeship system permitted the hearing of individual petitioners and this was extended to all colonial territories. In 1977, the General Assembly Fourth Committee voted to permit representatives of certain NLMs from Portugal's African territories to participate in its work dealing with such territories.[183] The General Assembly endorsed the concept of observer status for liberation movements recognised by the Organisation of African Unity in resolution 2918(XVII). In resolution 3247(XXIX), the Assembly accepted that NLMs recognised by the OAU or the Arab League could participate in Assembly sessions, in conferences arranged under the auspices of the Assembly and in meetings of the UN specialised agencies and the various Assembly organs.[184]

The inclusion of the regional recognition requirement was intended both to require a minimum level of effectiveness with regard to the organisation concerned before UN acceptance and to exclude in practice secessionist movements. The Economic and Social Committee of the UN has also adopted a similar approach and under its procedural rules it may invite any

---

[181] See *Oppenheim's International Law*, p. 165; Lauterpacht, *Jerusalem*, pp. 494–5; Brownlie, *Principles*, pp. 64–5 and T. C. Chen, *Recognition*, 1951. See also Cassese, *International Law*, p. 81.   [182] *Infra*, p. 795.

[183] See M. N. Shaw, 'The International Status of National Liberation Movements', 5 *Liverpool Law Review*, 1983, p. 19. See also Cassese, *International Law*, p. 90 and H. Wilson, *International Law and the Use of Force by National Liberation Movements*, Oxford, 1988.

[184] While the leader of the PAIGC was not permitted to speak at the Assembly in 1973, the leader of the PLO was able to address the body in 1974; see A/C.4/SR.1978 p. 23 and resolution 3237(XXIX).

NLM recognised by or in accordance with General Assembly resolutions to take part in relevant debates without a vote.[185]

The UN Security Council also permitted the Palestine Liberation Organisation (PLO) to participate in its debates with the same rights of participation as conferred upon a member state not a member of the Security Council, although this did raise serious constitutional questions.[186] Thus the possibility of observer status in the UN and related organs for NLMs appears to have been affirmatively settled in international practice. The question of international personality, however, is more complex and more significant, and recourse must be made to state practice.[187] Whether extensive state recognition of a liberation movement is of itself sufficient to confer such status is still a controversial issue.

The position of the PLO, however, began to evolve considerably with the Israel–PLO Declaration of Principles on Interim Self-Government Arrangements signed in Washington on 13 September 1993.[188] By virtue of this Declaration, the PLO team in the Jordanian–Palestinian delegation to the Middle East Peace Conference were accepted as representing the Palestinian people. It was agreed to establish a Palestinian Interim Self-Government Authority as an elected Council for the Palestinian people in the West Bank and Gaza (occupied by Israel since 1967) for a transitional period of up to five years leading to a permanent solution. Its jurisdiction was to cover the territory of the West Bank and Gaza, save for issues to be negotiated in the permanent status negotiations. Upon the entry into force of the Declaration, a transfer of authority was to commence from the Israeli military government and its civil administration. The Cairo Agreement of 4 May 1994[189] provided for the immediate withdrawal of Israeli forces from Jericho and the Gaza Strip and transfer of authority to a Palestinian Authority. This Authority was to have certain specified legislative, executive and judicial powers. The process continued with a transfer of further powers and responsibilities in a Protocol of 27 August 1995 and with the Interim Agreement on the West Bank and Gaza of 28 September 1995, under which an additional range of powers and responsibilities was transferred to the

---

[185] ECOSOC resolution 1949 (LVII), 8 May 1975, rule 73. See also as regards the Human Rights Commission, CHR/Res. 19(XXIX). The General Assembly and ECOSOC have also called upon the specialised agencies and other UN related organisations to assist the peoples and NLMs of colonial territories, see e.g. Assembly resolutions 33/41 and 35/29.

[186] See *Yearbook of the UN*, 1972, p. 70 and 1978, p. 297; S/PV 1859 (1975); S/PV 1870 (1976); *UN Chronicle*, April 1982, p. 16 and DUSPIL, 1975, pp. 73–75. See also Shaw, 'International Status'.

[187] See the *UN Headquarters Agreement* case, ICJ Reports, 1988, p. 12; 82 ILR, p. 225.

[188] 32 ILM, 1993, p. 1525. Note that letters of mutual recognition and commitment to the peace process were exchanged between the Prime Minister of Israel and the Chairman of the PLO on 9 September 1993. See e.g. Calvo-Goller, 'L'Accord du 13 Séptembre 1993 entre L'Israël et l'OLP: Le Régime d'Autonomie Prévu par la Déclaration Israël/OLP', AFDI, 1993, p. 435.   [189] 33 ILM, 1994, p. 622.

Palestinian Authority pending the election of the Council and arrangements were made for Israeli withdrawal from a number of cities and villages on the West Bank. With the increase in the territorial and jurisdictional competence of the Palestinian authority, the question of legal personality will no doubt arise.

As far as Namibia was concerned, the territory was regarded as having an international status[190] and there existed an NLM recognised as the authentic representative of the people[191] but it was, theoretically, administered by the UN Council for Namibia. This body was established in 1967 by the General Assembly in order to administer the territory and to prepare it for independence; it was disbanded in 1990. There were thirty-one UN member states on the Council, which was responsible to the General Assembly.[192] The Council sought to represent Namibian interests in international organisations and in conferences, and issued travel and identity documents to Namibians which were recognised by most states.[193] In 1974, the Council issued Decree No. 1 which sought to forbid the exploitation under South African auspices of the territory's resources, but little was in practice achieved by this Decree, which was not drafted in the clearest possible manner.[194] The status of the Council was unclear, but it was clearly recognised as having a role within the UN context and may thus have possessed some form of qualified personality.

International public companies

This type of entity, which may be known by a variety of names, for example, multinational public enterprises or international bodies corporate, is characterised in general by an international agreement providing for co-operation between governmental and private enterprises.[195] One writer, for example, defined such entities as corporations which

> have not been constituted by the exclusive application of one national law; whose members and directors represent several national sovereignties; whose legal personality is not based, or at any rate not entirely, on the decision of a national authority or the application of a national law; whose operations, finally, are governed, at least partially, by rules that do not stem from a single or even from several national laws.[196]

---

[190] The *Namibia* case, ICJ Reports, 1971, p. 16; 49 ILR, p. 3.
[191] Assembly resolution 3295(XXIX).
[192] The UK did not recognise the Council; see 408 HL Deb., col. 758, 23 April 1980.
[193] See e.g. Engers, 'The UN Travel and Identity Documents for Namibia', 65 AJIL, p. 571.
[194] See *Decolonisation*, no. 9, December 1977.
[195] See e.g. D. Fligler, *Multinational Public Enterprises*, 1967; Brownlie, *Principles*, pp. 67–9 and Ijalaye, *The Extension of Corporate Personality in International Law*, Leiden, 1978, pp. 57–146. See also P. Muchlinski, *Multinational Enterprises and the Law*, Oxford, 1995.
[196] Cited in Ijalaye, *Corporate Personality*, p. 69.

Such enterprises may vary widely in constitutional nature and in competences. Examples of such companies would include INTELSAT, established in 1973 as an intergovernmental structure for a global commercial telecommunications satellite system; Eurofima, established in 1955 by fourteen European states in order to lease equipment to the railway administrations of those states and the Bank of International Settlement, created in 1930 by virtue of a treaty between five states and the host country Switzerland. The personality question will depend upon the differences between municipal and international personality. If the entity is given a range of powers and is distanced sufficiently from municipal law, an international person may be involved, but it will require careful consideration of the circumstances.

Transnational corporations

Another possible candidate for international personality is the transnational or multinational enterprise. Various definitions exist of this important phenomenon in international relations.[197] They in essence constitute private business organisations comprising several legal entities linked together by parent corporations and are distinguished by size and multinational spread. In the years following the *Barcelona Traction* case,[198] an increasing amount of practice has been evident on the international plane dealing with such corporations. What has been sought is a set of guidelines governing the major elements of the international conduct of these entities.[199] However, progress has been slow and several crucial issues remain to be resolved, ranging from the legal effect, if any, of such a Code to the applicable tests for nationalisation and compensation.[200] Should such a Code come into effect containing duties directly imposed upon transnational corporations, as well as rights ascribed to them as against the host state, it would be

[197] See e.g. C. W. Jenks, *Transnational Law in a Changing Society* (eds. W. Friedman, L. Henkin and O. Lissitzyn), New York, 1972, p. 70; H. Baade, *Legal Problems of a Code of Conduct for Multinational Enterprises* (ed. N. Horn), Boston, 1980; J. Charney, 'Transnational Corporations and Developing Public International Law', *Duke Law Journal*, 1983, p. 748; F. Rigaux, 'Transnational Corporations', *International Law: Achievements and Prospects*, (ed. M. Bedjami), Dordrecht, 1991, p. 121 and Henkin, *et al.*, *International Law Cases and Materials*, p. 368.   [198] ICJ Reports, 1970, pp. 3, 46–7; 46 ILR, pp. 178, 220–1.

[199] See e.g. OECD Guidelines for Multinational Enterprises, 75 *US Dept. State Bull.*, p. 83 (1976) and ILO Tripartite Declaration of Principles concerning Multinational Enterprises and Social Policy, 17 ILM, pp. 423–30. See also Baade, *Legal Problems*, pp. 416–40.

[200] See the Draft Code of Conduct produced by the UN Commission on Transnational Corporations, 22 ILM, pp. 177–206, 23 ILM, p. 627 and *ibid.*, p. 602 (Secretariat report on outstanding issues); E/1990/94 (1990) and the World Bank Guidelines on the Treatment of Foreign Direct Investment, 31 ILM, 1992, p. 1366. See also the Andean Group commission decision 292 on a uniform code on Andean multinational enterprises, 30 ILM, 1991, p. 1295 and the Eastern and Southern African states charter on a regime of multinational industrial enterprises, *ibid.*, p. 696.

possible to regard them as international persons. This, however, has not yet occurred.[201]

The right of all peoples to self-determination[202]

The establishment of the legal right

This principle, which traces its origin to the concepts of nationality and democracy as evolved primarily in Europe, first appeared in major form after the First World War. Despite President Wilson's efforts, it was not included in the League of Nations Covenant and it was clearly not regarded as a legal principle.[203] However, its influence can be detected in the various provisions for minority protection[204] and in the establishment of the mandates system based as it was upon the sacred trust concept. In the ten years before the Second World War, there was relatively little practice regarding self-determination in international law. A number of treaties concluded by the USSR in this period noted the principle,[205] but in the *Aaland Islands* case it was clearly accepted by both the International Commission of Jurists and the Committee of Rapporteurs dealing with the situation that the principle of self-determination was not a legal rule of international law, but purely a political concept.[206] The situation, which concerned the Swedish inhabitants of an island alleged to be part of Finland, was resolved by the League's recognition of Finnish sovereignty coupled with minority guarantees.

The Second World War stimulated further consideration of the idea and the principle was included in the UN Charter. Article 1(2) noted as one of

---

[201] The *Third Restatement of US Foreign Relations Law*, St. Paul, 1987, p. 126 notes that the transnational corporation, while an established feature of international life, 'has not yet achieved independent status in international law'.

[202] See in general e.g. U. O. Umozurike, *Self-Determination in International Law*, 1972; Rigo-Sureda, *The Evolution of the Right of Self-Determination*, Leiden, 1973; M. Shukri, *The Concept of Self-Determination in the United Nations*, Leiden, 1967; M. Pomerance, *Self-Determination in Law and Practice*, Leiden, 1982; Shaw, 'National Liberation Movements', pp. 59–144; Crawford, 'Creation of Statehood', pp. 84–105; Rousseau, *Droit International Public*, vol. II, pp. 17–35; Wilson, *International Law*; Tunkin, *Theory*, pp. 60–9; *Modern Law of Self-Determination* (ed. Tomuschat), and Cassese, *International Law*. See also M. Koskenniemi, 'National Self-Determination Today' Problems of Legal Theory and Practice', 43 ICLQ, 1994, p. 241 and W. Ofuatey-Kodjoe, 'Self Determination' in *United Nations Legal Order* (eds. O. Schachter and C. Joyner), Cambridge, 1995, vol. I, p. 349.

[203] See A. Cobban, *The Nation-State and National Self-Determination*, London, 1969; Miller, *The Drafting of the Covenant*, New York, 1928, vol. II, pp. 12–13; S. Wambaugh, *Plebiscites since the World War*, Washington, 1933, vol. I, p. 42 and Pomerance, *Self Determination*.

[204] See e.g. I. Claude, *National Minorities*, 1955 and J. Lador-Lederer, *International Group Protection*, Leiden, 1968.

[205] See e.g. The Baltic States' treaties, Martens, *Recueil Général de Traités*, 3rd Series, XI, pp. 864, 877 and 888 and Cobban, *Nation-State*, pp. 187–218. See also Whiteman, *Digest*, vol. IV, p. 56.

[206] LNOJ Supp. No. 3, 1920, pp. 5–6 and Doc. B7/21/68/106[VII] pp. 22–3. See also Barros, *The Aaland Islands Question*, Leiden, 1968 and Verzijl, *International Law*, pp. 328–32.

the organisation's purposes the development of friendly relations among nations based upon respect for the principle of equal rights and self-determination and article 55 reiterated the phraseology. It is disputed whether the reference to the principle in these very general terms was sufficient to entail its recognition as a binding right, but the majority view is against this. Not every statement of a political aim in the Charter can be regarded as automatically creative of legal obligations. On the other hand, its inclusion in the Charter, particularly within the context of the statement of purposes of the UN, provided the opportunity for the subsequent interpretation of the principle both in terms of its legal effect and consequences and with regard to its definition. It is also to be noted that Chapters XI and XII of the Charter deal with non-self-governing and trust territories and may be seen as relevant within the context of the development and definition of the right to self-determination, although the term is not expressly used.[207]

Practice since 1945 within the UN, both generally as regards the elucidation and standing of the principle and more particularly as regards its perceived application in specific instances, can be seen as having ultimately established the legal standing of the right in international law. This may be achieved either by treaty or by custom or indeed, more controversially, by virtue of constituting a general principle of law. All these routes are relevant, as will be seen. The UN Charter is a multilateral treaty which can be interpreted by subsequent practice, while the range of state and organisation practice evident within the UN system can lead to the formation of customary law. The amount of material dealing with self-determination in the UN testifies to the importance of the concept and some of the more significant of this material will be briefly noted.

Resolution 1514 (XV), the Declaration on the Granting of Independence to Colonial Countries and Peoples, adopted in 1960 by eighty-nine votes to none, with nine abstentions, stressed that:

> all peoples have the right to self-determination; by virtue of that right they freely determine their political status and freely pursue their economic, social and cultural development.

Inadequacy of political, social, economic or educational preparedness was not to serve as a protest for delaying independence, while attempts aimed at the partial or total disruption of the national unity and territorial integrity of a country were deemed incompatible with the UN Charter. This Colonial

---

[207] See e.g. O'Connell, *International Law*, p. 312; N. Bentwich and A. Martin, *Commentary on the Charter of the UN*, New York, 1950, p. 7; D. Nincic, *The Problem of Sovereignty in the Charter and the Practice of States*, 1970, p. 221; H. Kelsen, *Law of the United Nations*, London, 1950, pp. 51–3 and H. Lauterpacht, *International Law and Human Rights*, The Hague, 1950, pp. 147–9. See also Judge Tanaka, *South West Africa* cases, ICJ Reports, 1966, pp. 288–9; 37 ILR, pp. 243, 451–2.

Declaration set the terms for the self-determination debate in its emphasis upon the colonial context and its opposition to secession, and has been regarded by some as constituting a binding interpretation of the Charter.[208] The Declaration was reinforced by the establishment of a Special Committee on Decolonisation, which now deals with all dependent territories and has proved extremely active, and by the fact that virtually all UN resolutions dealing with self-determination expressly refer to it. Indeed, the International Court has specifically referred to the Colonial Declaration as an 'important stage' in the development of international law regarding non-self-governing territories and as the 'basis for the process of decolonisation'.[209]

In 1966, the General Assembly adopted the International Covenants on Human Rights. Both these Covenants have an identical first article, declaring *inter alia* that '[a]ll peoples have the right to self-determination. By virtue of that right they freely determine their political status', while states parties to the instruments 'shall promote the realisation of the right of self-determination and shall respect that right in conformity with the provisions of the Charter of the United Nations'. The Covenants came into force in 1976 and thus constitute binding provisions as between the parties, but in addition they also may be regarded as authoritative interpretations of several human rights provisions in the Charter, including self-determination. The 1970 Declaration on Principles of International Law Concerning Friendly Relations can be regarded as constituting an authoritative interpretation of the seven Charter provisions it expounds. The Declaration states *inter alia* that 'by virtue of the principle of equal rights and self-determination of peoples enshrined in the Charter of the United Nations, all people have the right freely to determine . . . their political status' while all states are under the duty to respect this right in accordance with the Charter. The Declaration was specifically intended to act as an elucidation of certain important Charter provisions and was indeed adopted without opposition by the General Assembly.[210]

In addition to this general, abstract approach, the UN organs have dealt with self-determination in a series of specific resolutions with regard to particular situations and this practice may be adduced as reinforcing the conclusions that the principle has become a right in international law by virtue of a process of Charter interpretation. Numerous resolutions have

---

[208] See e.g. Brownlie, *Public International Law*, p. 595 and O. Asamoah, *The Legal Significance of the Declarations of the General Assembly of the United Nations*, The Hague, 1966, pp. 177–85. See also Shaw, *Title*, Chapter 2.

[209] The *Western Sahara* case, ICJ Reports, 1975, pp. 12, 31 and 32; 59 ILR, pp. 14, 49.

[210] Adopted in resolution 2625(XXV) without a vote. See e.g. R. Rosenstock, 'The Declaration of Principles of International Law Concerning Friendly Relations', 65 AJIL, 1971, pp. 16, 111 and 115.

been adopted in the General Assembly and also the Security Council.[211] It is also possible that a rule of customary law has been created since practice in the UN system is still state practice, but the identification of the *opinio juris* element is not easy and will depend upon careful assessment and judgment.

Judicial discussion of the principle of self-determination has been relatively rare and centres on the *Namibia*[212] and *Western Sahara*[213] advisory opinions by the International Court. In the former case, the Court emphasised that 'the subsequent development of international law in regard to non-self-governing territories as enshrined in the Charter of the United Nations made the principle of self-determination applicable to all of them'.[214] The *Western Sahara* case reaffirmed this point.[215] This case arose out of the decolonisation of that territory, controlled by Spain as the colonial power but subject to irredentist claims by Morocco and Mauritania. The Court was asked for an opinion with regard to the legal ties between the territory at that time and Morocco and the Mauritanian entity. The Court stressed that the request for an opinion arose out of the consideration by the General Assembly of the decolonisation of Western Sahara and that the right of the people of the territory to self-determination constituted a basic assumption of the questions put to the Court.[216] After analysing the Charter provisions and Assembly resolutions noted above, the Court concluded that the ties which had existed between the claimants and the territory during the relevant period of the 1880s were not such as to affect the application of resolution 1514(XV), the Colonial Declaration, in the decolonisation of the territory and in particular the right to self-determination. In other words, it is clear that the Court regarded the principle of self-determination as a legal one in the context of such territories.

The Court moved one step further in the *East Timor (Portugal* v. *Australia)* case[217] when it declared that 'Portugal's assertion that the right of peoples to self-determination, as it evolved from the Charter and from United Nations practice, has an *erga omnes* character, is irreproachable.' The Court emphasised that the right of peoples to self-determination was 'one of the essential principles of contemporary international law'.[218] However, in that

---

[211] See e.g. Assembly resolutions 1755(XVII); 2138(XXI); 2151(XXI); 2379(XXIII); 2383(XXIII) and Security Council Resolutions 183 (1963); 301 (1971); 377 (1975) and 384 (1975).   [212] ICJ Reports, 1971, p. 16; 49 ILR, p. 3.

[213] ICJ Reports, 1975, p. 12; 59 ILR, p. 30. See also M. N. Shaw, 'The Western Sahara Case', 49 BYIL, p. 119.   [214] ICJ Reports, 1971, pp. 16, 31; 49 ILR, pp. 3, 21.

[215] ICJ Reports, 1975, pp. 12, 31; 59 ILR, pp. 30, 48.

[216] *Ibid.*, p. 68; 59 ILR, p. 85. See in particular the views of Judge Dillard that 'a norm of international law has emerged applicable to the decolonisation of those non-self-governing territories which are under the aegis of the United Nations', ICJ Reports, 1975, pp. 121–2; 59 ILR, p. 138. See also Judge Petren, ICJ Reports, 1975, p. 110; 59 ILR, p. 127.

[217] ICJ Reports, 1995, pp. 90, 102.   [218] *Ibid.*

case, the Court, while noting that for both Portugal and Australia, East Timor (under Indonesian military occupation since the invasion of 1975) constituted a non-self-governing territory and pointing out that the people of East Timor had the right to self-determination, held that the absence of Indonesia from the litigation meant that the Court was unable to exercise its jurisdiction.[219]

The definition of self-determination

If the principle exists as a legal one, and it is believed that such is the case, the question arises then of its scope and application. As noted above, UN formulations of the principle from the 1960 Colonial Declaration to the 1970 Declaration on Principles of International Law and the 1966 International Covenants on Human Rights stress that it is the right of 'all peoples'. If this is so, then all peoples would become thereby to some extent subjects of international law as the direct repositories of international rights, and if the definition of 'people' used was the normal political-sociological one,[220] a major rearrangement of international law perceptions would have been created. In fact, that has not occurred and an international law concept of what constitutes a people for these purposes has been evolved, so that the 'self' in question must be determined within the accepted colonial territorial framework. Attempts to broaden this have not been successful and the UN has always strenuously opposed any attempt at the partial or total disruption of the national unity and territorial integrity of a country.[221] The UN has based its policy on the proposition that 'the territory of a colony or other non-self-governing territory has under the Charter a status separate and distinct from the territory of the state administering it' and that such status was to exist until the people of that territory had exercised the right to self-determination.[222] Self-determination has also been used in conjunction with the principle of territorial integrity so as to protect the territorial framework of the colonial period in the decolonisation process and to

---

[219] Ibid., pp. 105–6. The reason related to the principle that the Court is unable to exercise jurisdiction over a state without the consent of that state. The Court took the view that Portugal's claims against Australia could not be decided upon without an examination of the position of Indonesia, which had not consented to the jurisdiction of the Court. See further infra, Chapter 18, p. 757.

[220] See e.g. Cobban, Nation-State, p. 107, and K. Deutsche, Nationalism and Social Communications, New York, 1952. See also the Greco-Bulgarian Communities case, PCIJ, Series B, no. 17; 5 ILR, p. 4.

[221] See e.g. the Colonial Declaration 1960; the 1970 Declaration on Principles and Article III[3] of the OAU Charter.

[222] 1970 Declaration on Principles of International Law. Note also that resolution 1541(XV) declared that there is an obligation to transmit information regarding a territory 'which is geographically separate and is distinct ethnically and/or culturally from the country administering it'.

prevent a rule permitting secession from independent states from arising.[223] Self-determination as a concept is capable of developing further so as to apply to sovereign states in various ways including secession,[224] but that has not as yet convincingly happened.[225] It clearly applies within the context, however, of decolonisation of the European empires and thus provides the peoples of such territories with a degree of international personality.

The principle of self-determination provides that the people of the colonially defined territorial unit in question may freely determine their own political status. Such determination may result in independence, integration with a neighbouring state, free association with an independent state or any other political status freely decided upon by the people concerned.[226] Self-determination also has a role within the context of creation of statehood, preserving the sovereignty and independence of states, in providing criteria for the resolution of disputes, and in the area of the permanent sovereignty of states over natural resources.[227]

Individuals[228]

The question of the status in international law of individuals is closely bound up with the rise in the international protection of human rights. This section will be confined to some general comments about the former. The object theory in this regard maintains that individuals constitute only the subject-matter of intended legal regulation as such. Only states, and possibly international organisations, are subjects of the law.[229] This has been a theory of

---

[223] See e.g. T. M. Franck, *The Power of Legitimacy Among Nations*, Oxford, 1990, pp. 153 *et seq.*; Franck,'Fairness in the International Legal and Institutional System', 240 HR, 1993 III, pp. 13, 127–49; Higgins, *Problems*, Chapter 11 and Shaw, *Title*, Chapters 3 and 4.

[224] See further *infra*, Chapter 9, p. 354, with regard to the dissolution of independent states and claims to self-determination.

[225] But see further, *infra* Chapter 6, p. 215, with regard to the evolution of self-determination as a principle of human rights operating within independent states.

[226] ICJ Reports, 1975, pp. 12, 33 and 68. See also Judge Dillard, ibid., p. 122; 59 ILR, pp. 30, 50, 85, 138. See Assembly resolution 1541(XV) and the 1970 Declaration on Principles of International Law.

[227] Note that on 22 February 1991 Portugal instituted proceedings against Australia at the International Court of Justice alleging, *inter alia*, that Australia's agreement with Indonesia dealing with the exploration and exploitation of the continental shelf in the 'Timor Gap' has violated the right of the people of East Timor to self-determination. East Timor was a Portuguese colony that is now under the control of Indonesia. ICJ Press Communiqué No. 91/6, 22 February 1991. See *supra* p. 180.

[228] See e.g. *Oppenheim's International Law*, Chapter 8; Higgins, *Problems*, pp. 48–55; Brownlie, *Principles*, Chapter 24; O'Connell, *International law*, pp. 106–12; C. Norgaard, *Position of the Individual in International Law*, 1962; H. Lauterpacht, *Human Rights in International Law*, London, 1951, and *International Law; Collected Papers*, vol. II, 1975, p. 487, and *The Individual's Duties to the Community and the Limitations on Human Rights and Freedoms under Article 29 of the Universal Declaration of Human Rights*, study prepared by E. Daes, 1983, E/CN.4/Sub.2/432/Rev. 2. See also Chapter 6.

[229] See e.g. O'Connell, *International Law*, pp. 106–7.

limited value. The essence of international law has always been its ultimate concern for the human being and this was clearly manifest in the Natural Law origins of classical international law.[230] The growth of positivist theories, particularly in the nineteenth century, obscured this and emphasised the centrality and even exclusivity of the state in this regard. Nevertheless, modern practice does demonstrate that individuals have become increasingly recognised as participants and subjects of international law. This has occurred primarily but not exclusively through human rights law.

The link between the state and the individual for international law purposes has historically been the concept of nationality. This was and remains crucial particularly in the spheres of jurisdiction and the international protection of the individual by the state. It is often noted that the claim of an individual against a foreign state, for example, becomes subsumed under that of his national state.[231] Each state has the capacity to determine who are to be its nationals and this is to be recognised by other states in so far as it is consistent with international law, although in order for other states to accept this nationality there has to be a genuine connection between the state and the individual in question.[232]

Individuals as a general rule lack standing to assert violations of international treaties in the absence of a protest by the state of nationality,[233] although states may agree to confer particular rights on individuals which will be enforceable under international law, independently of municipal law. Under article 304(b) of the Treaty of Versailles 1919, for example, nationals of the Allied and Associated Powers could bring cases against Germany before the Mixed Arbitral Tribunal in their own names for compensation, while the Treaty of 1907 between five Central American states establishing the Central American Court of Justice provided for individuals to bring cases directly before the Court.[234]

This proposition was reiterated in the *Danzig Railway Officials* case[235] by the Permanent Court of International Justice. In that case, there had been an agreement between Poland and Danzig relating to the conditions of employment of Danzig railway officials working on the Polish rail system. Poland agreed that since an international treaty was involved and since the particular rights conferred had not been incorporated into its municipal law, any failure to enforce such rights would be a matter between itself and

---

[230] See e.g. Grotius, *De Jure Praedae Commentarius*, 1604, cited in Daes, *The Individual's Duties*, p. 44 and Lauterpacht, *Human Rights*, pp. 9, 70 and 74.
[231] See the *Panevezys–Saldutiskis* case, PCIJ, Series A/B, No. 76; 9 ILR, p. 308. See also the *Mavrommatis Palestine Concessions* case (Jurisdiction), PCIJ, Series A, No. 2 (1924); 2 ILR, p. 27. See also *infra*, Chapter 14.
[232] See the *Nottebohm* case, ICJ Reports, 1955, pp. 4, 22–3; 22 ILR, p. 349 and *infra*, Chapter 14.   [233] See e.g. *US v. Noriega*, 746 F.Supp. 1506, 1533 (1990); 99 ILR, pp. 143, 175.
[234] See Whiteman, *Digest*, vol. I, p. 39.   [235] PCIJ, Series B, No. 15 (1928); 4 ILR, p. 287.

Danzig alone and the individuals concerned would just have to make such representations as they could to Danzig. The Court dismissed this argument having regard to the particular circumstances of the treaty and the intentions at the time of agreement of the two parties to it. Whether a treaty does establish rights and duties as regards individuals will depend on the facts of the case and the intention of the parties.

Under the provisions concerned with minority protection in the 1919 Peace Treaties, it was possible for individuals to apply directly to an international court in particular instances. Similarly the tribunal created under the Upper Silesia Convention of 1922 decided that it was competent to hear cases by the nationals of a state against that state.[236]

Since then a wide range of other treaties have provided for individuals to have rights directly and have enabled individuals to have direct access to international courts and tribunals. One may mention as examples the European Convention on Human Rights, 1950; the European Communities treaties, 1957; the Inter-American Convention on Human Rights, 1969; the Optional Protocol to the International Covenant on Civil and Political Rights, 1966; the International Convention for the Elimination of All Forms of Racial Discrimination, 1965; and the Convention on the Settlement of Investment Disputes, 1965.

International criminal responsibility[237]

As far as obligations are concerned, international law has imposed direct responsibility upon individuals in certain specified matters.[238] In the cases of piracy and slavery,[239] offenders are guilty of a crime against international society and can thus be punished by international tribunals or by any state at all. Jurisdiction to hear the charge is not confined to, for example, the state on whose territory the act took place, or the national state of the offender.

The Treaty of Versailles 1919 noted that the German government recognised the right of the Allied and Associated Powers to bring individuals

---

[236] See e.g. *Steiner and Gross* v. *Polish State*, 4 ILR, p. 291.
[237] See e.g. Lauterpacht, *Human Rights*, p. 43; *Oppenheim's International Law*, p. 505; *International Criminal Law* (eds. Mueller and Wise), 1965, pp. 621–2; Glaser, *Droit International Pénal Conventionnel*, 2 vols., 1970 and 1978; V. Nanda, *International Criminal Law*, 2 vols., Boulder, CO, 1973; M. C. Bassiouni, *International Criminal Law*, 3 vols., Leyden, 1986–7; Bassiouni, *Crimes Against Humanity in International Criminal Law*, Dordrecht, 1992, Chapter 5; L. Sunga, *Individual Responsibility in International Law for Serious Human Rights Violations*, Dordrecht, 1992, and Brownlie, *Public International Law*, pp. 561–4.
[238] See the advisory opinion of the Inter-American Court of Human Rights in the *Re-Introduction of the Death Penalty in the Peruvian Constitution* case, 16 HRLJ, 1995, pp. 9, 14, noting that individual responsibility may only be invoked for violations that are defined in international instruments as crimes under international law.
[239] See e.g. Bassiouni, *Crimes Against Humanity*, *op. cit.*, pp. 193–6.

accused of crimes against the laws and customs of war before military tribunals (article 228) and established the individual responsibility of the Kaiser (article 227).[240] In the event, only a few trials were held before German courts in Leipzig.[241] A variety of other international instruments were also relevant in the establishment of individual responsibility with regard to specific issues.[242]

The Charter annexed to the Agreement for the Prosecution and Punishment of the Major War Criminals 1945 provided specifically for individual responsibility for crimes against peace, war crimes and crimes against humanity.[243] The Nuremberg Tribunal pointed out that 'international law imposes duties and liabilities upon individuals as well as upon states'. This was because 'crimes against international law are committed by men, not by abstract entities, and only by punishing individuals who commit such crimes can the provisions of international law be enforced'. Included in the relevant category for which individual responsibility was posited were crimes against peace, war crimes and crimes against humanity.[244]

The provisions of the Nuremberg Charter can now be regarded as part of international law, particularly since the General Assembly in 1946 affirmed the principles of this Charter and the decision of the Tribunal.[245] The Assembly also stated that genocide was a crime under international law bearing individual responsibility.[246] This was reaffirmed in the Genocide Convention of 1948, while the International Convention on the Suppression and Punishment of the Crime of Apartheid of 1973 declares apartheid to be an international crime involving direct individual criminal responsibility.[247]

---

[240] *Ibid.*, pp. 199–203.   [241] See Mullins, *The Leipzig Trials*, 1921.

[242] See e.g. the International Convention for the Protection of Submarine Telegraph Cables 1884; the Agreement for the Suppression of the Circulation of Obscene Publications 1910; the International Convention for the Suppression of the Circulation of and Traffic in Obscene Publications 1924; the Agreement Concerning the Suppression of Opium-Smoking 1931; Convention for the Suppression of the Illicit Traffic in Dangerous Drugs 1936 and the International Convention for the Suppression of Counterfeiting Currency 1929.

[243] See article 6, 39 AJIL, 1945, Suppl., p. 259. See also Brownlie, *Principles*, p. 562 and Lauterpacht, *Human Rights*, p. 6.

[244] See 41 AJIL, 1947, p. 220. See also I. Brownlie, *International Law and the Use of Force by States*, Oxford, 1963, p. 167. The Tokyo Charter, article 5, similarly provided for individual responsibility with regard to certain crimes, see e.g. Bassiouni, *Crimes Against Humanity*, p. 211; see also *ibid.*, pp. 212 *et seq.* with regard to the case law of the Tokyo Tribunal, for which also see Horowitz, *The Tokyo Trial*, International Conciliation No. 465 (1950), and trials held in various countries arising out of the events of the Second World War.

[245] Resolution 95(1). See also the International Law Commission's Report on Principles of the Nuremberg Tribunal, *Yearbook of the ILC*, 1950, vol. II, p. 195, and the Convention on the Non-Applicability of Statutory Limitations to War Crimes Against Humanity, 1968.

[246] Resolution 96(1).

[247] See also the International Law Commission's Draft Code of Offences, 1954, A/2693 and 45 AJIL, 1954, p. 123 (Suppl.), article 1 of which provided that 'offences against the peace and security of mankind, as defined in this Code, are crimes under international law, for which the responsible individuals shall be punishable'.

Individual responsibility has also been confirmed with regard to grave breaches of the four 1949 Geneva Red Cross Conventions and 1977 Protocols I and II dealing with armed conflicts. It is provided specifically that the High Contracting Parties undertake to enact any legislation necessary to provide effective penal sanctions for persons committing or ordering to be committed any of a series of grave breaches.[248] Such grave breaches include wilful killing, torture or inhuman treatment, extensive destruction and appropriation of property not justified by military necessity and carried out unlawfully and wantonly, unlawful deportation or transfer of protected persons and the taking of hostages.[249] Protocol I of 1977 to the 1949 Conventions extends the list to include, for example, making the civilian population the object of attack and launching an attack against works or installations containing dangerous forces in the knowledge that such attack will cause excessive loss of life or damage to civilians or their property when committed wilfully and causing death or serious injury; other activities such as transferring civilian population from the territory of an occupying power to that of an occupied area or deporting from an occupied area, apartheid and racial discrimination and attacking clearly recognised historic monuments, works of art or places of worship, may also constitute grave breaches when committed wilfully.[250] Any individual, regardless of rank or governmental status, would be personally liable for any war crimes or grave breaches committed.[251] Military necessity may not be pleaded as a defence[252] and the claim of superior orders will not provide a defence, although it may be taken in mitigation depending upon the circumstances.[253]

The International Law Commission in 1991 provisionally adopted a Draft Code of Crimes Against the Peace and Security of Mankind.[254] Under this Draft Code, individual criminal responsibility is provided for with regard to leading, planning or organising an act or threat of aggression (articles 15 and 16), leading or organising the commission or order-

---

[248] See article 49 of the First Geneva Convention; article 50 of the Second; article 129 of the Third Geneva Convention and article 146 of the Fourth Geneva Convention. See further *infra* Chapter 19, p. 806.

[249] See e.g. article 50 of the First Geneva Convention, article 51 of the Second Geneva Convention, article 130 of the Third Geneva Convention and article 147 of the Fourth Geneva Convention. See also L. C. Green, *The Contemporary Law of Armed Conflict*, Manchester, 1993, Chapter 18.   [250] See article 85 of Protocol I.

[251] See e.g. Green, *Armed Conflict*, p. 292.

[252] See e.g. *In re Lewinski (called von Manstein)*, 16 AD, p. 509.

[253] See Green, *Armed Conflict*, pp. 293–7; Green, *Superior Orders in National and International Law*, Leyden, 1976, and Y. Dinstein, *The Defence of 'Obedience to Superior Orders' in International Law*, Leyden, 1965. See also article 8 of the Nuremberg Charter, 39 AJIL, 1945, Suppl., p. 259, and Principle IV of the International Law Commission's Report on the Principles of the Nuremberg Tribunal 1950, *Yearbook of the ILC*, 1950, vol. II, p. 195.

[254] A/46/10 and 30 ILM, 1991, p. 1584.

ing the commission of an act of intervention in the internal or external affairs of a state by fomenting or assisting in subversive or terrorist activities (article 17), organising or leading the establishment or maintenance by force of colonial or alien domination (article 18), committing or ordering the commission of acts of genocide (article 19), organising or leading the commission of the crime of apartheid (article 20), committing or organising systematic or mass violations of human rights (article 21), committing or ordering the commission of an 'exceptionally serious war crime' (article 22),[255] committing or ordering as an agent or representative of a state the recruitment, use, financing or training of mercenaries (article 23), committing or ordering as an agent or representative of a state the organisation or other assistance of international terrorism (article 24), committing or ordering the commission of illicit trafficking in narcotic drugs (article 25) and wilful and severe damage to the environment (article 26). The fact that a state may also be responsible for the crimes is deemed not to affect the issue of individual responsibility and vice versa.

The Security Council in two resolutions on the Somali situation in the early 1990s unanimously condemned breaches of humanitarian law and stated that the authors of such breaches or those who had ordered their commission would be held 'individually responsible' for them.[256]

Events in the former Yugoslavia in particular[257] impelled a renewal of interest in the establishment of an international criminal court, which had long been under consideration.[258] In 1994, the International Law Commission adopted a Draft Statute for an International Criminal Court.[259] This statute provides for the Court to have jurisdiction over persons with respect to the crime of genocide, the crime of aggression, serious violations of the laws and customs applicable in armed conflict,

---

[255] The relationship between an 'exceptionally serious war crime' and a 'grave breach' as formulated in the 1949 Geneva Conventions and 1977 Protocols remains to be clarified. In 1995, the Rapporteur recommended to the International Law Commission that this category be abandoned and replaced by a new article 22 entitled 'War Crimes', see Report of the International Law Commission on the Work of its Forty-seventh Session, 1995, A/50/10, p. 52. However, the notion of an 'exceptionally serious war crime' is retained as such as a basis of individual responsibility in the context of war crimes without clear definition. Further discussions will follow. [256] Resolutions 794 (1992) and 814 (1993).

[257] But note also Security Council resolution 674 (1990) concerning Iraq's occupation of Kuwait. The resolution reaffirmed Iraq's liability under the Fourth Geneva Convention 1949 dealing with civilian populations of occupied areas. Such responsibility for grave breaches was also expressly stated to extend to 'individuals who commit or order the commission of grave breaches'. See e.g. the Special Section on Iraqi War Crimes, 31 Va JIL, 1991, p. 351.

[258] See e.g. B. Ferencz, 'An International Criminal Code and Court: Where They Stand and Where They're Going', 30 *Columbia Journal of Transnational Law*, 1992, p. 375.

[259] See Report of the ILC on the Work of its 46th Session, A/49/10, pp. 43 *et seq.* See also *infra* p. 471. See in particular J. Crawford, 'The ILC's Draft Statute for an International Criminal Court', 88 AJIL, 1994, p. 140.

crimes against humanity and 'crimes established under or pursuant to the treaty provisions listed in the Annex, which, having regard to the conduct alleged, constitute exceptionally serious crimes of international concern'.[260] An international agreement will be required for the proposed International Criminal Court to come into effect.

By way of contrast, two specific war crimes tribunals were established in recent years by the use of the authority of the UN Security Council to adopt decisions binding upon all member states of the organisation. This method was used in order both to enable the tribunal in question to come into operation as quickly as possible and to ensure that the parties most closely associated with the subject-matter of the war crimes alleged should be bound in a manner not dependent upon their consent (as would be necessary in the case of a court established by international agreement).

The Security Council adopted resolution 808 (1993) on 22 February 1993 and this resolution provided that 'an international tribunal shall be established for the prosecution of persons responsible for serious violations of international humanitarian law committed in the territory of the former Yugoslavia since 1991'.[261] The Secretary-General of the UN produced a report incorporating a draft statute and commentary,[262] which was adopted by the Security Council in resolution 827 (1993) acting under Chapter VII of the UN Charter, which allows the Council to take decisions binding upon all member states of the UN.

The International Tribunal for the Prosecution of Persons Responsible for Serious Violations of International Humanitarian Law Committed in the Territory of the Former Yugoslavia since 1 January 1991 (and until a date to be fixed upon the conclusion of peace) consists of two Trial Chambers and an Appeals Chambers, together with a Prosecutor and a Registry ser-

---

[260] Article 20. The Annex provides a list which *inter alia* includes grave breaches of the 1949 Geneva Conventions and article 85 of Protocol I, 1977; unlawful seizure of aircraft under the Hague Convention for the Suppression of Unlawful Seizure of Aircraft 1970; crimes contrary to the Montreal Convention for the Suppression of Unlawful Acts against the Safety of Civil Aviation 1971; hostage-taking under the International Convention against the Taking of Hostages 1979 and torture under the Convention against Torture 1984.

[261] See also Security Council resolutions 764 (1992), 771 (1992) and 820 (1993) in which grave concern was expressed with regard to breaches of international humanitarian law and the responsibilities of the parties reaffirmed. In particular, individual responsibility for the commission of grave breaches of the 1949 Conventions was emphasised. Under resolution 780 (1992), the Council established an impartial Commission of Experts to examine and analyse information concerning evidence of grave breaches of the Geneva Conventions and other violations of international humanitarian law committed in the territory of the former Yugoslavia. The Commission produced a report in early 1993 in which it concluded that grave breaches and other violations of international humanitarian law had been committed in the territory of the former Yugoslavia, including wilful killing, 'ethnic cleansing', mass killings, torture, rape, pillage and destruction of civilian property, the destruction of cultural and religious property and arbitrary arrests, see S/25274. See also M. C. Bassiouni, 'The United Nations Commission of Experts Established Pursuant to Security Council Resolution 780 (1992)', 88 AJIL, 1994, p. 784.   [262] S/25704 (1993).

vicing both the Chambers and the Prosecutor.[263] Articles 2 to 5 of the Statute lay down the crimes with regard to which the Tribunal can exercise jurisdiction. These encompass grave breaches of the Geneva Conventions of 1949 (article 2),[264] violations of the laws or customs of war (including use of weapons calculated to cause unnecessary suffering, wanton destruction of cities, towns and villages, and plunder of public or private property under article 3),[265] genocide (article 4)[266] and crimes against humanity (including murder, extermination, deportation and torture relating to the civilian population under article 5).

Article 6 of the Statute provides that the Tribunal has jurisdiction over natural persons, while article 7 establishes that persons who 'planned, instigated, ordered, committed or otherwise aided and abetted in the planning, preparation or execution' of crimes listed in article 2 to 5 shall be individually responsible for the crime.[267] This article also provides that the official position of any accused person is not to relieve a person of criminal responsibility nor mitigate punishment, while the fact that a subordinate committed the crime is not to relieve a superior of responsibility if the latter knew or had reason to know that the subordinate was about to or had committed the crime and the superior failed to take the necessary and reasonable measures to prevent the acts or to punish the perpetrators thereof. It is also stipulated that the fact that an accused person acted pursuant to an order of a government or of a superior will not relieve him of criminal responsibility, although this may constitute a mitigating factor if the Tribunal determines that justice so requires. The Appeal Chamber of the Tribunal in the *Tadic* case confirmed that customary international law had imposed criminal responsibility for serious violations of humanitarian law governing internal as well as international armed conflicts.[268]

Following events in Rwanda during 1994 and the mass slaughter that took

---

[263] See e.g. D. Shraga and R. Zacklin, 'The International Criminal Tribunal for the Former Yugoslavia', 5 EJIL, 1994, p. 360; M. C. Bassiouni, *Law of the International Criminal Tribunal for the Former Yugoslavia*, New York, 1995 and V. Morris and M. Scharf, *An Insider's Guide to the International Criminal Tribunal for the Former Yugoslavia*, New York, 1995, 2 vols.

[264] Note that in the *Tadiç* case, Case No. IT-94-1-AR72, p. 48, the Appeals Chamber of the International Tribunal concluded that article 2 only applies to crimes committed within the context of international armed conflicts.

[265] The Appeals Chamber concluded that article 3 was a general clause covering all violations of international humanitarian law not falling within article 2, 4 or 5, including therefore violations occurring in internal armed conflicts, see the *Tadiç* case, Case No. IT-94-1-AR72, p. 51. As to international and internal armed conflicts generally, see *infra*, Chapter 19, p. 815.

[266] Note that the Tribunal in November 1995 formally indicted two leaders of the Bosnian Serbs (Karadzic and Mladic) on charges *inter alia* of genocide following upon the capture of the Moslem 'safe haven' of Srebrenica, see IT-95-18-I.

[267] As of 6 September 1995, there were forty-three persons under indictment, see Tribunal Press Release CC/P10/17-E. See also 16 HRLJ, 1995, pp. 217-38.

[268] See IT-94-1-AR72, 2 October 1995, p. 70.

place,[269] the Security Council decided in resolution 955 (1994) to establish an International Tribunal for Rwanda, with the power to prosecute persons responsible for serious violations of international humanitarian law committed in the territory of Rwanda and Rwandan citizens responsible for such violations committed in the territory of neighbouring states between 1 January 1994 and 31 December 1994. The Statute of this Tribunal was annexed to the body of the Security Council resolution. It bears many similarities to the Statute of the Yugoslav Tribunal, consisting, for example, of two Trial Chambers, an Appeal Chamber, a Prosecutor[270] and a Registry (article 10). Articles 2 to 4 stipulate the crimes over which the Tribunal has jurisdiction. These are genocide (article 2), crimes against humanity (article 3) and violations of article 3 common to the Geneva Conventions 1949 and of Additional Protocol II (article 4).[271] Individual criminal responsibility is established for persons planning, ordering, committing or aiding the crimes listed, while provisions similar to the Statute of the Yugoslav Tribunal with regard to official positions, superior/subordinate relations and superior orders apply (article 6).[272]

This vast array of practice with regard to the international rights and duties of the individual under customary and treaty law clearly demonstrates that individuals are subjects of international law. It remains only to determine the nature and extent of this personality, while recognising that the current structure of international relations militates against anything other than a limited personality for individuals.

International organisations

The nature, characteristics and forms of international organisations will be surveyed in Chapter 21, but reference needs to be made to them at this stage. Such entities have played a crucial role in the sphere of international person-

---

[269] See e.g. UN Secretary-General Reports S/1994/879 and S/1994/906 and the Report of the Special Rapporteur for Rwanda of the UN Commission on Human Rights, S/1994/1157, annex I and annex II and the Report of the Commission of Experts, S/1994/1125. See also L. Sunga, 'The Commission of Experts on Rwanda and the Creation of the International Criminal Tribunal for Rwanda', 16 HRLJ, 1995, p. 121 and R. S. Lee, 'The Rwanda Tribunal', 9 *Leiden Journal of International Law*, 1996, p. 37.

[270] In fact, Justice Goldstone of South Africa was appointed Prosecutor for both the Yugoslav and Rwanda Tribunals.

[271] This provision differs from articles 2 and 3 of the Statute of the Yugoslav Tribunal in that the Rwanda conflict was seen purely as an internal armed conflict. Common article 3 and Protocol II are concerned with internal as distinct from international armed conflicts and the crimes listed include murder, torture, collective punishments, taking of hostages, acts of terrorism, rape and pillage.

[272] It should be particularly noted that in these instruments (the Draft Statute for an International Criminal Court and the Statutes for the Yugoslav and Rwanda Tribunals), as well as establishing individual criminal responsibility, the rights of the accused are given careful attention. See further *infra* Chapter 6.

ality. Since the nineteenth century a growing number of such organisations have appeared and thus raised the issue of international legal personality.[273] In principle it is now well established that international organisations may indeed possess objective international legal personality.[274] Whether that will be so in any particular instance will depend upon the particular circumstances of that case. Whether an organisation possesses personality in international law will hinge upon its constitutional status, its actual powers and practice. Significant factors in this context will include the capacity to enter into relations with states and other organisations and conclude treaties with them, and the status it has been given under municipal law. Such elements are known in international law as the indicia of personality.

The acquisition, nature and consequences of legal personality – some conclusions

The above survey of existing and possible subjects of international law demonstrates both the range of interaction upon the international scene by entities of all types and the pressures upon international law to come to terms with the contemporary structure of international relations. The International Court clearly recognised the multiplicity of models of personality in stressing that 'the subjects of law in any legal system are not necessarily identical in their nature or in the extent of their rights'.[275] There are, however, two basic categories – objective and qualified personality. In the former case, the entity is subject to a wide range of international rights and duties and it will be entitled to be accepted as an international person by any other international person with which it is conducting relations. In other words, it will operate *erga omnes*. The creation of objective international personality will of necessity be harder to achieve and will require the action in essence of the international community as a whole or a substantial element of it. The Court noted in the *Reparation* case that:

> fifty states, representing the vast majority of the members of the international community, have the power, in conformity with international law, to bring into being an entity possessing objective international personality and not merely personality recognised by them alone, together with capacity to bring international claims.[276]

The attainment of qualified personality, on the other hand, binding only the consenting subject, may arise more easily and it is clear that in this

---

[273] See O'Connell, *International Law*, p. 94.
[274] See the *Reparation for Injuries* case, ICJ Reports, 1949, p. 174; 16 ILR, p. 318. See also the *Interpretation of the Agreement of 25 March 1951 between the WHO and Egypt* case, ICJ Reports, 1980, pp. 73, 89–90; 62 ILR, pp. 450, 473–4.
[275] *Ibid.*, p. 178; 16 ILR, p. 321.   [276] *Ibid.*, p. 185; 16 ILR, p. 330.

respect at least theory ought to recognise existing practice. Any legal person may accept that another entity possesses personality in relation to itself and that determination will operate only *in personam*.

States are the original and major subjects of international law. Their personality derives from the very nature and structure of the international system. Statehood will arise as a result of the factual satisfaction of the stipulated legal criteria. The constitutive theory of recognition is not really acceptable, although recognition, of course, contributes valuable evidence of adherence to the required criteria. All states, by virtue of the principle of sovereign equality, will enjoy the same degree of international legal personality. It has been argued that some international organisations, rather than being derivative subjects of international law, will as sovereign or self-governing legal communities possess an inherent personality directly from the system and will thus constitute general and even objective subjects of international law. Non-sovereign persons, including non-governmental organisations and individuals, would be derived subjects possessing only such international powers as conferred exceptionally upon them by the necessary subjects of international law.[277] This view may be questioned, but it is true that the importance of practice via the larger international organisations cannot be underestimated.

Similarly, the role of the Holy See (particularly prior to 1929) as well as the UN experience demonstrates that the derivative denomination is unsatisfactory. The significance of this relates to their ability to extend their international rights and duties on the basis of both constituent instruments and subsequent practice and to their capacity to affect the creation of further international persons and to play a role in the norm-creating process.

Recognition, acquiescence and estoppel are important principles in the context of international personality, not only with regard to states and international organisations but throughout the range of subjects. They will affect not only the creation of new subjects but also the definition of their nature and rights and duties.

Personality may be acquired by a combination of treaty provisions and recognition or acquiescence by other international persons. For instance, the International Committee of the Red Cross, a private non-governmental organisation subject to Swiss law, was granted special functions under the 1949 Geneva Red Cross Conventions and has been accepted as being able to enter into international agreements under international law with international persons, such as with the EEC under the World Food Programme.[278]

---

[277] See e.g. F. Seyersted, 'International Personality of Intergovernmental Organisations', 4 *Indian Journal of International Law*, 1964, p. 19.
[278] See e.g. Whiteman, *Digest*, vol. I, p. 48 and *Yearbook of the ILC*, 1981, vol. II, p. 12.

Another possible method of acquiring international personality is by subjecting an agreement between a recognised international person and a private party directly to the rules of international law. This would have the effect of rendering the latter into an international person in the context of the arrangement in question so as to enable it to invoke in the field of international law the rights it derives from that arrangement.[279] While this currently may not be entirely acceptable to Third World states, this is probably because of a perception of the relevant rules of international law which may very well alter.[280] Personality may also be acquired by virtue of being directly subjected to international duties. This would apply to individuals in specific cases such as war crimes, piracy and genocide, and might in the future constitute the method by which transnational corporations may be accepted as international persons. One variation of the draft Code of Conduct under discussion would make the document a binding one and would impose duties directly upon such entities.[281]

Community needs with regard to the necessity to preserve international stability and life may well be of relevance in certain exceptional circumstances. In the case of non-state territorial entities that are not totally dominated by a state, there would appear to be a community need to ensure that at least the rules relating to the resort to force and the laws of war operate. Not to accept some form of qualified personality in this area might be to free such entities from having to comply with such rules, and that clearly would affect community requirements. Just as municipal law has sometimes to face the facts of the existence of particular entities for certain humanitarian purposes,[282] so also international law may have to come to terms with such bodies for such purposes.[283] The determining point here, it is suggested, must be the degree of effective control maintained by the entity in its territorial confines. However, even so, recognition may overcome this hurdle, as the recognition of Byelorussia and the Ukraine as non-sovereign state entities prior to the demise of the Soviet Union and the

---

[279] See in particular the *Texaco* v. *Libya* case, 53 ILR, pp. 389, 457–62.

[280] Note the intriguing suggestion raised in the study prepared for the Economic Commission for Asia and the Far East, that an agreement between autonomous public entities (not being subjects of international law) might create an international person; UNJYB, 1971, pp. 215–18. The study was very cautious about this possibility.

[281] See 22 ILM, 1983, p. 192.

[282] See e.g. *Hesperides Hotels* v. *Aegean Turkish Holidays Ltd.* [1978] QB 205; 73 ILR, p. 9; *Luigi Monta of Genoa* v. *Cechofracht Ltd.* [1956] 2 QB 552; 23 ILR, p. 71; *Re Al-Fin Corporation's Patent* [1970] Ch. 160; 52 ILR, p. 68 and *Reel* v. *Holder* [1981] 1 WLR 1226; 74 ILR, p. 105. See also J. G. Merrills, 'Recognition and Construction', 10 ICLQ, p. 476 and M. N, Shaw, 'Legal Acts of an Unrecognised Entity', 94 LQR, 1978, p. 500.

[283] See the *Namibia* case, ICJ Reports, 1971, pp. 16, 56, 134 and 149; 49 ILR, pp. 3, 46, 124, 139. See also Security Council resolutions 326 (1973); 328 (1973); 403 (1977); 406 (1977); 411 (1977); and 424 (1978) in which the Council condemned Rhodesian attacks against neighbouring states and recognised that the entity was subject to the norms relating to the use of force.

emergence of these entities as the independent states of Belarus and Ukraine demonstrated.[284]

All these entities may be easily contained within the category of qualified personality, possessing a limited range of rights and duties valid as against those accepting their personality. There are no preset rules governing the extent of rights and duties of international persons. This will depend upon the type of entity concerned, its claims and expectations, functions and attitude adopted by the international community. The exception here would be states which enter upon life with an equal range of rights and obligations. Those entities with objective personality will, it is suggested, benefit from a more elastic perception of the extent of their rights and duties in the form of a wider interpretation of implied powers through practice. However, in the case of qualified subjects implied powers will be more difficult to demonstrate and accept and the range of their rights and duties will be much more limited. The presumption, thus, will operate the other way.

The precise catalogue of rights and duties is accordingly impossible to list in advance; it will vary from case to case. The capacity to function on the international scene in legal proceedings of some description will not be too uncommon, while the power to make treaties will be less widespread. As to this the International Law Commission noted that 'agreements concluded between entities other than states or than international organisations seem too heterogeneous a group to constitute a general category, and the relevant body of international practice is as yet too exiguous for the characteristics of such a general category to be inferred from it'.[285] The extent to which subjects may be internationally responsible is also unclear, although in general such an entity will possess responsibility to the extent of its rights and duties; but many problem areas remain. Similarly controversial is the norm-creating role of such diverse entities, but the practice of all international persons is certainly relevant material upon which to draw in an elucidation of the rules and principles of international law, particularly in the context of the entity in question.

'International personality thus centres, not so much upon the capacity of the entity as such to possess international rights and duties, as upon the actual attribution of rights and/or duties on the international plane as determined by a variety of factors ranging from claims made to prescribed functions. Procedural capacity with regard to enforcement is important but not essential,[286] but in the case of non-individual entities the claimant will have

---

[284] See e.g. UKMIL, 49 BYIL, 1978, p. 340. Byelorussia and the Ukraine were separate members of the UN and parties to a number of conventions; *ibid.*

[285] *Yearbook of the ILC*, 1981, vol. II, pp. 125–6.

[286] See e.g. Norgaard, p. 35. See also the *Peter Pázmány University* case, PCIJ, Series A/B, No. 61 (1933); 7 ILR, p. 490.

to be in 'such a position that it possesses, in regard to its members, rights which it is entitled to ask them to respect'.[287] This, noted the International Court, expressed 'the essential test where a group, whether composed of states, of tribes or of individuals, is claimed to be a legal entity distinct from its members'.[288]

Finally, in examining the notion of international legal personality and the acquisition of the particular status of subject of international law, it cannot be overlooked that a wide variety of non-subjects exist and contribute to the evolution of the international system. Participation and personality are two concepts, but not to appreciate the general role played in the development of international relations and international law by individuals and entities of various kinds that are not international legal subjects as such (or acting beyond the limits of their particular legal capacity) would be an error.

[287] ICJ Reports, 1949, pp. 174, 178; 16 ILR, pp. 318, 321.
[288] ICJ Reports, 1975, pp. 12, 63; 59 ILR, pp. 14, 80.

CHAPTER 6

THE INTERNATIONAL PROTECTION OF HUMAN RIGHTS[1]

The nature of human rights

The preamble to the Universal Declaration of Human Rights adopted on 10 December 1948 emphasises that 'recognition of the inherent dignity and of the equal and inalienable rights of all members of the human family is the foundation of freedom, justice and peace in the world'. While there is widespread acceptance of the importance of human rights in the international structure, there is considerable confusion as to their precise nature and role in international law.[2] The question of what is meant by a 'right' is itself controversial and the subject of intense jurisprudential debate.[3] Some 'rights', for example, are intended as immediately enforceable binding commitments, others merely as specifying a possible future pattern of behaviour.[4] The problem of enforcement and sanctions with regard to human rights in international law is another issue which can affect the characterisation of the phe-

[1] See e.g. H. Lauterpacht, *International Law and Human Rights*, London, 1950; F. Newman and D. Weissbrodt, *International Human Rights*, Cincinnati, 2nd edn, 1996; M. S. McDougal, H. Lasswell and L. C. Chen, *Human Rights and World Public Order*, 1980; L. Sohn and T. Buergenthal, *International Protection of Human Rights*, 1973; P. Sieghart, *The International Law of Human Rights*, London, 1983; *The Human Rights Reader* (eds. W. Laqueur and B. Rubin), London, 1977; *Human Rights in International Law* (ed. T. Meron), 2 vols., Oxford, 1984; A. H. Robertson and J. G. Merrills, *Human Rights in the World*, 4th edn, Manchester, 1996; A. Cassese, *Human Rights in a Changing World*, London, 1990; *Human Rights in the 21st Century* (eds. K. E. Mahoney and P. Mahoney), Dordrecht, 1992; *Human Rights in the World Community* (eds. R. Claude and B. Weston), 2nd edn, Philadelphia, 1992; H. Hannum, *Guide to International Human Rights Practice*, 2nd edn, Philadelphia, 1992; S. Davidson, *Human Rights*, Buckingham, 1993; J. Donnelly, *International Human Rights*, 1993; *On Human Rights* (eds. S. Shute and S. Hurley), 1993; R. Higgins, *Problems and Process*, 1994, Oxford, Chapter 6; *Human Rights: An Agenda for the Next Century* (eds. L. Henkin and L. Hargrove), Washington, 1994 and H. Steiner and P. Alston, *International Human Rights in Context*, Oxford, 1996.
[2] See e.g. M. Moskowitz, *The Policies and Dynamics of Human Rights*, London, 1968, pp. 98–9 and McDougal *et al.*, *Human Rights*, pp. 63–8.
[3] See e.g. W. N. Hohfeld, 'Fundamental Legal Conceptions as Applied to Judicial Reasoning', 23 *Yale Law Journal*, 1913, p. 16 and R. Dworkin, *Taking Rights Seriously*, 1977. See also J. Shestack, 'The Jurisprudence of Human Rights' in Heron, *Human Rights in International Law*, vol. I, p. 69, and M. Cranston, *What Are Human Rights?*, London, 1973.
[4] Compare, for example, article 2 of the International Covenant on Civil and Political Rights 1966 with article 2 of the International Covenant on Economic, Social and Cultural Rights 1966.

nomenon. There are writers who regard the high incidence of non-compliance with human rights norms as evidence of state practice that argues against the existence of a structure of human rights principles in international law.[5] Although sight must not be lost of violations of human rights laws, such an approach is not only academically incorrect but also profoundly negative.[6] The concept of human rights is closely allied with ethics and morality. Those rights that reflect the values of a community will be those with the most chance of successful implementation. Of course, there is no necessary connection in particular instances, so that not all community values will be enshrined in law, nor will all legal rights reflect moral concerns, since many operate on a technical level as entitlements under specific conditions. However, this realisation does add to the uncertainty surrounding the definition of the nature and scope of rights. Positive rights may be taken to include those rights enshrined within a legal system, whether or not reflective of moral considerations, whereas a moral right does not necessarily exist as enforceable by law. One may easily discover positive rights. Deducing or inferring moral rights is another matter entirely and will depend upon the perception of the person seeking the existence of a particular right.[7] Rights may be seen as emanating from various sources, whether religious or the nature of man or the nature of society. The Natural Law view, as expressed in the traditional formulations of that approach or by virtue of the natural rights movement, is that certain rights exist as a result of a higher law than positive or man-made law. Such a higher law constitutes a universal and absolute set of principles governing all human beings in time and space. The natural rights approach of the seventeenth century, associated primarily with John Locke, founded the existence of such inalienable rights as the rights to life, liberty and property upon a social contract marking the end of the difficult conditions of the state of nature. This theory enabled recourse to be had to a superior type of law and thus was able to provide a powerful method of restraining arbitrary power.[8] Although this approach fell out of favour in the nineteenth century due to the problems of its non-empirical and diffuse methodology, it has proved of immense value this century in the establishment of human rights within the international community as universal

---

[5] See e.g. J. S. Watson, 'Legal Theory, Efficacy and Validity in the Development of Human Rights Norms in International Law', *University of Illinois Law Forum*, 1979, p. 609 and Watson, 'Autointerpretation, Competence and the Continuing Validity of Article 2(7) of the UN Charter', 71 AJIL, 1977, p. 60.

[6] See e.g. R. Higgins, 'Reality and Hope and International Human Rights: A Critique', 9 *Hofstra Law Review*, 1981, p. 1485.

[7] See M. Cranston, 'What are Human Rights?' in Lagner and Rubin, *The Human Rights Reader*, pp. 17, 19.

[8] See e.g. Lauterpacht; R. Tuck, *Natural Rights Theories*, 1979; J. Finnis, *Natural Law and Natural Rights*, 1980 and McDougal *et al.*, *Human Rights*, pp. 68–71. See also *supra*, Chapter 1.

principles. Positivism as a theory emphasised the authority of the state and as such left little place for rights in the legal system other than specific rights emanating from the constitutional structure of that system,[9] while the Marxist doctrine, although based upon the existence of certain immutable historical laws governing the development of society, nevertheless denied the existence of rights outside the framework of the legal order.[10] Modern rights theories cover a wide range of approaches, and this clearly emphasises the need to come to terms with the requirements of an evolving legal system that cannot be totally comprehended in terms of that system itself.[11]

Of particular interest is the work of the policy-oriented movement that seeks to identify, characterise and order a wide variety of relevant factors in the process of human rights creation and equipment. Eight interdependent values are noted (viz. demands relating to respect, power, enlightenment, well-being, health, skill, affection and rectitude) and various environmental influences stressed. Human dignity is seen as the key concept in relation to these values and to the ultimate goal of a world community in which a democratic distribution of values is sought.[12]

All these theories emphasise the complexity of the nature of the concept of human rights in the context of general legal and political processes, but also the importance and centrality of such notions. The broad issues are similarly raised within the framework of international law.

Ideological approaches to human rights in international law

The view adopted by the Western world with regard to international human rights law in general terms has tended to emphasise the basic civil and political rights of individuals, that is to say those rights that take the form of claims limiting the power of government over the governed. Such rights would include due process, freedom of expression, assembly and religion, and political participation in the process of government. The consent of the governed is seen as crucial in this process.[13] The approach of the Soviet Union was to note the importance of basic rights and freedoms for international peace and security, but to emphasise the role of the state. Indeed, the

---

[9] See e.g. D. Lloyd, *Introduction to Jurisprudence*, 4th edn, 1979, Chapter 4. See also H. Hart, *The Concept of Law*, 1960, and McDougal *et al.*, *Human Rights*, pp. 73–5 and *supra*, Chapters 1 and 2.

[10] See e.g. Lloyd, *Jurisprudence*, Chapter 10 and McDougal *et al.*, *Human Rights*, pp. 76–9. See also *infra*, p. 199.

[11] See e.g. J. Rawls, *A Theory of Justice*, Oxford, 1971; Cahn, *The Sense of Injustice*, 1949; R. Nozick, *Anarchy, State and Utopia*, Oxford, 1974 and Dworkin, *Taking Rights Seriously*. See also Davidson, *Human Rights*, Chapter 3.

[12] See McDougal *et al.*, *Human Rights*, especially pp. 82–93.

[13] See e.g. R. Hauser, 'A First World View', in *Human Rights and American Foreign Policy* (eds. D. P. Kommers and G. Loescher), Notre Dame, 1979, p. 85.

source of human rights principles was seen as the state. Tunkin wrote that the content of the principle of respect for human rights in international law may be expressed in three propositions:

(1) all states have a duty to respect the fundamental rights and freedoms of all persons within their territories; (2) states have a duty not to permit discrimination by reason of sex, race, religion or language; and (3) states have a duty to promote universal respect for human rights and to co-operate with each other to achieve this objective.[14]

In other words, the focus was not upon the individual (as in Western conceptions of human rights) but solely upon the state. Human rights were not directly regulated by international law and individuals were not subjects of international law. Indeed, human rights were implemented by the state and matters basically and crucially within the domestic affairs of state. As Tunkin emphasised, 'conventions on human rights do not grant rights directly to individuals'.[15] Having stressed the central function of the state, the point was also made that the context of the international human rights obligations themselves was defined solely by the state in the light of the socio-economic advancement of that state. Accordingly, the nature and context of those rights would vary from state to state, depending upon the social system of the state in question. It was the particular socio-economic system of a state that would determine the concrete expression of an international human rights provision.[16] In other words, the Soviet Union was able and willing to enter into many international agreements on human rights, on the basis that only a state obligation was incurred, with no direct link to the individual, and that such an obligation was one that the country might interpret in the light of its own socio-economic system. The supremacy or centrality of the state was the key in this approach. As far as the different kinds of human rights were concerned, the Soviet approach was to stress those dealing with economic and social matters and thus to minimise the importance of the traditional civil and political rights. However, a new approach to the question of international human rights began to emerge by the end of the 1980s. Vershchetin and Müllerson wrote that human rights activity was one of the most important components of a comprehensive system of international security and that the role of the individual was 'primary'.[17] In particular, it was stated that:

[14] G. Tunkin, *Theory of International Law*, London, 1974, p. 81. See also K. Tedin, 'The Development of the Soviet Attitude Towards Implementing Human Rights under the UN Charter', 5 HRJ, 1972, p. 399; Dean, 'Beyond Helsinki: The Soviet View of Human Rights in International Law', 21 Va JIL, 1980, p. 55 and P. Reddaway, 'Theory and Practice of Human Rights in the Soviet Union' in Kommers and Loescher, *Human Rights and American Foreign Policy*, p. 115.   [15] Tunkin, *Theory*, p. 83.   [16] *Ibid.*, pp. 82–3.
[17] V. Vereshchetin and R. Müllerson, 'International Law in an Interdependent World', 28 *Columbia Journal of Transnational Law*, 1990, pp. 291, 300.

Soviet legal scholarship has always emphasised that international human rights treaties obligate signatories to ensure the applicable rights and freedoms. However, until now, Soviet scholars have unjustifiably advocated that these documents do not represent rights directly enforceable by the individual. This approach has been excessively legalistic. A citizen of a state based on the rule of law has the right to demand that state agencies observe voluntarily adopted international obligations which directly affect the individual's interests. Human rights treaties establish state obligations to citizens, not just to other state parties to the international agreements.[18]

The general approach of the Third World states has combined elements of both the previous perceptions.[19] Concern with the equality and sovereignty of states, together with a recognition of the importance of social and economic rights has characterised the Third World view. Such countries, in fact constituting a wide range of nations with differing interests and needs, and at different stages of development, have been much influenced by decolonisation and the struggle to obtain it and by the phenomenon of apartheid in South Africa. In addition, economic problems have played a large role in focusing their attention upon general developmental issues. Accordingly, the traditional civil and political rights have tended to lose their priority in the concerns of Third World states.[20]

The development of international human rights law[21]

In the nineteenth century, the positivist doctrines of state sovereignty and domestic jurisdiction reigned supreme. Very few issues were regarded as of international concern as such. Virtually all matters that today would be classified as human rights issues were at that stage universally regarded as within the internal sphere of national jurisdiction. The major exceptions to this were related to piracy *jure gentium* and slavery. In the

---

[18] *Ibid.* Note that on 10 February 1989, the USSR recognised the compulsory jurisdiction of the International Court of Justice with regard to six human rights treaties, including the Genocide Convention 1948; the Racial Discrimination Convention 1965; the Convention on Discrimination against Women 1979 and the Torture Convention 1984.

[19] See e.g. R. Emerson, 'The Fate of Human Rights in the Third World', 27 *World Politics*, 1975, p. 201; G. Mower, 'Human Rights in Black Africa', 9 HRJ, 1976, p. 33; R. Zvobgo, 'A Third World View' in Kommers and Loescher, *Human Rights and American Foreign Policy*, p. 90 and M. Nawaz, 'The Concept of Human Rights in Islamic Law' in Symposium on International Law of Human Rights, 11 *Howard Law Journal*, 1965, p. 257.

[20] See generally T. Van Boven, 'Some Remarks on Special Problems Relating to Human Rights in Developing Countries', *Revue des Droits de l'Homme*, 1970, p. 383. See further *infra*, p. 293 on the Banjul Charter on Human and Peoples' Rights.

[21] See e.g. *The International Protection of Human Rights* (ed. E.Luard), London, 1967; Sohn and Buergenthal, *International Protection*; Lauterpacht, *International Law*; M. Moscowitz, *International Concern with Human Rights*, London, 1968 and M. Ganji, *The International Protection of Human Rights*, London, 1962.

latter case a number of treaties were entered into to bring about its abolition.[22] Concern also with the treatment of sick and wounded soldiers and with prisoners of war developed as from 1864 in terms of international instruments,[23] while states were required to observe certain minimum standards in the treatment of aliens.[24] In addition, certain agreements of a general welfare nature were beginning to be adopted by the turn of the century.[25] The nineteenth century also appeared to accept a right of humanitarian intervention, although its range and extent were unclear.[26]

An important change occurred with the establishment of the League of Nations in 1919.[27] Article 22 of the Covenant of the League set up the mandates system for peoples in ex-enemy colonies 'not yet able to stand by themselves in the strenuous conditions of the modern world'. The mandatory power was obliged to guarantee freedom of conscience and religion and a Permanent Mandates Commission was created to examine the reports the mandatory authorities had undertaken to make. The arrangement was termed 'a sacred trust of civilisation'. Article 23 of the Covenant provided for just treatment of the native populations of the territories in question.[28] The 1919 peace agreements with Eastern European and Balkan states included provisions relating to the protection of minorities, [29] providing essentially for equality of treatment and opportunities for collective activity.[30] These provisions were supervised by the League of Nations, to whom there was a right of petition.[31]

Part XIII of the Treaty of Versailles provided for the creation of the International Labour Organisation, among the purposes of which were the promotion of better standards of working conditions and support for the right of association.[32] The impact of the Second World War upon the

---

[22] See e.g. C. Greenidge, *Slavery*, London, 1958 and V. Nanda and M.C. Bassiouni, 'Slavery and the Slave Trade: Steps towards Eradication', 12 *Santa Clara Law Review*, 1972, p. 424. See also ST/SOA/4.

[23] See generally G. Best, *War and Law Since 1945*, Oxford, 1994 and *Studies and Essays on International Humanitarian Law and Red Cross Principles* (ed. C. Swinarski), The Hague, 1984. [24] See *infra*, Chapter 13.

[25] E.g. regarding the Prohibition of Night Work for Women in Industrial Employment and regarding the Prohibition of the Use of White Phosphorus in the Manufacture of Matches.

[26] See *infra*, Chapter 19, p. 802. [27] See *infra*, Chapter 21.

[28] See *supra*, Chapter 5, p. 160.

[29] See generally, P. Thornberry, 'Is There a Phoenix in the Ashes? – International Law and Minority Rights', 15 *Texas International Law Journal*, 1980, p. 421; C. A. Macartney, *National States and National Minorities*, London, 1934 and I. Claude, *National Minorities: An International Problem*, Cambridge, 1955. See also M. N. Shaw, 'The Definition of Minorities in International Law' in *Protection of Minorities and Human Rights* (eds. Y. Dinstein and M. Tabory), Dordrecht, 1992, p. 1,

[30] See e.g. the *Minority Schools in Albania* case, PCIJ, Series A/B, 1935, No. 64, p. 17.

[31] See Thornberry, 'Phoenix', pp. 433–54, and Jones, 'National Minorities: A Case Study in International Protection', 14 *Law and Contemporary Problems*, 1949, pp. 599, 610–24. See further *infra* p. 218. [32] See further *infra*, p. 249.

development of human rights law was immense as the horrors of the war and the need for an adequate international system to maintain international peace and protect human rights became apparent to all.

Some basic principles

Domestic jurisdiction[33]

The basic rule of international law providing that states have no right to encroach upon the preserve of other states' internal affairs is a consequence of the equality and sovereignty of states and is mirrored in article 2(7) of the UN Charter. It has, however, been subject to a process of reinterpretation in the human rights field[34] as this and the succeeding chapter will make apparent, so that states may no longer plead this rule as a bar to international concern and consideration of internal human rights situations.[35] It is, of course, obvious that where a state accepts the right of individual petition under an international procedure, it cannot thereafter claim that the exercise of such a right constitutes interference with its domestic affairs.[36]

The exhaustion of local remedies rule[37]

This rule flows from the above principle. It is a method of permitting states to solve their own internal problems in accordance with their own constitutional procedures before accepted international mechanisms can be invoked, and is well established in general international law.[38] However, where such internal remedies are non-existent or unduly and unreasonably prolonged or unlikely to bring effective relief, the resort to international

---

[33] See e.g. R. Higgins, *The Development of International Law Through the Political Organs of the United Nations*, Oxford, 1963; M. Rajan, *United Nations and Domestic Jurisprudence*, 2nd edn, 1961 and A. Cançado Trindade, 'The Domestic Jurisprudence of States in the Practice of the United Nations and Regional Organisations', 25 ICLQ, 1976, p. 715.

[34] Note that the question of the extent and content of domestic jurisdiction is a matter for international law, see *Nationality Decrees in Tunis and Morocco* cases, PCIJ, Series B, No. 4, 1923; 2 ILR, p. 349. See also *infra*, Chapter 12.

[35] See also the resolution of the Institut de Droit International, 1989, H/Inf (90) 1, p. 131.

[36] See e.g. *Miha v. Equatorial Guinea*, CCPR/C/51/D/414/1990, 10 August 1994, Human Rights Committee, para. 63.

[37] See e.g. A. Cançado Trindade, *The Application of the Rule of Exhaustion of Local Remedies in International Law*, Cambridge, 1983; C. Law, *The Local Remedies Rule in International Law*, 1961 and C. F. Amerasinghe, *Local Remedies in International Law*, Cambridge, 1990. See also C. F. Amerasinghe, 'The Rule of Exhaustion of Local Remedies and the International Protection of Human Rights', 17 *Indian Yearbook of International Affairs*, 1974, p. 3. See also *infra*, Chapter 14, p. 567.

[38] See e.g. the *Ambatielos* case, 23 ILR, p. 306; the *Finnish Ships* case, 3 RIAA, p. 1479 and the *Interhandel* case, ICJ Reports, 1959, pp. 26–7; 27 ILR, pp. 475, 490.

measures will not be required.[39] The existence of such a remedy must be certain not only in theory but also in practice.[40] A provision regarding the need to exhaust domestic remedies before the various international mechanisms may be resorted to appears in all the international and regional human rights instruments[41] and has been the subject of much consideration by the Human Rights Committee under the Optional Protocol procedure of the International Covenant on Civil and Political Rights,[42] and within the European Convention[43] and Inter-American Convention human rights systems.[44]

Priorities of rights

Certain rights may not be derogated from in the various human rights instruments even in times of war or other public emergency threatening the nation. In the case of the European Convention[45] these are the rights

---

[39] See e.g. the *Robert E. Brown* case, 6 RIAA, pp. 120; 2 ILR, p. 66. See also the *Salem* case, 2 RIAA, p. 1161; 6 ILR, p. 188 and the *Nielsen* case, 2 *Yearbook of the ECHR*, p. 413; 28 ILR, p. 210 and the *Second Cyprus* case (Greece v. UK), 2 *Yearbook of the ECHR*, p. 186. See also the cases cited in the succeeding footnotes.

[40] See e.g. *Johnston v. Ireland*, European Court of Human Rights, Series A, No. 112 (1986) and *Open Door and Dublin Well Woman v. Ireland*, European Court of Human Rights, Series A, No. 246 (1992).

[41] See e.g. article 41(c), Civil and Political Rights Covenant and article 2, Optional Protocol; article 11(3), Racial Discrimination Convention; article 26, European Convention; article 50, American Convention and article 50, Banjul Charter. See also ECOSOC resolution 1503 and UNESCO decision 104 EX/3.3, 1978, para. 14(IX).

[42] See e.g. the *Weinberger* case, Reports of the Human Rights Committee, A/36/40, p. 114 and A/44/40, p. 142 and the *Sara* case, A/49/40, Annex X, Section C, para. 8.3. States are required to provide evidence that there would be a reasonable prospect that available remedies would be effective, *Torres Ramirez v. Uruguay*, *Selected Decisions under the Optional Protocol*, CCPR/C/OP/1, 1985, p. 3. See also e.g. *Baboeram-Adhin v. Suriname*, A/40/40, p. 187: 94 ILR, p. 377; *Muhonen v. Finland*, A/40/40, p. 164: 94 ILR, p. 389 and *Solórzano v Venezuela*, A/41/40, p. 134: 94 ILR, p. 400. See also with regard to the UN Convention against Torture, *AE v. Switzerland*, CAT/C/14/D/24/1995.

[43] See as to the position under the European Convention on Human Rights, e.g. the *Nielsen* case; the *Second Cyprus* case (Greece v. UK), 2 *Yearbook of the ECHR*, p. 186; the *Donnelly* case, 16 *Yearbook of the ECHR*, p. 212; *Kjeldsen v. Denmark*, 15 *Yearbook of the ECHR*, p. 428; 58 ILR, p. 117; *Drozd and Janousek v. France and Spain*, 64 DR 97 (1989). See also D. J. Harris, M. O'Boyle and C. Warbrick, *Law of the European Convention on Human Rights*, London, 1995, p. 608; P. Van Dijk and G.Van Hoof, *Theory and Practice of the European Convention on Human Rights*, 2nd edn, Deventer, 1990, p. 81. The rule of exhaustion of domestic remedies applies also in inter-state cases, see *Cyprus v. Turkey*, 2 DR 125 at 137–8 (first and second applications) and 13 DR 85, 150–3 (third application), although not with regard to legislative measures nor with regard to administrative actions in certain circumstances, see e.g. the *Greek* case, 12 *European Yearbook of Human Rights*, p. 196.

[44] See e.g. article 46(1) a of the Inter-American Convention on Human Rights 1969 and article 37 of the Regulations of the Inter-American Commission on Human Rights. See also *Exceptions to the Exhaustion of Domestic Remedies in Cases of Indigency*, Advisory Opinion of the Inter-American Court of Human Rights, 1990, 12 HRLJ, 1991, p. 20 and *Annual Report of the Inter-American Commission on Human Rights 1993*, Washington, 1994, pp. 148, 185 and 266.

[45] Article 15. See generally, R. Higgins, 'Derogations Under Human Rights Treaties', 48 BYIL, 1976–7, p. 281.

to life (except in cases resulting from lawful acts of war), the prohibition on torture and slavery, and non-retroactivity of criminal offences.[46] In the case of the American Convention,[47] the following rights are non-derogable: the rights to judicial personality, life and humane treatment, freedom from slavery, freedom from *ex post facto* laws, freedom of conscience and religion, rights of the family, to a name, of the child, nationality and participation in government.[48] By article 4 of the International Covenant on Civil and Political Rights, the rights to life and recognition as a person before the law, the freedoms of thought, conscience and religion and the prohibition on torture, slavery, retroactivity of criminal legislation and imprisonment on grounds solely of inability to fulfil a contractual obligation are non-derogable.[49]

Such non-derogable rights clearly are regarded as possessing a special place in the hierarchy of rights.[50] In addition, it must be noted, many rights are subject to a limitation or clawback clause, whereby the absolute right provided for will not operate in certain situations.[51] Those rights therefore that are not so limited may be regarded as of particular value.[52]

Customary international law and human rights

In addition to the many international and regional treaty provisions concerning human rights to be noted in this and chapter 7,[53] certain human rights may now be regarded as having entered into the category of customary international law in the light of state practice. These would certainly include the prohibition of torture, genocide and slavery and the principle of non-discrimination.[54] In addition, human rights established under treaty may constitute obligations *erga omnes* for the states parties.[55]

---

[46] Articles 2, 3, 4(1) and 7.   [47] Article 27.

[48] Articles 3, 4, 5, 6, 9, 12, 17, 18, 19, 20 and 23.

[49] Articles 6, 7, 8(1) and (2), 11, 15, 16 and 18. Note that the Banjul Charter contains no specific derogations clause.

[50] The fact that a right may not be derogated from may constitute evidence that the right concerned is part of *jus cogens*.

[51] See e.g. articles 8–11 of the European Convention; articles 12–14, 15–16 and 21–22 of the American Convention and articles 12, 18, 19, 21 and 22 of the Civil and Political Rights Covenant. See also Higgins, 'Derogations'.   [52] See e.g. the due process rights.

[53] Note that questions relating to the interpretation of and reservations to human rights treaties will be noted in Chapter 16, *infra* pp. 647, while the issue of succession to human rights treaties will be noted in Chapter 17, *infra* p. 695.

[54] See e.g. *Third Restatement of US Foreign Relations Law*, St Paul, 1987, vol. II, pp. 161 *et seq.* and *Filartiga* v. *Pena-Irala*, 630 F.2d 876. See also T. Meron, *Human Rights and Humanitarian Norms as Customary Law*, Oxford, 1989 and the articles published in the Special Issue on Customary International Human Rights Law, 25 *Georgia Journal of International and Comparative Law*, 1995–6.   [55] See *infra* Chapter 14, p. 545.

The United Nations system – general[56]

There are a number of human rights provisions in the Charter.[57] Article 1 includes in the purposes of the organisation the promotion and encouragement of respect for human rights and fundamental freedoms for all without distinction as to race, sex, language or religion. Article 13(1) notes that the General Assembly shall initiate studies and make recommendations regarding the realisation of human rights for all, while article 55 provides that the United Nations shall promote universal respect for and observance of human rights. In a significant provision, article 56 states that:

> all members pledge themselves to take joint and separate action in co-operation with the organisation for the achievement of the purposes set forth in article 55.[58]

The mandate system was replaced by the trusteeship system, one of the basic objectives of which was, by article 76, the encouragement of respect for human rights, while, with regard to non-self-governing territories, the administering powers under article 73 of the Charter recognised the principle that the interests of the inhabitants were paramount, and accepted as a sacred trust the obligation to promote the well-being of the inhabitants. It can thus be seen that the Charter provisions on human rights were very general and vague. No enforcement procedures were laid down. Some have argued that the term 'pledge' in article 56 had the effect of converting the enumerated purposes of article 55 into legal obligations,[59] but this has been disputed.[60] Certainly, as of 1946, this would have been a difficult proposition to sustain, particularly in view of the hortatory language used in the provisions and the fact that the respect for human rights stipulation does not identify precise legal rights.[61] However, in the *Namibia* case of 1971, the Court noted that under the UN Charter:

[56] See generally D. W. Bowett, *The Law of International Institutions*, 4th edn, Manchester, 1982; Lauterpacht, *International Law*, pp. 145–220; *UN Action in the Field of Human Rights*, 1981; and *Human Rights: Thirty Years after the Universal Declaration* (ed. B. Ramcharan), Dordrecht, 1979.

[57] Largely as a result of lobbying by non-governmental organisations at the San Francisco Conference: see J. Humphrey, 'The United Nations Charter and the Universal Declaration of Human Rights' in *The International Protection of Human Rights* (ed. E. Luard), Oxford, Chapter 3.

[58] Under article 62, the Economic and Social Council has the power to make recommendations for the purpose of promoting respect for and observance of human rights.

[59] See e.g. Lauterpacht, *International Law*, pp. 47–9; Q. Wright, 'National Courts and Human Rights – the *Fujii* case', 45 AJIL, 1951, p. 73 and B. Sloan, 'Human Rights, the United Nations and International Law', 20 *Nordisk Tidsskrift for International Ret*, 1950, pp. 30–1. See also Judge Tanaka, *South West Africa* cases, ICJ Reports, 1966, pp. 6, 288–9; 37 ILR, pp. 243, 451–2.

[60] See M. O. Hudson, 'Integrity of International Instruments', 42 AJIL, 1948, pp. 105–8 and *Yearbook of the ILC*, 1949, p. 178. See also H. Kelsen, *The Law of the United Nations*, London, 1950, p. 29.

[61] See D. Driscoll, 'The Development of Human Rights in International Law' in Laqueur and Rubin, *The Human Rights Reader*, pp. 41, 43.

the former Mandatory had pledged itself to observe and respect, in a territory having international status, human rights and fundamental freedoms for all without distinction as to race. To establish instead and to enforce, distinctions, exclusions, restrictions and limitations, exclusively based on grounds of race, colour, descent or national or ethnic origin which constitute a denial of fundamental human rights is a flagrant violation of the purposes and principles of the Charter.[62]

It may be that this provision can only be understood in the light of the special, international status of that territory, but in the light of extensive practice since the 1940s in the general area of non-discrimination and human rights, the broader interpretation is to be preferred.

The Charter does contain a domestic jurisdiction provision. Article 2(7) provides that:

nothing contained in the present Charter shall authorise the United Nations to intervene in matters which are essentially within the domestic jurisdiction of any state

but as noted later[63] this has over the years been flexibly interpreted, so that human rights issues are no longer recognised as being solely within the domestic jurisdiction of states.

The elucidation, development and protection of human rights through the UN has proved to be a seminal event. A range of declarations and treaties has emerged coupled with the establishment of a variety of advisory services and implementation and enforcement mechanisms. Large numbers of studies and reports of various kinds have appeared, while the whole process has been accompanied by extensive debate and consideration in a variety of UN organs and committees. Notwithstanding a certain degree of cynicism, it can be concluded that the acceptance of the centrality of human rights concerns within the international community has been due in no small measure to the unceasing consideration of human rights issues within the framework of the United Nations.

The cornerstone of UN activity has been without doubt the Universal Declaration of Human Rights adopted by the UN General Assembly on 10 December 1948.[64] The Declaration was approved without a dissenting vote

---

[62] ICJ Reports, 1971, pp. 16, 57; 49 ILR, pp. 3, 47. See also I. Brownlie, *Principles of Public International Law*, 4th edn, Oxford, 1990, p. 569; E. Schwelb, 'The International Court of Justice and the Human Rights Clauses of the Charter', 66 AJIL, 1972, p. 337 and O. Schachter, 'The Charter and the Constitution', 4 *Vanderbilt Law Review*, 1951, p. 443.

[63] *Infra*, p. 454.

[64] See e.g. *Oppenheim's International Law* (eds. R. Y. Jennings and A. D. Watts), 9th edn, London, 1992, p. 1001; M. Whiteman, *Digest of International Law*, Washington, vol. V, p. 237; J. Humphrey, 'The Universal Declaration on Human Rights' in *Human Rights: Thirty Years after the Universal Declaration*, p. 21; J. Kunz, 'The United Nations Declaration of Human Rights', 43 AJIL, 1949, p. 316; E. Schwelb, 'The Influence of the Universal Declaration of Human Rights on International and National Law', PASIL, 1959, p. 217; A.

(Byelorussian SSR, Czechoslovakia, Poland, Ukrainian SSR, USSR, Yugoslavia and Saudi Arabia abstained). It was intended not as a legally binding document as such but, as its preamble proclaims, 'a common standard of achievement for all peoples and nations'. Its thirty articles cover a wide range of rights, from liberty and security of the person (article 3), equality before the law (article 7), effective remedies (article 8), due process (articles 9 and 10), prohibitions on torture (article 5) and arbitrary interference with privacy (article 12) to rights protecting freedom of movement (article 13), asylum (article 14), expression (article 19), conscience and religion (article 18) and assembly (article 20). One should also note that included in the Declaration are social and economic rights such as the right to work and equal pay (article 23), the right to social security (article 25) and the right to education (article 26).

Although clearly not a legally enforceable instrument as such, the question arises as to whether the Declaration has subsequently become binding either by way of custom[65] or general principles of law, or indeed by virtue of interpretation of the UN Charter itself by subsequent practice.[66] The Declaration has had a marked influence upon the constitutions of many states and upon the formulation of subsequent human rights treaties and resolutions.[67] It is also to be noted that in 1968, the Proclamation of Tehran at the conclusion of the UN sponsored International Conference on Human Rights stressed that the Declaration constituted 'an obligation for members of the international community'.[68] The Declaration has also been referred to in many cases,[69] and its importance within the context of United Nations human rights law should not be disregarded.[70] The intention had been that

Verdoodt, *Naissance et Signification de la Déclaration Universelle de Droits de l'Homme*, Paris, 1964 and *The Universal Declaration of Human Rights: A Commentary* (eds. A. Eide, G. Alfredsson, G. Melander, L. A. Rehof and A. Rosas), Dordrecht, 1992.

[65] Note that the Foreign and Commonwealth Office in a document issued in January 1991 on 'Human Rights in Foreign Policy' took the view that although the Declaration was 'not in itself legally binding, much of its content can now be said to form part of customary international law', UKMIL, 62 BYIL, 1991, p. 592.

[66] See e.g. *Oppenheim's International Law*, p. 1002.

[67] See e.g. E. Schwelb, 'Influence'; J. Humphrey, 'The International Bill of Rights: Scope and Implementation', 17 *William and Mary Law Review*, 1975, p. 527; *Oppenheim's International Law*, pp. 1002–5; Judge Tanaka, *South West Africa* cases, ICJ Reports, 1966, pp. 6, 288 and 293; 37 ILR, pp. 243, 451, 454 and the European Convention on Human Rights, 1950, *infra*, Chapter 7, p. 257.

[68] 23 GAOR, A/Conf. 32/41. See also the non-governmental Montreal Statement, 9 *Review of the International Commission of Jurists*, 1968, p. 94.

[69] See e.g. *In re Flesche*, 16 ILR, pp. 266, 269; *The State (Duggan)* v. *Tapley*, 18 ILR, pp. 336, 342; *Robinson* v. *Secretary-General of the UN*, 19 ILR, pp. 494, 496; *Extradition of Greek National* case, 22 ILR, pp. 520, 524 and *Beth El Mission* v. *Minister of Social Welfare*, 47 ILR, pp. 205, 207. See also *Corfu Channel* case, ICJ Reports, 1949, pp. 4, 22; 16 ILR, pp. 155, 158 and *Filartiga* v. *Pena-Irala*, 630, F.2d 876 (1980).

[70] The Vienna Declaration and Programme of Action adopted on 25 June 1993 at the UN Conference on Human Rights referred to the Declaration as the 'source of inspiration' and the 'basis for the United Nations in making advances in standard setting as contained in the

the Declaration would be followed immediately by a binding universal convention on human rights, but this process took considerably longer than anticipated. In the meantime, a number of important international conventions dealing with selective human rights issues were adopted, including the Genocide Convention[71] and the Convention on the Elimination of Racial Discrimination.[72]

The issue of human rights was extensively discussed at the UN World Conference on Human Rights at Vienna in 1993. The Vienna Declaration and Programme of Action, which was adopted, emphasised that all human rights were universal, indivisible and interdependent and interrelated. The protection of human rights was seen as a priority objective of the UN and the interrelationship of democracy, development and respect for human rights and fundamental freedoms underlined. Additional facilities for the UN Centre for Human Rights were called for as well as the establishment of a UN High Commissioner for Human Rights. The Declaration made particular reference *inter alia* to the problems of racial discrimination, minorities, indigenous peoples, migrant workers, the rights of women, the rights of the child, freedom from torture, the rights of disabled persons and human rights education.[73] The post of UN High Commissioner for Human Rights was indeed established several months later[74] and filled in April 1994. In General Assembly resolution 48/141, it is provided that the UN High Commissioner for Human Rights would be the UN official with principal responsibility for UN human rights activities. The High Commissioner is responsible for promoting and protecting the effective enjoyment by all of all civil, cultural, economic, political and social rights, providing through the UN Centre for Human Rights and other appropriate institutions, advisory services and other assistance including education and engaging in dialogue with all governments with a view to securing respect for human rights. The High Commissioner may also make recommendations to competent bodies of the UN system with a view to improving the promotion and protection of all human rights.[75] He has engaged in a series of visits to member states of the UN and has become involved in co-ordination activities.[76]

existing international human rights instruments', 32 ILM, 1993, pp. 1661, 1663. The private International Law Association adopted a resolution in 1994 in which it noted that 'the Universal Declaration of Human Rights is universally regarded as an authoritative elaboration of the human rights provisions of the United Nations Charter' and that 'many if not all of the rights elaborated in the Universal Declaration of Human Rights are widely recognised as constituting rules of customary international law', Report of the Sixty-sixth Conference, Buenos Aires, 1994, p. 29.   [71] See *infra* p. 209.
[72] See further *infra* p. 212.   [73] See 32 ILM, 1993, pp. 1661 *et seq.*
[74] See General Assembly resolution 48/141, 20 December 1993. See also A. Clapham, 'Creating the High Commissioner for Human Rights: The Outside Story', 5 EJIL, 1994, p. 556.
[75] See the first Report of the United Nations High Commissioner for Human Rights, 1995, A/49/36, p. 2.   [76] *Ibid.*, pp. 3 *et seq.*

The protection of the collective rights of groups and individuals[77]

International law since 1945 has focused primarily upon the protection of individual human rights, as can be seen from a perusal of the rights contained in the Universal Declaration of Human Rights. In recent years, however, more attention has been given to various expressions of the concept of collective rights, although it is often difficult to maintain a strict differentiation between individual and collective rights. Some rights are purely individual, such as the right to life or freedom of expression, others are individual rights that are necessarily expressed collectively, such as freedom of assembly or the right to manifest one's own religion. Some rights are purely collective, such as the right to self-determination or the physical protection of the group as such through the prohibition of genocide, others constitute collective manifestations of individual rights, such as the right of persons belonging to minorities to enjoy their own culture and practice their own religion or use their own language. In addition, the question of the balancing of the legitimate rights of the state, groups and individuals is in practice crucial and sometimes not sufficiently considered. States, groups and individuals have legitimate rights and interests that should not be ignored. All within a state have an interest in ensuring the efficient functioning of that state in a manner consistent with respect for the rights of groups and individuals, while the balancing of the rights of groups and individuals may itself prove difficult and complex.

Prohibition of genocide

The physical protection of the group as a distinct identity is clearly the first and paramount factor. The Convention on the Prevention and Punishment of the Crime of Genocide signed in 1948,[78] reaffirmed that genocide, whether committed in time of war or peace, was a crime under international

---

[77] See e.g. D. Sanders, 'Collective Rights', 13 *Human Rights Quarterly*, 1991, p. 368 and N. Lerner, *Group Rights and Discrimination*, Dordrecht, 1990.

[78] See e.g. N. Robinson, *The Genocide Convention*, London, 1960; R. Lemkin, *Axis Rule in Occupied Europe*, London, 1944; L. Kuper, *Genocide*, Harmondsworth, 1981 and *International Action Against Genocide*, Minority Rights Group Report no. 53, 1984; *Genocide and Human Rights* (ed. J. Porter), Washington, 1982 and I. Horowitz, *Taking Lives: Genocide and State Power*, New Brunswick, 1980. See also N. Ruhashyankiko, *Study on the Question of the Prevention and Punishment of the Crime of Genocide*, 1978, E/CN.4/Sub.2/416; B. Whittaker, *Revised and Updated Report on the Question of the Prevention and Punishment of the Crime of Genocide*, 1985, E/CN.4/Sub.2/1985/6; *Contemporary Practice of the United States Relating to International Law*, 79 AJIL, 1985, pp. 116 *et seq.*; M. N. Shaw, 'Genocide and International Law' in *International Law at a Time of Perplexity* (ed. Y. Dinstein), Dordrecht, 1989, p. 797 and Payam Akavan, 'Enforcement of the Genocide Convention through the Advisory Opinion Jurisdiction of the ICJ', 12 HRLJ, 1991, p. 285. As of early 1997, there were 123 ratifications to this Convention; ST/HR/4/Rev.12, 1995.

law. Genocide was defined as any of the following acts committed 'with intent to destroy, in whole or in part, a national, ethnical, racial or religious group as such':

> (a) killing members of the group; (b) causing serious bodily or mental harm to members of the group; (c) deliberately inflicting on the group conditions of life calculated to bring about its physical destruction in whole or in part; (d) imposing measures intended to prevent births within the group; (e) forcibly transferring children of the group to another group.

The Convention, which does not have an implementational system,[79] provides that persons charged with genocide shall be tried by a competent tribunal of the state in the territory of which the act was committed or by an international penal tribunal. Several points should be noted. First, the question of intent is such that states may deny genocidal activity by noting that the relevant intent to destroy in whole or in part was in fact absent.[80] Secondly, the groups protected do not include political groups.[81] Thirdly, the concept of cultural genocide is not included[82] and fourthly there is virtually no mention of means to prevent the crime.

The issue of genocide has, unfortunately, in the 1990s ceased to be an item of primarily historical concern. Events in the former Yugoslavia and in Rwanda have stimulated increasing anxiety in this context. The Statutes of both the International Tribunal for the Former Yugoslavia[83] and the International Tribunal for Rwanda,[84] established to deal with international crimes committed by individuals within defined geographic and chronological jurisdictional limits, have provided for the prosecution of individuals for the crime of genocide.[85]

---

[79] Note that Sub-Commission resolution 1994/11 recommended that the Commission on Human Rights request the General Assembly to consider with high priority with a view to its adoption, the draft statute for an international criminal court submitted by the International Law Committee. The resolution also suggested that states parties to the Genocide Convention should consider the drafting and adoption of a control mechanism in the form of a treaty committee charged in particular with monitoring compliance of states parties with the commitments undertaken under this Convention through the assessment of states' reports. The question of including a universal jurisdiction clause was raised as was the possibility of extending the application of the Convention to cover genocide of political groups.

[80] See Kuper, *Genocide*, pp. 32–5 and Lewis, 'The Camp at Cecilio Baez', in *Genocide in Paraguay* (ed. R. Arens), Philadelphia, 1976, p. 58. See also Ruhashyankiko, *Genocide*, p. 25.

[81] See e.g. Kuper, *Genocide*, footnote 47, pp. 25–30 and Ruhashyankiko, *Genocide*, p. 21. See also Robinson, *Genocide Convention*, p. 59.

[82] See e.g. Kuper, *Genocide*, footnote 47, p. 31; Robinson, *Genocide Convention*, p. 64 and Ruhashyankiko, *Genocide*, pp. 21 *et seq.*   [83] Article 4, see *supra* Chapter 5, p. 188.

[84] Article 2, see *supra*, Chapter 5, p. 189.

[85] See, for example, the indictments against Bosnian Serb leaders (Karadzic and Mladic) alleging *inter alia* genocide, see *Bulletin of the International Criminal Tribunal for the Former Yugoslavia*, 1995, p. 4 and IT-95–18–I. See also article 22(a) of the Draft Statute for an International Criminal Court produced by the International Law Commission in 1994, *supra*, Chapter 5, p. 187.

The question of state responsibility for the crime of genocide has also been raised. Article 19 of the International Law Commission Draft Articles on State Responsibility,[86] in particular, provides that an international crime for which a state may be liable may result from 'a serious breach on a widespread scale of an international obligation of essential importance for safeguarding the human being, such as those prohibiting . . . genocide . . .'.[87] The issue has come before the International Court of Justice in the *Case Concerning Application of the Convention on the Prevention and Punishment of the Crime of Genocide (Bosnia and Herzegovina v. Yugoslavia (Serbia and Montenegro))*.[88] In this case, Bosnia has alleged *inter alia* breaches of the Genocide Convention for which Yugoslavia (Serbia and Montenegro) is responsible. The Court in its Order of 8 April 1993 on the Request for the Indication of Provisional Measures[89] held that article IX of the Convention[90] provided a valid jurisdictional basis,[91] while reaffirming[92] the view expressed in the Advisory Opinion on *Reservations to the Genocide Convention*[93] that the crime of genocide 'shocks the conscience of mankind, results in great losses to humanity . . . and is contrary to moral law and to the spirit and aims of the United Nations'. The Court called upon both parties not to take any action that may aggravate or extend the dispute over the prevention or punishment of the crime of genocide. The government of Yugoslavia (Serbia and Montenegro) was requested to take all measures within its power to prevent commission of the crime of genocide, and was specifically called upon to ensure that 'any military, paramilitary or irregular armed units which may be directed or supported by it, as well as any organisations and persons which may be subject to its control, direction or influence, do not commit any acts of genocide'.[94] These provisional measures were reaffirmed by the Court in its Order on Provisional Measures of 13 September 1993 as measures which should be 'immediately and effectively implemented'.[95]

---

[86] See *Yearbook of the ILC*, 1980, vol. II, Part 2, pp. 30 *et seq.*
[87] See further *infra*, Chapter 14, p. 544.
[88] ICJ Reports, 1993, pp. 3 and 325; 95 ILR, pp. 1 and 43.
[89] ICJ Reports, 1993, pp. 3, 16; 95 ILR, pp. 1, 31. See also R. Maison, 'Les Ordonnances de la CIJ dans l'Affaire Relative à l'Application de la Convention sur la Prévention et la Répression du Crime du Génocide', 5 EJIL, 1994, p. 381.
[90] This provides that 'disputes between the Contracting Parties relating to the interpretation, application or fulfilment of the present Convention, including those relating to the responsibility of a state for genocide or for any of the other acts enumerated in article III, shall be submitted to the International Court of Justice at the request of any of the parties to the dispute'.
[91] The Court dismissed other suggested grounds for its jurisdiction in the case, ICJ Reports, 1993, p. 18; 95 ILR, p. 33.   [92] *Ibid.*, p. 23; 95 ILR, p. 38.
[93] ICJ Reports, 1951, pp. 15, 23 ; 18 ILR, pp. 364, 370, quoting the terms of General Assembly resolution 96(I) of 11 December 1946.
[94] ICJ Reports, 1993, pp. 3, 24; 95 ILR, pp. 1, 39.
[95] ICJ Reports, 1993, pp. 325, 350; 95 ILR, pp. 43, 68. See also the Separate Opinion of Judge Lauterpacht, *ibid.*, pp. 407, 431–2; 95 ILR, pp. 125, 149–50.

On 11 July 1996, the Court rejected the Preliminary Objections raised by Yugoslavia.[96] In particular, the Court emphasised that it followed from the object and purpose of the Genocide Convention that the rights and obligations contained therein were rights and obligations *erga omnes* and that the obligation upon each state to prevent and punish the crime of genocide was not dependent upon the type of conflict involved in the particular situation (whether international or domestic) and was not territorially limited by the Convention.[97] The type of state responsibility envisaged under article IX of the Convention did not exclude any form of state responsibility.[98] In addition, the Court observed that the Convention did not contain any clause the object or effect of which was to limit the scope of its jurisdiction *ratione temporis* so as to exclude events prior to a particular date.[99]

Prohibition of discrimination

Apart from the overwhelming requirement of protection from physical attack upon their very existence as a group, groups need protection from discriminatory treatment as such.[100] The norm of non-discrimination thus constitutes a principle relevant both to groups and individual members of groups.

The International Convention on the Elimination of All Forms of Racial Discrimination[101] was signed in 1965 and entered into force in 1969. It builds on the non-discrimination provisions in the UN Charter. Racial discrimination is defined as:

> any distinction, exclusion, restriction or preference based on race, colour, descent or national or ethnic origin which has the purpose or effect of nullifying or impairing the recognition, enjoyment or exercise, on an equal footing, of human rights and fundamental freedoms in the political, economic, social, cultural or any other field of public life.

States parties undertake to prohibit racial discrimination and guarantee equality for all in the enjoyment of a series of rights and to assure to all

---

[96] Now so called, rather than the former Yugoslavia (Serbia and Montenegro), as from, and in consequence of, the Dayton Peace Agreement initialled at Dayton, USA, on 11 November 1995 and signed in Paris on 14 December 1995.

[97] ICJ Reports, 1996, para. 31.   [98] ICJ Reports, 1996, para. 32.

[99] *Ibid.*, para. 34. See also the *Legality of the Threat or Use of Nuclear Weapons*, ICJ Reports, 1996, para. 26; 35 ILM, 1996, pp. 809, 820.

[100] See e.g. A. Bayefsky, 'The Principle of Equality or Non-discrimination in International Law', HRLJ, 1990, vol. 11, p. 1; J. Greenberg, 'Race, Sex and Religious Discrimination' in Meron, ed., *Human Rights in International Law*, p. 307; W. McKean, *Equality and Discrimination under International Law*, Oxford, 1983 and T. Meron, *Human Rights Law-Making in the United Nations*, 1986, Oxford, Chapters 1–3.

[101] See e.g. N. Lerner, *The UN Convention on the Elimination of All Forms of Racial Discrimination*, 2nd edn, Dordrecht, 1980. As of early 1997, there were 148 ratifications; ST/HR/4/Rev. 12, 1995.

within their jurisdiction effective protection and remedies regarding such human rights.[102] It is also fair to conclude that in addition to the existence of this Convention, the prohibition of discrimination on racial grounds is part of customary international law.[103] This conclusion may be reached on the basis *inter alia* of articles 55 and 56 of the UN Charter, articles 2 and 7 of the Universal Declaration on Human Rights, the International Covenants on Human Rights,[104] regional instruments on human rights protection[105] and general state practice. Discrimination on other grounds may also be contrary to customary international law, such as religion[106] and gender.[107] The International Covenant on Civil and Political Rights provides in article 2 (1) that all states parties undertake to respect and ensure to all individuals within their territories and within their jurisdictions the rights recognised in the Covenant 'without distinction of any kind such as race, colour, sex, language, religion, political or other opinion, national or

---

[102] See further *infra*, p. 232 with regard to the establishment of the Committee on the Elimination of Racial Discrimination. Note also the Convention on the Suppression and Punishment of the Crime of Apartheid 1973.

[103] See e.g. the Dissenting Opinion of Judge Tanaka in the *South West Africa* case, ICJ Reports, 1966, pp. 3, 293; 37 ILR, pp. 243, 455.   [104] See *infra* p. 234.   [105] See *infra* p. 255.

[106] See e.g. the Declaration on the Elimination of All Forms of Intolerance and of Discrimination Based on Religion or Belief, 1981, General Assembly resolution 36/55 and the appointment of a Special Rapporteur to examine situations inconsistent with the Declaration by the UN Commission on Human Rights, resolution 1986/20 of 10 March 1986. The initial one-year term has since been renewed and then extended to two-yearly then three-yearly terms, see e.g. resolutions 1988/55, 1990/27 and 1992/17. See Odio Benito, *Elimination of All Forms of Intolerance and Discrimination based on Religion or Belief*, New York, 1989 and Report on the Implementation of the Declaration on the Elimination of All Forms of Intolerance and of Discrimination Based on Religion or Belief, E/CN.4/1995/91, 1994. The UN Human Rights Committee has produced a General Comment on Article 18 concerning freedom of thought, conscience and religion, see General Comment 22, 1993, HRI/GEN/1/Rev.1, 1994. Note also S. Neff, 'An Evolving International Legal Norm of Religious Freedom: Problems and Prospects', 7 *California Western International Law Journal*, 1975, p. 543; A. Krishnaswami, *Study of Discrimination in the Matter of Religious Rights and Practices*, New York, 1960, E/CN.4/Sub.2/200/Rev.1; Lerner, 'Towards a Draft Declaration against Religious Intolerance and Discrimination', 11 *Israel Yearbook on Human Rights*, 1981, p. 82; B. Tahzib, *Freedom of Religion or Belief: Ensuring Effective International Legal Protection*, Dordrecht, 1995 and B. Dickson, 'The United Nations and Freedom of Religion', 44 ICLQ, 1995, p. 327.

[107] See the Convention on the Elimination of All Forms of Discrimination Against Women 1979, *infra* p. 240, Article 1 of the Convention provides that discrimination against women means any distinction, exclusion or restriction made on the basis of sex which has the effect or purpose of impairing or nullifying the recognition, enjoyment or exercise by women, irrespective of their marital status, on a basis of equality with men and women, of human rights and fundamental freedoms in the political, economic, social, cultural, civil or any other field. See e.g. McKean, *Equality*, Chapter 10, Bayefsky, 'Equality', and Meron, *Human Rights Law-Making*, Chapter 2. See also J. Morsink, 'Women's Rights in the Universal Declaration', 13 *Human Rights Quarterly*, 1991, p. 229; R. Cook, 'Women's International Human Rights Law', *Human Rights Quarterly*, 1993, p. 230; *Human Rights of Women* (ed. R. Cook), Philadelphia, 1994 and M. A. Freeman and A. S. Fraser, 'Women's Human Rights' in Henkin and Hargrove, *Human Rights: An Agenda for the Next Century*, p. 103. Note also the UN General Assembly Declaration on Elimination of Violence against Women, 33 ILM, 1994, p. 1049.

social origin, property, birth or other status'.[108] Article 26 stipulates that all persons are equal before the law and thus, 'the law shall prohibit any discrimination and guarantee to all persons equal and effective protection against discrimination on any ground such as race, colour, sex, language, religion, political or other opinion, national or social origin, property, birth or other status'.[109] The UN Human Rights Committee established under this Covenant[110] has noted in its General Comment 18 on Non-Discrimination[111] that non-discrimination 'constitutes a basic and general principle relating to the protection of human rights'. The Committee, while adopting the definition of the term 'discrimination' as used in the Racial Discrimination and Women's Discrimination Conventions, concludes that it should be understood to imply any distinction, exclusion, restriction or preference which is based on any ground such as race, colour, sex, language, religion, political or other opinion, national or social origin, property, birth or other status and which has the purpose or effect of nullifying or impairing the recognition, enjoyment or exercise by all persons, on an equal footing, of all rights and freedoms.

The principle of non-discrimination requires the establishment of equality in fact as well as formal equality in law. As the Permanent Court of International Justice noted in the *Minority Schools in Albania* case,[112] 'equality in law precludes discrimination of any kind; whereas equality in fact may involve the necessity of different treatment in order to attain a result which establishes an equilibrium between different situations'.[113] The appropriate test of acceptable differentiation in such circumstances will centre upon what is just or reasonable[114] or objectively and reasonably justified.[115] The

[108] See also, for example, articles 2(2) and 3 of the International Covenant on Economic, Social and Cultural Rights 1966. See M. C. Craven, *The International Covenant on Economic, Social and Cultural Rights*, Oxford, 1995, Chapter 4 and see further *infra*, p. 229.

[109] Note that this provision constitutes an autonomous or free-standing principle, whereas article 2(1) of that Covenant and articles 2 of the Universal Declaration of Human Rights, 14 of the European Convention on Human Rights and 2(1) of the Convention on the Rights of the Child prohibit discrimination in the context of specific rights and freedoms laid down in the instrument in question, see Bayefsky, 'Equality', pp. 3–4 and the Human Rights Committee's General Comment on Non-Discrimination, paragraph 12.

[110] See further *infra* p. 234.   [111] Adopted on 9 November 1989, CCPR/C/Rev.1/Add.1.

[112] PCIJ, Series A/B, No. 64, p. 19 (1935); 8 ILR, pp. 386, 389–90.

[113] See also the Human Rights Committee's General Comment on Non-Discrimination, paragraph 8.

[114] See Judge Tanaka's Dissenting Opinion in the *South West Africa* case, ICJ Reports, 1966, pp. 3, 306; 37 ILR, pp. 243, 464.

[115] See e.g. the *Belgian Linguistics* case, European Court of Human Rights, Series A, No. 6, 1986, para. 10; 45 ILR, pp. 114, 165. See also the *Amendments to the Naturalisation Provisions of the Constitution of Costa Rica* case, Inter-American Court of Human Rights, 1984, para. 56, 5 HRLJ, 1984, p. 172 and the Human Rights Committee's General Comment on Non-Discrimination, paragraph 13 which notes that 'not every differentiation of treatment will constitute discrimination, if the criteria for such differentiation are reasonable and objective and if the aim is to achieve a purpose which is legitimate under the Covenant'.

application of equality in fact may also require the introduction of affirmative action measures in order to diminish or eliminate conditions perpetuating discrimination. Such measures would need to be specifically targeted and neither absolute nor of infinite duration.[116]

The principle of self-determination as a human right[117]

The right to self-determination has already been examined in so far as it relates to the context of decolonisation.[118] The question arises whether this right which has been widely proclaimed has an application beyond the colonial context. Article 1 of both International Covenants on Human Rights provides that 'all peoples have the right to self-determination. By virtue of that right they freely determine their political status and freely pursue their economic, social and cultural development', while the Helsinki Final Act of 1975[119] refers to 'the principle of equal rights and self-determination . . . all peoples have the right, in full freedom, to determine, when and as they wish, their internal and external political status, without external interference, and to pursue as they wish their political, economic, social and cultural development'. Article 20 of the African Charter on Human and Peoples' Rights 1981[120] stipulates that 'all peoples shall have the right to existence. They shall have the unquestionable and inalienable right to self-determination. They shall freely determine their political status and shall pursue their economic and social development according to the policy they have chosen.' The 1970 Declaration on Principles of International Law Concerning Friendly Relations[121] referred to the colonial situation and noted that subjection of peoples to alien subjugation, domination and exploitation constituted a violation of the principle. A number of UN resolutions have discussed the relevance of self-determination also to situations of alien

---

[116] See the Human Rights Committee's General Comment on Non-Discrimination, paragraph 10. See also article 1(4) of the Racial Discrimination Convention, article 4(1) of the Women's Discrimination Convention and article 27 of the International Covenant on Civil and Political Rights.

[117] See e.g. W. Ofuatey-Kodjoe, 'Self Determination' in *United Nations Legal Order* (eds. O. Schachter and C. C. Joyner), Cambridge, 1995, vol. I, p. 349; A. Cassese, *Self-Determination of Peoples*, Cambridge, 1995; *Modern Law of Self-Determination* (ed. C. Tomuschat), Dordrecht, 1993; Higgins, *Problems*, Chapter 7; T. Franck, *The Power of Legitimacy Among Nations*, Oxford, 1990, pp. 153 *et seq.*; Franck, 'Fairness in the International and Institutional System', 240 HR, 1993 III, pp. 13, 125 *et seq.*; *The Rights of Peoples* (ed. J. Crawford), Oxford, 1988; *Peoples and Minorities in International Law* (eds. C. Brölmann, R. Lefeber and M. Zieck), Dordrecht, 1993; P. Thornberry, 'Self-Determination, Minorities, Human Rights: A Review of International Instruments', 38 ICLQ, 1989, p. 867 and M. Koskenniemi, 'National Self-Determination Today', 43 ICLQ, 1994, p. 241. See also M. Koskenniemi, '"National Self-Determination Today" Problems of Legal Theory and Practice', 43 ICLQ, 1994, p. 241 and R. McCorquodale, 'Self-Determination: A Human Rights Approach', 43 ICLQ, 1994, p. 857.

[118] See *supra* Chapter 5, p. 177.   [119] See further *infra* p. 281.

[120] See further *infra* p. 293.   [121] General Assembly resolution 2625(XXV).

occupation where the use of force has been involved.[122] The International Law Commission in 1988 expressed its view that the principle of self-determination was of universal application, [123] while the practice of the UN Human Rights Committee has been of particular significance.

Before this is briefly noted, one needs to refer to the crucial importance of the principle of territorial integrity.[124] This norm protects the territorial framework of independent states and is part of the overall concept of the sovereignty of states. In terms of the concept of the freezing of territorial boundaries as at the moment of independence (save by mutual consent), the norm is referred to as *uti possidetis juris*.[125] This posits that boundaries established and existing at the moment of independence cannot be altered unless the relevant parties consent to change. It is supported by international instruments[126] and by judicial pronouncement. In the *Burkina Faso/Mali* case,[127] the Chamber of the International Court of Justice emphasised that *uti possidetis* constituted a general principle, whose purpose was to prevent the independence and stability of new states from being endangered by fratricidal struggles provoked by the challenging of frontiers. This essential requirement of stability had induced newly independent states to consent to the respecting of colonial borders 'and to take account of it in the interpretation of the principle of self-determination of peoples'. The Arbitration Commission of the European Conference on Yugoslavia emphasised in Opinion No. 2[128] that 'it is well established that, whatever the circumstances, the right to self-determination must not involve changes to existing frontiers at the time of independence (*uti possidetis juris*) except where the states concerned agree otherwise'.

The principle of self-determination, therefore, applies beyond the colonial context, within the territorial framework of independent states.[129] It

---

[122] See for an examination of state practice, e.g. Cassese, *Self Determination*, pp. 90–9.

[123] *Yearbook of the ILC*, 1988, vol. II, Part 2, p. 64.

[124] General Assembly resolution 1514(XV) 1960 (the Colonial Declaration) underlines that 'any attempt at the partial or total disruption of the national unity and the territorial integrity of a country is incompatible with the purposes and principles of the Charter of the UN', while resolution 2625(XXV) 1970 (the Declaration on Principles of International Law Concerning Friendly Relations) emphasises that 'nothing in the foregoing paragraphs shall be construed as authorising or encouraging any action which would dismember or impair, totally or in part, the territorial integrity or political unity of sovereign or independent states'. See further *infra*, Chapter 8, p. 354.

[125] See further *infra*, Chapter 8, p. 356.

[126] See e.g. General Assembly resolutions 1514(XV) and 1541(XV) and Organisation of African Unity resolution 16(I) 1964.

[127] ICJ Reports, 1986, pp. 554, 566–7; 80 ILR, pp. 440, 470–1.

[128] §92 ILR, pp. 167, 168. See further *supra*, Chapter 5, p. 140.

[129] The clause in the 1970 Declaration on Principles of International Law Concerning Friendly Relations stating that nothing in the section on self-determination shall be construed as authorising or encouraging the dismembering or impairing of the territorial integrity of states conducting themselves in compliance with the principle of self-determination 'as described above and thus possessed of a government representing the whole

cannot be utilised as a legal tool for the dismantling of sovereign states. Its use, however, as a crucial principle of collective human rights[130] has been analysed by the Human Rights Committee in interpreting article 1 of the Civil and Political Rights Covenant.[131] In its General Comment on Self-Determination adopted in 1984,[132] the Committee emphasised that the realisation of the right was 'an essential condition for the effective guarantee and observance of individual human rights'. Nevertheless, the principle is seen as a collective one and not one that individuals could seek to enforce through the individual petition procedures provided in the First Optional Protocol to the Covenant.[133] The Committee takes the view, as Professor Higgins[134] noted,[135] that 'external self-determination requires a state to take action in its foreign policy consistent with the attainment of self-determination in the remaining areas of colonial or racist occupation. But internal self-determination is directed to their own peoples.' In the context of the significance of the principle of self-determination within independent states, the Committee has encouraged states parties to provide in their reports details about participation in social and political structures,[136] and

people belonging to the territory without distinction as to race, creed or colour' may be seen first, as establishing the primacy of the principle of territorial integrity and secondly, as indicating the content of self-determination within the territory. Whether it also can be seen as offering legitimacy to secession from an independent state in exceptional circumstances is the subject of much debate. Cassese, for example, concludes that 'a racial or religious group may attempt secession, a form of external self-determination, when it is apparent that internal self-determination is absolutely beyond reach. Extreme and unremitting persecution and the lack of any reasonable prospect for peaceful challenge may make secession legitimate', *Self Determination*, p. 120. See also R. Rosenstock, 'The Declaration on Principles of International Law', 65 AJIL, 1971, pp. 713, 732. It would appear that practice demonstrating the successful application of even this modest proposition is lacking.

[130] Note Brownlie's view that the principle of self-determination has a core of reasonable certainty and this consists in 'the right of a community which has a distinct character to have this character reflected in the institutions of government under which it lives', 'The Rights of Peoples in International Law' in Crawford, *The Rights of Peoples*, pp. 1, 5.
[131] See in particular D. McGoldrick, *The Human Rights Committee*, Oxford, 1994, Chapter 5; Cassese, *Self Determination*, pp. 59 *et seq.* and M. Nowak, *UN Covenant on Civil and Political Rights, CCPR Commentary*, Kehl, 1993, Part 1.
[132] General Comment 12, see HRI/GEN/1/Rev.1, p. 12, 1994.
[133] See the *Kitok* case, Report of the Human Rights Committee, A/43/40, pp. 221, 228; 96 ILR, pp. 637, 645; the *Lubicon Lake Band* case, A/45/40, vol. II, pp. 1, 27; 96 ILR, pp. 667, 702; *EP v. Colombia*, A/45/40, vol. II, pp. 184, 187 and *RL v. Canada* A/47/40, pp. 358, 365. [134] A member of the Committee from 1985–95.
[135] Higgins, 'Postmodern Tribalism and the Right to Secession' in Brölman *et al.*, *Peoples and Minorities in International Law*, p. 31.
[136] See e.g. the Report of Colombia, CCPR/C/64/Add.3, pp. 9 *et seq.*, 1991. In the Third Periodic Report of Peru, it was noted that the first paragraph of article 1 of the Covenant 'lays down the right of every people to self-determination. Under that right any people is able to decide freely on its political and economic condition or regime and hence establish a form of government suitable for the purposes in view. To this effect Peru adopted as its form of government the republican system which was embodied in the constitution of 1979, which stated that Peru was a democratic and social independent and sovereign republic based on work with a unitary representative and decentralised government', CCPR/C/83/Add.1, 1995, p. 4.

in engaging in dialogue with representatives of states parties, questions are regularly posed as to how political institutions operate and how the people of the state concerned participate in the governance of their state.[137] This necessarily links in with consideration of other articles of the Covenant concerning, for example, freedom of expression (article 19), freedom of assembly (article 21), freedom of association (article 22) and the right to take part in the conduct of public affairs and to vote (article 25). The right of self-determination, therefore, provides the overall framework for the consideration of the principles relating to democratic governance.[138]

The protection of minorities[139]

Various attempts were made in the post-World War One settlements, following the collapse of the German, Ottoman, Russian and Austro-Hungarian Empires and the rise of a number of independent nation-based states in Eastern and Central Europe, to protect those groups to whom sovereignty and statehood could not be granted.[140] Persons belonging to racial, religious or linguistic minorities were to be given the same treatment and the same civil and political rights and security as other nationals in the state in question. Such provisions constituted obligations of international concern and could not be altered without the assent of a majority of the League of Nations Council. The Council was to take action in the event of

---

[137] See e.g. with regard to Canada, A/46/40, p. 12. See also A/45/40, pp. 120–1, with regard to Zaire.

[138] See T. Franck, 'The Emerging Right to Democratic Governance', 86 AJIL, 1992, p. 46. See also P. Thornberry, 'The Democratic or Internal Aspect of Self-Determination' in *Modern Law of Self-Determination*, p. 101.

[139] See e.g. *Oppenheim's International Law*, pp. 972 *et seq.*; Nowak, *UN Covenant*, pp. 480 *et seq.*; R. Higgins, 'Minority Rights: Discrepancies and Divergencies Between the International Covenant and the Council of Europe System' in *Liber Amicorum for Henry Schermers*, Dordrecht, 1994, p. 193; Shaw, 'Definition of Minorities'; Thornberry, 'Phoenix', and 'Self-Determination, Minorities and Human Rights', 38 ICLQ, 1989, p. 867; F. Ermacora, 'The Protection of Minorities before the UN', 182 HR, 1983 IV, p. 251; G. Alfredson, 'Minority Rights and a New World Order' in *Broadening the Frontiers of Human Rights: Essays in Honour of A. Eide* (ed. D. Gomien), 1993; G. Alfredson and A. M. de Zayas, 'Minority Rights: Protection by the UN', HRLJ, 1993, p. 1; *Peoples and Minorities in International Law, The Protection of Ethnic and Linguistic Minorities in Europe* (eds. J. Packer and K. Myntti), Turku, 1993; *Documents on Autonomy and Minority Rights* (ed. Hannum), Dordrecht, 1993 and N. Rodley, 'Conceptual Problems in the Protection of Minorities: International Legal Developments', 17 HRQ , 1995, p. 48. See also the Capotorti Study on the Rights of Persons Belonging to Ethnic, Religious and Linguistic Minorities, E/CN.4/Sub.2/384/Rev.1, 1979.

[140] The minorities regime of the League consisted of five special minorities treaties binding Poland, the Serbo-Croat-Slovene state, Romania, Greece and Czechoslovakia; special minorities clauses in the treaties of peace with Austria, Bulgaria, Hungary and Turkey; five general declarations made on admission to the League by Albania, Latvia, Lithuania, Estonia and Iraq; a special declaration by Finland regarding the Aaland Islands and treaties relating to Danzig, Upper Silesia and Memel, see generally Thornberry, 'Self

any infraction of minorities' obligations. There also existed a petition procedure by minorities to the League, although they had no standing as such
before the Council or the Permanent Court of International Justice.[141]
However, the schemes of protection did not work well ultimately for a
variety of reasons ranging from the sensitivities of newly independent states
to international supervision of minority issues to overt exploitation of
minority issues by Nazi Germany in order to subvert neighbouring countries. After the Second World War, the focus shifted to the international
protection of universal individual human rights, although several instruments dealing with specific situations incorporated provisions concerning
the protection of minorities[142] and in 1947 the Sub-Commission on the
Prevention of Discrimination and the Protection of Minorities was established.[143] It was not, however, until the adoption of the International
Covenant on Civil and Political Rights in 1966 that the question of minority rights came back onto the international agenda. Article 27 of this
Covenant provides that 'in those states in which ethnic, religious or linguistic minorities exist, persons belonging to such minorities shall not be
denied the right, in community with the other members of their group, to
enjoy their own culture, to profess and practise their own religion, or to use
their own language'.

This modest and rather negative provision as formulated centres upon
'persons belonging' to minorities rather than upon minorities as such and
does not define the concept of minorities.[144] Nevertheless, the UN Human
Rights Committee has taken the opportunity to consider the issue in discussing states' reports, individual petitions and in a General Comment. In
commenting upon states' reports made pursuant to the International
Covenant, the Committee has made clear, for example, that the rights under
article 27 apply to all members of minorities within a state party's territory

Determination', pp. 38 *et seq.*
[141] In the early 1930s several hundred petitions were received but this dropped to virtually nil
by 1939; see Thornberry, pp. 434–6 and the Capotorti Report on the *Rights of Persons
belonging to Ethnic, Religious and Linguistic Minorities*, 1979, E/CN.4/Sub.2/384/Rev.1, pp.
20–2. See also Macartney, *National States*, pp. 370 *et seq.*; J. Stone, *International Guarantees
of Minority Rights*, London, 1932 and Richard, *Le Droit de Petition*, Paris, 1932.
[142] See e.g. Annex IV of the Treaty of Peace with Italy 1947; the Indian–Pakistan Treaty 1950
and article 7 of the Austrian State Treaty 1955. See also the provisions in the documents
concerning the independence of Cyprus, Cmnd. 1093, 1960.
[143] See further *infra*, p. 228.
[144] Attempts to define minorities have invariably focused upon the numerically inferior
numbers of minorities and their non-dominant position, the existence of certain objective
features differentiating them from the majority population (e.g. ethnic, religious or linguistic) coupled with the subjective wish of the minority concerned to preserve those
characteristics. See e.g. Shaw, 'Definition of Minorities', and the Capotorti Report, p. 96.
See also Council of Europe Assembly Recommendation 1255 (1955), H/Inf (95) 3, p. 88.
Note that the Human Rights Committee in the *Ballantyne* case held that English speaking
citizens in Quebec did not constitute a minority since the term minority applied to the
whole state and not a part of it, HRLJ, 1993, pp. 171, 176.

and not just nationals[145] and it has expressed concern with regard to the treatment of minorities within particular states.[146] In the *Lovelace* case,[147] the Committee decided that there had been a violation of article 27 with regard to an Indian woman who by having married a non-Indian had lost her rights by Canadian law to reside on the Tobique Reserve, something which she wished to do upon the collapse of her marriage. The Committee noted that statutory restrictions affecting the right to residence on a reserve of a person belonging to the minority concerned, had to have both a reasonable and objective justification and be consistent with the other provisions of the Covenant read as a whole. This had not been the case. There was no place outside the reserve where her right to access to her native culture and language could be conducted in community with other members of the minority in question. In the *Kitok* case,[148] the Committee took the view with regard to a petition by a member of the Sami community in Sweden that where the regulation of economic activity was an essential element in the culture of an economic community, its application to an individual could fall within article 27. It was emphasised that a restriction upon an individual member of a minority must be shown to have a reasonable and objective justification and to be necessary for the continued viability and welfare of the minority as a whole. In the *Lubicon Lake Band* case,[149] the Committee upheld the complaint that the Canadian government in allowing the Provincial Government of Alberta to expropriate the Band's territory for the benefit of private corporate interests violated article 27. It was held that the rights protected under article 27 included the right of persons in community with others to engage in economic and social activities which were part of the culture of the community to which they belonged.

The Committee adopted a General Comment on article 27 in 1994 after much discussion and hesitation due to fears that such a comment might be perceived to constitute an encouragement to secession.[150] The General Comment pointed to the distinction between the rights of persons belonging to minorities on the one hand and the right to self-determination and the right to equality and non-discrimination on the other. It was emphasised that the rights under article 27 did not prejudice the sovereignty and territorial integrity of states, although certain minority rights, in particular those pertaining to indigenous communities, might consist of a way of

---

[145] See e.g. comments upon Norway's third periodic report, A/49/40, p. 23 and Japan's third periodic report, *ibid.*, p. 25.

[146] See e.g. with regard to the third periodic report of Romania, *ibid.*, p. 29 and that of Mexico, *ibid.*, p. 35, and the fourth periodic report of Russia, CCPR/C/79/Add.54, p. 5 and of Ukraine, CCPR/C/79/Add.52, p. 4.

[147] I *Selected Decisions of the Human Rights Committee*, 1985, p. 83; 68 ILR, p. 17.

[148] A/43/40, p. 221; 96 ILR, pp. 637.   [149] A/45/40, vol. II, p. 1; 96 ILR, p. 667.

[150] General Comment No. 23, HRI/GEN/1/Rev.1, p. 38.

life closely associated with territory and the use of its resources, such as fishing, hunting and the right to live in reserves protected by law. The Committee in an important part of the General Comment underlined that persons belonging to a minority need not be nationals or permanent residents of the state concerned so that migrant workers or even visitors might be protected under article 27. Whether an ethnic, religious or linguistic minority exists was an objective question, not dependent upon a decision of the state party. Although article 27 is negatively formulated, the Committee pointed out that positive measures of protection were required not only against the acts of the state party itself, but also against the acts of other persons within the state party. Positive measures may also be necessary to protect the identity of the minority concerned and legitimate differentiation was permitted so long as it was based on reasonable and objective criteria.

The UN General Assembly adopted a Declaration on the Rights of Persons Belonging to National or Ethnic, Religious and Linguistic Minorities in December 1992.[151] Article 1 provides that states 'shall protect the existence and the national or ethnic, cultural, religious and linguistic indentity of minorities within their respective territories' and shall adopt appropriate legislative and other measures to achieve these ends. The Declaration states that persons belonging to minorities have the right to enjoy their own culture, practice and profess their own religion and to use their own language in private and in public without hindrance. Such persons also have the right to participate effectively in cultural, social, economic and public life. The UN Sub-Commission on Prevention of Discrimination and Protection of Minorities has been considering the question of minorities for many years and in 1994 agreed to establish a five person inter-sessional working group[152] to examine peaceful and constructive solutions to situations involving minorities and in particular to review the practical application of the Declaration, to provide recommendations to *inter alia* the Sub-Commission and the UN High Commissioner for Human Rights to protect minorities where there is a risk of violence, and generally to promote dialogue between minority groups in society and between those groups and governments. The issue of minority rights has been taken up recently, particularly by European states, primarily as a consequence of the demise of the Soviet Union and its empire in Eastern Europe and the reintegration of Eastern and Central European states within the political system of Western Europe. The specific response to questions of minority rights within the

---

[151] Resolution 47/135. See e.g. *The UN Minority Rights Declaration* (eds. A. Phillips and A. Rosas), London, 1993.
[152] E/CN.4/Sub.2/1994/56. This was authorised by the Commission on Human Rights on 3 March 1995, see resolution 1995/24. See also E/CN.4/Sub.2/1995/51.

Council of Europe and the Conference (as from 1995 Organisation) on Security and Co-operation in Europe are addressed below.[153]

As has been noted, the UN Human Rights Committee has pointed to the special position of indigenous peoples as minorities with a particular relationship to their traditional territory. It has been accepted that such communities form a specific category of minorities with special needs.[154] The International Labour Organisation adopted Convention No. 107 on Indigenous and Tribal Populations in 1957, an instrument with a predominantly assimilationist approach to the question of indigenous peoples. It was partially revised in Convention No. 169 on Indigenous and Tribal Peoples in Independent Countries 1989. The change in terminology from 'populations' to 'peoples' is instructive[155] and the latter Convention focuses far more upon the protection of the social, cultural, religious and spiritual values and practices of indigenous peoples. Unlike the prevailing approach to the definition of minorities generally which intermingles objective and subjective criteria, this Convention stipulates in article 1(2) that 'self-identification as indigenous or tribal shall be regarded as a fundamental criterion' for determining the groups to which the Convention applies. The Sub-Commission on Prevention of Discrimination and Protection of Minorities recommended that a study of discrimination against indigenous populations should be made and this was completed in 1984.[156] A definition of indigenous populations was suggested and various suggestions made as to future action. In 1982, the Sub-Commission established a Working Group on Indigenous Populations[157] and a Draft Declaration on the Rights of Indigenous Peoples was adopted in 1994.[158] This Draft Declaration notes that indigenous peoples have the right to self-determination (article 3) and the right to maintain and strengthen their distinctive political, economic, social and cultural characteristics, as well as their legal systems, while retain-

---

[153] *Infra*, p. 277.

[154] See e.g. S. Marquardt, 'International Law and Indigenous Peoples', 3 *International Journal on Group Rights*, 1995, p. 47; J. Berger and P. Hunt, 'Towards the International Protection of Indigenous Peoples' Rights', 12 NQHR, 1994, p. 405; C. Tennant, 'Indigenous Peoples, International Institutions, and the International Legal Literature from 1945–1993', 16 HRQ, 1994, p. 1; E. Stamatopoulou, 'Indigenous Peoples and the United Nations: Human Rights as a Developing Dynamic', 16 HRQ, 1994, p. 58; *The Rights of Peoples*; R. Barsh, 'Indigenous Peoples: An Emerging Object of International Law', 80 AJIL, 1986, p. 369; J. Anaya, *Indigenous Peoples in International Law*, Oxford, 1996 and G. Bennett, *Aboriginal Rights in International Law*, London, 1978.

[155] But note that the Convention provides that the use of the term 'peoples' is not to be construed as having any implication as regards the rights that may attach to the term under international law (article 1(3)).

[156] The Martinez Cobo Report, E/CN.4/Sub.2/1986/7 and Adds. 1–4.

[157] See E/CN.4/Sub.2/1982/33.

[158] See resolution 1994/45, E/CN.4/Sub.2/1994/56, p. 103. See also R. T. Coulter, 'The Draft UN Declaration on the Rights of Indigenous Peoples: What Is It? What Does It Mean?', 13 NQHR, 1995, p.

ing the right to participate fully in the life of the state (article 4). Indigenous peoples are deemed to have the collective right to live in freedom and security as distinct peoples (article 6) and the collective and individual rights to protection from ethnocide and cultural genocide (article 7). Their collective and individual rights to maintain and develop their distinct identities is particularly emphasised (article 8), while the Declaration lists their rights to practice their cultural traditions, and to education, access to media, health practices, together with a range of rights concerning their distinctive relationship to the land (articles 25–30).[159] A Voluntary Fund for Indigenous Populations was established in 1985[160] and a permanent forum for indigenous people is currently being sought.[161] The Sub-Commission is also studying the question of the heritage of indigenous people[162] and the issue of treaties, agreements and other constructive arrangements between states and indigenous populations.[163] The question of indigenous peoples is also under discussion within the Organisation of American States.[164]

Other suggested collective rights

The subject of much concern in recent years has been the question of a right to development.[165] In 1986, the UN General Assembly adopted the Declaration on the Right to Development.[166] This instrument reaffirms the interdependence and indivisibility of all human rights and seeks to provide a

---

[159] The Commission on Human Rights in resolution 1995/32, 3 March 1995, decided to establish an open-ended intersessional working group of the Commission to elaborate a draft declaration considering the draft submitted by the Sub-Commission. This was authorised by the Economic and Social Council in resolution 1995/32, 25 July 1995.

[160] See General Assembly resolution 40/131.

[161] See resolution 1995/39, E/CN.4/Sub.2/1995/51, p. 91. Note that 1993 was designated International Year of the World's Indigenous People, see E/CN.4/1994/AC.4/TN.4/2.

[162] See E/CN.4/Sub.2/1995/26, proposing a set of Principles and Guidelines for the Protection of the Heritage of Indigenous People.

[163] See e.g. resolution 1995/118, E/CN.4/Sub.2/1995/51, p. 99.

[164] See as to the Draft Declaration on the Rights of Indigenous Peoples adopted by the Inter-American Commission on Human Rights on 18 September 1995, *infra* p. 290.

[165] See e.g. *Le Droit au Développement au Plan International* (ed. R. J. Dupuy), Paris, 1980; A. Pellet, *Le Droit International du Développement*, 2nd edn, Paris, 1987; K. Mbaye, 'Le Droit du Developpement comme un Droit de l'Homme', 5 *Revue des Droits de l'Homme*, 1972, p. 503; *Report of the UN Secretary-General on the International Dimensions of the Right to Development as a Human Right*, E/CN.4/1334, 1979; O. Schachter, 'The Emerging International Law of Development', 15 *Columbia Journal of Transnational Law*, 1976, p. 1; R. Rich, 'The Right to Development as an Emerging Human Right', 23 *Va JIL*, 1983, p. 287; K. de Vey Mestdagh, 'The Right to Development', 28 NILR, 1981, p. 31; I. Brownlie, *The Human Right to Development*, Commonwealth Secretariat Human Rights Unit Occasional Paper, 1989; C. Weeramantry, 'The Right to Development', 25 *Indian Journal of International Law*, 1985, p. 482; P. Alston, 'Revitalising United Nations Work on Human Rights and Development', 18 *Melbourne University Law Review*, 1991, p. 216 and T. Kunanayakam, *Historical Analysis of the Principles Contained in the Declaration on the Right to Development*, HR/RD/1990/CONF.1, 1990.

[166] General Assembly resolution 41/128.

framework for a range of issues (article 9). The right to development is deemed to be an inalienable human right of all human beings and peoples to participate in and enjoy economic, social, cultural and political development (article 1), while states have the primary responsibility to create conditions favourable to its realisation (article 3) including the duty to formulate international development policies (article 4). States are particularly called upon to ensure *inter alia* equal opportunity for all in their access to basic resources, education, health services, food, housing, employment and the fair distribution of income. Effective measures are to be undertaken to ensure that women participate in the development process and appropriate economic and social reforms are to be carried out with a view to eradicating all social injustices (article 8). The question of encouraging the implementation of this Declaration was the subject of continuing UN attention,[167] with the reaffirmation of the right to development by the UN Vienna Declaration and Programme of Action 1993[168] and the establishment by the UN Commission on Human Rights of a Working Group on the Right to Development in the same year.[169] It should also be noted that Principle 3 of the Rio Declaration on Environment and Development 1992 stipulated that 'the right to development must be fulfilled so as to equitably meet developmental and environmental needs of present and future generations'.[170] While the general issue of development is clearly on the international agenda in the context of economic issues and broad human rights concerns, it is premature to talk in terms of a legal right in international law of groups or peoples or states to development.[171]

Other suggested collective rights have included the right to a healthy environment[172] and the right to peace.[173] The latter is a particularly amorphous concept in terms of a legal right, and, while it remains at the centre of international activity and a crucial aspiration, it cannot be regarded as a legal right of peoples or groups or individuals as such.

---

[167] Note e.g. the Global Consultation carried out in 1990, E/CN.4/1990/9/Rev.1, 1990, see R. Barsh, 'The Right to Development as a Human Right: Results of the Global Consultation', 13 HRQ, 1991, p. 322; the Report of the UN Secretary-General, E/CN.4/1992/10, 1991 and the Concrete Proposals of the UN Secretary-General, E/CN.4/1993/16, 1993.
[168] See 32 ILM, 1993, p. 1661.
[169] Resolution 1993/22. The first report of the Working Group was at the end of 1993, E/CN.4/1994/21.   [170] 31 ILM, 1992, p. 876. See also *infra* Chapter 15.
[171] Note that the Committee on Economic, Social and Cultural Rights has adopted a General Comment in which it is stated that international co-operation for development and thus the realisation of economic, social and cultural rights is an obligation for all states, General Comment 3 (1991), HRI/GEN/1/Rev.1, pp. 48, 52.
[172] See e.g. S. Prakash, 'The Right to the Environment. Emerging Implications in Theory and Praxis', 13 NQHR, 1995, p. 403. See further *infra*, Chapter 15 on International Environmental Law.
[173] See e.g. General Assembly resolutions 33/73 and 39/11. See also R. Bilder, 'The Individual and the Right to Peace', 11 *Bulletin of Peace Proposals*, 1982, p. 387 and J. Fried, 'The United Nations' Report to Establish a Right of the Peoples to Peace', 2 *Pace Yearbook of International Law*, 1990, p. 21.

The United Nations system – implementation[174]

The United Nations system has successfully generated a wide-ranging series of international instruments dealing with the establishment of standards and norms in the human rights field.[175] The question of implementation will now be addressed.

Political bodies – general

The General Assembly has power under article 13 of the Charter to initiate studies and make recommendations regarding *inter alia* human rights. Human rights items on its agenda may originate in Economic and Social Council (ECOSOC) reports or decisions taken by the Assembly at earlier sessions to consider particular matters, or are proposed for inclusion by the UN organs, the Secretary-General or member states. Most items on human rights go to the Assembly's Third Committee (Social, Humanitarian and Cultural Committee), but others may be referred to other committees such as the Sixth Committee (Legal) or the First Committee (Political and Security) or the Special Political Committee. The Assembly has also established subsidiary organs under Rule 161, several of which deal with human rights issues, such as the Special Committee on Decolonisation, the UN Council for Namibia, the Special Committee against Apartheid, the Special Committee to Investigate Israeli Practices in the Occupied Territories and the Committee on the Exercise of the Inalienable Rights of the Palestine People.[176] ECOSOC may under article 62 of the Charter make recommendations on human rights, draft conventions for the Assembly and call international conferences on human rights matters. It consists of fifty-four members of the UN elected by the General Assembly and hears

[174] See *United Nations Action in the Field of Human Rights*, New York, 1994; *The United Nations and Human Rights* (ed. P. Alston), Oxford, 1992; *Guide to International Human Rights Practice* (ed. H. Hannum), 2nd edn, Philadelphia, 1992; M. Tardu, *Human Rights: The International Petition System*, Leiden, 1979; *Human Rights: Thirty Years After the Universal Declaration*; *UN Law/Fundamental Rights*, (ed. A. Cassese), 1979; A.H. Robertson, 'The Implementation System: International Measures', in *The International Bill of Rights*, p. 332 and H. Golsong, 'Implementation of International Protection of Human Rights', 110 HR, p. 7. See also Lauterpacht, *International Law*, Chapter 11; F. Ermacora, 'Procedure to Deal with Human Rights Violations' 7 *Revue des Droits de l'Homme*, 1974, p. 670; Robertson and Merrills, *Human Rights*, and A. A. Cançado Trindade, 'Co-existence and Co-ordination of Mechanisms of International Protection of Human Rights', 202 HR, 1987, p. 9.
[175] See also e.g. the Slavery Convention 1926 and Protocol, 1953; the Supplementary Convention on the Abolition of Slavery, the Slave Trade and Institutions and Practices Similar to Slavery 1956; the Convention for the Suppression of the Traffic in Persons and of the Exploitation of the Prostitution of Others 1949; the Convention on the Status of Refugees 1951 and Protocol 1967; the Convention relating to the Status of Stateless Persons 1954 and the Convention on the Reduction of Statelessness 1961.
[176] See *UN Action*, Chapter 1. Note also the relevant roles of the other organs of the UN, the Security Council, Trusteeship Council, International Court and Secretariat, *ibid.*

annually the reports of a wide range of bodies including the UN High Commissioner for Refugees, the UN Children's Fund, the UN Conference on Trade and Development, the UN Environment Programme and the World Food Council. Of its subsidiary bodies, the Commission on Human Rights and the Commission on the Status of Women have the most direct connection with human rights issues.[177]

The Commission on Human Rights[178]

This was established in 1946 as a subsidiary organ of ECOSOC with extensive terms of reference, including making studies, preparing recommendations and drafting international instruments on human rights. Originally consisting of forty-three representatives of member states of the UN selected by ECOSOC on the basis of equitable geographic distribution,[179] that number was increased to fifty-three by resolution 1990/48 in May 1990. For its first twenty years, it took the view that it had no power to take any action with regard to complaints concerning human rights violations, despite receiving many via the Secretary-General.[180] However, in 1967, ECOSOC resolution 1235(XLII) authorised the Commission and its Sub-Commission on Prevention of Discrimination and Protection of Minorities to examine information relevant to gross violations of human rights contained in communications and to study such situations as revealed a consistent pattern of violations with a view to making recommendations to ECOSOC.[181] This constitutes the public debate function of the Commission relating to specific situations. The situations in question referred at first primarily to Southern Africa. In 1967, also, the Commission set up an *ad hoc* working group of experts on South Africa and has since established working groups on Chile; Situations revealing a Consistent Pattern of Gross Violations on Human Rights; Disappearances and the Right to Development. Special Rapporteurs have been appointed by the Commission to deal with situations in specific countries, such as, for example, Afghanistan, Cuba, El Salvador, Equatorial Guinea, Guatemala, Iran and Iraq. Special Rapporteurs have also been appointed to deal with

---

[177] *Ibid.*, pp. 13 *et seq.* See also Assembly resolutions 1991B(XVIII) and 2847(XXVI).

[178] See e.g. N. Rodley, 'United Nations Non-Treaty Procedures for Dealing with Human Rights Violations' in *Guide to International Human Rights Practice*, p. 60; Lauterpacht, *International Law*, Chapter 11; T. Buergenthal and Torney, *International Human Rights and International Education*, 1976, pp. 75 *et seq.* and Sieghart, *International Law*, p. 423. See also *UN Action*, p. 20 and H. Tolley, 'The Concealed Crack in the Citadel', 6 HRQ, 1984, p. 420. A Commission on the Status of Women was also created, see *UN Action*, p. 15 and *infra* p. 240.

[179] See ECOSOC resolutions 6(1), 1946; 9(II), 1946; 845(XXXII), 1961; 1147(XLI), 1966 and 1979/36, 1979.

[180] See e.g. Report of the First Session of the Commission, E/259, para. 22.

[181] See Tolley, 'Concealed Crack', pp. 421 *et seq.* and ECOSOC resolution 728F.

particular thematic concerns such as summary executions, torture, mercenaries, religious intolerance and the sale of children. In an attempt to provide some co-ordination, the first meeting of special rapporteurs and other mechanisms of the special procedures of the Commission took place in 1994.[182] A series of informal working groups have also been created to prepare drafts of international instruments, such as the Declaration on Religious Intolerance, the Convention against Torture and instruments on minority rights and the rights of the child.[183] The Commission also established a Group of Three pursuant to article IX of the Apartheid Convention to consider states' reports under that Convention. In 1970 a new procedure for dealing with human rights complaints was introduced in ECOSOC resolution 1503(XLVIII).[184] By virtue of this resolution, a working group of not more than five members was set up by the Sub-Commission to meet to consider communications and government replies and to pass on to the Sub-Commission those communications together with replies of governments that appeared to reveal 'a consistent pattern of gross and reliably attested violations of human rights'. The Sub-Commission would at that stage consider such material and refer to the Commission those situations appearing to reveal the necessary consistent pattern of gross and reliably attested violations of human rights. The five-person Commission Working Group on Situations examines these questions and reports to the full Commission which, in its turn, under resolution 1503 is empowered to study such situations and make recommendations to ECOSOC and, if it so decides, to establish an *ad hoc* committee of investigation with the express consent of the government concerned.[185] The procedure, it is fair to say, which is confidential until the final stage, has not fulfilled the initial high expectations. The confidentiality requirement and the highly political nature of the Commission itself have combined to frustrate hopes that had been raised.[186]

---

[182] See E/CN.4/1995/5. See also the report of the meeting of special rapporteurs/representatives/experts and chairpersons of working groups of the special procedures of the Commission on Human Rights and of the advisory services programme, May 1995, E/CN.4/1996/50.   [183] See e.g. *UN Action*, pp. 20–3.

[184] See e.g. P. Alston, 'The Commission on Human Rights' in *The United Nations and Human Rights*, pp. 126, 145 *et seq*. See also Newman and Weissbrodt, *Human Rights*, pp. 101 *et seq*. and M. Bossuyt, 'The Development of Special Procedures of the United Nations Commission on Human Rights', 6 HRLJ, 1985, p. 179.

[185] See also Sub-Committee resolution 1(XXIV), 1971.

[186] See e.g. T. Van Boven, 'Human Rights Fora at the United Nations', in *International Human Rights Law and Practice* (ed. Tuttle), 1978, p. 83; Möller, 'Petitioning the United Nations', 1 *Universal Human Rights*, 1979, p. 57; N. Rodley, 'Monitoring Human Rights by the UN System and Non-governmental Organisations' in *Human Rights and American Foreign Policy*, p. 157 and Tolley, 'Concealed Crack', pp. 429 *et seq*. Note that the Commission chairman now announces the names of the countries subject to complaints under resolution 1503, although no further details are disclosed: see e.g. E/CN.4/1984/77, p. 151, naming Albania, Argentina, Benin, Haiti, Indonesia, Malaysia, Pakistan, Paraguay, the Philippines, Turkey and Uruguay.

Nevertheless, many human rights issues are discussed publicly at sessions of the Commission and numerous resolutions are adopted,[187] although one cannot ignore the strong political currents that often prevent or mitigate criticism of particular states.[188] The events in Eastern Europe in 1989–90 led to an interesting change in the 1990 session of the Commission in that the earlier East-West axis of confrontation disappeared as the newly democratised states supported in the main Western positions criticising human rights violations. It was replaced by a growing North–South friction and this reflects an unfortunate trend.

Expert bodies established by UN organs

The Sub-Commission on Prevention of Discrimination and Protection of Minorities[189]

The Sub-Commission was established by the Commission in 1947 with wide terms of reference.[190] It is composed of twenty-six members elected by the Commission on the basis of nominations of experts made by the UN member states. Members serve in their individual capacity for four-year terms[191] and the composition must reflect an agreed geographical pattern.[192] The Sub-Commission produces a variety of studies by rapporteurs[193] and has established a number of subsidiary bodies. The Working Group on Communications functions within the framework of the resolution 1503 procedure noted in the previous sub-section, while the Working

---

[187] See generally, E/CN.4/1984/77 regarding the Commission's Fortieth Session.

[188] See e.g. the inability of the Commission in 1990 even to discuss draft resolutions relating to China and Iraq: E. Zoller, '46th Session of the United Nations Commission on Human Rights', 8(2) NQHR, 1990, pp. 140,142.

[189] See e.g. A. Eide, 'The Sub-Commission on Prevention of Discrimination and Protection of Minorities' in *The United Nations and Human Rights*, p. 211; Tolley, pp. 437 *et seq.*; J. Gardeniers, H. Hannum and C. Kruger, 'The UN Sub-Committee on Prevention of Discrimination and Protection of Minorities: Recent Developments', 4 HRQ, 1982, p. 353 and L. Garber and C. O'Conner, 'The 1984 UN Sub-Commission on Prevention of Discrimination and Protection of Minorities', 79 AJIL, 1985, p. 168. See also *UN Action*, pp. 23–4.

[190] See e.g. *UN Action*, p. 23. See also resolutions E/259, 1947; E/1371, 1949, and 17(XXXVII), 1981.

[191] See ECOSOC resolution 1986/35 with effect from 1988. Before this, the term was for three years and originally for two years.

[192] See ECOSOC resolution 1334(XLIV), 1968, and decision 1978/21, 1778.

[193] See e.g. the Capotorti Study, *supra* footnote 139 and the Ruhashyankiko Study, *supra* footnote 78. See also the Daes Study on the *Individual's Duties to the Community*, E/CN.4/Sub.2/432/Rev.2, 1983 and the Questiaux Study on *States of Emergency*, E/CN.4/Sub.2/1982/15, 1982. Note amongst other reports, the Sachar Study on *The Realisation of Economic, Social and Cultural Rights: The Right to Adequate Housing*, E/CN.4/Sub.2/1995/12, 1995. For the list of studies and reports completed at the 1995 session of the Sub-Committee and those ongoing and suggested, see E/CN.4/Sub.2/1995/51, pp. 201–4.

Groups on Contemporary Forms of Slavery[194] and the Working Group on the Rights of Indigenous Populations[195] prepare material within the areas of their concern. One should note in particular the adoption of the Draft Declaration on the Rights of Indigenous Peoples.[196] The Sessional Working Group on Detention, which has involved close collaboration with human rights non-governmental organisations, has produced a series of reports on particular rights.[197] The Sub-Commission has since 1987 produced an annual report listing all states that have proclaimed, extended or ended a state of emergency.[198]

The International Covenant on Economic, Social and Cultural Rights[199]

The International Covenant on Economic, Social and Cultural Rights[200] was adopted in 1966 and entered into force in 1976. Article 2 provides that each state party undertakes to take steps to the maximum of its available resources 'with a view to achieving progressively the full realisation of the rights recognised in the present Covenant'. In other words, an evolving programme is envisaged depending upon the goodwill and resources of states rather than an immediate binding legal obligation with regard to the rights in question. The rights included range from self-determination (article 1), the right to work (articles 6 and 7), the right to social security (article 9), adequate standard of living (article 11) and education (article 13) to the right to take part in cultural life and enjoy the benefits of scientific progress and its applications (article 15).

Under the Covenant itself, states parties were obliged to send periodic reports to ECOSOC (articles 16–25).[201] In 1978, a Sessional Working

---

[194] Resolution 11(XXVII), 1974, established the Working Group on Slavery. Its name was changed in 1988, see resolution 1988/42. See K. Zoglin, 'United Nations Action Against Slavery: A Critical Evaluation', 8 HRQ, 1986, p. 306. Note, for example, that a 35 Point Programme of Action for the Elimination of the Exploitation of Child Labour was adopted in 1991, see resolution 1990/31 and Commission resolution 1991/54. The Working Group is also concerned with the sexual exploitation of children, child labour and the question of child soldiers.

[195] See resolution 2(XXXIV), 1981. See also E/CN.4/Sub.2/1982/33. See also *supra* p. 222.

[196] See resolution 1994/45, E/CN.4/Sub.2/1994/56, p. 103. See also *supra* p. 222.

[197] See e.g. the Chernichenko and Treat Study on *The Administration of Justice and the Human Rights of Detainees: The Right to a Fair Trial*, E/CN.4/Sub.2/1994/24, 1994.

[198] See e.g. E/CN.4/Sub.2/1987/19/Rev.1; E/CN.4/Sub.2/1991/28 and E/CN.4/Sub.2/1995/20 and Corr. 1   [199] See e.g. Craven, *Covenant*.

[200] As of September 1996, it had 135 states parties.

[201] See articles 16–22 of the Covenant; Sieghart, pp. 427–29 and *UN Chronicle*, July 1982, pp. 68–70. See generally on implementation B. S. Ramcharan, 'Implementing the International Covenants on Human Rights' in *Human Rights: Thirty Years After the Universal Declaration*, p. 159; P. Alston, 'Out of the Abyss: The Challenge Confronting the New UN Committee on Economic, Social and Cultural Rights', 9 HRQ, 1987, p. 332; P. Alston and G. Quinn, 'The Nature and Scope of States Parties' Obligations under the International Covenant on Economic, Social and Cultural Rights', 9 HRQ, 1987, p. 156; P. Alston, 'The Committee on Economic, Social and Cultural Rights' in *The United Nations and Human*

Group was set up, consisting of fifteen members elected by ECOSOC from amongst states parties for three-year renewable terms. The Group met annually and reported to the Council. It was not a success, however, and in 1985 it was decided to establish a new committee of eighteen members, this time composed of independent experts.[202] Accordingly in 1987 the new Committee on Economic, Social and Cultural Rights commenced operation.[203] But it is to be especially noted that unlike, for example, the Racial Discrimination Committee, the Human Rights Committee and the Torture Committee, the Economic Committee is not autonomous and it is responsible not to the states parties but to a main organ of the United Nations. As will be seen by comparison with the other bodies, the Economic Committee has at its disposal only relatively weak means of implementation.

The implementation of this Covenant faces particular difficulties in view of the perceived vagueness of many of the principles contained therein, the relative lack of legal texts and judicial decisions, and the ambivalence of many states in dealing with economic, social and cultural rights. In addition, problems of obtaining relevant and precise information have loomed large, not least in the light of the fact that comparatively few non-governmental organisations focus upon this area.[204]

The Committee meets annually in Geneva for three-week sessions.[205] Its primary task lies in examining states' reports, drawing upon a list of questions prepared by its pre-sessional working group. The problem of overdue reports from states parties applies here as it does with regard to other human rights implementation committees. The Economic Rights Committee adopted a decision at its sixth session, whereby it established a procedure allowing for the consideration of the situation of particular states where those states had not produced reports for a long time, thus creating a rather valuable means of exerting pressure upon recalcitrant states parties.[206] Additional information may also be requested from states parties where this is felt necessary.[207] The Committee also prepares 'General Comments', the second of which on international technical assistance measures was adopted at its fourth session in 1990.[208] The third general comment adopted in 1991 is of particular interest and underlines that although the Covenant itself appears promotional and aspirational, nevertheless certain obligations of

Rights, p. 473 and B. Simma, 'The Implementation of the International Covenant on Economic, Social and Cultural Rights' in *The Implementation of Economic, Social and Cultural Rights* (ed. F. Matscher), 1991, p. 75.   [202] See ECOSOC resolution 1985/17.

[203] See P. Alston and B. Simma, 'First Session of the UN Committee on Economic, Social and Cultural Rights', 81 AJIL, 1987, p. 747 and 'Second Session of the UN Committee on Economic, Social and Cultural Rights', 82 AJIL, 1988, p. 603.

[204] See Alston, 'Economic Committee on Rights', p. 474.

[205] Although two sessions a year have been held in practice during 1993, 1994 and 1995.

[206] See e.g E/C.12/1994/20, p. 18.   [207] *Ibid.*, pp. 16–18.

[208] See HRI/GEN/Rev.1, p. 45.

immediate effect are imposed upon states parties. These include the non-discrimination provisions and the undertaking to take steps which should be taken within a reasonably short time after the Covenant has entered into force for the state concerned and which should be 'deliberate, concrete and targeted as clearly as possible towards meeting the obligations recognised in the Covenant'. The Committee also emphasised that international co-operation for development and thus for the realisation of economic, social and cultural rights was an obligation for all states.[209] General Comment 4, adopted in 1991, discussed the right to adequate housing,[210] while General Comment 5 adopted in 1994 dealt with the rights of persons with disabilities.[211] General Comment 6 adopted in 1995 concerned the economic, social and cultural rights of older persons.[212] The Committee also holds general discussions on particular rights in the form of a 'day of general discussion'.[213] It cannot hear individual petitions, nor has it an interstate complaints competence.[214]

Expert bodies established under particular treaties[215]

A number of expert committees have been established under particular treaties. They are not subsidiary organs of the UN, but autonomous, although in practice they are closely connected with it, being serviced, for example by the UN Secretariat through the UN Centre for Human Rights in Geneva.[216] These committees are termed 'UN Treaty Organs'.

---

[209] *Ibid.*, p. 48.   [210] *Ibid.*, p. 53.

[211] E/1995/22, p. 99. On disabilities and human rights, see also the final report of Leandro Despouy, Special Rapporteur on Human Rights and Disability, of the Sub-Commission on Prevention of Discrimination and Protection of Minorities, E/CN.4/Sub.2/1991/31; General Assembly resolution 3447(XXX) of 9 December 1975 adopting the Declaration of the Rights of Disabled Persons and General Assembly resolution 37/52 of 3 December 1982 adopting the World Programme of Action concerning Disabled Persons, A/37/351/Add.1 and Corr.1, Chapter VIII.   [212] E/C.12/1995/16, 1995.

[213] At the ninth session, for example, in the autumn of 1993, the Committee discussed the right to health, E/1994/23, p. 56, while at the tenth session in May 1994 the role of social safety nets as a means of protecting economic, social and cultural rights was discussed, see E/1995/22, p. 70. See also generally C. Dommen, 'Building from a Solid Basis: The Fourth Session of the Committee on Economic, Social and Cultural Rights', 8 NQHR, 1990, p. 199 and C. Dommen and M. C. Craven, 'Making Way for Substance: The Fifth Session of the Committee on Economic, Social and Cultural Rights', 9 NQHR, 1991, p. 93.

[214] Note, however, that at its seventh session in 1992, the Committee formally proposed that an optional protocol providing for some kind of petition procedure be drafted and adopted, see E/1993/22, pp. 87 *et seq.* and Craven, *Covenant*, pp. 98 *et seq.* See also E/C.12/1994/12 and E/C.12/1995/SR.50, December 1995.

[215] See e.g. S. Lewis-Anthony, 'Treaty-Based Procedures for Making Human Rights Complaints Within the UN System' in *Guide to International Human Rights Practice*, p. 41.

[216] This link with the Secretariat has been termed ambiguous, particularly in the light of the difficulties in performing the two functions carried out by the Secretariat (Charter-based political activies and expert activities), see e.g. T. Opsahl, 'The Human Rights Committee' in *The United Nations and Human Rights*, pp. 367, 388.

The Committee on the Elimination of Racial Discrimination[217]

Under Part II of the Convention on the Elimination of All Forms of Racial Discrimination, 1965, a Committee of eighteen experts was established consisting of persons serving in their personal capacity and elected by the states parties to the Convention.[218] States parties undertook to submit reports every two years regarding measures adopted to give effect to the provisions of the Convention to the Committee, which itself would report annually through the UN Secretary-General to the General Assembly. The Committee may make suggestions and general recommendations based on the examination of the reports and information received from the states parties, which are reported to the General Assembly together with any comments from states parties.[219] The Committee is also able to seek further information from states parties. For example, in 1993, the Committee concerned at events in the former Yugoslavia sought additional information on the implementation of the Convention as a matter of urgency.[220] This information was provided during the autumn of 1994 and the spring of 1995.[221] The Committee has also established a procedure to deal with states whose reports are most overdue. Under this procedure, the Committee proceeds to examine the situation in the state party concerned on the basis of the last report submitted.[222] Under article 11, one state party may bring a complaint against another state party and the Committee will seek to resolve the complaint. Should the matter not be so settled, either party may refer it back to the Committee and by article 12 an *ad hoc* Conciliation Commission may be established, which will report back to the Committee with any recommendation thought proper for the amicable solution of the dispute.[223]

In addition to hearing states' reports and interstate complaints, the Committee may hear also individual petitions under the article 14 procedure. This, however, is subject to the state complained of having made a declaration recognising the competence of the Committee to receive and

---

[217] See e.g. K. J. Partsch, 'The Committee on the Elimination of Racial Discrimination' in *The United Nations and Human Rights*, p. 339; T. Meron, *Human Rights Law-Making in the United Nations*, 1986, Oxford, Chapter 1; K. Das, 'The International Convention on the Elimination of All Forms of Racial Discrimination' in *The International Dimension of Human Rights* (eds. K. Vasak and P. Alston), 1982, p. 307; Lerner, *UN Convention*, and 'Curbing Racial Discrimination – Fifteen Years Cerd', 13 *Israel Yearbook on Human Rights*, 1983, p. 170; M.R. Burrowes, 'Implementing the UN Racial Convention – Some Procedural Aspects', 7 Australian YIL, p. 236 and T. Buergenthal, 'Implementing the UN Racial Convention', 12 *Texas International Law Journal*, 1977, p. 187.
[218] Rules of Procedure have been adopted, see CERD/C/35/Rev.3 (1986), and are revised from time to time, see, for example, A/48/18, p. 137.   [219] Articles 8 and 9 of the Convention.
[220] A/48/18, paras. 496–506.
[221] See e.g. CERD/C/248/Add.1 (Federal Republic of Yugoslavia); CERD/C/249/Add.1 (Croatia) and CERD/C/247/Add.1 (Bosnia and Herzegovina).
[222] See e.g. A/48/18, p. 20.   [223] Article 13.

consider such communications. If such a declaration has not been notified by a state, therefore, the Committee has no authority to hear a petition against the state. Indeed, article 14 only came into effect when ten states had made such declarations.[224] Under this procedure, consideration of communications is confidential and the Committee may be assisted by a five-person working group making recommendations to the full Committee. The Committee began hearing individual communications in 1984 and a number of important cases have now been completed.[225]

The Committee regularly meets twice a year and has interpreted articles of the Convention, discussed reports submitted to it, adopted decisions[226] and general recommendations,[227] obtained further information from states parties and co-operated closely with the International Labour Organisation and UNESCO. Many states have enacted legislation as a consequence of the work of the Committee and its record of impartiality is very good.[228] The Committee also receives copies of petitions and reports sent to UN bodies dealing with trust and non-self-governing territories in the general area of Convention matters and may make comments upon them.[229] The general article 9 reporting system appears to work well, with large numbers of reports submitted and examined, but some states have proved tardy in fulfilling their obligations.[230] The Committee has published guidelines for states parties as to the structure of their reports.[231]

The Committee, in order to speed up consideration of states' reports, has instituted the practice of appointing country rapporteurs, whose function it is to prepare analyses of reports of states parties.[232] The Committee has also called for additional technical assistance to be provided by the UN to help in the reporting process, while it has expressed serious concern that financial difficulties are beginning to affect its functioning.[233]

---

[224] The provision entered into force on 31 December 1982 upon the tenth declaration. As of 31 December 1995, twenty states had made the necessary declarations, ST/HR/4/Rev.13, 1996.

[225] See e.g. the Report of the Committee for its forty-eighth session, A/48/18, 1994, pp. 105 and 130.

[226] For example the decision adopted on 19 March 1993 requesting the governments of the Federal Republic of Yugoslavia (Serbia and Montenegro) and Croatia to submit further information concerning implementation of the Convention, see A/48/18, p. 112.

[227] See, for example, General Recommendation XII(42) encouraging successor states to declare that 'they continue to be bound' by the obligations of the Convention if predecessor states were parties to it and General Recommendation XIV(42) concerning non-discrimination, see A/48/18, pp. 113 et seq.   [228] See e.g. Lerner, UN Convention.

[229] Article 15. See, for example, A/48/18, p. 107.

[230] See e.g. A/38/18, pp. 14–24. Note, for example, that by late 1983 fifteen reminders had been sent to Swaziland requesting it to submit its fourth, fifth, sixth and seventh overdue periodic reports, ibid., p. 21. See also A/44/18, pp. 10–16.

[231] See CERD/C/70/Rev.1, 6 December 1983.

[232] See e.g. A/44/18, 1990, p. 7 and A/48/18, 1994, p. 149.   [233] A/44/18, p. 91.

The Human Rights Committee[234]

The International Covenant on Civil and Political Rights was adopted in 1966 and entered into force in 1976.[235] By article 2, all states parties undertake to respect and to ensure to all individuals within their territory and subject to their jurisdiction the rights recognised in the Covenant. These rights are clearly intended as binding obligations. They include the right of peoples to self-determination (article 1), the right to life (article 6), prohibitions on torture and slavery (articles 7 and 8), the right to liberty and security of the person (article 9), due process (article 14), freedom of thought, conscience and religion (article 18), freedom of association (article 22) and the rights of persons belonging to minorities to enjoy their own culture (article 27). A Human Rights Committee was established under Part IV of the Covenant.

It consists of eighteen independent and expert members, elected by the states parties to the Covenant for four-year terms, with consideration given to the need for equitable geographical distribution and representation of the different forms of civilisation and of the principal legal systems.[236] The Committee meets three times a year (in Geneva and New York) and operates by way of consensus.[237] The Covenant is primarily implemented by means of a reporting system, whereby states parties provide information on the measures adopted to give effect to the rights recognised in the Covenant. Initial reports are made within one year of the entry into force of the Covenant for the state in question and general guidelines have been issued.[238] The Committee has decided that subsequent reports would be required every five

---

[234] See e.g. M. Nowak, *UN Covenant on Civil and Political Rights: CCPR Commentary*, 1993, Strasbourg; D. McGoldrick, *The Human Rights Committee*, 1991, Oxford (revised paperback edition 1994); T. Opsahl, 'The Human Rights Committee' in *The United Nations and Human Rights*, p. 367; Robertson; D. Fischer, 'Reporting under the Convention on Civil and Political Rights: the First Five Years of the Human Rights Committee', 76 AJIL, 1982, p. 142; Ramcharan, 'Implementing the International Covenants on Human Rights'; E. Schwelb, 'The International Measures of Implementation of the International Covenant on Civil and Political Rights and of the Optional Protocol', 12 *Texas International Law Review*, 1977, p. 141; M. Nowak, 'The Effectiveness of the International Covenant on Civil and Political Rights – Stock-taking after the First Eleven Sessions of the UN Human Rights Committee', 2 HRLJ, 1981, p. 168 and 5 HRLJ, 1984, p. 199. See also M. Bossuyt, *Guide to the Travaux Préparatoires of the International Covenant on Civil and Political Rights*, The Hague, 1987; F. Jhabvala, 'The Practice of the Covenant's Human Rights Committee, 1976–82: Review of State Party Reports', 6 HRQ, 1984, p. 81 and P. R. Ghandhi, 'The Human Rights Committee and the Right of Individual Communication', 57 BYIL, 1986, p. 201.   [235] As of September 1996, there were 135 states parties.

[236] See articles 28–32 of the Covenant.

[237] See e.g. Nowak, 1981, 'Effectiveness', p. 169; 3 HRLJ, 1982, p. 209 and 1984, p. 202. See also A/36/40, annex VII, Introduction; CCPR/C/21/Rev.1 and A/44/40, p. 173.

[238] See article 40 and CCPR/C/5. Supplementary reports may be requested, see Rule 70(2) of the provisional rules of procedure, CCPR/C/3/Rev.1. See for the revised guidelines in 1991, A/46/40, Ax. VII.

years,[239] and the first of the second periodic reports became due in 1983. The reports are discussed by the Committee with representatives of the state concerned (following upon the precedent established by the Committee on the Elimination of Racial Discrimination).[240] The practice used to be that Committee members would informally receive information from sources other than the reporting state provided the source is not publicly identified. This enabled the Committee to be more effective than would otherwise have been the case.[241] However, no doubt due to the ending of Soviet control in Eastern Europe and the demise of the Soviet Union, there appears to be no problem now about acknowledging publicly the receipt of information from named non-governmental organisations.[242] The Committee may also seek additional information from the state concerned. For example, in October 1992, the Committee adopted a decision requesting the governments of the Federal Republic of Yugoslavia (Serbia and Montenegro), Croatia and Bosnia-Herzegovina to submit a short report concerning measures to prevent *inter alia* ethnic cleansing and arbitrary killings.[243] Such reports were forthcoming and were discussed with the states' representatives concerned and comments adopted. The Committee thereafter adopted an amendment to its rules of procedure permitting it to call for reports at any time deemed appropriate.[244] The Committee has also noted that the peoples within a territory of a former state party to the Covenant remain entitled to the guarantees of the Covenant.[245]

Under article 40(4), the Committee is empowered to make such 'general comments as it may deem appropriate'. After some discussion, a consensus was adopted in 1980, which permitted such comments provided that they promoted co-operation between states in the implementation of the Covenant, summarised the experience of the Committee in examining states' reports and drew the attention of states parties to matters relating to the improvement of the reporting procedure and the implementation of the

[239] See CCPR/C/18; CCPR/C/19 and CCPR/C/19/Rev.1. See also CCPR/C/20 regarding guidelines. Several states have been lax about producing reports, e.g. Zaire and the Dominican Republic, while the initial report of Guinea was so short as to be held by the Committee as not providing sufficient information: see Nowak, 1984, p. 200.

[240] See Buergenthal, 'Implementing', pp. 199–201, and Fischer, 'Reporting', p. 145.

[241] *Ibid.*, pp. 146–7.

[242] Such documents may now be officially distributed, rather than being informally made available to Committee members individually, see McGoldrick, *Human Rights Committee*, p. liii.

[243] CCPR/C/SR/1178/Add.1.

[244] New Rule 66(2), see CCPR/C/SR/1205/Add.1. See also S. Joseph, 'New Procedures Concerning the Human Rights Committee's Examination of State Reports', NQHR, 1995, p. 5.

[245] See with regard to former Yugoslavia, CCPR/C/SR.1178/Add.1, pp. 2–3 and CCPR/C/79/Add. 14–16. See with regard to the successor states of the USSR, CCPR/C/79/Add.38 (Azerbaijan). See also I. Boerefijn, 'Towards a Strong System of Supervision', 17 HRQ, 1995, p. 766.

Covenant. The aim of the Committee was to engage in a constructive dialogue with each reporting state, and the comments would be non-country-specific.[246] However, in 1992, the Committee decided that at the end of the consideration of each state party's report, specific comments would be adopted referring to the country in question and such comments would express both the satisfaction and the concerns of the Committee as approprate.[247] These specific comments are in a common format and refer to 'positive aspects' of the report and 'principal subjects for concern', as well as 'suggestions and recommendations'.[248]

The Committee has also adopted a variety of General Comments.[249] These comments are generally non-controversial. One interesting comment on article 6 (the right to life), however, emphasised the Committee's view that: 'the designing, testing, manufacture, possession and development of nuclear weapons are among the greatest threats to the right to life', and that the 'production, testing, possession and deployment and use of nuclear weapons should be prohibited and recognised as crimes against humanity'.[250]

In April 1989, the Committee adopted a General Comment on the rights of the child, as the process of adopting the Convention on the Rights of the Child neared its climax. It noted the importance of economic, social and cultural measures, such as the need to reduce infant mortality and prevent exploitation. Freedom of expression was referred to, as was the requirement that children be protected against discrimination on grounds such as race, sex, religion, national or social origin, property or birth. Responsibility for guaranteeing the necessary protection lies, it was stressed, with the family, society and the state, although primarily incumbent upon the family. Special attention needed to be paid to the right of every child to acquire a nationality.[251]

---

[246] CCPR/C/18.	[247] See A/47/40, p. 4.

[248] See, for example, the comments concerning Colombia in September 1992, CCPR/C/79/Add.2; Guinea in April 1993, CCPR/C/79/Add.20; Norway in November 1993, CCPR/C/79/Add.27; Morocco in November 1994, CCPR/C/79/Add.44; the Russian Federation in July 1995, CCPR/C/79/Add.54; Estonia in November 1995, CCPR/C/79/Add.59 and the United Kingdom in July 1995, CCPR/C/79/Add.55 and, relating to Hong Kong, in November 1995, CCPR/C/79/Add.57. Note that in September 1995, Mexico responded to the Committee's Concluding Comments upon its report by issuing Observations, CCPR/C/108.

[249] See e.g. T. Opsahl, 'The General Comments of the Human Rights Committee' in *Festschrift für Karl Josef Partsch zum 75*, 1989, p. 273.

[250] CCPR/C/21/Add.4, 14 November 1984. Note that the International Court of Justice gave an Advisory Opinion on 8 July 1996 at the request of the General Assembly of the UN concerning the *Legality of the Threat or Use of Nuclear Weapons*, in which it was noted that the right not to be arbitrarily deprived of one's life applied also in hostilities. Whether a particular loss of life was arbitrary within the terms of article 6 would depend on the situation and would be decided by reference to the law applicable in armed conflict and not deduced from the terms of the Covenant itself, ICJ Reports, 1996, para. 25; 35 ILM, 1996, pp. 809, 820.	[251] A/44/40, pp. 173–75.

In November 1989, an important General Comment was adopted on non-discrimination. Discrimination was to be understood to imply for the purposes of the Covenant:

> any distinction, exclusion, restriction or preference which is based on any ground such as race, colour, sex, language, religion, political or other opinion, national or social origin, property, birth or other status, and which has the purpose or effect of nullifying or impairing the recognition, enjoyment or exercise by all persons, on an equal footing, of all rights and freedoms.[252]

Identical treatment in every instance was not, however, demanded. The death sentence could not, under article 6(5) of the Covenant, be imposed on persons under the age of 18 or upon pregnant women. It was also noted that the principle of equality sometimes requires states parties to take affirmative action in order to diminish or eliminate conditions which cause or help to perpetuate discrimination prohibited by the Covenant. In addition, it was pointed out that not every differentiation constituted discrimination, if the criteria for such differentiation were reasonable and objective and if the aim was to achieve a purpose which was legitimate under the Covenant.[253] Important General Comments on Minorities[254] and Reservations[255] were adopted in 1994.

Under article 41 of the Covenant, states parties may recognise the competence of the Committee to hear interstate complaints. Both the complainant and object state must have made such declarations. The Committee will seek to resolve the issue and, if it is not successful, it may under article 42 appoint, with the consent of the parties, an *ad hoc* Conciliation Commission.[256]

The powers of the Human Rights Committee were extended by the Optional Protocol to the Civil and Political Rights Covenant with regard to ratifying states to include the competence to receive and consider individual communications, alleging violations of the Covenant by a state party to the Protocol.[257] The individual must have exhausted all available domestic remedies (unless unreasonably prolonged) and the same matter must not be in the process of examination under another international procedure.[258] The procedure under the Optional Protocol is divided into several stages. The

[252] CCPR/C/21/Rev.1/Add.1, p. 3.   [253] *Ibid.*, p. 4. See also *supra* p. 214.
[254] HRI/GEN/1/Rev.1, 1995. See further *supra* p. 220.
[255] CCPR/C/21/Rev.1/Add.6. See further *infra* p. 648.
[256] As of 31 December 1995, 41 states had made such declarations; see ST/HR/4/Rev.13, 1996. The inter-state procedure has not been used to date.
[257] Signed in 1966 and in force as from 23 March 1976. As of September 1996, 89 states had ratified the Optional Protocol. See also de Zayas, H. Möller and T. Opsahl, 'Application of the International Covenant on Civil and Political Rights under the Optional Protocol by the Human Rights Committee', 28 *German Yearbook of International Law*, 1985, p. 9 and *Selected Decisions of the Human Rights Committee under the Optional Protocol*, vol. I, 1985 and vol. II, 1990.   [258] Article 5, Optional Protocol.

gathering of basic information is done by the Secretary-General and laid before the Working Group on Communications of the Committee, which recommends whether, for example, further information is required from the applicant or the relevant state party and whether the communication should be declared inadmissible. The procedure before the Committee itself is divided into an admissibility and a merits stage. Interim decisions may be made by the Committee and ultimately a 'final view' communicated to the parties.[259]

An increasing workload, however, began to cause difficulties as the number of parties to the Optional Protocol increased. By September 1994, 587 communications concerning 44 states parties had been placed before the Committee, of which 193 had been concluded by final views having been issued and 201 declared inadmissible.[260] In order to deal with the growth in applications, the Committee decided at its thirty-fifth session to appoint a Special Rapporteur to process new communications as they were received (i.e. between sessions of the Committee) and this included requesting the state or individual concerned to provide additional written information or observations relevant to the question of the admissibility of the communication.[261] The Committee has also authorised its five-member Working Group on Communications to adopt a decision declaring a communication admissible, providing there is unanimity.[262] The Committee may also adopt interim measures of protection under rule 86 of its Rules of Procedure. This has been used primarily in connection with cases submitted by or on behalf of persons sentenced to death and awaiting execution. Such a request was made, for example, to Trinidad and Tobago in the *Ashby* case pending examination of the communication, but to no avail. After the individual was executed, the Committee adopted a decision expressing its indignation at the failure of the state party to comply with the request for interim measures and deciding to continue consideration of the case.[263]

The Committee, however, is not a court with the power of binding decision on the merits of cases. Indeed, in instances of non-compliance with its final views, the Optional Protocol does not provide for an enforcement mechanism, nor indeed for sanctions, although follow-up techniques are being developed in order to address such problems.[264]

---

[259] See Nowak, 1981, pp. 153 *et seq.* and 1981 Report of Human Rights Committee, A/36/40, pp. 85–91.   [260] A/49/40, vol. I, p. 63.

[261] A/44/40, pp. 139–40. See also rule 91 of the amended rules of procedure, *ibid.*, p. 180.
[262] *Ibid.*, p. 140.   [263] A/49/40, pp. 70–1.

[264] Note that in October 1990, the Committee appointed a Special Rapporteur to follow up cases, CCPR/C/SR.1002, p. 8. See rule 95 of the Rules of Procedure. In 1994, the Committee decided that every form of publicity would be given to follow-up activities, including separate sections in annual reports, the issuing of annual press communiqués and the institution of such practices in a new rule of procedure (rule 99) emphasising that follow-up activities were not confidential, A/49/40, pp. 84–6.

A variety of interesting decisions have so far been rendered. The first group of cases concerned complaints against Uruguay, in which the Committee found violations by that state of rights recognised in the Covenant.[265] In the *Lovelace* case, [266] the Committee found Canada in breach of article 27 of the Covenant protecting the rights of minorities, since its law provided that an Indian woman, whose marriage to a non-Indian had broken down, was not permitted to return to her home on an Indian reservation, and in the *Mauritian Women* case[267] a breach of Covenant rights was upheld where the foreign husbands of Mauritian women were liable to deportation whereas the foreign wives of Mauritian men would not have been. The Committee has also held that the Covenant's obligations cover the decisions of diplomatic authorities of a state party regarding citizens living abroad.[268] In the *Robinson* case,[269] the Committee considered whether a state was under an obligation itself to make provision for effective representation by counsel in a case concerning a capital offence, in circumstances where the counsel appointed by the author of the communication declines to appear. The Committee emphasised that it was axiomatic that legal assistance be available in capital cases and decided that the absence of counsel constituted unfair trial. The Committee has dealt with the death penalty issue in several cases[270] and has noted, for example, that such a sentence may only be imposed in accordance with due process rights.[271] The Committee has also taken the view that where the extradition of a person facing the death penalty may expose the person to violation of due process rights in the receiving state, the extraditing state may be in violation of the Covenant.[272] The Committee has also noted that execution by gas asphyxiation would violate the prohibition in article 7 of cruel and inhuman treatment.[273] The issue faced in the *Vuolanne* case[274] was whether the procedural safeguards in article 9(4) of the Covenant on Civil and Political Rights, whereby a person deprived of his liberty is to be allowed recourse to the courts, applied to military disciplinary detention. The Committee was very clear that it did.

---

[265] These cases are reported in 1 HRLJ, 1980, pp. 209 *et seq.* See for other cases, 2 HRLJ, 1981, pp. 130 *et seq.*; *ibid.*, pp. 340 *et seq.*; 3 HRLJ, 1982, p. 188; 4 HRLJ, 1983, pp. 185 *et seq.* and 5 HRLJ, 1984, pp. 191 *et seq.* See also Annual Reports of the Human Rights Committee, 1981–to date.

[266] 1981 Report of the Human Rights Committee, A/36/40, p. 166.   [267] *Ibid.*, p. 134.

[268] See e.g. the *Waksman* case, 1 HRLJ, 1980, p. 220 and the *Lichtensztejn* case, 5 HRLJ, 1984, p. 207.   [269] A/44/40, p. 241 (1989).

[270] Note that the death penalty is prohibited under the Second Optional Protocol, to which as of September 1996, twenty-nine states were parties.

[271] See e.g. the *Berry, Hamilton, Grant, Currie* and *Champagnie* cases against Jamaica, A/49/40, vol. II, pp. 20, 37, 50, 73 and 136.

[272] See the *Ng* case, concerning extradition from Canada to the US. The Committee found that there was no evidence of such a risk, A/49/40, vol. II, p. 189.   [273] *Ibid.*

[274] *Ibid.*, p. 249.

It is already apparent that the Committee has proved a success and is performing a very important role in the field of human rights protection.[275]

The Committee on the Elimination of Discrimination Against Women

The Commission on the Status of Women was established in 1946 as one of the functional commissions of ECOSOC and has played a role both in standard-setting and in the elaboration of further relevant instruments.[276] The Committee on the Elimination of All Forms of Discrimination Against Women was established under article 22 of the 1979 Convention on the Elimination of all Forms of Discrimination Against Women.[277] This Convention is implemented by means of states' reports. It is composed of twenty-three experts serving in individual capacities for four-year terms. It held its first regular session in October 1982 and at its second session examined the reports of seven states parties regarding measures taken to comply with the terms of the Convention. It reports annually to the UN General Assembly through ECOSOC.[278]

The Committee in addition to hearing states' reports may make suggestions and general recommendations, which are included in the report. For example, General Recommendation No. 5 called upon states parties to make more use of 'temporary special measures such as positive action, preferential treatment or quota systems to advance women's integration into education, the economy, politics and employment', while General Recommendation No. 8 provided that states parties should take further measures to ensure to women, on equal terms with men and without discrimination, the opportunity to represent their government at the international level.[279] General Recommendation No. 12 called upon states parties

---

[275] Note that the desirability of a third optional protocol to the Covenant, concerning the right to a fair trial and a remedy is currently being considered by the Commission on Human Rights, see E/CN.4/Sub.2.1994/24, Sub-Commission resolution 1994/35 and Commission resolution 1994/107.

[276] See ECOSOC resolutions 1/5 (1946), 2/11 (1946) and 48(IV) (1947). See also L. Reanda, 'The Commission on the Status of Women' in *The United Nations and Human Rights*, p. 265.

[277] This came into force in 1981 and as of September 1996 had fifty-four states parties. See R. Jacobson, 'The Committee on the Elimination of Discrimination against Women' in *The United Nations and Human Rights*, p. 444; A. Byrnes, 'The "Other" Human Rights Body: The Work of the Committee on the Elimination of Discrimination Against Women', 14 *Yale Journal of International Law*, 1989, p. 1; M. Galey, 'International Enforcement of Women's Rights', 6 HRQ, 1984, p. 463 and M. Wadstein, 'Implementation of the UN Convention on the Elimination of All Forms of Discrimination against Women', 6 NQHR, 1988, p. 5. See also R. Cook, 'Women's International Human Rights Law', 15 HRQ, 1993, p. 230; Cook, *Human Rights of Women*, 1994 and M. Freeman and A. Fraser, 'Women's Human Rights' in *Human Rights: An Agenda for the Next Century* (eds. L. Henkin and L. Hargrove), 1994, p. 103.

[278] See articles 17–21 of the Convention and the first Report of the Committee, A/38/45 and *UN Chronicle*, November 1983, pp. 65–86.   [279] A/43/38 (1988).

to include in their reports information on measures taken to deal with violence against women, while General Recommendation No. 14 called for measures to be taken to eradicate the practice of female circumcision. General Recommendation No. 19 (1992) dealt at some length with the problem of violence against women in general and specific terms and General Recommendation No. 21 is concerned with equality in marriage and family relations.[280]

The Committee, however, meets only for two weeks a year, which is clearly inadequate. There is no right of individual petition or interstate complaint under this Convention, although these issues are under consideration.[281] There is no doubt that much remains to be done in order to support and develop the work of this Committee.

In recent years, the question of women's rights has moved further up the international agenda. The Vienna Declaration and Programme of Action adopted in 1993 emphasised that the human rights of women should be brought into the mainstream of UN system-wide activity and that women's rights should be regularly and systematically addressed throughout the UN bodies and mechanisms.[282] In the light of this, the fifth meeting of Chairpersons of Human Rights Treaty Bodies in 1994 agreed that the enjoyment of the human rights of women by each treaty body within the competence of its mandate should be closely monitored. Each of the treaty bodies took steps to examine its guidelines with this in mind.[283] It should also be noted, for example, that the Special Rapporteur on Torture was called upon by the Commission on Human Rights in 1994 to examine questions concerning torture directed disproportionately or primarily against women.[284] In addition, the General Assembly adopted a Declaration on the Elimination of Violence Against Women in February 1994[285] and the

[280] HRI/GEN/1/Rev.1, 1994, pp. 72 et seq.
[281] See, for example, the Draft Optional Protocol to the Convention on the Elimination of All Forms of Discrimination Against Women adopted at a meeting at the University of Limburg, 1994; see R. Cook, 'The Elimination of Sexual Apartheid: Prospects for the Fourth World Conference on Women', ASIL Issue Papers on World Conferences, Washington, 1995, pp. 48 et seq.   [282] See Part II, Section 3, 32 ILM, 1993, p. 1678.
[283] See HRI/MC/1995/2. See also the Report of the Expert Group Meeting on the Development of Guidelines for the Integration of Gender Perspectives into Human Rights Activities and Programmes, E/CN.4/1996/105, 1995. This called inter alia for the use of gender inclusive language in human rights instruments and standards, the identification, collection and use of gender-disaggregated data, gender-sensitive interpretation of human rights mechanisms and education and the promotion of a system-wide co-ordination and collaboration on the human rights of women within the UN.
[284] See resolution 1994/37. See also the Report of the Special Rapporteur of January 1995, E/CN.4/1995/34, p. 8.
[285] Resolution 48/104, see 33 ILM, 1994, p. 1049. Note also the adoption of the Inter-American Convention on the Prevention, Punishment and Eradication of Violence Against Women in June 1994, ibid., p. 1534. See also infra p. 290. The Fourth World Conference on Women was held in Beijing in September 1995, see generally R. Cook, 'Elimination of Sexual Apartheid'.

242 INTERNATIONAL LAW

International Labour Organisation established the promotion of equality of opportunity and treatment of men and women in employment as a priority item in its programme and budget for 1994/5.[286] The Committee on the Rights of the Child has discussed the issue of the 'girl-child' and the question of an additional protocol to the Convention on the Rights of the Child concerning child prostitution is under consideration.[287]

The Committee against Torture[288]

The Convention against Torture and Other Cruel, Inhuman or Degrading Treatment or Punishment was signed on 10 December 1984 and entered into force in 1987.[289] It built particularly upon the Declaration on the Protection of All Persons from being subjected to Torture and Other Cruel, Inhuman and Degrading Treatment or Punishment adopted by the General Assembly in 1975. Other relevant instruments preceding the Convention were the Standard Minimum Rules for the Treatment of Prisoners, 1955; the Code of Conduct for Law Enforcement Officers, 1979 (article 5) and The Principles of Medical Ethics, 1982 (Principles 1 and 2).[290] Torture is defined in article 1 to mean:

[a]ny act by which severe pain or suffering, whether physical or mental, is intentionally inflicted on a person for such purposes as obtaining from him or a third person information or a confession, punishing him for an act he or a third person has committed or is suspected of having committed, or intimidating or coercing him or a third person, or for any reason based on discrimination of any kind, when such pain or suffering is inflicted by or at the instigation of or with the consent or the acquiescence of a public official or other person acting in an official capacity. It does not include pain or suffering arising only from, inherent in or incidental to lawful sanctions.

The states parties to the Convention are under duties *inter alia* to take measures to prevent such activities in territories under their jurisdiction

---

[286] E/CN.4/Sub.2/1994/5, p. 6.   [287] See further *infra*, p. 246.
[288] See e.g. A. Byrnes, 'The Committee Against Torture' in *The United Nations and Human Rights*, p. 509; N. Rodley, *The Treatment of Prisoners under International Law*, Oxford, 1987; J. Burgers and H. Danelius, *The United Nations Convention against Torture*, Boston, 1988; *Human Rights in International Law* (ed. Meron), 1984, pp. 126–30, 165–6, 511–15; S. Ackerman, 'Torture and Other Forms of Cruel and Unusual Punishment in International Law', 11 *Vanderbilt Journal of Transnational Law*, 1978, p. 653; *Torture in the Eighties*, Amnesty International, London, 1984; A. Dormenval, 'UN Committee Against Torture: Practice and Perspectives', 8 NQHR, 1990, p. 26; Z. Haquani, 'La Convention des Nations Unies Contre la Torture', 90 RGDIP, 1986, p. 127; N. Lerner, 'The UN Convention on Torture', 16 *Israel Yearbook on Human Rights*, 1986, p. 126 and R. St J. Macdonald, 'International Prohibitions against Torture and other Forms of Similar Treatment or Punishment' in *International Law at a Time of Perplexity* (ed. Y. Dinstein), Dordrecht, 1987, p. 385.   [289] As of September 1996, there were 99 states parties.
[290] Note also the Principles on the Protection of Persons under Detention or Imprisonment adopted by the General Assembly in 1989. See generally, *Human Rights: A Compilation of International Instruments*, United Nations, New York, vol. I (Part 1), 1993, Section H.

(article 2), not to return a person to a country where he may be subjected to torture (article 3), to make torture a criminal offence and establish jurisdiction over it (articles 4 and 5),[291] to prosecute or extradite persons charged with torture (article 7) and to provide a remedy for persons tortured (article 14). A Committee against Torture was provided for in Part II of the Convention.

This Committee was established under Part II of the Convention against Torture 1984 and commenced work in 1987. It consists of ten independent experts. In an interesting comment on the proliferation of international human rights committees and the dangers of inconsistencies developing, article 17(2) provides that in nominating experts, states parties should 'bear in mind the usefulness of nominating persons who are also members of the Human Rights Committee'.

The Committee receives states' reports (article 19), has an interstate complaint competence (article 21) and may hear individual communications (article 22). In both the latter cases, it is necessary that the state or states concerned should have made a declaration accepting the competence of the Committee.[292] Article 20 of the Convention provides that if the Committee receives 'reliable evidence' that torture is being systematically practised in the territory of a state party, it may invite the state in question to co-operate in examining the evidence. The Committee may designate one or more of its members to make a confidential inquiry. In doing so, it shall seek the co-operation of the state concerned and with the latter's agreement, such an inquiry may include a visit to its territory. The Committee will transmit the findings of the inquiry to the state, together with appropriate comments or suggestions. The proceedings up to this point are to be confidential, but the Committee may after consulting the state decide to include a summary account of the results in its annual report. This additional, if cautiously phrased, power may provide the Committee with a significant role. It remains to be seen whether this will happen.[293] It should be noted that states parties have the ability to 'opt-out' of this procedure if they so wish at the time of signature or ratification, or accession.[294]

The conduct of the reporting procedure bears much resemblance to the practice of the UN Human Rights Committee. Guidelines have been issued for states parties and the discussions with state representatives are held with a view to establishing a constructive dialogue. Many problems facing other

[291] See as far as the UK is concerned sections 134 and 135 of the Criminal Justice Act 1988.
[292] As of September 1996, there were thirty-nine declarations with regard to article 21, and thirty-seven declarations with regard to article 22.
[293] See E. Zoller, 'Second Session of the UN Commission against Torture', 7 NQHR, 1989, p. 250.   [294] Article 28(1).

treaty bodies also appear with regard to the Committee Against Torture, for example, overdue reports and problems relating to implementation of the Convention generally. The Committee may also make comments on states' reports.

The first three cases before the Committee under article 22 were admissibility decisions concerning Argentinian legislation exempting junior military officers from liability for acts of torture committed during the 1976–83 period and its compatibility with the Torture Convention.[295] The Committee noted that there existed a general rule of international law obliging all states to take effective measures to prevent and punish acts of torture. However, the Convention took effect only from its date of entry (26 June 1987) and could not be applied retroactively to cover the enactment of legislation prior to that date. Therefore, the communications were inadmissible. However, the Committee did criticise the Argentinian legislation and stated that Argentina was morally bound to provide a remedy to the victims of torture. The Committee has held that where substantial grounds exist for believing that the applicant would be in danger of being subjected to torture, the expulsion or return of the applicant by the state party concerned to the state in which he might be tortured would constitute a violation of article 3 of the Convention.[296] It has also been noted that where complaints of torture are made during court proceedings, it is desirable that they be elucidated by means of independent proceedings.[297] The question of an optional protocol to the Convention which would enable the Committee to conduct *inter alia* visits of an *ad hoc* nature is under consideration.[298]

In 1985, the United Nations Commission on Human Rights appointed a Special Rapporteur on Torture to examine questions relevant to torture and to seek and receive credible and reliable information on such questions and to respond to that information without delay.[299] The work of the Rapporteur includes the sending of urgent appeals and an increasing number of country visits. He is directed to co-operate closely with the Committee against Torture.[300] The Rapporteur also works with other UN officials. In 1994, for example, the rapporteur accompanied the Special Rapporteur on Rwanda on a visit to that country, while later that year the rapporteur accompanied the Special Rapporteur on Extrajudicial, Summary or Arbitrary Executions on a visit to Colombia.[301] The Rapporteur produces an annual report to the Commission on Human Rights.

---

[295] *O.R., M.M. and M.S.* v. *Argentina*, communications nos. 1–3/1988. Decisions of 23 November 1989. See 5 *Interights Bulletin*, 1990, p. 12.
[296] *Khan* v. *Canada*, CAT/C/13/D/15/1994.   [297] *Parot* v. *Spain*, CAT/C/14/D/6/1990.
[298] See e.g. 1992/43 and E/CN.4/1994/66.   [299] Resolution 1985/33.
[300] See e.g. Zoller, '46th Session'.   [301] See E/CN.4/1995/34, pp. 6–7.

The Committee on the Rights of the Child[302]

The Convention on the Rights of the Child was adopted by the General Assembly on 20 November 1989.[303] It provides that in all actions concerning children, the best interests of the child shall be a primary consideration. A variety of rights are stipulated including the inherent right to life (article 6); the right to a name and to acquire a nationality (article 7); the right to freedom of expression (article 13); the right to freedom of thought, conscience and religion (article 14); the right not to be subjected to arbitrary or unlawful interference with privacy, family, home or correspondence and the right to the enjoyment of the highest attainable standard of health (article 24).

States parties agree to take all appropriate measures to protect the child from all forms of physical and mental violence (article 19) and from economic exploitation (article 32) and the illicit use of drugs (article 33) and there are specific provisions relating to refugees and handicapped children. In addition, states parties agreed to respect the rules of international humanitarian law applicable to armed conflicts relevant to children (article 38). This provision was one response to the use of children in the Iran–Iraq war.

Article 43 of the Convention on the Rights of the Child 1989 provides for the establishment of a Committee. This Committee, which was elected in 1991, is composed of ten independent experts[304] and has the competence to hear states' reports (article 44). The Committee itself submits reports every two years to the General Assembly through ECOSOC. The Committee can recommend to the General Assembly that the Secretary-General be requested to undertake on its behalf studies on specific issues relating to the rights of the child, an innovation in the functions of such treaty bodies, and it can make suggestions and general recommendations (article 45). The Committee (like the Committee on Economic, Social and Cultural Rights) sets aside time for general discussions on particular topics in accordance with rule 75 of its provisional rules of procedure. For example, at its second session in 1992, the Committee discussed the question of children in armed

---

[302] See e.g. D. McGoldrick, 'The UN Convention on the Rights of the Child', 5 *International Journal of Law and the Family*, 1991, p. 132; M. Santos Pais, 'The Convention on the Rights of the Child and the Work of the Committee', 26 *Israel Law Review*, 1992, p. 16 and Santos Pais, 'Rights of Children and the Family' in *Human Rights: An Agenda for the Next Century*, p. 183. See also G. Van Bueren, *The International Law on the Rights of the Child*, Dordrecht, 1995 and *The United Nations Convention on the Rights of the Child* (ed. S. Detrick), Dordrecht, 1992.

[303] The Convention came into force on 2 September 1990. As of September 1996, there were 187 states parties, ST/HR/4/Rev.12, 1995. Note also the Declaration on the Rights of the Child adopted by the General Assembly in resolution 1386(XIV), 1959 and the proclamation of 1979 as the International Year of the Child in resolution 31/169.

[304] Note that the suggestion was made in 1995 for an increase in membership to eighteen. This suggestion is to be tabled before a special conference of states parties, see CRC/SP/18, 1995.

conflicts,[305] while at its fourth session, the problem of the economic exploitation of children was discussed.[306] A general discussion on the 'girl-child' was held at the eighth session of the Committee in 1995,[307] and one on the administration of juvenile justice at the ninth session.[308]

As part of the general reporting process, the Committee adopted an urgent action procedure at its second session. Provided that the state concerned has ratified the Convention, that the situation is serious and there is a risk of further violations, the Committee may send a communication to the state 'in a spirit of dialogue' and may request the provision of additional information or suggest a visit.[309] At its fourth session, the Committee established a working group to study ways and means whereby the urgent action procedure could be pursued effectively.[310] The Committee has produced a set of Guidelines concerning states reports[311] and a pre-sessional working group considers these reports and draws up a list of issues needing further clarification which is sent to the state concerned. As is the case with other reporting mechanisms, the representatives of the state whose report is being considered by the Committee is invited to send representatives to the appropriate meetings. After the process is completed, the Committee issues Concluding Observations in which both the positive aspects of the report considered and the problems identified are noted, together with suggestions and recommendations.[312] Various follow-up measures to the consideration of reports exist, but usually this consists of the request for the provision of further information.[313]

The Proposed Committee on the Protection of Migrant Workers[314]

The International Convention on the Protection of the Rights of All Migrant Workers and Members of their Families was adopted by the General

[305] A/49/41, pp. 94 et seq. This led to a recommendation to the General Assembly to request the Secretary-General to undertake a special study on the means to protect children in armed conflicts, see CRC/C/SR.72, p. 2 and resolution 48/157. A preliminary draft optional protocol on involvement of children in armed conflicts has been drafted, A/49/41, p. 130 and is currently under discussion by an open-ended working group of the Commission on Human Rights, see Commission resolution 1995/79 and ECOSOC resolution 1995/37. Note that the question of the protection of children in armed conflicts was referred to in the Vienna Declaration and Programme of Action 1993, Part II, B, 4, see 32 ILM, 1993, p. 1680. See also G. Van Bueren, 'The International Legal Protection of Children in Armed Conflicts', 43 ICLQ, 1994, p. 809.   [306] Ibid., pp. 99 et seq.
[307] See CRC/C/38, p. 47. Note that an open-ended working group of the Commission on Human Rights is currently considering a draft optional protocol to the Convention on the question of the sale of children, child prostitution and child pornography, see Commission resolution 1995/78 and ECOSOC resolution 1995/35.   [308] See CRC/C/43, p. 64.
[309] See CRC/C/SR.42, p. 2. and A/49/41, pp. 69–71.   [310] Ibid.   [311] See CRC/C/5.
[312] See e.g. A/49/41, pp. 20 et seq.; CRC/C/38, pp. 10 et seq and CRC/C/43, pp. 10 et seq.
[313] See e.g. CRC/C/27/Rev.3, 1995 detailing such measures up to mid-1995.
[314] See e.g. K. Samson, 'Human Rights Co-Ordination within the UN System' in The United Nations and Human Rights, pp. 620, 641 et seq.; S. Hune and J. Niessen, 'Ratifying the UN Migrant Workers Convention: Current Difficulties and Prospects', 12 NQHR, 1994, p.

Assembly and opened for signature in December 1990. The Convention will come into effect upon notification of twenty ratifications or accessions.[315] The Convention defines a migrant worker as 'a person who is to be engaged, is engaged, or has been engaged in a remunerated activity in a state of which he or she is not a national' (article 2). This includes, for example, frontier and seasonal workers, workers on offshore installations and specified-employment workers, but excludes employees of international organisations or official state employees abroad, refugees, stateless persons, students and workers on offshore installations who have not been admitted to take up residence and engage in a remunerated activity in the state of employment (article 3).

Migrant workers are entitled to equality of treatment with nationals in areas such as matters before courts and tribunals (article 18), terms of employment (article 25), freedom to join trades unions (article 26), medical treatment (article 28), access to education for their children (article 30) and respect for cultural identity (article 31). Migrant workers are protected from collective expulsion (article 22). Further provisions deal with additional rights for migrant workers and members of their families in a documented or regular situation (Part IV).

The Convention provides for the creation of a Committee of fourteen independent experts (Part VII). States parties will be required to provide reports on measures taken to give effect to the provisions of the Convention (article 73). An interstate complaints procedure is provided for in article 76, on the condition that the states concerned have made a declaration expressly recognising the competence of the Committee to hear such complaints, while under article 77 an individual complaints procedure can be used with regard to states that have made a declaration recognising the competence of the Committee in this regard.

Conclusions

Most international human rights conventions obligate states parties to take certain measures with regard to the provisions contained therein, whether by domestic legislation or otherwise.[316] Several treaties require states parties to make periodic reports.[317] The number of treaties establishing committees

---

393 and S. Hune and J. Niessen, 'The First UN Convention on Migrant Workers', 9 NQHR, 1991, p. 133.   [315] As of September 1996, there were seven states parties.

[316] See e.g. article 2 of the Civil and Political Rights Covenant 1966; article 1 of the European Convention on Human Rights 1950; articles 1 and 2 of the American Convention on Human Rights 1969; article 5 of the Genocide Convention 1948; article 4 of the Convention on the Suppression and Punishment of the Crime of Apartheid 1973 and article 3 of the Slavery Convention 1926.

[317] See in addition to the conventions mentioned *supra*, article 7 of the Apartheid Convention 1973. Several conventions provide for the communication of information to the UN Secretary-General, see e.g. article 33 of the Convention Relating to the Status of Stateless Persons 1954 and articles 35 and 36 of the Convention Relating to the Status of Refugees 1951.

specifically to oversee the implementation of particular conventions, however, is not large, although increasing, while relatively very few provide for the right of individual petition,[318] although consideration is now being given to the possibility of extending the right of individual petition to Committees that do not possess such competence, such as the Economic, Social and Cultural Rights Committee and the Committee on the Elimination of Discrimination Against Women.

The proliferation of committees raises problems concerned both with resources and with regard to consistency. The question of resources is a serious and ongoing difficulty. The Vienna Declaration and Programme of Action 1993 emphasised the necessity for a substantial increase in the resources for the human rights programme of the UN and particularly called for sufficient funding to be made available to the UN Centre for Human Rights, which *inter alia* provides the administrative support for the human rights organs and committees discussed in this chapter.[319] The various human rights committees themselves have pointed to the resource problem.[320] The Committee on the Elimination of Racial Discrimination and the Committee against Torture have recently changed their financing system so that as from January 1994, they are financed under the regular budget of the United Nations.[321] The Committee on Economic, Social and Cultural Rights has sought additional resources from the Economic and Social Council.[322] Nevertheless, the fact remains that human rights activity within the UN system is seriously underfunded.

The question of consistency in view of the increasing number of human rights bodies within the UN system has been partially addressed by the establishment of an annual system of meetings between the chairpersons of the treaty bodies.[323] Issues of concern have been discussed ranging from the need to encourage states to ratify all human rights treaties, concern about reservations made to human rights treaties,[324] attempts to establish that successor states are automatically bound by obligations under international human rights treaties from the date of independence irrespective of confirmation,[325] the formulation of new norms and instruments, and the

---

[318] See generally in addition to the above section, Tardu, *Human Rights*.

[319] See Part II, Section A of the Vienna Declaration and Programme of Action, 32 ILM, 1993, pp. 1674–5.

[320] See e.g. the Human Rights Committee, A/49/44, and the Committee Against Torture, A/50/44. See also the Report of the Secretary-General to the sixth meeting of Chairpersons of treaty bodies, HR/MC/1995/2, p. 13.

[321] See General Assembly resolution 47/111 and HRI/MC/1995/2, p. 14.   [322] *Ibid.*, p. 15.

[323] See General Assembly resolution 49/178, 1994, which endorsed the recommendation of the chairpersons that the meetings be held annually. The first meeting of the chairpersons of treaty bodies was held in 1984, A/39/484; the second in 1988, A/44/98; the third in 1990, A/45/636; the fourth in 1992, A/47/628; the fifth in 1994, A/49/537, and the sixth in 1995, HRI/MC/1995/2.   [324] See further Chapter 16, *infra* p. 647.

[325] See further Chapter 17, *infra*, p. 695.

promotion of human rights education to consideration of the continuing problem of overdue reports[326] and the role of non-governmental organisations.[327] The development of early warning and preventive procedures by committee are to be particularly noted. The Committee on the Elimination of Racial Discrimination, for example, under its urgent procedures, may since 1994 review the human rights situation in states parties that give rise to especial concern,[328] while the Human Rights Committee is able to request states parties to submit special urgent reports.[329]

The specialised agencies

The International Labour Organisation[330]

The ILO was created in 1919 and expanded in 1946.[331] The Declaration of Philadelphia of 1944 (which was incorporated in the ILO constitution in 1946) reaffirmed the basic principles of the organisation. These are: (a) that labour is not a commodity; (b) that freedom of expression and of association are essential to sustained progress; and (c) that poverty anywhere constitutes a danger to prosperity everywhere. The ILO is composed of a unique tripartite structure involving governments, workers and employers and consists of three organs; a General Conference of representatives of

---

[326] Both the Committee on the Elimination of Racial Discrimination and the Committee on Economic, Social and Cultural Rights have established procedures enabling them to examine the situation in the state concerned, see *supra* pp. 000 and 000. Other Committees have sought to hold meetings with the officials of the states concerned in order to encourage submission of overdue reports, HRI/MC/1995/2, p. 7.   [327] See e.g. HRI/MC/1995.
[328] See *supra* p. 232.
[329] See *supra* p. 235. See also *supra* p. 245 with regard to the procedures of the Committee on the Rights of the Child.
[330] See e.g. L. Betten, 'At its 75th Anniversary, the International Labour Organisation Prepares Itself for an Active Future', 12 NQHR, 1994, p. 425; L. Swepston, 'Human Rights Complaints Procedures of the International Labour Organisation' in *Guide to International Human Rights Practice*, p. 99; V. Leary, 'Lessons from the Experience of the International Labour Organisation' in *The United Nations and Human Rights*, p. 580; C. W. Jenks, 'Human Rights, Social Justice and Peace', in the *International Protection of Human Rights* (eds. A. Schou and A. Eide), Stockholm, 1968, p. 227, and *Social Justice in the Law of Nations*, Oxford, 1970; E. A. Landy, *The Effectiveness of International Supervision: Thirty Years of ILO Experience*, New York, 1966; N. Valticos, 'The Role of the ILO: Present Action and Future Perspectives' in *Human Rights: Thirty Years After the Universal Declaration*, p. 211, and 'The International Labour Organisation' in *The International Dimensions of Human Rights* (ed. K. Vasak), vol. I, 1982, p. 363; E. A. Landy, 'The Implementation Procedures of the International Labour Organisation', 20 *Santa Clara Law Review*, 1980, p. 633; F. Wolf, 'ILO Experience in Implementation of Human Rights', 10 *Journal of International Law and Economics*, 1975, p. 599; J. M. Servais, 'ILO Standards on Freedom of Association and Their Implementation', 123 *International Labour Review*, 1984, p. 765; N. Valticos, *Le Droit International Du Travail*, Paris, 1980 and Robertson and Merrills, *Human Rights*, p. 236. See also H. K. Nielsen, 'The Concept of Discrimination in ILO Convention No. 111', 43 ICLQ, 1994, p. 827.
[331] An agreement bringing the ILO into relationship with the UN as a specialised agency under article 63 of the UN Charter came into force on 14 December 1946, see General Assembly resolution 50(I).

member states (the International Labour Conference), the Governing Body and the International Labour Office.[332] The ILO constitution enables the organisation to examine and elaborate international labour standards, whether Conventions or Recommendations. The former are the more formal method of dealing with important matters, while the latter consist basically of guidelines for legislation. Between 1919 and 1994, 175 Conventions and 182 Recommendations were adopted by the ILO, all dealing basically with issues of social justice.[333] Under article 19 of the ILO constitution all members must submit Conventions and Recommendations to their competent national authorities within twelve to eighteen months of adoption. Under article 22, states which have ratified Conventions are obligated to make annual reports on measures taken to give effect to them to the International Labour Office.[334] Under article 19, members must also submit reports regarding both unratified Conventions and Recommendations to the Director-General of the International Labour Office at appropriate intervals as requested by the Governing Body, concerning the position of its law and practice in regard to the matters dealt with in the Convention or Recommendation showing the extent to which effect has been given, or is proposed to be given, to the provisions of the Convention or Recommendation, including a statement of the difficulties which prevent or delay ratification of the Convention concerned.[335] In 1926–7, a Committee of Experts on the Application of Conventions and Recommendations was established to consider reports submitted by member states. The comments of the twenty-member Committee, appointed by the Governing Body on the suggestion of the Director-General of the International Labour Office, on ratified Conventions take the form of 'observations' included in the printed report of the Committee in the case of more important issues, or 'requests' to the government concerned for information, which are not published in the report of the Committee. In the case of unratified Conventions and Recommendations a 'general survey' of the application of the particular instrument in question is carried out.[336] A

---

[332] See UN Action, p. 28. The tripartite structure means that the delegation of each member state to the International Labour Conference includes two representatives of the government, one representative of workers and one representative of the employers. There are fifty-six members of the Governing Body, with twenty-eight government representatives and fourteen each from employers' and workers' organisations.

[333] See Valticos, 'International Labour Organisation', p. 365, and Swepston, 'Human Rights Complaints Procedures of the International Labour Organisation', p. 100. See also E/CN.4/Sub.2/1994/5, p. 3.

[334] However, in practice the annual rule is relaxed, see Valticos, 'International Labour Organisation', p. 368. Governments are obliged by article 23(2) to communicate copies of the reports to employers' and workers' organisations.

[335] The latter provision does not, of course, apply in the case of Recommendations.

[336] Valticos, Le Droit, pp. 369–70 and Wolf, 'ILO Standards', pp. 608–10. See, for example, ILO, Freedom of Association and Collective Bargaining: General Survey, Geneva, 1983.

Committee on the Application of Conventions and Recommendations of the International Labour Conference is appointed at each of its annual sessions composed of tripartite representatives to discuss relevant issues based primarily upon the general report of the Committee of Experts.[337] It may also draw up a 'Special List' of cases to be drawn to the attention of the Conference.

Two types of procedure exist. Under articles 24 and 25, a representation may be made by employers' or workers' organisations to the Office to the effect that any of the members has failed to secure the effective observation of any Convention to which it is a party. These views are examined first by a committee of three of the Governing Body then by the Governing Body itself. States are invited to reply and both the original representation and the reply (if any) may be publicised by the Governing Body. There have not been many representations of this kind.[338] Under articles 26–29 and 31–33 any member may file a complaint against another member state that the effective observance of a ratified Convention has not been secured. The Governing Body may call for a reply by the object state or establish a commission of inquiry. Such a commission is normally composed of three experts and the procedure adopted is of a judicial nature. Recourse may be had by the parties to the International Court of Justice. Ultimately the Governing Body may recommend to the Conference such action as it considers wise and expedient. The complaints procedure was first used by Ghana against Portugal regarding the Abolition of Forced Labour Convention 1957 in its African territories.[339]

A special procedure regarding freedom of association was established in 1951, with a Committee on Freedom of Association which examines a wide range of complaints. It consists of nine members (three from each of the tripartite elements in the ILO). The Committee submits detailed reports to the Governing Body with proposed conclusions and suggested recommendations to be made to the state concerned, and a considerable case law has been build up.[340] A Fact-finding and Conciliation Commission has been created for more serious and politically delicate cases and operates with the consent of the state concerned. Accordingly, few questions have

---

[337] The Committee usually consists of 200 members.
[338] But see e.g. Official Bulletin of the ILO, 1956, p. 120 (Netherlands Antilles); ibid., 1967, p. 267 (Brazil) and ibid., 1972, p. 125 (Italy). See also ibid., 1978, (Czechoslovakia).
[339] See Official Bulletin of the ILO, 1962; ibid., 1963 (Liberia) and ibid., 1971 (Greece).
[340] See e.g. Von Potobsky, 'Protection of Trade Union Rights: Twenty Years Work of the Committee on Freedom of Association', 105 International Labour Review, 1972, p. 69. See also Servais, 'ILO Standards' and Freedom of Association: Digest of Decisions of the Freedom of Association Committee of the Governing Body of the ILO, 3rd edn, Geneva, 1985. By the end of 1991, over 1,600 cases had been considered by the Committee, see L. Swepston, 'Human Rights Complaints Procedures of the International Labour Organisation' in Guide to International Human Rights Practice, p. 109.

been dealt with,[341] although in 1992 a visit was made to South Africa and recommendations made to the ILO and ECOSOC. The government of that country sent a response to the Director-General of the ILO and at the request of ECOSOC the ILO Committee on Freedom of Association examined South Africa's report in 1994. The Committee's report, noting changes taking place in that country, was approved by the Governing Body and transmitted to ECOSOC.[342] In addition, a system of 'direct contacts' has been instituted, consisting of personal visits by ILO officials, or independent persons named by the Director-General, in order to assist in overcoming particular difficulties. These have included, for example, questions regarding freedom of association in Argentina in 1990 and the situation of Haitian workers on sugar plantations in the Dominican Republic in 1991.[343]

The United Nations Educational, Scientific and Cultural Organisation[344]

UNESCO came into being in November 1946 and was brought into relationship with the UN on 14 December that year.[345] The aim of the organisation, proclaimed in article 1 of its constitution, is to contribute to peace and security by promoting collaboration through education, science and culture 'in order to further universal respect for justice, for the rule of law and for the human rights and fundamental freedoms which are affirmed for the peoples of the world'. The organisation consists of a General Conference which meets every two years and in which all member states are represented, an Executive Board, elected by the conference, and a secretariat headed by a Director-General. Under article IV(4), member states undertake to submit Conventions and Resolutions to the competent national authorities within a year of adoption and may be required to submit reports on action taken.[346] Unlike the ILO, UNESCO has no constitution provision for reviewing complaints concerning the implementation of conventions pro-

---

[341] See Valticos, 'The International Labour Organisation', pp. 384 et seq. See also Official Bulletin of the ILO, 1966 (Japan); and Valticos, 'Un Double Type d'Enquête de l'OIT au Chili', AFDI, 1975, p. 483.   [342] E/CN.4/Sub.2/1994/5, p. 4.

[343] See N. Valticos, 'Une Nouvelle Forme d'Action Internationale: Les "Contacts Directs"', 27 AFDI, 1981, p. 481 and V. Leary, 'Lessons from the Experience of the International Labour Organisation' in The United Nations and Human Rights, p. 611.

[344] See e.g. S. Marks, 'The Complaints Procedure of the United Nations Educational, Scientific and Cultural Organisation' in Guide to International Human Rights Practice, p. 86; D. Weissbrodt and R. Farley, 'The UNESCO Human Rights Procedure: An Evaluation', 16 HRQ, 1994, p. 391; P. Alston, 'UNESCO's Procedures for Dealing with Human Rights Violations', 20 Santa Clara Law Review, 1980, p. 665; Saba, 'UNESCO and Human Rights' in The International Dimensions of Human Rights, vol. II, p. 401; Robertson and Merrills, Human Rights, p. 241 and UN Action, pp. 308 and 321.

[345] See General Assembly resolution 50(I).

[346] See for example the obligation to submit reports under article 7 of the 1960 Convention against Discrimination in Education, see also UN Action, p. 163.

cedure. However, in 1962 a Protocol instituting a Conciliation and Good Offices Commission was adopted to help resolve disputes arising between states parties to the 1960 Convention against Discrimination in Education. It entered into force in 1968 and the first meeting of the eleven-member Commission was in 1971. It aims to make available its good offices in order to reach a friendly settlement between the states parties to the convention in question. In 1978 the Executive Board of UNESCO adopted decision 104 EX/3.3, by which it established a procedure to handle individual communications alleging violations of human rights. Ten conditions for admissibility are laid down, including the requirement that the human rights violated must fall within UNESCO's competence in the fields of education, science, culture and information, and the need for the communication to be compatible with international human rights interests. The condition with regard to domestic remedies is rather different than is the case with other human rights organs, in that all the communication needs to do is to 'indicate whether an attempt has been made to exhaust domestic remedies . . . and the result of such an attempt, if any'. The investigating body is the Executive Board's Committee on Conventions and Recommendations, which is composed of twenty-four members and normally meets twice a year in private session.[347] The examination of communications is confidential. The Committee decides whether a communication is admissible and then makes a decision on the merits. The task of the Committee is to reach a 'friendly solution designed to advance the promotion of the human rights falling within UNESCO's fields of competence'.[348] Confidential reports are submitted to the Executive Board each session, which contain appropriate information plus recommendations.[349] It is also to be noted that under this procedure the Director-General generally has a role in seeking to strengthen the action of UNESCO in promoting human rights and initiating consultations in confidence to help reach solutions to particular human rights problems.[350] UNESCO published a report in 1993 concerning the operations of the procedure, noting that the Committee had examined 414 cases between 1978 and 1993, of which it settled 241 individual cases.[351] It is unclear how successful the procedure has been, in view of the strict confidentiality which

---

[347] Formerly the Committee on Conventions and Recommendations in Education, *ibid.*, pp. 321–2. See also A/CONF.157/PC/61/Add.6, 1993.
[348] Decision 104.EX/3.3, para. 14(k).
[349] In the April 1980 session, for example, forty-five communications were examined as to admissibility, of which five were declared inadmissible, thirteen admissible, twenty suspended and seven deleted from the agenda. Ten communications were examined on the merits, UNESCO Doc. 21 C/13, para. 65.   [350] *Ibid.*, paras 8 and 9.
[351] See UNESCO Doc. 141/EX/6 and Weissbrodt and Farley, 'UNESCO Human Rights Procedure', p. 391. It was noted that during this period, 129 individuals were either released or acquitted, 20 authorised to leave and 34 to return to the state concerned, 24 were able to resume banned employment or activity, and 11 were able to resume a banned publication or broadcast, *ibid.*

binds it,[352] the length of time taken to produce results and the high proportion of cases declared inadmissible.[353]

A special procedure to deal with disappeared persons has been established by the Committee. Communications dealing with such persons are placed on a Special List, if insufficient information is forthcoming from the government in question, and examined by the Committee.[354] In addition to *cases* concerning violations of human rights which are individual and specific, UNESCO may also examine *questions* of massive, systematic or flagrant violations of human rights resulting either from a policy contrary to human rights applied by a state or from an accumulation of individual cases forming a consistent pattern.[355] In the instance of such *questions*, the issue is to be discussed by the Executive Board of the General Conference in public.[356]

---

[352] See G. H. Dumont, 'UNESCO's Practical Action on Human Rights', 122 *International Social Sciences Journal*, 1989, p. 585 and K. Partsch, 'La Mise en Oeuvre des Droit de l'Homme par l'UNESCO', 36 AFDI, 1990, p. 482.

[353] Weissbrodt and Farley note that of sixty-four cases studied only five cases were declared admissible, 'The UNESCO Human Rights Procedure', p. 399. Of these, three concerned one particular country in Latin America. One case was considered over a nine and a half year period and another case was considered over eight and a half years.

[354] UNESCO doc.108 EX/CR/HR/PROC/2 Rev. (1979)

[355] Decision 104 ex/3.3, para. 10.   [356] *Ibid.*, para. 18.

THE REGIONAL PROTECTION OF
HUMAN RIGHTS

Europe[1]

The Council of Europe

The Council of Europe was founded in 1949 as a European organisation for encouraging and developing intergovernmental and interparliamentary co-operation. Its aim as laid down in article 1 of the Statute is to achieve a greater unity between member states for the purpose of safeguarding and realising the ideals and principles which are their common heritage and facilitating their economic and social progress. The principles of the Council of Europe as established in article 3 of the Statute include pluralist democracy, respect for human rights and the rule of law. A Committee of Ministers, consisting of the Foreign Ministers of member states, and a Parliamentary Assembly, consisting of delegations of members of national parliaments, constitute the principal organs of the Council of Europe, together with a Secretary-General and supporting secretariat. There also exists a Standing Conference of Local and Regional Authorities of Europe, consisting of national delegations of local and regional elected repre-sentatives. The Council of Europe also maintains a number of support and assistance programmes.[2] The demise of the Soviet empire in Eastern and Central Europe has been the primary reason for the great increase in member states over the last few years.[3] The process of joining the Council of Europe has provided the Council with some influence over prospective members and this has led both to expert advice and assistance being pro-ferred and to commitments being entered into in the field of human rights by applicants. For example, Parliamentary Assembly Opinion No. 191 on the Application for Membership by the Former Yugoslav Republic of

---

[1] See generally *Monitoring Human Rights in Europe* (eds. A. Bloed, Leicht, M. Nowak and A. Rosas), Dordrecht, 1993.   [2] See e.g. A/CONF.157/PC/66/Add.2, 1993.
[3] At the beginning of 1993, for example, there were twenty-six member states. By autumn 1996, there were forty member states, the most recent being Russia in early 1996 and Croatia in October 1996.

Macedonia[4] notes that the applicant entered into commitments relating to revision and establishment of new laws (for example, with respect to the organisation and functioning of the criminal justice system), amendment of the constitution in order to include the right to a fair trial, and agreement to sign a variety of international instruments including the European Convention on Human Rights, the European Convention on the Prevention of Torture, the Framework Convention for the Protection of National Minorities. In addition, the applicant agreed to co-operate fully in the monitoring process for implementation of Assembly Order No. 508 (1995) on the honouring of obligations and commitments by member states of the Council of Europe as well as in monitoring processes established by virtue of the Committee of Ministers Declaration of 10 November 1994. The Council of Europe has also moved beyond agreeing or noting commitments made at the time of application for membership and approval thereof to consideration of how those commitments have been honoured once an applicant has become a member state. The Committee of Ministers Declaration of 10 November 1994 provides a mechanism for examining state practice in this area and one may expect further developments in this context.[5]

Although a large number of treaties between member states have been signed under the auspices of the Council of Europe, undoubtedly the most important has been the European Convention on Human Rights.

[4] 16 HRLJ, 1995, p. 372. See also Parliamentary Assembly Opinion No. 190 on the Application of Ukraine for Membership, *ibid.*, p. 373 and Opinion Nos. 183 (1995) on the Application of Latvia for Membership, 188 (1995) on the Application of Moldova for Membership and 189 (1995) on the Application of Albania for Membership, H/INF (95) 3 pp. 77 *et seq.* Note that under Recommendation 1055 (1995), the Assembly decided to suspend the procedure concerning its statutory opinion on Russia's request for membership in the light of the situation in Chechnya. However, Russia joined the Council of Europe in early 1996.
[5] See further *infra* p. 267. Note also Assembly Order 508 (1995) on the Honouring of Obligations and Commitments by Member States of the Council of Europe, which seeks to strengthen the monitoring procedure of the Assembly established in 1993. Under Order No. 485 (1993), the Assembly instructed its Committee on Legal Affairs and Human Rights to report to it when problems arise on the situation of human rights in member states. Under the 1995 Order, the Committee on Legal Affairs and Human Rights and the Committee on Political Affairs were instructed to co-operate in monitoring closely the honouring of obligations and commitments in all member states, while the Committee on Relations with European Non-Member Countries would be asked for an opinion regarding member states that previously enjoyed special guest status prior to membership. The Committees are to report directly to the Assembly, which may sanction persistent failure to honour commitments and lack of co-operation in monitoring processes by the non-ratification of the credentials of a national parliamentary delegation. Beyond this, the Assembly may make a recommendation to the Committee of Ministers asking it to take appropriate measures under article 8 of the Statute of the Council of Europe, which concerns suspension of membership, see H/INF (95) 3, p. 110.

The European Convention on Human Rights[6]

The Convention was signed on 4 November 1950 and entered into force in September 1953.[7] Together with eleven Protocols, it covers a wide variety of primarily civil and political rights.[8] The preamble notes that the European states are like-minded and have a common heritage of political tradition, ideals, freedoms and the rule of law. The rights covered in the Convention itself include the right to life (article 2), prohibition of torture and slavery (articles 3 and 4), right to liberty and security of person (article 5), right to a fair and public hearing within a reasonable time by an independent and impartial tribunal established by law (article 6), prohibition of retroactive criminal legislation (article 7), right to respect for private and family life (article 8), freedom of thought, conscience and religion (article 9), freedom of expression (article 10), freedom of assembly and association (article 11), the right to marry and found a family (article 12), the right to an effective remedy before a national authority if one of the Convention rights or freedoms is violated (article 13) and a non-discrimination provision regarding the enjoyment of rights and freedoms under the Convention (article 14). In addition, several protocols have been added to the substantive rights protected under the Convention. Protocol I protects the rights of property, education and free elections by secret ballots, Protocol IV prohibits imprisonment for civil debt and protects *inter alia* the rights of free movement and choice of residence and the right to enter one's own country, Protocol VI provides for the abolition of the death penalty, while Protocol VII provides

---

[6] See e.g. F. G. Jacobs and R. C. A. White, *The European Convention on Human Rights*, 2nd edn, Oxford, 1996; D. J. Harris, M. O'Boyle and C. Warbrick, *Law of the European Convention on Human Rights*, London, 1995; *La Convention Européene des Droits de l'Homme* (eds. P. Imbert and L. Pettiti), Paris, 1995; M. Janis, R. Kay and A. Bradley, *European Human Rights Law: Text and Materials*, Oxford, 1995; L. J. Clements, *European Human Rights: Taking a Case under the Convention*, London, 1994; *The European System for the Protection of Human Rights* (eds. R. St J. Macdonald, F. Matscher and H. Petzold), Dordrecht, 1993; R. Beddard, *Human Rights and Europe*, 3rd edn, Cambridge, 1993; A. H. Robertson and J. G. Merrills, *Human Rights in Europe*, Manchester, 3rd edn, 1993; P. Van Dijk and G. J. H. Van Hoof, *Theory and Practice of the European Convention on Human Rights*, 2nd edn, Deventer, 1990; Ph. J. Velu and R. Ergel, *La Convention Européene des Droits de l'Homme*, Brussels, 1990; G. Cohen-Jonathan, *La Convention Européene des Droits de l'Homme*, Paris, 1989 and J. Fawcett, *The Application of the European Convention on Human Rights*, 2nd edn, Oxford, 1987. See also L. G. Loucaides, *Essays on the Developing Law of Human Rights*, Dordrecht, 1995; J. G. Merrills, *The Development of International Law by the European Court of Human Rights*, 2nd edn, Manchester, 1993, and A. Drzemczewski, *The European Human Rights Convention in Domestic Law*, Oxford, 1983.

[7] As of September 1996, there were thirty-three states parties to this Convention. See A. Drzemczewski, 'Ensuring Compatibility of Domestic Law with the European Convention on Human Rights Prior to Ratification: The Hungarian Model', 16 HRLJ, 1995, pp. 241, 247. Albania, Latvia, Moldova, Russia, Ukraine and 'the Former Yugoslav Republic of Macedonia' have yet to ratify the Convention.

[8] Economic and Social rights are covered in the European Social Charter, 1961. See *infra*, p. 272.

inter alia that an alien lawfully resident in a state shall not be expelled therefrom except in pursuance of a decision reached in accordance with the law,
that a person convicted of a criminal offence shall have the right to have that
conviction or sentence reviewed by a higher tribunal and that no one may
be tried or punished again in criminal proceedings for an offence for which
he has already been finally acquitted or convicted. Like other international
treaties, the European Convention imposes obligations upon states parties
to respect a variety of provisions. In this instance the Convention has also
been incorporated into the domestic legislation of all thirty-three current
states parties, apart from the UK and Ireland,[9] although the Convention
does not provide as to how exactly the states parties are to implement internally the relevant obligations.[10] However, it has been emphasised that:

> unlike international treaties of the classic kind, the Convention comprises
> more than mere reciprocal engagements between contracting states. It creates,
> over and above a network of mutual and bilateral undertakings, objective
> obligations, which in the words of the preamble, benefit from a 'collective
> enforcement'.[11]

In addition, a more teleological and flexible approach to the interpretation of the Convention has been adopted.[12] The Court has emphasised that
the Convention is a living instrument to be interpreted in the light of
present-day conditions and this approach applies not only to the substantive
rights protected under the Convention, but also to those provisions such as
articles 25 and 46 which govern the operation of the Convention's enforcement machinery.[13] In addition, the Court has noted that the object and
purpose of the Convention as an instrument for the protection of individuals requires that its provisions be interpreted and applied so as to make its
safeguards practical and effective.[14] It has also been emphasised that the
Convention constitutes a 'constitutional instrument of European public
order ("*ordre public*")'.[15] The Convention applies, of course, within the territory of contracting states, but the concept of 'jurisdiction' under article 1
has been interpreted to include the possibility of application to extradition

---

[9] See e.g. J. Polakiewicz and V. Jacob-Foltzer, 'The European Human Rights Convention in Domestic Law', 12 HRLJ, 1991, pp. 65 and 125 and Harris *et al.*, *Law of the European Convention*, p. 24, note 2.
[10] See e.g. the *Swedish Engine Drivers' Union* case, Series A, vol. 20, 1976, p. 18; 58 ILR, pp. 19, 36. See also the *Belgian Linguistics* case, Series A, vol. 6, 1968, p. 35; 45 ILR, pp. 136, 165.
[11] See article 1 and *Ireland* v. *UK*, Series A, vol. 25, 1978, pp. 90–1; 58 ILR, pp. 188, 290–1. See also *Loizidou* v. *Turkey*, Series A, vol. 310, 1995, pp. 22–3.
[12] See e.g. the *Tyrer* case, Series A, vol. 26, 1978; 58 ILR, p. 339, and see also the *Marckx* case, Series A, vol. 31, 1979; 58 ILR, p. 561. See also *infra*, Chapter 16, p. 659.
[13] See *Loizidou* v. *Turkey*, Series A, vol. 310, 1995, p. 23.
[14] See *Soering* v. *UK*, Series A, vol. 161, 1989, p. 34; *Artico* v. *Italy*, Series A, vol. 37, p. 16 and *Loizidou* v. *Turkey*, Series A, vol. 310, p. 23.
[15] *Loizidou* v. *Turkey*, Series A, vol. 310, pp. 24 and 27.

or expulsion of a person by a contracting state to the territory of a non-contracting state[16] and the situation where acts of the authorities of contracting states, whether performed within or outside national boundaries, produce effects outside their own territory.[17]

The Commission[18]

The number of members of the European Commission of Human Rights is equal to the number of contracting parties to the Convention.[19] The members of the Commission are elected by the Committee of Ministers from a list of names drawn up by the Bureau of the Consultative Assembly[20] of the Council of Europe. They serve for six-year terms in their individual capacity and are eligible for re-election.[21] By article 21(3) of the Convention (as amended by Protocol VIII), candidates for election to the Commission 'shall be of high moral character and must possess the qualifications required for appointment either to high judicial office or be persons of recognised competence in national or international law'. It is to the Commission that all applications, whether from individuals or states, must be addressed. The Commission constitutes a filtering system in deciding which applications may be declared admissible,[22] an organ for the establishment of the facts of the particular case[23] and a mechanism of conciliation and friendly settlement.[24] All deliberations of the Commission are confidential[25] and the Commission sits *in camera*.[26]

Article 24 provides for the right of interstate complaint and to date applications have been lodged with the Commission by states involving six situations.[27] Only one of these has to date reached the Court.[28] Such applications are a means of bringing to the fore an alleged breach of the

---

[16] See e.g. *Soering* v. *UK*, Series A, vol. 161, 1989, pp. 35–6.
[17] See e.g. *Drozd and Janousek* v. *France and Spain*, Series A, vol. 240, 1992, p. 29. In *Loizidou* v. *Turkey* (preliminary objections), Series A, vol. 310, p. 20, the Court emphasised that the responsibility of a contracting state may also arise 'when as a consequence of military action – whether lawful or unlawful – it exercises effective control of an area outside its national territory. The obligation to secure, in such an area, the rights and freedoms set out in the Convention, derives from the fact of such control whether it be exercised directly, through its armed forces, or through a subordinate local administration.' This was reaffirmed by the Court in *Loizidou* v. *Turkey* (merits) on 18 December 1996, para 52.
[18] See E. Fribergh and M. Villiger, 'The European Commission of Human Rights' in Macdonald *et al.*, *The European System*, p. 605 and Harris *et al.*, *Law of the European Convention*, p. 571. [19] As of September 1996, the number is thirty-three.
[20] Now termed the Parliamentary Assembly. [21] Articles 20–23. [22] Articles 25–27.
[23] See article 28(1)a. See also e.g. *Stocké* v. *Federal Republic of Germany*, Series A, vol. 199, 1991, p. 14; 95 ILR, pp. 327, 354. [24] Article 28(1)b.
[25] Rule 17 of the Rules of Procedure adopted in 1993.
[26] Article 33. This includes hearings as well as deliberations.
[27] Cyprus case *(Greece* v. *UK)*, 1956 and 1957, two applications; *Austria* v. *Italy*, 1960; five applications against Greece, 1967–70; *Ireland* v. *UK*, 1971; *Cyprus* v. *Turkey*, 1974–94, four applications, and five applications against Turkey, 1982.
[28] *Ireland* v. *UK*, Series A, vol. 25, 1978; 58 ILR, p. 188.

European public order, so that, for example, it is irrelevant whether the applicant state has been recognised by the respondent state.[29] Article 25 provides for the right of individual petition to the Commission and this has proved to be a crucial provision.[30] This right of individual petition will only exist where the state complained against has declared that it recognises the competence of the Commission to receive such petitions.[31] However, declarations under article 25 may be temporally limited, so that the state's acceptance of the right of individual petition will only apply for a fixed period, after which it will need to be renewed. This is permitted under article 25. The question of further limitation arose, for example, in the case of Turkey, who sought to limit its acceptance of the right of individual petition[32] to 'the boundaries of the territory to which the constitution of the Republic of Turkey is applicable'.[33] The Commission found that restrictions beyond temporal limitations were not acceptable[34] and this was upheld by the Court in the preliminary objections phase of *Loizidou* v. *Turkey*.[35] The Court emphasised that neither article 25 nor article 46 (dealing with the jurisdiction of the Court) permitted restrictions other than temporal ones. Not to adopt this approach would, the Court noted, have entailed a weakening of the Convention system for the protection of human rights, which constituted a European constitutional public order, and would run counter to the aim of greater unity in the maintenance and further realisation of human rights.[36] Acceptance of substantive or territorial restrictions attached to articles 25 and 46 would have meant that states would have been free to establish separate regimes of enforcement of Convention obligations. Such a result would be so far-reaching that it could not have been intended absent a specific power to that effect.[37] This judgment goes far in underlining the integrity of the Convention system and the centrality of its effectiveness as a constitutional pillar of the community of European states, notwithstanding the express intention of any one particular contracting party.[38]

---

[29] *Cyprus* v. *Turkey (Third Application)*, 13 DR 85 (1978).

[30] By the end of October 1995, nearly 88,000 provisional files had been opened by the Secretariat of the Commission and over 29,000 applications registered. Over 2, 300 applications had been declared admissible and over 600 cases referred to the Court. Friendly settlements had been reached in 280 cases.See Drzemczewski, 'Ensuring Compatibility', p. 241, note 1.

[31] All the contracting states have now made such a declaration and it is envisaged that states that are member states of the Council of Europe that are contemplating becoming contracting states to the Convention will do likewise.

[32] In its declaration of 28 January 1989.

[33] I.e. thereby excluding the Turkish-occupied part of Cyprus. See *Chrysostomos* v. *Turkey*, 68 DR 216, 228–9.   [34] *Chrysostomos* v. *Turkey*, 68 DR 216.   [35] Series A, vol. 310, 1995.

[36] *Ibid.*, pp. 20–7.   [37] *Ibid.*, p. 24.

[38] The Court, in dismissing the territorial limitations upon the Turkish declarations under articles 25 and 46, held that such declaration therefore took effect as valid declarations without such limitations, *ibid.*, pp. 27–9. Turkey had argued that if the limitations were not upheld, the declarations themselves would fall.

The Convention system does not contemplate an *actio popularis*.[39] Individuals cannot raise abstract issues, but must claim to be the victim of a violation of one or more of the Convention rights.[40] However, the Court has emphasised that:

> an individual may, under certain conditions, claim to be the victim of a violation occasioned by the mere existence of secret measures or of legislation permitting secret measures, without having to allege that such measures were in fact applied to him.[41]

A near relative of the victim, for example, could also raise an issue where the violation alleged was personally prejudicial or where there existed a valid personal interest.[42]

The Commission may only deal with a matter once all domestic remedies have been exhausted according to the generally accepted rules of international law and within a period of six months from the date on which the final decision was taken.[43] Such remedies must be effective. Where there are no domestic remedies to exhaust, the act or decision complained against will itself normally be taken as the 'final decision' for the purposes of article 26.[44] In addition, no petition may be dealt with which is anonymous or is substantially the same as a matter already examined, and any petition which is incompatible with the Convention, manifestly ill-founded[45] or an abuse of the right of petition is to be rendered inadmissible.[46]

In ascertaining whether an application is admissible, the Commission will appoint a Rapporteur, who will examine the application and report to the Commission on admissibility and upon the procedure to be adopted.[47] The application may be referred to a Committee of Three, if it is clearly

---

[39] See e.g. *X* v. *Austria*, 7 DR 87 (1976) concerning legislation on abortion.

[40] See e.g. *Pine Valley* v. *Ireland*, Series A, vol. 222, 1991; *Johnston* v. *Ireland*, Series A, vol. 112, 1986; *Marckx* v. *Belgium*, Series A, vol. 31, 1979; *Campbell and Cosans* v. *UK*, Series A, vol. 48, 1982; *Eckle* v. *Federal Republic of Germany*, Series A, vol. 51, 1982 and *Vijayanathan and Pusparajah* v. *France*, Series A, vol. 241–B, 1992.

[41] The *Klass* case, Series A, vol. 28, 1979, pp. 17–18; 58 ILR, pp. 423, 442. See also e.g. the *Marckx* case, Series A, vol. 31, 1979, pp. 12–14; 58 ILR, pp. 561, 576; the *Dudgeon* case, Series A, vol. 45, 1982, p. 18; 67 ILR, pp. 395, 410 and the *Belgian Linguistics* case, Series A, vol. 6, 1968; 45 ILR, p. 136.

[42] See e.g. Application 100/55, *X* v. *FRG*, 1 *Yearbook of the ECHR*, 1955–7, p. 162 and Application 1478/62, *Y* v. *Belgium*, *Yearbook of the ECHR*, 1963, p. 590.

[43] See further *infra*, p. 000.

[44] See e.g. *X* v. *UK*, 8 DR, pp. 211, 212–13 and *Cyprus* v. *Turkey*, *Yearbook of the European Convention on Human Rights*, 1978, pp. 240–2. Where, however, there is a permanent state of affairs which is still continuing, the question of the six months rule can only arise after the state of affairs has ceased to exist, see e.g. *De Becker* v. *Belgium*, 2 *Yearbook of the European Convention on Human Rights*, 1958, pp. 214, 244.

[45] See e.g. *Boyle and Rice* v. *UK*, Series A, vol. 131, 1988. This does not apply to inter-state cases.

[46] Articles 26 and 27. See Harris *et al.*, *Law of the European Convention*, pp. 608 *et seq.* and Van Dijk and Van Hoof, *Theory and Practice*, Chapter 2. See also e.g. the *Vagrancy* case, Series A, vol. 12, 1971; 56 ILR, p. 351.   [47] Rule 47.

inadmissible.[48] Unless this is the case, the application will be referred to a Chamber of the Commission, which will decide upon admissibility.[49] Where new points are raised at this stage, the plenary Commission may make the decision.[50] In urgent cases, the Commission may give precedence to a particular complaint and may indicate to the parties any interim measure deemed desirable.[51] One cause for concern has been the very high rate of petitions rendered inadmissible as well as the increasing numbers of applications coming before the Commission. Once a petition is accepted, the Commission examines the matter with the parties with a view to achieving a friendly settlement under article 28.[52] In considering a friendly settlement, the Commission must also have regard to the general interest as well as the interests of the parties to the dispute.[53] Where a friendly settlement is reached a brief report is sent to the states concerned, the Committee of Ministers and to the Secretary of the Council of Europe.[54] If a settlement is not reached, a more detailed report is transmitted under article 31 to the Committee of Ministers.[55] After the adoption of its report under article 31, the Commission meets in plenary session to decide whether or not to bring the case before the Court under article 48(a) of the Convention. Where it decides so to do, the Registry of the Court is informed within three months after the transmission of the Report to the Committee of Ministers. The latter body is informed, as are the parties to the application. Where the Commission decides not to take the case to the Court, the Committee, the Court and the parties are so informed.[56]

The Commission has gradually been transformed from a part-time into a semi-permanent body, meeting at least sixteen weeks per year, [57] and the role of the Chambers has developed markedly since their introduction. An

---

[48] See article 20(3) of the Convention, as amended by Protocol VIII (1985), which came into force in 1990. The Committee may, acting unanimously, declare an application inadmissible or strike it from the list of cases, when such a decision can be taken without further examination. See also Rules 27–29 and 47(2).

[49] Article 20 and Rule 49. However, where the petition raises a serious question affecting the interpretation or application of the Convention, the Commission will sit in plenary session, article 20(2). Chambers consist of at least seven members of the Commission (which number constitutes a quorum) and two Chambers were established under article 20(2) of the Convention for three-year terms, see Rules 24–26. In 1994, 90 per cent of all decisions declaring cases admissible were taken by Chambers, see Harris *et al.*, *Law of the European Convention*, p. 576.   [50] Rule 49(1).

[51] See Rules 33 and 36. The Court noted in *Cruz Varas* v. *Sweden*, Series A, vol. 201, 1991, that although the power to order binding interim measures could not be derived either directly or by way of inference from the Convention, where a party chose not to comply with such an indication of interim measures under Rule 36, it knowingly assumed the risk of being found in breach of article 3.   [52] A Rapporteur will also be appointed, see Rule 54,

[53] See Harris *et al.*, *Law of the European Convention*, pp. 599 *et seq.* and Van Dijk and Van Hoof, *Theory and Practice*, pp. 118 *et seq.* See also the *Tyrer* case, Series A, vol. 26, 1978, pp. 12–14; 58 ILR, pp. 339, 350 and the *Turkish* case, 44 DR 31, 38–9 (1985), where the settlement included a requirement for Turkey to report to the Commission on measures taken to ensure compliance with article 3 of the Convention.   [54] Article 30. See also Rule 62.

[55] See also Rules 57–60.   [56] Rule 61.   [57] Rule 16.

increase in the workload of the Commission is inevitable in the short term, given the recent accession to the Convention (and to article 25) of a substantial number of Eastern and Central European states. The terms of Protocol XI, however, provide for the abolition of the Commission as such, as part of the reorganisation of the structure of the enforcement organs of the Convention system.[58]

The Court[59]

The Court came into being in 1959 and consists of a number of judges equal to the number of member states of the Council of Europe.[60] Judges are elected by the Consultative Assembly [61] of the Council of Europe for a period of nine years[62] and must be of high moral character and either possess the qualifications required for appointment to high judicial office or be jurisconsults of recognised competence.[63] Judges sit in their individual capacity and may not hold any position incompatible with their independence and impartiality as members of the Court.[64] The Court, unlike the Commission, is a judicial body and its decisions are final and binding.[65] The jurisdiction of the Court extends to all cases involving the interpretation and application of the Convention,[66] but only as regards those states which have expressly recognised the jurisdiction of the Court under article 46.[67] All states parties have now done so. The admissibility of an application is a matter for the Commission and this therefore provides the framework for the jurisdiction of the Court, defining the issues of law and fact under consideration.[68] Thus, in general, issues cannot be raised before the Court that have not been raised before the Commission.[69] This applies especially with regard to findings of facts, while there is a certain necessary latitude with regard to questions of law, since the Court may take cognisance of relevant legal argumentation.[70] The decisions of the Court play a role not only as between the parties, but more generally as a method of elucidating, safeguarding and developing the rules of the Convention.[71] The operations of the Court are governed

[58] See *infra*, p. 270.
[59] See e.g. P. Mahoney and S. Prebensen, 'The European Court of Human Rights', in *The European System*, p. 621 and Harris *et al.*, *Law of the European Convention*, Chapter 24.
[60] Article 38 of the Convention. As of September 1996, there were forty member states of the Council of Europe.   [61] Now termed Parliamentary Assembly.
[62] Article 40. Judges may be re-elected.   [63] Article 39.
[64] Article 40(7), as amended by Protocol VIII.   [65] Articles 52 and 53.   [66] Article 45.
[67] Or where jurisdiction is accepted *ad hoc* under article 48, see *Tyrer* v. *UK*, Series A, vol. 26, 1978. See also Rule 34 of the Rules of the Court, 1994.
[68] See e.g. *Ireland* v. *UK*, Series A, vol. 25, 1978; 58 ILR, p. 188.
[69] See e.g. *Open Door and Dublin Well Woman* v. *Ireland*, Series A, vol. 246, 1992 and *Le Compte, Van Leuven and De Meyere* v. *Belgium*, Series A, vol. 43, 1981. See also *Brogan* v. *UK*, Series A, vol. 145, 1988.   [70] See e.g. *Handyside* v. *UK*, Series A, vol. 24, 1978; 58 ILR, p. 150.
[71] See e.g. *Ireland* v. *UK*, Series A, vol. 25, 1978; 58 ILR, p. 188.

by Rules of Procedure, the latest version being those adopted on 27 January 1994.[72]

The Court sits in Chambers of nine judges.[73] However, the Chamber may at any time relinquish jurisdiction in favour of a Grand Chamber where a pending case raises one or more serious questions affecting the interpretation of the Convention.[74] Jurisdiction must be relinquished where the resolution of such a question or questions might have a result inconsistent with a judgment previously delivered by the Court. The Grand Chamber comprises nineteen judges, including the President and Vice-President(s) of the Court, the other members of the Chamber which has relinquished jurisdiction, and additional judges appointed by the President by means of a separate drawing of lots.[75] The Grand Chamber may either retain jurisdiction over the whole case or after deciding the particular question or questions, order the case to be referred back to the Chamber with regard to the remainder of the case.[76] The Grand Chamber may exceptionally, when the issues raised are particularly serious or involve a significant change of existing case law, relinquish jurisdiction in favour of the plenary Court, comprising all the judges. The plenary Court may either retain jurisdiction over the whole case or after deciding the particular question or questions, order the case to be referred back to the Grand Chamber with regard to the remainder of the case.[77]

The Court may only deal with a case where a friendly settlement has not been reached and within three months of the transmission of the Commission's Report to the Committee of Ministers.[78] Under article 48, only the Commission, a contracting state whose national is alleged to be a victim, a contracting state which referred the case to the Commission or a contracting state against which the complaint has been lodged have the right to refer a case to the Court. In the large majority of cases, it is the Commission which refers a case to the Court. Germany and Cyprus have taken cases to the Court with regard to nationals, in situations where the states concerned have not been parties to the case.[79] It is to be noted, therefore, that the applicants themselves have not had the right to refer a case to

---

[72] It should be noted that the Rules appear in two forms. Rules of Court 'A' concern situations where the parties are not bound by Protocol IX, and Rules of Court 'B' concern situations where the parties are bound by Protocol IX. The latter Rules came into force the day after the Protocol came into force on 1 October 1994. Unless otherwise stated, references are to Rules of Court 'A'.

[73] Including a judge of the nationality of the state party concerned or, if none, a person of its choice. The names of the other judges are chosen by lot by the President of the Court, see article 43, as amended by Protocol VIII. The President or Vice-President also sits as an *ex officio* member of the Chamber, see Rule 21.

[74] See, for example, *Loizidou* v. *Turkey*, Series A, vol. 310, 1995.   [75] Rule 51(1) and (2).

[76] Rule 51(4).   [77] Rule 51(5).   [78] Article 47.

[79] See *Soering* v. *UK*, Series A, vol. 161, 1989, and *Loizidou* v. *Turkey*, Series A, vol. 310, 1995.

the Court.[80] However, article 5 of Protocol IX, which came into effect on 1 October 1994,[81] amended the terms of article 48[82] to include in the list of those able to refer a case to the Court, the 'person, non-governmental organisation or group of individuals having lodged the complaint with the Commission'. Where a case is referred to the Court under the new provision only, a special screening process operates. The case is first submitted to a three member 'screening panel' of the Court, including the judge elected in respect of the contracting state complained against. If the case does not appear to raise a serious question affecting the interpretation or application of the Convention and is seen as not warranting consideration by the Court for any other reason, the panel may by unanimous vote decide that it shall not be considered by the Court. In this case, the Committee of Ministers will decide whether or not there has been a violation of the Convention.[83] While there is no specific power in the Convention under which the Court may order interim measures of protection with binding effect,[84] the Court may under Rule 36 indicate to the state or applicant concerned advisable interim measures.[85] The Court may also note that interim measures suggested by the Commission remain recommended.[86] Despite initial reservations, [87] the Court is now willing to accept the possibility of third party interventions. Rule 37(2) provides that the President of the Court may, in the interests of the proper administration of justice, invite or grant leave to any contracting state which is not a party to the proceedings to submit written comments within a time-limit and on issues which he shall specify. Such an invitation or leave may be extended or granted to 'any person concerned other than the applicant'.[88] While the Court is not specifically given the power to order remedial measures under the Convention, article 50 does enable the Court to award 'just satisfaction' to an injured party if the domestic law of the state in question does not provide an adequate remedy. This has enabled the Court to grant damages as well as costs

[80] Although under Rules 30 and 33 of the 1982 Rules of Court, the person or persons originally lodging the petition under article 25 were allowed to appear separately before the Court. Cf. the *Lawless* case, Series A, vol. 1, 1961, p. 15; 31 ILR, pp. 290.
[81] As of September 1996, twenty-three states were bound by Protocol IX, see H/INF (96) 2, p. 16.   [82] I.e. for those states parties to Protocol IX,
[83] Article 48(2) of the Convention, as introduced by article 5 of Protocol IX. See also Rules 26–32 of Rules of Court 'B', applicable to cases concerning states bound by Protocol IX.
[84] The same applies as noted *supra* p. 000, to the Commission. See *Cruz Varas* v. *Sweden*, Series A, vol. 201, 1991.   [85] See e.g. *Soering* v. *UK*, Series A, vol. 161, 1989.
[86] See e.g. *Vijayanathan and Pusparajah* v. *France*, Series A, vol. 241–B, 1992.
[87] See e.g. *Winterwerp* v. *Netherlands*, Series A, vol. 33, 1979.Cf. *Young, James and Webster* v. *UK*, Series A, vol. 44, 1981.
[88] See for examples of third party interventions *Soering* v. *UK*, Series A, vol. 161, 1989; *Brannigan and McBride* v. *UK*, Series A, vol. 258–B, 1993; *Open Door and Dublin Well Woman* v. *Ireland*, Series A, vol. 246, 1992; *Hokkanen* v. *Finland*, Series A, vol. 295, 1994 and *McCann* v. *UK*, Series A, vol. 324, 1995. Leave was refused in *Modinos* v. *Cyprus*, Series A, vol. 259, 1993.

to the complainant.[89] The Court also possesses under Protocol II a very restricted capacity to give advisory opinions.[90]

The Court has dealt with an ever-increasing number of cases, delivering one judgment in its first year of operation in 1960, six in 1976, seventeen in 1986 and twenty-five in 1989. By the end of 1995, over 500 judgments had been delivered. The average length of proceedings before the Court is around one year, but to this one must add, of course, the period during which the Commission has been considering the particular case, in order to obtain a proper perception of the time taken for any given case. This as a general rule has meant a total duration of proceedings of between five and six years.

The Court has developed a jurisprudence of considerable importance.[91] In *Ireland* v. *UK*,[92] its only interstate case to date, the Court found that the five interrogation techniques used by the UK Forces in Northern Ireland amounted to a practice of inhuman and degrading treatment, contrary to article 3. In *McCann* v. *UK*,[93] the Court narrowly held that the killing by members of the security forces of three members of an IRA unit suspected of involvement in a bombing mission in Gibraltar violated the right to life under article 2. In *Golder* v. *UK*,[94] the Court inferred from article 6(1) a fundamental right of access to the courts and the Court has generally recognised a varying standard of the margin of appreciation allowed to domestic organs in dealing with internal law, so that in cases involving the protection of morals more scope would be left to domestic discretion than would be the case, for example, regarding the principle of contempt of court.[95] The Court has also developed a considerable jurisprudence in the field of due process[96] that is having a significant impact upon domestic law, not least in the UK. A brief reference to some further examples will suffice. In the *Marckx* case[97] the Court emphasised that Belgian legislation discriminating against illegit-

---

[89] See e.g. M. E. Mas, 'Right to Compensation under Article 50' in *The European System*, p. 775.

[90] At the request of the Committee of Ministers, provided that such opinions do 'not deal with any question relating to the content or scope of the rights or freedoms'. This competence has never been exercised.

[91] See also P. Mahoney, 'Judicial Activism and Judicial Self-Restraint in the European Court of Human Rights: Two Sides of the Same Coin', 11 HRLJ, 1990, p. 57.

[92] Series A, vol. 25, 1978; 58 ILR, p. 188.   [93] Series A, vol. 324, 1995.

[94] Series A, vol. 18, 1975; 57 ILR, p. 200.

[95] See e.g. *Handyside* v. *UK*, Series A, vol. 24, 1981; 58 ILR, p. 150; the *Dudgeon* case, Series A, vol. 45, 1982; 67 ILR, p. 395 and the *Sunday Times* case, Series A, vol. 30, 1979; 58 ILR, p. 491.

[96] See e.g. S. Trechsel, 'Liberty and Security of Person' in Macdonald, *The European System*, p. 277; P. Van Dijk, 'Access to Court', *ibid.*, p. 345; O. Jacot-Guillarmod, 'Rights Related to Good Administration (Article 6)', *ibid.*, p. 381; Harris *et al.*, *Law of the European Convention*, Chapter 6; Van Dijk and Van Hoof, *Theory and Practice*, pp. 294 *et seq.* and *Digest of Strasbourg Case law relating to the European Convention on Human Rights*, vol. II (article 6), 1984.   [97] Series A, No. 31, 1979; 58 ILR, p. 561.

imate children violated the Convention, while in the *Young, James and Webster* case[98] it was held that railway workers dismissed for refusing to join a trade union in the UK were entitled to compensation. In the *Brogan* case[99] the Court felt that periods of detention under anti-terrorist legislation in the UK before appearance before a judge or other judicial officer of at least four days violated the Convention. This decision, however, prompted a notice of derogation under article 15 of the Convention by the UK government.[100]

In the important *Soering* case[101] the Court unanimously held that the extradition of a German national from the UK to the United States, where the applicant feared he would be sentenced to death on a charge of capital murder and be subjected to the 'death row' phenomenon, would constitute a breach of article 3 of the Convention prohibiting torture and inhuman and degrading treatment and punishment.

The Committee of Ministers[102]

Unlike the other two organs of the Convention system, this is a political body. It is the executive organ of the Council of Europe[103] and consists of the Foreign Ministers, or their deputies, of all the member states.[104] Under article 15 of the Statute of the Council of Europe, the Committee of Ministers, acting on the recommendation of the Parliamentary Assembly or on its own initiative, considers the action required to further the aims of the Council of Europe, including the conclusion of conventions or agreements, and the adoption by governments of a common policy with regard to particular matters. Under article 16 of the Statute, it decides with binding effect all matters relating to the internal organisation and arrangements of the Council of Europe. Resolutions and recommendations on a wide variety of issues are regularly adopted.[105] The Committee of Ministers performs a variety of functions with regard to the protection of human rights. For example, in its Declaration on Compliance with Commitments Accepted by Member States of the Council of Europe, adopted on 10 November 1994,

---

[98] Series A, No. 44, 1981; 62 ILR, p. 359.   [99] Series A, No. 145, 1988.

[100] For the text, see e.g. 7 NQHR, 1989, p. 255. See also *Brannigan and McBride v. UK*, Series A, vol. 258–B, 1993.   [101] Series A, No. 161, 1989.

[102] See e.g. C. Ravaud, 'The Committee of Ministers' in Macdonald, *The European System*, p. 645; P. Leuprecht, 'The Execution of Judgments and Decisions', *ibid.*, p. 791; P. Leuprecht, 'The Protection of Human Rights by Political Bodies: The Example of the Committee of Ministers of the Council of Europe' in *Progress in the Spirit of Human Rights: Festschrift für Felix Ermacora* (eds. M. Nowak, D. Steurer and H. Tretter), Kehl, 1988, p. 95; Harris *et al.*, *Law of the European Convention*, Chapter 25; Van Dijk and Van Hoof, *Theory and Practice*, Chapter 4 and A. Tomkins, 'The Committee of Ministers: Its Roles under the European Convention on Human Rights', *European Human Rights Law Review*, 1995, p. 49.   [103] Article 13 of the Statute of the Council of Europe.

[104] Article 14 of the Statute of the Council of Europe.

[105] These are non-binding. Resolutions relate to the general work of the Council as such, while recommendations concern action which it is suggested should be taken by the governments of member states.

the Committee decided that it would consider the question of implementation of commitments concerning the situation of democracy, human rights
and the rule of law in any member state which may be referred to it by
member states, the Secretary-General or on the basis of a recommendation
of the Parliamentary Assembly. The Committee may request the Secretary-
General to make contacts, collect information or furnish advice, issue an
opinion or recommendation, forward a communication to the Parliamentary
Assembly or take any other decision within its statutory powers.[106] Within
the framework of the European Convention on Human Rights,[107] the
Committee, under article 42, for example, determines the amount of
compensation payable on a daily basis to judges of the Court,[108] while under
article 21 it is the Committee of Ministers which elects the members of the
Commission. However, more crucially, the Committee currently has two
specific and crucial roles with regard to the implementation of the
Convention. One of these roles is controversial, the other not. Under article
32, where a case is not taken to the Court within the required three-month
period,[109] the Committee makes a final decision on whether or not there has
been a violation, by a two-thirds majority vote. This has also been the case
where the state concerned has not accepted the jurisdiction of the Court
under article 46. The Committee of Ministers has adopted a series of Rules
for the Application of Article 32.[110] While exercising its functions under
article 32, the Committee is entitled to discuss the substance of any case on
which the Commission had submitted a report and it may consider written
or oral statements of the parties and hear witnesses.[111] The Committee may
also ask the Commission for information on particular points in the report
under consideration.[112] The report of the Commission will only be published
when the Committee has completed its consideration.[113] The Committee
meets in secret and its discussions are confidential. The Committee has particularly noted that the individual applicant has no right to be heard by it or
to have any written communication considered by it.[114] In the vast majority
of cases, the Committee accepts and endorses the report of the Commission,

---

[106] H/INF (95) 2, p. 146.

[107] See *infra* pp. 272–80, with regard to the role of the Committee of Ministers with regard to
the European Social Charter, the Convention on the Prevention of Torture and the
Framework Convention on National Minorities.

[108] Note generally that by article 58 of the Convention, the expenses of the Commission and
the Court are borne by the Council of Europe, while by article 37, the secretariat of the
Commission is provided by the Secretary-General of the Council of Europe.

[109] Under article 48.   [110] The most recent being adopted on 19 December 1991.

[111] Rule 1. The procedure adopted in any particular case, however, will be *ad hoc*, see Rule 4.
The Committee has accepted that it is not well equipped to take evidence etc. and ought
not normally undertake such tasks, see point 2 of the Appendix to the Rules.

[112] Rule 9.

[113] Rule 9 ter. Note that the Committee may by way of exception decide not to publish a report
of the Commission or part thereof.   [114] Point 3(c) of the Appendix to the Rules.

but, while there appears to have been no case where the Committee has decided the matter contrary to the opinion of the Commission, the Committee has in some instances refrained from making any decision. This has sometimes been because, for political reasons, the required two-thirds majority has not been attained.[115] This has provoked some disquiet, since in some cases it has been suggested that decisions have been unduly influenced by non-legal factors.[116] Particularly sensitive issues arise with regard to inter-state cases. In the *Greek* case, for example,[117] the Committee concluded that since Greece had denounced the Convention following the report of the Commission that the military junta of Greece had violated provisions of the Convention, no further action was required. The action of the Committee in the three *Cyprus* v. *Turkey* applications was particularly worrying. In the case of the first two applications,[118] the Committee adopted resolutions in 1977 and 1979 in which it noted that events which occurred in Cyprus violated the Convention and urged the parties to resume intercommunal talks. This was deemed sufficient to conclude its consideration of the case.[119] In the case of the third application,[120] the report of the Commission remained on the agenda of the Committee from 1983 until 1992, when it was finally decided to make public the report of the Commission, holding that this completed consideration of the case.[121] It is possible, although rare, for friendly settlements to occur while the Committee is deliberating. In such a case, the Committee may decide to discontinue its examination of the case, provided it is satisfied that the solution envisaged is based on respect for human rights as defined in the Convention.[122]

The judgments of the Court are final[123] and the decisions of the Court are binding upon the parties.[124] Under article 54, the judgments of the Court are transmitted to the Committee of Ministers, which supervises their execution. The Rules for the Application of Article 54, adopted in 1976, provide that once a judgment of the Court is transmitted to the Committee, the case is to be inscribed upon its agenda without delay. Where the judgment finds that there has been a violation of the Convention or an award of just satisfaction under article 50 has been made, the Committee under Rule 2 will invite the state concerned to inform it of measures taken to conform with the judgment. If the state concerned informs the Committee that it is not in a position to describe measures taken, the matter is automatically put

---

[115] See e.g. *East African Asians* v. *UK*, Resolution DH(77)2 and *Warwick* v. *UK*, Resolution DH(89)5. Note that the requirement for a two-thirds majority is deleted from article 32(1) under the terms of Protocol X, 1992. This Protocol will come into force three months after the date on which all parties to the Convention will have ratified it. As of 30 June 1995, twenty-one states have ratified this Protocol.

[116] See Van Dijk and Van Hoof, *Theory and Practice*, pp. 200 *et seq.* and Leuprecht, 'The Protection of Human Rights'. [117] Resolution DH(70)1. [118] 2 DR 125.

[119] Resolution DH(79)1. [120] 13 DR 85, Application No. 8007/77.

[121] Resolution DH(92)12. [122] Rule 6 bis. [123] Article 52. [124] Article 53.

on the agenda of a meeting of the Committee not more than six months later. The Committee will not regard its functions under article 54 as having been exercised until it has taken note of the information supplied in accordance with Rule 2, and when just satisfaction has been afforded, until it has satisfied itself that the state concerned has awarded this just satisfaction to the injured party.[125]

Future development of the European Convention System
The number of applications to the Commission has inevitably been increasing, not only as the system becomes more widely known throughout the member states, but also because Central and Eastern European states have joined the Council of Europe and accepted the Convention in recent years, and others have signalled their intention to apply. In the years to come, the Convention will probably have some forty states parties, thus imposing even further strain upon the administrative and judicial system. Various solutions have been suggested during the last ten years or so to these problems, including that of a merger of the Commission and the Court.[126] In 1992, the Parliamentary Assembly of the Council of Europe pronounced itself in favour of this idea[127] and the proposal for a single full-time Court was accepted by the member states of the Council in the Vienna Declaration of 9 October 1993.[128] Protocol XI to the Convention reflecting this decision was opened for signature on 11 May 1994 and it will enter into force one year after it has been ratified by all states parties.[129]

Several important changes will take place once Protocol XI is in force.[130] In the first place, under article 19 a single permanent Court will be established. Thus the current Court and Commission will cease to exist.[131] The new Court will consist of a number of judges equal to that of the contracting parties to the Convention[132] and judges will be elected by the Parliamentary Assembly of the Council of Europe for six-year terms.[133] Judges will be full time. To consider cases before it, the Court may sit in committees of three judges, in Chambers of seven judges and in a Grand Chamber of seventeen judges.[134] The plenary Court will be responsible for

---

[125] Rule 3.   [126] See e.g. 8 HRLJ, 1987, pp. 1 *et seq.*   [127] Recommendation 1194 (1992).
[128] See 14 HRLJ, 1993, p. 373.
[129] As of September 1996, there were twenty-one states parties to this Protocol.
[130] See e.g. H. Schermers, 'The Eleventh Protocol to the European Convention on Human Rights', 19 *European Law Review*, 1994, p. 367 and R. Bernhardt, 'Reform of the Control Machinery under the European Convention on Human Rights: Protocol No. 11', 89 AJIL, 1995, p. 145.
[131] Article 5 of Protocol XI. In addition, the terms of office of the Registrar and Deputy-Registrar will also cease.
[132] Article 20. This reference and those in the following footnotes are to the articles of the Convention as they will read after amendment by Protocol XI.
[133] Articles 22 and 23. Note that there will no longer be a prohibition on two judges having the same nationality. The terms of office of the judges will end at the age of 70.   [134] Article 27.

the election of the President and Vice-Presidents of the Court, the appointment of the Presidents of the Chambers, constituting Chambers and adopting rules of procedure.[135] A committee may under article 28, and by unanimous vote, declare inadmissible or strike out from its list of cases,[136] an individual application where such a decision can be taken without further examination. That decision is final. In other cases, a Chamber will decide on the admissibility and merits of both individual and inter-state applications, the decision on admissibility being taken separately unless the Court in exceptional circumstances decides otherwise.[137] Where a serious question affecting the interpretation of the Convention or its Protocols is raised in a case, or where the resolution of a question might lead to a result inconsistent with earlier case law, the Chamber may, unless one of the parties to the case objects, relinquish jurisdiction in favour of the Grand Chamber.[138] It is to be noted that the jurisdiction of the Court and its competence to give advisory opinions remain unaltered,[139] as do the criteria for admissibility.[140] The intervention of third parties will also remain in the new system. In all cases before a Chamber or the Grand Chamber, a contracting party, one of whose nationals is an applicant, shall have the right to submit written comments and to take part in hearings, while the President of the Court may, in the interest of the proper administration of justice, invite any contracting party which is not a party to the proceedings, or any person concerned who is not the applicant to submit written comments or take part in hearings.[141]

Once an application has been declared admissible, the Court will pursue the examination of the case and place itself at the disposal of the parties with a view to securing a friendly settlement.[142] If a friendly settlement is reached, the Court will strike the case out off its list.[143] Hearings before the Court will be in public unless the Court in exceptional circumstances decides otherwise. The Court will be able to afford just satisfaction to the injured party, if necessary, where a violation is found and the domestic law of the contracting party concerned allows only partial reparation to be made.[144] Under article 43, within a period of three months from the date of the judgment of the Chamber, any party to the case may, in exceptional cases, request that the case be referred to the Grand Chamber. A panel of five judges of the Grand Chamber will accept this request if the case raises a serious question

---

[135] Article 26.
[136] Note that the Court has the right to strike out an application at any stage of the proceedings where it concludes that the applicant does not intend to pursue his application or the matter has been resolved or for any other reason established by the Court, it is no longer justified to continue the examination of the application. However, the Court shall continue the examination of an application if respect for human rights as defined in the Convention and the Protocols thereto so requires, see article 37.   [137] Article 29.   [138] Article 30.
[139] See articles 32 and 47.   [140] Articles 33, 34 and 35.   [141] Article 36.
[142] Article 38. Proceedings in the latter case will be confidential.   [143] Article 39.
[144] Article 41.

affecting the interpretation or application of the Convention or Protocols, or a serious issue of general importance. If the panel does accept the request, the Grand Chamber will decide the case by means of a judgment. Judgments of the Grand Chamber will be final, as will those of a Chamber where the parties declare that they will not request that the case be referred to the Grand Chamber or three months after the date of judgment if reference to the Grand Chamber has not been requested or when the panel of the Grand Chamber rejects the request to refer. The final judgment will be published[145] and binding upon the parties[146] and will be transmitted to the Committee of Ministers, which shall supervise its execution.[147]

Thus several crucial changes to the current system will come about upon the entry into force of Protocol XI. Particularly to be noted are that the right of individual petition will become automatic, the new Court will be full-time, the function of the Committee of Ministers will be limited to the supervision of the execution of the judgments of the Court, the number of judges in a Chamber will be reduced from nine to seven, the right of third-party intervention will become part of the Convention itself rather than a Rule of Court and hearings will be public apart from the friendly settlement process. However, under new article 30, the parties to a case will be able to prevent the relinquishment of jurisdiction by a Chamber in favour of the Grand Chamber. In addition, where a case is referred to the Grand Chamber under article 43, the Grand Chamber will include the President of the Chamber and the judge who sat in respect of the state party concerned, who will thus be involved in a rehearing of a case that they have already heard. This unusual procedure can only be justified on the basis of the compromises necessary to create the new system, but it remains a source of some potential disquiet.

The European Social Charter[148]

The wide social and economic differences between the European states, coupled with the fact that economic and social rights often depend for their

---

[145] Article 44.   [146] Article 46(1).   [147] Article 46(2).

[148] See e.g. D. J. Harris, *The European Social Charter*, Charlottesville, 1984; D. J. Harris, 'A Fresh Impetus for the European Charter', 41 ICLQ, 1992, p. 659; D. J. Harris, 'The System of Supervision of the European Social Charter – Problems and Options for the Future' in *The Future of European Social Policy* (ed. L. Betten), 2nd edn, Leiden, 1991, p. 1; *25 Years of the European Social Charter* (eds. A. Ph. C. M. Jaspers and L. Betten), Leiden, 1988; H. Wiebringhaus, 'La Charte Sociale Européenne: 20 Ans Après la Conclusion du Traité', AFDI, 1982, p. 934; O. Kahn-Freund, 'The European Social Charter', in *European Law and the Individual* (ed. F. G. Jacobs), London, 1976; H. Wiebringhaus, 'La Charte Sociale Européenne et la Convention Européenne des Droits de l'Homme', VIII HRJ, 1975, p. 527; F. M. Van Asbeck, 'La Charte Sociale Européenne' in *Mélanges Rolin*, Paris, 1964, p. 427. See also Robertson and Merrills, *Human Rights in Europe*, p. 349.

realisation upon economic resources, has meant that this area of concern has lagged far behind that of civil and political rights. Seven years of negotiations were necessary before the Charter was signed in 1961.[149] The Charter consists of a statement of long-term objectives coupled with a list of more restricted rights. The Charter covers labour rights and trade union rights,[150] the protection of specific groups such as children, women, disabled persons and migrant workers,[151] social security rights,[152] and protection of the family.[153] In an attempt to deal with economic disparities within Europe, the Charter provides for a system whereby only ten of the forty-five paragraphs (including five 'key articles')[154] need to be accepted upon ratification.

The Charter is implemented by means of a Committee of Independent Experts, which receives every two years via the Secretary-General of the Council of Europe a report from contracting states on the way in which they are applying the Charter. Copies of these reports are sent to national organisations of employers and employees, whose comments the state in question must transmit to the Council of Europe. The reports of the governments and the comments of the Committee of Independent Experts are then examined by a Governmental Committee on the Social Charter, which reports to the Committee of Ministers of the Council of Europe. The conclusions of the experts are transmitted additionally to the Parliamentary Assembly of the Council of Europe, which sends its views to the Committee of Ministers, which in turn may make recommendations to each contracting party by a two-thirds majority.[155] The system works on the basis of two-yearly supervision cycles. The process is complicated and the conclusions of the Committee of Independent Experts have often been obscured by the Governmental Committee.[156]

A Protocol Amending the Social Charter was adopted in Turin in 1991 with the aim of improving the supervision mechanism by strengthening the role of the Committee of Independent Experts.[157] In particular, article 2 of

---

[149] As of September 1996, there were twenty states parties to the Charter, see 34 ILM, 1995, p. 1714. See also H/INF (96) 2, p. 21.   [150] Articles 1–6, 9–10.

[151] Articles 7–8, 15, 18–19.   [152] Articles 11–14.

[153] Articles 16–17. An Additional Protocol was signed in 1988 which added four more economic and social rights, guaranteeing the rights to equal opportunities in employment without discrimination based on sex; information and consultation of workers within the undertaking; participation in the determination and improvement of working conditions, and social protection of elderly persons. As of 17 July 1995, there were five ratifications, see 34 ILM, 1995, p. 1714. The Protocol entered into force on 4 September 1992.

[154] Out of the following seven rights: the rights to work, organise, bargain collectively, social security, social and medical assistance, and the rights of the family to special protection and of migrant workers and their families to protection and assistance; see article 20.

[155] See articles 27–29 of the Charter.

[156] See, for example, L. Betten, 'European Social Charter', 6 SIM Newsletter, 1988, p. 69.

[157] See 31 ILM, 1992, p. 155. As of 17 July 1995, there were ten ratifications, see 34 ILM, 1995, p. 1714.

the Protocol establishes in effect that the Committee has the exclusive competence to interpret and apply the Charter. It permits the Committee to request additional information directly from contracting parties and hold oral hearings with representatives of contracting parties either on its own initiative or at the request of the contracting party, while under article 4, the Governmental Committee will focus upon advising the Committee of Ministers on the basis of social, economic and other policy considerations in situations which should be the subject of recommendations to contracting parties. The Committee of Independent Experts is increased in size to at least nine members (from at least seven) elected by the Parliamentary Assembly for six-year periods, re-electable once. The Protocol also increases the role of non-governmental organisations concerned with economic and social rights, for example, by allowing such national organisations to send comments upon their states' reports directly to the Secretary-General (rather than via the contracting party) and by providing that the Secretary-General shall forward a copy of the reports of contracting parties to the international organisations which have consultative status with the Council of Europe and have particular competence in the matters covered in the Charter.[158] It is also to be noted that whereas under the Charter originally the Committee of Ministers could make recommendations by a two-thirds majority of members of the Committee, under the Protocol that majority becomes two-thirds of those voting, with entitlement to voting limited to contracting parties.[159]

The Final Resolution of the Conference adopting the Protocol also expressed the hope that a further protocol providing for a system of collective complaints might be drafted. An Additional Protocol to this effect was adopted on 9 November 1995.[160] This provides that international organisations of employers and trade unions, other international non-governmental organisations with consultative status with the Council of Europe placed on a list for this purpose by the Governmental Committee, and representative national organisations of employers and trade unions within the jurisdiction of the contracting party against which they have lodged a complaint, may submit complaints alleging unsatisfactory application of the Charter.[161] Contracting parties may also make a declaration recognising the right of any other representative national non-governmental organisation within its jurisdiction, which has particular competence in the matters governed by the Charter, to lodge complaints against it.[162] Such complaints are to be sent

---

[158] Article 1 of the Protocol, amending article 23 of the Charter. The reports of contracting parties under articles 21 and 22 of the Charter, as well as under article 23, are to be made available to the public on request.
[159] Article 5 of the Protocol, amending article 28 of the Charter.
[160] See 34 ILM, 1995, p. 1453. It requires five ratifications to come into force, article 14.
[161] Article 1.   [162] Article 2.

to the Secretary-General of the Council of Europe, who will notify the contracting party concerned and transmit the complaint immediately to the Committee of Independent Experts.[163] The Committee, once it has declared the complaint admissible, will produce a report presenting its conclusions, which will be sent to the Committee of Ministers.[164] On the basis of the report, the Committee of Ministers will adopt a resolution by a majority of those voting (entitlement being limited to contracting parties). The required majority rises to two-thirds where a recommendation to the contracting party is made where the Committee of Independent Experts has found that the Charter has not been applied satisfactorily. At the request of the contracting party concerned, the Committee of Ministers may decide, where the report raises new issues, by a two-thirds majority of the contracting parties to the Charter, to consult the Governmental Committee.[165] At the same time as the resolution is adopted, or no later than four months after it has been transmitted to the Committee of Ministers, the report will be transmitted to the Parliamentary Assembly and published.[166] The contracting party concerned will be required to submit information on measures taken to give effect to the recommendation of the Committee of Ministers, in its next report to the Secretary-General.[167]

The European Convention for the Prevention of Torture and Inhuman and Degrading Treatment or Punishment[168]

This innovative Convention was signed in 1987 and came into force on 1 February 1989.[169] The purpose of the Convention is to enable the

---

[163] Article 5.   [164] Article 8.   [165] Article 9.   [166] Article 8.

[167] Article 10. On 3 May 1996, the Revised European Social Charter was signed. This added to the list of rights contained in the 1961 Charter, twelve further rights including the rights to equal opportunity and equal treatment in matters of employment and occupation without discrimination on grounds of sex; the right to information and consultation; the right of elderly persons to social protection; the right of workers to the protection of their claims in the event of the insolvency of their employer; the right of workers' representatives to protection; the right to protection against poverty and social exclusion, and the right to housing (see articles 20–31). In addition, the number of articles in Part II by which parties are to consider themselves bound is to rise to at least six out of the following nine (articles 1, 5, 6, 7, 12, 13, 16, 19 and 20), while the total number of articles selected for binding purposes by parties rises to at least sixteen articles or sixty-three numbered paragraphs.

[168] See e.g. J. Murdoch, 'The Work of the Council of Europe's Torture Committee', 5 EJIL, 1994, p. 220; M. Evans and R. Morgan, 'The European Torture Committee: Membership Issues', 5 EJIL, 1994, p. 249; A. Cassese, 'A New Approach to Human Rights: The European Convention for the Prevention of Torture', 83 AJIL, 1989, p. 128; A. Cassese, 'Une Nouvelle Approche des Droits de l'Homme: La Convention Européene pour la Prévention de la Torture', 93 RGDIP, 1989, p. 6; M. Evans and R. Morgan, 'The European Convention on the Prevention of Torture: Operational Practice', 41 ICLQ, 1992, p. 590

[169] As of 31 July 1995, there were twenty-nine states parties to the Convention, see NQHR, 1995, p. 504. By Protocol No. 1, opened for signature in November 1993, non-member states of the Council of Europe will be allowed to accede to the Convention at the invitation of the Committee of Ministers, CPT/Inf (93) 17. All parties to the Convention need

supervision of persons deprived of their liberty and in particular to prevent the torture or other ill-treatment of such persons.[170] The Committee for the Prevention of Torture was established under the Convention,[171] placing, as it has noted, a 'proactive non-judicial mechanism alongside the existing reactive judicial mechanisms of the European Commission and European Court of Human Rights'.[172] The Committee is given a fact-finding and reporting function. The Committee is empowered to carry out both visits of a periodic nature and *ad hoc* visits to places of detention in order to examine the treatment of persons deprived of their liberty with a view to strengthening, if necessary, the protection of such persons from torture and from inhuman or degrading treatment or punishment. Periodic visits are carried out to all contracting parties on a regular basis, while *ad hoc* visits are organised when it appears to the Committee to be required in the circumstances.[173] Thus periodic visits are planned in advance. The real innovation of the Convention, however, lies in the competence of the Committee to visit places of detention when the situation so warrants.[174] When the Committee is not in session, the Bureau (i.e. the President and Vice-President of the Committee)[175] may in cases of urgency decide, on the Committee's behalf, on the carrying out of such an *ad hoc* visit.[176] States parties agree to permit visits to any place within its jurisdiction where persons are deprived of their liberty by a public authority,[177] although, in exceptional circumstances, the competent authorities of the state concerned may make representations to the Committee against a visit at the time or place proposed on grounds of national defence, public safety, serious disorder, the medical condition of a person or because an urgent interrogation relating to a serious crime is in progress.[178] The Committee may interview in private persons deprived of their liberty and may communicate freely with any person whom it believes can supply relevant information.[179]

After each visit, the Committee draws up a report for transmission to the

---

to ratify the Protocol for it to come into force, article 8. As of September 1996, twenty-one states had ratified the Protocol, see H/INF (96) 2, p. 22.

[170] The Committee established under the Convention described its function in terms of strengthening 'the *cordon sanitaire* that separates acceptable and unacceptable treatment or behaviour', see First General Report, CPT (91) 3, para. 3.

[171] See Resolution DH (89) 26 of the Committee of Ministers adopted on 19 September 1989 for the election of the members of the Committee. Note that under Protocol No. 2 to the Convention, the members of the Committee may be re-elected twice (rather than once as specified in article 5). The Protocol, which required the ratification of all contracting parties, has, as of September 1996, twenty-one ratifications, see H/INF (96) 2, p. 23.

[172] See Fifth General Report, CPT/Inf (95) 10, 1995, p. 3.

[173] See articles 1 and 7. See also the Rules of Procedure of the Committee, 1989, CPT/Inf (89) 2, especially Rules 29–35.

[174] Note that *ad hoc* visits have been made to Turkey (twice) and Northern Ireland, see Murdoch, 'Work of the Council of Europe's Torture Committee' p. 227.

[175] Rule 10 of the Rules of Procedure.   [176] Rule 31 of the Rules of Procedure.

[177] Article 2.   [178] Article 9(1).   [179] Article 8.

party concerned. That report will remain confidential[180] unless and until the state party concerned decides to make it public.[181] Where a state refuses to co-operate or to improve matters in the light of recommendations made, the Committee may decide, after the state has had an opportunity to make known its views, by a two-thirds majority, to issue a public statement.[182] The Committee makes an annual general report on its activities to the Committee of Ministers, which is transmitted to the Parliamentary Assembly and made public.[183] The relationship between the approach taken by the Committee as revealed in its published reports and the practice of the Commission and Court under the Human Rights Convention is particularly interesting and appears to demonstrate that the Committee had adopted a more flexible attitude to issues relating to detention and ill-treatment.[184]

The Council of Europe Framework Convention for the Protection of National Minorities[185]

The question of minorities is addressed in the European Convention on Human Rights only in terms of one possible ground of prohibited discrimination stipulated in article 14. However, the Council of Europe has been dealing with the issue of minorities in a more vigorous manner in more recent years. Resolution 192 (1988) of the Standing Conference of Local and Regional Authorities of Europe proposed the text of a European Charter for Regional or Minority Languages, while Recommendation 1134 (1990) of the Parliamentary Assembly on the Rights of Minorities called for either a protocol to the European Convention or special convention on this topic.[186] The Committee of Ministers adopted on 22 June 1992 the

---

[180] As does the information gathered by the Committee in relation to a visit and its consultations with the contracting state concerned, article 11(1).

[181] See Rules 40–42. Most reports have been published together with the comments of contracting states upon them, see e.g. Report to the Government of Liechtenstein, CPT/Inf (95) 7 and the Interim Report of the Government of Liechtenstein, CPT/Inf (95) 8; Report to the Government of Italy, CPT/Inf (95) 1 and the Response of the Government of Italy, CPT/Inf (95) 2; Report to the Government of the UK, CPT/Inf (94) 17 and the Response of the Government of the UK, CPT/Inf (94) 18; Report to the Government of Greece, CPT/Inf (94) 20 and the Response of the Government of Greece, CPT/Inf (94) 21. The Fifth General Report of the Committee revealed that twenty-one of the thirty-seven visit reports had been published and that there was good reason to believe that most of the remaining sixteen would be published soon, CPT/Inf (95) 10, p. 6. Note that during 1994, ten visit reports were adopted, while four periodic visits were made and five ad hoc visits made plus one follow-up visit to Turkey, see Fifth General Report, CPT/Inf (95) 10, pp. 4–5.

[182] Article 10(2). The only public statements to date have been those concerning police detention conditions in Turkey in 1992 and 1996 see e.g. CPT/Inf (93) 1, paras. 21 and 37.

[183] Article 12. This is subject to the rules of confidentiality in article 11.

[184] See e.g. Murdoch, 'The Work of the Council of Europe's Torture Committee', pp. 238 et seq.

[185] See generally, P. Thornberry and M. Estebanez, The Council of Europe and Minorities, Strasbourg, 1994.   [186] See also Recommendations 1177 (1992) and 1201 (1993).

European Charter for Regional or Minority Languages.[187] Under this Charter, a variety of measures to promote the use of regional or minority languages is suggested, for example, in the fields of education, court proceedings, public services, media, cultural facilities, economic and social life and transfrontier exchanges. Implementation is to be by periodic reports to the Secretary-General of the Council of Europe in a form to be prescribed by the Committee of Ministers.[188] Such reports will be examined by a committee of experts,[189] composed of one member per contracting party, nominated by the party concerned, appointed for a period of six years and eligible for re-appointment.[190] Bodies or associations legally established in a party may draw the attention of the committee of experts to matters relating to the undertakings entered into by that party and on the basis of states' reports, the committee will itself report to the Committee of Ministers. The committee of experts' report shall be accompanied by the comments which the parties have been requested to make and shall also contain the proposals of the committee of experts to the Committee of Ministers for the preparation of such recommendations of the latter body to one or more of the parties as may be required. The Secretary-General shall make a two-yearly detailed report to the Parliamentary Assembly on the application of the Charter.[191] It should also be noted that the Committee of Ministers may after the entry into force of the Charter invite any non-member state of the Council of Europe to accede to the Charter.[192]

At the Vienna Meeting of Heads of State and Government of the Council of Europe in October 1993, it was decided that a legal instrument would be drafted with regard to the protection of national minorities, and appendix II of the Vienna Declaration instructed the Committee of Ministers to work upon both a framework convention on national minorities and a draft protocol on cultural rights complementing the European Convention on Human Rights.[193] The Framework Convention for the Protection of National Minorities was adopted by the Committee of Ministers on 10 November 1994 and opened for signature on 1 February 1995.[194] The Framework Convention underlines the right to equality before the law of persons belonging to national minorities and prohibits discrimination based on belonging to a national minority. Contracting parties to the Framework

---

[187] It was opened for signature on 5 November 1992 and signed by eleven states at that time. By 1 January 1995, there were only two ratifications, see 16 HRLJ, 1995, p. 85.
[188] Article 15.   [189] Article 16.   [190] Article 17.   [191] Article 16.   [192] Article 20.
[193] See 14 HRLJ, 1993, pp. 373 *et seq.* See also the Explanatory Report to the Framework Convention for the Protection of National Minorities, 1995. An *ad hoc* Committee for the Protection of National Minorities (CAHMIN) was established. Note that in January 1996, it was decided to suspend the work of the Committee on the drafting of an Additional Protocol, see CAHMIN (95) 22 Addendum, 1996.
[194] As of September 1996, there were twenty-eight signatories and five ratifications, see H/INF (96) 2, p. 23.

Convention undertake to adopt, where necessary, adequate measures to promote in all areas of economic, social, political and cultural life, full and effective equality between persons belonging to a national minority and to the majority.[195] The parties agree to promote the conditions necessary for persons belonging to minorities to develop their culture and to preserve the essential elements of their identity, namely their religion, language, traditions and cultural heritage.[196] The collective expression of individual human rights of persons belonging to national minorities are to be respected,[197] while in areas inhabited by such persons traditionally or in substantial numbers, the parties shall endeavour to ensure as far as possible the condition which would make it possible to use the minority languages in relations between those persons and the administrative authorities.[198] By article 15, the parties agree to refrain from measures which alter the geographic proportions of the population in areas inhabited by persons belonging to national minorities. The implementation of this Framework Convention is to be monitored by the Committee of Ministers of the Council of Europe[199] with the assistance of an advisory committee of experts[200] and on the basis of periodic reports from contracting states.[201] Much will depend upon how this committee will be established and how it will function together with the Committee of Ministers. While the range of rights accorded to members of minorities is clearly greater than that envisaged in UN instruments,[202] its ambit is narrower in being confined to 'national minorities'. The Framework Convention itself provides no definition of that term, although Recommendation 1201 (1993) adopted by the Parliamentary Assembly and reaffirmed in Recommendation 1255 (1995) suggests that it refers to persons who reside on the territory of the state concerned and are citizens of it; maintain longstanding, firm and lasting ties with that state; display distinctive ethnic, cultural, religious or linguistic characteristics; are sufficiently representative, although smaller in numbers than the rest of the population of that state or of a region of that state; and are motivated by a concern to preserve together that which constitutes their common identity, including their culture, their traditions, their religion or their language. The

---

[195] Article 4.
[196] Article 5. The parties also agree to refrain from assimilation policies and practices where this is against the will of persons belonging to national minorities.
[197] E.g. the freedoms of peaceful assembly, association, expression and thought, conscience and religion, article 7. See also articles 8 and 9.
[198] Upon request and where such a request corresponds to a real need, article 10(2). Similarly with regard to the display of traditional local names, street names and other topographical indications intended for the public in the minority language, article 11(3), and with regard to adequate opportunities for being taught the minority language or for receiving instruction in that language, article 14(2).
[199] Article 24. Note that parties which are not members of the Council of Europe shall participate in the implementation mechanism according to modalities to be determined.
[200] Article 26.   [201] Article 25.   [202] See *supra* p. 218.

narrowing of regard to persons belonging to national minorities who are citizens of the state concerned is perhaps a matter of concern.[203]
The Council of Europe has adopted measures with regard to other areas
of human rights activities of some relevance to the above issues.[204]

The European Community[205]

The Treaty of Rome 1957 established the European Economic Community
and is not of itself a human rights treaty. However, the European Court of
Justice has held that subsumed within Community law are certain relevant
unwritten general principles of law, emanating from several sources.[206] The
Court noted in the *Internationale Handelsgesellschaft* case,[207] that 'respect for
fundamental rights forms an integral part of the general principles of law
protected by the Court of Justice', while in *Nold* v. *Commission*,[208] the Court
emphasised that measures incompatible with fundamental rights recognised
and protected by the constitutions of member states could not be upheld. It
was also held that international treaties for the protection of human rights
on which member states have collaborated or of which they are signatories,
could supply guidelines which should be followed within the framework of
Community law.[209] The European Convention on Human Rights is clearly
the prime example of this and it has been referred to on several occasions
by the Court.[210] Indeed the question has also been raised and considered

---

[203] See e.g. R. Higgins, 'Minority Rights Discrepancies and Divergencies Between the International Covenant and the Council of Europe System' in *Liber Amicorum for Henry Schermers*, Leiden, 1994.

[204] See e.g. the European Charter of Local Self-Government 1985; the European Convention on the Participation of Foreigners in Public Life at Local Level 1992; the European Outline Convention on Transfrontier Co-operation between Territorial Communities or Authorities 1980; the European Convention on the Legal Status of Migrant Workers 1977 and the European Convention on the Exercise of Children's Rights 1995.

[205] See e.g. *The European Union and Human Rights* (eds. N. Neuwahl and A. Rosas), Dordrecht, 1995; T. Hartley, *The Foundations of European Community Law*, Oxford, 3rd edn, 1994, Chapter 5; L. N. Brown and T. Kennedy, *The Court of Justice of the European Communities*, 4th edn, London, 1994, Chapter 15; M. Mendelson, 'The European Court of Justice and Human Rights', 1 *Yearbook of European Law*, 1981, p. 126 and H. Schermers, 'The European Communities Bound by Fundamental Human Rights', 27 *Common Market Law Review*, 1990, p. 249.

[206] See e.g. *Stauder* v. *City of Ulm* [1969] ECR 419; *Internationale Handelsgesellschaft* [1970] ECR 1125; *Nold* v. *EC Commission* [1974] ECR 491; *Kirk* [1984] ECR 2689 and *Johnston* v. *Chief Constable of the RUC* [1986] 3 CMLR 240. See also the Joint Declaration by the European Parliament, the Council and the Commission of 5 April 1979, *Official Journal*, 1977, C103/1; the Joint Declaration Against Racism and Xenophobia, 11 June 1986, *Official Journal*, 1986, C158/1 and the European Parliament's Declaration of Fundamental Rights and Freedoms, 1989, *EC Bulletin*, 4/1989.   [207] [1970] ECR 1125, 1134.

[208] [1974] ECR 491, 507.

[209] See e.g. *Hauer* v. *Land Rheinland-Pfaltz* [1979] ECR 3727 and *SPUC* v. *Grogan* [1991] ECR I-4685.

[210] See e.g. *Rutili* [1975] ECR 1219; *Valsabbia* v. *Commission* [1980] ECR 907; *Kirk* [1984] ECR 2689; *Dow Chemical Ibérica* v. *Commission* [1989] ECR 3165; *ERT* [1991] ECR I-2925 and *X* v. *Commission* [1992] ECR II-2195 and 16 HRLJ, 1995, p. 54.

without resolution as to whether the Community should itself accede to the European Convention on Human Rights.[211]

The Treaty on European Union (the Maastricht Treaty) 1992 amended the Treaty of Rome and established the European Union, founded on the European Communities supplemented by the policies and forms of co-operation established under the 1992 Treaty. Article F(2) of Title I noted that the Union 'shall respect fundamental rights', as guaranteed by the European Convention on Human Rights and as they result from common constitutional traditions, 'as general principles of Community law'. Under article K.1 of Title VI, the member states agreed that asylum, immigration, drug, fraud, civil and criminal judicial co-operation, customs co-operation and certain forms of police co-operation would be regarded as 'matters of common interest', which under article K.2 would be dealt with in compliance with the European Convention on Human Rights and the Convention relating to the Status of Refugees 1951. The provisions under Title V on the Common Foreign and Security Policy may also impact upon human rights, so that, for instance, the European Union sent its own human rights observers to Rwanda within this framework.[212] The Union, more generally, seeks in some measure to pay regard to human rights as internationally defined, in its activities.[213] There appears now to be a formal policy, for example, to include a human rights clause in co-operation agreements with third countries, which incorporates a provision for the suspension of the agreement in case of a breach of the essential elements of the agreement in question, including respect for human rights.[214] The European Parliament is also active in consideration of human rights issues.[215]

The OSCE (Organisation for Security and Co-operation in Europe)[216]

What was initially termed the 'Helsinki process', and which more formally was referred to as the Conference on Security and Co-operation in Europe,

---

[211] See e.g. 'Accession of the Communities to the European Convention on Human Rights', *EC Bulletin*, Suppl. 2/79.

[212] See J. Van Der Kaauw, 'European Union', NQHR, 1995, p. 173.

[213] See e.g. the Commission Report on the Implementation of Actions to Promote Human Rights and Democracy, 1994, COM 9(5) 191, 1995.

[214] See e.g. 13 NQHR, 1995, pp. 276 and 460.

[215] See e.g. the Annual Reports of the Parliament on Respect for Human Rights in the European Community, 14 HRLJ, 1993, p. 292.

[216] See, for example, A. Bloed, 'Monitoring the CSCE Human Dimension: In Search of its Effectiveness' in *Monitoring Human Rights in Europe* (ed. A. Bloed *et al.*), Dordrecht, 1993, p. 45 ; *The CSCE* (ed. A. Bloed), Dordrecht, 1993; *Human Rights, International Law and the Helsinki Accord* (ed. T. Buergenthal), Montclair, NJ, 1977; J. Maresca, *To Helsinki – the CSCE 1973–75*, Durham, 1987; T. Buergenthal, 'The Helsinki Process: Birth of a Human Rights System' in *Human Rights in the World Community* (eds. R. Claude and B. Weston), 2nd edn, Philadelphia, 1992, p. 256; *Essays on Human Rights in the Helsinki Process* (eds. A. Bloed and P. Van Dijk), Leiden, 1985; A. Bloed and P. Van Dijk, *The Human Dimension of*

developed out of the Final Act of the Helsinki meeting, which was signed on 1 August 1975 after two years of discussions by the representatives of the thirty-five participating states.[217] The Final Act[218] dealt primarily with questions of international security and state relations, and was seen as the method by which the post-war European territorial settlement would be finally accepted. In the Western view, the Final Act constituted a political statement and accordingly could not be regarded as a binding treaty. None the less, the impact of the Final Act on developments in Europe has far exceeded the impact of most legally binding treaties.

The Final Act set out in 'Basket I' a list of ten fundamental principles dealing with relations between participating states, principle 7 of which refers to 'respect for human rights and fundamental freedoms, including freedom of thought, conscience, religion and belief'. 'Basket III' dealt with Co-operation in Humanitarian and Other Fields and covered family reunification, free flow of information and cultural and educational co-operation.[219]

At the third 'follow-up' meeting at Vienna in January 1989, great progress regarding human rights occurred,[220] primarily as a result of the changed attitudes in the then USSR and in Eastern Europe, especially as regards the extent of the detailed provisions and the recognition of concrete rights and duties. The part entitled 'Questions Relating to Security in Europe' contained a Principles section, in which *inter alia* the parties confirmed their respect for human rights and their determination to guarantee their effective exercise. Paragraphs 13–27 contain in a detailed and concrete manner a list of human rights principles to be respected, ranging from due process rights to equality and non-discrimination and the rights of religious communities, and from the rights of minorities to the rights of refugees. The provision in which states agree to respect the right of their citizens to contribute actively, either individually or collectively, to the promotion and protection of human rights, constitutes an important innovation of great practical significance, as does the comment that states will respect the right of persons to observe and promote the implementation of CSCE provisions.

The part entitled 'Cooperation in Humanitarian and Other Fields' included an important section on Human Contacts in which the right to leave one's country and return thereto was reaffirmed. It was decided that

---

the Helsinki Process, Dordrecht, 1991; D. McGoldrick, 'Human Rights Developments in the Helsinki Process', 39 ICLQ, 1990, p. 923 and D. McGoldrick, 'The Development of the Conference on Security and Co-operation in Europe – From Process to Institution' in *Legal Visions of the New Europe* (eds. B. S. Jackson and D. McGoldrick), London, 1993, p. 135. See also *infra*, Chapter 18, p. 733.

[217] I.e. all the states of Western and Eastern Europe, except Albania, plus the United States and Canada.   [218] For the text, see, for example, 14 ILM, 1975, p. 1292.

[219] 'Basket II' covered co-operation in the fields of economics, science, technology, and the environment.   [220] See the text of the Concluding Document in 10 HRLJ, 1989, p. 270.

all outstanding human contacts applications would be resolved within six months and that thereafter there would be a series of regular reviews. Family reunion issues were to be dealt with in as short a time as possible and in normal practice within one month. The parties committed themselves to publishing all laws and statutory regulations concerning movement by individuals within their territory and travel between states, an issue that had caused a great deal of controversy, while the right of members of religions to establish and maintain personal contacts with each other in their own and other countries, *inter alia* through travel and participation in religious events, was proclaimed.[221]

In a further significant development, the Vienna Concluding Document contained a part entitled 'Human Dimension of the CSCE' in which some implementation measures were provided for. The participating states decided to exchange information and to respond to requests for information and to representations made to them by other participating states on questions relating to the human dimension of the CSCE. Bilateral meetings would be held with other participating states that so request, in order to examine such questions, while such questions could be brought to the attention of other participating states through diplomatic channels or raised at further 'follow-up' meetings or at meetings of the Conference on the Human Dimension. The procedure is confidential.[222] The Concluding Document of the Copenhagen meeting in 1990[223] constituted a further crucial stage in the development of the process. The participating states proclaimed support for the principles of the rule of law, free and fair elections, democracy, pluralism and due process rights. Paragraph 1 of Chapter 1 emphasised that the protection and promotion of human rights was one of the basic purposes of government. A variety of specific rights, including the freedoms of expression, assembly, association, thought, conscience and religion, and the rights to leave one's own country and return and to receive legal assistance, the rights of the child, the rights of national minorities and the prohibition of torture are proclaimed. Time-limits were imposed with regard to the Vienna Human Dimension mechanism.

The Charter of Paris, adopted at the Summit of Heads of State and of

---

[221] Paragraphs 18 and 32.

[222] The mechanism was used over one hundred times between 1989 and 1992, see Bloed and Van Dijk, *The Human Dimension*, p. 79 and McGoldrick, 'Conference on Security and Co-operation in Europe', p. 139. See also H. Tretter, 'Human Rights in the Concluding Document of the Vienna Follow-up Meeting of the Conference on Security and Co-operation in Europe of January 15, 1989', 10 HRLJ, 1989, p. 257; R. Brett, *The Development of the Human Dimension Machinery*, Essex University, 1992 and A. Bloed and P. Van Dijk, 'Supervisory Mechanisms for the Human Dimension of the CSCE: Its Setting-up in Vienna, its Present Functioning and its Possible Development towards a General Procedure for the Peaceful Settlement of Disputes' in Bloed and Van Dijk, *The Human Dimension, op. cit.*, p. 74.   [223] See 8 NQHR, 1990, p. 302 and Cm 1324 (1990).

Government in 1990,[224] called for more regular consultations at ministerial and senior official level and marked an important stage in the institutionalisation of the process, with a Council of Foreign Ministers, a Committee of Senior Officials and a secretariat being established. The section on Human Rights, Democracy and Rule of Law consisted of a list of human rights, including the right to effective remedies, full respect for which constituted 'the bedrock' for the construction of 'the new Europe'. The Moscow Human Dimension meeting of 1991[225] described the Human Dimension mechanism as an essential achievement of the CSCE process and it was strengthened. The time-limits provided for at Copenhagen were reduced[226] and a recourse list of experts was to be established,[227] with three experts being appointed by each participating state, in order to allow for CSCE missions to be created to assist states requesting such help in facilitating the resolution of a particular question or problem related to the human dimension of the CSCE. The observations of the missions of experts together with the comments of the state concerned were to be forwarded to CSCE states within three weeks of the submission of the observations to the state concerned and may be discussed by the Committee of Senior Officials, who could consider follow-up measures.[228] By the time of the Helsinki Conference in 1992, the number of participating states had risen to fifty-two,[229] and the political climate in Europe having changed dramatically after the establishment of democratic regimes in Eastern Europe, the ending of the Soviet Union and the rise of tensions in Yugoslavia and other parts of Eastern Europe. The participating states strongly reaffirmed that human dimension commitments were matters of direct and legitimate concern to all participating states and did not belong exclusively to the internal affairs of the states concerned, while gross violations of such commitments posed a special threat to stability. This reference of the link between human rights and international stability was to increase in the following years. At Helsinki, the CSCE was declared to be a regional arrangement in the sense of Chapter VIII of the UN Charter.[230] The post of High Commissioner on National Minorities

[224] See 30 ILM, 1991, p. 190.   [225] See 30 ILM, 1991, p. 1670 and Cm 1771 (1991).
[226] So that, for example, the written responses to requests for information were to occur within ten days, and the bilateral meetings to take place as a rule within one week of the date of request, Section I(1).
[227] The Council of Ministers of the CSCE subsequently decided that the Office of Democratic Institutions and Human Rights (formerly the Office for Free Elections) would be the appropriate institution establishing the resource list.
[228] A variety of missions have now been employed in, for example, Nagorno-Karabakh, Georgia, Chechnya, Moldova and Croatia.
[229] As of December 1995, there were fifty-four participating states (with the former Yugoslav Republic of Macedonia joining in October 1995 and the Federal Republic of Yugoslavia having been suspended in 1992).   [230] See further infra, p. 881.

was established in order to provide early warning and early action where appropriate, concerning tensions relating to national minority issues that have the potential to develop into a conflict within the CSCE area affecting peace, stability or relations between participating states.[231] The High Commissioner was also mandated to collect relevant information and make visits. Where the High Commissioner concludes that there is a *prima facie* risk of potential conflict in such situations, an early warning is to be issued, which will be conveyed promptly by the Chairman-in-Office of the CSCE to the Committee of Senior Officials. As far as the human dimension mechanism was concerned, the Conference decided to permit any participating state to provide information on situations and cases that are the subject of requests for information and it was also decided that in years in which a review conference was not being held, a three-week meeting at expert level of participating states would be organised in order to review implementation of the CSCE human dimension commitments. In addition, it was provided that the Office of Democratic Institutions and Human Rights would begin organising human dimension seminars.[232]

The next major step in the process took place at Budapest at the end of 1994.[233] The CSCE in recognition of the institutional changes underway in recent years changed its name to the OSCE (the Organisation for Security and Co-operation in Europe) and took a number of steps in the field of security and conflict management. The Conference emphasised that human rights, the rule of law and democratic institutions represented a crucial contribution to conflict prevention and that the protection of human rights constituted an 'essential foundation of democratic civil society'[234] and it was decided that human dimension issues would be regularly dealt with by the Permanent Council, with the Office of Democratic Institutions and Human Rights (based in Warsaw) acting as the main institution of the human dimension in an advisory capacity to the organisation, with enhanced roles in election monitoring and the despatch of missions.[235] States were encouraged to use the human dimension mechanism (now termed the Moscow Mechanism) and the Chairman-in-Office was encouraged to inform the Permanent Council of serious cases of alleged non-implementation of human dimension commitments. Thus, step by step over recent years, the Helsinki process has transformed itself into an institutional structure with a particular interest in describing and requiring the implementation of human

---

[231] See Section II of the Helsinki Decisions. Note that the High Commissioner deals with situations and not with individual complaints.   [232] Section VI of the Helsinki Decisions.
[233] See 5 HRLJ, 1994, p. 449.   [234] Section VIII of the Budapest Decisions.
[235] This group is responsible for the day to day operations of the OSCE and its members are the permanent representatives of the member states meeting weekly. It is based in Vienna.

rights.[236] Although some overlay with the Council of Europe system does exist, the fact that a large proportion of participating states are now either members of the Council of Europe, or seek to become so, should obviate the most acute dangers inherent in differing human rights systems. Nevertheless, as the Council of Europe system moves beyond the strictly legal enforcement stage and as the OSCE develops and strengthens its institutional mechanisms, some overlapping is inevitable. However, in general terms, the OSCE system remains politically based and expressed, while the essence of the Council of Europe system remains juridically focused.

The CIS Convention on Human Rights and Fundamental Freedoms[237]

The Commonwealth of Independent States, which links together the former Republics of the Soviet Union (with the exception of the three Baltic states) adopted a Convention on Human Rights in May 1995. Under this Convention, a standard range of rights is included, ranging from the right to life, liberty and security of person, equality before the judicial system, respect for private and family life, to freedom of religion, expression, assembly and the right to marry. The right to work is included (article 14) as is the right to social security, the right to education and the right of every minor child to special protective measures (article 17). The right of persons belonging to national minorities to express and develop their ethnic, linguistic, religious and cultural identity is protected (article 21), while everyone has the right to take part in public affairs, including voting (article 29). It is intended that the implementation of the Convention be monitored by the Human Rights Commission of the CIS (article 34). Under Section II of the Regulations of the Human Rights Commission, adopted in September 1993, states parties may raise human rights matters falling within the Convention with other states parties and if no satisfactory response is received within six months, the matter may be referred to the Commission. Domestic remedies need to be exhausted. Under Section III of the Regulations, the Commission may examine individual and collective applications submitted by any person or non-governmental organisation.

---

[236] Note that as a consequence of the Dayton Peace Agreement on Bosnia 1995, it was agreed that the OSCE would supervise elections in that country and would closely monitor human rights throughout Bosnia and would appoint an international human rights Ombudsman, see MC (5) Dec/1, 1995.   [237] See H/INF (95) 3, pp. 195 et seq.

The American Convention on Human Rights [238]

The American Convention, which came into force in 1978, contains a range of rights to be protected by the states parties.[239] The rights are fundamentally those protected by the European Convention, but with some interesting differences.[240] For example, under article 4 the right to life is deemed to start in general as from conception,[241] while the prohibition on torture and inhuman or degrading treatment is more extensively expressed and is in the context of the right to have one's physical, mental and moral integrity respected (article 5). In addition, articles 18 and 19 of the American Convention protect the right to a name and the specific rights of the child, article 23 provides for a general right to participation in the context of public affairs and article 26 provides for the progressive achievement of the economic, social and cultural rights contained in the Charter of the Organisation of American States 1948, as amended by the Protocol of Buenos Aires 1967.

The Inter-American Commission on Human Rights was created in 1959 and its first Statute approved by the OAS Council in 1960. In 1971, it was recognised as one of the principal organs of the OAS.[242] Under its original Statute, it had wide powers to promote the awareness and study of human rights in America and to make recommendations to member states. In 1965, the Statute was revised and the Commission's powers expanded to include *inter alia* the examination of communications. With the entry into force of the 1969 Convention, the Commission's position was further strengthened. The Commission has powers regarding all member states of the OAS, not just those that have ratified the Convention, and its Statute emphasises that the human rights protected include those enumerated in both the Convention and the American Declaration of the Rights and Duties of

---

[238] See generally T. Buergenthal and D. Shelton, *Protecting Human Rights in the Americas*, 4th edn, Strasbourg, 1995; D. Shelton, 'The Inter-American Human Rights System' in *Guide to International Human Rights Practice*, p. 119; T. Buergenthal, 'The Inter-American System for the Protection of Human Rights' in *Human Rights in International Law* (ed. T. Meron), Oxford, 1984, p. 439; and T. Buergenthal and R. Norris, *The Inter-American System*, 3 vols., 1983–4. See also A. H. Robertson and J. G. Merrills, *Human Rights in the World*, 4th edn, Manchester, 1996, Chapter 6; S. Davidson, *The Inter-American Court of Human Rights*, Aldershot, 1992; S. Davidson, 'Remedies for Violations of the American Convention on Human Rights', 44 ICLQ, 1995, p. 405 and C. Grossman, 'Proposals to Strengthen the Inter-American System of Protection of Human Rights', 32 German YIL, 1990, p. 264.

[239] As of February 1996, there were twenty-five ratifications, see NQHR, 1995, p. 502. See also *Annual Report of the Inter-American Commission on Human Rights 1995*, Washington, 1996, p. 229.

[240] See e.g. J. Frowein, 'The European and the American Conventions on Human Rights – A Comparison', 1 HRLJ, 1980, p. 44. See also the American Declaration of the Rights and Duties of Man, 1948.   [241] See e.g. 10 DR, 1977, p. 100.

[242] See e.g. C. Medina, 'The Inter-American Commission on Human Rights and the Inter-American Court of Human Rights: Reflections on a Joint Venture', 12 HRQ, 1990, p. 439.

Man.[243] Article 44 of the Convention provides that any person or group of persons or any non-governmental entity legally recognised in one or more of the OAS states may lodge petitions with the Commission alleging a violation of the Convention by a state party. Contrary to the European Convention, this right is automatic, whereas the right of inter-state complaint, again contrary to the European Convention, is under article 45 subject to a prior declaration recognising the competence of the Commission in this regard.[244] The admissibility requirements in articles 46 and 47 are very broadly similar to those in the European Convention, as is the procedure laid down in article 48 and the drawing up of a report in cases in which a friendly settlement has been achieved.[245] The Commission has dealt with a number of issues in the individual application procedure. During 1994, for example, just under 300 cases were opened and the total number of cases being processed by early 1995 was 641.[246]

The Commission has, unlike its European counterpart, a wide-ranging competence to publicise human rights matters by way of reports, studies, lectures and so forth. It may also make recommendations to states on the adoption of progressive measures in favour of human rights and conduct on-site investigations with the consent of the state in question.[247] It provides states generally with advisory services in the human rights field and submits an annual report to the OAS General Assembly. Many special reports have been published dealing with human rights in particular states, e.g. Argentina, Bolivia, Chile, Colombia, Cuba, Dominican Republic, El Salvador, Guatemala, Haiti, Nicaragua, Paraguay, Surinam and Uruguay.[248] The Commission has also devoted attention to certain themes, such as disappearances, torture, refugees and economic and social rights.[249] The Inter-American Court of Human Rights has declared that the Commission also has the authority to determine that any domestic law of a state party has violated the obligations assumed in ratifying or acceding to the Convention[250] and that the Commission may consequentially recom-

[243] See generally the *Basic Documents Pertaining to Human Rights in the Inter-American System*, Washington, 1992. The competence of the Commission to hear petitions relates to the rights in the Convention for states parties and to rights in the American Declaration for states not parties to the Convention.
[244] As of 31 July 1995, there were nine declarations, NQHR, 1995, p. 502.
[245] Articles 49–51. The Secretary-General of the OAS has played the role assigned in the European Convention to the Committee of Ministers.
[246] See *Annual Report 1994*, p. 39.
[247] In 1994, for example, with regard to Guatemala, Haiti, the Bahamas, Ecuador and Jamaica, see *Annual Report 1994*, pp. 21 *et seq.*
[248] See *ibid.*, Chapter IV, with regard to Colombia, Cuba, El Salvador and Guatemala.
[249] See e.g. *Annual Report 1992–3*, pp. 539 *et seq.* See also e.g. AG/Res.443, 1979 and AG/Res.666, 1983 and AG/Res.547, 1981, AG/Res.624, 1982 and AG/Res.644, 1983 (torture).
[250] *Some Powers of the Inter-American Commission on Human Rights*, Advisory Opinion OC-13/93 of 16 July 1993, Series A, No. 13, para. 26.

mend that states repeal or amend the law that is in violation of the Convention. For the Commission to be able to do this, the law may have come to its attention by any means, regardless of whether or not that law is applied in any specific case before the Commission.[251] In the light of this, the Commission in 1994 made a thorough study of the contempt laws (*leyes de desacato*), and concluded that many of these do not meet international human rights standards. The Commission recommended that all member states of the OAS that have such laws should repeal or amend them to bring them into line with international instruments, and with the obligations acquired under those instruments, so as to harmonise their laws with human rights treaties.[252]

In 1985, the OAS General Assembly adopted the Inter-American Convention to Prevent and Punish Torture,[253] while in 1988 an Additional Protocol on Economic, Social and Cultural Rights was signed.[254] Under article 19 of this instrument, states parties agree to provide periodic reports on the progressive measures undertaken to ensure respect for the rights set forth therein. Such reports will go to the Secretary-General of the OAS, who will send them to the Inter-American Economic and Social Council and the Inter-American Council for Education, Science and Culture, with a copy to both the Inter-American Commission on Human Rights and to the specialised agencies of the inter-American system. Violations by a state party of the rights to organise and join trades unions (article 8(a)) and to education (article 13) 'may give rise' to application of the system of individual or inter-state petition under the Inter-American Convention on Human Rights.

A Protocol on the Abolition of the Death Penalty was adopted on 8 June 1990[255] and a new Convention on Forced Disappearances of Persons was adopted on 9 June 1994.[256] Under article 13 of this Convention, states parties agree that the processing of petitions or communications presented

---

[251] *International Responsibility for Issuing and Applying Laws in Violation of the Convention,* Advisory Opinion OC-14/94 of 9 December 1994, Series A, No. 14, para. 39.

[252] *Annual Report 1994,* pp. 199 *et seq.*

[253] As of 31 July 1995, there were thirteen states parties to this Convention, which entered into force in February 1987. Under the Convention, states parties agree to inform the Inter-American Commission of measures taken in application of the Convention and the Commission 'will endeavour in its annual report to analyse the existing situation in the member states of the Organisation of American States in regard to the prevention and elimination of torture', article 17.

[254] As of February 1996, there were only five ratifications, see *Annual Report 1995,* p. 244. Eleven states parties are required for the Additional Protocol to come into force. See also L. Le Blanc, 'The Economic, Social and Cultural Rights Protocol to the American Convention and its Background', 10 NQHR, 1992, 130.

[255] As of February 1996, there were three ratifications of this instrument, *Annual Report 1995,* p. 245. The Protocol enters into force for states upon deposit of the instrument of ratification or accession, article 4. See also C. Cerna, 'US Death Penalty Tested Before the Inter-American Commission on Human Rights', 10 NQHR, 1992, p. 155.

[256] As of February 1995, there were no ratifications of this instrument, *Annual Report 1994,* p. 250. The Convention will enter into force after the second ratification.

to the Inter-American Commission alleging the forced disappearance of persons will be subject to the procedures established under the Inter-American Convention on Human Rights, the Statute and Regulations of the Commission and the Statute and Rules of the Court. Particular reference is made to precautionary measures.[257] Under article 14, when the Commission receives a petition or communication alleging forced disappearance, its Executive Secretariat shall urgently and confidentially address the respective government and shall request that government to provide as soon as possible information as to the whereabouts of the allegedly disappeared person. The OAS also adopted the Inter-American Convention on the Prevention, Punishment and Eradication of Violence Against Women in 1994. Article 10 provides that states parties are to include in their national reports to the Inter-American Commission of Women information on measures taken in this area, while, under article 11, both states parties and the Commission of Women may request of the Inter-American Court advisory opinions on the interpretations of this Convention. Article 12 provides a procedure whereby any person, group of persons or any non-governmental entity legally recognised in one or more member states of the OAS may lodge petitions with the Inter-American Commission on Human Rights alleging violations of the duties of states under article 7 to pursue without delay and by all appropriate means policies to prevent, punish and eradicate violence against women. The question of indigenous peoples has also been addressed and on 18 September 1995, the Inter-American Commission adopted a Draft Declaration on the Rights of Indigenous Peoples.[258]

The Commission itself consists of seven members elected in a personal capacity by the OAS General Assembly for four-year terms.[259] Where, in the case of petitions received, a friendly settlement has not been achieved, then

---

[257] Article 63(2) of the Convention states that in cases of extreme gravity and urgency, and when necessary to avoid irreparable damage to persons, the Court shall adopt such provisional measures as it deems pertinent in matters it has under consideration. With respect to a case not yet submitted to the Court, it may act at the request of the Commission. Article 19(c) of the Statute of the Commission provides that the Commission has the power to request the Court to take such provisional measures as it considers appropriate in serious and urgent cases which have not yet been submitted to it for consideration, whenever this becomes necessary to prevent irreparable injury to persons. Under article 29 of the Regulations of the Commission, the Commission may on its own initiative or at the request of a party take any action it considers necessary for the discharge of its functions. In particular, in urgent cases, when it becomes necessary to avoid irreparable damage to persons, the Commission may request that provisional measures be taken to avoid irreparable damage in cases where the denounced facts are true. Article 24 of the Rules of Procedure of the Inter-American Court provide that at any stage of the proceeding involving cases of extreme gravity and urgency and when necessary to avoid irreparable damage to persons, the Court, may, at the request of a party or on its own motion, order whatever provisional measures it deems appropriate, pursuant to article 63(2) of the Convention.

[258] OEA/Ser'L/V/II.90; Doc. 9, rev. 1, 1995.   [259] See articles 34–38 of the Convention.

under article 50 a report will be drawn up, together with such proposals and recommendations as are seen fit, and transmitted to the parties. A three-month period is then available during which the Commission or the state concerned (but not the individual concerned) may go to the Inter-American Court of Human Rights.[260] The Court consists of seven judges serving in an individual capacity and elected by an absolute majority of the states parties to the Convention in the OAS General Assembly for six-year terms.[261] The jurisdiction of the Court is subject to a prior declaration under article 62.[262] Under article 64, the Court also possesses an advisory jurisdiction with regard to the interpretation of the American Convention and other conventions concerning the protection of human rights in the American states.

The Court has dealt with a variety of important issues by way of advisory opinions. In *Definition of Other Treaties Subject to the Interpretation of the Inter-American Court*,[263] the Court took the view that the object of the Convention was to integrate the regional and universal systems of human rights protection and that, therefore, any human rights treaty to which American states were parties could be the subject of an advisory opinion. In *The Effect of Reservations*,[264] the Court stressed that human rights treaties involve the establishment of legal orders within which obligations were created towards all individuals within their jurisdiction and concluded that an instrument of ratification of adherence containing a reservation compatible with the object and purpose of the Convention does not require acceptance by the other states parties and the instrument thus enters into force as of the moment of deposit.[265] In a manner reminiscent of and clearly influenced by the European Court of Human Rights, the Inter-American Court stated that human rights treaties were different in nature from traditional multilateral treaties, since they focused not upon the reciprocal exchange of rights for the mutual benefit of the contracting states, but rather upon the protection of the basic rights of individuals. The obligations were *erga omnes*, rather than with regard to particular other states.[266]

In an important discussion of freedom of expression in the *Licensing of Journalists* case,[267] the Court advised that the compulsory licensing of journalists was incompatible with article 13, the freedom of expression

---

[260] Article 51. If this does not happen and the matter is not settled with the state concerned, the Commission by a majority vote may set forth its own opinion and conclusions on the matter, which may be published. See for example, *Annual Report 1983–4*, pp. 23–75.

[261] Articles 52–54. See also Davidson, *The Inter-American Court*; C. Cerna, 'The Structure and Functioning of the Inter-American Court of Human Rights (1979–1992)', 63 BYIL, 1992, p. 135 and Frost, 'The Evolution of the Inter American Court of Human Rights', 14 HRQ, 1992, p. 171.

[262] As of February 1996, there were seventeen declarations under article 62, see *Annual Report 1995*, p. 229.   [263] 22 ILM, 1983, p. 51; 67 ILR, p. 594.

[264] *Ibid.*, p. 33; 67 ILR, p. 559.   [265] para. 37. See article 74 of the Convention.

[266] *Ibid.*, para. 29. See also *supra* p. 258.   [267] 7 HRLJ, 1986, p. 74; 75 ILR, p. 31.

provision in the Convention, if it denied any person access to the full use of the media as a means of expressing opinions. The Court emphasised that freedom of expression could only be restricted on the basis of 'compelling governmental interest' and that the restriction must be 'closely tailored to the accomplishment of the legitimate governmental objective necessitating it'.[268] In the *Habeas Corpus* case,[269] the Court declared that the writ of habeas corpus was a non-suspendable 'judicial guarantee' for the protection of rights from which no derogation was permitted under the Convention under article 27. Reference was made to the 'inseparable bond between the principle of legality, democratic institutions and the rule of law'. The Court also emphasised that only democratic governments could avail themselves of the right to declare a state of emergency and then only under closely circumscribed conditions. The Court has also addressed the issue of the relationship between itself and the American Declaration of the Rights and Duties of Man 1948 in the *Interpretation of the American Declaration* case.[270] In an opinion likely to be of significance in view of the fact that, for example, the US is not a party to the Convention but as a member of the OAS has signed the Declaration, the Court stressed that in interpreting the Declaration regard had to be had to the current state of the Inter-American system and that, by a process of authoritative interpretation, the member states of the OAS have agreed that the Declaration contains and defines the human rights norms referred to in the OAS Charter.[271] Since the Charter was a treaty, the Court could, therefore, interpret the Declaration under article 64.[272] This rather ingenious argument is likely to open the door to a variety of advisory opinions on a range of important issues.

The exercise of the Court's contentious jurisdiction has, however, been less successful. In the *Gallardo* case,[273] the Court remitted the claim to the Commission declaring it inadmissible, noting that a state could not dispense with the processing of the case by the Commission, while in the *Velasquez Rodriguez*[274] and *Godinez Cruz*[275] cases the Court in 'disappearance' situations found that Honduras had violated the Convention.[276] In the former case, it was emphasised that states had a legal responsibility to prevent human rights violations and to use the means at its disposal to investigate and punish such violations. Where this did not happen, the state concerned

---

[268] *Ibid.*, para. 45. See also the *Sunday Times* case, European Court of Human Rights, Series A, vol. 30, 1979; 58 ILR, p. 150.   [269] 9 HRLJ, 1988, p. 94.

[270] 28 ILM, 1989, p. 378.

[271] *Ibid.*, pp. 388–9. See also T. Buergenthal, 'The Revised OAS Charter and the Protection of Human Rights, 69 AJIL, 1975, p. 828.

[272] The problem was that the Declaration clearly was not a treaty and article 64 provides for advisory opinions regarding the Convention itself and 'other treaties'.

[273] 20 ILM, 1981, p. 1424; 67 ILR, p. 578.   [274] 9 HRLJ, 1988, p. 212.

[275] H/Inf (90) 1, p. 80.

[276] Note also the award of compensation to the victims in both of these cases, *ibid.*, pp. 80–1.

had failed in its duty to ensure the full and free exercise of these rights within the jurisdiction.[277] It is to be hoped that the paucity of contentious cases will soon be remedied.[278]

The Banjul Charter on Human and Peoples' Rights[279]

This Charter was adopted by the Organisation of African Unity in 1981 and came into force in 1986. The Charter contains a wide range of rights, including in addition to the traditional civil and political rights, economic, social and cultural rights and various peoples' rights. In this latter category are specifically mentioned the rights to self-determination, development and a generally satisfactory environment.[280] The reference to the latter two concepts is unusual in human rights instruments and it remains to be seen both how they will be interpreted and how they will be implemented.

One question that is immediately posed with respect to the notion of 'peoples' rights' is to ascertain the definition of a people. If experience with the definition of self-determination in the context of the United Nations is any guide,[281] and bearing in mind the extreme sensitivity which African states have manifested with regard to the stability of the existing colonial borders,[282] then the principle is likely to be interpreted in the sense of independent states. This was confirmed in the *Katangese Peoples' Congress* v. *Zaire*,[283] where the Commission declared that Katanga was obliged to

[277] At paras. 174–6.
[278] Note that the Court utilised the provisional measures power under article 63(2) for the first time in January 1988, against Honduras, following the killing of a person due to testify before it and concerns expressed about the safety of other witnesses, H/Inf. (88) 1, p. 64. See also the provisional measures adopted by the Court against Peru, in similar circumstances, in August 1990, 11 HRLJ, 1990, p. 257.
[279] See e.g. E. Ankumah, *The African Commission on Human and Peoples' Rights*, Dordrecht, 1996; R. Gittleman, 'The African Charter on Human and Peoples' Rights: A Legal Analysis', 22 *Va JIL*, 1981, p. 667; Robertson and Merrills, *Human Rights in the World*, p. 200; U. O. Umozurike, 'The Protection of Human Rights under the Banjul (African) Charter on Human and Peoples' Rights', 1 *African Journal of International Law*, 1988, p. 65; A. Bello, 'The African Charter on Human and Peoples' Rights', 194 HR, 1985, p. 5; S. Neff, 'Human Rights in Africa', 33 ICLQ, 1984, p. 331; U. O. Umozurike, 'The African Charter on Human and Peoples' Rights', 77 AJIL, 1983, p. 902; B. Ramcharan, 'The Travaux Préparatoires of the African Commission on Human Rights', HRLJ, 1992, p. 307; W. Benedek, 'The African Charter and Commission on Human and Peoples' Rights: How to Make It More Effective', NQHR, 1993, p. 25; C. Flinterman and E. Ankumeh, 'The African Charter on Human and Peoples' Rights' in *Guide to International Human Rights Practice*, p. 159 and A. Danielsen and G. Oberleitner, '16th Session of the African Commission on Human and Peoples' Rights', 13 NQHR, 1995, p. 82. See also F. Ouguergouz, 'La Commission Africaine des Droits de l'Homme et des Peuples', AFDI, 1989, p. 557; K. Mbaye, *Les Droits de l'Homme en Afrique*, Paris, 1992 and M. Hamalengwa, C. Flintermann and E. Dankwa, *The International Law of Human Rights in Africa – Basic Documents and Annotated Bibliography*, Dordrecht, 1988.
[280] See articles 19–22.   [281] *Supra*, Chapter 5, p. 000.
[282] See e.g. M. N. Shaw, *Title to Territory in Africa: International Legal Issues*, Oxford, 1986.
[283] Case No. 75/92, see 13 NQHR, 1995, p. 478.

exercise a variant of self-determination that was compatible with the sovereignty and territorial integrity of Zaire.

The African Charter is the first human rights convention that details the duties of the individual to the state, society and family.[284] Included are the duties to avoid compromising the security of the state and to preserve and strengthen social and national solidarity and independence. It remains to be seen whether this distinctive approach brings with it more problems than advantages.

The Charter set up the African Commission on Human and Peoples' Rights, consisting of eleven persons appointed by the Conference of the Heads of State and Government of the OAU, to implement the Charter. The Commission has important educational and promotional responsibilities,[285] including undertaking studies, organising conferences, disseminating information and making recommendations to governments. This is quite unlike the European Commission, but rather more similar to the Inter-American Commission. The Commission may hear as of right inter-state complaints,[286] although the clear preference for friendly settlement is expressed, and other non-state communications.[287] No provision was made for a Court.[288] The Commission adopted Rules of Procedure in 1988.[289] In addition, there is an obligation upon states parties to produce reports every two years upon the measures taken to implement the rights under the Charter.[290] The Commission was given authority by the OAU to study the reports and make observations upon them and has indeed adopted guidelines. However, to date, it is fair to conclude that the reporting procedure has encountered serious problems, not least in that many states have failed to submit reports or adequate reports,[291] while the financial resources difficulties faced by the Commission have been significant.

---

[284] See articles 27–29.
[285] See article 45. See also A. Bello, 'The Mandate of the African Commission on Human and Peoples' Rights', 1 *African Journal of International Law*, 1988, p. 31.
[286] Articles 47–54. See also Rules 87 – 118 of the Rules of Procedure.   [287] Articles 55–59.
[288] However, a meeting of legal experts in 1995 in Cape Town, South Africa, adopted a draft protocol calling for the establishment of a Court, OAU/LEG/EXP/AFC/HPR (I) and 13 NQHR, 1995, p. 478.
[289] See 40 *The Review, International Commission of Jurists*, 1988, p. 26.   [290] Article 62.
[291] See e.g. G. Oberleitner and C. Welch, 'Africa: 15th Session African Commission on Human and Peoples' Rights', 12 NQHR, 1994, p. 333.

CHAPTER 8

RECOGNITION

International society is not an unchanging entity, but is subject to the ebb and flow of political life.[1] New states are created and old units fall away. New governments come into being within states in a manner contrary to declared constitutions whether or not accompanied by force. Insurgencies occur and belligerent administrations are established in areas of territory hitherto controlled by the legitimate government. Each of these events creates new facts and the question that recognition is concerned with revolves around the extent to which legal effects should flow from such occurrences. Each state will have to decide whether or not to recognise the particular eventuality and the kind of legal entity it should be accepted as.

Recognition involves consequences both on the international plane and within municipal law. If an entity is recognised as a state in, for example, the United Kingdom, it will entail the consideration of rights and duties that would not otherwise be relevant. There are privileges permitted to a foreign state before the municipal courts that would not be allowed to other institutions or persons.

It is stating the obvious to point to the very strong political influences that bear upon this topic.[2] In more cases than not the decision whether or not to recognise will depend more upon political considerations than upon exclusively legal factors. Recognition is not merely applying the relevant legal

[1] See generally, e.g. *Oppenheim's International Law* (eds. R. Y. Jennings and A. D. Watts), 9th edn, London, 1992; H. Lauterpacht, *Recognition in International Law*, Cambridge, 1947; T. C. Chen, *The International Law of Recognition*, London, 1951; J. Charpentier, *La Reconnaissance Internationale et l'Evolution du Droit des Gens*, Paris, 1956; T. L. Galloway, *Recognising Foreign Governments*, Washington, 1978; J. Verhoeven, *La Reconnaissance Internationale dans la Pratique Contemporaine*, Paris, 1975 and Verhoeven, 'La Reconnaissance Internationale, Déclin ou Renouveau?', AFDI, 1993, p. 7; J. Dugard, *Recognition and the United Nations*, Cambridge, 1987; H. Blix, 'Contemporary Aspects of Recognition', 130 HR, 1970–II, p. 587; J. Salmon, 'Reconnaissance d'Etat', 25 *Revue Belge de Droit International*, 1992, p. 226 and *Third US Restatement on Foreign Relations Law*, Washington, 1987, vol. I, pp. 77 *et seq*. See also Nguyen Quoc Dinh, P. Daillier and A. Pellet, *Droit International Public*, 3rd edn, Paris, 1994, pp. 529 *et seq.;* P. M. Dupuy, *Droit International Public*, 2nd edn, Paris, 1993, pp. 65 *et seq.* and L. Henkin, R. C. Pugh, O. Schachter and H. Smit, *International Law, Cases and Materials*, 3rd edn, St Paul, 1993, pp. 244 *et seq.*
[2] See e.g. H. A. Smith, *Great Britain and the Law of Nations*, London, vol. I, 1932, pp. 77–80.

consequences to a factual situation, for sometimes a state will not want such consequences to follow, either internationally or domestically.

To give one example, the United States refused for many years to recognise either the People's Republic of China or North Korea, not because it did not accept the obvious fact that these authorities exercised effective control over their respective territories, but rather because it did not wish the legal effects of recognition to come into operation.[3] It is purely a political judgment, although it has been clothed in legal terminology. In addition, there are a variety of options open as to what an entity may be recognised as. Such an entity may, for example, be recognised as a full sovereign state, or as the effective authority within a specific area or as a subordinate authority to another state.[4] Recognition is a statement by an international legal person as to the status in international law of another real or alleged international legal person. Although recognition in itself constitutes participation in the international legal process, it may also be important within the context of bilateral relations, in being a decision by which a recognised situation or person is accepted and thus rendered opposable to the recognising state.

Recognition of states

There are basically two theories as to the nature of recognition. The constitutive theory maintains that it is the act of recognition by other states that creates a new state and endows it with legal personality and not the process by which it actually obtained independence. Thus, new states are established in the international community as fully-fledged subjects of international law by virtue of the will and consent of already existing states.[5] The disadvantage of this approach is that an unrecognised 'state' may not be subject to the obligations imposed by international law and may accordingly be free from such restraints as, for instance, the prohibition on aggression. A further complication would arise if a 'state' were recognised by some but not other states. Could one talk then of, for example, partial personality?

The second theory, the declaratory theory, adopts the opposite approach

---

[3] See e.g. M. Kaplan and N. Katzenbach, *The Political Foundations of International Law*, New York, 1961, p. 109.

[4] See e.g. *Carl Zeiss Stiftung* v. *Rayner and Keeler* [1967] AC 853: 43 ILR, p. 23, where the Court took the view that the German Democratic Republic was a subordinate agency of the USSR, and the recognition of the Ciskei as a subordinate body of South Africa, *Gur Corporation* v. *Trust Bank of Africa Ltd* [1986] 3 All ER 449: 75 ILR, p. 675.

[5] See e.g. J. Crawford, *The Creation of States in International Law*, Oxford, 1979, pp. 17 *et seq.*; Henkin *et al.*, *International Law*, pp. 244 *et seq.* and J. Salmon, *La Reconnaissance d'Etat*, Paris, 1971. See also R. Rich and D. Turk, 'Symposium: Recent Developments in the Practice of State Recognition', EJIL, 1993, p. 36.

and is a little more in accord with practical realities.[6] It maintains that recognition is merely an acceptance by states of an already existing situation. A new state will acquire capacity in international law not by virtue of the consent of others but by virtue of a particular factual situation. It will be legally constituted by its own efforts and circumstances and will not have to await the procedure of recognition by other states. This doctrine owes a lot to traditional positivist thought on the supremacy of the state and the concomitant weakness or non-existence of any central guidance in the international community.

For the constitutive theorist, the heart of the matter is that fundamentally an unrecognised 'state' can have no rights or obligations in international law. The opposite stance is adopted by the declaratory approach, that emphasises the factual situation and minimises the power of states to confer legal personality.

Actual practice leads to a middle position between these two perceptions. The act of recognition by one state of another indicates that the former regards the latter as having conformed with the basic requirements of international law as to the creation of a state. Of course, recognition is highly political and is given in a number of cases for purely political reasons. This point of view was emphasised by the American representative on the Security Council during discussions on the Middle East in May 1948. He said that it would be:

> highly improper for one to admit that any country on earth can question the sovereignty of the United States of America in the exercise of the high political act of recognition of the *de facto* status of a state.

Indeed, he added that there was no authority that could determine the legality or validity of that act of the United States.[7] This American view that recognition is to be used as a kind of mark of approval was in evidence with regard to the attitude adopted towards Communist China for a generation.[8]

The United Kingdom, on the other hand, has often tended to extend recognition once it is satisfied that the authorities of the state in question have complied with the minimum requirements of international law, and have effective control which seems likely to continue over the country.[9] Recognition is constitutive in a political sense, for it marks the new entity

[6] See e.g. J. L. Brierly, *The Law of Nations*, 6th edn, Oxford, 1963, p. 138; I. Brownlie, *Principles of Public International Law*, 4th edn, Oxford, 1990, pp. 89–91; D. P. O'Connell, *International Law*, 2nd edn, London, 1970, vol. I, pp. 128 *et seq.* and Crawford, *Creation of States*, pp. 20 *et seq.* See also the *Tinoco* arbitration, 1 RIAA, p. 369; 2 ILR, p. 34 and *Wulfsohn* v. *Russian Republic*, 138 NE 24; 2 ILR, p. 39.
[7] See M. Whiteman, *Digest of International Law*, Washington, 1968, vol. II, p. 10.
[8] See generally D. Young, 'American Dealings with Peking', 45 *Foreign Affairs*, 1966, p. 77 and Whiteman, *Digest*, vol. II, pp. 551 *et seq.* See also A/CN.4/2, p. 53, cited in Crawford, *Creation of States*, p. 16.   [9] See Lauterpacht, *Recognition*, p. 6.

out as a state within the international community and is evidence of acceptance of its new political status by the society of nations. This does not imply
that the act of recognition is legally constitutive, because rights and duties
do not arise as a result of the recognition.

Practice over the last century or so is not unambiguous but does point to
the declaratory approach as the better of the two theories. States which for
particular reasons have refused to recognise other states, such as the Arab
world and Israel and the USA and certain communist nations,[10] rarely
contend that the other party is devoid of powers and obligations before international law and exists in a legal vacuum. The stance is rather that rights
and duties are binding upon them, and that recognition had not been
accorded for primarily political reasons. If the constitutive theory were
accepted it would mean, for example, in the context of the former Arab non-
recognition of Israel, that the latter was not bound by international law rules
of non-aggression and non-intervention. This has not been adopted in any
of the stances of non-recognition of 'states'.[11]

Of course, if an entity, while meeting the conditions of international law
as to statehood, went totally unrecognised, this would undoubtedly hamper
the exercise of its rights and duties, especially in view of the absence of diplomatic relations, but it would not seem in law to amount to a decisive argument against statehood itself.[12] For example, the Charter of the
Organisation of American States adopted at Bogotá in 1948 notes in its
survey of the fundamental rights and duties of states that:

> the political existence of the state is independent of recognition by other states.
> Even before being recognised the state has the right to defend its integrity and
> independence.[13]

And the Institut de Droit International emphasised in its resolution on
recognition of new states and governments in 1936 that the

> existence of the new state with all the legal effects connected with that exis-
> tence is not affected by the refusal of one or more states to recognise.[14]

In the period following the end of the First World War, the courts of the
new states of Eastern and Central Europe regarded their states as coming

---

[10] See 39 *Bulletin of the US Department of State*, 1958, p. 385.
[11] See e.g. the *Pueblo* incident, 62 AJIL, 1968, p. 756 and *Keesings Contemporary Archives*, p. 23129; Whiteman, *Digest*, vol. II, pp. 604 *et seq.* and 651; 'Contemporary Practice of the UK in International Law', 6 ICLQ, 1957, p. 507, and *British Practice in International Law* (ed. E. Lauterpacht), 1963 II, p. 90. See also N. Mugerwa, 'Subjects of International Law' in *Manual of International Law* (ed. M. Sørensen), London, 1968, pp. 247, 269.
[12] See *supra*, Chapter 5.
[13] Article 9. This became article 12 of the Charter as amended in 1967. See also the Montevideo Convention on Rights and Duties of States 1933, article 3.
[14] 39 *Annuaire de L'Institut de Droit International*, 1936, p. 300. See also *US Restatement*, pp. 77–8.

into being upon the actual declaration of independence and not simply as a result of the Peace Treaties. The Tribunal in one case pointed out that the recognition of Poland in the Treaty of Versailles was only declaratory of the state which existed '*par lui-même*'.[15] In addition, the Arbitration Commission established by the International Conference on Yugoslavia in 1991 stated in its Opinion No. 1 that 'the existence or disappearance of the state is a question of fact' and that 'the effects of recognition by other states are purely declaratory'.[16]

On the other hand, the constitutive theory is not totally devoid of all support in state practice. In some cases, the creation of a new state, or the establishment of a new government by unconstitutional means, or the occupation of a territory that is legally claimed will proceed uneventfully and be clearly accomplished for all to see and with little significant opposition. However, in many instances, the new entity or government will be insecure and it is in this context that recognition plays a vital role. In any event, and particularly where the facts are unclear and open to different interpretations, recognition by a state will amount to a declaration by that state of how it understands the situation, and such an evaluation will be binding upon it. It will not be able to deny later the factual position it has recognised, unless, of course, circumstances radically alter in the meantime. In this sense, recognition can be constitutive. Indeed, the Yugoslav Arbitration Commission noted in Opinion No. 8 that 'while recognition of a state by other states has only declarative value, such recognition, along with membership of international organisations, bears witness to these states' conviction that the political entity so recognised is a reality and confers on it certain rights and obligations under international law'.[17] By way of contrast, the fact of non-recognition of a 'new state' by a vast majority of existing states will constitute tangible evidence for the view that such an entity has not established its conformity with the required criteria of statehood.[18]

Another factor which leans towards the constitutive interpretation of recognition is the practice in many states whereby an unrecognised state or government cannot claim the rights available to a recognised state or government before the municipal courts. This means that the act of recognition itself entails a distinct legal effect and that after recognition a state or government would have enforceable rights within the domestic jurisdiction that it would not have had prior to the recognition.[19]

This theoretical controversy is of value in that it reveals the functions of

---

[15] *Deutsche Continental Gas-Gesellschaft* v. *Polish State*, 5 ILR, p. 11.
[16] 92 ILR, pp. 162, 165. See also the decision of the European Court of Human Rights in *Loizidou* v. *Turkey (Preliminary Objections)*, Series A, No. 310, 1995, at p. 14.
[17] 92 ILR, pp. 199, 201.
[18] See *Democratic Republic of East Timor* v. *State of the Netherlands*, 87 ILR, pp. 73, 74.
[19] See *infra*, p. 318.

recognition and emphasises the impact of states upon the development of
international law. It points to the essential character of international law,
poised as it is between the state and the international community. The
declaratory theory veers towards the former and the constitutive doctrine
towards the latter.

There have been a number of attempts to adapt the constitutive theory.
Lauterpacht maintained, for example, that once the conditions prescribed
by international law for statehood have been complied with, there is a duty
on the part of existing states to grant recognition. This is because, in the
absence of a central authority in international law to assess and accord legal
personality, it is the states that have to perform this function on behalf, as it
were, of the international community and international law.[20]

This operation is both declaratory, in that it is based upon certain definite
facts (i.e. the entity fulfils the requirements of statehood) and constitutive
in that it is the acceptance by the recognising state of the particular community as an entity possessing all the rights and obligations that are inherent in statehood. Before the act of recognition, the community that is hoping
to be admitted as a state will only have such rights and duties as have been
expressly permitted to it, if any.

The Lauterpacht doctrine is an ingenious bid to reconcile the legal elements in a coherent theory. It accepts the realities of new creations of states
and governments by practical (and occasionally illegal) means, and attempts
to assimilate this to the supremacy of international law as Lauterpacht saw
it. However, in so doing it ignores the political aspects and functions of
recognition, that is, its use as a method of demonstrating or withholding
support from a particular government or new community. The reality is that
in many cases recognition is applied to demonstrate political approval or disapproval. Indeed, if there is a duty to grant recognition, would the entity
involved have a right to demand this where a particular state or states is
proving recalcitrant? If this were so, one would appear to be faced with the
possibility of a non-state with as yet no rights or duties enforcing rights
against non-recognising states.

Nevertheless, state practice reveals that Lauterpacht's theory has not been
adopted.[21] The fact is that few states accept that they are obliged in every
instance to accord recognition. In most cases they will grant recognition, but
that does not mean that they have to, as history with regard to some communist nations and with respect to Israel illustrates. This position was supported in Opinion No. 10 of the Yugoslav Arbitration Commission in July
1992, which emphasised that recognition was 'a discretionary act that other

---

[20] *Recognition*, pp. 24, 55, 76–77.
[21] See e.g. H. Waldock, 'General Course on Public International Law', 106 HR, p. 154. See
also Mugerwa, 'Subjects', pp. 266–90.

states may perform when they choose and in a manner of their own choosing, subject only to compliance with the imperatives of general international law'.[22]

The approach of the United States was emphasised in 1976. The Department of State noted that:

[i]n the view of the United States, international law does not require a state to recognise another entity as a state; it is a matter for the judgment of each state whether an entity merits recognition as a state. In reaching this judgment, the United States has traditionally looked to the establishment of certain facts. These facts include effective control over a clearly defined territory and population; an organised governmental administration of that territory and a capacity to act effectively to conduct foreign relations and to fulfil international obligations. The United States has also taken into account whether the entity in question has attracted the recognition of the international community of states.[23]

The view of the UK government was expressed as follows:

The normal criteria which the government apply for recognition as a state are that it should have, and seem likely to continue to have, a clearly defined territory with a population, a government who are able of themselves to exercise effective control of that territory, and independence in their external relations. Other factors, including some United Nations resolutions, may also be relevant.[24]

Recent practice suggests that 'other factors' may in the light of the particular circumstances include human rights and other matters. The European Community adopted a Declaration on 16 December 1991 entitled 'Guidelines on the Recognition of New States in Eastern Europe and in the Soviet Union' in which a common position on the process of recognition of the new states was adopted. It was noted in particular that recognition required:

– respect for the provisions of the Charter of the United Nations and the commitments subscribed to in the Final Act of Helsinki and in the Charter of Paris, [25] especially with regard to the rule of law, democracy and human rights;

– guarantees for the rights of ethnic and national groups and minorities in accordance with the commitments subscribed to in the framework of CSCE;[26]

– respect for the inviolability of all frontiers which can only be changed by peaceful means and by common agreement;

[22] 92 ILR, pp. 206, 208. [23] DUSPIL, 1976, pp. 19–20.
[24] 102 HC Deb., col. 977, Written Answer, 23 October 1986. See also 169 HC Deb., cols. 449–50, Written Answer, 19 March 1990. As to French practice, see e.g. Journal Officiel, Débats Parl., A. N., 1988, p. 2324. [25] See *supra* Chapter 7, pp. 281–6.
[26] See *supra* Chapter 7, pp. 283–5.

– acceptance of all relevant commitments with regard to disarmament and nuclear non-proliferation as well as to security and regional stability;

– commitment to settle by agreement, including where appropriate by recourse to arbitration, all questions concerning state succession and regional disputes.[27]

On the same day that the Guidelines were adopted, the European Community also adopted a Declaration on Yugoslavia,[28] in which the Community and its member states agreed to recognise the Yugoslav republics fulfilling certain conditions. These were that such republics wished to be recognised as independent; that the commitments in the Guidelines were accepted; that provisions laid down in a draft convention under consideration by the Conference on Yugoslavia were accepted, particularly those dealing with human rights and the rights of national or ethnic groups; and that support would be given to the efforts of the Secretary-General of the UN and the Security Council and the Conference on Yugoslavia. The Community and its member states also required that the particular Yugoslav republic seeking recognition would commit itself prior to recognition to adopting constitutional and political guarantees ensuring that it had no territorial claims towards a neighbouring Community state.

The United States took a rather less robust position, but still noted the relevance of commitments and assurances given by the new states of Eastern Europe and the former USSR with regard to nuclear safety, democracy and free markets within the process of both recognition and the establishment of diplomatic relations.[29]

There are many different ways in which recognition can occur and it may apply in more than one kind of situation. It is not a single, constant idea but a category comprising a number of factors. There are indeed different entities which may be recognised, ranging from new states, to new governments, belligerent rights possessed by a particular group and territorial changes. Not only are there various objects of the process of recognition, but recognition may itself be *de facto* or *de jure* and it may arise in a variety of manners.

Recognition is an active process and should be distinguished from cognition, or the mere possession of knowledge, for example, that the entity

---

[27] UK Materials on International Law, 62 BYIL, 1991, pp. 559–60. On 31 December 1991, the European Community issued a statement noting that Armenia, Azerbaijan, Belarus, Kazakhstan, Moldova, Turkmenistan, Ukraine and Uzbekistan had given assurances that the requirements in the Guidelines would be fulfilled. Accordingly, the member states of the Community declared that they were willing to proceed with the recognition of these states, *ibid.*, p. 561. On 15 January 1992, a statement was issued noting that Kyrghyzstan and Tadzhikistan had accepted the requirements in the Guidelines and that they too would be recognised, UK Materials on International Law, 63 BYIL, 1992, p. 637.

[28] UK Materials on International Law, 62 BYIL, 1991, pp. 560–1.

[29] See the announcement by President Bush on 25 December 1991, vol. 2, Nos, 4 & 5 *Foreign Policy Bulletin*, 1992, p. 12 as cited in Henkin *et al.*, *International Law*, pp. 252–3.

involved complies with the basic international legal stipulations as to state-hood. Recognition implies both cognition of the necessary facts and an intention that, so far as the acting state is concerned, it is willing that the legal consequences attendant upon recognition should operate. For example, the rules as to diplomatic and sovereign immunities should apply as far as the envoys of the entity to be recognised are concerned. It is not enough for the recognising state simply to be aware of the facts, it must desire the coming into effect of the legal and political results of recognition. This is inevitable by virtue of the discretionary nature of the act of recognition, and is illustrated in practice by the lapse in time that often takes place between the events establishing a new state or government and the actual recognition by other states. Once given, courts have generally regarded recognition as retroactive so that the statehood of the entity recognised is accepted as of the date of statehood (which is a question of fact), not from the date of recognition.[30]

Recognition of governments[31]

The recognition of a new government is quite different from the recognition of a new state. As far as statehood is concerned the factual situation will be examined in terms of the accepted criteria.[32] Different considerations apply where it is the government which changes. Recognition will only really be relevant where the change in government is unconstitutional. In addition, recognition of governments as a category tends to minimise the fact that the precise capacity or status of the entity so recognised may be characterised in different ways. Recognition may be of a *de facto*[33] government or administration or of a government or administration in effective control of only part of the territory of the state in question. Recognition constitutes acceptance of a particular situation by the recognising state both in terms of the relevant factual criteria and in terms of the consequential legal repercussions, so that, for example, recognition of an entity as the government of a state implies

---

[30] See e.g. Chen, *Recognition*, pp. 172 *et seq.* See also the views of the Yugoslav Arbitration Commission as to the date of succession of the former Yugoslav republics, Opinion No. 11, 96 ILR, p. 719. Note that retroactivity of recognition is regarded by Oppenheim as a rule of convenience rather than of principle, see *Oppenheim's International Law, op. cit.*, p. 161.
[31] See e.g. I. Brownlie, 'Recognition in Theory and Practice', 53 BYIL, 1982, p. 197; C. Warbrick, 'The New British Policy on Recognition of Governments', 30 ICLQ, 1981, p. 568; M. J. Peterson, 'Recognition of Governments Should Not Be Abolished', 77 AJIL, 1983, p. 31; N. Ando, 'The Recognition of Governments Reconsidered', 28 *Japanese Annual of International Law*, 1985, p. 29; C. Symmons, 'United Kingdom Abolition of the Doctrine of Recognition: A Rose by Another Name', *Public Law*, 1981, p. 248; S. Talmon, 'Recognition of Governments: An Analysis of the New British Policy and Practice', 63 BYIL, 1992, p. 231; *Oppenheim's International Law*, p. 150; Nguyen Quoc Dinh *et al.*, *Droit International Public*, p. 541 and Galloway, *Foreign Governments*.
[32] See *supra*, Chapter 5, p. 139. [33] See further *infra* p. 308.

not only that this government is deemed to have satisfied the required conditions, but also that the recognising state will deal with the government as the governing authority of the state and accept the usual legal consequences of such status in terms of privileges and immunities within the domestic legal order.

Political considerations have usually played a large role in the decision whether or not to grant recognition. However, certain criteria have emerged to cover recognition of illegal changes in government.

Such criteria amounted to an acceptance of the realities of the transfer of power and suggested that once a new government effectively controlled the country and that this seemed likely to continue, recognition should not be withheld. The United Kingdom on a number of occasions adopted this approach.[34] It was declared by the Under-Secretary of State for Foreign Affairs in 1970 that the test employed was whether or not the new government enjoyed: 'with a reasonable prospect of permanence, the obedience of the mass of the population . . . effective control of much of the greater part of the territory of the state concerned'.[35]

It is this attitude which prompted such policies as the recognition of the communist government of China and the Russian-installed government of Hungary in 1956 after the failure of the uprising. However, this general approach cannot be regarded as an absolute principle in view of the British refusal over many years to recognise as states North Vietnam, North Korea and the German Democratic Republic.[36] The effective control of a new government over the territory of the state is thus an important guideline to the problem of whether to extend recognition or not, providing such control appears well established and likely to continue. But it was no more than that and in many cases appeared to yield to political considerations.

The *Tinoco* arbitration[37] constitutes an interesting example of the 'effective control' concept. In 1919, the government of Tinoco in Costa Rica was overthrown and the new authorities repudiated certain obligations entered into by Tinoco with regard to British nationals. Chief Justice Taft, the sole arbitrator, referred to the problems of recognition or non-recognition as relating to the Tinoco administration. He decided that since the administration was in effective control of the country, it was the valid government irrespective of the fact that a number of states, including the United Kingdom, had not recognised it. This was so despite his opinion that:

---

[34] See the Morrison statement, 485 HC Deb., cols. 2410–11, 21 March 1951.
[35] 799 HC Deb., col. 23, 6 April 1970. See also Foreign Office statements, 204 HL Deb., col. 755, 4 July 1957 and 742 HC Deb., cols. 6–7, Written Answer, 27 February 1967.
[36] See e.g. D. Greig, 'The Carl-Zeiss Case and the Position of an Unrecognised Government in English Law', 83 LQR, 1967, pp. 96, 128–30 and *Re Al-Fin Corporation's Patent* [1970] Ch. 160; 52 ILR, p. 68.   [37] 1 RIAA, p. 369 (1923); 2 ILR, p. 34.

the non-recognition by other nations of a government claiming to be a national personality, is usually appropriate evidence that it has not attained the independence and control entitling it by international law to be classed as such.[38]

Where recognition has been refused because of the illegitimacy or irregularity of origin of the government in question, rather than because of the lack of effectiveness of its control in the country, such non-recognition loses some of its evidential weight. In other words, where the degree of authority asserted by the new administration is uncertain, recognition by other states will be a vital factor. But where the new government is firmly established, non-recognition will not affect the legal character of the new government. The doctrine of effective control is an indication of the importance of the factual nature of any situation. But in those cases where recognition is refused upon the basis of the improper origins of the new government, it will have less of an impact than if recognition is refused because of the absence of effective control. Taft's view of the nature of recognition is an interesting amalgam of the declaratory and constitutive theories, in that recognition can become constitutive where the factual conditions (i.e. the presence or absence of effective control) are in dispute, but otherwise is purely declaratory or evidential.

A change in government, however accomplished, does not affect the identity of the state itself. The state does not cease to be an international legal person because its government is overthrown. That is not at issue. The recognition or non-recognition of a new administration is irrelevant to the legal character of the country. Accordingly one can see that two separate recognitions are involved and they must not be confused. Recognition of a state will affect its legal personality, whether by creating or acknowledging it, while recognition of a government affects the status of the administrative authority, not the state.

It is possible, however, for recognition of state and government to occur together in certain circumstances. This can take place upon the creation of a new state. Israel, to take one example, was recognised by the United States and the United Kingdom by the expedient of having its government recognised *de facto*.[39] Recognition of the government implies recognition of the state, but it does not work the other way.

It should be noted that recognition of a government has no relevance to the establishment of new persons in international law. Where it is significant is in the realm of diplomatic relations. If a government is unrecognised, there is no exchange of diplomatic envoys and thus problems can arise as to the enforcement of international rights and obligations.

Although the effective control doctrine is probably accepted as the most

[38] *Ibid.*, p. 380; 2 ILR, p. 37.   [39] See e.g. Whiteman, *Digest*, vol. II, p. 168.

reliable guide to recognition of governments, there have been other theories put forward, the most prominent amongst them being the Tobar doctrine or the so-called doctrine of legitimacy. This suggested that governments which came into power by extra-constitutional means should not be recognised, at least until the change had been accepted by the people.[40] This policy was applied particularly by the United States in relation to Central America and was designed to protect stability in that delicate area adjacent to the Panama Canal. Logically, of course, the concept amounts to the promotion of non-recognition in all revolutionary situations and it is, and was, difficult to reconcile with reality and political consideration. In American eyes it became transmuted into the Wilson policy of democratic legitimacy. Where the revolution was supported by the people, it would be recognised. Where it was not, there would be no grant of recognition. It was elaborated with respect to the Soviet Union until 1933, but gradually declined until it can now be properly accepted merely as a political qualification for recognition to be considered by the recognising state.[41]

A doctrine advocating the exact opposite, the automatic recognition of governments in all circumstances, was put forward by Estrada, the Mexican Secretary of Foreign Relations.[42] But this suffers from the same disadvantage as the legitimacy doctrine. It attempts to lay down a clear test for recognition in all instances excluding political considerations and exigencies of state and is thus unrealistic, particularly where there are competing governments.[43] It has also been criticised as minimising the distinction between recognition and maintenance of diplomatic relations.[44]

The problem, of course, was that recognition of a new government that has come to power in a non-constitutional fashion was taken to imply approval. Allied with the other factors sometimes taken into account in such recognition situations,[45] an unnecessarily complicated process had resulted. Accordingly, in 1977 the United States declared that:

---

[40] See e.g. Mugerwa, 'Subjects', p. 271, and 2 AJIL, 1908, Supp., p. 229.

[41] See e.g. Hackworth, *Digest of International Law*, vol. I, 1940, pp. 181 *et seq.* See also 17 AJIL, 1923, Supp., p. 118; O'Connell, *International Law*, pp. 137–9 and Whiteman, *Digest*, vol. II, p. 69.

[42] See e.g. 25 AJIL, 1931, Supp., p. 203; P. Jessup, 'The Estrada Doctrine', 25 AJIL, 1931, p. 719 and Whiteman, *Digest*, vol. II, p. 85. See also Talmon, 'Recognition of Governments', p. 263; Chen, *Recognition*, p. 116; O'Connell, *International Law*, pp. 134–5 and C. Rousseau, *Droit International Public*, Paris, vol. III, 1977, p. 555.

[43] See e.g. Peterson, 'Recognition', p. 42 and C. Rousseau, 'Chroniques des Faits Internationaux', 93 RGDIP, 1989, p. 923.   [44] Warbrick, 'New British Policy', p. 584.

[45] For example, the democratic requirement noted by President Wilson, President Rutherford Hayes' popular support condition and Secretary of State Seward's criterion of ability to honour international obligations, see statement by US Department of State, DUSPIL, 1977, pp. 19, 20. See also *Third US Restatement on Foreign Relations Law*, 1987, para. 203, note 1. The Organisation of American States adopted a resolution in 1965 recommending that states contemplating recognition of a new government should take into account whether that government proposes to hold elections within a reasonable time, 5 ILM, 1966, p. 155.

US practice has been to de-emphasise and avoid the use of recognition in cases of changes of governments and to concern ourselves with the question of whether we wish to have diplomatic relations with the new governments . . . The Administration's policy is that establishment of relations does not involve approval or disapproval but merely demonstrates a willingness on our part to conduct our affairs with other governments directly.[46]

In 1980, the UK government announced that it would no longer accord recognition to governments as distinct from states.[47] This was stated to be primarily due to the perception that recognition meant approval, a perception that was often embarrassing, for example, in the case of regimes violating human rights. There were, therefore, practical advantages in not according recognition as such to governments. This change to a policy of not formally recognising governments had in fact taken place in certain civil law countries rather earlier. Belgium[48] and France[49] appear, for example, to have adopted this approach in 1965. By the late 1980s, this approach was also adopted by both Australia[50] and Canada,[51] and indeed by other countries.[52]

The change, however, did not remove all problems, but rather shifted the focus from formal recognition to informal 'dealings'. The UK announced that it would continue to decide the nature of dealings with unconstitutional regimes:

> in the light of [an] assessment of whether they are able of themselves to exercise effective control of the territory of the state concerned, and seem likely to continue to do so.[53]

The change, therefore, is that recognition of governments is abolished but that the criterion for dealing with such regimes is essentially the same as the former test for the recognition of governments.[54] In that context, regard should also be had to the phrase 'of themselves'.[55]

---

[46] *Ibid.*, p. 20. See also DUSPIL *1981–8*, vol. I, 1993, p. 295. Note that Deputy Secretary of State Christopher stated in 1977 that unscheduled changes of government were not uncommon in this day and age and that 'withholding diplomatic relations from these regimes after they have obtained effective control penalises us', *ibid.*, p. 18. See also as regards Afghanistan and the continuation of diplomatic relations, 72 AJIL, 1978, p. 879. Cf. the special circumstances of the recognition of the government of China, DUSPIL, 1978, pp. 71–3 and DUSPIL, 1979, pp. 142 *et seq.* But cf. Petersen, 'Recognition'.
[47] See 408 HL Deb., cols. 1121–2, 28 April 1980. See also C. Symmons, 'United Kingdom Abolition of the Doctrine of Recognition of Governments: A Rose by Another Name?', *Public Law*, 1981, p. 249.   [48] See 11 *Revue Belge de Droit International*, 1973, p. 351.
[49] See 69 RGDIP, 1965, p. 1089. See also 83 RGDIP, 1979, p. 808, G. Charpentier, 'Pratique Française du Droit International', AFDI, 1981, p. 911 and Rousseau, *Droit International Public*, p. 555.
[50] See J. G. Starke, 'The New Australian Policy of Recognition of Foreign Governments', 62 *Australian Law Journal*, 1988, p. 390.   [51] See 27 Canadian YIL, 1989, p. 387.
[52] See e.g. the Netherlands, 22 Netherlands YIL, 1991, p. 237, and New Zealand, see *Attorney-General for Fiji* v. *Tobt Jones House Ltd* [1989] 2 NZLR 69 at 70–1.
[53] 408 HL Deb., cols.1121–22, 28 April 1980.
[54] See *Gur Corporation* v. *Trust Bank of Africa* [1987] 1 QB 599; 75 ILR, p. 675.
[55] See as regards the different approaches adopted to the Cambodian and Ugandan experiences, Symmons, 'United Kingdom', p. 250 and UKMIL 1979, 50 BYIL, 1979, p. 296. See

De facto and *de jure* recognition[56]

In addition to the fact that there are different entities to be recognised, recognition itself may take different forms. It may be either *de facto* or *de jure*. A more correct way of putting this might be to say that a government (or other entity or situation) may be recognised *de facto* or *de jure*.

Recognition *de facto* implies that there is some doubt as to the long-term viability of the government in question. Recognition *de jure* usually follows where the recognising state accepts that the effective control displayed by the government is permanent and firmly rooted and that there are no legal reasons detracting from this, such as constitutional subservience to a foreign power. *De facto* recognition involves a hesitant assessment of the situation, an attitude of wait and see, to be succeeded by *de jure* recognition when the doubts are sufficiently overcome to extend formal acceptance. To take one instance, the United Kingdom recognised the Soviet government *de facto* in 1921 and *de jure* in 1924.[57] A slightly different approach is adopted in cases of civil war where the distinction between *de jure* and *de facto* recognition is sometimes used to illustrate the variance between legal and factual sovereignty. For example, during the 1936–9 Spanish Civil War, the United Kingdom, while recognising the Republic government as the *de jure* government, extended *de facto* recognition to the forces under General Franco as they gradually took over the country. Similarly, the government of the Italian conquering forces in Ethiopia was recognised *de facto* by the UK in 1936, and *de jure* two years later.[58]

By this method a recognising state could act in accordance with political reality and its own interests while reserving judgment on the permanence of the change in government or its desirability or legality. It is able to safeguard the affairs of its citizens and institutions by this, because certain legal consequences will flow in municipal law from the recognition.[59]

There are in reality few meaningful distinctions between a *de facto* and a *de jure* recognition, although only a government recognised *de jure* may enter a claim to property located in the recognising state.[60] Additionally, it is generally accepted that *de facto* recognition does not of itself include the exchange of diplomatic relations.

also *supra*, Chapter 4, p. 134. See as to recognition of belligerency and insurgency e.g. O'Connell, *International Law*, pp. 148–53; Lauterpacht, *Recognition*, p. 270 and *Oppenheim's International Law*, pp. 161 *et seq*. See also further, *infra*, Chapter 19.
56 See e.g. *Oppenheim's International Law*, p. 154.
57 See e.g. O'Connell, *International Law*, p. 161. See also the Morrison statement, *supra*, note 34.   58 See *infra* pp. 314, 320.   59 See *infra*, p. 318.
60 See e.g. *Haile Selassie* v. *Cable and Wireless Ltd (No. 2)* [1939] 1 Ch. 182; 9 ILR, p. 94.

Premature recognition[61]

There is often a difficult and unclear dividing line between the acceptable recognition of a new state, particularly one that has emerged or is emerging as a result of secession, and intervention in the domestic affairs of another state by way of premature or precipitate recognition, such as, for example, the view taken by the Nigerian Federal Government with respect to the recognition of 'Biafra' by five states.[62] In each case, the state seeking to recognise will need to consider carefully the factual situation and the degree to which the criteria of statehood (or other relevant criteria with regard to other types of entity with regard to which recognition is sought) have been fulfilled. It is therefore a process founded upon a perception of fact. In the case of Croatia, it could be argued that the recognition of that state by the European Community and its member states (together with Austria and Switzerland) on 15 January 1992 was premature.[63] Croatia at that time, and for several years thereafter, did not effectively control some one-third of its territory. In addition, the Yugoslav Arbitration Commission had taken the view in Opinion No. 5 on 11 January 1992, that Croatia did not meet fully the conditions for recognition laid down in the European Community Guidelines of 16 December 1991,[64] since the Constitutional Act adopted by Croatia did not fully incorporate the required guarantees relating to human rights and minority rights.[65] It could also be argued that the recognition of Bosnia-Herzegovina on 6 April 1992 by the European Community and member states and on 7 April 1992 by the US was premature, particularly since the government of that state effectively controlled less than one-half of its territory, a situation that continued until the Dayton Peace Agreement of November 1995.[66] On

---

[61] See e.g. *Oppenheim's International Law*, pp. 143 *et seq.* and Nguyen Quoc Dinh *et al.*, *Droit International Public*, p. 535.

[62] See e.g. J. Stremlau, *The International Politics of the Nigerian Civil War, 1967–70*, Princeton, 1977, pp. 127–9, and D. Ijalaye, 'Was "Biafra" at any time a State in International Law?', 65 AJIL, 1971, p. 51. See also Lauterpacht, *Recognition*, pp. 7–8.

[63] See e.g. R. Müllerson, *International Law, Rights and Politics*, London, 1994, p. 130 and R. Rich, 'Recognition of States: The Collapse of Yugoslavia and the Soviet Union', 4 EJIL, 1993, p. 36.   [64] See *supra* p. 301.

[65] 92 ILR, pp. 179, 181. Note that the President of Croatia on 15 January 1992 announced that Croatia would abide by the necessary conditions and on 8 May 1992 its Constitution was amended. The amended Constitution was considered by the Arbitration Commission on 4 July 1992, which concluded that the requirements of general international law with regard to the protection of minorities had been satisfied, *ibid.*, p. 209. Note, however, the critical views of the UN Human Rights Committee with regard to the distinctions made in the Croatian Constitution between ethnic Croats and other citizens, see CCPR/C/79/Add.15, p. 3. Croatia became a member of the UN on 22 May 1992. See also M. Weller, 'The International Response to the Dissolution of the Socialist Federal Republic of Yugoslavia', 86 AJIL, 1992, p. 569.

[66] See e.g. Weller, 'International Response', Cf. the views of the UK Minister of State at the Foreign Office, UKMIL, 63 BYIL, 1992, p. 645. Note that Bosnia became a member of the UN on 22 May 1992.

the other hand, it could be argued that in the special circumstances of Former Yugoslavia, the international community (particularly by means of membership of the UN which is restricted to states) was prepared to accept a loosening of the traditional criteria of statehood, so that essentially international recognition compensated for lack of effectivity.

Recognition may also be overdue, in the sense that it occurs long after it is clear as a matter of fact that the criteria of statehood have been satisfied, but in such cases, different considerations apply since recognition is not compulsory and remains a political decision by states.[67]

Implied recognition[68]

Recognition itself need not be express, that is in the form of an open, unambiguous and formal communication but may be implied in certain circumstances.[69] This is due to the fact that recognition is founded upon the will and intent of the state that is extending the recognition. Accordingly, there are conditions in which it might be possible to declare that in acting in a certain manner, one state has by implication recognised another state or government. Because this facility of indirect or implied recognition is available, states may make an express declaration to the effect that a particular action involving another party is by no means to be interpreted as comprehending any recognition. This attitude was maintained by Arab countries with regard to Israel, and in certain other cases.[70] It automatically excludes any possibility of implied recognition but does suggest that without a definite and clear waiver, the result of some international actions may be recognition of a hitherto unrecognised entity in certain circumstances.

The point can best be explained by mentioning the kind of conditions which may give rise to the possibility of a recognition where no express or

---

[67] See e.g. with regard to the delays in recognising Macedonia, Henkin et al., International Law, op. cit., p. 253 and with regard to the recognition by Pakistan of Bangladesh in February 1974, Nguyen Quoc Dinh et al., Droit International Public, p. 536. Israel, of course, remained unrecognised by its Arab neighbours until long after its establishment in 1948. It was recognised in 1979 by Egypt and in 1995 by Jordan.

[68] See e.g. Oppenheim's International Law, p. 169; Lauterpacht, Recognition, pp. 369–408 and Chen, Recognition, pp. 201–16. See also Talmon, 'Recognition of Governments', pp. 255 et seq., and M. Lachs, 'Recognition and Modern Methods of International Co-operation', 35 BYIL, 1959, p. 252.

[69] Note that article 7 of the Montevideo Convention on Rights and Duties of States 1933 provides that 'the recognition of a state may be express or tacit. The latter results from any act which implies the intention of recognising the new state'. See also R. Higgins, The Development of International Law by the Political Organs of the United Nations, Oxford, 1963, pp. 140 et seq.

[70] See e.g. UK and North Vietnam, Cmd. 9763, p. 3, note 1 and e.g. Israel and Arab countries, International Convention on the Elimination of all Forms of Racial Discrimination, 1965, see Human Rights International Instruments, UN, ST/HR/4/rev.4, 1982. Note that Egypt withdrew its declarations regarding non-recognition of Israel with regard to this Convention on 18 January 1980, ibid., p. 86.

formal statement has been made. A message of congratulations to a new state upon attaining sovereignty will imply recognition of that state, as will the formal establishment of diplomatic relations.[71] But the maintenance of informal and unofficial contacts (such as those between the United States and Communist China during the 1960s and early 1970s in Warsaw) will not.[72] The issuing of a consular *exequatur*, the accepted authorisation permitting the performance of consular functions, to a representative of an unrecognised state will usually amount to a recognition of that state, though not in all cases.[73] A British Consul has operated in Taiwan, but the UK does not recognise the Taiwan government.[74] It is possible that the conclusion of a bilateral treaty between the recognising and unrecognised state, as distinct from a temporary agreement, might imply recognition, but the matter is open to doubt since there are a number of such agreements between parties not recognising each other. One would have to study the circumstances of the particular case to clarify the issue.[75] The making of claims by a state against an entity will not necessarily imply recognition.[76]

Recognition is not normally to be inferred from the fact that both states have taken part in negotiations and signed a multilateral treaty,[77] for example, the United Nations Charter. Practice shows that many of the member states or their governments are not recognised by other member states.[78] Although Israel and many Arab countries are UN members, this

---

[71] See O'Connell, *International Law*, pp. 154–5. Note that the UK stated that in the case of Namibia 'there was no formal recognition of statehood, but it was implicit in the establishment of diplomatic relations in March 1990', UKMIL, 63 BYIL, 1992, p. 642. Instructing an ambassador to make suitable, friendly contact with the new administration in question might also suffice, see UKMIL, 50 BYIL, 1979, p. 294.

[72] See e.g. *Pan American World Airways Inc v. Aetna Casualty and Surety Co.*, 13 ILM, 1974, pp. 1376, 1397.   [73] See *Oppenheim's International Law*, p. 171, note 9.

[74] Discussions with an unrecognised entity conducted by consular officers will not of itself imply recognition, see e.g. H. de Smith, *Great Britain and the Law of Nations*, London, 1932, vol. I, p. 79 and *Civil Air Transport Inc v. Central Air Transport Corporation* [1953] AC 70, 88–9. The establishment of an office in the UK, for example, of an unrecognised entity is not as such prohibited nor does it constitute recognition, see e.g. with regard to the PLO, HL Debs., vol. 483, cols. 1248–52, 27 January 1987 and UKMIL, 58 BYIL, 1987, p. 531. Note that under section 1 of the Diplomatic and Consular Premises Act 1987, the permission of the Foreign Secretary is required if the premises in question are to be regarded as diplomatic or consular.

[75] See e.g. *Republic of China v. Merchants' Fire Assurance Corporation of New York*, 30 F.2d 278 (1929); 5 ILR, p. 42 and *Clerget v. Banque Commerciale pour l'Europe du Nord*, 52 ILR, p. 310. See with regard to the special position as between the German Federal Republic and the German Democratic Republic, *Re Treaty on the Basis of Relations Between the Federal Republic of Germany and the German Democratic Republic*, 78 ILR, p. 150. See also Whiteman, *Digest*, vol. II, pp. 567 *et seq.*

[76] See e.g. with regard to Formosa/Taiwan, 6 ICLQ, 1957, p. 507 and with regard to Turkish-occupied northern Cyprus, HC Deb., vol. 957, col. 247. Written Answer, 8 November 1978.

[77] See e.g. UKMIL, 49 BYIL, 1978, p. 339. See also Whiteman, *Digest*, vol. II, pp. 563 *et seq.*

[78] See the Memorandum on the Legal Aspects of the Problem of Representation in the United Nations, S/1466, 1950 and 4 *International Organisation*, 1950, pp. 356, 359.

did not affect Arab non-recognition of the Israeli state.[79] However, where the state concerned has voted in favour of membership in the UN of the entity in question, it is a natural inference that recognition has occurred. The UK, for example, regarded its vote in favour of UN membership for the former Yugoslav republic of Macedonia as amounting to recognition of that entity as a state.[80] Indeed irrespective of recognition by individual states, there is no doubt that membership of the UN is powerful evidence of statehood since being a state is a necessary pre-condition to UN membership by virtue of article 4 of the UN Charter.[81]

In the case of common participation in an international conference, similar considerations apply, although the element of doubt has often stimulated non-recognising states to declare expressly that their presence and joint signature on any agreement issuing forth from the meeting is in no way to be understood as implying recognition. Such has been the case particularly with the Arab states over the years with regard to Israel.

State practice has restricted the possible scope of operation of this concept of implied recognition to a few instances only and all the relevant surrounding circumstances will have to be carefully evaluated before one can deduce from conduct the intention to extend recognition. States like to retain their control of such an important political instrument as recognition and are usually not keen to allow this to be inferred from the way they behave. They prefer recognition to be, in general, a formal act accorded after due thought.

Conditional recognition

The political nature of recognition has been especially marked with reference to what has been termed conditional recognition. This refers to the practice of making the recognition subject to fulfilment of certain conditions, for example, the good treatment of religious minorities, as occurred with regard to the independence of some Balkan countries in the late nineteenth century, or the granting of most-favoured-nation status to the recognised state. One well-known instance of this approach was the Litvinov agreement of 1933 whereby the United States recognised the Soviet government upon the latter undertaking to avoid acts prejudicial to the internal

---

[79] See e.g. Q. Wright, 'Some Thoughts about Recognition', 44 AJIL, 1950, p. 548. See also with regard to the Ukraine and Byelorussia, members of the UN prior to the demise of the USSR of which they were constituent republics, UKMIL, 55 BYIL, 1978, p. 339.

[80] See HC Debs., vol. 223, col. 241. Written Answer, 22 April 1993 and UKMIL, 64 BYIL, 1993, p. 601. Note that a similar view was taken with regard to the Democratic People's Republic of Korea, 62 BYIL, 1991, p. 559.

[81] See the *Conditions of Membership of the United Nations* case, ICJ Reports, 1948, pp. 57 *et seq.*: 15 ILR, p. 333.

security of the USA, and to come to a settlement of various financial claims.[82]

However, breach of the particular condition does not invalidate the recognition. It may give rise to a breach of international law and political repercussions but the law appears not to accept the notion of a conditional recognition as such. The status of any conditions will depend upon agreements specifically made by the particular parties.[83] It is, however, important to distinguish conditional recognition in this sense from the evolution of criteria for recognition generally although the two categories may in practice overlap. [84]

Collective recognition[85]

The expediency of collective recognition has often been noted. This would amount to recognition by means of an international decision, whether by an international organisation or not. It would, of course, signify the importance of the international community in its collective assertion of control over membership and because of this it has not been warmly welcomed, nor can one foresee its general application for some time to come. The idea has been discussed particularly since the foundation of the League of Nations and was re-emphasised with the establishment of the United Nations. However, it rapidly became clear that member states reserved the right to extend recognition to their own executive authorities and did not wish to delegate it to any international institution. The most that could be said is that membership of the United Nations constitutes powerful evidence of statehood. But that, of course, is not binding upon other member states who are free to refuse to recognise any other member state or government of the UN.[86]

Withdrawal of recognition[87]

Recognition once given may in certain circumstances be withdrawn. This is more easily achieved with respect to *de facto* recognition, as that is by its

[82] See e.g. *United States v. Pink* 315 US 203, 229 (1942) and Whiteman, *Digest*, vol. II, pp. 120 *et seq.*, and A. Kiss, *Répertoire de la Pratique Française en Matière de Droit International Public*, Paris, 1962–72, vol. III, pp. 40 *et seq.*
[83] See e.g. Lauterpacht, *Recognition*, Chapter 19. See also the Treaty of Berlin 1878 concerning Bulgaria, Montenegro, Serbia and Romania and the provisions dealing with freedom of religion, articles V, XXVII, XXXV and XLIII.
[84] See further *supra* p. 301, with regard to the approach of the European Community to the emergence of new states in Eastern Europe and out of the former USSR and Yugoslavia.
[85] See e.g. Higgins, *The Development of International Law*; Dugard, *Recognition*; Lauterpacht, *Recognition*, p. 400; Chen, *Recognition*, p. 211 and *Oppenheim's International Law*, pp. 177 *et seq.*
[86] See further *supra* p. 301, with regard to the approach of the European Community to the emergence of new states in Eastern Europe and out of the former USSR and Yugoslavia. This constituted a co-ordinated stand with regard to criteria for recognition by the Community and its member states rather than collective recognition as such.
[87] See Lauterpacht, *Recognition*, p. 349.

nature a cautious and temporary assessment of a particular situation. Where a *de facto* government loses the effective control it once exercised, the reason for recognition disappears and it may be revoked. It is in general a preliminary acceptance of political realities and may be withdrawn in accordance with a change in political factors.[88] *De jure* recognition, on the other hand, is intended to be more of a definitive step and is more difficult to withdraw.

Of course, where a government recognised *de jure* has been overthrown a new situation arises and the question of a new government will have to be faced, but in such instances withdrawal of recognition of the previous administration is assumed and does not have to be expressly stated, providing always that the former government is not still in existence and carrying on the fight in some way. Withdrawal of recognition of one government without recognising a successor is a possibility and indeed was the approach adopted by the UK and France, for example, with regard to Cambodia in 1979.[89] However, with the adoption of the new British policy on recognition with regard to governments,[90] the position is now that the UK government will neither recognise nor withdraw recognition of regimes.[91]

Withdrawal of recognition in other circumstances is not a very general occurrence but in exceptional conditions it remains a possibility. The United Kingdom recognised the Italian conquest of Ethiopia *de facto* in 1936 and *de jure* two years later. However, it withdrew recognition in 1940, with the intensification of fighting and the dispatch of military aid.[92] Recognition of belligerency will naturally terminate with the defeat of either party, while the loss of one of the required criteria of statehood would affect recognition. It is to be noted that the 1979 recognition of the People's Republic of China as the sole legal government of China entailed the withdrawal of recognition or 'derecognition' of the Republic of China (Taiwan). This was explained to mean that: 'so far as the formal foreign relations of the United States are concerned, a government does *not* exist in Taiwan any longer'.[93]

Nevertheless, this was not to affect the application of the laws of the United States with respect to Taiwan in the context of US domestic law.[94] To some extent in this instance the usual consequences of non-recognition have not flowed, but this has taken place upon the background of a formal

---

[88] Withdrawal of *de facto* recognition does not always entail withdrawal of *de jure* recognition, see with regard to Latvia, *Re Feivel Pikelny's Estate*, 32 BYIL, 1955–6, p. 288.

[89] See HC Debs., vol. 975, col. 723, 6 December 1979 and Warbrick, 30 ICLQ, 1981, p. 234. See also AFDI, 1980, p. 888.   [90] See *supra* p. 307.

[91] HL Debs., vol. 424, col. 551, 15 October 1981.

[92] See *Azazh Kebbeda v. Italian Government*, 9 *AD*, p. 93.

[93] US reply brief in the Court of Appeals in *Goldwater v. Carter*, 444 US 996 (1979), quoted in DUSPIL, 1979, pp. 143–4.

[94] Taiwan Relations Act, Pub. L. 96–8 Stat. 22 USC 3301–3316, s.4.

and deliberate act of policy. It does show how complex the topic of recognition has become.

The usual method of expressing disapproval with the actions of a particular government is to break diplomatic relations. This will adequately demonstrate aversion as, for example, the rupture in diplomatic relations between the UK and the USSR in 1927, and between some Arab countries and the United States in 1967, without entailing the legal consequences and problems that a withdrawal of recognition would initiate. But one must not confuse the ending of diplomatic relations with a withdrawal of recognition.

Since recognition is ultimately a political issue, no matter how circumscribed or conditioned by the law, it logically follows that, should a state perceive any particular situation as justifying a withdrawal of recognition, it will take such action as it regards as according with its political interests.

Non-recognition[95]

There has been developing since the 1930s a doctrine of non-recognition where under certain conditions a factual situation will not be recognised because of strong reservations as to the morality or legality of the actions that have been adopted in order to bring about the factual situation. It is a doctrine that has also been reinforced by the principle that legal rights cannot derive from an illegal situation (*ex injuria jus non oritur*).[96]

This approach was particularly stimulated by the Japanese invasion of Manchuria in 1931. The US Secretary of State declared in 1932 that the illegal invasion would not be recognised as it was contrary to the 1928 Pact of Paris (the Kellogg–Briand Pact) which had outlawed war as an instrument of national policy. The doctrine of not recognising any situation, treaty or agreement brought about by non-legal means was named the Stimson doctrine after the American Secretary of State who put it forward. It was reinforced not long afterwards by a resolution of the Assembly of the League of Nations stressing that League members should not recognise any situation, treaty or agreement brought about by means contrary to the League's Covenant or the Pact of Paris.[97]

However, state practice until the Second World War was not encouraging. The Italian conquest of the Empire of Ethiopia was recognised and the

---

[95] See e.g. Lauterpacht, *Recognition*, pp. 416–20 and *Oppenheim's International Law*, pp. 183 *et seq.* See also Langer, *Seizure of Territory*, 1947; Hackworth, *Digest*, vol. I, p. 334; I. Brownlie, *International Law and the Use of Force by States*, Oxford, 1963, Chapter 25; Dugard, *Recognition*, pp. 24 *et seq.* and 81 *et seq.* and Crawford, *Creation of States*, pp. 120 *et seq.*

[96] See e.g. *Oppenheim's International Law*, pp. 183–4 and the *Namibia* case, ICJ Reports, 1971, pp. 16, 46–7: 49 ILR, pp. 2, 36–7.

[97] LNOJ, Sp. Suppl. no. 101, p. 8. This principle was reiterated in a number of declarations subsequently, see e.g. 34 AJIL, 1940, Suppl. p. 197. See also O'Connell, *International Law*, pp. 143–6.

German takeover of Czechoslovakia accepted. The Soviet Union made a series of territorial acquisitions in 1940 ranging from areas of Finland to the Baltic states (of Lithuania, Estonia and Latvia) and Bessarabia. These were recognised *de facto* over the years by western powers (though not by the United States).[98]

The doctrine was examined anew after 1945. Article 2(4) of the UN Charter prohibits the threat or use of force *inter alia* against the territorial integrity of states, while the draft Declaration on the Rights and Duties of States, 1949, emphasised that territorial acquisitions by states were not to be recognised by other states where achieved by means of the threat or use of force or in any other manner inconsistent with international law and order. The Declaration on Principles of International Law, 1970, also included a provision to the effect that no territorial acquisition resulting from the threat or use of force shall be recognised as legal,[99] and resolution 242 (1967) on the solution to the Middle East conflict emphasised 'the inadmissibility of the acquisition of territory by war'.[100]

Rhodesia unilaterally proclaimed its independence in November 1965 and in the years of its existence did not receive official recognition from any state at all, although it did maintain diplomatic relations with South Africa and Portugal prior to the revolution of 1974. The day following the Rhodesian declaration of independence, the Security Council passed a resolution calling upon all states not to accord it recognition and to refrain from assisting it.[101] The Council imposed selective mandatory economic sanctions on Rhodesia and these were later made comprehensive.[102] Similar action was also taken with regard to the Bantustans, territories of South Africa declared by that state to be independent.[103] The Security Council also adopted resolution 541 in 1983, which deplored the purported secession of part of Cyprus occupied by Turkey in 1974 and terming the pro-

---

[98] *Ibid.*

[99] See also article 11 of the Montevideo Convention on the Rights and Duties of States 1933; article 17 of the Bogotá Charter of the OAS, 1948, and article 52 of the Vienna Convention on the Law of Treaties, 1969. Note also article 5(3) of the Consensus Definition of Aggression, 1974, adopted by the General Assembly in resolution 3314(XXIX).

[100] See also Security Council resolutions 476 (1980) and 478 (1980) declaring purported changes in the status of Jerusalem by Israel to be null and void, and resolution 491 (1981) stating that Israel's extension of its laws, jurisdiction and administration to the Golan Heights was without international legal effect.

[101] Security Council resolution 216 (1965). See also Security Council resolutions 217 (1965), 277 (1970) and 288 (1970).

[102] See e.g. Security Council resolutions 221 (1961), 232 (1966) and 253 (1968). See also M. N. Shaw, *Title to Territory in Africa: International Legal Issues*, Oxford, 1986, p. 160; R. Zacklin, *The United Nations and Rhodesia*, 1974 and J. Nkala, *The United Nations, International Law and the Rhodesian Crisis*, Oxford, 1985.

[103] See e.g. General Assembly resolution 31/6A and the Security Council statements of 21 September 1979 and 15 December 1981, Shaw, *Title to Territory*, p. 149. See also J. Dugard, *International Law, A South African Perspective*, Kenwyn, 1994, Chapter 5.

posed Turkish Cypriot state 'legally invalid'.[104] In 1990, the Security Council adopted resolution 662, which declared the Iraqi annexation of Kuwait 'null and void' and called on all states and institutions not to recognise the annexation.[105]

The role of non-recognition as an instrument of sanction as well as a means of pressure and a method of protecting the wronged inhabitants of a territory was discussed more fully in the Advisory Opinion of the International Court of Justice in the *Namibia* case, 1971, dealing with South Africa's presence in that territory. The Court held that since the continued South African occupancy was illegal, member states of the United Nations were obliged to recognise that illegality and the invalidity of South Africa's acts concerning Namibia and were under a duty to refrain from any actions implying recognition of the legality of or lending support or assistance to the South African presence and administration.[106]

The legal effects of recognition

In this section some of the legal results that flow from the recognition or non-recognition of an entity, both in the international sphere and within the municipal law of particular states, will be noted. Although recognition may legitimately be regarded as a political tool, it is one that nevertheless entails important consequences in the legal field.

Internationally

In the majority of cases, it can be accepted that recognition of a state or government is a legal acknowledgement of a factual state of affairs. Nevertheless, it should not be assumed that non-recognition of, for example, a state will deprive that entity of rights and duties before international law, excepting, of course, those situations where it may be possible to say that recognition is constitutive of the legal entity.

In general, the political existence of a state is independent of recognition by other states, and thus an unrecognised state must be deemed subject to the rules of international law. It cannot consider itself free from restraints as to aggressive behaviour, nor can its territory be regarded as *terra nullius*. States which have signed international agreements are entitled to assume that states which they have not recognised but which have similarly signed

---

[104] See *supra* Chapter 5, p. 166.   [105] See *infra* Chapter 20, p. 860.
[106] ICJ Reports, 1971, pp. 16, 54, 56; 49 ILR, pp. 2, 44, 46. Non-member states of the UN were similarly obliged, *ibid*. The non-recognition obligation did not extend, however, to certain acts of a humanitarian nature the effect of which could only be ignored to the detriment of the inhabitants of the territory, *ibid.*, p. 56. See also *supra*, Chapter 5, p. 161.

the agreement are bound by that agreement. For example, the United Kingdom treated the German Democratic Republic as bound by its signature of the 1963 Nuclear Test Ban Treaty even when the state was not recognised by the UK.

Non-recognition, with its consequent absence of diplomatic relations, may affect the unrecognised state in asserting its rights or other states in asserting its duties under international law, but will not affect the existence of such rights and duties. The position is, however, different under municipal law.

Internally

Because recognition is fundamentally a political act, it is reserved to the executive branch of government. This means that the judiciary must in general principle accept the discretion of the executive and give effect to its decisions. The courts cannot recognise a state or government. They can only accept and enforce the legal consequences which flow from the executive's political decision, although this situation has become more complex with the change in policy from express recognition of governments to acceptance of dealings with such entities.

To this extent, recognition is constitutive, because the act of recognition itself creates legal results within the domestic jurisdiction. In the United Kingdom and the United States particularly, the courts feel themselves obliged to accept the verdict of the executive branch of government as to whether a particular entity should be regarded as recognised or not. If the administration has recognised a state or government and so informs the judiciary by means of a certificate, the position of that state or government within the municipal structure is totally transformed.

It may sue in the domestic courts and be granted immunity from suit in certain instances. Its own legislative and executive acts will be given effect to in the courts of the recognising state and its own diplomatic representatives will be able to claim the various immunities accorded to the official envoys of a recognised state. In addition, it will be entitled to possession in the recognising state of property belonging to its predecessor.

The UK[107]

The English courts have adopted the attitude over many years that an entity unrecognised by the Foreign Office would be treated before the courts as if

---

[107] See e.g. Talmon, 'Recognition of Governments', pp. 275 *et seq.*; Greig, 'The Carl-Zeiss Case', and J. G. Merrills, 'Recognition and Construction', 20 ICLQ, 1971, p. 476.

it did not exist and accordingly it would not be able to claim immunity before the courts.[108] This meant in one case that ships of the unrecognised 'Provisional Government of Northern Russia' would not be protected by the courts from claims affecting them.[109] Similarly an unrecognised state or government is unable to appear before the courts as a plaintiff in an action. This particular principle prevented the revolutionary government of Berne in 1804 from taking action to restrain the Bank of England from dealing with funds belonging to the previous administration of the city.[110]

The leading case in English law on the issue of effects of recognition of an entity within the domestic sphere is *Luther* v. *Sagor*.[111] This concerned the operations and produce of a timber factory in Russia owned by the plaintiffs, which had been nationalised in 1919 by the Soviet government. In 1920 the defendant company purchased a quantity of wood from the USSR and this was claimed in England by the plaintiffs as their property since it had come from what had been their factory. It was argued by them that the 1919 Soviet decree should be ignored before the English courts since the United Kingdom had not recognised the Soviet government. The lower court agreed with this contention and the matter then came to the Court of Appeal.[112]

In the meantime the UK recognised the Soviet government *de facto* and the Foreign Office informed the Court of Appeal of this in writing. The result was that the higher court was bound to take note of the Soviet decree and accordingly the plaintiffs lost their case, since a court must give effect to the legislation of a recognised state or government. The Court also held that the fact that the Soviet government was recognised *de facto* and not *de jure* did not affect the issue. Another interesting point is that since the Foreign Office certificate included a statement that the former Provisional Government of Russia recognised by the UK had been dispersed during December 1917, the Court inferred the commencement of the Soviet government from that date.

The essence of the matter was that the Soviet government was now accepted as the sovereign government of the USSR as from December 1917. And since recognition once given is retroactive and relates back to the date that the authority of the government was accepted as being established, and not the date on which recognition is granted, the Soviet decree of 1919 was deemed to be a legitimate act of a recognised government. This was so even though at that date the Soviet government was not recognised by the United Kingdom.

---

[108] See e.g. *Halsbury's Laws of England*, London, 4th edn, vol. XVIII, 1977, p. 735.
[109] *The Annette* [1919] P.105; 1 ILR, p. 43.
[110] *The City of Berne* v. *The Bank of England* (1804) 9 Ves. Jun. 347.
[111] [1921] 1 KB 456; 1 ILR, p. 47.   [112] [1921] 3 KB 532; 1 ILR, p. 49.

The purpose of the retroactivity provision[113] is to avoid possible influence in the internal affairs of the entity recognised, since otherwise legislation made prior to recognition might be rejected. However, this will depend always upon the terms of the executive certificate by which the state informs its courts of the recognition. Should the Foreign Office insist that the state or government in question is to be recognised as a sovereign state or government as of the date of the action the courts would be bound by this.

As in the case with legislation, contracts made by an unrecognised government will not be enforced in English courts. Without the required action by the political authorities an unrecognised entity does not exist as a legal person before the municipal courts.

The case of *Luther* v. *Sagor* suggested that in general the legal consequences of a *de facto* recognition would be the same as a *de jure* one. This was emphasised in *Haile Selassie* v. *Cable and Wireless Ltd (No. 2)*,[114] but regarded as restricted to acts in relation to persons or property in the territory which the *de facto* government has been recognised as effectively controlling.

In other words, a different situation would ensue with regard to persons or property situated outside the territory of the state or government. In the *Haile Selassie* case, the Emperor of Ethiopia was suing a British company for money owing to him under an agreement. The problem was that when the action was brought, the UK had recognised the Italian forces as the *de facto* authority in Ethiopia while Haile Selassie was still recognised as the *de jure* sovereign. The Court held that since the case concerned a debt recoverable in England and not the validity of acts with regard to persons or property in Ethiopia, the *de jure* authority, Emperor Haile Selassie, was entitled to the sum due from the company, and the *de facto* control of the Italians did not affect this.

However, before the defendant's appeal was heard, the United Kingdom extended *de jure* recognition to the Italian authorities in Ethiopia. The Court of Appeal accepted that this related back to, and was deemed to operate as from the date of the *de facto* recognition. Since this had occurred prior to the case starting, it meant that the Italian government was now to be recognised as the *de jure* government of Ethiopia, before and during the time of the hearing of the action. Accordingly, Haile Selassie was divested of any right whatsoever to sue for the recovery of the money owing.

This problem of the relationship between a *de facto* government and a *de jure* government as far as English courts were concerned, manifested itself again during the Spanish Civil War.

---

[113] See e.g. *Oppenheim's International Law*, p. 161 and Whiteman, *Digest*, vol. II, pp. 728–45.
[114] [1939] 1 Ch. 182; 9 ILR, p. 94.

The case of the *Arantzazu Mendi*[115] concerned a private steam-ship registered in Bilbao in the Basque province of Spain. In June 1937, following the capture of that region by the forces of General Franco, the opposing Republican government issued a decree requisitioning all ships registered in Bilbao. Nine months later the Nationalist government of Franco also passed a decree taking control over all Bilbao vessels. In the meantime, the *Arantzazu Mendi* itself was in London when the Republican government issued a writ to obtain possession of the ship. The owners opposed this while accepting the Nationalists' requisition order.

It is an accepted rule of international law that a recognised state cannot be sued or otherwise brought before the courts of another state. Accordingly, the Nationalists argued that since their authority had been recognised *de facto* by the UK government over the areas they actually controlled, their decree was valid and could not be challenged in the English courts. Therefore, the action by the Republican government must be dismissed.

The case came before the House of Lords, where it was decided that the Nationalist government, as the *de facto* authority of much of Spain including the region of Bilbao, was entitled to be regarded as a sovereign state and was able to benefit from the normal immunities which follow therefrom. Thus, the action by the Republican government failed. The House of Lords pointed out that it did not matter that the territory over which the *de facto* authority was exercising sovereign powers was from time to time increased or diminished.[116] This case marks the high-point in the attribution of characteristics to a *de facto* authority and can be criticised for its over-generous assessment of the status of such an entity.[117]

The problems faced by the English court when the rights and obligations of a *de jure* government and a *de facto* government, claiming the same territory, appear to be in conflict have been briefly noted. Basically the actions of a *de facto* authority with regard to people and property within this sphere of control will be recognised in an English court, but where property is situated and recoverable in England, the *de jure* sovereign will have precedence. A similarly complicated situation arises where the interests of two recognised *de jure* governments of the same state are involved, as one supersedes the other. Problems can arise concerning the issue of retroactivity, that is, how far the court will relate back actions of a *de jure* government, since recognition is normally retroactive to the moment of inception of the particular state or government.

The matter was discussed in the *Gdynia Ameryka Linie* v. *Boguslawski*

---

[115] [1939] AC 256; 9 ILR, p. 60.   [116] See e.g. Lord Atkin, *ibid.*, pp. 264–5.
[117] See e.g. Lauterpacht, *Recognition*, pp. 288–94.

case.[118] During the Second World War the Polish government in exile stationed in London was recognised by the UK as the *de jure* government of Poland. However, on 28 June 1945 the communist provisional government was established with effective control of the country and at midnight on 5 July the UK recognised that government as the *de jure* government of Poland. A couple of days prior to this recognition, the Polish government in exile made an offer to Polish seamen of compensation in the event of leaving the merchant navy service. The money was to be paid by the particular employers to seamen not wanting to work for the communist provisional government. In the *Boguslawski* case the employers refused to pay the compensation to seamen requesting it, and argued that the UK recognition *de jure* of the provisional government was retroactive to 28 June, this being the date that the government effectively took control of the country. If this was the case, then acts of the government in exile after 28 June ceased to be of effect and thus the offers of compensation could not be enforced in the English courts.

The House of Lords emphasised the general proposition that recognition operates retroactively. However, they modified the statement by declaring that the courts had to give effect not only to acts done by the new government after recognition, but also to acts done before the recognition 'in so far as those acts related to matters under its control at the time when the acts were done'.[119] It was stated that while the recognition of the new government had certain retroactive effects, the recognition of the old government remained effective down to the date when it was in fact withdrawn. Problems might have arisen had the old government, before withdrawal of recognition, attempted to take action with respect to issues under the control of the new government. However, that was not involved in the present case.

In other words, and in the circumstances of the case, the principle of retroactivity of recognition was regarded as restricted to matters within the effective control of the new government. Where something outside the effective control of the new government is involved, it would appear that the recognition does not operate retroactively and that prior to the actual date of recognition one would have to accept and put into effect the acts of the previous *de jure* government.

This could lead to many complicated situations especially where a court was faced with conflicting courses of action, something which is not hard to envisage when one *de jure* government has been superseded by another. It could permit abuses of government such as where a government, knowing itself to be about to lose recognition, awards its supporters financial or other

---

[118] [1953] AC 11; 19 ILR, p. 72.   [119] Lord Reid, *ibid.*, pp. 44–5; 19 ILR, pp. 81, 83.

awards in decrees that may be enforced in English courts. What would happen if the new government issued contrary orders in an attempt to nullify the effect of the old government's decrees is something that was not examined in the *Boguslawski* case.

Another case which came before the courts in the same year was *Civil Air Transport Inc* v. *Central Air Transport Corporation*,[120] and it similarly failed to answer the question mentioned above. It involved the sale of aircraft belonging to the nationalist government of China, which had been flown to the British Crown Colony of Hong Kong. Such aircraft were sold to an American company after the communist government established effective control over the country but before it had been recognised by the UK. The Court accepted that the nationalist government had been entitled to the aircraft and pointed out that:

> retroactivity of recognition operates to validate acts of a *de facto* Government which has subsequently become the new *de jure* Government, and not to invalidate acts of the previous *de jure* Government.[121]

It is to be noted that the communist government did not attempt to nullify the sale to the American company. Had it done so, a new situation would have been created but it is as yet uncertain whether that would have materially altered the legal result.

The general doctrine adhered to by the UK with regard to recognition (and now diplomatic dealings) is that it will be accorded upon the evidence of effective control. It is used to acknowledge factual situations and not as a method of exhibiting approval or otherwise. However, this is not so in all cases and there are a number of governments in effective control of their countries and unrecognised by the UK. One major example was the former German Democratic Republic. Since the prime consequence of non-recognition is that the English courts will not give effect to any laws of an unrecognised entity, problems are thus likely to arise in ordinary international political and commercial life.

The issue came before the Court in the *Carl Zeiss Stiftung* v. *Rayner and Keeler Ltd (No. 2)* case.[122] It concerned the Carl Zeiss foundation which was run by a special board, reconstituted in 1952 as the Council of Gera. The problem was that it was situated in the German Democratic Republic (GDR) and the establishment of the Council of Gera as the governing body of the Carl Zeiss foundation was effected by a reorganisation of local government in the GDR. When Carl Zeiss brought a claim before the English courts, the issue was at once raised as to whether, in view of the UK

[120] [1953] AC 70; 19 ILR, pp. 85, 93, 110. See also F. A. Mann, 'Recognition of Sovereignty', 16 MLR, 1953, p. 226.   [121] [1953] AC 70, 90; 19 ILR, pp. 110, 113.
[122] [1967] AC 853; 43 ILR, p. 42. See also Greig, 'The Carl-Zeiss Case'.

non-recognition of the GDR, the governing body of the foundation could be accepted by the courts. The Court of Appeal decided that since the Foreign Office certified that the UK recognised 'the State and Government of the Union of Soviet Socialist Republics as *de jure* entitled to exercise governing authority in respect of that zone'[123] (i.e. the GDR, being the former Soviet zone of occupation) it was not possible to give effect to any rules or regulations laid down by the GDR. The House of Lords, however, extricated the English courts system from a rather difficult position by means of an elaborate fiction.

It stated that as a Foreign Office certificate is binding on the courts as to the facts it contains, it logically followed that the courts must recognise the USSR as the *de jure* governing authority of East Germany, irrespective of the creation of the GDR. The courts were not entitled to enter into a political examination of the actual situation but were obliged to accept and give effect to the facts set out in the Foreign Office certificate. Thus, the Soviet Union was the *de jure* sovereign and the GDR government must be accepted as a subordinate and dependent body.

Accordingly, the Court could recognise the existence of the Carl Zeiss Stiftung by virtue of the UK recognition of the *de jure* status of the Soviet Union, the GDR as an administrative body being relevant only as a legal creature of the USSR.

The problem brought out in the *Carl Zeiss* case and sidestepped there, was raised again in a series of cases concerning Rhodesia, following the unilateral declaration of independence by the Smith regime in 1965. Basically, if a government or state which exercises effective control over its own territory is unrecognised by the UK a strict enforcement of the 'no recognition, no existence' rule could lead to much hardship and inconvenience. Accordingly, in *Adams* v. *Adams*[124] a Rhodesian divorce decree was not recognised in an English court. However, in *Hesperides Hotels Ltd* v. *Aegean Turkish Holidays*,[125] concerning an action in trespass with respect to hotels owned by Greek Cypriots but run by Turkish Cypriots following the Turkish invasion of 1974, Lord Denning stated *obiter* that he believed that the courts could recognise the laws and acts of an unrecognised body in effective control of territory, at least with regard to laws regulating the day-to-day affairs of the people.[126] It is certainly an attractive approach, provided it is carefully handled and strictly limited to determinations of a humanitarian and non-sovereign nature. In many cases, the problems with regard to

---

[123] [1966] 1 Ch. 596; 43 ILR, p. 25.   [124] [1971] P.188; 52 ILR, p. 15.
[125] [1978] QB 205; 73 ILR, p. 9. See also M. N. Shaw, 'Legal Acts of an Unrecognised Entity', 94 LQR, 1978, p. 500.
[126] [1978] QB 205, 218; 73 ILR, pp. 9, 15. See also Steyn J, *Gur Corporation* v. *Trust Bank of Africa Ltd* [1986] 3 WLR 583, 589, 592; 75 ILR, p. 675.

whether an entity is or is not a 'state' arise in connection with the interpretation of a particular statutory provision. The approach of the courts has been to focus upon the construction of the relevant instrument rather than upon the Foreign Office certificate or upon any definition in international law of statehood.[127]

Some of the consequential problems of non-recognition were addressed in the Foreign Corporations Act 1991. This provides that a corporation incorporated in a territory not recognised by the UK government as a state would be regarded as having legal personality within the UK where the laws of that territory were applied by a settled court system. In other words, the territory would be treated for this purpose as if it were a recognised state, thereby enabling its legislation to be applied in this circumstance on the normal conflict of rules basis. The point should, however, be stressed that the legislation was not intended at all to impact upon recognition issues as such.[128]

Since the UK decision to abandon recognition of governments in 1980, the question arises as to the attitude of the courts on this matter. In particular, it appears that they may be called upon to examine the nature of the UK government's dealings with a new regime in order to determine its status for municipal law purposes.[129]

In *Gur Corporation* v. *Trust Bank of Africa*[130] the Court was in fact called upon to decide the status of Ciskei. This territory, part of South Africa, was one of the Bantustans granted 'independence' by South Africa. This was accomplished by virtue of the Status of Ciskei Act 1981. The preliminary issue that came before the Court in a commercial dispute was whether Ciskei had *locus standi* to sue or be sued in England. The Foreign and Commonwealth Office certified that Ciskei was not recognised as an independent sovereign state either *de facto* or *de jure* and that representations were made to South Africa in relation to matters occurring in Ciskei. The Court of Appeal held that it was able to take account of such declarations and legislation as were not in conflict with the certificates.

The effect of that, noted Lord Donaldson, was that the Status of Ciskei

---

[127] See e.g. *Re Al-Fin Corporation's Patent* [1970] Ch. 160; 52 ILR, p. 68; *Reel* v. *Holder* [1981] 1 WLR 1226; 74 ILR, p. 105 and *Caglar* v. *Bellingham*, 7 March 1996, Transcript at p. 21. See also Merrills, 'Recognition'.

[128] This legislation was adopted essentially to deal with the situation following *Arab Monetary Fund* v. *Hashim (No. 3)* [1991] 2 WLR, whereby the legal personality of a company not incorporated in a territory recognised as a state would not be recognised in English law. See UKMIL, 62 BYIL, 1991, pp. 565–8. See also the decision of the Special Commissioners in *Caglar* v. *Bellingham*, 7 March 1996, Transcript at p. 23, where it was emphasised that the intention of the legislation was not to affect at all the Government's policy on recognition, but to sever the connection with public international law and deal with issues of private international law.

[129] See 409 HL Deb., cols.1097–98 and Symmons, 'United Kingdom', pp. 254–60.

[130] [1987] 1 QB 599; 75 ILR, p. 675.

Act 1981 could be taken into account, except for those provisions declaring the territory independent and relinquishing South African sovereignty. This led to the conclusion that the Ciskei legislature was in fact exercising power by virtue of delegation from the South African authorities.[131] Accordingly, the government of Ciskei could sue or be sued in the English courts 'as being a subordinate body set up by the Republic of South Africa to act on its behalf'.[132] Clearly the Court felt that the situation was analogous to the *Carl Zeiss* case. Whether this was in fact so is an open question. It is certainly open to doubt whether the terms of the certificates in the cases were on all fours. In the *Gur* case, the executive was far more cautious and non-committal. Indeed, one of the certificates actually stated that the UK government did not have a formal position regarding the exercise of governing authority over the territory of Ciskei,[133] whereas in *Carl Zeiss* the certificate noted expressly that the USSR was recognised as *de jure* entitled to exercise governing authority in respect of the territory (the GDR).[134] The gap was bridged by construction and inference.

More widely, it is unclear to what extent the change in policy on recognition of governments has actually led to a change in attitude by the courts. There is no doubt that the attitude adopted by the government in certifying whether or not diplomatic dealings were in existence with regard to the entity in question is crucial. An assertion of such dealing would, it appears, be determinative.[135] The problem arises where the Foreign Office statement is more ambiguous than the mere assertion of dealings with the entity. The consequence is that a greater burden is imposed on the courts as an answer as to status is sought. On the one hand, the *Gur* case suggests that the courts are not willing to examine for themselves the realities of any given situation, but would seek to infer from the terms of any certificate what the answer ought to be.[136] One the other hand, Hobhouse J in the High Court in *Republic of Somalia* v. *Woodhouse Drake and Carey (Suisse) SA*[137] took the wider view that in deciding whether a regime was the government of a state, the court would have to take into account the following factors: (a) whether it is the constitutional government of the state; (b) the degree, nature and stability of administrative control, if any, that it of itself exercises over the territory of the state; (c) whether the UK government has any dealings with it, and if so the nature of those dealings; and (d) in marginal cases, the extent

---

[131] *Ibid.*, p. 623; 75 ILR, p. 696.

[132] *Ibid.*, p. 624. See also Nourse LJ, *ibid.*, pp. 624–66; 75 ILR, pp. 696–9.

[133] *Ibid.*, pp. 618–19; 75 ILR, p. 690.   [134] [1966] 1 Ch. 596; 43 ILR, p. 25.

[135] See e.g the *Arantzazu Mendi* [1939] AC 256, 264; 9 ILR, p. 60, and *Gur Corporation* v. *Trust Bank of Africa* [1987] 1 QB 599, 625; 75 ILR, p. 675. See also *Republic of Somalia* v. *Woodhouse Drake and Carey (Suisse) SA* [1993] QB 54, 65–6: 94 ILR, p. 620.

[136] See e.g. F. A. Mann, 'The Judicial Recognition of an Unrecognised State', 36 ICLQ, 1987, p. 349 and Beck, 'A South African Homeland Appears in the English Court: Legitimation of the Illegitimate?', p. 350.   [137] [1993] QB 54: 94 ILR, p. 608.

of international recognition that it has as the government of the state.[138] Part of the answer as to why a different emphasis is evident is no doubt due to the fact that, in the latter case, there were competing bodies claiming to be the government of Somalia and the situation on the ground as a matter of fact was deeply confused. It should also be noted that in the *Republic of Somalia* case, the court took the view that Foreign Office statements were no more than part of the evidence in the case, although likely to be the best evidence as to whether the government had dealings with the entity in question.[139]

The USA

The situation in the United States with regard to the recognition or non-recognition of foreign entities is similar to that pertaining in the UK, with some important differences. Only a recognised state or government can in principle sue in the US courts.[140] This applies irrespective of the state of diplomatic relations, providing there is no war between the two.[141] However, an unrecognised state or government may in certain circumstances be permitted access before the American courts. This would appear to depend on the facts of each case and a practical appreciation of the entity in question.[142] For example, in *Transportes Aeros de Angola* v. *Ronair*,[143] it was held that in the particular circumstances where the US State Department had clearly stated that allowing the plaintiff (a corporation owned by the unrecognised government of Angola) access to the Court would be consistent with the foreign policy interests of the United States, the jurisdictional bar placed upon the Court would be deemed to have been lifted.

As in the UK, a declaration by the executive will be treated as binding the courts, but in the United States, the courts appear to have a greater latitude. In the absence of the 'suggestion' clarifying how far the process of non-recognition is to be applied, the courts are more willing than their UK counterparts to give effect to particular acts of an unrecognised body. Indeed, in the *Carl Zeiss* case Lords Reid and Wilberforce referred in approving terms to the trend evident in decisions of US courts to give recognition to the 'actual facts or realities found to exist in the territory in question', in the interests of justice and common sense. Such recognition did not apply to every act, but in Lord Wilberforce's words, it did apply to

---

[138] *Ibid.*, p. 68: 94 ILR, p. 622.   [139] *Ibid.*, p. 65: 94 ILR, p. 619.
[140] See e.g. *Republic of Vietnam* v. *Pfizer* 556 F.2d 892 (1977); 94 ILR, p. 199.
[141] See *Banco Nacional de Cuba* v. *Sabbatino*, 376 US 398, 412; 35 ILR, p. 2 and *National Oil Corporation* v. *Libyan Sun Oil Co.*, 733 F.Supp 800 (1990); 94 ILR, p. 209.
[142] See *supra*, p. 314, regarding Taiwan after 1 January 1979. See also *Wulfsohn* v. *Russian Republic*, 234 NY 372 (1924); 2 ILR, p. 39.
[143] 544 F Supp 858, 863–4 (1982); 94 ILR, pp. 202, 208–9.

'private rights, or acts of everyday occurrence, or perfunctory acts of administration'.[144] How far this extends, however, has never been precisely defined.

It was the difficulties engendered by the American Civil War that first stimulated a reappraisal of the 'no recognition, no existence' doctrine. It was not possible to ignore every act of the Confederate authorities and so the idea developed that such rules adopted by the Confederate states as were not hostile to the Union or the authority of the central government, or did not conflict with the terms of the US Constitution, would be treated as valid and enforceable in the courts system.[145] The doctrine was developed in a case before the New York Court of Appeals, when, discussing the status of the unrecognised Soviet government, Judge Cardozo noted that an unrecognised entity which had maintained control over its territory, 'may gain for its acts and decrees a validity quasi-governmental, if violence to fundamental principles of justice or to our public policy might otherwise be done'.[146]

This thesis progressed rapidly in the period immediately preceding the American recognition of the USSR and led in *Salimoff* v. *Standard Oil Co of New York* [147] to the enforcement of a Soviet oil nationalisation decree, with the comment that: 'to refuse to recognise that Soviet Russia is a government regulating the internal affairs of the country, is to give to fictions an air of reality which they do not deserve'.

This decision, diametrically opposed to the *Luther* v. *Sagor* approach,[148] constituted a step towards the abolition of differences between the judicial treatment of the acts of recognised and unrecognised governments.

However, the limits of this broad doctrine were more carefully defined in *The Maret* case[149] where the Court refused to give effect to the nationalisation of an Estonian ship by the government of the unrecognised Soviet Republic of Estonia. However, the ship in dispute was located in an American port at the date of the nationalisation order, and there appears to be a difference in treatment in some cases depending upon whether the property was situated inside or outside the country concerned.

One can mention, in contrast to *The Maret*, the case of *Upright* v. *Mercury Business Machines*,[150] in which the non-recognition of the German Democratic Republic was discussed in relation to the assignment of a bill to the plaintiff by a state-controlled company of the GDR. The judge of the New York Supreme Court declared, in upholding the plaintiff's claim, that a foreign government, although unrecognised by the executive:

---

[144] [1967] AC 853, 954; 43 ILR, pp. 23, 66.
[145] See e.g. *Texas* v. *White*, 74 US 700 (1868).
[146] *Sokoloff* v. *National City Bank of New York*, 239 NY 158 (1924); 2 ILR, p. 44.
[147] 262 NY 220 (1933); 7 ILR, pp. 22, 26.
[148] [1921] 1 KB 456; 1 ILR, p. 47; *supra*, p. 319.   [149] 145 F.2d 431 (1944); 12 ILR, p. 29.
[150] 213 NYS (2d) 417 (1961); 32 ILR, p. 65.

may nevertheless have *de facto* existence which is judicially cognisable. The acts of such a *de facto* government may affect private rights and obligations arising either as a result of activity in, or with persons or corporations within, the territory controlled by such *de facto* government.

However, the creation of judicial entities by unrecognised states will not be allowed to circumvent executive policy. In *Kunstsammlungen zu Weimar* v. *Elicofon*,[151] the KZW was an East German governmental agency until 1969, when it was transformed into a separate juristic person in order to avoid the problems relating to unrecognised states in the above litigation. This concerned the recovery of pictures stolen from a museum during the American occupation of Germany.

As a branch of an unrecognised state, the KZW could not of course be permitted to sue in an American court, but the change of status in 1969 was designed to circumvent this. The Court, however, refused to accept this and emphasised that to allow the KZW to intervene in the case 'would render our government's non-recognition of the German Democratic Republic a meaningless gesture'.[152]

In *Ministry of Defense of the Islamic Republic of Iran* v. *Gould*,[153] the Court was faced with an action in which the unrecognised Iranian government sought to enforce an award. However, the US intervened and filed a statement of interest supporting Iran's argument and this proved of significant influence. This general approach was reinforced in *National Petrochemical* v. *The M/T Stolt Sheaf*,[154] where the Court stressed that the executive must have the power to deal with unrecognised governments and that therefore the absence of formal recognition did not necessarily result in a foreign government being barred from access to US courts.[155] However, where the executive has issued a non-recognition certificate and makes known its view that in the instant case the unrecognised party should not be permitted access to the courts, the courts appear very willing to comply.[156]

It is somewhat difficult to reconcile the various American cases or to determine the extent to which the acts of an unrecognised state or government may be enforced in the courts system of the United States. But two factors should be particularly noted. First of all, the declaration of the

[151] 358 F.Supp. 747 (1972); 61 ILR, p. 143.
[152] *Ibid.*, p. 757; 61 ILR, p. 154. See also *Federal Republic of Germany* v. *Elicofon*, 14 ILM, 1976, p. 806, following the US recognition of the GDR in which KZW was permitted to intervene in the litigation in progress. See also *Transportes Aereos de Angola* v. *Ronair*, 544 F.Supp. 858. [153] 1988 *Iranian Assets Litig. Rep.* 15, 313. See also 82 AJIL, 1988, p. 591.
[154] 860 F.2d 551 (1988). [155] *Ibid.*, p. 554.
[156] See e.g. *Republic of Panama* v. *Republic National Bank of New York*, 681 F.Supp. 1066 (1988) and *Republic of Panama* v. *Citizens & Southern International Bank*, 682 F.Supp. 1144 (1988). See also T. Fountain, 'Out From the Precarious Orbit of Politics: Reconsidering Recognition and the Standing of Foreign Governments to Sue in US Courts', 29 *Va JIL*, 1989, p. 473.

executive is binding. If that intimates that no effect is to be given to acts of the unrecognised entity, the courts will be obliged to respect this. It may also be the case that the State Department 'suggestions' will include some kind of hint or indication which, while not clearly expressed, may lead the courts to feel that the executive is leaning more one way than another in the matter of the government's status, and this may influence the courts. For example, in the *Salimoff* case[157] the terms of the certificate tended to encourage the court to regard the Soviet government as a recognised government, whereas in the case of *The Maret*[158] the tone of the executive's statement on the Soviet Republic of Estonia was decidedly hostile to any notion of recognition or enforcement of its decrees.

The second point is the location of the property in question. There is a tendency to avoid the enforcement of acts and decrees affecting property situated outside the unrecognised state or government and in any event the location of the property often introduces additional complications as regards municipal law provision.[159]

There is some uncertainty in the United States as to the operation of the retroactivity doctrine, particularly as it affects events occurring outside the country. There is a line of cases suggesting that only those acts of the unrecognised government performed in its own territory could be validated by the retroactive operation of recognition[160] while, on the other hand, there are cases illustrating the opposite proposition decided by the Supreme Court.[161]

---

[157] 262 NY 220 (1933); 7 ILR, p. 22.   [158] 145 F.2d 431 (1944); 12 ILR, p. 29.

[159] See e.g. *Civil Air Transport Inc* v. *Central Air Transport Corporation* [1953] AC 70; 19 ILR, p. 85.

[160] See e.g. *Lehigh Valley Railroad Co* v. *Russia*, 21 F.2d 396 (1927); 4 ILR, p. 58.

[161] See e.g. *US* v. *Pink*, 315 US 203 (1942); 10 ILR, p. 48, and *US* v. *Belmont*, 301 US 324 (1937); 8 ILR, p. 34.

TERRITORY

The concept of territory in international law

International law is based on the concept of the state. The state in its turn lies upon the foundation of sovereignty, which expresses internally the supremacy of the governmental institutions and externally the supremacy of the state as a legal person.[1] But sovereignty itself, with its retinue of legal rights and duties, is founded upon the fact of territory. Without territory a legal person cannot be a state.[2] It is undoubtedly the basic characteristic of a state and the one most widely accepted and understood. There are currently some 200 distinct territorial units, each one subject to a different territorial sovereignty and jurisdiction.

Since such fundamental legal concepts as sovereignty and jurisdiction can only be comprehended in relation to territory, it follows that the legal nature of territory becomes a vital part in any study of international law. Indeed, the principle whereby a state is deemed to exercise exclusive power over its territory can be regarded as a fundamental axiom of classical international law.[3] The development of international law upon the basis of the exclusive authority of the state within an accepted territorial framework meant that territory became 'perhaps the fundamental concept of international law'.[4] Most nations indeed developed through a close relationship with the land they inhabited.[5] One may note the central role of territory in the scheme of international

---

[1] See e.g. *Oppenheim's International Law* (eds. R. Y. Jennings and A. D. Watts), 9th edn, London, 1992, Chapter 5; R. Y. Jennings, *The Acquisition of Territory in International Law*, Manchester, 1963; J. H. W. Verzijl, *International Law in Historical Perspective*, Leiden, 1970, vol. III, pp. 297 *et seq.*; Nguyen Quoc Dinh, P. Daillier and A. Pellet, *Droit International Public*, 5th edn, Paris, 1994, pp. 444 *et seq.*; M. N. Shaw, 'Territory in International Law', 13 *Netherlands Yearbook of International Law*, 1982, p. 61; N. Hill, *Claims to Territory in International Law and Relations*, London, 1945; J. Gottman, *The Significance of Territory*, 1973 and W. Schoenborn, 'La Nature Juridique du Territoire', 30 HR, p. 85.

[2] See *Oppenheim's International Law*, p. 563.

[3] See L. Delbez, 'Du Territoire dans ses Rapports avec l'État', 39 *Revue Générale de Droit International Public*, 1932, p. 46. See also Hill, *Claims to Territory*, p. 3.

[4] D. P. O'Connell, *International Law*, London, 2nd edn, vol. I, 1970, p. 403. See also Jennings, *Acquisition*, p. 87 and Judge Huber, *The Island of Palmas* case, 2 RIAA, pp. 829, 838 (1928).

[5] See generally, Gottman, *Significance*.

law by remarking on the development of legal rules protecting its inviolability. The principle of respect for the territorial integrity of states is well founded as one of the linch-pins of the international system, as is the norm prohibiting interference within the internal affairs of other states.[6] A number of factors, however, have tended to reduce the territorial exclusivity of the state in international law. Technological and economic changes have had an impact as interdependence becomes more evident and the rise of such transnational concerns as human rights and self-determination have tended to impinge upon this exclusivity.[7] The growth of international organisations is another relevant factor, as is the development of the 'common heritage' concept in the context of the law of the sea and air law.[8] Nevertheless, one should not exaggerate the effects upon international law doctrine today of such trends.[9] Territorial sovereignty remains as a key concept in international law.

Since the law reflects political conditions and evolves, in most cases, in harmony with reality, international law has had to develop a series of rules governing the transfer and control of territory. Such rules, by the very nature of international society, have often (although not always) had the effect of legitimising the results of the exercise of power. The lack of a strong, central authority in international law has emphasised, even more than municipal legal structures, the way that law must come to terms with power and force.

The rules laid down by municipal legislation and judicial decisions regarding the transfer and control of land within a particular state are usually highly detailed, for they deal with one of the basic resources and wealth-creating factors of the nation. Land law has often reflected the power balance within a society, with feudal arrangements being succeeded by free market contracts and latterly the introduction of comprehensive provisions elaborating the rights and duties of landlords and their tenants, and the development of more sophisticated conveyancing techniques. A number of legal interests are capable of existing over land and the possibility exists of dividing ownership into different segments.[10]

The treatment of territory in international law has not reached this sophisticated stage for a number of reasons, in particular the horizontal

---

[6] See e.g. articles 2(4) and 2(7) of the UN Charter; the 1970 Declaration on Principles of International Law adopted by the UN General Assembly, resolution 2625(XXV) and article 1 of the 1974 Consensus Definition of Aggression adopted by the General Assembly, resolution 3314(XXIX).

[7] See e.g. R. Falk, 'A New Paradigm for International Legal Studies: Prospects and Proposals', 84 *Yale Law Journal*, 1975, pp. 969, 973, 1020. See also H. Lauterpacht, *International Law and Human Rights*, London, 1950 and C. W. Jenks, *The Common Law of Mankind*, London, 1958.

[8] See e.g. the Treaty on Outer Space, 1967 and the Convention on the Law of the Sea, 1982. See also Shaw, 'Territory', pp. 65–6; *infra*, p. 361.

[9] See e.g. the *Asylum* case, ICJ Reports, 1950, pp. 266, 275; 17 ILR, pp. 280, 283.

[10] See e.g. R. Megarry and H. W. R. Wade, *The Law of Real Property*, 5th edn, London, 1984.

system of territorial sovereignty that subsists internationally as distinct from the vertical order of land law that persists in most municipal systems.

One point that flows from this and is basic to an understanding of territory in international and domestic law, is the difference in the consequences that result from a change in the legal ownership of land in international law and in municipal law.

In international law a change in ownership of a particular territory involves also a change in sovereignty, in the legal authority governing the area. This means that the nationality of the inhabitants is altered, as is the legal system under which they live, work and conduct their relations, whereas in municipal law no such changes are involved in an alteration of legal ownership. Accordingly international law must deal also with all the various effects of a change in territorial sovereignty and not confine its attentions to the mere mechanism of acquisition or loss of territory.[11]

Territorial sovereignty

Judge Huber noted in the *Island of Palmas* case[12] that:

> sovereignty in relation to a portion of the surface of the globe is the legal condition necessary for the inclusion of such portion in the territory of any particular state.

Brierly defined territorial sovereignty in terms of the existence of rights over territory rather than the independence of the state itself or the relation of persons to persons. It was a way of contrasting 'the fullest rights over territory known to the law' with certain minor territorial rights, such as leases and servitudes.[13] Territorial sovereignty has a positive and a negative aspect. The former relates to the exclusivity of the competence of the state regarding its own territory,[14] while the latter refers to the obligation to protect the rights of other states.[15]

The international rules regarding territorial sovereignty are rooted in the Roman law provisions governing ownership and possession, and the classification of the different methods of acquiring territory is a direct descendant of the Roman rules dealing with property.[16] This has resulted in some confusion. Law, being so attached to contemporary life, cannot be

---

[11] See *infra*, Chapter 17, dealing with the problems of state succession.
[12] 2 RIAA, pp. 829, 838 (1928); 4 ILR, pp. 103, 104. See also the Report of the Commission of Jurists in the *Aaland Islands* case, LNOJ, Suppl. no. 3, p. 6.
[13] *The Law of Nations*, 6th edn, Oxford, 1963, p. 162.
[14] See Judge Huber, *Island of Palmas* case, 2 RIAA, pp. 829, 838 (1928); 4 ILR, pp. 103, 104.
[15] *Ibid.*, p. 839. See also Shaw, 'Territory', pp. 73 *et seq.* and S. Bastid, 'Les Problèmes Territoriaux dans la Jurisprudence de la Cour Internationale', 107 HR, pp. 360, 367.
[16] See e.g. Schoenborn, 'Nature Juridique', p. 96. See also O'Connell, *International Law*, pp. 403–4. Note in particular the Roman law distinction between *imperium* and *dominium*, Shaw, 'Territory', p. 74.

easily transposed into a different cultural milieu.[17] And, as shall be noted, the Roman method of categorising the different methods of acquiring territory faces difficulties when applied in international law.

The essence of territorial sovereignty is contained in the notion of title. This term relates to both the factual and legal conditions under which territory is deemed to belong to one particular authority or another. In other words, it refers to the existence of those facts required under international law to entail the legal consequences of a change in the juridical status of a particular territory.[18] As the International Court noted in the *Burkina Faso/Mali* case,[19] the word title comprehends both any evidence which may establish the existence of a right and the actual source of that right.[20]

One interesting characteristic that should be noted and which again points to the difference between the treatment of territory under international and municipal law is that title to territory in international law is more often than not relative rather than absolute.[21] Thus, a court, in deciding to which of contending states a parcel of land legally belongs, will consider all the relevant arguments and will award the land to the state which relatively speaking puts forward the better (or best) legal case. Title to land in municipal law is much more often the case of deciding in uncertain or contentious circumstances which party complies with the legal requirements as to ownership and possession, and in that sense title is absolute. It is not normally a question of examining the facts to see which claimant can under the law put forward a better claim to title.

Disputes as to territory in international law may be divided into different categories. The contention may be over the status of the country itself, that is, all the territory comprised in a particular state, as for example Arab claims against Israel at one time and claims formerly pursued by Morocco against Mauritania.[22] Or the dispute may refer to a certain area on the borders of two or more states, as for example Somali claims against the north-east of Kenya and south-east of Ethiopia.[23] Similarly, claims to territory may be based on a number of different grounds, ranging from the traditional method of occupation or prescription to the newer concepts such as self-determination, with various political and legal factors, for example, geographical contiguity, historical demands and economic elements possibly being relevant. These issues will be noted during the course of this chapter.

---

[17] See as regards the theories concerning the relationship between states and territory, *ibid.*, pp. 75–9.
[18] See e.g. Jennings, *Acquisition*, p. 4. See also I. Brownlie, *Principles of Public International Law*, 4th edn, Oxford, 1990, pp. 123–4.
[19] ICJ Reports, 1986, pp. 554, 564; 80 ILR, pp. 440, 459.
[20] This was reaffirmed in the *Land, Island and Maritime Frontier (El Salvador/Honduras)* case, ICJ Reports, 1992, pp. 351, 388; 97 ILR, pp. 266, 301.
[21] See e.g. the *Eastern Greenland* case, PCIJ, Series A/B, no. 53, 1933, p. 46; 6 ILR, p. 95.
[22] See *infra*, p. 355.   [23] See *infra*, p. 355.

Apart from territory actually under the sovereignty of a state, international law also recognises territory over which there is no sovereign. Such territory is known as *terra nullius*. In addition there is a category of territory called *res communis* which is (in contrast to *terra nullius*) generally not capable of being reduced to sovereign control. The prime instance of this is the high seas, which belong to no-one and may be used by all. Another example would be outer space. The concept of common heritage of mankind has also been raised and will be examined in this chapter.

New states and title to territory[24]

The problem of how a state actually acquires its own territory in international law is a difficult one and one that may ultimately only be explained in legal-political terms. While with long-established states one may dismiss the question on the basis of recognition and acceptance, new states pose a different problem, since under classical international law, until a new state is created, there is no legal person in existence competent to hold title. None of the traditional modes of acquisition of territorial title satisfactorily resolve the dilemma, which has manifested itself particularly in the post-Second World War period with the onset of decolonisation. The international community has traditionally approached the problem of new states in terms of recognition, rather than in terms of acquisition of title to territory. This means that states have examined the relevant situation and upon ascertainment of the factual conditions have accorded recognition to the new entity as a subject of international law. There has been relatively little discussion of the method by which the new entity itself acquires the legal rights to its lands. The stress has instead been on compliance with factual requirements as to statehood coupled with the acceptance of this by other states.[25]

One approach to this problem has been to note that it is recognition that constitutes the state, and that the territory of the state is, upon recognition, accepted as the territory of a valid subject of international law irrespective of how it may have been acquired.[26] While this theory is not universally or widely accepted,[27] it does nevertheless underline how the emphasis has been upon recognition of a situation and not upon the method of obtaining the rights in law to the particular territory.[28]

One major factor that is relevant is the crucial importance of the doctrine

---

[24] See Jennings, *Acquisition*, pp. 36 *et seq.*; J. G. Starke, 'The Acquisition of Title to Territory by Newly Emerged States', 41 BYIL, 1965–6, p. 411; J. Crawford, *The Creation of States in International Law*, Oxford, 1979 and M. N. Shaw, *Title to Territory in Africa: International Legal Issues*, Oxford, 1986, pp. 168–73.
[25] See e.g. *Oppenheim's International Law*, p. 677.   [26] *Ibid.*
[27] *Supra*, Chapter 8.
[28] See e.g. Jennings, *Acquisition*, p. 37 and Starke, 'Acquisition of Title', p. 413.

of domestic jurisdiction. This constitutes the legal prohibition on interference within the internal mechanisms of an entity and emphasises the supremacy of a state within its own frontiers. Many of the factual and legal processes leading up to the emergence of a new state are therefore barred from international legal scrutiny and this has proved a deterrent to the search for the precise method by which a new entity obtains title to the territory in question.[29]

In recent years, however, the scope of the domestic jurisdiction rule has been altered. Discussions in international conferences and institutions, such as the United Nations, have actively concerned themselves with conditions in non-independent countries and it has been accepted that territorial sovereignty in the ordinary sense of the words does not really exist over mandate or trust territories.[30] This is beginning to encourage a re-examination of the procedures of acquiring title. However, the plea of domestic jurisdiction does at least illustrate the fact that not only international law but also municipal law is involved in the process of gaining independence.

There are basically two methods by which a new entity may gain its independence as a new state; by constitutional means, that is by agreement with the former controlling administration in an orderly devolution of power, or by non-constitutional means, usually by force, against the will of the previous sovereign.

The granting of independence according to the constitutional provisions of the former power may be achieved either by agreement between the former power and the accepted authorities of the emerging state, or by a purely internal piece of legislation by the previous sovereign. In many cases a combination of both procedures is adopted. For example, the independence of Burma was preceded by a Burmese–United Kingdom agreement and treaty (June and October 1947) and by the Burma Independence Act of 1947 passed by the British legislature, providing for Burmese independence to take effect on 4 January 1948. In such cases what appears to be involved is a devolution or transfer of sovereignty from one power to another and the title to the territory will accordingly pass from the previous sovereign to the new administration in a conscious act of transference.

However, a different situation arises where the new entity gains its independence contrary to the wishes of the previous authority, whether by secession or revolution. It may be that the dispossessed sovereign may ultimately make an agreement with the new state recognising its new status, but, in the

---

[29] See Shaw, *Title to Territory*, pp. 168–9.
[30] See e.g. *International Status of South West Africa*, ICJ Reports, 1950, p. 128; 17 ILR, p. 47; the *South West Africa* cases, ICJ Reports, 1966, p. 6; 37 ILR, p. 243; the *Namibia* case, ICJ Reports, 1971, p. 16; 49 ILR, p. 2, and the *Western Sahara* case, ICJ Reports, 1975, p. 12; 59 ILR, p. 14. See further *supra*, Chapter 5, p. 160.

meantime, the new state might well be regarded by other states as a valid state under international law.[31]

The principle of self-determination is also very relevant here. Where a state gains its sovereignty in opposition to the former power, new facts are created and the entity may well comply with the international requirements as to statehood, such as population, territory and government. Other states will then have to make a decision as to whether or not to recognise the new state and accept the legal consequences of this new status. But at this point a serious problem emerges.

For a unit to be regarded as a state under international law it must conform with the legal conditions as to settled population, a definable area of land and the capacity to enter into legal relations. However, under traditional international law, until one has a state one cannot talk in terms of title to the territory, because there does not exist any legal person capable of holding the legal title. So to discover the process of acquisition of title to territory, one has first to point to an established state. A few ideas have been put forward to explain this. One theory is to concentrate upon the factual emergence of the new state and to accept that since a new state is in existence upon a certain parcel of land, international law should look no further but accept the reality of possession at the moment of independence as denoting ownership, that is, legal title.[32] While in most cases this would prove adequate as far as other states are concerned, it can lead to problems where ownership is claimed of an area not in possession and it does little to answer the questions as to the international legal explanation of territorial sovereignty. Another approach is to turn to the constitutive theory of recognition, and declare that by recognition not only is a new state in the international community created, but its title to the territory upon which it is based is conclusively determined.[33] The disadvantage of this attitude is that it presupposes the acceptance of the constitutive theory by states in such circumstances, something which is controversial.[34]

One possibility that could be put forward here involves the abandonment of the classical rule that only states can acquire territorial sovereignty, and the substitution of a provision permitting a people to acquire sovereignty over the territory pending the establishment of the particular state. By this method the complicated theoretical issues related to recognition are avoided. Some support for this view can be found in the provision in the 1970 Declaration on Principles of International Law that the territory of a colony or other non-self-governing entity possesses, under the United

---

[31] *Ibid.* See also D. Greig, *International Law*, 2nd edn, London, 1976, p. 156.
[32] See e.g. *Oppenheim's International Law*, p. 677 and Starke, 'Acquisition of Title', p. 413.
[33] See also Jennings, *Acquisition*, p. 37 and Starke, 'Acquisition of Title', p. 413.
[34] *Supra*, Chapter 8, p. 296.

Nations Charter, a status separate and distinct from that of the administering power, which exists until the people have exercised the right of self-determination.[35] However, the proposition is a controversial one and must remain tentative.[36]

The acquisition of additional territory

The classical technique of categorising the various modes of acquisition of territory is based on Roman law and is not altogether adequate.[37] Many of the leading cases do not specify a particular category or mode but tend to adopt an overall approach. Five modes of acquisition are usually detailed: occupation of *terra nullius*, prescription, cession, accretion and subjugation (or conquest); and these are further divided into original and derivative modes.[38]

Accretion[39]

This describes the geographical process by which new land is formed and becomes attached to existing land, as for example the creation of islands in a river mouth or the change in direction of a boundary river leaving dry land where it had formerly flowed. Where new land comes into being within the territory of a state, it forms part of the territory of the state and there is no problem. When, for example, an island emerged in the Pacific after an under-sea volcano erupted in January 1986, the UK government noted: 'We understand the island emerged within the territorial sea of the Japanese island of Iwo Jima. We take it therefore to be Japanese territory.'[40]

As regards a change in the course of a river forming a boundary, a different situation is created depending whether it is imperceptible and slight or a violent shift (*avulsion*). In the latter case, the general rule is that the boundary stays at the same point along the original river bed.[41] However, where a gradual move has taken place the boundary may be shifted.[42] If the river is navigable, the boundary will be the middle of the navigable channel,

---

[35] See the *Namibia* case, ICJ Reports, 1971, pp. 16, 31; 49 ILR, pp. 2, 21.
[36] See Shaw, *Title to Territory*, pp. 171–3.
[37] See O'Connell, *International Law*, p. 405.
[38] See *Oppenheim's International Law*, p. 677 and Brownlie, *Principles*, pp. 131–32.
[39] See e.g. C. C. Hyde, *International Law*, 2nd edn, 1947, vol. I, pp. 355–6; O'Connell, *International Law*, pp. 428–30, and *Oppenheim's International Law*, pp. 696–8.
[40] 478 HL Deb., col. 1005, Written Answer, 17 July 1986. See also A. J. Day, *Border and Territorial Disputes*, 2nd edn, London, 1987, p. 277, regarding a new island appearing after a cyclone in 1970 on a river boundary between India and Bangladesh. Title is disputed. See also *Georgia* v. *South Carolina* 111 L Ed 2d 309; 91 ILR, p. 439.
[41] See e.g. *Georgia* v. *South Carolina* 111 L Ed 2d 309, 334; 91 ILR, pp. 439, 458. See also the *Land, Island and Maritime Frontier Dispute (El Salvador/Honduras)*, ICJ Reports, 1992, pp. 351, 546.   [42] *Ibid.*

whatever slight alterations have occurred, while if the river is not navigable the boundary will continue to be the middle of the river itself. This aspect of acquiring territory is relatively unimportant in international law but these rules have been applied in a number of cases involving disputes between particular states of the United States of America.[43]

Cession[44]

This involves the peaceful transfer of territory from one sovereign to another (with the intention that sovereignty should pass) and has often taken place within the framework of a peace treaty following a war. Indeed the orderly transference of sovereignty by agreement from a colonial or administering power to representatives of the indigenous population could be seen as a form of cession.

Because cession has the effect of replacing one sovereign by another over a particular piece of territory, the acquiring state cannot possess more rights over the land than its predecessor had. This is an important point, so that where a third state has certain rights, for example, of passage over the territory, the new sovereign must respect them. It is expressed in the land law phrase that the burden of obligations runs with the land, not the owner. In other words the rights of the territorial sovereign are derived from a previous sovereign, who could not, therefore, dispose of more than he had.

This contrasts with, for example, accretion which is treated as an original title, there having been no previous legal sovereign over the land.

The *Island of Palmas* case[45] emphasised this point. It concerned a dispute between the United States and Holland. The claims of the United States were based on an 1898 treaty with Spain, which involved the cession of the island. It was emphasised by the arbitrator and accepted by the parties that Spain could not thereby convey to the Americans greater rights than it itself possessed.

The basis of cession lies in the intention of the relevant parties to transfer sovereignty over the territory in question.[46] Without this it cannot legally operate. Whether an actual delivery of the property is also required for a

[43] See e.g. *The Anna*, 5 C.Rob. 373 (1805); *Arkansas* v. *Tennessee*, 246 US 158 (1918); *Louisiana* v. *Mississippi*, 282 US 458 (1940); *Georgia* v. *South Carolina*, 111 L Ed 2d 309; 91 ILR, p. 439 and the *Chamizal* arbitration, 5 AJIL, 1911, p. 782. See also E. Lauterpacht, 'River Boundaries: Legal Aspects of the Shatt-Al-Arab Frontier', 9 ICLQ, 1960, pp. 208, 216.
[44] See e.g. *Oppenheim's International Law*, pp. 679–86, and O'Connell, *International Law*, pp. 436–40. [45] 2 RIAA, p. 829 (1928); 4 ILR, p. 103.
[46] Sovereignty over the territorial sea contiguous to and the airspace above the territory concerned would pass with the land territory, see the *Grisbadarna* case, 11 RIAA, p. 147 (1909) and the *Beagle Channel* case, HMSO, 1977; 52 ILR, p. 93. This suggests the corollary that a cession of the territorial sea or airspace would include the relevant land territory, see *Oppenheim's International Law*, p. 680. But see Brownlie, *Principles*, pp. 121–2.

valid cession is less certain. It will depend on the circumstances of the case. For example, Austria ceded Venice to France in 1866, and that state within a few weeks ceded the territory to Italy. The cession to the Italian state through France was nonetheless valid.[47] In the *Iloilo* case,[48] it was held that the cession of the Philippines to the United States took place, on the facts of the case, upon the ratification of the Treaty of Paris of 1898, even though American troops had taken possession of the town of Iloilo two months prior to this.

Although instances of cession usually occur in an agreement following the conclusion of hostilities,[49] it can be accomplished in other circumstances, such as the purchase of Alaska by the United States in 1867 from Russia or the sale by Denmark of territories in the West Indies in 1916 to the United States. It may also appear in exchanges of territories or pure gifts of territory.[50]

Conquest and the use of force

How far a title based on force can be regarded as a valid, legal right recognisable by other states and enforceable within the international system is a crucial question. Ethical considerations are relevant and the principle that an illegal act cannot give birth to a right in law is well established in municipal law and is an essential component of an orderly society.

However, international law has sometimes to modify its reactions to the consequences of successful violations of its rules to take into account the exigencies of reality. The international community has accepted the results of illegal aggression in many cases by virtue of recognition.

Conquest, the act of defeating an opponent and occupying all or part of its territory, does not of itself constitute a basis of title to the land.[51] It does give the victor certain rights under international law as regards the territory, the rights of belligerent occupation,[52] but the territory remains the legal possession of the ousted sovereign.[53] Sovereignty as such does not merely

---

[47] See *Oppenheim's International Law*, p. 681. Note also that in 1859 Austria ceded Lombardy to France, which then ceded it to Sardinia without having taken possession, see O'Connell, *International Law*, p. 438. Cf. *The Fama*, 5 C.Rob. 106, 115 (1804).

[48] 4 RIAA, p. 158 (1925); 3 ILR, p. 336.

[49] Note now that article 52 of the Vienna Convention on the Law of Treaties 1969 provides that a treaty is void if its conclusion has been procured by the threat or use of force in violation of the principles of international law embodied in the Charter of the United Nations. However, prior treaties of cession are subject to the rule of intertemporal law, see *infra*, p. 346.   [50] See for further examples *Oppenheim's International Law*, pp. 681–2.

[51] *Ibid.*, p. 699. See also S. Korman, *The Right of Conquest*, Oxford, 1996.

[52] See e.g. M. S. McDougal and F. P. Feliciano, *Law and Minimum World Public Order*, New Haven, 1961, pp. 733–6 and 739–44 and J. Stone, *Legal Controls of International Conflict*, London, 1959, pp. 744–51. See also E. Benveniste, *The International Law of Occupation*, Princeton, 1993.

[53] See generally *The Arab–Israeli Conflict* (ed. Moore), 4 vols., Princeton, 1974–89.

pass by conquest to the occupying forces, although complex situations may arise where the legal status of the territory occupied is, in fact, in dispute prior to the conquest.[54]

Conquest, of course, may result from a legal or illegal use of force. By the Kellogg–Briand Pact of 1928, war was outlawed as an instrument of national policy and by article 2(4) of the United Nations Charter all member states must refrain from the threat or use of force against the territorial integrity or political independence of any state. However, force will be legitimate when exercised in self-defence.[55] Whatever the circumstances, it is not the successful use of violence that in international law constituted the valid method of acquiring territory. Under the classical rules, formal annexation of territory following upon an act of conquest would operate to pass title. It was a legal fiction employed to mask the conquest and transform it into a valid method of obtaining land under international law.[56] However, it is doubtful whether an annexation proclaimed while war is still in progress would have operated to pass a good title to territory. Only after a war is concluded could the juridical status of the disputed territory be finally determined. This follows from the rule that has developed to the effect that the control over the relevant territory by the state purporting to annex must be effective and that there must be no reasonable chance of the former sovereign regaining the land.

These points were emphasised by the Nuremburg War Crimes Tribunal after the Second World War, in discussing the various purported German annexations of 1939 and 1940. The Tribunal firmly declared that annexations taking place before the conclusion of a war were ineffective and invalid in international law.[57] Intention to annex was a crucial aspect of the equation so that, for example, the conquest of Germany by the Allies in 1945 did not give rise to an implied annexation by virtue of the legislative control actually exercised (as it could have done) because the Allies had specifically ruled out such a course in a joint declaration.[58] It is, however, clear today that the acquisition of territory by force alone is illegal under international law. This may be stated in view of article 2(4) of the UN Charter and other practice. Security Council resolution 242, for example, emphasised the 'inadmissibility of the acquisition of territory by war', while the 1970 Declaration of Principles of International Law adopted by the UN General Assembly provides that:

---

[54] But cf. Y. Blum, 'The Missing Reversioner', in *ibid.* vol. II, p. 287.
[55] See article 51 of the UN Charter and *infra*, Chapter 19, p. 787.
[56] See e.g. *Oppenheim's International Law*, p. 699. See also O'Connell, *International Law*, pp. 431–6.   [57] *Ibid.*, p. 436. See also e.g. *Re Goering*, 13 ILR, p. 203 (1946).
[58] Cmd. 6648 (1945). See also *Oppenheim's International Law*, pp. 699–700.

the territory of a state shall not be the object of acquisition by another state
resulting from the threat or use of force. No territorial acquisition resulting
from the threat or use of force shall be recognised as legal.[59]

In Security Council resolution 662 (1990), adopted unanimously, the
Council decided that the declared Iraqi annexation of Kuwait 'under any
form and whatever pretext has no legal validity and is considered null and
void'. All states and institutions were called upon not to recognise the
annexation and to refrain from actions which might be interpreted as indirect recognition.[60]

Acquisition of territory following an armed conflict would require further
action of an international nature in addition to domestic legislation to
annex. Such further necessary action would be in the form either of a treaty
of cession by the former sovereign or international recognition.[61]

The exercise of effective control

It is customary in the literature to treat the modes of occupation and prescription as separate categories. However, there are several crucial factors
that link the concepts, so that the acquisition of territory by virtue of these
methods, based as they are upon the exercise of effective control, is best
examined within the same broad framework. The traditional definition of
these two modes will be noted first.

Occupation is a method of acquiring territory which belongs to no one
(*terra nullius*) and which may be acquired by a state in certain situations. The
occupation must be by a state and not by private individuals, it must be
effective and it must be intended as a claim of sovereignty over the area. The
high seas cannot be occupied in this manner for they are *res communis*, but
vacant land may be subjected to the sovereignty of a claimant state. It relates
primarily to uninhabited territories and islands, but may also apply to
certain inhabited lands.

The issue was raised in the *Western Sahara* case before the International
Court of Justice.[62] The question was asked as to whether the territory in
question had been *terra nullius* at the time of colonisation. It was emphasised

---

[59] See also article 5(3) of the Consensus Definition of Aggression adopted in 1974 by the UN
General Assembly. Similarly, by article 52 of the Vienna Convention on the Law of Treaties
1969, a treaty providing for the transfer of territory may be void for duress.

[60] See *The Kuwait Crisis – Basic Documents* (eds. E. Lauterpacht, C. Greenwood, M. Weller
and D. Bethlehem), Cambridge, 1991, p. 90.

[61] See, for example, Security Council resolution 497 (1981), condemning Israel's decision to
extend its laws, jurisdiction and administration onto the occupied Golan Heights. The UN
has also condemned Israel's policy of establishing settlements in the occupied territories, see
e.g. Security Council resolution 465 (1980). See further *infra*, Chapter 19, with regard to
self-determination and the use of force.

[62] ICJ Reports, 1975, p. 12; 59 ILR, p. 14. See also M. N. Shaw, 'The *Western Sahara* case',
49 BYIL, 1978, pp. 119, 127–34.

by the Court that the concept of *terra nullius* was a legal term of art used in connection with the mode of acquisition of territory known as 'occupation'.[63] The latter mode was defined legally as an original means of peaceably acquiring sovereignty over territory otherwise than by cession or succession.[64] In an important statement, the Court unambiguously asserted that the state practice of the relevant period (i.e. the period of colonisation) indicated that territories inhabited by tribes or peoples having a social and political organisation were not regarded as *terrae nullius*.[65]

The point should also be made that in fact the majority of territories brought under European control were regarded as acquired by means of cessions especially in Asia and Africa.[66] However, there were instances of title by occupation, for example Australia, and many sparsely inhabited islands.

Occupation, both in the normal sense of the word and in its legal meaning, was often preceded by discovery, that is the realisation of the existence of a particular piece of land.[67] But mere realisation or sighting was never considered (except for periods in the fifteenth and sixteenth centuries and this is not undisputed) as sufficient to constitute title to territory. Something more was required and this took the form of a symbolic act of taking possession, whether it be by the raising of flags or by solemn proclamations or by more sophisticated ritual expressions. As time passed, the conditions changed and the arbitrator in the *Island of Palmas* case pointed to the modern effect of discovery as merely giving an inchoate title which had to be completed within a reasonable time by the effective occupation of the relevant region. Discovery only put other states on notice that the claimant state had a prior interest in the territory which to become legally meaningful had to be supplemented by effective occupation within a certain period.[68]

Prescription[69] is a mode of establishing title to territory which is not *terra nullius* and which has been obtained either unlawfully or in circumstances wherein the legality of the acquisition cannot be demonstrated. It is the legitimisation of a doubtful title by the passage of time and the presumed

---

[63] ICJ Reports, 1975, pp. 12, 39; 59 ILR, pp. 14, 56.   [64] *Ibid.*
[65] *Ibid.* This ran counter to some writers of the period, see e.g. M. F. Lindley, *The Acquisition and Government of Backward Territory in International Law*, London, 1926, pp. 11–20; J. Westlake, *Chapters on the Principles of International Law*, London, 1894, pp. 141–42; Jennings, *Acquisition*, p. 20 and *Oppenheim's International Law*, p. 687, footnote 4.
[66] See Shaw, *Title to Territory*, Chapter 1 and C. H. Alexandrowicz, *The European-African Confrontation*, Leiden, 1973.
[67] See e.g. *Oppenheim's International Law*, pp. 689–90 and F. A. F. Von der Heydte, 'Discovery, Symbolic Annexation and Virtual Effectiveness in International Law', 29 AJIL, 1935, p. 448. See also A. S. Keller, O. J. Lissitzyn and F. J. Mann, *Creation of Rights of Sovereignty Through Symbolic Acts, 1400–1800*, New York, 1938.
[68] 2 RIAA, pp. 829, 846 (1928); 4 ILR, pp. 103, 108.
[69] See generally e.g. D. H. Johnson, 'Acquisitive Prescription in International Law', 27 BYIL, 1950, p. 332.

acquiescence of the former sovereign, and it reflects the need for stability felt within the international system by recognising that territory in the possession of a state for a long period of time and uncontested cannot be taken away from that state without serious consequences for the international order. It is the legitimisation of a fact. If it were not for some such doctrine, the title of many states to their territory would be jeopardised.[70]

Prescription differs from occupation, in that it relates to territory which has previously been under the sovereignty of a state. In spite of this, both concepts are similar in that they may require evidence of sovereign acts by a state over a period of time. And although distinct in theory, in practice these concepts are often indistinct since sovereignty over an area may lapse and give rise to doubts whether an abandonment has taken place,[71] rendering the territory *terra nullius*.

In fact, most cases do not fall into such clear theoretical categories as occupation or prescription. Particular modes of acquisition that can be unambiguously related to the classic definitions tend not to be specified. Most cases involve contesting claims by states, where both (or possibly all) the parties have performed some sovereign acts. As in the instance of occupation, so prescription too requires that the possession forming the basis of the title must be by virtue of the authority of the state or *à titre de souverain*, and not a manifestation of purely individual effort unrelated to the state's sovereign claims. And this possession must be public so that all interested states can be made aware of it.

This latter requirement also flows logically from the necessity for the possession to be peaceful and uninterrupted, and reflects the vital point that prescription rests upon the implied consent of the former sovereign to the new state of affairs. This means that protests by the dispossessed sovereign may completely block any prescriptive claim.[72]

In the *Chamizal* arbitration[73] between the United States and Mexico, the Rio Grande River forming the border between the parties changed course and the United States claimed the ground between the old and the new river beds partly on the basis of peaceful and uninterrupted possession. This claim was dismissed in view of the constant protests by Mexico and in the light of a Convention signed by both parties that there existed a dispute as to the boundary which had to be resolved. The fact that Mexico did not go

---

[70] As noted in the *Grisbadarna* case, 'it is a settled principle of the law of nations that a state of things which actually exists and has existed for a long time should be changed as little as possible', J. B. Scott, *Hague Court Reports*, vol. I, 1916, pp. 121, 130.

[71] For abandonment of territory, the fact of the loss plus the intention to abandon is required. This is very rare; see e.g. the *Delagoa Bay* case, C. Parry, *British Digest of International Law*, Cambridge, vol. V, 1965, p. 535 and the *Frontier Land* case, ICJ Reports, 1959, p. 209. See also Brownlie, *Principles*, p. 145.   [72] See Johnson, 'Acquisitive Prescription', pp. 343–8.

[73] 5 AJIL 1911, p. 782. See also the *Minquiers and Ecrehos* case, ICJ Reports, 1953, pp. 47, 106–8; 20 ILR, pp. 94, 142–4.

to war over the issue was not of itself sufficient to make the possession of the tract of land by the United States peaceful.

Thus acquiescence in the case of prescription, whether express or implied from all the relevant circumstances, is essential, whereas in the case of occupation it is merely an evidential point reinforcing the existence of an effective occupation, but not constituting the essence of the legal claim.

Precisely what form the protest is to take is open to question but resort to force is not acceptable in modern international law, especially since the 1928 Kellogg–Briand Pact and article 2(4) of the United Nations Charter.[74] The bringing of a matter before the United Nations or the International Court of Justice will be conclusive as to the existence of the dispute and thus of the reality of the protests, but diplomatic protests will probably be sufficient. This, however, is not accepted by all academic writers, and it may well be that in serious disputes further steps should be taken such as severing diplomatic relations or proposing arbitration or judicial settlement.[75]

The requirement of a 'reasonable period' of possession is similarly imprecise and it is not possible to point to any defined length of time.[76] It will depend, as so much else, upon all the circumstances of the case, including the nature of the territory and the absence or presence of any competing claims.

In the *Minquiers and Ecrehos* case[77] concerning disputed sovereignty over a group of islets and rocks in the English Channel, claimed by both France and the United Kingdom, the International Court of Justice exhaustively examined the history of the region since 1066. However, its decision was based primarily on relatively recent acts relating to the exercise of jurisdiction and local administration as well as the nature of legislative enactments referable to the territory in question. And upon these grounds, British sovereignty was upheld. The sovereign acts of the United Kingdom relating to the islets far outweighed any such activities by the French authorities and accordingly the claims of the latter were dismissed.

As in other cases, judgment was given not on the basis of clearly defined categories of occupation or prescription, but rather in the light of the balance of competing state activities.

De Visscher has attempted to render the theoretical classifications more consonant with the practical realities by the introduction of the concept of historical consolidation.[78] This idea is founded on proven long use, which

---

[74] *Supra*, p. 341 and *infra*, Chapter 19.
[75] See e.g. Johnson, 'Acquisitive Prescription', pp. 353–4 and I. MacGibbon, 'Some Observations on the Part of Protest in International Law', 30 BYIL, 1953, p. 293. Cf. Brownlie, *Principles*, p. 157, who notes that 'if acquiescence is the crux of the matter (and it is believed that it is) one cannot dictate what its content is to be'.
[76] In the *British Guiana–Venezuela Boundary* case, the parties agreed to adopt a fifty-year adverse holding rule, 89 BFSP, 1896, p. 57.   [77] ICJ Reports, 1953, p. 47; 20 ILR, p. 94.
[78] *Theory and Reality in Public International Law*, 1968, p. 209.

346 INTERNATIONAL LAW

reflects a complex of interests and relations resulting in the acquisition of territory (including parts of the sea). Such a grouping of interests and relations is considered by the courts in reaching a decision as of more importance than the mere passage of time and historical consolidation may apply to *terra nullius* as well as to territories previously occupied. Thus it can be distinguished from prescription. It differs from occupation in that the concept has relevance to the acquisition of parts of the sea, as well as of land. And it may be brought into existence not only by acquiescence and consent, but also by the absence of protest over a reasonable period by relevant states.[79]

However, de Visscher's discussion, based on the *Anglo-Norwegian Fisheries* case[80] does fail to note the important distinction between the acquisition of territory in accordance with the rules of international law, and the acquisition of territory as a permitted exception to the generally accepted legal principles. The passage in the *Anglo-Norwegian Fisheries* case relied upon[81] is really concerned with general acquiescence with regard to a maritime area, while the criticism has been made[82] that de Visscher has overemphasised the aspect of 'complex of interests and relations which *in themselves* have the effect of attaching a territory or an expanse of sea to a given state'.[83] Effectiveness, therefore, rather than consolidation would be the appropriate term. Both occupation and prescription rely primarily upon effective possession and control. The element of time is here also relevant as it affects the effectiveness of control.

Intertemporal law[84]

One question that arises is the problem of changing conditions related to particular principles of international law, in other words the relevant time period at which to ascertain the legal rights and obligations in question. This can cause considerable difficulties since a territorial title may be valid under, for example, sixteenth-century legal doctrines but ineffective under nineteenth-century developments. The general rule in such circumstances is that in a dispute the claim or situation in question (or relevant treaty, for

[79] *Ibid.*   [80] ICJ Reports, 1951, pp. 116, 138; 18 ILR, pp. 86, 100.   [81] *Ibid.*
[82] See Jennings, *Acquisition*, pp. 25–6. See also D. H. Johnson, 'Consolidation as a Root of Title in International Law', *Cambridge Law Journal*, 1955, pp. 215, 223.
[83] De Visscher, *Theory and Reality*, p. 209. Emphasis added. See further *infra*, p. 395.
[84] See e.g. the *Western Sahara* case, ICJ Reports, 1975, pp. 12, 38–39; 59 ILR, pp. 14, 55. See also Shaw, '*Western Sahara* case', pp. 152–3; Jennings, *Acquisition*, pp. 28–31; T. O. Elias, 'The Doctrine of Intertemporal Law', 74 AJIL, 1980, p. 285; Brownlie, *Principles*, pp. 129–30; *Oppenheim's International Law*, pp. 1281–2; G. Fitzmaurice, *The Law and Procedure of the International Court of Justice*, Cambridge, 1986, vol. I, p. 135 and H. Thirlway, 'The Law and Procedure of the International Court of Justice 1960–1989', 60 BYIL, 1989, pp. 4, 128.

example)[85] has to be examined according to the conditions and rules in existence at the time it was made and not at a later date. This meant, for example, that in the *Island of Palmas* case,[86] the Spanish claim to title by discovery, which the United States declared it had inherited, had to be tested in the light of international legal principles in the sixteenth century when the discovery was made.

But it was also noted in this case that while the creation of particular rights was dependent upon the international law of the time, the continued existence of such rights depended upon their according with the evolving conditions of a developing legal system, although this stringent test would not be utilised in the case of territories with an 'established order of things'.[87] This proviso has in practice been carefully and flexibly interpreted within the context of all the relevant rules relating to the acquisition of territory including recognition and acquiescence.[88] However, the Court in the *Aegean Sea Continental Shelf* case[89] declared that the phrase 'disputes relating to the territorial status of Greece' contained in a Greek reservation to the 1928 Kellogg–Briand Pact had to be interpreted 'in accordance with the rules of international law as they exist today, and not as they existed in 1931'. The evolution of international law concerning the continental shelf, therefore, had to be considered, so that the territorial status of Greece was taken to include its continental shelf, although that concept was completely unknown in the 1920s. How far this aspect of the principle of international law may be extended is highly controversial. The better view is to see it as one element in the bundle of factors relevant to the determination of effective control, but one that must be applied with care.

Exercise of authority

The exercise of effective authority, therefore, is the crucial element. As Max Huber argued, 'the actual continuous and peaceful display of state functions is in case of dispute the sound and natural criterion of territorial sovereignty'.[90]

---

[85] See e.g. the *Rights of Passage* case, ICJ Reports, 1960, pp. 6, 37.

[86] 2 RIAA, pp. 829, 845 (1928); 4 ILR, p. 103.

[87] *Ibid.*, pp. 839–45. See P. Jessup, 'The Palmas Island Arbitration', 22 AJIL, 1928, p. 735. See also M. Sørensen, 'Le Problème Dit du Droit Intertemporal dans l'Ordre International', *Annuaire de l'Institut de Droit International*, Basle, 1973, pp. 4 *et seq*, and subsequent discussions, *ibid.*, at pp. 50 *et seq.* and the Resolution adopted by the Institut de Droit International, *Annuaire de l'Institut de Droit International*, 1975, pp. 536 *et seq.*

[88] Note that the 1970 Declaration on Principles of International Law provides that the concept of non-acquisition of territory by force was not to be affected *inter alia* by any international agreement made prior to the Charter and valid under international law.

[89] ICJ Reports, 1978, pp. 3, 33–4; 60 ILR, pp. 562, 592. See Elias, 'Intertemporal Law', pp. 296 *et seq.* See also the Indian argument regarding the invalidity of Portugal's title to Goa, SCOR, S/PV-987, 11, 18 December 1961. [90] 2 RIAA, pp. 829, 840 (1928).

However, control, although needing to be effective, does not necessarily have to amount to possession and settlement of all of the territory claimed. Precisely what acts of sovereignty are necessary to found title will depend in each instance upon all the relevant circumstances of the case, including the nature of the territory involved, the amount of opposition (if any) that such acts on the part of the claimant state have aroused, and international reaction.

Indeed in international law many titles will be deemed to exist not as absolute but as relative concepts. The state succeeding in its claim for sovereignty over *terra nullius* over the claims of other states will in most cases have proved not an absolute title, but one relatively better than that maintained by competing states.

In the *Island of Palmas* arbitration[91] the dispute concerned sovereignty over a particular island in the Pacific. The United States declared that since by a Treaty of 1898 Spain had ceded to it all Spanish rights possessed in that region and since that included the island discovered by Spain, the United States of America therefore had a good title. The Netherlands, on the other hand, claimed the territory on the basis of the exercise of various rights of sovereignty over it since the seventeenth century. The arbitrator, Max Huber, in a judgment which discussed the whole nature of territorial sovereignty, dismissed the American claims derived from the Spanish discovery as not effective to found title.[92] Huber declared that the Netherlands possessed sovereignty on the basis of 'the actual continuous and peaceful display of state functions' evidenced by various administrative acts performed over the centuries.[93] It was also emphasised that manifestations of territorial sovereignty may assume different forms, according to conditions of time and place. Indeed, 'the intermittence and discontinuity compatible with the maintenance of the right necessarily differ according as inhabited or uninhabited regions are involved'. Additionally, geographical factors were relevant.[94]

The *Clipperton Island* arbitration[95] concerned a dispute between France and Mexico over an uninhabited island. The arbitrator emphasised that the actual, and not the nominal, taking of possession was a necessary condition of occupation, but noted that such taking of possession may be undertaken in different ways depending upon the nature of the territory concerned. In this case, a proclamation of sovereignty by a French Naval Officer later published in Honolulu was deemed sufficient to create a valid title. Relevant to

---

[91] *Ibid.*   [92] *Ibid.*, p. 846.   [93] *Ibid.*, pp. 867–71.
[94] *Ibid.*, p. 840. See also in this context, the American claim to the Howland, Baker and Jarvis Islands in the Pacific Ocean, where it was argued that the administration of the islands as part of the US Wildlife Refuge System constituted sufficient occupation, DUSPIL, 1975, pp. 92–4.   [95] 26 AJIL, 1932, p. 390; 6 ILR, p. 105.

this decision was the weakness of the Mexican claims to the guano-rich island, as well as the uninhabited and inhospitable nature of the territory. These two cases, together with the *Eastern Greenland*[96] case, reveal that the effectivity of the occupation may indeed be relative and may in certain rare circumstances be little more than symbolic. In the *Eastern Greenland* case before the Permanent Court of International Justice, both Norway and Denmark claimed sovereignty over Eastern Greenland. Denmark had colonies in other parts of Greenland and had granted concessions in the uninhabited Eastern sector. In addition, it proclaimed that all treaties and legislation regarding Greenland covered the territory as a whole, as for example its establishment of the width of the territorial sea, and it sought to have its title to all of the territory recognised by other states. The Court felt that these acts were sufficient upon which to base a good title and were superior to various Norwegian actions such as the wintering of expeditions and the erection of a wireless station in Eastern Greenland, against which Denmark had protested. It is also to be noted that it was not until 1931 that Norway actually claimed the territory.

Such activity in establishing a claim to territory must be performed by the state or by individuals whose actions are subsequently ratified by their state, or by corporations or companies permitted by the state to engage in such operations. Otherwise, any acts undertaken are of no legal consequence.[97]

Another relevant factor, although one of uncertain strength, is the requirement of the intention by the state in performing various activities to assert claim in its sovereign capacity. In other words the facts are created pursuant to the will of the state to acquire sovereignty. This point was stressed in the *Eastern Greenland* case,[98] but appears not to have been considered as of first importance in the *Island of Palmas* case[99] or in the *Minquiers and Ecrehos* case, [100] where concern centred upon the nature and extent of the actual actions carried out by the contending states. Whatever the precise role of this subjective element, some connection between the actions undertaken and the assertion of sovereignty is necessary.

Account will also be taken of the nature of the exercise of the sovereignty in question, so that in the *Rann of Kutch* case, it was noted that:

> the rights and duties which by law and custom are inherent in and characteristic of sovereignty present considerable variations in different circumstances according to time and place, and in the context of various political systems.[101]

[96] PCIJ, Series A/B, No. 53, 1933, p. 46; 6 ILR, p. 95.
[97] See Judge McNair, the *Anglo-Norwegian Fisheries* case, ICJ Reports, 1951, pp. 116, 184; 18 ILR, pp. 86, 113 and *ibid.*, *International Law Opinions*, 1956, vol. I, p. 21. See also O'Connell, *International Law*, pp. 417–19.
[98] PCIJ, Series A/B, No. 53, 1933, p. 46; 6 ILR, p. 95.
[99] 2 RIAA, p. 829 (1928); 4 ILR, p. 103.   [100] ICJ Reports, 1953, p. 47; 20 ILR, p. 94.
[101] Annex I, 7 ILM, 1968, pp. 633, 674; 50 ILR, p. 2.

Similarly, the Court was willing to take into account the special character-istics of the Moroccan state at the relevant time in the *Western Sahara* case[102] in the context of the display of sovereign authority, but it was the exercise of sovereignty which constituted the crucial factor.

Recognition, acquiescence and estoppel

These three principles have a common foundation in that they all rest to a stronger or weaker extent upon the notion of consent.[103] They reflect expressly or impliedly the presumed will of a state, which in turn may in some situations prove of great importance in the acquisition of title to terri-tory. However, there are significant theoretical differences between the three concepts, even if in practice the dividing lines are often blurred. In any event, they flow to some extent from the fundamental principles of good faith and equity.

Recognition is a positive act by a state accepting a particular situation and even though it may be implied from all the relevant circumstances, it is nev-ertheless an affirmation of the existence of a specific factual state of affairs.[104] Acquiescence, on the other hand, occurs in circumstances where a protest is called for and does not happen[105] or does not happen in time in the circumstances.[106] In other words, a situation arises which would seem to require a response denoting disagreement and since this does not transpire, the state making no objection is understood to have accepted the new situa-tion.[107] The idea of estoppel in general is that a party which has made or consented to a particular statement upon which another party relies in sub-sequent activity to its detriment or the other's benefit cannot thereupon change its position. This rests also upon the notion of preclusion.[108]

While, of course, the consent of a ceding state to the cession is essential, the attitude adopted by other states is purely peripheral and will not affect the legality of the transaction. Similarly, in cases of the acquisition of title over *terra nullius*, the acquiescence of other states is not strictly relevant

---

[102] ICJ Reports, 1975, pp. 12, 43–4; 59 ILR, pp. 14, 60. See also the *Dubai/Sharjah Border Arbitration*, 91 ILR, pp. 543, 585–90.

[103] Consent, of course, is the basis of cession, *supra*, p. 339.

[104] See e.g. the *Eastern Greenland* case, PCIJ, Series A/B, No. 53, 1933, pp. 46, 51–2; 6 ILR, pp. 95, 100, and the *Western Sahara* case, ICJ Reports, 1975, pp. 12, 49–57; 59 ILR, pp. 14, 66. See also G. Schwarzenberger, 'Title to Territory: Response to a Challenge', 51 AJIL, 1957, p. 308.   [105] See Brownlie, *Principles*, p. 160.

[106] See the *Land, Island and Maritime Frontier (El Salvador/Honduras)* case, ICJ Reports, 1992, pp. 351, 577; 97 ILR, pp. 266, 493.

[107] See e.g. the *Libya/Chad* case, ICJ Reports, 1994, pp. 6, 35; 100 ILR, pp. 1, 34, where the Court noted that 'If a serious dispute had indeed existed regarding frontiers, eleven years after the conclusion of the 1955 Treaty, one would expect it to have been reflected in the 1966 Treaty'.

[108] See e.g. the *Gulf of Maine* case, ICJ Reports, 1984, p. 305; 71 ILR, p. 74.

although of useful evidential effect. However, where two or more states have asserted competing claims the role of consent by third parties is much enhanced. In the *Eastern Greenland* case,[109] the International Court noted that Denmark was entitled to rely upon treaties made with other states (apart from Norway) in so far as these were evidence of recognition of Danish sovereignty over all of Greenland.

Recognition and acquiescence are also important in cases of acquisition of control contrary to the will of the former sovereign. Where the possession of the territory is accompanied by emphatic protests on the part of the former sovereign, no title by prescription can arise for such title is founded upon the acquiescence of the dispossessed state, and in such circumstances, consent by third states is of little consequence. However, over a period of time recognition may ultimately validate a defective title, although much will depend upon the circumstances including the attitude of the former sovereign. Where the territory involved is part of the high seas (i.e. *res communis*) acquiescence by the generality of states may affect the subjection of any part of it to another's sovereignty, particularly by raising an estoppel.[110]

Acquiescence and recognition[111] are also relevant where the prescriptive title is based on what is called immemorial possession, that is, the origin of the particular situation is shrouded in doubt and may have been lawful or unlawful but is deemed to be lawful in the light of general acquiescence by the international community or particular acquiescence by a relevant other state. Accordingly, acquiescence may constitute evidence reinforcing a title based upon effective possession and control, rendering it definitive.[112]

Estoppel is a legal technique whereby states deemed to have consented to a state of affairs cannot afterwards alter their position.[113] Although it cannot found title by itself, it is of evidential and often of practical importance. Estoppel may arise either by means of a prior recognition or acquiescence, but the nature of the consenting state's interest is vital. Where, for example, two states put forward conflicting claims to territory, any acceptance by one of the other's position will serve as a bar to a renewal of contradictory assertions. This was illustrated in the *Eastern Greenland* case,[114] where the Court regarded the Norwegian acceptance of treaties with Denmark, which

[109] PCIJ, Series A/B, No. 53, 1933, pp. 46, 51–2; 6 ILR, pp. 95, 100.
[110] See the *Anglo-Norwegian Fisheries* case, ICJ Reports, 1951, p. 116; 18 ILR, p. 86.
[111] Note also the role of recognition in the context of new states and territory, *supra*, p. 335.
[112] See the *Land, Island and Maritime Frontier (El Salvador/Honduras)* case, ICJ Reports, 1992, pp. 351, 579; 97 ILR, pp. 266, 495.
[113] See e.g. D. W. Bowett, 'Estoppel before International Tribunals and its Relation to Acquiescence', 33 BYIL, 1975, p. 176; Thirlway, 'Law and Procedure', p. 29; A. Martin, *L'Estoppel en Droit International Public*, Paris, 1979; C. Dominicé, 'A Propos du Principe de l'Estoppel en Droit des Gens' in *Recueil d'Études de Droit International en hommage à Paul Guggenheim*, Geneva, 1968, p. 327 and I. Sinclair, 'Estoppel and Acquiescence' in *Fifty Years of the International Court of Justice* (eds. A. V. Lowe and M. Fitzmaurice), Cambridge, 1996, p. 104. [114] PCIJ, Series A/B, No. 53, 1933, pp. 46, 68; 6 ILR, pp. 95, 102.

incorporated Danish claims to all of Greenland, as preventing Norway from contesting Danish sovereignty over the area.

The leading case on estoppel is the *Temple of Preah Vihear*[115] which concerned a border dispute between Cambodia and Thailand. The frontier was the subject of a treaty in 1904 between Thailand and France (as sovereign over French Indo-China which included Cambodia) which provided for a delimitation commission. The border was duly surveyed but was ambiguous as to the siting of the Preah Vihear temple area. Thailand called for a map from the French authorities and this placed the area within Cambodia. The Thai government accepted the map and asked for further copies.[116] A number of other incidents took place, including a visit by a Thai prince to the temple area for an official reception, with the French flag clearly flying there, which convinced the International Court that Thailand had tacitly accepted French sovereignty over the disputed area.[117] In other words, Thailand was estopped by its conduct from claiming that it contested the frontier in the temple area. However, it is to be noted that estoppel in that case was one element in a complexity of relevant principles which included prescription and treaty interpretation. The case also seemed to show that in situations of uncertainty and ambiguity, the doctrines of acquiescence and estoppel come into their own,[118] but it would not appear correct to refer to estoppel as a rule of substantive law.[119]

The extent to which silence as such may create an estoppel is unclear and much will depend upon the surrounding circumstances, in particular the notoriety of the situation, the length of silence maintained in the light of that notoriety and the type of conduct that would be seen as reasonable in the international community in order to safeguard a legal interest.[120]

Conclusions

It will be clear from the above that apart from the modes of acquisition that rely purely on the consent of the state and the consequences of sovereignty (cession or accretion), the method of acquiring additional territory is by the sovereign exercise of effective control. Both occupation and prescription are

---

[115] ICJ Reports, 1962, p. 6; 33 ILR, p. 48. See D. H. Johnson, 'The Case Concerning the Temple of Preah Vihear', 11 ICLQ, 1962, p. 1183 and J. P. Cot, 'Cour Internationale de Justice: Affaire du Temple de Préah Vihéar', AFDI, 1962, p. 217.

[116] ICJ Reports, 1962, pp. 6, 23; 33 ILR, pp. 48, 62.   [117] *Ibid.*, pp. 30–2; 33 ILR, p. 68.

[118] See also the *Award of the King of Spain* case, ICJ Reports, 1960, p. 192; 30 ILR, p. 457.

[119] See e.g. Jennings, *Acquisition*, pp. 47–51.

[120] See e.g. the *Anglo-Norwegian Fisheries* case, ICJ Reports, 1951, pp. 116, 139; 18 ILR, pp. 86, 101, the *North Sea Continental Shelf* cases, ICJ Reports, 1969, pp. 3, 26; 41 ILR, pp. 29, 55, the *Gulf of Maine* case, ICJ Reports, 1984, pp. 246, 308; 71 ILR, pp. 74, 135 and the *ELSI* case, ICJ Reports, 1989, pp. 15, 44; 84 ILR, pp. 311, 350. See also M. Koskenniemi, 'L'Affaire du Passage par le Great Belt', AFDI, 1992, p. 905.

primarily based upon effective possession and although the time element is a factor in prescription, this in fact is really concerned with the effectiveness of control.

The principle of effective control applies in different ways to different situations, but its essence is that 'the continuous and peaceful display of territorial sovereignty . . . is as good as title'.[121] Such control has to be deliberate sovereign action, but what will amount to effectiveness is relative and will depend upon, for example, the geographical nature of the region, the existence or not of competing claims and other relevant factors, such as international reaction.[122] It will not be necessary for such control to be equally effective throughout the region.[123] The doctrine of effectiveness has displaced earlier doctrines relating to discovery and symbolic annexation as in themselves sufficient to generate title.[124] Effectiveness has also a temporal as well as a spatial dimension as the doctrine of intertemporal law has emphasised, while clearly the public or open nature of the control is essential. The acquiescence of a party directly involved is also a very important factor in providing evidence of the effectiveness of control. Where a dispossessed sovereign disputes the control exercised by a new sovereign, title can hardly pass. Effectiveness is related to the international system as a whole, so that mere possession by force is not the sole determinant of title. This factor also emphasises and justifies the role played by recognition.

Bilateral recognition is important as evidence of effective control and should be regarded as part of that principle. International recognition, however, involves not only a means of creating rules of international law in terms of practice and consent of states, but may validate situations of dubious origin. A series of recognitions could validate an unlawful acquisition of territory and could similarly prevent effective control from ever hardening into title.[125] The significance of UN recognition is self-evident.[126] Acquisition of title, therefore, rests upon the interplay of a number of rules, particularly effectiveness, sovereignty, recognition and acquiescence.

---

[121] Judge Huber, *Island of Palmas* case, 2 RIAA, pp. 829, 839 (1928); 4 ILR, p. 103.
[122] *Ibid.*, p. 840. See also the *Eastern Greenland* case, PCIJ, Series A/B, no. 53, 1933, p. 46; 6 ILR, p. 95; the *Clipperton Island* case, 26 AJIL, 1932, p. 390; 6 ILR, p. 105 and the *Minquiers and Ecrehos* case, ICJ Reports, 1953, p. 47; 20 ILR, p. 94.
[123] See e.g. the *Island of Palmas* case, 2 RIAA, pp. 829, 840 (1928).
[124] See in this context article 35 of the General Act of the Congress of Berlin, 1885, in which the parties recognised the obligation to 'ensure the establishment of authority in the regions occupied by them on the coast of the African continent'.
[125] See e.g as to Rhodesia, the Bantustans, Namibia and Kuwait, *supra*, pp. 316–17.
[126] See particularly Security Council resolution 687 (1991) in which the international boundary between Kuwait and Iraq was deemed to be that agreed by both parties in 'Minutes' agreed in 1963. This boundary was then formally guaranteed by the Council in Section A, paragraph 4 of this resolution. See e.g. M. H. Mendelson and S. C. Hulton, 'The Iraq–Kuwait Boundary', 64 BYIL, 1993, p. 135. See also Security Council resolution 833 (1993) and S/26006.

Where a particular dispute goes to judicial settlement, the award produced will constitute a recognition of the legal situation binding as between the parties and of significant persuasive force as far as third parties are concerned. This decision may be dispositive in the sense that a definitive choice may be made as between rival claims to territory, both legally based, and to that extent title may be founded upon the decision.[127]

Territorial integrity, self-determination and sundry claims

There are a number of other concepts which may be of some relevance in territorial situations ranging from self-determination to historical and geographical claims. These may not necessarily be legal principles as such but rather purely political or moral expressions. Although they may be extremely persuasive within the international political order, they would not necessarily be juridically effective. Other legal principles may generate further legal rules, such is the case with the principle of territorial integrity.

The principle of the territorial integrity of states is well established and is protected by a series of consequential rules prohibiting interference within the domestic jurisdiction of states as, for example, article 2(7) of the United Nations Charter and forbidding the threat or use of force against the territorial integrity and political independence of states, particularly article 2(4) of the United Nations Charter. This principle has been particularly emphasised by Third World states and also by other regions.[128]

However, it does not apply where the territorial dispute centres upon uncertain frontier demarcations. In addition, the principle appears to conflict on the face of it with another principle of international law, that of the self-determination of peoples.[129]

This principle, noted in the United Nations Charter and emphasised in the 1960 Colonial Declaration, the 1966 International Covenant on Human Rights and the 1970 Declaration on Principles of International Law can be regarded as a rule of international law in the light of, *inter alia*, the number and character of United Nations declarations and resolutions and actual state practice in the process of decolonisation. However, it has been interpreted as referring only to the inhabitants of non-independent territories.

---

[127] See e.g. Brownlie, Principles, p. 137 and H. Post, 'Adjudication as a Mode of Acquisition of Territory?' in *Fifty Years of the International Court of Justice* (eds. A. V. Lowe and M. Fitzmaurice), Cambridge, 1996, p. 237.

[128] See generally, Shaw, *Title to Territory*, Chapter 5. But see as regards Europe, Principle III of the Helsinki Final Act, 14 ILM, 1975, p. 1292 and the Guidelines on Recognition on New States in Eastern Europe and the Soviet Union adopted by the European Community and its member states on 16 December 1991, 92 ILR, p. 173.

[129] See *Burkina Faso* v. *Mali*, ICJ Reports, 1986, pp. 554, 565; 80 ILR, p. 469.

It has been rejected as a principle conferring the right to secede upon identifiable groups within already independent states.[130] Accordingly self-determination fits in with the concept of territorial integrity[131] as it cannot apply once a colony or trust territory attains sovereignty and independence. Probably the most prominent exponent of the relevance of self-determination to post-independence situations is Somalia with its claims to those parts of Ethiopia and Kenya populated by Somali tribes, but that country has received very little support for its demands.[132]

Self-determination may be of some use in resolving cases of disputed frontier lines on the basis of the wishes of the inhabitants, but cannot be used to further larger territorial claims in defiance of internationally accepted boundaries of sovereign states.

Geographical claims have been raised throughout history.[133] France for long maintained that its natural frontier in the east was the west bank of the Rhine, and the European powers in establishing their presence upon African coastal areas often claimed extensive hinterland territories. Much utilised also was the doctrine of contiguity, whereby areas were claimed on the basis of the occupation of territories of which they formed a geographical continuation. However, such claims, although relevant in discussing the effectivity and limits of occupation, are not able in themselves to found title, and whether or not such claims will be taken into account at all will depend upon the nature of the territory and the strength of competing claims.[134]

Of some similarity are claims based upon historical grounds.[135] This was one of the grounds upon which Iraq sought to justify its invasion and annexation of the neighbouring state of Kuwait in August 1990,[136] although the response of the United Nations demonstrated that such arguments were unacceptable to the world community as a whole.[137] Morocco too has made extensive claims to Mauritania, Western Sahara and parts of Algeria as

[130] See *supra*, Chapter 5, p. 177. Self-determination does have a continuing application in terms of human rights situations within the territorial framework of independent states, *supra*, Chapter 6, p. 215.
[131] This analysis is supported by *Burkina Faso* v. *Mali*, ICJ Reports, 1986, pp. 554; 80 ILR, p. 459. [132] Shaw, *Title to Territory*, Chapter 5. See also the Moroccan approach, *ibid.*
[133] See e.g. Shaw, *Title to Territory*, p. 195; Jennings, *Acquisition*, p. 74 and Hill, *Claims to Territory*, pp. 77–80.
[134] See the *Eastern Greenland* case, PCIJ, Series A/B, no. 53, 1933, p. 46; 6 ILR, p. 95 and the *Western Sahara* case, ICJ Reports, 1975, pp. 12, 42–43; 59 ILR, pp. 14, 59. See generally, B. Feinstein, 'Boundaries and Security in International Law and Practice', 3 Finnish YIL, 1992, p. 135.
[135] See e.g. Shaw, *Title to Territory*, pp. 193–4; Jennings, *Acquisition*, pp. 76–8 and Hill, *Claims to Territory*, pp. 81–91.
[136] See *Keesing's Record of World Events*, p. 37635, London, 1990. Note that Iraq made a similar claim to Kuwait in the early 1960s, although not then taking military action, see Jennings, *Acquisition*, p. 77, note 2.
[137] See e.g. Security Council resolution 662 (1990); *The Kuwait Crisis: Basic Documents*, p. 90.

territories historically belonging to the old Moroccan empire.[138] But such arguments are essentially political and are of but little legal relevance. The International Court of Justice in the *Western Sahara* case[139] of 1975 accepted the existence of historical legal ties between the tribes of that area and Morocco and Mauritania, but declared that they were not of such a nature as to override the right of the inhabitants of the colony to self-determination and independence.

The doctrine of uti possidetis

The influence of the principle of territorial integrity may be seen in the Latin American idea of *uti possidetis*, whereby the administrative divisions of the Spanish empire in South America were deemed to constitute the boundaries for the newly independent successor states, thus theoretically excluding any gaps in sovereignty which might precipitate hostilities and encourage foreign intervention.[140] It is more accurately reflected in the practice of African states, explicitly stated in a resolution of the Organisation of African Unity in 1964, which declared that colonial frontiers existing as at the date of independence constituted a tangible reality and that all member states pledged themselves to respect such borders.[141]

Practice in Africa has reinforced the approach of emphasising the territorial integrity of the colonially defined territory, witness the widespread disapproval of the attempted creation of secessionist states whether in the former Belgian Congo, Nigeria or Sudan. Efforts to prevent the partition of the South African controlled territory of Namibia into separate Bantustans as a possible prelude to a dissolution of the unity of the territory are a further manifestation of this.[142]

The question of *uti possidetis* was discussed by a Chamber of the International Court in *Burkina Faso* v. *Republic of Mali*,[143] where the *compromis* (or special agreement) by which the parties submitted the case to the

[138] Shaw, *Title to Territory*, pp. 193–4. Note also the claims advanced by Indonesia to West Irian, *ibid.*, p. 22.   [139] ICJ Reports, 1975, p. 12; 59 ILR, p. 14.

[140] See the *Colombia-Venezuela* arbitral award, 1 RIAA, pp. 223, 228 (1922); 1 ILR, p. 84; the *Beagle Channel* case, HMSO, 1977; 52 ILR, p. 93; A. O. Cukwurah, *The Settlement of Boundary Disputes in International Law*, Manchester, 1967, p. 114 and P. De La Pradelle, *La Frontière*, Paris, 1928, pp. 86–7. See also M. N. Shaw, 'The Heritage of States: The Principle of *Uti Possidetis Juris* Today', 67 BYIL, 1996; J. M. Sorel and R. Mehdi, 'L'*Uti Possidetis* Entre la Consécration Juridique et la Pratique: Essai de Réactualisation', AFDI, 1994, p. 11; *Oppenheim's International Law*, pp. 669–70 and D. Bardonnet, 'Les Frontières Terrestres et la Relativité de leur Tracé', 153 HR, 1976 V, p. 9.

[141] AHG/Res.16(1). See Shaw, *Title to Territory*, pp. 185–7. See also the Separate Opinion by Judge Ajibola in the *Libya/Chad* case, ICJ Reports, pp. 6, 83 *et seq.*; 100 ILR, pp. 1, 81 *et seq.*

[142] *Ibid.*, Chapter 5. The principle has also been noted in Asian practice, see e.g. the *Temple of Preah Vihear* case, ICJ Reports, 1962, p. 6; 33 ILR, p. 48 and the *Rann of Kutch* case, 7 ILM, 1968, p. 633; 50 ILR, p. 2.   [143] ICJ Reports, 1986, p. 554; 80 ILR, p. 459.

Court specified that the settlement of the dispute should be based upon respect for the principle of the 'intangibility of frontiers inherited from colonisation'.[144] It was noted, however, that the principle had in fact developed into a general concept of contemporary customary international law and was unaffected by the emergence of the right of peoples to self-determination.[145] In the African context particularly, the obvious purpose of the principle was 'to prevent the independence and stability of new states being endangered by fratricidal struggles provoked by the challenging of frontiers following the withdrawal of the administering power'.[146] The application of the principle has the effect of freezing the territorial title existing at the moment of independence to produce what the Chamber described as the 'photograph of the territory' at the critical date.[147] The Chamber, however, went further than emphasising the application of the principle to Africa. It declared that the principle applied generally and was logically connected with the phenomenon of independence wherever it occurred in order to protect the independence and stability of new states.[148] *Uti possidetis* was defined as follows:

> The essence of the principle lies in its primary aim of securing respect for the territorial boundaries at the moment when independence is achieved. Such territorial boundaries might be no more than delimitations between different administrative divisions or colonies all subject to the same sovereign. In that case, the application of the principle of *uti possidetis* resulted in administrative boundaries being transformed into international frontiers in the full sense of the term.[149]

The application of this principle beyond the purely colonial context was underlined particularly with regard to the Former USSR[150] and the Former Yugoslavia. In the latter case, the Yugoslav Arbitration Commission established by the European Community and accepted by the states of the Former Yugoslavia made several relevant comments. In Opinion No. 2, the Arbitration Commission declared that 'whatever the circumstances, the right to self-determination must not involve changes to existing frontiers at the time of independence (*uti possidetis juris*) except where the states

---

[144] *Ibid.*, p. 557; 80 ILR, p. 462.   [145] *Ibid.*, p. 565; 80 ILR, p. 469.   [146] *Ibid.*

[147] *Ibid.*, p. 568; 80 ILR, p. 473.   [148] *Ibid.*, p. 565; 80 ILR, p. 470.

[149] *Ibid.*, p. 566; 80 ILR, p. 459. This was reaffirmed by the Court in the *Land, Island and Maritime Frontier Dispute (El Salvador/Honduras)* case, ICJ Reports, 1992, pp. 351, 386–7; 97 ILR, pp. 266, 299–300. The Court in the latter case went on to note that '*uti possidetis juris* is essentially a retrospective principle, investing as international boundaries administrative limits intended originally for quite other purposes', *ibid.*, p. 388; 79 ILR, p. 301. See also M. N. Shaw, 'Case Concerning the Land, Island and Maritime Frontier Dispute', 42 ICLQ, 1993, p. 929.

[150] See e.g. R. Yakemtchouk, 'Les Conflits de Territoires et de Frontières dans les Etats de l'Ex-URSS', AFDI, 1993, p. 401. See also with regard to the application of *uti possidetis* to the dissolution of the Czech and Slovak Federal Republic, J. Malenovsky, 'Problèmes Juridiques Liés à la Partition de la Tchécoslovaquie', AFDI, 1993, p. 328.

concerned agree otherwise'.[151] In Opinion No. 3, the Arbitration Commission emphasised that except where otherwise agreed, the former boundaries[152] became frontiers protected by international law. This conclusion, it was stated, derived from the principle of respect for the territorial status quo and from the principle of *uti possidetis*.[153]

Beyond uti possidetis

The principle of *uti possidetis* is not able to resolve all territorial or boundary problems.[154] Where there is a relevant applicable treaty, then this will dispose of the matter completely.[155] Indeed, once defined in a treaty, an international frontier achieves permanence so that even if the treaty itself were to cease to be in force, the continuance of the boundary would be unaffected and may only be changed with the consent of the states directly concerned.[156] On the other hand, where the line which is being transformed into an international boundary by virtue of the principle cannot be conclusively identified by recourse to authoritative material, then the principle of *uti possidetis* must allow for the application of other principles and rules. Essentially these other principles focus upon the notion of *effectivités* or effective control. The issue was extensively analysed by the International Court in the *Burkino Faso* v. *Mali* case[157] and later in the *Land, Island and Maritime Frontier Dispute (El Salvador/Honduras; Nicaragua Intervening)* case.[158] The Court noted the possible relevance of colonial *effectivités*,

[151] 92 ILR, p. 168. See also A. Pellet, 'Note sur la Commission d'Arbitrage de la Conférence Européenne pour la Paix en Yugoslavie', AFDI, 1991, p. 329 and Pellet, 'Activité de la Commission d'Arbitrage de la Conférence Européenne pour la Paix en Yugoslavie', AFDI, 1992, p. 220.

[152] The Arbitration Commission was here dealing specifically with the internal boundaries between Serbia and Croatia and Serbia and Bosnia-Herzegovina.

[153] 92 ILR, p. 171. The Arbitration Commission specifically cited here the views of the International Court in the *Burkina Faso* v. *Mali* case, see *supra*, p. 357. Note also that the Under-Secretary of State of the Foreign and Commonwealth Office stated in January 1992 that 'the borders of Croatia will become the frontiers of independent Croatia, so there is no doubt about that particular issue. That has been agreed amongst the Twelve, that will be our attitude towards those borders. They will just be changed from being republican borders to international frontiers', UKMIL, 63 BYIL, 1992, p. 719.

[154] Note that the International Court has emphasised that the principle of *uti possidetis* applies to territorial as well as boundary problems, see the *Land, Island and Maritime Frontier Dispute (El Salvador/Honduras)* case, ICJ Reports, 1992, pp. 351, 387; 97 ILR, pp. 266, 300.

[155] See the *Libya/Chad* case, ICJ Reports, 1994, pp. 6, 38–40; 100 ILR, pp. 1, 37–9. See also *Oppenheim's International Law*, p. 663. Note that by virtue of article 11 of the Convention on Succession of States in respect of Treaties 1978, a succession of states does not as such affect a boundary established by a treaty or obligations or rights established by a treaty and relating to the regime of a boundary. Article 62 of the Vienna Convention on the Law of Treaties 1969 provides that the doctrine of *rebus sic stantibus* does not apply to boundary treaties, see *infra*, Chapter 16.

[156] *Libya/Chad* case, ICJ Reports, 1994, p. 37; 100 ILR, p. 36.

[157] ICJ Reports, 1986, p. 554; 80 ILR, p. 440.

[158] ICJ Reports, 1992, p. 351; 97 ILR, p. 266. See also Shaw, 'Concerning the Land'.

immediate post-colonial *effectivités* and more recent *effectivités*. Each of these might be relevant in the context of seeking to determine the *uti possidetis* pre-independence line. In the case of colonial *effectivités*, i.e. the conduct of the colonial administrators as proof of the effective exercise of territorial jurisdiction in the area during the colonial period, the Court in the former case distinguished between certain situations. Where the act concerned corresponded to the title comprised in the *uti possidetis juris*, then the *effectivité* simply confirmed the exercise of the right derived from a legal title. Where the act did not correspond with the law as described, i.e. the territory subject to the dispute was effectively administered by a state other than the one possessing the legal title, preference would be given to the holder of the title. In other words, where there was a clear *uti possidetis* line, this would prevail over inconsistent practice. Where, however, there was no clear legal title, then the *effectivités* 'play an essential role in showing how the title is interpreted in practice'.[159] It would then become a matter for evaluation by the Court with regard to each piece of practice adduced. This approach was reaffirmed in the *Land, Island and Maritime Frontier Dispute* case with regard to the grant of particular lands to individuals or to Indian communities or records of such grants.[160] The Court also noted that it could have regard in certain instances to documentary evidence of post-independence *effectivités* when it considered that they afforded indications with respect to the *uti possidetis* line, provided that there was a relationship between the *effectivités* concerned and the determination of the boundary in question.[161] Such post-independence practice could be examined not only in relation to the identification of the *uti possidetis* line but also in the context of seeking to establish whether any acquiescence could be demonstrated both as to where the line was and as to whether any changes in that line could be proved to have taken place.[162] This post-independence practice could even be very recent practice and was not confined to immediate post-independence practice.

Where the *uti possidetis* line could be determined neither by authoritative decisions by the appropriate authorities at the relevant time nor by subsequent practice with regard to a particular area, recourse to equity[163] might be necessary. What this might involve would depend upon the circumstances. In the *Burkina Faso/Mali* case, it meant that a particular frontier pool would be equally divided between the parties;[164] in the *Land, Island and Maritime Frontier Dispute* case, it meant that resort could be had to an

---

[159] ICJ Reports, 1986, pp. 554, 586–7; 80 ILR, pp. 440, 490–1.
[160] ICJ Reports, 1992, pp. 351, 389; 97 ILR, pp. 266, 302.
[161] *Ibid.*, p. 399; 80 ILR, p. 312.
[162] See e.g. *ibid.*, pp. 408, 485, 514, 525, 563 and 565; 97 ILR, pp. 321, 401, 430, 441, 479 and 481.   [163] I.e. equity *infra legem* or within the context of existing legal principles.
[164] ICJ Reports, 1986, pp. 554, 633; 80 ILR, pp. 440, 535.

unratified delimitation of 1869.[165] It was also noted that the suitability of topographical features in providing an identifiable and convenient boundary was a material aspect.[166]

International boundary rivers[167]

Special rules have evolved in international law with regard to boundary rivers. In general, where there is a navigable channel, the boundary will follow the middle line of that channel (the *thalweg* principle).[168] Where there is no such channel, the boundary line will, in general, be the middle line of the river itself or of its principal arm.[169] These respective boundary lines would continue as median lines (and so would shift also) if the river itself changed course as a result of gradual accretion on one bank or degradation of the other bank. Where, however, the river changed course suddenly and left its original bed for a new channel, the international boundary would continue to be the middle of the deserted river bed.[170] It is possible for the boundary to follow one of the banks of the river, thus putting it entirely within the territory of one of the states concerned where this has been expressly agreed, but this is unusual.[171]

The Falkland Islands[172]

The long dispute between the UK and Argentina over the Falkland Islands (or Las Malvinas) well illustrates the complex factors involved in resolving

---

[165] ICJ Reports, 1992, pp. 351, 514–15; 97 ILR, pp. 266, 430–1.

[166] *Ibid.*, p. 396; 97 ILR, p. 309.

[167] See e.g. *Oppenheim's International Law*, pp. 664–6; S. W. Boggs, *International Boundaries*, 1940; L. J. Bouchez, 'International Boundary Rivers', 12 ICLQ, 1963, p. 789; A. Patry, 'Le Régime des Cours d'eau Internationaux', 1 Canadian YIL, 1963, p. 172; Verzijl, *International Law*, vol. III, pp. 537 *et seq.*; H. Dipla, 'Les Règles de Droit International en Matière de Délimitation Fluviale: Remise en Question ?', 89 RGDIP, 1985, p. 589; H. Ruiz Fabri, 'Règles Coutumières Générales et Droit International Fluvial', AFDI, 1990, p. 818 and F. Schroeter, 'Les Systèmes de Délimitation dans les Fleuves Internationaux', AFDI, 1992, p. 948.

[168] See e.g. *State of New Jersey* v. *State of Delaware* 291 US 361 (1934). See as to the use of the *thalweg* principle with regard to wadis (dried river beds), Mendelson and Hutton, 'Iraq–Kuwait Boundary', pp. 160 *et seq.*

[169] See e.g. the *Argentine–Chile Frontier* case, 38 ILR, pp. 10, 93. See also article 2 A(1) of Annex I(a) of the Israel–Jordan Treaty of Peace 1994.

[170] See e.g. the *Chamizal* case, 11 RIAA, p. 320.

[171] See e.g. the Iran–Iraq agreements of 1937 and 1975. See E. Lauterpacht, 'River Boundaries: Legal Aspects of the Shatt-al-Arab Frontier', 9 ICLQ, 1960, p. 208; K. H. Kaikobad, *The Shatt-al-Arab Boundary Question*, Oxford, 1980 and Kaikobad, 'The Shatt-al-Arab River Boundary: A Legal Reappraisal', 56 BYIL, 1985, p. 49.

[172] See e.g. J. Goebel, *The Struggle for the Falklands*, New Haven, 1927; F. L. Hoffmann and O. M. Hoffmann, *Sovereignty in Dispute*, Boulder, CO,1984; The Falkland Islands Review, Cmnd. 8787 (1983); Chatham House, *The Falkland Islands Dispute – International Dimensions*, London, 1982; W. M. Reisman, 'The Struggle for the Falklands', 93 *Yale Law Journal*, 1983, p. 287 and M. Hassan, 'The Sovereignty Dispute over the Falkland Islands', 23 *Va JIL* 1982, p. 53. See also House of Commons Foreign Affairs Committee, Session 1983/4, 5th Report, 2681, and Cmnd. 9447 (1985).

issues as to title to territory. The islands were apparently discovered by a British sea captain in 1592, but it is only in 1764 that competing acts of sovereignty commenced. In that year the French established a settlement on East Falklands and in 1765 the British established one on West Falklands. In 1767 the French sold their settlement to Spain. The British settlement was conquered by the Spaniards in 1770 but returned the following year. In 1774 the British settlement was abandoned for economic reasons, but a plaque asserting sovereignty was left behind. The Spaniards left in 1811. In 1816, the United Provinces of the River Plate (Argentina) declared their independence from Spain and four years later took formal possession of the islands. In 1829 the British protested and two years later, an American warship evicted Argentinian settlers from the islands, following action by the Argentinian Governor of the territory against American rebels: in 1833 the British captured the islands and have remained there ever since. The question has arisen therefore as to the basis of British title. It was originally argued that this lay in a combination of discovery and occupation, but this would be questionable in the circumstances.[173] It would perhaps have been preferable to rely on conquest and subsequent annexation for in the 1830s this was perfectly legal as a method of acquiring territory,[174] but for political reasons this was not claimed. By the 1930s the UK approach had shifted to prescription as the basis of title,[175] but of course this was problematic in the light of Argentinian protests made intermittently throughout the period since 1833.

The principle of self-determination as applicable to a recognised British non-self-governing territory has recently been much relied upon by the UK government,[176] but something of a problem is posed by the very small size of the territory's population (some 1,800) although this may not be decisive.

It would appear that conquest formed the original basis of title, irrespective of the British employment of other principles. This, coupled with the widespread recognition by the international community, including the United Nations, of the status of the territory as a British Colony would appear to resolve the legal issues, although the matter is not uncontroversial.

'The common heritage of mankind'

The proclamation of certain areas as the common heritage of mankind has raised the question as to whether a new form of territorial regime has been

[173] See A. D. McNair, *International Law Opinions*, vol. I, 1956, pp. 299–300.
[174] See e.g. Lindley, *The Acquisition*, pp. 160–5 and *supra*, p. 340.
[175] See e.g. Beck, *The Guardian*, 26 July 1982, p. 7.
[176] See e.g. The Prime Minister, HC Deb., col. 946, 13 May 1982.

or is in process of being created.[177] In 1970, the UN General Assembly adopted a Declaration of Principles Governing the Seabed and Ocean Floor in which it was noted that the area in question and its resources were the common heritage of mankind. This was reiterated in articles 136 and 137 of the 1982 Convention on the Law of the Sea, in which it was provided that no sovereign or other rights would be recognised with regard to the area (except in the case of minerals recovered in accordance with the Convention) and that exploitation could only take place in accordance with the rules and structures established by the Convention.[178] Article XI of the 1979 Moon Treaty emphasises that the moon and its natural resources are the common heritage of mankind, and thus incapable of national appropriation and subject to a particular regime of exploitation.[179] As is noted in the next section, attempts are currently being made to establish a common heritage regime over the Antarctic. There are certain common characteristics relating to the concept. Like *res communis*, the areas in question are incapable of national appropriation. Sovereignty is not an applicable principle and the areas in question would not be 'owned', nor would any jurisdictional rights exist outside the framework of the appropriate common heritage regime institutional arrangements. However, while a *res communis* regime permits freedom of access, exploration and exploitation, a common heritage regime as envisaged in the examples noted above would strictly regulate exploration and exploitation, would establish management mechanisms and would employ the criterion of equity in distributing the benefits of such activity.

It is too early to predict the success or failure of this concept. The 1982 Law of the Sea Convention has only very recently entered into force, while the Moon Treaty has the bare minimum of ratifications and its exploitation provisions are not yet operative. As a legal concept within the framework of the specific treaties concerned, it provides an interesting contrast to traditional *jus communis* rules, although the extent of the management structures required to operate the regime may pose considerable problems.[180]

---

[177] See e.g. A. Cassese, *International Law in a Divided World*, Oxford, 1986, Chapter 14; Larschan and Brennan, 'The Common Heritage of Mankind Principle in International Law', 21 *Columbia Journal of International Law*, 1983, p. 305; R. Wolfrum, 'The Principle of the Common Heritage of Mankind', *ZaöRV* 1983, p. 312; S. Gorove, 'The Concept of Common Heritage of Mankind', 9 *San Diego Law Review*, 1972, p. 390 and C. Joyner, 'Legal Implications of the Common Heritage of Mankind', 35 ICLQ, 1986, p. 190.

[178] See further *infra*, Chapter 11, p. 445.   [179] See further *infra*, Chapter 10, p. 383.

[180] Questions have arisen as to whether the global climate could be regarded as part of the common heritage of mankind. However, international environmental treaties have not used such terminology, but have rather used the phrase 'common concern of mankind', which is weaker and more ambiguous, see e.g. the Convention on Biological Diversity 1992. See A. Boyle, 'International Law and the Protection of the Global Atmosphere' in *International Law and Global Climate Change* (eds. D. Freestone and R. Churchill), London, 1991, Chapter 1 and P. Birnie and A. Boyle, *International Law and the Environment*, Oxford, 1992, p. 120.

The Polar regions[181]

The Arctic region is of some strategic importance, constituting as it does a vast expanse of inhospitable territory between North America and the Soviet Union. It consists to a large extent of ice packs beneath which submarines may operate.

Denmark possesses Greenland and its associated islands within the region,[182] while Norway has asserted sovereign rights over Spitzbergen and other islands. The Norwegian title is based on occupation and long exploitation of mineral resources and its sovereignty was recognised by nine nations in 1920, although the Soviet Union had protested.[183]

More controversial are the respective claims made by Canada[184] and the former USSR.[185] Use has been made of the concept of contiguity to assert claims over areas forming geographical units with those already occupied, in the form of the so-called sector principle. This is based on meridians of longitude as they converge at the North Pole and as they are placed on the coastlines of the particular nations, thus producing a series of triangular sectors with the coasts of the Arctic states as their baselines.

The other Arctic states of Norway, Finland, Denmark and the United States have abstained from such assertions. Accordingly it is exceedingly doubtful whether the sector principle can be regarded as other than a political proposition.[186] Part of the problem is that such a large part of this region consists of moving packs of ice. The former USSR made some claims to relatively immovable ice formations as being subject to its national sovereignty,[187] but the overall opinion remains that these are to be treated as part of the high seas open to all.[188]

Occupation of the land areas of the Arctic region may be effected by states

---

[181] See e.g. O'Connell, *International Law*, pp. 448–50 and Balch, 'The Arctic and Antarctic Regions and the Law of Nations', 4 AJIL, 1910, p. 165; Hayton, 'Polar Problems and International Law', 52 AJIL, 1958, p. 746 and M. Whiteman, *Digest of International Law*, Washington, 1962, vol. II, pp. 1051–61. See also Lakhtine, 'Rights over the Arctic', 24 AJIL, 1930, p. 703; Mouton, 'The International Regime of the Polar Regions, ' 101 HR, p. 169; F. Auburn, *Antarctic Law and Politics*, 1982; *International Law for Antarctica* (eds. Francioni and Scovazzi), 1987; A. D. Watts, *International Law and the Antarctic Treaty System*, Cambridge, 1992; Sahuvic, *The International Law of Antarctic*, 1991; C. Joyner, *Antarctica and the Law of the Sea*, 1992; *The Antarctic Environment and International Law* (eds. P. Sands, J. Verhoeven and Bruce), 1992 and Franckx, *Maritime Claims in the Arctic*, 1993.   [182] See Hackworth, *Digest of International Law*, vol. I, 1940.
[183] *Ibid.*, pp. 465 *et seq.* See also O'Connell, *International Law*, p. 499.
[184] Hackworth, *Digest*, p. 463. But note Canadian Government statements denying that the sector principle applies to the ice, see e.g. 9 ILM, 1970, pp. 607, 613. See also I. Head, 'Canadian Claims to Territorial Sovereignty in the Arctic Regions', 9 *McGill Law Journal*, 1962–3, p. 200.   [185] Hackworth, *Digest*, p. 461.
[186] See e.g. *Oppenheim's International Law*, 'Rights', p. 693.
[187] See e.g. Lakhtine, 'Rights', p. 461.   [188] See e.g. Balch, 'The Arctic', pp. 265–6.

by relatively little activity in view of the decision in the *Eastern Greenland* case[189] and the nature of the territory involved.

Claims have been made by seven nations (Argentina, Australia, Chile, France, New Zealand, Norway and the United Kingdom) to the Antarctic region, which is an ice-covered land mass in the form of an island.[190] Such claims have been based on a variety of grounds ranging from mere discovery to the sector principle employed by the South American states, and most of these are of rather dubious quality. Significantly, the United States of America has refused to recognise any claims at all to Antarctica and although the American Admiral Byrd discovered and claimed Marie Byrd Land for his country, the United States refrained from adopting the claim.[191] Several states have recognised the territorial aspirations of each other in the area, but one should note that the British, Chilean and Argentinian claims overlap.[192]

However, in 1959 the Antarctic Treaty was signed by all states concerned with territorial claims or scientific exploration in the region. Its major effect apart from the demilitarisation of Antarctica, is to suspend, although not to eliminate, territorial claims during the life of the treaty. Article IV(2) declares that:

> no acts or activities taking place while the present treaty is in force shall constitute a basis for asserting, supporting or denying a claim to territorial sovereignty in Antarctica or create any rights of sovereignty in Antarctica. No new claim or enlargement of an existing claim, to territorial sovereignty in Antarctica shall be asserted while the present treaty is in force.

Since the treaty does not provide for termination, an on-going regime has been created which because of its inclusion of all interested parties appears to have established an international regime binding on all. Subsequent meetings of the parties have resulted in a number of recommendations including proposals for the protection of flora and fauna in the region, and other environmental preservation measures.[193]

Of the forty-two parties to the treaty in 1996, twenty-six had consultative status. Full participation in the work of the consultative meetings of the parties is reserved to the original parties to the treaty and those contracting parties which demonstrate substantial scientific research activity in the area. Under article XII, any party entitled to participate in the consultative meet-

---

[189] PCIJ, Series A/B, no. 53, 1933, p. 46; 6 ILR, p. 95.

[190] See e.g. O'Connell, *International Law*, pp. 450–3; Mouton, 'Polar Regions', and G. Triggs, 'Australian Sovereignty in Antarctica – Part I', 13 *Melbourne University Law Review*, 1981, p. 123. See also UKMIL, 54 BYIL, 1983, pp. 488 *et seq.*

[191] See Hackworth, *Digest*, p. 457. See also DUSPIL, 1975, pp. 107–11 and Whiteman, *Digest*, vol. II, pp. 250–4, 1254–6 and 1262.   [192] See e.g. Cmd. 5900.

[193] See e.g. the 1980 Convention on the Conservation of Antarctic Marine Living Resources. See also Howard, 'The Convention on the Conservation of Antarctic Marine Living Resources: A Five Year Review', 38 ICLQ, 1989, p. 104.

ings may call for a review conference thirty years after the date the treaty came into force, that is in 1991.

The issue of a mineral resources regime has been under discussion since 1979 by the consultative parties and a series of special meetings on the subject held.[194] This resulted in the signing in June 1988 of the Convention on the Regulation of Antarctic Minerals Resource Activities.[195] The Convention provided for three stages of mineral activity, being defined as prospecting, exploration and development. Four institutions were to be established, once the treaty came into force (following sixteen ratifications or accessions, including the US, the former USSR and claimant states). The Commission was to consist of the consultative parties, any other party to the Convention engaged in substantive and relevant research in the area and any other party sponsoring mineral resource activity. A Scientific, Technical and Environmental Advisory Committee consisting of all parties to the Convention was to be established, as were Regulatory Committees, in order to regulate exploration and development activity in a specific area. Such committees would consist of ten members of the Commission, including the relevant claimant and additional claimants up to a maximum of four, the US, the former USSR and representation of developing countries. A system for Special Meetings of Parties, consisting of all parties to the Convention, was also provided for.

A framework for decision-making had thus been established and procedures provided for and several countries signed the Convention.[196] However, opposition to the Convention began to grow. The signing of the 1988 Convention on mineral resource activities stimulated opposition and in resolution 43/83, adopted by the General Assembly that year, 'deep regret' was expressed that such a convention should have been signed despite earlier resolutions calling for a moratorium on negotiations to create a minerals regime in the Antarctic. France and Australia proposed at the October 1989 meeting of the signatories of the Antarctic Treaty that all mining be banned in the area, which should be designated a global 'wilderness reserve'.[197]

At a meeting of the consultative parties to the Antarctic Treaty in April 1991 the Protocol on Environmental Protection to the Antarctic Treaty was adopted, article 7 of which prohibited any activity relating to mineral resources other than scientific research. This prohibition is to continue unless there is in force a binding legal regime on Antarctic mineral resource

[194] See e.g. *Keesings Contemporary Archives*, p. 32834 and 21(9) *UN Chronicle*, 1984, p. 45.
[195] See e.g. C. Joyner, 'The Antarctic Minerals Negotiating Process', 81 AJIL, 1987, p. 888.
[196] See e.g. the Antarctic Minerals Act 1989, which provided for a UK licensing system for exploration and exploitation activities in Antarctica.
[197] See *Keesing's Record of World Events*, p. 36989, 1989.

activities that includes an agreed means of determining whether and if so under which conditions any such activities would be acceptable. A review conference with regard to the operation of the Protocol may be held after it has been in force for fifty years if so requested.[198] In addition, a Committee for Environmental Protection has been established.[199] This effectively marks the end of the limited mining approach, which had led to the signing of the Convention on the Regulation of Antarctic Mineral Resource Activities.

An initiative has been developing at the United Nations, headed by Malaysia, to consider establishing a common heritage of mankind regime over Antarctica. An extensive report on the area was issued by the Secretary-General of the UN in November 1984, detailing the operations of the regime created under the 1959 Treaty, and the subject is being further considered by the General Assembly. The parties to the treaty have emphasised the success of the system and the participation in it of the major powers. The possible disadvantages of a common heritage international regime have also been referred to, while the proponents of the common heritage regime have stressed the need for exploitation of the area in the interests of all mankind.[200]

Leases and servitudes[201]

This section is concerned with various legal rights exercisable by states over the territory of other states, which fall short of absolute sovereignty. Such rights are attached to the land and so may be enforced even though the ownership of the particular territory subject to the rights has passed to another sovereign. They are in legal terminology formulated as rights *in rem*.

Leases of land rose into prominence in the last century as a way of obtaining control of usually strategic points without the necessity of actually annexing the territory. Leases were used extensively in the Far East, as for example Britain's rights over the New Territories amalgamated with Hong Kong,[202] and sovereignty was regarded as having passed to the lessee for the duration of the lease, upon which event it would revert to the original sovereign who made the grant.

[198] Article 25.
[199] *The Guardian*, 30 April 1991, p. 20. See also C. Redgewell, 'Environmental Protection in Antarctica: The 1991 Protocol', 43 ICLQ, 1994, p. 599.
[200] *Ibid*. See also Assembly resolutions 38/77 and 39/152, and A/39/583.
[201] See e.g. *Oppenheim's International Law*, pp. 670 *et seq.*; Reid, *International Servitudes*, 1932 and Vali, *Servitudes in International Law*, 2nd edn, 1958. See also Parry, *Digest*, vol. IIB, 1967, pp. 373 *et seq.*, and article 12, Vienna Convention on Succession of States in Respect of Treaties, 1978.
[202] See 50 BFSP, 1860, p. 10 and 90 BFSP, 1898, p. 17. See now 23 ILM, 1984, pp. 1366 *et seq.* for the UK–China agreement on Hong Kong. See also Cmnd. 9543 (1985) and the 1985 Hong Kong Act, providing for the termination of British sovereignty and jurisdiction over the territory as from 1 July 1997.

An exception to this usual construction of a lease in international law as limited to a defined period, occurred with regard to the Panama Canal, with the strip of land through which it was constructed being leased to the United States in 1903 'in perpetuity'. However, by the 1977 Panama Canal Treaty, sovereignty over the Canal Zone was transferred to Panama. The United States will have certain operating and defensive rights until the treaty ends in 1999.[203]

A servitude exists where the territory of one state is under a particular restriction in the interests of the territory of another state. Such limitations are bound to the land as rights *in rem* and thus restrict the sovereignty of the state concerned, even if there is a change in control of the relevant territory, for instance upon merger with another state or upon decolonisation.[204]

Examples of servitudes would include the right to use ports or rivers in, or a right of way across, the territory so bound, or alternatively an obligation not to fortify particular towns or areas in the territory.[205]

Servitudes may exist for the benefit of the international community or a large number of states. To give an example, in the *Aaland Islands* case in 1920, a Commission of Jurists appointed by the Council of the League of Nations declared that Finland since its independence in 1918 had succeeded to Russia's obligations under the 1856 treaty not to fortify the islands. And since Sweden was an interested state in that the islands are situated near Stockholm, it could enforce the obligation although not a party to the 1856 treaty. This was because the treaty provisions had established a special international regime with obligations enforceable by interested states and binding upon any state in possession of the islands.[206]

The situation of the creation of an international status by treaty, which is to be binding upon all and not merely upon the parties to the treaty, is a complex one and it is not always clear when it is to be presumed. However, rights attached to territory for the benefit of the world community were created with respect to the Suez and Panama Canals.

Article 1 of the Constantinople Convention of 1888[207] declared that 'the Suez Maritime Canal shall always be free and open in time of war as in time of peace, to every vessel of commerce or of war without distinction of flag' and this international status was in no way affected by the Egyptian nationalisation of the Canal Company in 1956. Egypt stressed in 1957 that it was willing to respect and implement the terms of the Convention, although in fact it consistently denied use of the canal to Israeli ships and vessels bound

[203] See e.g. 72 AJIL, 1978, p. 225. This superseded treaties of 1901, 1903, 1936 and 1955 governing the Canal. See also A. Rubin, 'The Panama Canal Treaties', YBWA, 1981, p. 181. [204] See the *Rights of Passage* case, ICJ Reports, 1960, p. 6; 31 ILR, p. 23.
[205] See e.g. J. B. Brierly, *The Law of Nations*, 6th edn, Oxford, 1963, p. 191.
[206] LNOJ, Sp. Suppl. No. 3, 1920, pp. 3, 16–19.
[207] See e.g. O'Connell, *International Law*, pp. 582–7.

for its shores or carrying its goods.[208] The canal was reopened in 1975 following the disengagement agreement with Israel, after a gap of eight years.[209] Under article V of the 1979 Peace Treaty between Israel and Egypt, it was provided that ships of Israel and cargoes destined for or coming from Israel were to enjoy 'the right of free passage through the Suez Canal . . . on the basis of the Constantinople Convention of 1888, applying to all nations'.

In the *Wimbledon* case,[210] the Permanent Court of International Justice declared that the effect of article 380 of the Treaty of Versailles 1919 maintaining that the Kiel Canal was to be open to all the ships of all countries at peace with Germany was to convert the canal from an internal to an international waterway 'intended to provide under treaty guarantee easier access to the Baltic for the benefit of all nations of the world'.

Some of the problems relating to the existence of servitudes have arisen by virtue of the *North Atlantic Fisheries* arbitration.[211] This followed a treaty signed in 1818 between the United Kingdom and the United States, awarding the inhabitants of the latter country 'forever . . . the liberty to take fish of every kind' from the southern coast of Newfoundland. The argument arose as to Britain's capacity under the treaty to issue fishing regulations binding American nationals. The arbitration tribunal decided that the relevant provision of the treaty did not create a servitude, partly because such a concept was unknown by American and British statesmen at the relevant period (i.e. 1818). However, the terms of the award do leave open the possibility of the existence of servitudes, especially since the tribunal did draw a distinction between economic rights (as in the case) and a grant of sovereign rights which could amount to a servitude in international law.[212]

---

[208] See Security Council Doc. S/3818, 51 AJIL, p. 673.
[209] See DUSPIL, 1974, pp. 352–4 and 760.
[210] PCIJ, Series A, No. 1, 1923, p. 24; 2 ILR, p. 99. See generally R. Baxter, *The Law of International Waterways*, 1964.   [211] 11 RIAA, p. 167 (1910).
[212] See as to land-locked states, *infra*, Chapter 11, p. 416.

AIR LAW AND SPACE LAW

Air law[1]

Theories[2]

There were a variety of theories prior to the First World War with regard to the status of the airspace above states and territorial waters. One view was that the airspace was entirely free, another that there was, upon an analogy with the territorial sea, a band of 'territorial air' appertaining to the state followed by a higher free zone, a third approach was that all the airspace above a state was entirely within its sovereignty, while a fourth view modified the third approach by positing a right of innocent passage through the air space for foreign civil aircraft.[3] There was a particular antagonism between the French theory of freedom of the air and the British theory of state sovereignty,[4] although all agreed that the airspace above the high seas and *terrae nullius* was free and open to all.

However, the outbreak of the First World War with its recognition of the security implications of use of the air changed this.

The approach that then prevailed, with little dissension, was based upon the extension of state sovereignty upwards into airspace. This was acceptable both from the defence point of view and in the light of evolving state practice regulating flights over national territory.[5] It was reflected in the

---

[1] See generally B. Cheng, *The Law of International Air Transport*, London, 1962; Shawcross and Beaumont, *Air Law*, 4th edn, London, regularly up-dated; A. Lowenfield, *Aviation Law: Cases and Materials*, 1981; N. Matte, *Traité de Droit Aérien-Aéronautique*, 3rd edn, Paris, 1980 and Matte, *Treatise on Air-Aeronautical Law*, 1981; R. Y. Jennings, 'Some Aspects of the International Law of the Air', 75 HR, 1949, p. 5 and B. Cheng and R. Austin, 'Air Law' in *The Present State of International Law* (ed. M. Bos), 1973, p. 183. See also *Air and Space Law: De Lege Ferenda* (eds. Zwaan and Mendes de Leon), 1992; J. Naveau, *International Air Transport in a Changing World*, Brussels, 1989; M. Folliot, *Les Relations Aériennes Internationales*, Paris, 1985; I. H. Diederiks-Verschoor, *An Introduction to Air Law*, Deventer, 1983; K. G. Park, *La Protection de la Souveraineté Aérienne*, Paris, 1991; M. Zylicks, *International Air Transport Law*, Dordrecht, 1992; *Oppenheim's International Law* (eds. R. Y. Jennings and A. D. Watts), 9th edn, London, 1992, pp. 650 *et seq.* and Nguyen Quoc Dinh, P. Daillier and A. Pellet, *Droit International Public*, 5th edn, Paris, 1994, p. 1150 *et seq.*
[2] See e.g. *Oppenheim's International Law*, pp. 650–1 and Matte, *Treatise*, Chapters 4 and 5.
[3] See Matte, *Treatise*, Chapter 5.   [4] *Ibid.*, p. 83.   [5] *Ibid.*, pp. 91–6.

1919 Paris Convention for the Regulation of Aerial Navigation, which recognised the full sovereignty of states over the airspace above their land and territorial sea.[6]

Sovereignty was understood to extend for an unlimited distance into the airspace (*usque ad coelum*),[7] although this has been modified by the new law of outer space.

One question that did arise immediately concerned the apparent similarity of treatment as regards sovereignty between the airspace and the territorial sea and centred upon the right of passage that exists through territorial waters. It questioned whether there existed a right of passage through the airspace above states. This issue had, of course, tremendous implications for the development of aerial transport and raised the possibility of some erosion of state exclusivity. However, it is now accepted that no such right may be exercised in customary international law.[8] Aircraft may only traverse the airspace of states with the agreement of those states, and where that has not been obtained an illegal intrusion will be involved which will justify interception, though not (save in very exceptional cases) actual attack.[9] This is discussed later.

The structure

The present regime concerning air navigation developed from the 1944 Chicago Conference and the conventions adopted there.

The Chicago Convention on International Civil Aviation, which does not apply to state aircraft (for example, military, customs and police aircraft),[10] emphasises the complete and exclusive sovereignty of states over their airspace[11] and article 6 reinforces this by providing that no scheduled international air service may be operated over or into the territory of a contracting state without that state's special authorisation. However, the states parties

---

[6] Article 1. Each party also undertook to accord in peace time freedom of innocent passage to the private aircraft of other parties so long as they complied with the rules made by or under the authority of the Convention. Articles 5–10 also provided that the nationality of aircraft would be based upon registration and that registration would take place in the state of which their owners were nationals. An International Commission for Air Navigation was also established. See also the 1978 American Convention on Commercial Aviation.

[7] Based upon common law principles, see e.g. *Co. Litt.* 4 and Blackstone, *Commentaries*, vol. II, Chapter 2, p. 18.

[8] See e.g. *Oppenheim's International Law*,p. 652. It should, however, be noted that articles 38 and 39 of the Convention on the Law of the Sea 1982 provides for a right of transit passage through straits used for international navigation between one part of the high seas or an exclusive economic zone and another part of the high seas or an exclusive economic zone for aircraft as well as ships. Note also that under article 53 of this Convention, aircraft have a right of overflight with regard to designated air routes above archipelagic waters.

[9] See also *Pan Am Airways* v. *The Queen* (1981) 2 SCR 565; 90 ILR, p. 213, with regard to the exercise of sovereignty over the airspace over the high seas.   [10] Article 3.

[11] Article 1. This includes the airspace above territorial waters, article 2.

to the Convention qualified their sovereignty by agreeing in article 5 that aircraft of other contracting states:

> not engaged in scheduled international air service, shall have the right . . . to make flights into or in transit non-stop across [their territory and to make stops for non-traffic purposes without the necessity of obtaining prior permission and subject to the right of the state flown over to require landing.[12]

This provision has in practice been viewed as an exception to the general principle enumerated in article 6 of the Convention, particularly since states have required that permission be obtained prior to the acceptance of charter flights over or into their territory, even though such flights do not really come within the meaning of article 6 or within the definition of scheduled international air services put forward by the Council of the International Civil Aviation Organisation in 1952. It is one more example of state practice modifying the original interpretation of a treaty stipulation.[13] By article 17, aircraft have the nationality of the state in which they are registered, although the conditions for registration are a matter for domestic law.[14]

The Chicago International Air Services Transit Agreement, 1944, dealing with scheduled international air services, specified that contracting states recognised the privileges of such services to fly across their territories without landing and to land for non-traffic purposes. This 'two freedoms' agreement, as it has been termed, was accompanied by a 'five freedoms' agreement, the 1944 Chicago International Air Transport Agreement, which added to the aforementioned provisions extensive privileges of taking on and putting down passengers, mail and cargo in the territories of contracting states. However, this agreement was not ratified by many countries and the USA withdrew from it in 1946[15] because it was felt that too much of commercial value had been granted away. Thus, that agreement is of little importance today.

This has meant in actual practice that the regulation of international scheduled services has been achieved by an extensive network of bilateral agreements such as the UK-USA Bermuda Agreement of 1946,[16] since the

---

[12] Note also that under article 9, states may for reasons of military necessity or public safety prohibit or restrict the aircraft of other states on a non-discriminatory basis from flying over certain areas of its territory.

[13] The distinction between scheduled and non-scheduled international air services is not entirely clear, see here D. P. O'Connell, *International Law*, London, 2nd edn, 1970, vol. I, p. 521. See also the non-binding ICAO Council definition of 1952, Doc. 7278–C/841, quoted in D. W. Greig, *International Law*, London, 2nd edn, 1976, p. 349. Note that under article 68, each contracting state to the convention may designate the route to be followed within its territory by any international air service and the airports which any such service may use, see also *International Law Asssociation: Report of the 63rd Conference at Warsaw*, London, 1988, pp. 835 *et seq.*

[14] See article 19.   [15] See *Oppenheim's International Law*, p. 656.

[16] Replaced by the Bermuda II agreement of 1977. See e.g. Matte, *Treatise*, pp. 229–50. See also the *Heathrow Airport User Charges Arbitration*, 102 ILR, p. 215.

agreed 'two freedoms' only relate to transit and not traffic rights. The hard bargaining that goes on in negotiations between states to arrange the operation of the remaining 'three freedoms' attests to the commercial as well as strategic significance connected with such privileges. But the technological advances of advanced design and 'jumbo' jets as well as the proliferation of state airlines has put this somewhat unwieldy system under great strain.

The Chicago Conference also led to the creation of the International Civil Aviation Organisation (ICAO), a UN specialised agency based in Canada, which concentrates upon technical and administrative co-operation between states in the field of civil aviation, ranging from the adoption of agreed safety standards to the encouragement of the expansion of navigational facilities.[17] ICAO's aims and objectives are to develop the principles and techniques of international air navigation and to foster the planning and development of international air transport.[18] It has a range of powers from legal to technical and administrative and it consists of an Assembly, a Council and such other bodies as may be necessary.[19]

In the main, the Chicago Conference reaffirmed the principles agreed in the 1919 Convention with regard to, for example, the sovereignty of the state over its airspace and the need for permission to operate scheduled international air services. Air cabotage, i.e. the right to carry traffic between points within the territory of a state, can be reserved exclusively to the state as may traffic between the metropolitan and colonial areas. The Chicago Conference system was to some extent undermined by the growth of bilateral agreements[20] as the means to regulate international air transport, but many common principles may be discerned in such agreements based as they are upon the Bermuda model.

The Bermuda principles,[21] in general, provide that the air transport facilities available to the travelling public should bear a close relationship to the requirements of the public; that there shall be a fair and equal opportunity for the carriers of the two nations to operate on any route between their respective territories; that in the operation by the air carriers of either

---

[17] *Ibid.*, pp. 187–201.   [18] Article 44 of the Chicago Convention 1944.
[19] Article 43. There are, for example, Committees dealing with Air Transport, Joint Support of Air Navigation Services and Legal Matters, and an Air Navigation Commission. Note the standard-setting work of ICAO, e.g. the 1948 Convention on the International Recognition of Rights in Aircraft and the 1955 Protocol to the 1929 Warsaw Convention. See generally Shawcross and Beaumont, *Air Law*, DII (2)-(19) and F. Kirgis, 'Aviation' in *United Nations Legal Order* (eds. O. Schachter and C. C. Joyner), Cambridge, 1995, vol. II, p. 825. Note also the mechanisms available to settle international aviation disputes, see article 84 and T. Buergenthal, *Law Making in the International Civil Aviation Organisation*, Syracuse, 1969, Part III and the *Jurisdiction of the ICAO Council (India v. Pakistan)* case, ICJ Reports, 1972, p. 46: 48 ILR, p. 331.
[20] See e.g. *Cumulative* DUSPIL *1981–8*, vol. II, Washington, 1994, pp. 2175 *et seq.*
[21] See e.g. Jennings, 'Some Aspects', pp. 529 *et seq.* and J. Dutheil de la Rochère, 'Aspects Nouveaux du Bilatéralisme Aérien', AFDI, 1982, p. 914.

government of the trunk services described in the Annex of the Agreement, the interest of the air carriers of the other government shall be taken into consideration, so as not to affect unduly the services which the latter provides on all or part of the same routes; and that it is the understanding of both governments that services provided by a designated air carrier under the Agreement and its Annex shall retain, as their primary objective, the provision of capacity adequate to the traffic demands between the country of which the carrier is a national and the country of ultimate destination of the traffic. The right to embark or to disembark on such services of international traffic destined for and coming from third countries at a point or points on the routes specified in the Annex to the Agreement, shall be applied in accordance with the general principles of orderly development to which both governments subscribe and shall be subject to the general principle that capacity should be related:

(a) to traffic requirements between the country of origin and the countries of destination;
(b) to the requirements of through airline operation; and
(c) to the traffic requirements of the area through which the airline passes after taking account of local and regional services; and that it is the intention of both governments that there should be regular and frequent consultation between their respective aeronautical authorities and that there should thereby be close collaboration in the observation of the principles and the implementation of the provisions outlined therein and in the Agreement and its Annex.[22]

The UK denounced the Bermuda Agreement in 1976 on grounds of inequity of share in the North Atlantic traffic and in 1977 a new agreement with the USA, Bermuda II, was signed.[23] The basic principles of Bermuda I were reaffirmed, but with new regulation techniques. British airlines were allowed new non-stop services and the freedom to combine their US points on each route as they choose. The problem of 'excess capacity' was dealt with by a consultative process and a Tariff Working Group was established.[24]

In addition to the International Civil Aviation Organisation there also exists the International Air Transport Association which consists of most of the airline companies acting together to establish uniform fares and tariffs

---

[22] See Matte, *Treatise*, pp. 591–5.
[23] See DUSPIL, 1977, pp. 638–41. See generally as to dispute settlement in such cases, B. Cheng, 'Dispute Settlement in Bilateral Air Transport Agreements' in *Settlement of Space Law Disputes* (ed. Böckstiegel), 1980, p. 97. See also Shawcross and Beaumont, *Air Law*, DIV.
[24] Note also the US–UK dispute over Heathrow Airport User Charges, see *Cumulative DUSPIL 1981–8*, vol. III, Washington, 1995, pp. 3137 *et seq.* and S. Witten, 'The US–UK Arbitration Concerning Heathrow Airport User Charges', 89 AJIL, 1995, p. 174. See also the *Heathrow Airport User Charges Arbitration*, 102 ILR, p. 215.

subject to governmental approval. It is also an important forum for discussion of relevant topics such as hijacking and attacks upon civil aircraft.

The Warsaw Convention System[25]

An issue which has become of great importance in recent years relates to the liability of civil airline companies for death or injury suffered by passengers. The 1929 Warsaw Convention for the Unification of Certain Rules relating to International Carriage by Air established upper limits for such liability as well as dealing with other questions of responsibility and insurance. The Convention was modified by the Hague Amendment of 1955, but as this proved unacceptable to the United States a subsequent Agreement in Montreal was signed in 1966 raising the limits of liability as regards airlines flying in or to the USA.

Article 20 of the Convention lays down the general rule that the carrier is not liable if he proves that he and his agents have taken all necessary measures to avoid the damage or that it was impossible for him or them to take such measures. The standard of proof is high.[26] Article 22 provides for limits to the carrier's liability, defined in terms of gold French francs (or Poincaré francs),[27] but liability is unlimited under article 25 if damage[28] results from the wilful misconduct of the carrier or of one of his agents.[29] Some help would undoubtedly be provided by the entry into force of the Montreal Additional Protocols 1975, which seek *inter alia* to substitute Special Drawing Rights for the gold franc, and the Guatemala Protocol 1971, which seeks to introduce absolute liability with increased limits in passenger and baggage cases. The ICAO Council and its Legal Committee did indeed discuss a plan to encourage the ratification of the Montreal Protocols in early 1990.[30]

But the situation respecting the airlines' liability outside the US is not at all satisfactory and the limits are low. This has meant that claimants are often tempted to sue not the airlines but, for example, the aircraft

---

[25] See e.g. Matte, *Treatise*, pp. 377–496 and Miller, *Liability in International Air Transport*, 1977. See also the 1961 Guadalajara Convention, which deals with international carriage by air performed by a person other than the contracting carrier. See generally Shawcross and Beaumont, *Air Law*, DVII; *Cumulative* DUSPIL *1981–8*, vol. II, Washington, 1994, pp. 2218 *et seq.* and Goldhirsch, *The Warsaw Convention Annotated*, 1988.

[26] See e.g. *Grein* v. *Imperial Airways Ltd*, [1937] 1 KB 50; 8 ILR, p. 453; *Ritts* v. *American Overseas Airlines*, US Av R, 1949, p. 65 and *American Smelting and Refining Co* v. *Philippine Airlines Inc*, US and C Av R, 1954, p. 221; 21 ILR, p. 286.

[27] See e.g. *TWA Inc.* v. *Franklin Mint Corporation*, 23 ILM, 1984, p. 814.

[28] Damage in this instance has been interpreted to include loss, see *Fothergill* v. *Monarch Airlines* [1980] 2 All ER 696; 74 ILR, p. 627.

[29] Dissatisfaction with the Warsaw system has led some municipal courts into the realms of judicial creativity, see e.g. *Chen* v. *Korean Air Lines Ltd*, 109 S Ct 1676 (1989) and *Coccia* v. *Turkish Airlines* [1985] Dir Mar 751 (Italian Constitutional Court).

[30] See Shawcross and Beaumont, *Air Law*, DVII (57).

manufacturers in the hope of obtaining higher levels of compensation. However, here problems centre upon the choice of courts before which to bring the issue, since the sums available in personal injury cases vary considerably from country to country and the grounds for liability are not the same in all jurisdictions.

The whole position was graphically illustrated by the Turkish Airlines tragedy in 1974. The crash of the American-built plane near Paris and the loss of over three hundred lives emphasised the complexity of injustice of the situation respecting the amounts of compensation available for the death or injuries caused to passengers.

The sums that could have been obtained from Turkish Airlines were limited by the terms of the Warsaw Convention as amended, and accordingly the claimants turned to the American manufacturer of the defective aircraft. But the position was that if the case were brought in the UK, substantially less could have been obtained than if the matter came before the American courts, which have a much more progressive system of absolute liability and higher compensation limits with respect to personal injuries. In the end, a group of Britons succeeded in bringing their cases before Californian judges and were awarded satisfactory levels of compensation, in line with the American approach.[31]

The general significance of air transportation for the world community can be seen in the developing provisions relating to hijacking. The airspace has become a vital means of communication and the various attacks upon aircraft condemned as threatening this freedom of the air. The international community has adopted a series of conventions outlawing hijacking and stipulating methods of enforcement, though with a limited degree of success. Nevertheless, it is likely that the law relating to hijacking will eventually turn that offence into a universal one on similar lines to piracy on the high seas.[32]

The Montreal Convention for the Suppression of Unlawful Acts against the Safety of Civil Aviation 1971 makes it an offence unlawfully and intentionally, inter alia, to perform an act of violence against a person on board an aircraft in flight where the act is likely to endanger the safety of the aircraft; to destroy an aircraft in service or to so damage it as to make flight

---

[31] See e.g. DUSPIL, 1975, pp. 459–61 and *In re Paris Air Crash of March 2, 1974*, 399 F.Supp. 732 (1975). See also *Holmes* v. *Bangladesh Bimani Corporation* [1989] 1 AC 1112: 87 ILR, p. 365, where the House of Lords held that sovereign states retained the right to legislate for domestic carriage by air within their own boundaries and a presumption existed that a positive connection with UK territory was required for UK rules to be applicable to a contract for carriage by air. The Air Law Committee of the ILA has suggested three principles – (1) There should be an integrated system of civil aviation liability in international carriage by air and in respect of surface damage; (2) Claims should be channelled through the carrier and operator of the aircraft; and (3) Compensation for personal injuries shall be based on the principle of absolute, unlimited and secured liability, see International Law Association, *Report of the Sixteenth Conference at Montreal, 1982*, London, p. 553.

[32] See further, *infra*, Chapter 12, p. 470.

unsafe or impossible; to destroy, damage or interfere with the operation of air navigation facilities or to communicate knowingly false information if this is likely to endanger an aircraft in flight.

The ambit of this convention was extended by the Montreal Protocol 1988 to include acts of violence against a person at an airport serving international civil aviation which cause or are likely to cause serious injury or death; destroying or seriously damaging the facilities of such an airport or aircraft not in service located thereon and disrupting the services of the airport.[33]

The terrorist attacks of the 1970s in particular gave rise to a series of cases, which have established, for example, that recovery for mental distress arising out of an airplane hijack was possible under the Warsaw Convention as amended by the Montreal Agreement of 1966[34] and that a carrier remains liable for injuries to passengers that occurred in a terrorist attack at Hellenikon Airport, Athens, at the departure gate of the terminal.[35] However, there was no liability in the case of an attack in the baggage retrieval area of an air terminal building while the passengers were waiting for their luggage as this was not 'disembarking' within the meaning of article 17.[36]

The question of liability for damage caused by aircraft to persons on the surface has also been dealt with. The Rome Convention on Damage Caused by Foreign Aircraft to Third Parties on the Surface, 1952, and the Montreal Protocol of 1978, provide for compensation to be paid upon proof only of damage caused by an aircraft in flight or by any person or thing falling therefrom. It is the operator of the aircraft that bears the responsibility and under the 1952 Convention the registered owner of the aircraft is presumed to be the operator. The extent of liability is stipulated and one of the reasons for the low level of ratification has been the relatively limited level of compensation provided for. The system is based upon strict liability and on clear connection being established between the damage and the act causing the injury.

Unauthorised aerial intrusion and the downing of civilian airliners[37]

The International Court has emphasised that the principle of respect for territorial sovereignty is directly infringed by the unauthorised overflight of a

---

[33] See the Aviation and Maritime Security Act 1990. Note that the ICAO Convention on the Marking of Plastic Explosives for the Purpose of Detection 1991 calls upon all states to take measures to prohibit the manufacture of unmarked explosives and established an International Explosives Technical Commission.

[34] *Krystal* v. *BOAC*, 403 F.Supp. 1322 (1975).

[35] *Day* v. *TWA Inc*, 528 F.2d 31 (1975), cert. denied 429 US 890.

[36] *Hernandez* v. *Air France*, 545 F.2d 279 (1976). See also *Mangrui* v. *Compagnie Nationale Air France*, 549 F.2d 1256 (1977), cert. denied, 45 Law Week 3801 (1977). See also e.g. *Korean Airlines* v. *Entiope*, RGDIP, 1983, p. 231; 89 ILR, p. 23 and *Haddad* v. *Société Air France*, RGDIP, 1983, p. 468; 89 ILR, p. 26 and *Air Inter* v. *Bornier*, AFDI, 1983, p. 848.

[37] See e.g. O. Lissitzyn, 'The Treatment of Aerial Intruders in Recent Practice and International Law', 47 AJIL, 1953, p. 554; Greig, *International Law*, pp. 356–60; F. Hassan,

state's territory by aircraft belonging to, or under the control of, the government of another state.[38] Such unauthorised overflight would justify interception and a demand to land. However, a number of incidents have occurred since 1945 of the destruction of foreign aerial intruders. In 1955 a civil airliner of El Al Israel Airlines was shot down while intruding into Bulgarian airspace by Bulgarian warplanes. An action was commenced before the International Court of Justice which, however, dismissed the case on grounds of lack of jurisdiction. The Israeli Memorials emphasised that a state faced with an unauthorised aerial intrusion may deal with it in one or both of two ways: first, by informing the intruder that it is performing an unauthorised act (and this may include compelling it to land); secondly, by taking diplomatic action.[39]

In 1973, Israeli jets shot down a Libyan airliner straying several score miles into Israeli-occupied Sinai. It was alleged that the airliner had been warned to land but had refused to comply with the order. After an investigation the Council of ICAO condemned Israel's action and declared that 'such actions constitute a serious danger against the safety of international civil aviation'. Israel's attitude was criticised as a 'flagrant violation of the principles enshrined in the Chicago Convention'.[40]

On 1 September 1983, Soviet jets shot down a Korean Airlines airplane which had strayed several hundred miles into sensitive Soviet airspace causing the deaths of 269 persons.[41] A week later, the USSR vetoed a draft Security Council resolution which reaffirmed the rules of international law prohibiting acts of violence against the safety of international civil aviation.[42] The Council of ICAO directed on 16 September that an investigation be held and that the Air Navigation Commission should review the Chicago Convention and related documents to prevent a recurrence of such a tragic incident and to seek to improve methods of communication between civil and military aircraft and air traffic control services.[43]

After the submission of the report,[44] the Council of ICAO adopted a

---

'The Shooting Down of Korean Airlines Flight 007 By the USSR and the Furtherance of Air Safety for Passengers', 33 ICLQ 1984, p. 712 and J. Dutheil de la Rochère, 'L'Affaire de l'Accident du Boeing 747 de Korean Airlines', AFDI, 1983, p. 749. See also Matte, *Treatise*, pp. 175–7 and *Cumulative* DUSPIL *1981–8*, vol. II, Washington, 1994, pp. 2167 *et seq.* [38] The *Nicaragua v. US* case, ICJ Reports, 1986, pp, 3, 128; 76 ILR, pp. 349, 462.

[39] *Aerial Incident* case, ICJ Reports, 1959, pp. 127, 130; 27 ILR, p. 557.

[40] 12 ILM, 1973, p. 1180. Israel apologised for the incident and paid compensation to the victims. See also DUSPIL, 1973, pp. 312–13. As to the Chicago Convention, see *supra*, p. 370.

[41] See the Report of the Secretary-General of ICAO, 23 ILM, 1984, p. 864. See also 88 ILR, p. 55 and *Cumulative* DUSPIL *1981–8*, vol. II, Washington, 1994, pp. 2199 *et seq.*

[42] 22 ILM, 1983, p. 1148.

[43] See M. N. Leich, 'Destruction of Korean Airliner: Action by International Organisations', 78 AJIL, 1984, pp. 244–5.   [44] 23 ILM, 1984, p. 864.

resolution condemning the shooting down of the Korean airliner.[45] In addition, an amendment to the Chicago Convention was adopted.[46] This amendment was to article 3 of the Convention, which had laid down as one of its general principles that contracting states undertook to have due regard for the safety of navigation of civil aircraft. In addition to the general provision in article 3, Annex II to the Convention had provided for detailed procedures to be followed in cases of interception, procedures which were apparently not complied with in the case of the Korean Airlines tragedy.[47] Annex II also provided that 'intercepting aircraft should refrain from the use of weapons in all cases of interception of civil aircraft'. Despite this provision and ICAO Council action in 1973 regarding Israel's attack on a Libyan airliner over Sinai, the need was felt to strengthen the general principle in article 3 itself in order to add greater force to the concern felt. New article 3 *bis* provides that:

> (a) The contracting states recognise that every state must refrain from resorting to the use of weapons against the civil aircraft in flight, and that in case of interception, the lives of persons on board and the safety of aircraft must not be endangered. This provision shall not be interpreted as modifying in any way the rights and obligations of states set forth in the Charter of the United Nations.

The right of states to require a civil aircraft to land at a designated airport, where the aircraft is flying above its territory without authority or where there are reasonable grounds to conclude that it is being used for any purpose inconsistent with the Convention, was reaffirmed in subsection (b). There are several points that may be made with regard to the amendment. First, it is to be noted that reference is made to 'weapons' not force in the prohibition provision. Presumably this means that force may be used against civil aircraft in flight in pursuance of an interception, provided that weapons are not actually fired. Second, the wording appears to suggest that national as well as foreign civil aircraft fall within the scope of the provision, but the restriction to aircraft 'in flight' leads one to assume that the need to distinguish this kind of situation from the recapture of hijacked aircraft on the ground was felt. Finally, the provision in subsection (b) stipulating when states may require aircraft to land appears to be more restrictive than article 4 of the 1963 Tokyo Convention on Offences and Certain Other Acts

---

[45] *Ibid.*, p. 937. Note also that an ICAO investigation in June 1993 concluded that the evidence obtained supported the first hypothesis listed in the 1983 Report, i.e. that the flight crew had mistakenly flown on a constant magnetic heading because it had not been realised that the autopilot had been left in use. It was also concluded that the USSR Command Centre had assumed that the aircraft was a US RC-135 aircraft, see 33 ILM, 1994, p. 310.

[46] *Ibid.*, p. 705. This amendment, the Montreal Protocol 1984, required ratification by two-thirds of the ICAO membership before coming into force.

[47] *Ibid.*, p. 864 and de la Rochère, 'L'accident du Boeing 747'.

Committed on Board Aircraft, which permits interference in five defined situations, i.e. where:

(a) the offence has effect on the territory of such state;
(b) the offence has been committed by or against a national or permanent resident of such state;
(c) the offence is against the security of such state;
(d) the offence consists of a breach of any rules or regulations relating to the flight or manoeuvre of aircraft in force in such state;
(e) the exercise of jurisdiction is necessary to ensure the observance of any obligation of such state under a multilateral international agreement.

Article 82 of the Chicago Convention provides for the abrogation of all inconsistent obligations and understandings among ICAO members and it is a moot point whether this means that article 3 *bis* (when in force) would override the Tokyo provisions,[48] although it should be noted that the Tokyo Convention deals only with offences committed on board the aircraft.

Under article 25 of the Chicago Convention, an aircraft in distress is to be given necessary assistance, but this relies upon the fact of distress being evident or made known to the intercepting forces. In such a situation resort to the use of force would be illegal.

It is also clear that the doctrine of self-defence may be of relevance in certain situations, for example, if the intruding aircraft was clearly involved in an act of aggression or terrorism. The intercepting forces may have to take action, within the parameters of proportionality,[49] to forestall that threat and force may be necessary. However, a civilian airliner is unlikely to pose this level of threat justifying a shooting down. It appears that the USSR believed that the airliner was an American spy plane.[50] Even if that were true or if the belief were genuine, it would seem that the actions taken to require it to land were inadequate and the course actively embarked upon beyond the bounds of proportionality.

The general issue was again raised by the shooting down by the USS warship *Vincennes* in July 1988 of an Iranian civil airliner over the Persian Gulf, although it should be noted in this case that there was, of course, no unauthorised aerial intrusion into domestic airspace.[51] Both the US Defence Department and the ICAO reports into the incident in essence

---

[48] See e.g. B. Cheng, 'The Destruction of KAL Flight KE007, and Article 3 *bis* of the Chicago Convention' in *Air Worthy* (eds. Van Gravesande and Van der Veen Vonk), 1985, p. 49.
[49] As to self-defence and proportionality, see *infra*, Chapter 19.
[50] See 22 ILM, 1983, pp. 1126–8 and *supra*, footnote 45.
[51] See e.g. *Keesing's Record of World Events*, pp. 36064, 36169, 36631 and 37423, and 'Agora: The Downing of Iran Air Flight 655', 83 AJIL, 1989, p. 318. See also 28 ILM, 1989, p. 896.

placed the blame for the incident upon the warship.[52] Mistakes made as to the identification of the aircraft and with regard to the warnings issued to it combined with the tense atmosphere in that region during the Iran-Iraq war to create the disaster. Suggestions have been made that the US should not be regarded as legally responsible, since proof of fault beyond reasonable doubt has yet to be established and the fact that the incident took place in a war zone is of the utmost relevance in assessing this.[53] However, it is undisputed that the airliner was shot down by a US warship and this is certainly contrary to article 3 *bis*, which could well now be regarded as a principle of customary law. While self-defence may well have been an initial consideration, its application is circumscribed by the principles of necessity and proportionality. The incident came before the International Court of Justice upon Iran's application on 17 May 1989, but was removed from the Court's list upon notification of a full and final settlement between the US and Iran.[54]

Following the Iraqi invasion of Kuwait on 2 August 1990, the Security Council adopted a series of resolutions. Resolution 670 (1990) declared that permission to any aircraft to take off should be denied by all states from their territory where the aircraft was carrying any cargo to or from Iraq or Kuwait other than food in humanitarian circumstances or supplies strictly for medical purposes or solely for the UN Iran-Iraq Military Observer Group. All states were called upon to deny permission to overfly their territory to any aircraft destined to land in Iraq or Kuwait, unless it had been inspected to ensure it had no cargo on board which was in violation of Security Council resolution 661 (1990) establishing sanctions against Iraq, or unless the particular flight had been approved by the Sanctions Committee or had been certified by the UN as being solely for the purposes of the Military Observer Group. The Council would consider measures directed at states which evaded these provisions. However, this would not permit the shooting down of civilian airliners suspected of breaking the UN sanctions against Iraq.

The situation is different with regard to military aircraft intruding without authorisation into foreign airspace. The self-defence argument may be stronger and the burden of proof thus lower, but it is questionable whether the need for a prior warning has been dispensed with.[55]

---

[52] *Keesing's Record of World Events*, and 83 AJIL, 1989, p. 332. See also Security Council resolution 616 (1988).

[53] See e.g. H. Maier, 'Ex Gratia Payments and the Iranian Airline Tragedy', 83 AJIL, 1989, p. 325.   [54] See Court's Order of 22 February 1996.

[55] See e.g. O. Lissitzyn, Editorial Comment, 56 AJIL, 1962, pp. 135, 138. See further *infra*, Chapter 19.

The law of outer space[56]

The fundamental principle of air law relates to the complete sovereignty of the subjacent state. This is qualified by the various multilateral and bilateral conventions which permit airlines to cross and land in the territories of the contracting states under recognised conditions and in the light of the accepted regulations. But there is also another qualification and one that substantially modifies the *usque ad coelum* concept, whereby sovereignty extended over the airspace to an unlimited height. This centres upon the creation and development of the law of outer space.

Ever since the USSR launched the first earth satellite in 1957, the pace of space exploration has developed at an ever-increasing rate. Satellites now control communications and observation networks, while landings have been made on the moon and information-seeking space probes dispatched to survey planets like Venus and Saturn. The amount of new knowledge obtained and collated by the various American, Soviet and European programmes has been vast and has demonstrated man's capacity to embark upon the discovery of his space environment.

The research material gathered upon such diverse matters as earth resources, ionospheric activities, solar radiation, cosmic rays and the general structure of space and planet formations has stimulated further efforts to understand the nature of space and the cosmos.[57]

This immense increase in available information has also led to the development of the law of outer space, formulating generally accepted principles to regulate the interests of the various states involved as well as taking into account the concern of the international community as a whole.

---

[56] See e.g. C. Q. Christol, *Space Law*, Deventer, 1991; J. E. S. Fawcett, *Outer Space*, Oxford, 1984; D. Goedhuis, 'The Present State of Space Law' in *The Present State of International Law* (ed. Bos), London, 1973, p. 201; S. Gorove, 'International Space Law in Perspective', 181 HR, p. 349; Gorove, *Developments in Space Law*, Dordrecht, 1991; M. Marcoff, *Traité de Droit International Public de l'Espace*, Fribourg, 1973; Marcoff, 'Sources du Droit International de l'Espace', 168 HR, p. 9; N. Matte, *Aerospace Law*, 1969; *Le Droit de l'Espace* (ed. J. Dutheil de la Rochère), Paris, 1988; P. M. Martin, *Droit International des Activités Spatiales*, Masson, 1992; B. Cheng, 'The 1967 Space Treaty', *Journal de Droit International*, 1968, p. 532; Cheng, 'The Moon Treaty', 33 *Current Legal Problems*, 1980, p. 213; Cheng, 'The Legal Status of Outer Space', *Journal of Space Law*, 1983, p. 89 and Cheng, 'The UN and the Development of International Law Relating to Outer Space', 16 *Thesaurus Acroasium*, 1990, Thessaloniki, p. 49. See also *Oppenheim's International Law*, Chapter 7; R. G. Steinhardt, 'Outer Space' in *United Nations Legal Order* (eds. O. Schachter and C. C. Joyner), Cambridge, 1995, vol. II, p. 753; *Manual on Space Law* (eds. N. Jasentulajana and R. Lee), 4 vols., New York, 1979 and *Space Law – Basic Documents* (eds. K. H. Böckstiegel and M. Berkö), Dordrecht, 1991. Note in particular the role of the UN Committee on the Peaceful Uses of Outer Space, established in 1958 and now consisting of representatives of fifty-three states. The Committee has a Legal Sub-Committee and a Scientific and Technical Sub-Committee, see in particular C. Q. Christol, *The Modern International Law of Outer Space*, 1982, New York, pp. 13–20.

[57] See e.g. Fawcett, *Outer Space*, Chapter 7.

The definition and delimitation of outer space

It soon became apparent that the *usque ad coelum* rule, providing for state sovereignty over territorial airspace to an unrestricted extent, was not viable where space exploration was concerned. To obtain the individual consents of countries to the passage of satellites and other vehicles orbiting more than one hundred miles above their surface would prove cumbersome in the extreme and in practice states have acquiesced in such traversing. This means that the sovereignty of states over their airspace is limited in height at most to the point where the airspace meets space itself. Precisely where this boundary lies is difficult to say and will depend upon technological and other factors, but figures between fifty and one hundred miles have been put forward.

As conventional aircraft are developed to attain greater heights, so states will wish to see their sovereignty extend to those heights and, as well as genuine uncertainty, this fear of surrendering what may prove to be in the future valuable sovereign rights has prevented any agreement on the delimitation of this particular frontier.[58]

The regime of outer space

Beyond the point separating air from space, states have agreed to apply the international law principles of *res communis*, so that no portion of outer space may be appropriated to the sovereignty of individual states.

This was made clear in a number of General Assembly resolutions following the advent of the satellite era in the late 1950s. For instance, UN General Assembly resolution 1962 (XVII) adopted in 1963 lays down a series of applicable legal principles which include the provisions that outer space and celestial bodies were free for exploration and use by all states on a basis of equality and in accordance with international law, and that outer space and celestial bodies were not subject to national appropriation by any means.[59] Such resolutions constituted in the circumstances expressions of state practice and *opinio juris* and thus part of customary law.[60]

---

[58] See generally Christol, *Modern International Law*, Chapter 10 and see also e.g. UKMIL, 64 BYIL, 1993, p. 689. A variety of suggestions have been put forward regarding the method of delimitation, ranging from the properties of the atmosphere to the lowest possible orbit of satellites. They appear to fall within either a spatial or functional category, see *ibid.*, and UN Doc. A/AC.105/C.2/7/Add.1, 21 January 1977. Some states have argued for a 110 km. boundary, see e.g. USSR, 21(4) *UN Chronicle*, 1984, p. 37; others feel it is premature to establish such a fixed delimitation, e.g. USA and UK, *ibid.* See also 216 HL Deb., 1958–9, col. 975, and D. Goedhuis, 'The Problems of the Frontiers of Outer Space and Airspace', 174 HR, p. 367.

[59] See also General Assembly resolutions 1721(XVI) and 1884(XVIII).

[60] See *supra*, Chapter 3, and B. Cheng, 'United Nations Resolutions on Outer Space: "Instant" International Customary Law?', 5 *Indian Journal of International Law*, 1965, p. 23.

The legal regime of outer space was clarified by the signature in 1967 of the Treaty on Principles Governing the Activities of States in the Exploration and Use of Outer Space, including the Moon and Other Celestial Bodies. This reiterates that outer space, including the moon and other celestial bodies, is not subject to national appropriation by any means and emphasises that the exploration and use of outer space must be carried out for the benefit of all countries. The Treaty does not provide a precise boundary between airspace and outer space but it provides the framework for the international law of outer space.[61]

Article IV provides that states parties to the Treaty agree:

> not to place in orbit around the earth any objects carrying nuclear weapons or any other kinds of weapons of mass destruction, install such weapons on celestial bodies, or station such weapons in outer space in any other manner.

There are, however, disagreements as to the meaning of this provision.[62] The article bans only nuclear weapons and weapons of mass destruction from outer space, the celestial bodies and from orbit around the earth, but article I does emphasise that the exploration and use of outer space 'shall be carried out for the benefit and in the interests of all countries' and it has been argued that this can be interpreted to mean that any military activity in space contravenes the treaty.[63]

Under article IV, only the moon and other celestial bodies must be used exclusively for peaceful purposes, although the use of military personnel for scientific and other peaceful purposes is not prohibited. There are minimalist and maximalist interpretations as to how these provisions are to be understood. The former, for example, would argue that only aggressive military activity is banned, while the latter would prohibit all military behaviour.[64]

Under article VIII, states retain jurisdiction and control over personnel and vehicles launched by them into space and under article VII they remain responsible for any damage caused to other parties to the Treaty by their space objects.

This aspect of space law was further developed by the Convention on International Liability for Damage Caused by Space Objects signed in

---

[61] See e.g. Christol, *Modern International Law*, Chapter 2. See also *Oppenheim's International Law*, p. 828 and Nguyen Quoc Dinh et al., *Droit International Public*, pp. 1160 *et seq.*

[62] The issue became particularly controversial in the light of the US Strategic Defence Initiative, ('Star Wars'), which aimed to develop a range of anti-satellite and anti-missile weapons based in space. The UN Committee on the Peaceful Uses of Outer Space considered the issue, although without the participation of the US, which objected to the matter being considered, see e.g. 21(6) *UN Chronicle*, 1984, p. 18.

[63] See e.g. Marcoff, *Traité*, 1973, pp. 361 *et seq.*

[64] See e.g. Christol, *Modern International Law*, pp. 25–6. See also Goedhuis, 'Legal Issues Involved in the Potential Military Uses of Space Stations' in *Liber Amicorum for Rt Hon Richard Wilberforce* (eds. Bos and Brownlie), Oxford, 1987, p. 23 and Gorove, *Developments*, Part VI.

1972, article XII of which provides for the payment of compensation in accordance with international law and the principles of justice and equity for any damage caused by space objects. Article II provides for absolute liability to pay such compensation for damage caused by a space object on the surface of the earth or to aircraft in flight, whereas article III provides for fault liability for damage caused elsewhere or to persons or property on board a space object.[65] This Convention was invoked by Canada in 1979 following the damage allegedly caused by Soviet Cosmos 954.[66] As a reinforcement to this evolving system of state responsibility, the Convention on the Registration of Objects Launched into Outer Space was adopted by the General Assembly in 1974 and opened for signature the following year, coming into force in 1976. This laid down a series of stipulations for the registration of information regarding space objects, such as, for example, their purpose, location and parameters, with the United Nations Secretary-General.[67] In 1993, the UN General Assembly adopted Principles Relevant to the Use of Nuclear Power Sources in Outer Space.[68] Under these Principles, the launching state is, prior to the launch, to ensure that a thorough and comprehensive safety assessment is conducted and made publicly available. Where a space object appears to malfunction with a risk of re-entry of radioactive materials to the earth, the launching state is to inform states concerned and the UN Secretary-General and respond promptly to requests for further information or consultations sought by other states. Principle 8 provides that states shall bear international responsibility for national activities involving the use of nuclear power sources in outer space, whether such activities are carried out by governmental agencies or by non-governmental agencies. Principle 9 provides that each state which launches or procures the launching of a space object and each state from whose territory or facility a space object is launched

---

[65] See e.g. the Exchange of Notes between the UK and Chinese governments with regard to liability for damages arising during the launch phase of the Asiasat Satellite in 1990 in accordance with *inter alia* the 1967 and 1972 conventions, UKMIL, 64 BYIL, 1993, p. 689.

[66] The claim was for $6,401,174.70. See 18 ILM, 1979, pp. 899 *et seq*. See also Christol, *Modern International Law*, pp. 59 *et seq* and *ibid.*, 'International Liability for Damage Caused by Space Objects', 74 AJIL, 1980, p. 346. Note also that under article 3 of the 1967 Treaty, all states parties to the Treaty agree to carry on activities 'in accordance with international law', which clearly includes rules relating to state responsibility. See also Gorove, *Developments*, Part V and B. Hurwitz, *State Liability for Outer Space Activities in Accordance with the 1972 Convention on International Liability for Damage Caused by Space Objects*, Dordrecht, 1992.

[67] The International Law Association adopted in 1994 the 'Buenos Aires International Instrument on the Protection of the Environment from Damage Caused by Space Debris'. This provides that each state or international organisation party to the Instrument that launches or procures the launching of a space object is internationally liable for damage arising therefrom to another state, persons or objects, or international organisation party to the Instrument as a consequence of space debris produced by any such object, see *Report of the 66th Conference at Buenos Aires*, 1994, London, p. 7.   [68] Resolution 47/68.

shall be internationally liable for damage caused by such space object or their component parts.

The Agreement on the Rescue of Astronauts, the Return of Astronauts and the Return of Objects Launched into Outer Space was signed in 1968 and this sets out the legal framework for the provision of emergency assistance to astronauts. It provides for immediate notification of the launching authority or, if that is not immediately possible, a public announcement regarding space personnel in distress as well as the immediate provision of assistance. It also covers search and rescue operations as well as a guarantee of prompt return. The Convention also provides for recovery of space objects.[69]

In 1979, the Agreement Governing the Activities of States on the Moon and other Celestial Bodies was adopted.[70] This provides for the demilitarisation of the moon and other celestial bodies, although military personnel may be used for peaceful purposes and reiterates the principle established in the 1967 Outer Space Treaty. Under article IV, the exploration and the use of the moon shall be the province of all mankind and should be carried out for the benefit of all. Article XI emphasises that the moon and its natural resources are the common heritage of mankind and are not subject to national appropriation by any means. That important article emphasises that no private rights of ownership over the moon or any part of it or its natural resources in place may be created, although all states parties have the right to exploration and use of the moon. The states parties also agreed under article XI (5) and (7) to establish an international regime to govern the exploitation of the resources of the moon, when this becomes feasible.[71]

---

[69] The UK Outer Space Act 1986, for example, provides a framework for private sector space enterprises by creating a licensing system for outer space activities and by establishing a system for indemnification for damage suffered by third parties or elsewhere. The Act also establishes a statutory register of the launch of space objects. Note also that the US has signed a number of agreements with other states providing for assistance abroad in the event of an emergency landing of the Space Shuttle. These agreements also provide for US liability to compensate for damage and loss caused as a result of an emergency landing, in accordance with the 1972 treaty, see *Cumulative DUSPIL 1981–8*, vol. II, Washington, 1994, p. 2269. In 1988 an Agreement on Space Stations was signed between the US, the governments of the member states of the European Space Agency, Japan and Canada. This provides *inter alia* for registration of flight elements as space objects under the Registration Convention of 1975, each state retaining jurisdiction over the elements it so registers and personnel in or on the Space Station who are its nationals. There is also an interesting provision (article 22) permitting the US to exercise criminal jurisdiction over misconduct committed by a non-US national in or on a non-US element of the manned base or attached to the manned base, which endangers the safety of the manned base or the crew members thereon. Before proceeding to trial with such a prosecution, the US shall consult with the partner state whose nationality the alleged perpetrator holds, and shall either have received the agreement of that partner to the prosecution or failed to have received an assurance that the partner state intends to prosecute.

[70] This came into force in July 1984, see C. Q. Christol, 'The Moon Treaty Enters into Force', 79 AJIL, 1985, p. 163.

[71] See e.g. Cheng, 'The Moon Treaty', pp. 231–2, and Christol, *Modern International Law*, Chapters 7 and 8.

The main purposes of the international regime to be established are to include:

(a) The orderly and safe development of the natural resources of the moon;
(b) The rational management of those resources;
(c) The expansion of opportunities in the use of those resources; and
(d) An equitable sharing by all states parties in the benefits derived from those resources, whereby the interests and need of the developing countries, as well as the efforts of those countries which have contributed either directly or indirectly to the exploration of the moon, shall be given special consideration.

Several points are worth noting. First, the proposed international regime is only to be established when exploitation becomes feasible. Second, it appears that until the regime is set up, there is a moratorium on exploitation, although not on 'exploration and use', as recognised by articles XI(4) and VI(2). This would permit the collection of samples and their removal from the moon for scientific purposes. Thirdly, it is to be noted that private ownership rights of minerals or natural resources not in place are permissible under the Treaty.[72]

Telecommunications[73]

Arguably the most useful application of space exploitation techniques has been the creation of telecommunications networks. This has revolutionised communications and has an enormous educational as well as entertainment potential.[74]

The legal framework for the use of space in the field of telecommunications is provided by the various INTELSAT (international telecommunications satellites) agreements which enable the member states of the International Telecommunications Union to help develop and establish the system, although much of the work is in fact carried out by American corporations, particularly COMSAT. In 1971 the communist countries established their own network of telecommunications satellites, called INTER-SPUTNIK. The international regime for the exploitation of the orbit/spectrum resource[75] has built upon the 1967 Treaty, the 1973

---

[72] See infra, Chapter 11, p. 445, regarding the 'common heritage' regime envisaged for the deep seabed under the 1982 Convention on the Law of the Sea.
[73] See e.g. A. Matteesco-Matté, Les Télécommunications par Satellites, Paris, 1982; M. L. Smith, International Regulation of Satellite Communications, Dordrecht, 1990 and J. M. Smits, Legal Aspects of Implementing International Telecommunications Links, Dordrecht, 1992.
[74] See e.g. the use by India of US satellites to beam educational television programmes to many thousands of isolated settlements that would otherwise not have been reached, DUSPIL, 1976, pp. 427–8.   [75] See Christol, Space Law, Chapter 11.

Telecommunications Convention and Protocol and various International Telecommunication Union Radio Regulations. Regulation of the radio spectrum is undertaken at the World Administrative Radio Conferences and by the principal organs of the ITU.

However, there are a number of problems associated with these ventures ranging from the allocation of radio wave frequencies to the dangers inherent in direct broadcasting via satellites to willing and unwilling states alike. Questions such as the control of material broadcast by such satellites and the protection of minority cultures from 'swamping' have yet to be answered, but are being discussed in various UN organs, for instance UNESCO and the Committee on the Peaceful Uses of Outer Space.[76]

Two principles are relevant in this context: freedom of information, which is a right enshrined in many international instruments,[77] and state sovereignty. A number of attempts have been made to reconcile the two.

In 1972, UNESCO adopted a Declaration of Guiding Principles on the Use of Satellite Broadcasting, in which it was provided that all states had the right to decide on the content of educational programmes broadcast to their own peoples, while article IX declared that prior agreement was required for direct satellite broadcasting to the population of countries other than the country of origin of the transmission. Within the UN support for the consent principle was clear, but there were calls for a proper regulatory regime, in addition.[78]

In 1983, the General Assembly adopted resolution 37/92 entitled 'Principles Governing the Use by States of Artificial Earth Satellites for International Direct Television Broadcasting'. This provides that a state intending to establish or authorise the establishment of a direct television broadcasting satellite service must first notify the proposed receiving state or states and then consult with them. A service may only be established after this and on the basis of agreements and/or arrangements in conformity with the relevant instruments of the International Telecommunications Union. However, the value of these principles is significantly reduced in the light of the fact that nearly all the western states voted against the resolution.[79]

ITU regulations call for technical coordination between the sending and receiving states as to frequency and orbital positioning before any direct

---

[76] See Christol, *Modern International Law*, footnote 49, Chapter 12 and N. Matte, 'Aerospace Law: Telecommunications Satellites', 166 HR, p. 119. See also the study requested by the 1982 Conference, A/AC.107/341 and the European Convention on Transfrontier Television 1988 and EEC Directive 89/552 on the Pursuit of Television Broadcasting Activities. See also Gorove, *Developments*, Part II, Chapter 5.

[77] See e.g. article 19, International Covenant on Civil and Political Rights, 1966; article 10, Universal Declaration on Human Rights, 1948 and article 10, European Convention on Human Rights, 1950.

[78] See e.g. *Space Activities and Emerging International Law*, p. 438. See also A/8771 (1972).

[79] These included France, West Germany, the UK, US and Japan.

broadcasting by satellite can be carried out and thus do not affect regulation of the conduct of the broadcast activity as such, although the two elements are clearly connected.[80] The question of remote sensing has also been under consideration for many years by several bodies, including the UN Committee on the Peaceful Uses of Outer Space. Remote sensing refers to the detection and analysis of the earth's resources by sensors carried in aircraft and spacecraft and covers, for example, meteorological sensing, ocean observation, military surveillance and land observation. It clearly has tremendous potential, but the question of the uses of the information received is highly controversial.[81] In 1986, the General Assembly adopted fifteen principles relating to remote sensing.[82] These range from the statement that such activity is to be carried out for the benefit and in the interests of all countries, taking into particular account the needs of developing countries, to the provision that sensing states should promote international co-operation and environmental protection on earth. There is, however, no requirement of prior consent from states that are being sensed,[83] although there consultations in order to enhance participation are called for. One key issue relates to control over the dissemination of information gathered by satellite. Some have called for the creation of an equitable regime for the sharing of information[84] and there is concern over the question of access to data about states by those, and other states. The USSR and France, for example, jointly proposed the concept of the inalienable right of states to dispose of their natural resources and of information concerning those resources,[85] while the US in particular points to the practical problems this would cause and the possible infringement of freedom of information. The UN Committee on the Peaceful Uses of Outer Space has been considering the problem for many years and general agreement has proved elusive.[86] The Principles on Remote Sensing provide that the sensed state shall have access to the primary and processed data produced upon a non-discriminatory basis and on reasonable cost terms. States conducting such remote sensing are to bear international responsibility for their activities.

[80] See *Space Activities and Emerging International Law*, pp. 453 *et seq*. See also Chapman and Warren, 'Direct Broadcasting Satellites: The ITU, UN and the Real World', 4 *Annals of Air and Space Law*, 1979, p. 413.
[81] See e.g. Christol, *Modern International Law*, Chapter 13 and 21(4) *UN Chronicle*, 1984, p. 32. See also the Study on Remote Sensing, A/AC.105/339 and Add.1, 1985 and Gorove, *Developments*, Part VII.   [82] General Assembly resolution 41/65.
[83] Note that the 1967 Outer Space Treaty provides for freedom of exploration and use, although arguments based *inter alia* on permanent sovereignty over natural resources and exclusive sovereignty over airspace have been put forward, see e.g. A/AC.105/171, Annex IV (1976) and A/AC.105/C.2/SR.220 (1984).
[84] See e.g. Gotlieb, 'The Impact of Technology on the Development of Contemporary International Law', 170 HR, p. 115.   [85] A/AC.105/C.2/L.99 (1974).
[86] See e.g. A/AC.105/320, Annex IV (1983).

The increase in the use of satellites for all of the above purposes has put pressure upon the geostationary orbit. This is the orbit 22, 300 miles directly above the equator, where satellites circle at the same speed as the earth rotates. It is the only orbit capable of providing continuous contact with ground stations via a single satellite. The orbit is thus a finite resource.[87] However, in 1976, Brazil, Colombia, the Congo, Ecuador, Indonesia, Kenya, Uganda and Zaire signed the Bogotá Declaration under which they stated that 'the segments of geostationary synchronous orbit are part of the territory over which equatorial states exercise their sovereignty'.[88]

Other states have vigorously protested against this and it therefore cannot be taken as other than an assertion and a bargaining counter.[89] Nevertheless, the increase in satellite launches and the limited nature of the geostationary orbit facility calls for urgent action to produce an acceptable series of principles governing its use.

---

[87] See e.g. article 33 of the 1973 International Telecommunications Convention and Christol, *Modern International Law*, pp. 451 *et seq.* See also the Study on the Feasibility of Closer Spacing of Satellites in the Geostationary Orbit, A/AC.105/340 (1985) and A/AC105/404 (1988). See also Gorove, *Developments*, Part II, Chapters 3 and 4.

[88] *Ibid.*, pp. 891–5. See also ITU Doc. WARC-155 (1977) 81–E.

[89] See e.g. DUSPIL, 1979, pp. 1187–8.

CHAPTER 11

THE LAW OF THE SEA

The seas have historically performed two important functions: first, as a medium of communication, and secondly as a vast reservoir of resources, both living and non-living. Both of these functions have stimulated the development of legal rules.[1]

The seas were at one time thought capable of subjection to national sovereignties. The Portuguese in particular in the seventeenth century proclaimed huge tracts of the high seas as part of their territorial domain, but these claims stimulated a response by Grotius who elaborated the doctrine of the open seas, whereby the oceans as *res communis* were to be accessible to all nations but incapable of appropriation.[2] This view prevailed, partly because it accorded with the interests of the North European states, which demanded freedom of the seas for the purposes of exploration and expanding commercial intercourse with the East.

The freedom of the high seas rapidly became a basic principle of international law, but not all the seas were so characterised. It was permissible for a coastal state to appropriate a maritime belt around its coastline as territorial waters, or territorial sea, and treat it as an indivisible part of its domain. Much of the history of the law of the sea has centred on the extent of the

---

[1] See e.g. E. D. Brown, *The International Law of the Sea*, 2 vols., Aldershot, 1994; M. Rémond-Gouilloud, *Droit Maritime*, Paris, 1993; *Oppenheim's International Law* (eds. R. Y. Jennings and A. D. Watts), 9th edn, London, 1992, Chapter 6; Nguyen Quoc Dinh, P. Daillier and A. Pellet, *Droit International Public*, 5th edn, Paris, 1994, p. 1041; P. Allott, 'Mare Nostrum: A New International Law of the Sea', 86 AJIL, 1992, p. 764; T. Treves, 'Codification du Droit International et Pratique des États dans le Droit de la Mer', 223 HR, 1990 IV, p. 9; R. R. Churchill and A. V. Lowe, *The Law of the Sea*, 2nd edn, Manchester, 1988; R. J. Dupuy and D. Vignes, *Traité du Nouveau Droit de la Mer*, Brussels, 1985; *Le Nouveau Droit International de la Mer* (eds. D. Bardonnet and M. Virally), Paris, 1983; D. P. O'Connell, *The International Law of the Sea*, 2 vols., Oxford, 1982–4; C. J. Colombos, *The International Law of the Sea*, 6th edn, London, 1967; M. S. McDougal and W. T. Burke, *The Public Order of the Oceans*, New Haven, 1962; *New Directions in the Law of the Sea*, Dobbs Ferry, vols. I–VI, (eds. Churchill, Nordquist and Lay), 1973–7; *ibid.*, vols. 7–11 (eds. Nordquist and Simmons), 1980–1 and S. Oda, *The Law of the Sea in Our Time*, 2 vols., Leiden, 1977. See also the series *Limits in the Seas*, published by the Geographer of the US State Department.

[2] *Mare Liberum*, 1609. See also O'Connell, *International Law*, vol. I, pp. 9 *et seq.* The closed seas approach was put by e.g. J. Selden, *Mare Clausum*, 1635.

territorial sea or the precise location of the dividing line between it and the high seas and other recognised zones.

The original stipulation linked the width of the territorial sea to the ability of the coastal state to dominate it by military means from the confines of its own shore. But the present century has witnessed continual pressure by states to enlarge the maritime belt and thus subject more of the oceans to their exclusive jurisdiction.

Beyond the territorial sea, other jurisdictional zones have been in process of development. Coastal states may now exercise particular jurisdictional functions in the contiguous zone, and the trend of international law today is moving rapidly in favour of even larger zones in which the coastal state may enjoy certain rights to the exclusion of other nations, such as fishery zones and more recently exclusive economic zones.

This gradual shift in the law of the sea towards the enlargement of the territorial sea (the accepted limit is now a width of 12 miles in contrast to 3 miles some thirty years ago), coupled with the continual assertion of jurisdictional rights over portions of what were regarded as high seas, reflects a basic change in emphasis in the attitude of states to the sea.

The predominance of the concept of the freedom of the high seas has been modified by the realisation of resources present in the seas and seabed beyond the territorial seas. Parallel with the developing tendency to assert ever greater claims over the high seas, however, has been the move towards proclaiming a 'common heritage of mankind' regime over the seabed of the high seas. The law relating to the seas, therefore, has been in a state of flux for several decades as the conflicting principles have manifested themselves.

A series of conferences have been held, which led to the four 1958 Conventions on the Law of the Sea and then to the 1982 Convention on the Law of the Sea.[3] The 1958 Convention on the High Seas was stated in its Preamble to be 'generally declaratory of established principles of international law', while the other three 1958 instruments can be generally accepted as containing both reiterations of existing rules and new rules.

The pressures leading to the Law of the Sea Conference, that lasted between 1974 and 1982 and involved a very wide range of states and international organisations, included a variety of economic, political and strategic factors. Many Third World states wished to develop the exclusive economic zone idea, by which coastal states would have extensive rights over a 200 mile zone beyond the territorial sea, and were keen to establish international control over the deep seabed, so as to prevent the technologically

---

[3] The 1958 Convention on the Territorial Sea and the Contiguous Zone came into force in 1964; the 1958 Convention on the High Seas came into force in 1962; the 1958 Convention on Fishing and Conservation of Living Resources came into force in 1966 and the 1958 Convention on the Continental Shelf came into force in 1964.

advanced states from being able to extract minerals from this vital and vast source freely and without political constraint. Western states were desirous of protecting their navigation routes by opposing any weakening of the freedom of passage through international straits particularly, and wished to protect their economic interests through free exploitation of the resources of the high seas and the deep seabed.

It was soon recognised that this Conference would be a highly political one. Unlike many other such conferences, such as the 1958 and 1960 conferences, for example, this one did not operate on the basis of a pre-existing report or other established document, and the question was dealt with in the United Nations framework via the First (Political and Security) Committee rather than the Sixth (Legal) Committee.[4]

Within the Conference itself, a variety of coalitions or groupings of states attending manifested themselves. The 'Group of 77', consisting of well over 100 developing states, and the Western and communist groups were particular examples. In addition, alliances of states with especial interests were very much in evidence. Examples here would include the land-locked and geographically disadvantaged states, archipelagic states and coastal states. The effect of this kaleidoscopic range of interests was very marked and led on to the 'package deal' concept of the final draft. According to this approach, for example, the Third World accepted passage through straits and enhanced continental shelf rights beyond the 200 mile limit from the coasts in return for the internationalisation of deep sea mining.[5]

The 1982 Convention contains 320 articles and 9 Annexes. It was adopted by 130 votes to 4, with 17 abstentions. The Convention entered into force on 16 November 1994, 12 months after the required 60 ratifications. In order primarily to meet Western concerns with regard to the International Seabed Area (Part XI of the Convention), an Agreement relating to the Implementation of Part XI of the 1982 Convention was adopted on 29 July 1994.[6]

Many of the provisions in the 1982 Convention repeat principles enshrined in the earlier instruments and others have since become customary rules, but many new rules were proposed. Accordingly, a complicated series of relationships between the various states exists in this field, based on customary rules and treaty rules.[7] All states are *prima facie* bound by the accepted customary rules, while only the parties to the five treaties involved

[4] See Churchill and Lowe, *Law of the Sea*, p. 14.
[5] See, e.g. H. Caminos and M. R. Molitor, 'Progressive Development of International Law and the Package Deal', 79 AJIL, 1985, p. 871.   [6] See further *infra*, p. 448.
[7] See the *North Sea Continental Shelf* cases, ICJ Reports, 1969, pp. 3, 39; 41 ILR, pp. 29, 68; the *Fisheries Jurisdiction (UK v. Iceland)* case, ICJ Reports, 1974, p. 1; 55 ILR, p. 238 and the *Anglo-French Continental Shelf* case, Cmnd. 7438, 1978; 54 ILR, p. 6. See also *supra*, Chapter 3, p. 75.

will be bound by the new rules contained therein, and since one must envisage some states not adhering to the 1982 Conventions, the 1958 rules will continue to be of importance.[8] During the twelve year period between the signing of the Convention and its coming into force, the influence of its provisions was clear in the process of law creation by state practice.[9]

The territorial sea

Internal waters[10]

Internal waters are deemed to be such parts of the seas as are not either the high seas or relevant zones or the territorial sea, and are accordingly classed as appertaining to the land territory of the coastal state. Internal waters, whether harbours, lakes or rivers, are such waters as are to be found on the landward side of the baselines from which the width of the territorial and other zones is measured,[11] and are assimilated with the territory of the state. They differ from the territorial sea primarily in that there does not exist any right of innocent passage from which the shipping of other states may benefit. There is an exception to this rule where the straight baselines enclose as internal waters what had been territorial waters.[12]

In general, a coastal state may exercise its jurisdiction over foreign ships within its internal waters to enforce its laws, although the judicial authorities of the flag state (i.e. the state whose flag the particular ship flies) may also act where crimes have occurred on board ship. This concurrent jurisdiction may be seen in two cases.

In *R* v. *Anderson*,[13] in 1868, the Court of Criminal Appeal in the UK declared that an American national who had committed manslaughter on board a British vessel in French internal waters was subject to the jurisdiction of the British courts, even though he was also within the sovereignty of French justice (and American justice by reason of his nationality), and thus could be correctly convicted under English law. The US Supreme Court held in *Wildenhus'* case[14] that the American courts had jurisdiction to try a

---

[8] Note that by article 311(1) of the 1982 Convention, the provisions of this convention will prevail as between the states parties over the 1958 conventions.

[9] See e.g. J. R. Stevenson and B. H. Oxman, 'The Future of the UN Convention on the Law of the Sea', 88 AJIL, 1994, p. 488.

[10] See e.g. Brown, *International Law of the Sea*, Chapter 5; O'Connell, *International Law of the Sea*, vol. I, Chapter 9 and Churchill and Lowe, *Law of the Sea*, Chapter 3.

[11] Article 5(1) of the 1958 Convention on the Territorial Sea and article 8(1) of the 1982 Convention. Note the exception in the latter provision with regard to archipelagic states, *infra*, p. 399. See also *Regina* v. *Farnquist* (1981) 54 CCC (2d) 417; 94 ILR, p. 238.

[12] Article 5(2) of the 1958 Convention on the Territorial Sea and article 8(2) of the 1982 Convention. See *infra*, p. 394.   [13] 1 Cox's Criminal Cases 198.

[14] 120 US 1 (1887). See also *Armament Dieppe SA* v. *US*, 399 F.2d 794 (1968).

crew member of a Belgian vessel for the murder of another Belgian national, when the ship was docked in the port of Jersey City in New York.[15]

A merchant ship in a foreign port or in foreign internal waters is automatically subject to the local jurisdiction (unless there is an express agreement to the contrary), although where purely disciplinarian issues related to the ship's crew are involved, which do not concern the maintenance of peace within the territory of the coastal state, then such matters would by courtesy be left to the authorities of the flag-ship to regulate.[16] Although some writers have pointed to theoretical differences between the Common Law and French approaches, in practice the same fundamental proposition applies.[17]

However, a completely different situation operates where the foreign vessel involved is a warship. In such cases, the authorisation of the captain or of the flag-state is necessary before the coastal state may exercise its jurisdiction over the ship and its crew. This is due to the status of the warship as a direct arm of the sovereign of the flag-state.[18]

Baselines[19]

The width of the territorial sea is defined from the low-water mark around the coasts of the state. This is the traditional principle under customary international law and was reiterated in article 3 of the Geneva Convention on the Territorial Sea and the Contiguous Zone in 1958 and article 5 of the 1982 Convention, and the low-water line along the coast is defined 'as marked on large-scale charts officially recognised by the coastal state'.[20]

In the majority of cases, it will not be very difficult to locate the low-water line which is to act as the baseline for measuring the width of the territorial sea.[21] Sometimes, however, the geography of the state's coasts will be such

---

[15] See the Madrid incident, where US officials asserted the right to interview a potential defector from a Soviet ship in New Orleans, 80 AJIL, 1986, p. 622.

[16] See e.g. *NNB* v. *Ocean Trade Company*, 87 ILR, p. 96, where the Court of Appeal of The Hague held that a coastal state had jurisdiction over a foreign vessel where the vessel was within the territory of the coastal state and a dispute arose affecting not only the internal order of the ship but also the legal order of the coastal state concerned. The dispute concerned a strike on board ship taken on the advice of the International Transport Workers' Federation.

[17] See e.g. Churchill and Lowe, *Law of the Sea*, pp. 54–7. See also J. L. Lenoir, 'Criminal Jurisdiction over Foreign Merchant Ships', 10 *Tulane Law Review*, 1935, p. 13. See with regard to the right of access to ports and other internal waters, A. V. Lowe, 'The Right of Entry into Maritime Ports in International Law', 14 *San Diego Law Review*, 1977, p. 597, and O'Connell, *International Law of the Sea*, vol. II, Chapter 22. See also the Dangerous Vessels Act 1985.

[18] See *The Schooner Exchange* v. *McFaddon*, 7 Cranch 116 (1812). See also 930 HC Deb., col. 450, Written Answers, 29 April 1977.

[19] See e.g. W. M. Reisman and G. S. Westerman, *Straight Baselines in International Maritime Boundary Delimitation*, New York, 1992.

[20] See e.g. Churchill and Lowe, *Law of the Sea*, Chapter 2 and O'Connell, vol. I, Chapter 5. See also *Oppenheim's International Law*, p. 607.

[21] See the *Dubai/Sharjah Border Award*, 91 ILR, pp. 543, 660–3, where the Arbitral Tribunal took into account the outermost permanent harbour works of the two states as part of the coast for the purpose of drawing the baselines.

as to cause certain problems, for instance, where the coastline is deeply indented or there are numerous islands running parallel to the coasts, or where there exist bays cutting into the coastlines. Special rules have evolved to deal with this issue, which is of importance to coastal states, particularly where foreign vessels regularly fish close to the limits of the territorial sea. A more rational method of drawing baselines might have the effect of enclosing larger areas of the sea within the state's internal waters, and thus extend the boundaries of the territorial sea further than the traditional method might envisage.

This point was raised in the *Anglo-Norwegian Fisheries* case,[22] before the International Court of Justice. The case concerned a Norwegian decree delimiting its territorial sea along some 1,000 miles of its coastline. However, instead of measuring the territorial sea from the low-water line, the Norwegians constructed a series of straight baselines linking the outermost parts of the land running along the skjaergaard (or fringe of islands and rocks) which parallels the Norwegian coastline. This had the effect of enclosing within its territorial limits parts of what would normally have been the high seas if the traditional method had been utilised. As a result certain disputes involving British fishing boats arose, and the United Kingdom challenged the legality of the Norwegian method of baselines under international law. The Court held that it was the outer line of the skjaergaard that was relevant in establishing the baselines, and not the low-water line of the mainland. This was dictated by geographic realities. The Court noted that the normal method of drawing baselines that are parallel to the coast (the *tracé parallèle*) was not applicable in this case because it would necessitate complex geometrical constructions in view of the extreme indentations of the coastline and the existence of the series of islands fringing the coasts.[23]

Since the usual methods did not apply, and taking into account the principle that the territorial sea must follow the general direction of the coasts, the concept of straight baselines drawn from the outer rocks could be considered.[24] The Court also made the point that the Norwegian system had been applied consistently over many years and had met no objections from other states, and that the UK had not protested until many years after it had first been introduced.[25] In other words, the method of straight baselines operated by Norway:

---

[22] ICJ Reports, 1951, p. 116; 18 ILR, p. 86.

[23] *Ibid.*, p. 128; 18 ILR, p. 91. Note also the Court's mention of the *courbe tangente* method of drawing arcs of circles from points along the low-water line, *ibid.*

[24] *Ibid.*, p. 129; 18 ILR, p. 92. Other states had already used such a system, see e.g. H. Waldock, 'The Anglo-Norwegian Fisheries Case', 28 BYIL, 1951, pp. 114, 148. See also I. Brownlie, *Principles of Public International Law*, 4th edn, Oxford, 1990, p. 183.

[25] ICJ Reports, 1951, p. 138; 18 ILR, p. 101. Cf. Judge McNair, *ibid.*, pp. 171–80; 18 ILR, p. 123.

had been consolidated by a constant and sufficiently long practice, in the face of which the attitude of governments bears witness to the fact that they did not consider it to be contrary to international law.[26]

Thus, although noting that Norwegian rights had been established through actual practice coupled with acquiescence, the Court regarded the straight baseline system itself as a valid principle of international law, in view of the special geographic conditions of the area. The Court provided criteria for determining the acceptability of any such delimitations. The drawing of the baselines had not to depart from the general direction of the coast, in view of the close dependence of the territorial sea upon the land domain; the baselines had to be drawn so that the sea area lying within them had to be sufficiently closely linked to the land domain to be subject to the regime of internal waters and it was permissible to consider in the process 'certain economic interests peculiar to a region, the reality and importance of which are evidenced by long usage'.[27]

These principles emerging from the *Fisheries* case were accepted by states as part of international law within a comparatively short period.

Article 4 of the Geneva Convention on the Territorial Sea 1958 declared that the straight baseline system could be used in cases of indented coastlines or where there existed a skjaergaard, provided that the general direction of the coast was followed and that there were sufficiently close links between the sea areas within the lines and the land domain to be subject to the regime of internal waters. In addition, particular regional economic interests of long standing may be considered where necessary.[28]

A number of states now use the system including, it should be mentioned, the United Kingdom as regards areas on the west coast of Scotland.[29]

Where the result of the straight baseline method is to enclose as internal waters areas previously regarded as part of the territorial sea or high seas, a right of innocent passage shall be deemed to exist in such waters by virtue of article 5(2) of the 1958 Convention.[30]

Bays[31]

Problems also arise as to the approach to be adopted with regard to bays, in particular whether the waters of wide-mouthed bays ought to be treated as

---

[26] *Ibid.*, p. 139; 18 ILR, p. 102.   [27] *Ibid.*, p. 133; 18 ILR, p. 95.
[28] See also article 7 of the 1982 Convention.
[29] Territorial Waters Order in Council, 1964, article 3, s.1, 1965, Part III, s.2, p. 6452A. See also the Territorial Sea (Limits) Order 1989 regarding the Straits of Dover. See generally as regards state practice, Churchill and Lowe, *Law of the Sea*, pp. 31–3 and M. Whiteman, *Digest of International Law*, Washington, vol. IV, pp. 21–35.
[30] See also article 8(2) of the 1982 Convention.
[31] See e.g. Brown, *International Law of the Sea*, p. 28, Churchill and Lowe, *Law of the Sea*, pp. 33–8 and O'Connell, *International Law of the Sea*, vol. I, p. 209. See also G. Westerman, *The Juridical Bay*, Oxford, 1987.

other areas of the sea adjacent to the coast, so that the baseline of the territorial sea would be measured from the low-water mark of the coast of the
bay, or whether the device of the straight baseline could be used to 'close
off' the mouth of the bay of any width and the territorial limit measured from
that line.

It was long accepted that a straight closing line could be used across the
mouth of bays, but there was considerable disagreement as to the permitted
width of the bay beyond which this would not operate.[32] The point was
settled in article 7 of the 1958 Convention on the Territorial Sea. This
declared that:

> if the distance between the low-water marks of the natural entrance points of
> a bay does not exceed twenty-four miles, a closing line may be drawn between
> these two low-water marks, and the waters enclosed thereby shall be consid-
> ered as internal waters,

otherwise a straight baseline of 24 miles may be drawn.[33]

This provision, however, does not apply to historic bays. These are bays
the waters of which are treated by the coastal state as internal in view of historic rights supported by general acquiescence rather than any specific principle of international law.[34] A number of states have claimed historic bays,
for example, Canada with respect to Hudson Bay (although the US has
opposed this),[35] and certain American states as regards the Gulf of
Fonseca.[36] The question of this Gulf came before the International Court in
the *Land, Island and Maritime Frontier Dispute (El Salvador/Honduras;
Nicaragua intervening)*.[37] The Court noted that the states concerned and
commentators were agreed that the Gulf was an historic bay, but this was
defined in terms of the particular historical situation of that Gulf, especially
as it constituted a pluri-state bay, for which there were no agreed and codified general rules of the kind well established for single state bays.[38] In the
light of the particular historical circumstances and taking particular note of
the 1917 decision, the Court found that the Gulf, beyond a long accepted
3 mile maritime belt for the coastal states, constituted historic waters subject
to the co-ownership or a condominium of the three coastal states.[39] The
Court continued by noting that the vessels of other states would enjoy a right
of innocent passage in the waters beyond the coastal belt in order to ensure

---

[32] See e.g. the *North Atlantic Coast Fisheries* case, 11 RIAA, p. 167 (1910) and the *Anglo-Norwegian Fisheries* case, ICJ Reports, 1951, p. 116; 18 ILR, p. 86, to the effect that no general rules of international law had been uniformly accepted.

[33] See also article 10 of the 1982 Convention.

[34] See the *Tunisia/Libya Continental Shelf* case, ICJ Reports, 1982, pp. 18, 74; 67 ILR, pp. 4, 67. [35] See Whiteman, *Digest*, vol. IV, pp. 250–7.

[36] See *El Salvador v. Nicaragua*, 11 AJIL, 1917, p. 674.

[37] ICJ Reports, 1992, p. 351; 97 ILR, p. 266.

[38] *Ibid.*, p. 589; 97 ILR, p. 505. But cf. the dissenting opinion of Judge Oda, *ibid.*, p. 745; 97 ILR, p. 661. [39] *Ibid.*, p. 601; 97 ILR, p. 517.

access to any one of the three coastal states.[40] Having decided that the three states enjoyed a condominium within the Gulf, the Court concluded that there was a tripartite presence at the closing line of the Gulf.[41]

The United States Supreme Court has taken the view that where waters are outside the statutory limits for inland waters, the exercise of sovereignty required to establish title to a historic bay amounted to the exclusion of all foreign vessels and navigation from the area claimed. The continuous authority exercised in this fashion had to be coupled with the acquiescence of states. This was the approach in the *US* v. *State of Alaska* case[42] concerning the waters of Cook Inlet. The Supreme Court held that Alaska had not satisfied the terms and that the Inlet had not been regarded as a historic bay under Soviet, American or Alaskan sovereignty. Accordingly, it was the Federal State and not Alaska which was entitled to the subsurface of Cook Inlet.[43]

In response to the Libyan claim to the Gulf of Sirte (Sidra) as an historic bay and consequent drawing of a closing line of nearly 300 miles in length in 1973, several states immediately protested, including the US and the states of the European Community.[44] The US in a note to Libya in 1974 referred to 'the international law standards of past open, notorious and effective exercise of authority, and the acquiescence of foreign nations'[45] and has on several occasions sent naval and air forces into the Gulf in order to maintain its opposition to the Libyan claim and to assert that the waters of the Gulf constitute high seas.[46] Little evidence appears, in fact, to support the Libyan contention.

Islands[47]

As far as islands are concerned, the general provisions noted above regarding the measurement of the territorial sea apply. Islands are defined in the

---

[40] *Ibid.*, p. 605; 97 ILR, p. 521.
[41] *Ibid.*, pp. 608–9; 97 ILR, pp. 524–5. See also M. N. Shaw, 'Case Concerning the Land, Island and Maritime Frontier Dispute (*El Salvador/Honduras: Nicaragua Intervening*), Judgment of 11 September 1992', 42 ICLQ, 1993, p. 929 and Gioia, 'The Law of Multinational Bays and the Case of the Gulf of Fonseca', Netherlands YIL, 1993, p. 81.
[42] 422 US 184 (1975). See also Bouchez, *The Regime of Bays in International Law*, 1963 and the *Tunisia–Libya Continental Shelf* case, ICJ Reports, 1982, pp. 18, 74; 67 ILR, pp. 4, 67.
[43] See also *United States* v. *California*, 381 US 139 (1965); *United States* v. *Louisiana (Louisiana Boundary Case)*, 394 US 11 (1969); *United States* v. *Maine (Rhode Island and New York Boundary Case)*, 471 US 375 (1985) and *Alabama and Mississippi Boundary Case, United States* v. *Louisiana*, 470 US 93 (1985).
[44] See Churchill and Lowe, *Law of the Sea*, pp. 37–8 and UKMIL, 57 BYIL, 1986, pp. 579–80. See also Francioni, 'The Gulf of Sidra Incident (*United States* v. *Libya*) and International Law', 5 *Italian Yearbook of International Law*, 1980–1, p. 85.
[45] See 68 AJIL, 1974, p. 510. See also *Cumulative DUSPIL 1981–8*, vol. II, Washington, 1994, p. 1810.   [46] See e.g. UKMIL, 57 BYIL, 1986, pp. 581–2.
[47] See e.g. H. W. Jayewardene, *The Regime of Islands in International Law*, 1990; D. W. Bowett, *The Legal Regime of Islands in International Law*, New York, 1979; C. Symmons, *The*

1958 Convention on the Territorial Sea as consisting of 'a naturally-formed area of land, surrounded by water, which is above water at high tide',[48] and they can have a maritime belt.[49] Where only low tide elevations are involved, that is areas of land visible at low tide but submerged at high tide, they cannot have a territorial sea of their own. But they may be used as baselines if within the territorial sea of a coastal state and they may be utilised as a point on a straight baseline if installations permanently above sea level (for example, a lighthouse) have been constructed upon them.

Although islands may serve as the base for the measurement of the territorial sea, contiguous zone, exclusive economic zone and continental shelf, article 121(3) of the 1982 Convention notes that 'rocks which cannot sustain human habitation or economic life of their own shall have no exclusive economic zone or continental shelf'.[50] Article 121(3) begs a series of questions, such as the precise dividing line between rocks and islands, for example, and as to the actual meaning of an 'economic life of their own', for another.

Archipelagic states[51]

Problems have arisen as a result of efforts by states comprising a number of islands to draw straight baselines around the outer limits of their islands, thus 'boxing in' the whole territory. Indonesia in particular has resorted to this method, against the protests of a number of states since it tends to reduce previously considered areas of the high seas extensively

Maritime Zone of Islands in International Law, The Hague, 1979; J. Simonides, 'The Legal Status of Islands in the New Law of the Sea', 65 *Revue de Droit International*, 1987, p. 161 and R. O'Keefe, 'Palm-Fringed Benefits: Island Dependencies in the New Law of the Sea', 45 ICLQ, 1996, p. 408.

[48] Article 10(1). See also article 121(1) of the 1982 Convention.
[49] Article 121(2) of the 1982 Convention. See also the *Jan Mayen (Denmark v. Norway)* case, ICJ Reports, 1993, pp. 37, 64–5 ; 99 ILR, pp. 395, 432–3. Article 10(2) of the 1958 Convention on the Territorial Sea referred only to the territorial sea of islands.
[50] See the *Jan Mayen* report, 20 ILM, 1981, pp. 797, 803; 62 ILR, pp. 108, 114 and the Declaration by Judge Evensen in the *Jan Mayen (Denmark v. Norway)* case, ICJ Reports, 1993, pp. 37, 84–5 ; 99 ILR, pp. 395, 452–3. Note as regards Rockall and the conflicting UK, Irish, Danish and Icelandic views, Symmons, *Maritime Zone*, pp. 117–18, 126 and E. D. Brown, 'Rockall and the Limits of National Jurisdiction of the United Kingdom', 2 *Marine Policy*, 1978, pp. 181–211 and 275–303. See also 878, HC Deb., col. 82, Written Answers and *The Times*, 8 May 1985, p. 6 (Danish claims) and *The Guardian*, 1 May 1985, p. 30 (Icelandic claims). The UK Minister of State declared that the twelve-mile territorial sea around Rockall was consistent with the terms of the 1982 Convention and that there was no reason to believe that this was not accepted by the international community, apart from the Republic of Ireland, UKMIL, 60 BYIL, 1989, p. 666.
[51] See e.g. Brown, *International Law of the Sea*, Chapter 8; Churchill and Lowe, *Law of the Sea*, Chapter 6; O'Connell, *International Law of the Sea*, vol. I, Chapter 6; Bowett, *Legal Regime*, Chapter 4; C. F. Amerasinghe, 'The Problem of Archipelagos in the International Law of the Sea', 23 ICLQ, 1974, p. 539 and D. P. O'Connell, 'Mid-Ocean Archipelagos in International Law', 45 BYIL, 1971, p. 1.

used as shipping lanes to the sovereignty of the archipelago state concerned.[52]

There has been a great deal of controversy as to which international law principles apply in the case of archipelagos and the subject was not expressly dealt with in the 1958 Geneva Convention.[53] Article 47 of the 1982 Convention, however, provides that an archipelagic state[54] may draw straight archipelagic baselines joining the outermost points of the outermost islands and drying reefs of the archipelago, which would then serve as the relevant baselines for other purposes. There are a number of conditions before this may be done, however, and article 47 provides as follows:

1. An archipelagic state may draw straight archipelagic baselines joining the outermost points of the outermost islands and drying reefs of the archipelago provided that within such baselines are included the main islands and in areas in which the ratio of the area of the water to the area of the land, including atolls, is between 1 to 1 and 9 to 1.
2. The length of such baselines shall not exceed 100 nautical miles, except that up to 3 per cent of the total number of baselines enclosing any archipelago may exceed that length, up to a maximum length of 125 nautical miles.
3. The drawing of such baselines shall not depart to any appreciable extent from the general configuration of the archipelago.
4. Such baselines shall not be drawn from low-tide elevations, unless lighthouses or similar installations which are permanently above sea level have been built on them or where a low-tide elevation is situated wholly or partly at a distance not exceeding the breadth of the territorial sea from the nearest island.
5. The system of such baselines shall not be applied by an archipelagic state in such a manner as to cut off from the high seas or the exclusive economic zone the territorial sea of another state.
6. If a part of the archipelagic waters of an archipelagic state lies between two parts of an immediately adjacent neighbouring state, existing rights and all other legitimate interests which the latter state has traditionally exercised in such waters and all rights stipulated by agreement between those states shall continue and be respected.
7. For the purpose of computing the ratio of water to land under paragraph 1, land areas may include waters lying within the fringing reefs of islands and atolls, including that part of a steep-sided oceanic plateau which is enclosed or nearly

[52] *Ibid.*, pp. 23–4, 45–7 and 51 and Whiteman, *Digest*, vol. IV, p. 284. See also the Indonesian Act No. 4 of 18 February 1960 Concerning Indonesian Waters, extracted in Brown, *International Law of the Sea*, vol. II, p. 98; the Philippines Act to Define the Baselines of the Territorial Sea of the Philippines, Act No. 3046 of 17 June 1961, and the Philippines Declaration with respect to the 1982 Convention, *ibid.*, pp. 100–1 (with objections from the USSR and Australia, *ibid.*, pp. 101–2). See as to the US objection to the Philippines Declaration, *Cumulative* DUSPIL *1981–8*, Washington, 1994, vol. II, p. 1066.
[53] But see as regards 'coastal archipelagos', article 4 of the 1958 Convention on the Territorial Sea.
[54] Defined as 'a state constituted wholly by one or more archipelagos and may include other islands', see article 46(a). Article 46(b) defines archipelagos as 'a group of islands, including parts of islands, interconnecting waters and other natural features which are so closely interrelated that such islands, waters and other natural features form an intrinsic geographical, economic and political entity, or which historically have been regarded as such'.

enclosed by a chain of limestone islands and drying reefs lying on the perimeter of the plateau.

8. The baselines drawn in accordance with this article shall be shown on charts of a scale or scales adequate for ascertaining their position. Alternatively, lists of geographic co-ordinates of points, specifying the geodetic datum, may be substituted.

9. The archipelagic states shall give due publicity to such charts or lists of geographical co-ordinates and shall deposit a copy of each such chart or list with the Secretary-General of the United Nations.

All the waters within such baselines are archipelagic waters[55] over which the state has sovereignty,[56] but existing agreements, traditional fishing rights and existing submarine cables must be reported.[57] In addition, ships of all states shall enjoy the rights of innocent passage through archipelagic waters[58] and all the ships and aircraft are to enjoy a right of archipelagic sea lanes passage through such lanes and air routes designated by the archipelagic state for 'continuous and expeditious passage'.[59]

In response to a reported closure in 1988 of the Straits of Sunda and Lombok by Indonesia, the US stressed that the archipelagic provisions of the 1982 Convention reflected customary international law and that those straits were subject to the regime of archipelagic sea lanes passage. Accordingly, it was pointed out that any interference with such passage would violate international law.[60]

The width of the territorial sea[61]

There has historically been considerable disagreement as to how far the territorial sea may extend from the baselines. Originally, the 'cannon-shot' rule defined the width required in terms of the range of shore-based artillery, but at the turn of the nineteenth century, this was transmuted into the 3 mile rule. This was especially supported by the United States and the United Kingdom, and any detraction had to be justified by virtue of historic rights and general acquiescence as, for example, the Scandinavian claim to 4 miles.[62]

However, the issue was much confused by the claims of many coastal states to exercise certain jurisdictional rights for particular purposes, for example, fisheries, customs and immigration controls. It was not until after

---

[55] Article 50 provides that within its archipelagic waters, the archipelagic state may draw closing lines for the delimitation of internal waters.   [56] Article 49.   [57] Article 51.
[58] Article 52.
[59] Article 53. For recent state practice, see Churchill and Lowe, *Law of the Sea*, pp. 106–8.
[60] 83 AJIL, 1989, pp. 559–61. See also *Cumulative DUSPIL 1981–8*, Washington, 1994, vol. II, p. 2060.
[61] See e.g. Brown, *International Law of the Sea*, p. 43; Churchill and Lowe, *Law of the Sea*, pp. 65–8 and O'Connell, *International Law of the Sea*, vol. I, Chapter 4. See also *Oppenheim's International Law*, p. 611.
[62] See e.g. H. S. K. Kent, 'Historical Origins of the Three-mile Limit', 48 AJIL, 1954, p. 537 and *The Anna* (1805) 165 ER 809. See also *US* v. *Kessler*, 1 Baldwin's C C Rep. 15 (1829).

402INTERNATIONAL LAW

the First World War that a clear distinction was made between claims to enlarge the width of the territorial sea and claims over particular zones. Recently the 3 mile rule has been discarded as a rule of general application to be superseded by contending assertions. The 1958 Geneva Convention on the Territorial Sea did not include an article on the subject because of disagreements among the states, while the 1960 Geneva Conference failed to accept a United States–Canadian proposal for a 6 mile territorial sea coupled with an exclusive fisheries zone for a further 6 miles by only one vote.[63]

Article 3 of the 1982 Convention, however, notes that all states have the right to establish the breadth of the territorial sea up to a limit not exceeding 12 nautical miles from the baselines. This clearly accords with the evolving practice of states.[64] The UK adopted a 12 mile limit in the Territorial Sea Act 1987, for instance, as did the US by virtue of Proclamation No. 5928 in December 1988.

Delimitation of the territorial sea between states with opposite or adjacent coasts

Article 15 of the 1982 Convention, following basically article 12 of the Geneva Convention on the Territorial Sea 1958, provides that where no agreement has been reached, neither state may extend its territorial sea beyond the median point every point of which is equidistant from the nearest point on the baselines from which the territorial sea is measured. This provision, however, does not apply where it is necessary by reason of historic title or other special circumstances to delimit the territorial sea of the two states in a different way.[65]

The juridical nature of the territorial sea[66]

There have been a number of theories as to the precise legal character of the territorial sea of the coastal state, ranging from treating the territorial sea as part of

---

[63] See O'Connell, *International Law of the Sea*, footnote 1, vol. I, pp. 163–4.
[64] The notice issued by the Hydrographic Department of the Royal Navy on 1 January 1995 shows that 136 states or territories claim a 12 mile territorial sea, UKMIL, 65 BYIL, 1994, pp. 642–7, with 19 states or territories claiming less than this. Only 13 states claimed more than 12 miles. A Summary of National Maritime Claims issued by the Office of Ocean Affairs of the US Department of State shows that as of 31 January 1996, 129 states claimed a territorial sea of 12 miles or under, with 16 states claiming a larger territorial sea. See also Churchill and Lowe, *Law of the Sea*, pp. 189–90, with regard to the position in June 1987 and Brownlie, *Principles*, pp. 189–90, footnote 53.
[65] See *infra* p. 413 with regard to delimitation of the exclusive economic zone and *infra* p. 436 with regard to delimitation of the continental shelf of opposite and adjacent states.
[66] See Brown, *International Law of the Sea*, Chapter 6; O'Connell, *International Law of the Sea*, vol. I, Chapter 3. See also Brownlie, *Public International Law*, p. 194 and Churchill and Lowe, *Law of the Sea*, Chapter 4.

the *res communis*, but subject to certain rights exercisable by the coastal state, to regarding the territorial sea as part of the coastal state's territorial domain subject to a right of innocent passage by foreign vessels.[67] Nevertheless, it cannot be disputed that the coastal state enjoys sovereign rights over its maritime belt and extensive jurisdictional control, having regard to the relevant rules of international law. The fundamental restriction upon the sovereignty of the coastal state is the right of other nations to innocent passage through the territorial sea, and this distinguishes the territorial sea from the internal waters of the state, which are fully within the unrestricted jurisdiction of the coastal nation.

Articles 1 and 2 of the Convention on the Territorial Sea 1958[68] provide that the coastal state's sovereignty extends over its territorial sea and to the airspace and seabed and subsoil thereof, subject to the provisions of the Convention and of international law. The territorial sea forms an undeniable part of the land territory to which it is bound, so that a cession of land will automatically include any band of territorial waters.[69]

The coastal state may, if it so desires, exclude foreign nationals and vessels from fishing within its territorial sea and (subject to agreements to the contrary) from coastal trading (known as cabotage), and reserve these activities for its own citizens.

Similarly the coastal state has extensive powers of control relating to, amongst others, security and customs matters. It should be noted, however, that how far a state chooses to exercise the jurisdiction and sovereignty to which it may lay claim under the principles of international law will depend upon the terms of its own municipal legislation, and some states will not wish to take advantage of the full extent of the powers permitted them within the international legal system.

The right of innocent passage

The right of foreign merchant ships (as distinct from warships) to pass unhindered through the territorial sea of a coast has long been an accepted principle in customary international law, the sovereignty of the coast state notwithstanding. However, the precise extent of the doctrine is blurred and open to contrary interpretation, particularly with respect to the requirement that the passage must be 'innocent'.[70]

---

[67] O'Connell, *International Law of the Sea*, pp. 60–7.
[68] See also article 2 of the 1982 Convention.
[69] See the *Grisbadarna* case, 11 RIAA, p. 147 (1909) and the *Beagle Channel* case, HMSO, 1977; 52 ILR, p. 93. See also Judge McNair, *Anglo-Norwegian Fisheries* case, ICJ Reports, 1951, pp. 116, 160; 18 ILR, pp. 86, 113.
[70] See Brown, *International Law of the Sea*, pp. 53 *et seq.*; Churchill and Lowe, *Law of the Sea*, pp. 68–77 and O'Connell, *International Law of the Sea*, Chapter 7. See also *Oppenheim's International Law*, p. 615.

The doctrine was elaborated in article 14 of the Convention on the Territorial Sea 1958, which emphasised that the coastal state must not hamper innocent passage and must publicise any dangers to navigation in the territorial sea of which it is aware. Passage is defined as navigation through the territorial sea for the purpose of crossing that sea without entering internal waters or of proceeding to or from that sea without entering internal waters or of proceeding to or from internal waters. It may include temporary stoppages, but only if they are incidental to ordinary navigation or necessitated by distress or *force majeure*.[71]

The coastal state may not impose charges for such passage unless they are in payment for specific services, and ships engaged in passages are required to comply with the coastal state's regulations covering for example navigation in so far as they are consistent with international law.

Passage ceases to be innocent under article 14(4) of the 1958 Convention where it is 'prejudicial to the peace, good order or security of the coastal state' and in the case of foreign fishing vessels when they do not observe such laws and regulations as the coastal state may make and publish to prevent these ships from fishing in the territorial sea. In addition, submarines must navigate on the surface and show their flag.

Where passage is not innocent, the coastal state may take steps to prevent it in its territorial sea and where ships are proceeding to internal waters, it may act to forestall any breach of the conditions to which admission of such ships to internal water is subject. Coastal states have the power temporarily to suspend innocent passage of foreign vessels where it is essential for security reasons provided such suspension has been published and provided it does not cover international straits.

Article 19(2) of the 1982 Convention has developed the notion of innocent passage contained in article 14(4) of the 1958 Convention by the provision of examples of prejudicial passage such as the threat or use of force; weapons practice; spying; propaganda; breach of customs, fiscal, immigration or sanitary regulations; wilful and serious pollution; fishing; research or survey activities and interference with coastal communications or other facilities. In addition a wide-ranging clause also includes 'any activity not having a direct bearing on passage'. This would appear to have altered the burden of proof from the coastal state to the other party with regard to innocent passage as well as being somewhat difficult to define. By virtue of article 24 of the 1982 Convention, coastal states must not hamper the innocent passage of foreign ships, either by imposing requirements upon them which would have the practical effect of denying or impairing the right or by discrimination.

---

[71] See articles 17 and 18 of the 1982 Convention.

Article 17 of the Geneva Convention on the Territorial Sea 1958 provided that foreign ships exercising the right of innocent passage were to comply with the laws and regulations enacted by the coastal state, in particular those relating to transport and navigation. This was developed in article 21(1) of the 1982 Convention, which expressly provided that the coastal state could adopt laws and regulations concerning innocent passage with regard to:

(a) the safety of navigation and the regulation of maritime traffic;
(b) the protection of navigational aids and facilities and other facilities or installations;
(c) the protection of cables and pipelines;
(d) the conservation of the living resources of the sea;
(e) the prevention of infringement of the fisheries laws and regulations of the coastal state;
(f) the preservation of the environment of the coastal state and the prevention, reduction and control of pollution thereof;
(g) marine scientific research and hydrographic surveys;
(h) the prevention of infringement of the customs, fiscal, immigration or sanitary laws and regulations of the coastal state.

Breach of such laws and regulations will render the offender liable to prosecution, but will not make the passage non-innocent as such, unless article 19 has been infringed.[72]

One major controversy of considerable importance revolves around the issue of whether the passage of warships in peace-time is or is not innocent.[73] The question was further complicated by the omission of an article on the problem in the 1958 Convention on the Territorial Sea, and the discussion of innocent passage in a series of articles headed 'Rules applicable to all ships'. This has led some writers to assert that this includes warships by inference, but other authorities maintain that such an important issue could not be resolved purely by omission and inference, especially in view of the reservations by many states to the Convention rejecting the principle of innocent passage for warships and in the light of comments in the various preparatory materials to the 1958 Geneva Convention.[74]

It is primarily the Western states, with their preponderant naval power, that have historically maintained the existence of a right of innocent passage for warships, to the opposition of the communist and Third World nations. However, having regard to the rapid growth in their naval capacity in recent

---

[72] Under article 22 of the 1982 Convention, the coastal state may establish designated sea lanes and traffic separation schemes in its territorial sea. See UKMIL, 64 BYIL, 1993, p. 688 for details of traffic separation schemes around the UK.
[73] See e.g. O'Connell, *International Law of the Sea*, footnote 1, pp. 274–97. See also *Oppenheim's International Law*, p. 618.
[74] *Ibid.*, pp. 290–2. See also Brownlie, *Public International law*, pp. 197–8.

years and the ending of the Cold War, Soviet attitudes have undergone somewhat of a modification.[75]

In September 1989, the US and the USSR issued a joint 'Uniform Interpretation of the Rules of International Law Governing Innocent Passage'.[76] This reaffirms that the relevant rules of international law are stated in the 1982 Convention. It then provides that:

> [a]ll ships, including warships, regardless of cargo, armament or means of propulsion, enjoy the right of innocent passage through the territorial sea in accordance with international law, for which neither prior notification nor authorisation is required.

The statement notes that where a ship in passage through the territorial sea is not engaged in any of the activities laid down in article 19(2), it 'is in innocent passage' since that provision is exhaustive. Ships in passage are under an obligation to comply with the laws and regulations of the coastal state adopted in conformity with articles 21, 22, 23 and 25 of the 1982 Convention, provided such laws and regulations do not have the effect of denying or impairing the exercise of the right of innocent passage. This important statement lends considerable weight to the view that warships have indeed a right of innocent passage through the territorial sea and one that does not necessitate prior notification or authorisation.[77]

Jurisdiction over foreign ships[78]

Where foreign ships are in passage through the territorial sea, the coastal state may only exercise its criminal jurisdiction as regards the arrest of any person or the investigation of any matter connected with a crime committed on board ship in defined situations. These are enumerated in article

---

[75] See also Churchill and Lowe, *Law of the Sea*, pp. 54–6. The issue was left open at the Third UN Conference on the Law of the Sea and does not therefore appear in the 1982 Convention. Note, however, that Western and communist states both proposed including a reference to warships in early sessions of the Conference, see UNCLOS III, Official Records, vol. III, pp. 183, 203, 192 and 196. See also article 29(2) of the 1975 Informal Single Negotiating Text. The right of warships to innocent passage was maintained by the US following an incident during which four US warships sailed through Soviet territorial waters off the Crimean coast, see *The Times*, 19 March, 1986, p. 5.

[76] See 84 AJIL, 1990, p. 239.

[77] See also *Cumulative DUSPIL 1981–8*, vol. II, Washington, 1994, pp. 1844 *et seq.* and UKMIL, 65 BYIL, 1994, pp. 642–7. See also *Cumulative DUSPIL 1981–8*, vol. II, Washington, 1994, p. 1854 with regard to the claim by some states that the passage of nuclear-powered ships or ships carrying nuclear substances through territorial waters requires prior authorisation or prior consent. See also UKMIL, 62 BYIL, 1991, pp. 632–3 with regard to UK views on claims concerning prior authorisation or consent with regard to the passage of ships carrying hazardous wastes.

[78] See e.g. O'Connell, *International Law of the Sea*, footnote 1, Chapter 23 and 24. See also *Oppenheim's International Law, op. cit.*, p. 620 and Brown, *Principles*, p. 62 Note that these rules are applicable to foreign ships and government commercial ships.

27(1) of the 1982 Convention, reaffirming article19(1) of the 1958 Convention on the Territorial Sea, as follows:

(a) if the consequences of the crime extend to the coastal state; or (b) if the crime is of a kind likely to disturb the peace of the country or the good order of the territorial sea; or (c) if the assistance of the local authorities has been requested by the master of the ship or by a diplomatic agent or consular officer of the country of the flag state; or (d) if such measures are necessary for the suppression of illicit traffic in narcotic drugs or pyschotropic substances.[79]

However, if the ship is passing through the territorial sea having left the internal waters of the coastal state, then the coastal state may act in any manner prescribed by its laws as regards arrest or investigation on board ship and is not restricted by the terms of article 27(1). But the authorities of the coastal state cannot act where the crime was committed before the ship entered the territorial sea, providing the ship is not entering or has not entered internal waters.

Under article 28 of the 1982 Convention, the coastal state should not stop or divert a foreign ship passing through its territorial sea for the purpose of exercising civil jurisdiction in relation to a person on board ship, nor levy execution against or arrest the ship, unless obligations are involved which were assumed by the ship itself in the course of or for the purpose of its voyage through waters of the coastal state, or unless the ship is passing through the territorial sea on its way from internal waters. The above rules do not, however, prejudice the right of a state to levy execution against or to arrest, for the purpose of any civil proceedings, a foreign ship lying in the territorial sea or passing through the territorial sea after leaving internal waters.[80]

Warships and other government ships operated for non-commercial purposes are immune from the jurisdiction of the coastal state, although they may be required to leave the territorial sea immediately for breach of rules governing passage and the flag-state will bear international responsibility in cases of loss or damage suffered as a result.[81]

International straits[82]

Article 16(4) of the 1958 Convention on the Territorial Sea declares that:

there shall be no suspension of the innocent passage of foreign ships through straits which are used for international navigation between one part of the high sea and another part of the high seas or the territorial sea of a foreign state.

---

[79] The latter phrase was added by article 27(1) of the 1982 Convention.
[80] See also article 20 of the 1958 Convention.
[81] Articles 29–32 of the 1982 Convention. See also articles 21–23 of the 1958 Convention.
[82] See e.g. Brown, *International Law of the Sea*, Chapter 7; Churchill and Lowe, *Law of the Sea*, Chapter 5; O'Connell, *International Law of the Sea*, 1, vol. I, Chapter 8; R. Lapidoth, *Les Détroits en Droit International*, Paris, 1972; T. L. Koh, *Straits in International Navigation*,

This provision should be read in conjunction with the decision in the *Corfu Channel* case.[83] In this case, British warships passing through the straits were fired upon by Albanian guns. A number of months later, an augmented force of cruisers and destroyers sailed through the North Corfu Channel and two of them were badly damaged after striking mines. This impelled the British authorities to sweep the Channel three weeks later, and clear it of some twenty mines of German manufacture. The Court in a much-quoted passage emphasised that:

> states in time of peace have a right to send their warships through straits used for international navigation between two parts of the high seas without the previous authorisation of a coastal state, provided that the passage is innocent.[84]

It was also noted that the minesweeping operation was in no way 'innocent' and was indeed a violation of Albania's sovereignty, although the earlier passages by British naval vessels were legal.[85]

The 1982 Convention established a new regime for straits used for international navigation. The principle is reaffirmed that the legal status of the waters of the straits in question is unaffected by the provisions dealing with passage.[86]

A new right of transit passage is posited with respect to straits used for international navigation between one part of the high seas or an exclusive economic zone and another part of the high seas or an exclusive economic zone.[87] It involves the exercise of the freedom of navigation and overflight solely for the purpose of continuous and expeditious transit of the strait and does not preclude passage through the strait to enter or leave a state bordering that strait.[88] States bordering the straits in question are not to hamper or suspend transit passage.[89]

There are two exceptions to the right, under article 36 where a route exists through the strait through the high seas or economic zone of similar navigational convenience and under article 38(1) in the case of a strait formed by

London, 1982; J. N. Moore, 'The Regime of Straits and the Third United Nations Conference on the Law of the Sea', 74 AJIL, 1980, p. 77; W. M. Reisman, 'The Regime of Straits and National Security', *ibid.*, p. 48; H. Caminos, 'Le Régime des Détroits dans la Convention des Nations Unies de 1982 sur le Droit de la Mer', 205 HR, 1987 V, p. 9 and S. N. Nandan and D. H. Anderson, 'Straits Used for International Navigation: A Commentary on Part III of the UN Convention on the Law of the Sea 1982', 60 BYIL, 1989, p. 159. See also *Oppenheim's International Law, op. cit.*, p. 633 and Nguyen Quoc Dinh *et al., Droit International Public*, p. 1072.   [83] ICJ Reports, 1949, p. 4; 16 ILR, p. 155.
[84] *Ibid.*, p. 28; 16 ILR, p. 161. The Court emphasised that the decisive criterion regarding the definition of 'strait' was the geographical situation of the strait as connecting two parts of the high seas, coupled with the fact that it was actually used for international navigation, *ibid.*
[85] *Ibid.*, pp. 30–1, 33; 16 ILR, pp. 163, 166. Note the final settlement of the case, UKMIL, 63 BYIL, 1992, p. 781.   [86] Articles 34 and 35.
[87] Article 37. See also R. P. Anand, 'Transit Passage and Overflight in International Straits', 26 IJIL, 1986, p. 72 and *Oppenheim's International Law*, p. 636.   [88] Article 38.
[89] Article 44.

an island of a state bordering the strait and its mainland, where there exists seaward of the island a route through the high seas or economic zone of similar navigational convenience.

Ships and aircraft in transit must observe the relevant international regulations and refrain from all activities other than those incidental to their normal modes of continuous and expeditious transit, unless rendered necessary by *force majeure* or by distress.[90]

Under article 45, the regime of innocent passage will apply with regard to straits used for international navigation excluded from the transit passage provisions by article 38(1) and to international straits between a part of the high seas or economic zone and the territorial sea of a foreign state. Such innocent passage is not to be suspended.[91]

It is unclear whether the right of transit passage has passed into customary law. Practice is as yet ambiguous.[92] Some states have provided explicitly for rights of passage through international straits. When the UK extended its territorial sea in 1987 to 12 miles, one of the consequences was that the high sea corridor through the Straits of Dover disappeared. The following year an agreement was signed with France which related to the delimitation of the territorial sea in the Straits of Dover and a joint declaration was issued in which both governments recognised:

> rights of unimpeded transit passage for merchant vessels, state vessels and, in particular, warships following their normal mode of navigation, as well as the right of overflight for aircraft, in the Straits of Dover. It is understood that, in accordance with the principles governing this regime under the rules of international law, such passage will be exercised in a continuous and expeditious manner.[93]

A number of straits are subject to special regimes, which are unaffected by the above provisions.[94] One important example is the Montreux Convention of 1936 governing the Bosphorus and Dardanelles Straits. This provides for complete freedom of transit or navigation for merchant vessels during peacetime and for freedom of transit during daylight hours for some warships, giving prior notification to Turkey.[95]

---

[90] Article 39. Under articles 41 and 42, the coastal state may designate sea lanes and traffic separation schemes through international straits.
[91] See as to the differences between the regimes of innocent passage through the territorial sea, transit passage and archipelagic sea lanes passage, Nandan and Anderson, 'Straits', p. 169.
[92] See Churchill and Lowe, *Law of the Sea*, p. 94, but cf. O. Schachter, 'International Law in Theory and Practice', 178 HR, 1982, pp. 9, 281.
[93] Cmnd. 557. See also 38 ICLQ, 1989, pp. 416–17 and AFDI, 1988, p. 727.
[94] Article 35(c).
[95] See e.g. Churchill and Lowe, *Law of the Sea*, pp. 94–6. See also UKMIL, 57 BYIL, 1986, p. 581 and F. A. Vali, *The Turkish Straits and NATO*, Stanford, 1972. Note that the dispute as to the status of the Strait of Tiran and the Gulf of Aqaba between Israel and its Arab neighbours was specifically dealt with in the treaties of peace. Article 5 (2) of the Israel–Egypt Treaty of Peace 1979 and article 14 (3) of the Israel–Jordan Treaty of Peace

The contiguous zone[96]

Historically some states have claimed to exercise certain rights over partic-ular zones of the high seas. This has involved some diminution of the prin-ciple of the freedom of the high seas as the jurisdiction of the coastal state has been extended into areas of the high seas contiguous to the territorial sea, albeit for defined purposes only. Such restricted jurisdiction zones have been established or asserted for a number of reasons, for instance, to prevent infringement of customs, immigration or sanitary laws of the coastal state, or to conserve fishing stocks in a particular area, or to enable the coastal state to have exclusive or principal rights to the resources of the proclaimed zone. In each case they enable the coastal state to protect what it regards as its vital or important interests without having to extend the boundaries of its territorial sea further into the high seas. It is thus a compromise between the interests of the coastal state and the interests of other maritime nations seeking to maintain the status of the high seas, and it marks a balance of competing claims.

The extension of rights beyond the territorial sea has, however, been seen not only in the context of preventing the infringement of particular domes-tic laws, but also increasingly as a method of maintaining and developing the economic interests of the coastal state regarding maritime resources.

The idea of a contiguous zone (i.e. zone bordering upon the territorial sea) was virtually formulated as an authoritative and consistent doctrine in the 1930s by the French writer Gidel, [97] and it appeared in the Convention on the Territorial Sea. Article 24 declared that:

> In a zone of the high seas contiguous to its territorial sea, the coastal state may exercise the control necessary to:
>
> (a) Prevent infringement of its customs, fiscal, immigration or sanitary regu-lations within its territory or territorial sea;
>
> (b) Punish infringement of the above regulations committed within its ter-ritory or territorial sea.

1994 both affirm that the Strait and Gulf are international waterways open to all nations for unimpeded and non-suspendable freedom of navigation and overflight. As to the US–USSR Agreement on the Bering Straits Region, see 28 ILM, 1989, p. 1429. See also as to the Great Belt dispute between Finland and Denmark, M. Koskenniemi, 'L'Affaire du Passage par le Grand-Belt', AFDI, 1992, p. 905. See as to other particular straits, e.g. S. C. Truver, *Gibraltar and the Mediterranean*, Alphen, 1982; M. A. Morris, *The Strait of Magellan*, Dordrecht, 1989; G. Alexander, *The Baltic Straits*, Alphen, 1982 and M. Leiffer, *Malacca, Singapore and Indonesia*, Alphen, 1978.

[96] See A. V. Lowe, 'The Development of the Concept of the Contiguous Zone', 52 BYIL, 1981, p. 109; Brown, *International Law of the Sea*, Chapter 9; Churchill and Lowe, *Law of the Sea*, Chapter 7 and O'Connell, *International Law of the Sea*, vol. II, Chapter 27. See also S. Oda, 'The Concept of the Contiguous Zone', ICLQ, 1962, p. 131; *Oppenheim's International Law*, p. 625 and Nguyen Quoc Dinh *et al.*, *Droit International Public*, p. 1077.

[97] A. Gidel, 'La Mer Territoriale et la Zone Contigue', 48 HR, p. 241.

Thus, such contiguous zones were clearly differentiated from claims to full sovereignty as parts of the territorial sea, by being referred to as part of the high seas over which the coastal state may exercise particular rights. Unlike the territorial sea, which is automatically attached to the land territory of the state, contiguous zones have to be specifically claimed.

While sanitary and immigration laws are relatively recent additions to the rights enforceable over zones of the high seas and may be regarded as stemming by analogy from customs regulations, in practice they are really only justifiable since the 1958 Convention. On the other hand, customs zones have a long history and are recognised in customary international law as well. Many states, including the UK and the USA, have enacted legislation to enforce customs regulations over many years, outside their territorial waters and within certain areas, in order to suppress smuggling which appeared to thrive when faced only with territorial limits of 3 or 4 miles.[98]

Contiguous zones, however, were limited to a maximum of 12 miles from the baselines from which the territorial sea is measured. So if the coastal state already claimed a territorial sea of 12 miles, the question of contiguous zones would not arise.

This limitation, plus the restriction of jurisdiction to customs, sanitary and immigration matters, is the reason for the decline in relevance of the contiguous zones in international affairs in recent years. Under article 33 of the 1982 Convention, however, a coastal state may claim a contiguous zone (for the same purpose as the 1958 provisions) up to 24 nautical miles from the baselines. In view of the accepted 12 mile territorial sea limit, such an extension was required in order to preserve the concept. One crucial difference is that while under the 1958 system the contiguous zone was part of the high seas, under the 1982 Convention it would form part of the exclusive economic zone complex.[99] This will clearly have an impact upon the nature of the zone.

The exclusive economic zone[100]

This zone has developed out of earlier, more tentative claims, particularly relating to fishing zones,[101] and as a result of developments in the negotiating

---

[98] E.g. the British Hovering Acts of the eighteenth and nineteenth century. See O'Connell, footnote 1, vol. 2, pp. 1034–8 and the similar US legislation, *ibid.*, pp. 1038 *et seq.*

[99] See article 55, which states that the exclusive economic zone is 'an area beyond and adjacent to the territorial seas'.

[100] See e.g. Brown, *International Law of the Sea*, Chapters 10 and 11; Churchill and Lowe, *Law of the Sea*, Chapter 9; D. J. Attard, *The Exclusive Economic Zone in International Law*, Oxford, 1986; O'Connell, *International Law of the Sea*, footnote 1, vol. 1, Chapter 15; *Oppenheim's International Law, op. cit.*, p. 782 and Nguyen Quoc Dinh *et al.*, *Droit International Public*, p. 1079. See also F. Orrego Vicuña, 'La Zone Économique Exclusive', 199 HR, 1986 IV, p. 9; *ibid.*, *The Exclusive Economic Zone, Regime and Legal Nature under International Law*, Cambridge, 1989, and B. Kwiatkowska, *The 200 Mile Exclusive Economic Zone in the New Law of the Sea*, Dordrecht, 1989.   [101] O'Connell, *International Law of the Sea*, Chapter 14.

processes leading to the 1982 Convention.[102] It marks a compromise between those states seeking a 200 mile territorial sea and those wishing a more restricted system of coastal state power.

One of the major reasons for the call for a 200 mile exclusive economic zone has been the controversy over fishing zones. The 1958 Geneva Convention on the Territorial Sea did not reach agreement on the creation of fishing zones and article 24 of the Convention does not give exclusive fishing rights in the contiguous zone. However, increasing numbers of states have claimed fishing zones of widely varying widths. The European Fisheries Convention, 1964, which was implemented in the UK by the Fishing Limits Act, 1964, provided that the coastal state has the exclusive right to fish and exclusive jurisdiction in matters of fisheries in a 6 mile belt from the baseline of the territorial sea; while within the belt between 6 and 12 miles from the baseline, other parties to the Convention have the right to fish, provided they had habitually fished in that belt between January 1953 and December 1962. This was an attempt to reconcile the interests of the coastal state with those of other states who could prove customary fishing operations in the relevant area. In view of the practice of many states in accepting at one time or another a 12 mile exclusive fishing zone, either for themselves or for some other states, it seems clear that there has already emerged an international rule to that effect.

Indeed, the International Court in the *Fisheries Jurisdiction* cases[103] stated that the concept of the fishing zone, the area in which a state may claim exclusive jurisdiction independently of its territorial sea for this purpose, had crystallised as customary law in recent years and especially since the 1960 Geneva Conference, and that 'the extension of that fishing zone up to a 12 mile limit from the baselines appears now to be generally accepted'. That much is clear, but the question was whether international law recognised such a zone in excess of 12 miles.

In 1972, concerned at the proposals regarding the long-term effects of the depletion of fishing stocks around its coasts, Iceland proclaimed unilaterally a 50 mile exclusive fishing zone. This precipitated prolonged and acrimonious exchanges between that state, which depends upon fishing for some 90 per cent of its foreign earnings, and the UK and West Germany. The latter states referred the issue to the ICJ and specifically requested the Court to decide whether or not Iceland's claim was contrary to international law.

The Court did not answer that question and held that Iceland's fishing regulations extending the zone were not binding upon the UK and West Germany, since they had in no way acquiesced in them. Indeed, they had vigorously protested and brought the matter before the Court. However, by

---

[102] *Ibid.*, pp. 559 *et seq.*   [103] ICJ Reports, 1974, pp. 8, 175; 55 ILR, pp. 238.

implication the ICJ based its judgment on the fact that there did not exist any rule of international law permitting the establishment of a 50 mile fishing zone. Similarly, it appeared that there was no rule prohibiting claims beyond 12 miles and that the validity of such claims would depend upon all relevant facts of the case and the degree of recognition by other states. The Court emphasised instead the notion of preferential rights, which it regarded as a principle of customary international law. Such rights arose where the coastal state was 'in a situation of special dependence on coastal fisheries'.[104] However, this concept was overtaken by developments at the UN Conference and the 1982 Convention. Article 55 of the 1982 Convention provides that the exclusive economic zone is an area beyond and adjacent to the territorial sea, subject to the specific legal regime established under the Convention.

Under article 56, the coastal state in the economic zone has *inter alia*:

(a) sovereign rights for the purpose of exploring and exploiting, conserving and managing the natural resources, whether living[105] or non-living of the waters superjacent to the seabed and of the seabed and its subsoil and with regard to other activities for the economic exploitation and exploration of the zone, such as the production of energy from the water, currents and winds;
(b) jurisdiction with regard to (i) the architecture and use of artificial islands, installations and structures;[106] (ii) marine scientific research;[107] (iii) the protection and preservation of the marine environment.[108]

Article 57 provides that the zone shall not extend beyond 200 nautical miles from the baselines from which the breadth of the territorial sea is measured.

Article 58 lays down the rights and duties of other states in the exclusive economic zone. These are basically the high seas freedom of navigation, overflight and laying of submarine cables and pipelines. It is also provided that in exercising their rights and performing their duties, states should have due regard to the rights, duties and laws of the coastal state. In cases of conflict over the attribution of rights and jurisdiction in the zone the resolution is to be on the basis of equity and in the light of all the relevant circumstances.[109]

The delimitation of economic zones between states with opposite or adjacent coasts is to be effected by agreement on the basis of international law, as referred to in article 38 of the Statute of the ICJ, 'in order to achieve an equitable solution'.[110] Since this phrase is identical to the provision on

---

[104] ICJ Reports, 1974, pp. 23–9; 55 ILR, p. 258.   [105] See also articles 61–69.
[106] See also article 60.
[107] See further Part XIII of the Convention and see Churchill and Lowe, *Law of the Sea*, Chapter 15.
[108] See further Part XII of the Convention and see Churchill and Lowe, *Law of the Sea*, Chapter 14.   [109] Article 59.   [110] Article 74.

delimitation of the continental shelf,[111] it is not surprising that cases have arisen in which states have sought a single maritime boundary, applying both to the continental shelf and the economic zone. In the *Gulf of Maine* case,[112] the Chamber of the International Court took the view that the criteria for a single maritime boundary were those that would apply to both the continental shelf and economic zones (in this case a fisheries zone) and not criteria that relate to one only of these areas.[113] Nevertheless, the overall requirement for the establishment of such a boundary is the need to achieve an equitable solution and this brings into consideration a range of factors that may or may not be deemed relevant or decisive by the Court. It is in the elucidation of such factors that difficulties have been encountered and it would be overoptimistic to assert that the situation is clear. In the *Gulf of Maine* case, the Court emphasised that the relevant criteria had to be essentially determined 'in relation to what may be properly called the geographical features of the area', but what these are is subject to some controversy and did not appear to cover scientific and other facts relating to fish stocks, oil exploration, scientific research or common defence arrangements.[114] In the *Guinea/Guinea Bissau Maritime Delimitation* case,[115] the Tribunal was called upon to draw a single line dividing the territorial sea, economic zone and continental shelf of the two states concerned. In the case of the latter two zones, the Tribunal noted that the use of the equidistance method was unsatisfactory since it exaggerated the importance of insignificant coastal features. Rather one had to consider the whole coastline of West Africa.[116] The Tribunal also considered that the evidence with regard to the geological and geomorphological features of the continental shelf was unsatisfactory,[117] while general economic factors were rejected as being unjust and inequitable, since they were based upon an evaluation of data that was constantly changing.[118] The question of a single maritime boundary arose again in the *St Pierre and Miquelon (Canada/France)* case,[119] where the Tribunal was asked to establish a single delimitation as between the parties

---

[111] See *infra*, p. 436. Note that the International Court declared that 'the identity of the language which is employed, even though limited of course to the determination of the relevant principles and rules of international law, is particularly significant', the *Gulf of Maine* case, ICJ Reports, 1984, pp. 246, 295: 71 ILR, pp. 74, 122. The Court declared in the *Jan Mayen Maritime Delimitation (Denmark v. Norway)* case, ICJ Reports, 1993, pp. 37, 59; 99 ILR, pp. 395, 427, that the statement in article 74(1) and the corresponding provision in article 83(1) with regard to the aim of any delimitation process being an equitable solution, 'reflects the requirements of customary law as regards the delimitation both of continental shelf and of exclusive economic zones'. [112] ICJ Reports, 1984, p. 246: 71 ILR, p. 74.
[113] *Ibid.*, p. 326; 71 ILR, p. 153. [114] *Ibid.*, p. 278; 71 ILR, p. 105. [115] 77 ILR, p. 635.
[116] *Ibid.*, pp. 679–81. [117] *Ibid.*, pp. 685–7. [118] *Ibid.*, pp. 688–9.
[119] 31 ILM, 1992, p. 1145; 95 ILR, p. 645. See also M. D. Evans, 'Less Than an Ocean Apart: the St Pierre and Miquelon and Jan Mayen Islands and the Delimitation of Maritime Zones', 43 ICLQ, 1994, p. 678; K. Highet, 'Delimitation of the Maritime Areas Between Canada and France', 87 AJIL, 1993, p. 452 and H. Ruiz Fabri, 'Sur la Délimitation des Espaces Maritimes entre le Canada et la France', 97 RGDIP, 1993, p. 67.

governing all rights and jurisdiction that the parties may exercise under international law in these maritime areas. In such cases, the Tribunal, following the *Gulf of Maine* decision, took the view that in a single or all purpose delimitation, article 6 of the Geneva Convention on the Continental Shelf 1958, which governed the delimitation of the continental shelf, did not have mandatory force as regards the establishment of that single maritime line.[120]

However, where there did not exist a special agreement between the parties asking the Court to determine a single maritime boundary applicable both to the continental shelf and the economic zone, the Court declared in the *Jan Mayen Maritime Delimitation (Denmark v. Norway)* case[121] that the two strands of the applicable law had to be examined separately. These strands related to the effect of article 6 of the Geneva Convention on the Continental Shelf 1958 upon the continental shelf and the rules of customary international law with regard to the fishery zone.[122]

A wide variety of states have in the last decade claimed exclusive fishing or economic zones of 200 miles.[123] It would appear that such is the number and distribution of these states, that the existence of the exclusive economic zone as a rule of customary law is firmly established. This is underlined by the comment of the International Court of Justice in the *Libya/Malta Continental Shelf* case[124] that 'the institution of the exclusive economic zone . . . is shown by the practice of states to have become a part of customary law'.[125]

In addition to such zones, some other zones have been announced by states over areas of the seas. Canada has, for example, claimed a 100 mile deep zone along her Arctic coastline as a special, pollution-free

[120] *Ibid.*, p. 1163; 95 ILR, p. 663.
[121] ICJ Reports, 1993, p. 37; 99 ILR, p. 395. See also M. D. Evans, 'Case Concerning Maritime Delimitation in the Area Between Greenland and Jan Mayen (*Denmark v. Norway*)', 43 ICLQ, 1994, p. 697.
[122] But see the Separate Opinion of Judge Oda, who took the view that the regime of the continental shelf was independent of the concept of the exclusive economic zone and that the request to draw a single maritime boundary was misconceived, *ibid.*, pp. 96–7; 99 ILR, pp. 464–5.
[123] The Hydrographic Department of the Royal Navy noted that as of 1 January 1995, ninety-eight states had proclaimed 200 mile economic zones (three of which are UK dependencies), see UKMIL, 65 BYIL, 1994, pp. 642–7. The Office of Ocean Affairs of the US State Department has given a figure of ninety-six states as of 31 January 1996. See also Churchill and Lowe, *Law of the Sea*, p. 353, and AFDI, 1978, pp. 851, 858–65. See also the US Declaration of an Exclusive Economic Zone in March 1983, which did not, however, assert a right of jurisdiction over marine scientific research over the zone, 22 ILM, 1983, pp. 461 *et seq.* On 22 September 1992, eight North Sea littoral states and the European Commission adopted a Ministerial Declaration on the Coordinated Extension of Jurisdiction in the North Sea in which it was agreed that these states would establish exclusive economic zones if they had not already done so, UKMIL, 63 BYIL, 1992, p. 755.
[124] ICJ Reports, 1985, p. 13; 81 ILR, p. 238.
[125] *Ibid.*, p. 33; 81 ILR, p. 265. See also the *Tunisia/Libya* case, ICJ Reports, 1982, pp. 18, 74: 67 ILR, pp. 4, 67.

zone.[126] Certain states have also asserted rights over what have been termed security or neutrality zones,[127] but these have never been particularly well received and are rare.

In an unusual arrangement, pursuant to a US–USSR Maritime Boundary Agreement of 1 June 1990, it was provided that each party would exercise sovereign rights and jurisdiction derived from the exclusive economic zone jurisdiction of the other party in a 'special area' on the other party's side of the maritime boundary in order to ensure that all areas within 200 miles of either party's coast would fall within the resource jurisdiction of one party or the other. It would appear that jurisdiction over three special areas within the USSR's 200 mile economic zone and one special area within the US's 200 mile economic zone were so transferred.[128]

Land-locked states[129]

Article 3 of the Geneva Convention on the High Seas 1958 provided that 'in order to enjoy freedom of the seas on equal terms with coastal states, states having no sea coast should have free access to the sea'.[130] Article 125 of the 1982 Convention on the Law of the Sea is formulated as follows:

1. Land-locked states shall have the right of access to and from the sea for the purpose of exercising the rights provided for in this Convention including those relating to the freedom of the high seas and the common heritage of mankind. To this end, land-locked states shall enjoy freedom of transit through the territory of transit states by all means of transport.
2. The terms and modalities for exercising freedom of transit shall be agreed between the land-locked states and the transit state concerned through bilateral, subregional or regional agreements.
3. Transit states, in the exercise of their full sovereignty over their territory, shall have the right to take all measures necessary to ensure that the rights and facilities provided for in this Part for land-locked states shall in no way infringe their legitimate interests.

[126] See O'Connell, *International Law of the Sea*, footnote 1, vol. II, pp. 1022–5. See also the Canadian Arctic Water Pollution Prevention Act 1970. The US has objected to this jurisdiction, see e.g. *Keesings Contemporary Archives*, pp. 23961 and 24129. The Canadian claim was reiterated in September 1985, *ibid.*, p. 33984.
[127] O'Connell, *International Law of the Sea*, vol. I, p. 578, note 95 regarding North Korea's proclamation of a fifty-mile security zone in 1977. See also *Cumulative* DUSPIL *1981–8*, vol. II, Washington, 1994, pp. 1750 *et seq.* detailing US practice objecting to peacetime security or military zones. Note also the establishment of the 'exclusion zone' around the Falkland Islands in 1982, see HC Deb., 28 April 1982, cols.296–7. See e.g. R. P. Barston and P. W. Birnie, 'The Falkland Islands/Islas Malvinas Conflict. A Question of Zones', 7 *Marine Policy*, 1983, p. 14.   [128] 84 AJIL, 1990, pp. 885–7.
[129] See e.g. L. Caflisch, 'Land-locked States and their Access to and From the Sea', 49 BYIL, 1978, p. 71 and I. Delupis, 'Landlocked States and the Law of the Sea', 19 *Scandinavian Studies in Law*, 1975, p. 101. See also Churchill and Lowe, *Law of the Sea*, Chapter 18.
[130] See also the Convention on Transit Trade of Land-Locked States 1965.

It will thus be seen that there is no absolute right of transit, but rather that transit depends upon arrangements to be made between the land-locked and transit states. Nevertheless, the affirmation of a right of access to the sea coast is an important step in assisting land-locked states. Articles 127 to 130 of the 1982 Convention set out a variety of terms for the operation of transit arrangements, while article 131 provides that ships flying the flag of land-locked states shall enjoy treatment equal to that accorded to other foreign ships in maritime ports. Ships of all states, whether coastal states or land-locked states, have the right of innocent passage in the territorial sea and freedom of navigation in the waters beyond the territorial sea.[131]

It is also to be noted that land-locked states have the right to participate upon an equitable basis in the exploitation of an appropriate part of the surplus of the living resources of the economic zones of coastal states of the same subregion or region, taking into account relevant economic and geographical factors.[132] Geographically disadvantaged states have the same right.[133] The terms and modalities of such participation are to be established by the states concerned through bilateral, subregional or regional agreements, taking into account a range of factors including the need to avoid effects detrimental to fishing communities or fishing industries of the coastal state and the nutritional needs of the respective states.[134]

With regard to provisions concerning the international seabed regime, article 148 of the 1982 Convention provides that the effective participation of developing states in the International Seabed Area shall be promoted, having due regard to their special interests and needs, and in particular to the special need of land-locked and geographically disadvantaged among them to overcome obstacles arising from their disadvantaged location, including remoteness from the Area and difficulty of access to and from it.[135]

---

[131] See e.g. article 14(1) of the Geneva Convention on the Territorial Sea 1958; article 2(1) and 4 of the Geneva Convention on the High Seas 1958 and articles 17, 38(1), 52(1), 53(2), 58(1), 87 and 90 of the 1982 Convention.

[132] Articles 69(1) of the 1982 Convention.

[133] Article 70(1). Geographically disadvantaged states are defined in article 70(2) as 'coastal states, including states bordering enclosed or semi-enclosed seas, whose geographical situation makes them dependent upon the exploitation of the living resources of the exclusive economic zones of other states in the subregion or region for adequate supplies of fish for the nutritional purposes of their populations or parts thereof, and coastal states which can claim no exclusive economic zone of their own'.

[134] See articles 69(2) and 70(2). Note also articles 69(4) and 70(5) restricting such rights of participation of developed landlocked states to developed coastal states of the same sub-region or region. By article 71, the provisions of articles 69 and 70 do not apply in the case of a coastal state whose economy is overwhelmingly dependent on the exploitation of the living resources of its exclusive economic zone.

[135] See also articles 152, 160 and 161.

The high seas[136]

The closed seas concept proclaimed by Spain and Portugal in the fifteenth and sixteenth centuries, and supported by the Papal Bulls of 1493 and 1506 dividing the seas of the world between the two powers, was replaced by the notion of the open seas and the concomitant freedom of the high seas during the eighteenth century.

The essence of the freedom of the high seas is that no state may acquire sovereignty over parts of it.[137] This is the general rule, but it is subject to the operation of the doctrines of recognition, acquiescence and prescription, where, by long usage accepted by other nations, certain areas of the high seas bounding on the territorial waters of coastal states may be rendered subject to that state's sovereignty. This was emphasised in the *Anglo-Norwegian Fisheries* case.[138]

The high seas were defined in Article 1 of the Geneva Convention on the High Seas 1958 as all parts of the sea that were not included in the territorial sea or in the internal waters of a state. This reflected customary international law, although as a result of developments the definition in article 86 of the 1982 Convention includes: 'all parts of the sea that are not included in the exclusive economic zone, in the territorial sea or in the internal waters of a state, or in the archipelagic waters of an archipelagic state'.

Article 87 of the 1982 Convention (developing article 2 of the 1958 Geneva Convention on the High Seas) provides that the high seas are open to all states and that the freedom of the high seas is exercised under the conditions laid down in the Convention and by other rules of international law. It includes *inter alia* the freedoms of navigation, overflight, the laying of submarine cables and pipelines,[139] the construction of artificial islands and other installations permitted under international law,[140] fishing, and the conduct of scientific research.[141] Such freedoms are to be exercised with due regard for the interests of other states in their exercise of the freedom of the high seas, and also with due regard for the rights under the Convention regarding activities in the International Seabed Area.[142]

Australia and New Zealand alleged before the ICJ, in the *Nuclear Tests*

---

[136] See e.g. Brown, *International Law of the Sea*, Chapter 14; O'Connell, *International Law of the Sea*, vol. II, Chapter 21, and Churchill and Lowe, *Law of the Sea*, Chapter 11. See also *Oppenheim's International Law*, pp. 710 *et seq.* and Nguyen Quoc Dinh *et al.*, *Droit International Public*, p. 1097.

[137] See article 2 of the 1958 High Seas Convention and article 89 of the 1982 Convention.

[138] ICJ Reports, 1951, p. 116; 18 ILR, p. 86. See *supra*, p. 395.

[139] Subject to Part VI of the Convention, dealing with the continental shelf.

[140] Subject to Part VI of the Convention, dealing with the continental shelf.

[141] Subject to Part VI of the Convention, dealing with the continental shelf, and Part XIII, dealing with marine scientific research.   [142] *Infra*, p. 444.

THE LAW OF THE SEA 419

case,[143] that French nuclear testing in the Pacific infringed the principle of the freedom of the seas, but this point was not decided by the Court. The 1963 Nuclear Test Ban Treaty prohibited the testing of nuclear weapons on the high seas as well as on land, but France was not a party to the treaty, and it appears not to constitute a customary rule binding all states, irrespective of the treaty.[144] Nevertheless, article 88 of the 1982 Convention provides that the high seas shall be reserved for peaceful purposes.

Principles that are generally acknowledged to come within article 2 include the freedom to conduct naval exercises on the high seas and the freedom to carry out research studies.

The freedom of navigation[145] is a traditional and well-recognised facet of the doctrine of the high seas, as is the freedom of fishing.[146] This was reinforced by the declaration by the Court in the *Fisheries Jurisdiction* cases[147] that Iceland's unilateral extension of its fishing zones from 12 to 50 miles constituted a violation of article 2 of the High Seas Convention, which is, as the preamble states, 'generally declaratory of established principles of international law'. The freedom of the high seas applies not only to coastal states but also to states that are land-locked.[148]

The question of freedom of navigation on the high seas in times of armed conflict was raised during the Iran–Iraq war, which during its latter stages involved attacks upon civilian shipping by both belligerents. Rather than rely on the classical and somewhat out-of-date rules of the laws of war at sea,[149] the UK in particular has analysed the issue in terms of the UN Charter. The following statement was made:[150]

The UK upholds the principle of freedom of navigation on the high seas and condemns all violations of the law of armed conflicts including attacks on mer-

[143] ICJ Reports, 1974, pp. 253 and 457; 57 ILR, pp. 350, 605. See also the Order of the International Court of Justice of 22 September 1995 in the *Request for an Examination of the Situation in Accordance with Paragraph 63 of the Court's Judgment of 20 December 1974 in the* Nuclear Tests (New Zealand v. France case), ICJ Reports, 1995, p. 288, where the Court refused to accede to a request by New Zealand to re-examine the 1974 judgment in view of the resumption by France of underground nuclear testing in the South Pacific.
[144] Note, however, the development of regional agreements prohibiting nuclear weapons, see the Treaty of Tlatelolco for the Prohibition of Nuclear Weapons in Latin America 1967, which extends the nuclear weapons ban to the territorial sea, airspace and any other space over which a state party exercises sovereignty in accordance with its own legislation; the Treaty of Rarotonga establishing a South Pacific Nuclear-Free Zone 1985; the African Nuclear Weapon-Free Treaty 1995 and the Treaty on the Southeast Asia Nuclear Weapon-Free Zone 1995.
[145] See the *Corfu Channel* case, ICJ Reports, 1949, pp. 4, 22; 16 ILR, p. 155, and *Nicaragua v. United States*, ICJ Reports, 1986, pp. 14, 111–12; 76 ILR, pp. 349, 445.
[146] See the *Anglo-Norwegian Fisheries* case, ICJ Reports, 1951, pp. 116, 183; 18 ILR, pp. 86, 131. See also *infra* p. 428.   [147] ICJ Reports, 1974, p. 3.   [148] *Supra*, p. 416.
[149] See e.g. Churchill and Lowe, *Law of the Sea*, Chapter 17 and C. J. Colombos, *International Law of the Sea*, 6th edn, London, 1967, Part II.
[150] *Parliamentary Papers*, 1987–88, HC, Paper 179–II, p. 120 and UKMIL, 59 BYIL, 1988, p. 581.

chant shipping. Under article 51 of the UN Charter, a state actively engaged in armed conflict (as in the case of Iran and Iraq) is entitled in exercise of its inherent right of self-defence to stop and search a foreign merchant ship on the high seas if there is reasonable ground for suspecting that the ship is taking arms to the other side for use in the conflict. This is an exceptional right: if the suspicion proves to be unfounded and if the ship has not committed acts calculated to give rise to suspicion, then the ship's owners have a good claim for compensation for loss caused by the delay. This right would not, however, extend to the imposition of a maritime blockade or other forms of economic warfare.

Jurisdiction on the high seas[151]

The foundation of the maintenance of order on the high seas has rested upon the concept of the nationality of the ship, and the consequent jurisdiction of the flag state over the ship. It is, basically, the flag state that will enforce the rules and regulations not only of its own municipal law but of international law as well. A ship without a flag will be deprived of many of the benefits and rights available under the legal regime of the high seas.

Each state is required to elaborate the conditions necessary for the grant of its nationality to ships, for the registration of ships in its territory and for the right to fly its flag.[152] The nationality of the ship will depend upon the flag it flies, but article 5 of the High Seas Convention also stipulates that there must be a 'genuine link' between the state and the ship, and 'in particular the state must effectively exercise its jurisdiction and control in administrative, technical and social matters over ships flying its flag'.[153] This provision was intended to check the use of flags of convenience operated by states such as Liberia and Panama which would grant their nationality to ships requesting such because of low taxation and the lack of application of most wage and social security agreements. This enabled the ships to operate at very low costs indeed.

However, what precisely the 'genuine link' consists of and how one may regulate any abuse of the provisions of article 5 are unresolved questions. Some countries, for example the United States, maintain that the requirement of a 'genuine link' really only amounts to a duty to exercise jurisdiction over the ship in an efficacious manner, and is not a precondition for the grant, or the acceptance by other states of the grant, of nationality.[154]

An opportunity did arise in 1960 to discuss the meaning of the provision of the *IMCO* case.[155] The International Court was called upon to define

---

[151] See e.g. *Oppenheim's International Law*, p. 731.
[152] Article 5 of the 1958 High Seas Convention and article 91 of the 1982 Convention.
[153] Note that the latter requirement was omitted in the 1982 Convention, see article 91.
[154] See Churchill and Lowe, *Law of the Sea*, pp. 205–9.
[155] ICJ Reports, 1960, p. 150; 30 ILR, p. 426.

'largest ship-owning nations' for the purposes of the constitution of a committee of the Inter-Governmental Maritime Consultative Organisation. It was held that the term referred only to registered tonnage so as to enable Liberia and Panama to be elected to the committee. Unfortunately, the opportunity was not taken of considering the problems of flags of convenience or the meaning of the 'genuine link' in the light of the true ownership of the ships involved, and so the doubts and ambiguities remain.

The UN Conference on Conditions of Registration of Ships, held under the auspices of the UN Conference on Trade and Development, convened in July 1984 and an agreement was signed in 1986. It attempts to deal with the flags of convenience issue, bearing in mind that nearly one-third of the world's merchant fleet by early 1985 flew such flags. It specifies that flag states should provide in their laws and regulations for the ownership of ships flying their flags and that those should include appropriate provision for participation by nationals as owners of such ships, and that such provisions should be sufficient to permit the flag state to exercise effectively its jurisdiction and control over ships flying its flag.[156]

The issue of the genuine link arose in the context of the Iran–Iraq war and in particular Iranian attacks upon Kuwaiti shipping. This prompted Kuwait to ask the USSR and the US to reflag Kuwaiti tankers. The US agreed in early 1987 to reflag eleven such tankers under the US flag and to protect them as it did other US-flagged ships in the Gulf.[157] The UK also agreed to reflag some Kuwaiti tankers, arguing that only satisfaction of Department of Trade and Industry requirements was necessary.[158] Both states argued that the genuine link requirement was satisfied and in view of the ambiguity of state practice as to the definition of genuine link in such instances, it is hard to argue that the US and UK acted unlawfully.

Ships are required to sail under the flag of one state only and are subject to its exclusive jurisdiction (save in exceptional cases). Where a ship does sail under the flags of more than one state, according to convenience, it may be treated as a ship without nationality and will not be able to claim any of the nationalities concerned.[159] A ship that is stateless, and does not fly a flag, may be boarded and seized on the high seas. This point was accepted by the Privy Council in the case of *Naim Molvan* v. *Attorney-General for Palestine*,[160]

---

[156] *Keesings Contemporary Archives*, p. 33952.
[157] See 26 ILM, 1987, pp. 1429–30, 1435–40 and 1450–2. See also 37 ICLQ, 1988, pp. 424–5 and Nordquist and Wachenfeld, 'Legal Aspects of Reflagging Kuwaiti Tankers and Laying of Mines in the Persian Gulf', 31 German YIL, 1988, p. 138.
[158] See e.g. 119 HC Deb., col. 645, 17 July 1987.
[159] Article 6 of the 1958 Convention and article 92 of the 1982 Convention.
[160] [1948] AC 351; 13 ILR, p. 51. See also e.g. *US* v. *Dominguez*, 604 F.2d 304 (1979); *US* v. *Cortes*, 588 F.2d 106 (1979); *US* v. *Monroy*, 614 F.2d 61 (1980) and *US* v. *Marino-Garcia*, 679 F.2d 1373 (1982). In the latter case, the Court referred to stateless vessels as 'international pariahs', *ibid.*, p. 1383.

which concerned the seizure by the British navy of a stateless ship attempting to convey immigrants into Palestine.

The basic principle relating to jurisdiction on the high seas is that the flag state alone may exercise such rights over the ship.[161] This was elaborated in the *Lotus* case,[162] where it was held that 'vessels on the high seas are subject to no authority except that of the state whose flag they fly'.[163] This exclusivity is without exception regarding warships and ships owned or operated by a state where they are used only on governmental non-commercial service. Such ships have, according to articles 95 and 96 of the 1982 Convention, 'complete immunity from the jurisdiction of any state other than the flag state'.[164]

Exceptions to the exclusivity of flag state jurisdiction

However, this basic principle is subject to exceptions regarding other vessels, and the concept of the freedom of the high seas is similarly limited by the existence of a series of exceptions.

1. Right of visit

Since the law of the sea depends to such an extent upon the nationality of the ship, it is well recognised in customary international law that warships have a right of approach to ascertain the nationality of ships. However, this right of approach to identify vessels does not incorporate the right to board or visit ships. This may only be undertaken, in the absence of hostilities between the flag states of the warship and a merchant vessel and in the absence of special treaty provisions to the contrary, where the ship is engaged in piracy or the slave trade, or, though flying a foreign flag or no flag at all, is in reality of the same nationality as the warship or of no nationality. But the warship has to operate carefully in such circumstances, since it may be liable to pay compensation for any loss or damage sustained if its suspicions are unfounded and the ship boarded has not committed any act justifying them. Thus, international law has settled for a narrow exposition of the right of approach, in spite of earlier tendencies to expand this right, and the above provisions were incorporated into article 22 of the High Seas Convention. Article 110 of the 1982 Convention added to this list a right of visit where the ship is engaged in unauthorised broadcasting and the flag state of the warship has under article 109 of the Convention jurisdiction to prosecute the offender.

[161] See article 6 of the 1958 Convention and article 92 of the 1982 Convention.
[162] PCIJ, Series A, No. 10, 1927, p. 25; 4 ILR, p. 153.
[163] Note that duties of the flag state are laid down in articles 94, 97, 98, 99, 113 and 115 of the 1982 Convention.   [164] See articles 8 and 9 of the High Seas Convention 1958.

2. Piracy[165]

The most formidable of the exceptions to the exclusive jurisdiction of the flag state and to the principle of the freedom of the high seas is the concept of piracy. Piracy is strictly defined in international law and was declared in article 101 of the 1982 Convention to consist of any of the following acts:

> (a) Any illegal acts of violence, detention or any act of depredation, committed for private ends by the crew or the passengers of a private ship or private aircraft and directed: (i) on the high seas, against another ship or aircraft, or against persons or property on board such ship or aircraft; (ii) against a ship, aircraft, persons or property in a place outside the jurisdiction of any state; (b) Any act of voluntary participation in the operation of a ship or of an aircraft with knowledge of facts making it a pirate ship or aircraft; (c) Any act of inciting or of intentionally facilitating an act described in subparagraph (a) or (b).[166]

The essence of piracy under international law is that it must be committed for private ends. In other words, any hijacking or takeover for political reasons is automatically excluded from the definition of piracy. Similarly, any acts committed on the ship by the crew and aimed at the ship itself or property or persons on the ship do not fall within this category.

Any and every state may seize a pirate ship or aircraft whether on the high seas or on *terra nullius* and arrest the persons and seize the property on board. In addition, the courts of the state carrying out the seizure have jurisdiction to impose penalties, and may decide what action to take regarding the ship or aircraft and property, subject to the rights of third parties that have acted in good faith.[167] The fact that every state may arrest and try persons accused of piracy makes that crime quite exceptional in international law, where so much emphasis is placed upon the sovereignty and jurisdiction of each particular state within its own territory.

3. The slave trade[168]

Although piracy may be suppressed by all states, most offences on the high seas can only be punished in accordance with regulations prescribed by the municipal legislation of states, even where international law requires such

---

[165] See e.g. Brown, *International Law of the Sea*, p. 299; *Oppenheim's International Law*, p. 746 and B. H. Dubner, *The Law of International Sea Piracy*, The Hague, 1979.

[166] See also article 15 of the High Seas Convention 1958. Note that article 105 of the 1982 Convention deals with the seizure of pirate boats or aircraft, while article 106 provides for compensation in the case of seizure without adequate grounds. See also *Athens Maritime Enterprises Corporation v. Hellenic Mutual War Risk Association* [1983] 1 All ER 590; 78 ILR, p. 563.

[167] See article 19 of the 1958 Convention and article 105 of the 1982 Convention.

[168] See e.g. Brown, *International Law of the Sea*, p. 309.

rules to be established. Article 99 of the 1982 Convention provides that every state shall take effective measures to prevent and punish the transport of slaves in ships authorised to fly its flag and to prevent the unlawful use of its flag for that purpose. Any slave taking refuge on board any ship, whatever its flag, shall *ipso facto* be free.[169] Under article 110, warships may board foreign merchant ships where they are reasonably suspected of engaging in the slave trade; offenders must be handed over to the flag state for trial.[170]

4. Unauthorised broadcasting[171]

Under article 109 of the 1982 Convention, all states are to cooperate in the suppression of unauthorised broadcasting from the high seas. This is defined to mean transmission of sound or TV from a ship or installation on the high seas intended for reception by the general public, contrary to international regulations but excluding the transmission of distress calls. Any person engaged in such broadcasting may be prosecuted by the flag state of the ship, the state of registry of the installation, the state of which the person is a national, any state where the transmission can be received or any state where authorised radio communication is suffering interference.

Any of the above states having jurisdiction may arrest any person or ship engaging in unauthorised broadcasting on the high seas and seize the broadcasting apparatus.[172]

5. Hot pursuit[173]

The right of hot pursuit of a foreign ship is a principle designed to ensure that a vessel which has infringed the rules of a coastal state cannot escape punishment by fleeing to the high seas. In reality it means that in certain defined circumstances a coastal state may extend its jurisdiction onto the

---

[169] See also article 13 of the High Seas Convention 1958.

[170] See also article 22 of the High Seas Convention 1958. Several international treaties exist with the aim of suppressing the slave trade and some provide for reciprocal rights of visits and search on the high seas, see e.g. Churchill and Lowe, *International Law of the Sea*, pp. 171–2. Note also that under article 108 of the 1982 Convention all states are to co-operate in the suppression of the illicit drug trade.

[171] See e.g. J. C. Woodliffe, 'The Demise of Unauthorised Broadcasting from Ships in International Waters', 1 *Journal of Estuarine and Coastal Law*, 1986, p. 402 and Brown, *International Law of the Sea*, p. 312.

[172] See also article 110 of the 1982 Convention. In addition, see the European Agreement for the Prevention of Broadcasting transmitted from Stations outside National Territories.

[173] See e.g. N. Poulantzas, *The Right of Hot Pursuit in International Law*, Leiden, 1969 and *Oppenheim's International Law, op. cit.*, p. 739. See also W. C. Gilmore, 'Hot Pursuit: The Case of *R v. Mills and Others*', 44 ICLQ, 1995, p. 949.

high seas in order to pursue and seize a ship which is suspected of infringing its laws. The right, which has been developing in one form or another since the nineteenth century,[174] was comprehensively elaborated in article 111 of the 1982 Convention, building upon article 23 of the High Seas Convention 1958.

It notes that such pursuit may commence when the authorities of the coastal state have good reason to believe that the foreign ship has violated its laws. The pursuit must start while the ship, or one of its boats, is within the internal waters, territorial sea or contiguous zone of the coastal state and may only continue outside the territorial sea or contiguous zone if it is uninterrupted. However, if the pursuit commences while the foreign ship is in the contiguous zone, then it may only be undertaken if there has been a violation of the rights for the protection of which the zone was established. The right may similarly commence from the archipelagic waters. In addition, the right will apply *mutatis mutandis* to violations in the exclusive economic zone or on the continental shelf (including safety zones around continental shelf installations) of the relevant rules and regulations applicable to such areas.

Hot pursuit only begins when the pursuing ship has satisfied itself that the ship pursued or one of its boats is within the limits of the territorial sea or as the case may be in the contiguous zone, or economic zone or on the continental shelf.

It is essential that prior to the chase a visual or auditory signal to stop has been given at a distance enabling it to be seen or heard by the foreign ship and pursuit may only be exercised by warships or military aircraft or by specially authorised government ships or places. The right of hot pursuit ceases as soon as the ship pursued has entered the territorial waters of its own or a third state.

6. Collisions

Where ships are involved in collisions on the high seas, article 11 of the High Seas Convention declares, overruling the decision in the *Lotus* case,[175] that penal or disciplinary proceedings may only be taken against the master or other persons in the service of the ship by the authorities of either the flag state or the state of which the particular person is a national. It also provides that no arrest or detention of the ship, even for investigation purposes, can be ordered by other than the authorities of the flag state. This was reaffirmed in article 97 of the 1982 Convention.

---

[174] See e.g. the *I'm Alone* case, 3 RIAA, p. 1609 (1935); 7 ILR, p. 203.
[175] PCIJ, Series A, No. 10, 1927, p. 25; 4 ILR, p. 153.

7. Treaty rights

In many cases, states may by treaty permit each other's warships to exercise certain powers of visit and search as regards vessels flying the flags of the signatories to the treaty. For example, most of the agreements in the last century relating to the suppression of the slave trade provided that warships of the parties to the agreements could search and sometimes detain vessels suspected of being involved in the trade, where such vessels were flying the flags of the treaty states.[176] The Convention for the Protection of Submarine Cables of 1884 gave the warships of contracting states the right to stop and ascertain the nationality of merchant ships that were suspected of infringing the terms of the Convention, and other agreements dealing with matters as diverse as arms trading and liquor smuggling contained like powers.[177]

Pollution[178]

Article 24 of the 1958 Convention on the High Seas called on states to draw up regulations to prevent the pollution of the seas by the discharge of oil or the dumping of radioactive waste, while article 1 of the Convention on the Fishing and Conservation of the Living Resources of the High Seas, of the same year, declared that all states had the duty to adopt, or co-operate with other states in adopting, such measures as may be necessary for the conservation of the living resources of the high seas. Although these provisions have not proved an unqualified success, they have been reinforced by an interlocking series of additional agreements covering the environmental protection of the seas.

The International Convention relating to Intervention on the High Seas in Cases of Oil Pollution Casualties, signed in 1969 and in force as of June 1975, provides that the parties to the Convention may take such measures on the high seas:

> as may be necessary to prevent, mitigate or eliminate grave and imminent danger to their coastline or related interests from pollution or threat of pollution of the sea by oil, following upon a maritime casualty or acts related to such a casualty, which may reasonably be expected to result in major harmful consequences.

[176] See e.g. Churchill and Lowe, *International Law of the Sea*, pp. 171–2 and 175.
[177] See the UK–US Agreement on Vessels Trafficking in Drugs 1981 and *US* v. *Biermann*, 83 AJIL, 1989, p. 99.
[178] See Brown, *International Law of the Sea*, Chapter 15; Churchill and Lowe, *Law of the Sea*, Chapter 15, and O'Connell, *International Law of the Sea*, footnote 1, vol. II, Chapter 25. See *infra*, Chapter 15.

This provision came as a result of the *Torrey Canyon* incident in 1967[179] in which a Liberian tanker foundered off the Cornish coast, spilling massive quantities of oil and polluting large stretches of the UK and French coastlines. As a last resort to prevent further pollution, British aircraft bombed the tanker and set it ablaze. The Convention on Intervention on the High Seas provided for action to be taken to end threats to the coasts of states, while the Convention on Civil Liability for Oil Pollution Damage, also signed in 1969 and which came into effect in June 1975, stipulated that the owners of ships causing oil pollution damage were to be liable to pay compensation. The latter agreement was supplemented in 1971 by the Convention on the Establishment of an International Fund for Compensation for Oil Pollution Damage which sought to provide for compensation in circumstances not covered by the 1969 Convention and aid ship owners in their additional financial obligations.

These agreements are only a small part of the web of treaties covering the preservation of the sea environment. Other examples include the 1954 Convention for the Prevention of Pollution of the Seas by Oil, with its series of amendments designed to ban offensive discharges, the 1971 Oslo Convention for the Prevention of Marine Pollution by Dumping from Ships and Aircraft and the subsequent London Convention on the Dumping of Wastes at Sea the following year, the 1973 Convention for the Prevention of Pollution from Ships and the 1974 Paris Convention for the Prevention of Marine Pollution from Land-Based Sources.[180]

Under the 1982 Convention nearly fifty articles are devoted to the protection of the marine environment. Flag states still retain the competence to legislate for their ships, but certain minimum standards are imposed upon them.[181] It is also provided that states are responsible for the fulfilment of their international obligations concerning the protection and preservation of the marine environment and are liable in accordance with international law. States must also ensure that recourse is available in accordance with their legal systems for prompt and adequate compensation or other relief regarding damage caused by pollution of the marine environment by persons under their jurisdiction.[182]

States are under a basic obligation to protect and preserve the marine environment.[183] Article 194 also provides that:

[179] 6 ILM, 1967, p. 480. See also the *Amoco Cadiz* incident in 1978, e.g. Churchill and Lowe, *Law of the Sea*, p. 241, and the *Aegean Sea* and *Braer* incidents in 1992–3, see e.g. G. Plant, ' "*Safer Ships, Cleaner Seas*": Lord Donaldson's Inquiry, The UK Government's Response and International Law', 44 ICLQ, 1995, p. 939.
[180] Also a variety of regional and bilateral agreements have been signed, *ibid.*, pp. 263–4.
[181] See article 211. See also generally articles 192–238, covering *inter alia* global and regional co-operation, technical assistance, monitory and environmental assessment, and the development of the enforcement of international and domestic law preventing pollution.
[182] Article 235.   [183] Article 192.

1. States shall take, individually or jointly as appropriate, all measures consistent with this Convention that are necessary to prevent, reduce and control pollution of the marine environment from any source, using for this purpose the best practicable means at their disposal and in accordance with their capabilities, and they shall endeavour to harmonise their policies in this connection.

2. States shall take all measures necessary to ensure that activities under their jurisdiction or control are so conducted as not to cause damage by pollution to other states and their environment, and that pollution arising from incidents or activities under their jurisdiction or control does not spread beyond the areas where they exercise sovereign rights in accordance with this Convention.

3. The measures taken pursuant to this Part shall deal with all sources of pollution of the marine environment. These measures shall include, *inter alia*, those designed to minimise to the fullest possible extent:

(a) the release of toxic, harmful, or noxious substances, especially those which are persistent, from land-based sources, from or through the atmosphere or by dumping;

(b) pollution from vessels, in particular measures for preventing accidents and dealing with emergencies, ensuring the safety of operations at sea, preventing intentional and unintentional discharges, and regulating the design, construction, equipment, operation and manning of vessels;

(c) pollution from installations and devices used in exploitation of the natural resources of the seabed and subsoil, in particular measures for preventing accidents and dealing with emergencies, ensuring the safety of operations at sea, and regulating the design, construction, equipment, operation and manning of such installations or devices;

(d) pollution from other installations and devices operating in the marine environment, in particular for preventing accidents and dealing with emergencies, ensuring the safety of operations at sea, and regulating the design, construction, equipment, operation and manning of such installations or devices.

4. In taking measures to prevent, reduce or control pollution of the marine environment, states shall refrain from unjustifiable interference with activities carried out by other states in the exercise of their rights and in pursuance of their duties in conformity with this Convention.

Straddling stocks[184]

The freedom to fish on the high seas is one of the fundamental freedoms of the high seas, but it is not total or absolute.[185] The development of exclu-

[184] See e.g. Brown, *International Law of the Sea*, p. 226; W. T. Burke, *The New International Law of Fisheries*, Oxford, 1994; H. Gherari, 'L'Accord de 4 août 1995 sur les Stocks Chevauchants et les Stocks de Poisson Grands Migrateurs', 100 RGDIP, 1996, p. 367; B. Kwiatkowska, 'Creeping Jurisdiction beyond 200 miles in the Light of the 1982 Law of the Sea Convention and State Practice', 22 *Ocean Development and International Law*, 1991, p. 167; E. Miles and W. T. Burke, 'Pressures on the UN Convention on the Law of the Sea 1982 Arising from New Fisheries Conflicts: The Problem of Straddling Stocks', 20 *Ocean Development and International Law*, 1989, p. 352 and E. Meltzer, 'Global Overview of Straddling and Highly Migratory Fish Stocks: The Nonsustainable Nature of High Seas Fisheries', 25 *Ocean Development and International Law*, 1994, p. 256.
[185] See article 2 of the High Seas Convention 1958 and articles 1 and 6 of the Geneva Convention on Fishing and Conservation of the Living Resources of the High Seas 1958,

sive economic zones has meant that the area of high seas has shrunk appreciably, so that the bulk of fish stocks are now to be found within the economic zones of coastal states. In addition, the interests of such coastal states have extended to impinge more clearly upon the regulation of the high seas.

Article 56(1) of the 1982 Convention provides that coastal states have sovereign rights over their economic zones for the purpose of exploring and exploiting, conserving and managing the fish stocks of the zones concerned. Such rights are accompanied by duties as to conservation and management measures in order to ensure that the fish stocks in exclusive economic zones are not endangered by overexploitation and that such stocks are maintained at, or restored to, levels which can produce the maximum sustainable yield.[186] Where the same stock or stocks of associated species occur within the exclusive economic zones of two or more coastal states, these states shall seek either directly or through appropriate subregional or regional organisations to agree upon the measures necessary to co-ordinate and ensure the conservation and development of such stocks.[187]

Article 116(b) of the 1982 Convention states that the freedom to fish on the high seas is subject to the rights and duties as well as the interests of coastal states as detailed above, while the 1982 Convention lays down a general obligation upon states to co-operate in taking such measures for their respective nationals as may be necessary for the conservation of the living resources of the high seas and a variety of criteria are laid down for the purpose of determining the allowable catch and establishing other conservation measures.[188]

A particular problem is raised with regard to straddling stocks, that is stocks of fish that straddle both exclusive economic zones and high seas, for if the latter were not in some way regulated, fishery stocks regularly present in the exclusive economic zone could be depleted by virtue of unrestricted fishing of those stocks while they were present on the high seas. Article 63(2) of the 1982 Convention stipulates that where the same stock or stocks of associated species occur both within the exclusive economic zone and in an area beyond and adjacent to the zone (ie. the high seas), the coastal state and the states fishing for such stocks in the adjacent area shall seek, either

and article 116 of the 1982 Convention. In particular, the freedom to fish is subject to a state's treaty obligations, to the interests and rights of coastal states and to the requirements of conservation. See also *supra* p. 412 with regard to the *Fisheries Jurisdiction* case.
[186] Article 61. See also article 62.
[187] Article 63(1). This is without prejudice to the other provisions of this part of the 1982 Convention.
[188] See articles 117–20. A series of provisions in the 1982 Convention apply with regard to particular species, e.g. article 64 concerning highly migratory species (such as tuna); article 65 concerning marine mammals (such as whales, for which see also the work of the International Whaling Commission); article 66 concerning andromous species (such as salmon); article 67 concerning catadromous species (such as eels) and article 68 concerning sedentary species (which are regarded as part of the natural resources of a coastal state's continental shelf, see article 77 (4)).

directly or through appropriate subregional or regional organisations, to agree upon the measures necessary for the conservation of these stocks in the adjacent area.

The provisions in the 1982 Convention, however, were not deemed to be fully comprehensive[189] and as problems of straddling stocks grew more apparent,[190] a Straddling Stocks Conference was set up in 1993 and produced an agreement two years later. The Agreement emphasises the need to conserve and manage straddling fish stocks and highly migratory species and calls in particular for the application of the precautionary approach.[191] Coastal states and states fishing on the high seas shall pursue co-operation in relation to straddling and highly migratory fish stocks either directly or through appropriate subregional or regional organisations and shall enter into consultations in good faith and without delay at the request of any interested state with a view to establishing appropriate arrangements to ensure conservation and management of the stocks.[192] Much emphasis is placed upon subregional and regional organisations and article 10 provides that in fulfilling their obligation to co-operate through such organisations or arrangements, states shall *inter alia* agree on measures to ensure the long-term sustainability of straddling and highly migratory fish stocks and agree as appropriate upon participatory rights such as allocations of allowable catch or levels of fishing effort. In particular, the establishment of co-operative mechanisms for effective monitoring, control, surveillance and enforcement; decision-making procedures facilitating the adoption of such measures of conservation and management, and the promotion of the peaceful settlement of disputes is called for. The focus in terms of implementation is upon the flag state. Article 18 provides that flag states shall take such measures as may be necessary to ensure that its vessels comply with subregional and regional conservation and management measures, while article 19 provides that flag states must enforce such measures irrespective of where violations occur and investigate immediately any alleged violation. Article 21 deals specifically with subregional and regional co-operation in enforcement and provides that in any area of the high seas covered by such an organisation or arrangement, a state party who is also a member or participant in such an organisation or arrangement, may board and inspect fishing vessels flying the flag of another state party to the Agreement. This

---

[189] See e.g. Burke, 'Pressures', pp. 348 *et seq.* and B. Kwiatowska, 'The High Seas Fisheries Regime: At a Point of No Return ?', 8 *International Journal of Marine and Coastal Law*, 1993, p. 327.

[190] E.g. with regard to the Grand Banks of Newfoundland, the Bering Sea, the Barents Sea, the Sea of Okhotsk and off Patagonia and the Falklands, see D. H. Anderson, 'The Straddling Stocks Agreement of 1995 – An Initial Assessment', 45 ICLQ, 1996, p. 463.

[191] See articles 5 and 6 of the Straddling Stocks Agreement. See also with regard to this approach, *infra*, Chapter 15, p. 604.   [192] Article 8.

applies whether that state party is or is not a member of or a participant in such a subregional or regional organisation or arrangement. The boarding and visiting powers are for the purpose of ensuring compliance with the conservation and management measures established by the organisation or arrangement. Where, following a boarding and inspection, there are clear grounds for believing that a vessel has engaged in activities contrary to the relevant conservation and management measures, the inspecting state shall secure evidence and promptly notify the flag state. The flag state must respond within three working days and either fulfill its investigation and enforcement obligations under article 19 or authorise the inspecting state to investigate. In the latter case, the flag state must then take enforcement action or authorise the inspecting state to take such action. Where there are clear grounds for believing that the vessel has committed a serious violation and the flag state has failed to respond or take action as required, the inspectors may remain on board and secure evidence and may require the master to bring the vessel into the nearest appropriate port.[193] Article 23 provides that a port state has the right and duty to take measures in accordance with international law to promote the effectiveness of subregional, regional and global conservation and management measures.

One of the major regional organisations existing in this area is the North Atlantic Fisheries Organisation (NAFO), which came into being following the Northwest Atlantic Fisheries Convention 1978. The organisation has established a Fisheries Commission with responsibility for conservation measures in the area covered by this Convention. The European Community is a party to the Convention, although it has objected on occasions to NAFO's total catch quotas and the share-out of such quotas among state parties. In particular, a dispute developed with regard to the share-out of Greenland halibut, following upon a decision by NAFO to reduce the EC share of this fishery in 1995.[194] The EC formally objected to this decision using NAFO procedures and established its own halibut quota, which was in excess of the NAFO quota. In May 1994, Canada had amended its Coastal Fisheries Protection Act 1985 in order to enable it to take action to prevent further destruction of straddling stocks and by virtue of which any vessel from any nation fishing at variance with good conservation rules could be rendered subject to Canadian action. In early 1995, regulations were issued in order to protect Greenland halibut outside Canada's 200 mile limit from overfishing. On 9 March 1995, Canadian officers boarded a Spanish vessel fishing on the high seas on the Grand Banks some 245 miles off the Canadian coast. The captain was arrested and the vessel seized and towed

---

[193] See also article 22.
[194] See e.g. P. G. G. Davies, 'The EC/Canadian Fisheries Dispute in the Northwest Atlantic', 44 ICLQ, 1995, p. 927.

to a Canadian harbour. Spain commenced an application before the International Court on 28 March 1995.[195] A month later, an agreement between the EC and Canada was reached, under which the EC obtained an increased quota for Greenland halibut and Canada stayed charges against the vessel and agreed to repeal the provisions of the regulation banning Spanish and Portuguese vessels from fishing in the NAFO regulatory area. Improved control and enforcement procedures were also agreed.[196] Nevertheless, a serious general issue remains and that is the effective enforcement of conservation measures covering straddling stocks on the high seas.

The continental shelf[197]

The continental shelf is a geological expression referring to the ledges that project from the continental land mass into the seas and which are covered with only a relatively shallow layer of water (some 150–200 metres) and which eventually fall away into the ocean depths (some thousands of metres deep). These ledges or shelves take up some 7 to 8 per cent of the total area of ocean and their extent varies considerably from place to place. Off the western coast of the United States, for instance, it is less than 5 miles wide, while on the other hand the whole of the underwater area of the North Sea and Persian Gulf consists of shelf.

The vital fact about the continental shelves is that they are rich in oil and gas resources and quite often are host to extensive fishing grounds. This stimulated a round of appropriations by coastal states in the years following the Second World War, which gradually altered the legal status of the continental shelf from being part of the high seas and available for exploitation by all states until its current recognition as exclusive to the coastal state.

The first move in this direction, and the one that led to a series of similar and more extensive claims, was the Truman Proclamation of 1945.[198] This pointed to the technological capacity to exploit the riches of the shelf and the need to establish a recognised jurisdiction over such resources, and declared that the coastal state was entitled to such jurisdiction for a number of reasons. First, because utilisation or conservation of the resources of the

---

[195] ICJ Communiqué No. 95/8.
[196] See European Commission Press Release, WE/15/95, 20 April 1995.
[197] See e.g. Brown, *International Law of the Sea*, Chapters 10 and 11; O'Connell, *International Law of the Sea*, vol. I, Chapter 13; Churchill and Lowe, *Law of the Sea*, Chapter 8; Z. J. Slouka, *International Custom and the Continental Shelf*, The Hague, 1968; C. Vallée, *Le Plateau Continental dans le Droit International Positif*, Paris, 1971; V. Marotta Rangel, 'Le Plateau Continental dans la Convention de 1982 sur le Droit de la Mer', 194 HR, 1985 V, p. 269 and H. Lauterpacht, 'Sovereignty over Submarine Areas', 27 BYIL, 1950, p. 376. See also *Oppenheim's International Law*, op. cit., p. 764 and Nguyen Quoc Dinh *et al.*, *Droit International Public*, p. 1087.   [198] Whiteman, *Digest*, vol. IV, p. 756.

subsoil and seabed of the continental shelf depended upon co-operation from the shore. Secondly, because the shelf itself could be regarded as an extension of the land mass of the coastal state, and its resources were often merely an extension into the sea of deposits lying within the territory. And finally, because the coastal state, for reasons of security, was profoundly interested in activities off its shores which would be necessary to utilise the resources of the shelf.

Accordingly, the US government proclaimed that it regarded the 'natural resources of the subsoil and seabed of the continental shelf beneath the high seas but contiguous to the coasts of the United States as appertaining to the United States, subject to its jurisdiction and control'. However, this would in no way affect the status of the waters above the continental shelf as high seas. This proclamation precipitated a whole series of claims by states to their continental shelves, some in similar terms to the US assertions, and others in substantially wider terms. Argentina and El Salvador, for example, claimed not only the shelf but also the waters above and the airspace. Chile and Peru, having no continental shelf to speak of, claimed sovereignty over the seabed, subsoil and waters around their coasts to a limit of 200 miles, although this occasioned vigorous protests by many states.[199] The problems were discussed over many years leading to the 1958 Geneva Convention on the Continental Shelf.[200]

In the *North Sea Continental Shelf* cases,[201] the Court noted that:

> the rights of the coastal state in respect of the area of continental shelf that constitutes a natural prolongation of its land territory into and under the sea exist *ipso facto* and *ab initio*, by virtue of its sovereignty over the land, and as an extension of it in an exercise of sovereign rights for the purpose of exploring the seabed and exploiting its natural resources. In short there is here an inherent right.

The development of the concept of the exclusive economic zone has to some extent confused the issue, since under article 56 of the 1982 Convention the coastal state has sovereign rights over all the natural resources of its exclusive economic zone, including the seabed resources.[202] Accordingly, states possess two sources of rights with regard to the seabed,[203] although claims with regard to the economic zone, in contrast to the continental shelf, need to be specifically maintained. It is also possible,

[199] *Ibid.*, pp. 794–9 and see also *Oppenheim's International Law*, pp. 768–9.
[200] Note that in the *Abu Dhabi* case, the arbitrator declared that the doctrine of the continental shelf in 1951 was not yet a rule of international law, 18 ILR, p. 144. See also to the same effect (with regard to 1949), *Reference Re: The Seabed and Subsoil of the Continental Shelf Offshore Newfoundland*, 5 DLR (46), p. 385 *per* Supreme Court of Canada (1984).
[201] ICJ Reports, 1969; pp. 3, 22; 41 ILR, pp. 29, 51.   [202] See *supra*, p. 411.
[203] Note that the International Court in the *Libya/Malta Continental Shelf* case, ICJ Reports, 1985, pp. 13, 33; 81 ILR, pp. 238, 265, stated that the two concepts were 'linked together in modern law'.

as will be seen, that the geographical extent of the shelf may be different from that of the 200 mile economic zone.

Definition

Article 1 of the 1958 Convention on the Continental Shelf defined the shelf in terms of its exploitability rather than relying upon the accepted geological definition, noting that the expression referred to the seabed and subsoil of the submarine areas adjacent to the coast but outside the territorial sea to a depth of 200 metres or 'beyond that limit to where the depth of the superjacent waters admits of the exploitation of the natural resources of the said areas'.

This provision caused problems, since developing technology rapidly reached a position to extract resources to a much greater depth than 200 metres, and this means that the outer limits of the shelf, subject to the jurisdiction of the coastal state, were consequently very unclear. Article 1 was, however, regarded as reflecting customary law by the Court in the *North Sea Continental Shelf* case.[204] It is also important to note that the basis of title to continental shelf is now accepted as the geographical criterion, and not reliance upon, for example, occupation or effective control. The Court emphasised this and declared that:

> The submarine areas concerned may be deemed to be actually part of the territory over which the coastal state already has dominion in the sense that although covered with water, they are a prolongation or continuation of that territory, an extension of it under the sea.[205]

This approach has, however, been somewhat modified. Article 76(1) of the 1982 Convention provides as to the outer limit of the continental shelf that:

> [t]he continental shelf of a coastal state comprises the seabed and subsoil of the submarine areas that extend beyond its territorial sea throughout the natural prolongation of its land territory to the outer edge of the continental margin, or to a distance of 200 nautical miles from the baselines from which the breadth of the territorial sea is measured where the outer edge of continental margin does not extend up to that distance.[206]

Thus, an arbitrary, legal and non-geographical definition is provided. Where the continental margin actually extends beyond 200 miles, geographical factors are to be taken into account in establishing the limit, which in any event shall not exceed either 350 miles from the baselines or 100 miles

[204] ICJ Reports, 1969, pp. 3, 39; 41 ILR, pp. 29, 68.   [205] *Ibid.*, p. 31; 41 ILR, p. 60.
[206] See article 76(3) for a definition of the continental margin. See also D. N. Hutchinson, 'The Seaward Limit to Continental Shelf', 56 BYIL, 1985, p. 133 and Brown, *International Law of the Sea*, p. 140.

from the 2,500 metre isobath.[207] Where the shelf does not extend as far as 200 miles from the coast, natural prolongation is complemented as a guiding principle by that of distance.[208]

The rights of the coastal state[209]

The coastal state may exercise sovereign rights over the continental shelf for the purposes of exploring it and exploiting its natural resources under article 77 of the 1982 Convention and such rights are exclusive in that no other state may undertake such activities without the express consent of the coastal state. These sovereign rights (note the Convention does not talk in terms of 'sovereignty' but of 'sovereign rights') do not depend upon occupation or express proclamation.[210] The Truman concept of resources, which referred only to mineral resources, has been extended to include organisms belonging to the sedentary species.[211] However, this vague description did lead to disputes between France and Brazil over lobster, and between the USA and Japan over the Alaskan King Crab in the early 1960s.[212]

The Convention expressly states that the rights of the coastal state do not affect the status of the superjacent waters as high seas, or that of the airspace above the waters.[213] This is stressed in succeeding articles which note that, subject to its right to take reasonable measures for exploration and exploitation of the continental shelf, the coastal state may not impede the laying or maintenance of cables or pipelines on the shelf. In addition, such exploration and exploitation must not result in any unjustifiable interference with navigation, fishing or the conservation of the living resources of the sea.[214]

The coastal state may, under article 80 of the 1982 Convention,[215] construct and maintain installations and other devices necessary for exploration on the continental shelf and is entitled to establish safety zones around such installations to a limit of 500 metres, which must be respected by ships of all nationalities. Within such zones, the state may take such measures as are

[207] Article 76(4), (5), (6), (7), (8) and (9). See also Annex II to the Final Act.
[208] See the *Libya/Malta Continental Shelf* case, ICJ Reports, 1985, pp. 13, 33–4; 81 ILR, pp. 238, 265–6. See also the *Tunisia/Libya* case, ICJ Reports, 1982, pp. 18, 61; 67 ILR, pp. 4, 54 and the *Gulf of Maine* case, ICJ Reports, 1984, pp. 246, 277; 71 ILR, pp. 57, 104.
[209] See *Oppenheim's International Law*, p. 773.
[210] See also article 2 of the Continental Shelf Convention 1958.
[211] See articles 77(4) of the 1982 Convention and article 2(4) of the 1958 Convention.
[212] See e.g. O'Connell, *International Law of the Sea*, vol. I, pp. 501–2.
[213] Articles 78 of the 1982 Convention and article 3 of the 1958 Convention. Note that the reference to 'high seas' in the latter is omitted in the former for reasons related to the new concept of the exclusive economic zone.
[214] Articles 78 and 79 of the 1982 Convention and articles 4 and 5 of the 1958 Convention.
[215] Applying *mutatis mutandis* article 60, which deals with the construction of artificial islands, installations and structures in the exclusive economic zone. See also article 5 of the 1958 Convention.

necessary for their protection. But although under the jurisdiction of the coastal state, these installations are not to be considered as islands. This means that they have no territorial sea of their own and their presence in no way affects the delimitation of the territorial waters of the coastal state. Such provisions are, of course, extremely important when considering the status of oil rigs situated, for example, in the North Sea. To treat them as islands for legal purposes would cause difficulties.[216]

Where the continental shelf of a state extends beyond 200 miles, article 82 of the 1982 Convention provides that the coastal state must make payments or contributions in kind in respect of the exploitation of the non-living resources of the continental shelf beyond the 200 mile limit. The payments are to be made annually after the first five years of production at the site in question on a sliding scale up to the twelfth year, after which it is to remain at 7 per cent. These payments and contributions are to be made to the International Seabed Authority, which shall distribute them amongst state parties on the basis of 'equitable sharing criteria, taking into account the interests and needs of developing states particularly the least developed and the landlocked among them'.[217]

Delimitation of the continental shelf between opposite and adjacent states[218]

The question of the delimitation of the continental shelf has occasioned considerable debate and practice from the 1958 and 1982 Conventions to case law and a variety of treaties. While delimitation is in principle an aspect of territorial sovereignty, where other states are involved agreement is required. Most difficulties in this area are indeed resolved by agreement and the guiding principle of international law now is that disputes over conti-

---

[216] See also N. Papadakis, *The International Legal Regime of Artificial Islands*, Leiden, 1977.
[217] Note also that by article 82(3) a developing state which is a net importer of the mineral resource in question is exempt from such payments and contributions.
[218] See Churchill and Lowe, *Law of the Sea*, Chapter 10; E. D. Brown, *Sea-Bed Energy and Mineral Resources and the Law of the Sea*, London, 1984–86, vols. I and III; M. D. Evans, *Relevant Circumstances and Maritime Delimitation*, Oxford, 1989, and P. Weil, *The Law of Maritime Delimitation – Reflections*, Cambridge, 1989. See also *International Maritime Boundaries* (eds. J. Charney and L. Alexander), Washington, 1993; P. Cahier, 'Les Sources du Droit Relatif à la Délimitation du Plateau Continental', *Mélanges Virally*, 1991, p. 175; L. D. M. Nelson, 'The Roles of Equity in the Delimitation of Maritime Boundaries', 84 AJIL, 1990, p. 837; B. Kwiatowska, 'Judge Shigeru Oda's Opinions in Law-of-the-Sea Cases: Equitable Maritime Boundary Delimitation', 36 German YIL, 1993, p. 225; H. Thirlway, 'The Law and Procedure of the International Court of Justice 1960–89', 64 BYIL, 1993, p. 1; J. I. Charney, 'Progress in International Maritime Boundary Delimitation Law', 88 AJIL, 1994. p. 227; J. I. Charney, 'Central East Asian Maritime Boundaries and the Law of the Sea', 89 AJIL, 1995, p. 724; *Oppenheim's International Law*, p. 776 and Nguyen Quoc Dinh *et al.*, *Droit International Public*, p. 1091.

nental shelf boundaries are to be settled by agreement in accordance with equitable principles.[219]

Article 6 of the Continental Shelf Convention 1958 declared that in the absence of agreement and unless another boundary line was justified by special circumstances, the boundary should be determined 'by application of the principle of equidistance from the nearest points of the baselines from which the breadth of the territorial sea of each state is measured', that is to say by the introduction of the equidistance or median line which would operate in relation to the sinuosities of the particular coast lines.

This provision was considered in the *North Sea Continental Shelf* cases[220] between the Federal Republic of Germany on the one side and Holland and Denmark on the other. The problem was that the application of the equidistance principle of article 6 would give Germany only a small share of the North Sea continental shelf, in view of its concave northern shoreline between Holland and Denmark. The question arose as to whether the article was binding upon the Federal Republic of Germany at all, since it had not ratified the 1958 Continental Shelf Convention.

The Court held that the principles enumerated in article 6 did not constitute rules of international customary law and therefore Germany was not bound by them.[221] The Court declared that the relevant rule was that:

> delimitation is to be effected by agreement in accordance with equitable principles, and taking account of all the relevant circumstances, in such a way as to leave as much as possible to each party all those parts of the continental shelf that constitute a natural prolongation of its land territory into and under the sea, without encroachment on the natural prolongation of the land territory of the others.[222]

The Court, therefore, took the view that delimitation was based upon a consideration and weighing of relevant factors in order to produce an equitable result. Included amongst the range of factors was the element of a reasonable degree of proportionality between the lengths of the coastline and the extent of the continental shelf.[223]

In the *Anglo-French Continental Shelf* case,[224] both states were parties to

---

[219] The International Court noted in the *Gulf of Maine* case, ICJ Reports, 1984, pp. 246, 299; 77 ILR, pp. 57, 126, that 'no maritime delimitation between states with opposite or adjacent coasts may be effected unilaterally by one of those states. Such delimitation must be sought and effected by means of an agreement, following negotiations conducted in good faith and with the genuine intention of achieving a positive result. Where, however, such agreement cannot be achieved, delimitation should be effected by recourse to a third party possessing the necessary competence.'   [220] ICJ Reports, 1969, p. 3; 41 ILR, p. 29.
[221] See *supra*, Chapter 3, p. 67.   [222] ICJ Reports, 1969, pp. 3, 53; 41 ILR, pp. 29, 83.
[223] ICJ Reports, 1969, pp. 3; 52; 41 ILR, pp. 29. 82. See also *infra* p. 441.
[224] Cmnd. 7438 (1978); 54 ILR, p. 6. See also D. W. Bowett, 'The Arbitration between the United Kingdom and France Concerning the Continental Shelf Boundary in the English Channel of South-Western Approaches', 49 BYIL, 1978, p. 1.

the 1958 Convention, so that article 6 applied.[225] It was held that article 6 contained one overall rule, 'a combined equidistance-special circumstances rule', which in effect:

> gives particular expression to a general norm that, failing agreement, the boundary between states abutting on the same continental shelf is to be determined on equitable principles.[226]

The choice of method of delimitation, whether by the equidistance or any other method, depended upon the relevant circumstances of the case. The fundamental norm under both customary law and the 1958 Convention was that the delimitation had to be in accordance with equitable principles.[227] The Court took into account 'special circumstances' in relation to the situation of the Channel Islands which justified a delimitation other than the median line proposed by the UK.[228] In addition, the situation of the Scilly Isles was considered and they were given only 'half-effect' in the delimitation in the Atlantic area since

> what equity calls for is an appropriate abatement of the disproportionate effects of a considerable projection on the Atlantic continental shelf of a somewhat attenuated projection of the coast of the United Kingdom.[229]

In the *Tunisia/Libya Continental Shelf* case,[230] the Court, deciding on the basis of custom as neither state was a party to the 1958 Convention, emphasised that 'the satisfaction of equitable principles is, in the delimitation process, of cardinal importance'. The concept of natural prolongation was of some importance depending upon the circumstances, but not on the same plane as the satisfaction of equitable principles.[231] The Court also employed the 'half-effect' principle for the Kerkennah Islands,[232] and emphasised that each continental shelf dispute had to be considered on its own merits having regard to its peculiar circumstance. No attempt should be made to 'overconceptualise the application of the principles and rules relating to the continental shelf'.[233]

The view of the Court that 'the principles are subordinate to the goal' and

---

[225] Although subject to a French reservation regarding the Bay of Granville to which the UK had objected, Cmnd. 7438 (1978), p. 50; 54, ILR, p. 57.

[226] *Ibid.*, p. 48; 54 ILR, p. 55.   [227] *Ibid.*, pp. 59–60; 54 ILR, p. 66.

[228] *Ibid.*, p. 94; 54 ILR, p. 101. This arose because of the presence of the British islands close to the French coast, which if given full effect would substantially reduce the French continental shelf. This was *prima facie* a circumstance creative of inequity, *ibid.*

[229] *Ibid.*, pp. 116–17; 54 ILR, p. 123.

[230] ICJ Reports, 1982, p. 18; 67 ILR, p. 4. See also Herman, 'The Court Giveth and the Court Taketh Away', 33 ICLQ, 1984, p. 825.

[231] ICJ Reports, 1982, p. 47; 67 ILR, p. 40. See also *Ibid.*, p. 60; 67 ILR, p. 53.

[232] *Ibid.*, p. 89; 67 ILR, p. 82. This was specified in far less constrained terms than in the *Anglo-French Continental Shelf* case, Cmnd. 7438, pp. 116–17; 54 ILR, p. 123. See e.g. Judge Gros' dissenting opinion, ICJ Reports, 1982, pp. 18, 150; 67 ILR, p. 143.

[233] *Ibid.*, p. 92; 67 ILR, p. 85.

that '[t]he principles to be indicated . . . have to be selected according to their appropriateness for reaching an equitable result'[234] has led to criticism that the carefully drawn restriction on equity in the *North Sea Continental Shelf* cases[235] has been overturned and the element of predictability minimised. The dangers of an equitable solution based upon subjective assessments of the facts, regardless of the law of delimitation, were pointed out by Judge Gros in his dissenting opinion.[236]

The Court in the *North Sea Continental Shelf* cases[237] in general discussed the relevance of the use of equitable principles in the context of the difficulty of applying the equidistance rule in specific geographical situations where inequity might result. In such a case, recourse may be had to equitable principles, provided a reasonable result was reached.

In the *Anglo-French Continental Shelf* case,[238] it was emphasised that:

> the appropriateness of the equidistance method or any other method for the purpose of effecting an equitable delimitation is a function or reflection of the geographical and other relevant circumstances of each particular case.

The methodological aspect here is particularly important, based as it is upon the requisite geographical framework.

A rigorous approach is rather less apparent in the *Tunisia/Libya* case, but the emphasis upon the solution, perhaps to the detriment of the method of reaching it, is reflected in recent cases. Indeed, article 83 of the 1982 Convention simply provides that delimitation 'shall be effected by agreement on the basis of international law . . . in order to achieve an equitable solution'.

In the *Gulf of Maine* case,[239] which dealt with the delimitation of both the continental shelf and fisheries zones of Canada and the United States,[240] the Chamber of the ICJ produced two principles reflecting what general international law prescribes in every maritime delimitation. First, there could be no unilateral delimitations. Delimitations had to be sought and effected by agreement between the parties or if necessary with the aid of third parties. Secondly, it held that 'delimitation is to be effected by the application of equitable criteria and by the use of practical methods capable of ensuring, with regard to the geographic configuration of the area and other relevant circumstances, an equitable result'.[241] The Court took as its starting point

---

[234] *Ibid.*, p. 59; 67 ILR, p. 52.   [235] ICJ Reports, 1969, pp. 3, 49–50; 41 ILR, pp. 29, 79.
[236] ICJ Reports, 1982, pp. 18, 153; 67 ILR, pp. 4, 146.
[237] ICJ Reports, 1969, pp. 3, 35–6; 41 ILR, pp. 29, 64.
[238] Cmnd. 7438, p. 59; 54 ILR, p. 66.
[239] ICJ Reports, 1984, p. 246; 71 ILR, p. 74. See also J. Schneider, 'The Gulf of Maine Case: The Nature of an Equitable Result', 79 AJIL, 1985, p. 539.
[240] A 'single maritime boundary' was requested by the parties, ICJ Reports, 1984, pp. 246, 253; 71 ILR, p. 80. See also *supra* p. 414.
[241] *Ibid.*, pp. 299–300; 71 ILR, pp. 126–7. This was regarded as the fundamental norm of customary international law governing maritime delimitation, *ibid.*, p. 300.

the criterion of the equal division of the areas of convergence and over-lapping of the maritime projections of the coastlines of the states concerned, a criterion regarded as intrinsically equitable. This, however, had to be combined with the appropriate auxiliary criteria in the light of the relevant circumstances of the area itself. As regards the practical methods necessary to give effect to the above criteria, like the criteria themselves these had to be based upon geography and the suitability for the delimitation of both the seabed and the superjacent waters. Thus, it was concluded, geometrical methods would serve.[242] It will be noted that the basic rule for delimitation of the continental shelf is the same as that for the exclusive economic zone,[243] but the same boundary need not necessarily result.[244] The Chamber in the *Gulf of Maine* case indeed strongly emphasised 'the unprecedented aspect of the case which lends it its special character', in that a single line delimiting both the shelf and fisheries zone was called for by the parties. Criteria found equitable with regard to a shelf delimitation need not necessarily possess the same properties with regard to a dual delimitation.[245] The above principles were reflected in the arbitral award in the *Guinea/Guinea-Bissau Maritime Delimitation* case in 1985.[246] The Tribunal emphasised that the aim of any delimitation process was to achieve an equitable solution having regard to the relevant circumstances.[247] In the instant case, the concepts of natural prolongation and economic factors were in the circumstances of little assistance.[248]

In the *Libya/Malta Continental Shelf* case,[249] the International Court, in deciding the case according to customary law since Libya was not a party to the 1958 Convention on the Continental Shelf, emphasised the distance criterion. This arose because of the relevance of the economic zone concept, which was now held to be part of customary law, and the fact that an economic zone could not exist without rights over the seabed and subsoil similar to those enjoyed over a continental shelf. Thus the 200 mile limit of the zone had to be taken into account with regard to the delimitation of the continental shelf.[250] The fact that the law now permitted a state to claim a

---

[242] *Ibid.*, pp. 328–9; 71 ILR, p. 155. Note that the Chamber gave 'half-effect' to Seal Island for reasons of equity, *ibid.*, p. 337; 71 ILR, p. 164.

[243] Article 74 of the 1982 Convention and *supra*, p. 413.

[244] See e.g. the Australia–Papua New Guinea Maritime Boundaries Treaty of 1978, cited in Churchill and Lowe, *Law of the Sea*, p. 160.

[245] ICJ Reports, 1984, pp. 246, 326; 71 ILR, p. 153.

[246] See 25 ILM, 1986, p. 251; 77 ILR, p. 636. The tribunal consisted of Judge Lachs, President and Judges Mbaye and Bedjaoui.   [247] *Ibid.*, p. 289; 77 ILR, pp. 675–6.

[248] *Ibid.*, pp. 300–2; 77 ILR, p. 686. It should be noted that the delimitation concerned a single line delimiting the territorial waters, continental shelves and economic zones of the respective countries.   [249] ICJ Reports, 1985, p. 13; 81 ILR, p. 239.

[250] The Court emphasised that this did not mean that the concept of the continental shelf had been absorbed by that of the economic zone, but that greater importance had to be attributed to elements, such as distance from the coast, which are common to both, p. 33; 81 ILR, p. 265.

shelf of up to 200 miles from its coast, irrespective of geological character-istics, also meant that there was no reason to ascribe any role to geological or geographical factors within that distance.[251]

Since the basis of title to the shelf up to the 200 mile limit is recognised as the distance criterion, the Court felt that the drawing of a median line between opposite states was the most judicious manner of proceeding with a view to the eventual achievement of an equitable result. This provisional step had to be tested in the light of equitable principles in the context of the relevant circumstances.[252] The Court also followed the example of the *Tunisia/Libya* case[253] in examining the role of proportionality and in treating it as a test of the equitableness of any line.

However, the Court did consider the comparability of coastal lengths in the case as part of the process of reaching an equitable boundary, and used the disparity of coastal lengths of the parties as a reason for adjusting the median line so as to attribute a larger shelf area to Libya.[254] The general geographical context in which the islands of Malta exist as a rela-tively small feature in a semi-enclosed sea was also taken into account in this context.[255]

The Court in its analysis also referred to a variety of well-known exam-ples of equitable principles, including abstention from refashioning nature, non-encroachment by one party on areas appertaining to the other, respect due to all relevant circumstances and the notions that equity did not neces-sarily mean equality and that there could be no question of distributive justice.[256] The Court, however, rejected Libya's argument that a state with a greater landmass would have a greater claim to the shelf and dismissed Malta's view that the relative economic position of the two states was of rel-evance.[257]

In conclusion, the Court reiterated in the operative provisions of its judg-ment, the following circumstances and factors that needed to be taken in account in the case:

(1) the general configuration of the coasts to the parties, their oppositeness, and their relationship to each other within the general context;
(2) the disparity in the lengths of the relevant coasts of the parties and the distance between them;
(3) the need to avoid in the delimitation any excessive disproportion between the extent of the continental shelf areas appertaining to the

---

[251] *Ibid.* [252] *Ibid.*, p. 47; 81 ILR, p. 279. [253] *Supra*, p. 438.
[254] ICJ Reports, 1985, pp. 48–50; ILR, p. 280. [255] *Ibid.*, p. 52; 81 ILR, p. 284.
[256] *Ibid.*, pp. 39–40; 81 ILR, p. 271.
[257] *Ibid.*, pp. 40–1; 81 ILR, p. 272. The Court also noted that an equitable boundary between the parties had in the light of the general geographical situation to be south of a notional median line between Libya and Sicily, *ibid.*, p. 51; 81 ILR, p. 283.

coastal state and the length of the relevant part of its coast, measured in the general direction of the coastlines.[258]

In the *St Pierre and Miquelon* case,[259] the Court of Arbitration emphasised that the delimitation process commenced with the identification of the geographical context of the dispute in question and indeed pointed out that geographical features were at the heart of delimitation.[260] The identification of the relevant coastlines in each particular case, however, generates specific problems. Accordingly, the way in which the geographical situation is described may suggest particular solutions, so that the seemingly objective process of geographical identification may indeed constitute a crucial element in the adoption of any particular juridical answer. In the *St Pierre and Miquelon* case, the Court divided the area into two zones, the southern and western zones. In the latter case, any seaward extension of the islands beyond their territorial sea would cause some degree of encroachment and cut off to the seaward projection towards the south from points located in the southern shore of Newfoundland. The Court felt here that any enclaving of the islands within their territorial sea would be inequitable and the solution proposed was to grant the islands an additional 12 miles from the limits of the territorial sea as an exclusive economic zone.[261] In the case of the southern zone, where the islands had a coastal opening seawards unobstructed by any opposite or laterally aligned Canadian coast, the Court held that France was entitled to an outer limit of 200 nautical miles, provided that such a projection was not allowed to encroach upon or cut off a parallel frontal projection of the adjacent segments of the Newfoundland southern coast. In order to achieve this, the Court emphasised the importance of the breadth of the coastal opening of the islands towards the south, thus resulting in a 200 mile, but narrow, corridor southwards from the islands as their economic zone.[262] Having decided upon the basis of geographical considerations, the Court felt it necessary to assure itself that the delimitation proposed was not 'radically inequitable'.[263] This it was able to do on the basis of facts submitted by the parties. The Court also considered the criterion of proportionality and satisfied itself that there was no disproportion in the areas appertaining to each of the parties.[264]

In the *Jan Mayen (Denmark v. Norway)* case,[265] the question of the

---

[258] *Ibid.*, pp. 56–8; 81 ILR, p. 288.
[259] 31 ILM, 1992, p. 1145; 95 ILR, p. 645. See also *supra* p. 414.
[260] *Ibid.*, pp. 1160–1; 95 ILR, p. 660–3.   [261] *Ibid.*, pp. 1169–70; 95 ILR, p. 671.
[262] *Ibid.*, pp. 1170–1; 95 ILR, p. 671–3.
[263] *Ibid.*, p. 1173; 95 ILR, p. 675. The phrase comes from the *Gulf of Maine* case, ICJ Reports, 1984, pp. 246, 342; 71 ILR, pp. 74, 169, where it was defined as 'likely to entail catastrophic repercussions for the livelihood and economic well-being of the population of the parties concerned'.   [264] *Ibid.*, p. 1176; 95 ILR, p. 678.
[265] ICJ Reports, 1993, p. 37; 99 ILR, p. 395. See also *supra* p. 415.

delimitation of the continental shelf between the islands of Greenland and Jan Mayen was governed in the circumstances by article 6 of the 1958 Convention, accepted as substantially identical to customary law in requiring an equitable delimitation.[266] The International Court noted that since a delimitation between opposite coasts was in question, one needed to begin by taking provisionally the median line and then enquiring whether 'special circumstances'[267] required another boundary line.[268] In particular, one needed to take into account the disparity between the respective coastal lengths of the relevant area and since, in this case, that of Greenland was more than nine times that of Jan Mayen, an unqualified use of equidistance would produce a manifestly disproportionate result.[269] In addition, the question of equitable access to fish stocks for vulnerable fishing communities needed to be considered. Since the principal resource in the area was cappelin, which was centred on the southern part of the area of overlapping claims, the adoption of a median line would mean that Denmark could not be assured of equitable access to the cappelin. This was a further reason for adjusting the median line towards the Norwegian island of Jan Mayen.[270] However, there was no need to consider the presence of ice as this did not materially affect access to fishery resources,[271] nor the limited population of Jan Mayen nor socio-economic factors nor security matters in the circumstances.[272]

In discussing the variety of applicable principles, a distinction has traditionally been drawn between opposite and adjacent states for the purposes of delimitation. In the former case, the Court has noted that there is less difficulty in applying the equidistance method than in the latter, since the distorting effect of an individual geographical feature in the case of adjacent states is more likely to result in an inequitable delimitation. Accordingly, greater weight is to be placed upon equidistance in a delimitation of the shelf between opposite states in the context of equitable considerations,[273] than

---

[266] Ibid., p. 58; 99 ILR, p. 426. But see the Separate Opinion of Judge Oda, Ibid., pp. 102–14; 99 ILR, pp. 470–82.
[267] The Court noted that the category of 'special circumstances' incorporated in article 6 was essentially the same as the category of 'relevant circumstances' developed in customary international law since both were designed to achieve an equitable solution, ibid., p. 62; 99 ILR, p. 430.   [268] Ibid., pp. 59–61; 99 ILR, pp. 427–9.
[269] Ibid., pp. 65–9; 99 ILR, pp. 433–7.
[270] Ibid., pp. 70–2; 99 ILR, pp. 438–40. But see the Separate Opinion of Judge Schwebel, ibid., pp. 118–20; 99 ILR, pp. 486–8.   [271] Ibid., pp. 72–3; 99 ILR, pp. 440–1.
[272] Ibid., pp. 73–5; 99 ILR, pp. 441–3. But see the Separate Opinion by Judge Oda, ibid., pp. 114–17; 99 ILR, pp. 482–5. Note also the discussion of equity in such situations in the Separate Opinion of Judge Weeramantry, ibid., pp. 211 et seq.; 99 ILR, pp. 579 et seq.
[273] See North Sea Continental Shelf cases, ICJ Reports, 1969, pp. 3, 36–7; 41 ILR, pp. 29, 65; the Anglo-French Continental Shelf case, Cmnd. 7438, pp. 58–9; 54 ILR, p. 65; the Tunisia/Libya Continental Shelf case, ICJ Reports, 1982, pp. 18, 88; 67 ILR, pp. 4, 81; the Gulf of Maine case, ICJ Reports, 1984, pp. 246, 325; 71 ILR, pp. 74 and the Jan Mayen case, ICJ Reports, 1993, p. 37; 99 ILR, p. 395. 152. See also article 6 of the Continental Shelf Convention, 1958.

in the case of adjacent states where the range of applicable equitable principles may be more extensive and the relative importance of each particular
principle less clear. Article 83 of the 1982 Convention, however, makes no
distinction between delimitations on the basis of whether the states are in an
opposite or adjacent relationship. The same need to achieve an equitable
solution on the basis of international law is all that is apparent. Now that the
1982 Convention is in force, it will be interesting to note whether the distinction is totally eliminated or reappears within the framework of the phrase
'international law'.

The weight to be given to the criterion of proportionality between the
length of the coastline and the area of continental shelf has also been the
subject of some consideration and opinions have varied. It is a factor that
must be cautiously applied.[274] It is as well to note that in the process of considering all the relevant factors in the attempt to reach an equitable solution,
one is not seeking to do justice generally but to operate within the framework of legal rules, which themselves permit consideration of equitable
matters.[275]

The international seabed[276]

Introduction

In recent years the degree of wealth contained beneath the high seas has
become more and more apparent. It is estimated that some 175 billion dry
tonnes of mineable manganese nodules are in existence scattered over some
15 per cent of the seabed. This far exceeds the land-based reserves of the

---

[274] The Court in the *North Sea Continental Shelf* cases, in discussing this issue, called for a reasonable degree of proportionality, ICJ Reports, 1969, pp. 3, 52; 41 ILR, pp. 29, 82, while
in the *Anglo-French Continental Shelf* case the Tribunal emphasised that it was disproportion rather than proportionality that was relevant in the context of the equities, Cmnd.
7438, pp. 60–1; 54 ILR, pp. 6, 67. But cf. the *Tunisia/Libya Continental Shelf* case, ICJ
Reports, 1982, pp. 18, 75; 67 ILR, pp. 4, 75. See also the *Libya/Malta Continental Shelf*
case, ICJ Reports, 1985, pp. 48–50; 81 ILR, p. 280.

[275] Since the rule for delimitation of the economic zone in article 74 of the 1982 Convention
is the same as for the continental shelf, one must assume that the same range of factors as
noted above would similarly be relevant. However, it should be noted that treaty practice
demonstrates that the equidistance principle tends to predominate, see Churchill and
Lowe, *Law of the Sea*, pp. 160–1.

[276] See e.g.Brown, *International Law of the Sea*, Chapter 17; O'Connell, *International Law of
the Sea*, footnote 1, vol. I, Chapter 12; Churchill and Lowe, *Law of the Sea*, Chapter 12; E.
Luard, *The Control of the Seabed*, Oxford, 1974; B. Buzan, *Seabed Politics*, New York, 1976;
T. G. Kronmiller, *The Lawfulness of Deep Seabed Mining*, 2 vols., New York, 1980, E. D.
Brown, *Sea-Bed Energy and Mineral Resources and the Law of the Sea*, 3 vols., London, 1986;
A. M. Post, *Deepsea Mining and the Law of the Sea*, The Hague, 1983; A. D. Henchoz,
*Règlementations Nationales et Internationales de l'Exploration et de l'Exploitation des Grans
Fonds Marins*, Zurich, 1992; *Oppenheim's International Law*, p. 812 and Nguyen Quoc Dinh
et al., *Droit International Public*, p. 1119.

metals involved (primarily manganese, nickel, copper and cobalt).[277] While this source of mineral wealth is of great potential importance to the developed nations possessing or soon to possess the technical capacity to mine such nodules, it poses severe problems for developing states, particularly those who are dependent upon the export earnings of a few categories of minerals. Zaire, for example, accounts for over one-third of total cobalt production, while Gabon and India each account for around 8 per cent of total manganese production.[278] By the early 1990s, there appeared to be six major deep sea mining consortia with the participation of numerous American, Japanese, Canadian, British, Belgian, West German, Dutch and French companies.[279] The technology to mine is at an advanced stage and some basic investment has been made, although it is unlikely that there will be considerable mining activity for several years to come.

In 1969, the UN General Assembly adopted resolution 2574(XXIV) calling for a moratorium on deep seabed activities and a year later a Declaration of Principles Governing the Seabed and Ocean Floor and the Subsoil Thereof, beyond the Limits of National Jurisdiction ('the Area') was adopted. This provided that the Area and its resources were the 'common heritage of mankind' and could not be appropriated and that no rights at all could be acquired over it except in conformity with an international regime to be established to govern its exploration and exploitation.

The 1982 Law of the Sea Convention (Part XI)

Under the Convention, the Area[280] and its resources are deemed to be the common heritage of mankind and no sovereign or other rights may be recognised. Minerals recovered from the Area in accordance with the Convention are alienable, however.[281] Activities in the Area are to be carried out for the benefit of mankind as a whole by or on behalf of the International Seabed Authority (the Authority) established under the Convention.[282] The Authority[283] is to provide for the equitable sharing of such benefits.[284] Activities in the Area are to be carried out under article 153 by the

[277] See e.g. *Seabed Mineral Resource Development*, UN Dept. of International Economic and Social Affairs, 1980, ST/ESA/107, pp. 1–2.   [278] *Ibid.*, p. 3.   [279] *Ibid.*, pp. 10–12.
[280] Defined in article 1 as the 'seabed and ocean floor and subsoil thereof beyond national jurisdiction'. This would start at the outer edge of the continental margin or at least at a distance of 200 nautical miles from the baselines.   [281] Articles 136 and 137.
[282] Articles 137 and 140. See also articles 156 and 157.
[283] The Authority is to consist of an Assembly (composed of all members of the Authority, i.e. all states parties to the Convention); a Council (thirty-six members elected by the Assembly in accordance with certain criteria) acting as the executive organ and having an Economic Planning Commission and a Legal and Technical Commission and a Secretariat, see articles 158–169. The Enterprise which will be the organ of the Authority actually carrying out activities in the Area is also to be established, see article 170.
[284] Article 140. See also article 150.

Enterprise (i.e. the organ of the Authority established as its operating arm) and by states parties or state enterprises, or persons possessing the nationality of state parties or effectively controlled by them, acting in association with the Authority. The latter 'qualified applicants' will be required to submit formal written plans of work to be approved by the Council after review by the Legal and Technical Commission.[285]

This plan of work is to specify two sites of equal estimated commercial value. The Authority may then approve a plan of work relating to one of these sites and designate the other as a 'reserved site' which may only be exploited by the Authority, via the Enterprise or in association with developing states.[286]

Resolution I of the Conference established a Preparatory Commission to make arrangements for the operation of the Authority and the International Tribunal for the Law of the Sea. It is currently preparing rules and regulations and carrying out research.[287]

Resolution II of the Conference makes special provision for eight 'pioneer investors', four from France, Japan, India and the USSR and four from Belgium, Canada, the Federal Republic of Germany, Italy, Japan, the Netherlands, the UK and the USA, and possibly others from developing states, to be given pioneer status. Each investor must have invested at least $30 million in preparation for seabed mining at least 10 per cent of which must be invested in a specific site. Sponsoring states must provide certification that this has happened.[288] Such pioneer investors will be able to carry out exploration activities pending entry into force of the Convention and will have priority over the other applicants (apart from the Enterprise) in the allocation of exploitation contracts.[289] India, France, Japan and the USSR were registered as pioneer investors in 1987 on behalf of various consortia.[290] China was registered as a pioneer investor in March 1991,[291] while the multinational Interoceanmetal Joint Organisation was registered as a pioneer

---

[285] See also Annex III, articles 3 and 4. Highly controversial requirements for transfer of technology are also included, *ibid.*, article 5.

[286] *Ibid.*, articles 8 and 9. The production policies of the Authority are detailed in article 151 of the Convention.

[287] 21(4) *UN Chronicle*, 1984, pp. 44 *et seq.* See also 25 ILM, 1986, p. 1329 and 26 ILM, 1987, p. 1725.   [288] See Churchill and Lowe, *Law of the Sea*, p. 195.

[289] See 21(4) *UN Chronicle*, 1984, pp. 45–7.

[290] See LOS/PCN/97–99 (1987). See also the Understanding of 5 September 1986 making various changes to the rules regarding pioneer operations, including extending the deadline by which the $30 million investment had to be made and establishing a Group of Technical Experts, LOS/PCN/L.41/Rev.1. See also Brown, *International Law of the Sea*, pp. 448–54. An Understanding of 30 August 1990 dealt with training costs, transfer of technology, expenditure on exploration and the development of a mine site for the Authority, *ibid.*, pp. 454–5, while an Understanding of 22 February 1991 dealt with the avoidance of overlapping claims signed by China on the one hand and seven potential pioneer investor states on the other (Belgium, Canada, Italy, the Netherlands, Germany, the UK and the US), *ibid.*, p. 455.   [291] Brown, *Seabed Energy*, p. 455.

investor in August that year.[292] Several sites have been earmarked for the Authority, all on the Clarion-Clipperton Ridge in the East Central Pacific. The regime for the deep seabed, however, was opposed by the United States in particular and as a consequence it voted against the adoption of the 1982 Convention. The UK also declared that it would not sign the Convention until a satisfactory regime for deep seabed mining was established.[293] Concern was particularly expressed regarding the failure to provide assured access to seabed minerals, lack of a proportionate voice in decision-making for countries most affected and the problems that would be caused by not permitting the free play of market forces in the development of seabed resources.[294]

The Reciprocating States Regime

As a result of developments in the Conference on the Law of the Sea, many states began to enact domestic legislation with the aim of establishing an interim framework for exploration and exploitation of the seabed pending an acceptable international solution. The UK Deep Sea Mining (Temporary Provisions) Act, 1981, for example, provides for the granting of exploration licences (but not in respect of a period before 1 July 1981) and exploitation licences (but not in a period before 1 January 1988). The Act also provides for a Deep Sea Mining Levy to be paid by the holder of an exploitation licence into a Deep Sea Mining Fund. This fund may be paid over to an international organisation for the deep seabed if an agreement to create this has come into force for the UK. If this has not occurred within ten years, the fund will be wound up and paid into the Consolidated Fund. Section 3(1) provides that countries with similar legislation[295] may be designated as 'reciprocating countries', which would allow for mutual recognition of licences.

A 1982 Agreement[296] calls for consultations to avoid overlapping claims under national legislation and for arbitration to resolve any dispute, while a 1984 Agreement[297] provides that no party shall issue

---

[292] *Ibid.*, p. 456. This organisation consisted of Bulgaria, Czechoslovakia, Poland, the USSR and Cuba.
[293] See e.g. *The Times*, 16 February 1984, p. 4 and HC Debs., vol. 33, col. 404 (2 December 1982). [294] See e.g. the US delegate, *UN Chronicle*, June 1982, p. 16.
[295] A number of countries adopted similar, unilateral legislation, e.g. the US in 1980, 19 ILM, 1980, p. 1003; 20 ILM, 1981, p. 1228 and 21 ILM, 1982, p. 867; West Germany, 20 ILM, 1981, p. 393 and 21 ILM, 1982, p. 832; the USSR, 21 ILM, 1982, p. 551; France, 21 ILM, 1982, p. 808; Japan, 22 ILM, 1983, p. 102 and Italy in 1985, see Brown, *International Law of the Sea*, pp. 456 *et seq.*
[296] The 1982 Agreement Concerning Interim Arrangements Relating to Polymetallic Nodules of the Deep Seabed (France, West Germany, UK, US), 21 ILM, 1982, p. 950.
[297] Provisional Understanding Regarding Deep Seabed Mining (Belgium, France, West Germany, Italy, Japan, Netherlands, UK, USA), 23 ILM, 1984, p. 1354. This was signed on 3 August 1984 and entered into force 2 September 1984.

an authorisation in respect of an application or seek registration of an area included in another application properly filed[298] and under consideration by another party; or within an area claimed in another application filed in conformity with national law and the instant Agreement before 3 April 1984 or earlier than the application or request for registration and which is still under consideration by another party; or within an authorisation granted by another party in conforming with the instant Agreement.

It is also provided that no party shall itself engage in deep seabed operations in an area for which it shall not issue an authorisation or seek registration, in accordance with the above provisions of the Agreement.

The Preparatory Commission, however, adopted a declaration in 1985 stating that any claim, agreement or action regarding the Area and its resources undertaken outside the Commission itself, which is incompatible with the 1982 Convention and its related resolutions, 'shall not be recognised'.[299] Nevertheless, the Agreement on the Resolution of Practical Problems with respect to Deep Sea Mining Areas was signed in 1987 between Belgium, Italy, the Netherlands, Canada and the USSR, to which were attached Exchanges of Notes involving also the USA, UK and the Federal Republic of Germany.[300] It constituted an attempt to prevent overlapping claims as between states within the Convention system and other states with regard to the Clarion-Clipperton Zone of the North-East Pacific, there being a particular problem, for example, between overlapping French and USSR claims.[301]

The 1994 Agreement on Implementation of the Seabed Provisions of the Convention on the Law of the Sea[302]

Attempts to ensure the universality of the 1982 Convention system and thus prevent the development of conflicting deep seabed regimes began in earnest in 1990 in consultations sponsored by the UN Secretary-General, with more flexibility being shown by states.[303] Eventually, the

---

[298] I.e. in conformity with the agreement for voluntary conflict resolution reached on 18 May 1983 and 15 December 1983.

[299] See *Law of the Sea Bulletin*, no. 6, October 1985, p. 85.   [300] 26 ILM, 1987, p. 1502.

[301] See also 25 ILM, 1986, p. 1326 and 26 ILM, 1987, p. 1725.

[302] 33 ILM, 1994, p. 1309. See also B. H. Oxman, 'The 1994 Agreement and the Convention', 88 AJIL, 1994, p. 687; L. B. Sohn, 'International Law Implications of the 1994 Agreement', *ibid.*, p. 696; J. I. Charney, 'US Provisional Application of the 1994 Deep Seabed Agreement'. *Ibid.*, p. 705; D. H. Anderson, 'Further Efforts to Ensure Universal Participation in the United Nations Convention on the Law of the Sea', 43 ICLQ, 1994, p. 886 and Report of the UN Secretary-General, A/50/713, 1 November 1995.

[303] See e.g. D. H. Anderson, 'Efforts to Ensure Universal Participation in the United Nations Convention on the Law of the Sea', 42 ICLQ, 1993, p. 654 and Brown, *Seabed Energy*, p. 462.

1994 Agreement emerged. The states parties undertake in article 1 to implement Part XI of the 1982 Convention in accordance with the Agreement. By article 2, the Agreement and Part XI are to be interpreted and applied together as a single instrument and in the event of any inconsistency, the provisions in the former document are to prevail. States can only express their consent to become bound by the Agreement if they at the same time or previously express their consent to be bound by the Convention. Thus, conflicting systems operating with regard to the seabed become impossible. The Agreement also provides in article 7 for provisional application if it has not come into force[304] on 16 November 1994 (the date on which the Convention came into force). The Agreement may thus be provisionally applied by states that have consented to its adoption in the General Assembly, unless they otherwise notify the depositary (the UN Secretary-General) in writing; states and entities signing the agreement, unless they otherwise notify the depositary in writing; states and entities which consent to its provisional application by so notifying the depositary in writing and states which accede to the Agreement.

The Annex to the Agreement addresses a number of issues raised by developed states. In particular, it is provided that all organs and bodies established under the Convention and Agreement are to be cost-effective and be based upon an evolutionary approach taking into account the functional needs of such organs or bodies; a variety of institutional arrangements are detailed with regard to the work of the International Seabed Authority (section 1); the work of the Enterprise is to be carried out initially by the Secretariat of the Authority and the Enterprise shall conduct its initial deep seabed mining operations through joint ventures that accord with sound commercial principles (section 2); decision-making in the Assembly and Council of the Authority is to comply with a series of specific rules[305] (section 3); the Assembly upon the recommendation of the Council may conduct a review at any time of matters referred to in article 155(1) of the Convention, notwithstanding the provisions of that article as a whole (section 4) and transfer of technology to the Enterprise and developing states is to be sought on fair and reasonable

---

[304] Under article 6, the Agreement comes into force thirty days after the date on which forty states have established their consent to be bound under procedures detailed in article 4 and 5 (i.e. signature subject or not subject to ratification, signature under a simplified procedure or accession).

[305] Note especially the increase in the role of the Council vis-à-vis the Assembly with regard to general policy matters. Note also that the Agreement guarantees a seat on the Council for the state 'on the date of entry into force of the Convention having the largest economy in terms of gross domestic product', i.e. the US (section 3, para. 15 a), and establishes groups of states on the Council of states with particular interests (section 3, paras. 10 and 15).

commercial terms on the open market or through joint-venture arrangements (section 5).[306]

The coming into force of the 1982 Convention, as amended, is now accomplished and a major piece of international legislation eventually successfully completed.

Settlement of disputes[307]

The 1982 Convention contains detailed provisions regarding the resolution of law of the sea disputes. Under Part XV, where a dispute arises, the parties are to proceed 'expeditiously to an exchange of views regarding its settlement by negotiation or other peaceful means'. The parties may resort if they wish to conciliation procedures under article 284, in which case a conciliation commission will be established, whose report will be non-binding.[308] Where no settlement is reached, recourse may be had to other procedures.[309] Upon signing, ratifying or acceding to the Convention, or at any time thereafter, a state may choose one of the following means of dispute settlement: the International Tribunal for the Law of the Sea,[310] the International Court of Justice, an arbitral tribunal under Annex VII[311] or a special arbitral tribunal under Annex VIII for specific disputes.[312]

There is also provision for a Seabed Disputes Chamber of the Tribunal,[313] which under article 187 shall have jurisdiction with regard to matters concerning the Deep Seabed and the International Seabed Authority.

There is a general obligation under article 279 for states to settle disputes by peaceful means, but they are able to choose methods other than those specified in the Convention.[314] States of the European Community, for

---

[306] Thus, the provisions in the Convention on the mandatory transfer of technology are not to apply (section 5, para. 2). Note also that provisions in the Convention regarding production ceiling and limitations, participation in commodity agreements etc. are not to apply (section 6, para. 7).

[307] See e.g. J. G. Merrills, *International Dispute Settlement*, 2nd edn, Cambridge, 1991, Chapter 8; Churchill and Lowe, *Law of the Sea*, Chapter 19 and A. O. Adede, 'Settlement of Disputes Arising Under the Law of the Sea Convention', 69 AJIL, 1975, p. 798 and 72 AJIL, 1978, p. 84. See also generally *infra*, Chapter 18.   [308] See Annex V.

[309] See articles 286 and 287

[310] Annex VI. The Tribunal is composed of twenty-one independent members elected by the states parties, with no two members being nationals of the same state and with no fewer than three members from each geographical group as established by the UN General Assembly. The election was held on 1 August 1996. Concern has been expressed as to the impact upon the International Court of Justice of the establishment of the Tribunal, see e.g. S. Oda, 'Dispute Settlement Prospects in the Law of the Sea', 44 ICLQ, 1995, p. 862 and G. Guillaume, *ibid.*, p. 848, but cf. S. Rosenne, 'Establishing the International Tribunal for the Law of the Sea', 89 AJIL, 1995, p. 806.   [311] Annex VII.

[312] I.e. relating to fisheries, protection and preservation of the marine environment, marine scientific research, or navigation, including pollution from vessels and by dumping, see article 1, Annex VIII.   [313] See Annex VI, Section 4.   [314] Article 280.

example, have agreed to submit fisheries disputes amongst member states to the European Court of Justice under the EEC Treaty. Outside the framework of the 1982 Convention, states may adopt a variety of means of resolving disputes, ranging from negotiations, inquiries,[315] conciliation,[316] arbitration,[317] and submission to the International Court of Justice.[318]

---

[315] E.g. the *Red Crusader* incident, 35 ILR, p. 485.

[316] E.g. the *Jan Mayen Island Continental Shelf* dispute, 20 ILM, 1981, p. 797; 62 ILR, p. 108.

[317] E.g. the *Anglo-French Continental Shelf* case, Cmnd. 7438; 54 ILR, p. 6.

[318] E.g. the *Anglo-Norwegian Fisheries* case, ICJ Reports, 1951, p. 116; 18 ILR, p. 84; the *North Sea Continental Shelf* cases, ICJ Reports, 1969, p. 16; 41 ILR, p. 29 and others referred to in this Chapter.

CHAPTER 12

JURISDICTION

Jurisdiction concerns the power of the state to affect people, property and circumstances and reflects the basic principles of state sovereignty, equality of states and non-interference in domestic affairs.[1] Jurisdiction is a vital and indeed central feature of state sovereignty, for it is an exercise of authority which may alter or create or terminate legal relationships and obligations. It may be achieved by means of legislative action or by executive action or by judicial action. In each case, the recognised authorities of the state as determined by the legal system of that state perform certain functions permitted them which affect the life around them in various ways. In the UK, Parliament passes binding statutes, the courts make binding decisions and the administrative machinery of government has the power and jurisdiction (or legal authority) to enforce the rules of law. These differences, particularly between the capacity to make law (the prescriptive jurisdiction) and the capacity to ensure compliance with such law (the enforcement jurisdiction), are basic to an understanding of the legal competence of a state. This is to some extent because jurisdiction, although primarily territorial, may be based on other grounds, for example nationality, while enforcement is restricted by territorial factors.

To give an instance, if a man kills somebody in Britain and then manages to reach Holland, the British courts have jurisdiction to try him, but they cannot enforce it by sending officers to Holland to apprehend him. They must apply to the Dutch authorities for his arrest and despatch to Britain. If, on the other hand, the murderer remains in Britain then he may be

---

[1] See e.g. M. Akehurst, 'Jurisdiction in International Law', 46 BYIL, 1972–3, p. 145; F. A. Mann, 'The Doctrine of Jurisdiction in International Law', 111 HR, p. 1 and Mann, 'The Doctrine of Jurisdiction in International Law Revisited After Twenty Years', 186 HR, p. 9; D. W. Bowett, 'Jurisdiction: Changing Problems of Authority over Activities and Resources', 53 BYIL, 1982, p. 1; R. Y. Jennings, 'Extraterritorial Jurisdiction and the United States Antitrust Laws', 33 BYIL, 1957, p. 146; *Oppenheim's International Law* (eds. R. Y. Jennings and A. D. Watts), 9th edn, London, 1992, pp. 456 *et seq.*; L. Henkin, R. C. Pugh, O. Schachter and H. Smit, *International Law Cases and Materials*, 3rd edn, St Paul, 1993, Chapter 12; O. Schachter, *International Law in Theory and Practice*, Dordrecht, 1991, Chapter XII and R. Higgins, *Problems and Process*, Oxford, 1994, Chapter 4. See also *Third US Restatement of Foreign Relations Law*, 1987, vol. I, Part IV.

arrested and tried there, even if it becomes apparent that he is a German national. Thus, while prescriptive jurisdiction (or the competence to make law) may be exercised as regards events happening within the territorial limits irrespective of whether or not the actors are nationals or not, and may be founded on nationality as in the case of a British subject suspected of murder committed abroad who may be tried for the offence in the UK (if he is found in the UK, of course) enforcement jurisdiction is another matter entirely and is essentially restricted to the presence of the suspect in the territorial limits.[2]

However, there are circumstances in which it may be possible to apprehend a suspected murderer, but the jurisdictional basis is lacking. For example, if a Frenchman has committed a murder in Germany he cannot be tried for it in Britain, notwithstanding his presence in the country, although, of course, both France and Germany may apply for his extradition and return to their respective countries from Britain.

Thus, while jurisdiction is closely linked with territory it is not exclusively so tied. Many states have jurisdiction to try offences that have taken place outside their territory, and in addition certain persons, property and situations are immune from the territorial jurisdiction in spite of being situated or taking place there. Diplomats, for example, have extensive immunity from the laws of the country in which they are working[3] and various sovereign acts by states may not be questioned or overturned in the courts of a foreign country.[4]

The whole question of jurisdiction is complex, not least because of the relevance also of constitutional issues and conflict of laws rules. International law tries to set down rules dealing with the limits of a state's exercise of governmental functions while conflict of laws (or private international law) will attempt to regulate in a case involving a foreign element whether the particular country has jurisdiction to determine the question, and secondly, if it has, then the rules of which country will be applied in resolving the dispute.

The grounds for the exercise of jurisdiction are not identical in the cases of international law and conflict of laws rules. In the latter case, specific subjects may well be regulated in terms of domicile or residence (for instance, as regards the recognition of foreign marriages or divorces) but such grounds would not found jurisdiction where international law matters were concerned.[5] Although it is by no means impossible or in all cases difficult to

---

[2] Reference has also been made to the jurisdiction to adjudicate, whereby persons or things are rendered subject to the process of a state's court system, see *Third US Restatement of Foreign Relations Law*, p. 232. [3] *Infra*, Chapter 13, p. 523. [4] *Ibid.*, p. 491.
[5] See generally, G. C. Cheshire and P. M. North, *Private International Law*, 12th edn, 1992. Questions also arise as to the conditions required for leave for service abroad, see e.g. *Al-Adsani* v. *Government of Kuwait and Others*, 100 ILR, p. 465.

keep apart the categories of international law and conflict of laws, nevertheless the often different definitions of jurisdiction involved are a confusing factor.

One should also be aware of the existence of disputes as to jurisdictional competence within the area of constitutional matters. These problems arise in federal court structures, as in the United States, where conflicts as to the extent of authority of particular courts may arise.

While the relative exercise of powers by the legislative, executive and judicial organs of government is a matter for the municipal legal and political system, the extraterritorial application of jurisdiction will depend upon the rules of international law and in this chapter we shall examine briefly the most important of these rules.

The principle of domestic jurisdiction[6]

It follows from the nature of the sovereignty of states that while a state is supreme internally, that is within its own territorial frontiers, it must not intervene in the domestic affairs of another nation. This duty of non-intervention within the domestic jurisdiction of states provides for the shielding of certain state activities from the regulation of international law. State functions which are regarded as beyond the reach of international legal control and within the exclusive sphere of state management include the setting of conditions for the grant of nationality and the elaboration of the circumstances in which aliens may enter the country.

However, the influence of international law is beginning to make itself felt in areas hitherto regarded as subject to the state's exclusive jurisdiction. For example, the treatment by a country of its own nationals is now viewed in the context of international human rights regulations, although in practice the effect of this has often been disappointing.[7]

Domestic jurisdiction is a relative concept, in that changing principles of international law have had the effect of limiting and reducing its extent[8] and in that matters of internal regulation may well have international repercussions and thus fall within the ambit of international law. This latter point has been emphasised by the International Court of Justice.

In the *Anglo-Norwegian Fisheries* case[9] it was stressed that:

> [a]lthough it is true that the act of delimitation [of territorial waters] is necessarily a unilateral act, because only the coastal state is competent to undertake

---

[6] See e.g. I. Brownlie, *Principles of Public International Law*, 4th edn, Oxford, 1990, p. 291 and M. S. Rajan, *United Nations and Domestic Jurisdiction*, 2nd edn, 1961. See further *supra*, Chapter 4.   [7] *Supra*, Chapters 6 and 7.

[8] Whether a matter is or is not within the domestic jurisdiction of states is itself a question for international law, see *Nationality Decrees in Tunis and Morocco* case, PCIJ, Series B, No. 4, 1923, pp. 7, 23–4; 2 ILR, pp. 349, 352.   [9] ICJ Reports, 1951, p. 116; 18 ILR, p. 86.

it, the validity of the delimitation with regard to other states depends upon international law.[10]

The principle was also noted in the *Nottebohm* case,[11] where the Court remarked that while a state may formulate such rules as it wished regarding the acquisition of nationality, the exercise of diplomatic protection upon the basis of nationality was within the purview of international law.

In addition, no state may plead its municipal laws as a justification for the breach of an obligation of international law.[12]

Accordingly, the dividing line between issues firmly within domestic jurisdiction on the one hand, and issues susceptible to international legal regulation on the other is by no means as inflexible as at first may appear. Article 2(7) of the UN Charter declares that:

> [n]othing contained in the present Charter shall authorise the United Nations to intervene in matters which are essentially within the domestic jurisdiction of any state or shall require the members to submit such matters to settlement under the present Charter.

This paragraph, intended as a practical restatement and reinforcement of domestic jurisdiction, has constantly been reinterpreted in the decades since it was first enunciated. It has certainly not prevented the United Nations from discussing or adopting resolutions relating to the internal policies of member states and the result of forty years of practice has been the further restriction and erosion of domestic jurisdiction.

In the late 1940s and 1950s, the European colonial powers fought a losing battle against the United Nations debate and adoption of resolutions concerning the issues of self-determination and independence for their colonies. The involvement of the United Nations in human rights matters is constantly deepening and until their disappearance South Africa's domestic policies of apartheid were continually criticised and condemned. The expanding scope of United Nations concern has succeeded in further limiting the extent of the doctrine of domestic jurisdiction.[13] Nevertheless, the concept does retain validity in recognising the basic fact that state sovereignty within its own territorial limits is the undeniable foundation of international law as it has evolved, and of the world political and legal system.[14]

---

[10] *Ibid.*, p. 132; 18 ILR, p. 95.   [11] ICJ Reports, 1955, pp. 4, 20–1; 22 ILR, pp. 349, 357.

[12] *Supra*, Chapter 4, p. 102.

[13] See e.g. R. Higgins, *The Development of International Law Through the Political Organs of the United Nations*, Oxford, 1963. See also the view of the British Foreign Secretary on 27 January 1993 that article 2(7) was 'increasingly eroded as humanitarian concerns prevail over the respect for each nation's right to manage or mis-manage its affairs and its subjects', UKMIL, 64 BYIL, 1993, p. 599.

[14] Note also the importance of the doctrine of the exhaustion of local remedies, see *supra*, Chapter 6, p. 202.

Legislative, executive and judicial jurisdiction

Legislative jurisdiction[15] refers to the supremacy of the constitutionally recognised organs of the state to make binding laws within its territory. Such acts of legislation may extend abroad in certain circumstances.[16] The state has legislative exclusivity in many areas. For example, a state lays down the procedural techniques to be adopted by its various organs, such as courts, but can in no way seek to alter the way in which foreign courts operate. This is so even though an English court might refuse to recognise a judgment of a foreign court on the grounds of manifest bias. An English law cannot then be passed purporting to alter the procedural conditions under which the foreign courts operate.

International law accepts that a state may levy taxes against persons not within the territory of that state, so long as there is some kind of real link between the state and the proposed taxpayer, whether it be, for example, nationality or domicile.[17] A state may nationalise foreign owned property situated within its borders,[18] but it cannot purport to take over foreign owned property situated abroad. It will be obvious that such a regulation could not be enforced abroad, but the reference here is to the prescriptive jurisdiction, or capacity to pass valid laws.

The question of how far a court will enforce foreign legislation is a complicated one within, basically, the field of conflict of laws, but in practice it is rare for one state to enforce the penal or tax laws of another state.[19]

Although legislative supremacy within a state cannot be denied, it may be challenged. A state that adopts laws that are contrary to the provisions of international law, for example as regards the treatment of aliens or foreign property within the country, will render itself liable for a breach of international law on the international scene, and will no doubt find itself faced with protests and other action by the foreign state concerned. It is also possible that a state which abuses the rights it possesses to legislate for its nationals abroad may be guilty of a breach of international law. For example, if France were to order its citizens living abroad to drive only French cars, this would most certainly infringe the sovereignty and independence of the states in

---

[15] See e.g. Akehurst, 'Jurisdiction', pp. 179 *et seq.*   [16] See further *infra*, p. 483.
[17] Akehurst, 'Jurisdiction', pp. 179–80.   [18] See *infra*, Chapter 14, p. 573.
[19] See e.g. Cheshire and North, *Private International Law*, Chapter 8. English courts in general will not enforce the penal laws of foreign states. It will be for the court to decide what a foreign penal law is. See also *Huntington* v. *Attrill* [1893] AC 150, and Marshall CJ, *The Antelope*, 10 Wheat, 123 (1825). As far as tax laws are concerned see *Government of India* v. *Taylor* [1955] AC 491; 22 ILR, p. 286. See in addition *Attorney-General of New Zealand* v. *Ortiz* [1982] 3 All ER 432; 78 ILR, p. 608, particularly Lord Denning, and *ibid.* [1983] 3 All ER 93 (House of Lords); 78 ILR, p. 631. See also *Williams & Humbert* v. *W & H Trade Marks* [1985] 2 All ER 619 and [1986] 1 All ER 129 (House of Lords); 75 ILR, p. 269 and *Re State of Norway's Application* [1986] 3 WLR 452 and [1989] 1 All ER 745, 760–2 (House of Lords).

which such citizens were residing and would constitute an illegitimate exercise of French legislative jurisdiction.[20]

Executive jurisdiction relates to the capacity of the state to act within the borders of another state.[21] Since states are independent of each other and possess territorial sovereignty,[22] it follows that generally state officials may not carry out their functions on foreign soil (in the absence of express consent by the host state)[23] and may not enforce the laws of their state upon foreign territory. It is also contrary to international law for state agents to apprehend persons or property abroad. The seizure of the Nazi criminal Eichmann by Israeli agents in Argentina in 1960 was a clear breach of Argentina's territorial sovereignty and an illegal exercise of Israeli jurisdiction.[24] Similarly, the unauthorised entry into a state of military forces of another state is clearly an offence under international law.

Judicial jurisdiction[25] concerns the power of the courts of a particular country to try cases in which a foreign factor is present. There are a number of grounds upon which the courts of a state may claim to exercise such jurisdiction. In criminal matters these range from the territorial principle to the universality principle and in civil matters from the mere presence of the defendant in the country to the nationality and domicile principles. It is judicial jurisdiction which forms the most discussed aspect of jurisdiction and criminal questions the most important manifestation of this.

Civil jurisdiction[26]

Although jurisdiction in civil matters is enforced in the last resort by the application of the sanctions of criminal law, there are a number of differences between civil and criminal issues in this context.

In general it is fair to say that the exercise of civil jurisdiction has been claimed by states upon far wider grounds than has been the case in criminal matters, and the resultant reaction by other states much more muted.[27] This is partly due to the fact that public opinion is far more easily roused where a person is tried abroad for criminal offences than if a person is involved in a civil case.

In common law countries, such as the United States and Britain, the usual basis for jurisdiction in civil cases remains service of a writ upon the

[20] See Mann, 'Jurisdiction', pp. 36–62.   [21] See Akehurst, 'Jurisdiction', p. 147.
[22] See e.g. *Lotus* case, PCIJ, Series A, No. 10, 1927, p. 18; 4 ILR, p. 153 and the *Island of Palmas* case, 2 RIAA, pp. 829, 838 (1928); 4 ILR, p. 103.
[23] This cannot, of course, be taken too far. An official would still be entitled, for example, to sign a contract, see Akehurst, 'Jurisdiction', p. 147.   [24] See further, *infra*, p. 472.
[25] See e.g. Akehurst, 'Jurisdiction', pp. 152 *et seq.*
[26] *Ibid.*, pp. 170 *et seq.*; Mann, 'Jurisdiction', pp. 49–51 and Brownlie, *Public International Law*, p. 299. See also Bowett,pp. 1–4.   [27] See e.g. Akehurst, 'Jurisdiction', pp. 152 *et seq.*

defendant within the country, even if the presence of the defendant is purely temporary and coincidental.[28] In continental European countries on the other hand, the usual ground for jurisdiction is the habitual residence of the defendant in the particular state.

Many countries, for instance Holland, Denmark and Sweden, will allow their courts to exercise jurisdiction where the defendant in any action possesses assets in the state, while in matrimonial cases the commonly accepted ground for the exercise of jurisdiction is the domicile or residence of the party bringing the action.[29]

In view of, for example, the rarity of diplomatic protests and the relative absence of state discussions, some writers have concluded that customary international law does not prescribe any particular regulations as regards the restriction of courts' jurisdiction in civil matters.[30]

Criminal jurisdiction[31]

The application by municipal courts of their own powers and the rules of their state to cases involving foreign persons, property or events is a crucial topic although complicated by the convergence of principles from international law and conflict of laws. A number of definite principles upon which to base jurisdiction have emerged, with varying degrees of support and of different historical legitimacy.

The territorial principle

This concept reflects one aspect of the sovereignty exercisable by a state in its territorial home, and is the indispensable foundation for the application of the series of legal rights that a state possesses.[32] That a country should be able to prosecute for offences committed upon its soil is a logical manifestation of a world order of independent states and is entirely reasonable since the authorities of a state are responsible for the conduct of law and the main-

---

[28] See e.g. *Maharanee of Baroda* v. *Wildenstein* [1972] 2 All ER 689. See also the Civil Jurisdiction and Judgments Act, 1982.
[29] See, for example, the 1970 Hague Convention on the Recognition of Divorces and Legal Separations.
[30] See e.g. Akehurst, 'Jurisdiction', p. 177. Cf. Mann, 'Jurisdiction', pp. 49–51 and see also Brownlie, *Public International Law*, p. 299, and Bowett, 'Jurisdiction', pp. 3–4.
[31] See e.g. Akehurst, 'Jurisdiction', pp. 152 *et seq.*; Mann, 'Jurisdiction', pp. 82 *et seq.* and D. P. O'Connell, *International Law*, 2nd edn, London, 1970, vol. II, pp. 823–31.
[32] See Lord Macmillan, *Compania Naviera Vascongado* v. *Cristina SS* [1938] AC 485, 496–7; 9 ILR, pp. 250, 259. Note also Bowett's view that the 'dynamism and adaptability of the principle in recent years has been quite remarkable', 'Jurisdiction', p. 5 and Marshall, CJ in *The Schooner Exchange* v. *McFaddon* (7 Cranch) 116, 136 (1812) to the effect that '[t]he jurisdiction of the nation within its own territory is necessarily exclusive and absolute'. Donaldson LJ also pointed to the general presumption in favour of the territoriality of jurisdiction, *R* v. *West Yorkshire Coroner, ex p. Smith* [1983] QB 335, 358.

tenance of good order within that state. It is also highly convenient since in practice the witnesses to the crime will be situated in the country and more often than not the alleged offender will be there too.

Thus, all crimes committed (or alleged to have been committed) within the territorial jurisdiction of a state may come before the municipal courts and the accused if convicted may be sentenced. This is so even where the offenders are foreign citizens.[33]

The principle whereby criminal jurisdiction is based upon the territory of the state claiming to try the offence is the principal ground for the exercise of jurisdiction, although not the exclusive one. There are others, such as nationality, but the majority of prosecutions occurring where a crime has been involved take place because the crime was committed within the territory of the state.

However, the territorial concept is more extensive than at first appears since it encompasses not only crimes committed on the territory of a state but also crimes in which only part of the offence has occurred in the state, for example where a person fires a weapon across a frontier killing somebody.

Both the state where the gun was fired and the state where the injury actually took place have jurisdiction to try the offender, the former under the so-called objective territorial principle. Of course, which of the states will in the event exercise its jurisdiction will depend upon where the offender is situated, but the point remains that both the state where the offence was commenced and the state where the offence was concluded may validly try the offender.[34] For example, the Scottish Solicitor General made it clear that Scottish courts had jurisdiction with regard to the alleged bombers of the airplane which exploded over the Scottish town of Lockerbie as the locus of the offences.[35]

Such a situation would also apply in cases of offences against immigration regulations and in cases of conspiracy where activities have occurred in each of two, or more, countries.[36]

---

[33] See e.g. *Holmes* v. *Bangladesh Binani Corporation* [1989] 1 AC 1112, 1137; 87 ILR, pp. 365, 380–1, per Lord Griffiths.

[34] See e.g. the *Lotus case*, PCIJ, Series A, No. 10, 1927, pp. 23, 30; 4 ILR, pp. 153, 159 and Judge Moore, *ibid.*, p. 73; the Harvard Research Draft Convention on Jurisdiction with Respect to Crime, 29 AJIL, 1935, Suppl., p. 480 (article 3) and Akehurst, 'Jurisdiction', pp. 152–3. See Lord Wilberforce, *DPP* v. *Doot* [1973] AC 807, 817; 57 ILR, pp. 117, 119 and *R* v. *Berry* [1984] 3 All ER 1008. See also *Strassheim* v. *Dailey*, 221 US 280 (1911); *US* v. *Columba-Colella*, 604 F.2d 356 and *US* v. *Perez-Herrera*, 610 F.2d 289.

[35] Before the International Court in oral pleadings at the provisional measures phase of the *Lockerbie* case, CR 92/3, pp. 11–12, UKMIL, 63 BYIL, 1992, p. 722.

[36] See e.g. *Board of Trade* v. *Owen* [1957] AC 602, 634 and *DPP* v. *Stonehouse* [1977] 2 All ER 909, 916; 73 ILR, p. 252. See also the Home Secretary speaking as to the Criminal Justice Bill on 14 April 1993, and noting that the effect of the proposed legislation would be to ensure that where a fraud had a significant connection with the UK, British courts would

The nature of territorial sovereignty in relation to criminal acts was examined in the *Lotus* case.[37] The relevant facts may be summarised as follows. The French steamer, the *Lotus*, was involved in a collision on the high seas with the *Boz-Kourt*, a Turkish collier. The latter vessel sank and eight sailors and passengers died as a result. Because of this the Turkish authorities arrested the French officer of the watch (at the time of the incident) when the *Lotus* reached a Turkish port.

The French officer was charged with manslaughter and France protested strongly against this action, alleging that Turkey did not have the jurisdiction to try the offence. The case came before the Permanent Court of International Justice, which was called upon to decide whether there existed an international rule prohibiting the Turkish exercise of jurisdiction.

Because the basis of international law is the existence of sovereign states, the Court regarded it as axiomatic that restrictions upon the independence of states could not be presumed.[38] However, a state was not able to exercise its power outside its frontiers in the absence of a permissive rule of international law. But, continued the Court, this did not mean that 'international law prohibits a state from exercising jurisdiction in its own territory, in respect of any case which relates to acts which have taken place abroad and in which it cannot rely on some permissive rule of international law'. In this respect, states had a wide measure of discretion limited only in certain instances by prohibitive rules.[39]

Because of this, countries had adopted a number of different rules extending their jurisdiction beyond the territorial limits so that 'the territoriality of criminal law, therefore, is not an absolute principle of international law and by no means coincides with territorial sovereignty'.[40]

The Court rejected the French claim that the flag state had exclusive jurisdiction over the ship on the high seas, saying that no rule to that effect had emerged in international law, and stated that the damage to the Turkish vessel was equivalent to affecting Turkish territory so as to enable that country to exercise jurisdiction on the objective territorial principle, unrestricted by any rule of international law prohibiting this.[41]

The general pronouncements by the Court leading to the dismissal of the French contentions have been criticised by writers for a number of

---

have jurisdiction, whether or not the final element of the crime occurred within the country, UKMIL, 64 BYIL, 1993, pp. 646–7. See G. Gilbert, 'Crimes Sans Frontières: Jurisdictional Problems in English Law', 63 BYIL, 1992, pp. 415, 430 *et seq.* Note also Akehurst, who would restrict the operation of the doctrine so that jurisdiction could only be claimed by the state where the primary effect is felt, 'Jurisdiction', p. 154.

[37] PCIJ, Series A, no. 10, 1927; 4 ILR, p. 153. See e.g. Mann, 'Jurisdiction', pp. 33–6, 39, 92–3; J. W. Verzijl, *The Jurisprudence of the World Court*, Leiden, 1965, vol. I, pp. 73–98 and Schachter, *International Law*, p. 250. See also *Oppenheim's International Law*, p. 478.

[38] PCIJ, Series A, No. 10, 1927, pp. 18–19; 4 ILR, p. 155.   [39] *Ibid.*, p. 19; 4 ILR, p. 156.

[40] *Ibid.*, p. 20.   [41] *Ibid.*, p. 24; 4 ILR, p. 158.

years, particularly with respect to its philosophical approach in treating states as possessing very wide powers of jurisdiction which could only be restricted by proof of a rule of international law prohibiting the action concerned.[42] It is widely accepted today that the emphasis lies the other way around.[43]

It should also be noted that the *Lotus* principle as regards collisions at sea has been overturned by article 11(1) of the High Seas Convention 1958, which emphasised that only the flag state or the state of which the alleged offender was a national has jurisdiction over sailors regarding incidents occurring on the high seas.

The territorial principle covers crimes committed not only upon the land territory of the state but also upon the territorial sea and in certain cases upon the contiguous and other zones and on the high seas where the state is the flag state of the vessel.[44]

As modern communications develop, so states evolve new methods of dealing with new problems. In the case of the Channel Tunnel, for example, providing a land link between the UK and France, these countries entered into an agreement whereby each state was permitted to exercise jurisdiction within the territory of the other. The Protocol concerning Frontier Controls and Policing, Co-operation in Criminal Justice, Public Safety and Mutual Assistance relating to the Channel Fixed Link was signed on 25 November 1991.[45] Under this Protocol, French and UK frontier control officers are empowered to work in specified parts of one another's territory. These areas are termed 'control zones' and are located at Cheriton, Coquelles, on board through trains and at international railway stations. The frontier control laws and regulations of one state thus apply and may be enforced in the other. In particular, the officers of the adjoining state shall in their exercise of national powers be permitted in the control zone in the host state to detain or arrest persons in accordance with the frontier control laws and regulations of the adjoining state. Article 38(2) of the Protocol provides that within the Fixed Link (i.e. the Tunnel), each state shall have jurisdiction and shall apply its own law when it cannot be ascertained with certainty where an offence has been committed or when an offence committed in the territory of one state is related to an offence committed in the territory of the other state or when an offence has begun in or has been continued into its own

---

[42] See e.g. G. Fitzmaurice, 'The General Principles of International Law Considered from the Standpoint of the Rule of Law', 92 HR, pp. 1, 56–7 and H. Lauterpacht, *International Law: Collected Papers*, Cambridge, vol. I, 1970, pp. 488–9.
[43] See e.g. the *Anglo-Norwegian Fisheries* case ICJ Reports, 1951, p. 116; 18 ILR, p. 86 and the *Nottebohm* case, ICJ Reports, 1955, p. 4; 22 ILR, p. 349.
[44] See *supra*, Chapter 11, pp. 406–7, 410–11, 413 and 420–2.
[45] The Protocol was brought into force in the UK by the Channel Tunnel (International Arrangements) Order 1993, see e.g. UKMIL, 64 BYIL, 1993, p. 647.

territory.[46] However, it is also provided that the state which first receives the person suspected of having committed such an offence shall have priority in exercising jurisdiction.

Another example of such cross-state territorial jurisdictional arrangements may be found in the Israel–Jordan Treaty of Peace 1994. Annex 1 (b) and (c) of the Treaty, relating to the Naharayim/Baqura Area and the Zofar/Al-Ghamr Area respectively, provides for a special regime on a temporary basis. Although each area itself is recognised as under Jordan's sovereignty, with Israeli private land ownership rights and property interests, Jordan undertakes to grant unimpeded entry to, exit from, land usage and movement within the area to land-owners and to their invitees or employees and not to apply its customs or immigration legislation to such persons. In particular, Jordan undertakes to permit with minimum formality the entry of uniformed Israeli police officers for the purpose of investigating crime or dealing with other incidents solely involving the land-owners, their invitees or employees. Jordan undertakes also not to apply its criminal laws to activities in the area involving only Israeli nationals, while Israeli laws applying to the extraterritorial activities of Israelis may be applied to Israelis and their activities in the area. Israel could also take measures in the area to enforce such laws.[47]

Thus although jurisdiction is primarily and predominantly territorial, it is not inevitably and exclusively so and states are free to consent to arrangements whereby jurisdiction is exercised outside the national territory and whereby jurisdiction by other states is exercised within the national territory.[48]

The nationality principle[49]

Since every state possesses sovereignty and jurisdictional powers and since every state must consist of a collection of individual human beings, it is

---

[46] This is in addition to the normal territorial jurisdiction of the states within their own territory up to the frontier in the Tunnel under the sea, article 38(1).

[47] See also e.g. the treaties of 1903 and 1977 between the US and Panama concerning jurisdictional rights over the Panama Canal Zone and the NATO Status of Forces Agreement 1951 regulating the exercise of jurisdiction of NATO forces based in other NATO states.

[48] Jurisdiction, and its concomitant international responsibility for acts done in the exercise of that jurisdiction, may also exist on the basis of actual control of the territory in question in specific contexts. See e.g. *Loizidou* v. *Turkey*, European Court of Human Rights, Series A, No. 310, 1995, p. 20. For the European Convention on Human Rights, see *supra* Chapter 7 and for international responsibility, see *infra* Chapter 14.

[49] Akehurst, 'Jurisdiction', pp. 156–7; Harvard Research Draft Convention on Jurisdiction with Respect to Crime, 29 AJIL, 1935, Suppl., pp. 519 *et seq.*; Whiteman, *Digest*, vol. VIII, pp. 1–22, 64–101, 105–13, 119–87; R. Donner, *The Regulation of Nationality in International Law*, 2nd edn, New York, 1995; H. Silving, 'Nationality in Comparative Law', 5 *American Journal of Comparative Law*, 1956, p. 410 and Brownlie, *Public International Law*, p. 303 and Chapter 18. See also Nguyeyen Quoc Dinh, P. Daillier and A. Pellet, *Droit International Public*, 5th edn, Paris, 1994, pp. 474 *et seq.* and, *infra*, Chapter 14, p. 562.

essential that a link between the two be legally established. That link connecting the state and the people it includes in its territory is provided by the concept of nationality.

By virtue of nationality, a person becomes entitled to a series of rights ranging from obtaining a valid passport enabling travel abroad to being able to vote. In addition, nationals may be able to undertake various jobs (for example in the diplomatic service) that a non-national may be barred from. Nationals are also entitled to the protection of their state and to various benefits prescribed under international law. On the other hand, states may not mistreat the nationals of other states nor, ordinarily, conscript them into their armed forces, nor prosecute them for crimes committed outside the territory of the particular state.

The concept of nationality is important since it determines the benefits to which persons may be entitled and the obligations (such as conscription) which they must perform.

The problem is that there is no coherent, accepted definition of nationality in international law and only conflicting descriptions under the different municipal laws of states. Not only that, but the rights and duties attendant upon nationality vary from state to state.

Generally, international law leaves the conditions for the grant of nationality to the domestic jurisdiction of states.

This was the central point in the *Nationality Decrees in Tunis and Morocco* case.[50] This concerned a dispute between Britain and France over French nationality decrees which had the effect of giving French nationality to the children of certain British subjects. The Court, which had been requested to give an advisory opinion by the Council of the League of Nations, declared that:

> [t]he question of whether a certain matter is or is not solely within the jurisdiction of a state is an essentially relative question, it depends upon the development of international relations. Thus, in the present state of international law, questions of nationality are, in the opinion of this court, in principle within this reserved domain.[51]

However, although states may prescribe the conditions for the grant of nationality, international law is relevant, especially where other states are involved. As was emphasised in article I of the 1930 Hague Convention on the Conflict of Nationality Laws:

> it is for each state to determine under its own law who are its nationals. This law shall be recognised by other states in so far as it is consistent with international conventions, international custom and the principles of law generally recognised with regard to nationality.

---

[50] PCIJ, Series B, No. 4, 1923; 2 ILR, p. 349.   [51] *Ibid.*, p. 24.

The International Court of Justice noted in the *Nottebohm* case[52] that according to state practice, nationality was:

a legal bond having as its basis a social fact of attachment, a genuine connection of existence, interests and sentiments, together with the existence of reciprocal rights and duties.

It was a legal manifestation of the link between the person and the state granting nationality and a recognition that the person was more closely connected with that state than with any other.[53]

Since the concept of nationality provides the link between the individual and the benefits of international law, it is worth pointing to some of the basic ideas associated with the concept, particularly with regard to its acquisition.[54]

In general, the two most important principles upon which nationality is founded in states are first by descent from parents who are nationals (*jus sanguinis*) and second by virtue of being born within the territory of the state (*jus soli*).

It is commonly accepted that a child born of nationals of a particular state should be granted the nationality of that state by reason of descent. This idea is particularly utilised in continental European countries, for example, France, Germany and Switzerland, where the child will receive the nationality of his father, although many municipal systems do provide that an illegitimate child will take the nationality of his mother. On the other hand, in common law countries such as Britain and the US the doctrine of the *jus sanguinis* is more restricted, so that where a father has become a national by descent it does not always follow that that fact alone will be sufficient to make the child a national.

The common law countries have tended to adopt the *jus soli* rule, whereby any child born within the territorial limits of the state automatically becomes a national thereof.[55] The British Nationality Act of 1948, for example, declared that 'every person born within the United Kingdom and Colonies . . . shall be a citizen of the United Kingdom and Colonies by birth'.[56] There is an exception to this, however, which applies to virtually every country applying the *jus soli* rule, and that is with regard to persons entitled to immunity from the jurisdiction of the state. In other words, the children of diplomatic personnel born within the country do not automatically acquire its

---

[52] ICJ Reports, 1955, pp. 4, 23; 22 ILR, pp. 349, 360. See also *infra*, p. 563.
[53] See *infra* Chapter 14, p. 565 as to dual nationality and state responsibility for injuries to aliens.
[54] See e.g. Brownlie, *Principles*, pp. 386–9; P. Weiss, *Nationality and Statelessness in International Law*, London, 1956 and Van Panhuys, *The Role of Nationality in International Law*, 1959.
[55] See e.g. *United States* v. *Wong Kim Ark*, 169 US 649 (1898).
[56] But see now the British Nationality Act of 1981.

nationality.[57] Precisely how far this exception extends varies from state to state. Some countries provide that this rule applies also to the children of enemy alien fathers[58] born in areas under enemy occupation.[59]

Nationality may also be acquired by the wives of nationals, although here again the position varies from state to state. Some states provide for the automatic acquisition of the husband's nationality, others for the conditional acquisition of nationality and others merely state that the marriage has no effect as regards nationality. Problems were also caused in the past by the fact that many countries stipulated that a woman marrying a foreigner would thereby lose her nationality.

The Convention of 1957 on the Nationality of Married Women provides that contracting states accept that the marriage of one of its nationals with an alien shall not automatically affect the wife's nationality, although a wife may acquire her husband's nationality by special procedures should she so wish.

It should be noted also that article 9 of the Convention on the Elimination of All Forms of Discrimination against Women 1979 provides that states parties shall grant women equal rights with men to acquire, change or retain their nationality and that in particular neither marriage to an alien nor change of nationality by the husband during marriage shall automatically change the nationality of the wife, render her stateless or force upon her the nationality of the husband. It is also provided that women shall have equal rights with men with respect to the nationality of their children. As far as children themselves are concerned, article 24(3) of the International Covenant on Civil and Political Rights 1966 stipulated that every child has the right to acquire a nationality, while this is reaffirmed in article 7 of the Convention on the Rights of the Child 1989.

Nationality may be obtained by an alien by virtue of a naturalisation process usually involving a minimum period of residence, but the conditions under which this takes place vary considerably from country to country.[60]

Civil jurisdiction, especially as regards matters of personal status, in a number of countries depends upon the nationality of the parties involved. So that, for example, the appropriate matrimonial law in any dispute for a Frenchman anywhere would be French law. However, common law countries tend to base the choice of law in such circumstances upon the law of the state where the individual involved has his permanent home (domicile).

---

[57] See e.g. *In Re Thenault*, 47 F.Supp. 952 (1942) and article 12, Convention on Conflict of Nationality Law, 1930. See also article II, Optional Protocol on Acquisition of Nationality, (UN Conference on Diplomatic Law), 1961.

[58] But see *Inglis* v. *Sailor's Snug Harbour*, 3 Peters 99 (1830), US Supreme Court.

[59] Note the various problems associated with possible extensions of the *jus soli* rule, e.g. regarding births on ships, see Brownlie, *Public International Law*, pp. 388–9. See also *Lam Mow* v. *Nagle*, 24 F.2d 316 (1928); 4 ILR, pp. 295, 296. [60] See e.g. Weiss, *Nationality*, p. 101.

Many countries, particularly those with a legal system based upon the continental European model, claim jurisdiction over crimes committed by their nationals, notwithstanding that the offence may have occurred in the territory of another state.[61] Common law countries tend, however, to restrict the crimes over which they will exercise jurisdiction over their nationals abroad to very serious ones. The English courts, for instance, generally limit such claims to treason, murder and bigamy committed by British nationals abroad.[62] But the common law countries have never protested against the extensive use of the nationality principle to found jurisdiction in criminal matters by other states. Under section 21 of the Antarctic Act 1994, when a UK national does or omits to do anything in Antarctica which would have constituted an offence if committed in the UK, then such person will be deemed to have committed an offence and be liable to be prosecuted and punished if convicted. In addition, the War Crimes Act 1991 provides for jurisdiction against a person who was on 8 March 1990 or subsequently became a British citizen or resident in the UK. Proceedings for murder, manslaughter or culpable homicide may be brought against that person in the UK, irrespective of his nationality at the time of the alleged offence, if the offence was committed during the Second World War in a place that was part of Germany or under German occupation and constituted a violation of the laws and customs of war.[63]

It should be noted finally that by virtue of article 91 of the 1982 Convention on the Law of the Sea, ships have the nationality of the state whose flag they are entitled to fly. Each state is entitled to fix the conditions for the grant of its nationality to ships, for the registration of ships in its territory and for the right to fly its flag. However, there must be a genuine link between the state and the ship.[64] By article 17 of the Chicago Convention on International Civil Aviation 1944 aircraft have the nationality of the state

---

[61] See e.g. Gilbert, 'Crimes', p. 417. See also *re Gutierrez*, 24 ILR, p. 265, *Public Prosecutor v. Antoni*, 32 ILR, p. 140 and *Serre et Régnier, Recueil Dalloz Sirey (Jurisprudence)*, 1991, p. 395.

[62] See e.g. the Official Secrets Acts, 1911 (s.10); 1970 (s.8) and 1989 (s.15); the Offences Against the Person Act, 1861, ss.9 and 57 and the Merchant Shipping Act, 1894, s.686 (1) and *R v. Kelly* [1982] AC 665; 77 ILR, p. 284. See also the Suppression of Terrorism Act 1978, s. 4. Whether this list may now be extended to cover, for example, the problem of UK nationals participating in 'child sex tourism' in other countries is currently under discussion, see e.g. *The Times*, 24 July 1996, p. 2. Note that in *Skiriotes v. Florida*, 313 US 69, 73 (1941); 10 ILR, pp. 258, 260, Hughes CJ declared that 'the United States is not debarred by any rule of international law from governing the conduct of its own citizens upon the high seas or even in foreign countries when the rights of other nations or their nationals are not infringed'. See also DUSPIL, 1976, pp. 449–57, regarding legislation to subject US nationals and citizens to US district court jurisdiction for crimes committed outside the US, particularly regarding Antarctica.

[63] See also with regard to the nationality of ships and aircraft, *supra* Chapter 11, p. 420 and *infra* p. 475. See further as to the nationality of claims, *infra* Chapter 14, p. 562.

[64] See also article 5 of the Geneva Convention on the High Seas 1958.

in which they are registered, although the conditions for registration are a matter for domestic law.[65]

The passive personality principle[66]

Under this principle, a state may claim jurisdiction to try an individual for offences committed abroad which have affected or will affect nationals of the state.

The leading case on this particular principle is the *Cutting* case in 1886[67] which concerned the publication in Texas of a defamatory statement by an American citizen of a Mexican. Cutting was arrested while in Mexico and convicted of the offence (a crime under Mexican law) with Mexico maintaining its right to jurisdiction upon the basis of the passive personality principle. The United States strongly protested against this, but there was an inconclusive end to the incident, the charges being withdrawn by the injured party.[68]

A strong attack on this principle was made by Judge Moore, in a dissenting opinion in the *Lotus* case,[69] since the Turkish criminal code provided for jurisdiction where harm resulted to a Turkish national. However, the Court did not resolve the issue and concentrated upon the objective territorial jurisdiction principle.[70]

The overall opinion has been that the passive personality principle is rather a dubious ground upon which to base claims to jurisdiction under international law and it has been strenuously opposed by the US[71] and the UK, although a number of states apply it.

However, article 9 of the International Convention against the Taking of Hostages 1979, in detailing the jurisdictional bases that could be established with regard to the offence, included the national state of a hostage 'if that state considers it appropriate'.[72] The possibility of using the passive personality concept was taken up by the US in 1984 in the Comprehensive

---

[65] See article 19.
[66] See e.g. Akehurst, 'Jurisdiction', pp. 162–6; Mann, 'Jurisdiction', pp. 40–1; E. Beckett, 'The Exercise of Criminal Jurisdiction over Foreigners', 6 BYIL, 1925, p. 44 and Beckett, 'Criminal Jurisdiction over Foreigners', 8 BYIL, 1927, p. 108; W. W. Bishop, 'General Course of Public International Law, 1965', 115 HR, pp. 151, 324 and Higgins, *Problems*, p. 65. See also the *Eichmann* case, 36 ILR, pp. 5, 49–57, 304.
[67] J. B. Moore, *Digest of International Law*, Washington, vol. II, 1906, p. 228.
[68] See *US Foreign Relations*, 1886, p. viii; *ibid.*, 1887, p. 757 and *ibid.*, 1888, vol. II, p. 1114.
[69] PCIJ, Series A, No. 10, 1927, p. 92; 4 ILR, p. 153.
[70] *Ibid.*, pp. 22–3. See also O'Connell, *Law of the Sea*, vol. II, pp. 901–2 and Higgins, *Problems*, pp. 65–6.
[71] See, for example, US protests to Greece, concerning the service of summonses by Greek Consuls in the US on US nationals involved in accidents with Greek nationals occurring in the United States, DUSPIL, 1973, pp. 197–8 and DUSPIL, 1975, pp. 339–40.
[72] See *Rees v. Secretary of State for the Home Department* [1986] 2 All ER 321. See generally, J. J. Lambert, *Terrorism and Hostages in International Law*, Cambridge, 1990. See also article 3(1)c of the Convention on the Prevention and Punishment of Crimes against Internationally Protected Persons 1973 and article 5(1)c of the Convention against Torture 1984.

Crime Control Act[73] *inter alia* implementing the Convention and in the provision extending the special maritime and territorial jurisdiction of the US to include '[a]ny place outside the jurisdiction of any nation with respect to an offence by or against a national of the United States'.[74] In 1986, following the *Achille Lauro* incident,[75] the US adopted the Omnibus Diplomatic Security and Anti-Terrorism Act,[76] inserting into the criminal code a new section which provided for US jurisdiction over homicide and physical violence outside the US where a national of the US is the victim. The section is less sweeping than it appears, since the written certification of the Attorney General is required, before a prosecution may commence by the US, to the effect that the offence was intended to coerce, intimidate or retaliate against a government or a civilian population.

In *US* v. *Yunis (No. 2)*[77] the issue concerned the apprehension of a Lebanese citizen by US agents in international waters and his prosecution in the US for alleged involvement in the hijacking of a Jordanian airliner. The only connection between the hijacking and the US was the fact that several American nationals were on that flight. The Court accepted that both the universality principle[78] and the passive personality principle provided an appropriate basis for jurisdiction in the case. It was stated that although the latter principle was the most controversial of the jurisdictional principles in international law, 'the international community recognises its legitimacy'.[79] It was pointed out that although the US had historically opposed the passive personality principle, it had been accepted by the US and the international community in recent years in the sphere of terrorist and other internationally condemned crimes.[80]

The protective principle[81]

This principle provides that states may exercise jurisdiction over aliens who have committed an act abroad which is deemed prejudicial to the

---

[73] See new section 1203 of the Criminal Code, 18 USC para. 1203, Pub.L. No. 98–473, ch. 19, para. 2002(a), 98 Stat. 1976, 2186.
[74] Pub.L. No. 98–473, para. 1210, 98 Stat. at 2164. Note also article 689(1) of the French Code de Procédure Pénal adopted in 1975.   [75] See *infra*, p. 477.
[76] Pub.L. No. 99–399, tit. XII, para. 1202(a), 100 Stat. 853, 896. See e.g. C. Blakesley, 'Jurisdictional Issues and Conflicts of Jurisdiction' in *Legal Responses to International Terrorism* (ed. M. C. Bassiouni), Charlottesville, 1988.
[77] 681 F.Supp. 896 (1988); 82 ILR, p. 344. See also *US* v. *Yunis (No. 3)*, 924 F 2d 1086, 1091; 88 ILR, pp. 176, 181.   [78] *Infra*, p. 470.   [79] *Ibid.*, p. 901; 82 ILR, p. 349.
[80] *Ibid.*, p. 902; 82 ILR, p. 350. Note that a comment to paragraph 402 of the *Third Restatement of US Foreign Relations Law*, vol. I, p. 240, states that the passive personality principle 'is increasingly accepted as applied to terrorist and other organised attacks on a state's nationals by reason of their nationality, or to assassinations of a state's diplomatic representatives or other officials'. See also *US* v. *Benitez*, 741 F.2d 1312, 1316 (1984), *cert. denied*, 471 US 1137, 105 S.Ct.2679 (1985).
[81] See e.g. Akehurst, 'Jurisdiction', pp. 157–9; Harvard Research, pp. 543–63 and M. Sahovic and W. W. Bishop, 'The Authority of the State: its Range with Respect to Persons and Places'

security of the particular state concerned. It is a well-established concept, although there are uncertainties as to how far it extends in practice
and particularly which acts are included within the net of the claimed
jurisdiction.[82]

The principle is justifiable on the basis of protection of a state's vital interests, since the alien might not be committing an offence under the law of the
country where he is residing and extradition might be refused if it encom-
passed political offences.

However, it is clear that it is a principle that can easily be abused, although
usually centred upon immigration and various economic offences, since far
from protecting important state functions it could easily be manipulated to
subvert foreign governments. Nevertheless, it exists partly in view of the
insufficiency of most municipal laws as far as offences against the security
and integrity of foreign states are concerned.[83]

This doctrine seems to have been applied in the British case of *Joyce* v.
Director of Public Prosecutions,[84] involving the infamous pro-Nazi propa-
gandist 'Lord Haw-Haw'. Joyce was born in America, but in 1933 fraudulently acquired a British passport by declaring that he had been born in
Ireland. In 1939, he left Britain and started working for German radio.
The following year, he claimed to have acquired German nationality. The
case turned on whether the British court had jurisdiction to try him after
the war, on a charge of treason. The House of Lords decided that jurisdiction did exist in this case. Joyce had held himself out to be a British subject
and had availed himself of the protection (albeit fraudulently) of a British
passport. Accordingly he could be deemed to owe allegiance to the
Crown, and be liable for a breach of that duty. The fact that the treason
occurred outside the territory of the UK was of no consequence since
states were not obliged to ignore the crime of treason committed against
it outside its territory. Joyce was convicted and suffered the penalty for his
actions.[85]

The protective principle is often used in treaties providing for multiple
jurisdictional grounds with regard to specific offences.[86]

in *Manual of Public International Law* (ed. Sørensen), London, 1968, pp. 311, 362–5. See
also M. S. McDougal, H. Lasswell and V. Vlasic, *Law and Public Order in Space*, New Haven,
1963, pp. 699–701.
[82] See e.g. *In re Urios*, 1 ILR, p. 107 and article 694(1) of the French Code de Procédure Pénal.
[83] See e.g. *Rocha* v. *US*, 288 F.2d 545 (1961); 32 ILR, p. 112; *US* v. *Pizzarusso*, 62 AJIL, 1968,
p. 975, and *US* v. *Rodriguez*, 182 F.Supp. 479 (1960). See also the *Italian South Tyrol
Terrorism* case, 71 ILR, p. 242.   [84] [1946] AC 347; 15 ILR, p. 91.
[85] See with regard to US practice, *Rocha* v. *United States*, 182 F Supp 479 (1960); *United States*
v. *Pizzarusso*, 388 F 2d 8 (1968) and *United States* v. *Layton*, 509 F.Supp 212 (1981). See
also *Third US Restatement on Foreign Relations Law*, vol. I, pp. 237 *et seq.* and the Omnibus
Diplomatic Security and Anti-Terrorism Act 1986.
[86] See e.g. the Hostages Convention 1979; the aircraft hijacking conventions and the Safety of
United Nations and Associated Personnel Convention 1994, see *infra* pp. 474 *et seq.*

The universality principle[87]

Under this principle, each and every state has jurisdiction to try particular offences. The basis for this is that the crimes involved are regarded as particularly offensive to the international community as a whole. There are two categories that clearly belong to the sphere of universal jurisdiction. These are piracy and war crimes. However, there is a growing number of other offences which by international treaty may be subject to the jurisdiction of contracting parties.

Piracy

Universal jurisdiction over piracy has been accepted under international law for many centuries and constitutes a long-established principle of the world community.[88] All states may both arrest and punish pirates, provided of course that they have been apprehended on the high seas [89] or within the territory of the state concerned. The punishment of the offenders takes place whatever their nationality and wherever they happened to carry out their criminal activities.

Piracy under international law (or piracy *jure gentium*) must be distinguished from piracy under municipal law. Offences that may be characterised as piratical under municipal laws do not necessarily fall within the definition of piracy in international law, and thus are not susceptible to universal jurisdiction (depending of course upon the content and form of international conventions). Piracy *jure gentium* was defined in article 15 of the High Seas Convention 1958 (and reaffirmed in article 101 of the 1982 Convention on the Law of the Sea) as illegal acts of violence, detention or depredation committed for private ends by the crew or passengers of a private ship or private aircraft and directed against another ship or aircraft (or persons or property therein) on the high seas or *terra nullius*.[90] Attempts to commit such acts are sufficient to constitute piracy and it is not essential for the attempt to have been successful.[91]

---

[87] See e.g. Akehurst, 'Jurisdiction', pp. 160–6; Bowett, 'Jurisdiction', pp. 11–14; Harvard Research, pp. 563–92; Jennings, 'Extraterritorial', p. 156; Gilbert, 'Crimes', p. 423 and Randall, 'Universal Jurisdiction under International Law', 66 *Texas Law Review*, 1988, p. 785. See also M. C. Bassiouni, *Crimes Against Humanity in International Criminal Law*, Dordrecht, 1992;

[88] See e.g. *In re Piracy Jure Gentium* [1934] AC 586; 7 ILR, p. 213. See also D. H. Johnson, 'Piracy in Modern International Law', 43 *Transactions of the Grotius Society*, London, 1957, p. 63 and G. E. White, 'The Marshall Court and International Law: The Piracy Cases', 83 AJIL, 1989, p. 727.

[89] Article 105 of the 1982 Convention on the Law of the Sea (reproducing article 19 of the Geneva Convention on the High Seas 1958).   [90] See further, *supra*, Chapter 11, p. 423.

[91] *In re Piracy Jure Gentium* [1934] AC 586; 7 ILR, p. 213.

War crimes, crimes against peace and crimes against humanity

In addition to piracy, war crimes are now accepted by most authorities as subject to universal jurisdiction, though of course the issues involved are extremely sensitive and highly political.[92] While there is little doubt about the legality and principles of the war crimes decisions emerging after the Second World War, a great deal of controversy arose over suggestions of war crimes guilt appertaining to American personnel connected with the Vietnam war,[93] and Pakistani soldiers involved in the Bangladesh war of 1971.

Article 6 of the Charter of the International Military Tribunal of 1945 referred to crimes against peace, violations of the law and customs of war and crimes against humanity as offences within the jurisdiction of the Tribunal for which there was to be individual responsibility.[94] This article can now be regarded as part of international law. In a resolution unanimously approved by the General Assembly of the United Nations in 1946, the principles of international law recognised by the Charter of the Nuremberg Tribunal and the judgment of the Tribunal were expressly confirmed.[95] The General Assembly in 1968 adopted a Convention on the Non-Applicability of Statutory Limitations to War Crimes and Crimes Against Humanity, reinforcing the general conviction that war crimes form a distinct category under international law, susceptible to universal jurisdiction,[96] while the four Geneva 'Red Cross' Conventions of 1949 also contain provisions for universal jurisdiction over grave breaches.[97] Such grave breaches include wilful killing, torture or inhuman treatment, unlawful deportation of protected persons and the taking of hostages. The list was extended in Protocol I of 1977 to the 1949 Conventions to include, for example, attacking civilian populations.[98]

[92] See e.g. Akehurst, 'Jurisdiction', p. 160; Sahovic and Bishop, 'Authority', pp. 367–8; A. Cowles, 'Universality of Jurisdiction over War Crimes', 33 *California Law Review*, 1945, p. 177; Brownlie, *Public International Law*, pp. 304–5; Bowett, 'Jurisdiction', p. 12; Higgins, *Problems*, p. 56; Mann, 'Doctrine of Jurisdiction', p. 93 and Bassiouni, *Crimes*, p. 510. See also the *Eichmann* case, 36 ILR, p. 5 and p. 277 and the UN War Crimes Commission, 15 *Law Reports of Trials of War Criminals*, 1949, p. 26. See further, *supra* Chapter 5, p. 184.

[93] See e.g. *Calley* v. *Calloway*, 382 F.Supp. 650 (1974), rev'd 519 F.2d 184 (1975), cert. denied 425 US 911 (1976).

[94] See also article 228 of the Treaty of Versailles 1919, *supra* Chapter 5, p. 185.

[95] Resolution 95(I). See also *Yearbook of the ILC*, 1950 II p. 195; 253 HL Deb., col. 831, 2 December 1963; the *British Manual of Military Law*, 1958, Part III, para. 637; Brownlie, *Public International Law*, p. 562 and P. Weiss, 'Time Limits for the Prosecution of Crimes against International Law', 53 BYIL, 1982, pp. 163, 188 *et seq.*

[96] See e.g. Weiss, 'Time Limits'.

[97] See article 49 of the First Geneva Convention; article 50 of the Second Geneva Convention; article 129 of the Third Geneva Convention and article 146 of the Fourth Geneva Convention. See also e.g. G. I. D. Draper, *The Red Cross Conventions*, 1958, p. 105. Cf. Bowett, 'Jurisdiction', p. 12.   [98] See further, Chapter 5, p. 186 and Chapter 19, pp. 806 *et seq.*

The universality principle was to some extent applied in the *Eichmann* case[99] before the District Court of Jerusalem and the Supreme Court of Israel in 1961. Eichmann was prosecuted and convicted under an Israeli law of 1951 for war crimes, crimes against the Jewish people and crimes against humanity. The District Court declared that far from limiting states' jurisdiction with regard to such crimes, international law was actually in need of the legislative and judicial organs of every state to give effect to its criminal interdictions and bring the criminals to trial. The fact that the crimes were committed prior to the establishment of the state of Israel did not prevent the correct application of its powers pursuant to universal jurisdiction under international law. Israel's municipal law merely reflected the reiterated offences existing under international law.

Nuremberg practice demonstrates that crimes against peace consist of the commission by the authorities of a state of an act of aggression. In theory this is not controversial, but in practice serious problems are likely to arise within the framework of universal jurisdiction. However, whether this category can be expanded to include support for international terrorism is open to question. Crimes against humanity clearly cover genocide and related activities. They differ from war crimes in applying beyond the context of an international armed conflict, but cover essentially the same substantive offences.[100] The UN Secretary-General's Report on the Establishment of an International Tribunal for the Former Yugoslavia[101] noted in the commentary to article 5 of what became the Statute of the Tribunal[102] that 'crimes against humanity are aimed at any civilian population and are prohibited regardless of whether they are committed in an armed conflict, international or internal in character' and that 'crimes against humanity refer to inhumane acts of a very serious nature, such as wilful killing, torture or rape, committed as part of a widespread or systematic attack against any civilian population on national, political, ethnic, racial or religous grounds'.[103]

The International Law Commission provisionally adopted a Draft Code of Crimes Against the Peace and Security of Mankind in 1991.[104] Article 6 of the Draft provides that a state in whose territory an individual alleged to

[99] 36 ILR, pp. 5 and 277. See also the *Barbie* cases, 78 ILR, pp. 78, 125, 136 and *Demjanjuk v. Petrovsky*, 776 F.2d 571 (1985); 79 ILR, p. 534. See also *Keesing's Record of World Events*, p. 36189 regarding the *Demjanjuk* case in Israel.

[100] See e.g. Brownlie, *Public International Law*, p. 562; L. C. Green, *The Contemporary Law of Armed Conflict*, Manchester, 1993, Chapter 18; E. Schwelb, 'Crimes Against Humanity', 23 BYIL, 1946, p. 178. See also the Commentary to article 20 of the Draft Statute for an International Criminal Court which refers to the concept as a term of art, *Report of the International Law Commission*, A/49/10, 1994, p. 75.

[101] S/25704, 1993, at paragraphs 47–8.   [102] Security Council resolution 827 (1993).

[103] See article 3 of the Statute of the International Tribunal for Rwanda 1994, Security Council resolution 955 (1994). See also the *Barbie* case, 100 ILR, p. 330 and the *Touvier* case, *ibid.*, p. 337.

[104] A/46/10 and 30 ILM, 1991, p. 1584. This had been under consideration since 1982, see General Assembly resolution 36/106 of 10 December 1981. A Draft Code was formulated

have committed a crime against the peace and security of mankind is present shall either try or extradite him.[105] The Crimes against the Peace and Security of Mankind, for which there is individual responsibility, include aggression (article 15); genocide (article 19); apartheid (article 20); exceptionally serious war crimes (article 22); recruitment, use, financing and training of mercenaries (article 23); international terrorism (article 24); illicit traffic in narcotic drugs (article 25) and wilful and severe damage to the environment (article 26). The Draft is not to be taken as an agreed and binding text and many of the suggestions made for categories of universal jurisdiction are controversial.

The fact that a particular activity may be seen as an international crime does not of itself establish universal jurisdiction and state practice does not appear to have moved beyond war crimes, crimes against peace and crimes against humanity in terms of permitting the exercise of such jurisdiction. In particular, references to, for example, apartheid, mercenaries and environmental offences in this context must be taken as *de lege ferenda*.

Treaties providing for jurisdiction

In addition to the accepted universal jurisdiction to apprehend and try pirates and war criminals, there are a number of treaties which provide for the suppression by the international community of various activities, ranging from the destruction of submarine cables to drug trafficking and slavery.[106] These treaties provide for the exercise of state jurisdiction but not for universal jurisdiction. Some conventions establish what might be termed a quasi-universal jurisdiction in providing for the exercise of jurisdiction upon a variety of bases by as wide a group of state parties as possible.

For instance, the 1948 Genocide Convention declares that persons charged with genocide shall be tried by a competent tribunal of the state in the territory of which the offence was committed or 'by such international penal tribunal as may have jurisdiction with respect to those contracting parties which shall have accepted its jurisdiction'[107] and treaties relating to currency counterfeiting and drug trafficking[108] require the state claiming

---

in 1954 by the ILC and submitted to the UN General Assembly, see *Yearbook of the ILC*, 1954, vol. II, p. 150. The General Assembly postponed consideration of it until a definition of aggression had been formulated, resolution 897(IX). This was achieved in 1974, see resolution 3314(XXIX). See also *supra* Chapter 5, p. 184.

[105] The Draft includes a comment noting that this article will be reviewed if an international criminal court is established. [106] See e.g. Akehurst, 'Jurisdiction', pp. 160–1.

[107] See further, *supra*, Chapter 6, p. 209. See also the 1984 Convention against Torture, which similarly calls upon states either to prosecute an alleged offender or extradite him to a state which will prosecute him *(aut dedire aut punire)*.

[108] See also the 1979 Convention against the Taking of Hostages and e.g. the UK Taking of Hostages Act, 1982.

jurisdiction to have adopted municipal legislation accepting the prosecution of aliens for offences committed abroad.

Other examples of the recognition of a quasi-universal jurisdiction occur with regard to the offence of hijacking and crimes against diplomats and other internationally protected persons.[109] These offences are not like piracy *jure gentium*, in that all states automatically possess under international law the capacity to apprehend and try those suspected of them; rather, they stem from international treaties providing that jurisdiction with respect to them may be based upon any of several grounds. These treaties have several common features, including requiring that the violation in question be rendered an offence in domestic law, calling upon states parties in whose territory the alleged offender is found either to prosecute or extradite such person and providing for the exercise of jurisdiction upon a variety of bases, ranging from territoriality to nationality and passive personality grounds.

The Convention on the Prevention and Punishment of Crimes against Internationally Protected Persons, including Diplomatic Agents, was adopted in 1973 by the General Assembly of the United Nations and came into force in 1977. This stipulates that contracting states should make acts such as assaults upon the person, premises and transport of such persons a crime under their domestic law (article 2).[110] This, of course, will require little if any revision of existing penal statutes. Each state is to establish its jurisdiction over these crimes when committed in its territory or on board ships or aircraft registered in its territory, or when the alleged offender is a national or when the crimes have been committed against an internationally protected person functioning on behalf of that state (article 3). A person is regarded as internationally protected where he is a head of state or government, or foreign minister abroad, or state representative or official of an international organisation (article 1).

The International Convention against the Taking of Hostages 1979 came into force in 1983 and, like the Internationally Protected Persons Treaty, requires each state party to make the offence punishable under national law,[111] and provides that states parties must either extradite or prosecute an alleged offender found on their territory and incorporate the offence of hostage-taking into existing and future extradition treaties. The grounds

---

[109] Note that the International Law Commission's Draft Statute for an International Criminal Court proposes that the court would have jurisdiction in certain conditions with regard to a range of 'treaty crimes' arising out of the Geneva Conventions of 1949 and Protocol I thereto; the Hague Convention 1970; the Montreal Convention 1971; the Apartheid Convention 1973; the Internationally Protected Persons Convention 1973; the Hostages Convention 1979; the Torture Convention 1984; the Safety of Maritime Navigation Convention and Protocol 1988 and the Convention against Illicit Traffic in Narcotic Drugs and Psychotropic Substances 1988, see *Report of the International Law Commission*, A/49/10, 1994, pp. 141 *et seq.* [110] See e.g. the UK Internationally Protected Persons Act 1978.
[111] See e.g. the UK Taking of Hostages Act 1982.

upon which a state party may exercise jurisdiction are laid down in article 5 and cover offences committed in its territory or on board a ship or aircraft registered in that state; by any of its nationals, or if that state considers it appropriate, by stateless persons having their habitual residence in its territory; in order to compel that state to do or abstain from doing any act; or with respect to a hostage who is a national of that state, if that state considers it appropriate.

The Convention on the Safety of United Nations and Associated Personnel 1994 provides that attacks upon UN or associated personnel or property be made a crime under national law by each state party (article 9) and that jurisdiction should be established with regard to such offences when the crime is committed in the territory of that state or on board a ship or aircraft registered in that state or when the alleged offender is a national of that state. States parties may also establish their jurisdiction over any such crimes when either committed by a stateless person whose habitual residence is in the state concerned, or with regard to a national of that state, or in an attempt to compel that state to do or to abstain from doing any act (article 10). In addition, the state in whose territory the alleged offender is present shall either prosecute or extradite such person (article 14).

As far as the hijacking of and other unlawful acts connected with aircraft is concerned, the leading treaties are the Tokyo Convention on Offences and Certain Other Acts Committed on Board Aircraft, 1963; the Hague Convention for the Suppression of Unlawful Seizure of Aircraft, 1970 and the Montreal Convention for the Suppression of Unlawful Acts against the Safety of Civil Aviation, 1971. The latter two instruments arose as a result of the wave of aircraft hijacking and attacks upon civilian planes that took place in the late 1960s, and tried to deal with the problem of how to apprehend and punish the perpetrators of such deeds.

The Tokyo Convention applies to both general offences and acts which, whether or not they are offences, may or do jeopardise the safety of the aircraft or of persons or property therein or which jeopardise good order and discipline on board. It provides for the jurisdiction of the contracting state over aircraft registered therein while the aircraft is in flight, or on the surface of the high seas or on any other area outside the territory of any state. Contracting states are called upon to take the necessary measures to establish jurisdiction by municipal law over such aircraft in such circumstances. In addition, the Convention permits interference with an aircraft in flight in order to establish criminal jurisdiction over an offence committed on board in certain specific circumstances by contracting states not being the state of registration. The circumstances specified are where the offence has effect on the territory of such state; has been committed by or against a national or permanent resident of such state; is against the security of such state;

consists of a breach of any rules or regulations relating to the flight or manoeuvre of aircraft in force in such state or where the exercise of jurisdiction is necessary to ensure the observance of any obligation of such state under a multilateral international agreement.[112] No obligation to extradite is provided for.

The Hague Convention provides that any person who, on board an aircraft in flight, is involved in the unlawful seizure of that aircraft (or attempts the same), commits an offence which contracting states undertake to make punishable by severe penalties. Each contracting state is to take such measures as may be necessary to establish its jurisdiction over the offence or related acts of violence when the offence is committed on board an aircraft registered in that state; when the aircraft in question lands in its territory with the alleged offender still on board or when the offence is committed on board an aircraft leased without a crew to a lessee who has his principal place of business, or if the lessee has no such place of business, his permanent residence, in that state. The Convention also provides that contracting states in the territory of which an alleged offender is found must either extradite or prosecute him.

The Montreal Convention contains similar rules as to jurisdiction and extradition as the Hague Convention but is aimed at controlling and punishing attacks and sabotage against civil aircraft in flight and on the ground rather than dealing with hijacking directly.[113] A Protocol to the Montreal Convention was signed in 1988. This provides for the suppression of unlawful acts of violence at airports serving international civil aviation which cause or are likely to cause serious injury, and acts of violence which destroy or seriously damage the facilities of an airport serving international civil aviation or aircraft not in service located thereon or disrupt the service of the airport.[114]

The wide range of jurisdictional bases is to be noted, although it would appear that universality as such is not included. Nevertheless, condemnation of this form of activity is widespread and it is likely that hijacking has become an international crime of virtually universal jurisdiction in practice.[115]

[112] Article 4. See S. Shuber, *Jurisdiction over Crimes on Board Aircraft*, The Hague, 1973; C. C. Joyner, *Aerial Hijacking as an International Crime*, 1974 and McWhinney, *Aerial Piracy and International Terrorism*, 2nd edn, Dordrecht, 1987. See also the US Anti-Hijacking Act of 1974, and *supra*, Chapter 10, p. 376.

[113] Note that neither the Tokyo nor the Hague Conventions apply to aircraft used in military, customs or police services, see articles 1(4) and 3(2) respectively.

[114] Note the Hindawi episode, where the European Community imposed sanctions upon Syria in a situation where it emerged during a court case in the UK that an attempt to smuggle a bomb on an Israeli airliner in 1986 in London had been supported by Syrian intelligence; see *Keesing's Contemporary Archives*, pp. 34771–2 and pp. 34883–4.

[115] See *US* v. *Yunis (No. 2)*, 681 F.Supp. 896, 900–1 (1988); 82 ILR, pp. 344, 348. See also *US* v. *Yunis (No. 3)*, 924 F.2d 1086, 1091 (1991); 88 ILR, pp. 176, 181.

Of course questions as to enforcement will arise where states fail either to respect their obligations under the above Conventions or if they are not parties to them then to respect customary law on the reasonable assumption that state practice now recognises hijacking as an unlawful act.[116]

A number of possibilities exist, in addition to recourse to the United Nations and the relevant international air organisations.[117] Like-minded states may seek to impose sanctions upon errant states. The 1978 Bonn Declaration, for example, agreed that 'in cases where a country refuses the extradition or prosecution of those who have hijacked an aircraft and/or does not return such aircraft' action would be taken to cease all flights to and from that country and its airlines.[118] Bilateral arrangements may also be made, which provide for the return of, or prosecution of, hijackers.[119] States may also, of course, adopt legislation which enables them to prosecute alleged hijackers found in their territory,[120] or more generally seeks to combat terrorism. The 1984 US Act to Combat International Terrorism, for example, provides for rewards for information concerning a wide range of terrorist acts primarily (although not exclusively) within the territorial jurisdiction of the US.

Other acts of general self-help have also been resorted to. In 1973, for example, Israeli warplanes intercepted a civil aircraft in Lebanese airspace in an unsuccessful attempt to apprehend a guerrilla leader held responsible for the killing of civilians aboard hijacked aircraft. Israel was condemned for this by the UN Security Council[121] and the International Civil Aviation Organisation.[122]

On the night of 10–11 October 1985, an Egyptian civil aircraft carrying the hijackers of the Italian cruise ship *Achille Lauro* was intercepted over the Mediterranean Sea by US Navy fighters and compelled to land in Sicily. The US justified its action generally by reference to the need to combat international terrorism, while the UK Foreign Secretary noted it was relevant to take into account the international agreements on hijacking and hostage-taking.[123] However, nothing in these conventions, it is suggested, would

---

[116] See e.g. General Assembly resolution 2645(XXV) and Security Council resolution 286 (1970). [117] See *supra*, Chapter 10, p. 376 and *infra*, Chapter 19, p. 803.
[118] See UKMIL, 49 BYIL, 1978, p. 423. The states making the Declaration were the UK, France, US, Canada, West Germany, Italy and Japan.
[119] See e.g. the US–Cuban Memorandum of Understanding on Hijacking of Aircraft and Vessels and Other Offences, 1973.
[120] See e.g. the US Anti-Hijacking Act of 1974 and the UK Civil Aviation Act, 1982, s.92 and the Aviation Security Act, 1982. [121] Resolution 337 (1973).
[122] ICAO Doc. 9050–LC/169–1, at p. 196 (1973).
[123] See *Keesing's Contemporary Archives*, p. 34078 and *The Times*, 6 February 1986, p. 4. In this context, one should also note the hijack of a TWA airliner in June 1985, the murder of a passenger and the prolonged detention in the Lebanon of the remaining passengers and the crew, see *Keesing's Contemporary Archives*, p. 34130. See also A. Cassese, *Violence and Law in the Modern Age*, Cambridge, 1988, Chapter 4.

appear to justify an interception of a civilian aircraft over the high seas or over any area other than the territory of the intercepting state and for specified reasons. The apprehension of terrorists is to be encouraged, but the means must be legitimate. On 4 February 1986, the Israeli Airforce intercepted a Libyan civil aircraft en route from Libya to Syria in an attempt to capture terrorists, arguing that the aircraft in question was part of a terrorist operation.[124]

Nevertheless, there may be circumstances where an action taken by a state as a consequence of hostile hijacking or terrorist operations would be justifiable in the context of self-defence.[125]

Illegal apprehension of suspects and the exercise of jurisdiction[126]

It would appear that unlawful apprehension of a suspect by state agents acting in the territory of another state is not a bar to the exercise of jurisdiction. Such apprehension would, of course, constitute a breach of international law and the norm of non-intervention,[127] unless the circumstances were such that the right of self-defence could be pleaded.[128] It could be argued that the seizure, being a violation of international law, would only be compounded by permitting the abducting state to exercise jurisdiction[129] but international practice on the whole demonstrates otherwise.[130] In most cases a distinction is clearly drawn between the apprehension and jurisdiction to prosecute and one should also distinguish situations where the apprehension has taken place on or over the high seas from cases where it has occurred without consent on the territory of another state. A further distinction that has been made relates to situations where the abduction has taken place from a state with which the apprehending state has an extradi-

---

[124] See *The Times*, 5 February 1986, p. 1.
[125] See e.g. as to the 1976 Entebbe incident, *infra*, Chapter 19, p. 791.
[126] See e.g. F. Morgenstern, 'Jurisdiction in Seizures Effected in Violation of International Law', 29 BYIL, 1952, p. 256; P. O'Higgins, 'Unlawful Seizure and Irregular Extradition', 36 BYIL, 1960, p. 279; A. Lowenfeld, 'US Law Enforcement Abroad: The Constitution and International Law', 83 AJIL, 1989, p. 880; Lowenfeld, 'US Law Enforcement Abroad: The Constitution and International Law, Continued', 84 AJIL, 1990, p. 444; Lowenfeld, 'Kidnapping by Government Order: A Follow-Up', 84 AJIL, 1990, p. 712 and Lowenfeld, 'Still More on Kidnapping', 85 AJIL, 1991, p. 655. See also F. A. Mann, 'Reflections on the Prosecution of Persons Abducted in Breach of International Law' in *International Law at a Time of Perplexity* (ed. Y. Dinstein), Dordrecht, 1989, p. 407 and Higgins, *Problems*, p. 69.
[127] See e.g. article 2(4) of the United Nations Charter and *Nicaragua* v. *US*, ICJ Reports, 1986, p. 110; 76 ILR, 349. See further *infra*, Chapter 19, p. 797.
[128] Note, in particular, the view of the Legal Adviser of the US Department of State to the effect that '[w]hile international law therefore permits extraterritorial "arrests" in situations which permit a valid claim of self-defence, decisions about any extraterritorial arrest entail grave potential implications for US personnel, for the United States, and for our relations with other states', 84 AJIL, 1990, pp. 725, 727.   [129] See Mann, 'Jurisdiction', p. 415.
[130] See e.g. the *Eichmann* case, 36 ILR, pp. 5 and 277.

tion treaty which governs the condition under which movement of alleged offenders occur between the two. A final distinction may be drawn as between cases depending upon the type of offences with which the offender is charged, so that the problem of the apprehension interfering with the prosecution may be seen as less crucial in cases where recognised international crimes are alleged.[131] Of course, any such apprehension would constitute a violation of the human rights of the person concerned, but whether that would impact upon the exercise of jurisdiction as such is the key issue here.

Variations in approaches are evident between states. The US Court of Appeals in *US* v. *Toscanino*[132] held that the rule that jurisdiction was unaffected by an illegal apprehension[133] should not be applied where the presence of the defendant has been secured by force or fraud, but this approach has, it seems, been to a large extent eroded. In *US ex rel. Lujan* v. *Gengler*[134] it was noted that the rule in *Toscanino* was limited to cases of 'torture, brutality and similar outrageous conduct'.[135] The issue came before the US Supreme Court in *US* v. *Alvarez-Machain*,[136] which took the view that the issue essentially revolved around a strict interpretation of the relevant extradition treaty between Mexico and the US. The Court noted that where the terms of an extradition treaty in force between the states concerned prohibited abduction then jurisdiction could not be exercised. Otherwise the rule in *Ker* would apply and the prosecution would proceed. This applied even though there were some differences between the cases, in that, unlike the situation in *Ker*, the US government had been involved in the abduction and the state from whose territory the apprehension took place had protested.[137]

In the UK, the approach has appeared to alter somewhat. In *R* v. *Plymouth Justices, ex parte Driver*,[138] it was noted that once a person was in lawful

[131] See Higgins, 'Jurisdiction', p. 69.   [132] 500 F.2d 267 (1974); 61 ILR, p. 190.

[133] See in particular *Ker* v. *Illinois*, 119 US 436 (1886) and *Frisbie* v. *Collins*, 342 US 519 (1952). These cases have given rise to the reference to the Ker–Frisbie doctrine.

[134] 510 F.2d 62 (1975); 61 ILR, p. 206. See also *US* v. *Lira*, 515 F.2d 68 (1975); Lowenfeld, 'US Law Enforcement Abroad, Continued', 1990, p. 712; *Afouneh* v. *Attorney-General*, 10 ILR, p. 327 and *re Argoud*, 45 ILR, p. 90.

[135] This approach was reaffirmed in *US* v. *Yunis* both by the district court, 681 F.Supp. 909, 918–21 (1988) and by the Court of Appeals, 30 ILM, 1991, pp. 403, 408–9.

[136] 119 L Ed 2d 441 (1992); 95 ILR, p. 355. See also M. Halberstam, 'In Defence of the Supreme Court Decision in *Alvarez-Machain*', 86 AJIL, 1992, p. 736 and M. J. Glennon, 'State-Sponsored Abduction: A Comment on *United States* v. *Alvarez-Machain*', *ibid.*, p. 746.

[137] 119 L Ed 2d 441 (1992), 451; 95 ILR, p. 363. See also the dissenting opinion, which took the view that the abduction had in fact violated both international law and the extradition treaty, *ibid.*, 456–79; 95 ILR, pp. 369–79.

[138] [1986] 1 QB 95; 77 ILR, p. 351. See also *Ex Parte Susannah Scott* (1829) 9 B & C 446; *Sinclair* v. *HM Advocate* (1890) 17 R (J) 38 and *Rex* v. *Officer Commanding Depot Battalion RASC Colchester, ex p. Elliott* [1949] 1 All ER 373. Cf. *Reg* v. *Bow Street Magistrates, ex p. Mackerson* (1981) 75 Cr App R 24.

custody within the jurisdiction, the court had no power to inquire into the circumstances in which he had been brought into the jurisdiction. However, in *R* v. *Horseferry Road Magistrates' Court, ex p. Bennett*,[139] the House of Lords declared that where an extradition treaty existed with the relevant country under which the accused could have been returned, 'our courts will refuse to try him if he has been forcibly brought within our jurisdiction in disregard of those procedures by a process to which our own police, prosecuting or other executive authorities have been a knowing party'.[140]

The US Alien Tort Claims Act[141]

Under this Act, the First Congress established original district court jurisdiction over all causes where an alien sues for a tort 'committed in violation of the law of nations or a treaty of the United States'. In *Filartiga* v. *Pena-Irala*,[142] the US Court of Appeals for the Second Circuit interpreted this provision to permit jurisdiction over a private tort action by a Paraguayan national against a Paraguayan police official for acts of torture perpetrated in that state, it being held that torture by a state official constituted a violation of international law. This amounted to an important move in the attempt to exercise jurisdiction in the realm of international human rights violations, although one clearly based upon a domestic statute permitting such court competence. The relevant issues in such actions would thus depend upon the definition of the 'law of nations' in particular cases.[143]

In *Tel-Oren* v. *Libyan Arab Republic*,[144] however, the Court dismissed an action under the same statute brought by survivors and representatives of persons murdered in an armed attack on an Israeli bus in 1978 for lack of subject-matter jurisdiction. The three judges differed in their reasoning. Judge Edwards held that the law of nations did not impose liability on non-state entities like the PLO. Judge Bork, in a departure from the *Filartiga* principles, declared that 'an explicit grant of a cause of action [had to exist]

---

[139] [1993] 3 WLR 90; 95 ILR, p. 380.
[140] *Ibid.*, 105; 95 ILR, p. 393, per Lord Griffiths. See also Lord Bridge, *ibid.*, 110; 95 ILR, p. 399 and Lord Slynn, *ibid.*, 125; 95 ILR, p. 416. The House of Lords was also influenced by the decision of the South Africa Supreme Court in *State* v. *Ebrahim*, 95 ILR, p. 417, where the conviction and sentence before a South African court of a person were set aside as a consequence of his illegal abduction by state officials from Swaziland. This view was based both on Roman-Dutch and South African common law and on international law.
[141] 28 USC, para. 1350 (1982), originally enacted as part of the Judiciary Act of 1789. See also 28 USC, para. 1331, and *supra*, Chapter 4, p. 116.
[142] 630 F.2d 876 (2d Cir. 1980); 77 ILR, p. 169. See also *ibid.*, 577 F.Supp. 860 (1984); 77 ILR, p. 185, awarding punitive damages.
[143] In establishing the content of the 'law of nations', the courts must interpret international law as it exists today, 630 F.2d 876, 881 (1980); 77 ILR, pp. 169, 175.
[144] 726 F.2d 774 (1984); 77 ILR, p. 204. See also 'Agora', 79 AJIL, 1985, pp. 92 *et seq.* for a discussion of the case.

before a private individual [will] be allowed to enforce principles of international law in a federal tribunal',[145] while Senior Judge Robb held that the case was rendered non-justiciable by the political question doctrine. Further restrictions upon the *Filartiga* doctrine have also been manifested. It has, for example, been held that the Alien Tort Claims Act does not constitute an exception to the principle of sovereign immunity so that a foreign state could not be sued,[146] while it has also been held that US citizens could not sue for violations of the law of nations under the Act.[147]

In *Sanchez-Espinoza* v. *Reagan*,[148] suit was brought against a variety of present and former US executive officials for violation *inter alia* of domestic and international law with regard to the US support of the 'contra' guerrillas fighting against the Nicaraguan government. The Alien Tort Claims Act was cited, but the Court of Appeals noted that the statute arguably only covered private, non-governmental acts that violated a treaty or customary international law and, relying on *Tel-Oren*, pointed out that customary international law did not cover private conduct 'of this sort'.[149] Thus the claim for damages could only be sustained to the extent that the defendants acted in an official capacity and even if the Alien Tort Claims Act applied to official state acts, the doctrine of domestic sovereign immunity precluded the claim. In *Kadic* v. *Karadzic*,[150] the US Court of Appeals emphasised the 'liability of private persons for certain violations of customary international law and the availability of the Alien Tort Act to remedy such violations'.[151] In particular, it was noted that the proscription of genocide and war crimes and other violations of international humanitarian law applied both to state and non-state actors, although torture and summary execution (when not perpetrated in the course of genocide or war crimes) were proscribed by international law only when committed by state officials or under colour of law.[152] Even in this case, it may be that all that was required was 'the semblance of official authority' rather than establishing statehood under the formal criteria of international law.[153] The Court also held that the Torture Victim Protection Act 1992, which provides a cause of action for torture and extrajudicial killing by an individual 'under actual or apparent authority, or colour of law, of any foreign nation', was not itself a jurisdictional statute and depended upon the establishment of jurisdiction under either the Alien Tort Act or under the general federal question jurisdiction of section 1331.[154]

The Alien Tort Act was relied upon again in the *Amerada Hess* case which

---

[145] 726 F.2d 774 (1984), p. 801; 77 ILR, p. 230.
[146] *Siderman* v. *Republic of Argentina*, 965 F.2d 699 (1992).
[147] *Handel* v. *Artukovic*, 601 F.Supp. 1421 (1985); 79 ILR, p. 397.
[148] 770 F.2d 202 (1985); 80 ILR, p. 586.   [149] *Ibid.*, pp. 206–7; 80 ILR, pp. 590–1.
[150] 34 ILM, 1995, p. 1592.   [151] *Ibid.*, p. 1600.   [152] *Ibid.*, pp. 1602–6.
[153] *Ibid.*, p. 1607.   [154] *Ibid.*, pp. 1607–8.

concerned the bombing of a ship in international waters by Argentina during the Falklands war and where it was claimed that the federal courts had jurisdiction under the Act. A divided Court of Appeals[155] held that the Act provided, and the Foreign Sovereign Immunities Act did not preclude,[156] federal subject matter jurisdiction over suits in tort by aliens against foreign sovereigns for violations of international law. However, the Supreme Court unanimously disagreed.[157] It was noted that the Act did not expressly authorise suits against foreign states and that at the time the Foreign Sovereign Immunities Act was enacted, the 1789 Act had never provided the jurisdictional basis for a suit against a foreign state.[158] Since the Congress had decided to deal comprehensively with sovereign immunity in the Foreign Sovereign Immunity Act, it appeared to follow that this Act alone provided the basis for federal jurisdiction over foreign states. This basis was thus exclusive. The Court did note, however, that the Alien Tort Claims Act was unaffected by the Foreign Sovereign Immunities Act in so far as non-state defendants were concerned.[159]

Extradition[160]

The practice of extradition enables one state to hand over to another suspected or convicted criminals who have fled abroad. It is based upon bilateral treaty law and does not exist as an obligation upon states in customary law.[161] It is usual to derive from existing treaties on the subject certain general principles, for example that of double criminality, i.e. that the crime involved should be a crime in both states concerned[162] and that of specialty, i.e. a person surrendered may be tried and punished only for the offence for which extradition had been sought and granted.[163] In general, offences of a political character have been excluded,[164] but this would not cover terrorist

---

[155] *Amerada Hess Shipping Corp.* v. *Argentine Republic*, 830 F.2d 421 (1987); 79 ILR, p. 8.
[156] See *infra*, Chapter 13, p. 499.
[157] *Argentine Republic* v. *Amerada Hess Shipping Corp.*, 109 S. Ct. 683 (1989); 81 ILR, p. 658.
[158] *Ibid.*, p. 689; 81 ILR, pp. 664–5.   [159] *Ibid.*, p. 690.
[160] See e.g. I. A. Shearer, *Extradition in International Law*, Leiden, 1971; M. C. Bassiouni, *International Extradition and World Public Order*, Leiden, 1974; Stanbrook and Stanbrook, *The Law and Practice of Extradition*, Chichester, 1980; M. Forde, *The Law of Extradition in the UK*, London, 1995; A. Jones, *Jones on Extradition*, London, 1995; G. Gilbert, *Aspects of Extradition Law*, Dordrecht, 1991; *International Law Cases and Materials*, (Henkin et al.), p. 1111 and *Oppenheim's International Law*, p. 958. See also Study of the Secretariat on Succession of States in Respect of Bilateral Treaties, *Yearbook of the ILC*, 1970 II, pp. 102, 105.
[161] See e.g. the Joint Declaration of Judges Evensen, Tarassov, Guillaume and Aguilar Maudsley, the *Lockerbie* case, ICJ Reports, 1992, pp. 3, 24; 94 ILR, pp. 478, 507 and the Dissenting Opinion of Judge Bedjaoui, *ibid.*, p. 38; 94 ILR, p. 521.
[162] But see now the House of Lords decisions in *Government of Denmark* v. *Nielsen* [1984] 2 All ER 81; 74 ILR, p. 458 and *United States Government* v. *McCaffery* [1984] 2 All ER 570.
[163] See e.g. *Oppenheim's International Law*, p. 961.   [164] *Ibid.*, p. 962.

activities.[165] As noted above, it is common for many treaties laying down multiple bases for the exercise of jurisdiction to insist that states parties in whose territory the alleged offender is present, either prosecute or extradite such person.[166] In addition, many treaties provide for the automatic inclusion within existing bilateral extradition treaties between states parties to such treaties of the offence concerned.[167] Many states will not allow the extradition of nationals to another state,[168] but this is usually in circumstances where the state concerned has wide powers to prosecute nationals for offences committed abroad.

Extraterritorial jurisdiction[169]

Claims have arisen in the context of economic issues whereby some states, particularly the United States, seek to apply their laws outside their territory[170] in a manner which may precipitate conflicts with other states. Where the claims are founded upon the territorial and nationality theories of

[165] See e.g. the European Convention on the Suppression of Terrorism, 1976, article 1 of which provides a list of offences which are not to be regarded as political offences or inspired by political motives. See also the *McMullen* case, 74 AJIL, 1980, p. 434; the *Eain* case, *ibid.*, p. 435; *Re Piperno, ibid.*, p. 683 and *US* v. *Mackin*, 668 F.2d 122 (1981); 79 ILR, p. 459. A revised directive on international extradition was issued by the US Department of State in 1981; see 76 AJIL, 1982, pp. 154–9. Note also the view of the British Home Secretary, *The Times*, 25 June 1985, p. 1, that the political offences 'loophole' as it applied to violent offences was not suitable to extradition arrangements between the democratic countries 'sharing the same high regard for the fundamental principles of justice and operating similar independent judicial systems'. The English law relating to extradition has now been consolidated in the Extradition Act 1989. See also *Government of Belgium* v. *Postlethwaite* [1987] 2 All ER 985 and *R* v. *Chief Metropolitan Magistrate, ex parte Secretary of State for the Home Department*, [1988] 1 WLR 1204.   [166] *Supra* p. 474.
[167] See e.g. article 8 of the Hague Convention for the Suppression of the Unlawful Seizure of Aircraft 1970, article 8 of the Montreal Convention for the Suppression of Unlawful Acts against the Safety of Civil Aviation 1971, article 8 of the Internationally Protected Persons Convention 1973 and article 4 of the European Convention for the Suppression of Terrorism.
[168] See e.g. article 3(1) of the French Extradition Law of 1927, and article 16 of the Basic Law of the Federal Republic of Germany.
[169] See e.g. *Extraterritorial Jurisdiction* (ed. A. V. Lowe), London, 1983; D. Rosenthal and W. Knighton, *National Laws and International Commerce*, London, 1982; Meesen, 'Antitrust Jurisdiction under Customary International Law', 78 AJIL, 1984, p. 783; A. V. Lowe, 'Blocking Extraterritorial Jurisdiction; The British Protection of Trading Interests Act, 1980', 75 AJIL, 1981, p. 257; Akehurst, 'Jurisdiction', pp. 190 *et seq.*; *Extraterritorial Application of Law and Responses Thereto* (ed. C. Olmstead), 1984; B. Stern, 'L'Extra-territorialité "Revisitée": Où Il est Question des Affaires Alvarez-Machain, Pâte de Bois et de Quelques Autres', AFDI, 1992, p. 239; Higgins, *Problems* p. 73 and *Oppenheim's International Law*, p. 466. See also P. Torremans, 'Extraterritorial Application of EC and US Competition Law', 21 *European Law Review*, 1996, p. 280.
[170] Note there is a general presumption against the extraterritorial application of legislation, see e.g. the House of Lords decision in *Holmes* v. *Bangladesh Biman Corporation* [1989] 1 AC 1112, 1126; 87 ILR, p. 365, 369 per Lord Bridge and *Air India* v. *Wiggins* [1980] 1 WLR 815, 819; 77 ILR, pp. 276, 279, per Lord Bridge, and the US Supreme Court decision in *EEOC* v. *Arabian American Oil Company and Aramco Services*, 113 L Ed 2d 274, 282 (1991); 90 ILR, pp. 617, 622.

INTERNATIONAL LAW

jurisdiction, problems do not often arise, but claims made upon the basis of the so-called 'effects' doctrine have provoked considerable controversy. This goes beyond the objective territorial principle to a situation where the state assumes jurisdiction on the grounds that the behaviour of a party is producing 'effects' within its territory. This is so even though all the conduct complained of takes place in another state.[171] The effects doctrine has been energetically maintained particularly by the US in the area of antitrust regulation.[172] The classic statement of the American doctrine was in *US v. Aluminum Co. of America*,[173] in which the Court declared that:

> any state may impose liabilities, even upon persons not within its allegiance, for conduct outside its borders that has consequences within its borders which the state reprehends.[174]

The doctrine was to some extent modified by the requirement of intention and the view that the effect should be substantial, but the wide-ranging nature of the concept aroused considerable opposition outside the US, as did American attempts to take evidence abroad under very broad pre-trial discovery provisions in US law[175] and the possibility of treble damage awards.[176] The US courts, perhaps in view of the growing opposition of foreign states, modified their approach in the *Timberlane Lumber Co. v. Bank*

---

[171] The true 'effects' doctrine approach should be distinguished from other heads of jurisdiction such as the objective territorial principle, where part of the offence takes place within the jurisdiction, see e.g. *US v. Noriega*, 808 F Supp 791 (1992); 99 ILR, p. 143. In many cases the disputes have centred upon nationality questions, the US regarding subsidiaries of US companies abroad as of US nationality even where such companies have been incorporated abroad, while the state of incorporation has regarded them as of its nationality and thus subject not to US law but to its law, see e.g. Higgins, *Problems*, p. 73.

[172] See e.g. the US Sherman Antitrust Act, 1896, 15 USC, para. 1 *et seq.* See also the controversies engendered by the US freezing of Iranian assets in 1979 and the embargo imposed under the Export Administration Act in 1981 and 1982 on equipment intended for use on the Siberian gas pipeline, R. Edwards, 'Extraterritorial Application of the US Iranian Assets Control Regulations', 75 AJIL, 1981, p. 870; J. Bridge, 'The Law and Politics of United States Foreign Policy Export Controls', 4 *Legal Studies*, 1984, p. 2 and A. V. Lowe, 'Public International Law and the Conflict of Laws', 33 ICLQ, 1984, p. 575.

[173] 148 F.2d 416 (1945).

[174] *Ibid.*, p. 443. This approach was reaffirmed in a series of later cases, see e.g. *US v. Timken Roller Bearing Co.*, 83 F.Supp. 284 (1949) affirmed 341 US 593 (1951); *US v. The Watchmakers of Switzerland Information Center, Inc.* cases, s.77, p. 414 (1963); 22 ILR, p. 168 and *US v. General Electric Co*, 82 F.Supp. 753 (1949) and 115 F.Supp. 835 (1953). See also *Hazeltine Research Inc.* v. *Zenith Radio Corporation*, 239 F.Supp. 51 (1965), affirmed 395 US 100 (1969).

[175] See e.g. the statement of the UK Attorney-General that 'the wide investigating procedures under the United States antitrust legislation against persons outside the United States who are not United States citizens constitute an 'extraterritorial' infringement of the proper jurisdiction and sovereignty of the United Kingdom', *Rio Tinto Zinc* v. *Westinghouse Electric Corporation* [1978] 2 WLR 81; 73 ILR, p. 296. See also *Extraterritorial Jurisdiction*, pp. 159–60 and 165–71. But see *Société Internationale* v. *Rogers*, 357 US 197 (1958); 26 ILR, p. 123; *US v. First National City Bank*, 396 F.2d 897 (1968); 38 ILR, p. 112; *In re Westinghouse Electric Corporation*, 563 F.2d 992 (1977) and *In re Uranium Antitrust Litigation*, 480 F.Supp. 1138 (1979).

[176] See e.g. Meessen, 'Antitrust Jurisdiction', p. 794.

of America[177] and *Mannington Mills* v. *Congoleum Corporation*[178] cases. It was stated that in addition to the effects test of the earlier cases, the courts had to take into account a balancing test, 'a jurisdictional rule of reason', involving a consideration of other nations' interests and the full nature of the relationship between the actors concerned and the US.[179] A series of factors that needed to be considered in the process of balancing was put forward in the latter case.[180] The view taken by the Third Restatement of Foreign Relations Law,[181] it should be noted, is that a state may exercise jurisdiction based on effects in the state, when the effect or intended effect is substantial and the exercise of jurisdiction is reasonable. It is noted that the principle of reasonableness calls for limiting the exercise of jurisdiction so as to minimise conflict with the jurisdiction of other states, particularly the state where the act takes place.[182] However, the assumption by the courts of a basically diplomatic function, that is, weighing and considering the interests of foreign states, stimulated criticism.[183]

The US courts have recently modified their approach. In *Laker Airways* v. *Sabena*,[184] the Court held *inter alia* that once US antitrust law was declared applicable, it could not be qualified or ignored by virtue of comity. The judicial interest balancing under the *Timberlane* precedent should not be engaged in since the courts on both sides of the Atlantic were obliged to follow the directions of the executive. Accordingly, the reconciliation of conflicting interests was to be undertaken only by diplomatic negotiations. Quite how such basic and crucial differences of opinion over the effects doctrine can be resolved is open to question and international fora have been suggested as the most appropriate way forward.[185]

In the *Hartford Fire Insurance Co.* v. *California* case before the US Supreme

---

[177] 549 F.2d 597 (1976); 66 ILR, p. 270.   [178] 595 F.2d 1287 (1979); 66 ILR, p. 487.
[179] See particularly Brewster, *Antitrust and American Business Abroad*, 1958.
[180] 595 F.2d 1287, 1297 (1979); 66 ILR, pp. 487, 496. See also the *Timberlane* case, 549 F.2d 597, 614 (1976); 66 ILR, pp. 270, 285. The need for judicial restraint in applying the effects doctrine in the light of comity was emphasised by the State Department, see 74 AJIL, 1980, pp. 179–83. See also the US Foreign Trade Antitrust Improvements Act, 1982, where jurisdiction was said to be dependent on 'direct, substantial and reasonably foreseeable effect'.   [181] *Op. cit.*, para. 402, p. 239 and para. 403, p. 250.
[182] See also the US Department of Justice, *Antitrust Enforcement Guidelines for International Operations*, 1988, pp. 31–2. But see now the Supreme Court's decision in *Hartford Fire Insurance Co* v. *California*, 113 S.Ct.2891 (1993) discussed *infra* p. 486.
[183] See e.g. H. Maier, 'Interest Balancing and Extraterritorial Jurisdiction', 31 *American Journal of Comparative Law*, 1983, p. 579 and *ibid.*, 'Resolving Extraterritorial Conflicts or There and Back Again', 25 *Va JIL*, 1984, p. 7; Fugate, 'Antitrust Aspect of the Revised Restatement of Foreign Relations Law', *ibid.*, p. 49 and Bowett, 'Jurisdiction', pp. 21–2. See also *Extraterritorial Jurisdiction*, pp. 58–62.
[184] 731 F.2d 909 (1984). However, cf. the continuation of the *Timberlane* litigation, 749 F.2d 1378 (1984), which reaffirms the approach of the first *Timberlane* case.
[185] See e.g. Bowett, 'Jurisdiction', pp. 24–6 and Meessen, 'Antitrust', pp. 808–10. See also *Extraterritorial Jurisdiction*, Part 3.

Court,[186] Judge Souter writing for the majority stated that it was well established that the relevant US legislation (the Sherman Act) 'applies to foreign conduct that was meant to produce and did in fact produce some substantial effect in the United States'.[187] It was felt that a person subject to regulation by two states (here the UK with regard to the London reinsurance market and the US) could comply with the laws of both and there was no need in this case to address other considerations concerning international comity.[188] The dissenting opinion in this case took the view that such exercise of extraterritorial jurisdiction was subject to the test of reasonableness,[189] a view that the majority did not embrace.

Foreign states had started reacting to the effects doctrine by the end of the 1970s and early 1980s by enacting blocking legislation. Under the UK Protection of Trading Interests Act 1980, for example, the Secretary of State in dealing with extraterritorial actions by a foreign state may prohibit the production of documents or information to the latter's courts or authorities. In addition, a UK national or resident may sue in an English court for recovery of multiple damages paid under the judgment of a foreign court.[190]

The Protection of Trading Interests Act was used in connection with the action by the liquidator of Laker Airways to sue various major airlines, the Midland Bank and McDonnell Douglas in the US for conspiracy to violate the anti-trust laws of the United States. Two of the airlines, British Airways and British Caledonian, sought to prevent this suit in the US by bringing an action to restrain the liquidator in the UK. Thus, the effects doctrine was not actually in issue in the case, which centred upon the application of the US anti-trust law in connection with alleged conspiratorial activities in the US. The UK government, holding the view that the Bermuda Two agreement regulating transatlantic airline activity[191] prohibited anti-trust actions against UK airlines, issued instructions under the 1980 Act forbidding compliance with any requirement imposed pursuant to US anti-trust measures,

[186] 113 S.Ct.2891 (1993). See e.g. A. F. Lowenfeld, 'Conflict, Balancing of Interest, and the Exercise of Jurisdiction to Prescribe: Reflections of the *Insurance Antitrust Case*', 89 AJIL, 1995, p. 42; P. R. Trimble, 'The Supreme Court and International Law: The Demise of *Restatement* Section 403', *ibid.*, p. 53 and L. Kramer, 'Extraterritorial Application of American Law after the *Insurance Antitrust Case*: A Reply to Professors Lowenfeld and Trimble', *ibid.*, p. 750.   [187] Kramer, 'Extraterritorial', at 2909.   [188] *Ibid.*, p. 2911.
[189] *Ibid.*, p. 2921.
[190] See Lowe, 'Conflict of Laws', pp. 257–82; 50 BYIL, 1979, pp. 357–62 and 21 ILM, 1982, pp. 840–50. See also the Australian Foreign Proceedings (Prohibition of Certain Evidence) Act 1976, the Danish Limitation of Danish Shipowners' Freedom to Give Information to Authorities of Foreign Countries 1967 and the Finnish Law Prohibiting a Shipowner in Certain Cases to Produce Documents 1968. In some cases, courts have applied aspects of domestic law to achieve the same aim, see. e.g. the *Fruehauf* case, 5 ILM, 1966, p. 476. Several states have made diplomatic protests at extraterritorial jurisdictional claims, see e.g. *Report of the 51st Session of the International Law Association*, 1964, pp. 565 *et seq.*
[191] See *supra*, Chapter 10, p. 373.

including the provision of information.[192] The Court of Appeal felt that the order and directions required them in essence to prevent the *Laker* action in the US,[193] but the House of Lords disagreed.[194] It was held that the order and directions did not affect the appellant's right to pursue the claim in the US because the 1980 Act was concerned with 'requirements' and 'prohibitions' imposed by a foreign court,[195] so that the respondents would not be prohibited by the direction from paying damages on a 'judgment' given against them in the US.[196] In fact the Court refused to restrain the US action.

The Court also refused to grant judicial review of the order and directions, since the appellant had failed to show that no reasonable minister would have issued such order and directions, this being the requisite test in ministerial decisions concerning international relations.[197] The case, however, did not really turn on the 1980 Act but it was the first time the issue has come before the courts.[198]

The dispute over extraterritoriality between the US and many other states has been apparent across a range of situations since the freezing of Iranian assets and the Siberian pipeline episode. The operation of the Western supervision of technological exports to the communist bloc through COCOM was also affected, while that system still existed, since the US sought to exercise jurisdiction with respect to exports from third states to communist states.[199] The adoption of legislation in the US imposing sanctions on Cuba and Iran and Libya has also stimulated opposition in view of the extraterritorial reach of such measures. The extension of sanctions against Cuba in the Cuban Democracy Act of 1992, for example, prohibited the granting of licences under the US Cuban Assets Control Regulations for certain transactions between US owned or controlled firms in the UK and Cuba and this led to the adoption of an order under the Protection of

192 The Protection of Trading Interests (US Anti-Trust Measures) Order 1983. Two directions were issued as well.
193 *British Airways Board v. Laker Airways Ltd* [1983] 3 All ER 375; 74 ILR, p. 36.
194 [1984] 3 All ER 39; 74 ILR, p. 65. But see also *Midland Bank plc v. Laker Airways Ltd* [1986] 2 WLR 707.   195 S.1(3).   196 [1984] 3 All ER 39, 55–56; 74 ILR, p. 84.
197 *Ibid.*, pp. 54–5; 74 ILR, p. 83. See also *Associated Provincial Picture Houses Ltd v. Wednesbury Corp.* [1947] 2 All ER 680.
198 See also the statement by the Minister of State, Department of Trade and Industry listing the statutory instruments, orders and directions made under the Protection of Trading Interests Act, HC Deb., vol. 220, Written Answers, cols. 768–70, 12 March 1993; UKMIL, 64 BYIL, 1993, pp. 644–6.
199 See the the US and the UK agreement in 1984 to consult should problems appear to arise with regard to the application of US export controls to individuals or businesses in the UK, or if the UK were contemplating resorting to the Protection of Trading Interests Act in relation to such controls, 68 HC Deb., col. 332, Written Answer, 23 November 1984 and 88 HC Deb., col. 373, Written Answer, 6 December 1985. See also Current Legal Developments, 36 ICLQ, 1987, p. 398.
200 See UKMIL, 64 BYIL, 1993, p. 643. The proposed adoption of this legislation led to UK protests as well, see UKMIL, 63 BYIL, 1992, pp. 726 *et seq.*

Trading Interests Act 1980 by the UK government.[200] The adoption of the Helms-Burton legislation in March 1996, amending the 1992 Act by further tightening sanctions against Cuba, provided *inter alia* for the institution of legal proceedings before the US courts against foreign persons or companies deemed to be 'trafficking' in property expropriated by Cuba from American nationals.[201] In addition, the legislation enables the US to deny entry into the country of senior executives (and their spouses and minors) of companies deemed by the US State Department to be so 'trafficking'. This legislation, together with the adoption of the D'Amato Act in mid-1996,[202] led to protests from many states, including the UK and Canada.[203] The Inter-American Juridical Committee of the Organisation of American States, 'directed' by the OAS General Assembly 'to examine and decide upon the validity under international law' of the Helms-Burton legislation,[204] unanimously concluded that:

> the exercise of such jurisdiction over acts of 'trafficking in confiscated property' does not conform with the norms established by international law for the exercise of jurisdiction in each of the following respects:
>
> (a) A prescribing state does not have the rights to exercise jurisdiction over acts of 'trafficking' abroad by aliens unless specific conditions are fulfilled which do not appear to be satisfied in this situation.
>
> (b) A prescribing state does not have the rights to exercise jurisdiction over acts of 'trafficking' abroad by aliens under circumstances where neither the alien nor the conduct in question has any connection with its territory and where no apparent connection exists between such acts and the protection of its essential sovereign interests.[205]

The European Community, in particular, has taken a strong stance on the US approach. It declared in a letter to the Congressional Committee considering changes in the US export control legislation in March 1984 that:

---

[201] This part of the legislation was suspended by the President for six months as from July 1996, see as to the legislation, 35 ILM, 1996, p. 357.

[202] Intended to impose sanctions on persons or entities participating in the development of the petroleum resources of Iran or Libya. As to the legislation concerning Iran and Libya, see 35 ILM, 1996, p. 1273.

[203] Canada also announced that legislation would be introduced under the Foreign Extraterritorial Measures Act 1985 to help protect Canadian companies against the US Act, see Canadian Foreign Affairs Ministry Press Release No. 115, 17 June 1996. Note that the UN General Assembly, in resolution 50/10, 1995, called upon the US to end its embargo against Cuba. See also A. F. Lowenfeld, 'Congress and Cuba: The Helms-Burton Act', 90 AJIL, 1996, p. 419 and B. M. Clagett, 'Title III of the Helms-Burton Act is Consistent with International Law', *ibid.*, p. 434.

[204] OAS Doc. OEA/SER.P AG/doc.3375/96, 4 June 1996.

[205] CJI/SO/II/doc.67/96 rev. 5, para. 9, 23 August 1996; 35 ILM, 1996, pp. 1329, 1334. It should be noted that under article 98 of the Charter of the OAS, Opinions of the Committee have no binding effect.

[206] Cited in Current Legal Developments, p. 399. See also UKMIL, 56 BYIL, 1985, pp. 480–1.

US claims to jurisdiction over European subsidiaries of US companies and over goods and technology of US origin located outside the US are contrary to the principles of international law and can only lead to clashes of both a political and legal nature. These subsidiaries, goods and technology must be subject to the laws of the country where they are located.[206]

There was an attempt to solve such extraterritoriality conflicts in the Agreement Regarding the Application of Competition Laws signed by the European Commission on 23 September 1991 with the US.[207] This called *inter alia* for notification and co-ordination of such activities, with emphasis placed upon the application of comity. However, the European Court of Justice held that the Commission had acted *ultra vires* in concluding such an agreement.[208] The Agreement was reintroduced in the Decision of the Council and the Commission of 10 April 1995, which rectified certain competence problems arising as a result of the decision.[209] Nevertheless, it remains of uncertain value, not least because the question of private law suits in the US is not dealt with. The root problems of conflict have not been eradicated at all.

The adoption in 1992 of US legislation amending the Cuban Assets Control Regime stimulated a *démarche* from the European Community protesting against the extraterritorial application of US law,[210] as did the adoption of the Helms–Burton Act of 1996.[211]

However, the European Community itself has wrestled with the question of exercising jurisdiction over corporations not based in the Community in the field of competition law.[212] In *ICI* v. *Commission*,[213] the European Court of Justice established jurisdiction with regard to a series of restrictive agreements to fix the price of dyestuffs on the ground that the defendant undertakings had corporate subsidiaries that were based within the Community, and declined to follow the Advocate General's suggestion[214] that jurisdiction should be founded upon direct and immediate, reasonably foreseeable and substantial effect.

The *Wood Pulp* case[215] concerned a number of non-EC companies and an association of US companies alleged to have entered into a price-fixing arrangement. The European Commission had levied fines on the jurisdictional basis that the effects of the price agreements and practices were direct,

---

[207] See 30 ILM, 1991, p. 1487. See also Torremans, 'Extraterritorial', pp. 289 *et seq.*
[208] Case C-327/91, *French Republic* v. *Commission of the European Communities* [1994] ECR I-3641.   [209] [1995] OJL 95/45.   [210] See UKMIL, 63 BYIL, 1992, p. 725,
[211] See e.g. European Commission Press Release WE 27/96, 18 July 1996 and 35 ILM, 1996, p. 397.
[212] But not the UK, see e.g. *Attorney General's Reference (No. 1 of 1982)*, [1983] 3 WLR 72, where the Court of Appeal refused to extend the scope of local jurisdiction over foreign conspiracies based on the effects principle.   [213] [1972] ECR 619; 48 ILR, p. 106.
[214] *Ibid.*, pp. 693–4.   [215] *A. Ahlstrom Oy* v. *Commission* [1988] 4 CMLR 901.
[216] *Ibid.*, p. 916.

substantial and intended within the EC.[216] An action was then commenced before the European Court of Justice for annulment of the Commission's decision under article 173 of the EEC Treaty. Advocate General Darmon argued that international law permitted a state (and therefore the EC) to apply its competition laws to acts done by foreigners abroad if those acts had direct, substantial and foreseeable effects within the state concerned.[217]

The Court, however, took the view that the companies concerned had acted within the EC and were therefore subject to Community law. It was noted that where producers from third states sell directly to purchasers within the Community and engage in price competition in order to win orders from those customers, that constitutes competition within the Community, and, where such producers sell at prices that are actually co-ordinated, that restricts competition within the Community within the meaning of article 85 of the EEC Treaty. It was stressed that the decisive factor was the place where the price-fixing agreement was actually implemented, not where the agreement was formulated.[218] In other words, the Court founded its jurisdiction upon an interpretation of the territoriality principle, if somewhat stretched. It did not take the opportunity presented to it by the opinion of the Advocate General of accepting the effects principle of jurisdiction. Nevertheless, the case does appear to suggest that price-fixing arrangements intended to have an effect within the Community that are implemented there would be subject to the jurisdiction of the Community, irrespective of the nationality of the companies concerned and of the place where the agreement was reached.[219]

---

[217] *Ibid.*, p. 932.

[218] *Ibid.*, pp. 940–1. Note that the Court held that the association of US companies (KEA) was not subject to Community jurisdiction on the ground that it had not played a separate role in the implementation within the Community of the arrangements in dispute, *ibid.*, pp. 942–3.

[219] See e.g. Lange and Sandage, 'The *Wood Pulp* Decision and its Implications for the Scope of EC Competition Law', 26 *Common Market Law Review*, 1989, p. 137 and L. Collins, *European Community Law in the United Kingdom*, 4th edn, London, 1990, p. 7.

IMMUNITIES FROM JURISDICTION

In chapter 12, the circumstances in which a state may seek to exercise its jurisdiction in relation to civil and criminal matters were considered. In this chapter the reverse side of this phenomenon will be examined, that is those cases in which jurisdiction cannot be exercised as it normally would because of special factors. In other words, the concern is with immunity from jurisdiction and those instances where there exist express exceptions to the usual application of a state's legal powers.

The concept of jurisdiction revolves around the principles of state sovereignty, equality and non-interference. Domestic jurisdiction as a notion attempts to define an area in which the actions of the organs of government and administration are supreme, free from international legal principles and interference. Indeed, most of the grounds for jurisdiction can be related to the requirement under international law to respect the territorial integrity and political independence of other states.

Immunity from jurisdiction, whether as regards the state itself or as regards its diplomatic representatives, is grounded in this requirement. Although constituting a derogation from the host state's jurisdiction, in that, for example, the UK cannot exercise jurisdiction over foreign ambassadors within its territory, it is to be construed nevertheless as an essential part of the recognition of the sovereignty of foreign states, as well as an aspect of the legal equality of all states.

Sovereign immunity[1]

Sovereignty until comparatively recently was regarded as appertaining to a particular individual in a state and not as an abstract manifestation of the

[1] See generally e.g. G. M. Badr, *State Immunity*, The Hague, 1984; S. Sucharitkul, *State Immunities and Trading Activities in International Law*, Leiden, 1959 and Sucharitkul, 'Immunities of Foreign States before National Authorities', 149 HR, p. 87; I. Sinclair, 'The Law of Sovereign Immunity: Recent Developments', 167 HR, p. 113; UN Legislative Series, *Materials on Jurisdictional Immunities of States and Their Property*, New York, 1982; 10 Netherlands YIL, 1979; H. Lauterpacht, 'The Problem of Jurisdictional Immunities of Foreign States', 28 BYIL, 1951, p. 220 and R. Higgins, 'Certain Unresolved Aspects of the

existence and power of the state.[2] The sovereign was a definable person, to whom allegiance was due. As an integral part of this mystique, the sovereign could not be made subject to the judicial processes of his country. Accordingly, it was only fitting that he could not be sued in foreign courts. The idea of the personal sovereign would undoubtedly have been undermined had courts been able to exercise jurisdiction over foreign sovereigns. This personalisation was gradually replaced by the abstract concept of state sovereignty, but the basic mystique remained. In addition, the independence and equality of states made it philosophically as well as practically difficult to permit municipal courts of one country to manifest their power over foreign sovereign states, without their consent.

The classic case illustrating this relationship between territorial jurisdiction and sovereign immunity is *The Schooner Exchange* v. *McFaddon*,[3] decided by the US Supreme Court. Chief Justice Marshall declared that the jurisdiction of a state within its own territory was exclusive and absolute, but it did not encompass foreign sovereigns. He noted that the:

> perfect equality and absolute independence of sovereigns . . . have given rise to a class of cases in which every sovereign is understood to waive the exercise of a part of that complete exclusive territorial jurisdiction, which has been stated to be the attribute of every nation.[4]

It therefore followed that as concerned the case under litigation, 'national ships of war entering the port of a friendly power open for their reception, are to be considered as exempted by the consent of that power from its jurisdiction'. Such rules would not apply to private ships which are susceptible to foreign jurisdiction abroad.

Sovereign immunity is closely related to two other legal doctrines, non-justiciability and act of state. Reference has been made earlier to the interaction between the various principles,[5] but it is worth noting here that the concepts of non-justiciability and act of state posit an area of international activity of states that is simply beyond the competence of the domestic tribunal in its assertion of jurisdiction, for example, that the courts would not adjudicate upon the transactions of foreign sovereign

---

Law of State Immunity', 29 NILR, 1982, p. 265; J. Crawford, 'International Law of Foreign Sovereigns: Distinguishing Immune Transactions', 54 BYIL, 1983, p. 75; C. J. Lewis, *State and Diplomatic Immunity*, 3rd edn, London, 1990; C. H. Schreuer, *State Immunity: Some Recent Developments*, Cambridge, 1988 and *Oppenheim's International Law* (eds. R. Y. Jennings and A. D. Watts), 9th edn, London, 1992, p. 341.See also the cases on sovereign immunity collected in ILR, vols. 63–5; ILA, *Report of the Sixtieth Conference*, London, 1982, p. 325 and *Report of the Sixty-sixth Conference*, London, 1994, p. 452; *Annuaire de l'Institut de Droit International*, vol. 64 I, 1991, p. 84, and Report of the International Law Commission, 1991, A/46/10, p. 8.
[2] See A. D. Watts, 'The Legal Position in International Law of Heads of State, Heads of Governments and Foreign Ministers', 247 HR, 1994 III, p. 13.   [3] 7 Cranch 116 (1812).
[4] *Ibid.*, p. 137.   [5] *Supra*, Chapter 4, p. 129.

states.[6] On the other hand the principle of jurisdictional immunity asserts that in particular situations a court is prevented from exercising the jurisdiction that it possesses. Thus, immunity from jurisdiction does not mean exemption from the legal system of the territorial state in question. The two concepts are distinct. In *International Association of Machinists & Aerospace Workers* v. *OPEC*,[7] it was declared that the two concepts were similar in that they reflect the need to respect the sovereignty of foreign states, but that they differed in that the former went to the jurisdiction of the court and was a principle of international law, whereas the latter constituted a prudential doctrine of domestic law having internal constitutional roots.

In practice, however, the distinction is not always so evident and arguments presented before the court founded both upon non-justiciability and sovereign immunity are to be expected. It is also an interesting point to consider the extent to which the demise of the absolute immunity approach has affected the doctrine of non-justiciability.

As far as the act of state doctrine is concerned in particular in this context, some disquiet has been expressed by courts that the application of that principle may in certain circumstances have the effect of reintroducing the absolute theory of sovereign immunity. In *Letelier* v. *Republic of Chile*,[8] for example, Chile argued that even if its officials had ordered the assassination of Letelier in the US, such acts could not be the subject of discussion in the US courts as the orders had been given in Chile. This was not accepted by the Court since to do otherwise would mean emasculating the Foreign Sovereign Immunities Act by permitting a state to bring back the absolute immunity approach 'under the guise of the act of state doctrine'.[9] In somewhat different circumstances, Kerr LJ signalled his concern in *Maclaine Watson* v. *The International Tin Council*[10] that the doctrine of non-justiciability might be utilised to by-pass the absence of sovereign immunity with regard to a state's commercial activities.

Of course, once a court has determined that the relevant sovereign

---

[6] See e.g. *Buttes Gas and Oil Co.* v. *Hammer (No. 3)*, [1982] AC 888; 64 ILR, p. 332; *Buck* v. *Attorney-General* [1965] 1 Ch. 745; 42 ILR, p. 11 and Goff J, *I° Congreso del Partido* [1978] 1 QB 500, 527–8; 64 ILR, pp. 154, 178–9. See also Sinclair, 'Sovereign Immunity', p. 198. See further *supra* p. 129.

[7] 649 F.2d 1354, 1359; 66 ILR, pp. 413, 418. Reaffirmed in *Asociacion de Reclamantes* v. *The United Mexican States*, 22 ILM, 1983, pp. 625, 641–2. See also *Ramirez* v. *Weinberger*, 23 ILM, 1984, p. 1274; *Goldwater* v. *Carter*, 444 US 996 (1979) and *Empresa Exportadora de Azucar* v. *Industria Azucarera Nacional SA* [1983] 2 LL. R, 171; 64 ILR, p. 368.

[8] 488 F.Supp. 665 (1980); 63 ILR, p. 378. Note that the US Court of Appeals has held that the Foreign Sovereign Immunities Act 1976 does not supersede the act of state doctrine, see *Helen Liu* v. *Republic of China*, 29 ILM, 1990, p. 192.

[9] *Ibid.*, p. 674. See also the view expressed in *Siderman* v. *Republic of Argentina*, 965 F.2d 699 (1992), that the jurisdictional question of sovereign immunity logically precedes the issue of act of state. [10] [1988] 3 WLR 1169, 1188; 80 ILR, pp. 191, 209.

immunity legislation permits it to hear the case, it may still face the act of state argument. Such legislation implementing the restrictive immunity approach does not supplant the doctrine of act of state or non-justiciability,[11] although by accepting that the situation is such that immunity does not apply the scope for the non-justiciability plea is clearly much reduced.[12]

The absolute immunity approach

The relatively uncomplicated role of the sovereign and of government in the eighteenth and nineteenth centuries logically gave rise to the concept of absolute immunity, whereby the sovereign was completely immune from foreign jurisdiction in all cases regardless of circumstances. However, the unparalleled growth in the activities of the state, especially with regard to commercial matters, has led to problems and in most countries to a modification of the above rule. The number of governmental agencies and public corporations, nationalised industries and other state organs created a reaction against the concept of absolute immunity, partly because it would enable state enterprises to have an advantage over private companies. Accordingly many states began to adhere to the doctrine of restrictive immunity, under which immunity was available as regards governmental activity, but not where the state was engaging in commercial activity. Governmental acts with regard to which immunity would be granted are termed acts *jure imperii*, while those relating to private or trade activity are termed acts *jure gestionis*.

The leading practitioner of the absolute immunity approach has been the United Kingdom, and this position was established in a number of important cases.[13]

In the *Parlement Belge* case,[14] the Court of Appeal emphasised that the principle to be deduced from all the relevant preceding cases was that every state

> declines to exercise by means of its courts any of its territorial jurisdiction over the person of any sovereign or ambassador of any other state, or over the public property of any state which is destined to public use . . . though such sovereign, ambassador or property be within its jurisdiction.[15]

---

[11] See *International Association of Machinists & Aerospace Workers* v. *OPEC*, 649 F.2d 1354, 1359–60; 66 ILR, pp. 413, 418. See also *Liu* v. *Republic of China*, 29 ILM, 1990, pp. 192, 205.

[12] See the interesting discussion of the relationship between non-justiciability and immunity by Evans J. in *Australia and New Zealand Bank* v. *Commonwealth of Australia*, 1989, Transcript, pp. 59–60.

[13] But note a series of early cases which are not nearly so clear in their adoption of a broad absolute immunity doctrine, see e.g. *The Prins Frederik* (1820) 2 Dod. 451; *Duke of Brunswick* v. *King of Hanover* (1848) 2 HLC 1 and *De Haber* v. *Queen of Portugal* (1851) 17 Cl B 171. See also Phillimore J in *The Charkieh* (1873) LR 4A and E 59.

[14] (1880) 5 PD 197.

[15] Brett LJ, *ibid.*, pp. 214–15. Note of course, that the principle relates to public property destined to public, not private use.

The wide principle expressed in this case gave rise to the question as to what kind of legal interest it was necessary for the foreign sovereign to have in property so as to render it immune from the jurisdiction of the British courts. Commonly regarded as the most extreme expression of the absolute immunity doctrine is the case of the *Porto Alexandre*.[16] This concerned a Portuguese requisitioned vessel against which a writ was issued in an English court for non-payment of dues for services rendered by tugs near Liverpool. The vessel was exclusively engaged in private trading operations, but the Court felt itself constrained by the terms of the *Parlement Belge* principle to dismiss the case in view of the Portuguese government interest.

Differences of opinion as to the application of the immunity rules were revealed in the House of Lords in the *Cristina* case.[17] This followed a Spanish Republican Government decree requisitioning ships registered in Bilbao which was issued while the *Cristina* was on the high seas. On its arrival in Cardiff the Republican authorities took possession of the ship, whereupon its owners proceeded to issue a writ claiming possession. The case turned on the argument to dismiss the case, by the Republican government, in view of its sovereign immunity. The majority of the House of Lords accepted this in view of the requisition decree taking over the ship. However, two of the Lords criticised the *Porto Alexandre* decision and doubted whether immunity covered state trading vessels,[18] while Lord Atkin took more of a fundamentalist absolute approach.[19]

In *Krajina* v. *Tass Agency*[20] the Court of Appeal held that the Agency was a state organ of the USSR and was thus entitled to immunity from local jurisdiction. This was followed in *Baccus SRL* v. *Servicio Nacional del Trigo*,[21] where the Court felt that the defendants, although a separate legal person under Spanish law, were in effect a department of state of the Spanish government. How the entity was actually constituted was regarded as an internal matter, and it was held entitled to immunity from suit.

A different view from the majority was taken by Lord Justice Singleton who, in a dissenting opinion, condemned what he regarded as the extension of the doctrine of sovereign immunity to separate legal entities.[22]

There is some limitation to the absolute immunity rule to the extent that a mere claim by a foreign sovereign to have an interest in the contested property would have to be substantiated before the English court would grant immunity. Since this involves some submission by the foreign sovereign to

---

16 [1920] P.30; 1 ILR, p. 146. See e.g. Sinclair, 'Law', p. 126. See also *The Jupiter*, [1924] P.236, 3 ILR, p. 136.   17 [1938] AC 485; 9 ILR, p. 250.
18 See e.g. Lord Macmillan, [1938] AC 485, p. 498; 9 ILR, p. 260.
19 *Ibid.*, p. 490. See also *Berizzi Bros. Co* v. *SS Pesaro*, 271 US 562 (1926); 3 ILR, p. 186 and *The Navemar*, 303 US 68 (1938); 9 ILR, p. 176.
20 [1949] 2 All ER 274; 16 ILR, p. 129. See also Cohen LJ, *ibid.*, p. 281.
21 [1957] 1 QB 438; 23 ILR, p. 160.   22 *Ibid.*, p. 461; 23 ILR, p. 169.

the local jurisdiction, immunity is not unqualifiedly absolute. Once the court is clear that the claim by the sovereign is not merely illusory or founded on a manifestly defective title, it will dismiss the case. This was brought out in *Juan Ysmael* v. *Republic of Indonesia*[23] in which the asserted interest in a vessel by the Indonesian government was regarded as manifestly defective so that the case was not dismissed on the ground of sovereign immunity.[24]

American cases, however, have shown a rather different approach, one that distinguishes between ownership on the one hand and possession and control on the other. In two cases particularly, immunity was refused where the vessels concerned, although owned by the states claiming immunity, were held subject to the jurisdiction since at the relevant time they were not in the possession or control of these states.[25]

Since the courts will not try a case in which a foreign state is the defendant, it is necessary to decide what a foreign state is in each instance. Where doubts are raised as to the status of a foreign entity and whether or not it is to be regarded as a state for the purposes of the municipal courts, the executive certificate issued by the UK government will be decisive.

The case of *Duff Development Company* v. *Kelantan*[26] is a good example of this point. Kelantan was a Malay state under British protection. Both its internal and external policies were subject to British direction and it could in no way be described as politically independent. However, the UK government had issued an executive certificate to the effect that Kelantan was an independent state and that the Crown neither exercised nor claimed any rights of sovereignty or jurisdiction over it. The House of Lords, to whom the case had come, declared that once the Crown recognised a foreign ruler as sovereign, this bound the courts and no other evidence was admissible or needed. Accordingly, Kelantan was entitled to sovereign immunity from the jurisdiction of the English courts.

The restrictive approach

A number of states in fact started adopting the restrictive approach to immunity, permitting the exercise of jurisdiction over non-sovereign acts, at

---

[23] [1955] AC 72; 21 ILR, p. 95. See also *USA and France* v. *Dollfus Mieg et Compagnie* [1952] AC 582; 19 ILR, p. 163.

[24] See Higgins, 'Unresolved Aspects', p. 273, who raises the question as to whether this test would be rigorous in an era of restrictive immunity. See also R. Higgins, *Problems and Process*, Oxford, 1994, Chapter 5.

[25] *The Navemar*, 303 US 68 (1938); 9 ILR, p. 176 and *Republic of Mexico* v. *Hoffman*, 324 US 30 (1945); 12 ILR, p. 143.

[26] [1924] AC 797; 2 ILR, p. 124. By s.21 of the State Immunity Act, 1978, an executive certificate is deemed to be conclusive as to e.g. statehood in this context. See also *Trawnik* v. *Gordon Lennox* [1985] 2 All ER 368 as to the issue of a certificate under s. 21 on the status of the Commander of UK forces in Berlin.

a relatively early stage.[27] The Supreme Court of Austria in 1950, in a comprehensive survey of practice, concluded that in the light of the increased activity of states in the commercial field the classic doctrine of absolute immunity had lost its meaning and was no longer a rule of international law.[28] In 1952, in the Tate letter, the United States Department of State declared that the increasing involvement of governments in commercial activities coupled with the changing views of foreign states to absolute immunity rendered a change necessary and that thereafter 'the Department [will] follow the restrictive theory of sovereign immunity'.[29] This approach was also adopted by the courts, most particularly in *Victory Transport Inc.* v. *Comisaria General de Abasteciementos y Transportes.*[30] In this case, the Court, in the absence of a State Department 'suggestion' as to the immunity of the defendants, a branch of the Spanish Ministry of Commerce, affirmed jurisdiction since the chartering of a ship to transport wheat was not strictly a political or public act. The restrictive theory approach was endorsed by four Supreme Court Justices in *Alfred Dunhill of London Inc.* v. *Republic of Cuba.*[31]

As far as the UK was concerned, the adoption of the restrictive approach occurred rather later.[32]

In the *Philippine Admiral* case,[33] the vessel which was owned by the Philippine government had writs issued against it in Hong Kong by two shipping corporations. The Privy Council, hearing the case on appeal from the Supreme Court of Hong Kong, reviewed previous decisions on sovereign immunity and concluded that it would not follow the *Porto Alexandre* case.[34] Lord Cross gave four reasons for not following the earlier case. First, that the Court of Appeal wrongly felt that they were bound by the *Parlement Belge*[35] decision. Secondly, that the House of Lords in *The*

---

[27] See e.g. Belgium and Italy, Lauterpacht, 'Problem'; Badr, *State Immunity*, Chapter 2; Sinclair, 'Sovereign Immunity'; I. Brownlie, *Principles of Public International Law*, 4th edn, Oxford, 1990, p. 327 and the Tate letter, 26 *Department of State Bulletin*, 984 (1952). See also the Brussels Convention on the Immunity of State-owned Ships, 1926, which assimilated the position of such ships engaged in trade to that of private ships regarding submission to the jurisdiction and the 1958 Conventions on the Territorial Sea and on the High Seas. See now articles 31, 32, 95 and 96 of the 1982 Convention on the Law of the Sea.

[28] *Dralle* v. *Republic of Czechoslovakia*, 17 ILR, p. 155. This case was cited with approval by the West German Supreme Constitutional Court in *The Empire of Iran*, 45 ILR, p. 57 and by the US Court of Appeals in *Victory Transport Inc.* v. *Comisaria General de Abasteciementos y Transportes*, 35 ILR, p. 110.   [29] 26 *Department of State Bulletin*, 984 (1952).

[30] 35 ILR, p. 110. See also e.g. *National City Bank of New York* v. *Republic of China*, 22 ILR, p. 210 and *Rich* v. *Naviera Vacuba*, 32 ILR, p. 127.

[31] 15 ILM, 1976, pp. 735, 744, 746–7; 66 ILR, pp. 212, 221, 224.

[32] See for some early reconsiderations, Lord Denning in *Rahimtoola* v. *Nizam of Hyderabad* [1958] AC 379, 422; 24 ILR, pp. 175, 190.

[33] [1976] 2 WLR 214; 64 ILR, p. 90. Sinclair, 'Sovereign Immunity' describes this as an 'historic landmark', p. 154. See also R. Higgins, 'Recent Developments in the Law of Sovereign Immunity in the United Kingdom', 71 AJIL, 1977, pp. 423, 424.

[34] [1920] P.30; 1 ILR, p. 146.   [35] (1880) 5 PD 197.

Cristina[36] had been divided on the issue of immunity for state owned vessels engaged in commerce. Thirdly, that the trend of opinion was against the absolute immunity doctrine; and fourthly that it was 'wrong' to apply the doctrine since states could in the western world be sued in their own courts on commercial contracts and there was no reason why foreign states should not be equally liable to be sued.[37] Thus, the Privy Council held that in cases where a state owned merchant ship involved in ordinary trade was the object of a writ, it would not be entitled to sovereign immunity and the litigation would proceed.

In the case of *Thai-Europe Tapioca Service Ltd* v. *Government of Pakistan*,[38] a German owned ship on charter to carry goods from Poland to Pakistan had been bombed in Karachi by Indian planes during the 1971 war. Since the agreement provided for disputes to be settled by arbitration in England, the matter came eventually before the English courts. The cargo had previously been consigned to a Pakistani corporation, and that corporation had been taken over by the Pakistani government. The shipowners sued the government for the sixty-seven-day delay in unloading that had resulted from the bombing. The government pleaded sovereign immunity and sought to have the action dismissed.

The Court of Appeal decided that since all the relevant events had taken place outside the jurisdiction and in view of the action being *in personam* against the foreign government rather than against the ship itself, the general principle of sovereign immunity would have to stand.

Lord Denning declared in this case that there were certain exceptions to the doctrine of sovereign immunity. It did not apply where the action concerned land situated in the UK or trust funds lodged in the UK or debts incurred in the jurisdiction for services rendered to property in the UK, nor was there any immunity when a commercial transaction was entered into with a trader in the UK 'and a dispute arises which is properly within the territorial jurisdiction of our courts'.[39]

This unfortunate split approach, absolute immunity for actions *in personam* and restrictive immunity for actions *in rem* did not, however, last long. In *Trendtex Trading Corporation Ltd* v. *Central Bank of Nigeria*,[40] all three judges of the Court of Appeal accepted the validity of the restrictive approach as being consonant with justice, comity and international practice.[41] The problem of precedent was resolved for two of the judges by declaring that international law knew no doctrine of *stare*

---

[36] [1938] AC 485; 9 ILR, p. 250.
[37] [1976] 2 WLR 214, 232; 64 ILR, pp. 90, 108. Note that Lord Cross believed that the absolute theory still obtained with regard to actions *in personam*, *ibid.*, p. 233.
[38] [1975] 1 WLR 1485; 64 ILR, p. 81.   [39] *Ibid.*, pp. 1490–1; 64 ILR, p. 84.
[40] [1977] 2 WLR 356; 64 ILR, p. 122.
[41] *Ibid.*, pp. 366–7 (Denning MR), 380 (Stephenson LJ) and 385–86 (Shaw LJ).

decisis.[42] The clear acceptance of the restrictive theory of immunity in *Trendtex* was reaffirmed in later cases,[43] particularly by the House of Lords in the *I° Congreso del Partido* case[44] and in *Alcom Ltd* v. *Republic of Colombia.*[45] The majority of states now have tended to accept the restrictive immunity doctrine[46] and this has been reflected in domestic legislation.[47] In particular, the US Foreign Sovereign Immunities Act, 1976,[48] provides in section 1605 for the grounds upon which a state may be subject to the jurisdiction (as general exceptions to the jurisdiction immunity of a foreign state), while the UK State Immunity Act, 1978,[49] similarly provides for a general rule of immunity from the jurisdiction of the courts with a range of exceptions thereto.[50]

The former Soviet Union and some other communist countries generally adhered to the absolute immunity theory, although in practice they entered into many bilateral agreements permitting the exercise of jurisdiction in cases where a commercial contract had been signed on the territory of the other state party.[51]

---

[42] *Ibid.*, pp. 365–6 and 380. But cf. Stephenson LJ, *ibid.*, p. 381. See further *supra*, Chapter 4, p. 109.

[43] See e.g. *Hispano Americana Mercantil SA* v. *Central Bank of Nigeria* [1979] 2 LL. R 277; 64 ILR, p. 221.

[44] [1981] 2 All ER 1064; 64 ILR, p. 307, a case concerned with the pre-1978 Act common law. See also *Planmount Ltd* v. *Republic of Zaire* [1981] 1 All ER 1110; 64 ILR, p. 268.

[45] [1984] 2 All ER 6; 74 ILR, p. 179.

[46] See e.g. the *Administration des Chemins de Fer du Gouvernement Iranien* case, 52 ILR, p. 315 and the *Empire of Iran* case, 45 ILR, p. 57; see also Sinclair, 'Sovereign Immunity'; Badr, *State Immunity*; and UN *Materials*. Note also *Abbott* v. *Republic of South Africa*, BJC 135, p. 155 (1992) before the Spanish Constitutional Court.

[47] See e.g. the Singapore State Immunity Act 1979; The Pakistan State Immunity Ordinance 1981; the South African Foreign States Immunities Act 1981; the Canadian State Immunity Act 1982 and the Australian Foreign States Immunities Act 1985.

[48] See e.g. G. Delaume, 'Public Debt and Sovereign Immunity; The Foreign Sovereign Immunities Act of 1976', 71 AJIL, 1977, p. 399; Sinclair, 'Sovereign Immunity', pp. 243 *et seq.* and D. Weber, 'The Foreign Sovereign Immunities Act of 1976', 3 *Yale Studies in World Public Order*, 1976, p. 1.

[49] See e.g. D. W. Bowett, 'The State Immunity Act 1978', 37 *Cambridge Law Journal*, 1978, p. 193; R. C. A. White, 'The State Immunity Act 1978', 42 MLR, 1979, p. 72; Sinclair, 'Sovereign Immunity', pp. 257 *et seq.* and M. N. Shaw, 'The State Immunity Act 1978', *New Law Journal*, 23 November 1978, p. 1136.

[50] See also the 1972 European Convention on State Immunity. The Additional Protocol to the European Convention, which establishes a European Tribunal in matters of State Immunity to determine disputes under the Convention, came into force on 22 May 1985. It will initially be composed of the same members as the European Court of Human Rights, see Council of Europe Press Release, C(85)39. See generally UN *Materials*, Part I 'National Legislation', and Badr, *State Immunity*, Chapter 3. See also the Inter-American Draft Convention on Jurisdictional Immunity of States, 22 ILM, 1983, p. 292. Note that the large number of cases precipitated by the 1979 Iran Hostages Crisis and the US freezing of assets were argued on the basis of the restrictive theory, before being terminated, see e.g. R. Edwards, 'Extraterritorial Application of the US Iranian Assets Control Regulations', 75 AJIL, 1981, p. 870. See also *Dames and Moore* v. *Regan*, 101 S. Ct. 1972 (1981); 72 ILR, p. 270.

[51] See for a number of examples, UN *Materials*, pp. 134–50. See also Boguslavsky, 'Foreign State Immunity; Soviet Doctrine and practice', 10 Netherlands YIL, 1979, p. 167. See as to Philippines practice, *USA* v. *Ruiz and De Guzman*, 102 ILR, p. 122; *USA* v. *Guinto, Valencia and Others*, *ibid.*, p. 132 and *The Holy See* v. *Starbright Sales Enterprises*, *ibid.*, p. 163.

Sovereign and non-sovereign acts

With the acceptance of the restrictive theory, it becomes crucial to analyse the distinction between those acts that will benefit from immunity and those that will not. In the *Victory Transport* case,[52] the Court declared that it would (in the absence of a State Department suggestion)[53] refuse to grant immunity, unless the activity in question fell within one of the categories of strictly political or public acts; viz. internal administrative acts, legislative acts, acts concerning the armed forces or diplomatic activity and public loans.

However, the basic approach of recent legislation[54] has been to proclaim a rule of immunity and then list the exceptions, so that the onus of proof falls on the other side of the line.[55] This approach is mirrored in the Draft Articles on Jurisdictional Immunities of States and Their Property adopted by the International Law Commission in 1991.[56] Article 5 notes that:

> A state enjoys immunity in respect of itself and its property, from the jurisdiction of the courts of another state subject to the provisions of the present articles.

In such circumstances, the way in which the 'state' is defined for sovereign immunity purposes becomes important. Article 2(1) b of the ILC Draft, as well as referring to the uncontentious elements,[57] includes political subdivisions of the state acting in the exercise of sovereign authority, and agencies and instrumentalities of the state and other entities to the extent that they are entitled to perform acts in the exercise of sovereign authority. It may be that some refining will be required before an international treaty emerges. In particular, the apparent presumption of immunity for such entities may prove troublesome. What needs to be borne in mind is that the key in such

---

[52] 336 F.2d 354(1964); 35 ILR, p. 110. See also P. Lalive, 'L'Immunité de Juridiction des Etats et des Organisations Internationales', 84 HR, p. 205 and Lauterpacht, 'Problem', pp. 237–9.

[53] Note that since the 1976 Foreign Sovereign Immunities Act, the determination of such status is a judicial, not executive act.

[54] See e.g. s.1 of the State Immunity Act 1978; s.1604 of the US Foreign Sovereign Immunities Act 1976 and s. 9 of the Australian Foreign States Immunities Act 1985. See also *Saudi Arabia v. Nelson*, 123 L Ed 2d 47 (1993); 100 ILR, p. 544.

[55] See also article 15 of the European Convention on State Immunity 1972. Article II of the Revised Draft Articles for a Convention on State Immunity adopted by the International Law Association in 1994, *Report of the Sixty-sixth Conference*, 1994, p. 22, provides that: 'In principle, a foreign state shall be immune from the adjudicatory jurisdiction of a forum state for acts performed by it in the exercise of its sovereign authority, i.e. *jure imperii*. It shall not be immune in the circumstances provided in article III.'

[56] See Report of the International Law Commission 1991, p. 37. There is extensive state practice on whether immunity should be seen as a derogation from territorial sovereignty and thus to be justified in each particular case, or as a rule of international law as such, thus not requiring substantiation in each and every case, see *Yearbook of the ILC*, 1980, vol. II, part 2, pp. 142 *et seq.*

[57] I.e. 'the state and its various organs of government' and (perhaps to a lesser extent) the 'constituent units of a federal state'.

circumstances is whether or not such an entity, however termed, exercises as a matter of fact elements of sovereign authority.[58] With the adoption of the restrictive theory of immunity, the appropriate test becomes whether the activity in question is of itself sovereign (*jure imperii*) or non-sovereign (*jure gestionis*). In determining this, the predominant approach has been to focus upon the nature of the transaction rather than its purpose.[59] However, it should be noted that article 2(2) of the ILC Draft provides that:

> In determining whether a contract or transaction is a 'commercial transaction' . . . reference should be made primarily to the nature of the contract or transaction, but its purpose should also be taken into account if, in the practice of the state which is a party to it, that purpose is relevant to determining the non-commercial character of the contract or transaction.[60]

The reason for the modified 'nature' test was in order to provide an adequate safeguard and protection for developing countries, particularly as they attempt to promote national economic development. The ILC Commentary to this draft article notes that a two stage approach is posited, to be applied successively. First, reference should be made primarily to the nature of the contract or transaction and if it is established that it is non-commercial or governmental in nature, no further inquiry would be needed. If, however, the contract or transaction appeared to be commercial, then reference to its purpose should be made in order to determine whether the contract or transaction was truly sovereign or not. States should be given an opportunity to maintain that in their practice a particular contract or transaction should be treated as non-commercial since its purpose is clearly public and supported by reasons of state. Examples given include the procurement of medicaments to fight a spreading epidemic, and food supplies.[61] This approach, a modification of earlier drafts,[62] is not uncontroversial and some care is required. It would, for example, be unhelpful if the purpose criterion were to be adopted in a manner which would permit it to be used to effect a considerable retreat from the restrictive immunity approach. This is not to say, however, that no consideration

---

[58] See also e.g. A/C.6/48/L.4, 1993.
[59] See e.g. s.1603(d) of the US Foreign Sovereign Immunities Act of 1976. The Section-by-Section analysis of the Act emphasises that 'the fact that goods or services to be procured through a contract are to be used for a public purpose is irrelevant; it is the initially commercial nature of an activity or transaction that is critical', reproduced in UN *Materials*, pp. 103, 107. See also the *Empire of Iran* case, 45 ILR, pp. 57, 80–1; *Trendtex Trading Corporation Ltd* v. *Central Bank of Nigeria* [1977] 2 WLR 356; 64 ILR, p. 122; *Non-resident Petitioner* v. *Central Bank of Nigeria*, 16 ILM, 1977, p. 501 (a German case) and *Planmount Ltd* v. *Republic of Zaire* [1981] 1 All ER 1110; 64 ILR, p. 268. See also article I of the Revised Draft Articles for a Convention on State Immunity adopted by the International Law Association in 1994, *Report of the Sixty-sixth Conference*, 1994, p. 23.
[60] See Report of the International Law Commission 1991, p. 13.   [61] *Ibid.*, pp. 29–30.
[62] *Yearbook of the ILC*, 1983, vol. II, Part 2.

whatsoever of the purpose of the transaction in question should be undertaken.

Lord Wilberforce in *I° Congreso del Partido*[63] emphasised that in considering whether immunity should be recognised one had to consider the whole context in which the claim is made in order to identify the 'relevant act' which formed the basis of that claim. In particular, was it an act *jure gestionis*, or in other words 'an act of a private law character such as a private citizen might have entered into'?[64] This use of the private law/public law dichotomy, familiar to civil law systems, was particularly noticeable, although different states draw the distinction at different points.[65] It should also be noted, however, that this distinction is less familiar to common law systems. In addition, the issues ascribed to the governmental sphere as distinct from the private area rest upon the particular political concept proclaimed by the state in question, so that a clear and comprehensive international consensus regarding the line of distinction is unlikely.[66] The characterisation of an act as *jure gestionis* or *jure imperii* will also depend upon the perception of the issue at hand by the courts. Lord Wilberforce also noted that while the existence of a governmental purpose or motive could not convert what would otherwise be an act *jure gestionis* or an act of private law into one done *jure imperii*,[67] purpose may be relevant if throwing some light upon the nature of what was done.[68]

The importance of the contextual approach at least as the starting point of the investigation was also emphasised by the Canadian Supreme Court in *United States of America* v. *The Public Service Alliance of Canada and Others (Re Canada Labour Code)*.[69] It was noted that the contextual approach was the only reasonable basis for applying the restrictive immunity doctrine for the alternative was to attempt the impossible, 'an antiseptic distillation of a "once-and-for-all" characterisation of the activity in question, entirely divorced from its purpose'.[70] The issue was also considered by the Supreme Court of Victoria, Australia, in *Reid* v. *Republic of Nauru*,[71] which stated that in some situations the separation of act, motive and purpose might not be possible. The motive or purpose underlying particular conduct may constitute part of the definition of the act itself in some cases, while in others the nature or quality of the act performed might not be ascertainable without reference to the context within which it is carried out. The Court also made the point that a relevant factor was the perception held or policy adopted in

---

[63] [1983] AC 244, 267; 64 ILR, pp. 307, 318.   [64] *Ibid.*, p. 262; 64 ILR, p. 314.
[65] See e.g. Sinclair, 'Sovereign Immunity', pp. 210–13 and the *Empire of Iran* case, 45 ILR, pp. 57, 80. See also article 7 of the European Convention on State Immunity 1972.
[66] See e.g. Crawford, 'International law', p. 88; Lauterpacht, 'Problem', pp. 220, 224–6 and Brownlie, *Principles*, pp. 330–1.   [67] [1983] AC at 267; 64 ILR, p. 318.
[68] *Ibid.*, p. 272; 64 ILR, p. 323.   [69] (1992) 91 DLR (4th) 449; 94 ILR, p. 264.
[70] *Ibid.*, 463; 94 ILR, p, 278.   [71] [1993] 1 VR 251; 101 ILR, p. 193.

each particular country as to the attributes of sovereignty itself.[72] The point that 'unless we can inquire into the purpose of such acts, we cannot determine their nature' was also made by the US Court of Appeals in *De Sanchez v. Banco Central de Nicaragua and Others*.[73]

The particular issue raised in the *Congreso* case was whether immunity could be granted where, while the initial transaction was clearly commercial, the cause of the breach of the contract in question appeared to be an exercise of sovereign authority. In that case, two vessels operated by a Cuban state-owned shipping enterprise and delivering sugar to a Chilean company were ordered by the Cuban government to stay away from Chile after the Allende regime had been overthrown. The Cuban government pleaded sovereign immunity on the grounds that the breach of the contract was occasioned as a result of a foreign policy decision. The House of Lords did not accept this and argued that once a state had entered the trading field, it would require a high standard of proof of a sovereign act for immunity to be introduced. Lord Wilberforce emphasised that:

> in order to withdraw its action from the sphere of acts done *jure gestionis*, a state must be able to point to some act clearly done *jure imperii*[74]

and that the appropriate test was to be expressed as follows:

> it is not just that the purpose or motive of the act is to serve the purposes of the state, but that the act is of its own character a governmental act, as opposed to an act which any private citizen can perform.[75]

In the circumstances of the case, that test had not been satisfied. One of the two ships, the *Playa Larga*, had been owned at all relevant times by the Cuban government, but the second ship, the *Marble Islands*, was owned by a trading enterprise not entitled to immunity. When this ship was on the high seas, it was taken over by the Cuban government and ordered to proceed to North Vietnam, where its cargo was eventually donated to the people of that country. The Court was unanimous in rejecting the plea of immunity with regard to the *Playa Larga*, but was split over the second ship.

Two members of the House of Lords, Lord Wilberforce and Lord Edmund-Davies, felt that the key element with regard to the *Marble Islands*, as distinct from the *Playa Larga*, where the government had acted as owner of the ship and not as governmental authority, was that the Republic of Cuba directed the disposal of the cargo in North Vietnam. This was not part of any commercial arrangement which was conducted by the demise charterer, who was thus responsible for the civil wrongs committed. The acts of

---

[72] *Ibid.*, p. 253; 101 ILR, pp. 195–6.   [73] 770 F 2d 1385, 1393 (1985); 88 ILR, pp. 75, 85.
[74] [1981] 2 All ER 1064, 1075; 64 ILR, p. 320.
[75] *Ibid.*, quoting the judge at first instance [1978] 1 All ER 1169, 1192; 64 ILR, p. 179.

the government were outside this framework and accordingly purely governmental.[76]

However, the majority held that the Cuban government had acted in the context of a private owner in discharging and disposing of the cargo in North Vietnam and had not regarded itself as acting in the exercise of sovereign powers. Everything had been done in purported reliance upon private law rights in that the demise charterers had sold the cargo to another Cuban state enterprise by ordinary private law sale and in purported reliance upon the bill of lading which permitted the sale in particular instances. It was the purchaser who donated the cargo to the Vietnamese people.[77]

In many respects, nevertheless, the minority view is the more acceptable one, in that in reality it was the Cuban government's taking control of the ship and direction of it and its cargo that determined the issue and this was done as a deliberate matter of state policy. The fact that it was accomplished by the private law route rather than, for example, by direct governmental decree should not settle the issue conclusively. In fact, one thing that the case does show is how difficult it is in reality to distinguish public from private acts.[78]

In *Littrell* v. *United States of America (No. 2)*,[79] Hoffman LJ in the Court of Appeal emphasised that it would be facile in the case which concerned medical treatment for a US serviceman on an American base in the UK, to regard the general military context as such as determinative. One needed to examine carefully all the relevant circumstances in order to decide whether a sovereign or a non-sovereign activity had been involved. Important factors to be considered included where actually the activity took place, whom it involved and what kind of act itself was involved. The problem of sovereign immunity with regard to foreign bases was also addressed by the Canadian Supreme Court in *United States of America* v. *The Public Service Alliance of Canada (Re Canada Labour Code)*.[80] The Court emphasised that employment at the base was a multifaceted activity and could neither be labelled as such as sovereign or commercial in nature. One had to determine which aspects of the activity were relevant to the proceedings at hand and then to assess the impact of the proceedings on these attributes as a whole.[81] The closer the activity in question was to undisputable sovereign acts, such as managing and operating an offshore military base, the more likely would it be that immunity would be recognised.

In *Kuwait Airways Corporation* v. *Iraqi Airways Co.*,[82] Lord Goff, giving the leading judgment in the House of Lords, adopted Lord Wilberforce's statement of principle in *Congreso* and held that 'the ultimate test of what con-

<hr>

[76] [1981] 2 All ER 1064, 1077 and 1081; 64 ILR, pp. 321, 327.
[77] *Ibid.*, pp. 1079–80, 1082 and 1083; 64 ILR, pp. 325, 328, 329.
[78] Note that if the State Immunity Act, 1978 had been in force when the cause of action arose in this case, it is likely that the claim of immunity would have completely failed, see s.10.
[79] [1995] 1 WLR 82, 95.   [80] (1992) 91 DLR (4th) 449; 94 ILR, p. 264.
[81] *Ibid.*, 466; 94 ILR, p. 281.   [82] [1995] 1 WLR 1147, 1160.

stitutes an act *jure imperii* is whether the act in question is of its own character a governmental act, as opposed to an act which any private citizen can perform'.[83] In that case, the Court was faced with the question as to whether Iraqi Airways was entitled to claim immunity with regard to the seizure, retention and use of aircraft belonging to Kuwait Airways consequent upon the invasion of Kuwait by Iraq. The Court held that Iraqi Airways involvement in the initial seizure of the aircraft was to be characterised as a sovereign activity and thus immune. However, once Iraq had adopted legislation purporting to dissolve Kuwait Airways and vest all its property in Iraqi Airways, the situation was deemed to have changed so that the subsequent retention and use of the aircraft were not acts *jure imperii* but fresh acts of conversion for which no immunity could be claimed. The fact that the initial act was an act *jure imperii* did not determine as such the characterisation of subsequent acts.[84]

In *Saudi Arabia* v. *Nelson*,[85] the US Supreme Court held that the alleged wrongful arrest, imprisonment and torture by the Saudi government of Nelson would amount to abuse of the power of its police by that government and 'a foreign state's exercise of the power of its police has long been understood for the purposes of the restrictive theory as peculiarly sovereign'. The English Court of Appeal in *Al-Adsani* v. *Government of Kuwait*[86] rejected an argument that the term 'immunity' in domestic legislation meant immunity from sovereign acts that were in accordance with international law, thus excluding torture for which immunity could not be claimed. The Court held that the State Immunity Act provided for immunity for states apart from specific listed express exceptions, and there was no room for implied exceptions to the general rule.

Commercial acts

Of all state activities for which immunity is no longer to be obtained, that of commercial transactions is the primary example and the definition of such activity is crucial.[87]

---

[83] Note that in *Sengupta* v. *Republic of India*, 65 ILR, pp. 325, 360, it was emphasised that in deciding whether immunity applied one had to consider whether it was the kind of contract an individual might make, whether it involved the participation of both parties in the public functions of the state, the nature of the alleged breach and whether the investigation of the claim would involve an investigation into the public or sovereign acts of the foreign state.

[84] *Ibid.*, 1162–3.   [85] 123 L Ed 2d 47, 61 (1993); 100 ILR, pp. 544, 533.

[86] (1996) 1 Lloyds Reports 104. But see Evans LJ in *Al-Adsani* v. *Government of Kuwait* 100 ILR, p. 465, which concerned leave to serve proceedings upon the Government of Kuwait and in which it had been held that there was a good arguable case that under the State Immunity Act there was no immunity for a state in respect of alleged acts of torture.

[87] In his discussion of the development of the restrictive theory of sovereign or state immunity in *Alcom* v. *Republic of Colombia* [1984] 2 All ER 6, 9; 74 ILR, pp. 180, 181, Lord Diplock noted that the critical distinction was between what a state did in the exercise of its sovereign authority and what it did in the course of commercial activities. The former enjoyed immunity, the latter did not. See also Schreuer, *State Immunity*, Chapter 2.

Section 3(3) of the State Immunity Act 1978 defines the term 'commercial transaction' to mean:

(a) any contract for the supply of goods or services;
(b) any loan or other transaction for the provision of finance and any guarantee or indemnity in respect of any such transaction or of any other financial obligation; and
(c) any other transaction or activity (whether of a commercial, industrial, financial, professional or other similar character) into which a state enters or in which it engages otherwise than in the exercise of sovereign authority.

Thus a wide range of transactions is covered[88] and as Lord Diplock pointed out,[89] the 1978 Act does not adopt the straightforward dichotomy between acts *jure imperii* and those *jure gestionis*. Any contract falling within section 3 would be subject to the exercise of jurisdiction and the distinction between sovereign and non-sovereign acts in this context would not be relevant, except in so far as transactions falling within section 3(3)c were concerned, in the light of the use of the term 'sovereign authority'. The Act contains no reference to the public/private question, but the *Congreso* case (dealing with the pre-Act law) would seem to permit examples from foreign jurisdictions to be drawn upon in order to determine the nature of 'the exercise of sovereign authority'.

Section 3(1) of the State Immunity Act provides that a state is not immune as respects proceedings relating to:

(a) a commercial transaction entered into by the state; or
(b) an obligation of the state which by virtue of a contract (whether a commercial transaction or not) falls to be performed wholly or partly in the United Kingdom.[90]

The scope of section 3(1)a was discussed by the court in *Australia and New Zealand Banking Group* v. *Commonwealth of Australia*.[91] This case arose out of the collapse of the International Tin Council in 1985. The ensuing litigation sought, by various routes, to ascertain whether the member states of the ITC (which was itself an international organisation with separate personality) could be held liable themselves for the debts of that organisation – a prospect vigorously opposed by the states concerned. The case in question concerned an attempt by the brokers and banks to hold the member

---

[88] Thus, for example, the defence of sovereign immunity was not available in an action relating to a contract for the repair of an ambassador's residence, *Planmount Ltd* v. *Republic of Zaire* [1981] 1 All ER 1110; 64 ILR, p. 268.
[89] *Alcom* v. *Republic of Colombia* [1984] 2 All ER 6, 10; 74 ILR, p. 183.
[90] Note that by s.3(3), s.3(1) does not apply to a contract of employment between a state and an individual.   [91] 1989, Transcript, pp. 52 *et seq.*

states of the ITC liable in tort for losses caused by misrepresentation and fraudulent trading.

It was argued by the defendants that as far as section 3(1) was concerned, the activity in question not only had to be commercial within the Act's definition but also undertaken 'otherwise than in the exercise of sovereign authority'. Evans J saw little difference in practice between the two terms in the context.[92] The defendants also argued that the term 'activity' meant something more than a single act or sequence of acts. Evans J did not accept this, but did emphasise that the activity in question had to be examined in context. It was held that both the trading and loan contracts under discussion in the case were commercial and that if it could be demonstrated that the member states of the ITC had authorised them, such authorisation would amount to commercial activity within the meaning of section 3.[93]

The scope of section 3(1)b was discussed by the Court of Appeal in *Maclaine Watson* v. *Department of Trade and Industry*,[94] which concerned the direct action by the brokers and banks against the member states of the ITC in respect of liability for the debts of the organisation on a contractual basis. It was held that the 'contract' referred to need not have been entered into by the state as such. That particular phrase was absent from section 3(1)b. Accordingly, the member states would not have been able to benefit from immunity in the kind of secondary liability of a guarantee nature that the plaintiffs were *inter alia* basing their case upon.[95] This view was adopted in the tort action against the member states[96] in the more difficult context where the obligation in question was a tortious obligation on the part of the member states, that is the authorisation or procuring of a misrepresentation inducing the creditors concerned to make a contract with another party (the ITC).[97]

Section 1603(d) of the US Foreign Sovereign Immunities Act, 1976 defines 'commercial activity' as 'a regular course of commercial conduct or a particular commercial transaction or act'. It is also noted that the commercial character of an activity is to be determined by reference to the nature of the activity rather than its purpose. The courts have held that the purchases of food were commercial activities[98] as were purchases of cement,[99] the sending by a government ministry of artists to

---

[92] *Ibid.*, p. 54.   [93] *Ibid.*, pp. 56–7.   [94] [1988] 3 WLR 1033; 80 ILR, p. 49.
[95] *Ibid.*, pp. 1104–5 (Kerr LJ) and 1130 (Nourse LJ); 80 ILR, pp. 119, 148.
[96] *Australia and New Zealand Banking Group* v. *Commonwealth of Australia* 1989, Transcript pp. 57–9.
[97] It should be noted that Evans J reached his decision on this point only with considerable hesitation and reluctance, *ibid.*, p. 59.
[98] See e.g. *Gemini Shipping* v. *Foreign Trade Organisation for Chemicals and Foodstuffs*, 63 ILR, p. 569 and *ADM Milling Co.* v. *Republic of Bolivia*, 63 ILR, p. 56.
[99] *NAC* v. *Federal Republic of Nigeria*, 63 ILR, p. 137.

perform in the US under a US impresario[100] and activities by state air-lines.[101]

The issuance of foreign governmental Treasury notes has also been held to constitute a commercial activity, but one which once validly statute-barred by passage of time cannot be revived or altered.[102]

In *Callejo* v. *Bancomer*,[103] a case in which a Mexican bank refused to redeem a certificate of deposit, the District Court dismissed the action on the ground that the bank was an instrumentality of the Mexican government and thus benefited from sovereign immunity, although the Court of Appeals decided the issue on the basis that the act of state doctrine applied since an investigation of a sovereign act performed wholly within the foreign govern-ment's territory would otherwise be required. In other cases, US courts have dealt with the actions of Mexican banks consequent upon Mexican exchange control regulations on the basis of sovereign immunity.[104] However, the Supreme Court in *Republic of Argentina* v. *Weltover Inc.*,[105] held that the act of issuing Government Bonds was a commercial activity and the unilateral rescheduling of payment of these bonds also constituted a com-mercial activity. The Court noting that the term 'commercial' was largely undefined in the legislation, took the view that its definition related to the meaning it had under the restrictive theory of sovereign immunity and par-ticularly as discussed in *Alfred Dunhill* v. *Republic of Cuba*.[106] Accordingly, 'when a foreign government acts, not as regulator of a market, but in the manner of a private player within it, the foreign sovereign's actions are "commercial" within the meaning of the FSIA . . . the issue is whether the particular actions that the foreign state performs (whatever the motives behind them) are the *type* of actions by which a private party engages in "trade or traffic or commerce"'. In this case, the bonds in question were debt instruments that could be held by private persons and were negotiable and could be traded on the international market.[107]

The purchase of military equipment by Haiti for use by its army,[108] and a military training agreement whereby a foreign soldier was in the US were

[100] *United Euram Co.* v. *USSR*, 63 ILR, p. 228.   [101] *Argentine Airlines* v. *Ross*, 63 ILR, p. 195.
[102] *Schmidt* v. *Polish People's Republic*, 742 F.2d 67(1984). See also *Jackson* v. *People's Republic of China*, 596 F.Supp. 386 (1984); *Amoco Overseas Oil Co.* v. *Compagnie Nationale Algérienne*, 605 F.2d 648 (1979); 63 ILR, p. 252 and *Corporacion Venezolana de Fomenta* v. *Vintero Sales*, 629 F.2d 786 (1980); 63 ILR, p. 477.   [103] 764 F.2d 1101 (1985).
[104] See e.g. *Braka* v. *Nacional Financiera*, No. 83–4161 (SDNY 9 July 1984) and *Frankel* v. *Banco Nacional de Mexico*, No. 82–6457 (SDNY 31 May 1983) cited in 80 AJIL, 1986, p. 172, note 5.   [105] 119 L Ed 2d 394 (1992); 100 ILR, p. 509.
[106] 425 US 682; 66 ILR, p. 212. Here, the plurality stated that a foreign state engaging in com-mercial activities was exercising only those powers that can be exercised by private citizens, *ibid.*, 704.
[107] 119 L Ed 2d 394, 405; 100 ILR, p. 515. Reaffirmed in *Saudi Arabia* v. *Nelson*, 123 L Ed 2d 47, 61 (1993); 100 ILR, 545, 553.
[108] *Aerotrade Inc.* v. *Republic of Haiti*, 63 ILR, p. 41.

held not to be commercial activities.[109] It has also been decided that Somalia's participation in an Agency for International Development programme constituted a public or governmental act,[110] while the publication of a libel in a journal distributed in the US was not a commercial activity where the journal concerned constituted an official commentary of the Soviet government.[111]

Many cases before the US courts have, however, centred upon the jurisdictional requirements of section 1605(a), which states that a foreign state is not immune in any case in which the action is based upon a commercial activity carried on in the US by a foreign state; or upon an act performed in the US in connection with a foreign state's commercial activity elsewhere; or upon an act outside the territory of the US in connection with a foreign state's commercial activity elsewhere, when that act causes a direct effect in the US.[112]

In *Zedan v. Kingdom of Saudi Arabia*,[113] for example, the US Court of Appeals in discussing the scope of section 1605(a)(2) emphasised that the commercial activity in question taking place in the US had to be substantial, so that a telephone call in the US which initiated a sequence of events which resulted in the plaintiff working in Saudi Arabia was not sufficient. Additionally, where an act is performed in the US in connection with a commercial activity of a foreign state elsewhere, this act must in itself be sufficient to form the basis of a cause of action,[114] while the direct effect in the US provision of an act abroad in connection with a foreign state's commercial activity elsewhere was subject to a high threshold. As the Court noted[115] in cases where this clause was held to have been satisfied, 'something legally significant actually happened in the United States'.[116]

---

[109] *Castro v. Saudi Arabia*, 63 ILR, p. 419.

[110] *Transamerican Steamship Corp v. Somali Democratic Republic*, 590 F.Supp. 968 (1984) and 767 F.2d 998. This is based upon the legislative history of the 1976 Act, see the H.R. Rep. No. 1487, 94th Cong., 2d Sess. 16 (1976).

[111] *Yessenin-Volpin v. Novosti Press Agency*, 443 F.Supp. 849 (1978); 63 ILR, p. 127. See also Schreuer, *State Immunity*, pp. 42–3, providing a list of criteria with respect to identifying commercial transactions.

[112] See e.g. *International Shoe Co v. Washington*, 326 US 310 (1945); *McGee v. International Life Insurance Co.*, 355 US 220 (1957); *Libyan-American Oil Co v. Libya*, 482 F.Supp. 1175 (1980); 62 ILR, p. 220; *Perez et al. v. The Bahamas*, 482 F.Supp. 1208 (1980); 63 ILR, p. 350 and *Thos. P. Gonzalez Corp v. Consejo Nacional de Produccion de Costa Rica*, 614 F.2d 1247 (1980); 63 ILR, p. 370, aff'd 652 F.2d 186 (1982).   [113] 849 F.2d 1511 (1988).

[114] *Ibid.* Note that the Supreme Court in *Saudi Arabia v. Nelson*, 123 L Ed 2d 47, 58–9; 100 ILR, pp. 545, 550–1, held that the phrase 'based on' appearing in the section, meant 'those elements of a claim that, if proven, would entitle a plaintiff to relief under his theory of the case'.   [115] *Ibid.*, p. 1515.

[116] Referring to the cases of *Transamerican Steamship Corp v. Somali Democratic Republic*, 767 F.2d 998, 1004, where demand for payment in the US by an agency of the Somali government and actual bank transfers were held to be sufficient, and *Texas Trading & Milling Corp. v. Federal Republic of Nigeria*, 647 F.2d 300, 312; 63 ILR, pp. 552, 563, where refusal to pay letters of credit issued by a US bank and payable in the US to financially injured claimant was held to suffice.

However, in *Republic of Argentina* v. *Weltover Inc.*,[117] the Court rejected the suggestion that section 1605 (a)(2) contained any unexpressed requirement as to substantiality or foreseeability and supported the Court of Appeals' view that an effect was direct if it followed as an immediate consequence of the defendant's activity.[118] In the case, it was sufficient that the respondents had designated their accounts in New York as the place of payment and Argentina had made some interest payments into them prior to the rescheduling decision.

It is interesting to note the approach adopted in the ILC Draft on Jurisdictional Immunities. Article 10 provides for immunity where a state engages in a 'commercial transaction' with a foreign natural or juridical person (but not another state) in a situation where by virtue of the rules of private international law a dispute comes before the courts of another state. Article 2(1)c provides that the term 'commercial transaction' means:

> (i) any commercial contract or transaction for the sale or purchase of goods or the supply of services;
> (ii) any contract for a loan or other transaction of a financial nature, including any obligation of guarantee in respect of any such loan or of indemnity in respect of any such loan or transaction;
> (iii) any other contract or transaction, whether of a commercial, industrial, trading or professional nature, but not including a contract of employment of persons.[119]

This definition is essentially the same as that suggested in previous drafts, with the difference that the reference is to 'commercial transactions' and not 'commercial contract'.[120]

Other non-immunity areas

Domestic and international instruments prohibit sovereign immunity in cases of tortious activity.[121] Article 11 of the European Convention on State Immunity 1972, for example, refers to 'redress for injury to the person or damage to tangible property, if the facts which occasioned the injury or damage occurred in the territory of the state of the forum, and if the author of the injury or damage was present in that territory at the time when those facts occurred'. Section 4 of the State Immunity Act 1978 provides that a state is not immune as respects proceedings in respect of death or personal injury, or damage to or loss of tangible property, caused by an act or omission in the

---

[117] 119 L Ed 2d 394 (1992); 100 ILR, p. 509.
[118] *Ibid.*, 407;100 ILR, p. 517, citing 941 F 2d at 152.
[119] Report of the International Law Commission, 1991, pp. 13 and 69. See also *supra* p. 000, with regard to the definition of 'commercial transaction' contained in Draft Article 2 (2).
[120] See *Yearbook of the ILC*, 1986, vol. II, part 2, p. 8.
[121] See e.g. Schreuer, *State Immunity*, Chapter 3.

UK,[122] while section 1605(a)(5) of the US Foreign Sovereign Immunities Act 1976, although basically similar, does include exceptions relating to the exercise of the state's discretionary functions and to claims arising out of malicious prosecution, abuse of process, libel, slander, misrepresentation, deceit or interference with contractual rights. In *Letelier* v. *Chile*,[123] the Court rejected a claim that the torts exception in this legislation referred only to private acts and held that it could apply to political assassinations.

Sections 4–11 of the UK Act detail the remainder of the wide-ranging non-immunity areas and include contracts of employment made in the UK or where the work is to be performed wholly or in part in the UK (section 4);[124] proceedings relating to immovable property (section 6); patents, trademarks, designs, plant breeders' rights or copyrights (section 7); proceedings relating to a state's membership of a body corporate, an unincorporated body or partnership, with members other than states which is incorporated or constituted under UK law or is controlled from or has its principal place of business in the UK (section 8); where a state has agreed in writing to submit to arbitration and with respect to proceedings in the UK courts relating to that arbitration (section 9); Admiralty proceedings with regard to state owned ships used or intended for use for commercial purposes (section 10) and proceedings relating to liability for various taxes, such as VAT (section 11). This, together with generally similar provisions in the legislation of other states,[125] demonstrates how restricted the concept of sovereign acts is now becoming in practice in the context of sovereign immunity, although definitional problems remain.

The personality issue[126]

Whether the absolute or restrictive theory is applied, the crucial factor is to determine the entity entitled to immunity. If the entity, in very general terms, is not part of the apparatus of state, then no immunity can arise. Shaw LJ in *Trendtex Trading Corporation Ltd* v. *Central Bank of Nigeria*[127]

---

[122] See also s. 6 of the Canadian State Immunity Act 1982; s. 6 of the South African Foreign Sovereign Immunity Act 1981; s. 7 of the Singapore State Immunity Act 1979 and s. 13 of the Australian Foreign States Immunities Act 1985. See also article 12 of the ILC Draft Articles, Report of the International Law Commission, 1991, p. 102.

[123] 488 F.Supp. 665 (1980); 63 ILR, p. 378.

[124] See e.g. *Sengupta* v. *Republic of India*, 65 ILR, p. 325. See also *United States of America* v. *The Public Service Alliance of Canada (Re Canada Labour Code)* (1992) 91 DLR (4th) 449; 94 ILR, p. 264.

[125] See e.g. section 1605 of the US Foreign Sovereign Immunities Act, 1976 and sections 10–21 of the Australian Foreign States Immunities Act 1985. Note in particular the inclusion in the US legislation of an exception to immunity with regard to rights in property taken in violation of international law, s. 1605 (a)(3), which does not appear in other domestic legislation. [126] See e.g. Schreuer, *State Immunity*, Chapter 5.

[127] [1977] 2 WLR 356, 383; 64 ILR, pp. 122, 147.

cautioned against too facile an attribution of immunity particularly in the light of the growth of governmental functions, since its acceptance resulted in a significant disadvantage to the other party.

A department of government would, however, be entitled to immunity, even if it had a separate legal personality under its own law.[128] The issue was discussed in detail in the *Trendtex* case. It was emphasised that recourse should be had to all the circumstances of the case. The fact of incorporation as a separate legal identity was noted in *Baccus SrL* v. *Servicio Nacional del Trigo*[129] and both Donaldson J at first instance and Denning MR emphasised this.[130] The question arises in analysing whether a body is a corporation or not, and indeed whether it is or is not an arm of government, as to which law is relevant. Each country may have its own rules governing incorporation, and similarly with regard to government departments. Should English law therefore merely accept the conclusions of the foreign law? The majority of the Court in *Baccus* was of the view that foreign law was decisive in questions relating to incorporation and whether corporateness was consistent with the recognition of immunity, and to a certain extent this was accepted in *Trendtex*. Shaw LJ declared that 'the constitution and powers of Nigerian corporation) must be viewed in the light of the domestic law of Nigeria'.[131] However, the status on the international scene of the entity in question must be decided, it was held, by the law of the country in which the issue as to its status has been raised. The Court had to determine whether the Nigerian Bank could constitute a government department as understood in English law.[132] It was also noted that where a material difference existed between English law and the foreign law, this would be taken into account, but the Court was satisfied that this was not the case in *Trendtex*.

This position of pre-eminence for English law must not be understood to imply the application of decisions of English courts relating to immunities granted internally. These could be at best only rough guides to be utilised depending on the circumstances of each case. If the view taken by the foreign law was not conclusive, neither was the attitude adopted by the foreign government. It was a factor to be considered, again, but no more than that. In this, the Court followed *Krajina* v. *Tass Agency*.[133] The point was also made that the evidence provided by Nigerian officials, including the High Commissioner, that the Bank was a government organ, was not conclusive. This was because the officials might very well be applying a test of governmental control which would not be decisive for the courts of this country.[134]

[128] *Baccus SrL* v. *Servicio Nacional del Trigo* [1957] 1 QB 438; 23 ILR, p. 160.
[129] *Ibid.*, p. 467.   [130] [1977] 2 WLR 356, 370; 64 ILR, p. 133.
[131] *Ibid.*, p. 385; 64 ILR, p. 149.   [132] *Ibid.*, pp. 385 and 175.   [133] [1949] 2 All ER 274.
[134] [1977] 2 WLR 356, 370 and 374; 64 ILR, p. 137, 139.

Of more importance was the legislative intention of the government in creating and regulating the entity and the degree of its control. Stephenson LJ in fact based his decision upon this point. An express provision in the creative legislation to the effect that the Bank was an arm of government was not necessary, but the Bank had to prove that the intention to make it an organ of the Nigerian state was of necessity to be implied from the enabling Central Bank of Nigeria Act, 1958 and subsequent decrees. This the Bank had failed to do and Stephenson LJ accordingly allowed the appeal.[135] It could be argued that the judge was placing too much stress upon this aspect, particularly in the light of the overall approach of the Court in applying the functional rather than the personality test. In many ways, Stephenson LJ was also looking at the attributes of the Bank but from a slightly different perspective. He examined the powers and duties of the entity and denied it immunity since the intention of the government to establish the Bank as an arm of itself could not be clearly demonstrated. The other judges were concerned with the functions of the Bank as implying governmental status *per se*.

The Court clearly accepted the functional test as the crucial guide to the determination of sovereign immunity. In this it was following the modern approach which has precipitated the change in emphasis from the personality of the entity for which immunity is claimed to the nature of the subject matter. This functional test looks to the powers, duties and control of the entity within the framework of its constitution and activities.

In such difficult borderline decisions, the proposition put forward by Shaw LJ is to be welcomed. He noted that:

> where the issue of status trembles on a fine edge, the absence of any positive indication that the body in question was intended to possess sovereign status and its attendant privileges must perforce militate against the view that it enjoys that status or is entitled to those privileges.[136]

In *Czarnikow Ltd v. Rolimpex*,[137]the House of Lords accepted as correct the findings of the arbitrators that although Rolimpex had been established by the Polish government and was controlled by it, it was not so closely connected with the government as to be an organ or department of the state. It had separate legal personality and had considerable freedom in day-to-day commercial activities.

Under section 14 of the State Immunity Act of 1978, a state is deemed to include the sovereign or other head of state in his public capacity,[138] the government and any department of that government, but not any entity 'which is distinct from the executive organs of the government of the state

---

[135] *Ibid.*, pp. 374–6. See also Shaw LJ, *ibid.*, p. 384; 64 ILR, p. 149.   [136] *Ibid.*
[137] [1979] AC 351, 364 (Lord Wilberforce) and 367 (Viscount Dilhorne).
[138] See also e.g. *Re Honecker*, 80 ILR, p. 365.

and capable of suing or being sued'. This modifies the *Baccus* and *Trendtex* approaches to some extent. Such a separate entity would only be immune if the proceedings related to acts done 'in the exercise of sovereign authority' and the circumstances are such that a state would have been so immune. The US Foreign Sovereign Immunities Act of 1976 provides in section 1603 that 'foreign state' includes a political subdivision of such a state and its agencies or instrumentalities. This is defined to mean any entity which is a separate legal person and which is an organ of a foreign state or political subdivision thereof or a majority of whose shares or other ownership interest is owned by a foreign state or political subdivision thereof or a majority of whose shares or other ownership interest is owned by a foreign state or political subdivision thereof and which is neither a citizen of a state of the United States nor created under the laws of any third country.[139] This issue of personality has occasioned problems and some complex decisions.[140]

In *First National City Bank* v. *Banco Para el Comercio Exterior de Cuba (Bancec)*,[141] for example, the Supreme Court suggested a presumption of separateness for state entities, under which their separate legal personalities were to be recognised unless applicable equitable principles mandated otherwise or the parent entity so completely dominated the subsidiary as to render it an agent of the parent.[142]

In *Republic of the Philippines* v. *Marcos (No. 1)*,[143] the US Court of Appeals for the Second Circuit held that the Marcoses, the deposed leader of the Philippines and his wife, were not entitled to claim sovereign immunity, but went on to note that even if they were to have standing it was uncertain that the immunity of a foreign state would go so far as to render a former head of state immune as regards his private acts. In a further decision on the same general issue of immunity and the Marcoses, the Court of Appeals for the Fourth Circuit held in *In Re Grand Jury Proceedings, Doe No. 770*[144] that head of state immunity was primarily an attribute of state sovereignty, not an individual right, and that accordingly full effect should be given to the revocation by the Philippines government of the immunity of the Marcoses. In *US*

[139] See e.g. *Gittler* v. *German Information Centre*, 408 NYS 2d 600 (1978); 63 ILR, p. 170; *Carey* v. *National Oil Co.*, 453 F.Supp. 1097 (1978); 63 ILR, p. 164 and *Yessenin-Volpin* v. *Novosti Press Agency*, 443 F.Supp. 849 (1978); 63 ILR, p. 127. See also Sinclair, 'Sovereign Immunity', pp. 248–9 and 258–9. Note in addition, articles 6 and 7 of the European Convention on State Immunity, 1972.
[140] See also article 2(1) b of the ILC Draft Articles, in which the term 'state' is defined to include 'political subdivisions of the state which are entitled to perform acts in the exercise of sovereign authority' and 'agencies or instrumentalities of the state and other entities, to the extent that they are entitled to perform acts in the exercise of the sovereign authority of the state'. This formulation has raised controversy in appearing to establish a presumption of immunity for such entities, see Report of the International Law Commission, 1991, p. 13.   [141] 462 US 611 (1983); 80 ILR, p. 566.
[142] See also *Foremost-McKesson Inc* v. *Islamic Republic of Iran*, 905 F.2d 438 (1990).
[143] 806 F.2d 344 (1986); 81 ILR, p. 581.   [144] 817 F.2d 1108 (1987); 81 ILR, p. 599.

v. *Noriega*,[145] the District Court noted that head of state immunity was grounded in customary international law, but in order to assert such immunity, a government official must be recognised as head of state and this had not happened with regard to General Noriega.[146]

One particular issue that has caused controversy in the past relates to the status of component units of federal states.[147] There have been cases asserting immunity[148] and denying immunity[149] in such circumstances. In *Mellenger v. New Brunswick Development Corporation*,[150] Lord Denning emphasised that since under the Canadian constitution:

> (each) provincial government, within its own sphere, retained its independence and autonomy directly under the Crown . . . It follows that the Province of New Brunswick is a sovereign state in its own right and entitled if it so wishes to claim sovereign immunity.

However, article 28 of the European Convention on State Immunity 1972 provides that constituent states of a federal state do not enjoy immunity, although this general principle is subject to the proviso that federal state parties may declare by notification that their constituent states may invoke the benefits and carry out the obligations of the Convention.[151]

The State Immunity Act follows this pattern in that component units of a federation are not entitled to immunity. However, section 14(5) provides that the Act may be made applicable to the 'constituent territories of a federal state by specific Order in Council'.[152] Article 2 (1) b of the ILC Draft Articles, it should be noted, includes within its definition of state, 'constituent units of a federal state'.[153]

---

[145] 746 F.Supp. 1506, 1519 (1990); 99 ILR, p. 143, 161.

[146] See also Watts, 'Legal Position', pp. 52 *et seq.*

[147] See e.g. Bernier, *International Legal Aspects of Federalism*, 1973, pp. 121 *et seq.* and Sucharitkul, *State Immunities*, p. 106

[148] See e.g. *Feldman* c. *Etat de Bahia, Pasicrisie Belge*, 208, II, 55; *Etat de Céara* c. *Dorr et autres*, 4 ILR, p. 39; *Etat de Céara* c. *D'Archer de Montgascon*, 6 ILR, p. 162 and *Dumont* c. *Etat d'Amazonas*, 15 ILR, p. 140. See also *Etat de Hesse* c. *Jean Negev*, 74 *Revue Générale de Droit International Public*, 1970, p. 1108.

[149] See e.g. *Sullivan* v. *State of Sao Paulo*, 122 F.2d 355 (1941); 10 ILR, p. 178.

[150] [1971] 2 All ER 593, 595; 52 ILR, pp. 322, 324. See also *Swiss–Israel Trade Bank* v. *Salta*, 55 ILR, p. 411.

[151] See e.g. I. Sinclair, 'The European Convention on State Immunity', 22 ICLQ, 1973, pp. 254, 279–80.

[152] An Order in Council has been made with respect to the constituent territories of Austria, S.I. 1979 no. 457, and Germany, S.I. 1993, no. 2809. The Act may also be extended to dependent territories, see e.g. the State Immunity (Overseas Territories) Order, 1979, S.I. 1979 no. 458 and the State Immunity (Jersey) Order, 1985, S.I. 1985 no. 1642.

[153] See Report of the International Law Commission, 1991, p. 13. Note that article I of the Revised Draft Articles for a Convention on State Immunity adopted by the International Law Association in 1994 defines the term 'foreign state' to include the government of the state, any other state organs and agencies and instrumentalities of the state not possessing legal personality distinct from the state. No specific reference to units of federal states is made. In 1996, a further amendment wad adopted, providing that re immunity would be available in an action for damages against a foreign state for injury or death caused by certain human rights violations or terrorist activities.

The issue of the status of the European Community in this context was raised in the course of the ITC litigation as the EEC was a party to the sixth International Tin Agreement 1982 under which the ITC was constituted. The Court of Appeal in *Maclaine Watson* v. *Department of Trade and Industry*[154] held that the EEC's claim to sovereign immunity was untenable. It had been conceded that the EEC was not a state and thus could not rely on the State Immunity Act 1978, but it was argued that the Community was entitled to immunity analogous to sovereign immunity under the rules of common law. This approach was held by Kerr LJ to be 'entirely misconceived'.[155] Although the EEC had personality in international law and was able to exercise powers and functions analogous to those of sovereign states, this did not lead on to immunity as such. This was because sovereign immunity was 'a derogation from the normal exercise of jurisdiction by the courts and should be accorded only in clear cases',[156] while the concept itself was based upon the equality of states. The EEC Treaty 1957 and the Merger Treaty 1965 themselves made no claim for general immunity and nothing else existed upon which such a claim could be based.[157]

Waiver of immunity

It is possible, of course, for a state to waive expressly or impliedly its immunity from the jurisdiction of the court. Express waiver of immunity from jurisdiction, however, does not of itself mean waiver of immunity from execution.[158] In the case of implied waiver, some care is required. Section 2 of the State Immunity Act provides for loss of immunity upon submission to the jurisdiction, either by a prior written agreement[159] or after the particular dispute has arisen. A state is deemed to have submitted to the jurisdiction where the state has instituted proceedings or has intervened or

---

[154] [1988] 3 WLR 1033; 80 ILR, p. 49.   [155] *Ibid.*, p. 1107; 80 ILR, p. 122.
[156] *Victory Transport* v. *Comisaria General de Abastecimientos y Transportes*, 336 F.2d 354 (1964) cited with approval by Ackner LJ in *Empresa Exportadora de Azucar* v. *Industria Azucarera Nacional* [1983] 2 LL. Rep. 171, 193 and Lord Edmund-Davies in *I° Congreso del Partido* [1983] 1 AC 244, 276.
[157] [1988] 3 WLR 1033, 1108–12; 80 ILR, pp. 49, 123. Nourse and Ralph Gibson LLJ agreed with Kerr LJ completely on this issue, *ibid.*, pp. 1131 and 1158; 80 ILR, pp. 150, 180.
[158] See e.g. article 18(2) of the ILC Draft Articles on Jurisdictional Immunities, Report of the International Law Association, 1991, p. 000. Note, however, that the issue will turn upon the interpretation of the terms of the waiver, see *A Company* v. *Republic of X* [1990] 2 Lloyd's Rep 520; 87 ILR, p. 412. However, it is suggested that the principle that waiver of immunity from jurisdiction does not of itself constitute a waiver of immunity from the grant of relief by the courts is of the nature of a presumption, thus placing the burden of proof to the contrary upon the private party and having implications with regard to the standard of proof required.
[159] Overruling *Kahan* v. *Pakistan Federation* [1951] 2 KB 1003; 18 ILR, p. 210.

taken any step in the proceedings.[160] If a state submits to proceedings, it is deemed to have submitted to any counterclaim arising out of the same legal relationship or facts as the claim.[161] A provision in an agreement that it is to be governed by the law of the UK is not to be taken as a submission. By section 9, a state which has agreed in writing to submit a dispute to arbitration is not immune from proceedings in the courts which relate to the arbitration.[162] The issue of waiver is also a key factor in many US cases.[163]

Pre-judgment attachment[164]

Section 1610(d) of the US Foreign Sovereign Immunities Act, 1976 prohibits the attachment of the property of a foreign state before judgment unless that state has explicitly waived its immunity from attachment prior to judgment and the purpose of the attachment is to secure satisfaction of a judgment that has been or may be entered against the foreign state. A variety of cases in the US have arisen over whether general waivers contained in treaty provisions may be interpreted as permitting pre-judgment attachment, in order to prevent the defendant from removing his assets from the jurisdiction. The courts generally require clear evidence of the intention to waive pre-judgment attachment, although that actual phrase need not necessarily be used.[165]

---

[160] But not where the intervention or step taken is only for the purpose of claiming immunity, or where the step taken by the state is in ignorance of facts entitling it to immunity if those facts could not reasonably have been ascertained and immunity is claimed as soon as reasonably practicable, s.2(5). See also article 1 of the European Convention on State Immunity and article 8 of the ILC Draft Articles on Jurisdictional Immunities, see Report of the International Law Commission, 1991, p. 53.

[161] See also article 1 of the European Convention on State Immunity 1972 and article 9 of the ILC Draft Articles on Jurisdictional Immunities, see Report of the International Law Commission, 1991, p. 60.

[162] See also article 12 of the European Convention on State Immunity 1972 and article 17 of the ILC Draft Articles on Jurisdictional Immunities, see Report of the International Law Commission, 1991, p. 128

[163] Section1605(a)(1) of the US Foreign Sovereign Immunities Act, 1976 provides that a foreign state is not immune where it has waived its immunity either expressly or by implication, notwithstanding any withdrawal of the waiver which the foreign state may purport to effect, except in accordance with the terms of the waiver, see e.g. *Siderman* v. *Republic of Argentina*, 965 F 2s 699 (1992). It should also be noted that a substantial number of bilateral treaties expressly waive immunity from jurisdiction. This is particularly the case where the states maintaining the absolute immunity approach are concerned, see e.g. UN *Materials*, Part III.

[164] See e.g. J. Crawford, 'Execution of Judgments and Foreign Sovereign Immunity', 75 AJIL, 1981, pp. 820, 867 *et seq.* and Schreuer, *State Immunity*, p. 162.

[165] See e.g. *Behring International Inc.* v. *Imperial Iranian Air Force*, 475 F.Supp. 383 (1979); 63 ILR, p. 261; *Reading & Bates Corp.* v. *National Iranian Oil Company*, 478 F.Supp. 724 (1979); 63 ILR, p. 305; *New England Merchants National Bank* v. *Iran Power Generation and Transmission Company*, 19 ILM, 1980, p. 1298; 63 ILR, p. 408; *Security Pacific National Bank* v. *Government of Iran*, 513 F.Supp. 864 (1981); *Libra Bank Ltd* v. *Banco Nacional de Costa Rica*, 676 F.2d 47 (1982); 72 ILR, p. 119; *S & S Machinery Co.* v. *Masinexportimport*, 706 F.2d 411 (1981) and *O'Connell Machinery* v. *M.V. Americana*, 734 F.2d 115 (1984).

Under the UK State Immunity Act, 1978, no relief may be given against a state by way of injunction or order for specific performance, recovery of land or recovery of any property without the written consent of that state.[166] The question has therefore arisen as to whether a *Mareva* injunction,[167] ordering that assets remain within the jurisdiction pending the outcome of the case, may be obtained, particularly since this type of injunction is inter-locutory and obtained *ex parte*. It is suggested that an application for a *Mareva* injunction may indeed be made *ex parte* since immunity may not apply in the circumstances of the case. In applying for such an injunction, a plaintiff is under a duty to make full and frank disclosure and the standard of proof is that of a 'good and arguable case', explaining, for example, why it is contended that immunity would not be applicable. It is then for the defendant to seek to discharge the injunction by arguing that these criteria have not been met. The issue as to how the court should deal with such a situation was discussed in *A Company* v. *Republic of X*.[168] Saville J noted that the issue of immunity had to be finally settled at the outset so that when a state sought to discharge a *Mareva* injunction on the grounds of immunity, the Court could not allow the injunction to continue on the basis that the plaintiff has a good arguable case that immunity does not exist, for if immunity did exist 'then the court simply has no power to continue the injunction'. Accordingly, a delay between the granting of the injunction *ex parte* and the final determination by the court of the issue was probably unavoidable.[169] The situation is generally the same in other countries.[170]

Immunity from execution[171]

Immunity from execution is to be distinguished from immunity from jurisdiction, particularly since it involves the question of the actual seizure of assets appertaining to a foreign state. As such it poses a considerable challenge to relations between states and accordingly states have proved unwilling to restrict immunity from enforcement judgment in contradistinction to the

---

See also article 23 of the European Convention on State Immunity prohibiting such action and article 18 of the ILC Draft Articles on Jurisdictional Immunities, see Report of the International Law Commission, 1991, p. 134.   [166] S.13(2).

[167] See *Mareva Compania Naviera* v. *International Bulkcarriers* [1975] 2 LL. R 509. See also S. Gee, *Mareva Injunctions & Anton Piller Relief*, 2nd edn, London, 1990, especially at p. 22.

[168] [1990] 2 Lloyd's Rep 520; 87 ILR, p. 412.

[169] *Ibid.*, 525: 87 ILR, p. 417, citing *McLean Watson* v. *Department of Trade and Industry* [1988] 3 WLR 1033 at 1103–4 and 1157–8.

[170] But see the case of *Condor and Filvem* v. *Minister of Justice*, 101 ILR, p. 394, before the Italian Constitutional Court in 1992.

[171] See e.g. Schreuer, *State Immunity*, Chapter 6; Sinclair, 'Sovereign Immunity', Chapter IV; Crawford, 'International Law'; H. Fox, 'Enforcement Jurisdiction, Foreign State Property and Diplomatic Immunity', 34 ICLQ, 1985, p. 115 and various articles in 10 *Netherlands Yearbook of International Law*, 1979.

situation concerning jurisdictional immunity. Article 23 of the European Convention on State Immunity 1972 prohibits any measures of execution or preventive measures against the property of a contracting state in the absence of written consent in any particular case. However, the Convention provides for a system of mutual enforcement of final judgments rendered in accordance with its provisions[172] and an Additional Protocol provides for proceedings to be taken before the European Tribunal of State Immunity, consisting basically of members of the European Court of Human Rights. Article 18 of the ILC Draft Articles on Jurisdictional Immunities provides that no measures of constraint may be taken against the property of a state unless that state has expressly consented either by international agreement, or by an arbitration agreement or written contract, or by a declaration before the Court or by a written communication after a dispute between the parties has arisen. In addition, the state must have allocated property for the satisfaction of the claim in question or the property is specifically in use or intended for use by the state for other than government non-commercial purposes and is in the territory of the state of the forum and has a connection with the claim concerned or with the agency or instrumentality against which the proceeding was directed.[173]

Section 13(2)b of the UK State Immunity Act provides, for instance, that 'the property of a state shall not be subject to any process for the enforcement of a judgment or arbitration award or, in an action *in rem*, for its arrest, detention or sale'. Such immunity may be waived by written consent but not by merely submitting to the jurisdiction of the courts,[174] while there is no immunity from execution in respect of property which is for the time being in use or intended for use for commercial purposes.[175] It is particularly to be noted that this latter stipulation is not to apply to a state's central bank or other monetary institution.[176] Thus, a *Trendtex* type of situation could not arise again in the same form. It is also interesting that the corresponding provision in the US Foreign Sovereign Immunities Act of 1976 is more restrictive with regard to immunity from execution.[177]

---

[172] Article 20. [173] See Report of the International Law Commission, 1991, p. 134.
[174] S.13(3). See also s. 14 of the South African Foreign Sovereign Immunity Act 1981; s. 14 of the Pakistan State Immunity Ordinance 1981; s. 15 of the Singapore State Immunity Act 1979 and s. 31 of the Australian Foreign States Immunities Act 1985. [175] S.13(4).
[176] S.14(4).
[177] Section 1610. Thus, for example, there would be no immunity with regard to property taken in violation of international law. See also *First National City Bank v. Banco Para El Comercio Exterior de Cuba*, 462 US 611 (1983); *Letelier v. Republic of Chile*, 748 F.2d 790 (1984) and *Foxworth v. Permanent Mission of the Republic of Uganda to the United Nations*, 796 F.Supp. 761 (1992); 99 ILR, p. 138. See also G. R. Delaume, 'The Foreign Sovereign Immunities Act and Public Debt Litigation: Some Fifteen Years Later', 88 AJIL, 1994, pp. 257, 266. Note that in 1988, the legislation was amended to include a provision, which provides that with regard to measures of execution following confirmation of an arbitral award, all the commercial property of the award debtor was open to execution, new s. 1610 (a)(6), *ibid*. In 1996, a further amendment was adopted, providing that no immunity would be available in an action for damages against a foreign state for injury or death caused by certain human rights violations or terrorist actions.

In 1977, the West German Federal Constitutional Court in the *Philippine Embassy* case[178] declared that:

> forced execution of judgment by the state of the forum under a writ of execution against a foreign state which has been issued in respect of non-sovereign acts . . . of that state, or property of that state which is present or situated in the territory of the state of the forum is inadmissible without the consent of the foreign state if . . . such property serves sovereign purposes of the foreign state.

In particular it was noted that:

> claims against a general current bank account of the embassy of a foreign state which exists in the state of the forum and the purpose of which is to cover the embassy's costs and expenses are not subject to forced execution by the state of the forum.[179]

This was referred to approvingly by Lord Diplock in *Alcom Ltd* v. *Republic of Colombia*,[180] a case which similarly involved the attachment of a bank account of a diplomatic mission. The House of Lords unanimously accepted that the general rule in international law was not overturned in the State Immunity Act. In *Alcom*, described as involving a question of law of 'outstanding international importance',[181] it was held that such a bank account would not fall within the section 13(4) exception relating to commercial purposes, unless it could be shown by the person seeking to attach the balance that 'the bank account was earmarked by the foreign state solely . . . for being drawn on to settle liabilities incurred in commercial transactions'.[182] The onus of proof lies upon the applicant. It is also to be noted that under section 13(5) of the Act, a certificate by a head of mission to the effect that property was not in use for commercial purposes was sufficient evidence of that fact, unless the contrary was proven.[183] The question of determining property used for commercial purposes is a significant and complex one that will invariably depend upon an analysis of various factors, as seen in the light of the law of the forum state,[184] for example the present and future use of the funds and their origin.[185]

[178] See UN *Materials*, p. 297; 65 ILR, pp. 146, 150.
[179] UN *Materials*, pp. 300–1; 65 ILR, p. 164.
[180] [1984] 2 All ER 6; 74 ILR, p. 180, overturning the Court of Appeal Decision [1984] 1 All ER 1; 74 ILR, p. 170.   [181] [1984] 2 All ER 14; 74 ILR, p. 189.
[182] *Ibid.*, p. 13; 74 ILR, p. 187. But cf. *Birch Shipping Corporation* v. *Embassy of the United Republic of Tanzania*, 507 F.Supp. 311 (1980); 63 ILR, p. 524. But see the decision of the Swiss Federal Tribunal in 1990 in *Z* v. *Geneva Supervisory Authority for the Enforcement of Debts and Bankruptcy*, 102 ILR, p. 205, holding that funds allocated for the diplomatic service of a foreign state were immune from attachment.
[183] Such certificate had been issued by the Colombian Ambassador. See *infra* p. 531, with regard to diplomatic immunities.
[184] See the West German Federal Constitutional Court decision in the *National Iranian Oil Co.* case, 22 ILM, 1983, p. 1279.
[185] See e.g. *Eurodif Corporation* v. *Islamic Republic of Iran*, 23 ILM, 1984, p. 1062.

In *Benamar* v. *Embassy of the Democratic and Popular Republic of Algeria,*[186] the Italian Supreme Court reaffirmed the rule that customary international law forbids measures of execution against the property of foreign states located in the territory of the state seeking to exercise jurisdiction and used for sovereign purposes, and held that it lacked jurisdiction to enforce a judgment against a foreign state by ordering execution against bank accounts standing in the name of that state's embassy. This approach appears to have been modified in *Condor and Filvem* v. *Minister of Justice*[187] before the Italian Constitutional Court in 1992. The Court held that it could no longer be affirmed that there existed an international customary rule forbidding absolutely coercive measures against the property of foreign states. In order for immunity against execution not to apply, it is necessary not only to demonstrate that the activity or transaction concerned was *jure gestionis*, but also to show that the property to which the request for execution refers is not destined to accomplish public functions (*jure imperii*) of the foreign state.[188]

The burden and standard of proof

Since section 1 of the State Immunity Act stipulates that a state is immune from the jurisdiction of the courts of the UK except as provided in the following sections, it is clear that the burden of proof lies upon the plaintiff to establish that an exception to immunity applies.[189]

As far as the standard of proof is concerned, the Court of Appeal in *Maclaine Watson* v. *Department of Trade and Industry*[190] held that whenever a claim of immunity is made, the court must deal with it as a preliminary issue and on the normal test of balance of probabilities.[191] It would be insufficient to apply the 'good arguable case' test usual in Order 11[192] cases with regard to leave to serve.[193] To have decided otherwise would have meant that the state might have lost its claim for immunity upon the more impressionistic 'good arguable case' basis, which in practice is decided upon affidavit evidence only, and would have been precluded from pursuing its claim at a later stage since that could well be construed as submission to the jurisdiction under section 2(3) of the State Immunity Act.

The question of service of process upon a foreign state arose in *Westminster City Council* v. *Government of the Islamic Republic of Iran,*[194] where Peter

---

[186] 84 AJIL, 1990, p. 573; 87 ILR, p. 56. See also *Libya* v. *Rossbeton SRL, ibid.*, p. 63.
[187] 101 ILR, p. 394.   [188] *Ibid.*, pp. 401–2.
[189] See also Staughton J in *Rayner* v. *Department of Trade and Industry* [1987] BCLC 667.
[190] [1988] 3 WLR 1033, 1103 and 1157; 80 ILR, pp. 49, 118, 179.
[191] This would be done procedurally under Order 12, Rule 8 of the Rules of the Supreme Court, 1991. See also *A Company* v. *Republic of X* 87 ILR, pp. 412, 417.
[192] Rules of the Supreme Court, 1991.
[193] See e.g. *Vitkovice Horni* v. *Korner* [1951] AC 869.   [194] [1986] 3 All ER 284.

Gibson J held that without prior service upon the Iranian government, the court was unable to deal with the substantive issue before it which concerned the attempt by the Westminster City Council to recover from the Iranian government charges incurred by it in rendering the Iranian embassy safe after it had been stormed in the famous 1980 siege. In the absence of diplomatic relations between the UK and Iran at that time and in the absence of Iranian consent, there appeared to be no way to satisfy the requirement in section 12 of the State Immunity Act that 'any writ or other document required to be served for instituting proceedings against a state shall be served by being transmitted through the Foreign and Commonwealth Office to the Ministry of Foreign Affairs of the state'. The question also arose in *Kuwait Airways Corporation* v. *Iraqi Airways*.[195] Since at the relevant time there was no British diplomatic presence in Baghdad, the necessary documents were lodged pursuant to Order 11, Rule 7 at the Central Office, whence they were sent to the Foreign and Commonwealth Office and thence to the Iraqi Embassy in London with a request for transmission to Baghdad. The House of Lords held that since the writ was not forwarded to the Iraqi Ministry of Foreign Affairs in Baghdad, the writ was not served as required under section 12(1) of the 1978 Act.[196]

Conclusion

Although sovereign immunity is in various domestic statutes proclaimed as a general principle, subject to wide-ranging exceptions, it is, of course, itself an exception to the general rule of territorial jurisdiction. The enumeration of non-immunity situations is so long, that the true situation of a rapidly diminishing exception to jurisdiction should be appreciated. In many instances, it has only been with practice that it has become apparent how much more extensive the submission to jurisdiction has become under domestic legislation. In *Letelier* v. *Republic of Chile*,[197] for example, section 1605(a)5 providing for foreign state liability for injury, death and loss of property occurring in the US was used to indict the secret service of Chile with regard to the murder of a former Chilean foreign minister in Washington. Similarly in *Verlinden* v. *Central Bank of Nigeria*,[198] the Supreme Court permitted a Dutch company to sue the Central Bank of Nigeria in the US,[199] although the *Tel-Oren*[200] case may mark a modification of this

---

[195] [1995] 1 WLR 1147.   [196] *Ibid.*, p. 1156 (per Lord Goff).
[197] 488 F.Supp. 665 (1980); 63 ILR, p. 378.   [198] 22 ILM, 1983, p. 647; 79 ILR, p. 548.
[199] Nevertheless, it would appear that the Foreign Sovereign Immunities Act of 1976 does require some minimum jurisdictional links, see generally *International Shoe Co* v. *Washington*, 326 US 310 (1945) and *Perez* v. *The Bahamas*, 482 F.Supp. 1208 (1980); 63 ILR, p. 350, cf. State Immunity Act of 1978.
[200] 726 F.2d 774 (1984); 77 ILR, p. 193. See further, *supra*, p. 480.

approach. The principle of diplomatic immunity may often be relevant in a sovereign immunity case. This is considered in the next section.

Diplomatic law[201]

Rules regulating the various aspects of diplomatic relations constitute one of the earliest expressions of international law. Whenever in history there has been a group of independent states co-existing, special customs have developed on how the ambassadors and other special representatives of other states were to be treated.[202] Diplomacy as a method of communication between various parties, including negotiations between recognised agents, is an ancient institution and international legal provisions governing its manifestations are the result of centuries of state practice. The special privileges and immunities related to diplomatic personnel of various kinds grew up partly as a consequence of sovereign immunity and the independence and equality of states, and partly as an essential requirement of an international system. States must negotiate and consult with each other and with international organisations and in order to do so need diplomatic staffs. Since these persons represent their states in various ways, they thus benefit from the legal principle of state sovereignty. This is also an issue of practical convenience.

Diplomatic relations have traditionally been conducted through the

[201] See e.g. P. Cahier, *Le Droit Diplomatique Contemporain*, Geneva, 1962; M. Hardy, *Modern Diplomatic Law*, Manchester, 1968; Do Naslimento e Silva, *Diplomacy in International Law*, Leiden, 1973; E. Denza, *Diplomatic Law*, London, 1976; *Satow's Guide to Diplomatic Practice* (ed. P. Gore-Booth), 5th edn, London, 1979; B. Sen, *A Diplomat's Handbook of International Law and Practice*, 3rd edn, The Hague, 1988; J. Brown, 'Diplomatic Immunity: State Practice under the Vienna Convention on Diplomatic Relations', 37 ICLQ, 1988, p. 53; Société Français de Droit International, *Aspects Récents du Droit des Relations Diplomatiques*, Paris, 1989; G. V. McClanahan, *Diplomatic Immunity*, London, 1989; B. S. Murty, *The International Law of Diplomacy*, Dordrecht, 1989; L. Dembinski, *The Modern Law of Diplomacy*, Dordrecht, 1990; J. Salmon, *Manuel de Droit Diplomatique*, Brussels, 1994; J. C. Barker, *The Abuse of Diplomatic Privileges and Immunities*, Aldershot, 1996; C. E. Wilson, *Diplomatic Privileges and Immunities*, Tucson, 1967; J. Salmon, 'Immunités et Actes de la Fonction', AFDI, 1992, p. 313; M. Whiteman, *Digest of International Law*, Washington, vol. VII; *Third US Restatement of Foreign Relations Law*, St Paul, 1987, pp. 455 *et seq.* House of Commons Foreign Affairs Committee, *The Abuse of Diplomatic Immunities and Privileges*, 1984 and the UK Government Response to the *Report*, Cmnd. 9497. and *Memorandum on Diplomatic Privileges and Immunities in the United Kingdom*, UKMIL, 63 BYIL, 1992, p. 688. See also R. Higgins, 'The Abuse of Diplomatic Privileges and Immunities: Recent United Kingdom Experience', 79 AJIL, 1985, p. 641 and Higgins, *Problems and Process*, Oxford, 1994, p. 86; A. James, 'Diplomatic Relations and Contacts', 62 BYIL, 1991, p. 347; Nguyen Quoc Dinh, P. Daillier and A. Pellet, *Droit International Public*, 5th edn, Paris, 1994, p. 708 and *Oppenheim's International Law*, Chapters 10 and 11.
[202] See e.g. G. Mattingley, *Renaissance Diplomacy*, London, 1955. See as to the position of Heads of State and other senior figures, A. Watts, 'The Legal Position in International Law of Heads of State, Heads of Government and Foreign Ministers', 247 HR, 1994 III, p. 13.

medium of ambassadors[203] and their staffs, but with the growth of trade and commercial intercourse the office of consul was established and expanded. The development of speedy communications stimulated the creation of special missions designed to be sent to particular areas for specific purposes, often with the head of state or government in charge. To some extent, however, the establishment of telephone, telegraph, telex and fax services has lessened the importance of the traditional diplomatic personnel by strengthening the centralising process. Nevertheless, diplomats and consuls do retain some useful functions in the collection of information and pursuit of friendly relations, as well as providing a permanent presence in foreign states, with all that that implies for commercial and economic activities.[204]

The field of diplomatic immunities is one of the most accepted and uncontroversial of international law topics, as it is in the interest of all states ultimately to preserve an even tenor of diplomatic relations, although not all states act in accordance with this. As the International Court noted in the *US Diplomatic and Consular Staff in Tehran* case:[205]

> the rules of diplomatic law, in short, constitute a self-contained regime, which on the one hand, lays down the receiving state's obligations regarding the facilities, privileges and immunities to be accorded to diplomatic missions and, on the other, foresees their possible abuse by members of the mission and specifies the means at the disposal of the receiving state to counter any such abuse.[206]

The Vienna Convention on Diplomatic Relations 1961

This treaty, which came into force in 1964,[207] emphasises the functional necessity of diplomatic privileges and immunities for the efficient conduct of international relations[208] as well as pointing to the character of the diplomatic mission as representing its state.[209] It both codified existing laws and established others.[210]

---

[203] See as to the powers of ambassadors, *First Fidelity Bank NA* v. *Government of Antigua and Barbuda Permanent Mission*, 877 F 2d 189 (1989); 99 ILR, p. 125
[204] See generally *Satow's Guide*, Chapter 1.
[205] ICJ Reports, 1980, p. 3; 61 ILR, p. 504. Hereinafter, the *Iran* case.
[206] *Ibid.*, p. 40; 61 ILR, p. 566.
[207] The importance of the Convention was stressed in the *Iran* case, ICJ Reports, 1980, pp. 330–430; 61 ILR, p. 556. Many of its provisions are incorporated into English law by the Diplomatic Privileges Act, 1964.
[208] See also *767 Third Avenue Associates* v. *Permanent Mission of the Republic of Zaire to the United Nations*, 988 F 2d 295 (1993); 99 ILR, p. 194.
[209] See *Yearbook of the ILC*, 1958 vol. II, pp. 94–5. The extraterritorial theory of diplomatic law, according to which missions constituted an extension of the territory of the sending state, was of some historic interest but not of practical use, *ibid.* See also *Radwan* v. *Radwan* [1973] Fam. 24; 55 ILR, p. 579 and *McKeel* v. *Islamic Republic of Iran*, 722 F.2d 582 (1983); 81 ILR, p. 543. Note that in *US* v. *Kostadinov*, 734 F 2d 906, 908 (1984); 99 ILR, pp. 103, 107, the term 'mission' in the Convention was defined not as the premises occupied by diplomats, but as a group of people sent by one state to another.
[210] See e.g. the *Iran* case, ICJ Reports, 1980, pp. 3, 24; 61 ILR, p. 550.

There is no right as such under international law to diplomatic relations, and they exist by virtue of mutual consent.[211] If one state does not wish to enter into diplomatic relations, it is not legally compelled so to do. Accordingly, the Convention specifies in article 4 that the sending state must ensure that the consent (or *agrément*) of the receiving state has been given for the proposed head of its mission, and reasons for any refusal of consent do not have to be given. Similarly, by article 9 the receiving state may at any time declare any member of the diplomatic mission *persona non grata* without having to explain its decision, and thus obtain the removal of that person. However, the principle of consent as the basis of diplomatic relations may be affected by other rules of international law. For example, the Security Council in resolution 748 (1992), which imposed sanctions upon Libya, decided that 'all states shall: (a) significantly reduce the number and level of the staff at Libyan diplomatic missions and consular posts and restrict or control the movement within their territory of all such staff who remain . . .'.

The main functions of a diplomatic mission are specified in article 3 and revolve around the representation and protection of the interests and nationals of the sending state, as well as the promotion of information and friendly relations.

Article 13 provides that the head of the mission is deemed to have taken up his functions in the receiving state upon presentation of credentials. Heads of mission are divided into three classes by article 14, viz. ambassadors or nuncios accredited to Heads of State and other heads of mission of equivalent rank; envoys, ministers and internuncios accredited to Heads of State and chargés d'affaires accredited to Ministers of Foreign Affairs.[212] It is customary for a named individual to be in charge of a diplomatic mission. When in 1979, Libya designated its embassies as 'People's Bureaux' to be run by revolutionary committees, the UK insisted upon and obtained the nomination of a named person as the head of the mission.[213]

The inviolability of the mission

In order to facilitate the operations of normal diplomatic activities, article 22 of the Convention specifically declares that the premises of the mission are inviolable and that agents of the receiving state are not to enter them without the consent of the head of the mission. This appears to be an

---

[211] Article 2.
[212] The rules as to heads of missions are a modern restatement of the rules established in 1815 by the European powers, see Denza, *Diplomatic Law*, p. 58.
[213] Comment by Sir Antony Acland, Minutes of Evidence Taken Before the Foreign Affairs Committee, *Report*, p. 20. See also DUSPIL, 1979, pp. 571–73.

absolute rule[214] and in the Sun Yat Sen incident in 1896, the Court refused to issue a writ of habeas corpus with regard to a Chinese refugee held against his will in the Chinese legation in London.[215] Precisely what the legal position would be in the event of entry without express consent because, for example, of fire fighting requirements or of danger to persons within that area, is rather uncertain and justification might be pleaded by virtue of implied consent, but it is a highly controversial area.[216] The receiving state is under a special duty to protect the mission premises from intrusion or damage or 'impairment of its dignity'. By the same token, the premises of a mission must not be used in a way which is incompatible with the functions of the mission.[217]

In 1979, the US Embassy in Tehran, Iran, was taken over by several hundred demonstrators. Archives and documents were seized and fifty diplomatic and consular staff were held hostage. In 1980, the International Court declared that, under the 1961 Convention (and the 1963 Convention on Consular Relations):

> Iran was placed under the most categorical obligations, as a receiving state, to take appropriate steps to ensure the protection of the United States Embassy and Consulates, their staffs, their archives, their means of communication and the free movement of the members of their staffs.[218]

These were also obligations under general international law.[219] The Court in particular stressed the seriousness of Iran's behaviour and the conflict between its conduct and its obligations under 'the whole corpus of the international rules of which diplomatic and consular law is comprised, rules the fundamental character of which the Court must here again strongly affirm'.[220]

On 17 April 1984, a peaceful demonstration took place outside the

---

[214] See e.g. *767 Third Avenue Associates v. Permanent Mission of the Republic of Zaire to the United Nations*, 988 F.2d 295 (1993); 99 ILR, p. 194.

[215] A. D. McNair, *International Law Opinions*, Oxford, 1956, vol. I, p. 85. The issue was resolved by diplomatic means.

[216] The original draft of the article would have permitted such emergency entry, but this was rejected, see Denza, *Diplomatic Law*, pp. 82–4. In 1973 an armed search of the Iraqi embassy in Pakistan took place and considerable quantities of arms were found. As a result the Iraqi ambassador and an attaché were declared *personae non grata*, *ibid.*, p. 84.

[217] Article 41(3) of the Vienna Convention.

[218] The *Iran* case, ICJ Reports, 1980, pp. 3, 30–1; 61 ILR, p. 556. This the Iranians failed to do, *ibid.*, pp. 31–2. The Court emphasised that such obligations concerning the inviolability of the members of a diplomatic mission and of the premises, property and archives of the mission continued even in cases of armed conflict or breach of diplomatic relations, *ibid.*, p. 40. See also DUSPIL, 1979, pp. 577 *et seq.*; K. Gryzbowski, 'The Regime of Diplomacy and the Tehran Hostages', 30 ICLQ, 1981, p. 42 and L. Gross, 'The Case Concerning United States Diplomatic and Consular Staff in Tehran: Phase of Provisional Measures', 74 AJIL, 1980, p. 395.   [219] See e.g. *Belgium v. Nicod and Another*, 82 ILR, p. 124.

[220] The *Iran* case, ICJ Reports, 1980, p. 42; 61 ILR, p. 568. The Court particularly instanced articles 22, 25, 26 and 27 and analogous provisions in the 1963 Consular Relations Convention, *ibid.*

Libyan Embassy in London. Shots from the Embassy were fired that resulted in the death of a policewoman. After a siege, the Libyans inside left and the building was searched in the presence of a Saudi Arabian diplomat. Weapons and other relevant forensic evidence were found.[221] The issue raised here, in the light of article 45(a) which provides that after a break in diplomatic relations, 'the receiving state must . . . respect and protect the premises of the mission', is whether that search was permissible. The UK view is that article 45(a) does not mean that the premises continue to be inviolable[222] and this would clearly appear to be correct. There is a distinction between inviolability under article 22 and respect and protection under article 45(a).

The suggestion has also been raised that the right of self-defence may also be applicable in this context. It was used to justify the search of personnel leaving the Libyan Embassy[223] and the possibility was noted that in certain limited circumstances it may be used to justify entry into an embassy.[224]

A rather different issue arises where mission premises have been abandoned. The UK enacted the Diplomatic and Consular Premises Act in 1987, under which states wishing to use land as diplomatic or consular premises are required to obtain the consent of the Secretary of State. Once such consent has been obtained (although this is not necessary in the case of land which had this status prior to the coming into force of the Act), it could be subsequently withdrawn. The Secretary of State has the power to require that the title to such land be vested in him where that land has been lying empty, or without diplomatic occupants, and could cause damage to pedestrians or neighbouring buildings because of neglect, providing that he is satisfied that to do so is permissible under international law (section 2). By section 3 of the Act, the Secretary of State is able to sell the premises, deduct certain expenses and transfer the residue to the person divested of his interest.

This situation occurred with respect to the Cambodian Embassy in London, whose personnel closed the building after the Pol Pot take-over of Cambodia in 1975, handing the keys over to the Foreign Office.[225] In 1979, the UK withdrew its recognition of the Cambodian government after the Vietnamese invasion and since that date has had no dealings with any

---

[221] See Foreign Affairs Committee, *Report*, p. xxvi.
[222] Memorandum by the Foreign and Commonwealth Office, Foreign Affairs Committee, *Report*, p. 5.
[223] *Ibid.*, p. 9. Such a search was declared essential for the protection of the police, *ibid.* Note the reference to self-defence is both to domestic and international law, *ibid.*
[224] See the comments of the Legal Adviser to the FCO, Minutes of Evidence, Foreign Affairs Committee, *Report*, p. 28. Of course, entry can be made into the building with the consent of the receiving state, as for example when Iran requested the UK to eject militants who had taken over their London Embassy in 1980.
[225] See C. Warbrick, 'Current Developments', 38 ICLQ, 1989, p. 965.

authority as the government of that country. Squatters moved in shortly thereafter. These premises were made subject to section 2 of the Diplomatic and Consular Premises Act in 1988[226] and the Secretary of State vested the land in himself. This was challenged by the squatters and in *R v. Secretary of State for Foreign and Commonwealth Affairs, ex parte Samuel*,[227] Henry J held that the Secretary of State had acted correctly and in accordance with the duty imposed under article 45 of the Vienna Convention. The Court of Appeal dismissed an appeal,[228] holding that the relevant section merely required that the Secretary of State be satisfied that international law permitted such action.[229]

In *Westminster City Council v. Government of the Islamic Republic of Iran*,[230] the issue concerned the payment of expenses arising out of repairs to the damaged and abandoned Iranian embassy in London in 1980. The council sought to register a land charge, but the question of the immunity of the premises under article 22 of the Vienna Convention was raised. Although the Court felt that procedurally it was unable to proceed,[231] reference was made to the substantive issue and it was noted that the premises had ceased to be diplomatic premises in the circumstances and thus the premises were not 'used' for the purpose of the mission as required by article 22, since that phrase connoted the present tense. The inviolability of diplomatic premises, however, must not be confused with extraterritoriality. Such premises do not constitute part of the territory of the sending state.[232]

Whether a right of diplomatic asylum exists within general international law is doubtful and in principle refugees are to be returned to the authorities of the receiving state in the absence of treaty or customary rules to the contrary. The International Court in the *Asylum* case between Colombia and Peru[233] emphasised that a decision to grant asylum involves a derogation from the sovereignty of the receiving state 'and constitutes an intervention in matters which are exclusively within the competence of that state. Such a derogation from territorial sovereignty cannot be recognised unless its legal basis is established in each particular case'. Where treaties exist

[226] See s.2 of the Diplomatic and Consular Premises (Cambodia) Order, SI 30, 1988.
[227] *The Times*, 10 September 1988.
[228] *The Times*, 17 August 1989; 83 ILR, p. 232. Note that in *Secretary of State for Foreign and Commonwealth Affairs v. Tomlin, The Times*, 4 December 1990; [1990] 1 All ER 920, the Court of Appeal held that in this situation, the extended limitation period of thirty years under s.15(1) of and Schedule 1 to the Limitation Act 1980 was applicable and the squatters could not rely on twelve years' adverse possession.
[229] Note that in the US, embassies temporarily abandoned due to broken relations may be sequestered and turned to other uses pending resumption of relations. This has been the case with regard to Iranian, Cambodian and Vietnamese properties that have been in the custody of the Office of Foreign Missions, see McClanahan, *Diplomatic Immunity*, pp. 53 and 110. See also the US Foreign Missions Act 1982.   [230] [1986] 3 All ER 284.
[231] See *supra* p. 521.
[232] See e.g. *Persinger v. Islamic Republic of Iran*, 729 F.2d 835 (1984). See also *Swiss Federal Prosecutor v. Kruszyk*, 102 ILR, p. 176.   [233] ICJ Reports, 1950, pp. 266, 274–5.

regarding the grant of asylum, the question will arise as to the respective competences of the sending and receiving state or the state granting asylum and the territorial state. While the diplomats of the sending state may provisionally determine whether a refugee meets any condition laid down for the grant of asylum under an applicable treaty this would not bind the receiving state, for 'the principles of international law do not recognise any rule of unilateral and definitive qualification by the state granting asylum'.[234] It may be that in law a right of asylum will arise for 'urgent and compelling reasons of humanity',[235] but the nature and scope of this is unclear.

The diplomatic bag

Article 27 provides that the receiving state shall permit and protect free communication on behalf of the mission for all official purposes. Such official communication is inviolable and may include the use of diplomatic couriers and messages in code and in cipher, although the consent of the receiving state is required for a wireless transmitter.[236]

Articles 27(3) and (4) deal with the diplomatic bag,[237] and provide that it shall not be opened or detained and that the packages constituting the diplomatic bag 'must bear visible external marks of their character and may contain only diplomatic documents or articles intended for official use'. The need for a balance in this area is manifest. On the one hand, missions require a confidential means of communication, while on the other the need to guard against abuse is clear. Article 27, however, lays the emphasis upon the former.[238] This is provided that article 27(4) is complied with. In the Dikko incident on 5 July 1984, a former Nigerian minister was kidnapped in London and placed in a crate to be flown to Nigeria. The crate was opened at Stansted Airport, although accompanied by a person claiming diplomatic status. The crate[239] did not contain an official seal and was thus clearly not a diplomatic bag.[240]

---

[234] *Ibid.*, p. 274.   [235] *Oppenheim's International Law*, p. 1084.
[236] There was a division of opinion at the Vienna Conference between the developed and developing states over this issue. The former felt that the right to install and use a wireless did not require consent, see Denza, *Diplomatic Law*, pp. 121–3.
[237] Defined in article 3(2) of the Draft Articles on the Diplomatic Courier and the Diplomatic Bag adopted by the International Law Commission in 1989 as 'the packages containing official correspondance, and documents or articles intended exclusively for official use, whether accompanied by diplomatic courier or not, which are used for the official communication referred to in article 1 and which bear visible external marks of their character' as a diplomatic bag, see *Yearbook of the ILC*, 1989, vol. II, part 2, p. 15.
[238] This marked a shift from earlier practice, *ibid.*
[239] An accompanying crate contained persons allegedly part of the kidnapping operation.
[240] See Foreign Affairs Committee, *Report*, pp. xxxiii–xxxiv. Note also the incident in 1964 when an Israeli was found bound and drugged in a crate marked 'diplomatic mail' at Rome Airport. As a result, the Italians declared one Egyptian official at the embassy *persona non grata* and expelled two others, *Keesings Contemporary Archives*, p. 20580. In 1980, a crate

In view of suspicions of abuse, the question has arisen as to whether electronic screening, not involving opening or detention, of the diplomatic bag is legitimate. The UK appears to take the view that electronic screening of this kind would be permissible, although it claims not to have carried out such activities, but other states do not accept this.[241] It is to be noted that after the Libyan Embassy siege in April 1984, the diplomatic bags leaving the building were not searched.[242] However, Libya had entered a reservation to the Vienna Convention, reserving its right to open a diplomatic bag in the presence of an official representative of the diplomatic mission concerned. In the absence of permission by the authorities of the sending state, the diplomatic bag was to be returned to its place of origin. Kuwait and Saudi Arabia made similar reservations which were not objected to.[243] This is to be contrasted with a Bahraini reservation to article 27(3) which would have permitted the opening of diplomatic bags in certain circumstances.[244] The Libyan reservation could have been relied upon by the UK in these conditions.

It is also interesting to note that after the Dikko incident, the UK Foreign Minister stated that the crates concerned were opened because of the suspicion of human contents. Whether the crates constituted diplomatic bags or not was a relevant consideration with regards to a right to search, but: 'the advice given and the advice which would have been given had the crate constituted a diplomatic bag took fully into account the overriding duty to preserve and protect human life'.[245]

This appears to point to an implied exception to article 27(3) in the interests of humanity. It is to be welcomed, provided, of course, it is applied solely and strictly in these terms.

The issue of the diplomatic bag has been considered by the International Law Commission, in the context of article 27 and analogous provisions in the 1963 Consular Relations Convention, the 1969 Convention on Special Missions and the 1975 Convention on the Representation of States in their Relations with International Organisations. Article 28 of the Draft Articles on the Diplomatic Courier and the Diplomatic Bag, as finally adopted by

---

bound for the Moroccan Embassy in London split open at Harwich to reveal £500, 000 worth of drugs, *The Times*, 13 June 1980. In July 1984, a lorry belonging to the USSR was opened for inspection by West German authorities on the grounds that a lorry itself could not be a bag. The crates inside the lorry were accepted as diplomatic bags and not opened, Foreign Affairs Committee, *Report*, p. xiii, note 48.

[241] See the Legal Adviser, FCO, Foreign Affairs Committee, *Report*, p. 23. See also 985, HC Deb., col. 1219, 2 June 1980, and Cmnd. 9497.

[242] Foreign Affairs Committee, *Report*, p. xxx.

[243] Except by France, see Denza, *Diplomatic Law*, p. 128. The UK did not object and regarded the reservations in fact as reflective of customary law prior to the Convention, Memorandum of the FCO, Foreign Affairs Committee, *Report*, p. 4.

[244] This was objected to, *ibid.*, and see Denza, *Diplomatic Law*, p. 128.

[245] See Foreign Affairs Committee, *Report*, p. 50.

the International Law Commission in 1989, provides that the diplomatic bag shall be inviolable wherever it may be. It is not to be opened or detained and 'shall be exempt from examination directly or through electronic or other technical device'. However, in the case of the consular bag, it is noted that if the competent authorities of the receiving or transit state have serious reason to believe that the bag contains something other than official correspondence and documents or articles intended exclusively for official use, they may request that the bag be opened in their presence by an authorised representative of the sending state. If this request is refused by the authorities of the sending state, the bag is to be returned to its place of origin.[246] It was thought that this preserved existing law. Certainly, in so far as the consular bag is concerned, the provisions of article 35(3) of the Vienna Convention on Consular Relations are reproduced, but the stipulation of exemption from electronic or other technical examination does not appear in the Vienna Convention on Diplomatic Relations and the view of the Commission that this is mere clarification[247] is controversial.[248]

As far as the diplomatic courier is concerned, that is, a person accompanying a diplomatic bag, the Draft Articles provide for a regime of privileges, immunities and inviolability that is akin to that governing diplomats. He is to enjoy personal inviolability and is not liable to any form of arrest or detention (draft article 10), his temporary accommodation is inviolable (draft article 17), and he will benefit from immunity from the criminal and civil jurisdiction of the receiving or transit state in respect of all acts performed in the exercise of his functions (draft article 18). In general, his privileges and immunities last from the moment he enters the territory of the receiving or transit state until he leaves such state (draft article 21).[249]

Diplomatic immunities – property

Under article 22 of the Vienna Convention, the premises of the mission are inviolable[250] and together with their furnishings and other property thereon and the means of transport are immune from search, requisition, attachment or execution. By article 23, a general exception from taxation in

---

[246] Draft article 28(2). See *Yearbook of the ILC*, 1989, vol. II, part 2, pp. 42–3. See also S. McCaffrey, 'The Forty-First Session of the International Law Commission', 83 AJIL, 1989, p. 937. [247] *Yearbook of the ILC*, 1989, vol. II, part 2, p. 43.
[248] See e.g. *Yearbook of the ILC*, 1980, vol. II, pp. 231 *et seq.*; *ibid.*, 1981, vol. II, pp. 151 *et seq.* and *ibid.*, 1985, vol. II, Part 2, pp. 30 *et seq.* See also A/38/10 (1983) and the Memorandum by Sir Ian Sinclair, member of the ILC, dealing with the 1984 session on this issue, Foreign Affairs Committee, *Report*, p. 79 *et seq.*
[249] See e.g. McClanahan, *Diplomatic Immunity*, p. 64 and *Yearbook of the ILC*, 1985, vol. II, Part 2, pp. 36 *et seq.*
[250] By article 30(1) of the Convention, the private residence of a diplomatic agent shall enjoy the same inviolability and protection as the premises of the mission.

respect of the mission premises is posited. The Court in the *Philippine Embassy* case explained that in the light of customary and treaty law, 'property used by the sending state for the performance of its diplomatic functions in any event enjoys immunity even if it does not fall within the material or spatial scope' of article 22.[251] It should also be noted that the House of Lords in *Alcom Ltd* v. *Republic of Colombia*[252] held that under the State Immunity Act 1978 a current account at a commercial bank in the name of a diplomatic mission would be immune unless the plaintiff could show that it had been earmarked by the foreign state solely for the settlement of liabilities incurred in commercial transactions. An account used to meet the day-to-day running expenses of a diplomatic mission would therefore be immune. This approach was also based upon the obligation contained in article 25 of the Vienna Convention on Diplomatic Relations, which provided that the receiving state 'shall accord full facilities for the performance of the functions of the mission'. The House of Lords noted that the negative formulation of this principle meant that neither the executive nor the legal branch of government in the receiving state must act in such manner as to obstruct the mission in carrying out its functions.[253]

Section 16 of the State Immunity Act provides, however, that the exemption from immunity in article 6 relating to proceedings involving immovable property in the UK did not extend to proceedings concerning 'a state's title to or its possession of property used for the purposes of a diplomatic mission'. It was held in *Intpro Properties (UK) Ltd* v. *Sauvel*[254] by the Court of Appeal that the private residence of a diplomatic agent, even where used for embassy social functions from time to time, did not constitute use for the purposes of a diplomatic mission and that in any event the proceedings did not concern the French government's title to or possession of the premises, but were merely for damages for breach of a covenant in a lease. Accordingly, there was no immunity under section 16.

It is to be noted that by article 24 of the Vienna Convention, the archives and documents of the mission are inviolable at any time and wherever they may be.[255]

The question of the scope of article 24 was discussed by the House of Lords in *Shearson Lehman* v. *Maclaine Watson (No. 2)*,[256] which concerned the intervention by the International Tin Council in a case on the grounds that certain documents it was proposed to adduce in evidence were inadmissible. This argument was made in the context of article 7 of the

[251] See UN *Materials*, pp. 297, 317; 65 ILR, pp. 146, 187.
[252] [1984] 2 All ER 6; 74 ILR, p. 180.   [253] *Ibid.*, p. 9; 74 ILR, p. 182.
[254] [1983] 2 All ER 495; 64 ILR, p. 384.
[255] This goes beyond previous customary law, see e.g. *Rose* v. *R* [1947] 3 DLR 618.
[256] [1988] 1 WLR 16; 77 ILR, p. 145.

International Tin Council (Immunities and Privileges) Order 1972 which
stipulates that the ITC should have the 'like inviolability of official archives
as . . . is accorded in respect of the official archives of a diplomatic mission'.
Lord Bridge interpreted the phrase 'archives and documents of the mission'
in article 24 as referring to the archives and documents 'belonging to or held
by the mission'.[257] Such protection was not confined to executive or judicial
action by the host state, but would cover, for example, the situation where
documents were put into circulation by virtue of theft or other improper
means.[258]

Diplomatic immunities – personal

The person of a diplomatic agent[259] is inviolable under article 29 of the
Vienna Convention and he may not be detained or arrested. This principle
is the most fundamental rule of diplomatic law.[260] Article 30(1) provides for
the inviolability of the private residence of a diplomatic agent, while article
30(2) provides that his papers, correspondence and property[261] are inviolable. Section 4 of the Diplomatic Privileges Act 1964 stipulates that where
a question arises as to whether a person is or is not entitled to any privilege
or immunity under the Act, which incorporates many of the provisions of
the Vienna Convention, a certificate issued by or under the authority of the
Secretary of State stating any fact relating to that question shall be conclusive evidence of that fact.

As far as criminal jurisdiction is concerned, diplomatic agents enjoy complete immunity from the legal system of the receiving state.[262] This provision noted in article 31(1) merely reflects the accepted position under
customary law. The only remedy the host state has in the face of offences
alleged to have been committed by a diplomat is to declare him *persona non
grata* under article 9.[263]

---

[257] *Ibid.*, p. 24; 77 ILR, p. 150.
[258] *Ibid.*, p. 27; 77 ILR, p. 154. See also *Fayed* v. *Al-Tajir* [1987] 2 All ER 396.
[259] Defined in article 1(e) as the head of the mission or a member of the diplomatic staff of the
mission. See *supra* p. 492, with regard to Head of State immunities. See also *US* v. *Noriega*,
746 F.Supp. 1506, 1523–5; 99 ILR, pp. 145, 165–7.
[260] See Denza, *Diplomatic Law*, p. 135. See also the 1973 Convention on the Prevention and
Punishment of Crimes against Internationally Protected Persons, including Diplomatic
Agents. [261] Except that this is limited by article 31, see *infra* p. 534.
[262] See *Dickinson* v. *Del Solar* [1930] 1 KB 376; 5 ILR, p. 299. See also Denza, *Diplomatic Law*,
pp. 149–82.
[263] However, the US has tackled the problem of unpaid parking fines by adopting Section 574
of the Foreign Operations, Export Financing and Related Programs Appropriations Act
1994, under which 110 per cent of unpaid parking fines and penalties must be withheld
from that state's foreign aid. In addition, the State Department announced in December
1993 that registration renewal of vehicles with unpaid or unadjudicated parking tickets of
more than one year old would be withheld, thus rendering the use of such vehicles illegal
in the US, see 'Contemporary Practice of the United States Relating to International Law',

Article 31(1) also specifies that diplomats are immune from the civil and administrative jurisdiction of the state in which they are serving, except in three cases. First, where the action relates to private immovable property situated within the host state (unless held for mission purposes),[264] secondly in litigation relating to succession matters in which the diplomat is involved as a private person (for example as an executor or heir) and finally, with respect to unofficial professional or commercial activity engaged in by the agent.[265] In a document issued by the Foreign Office in 1987, entitled *Memorandum on Diplomatic Privileges and Immunities in the United Kingdom*,[266] it was noted that a serious view was taken of any reliance on diplomatic immunity from civil jurisdiction to evade a legal obligation and that such conduct could call into question the continued acceptability in the UK of a particular diplomat.[267]

Article 37 provides that the members of a family of a diplomatic agent forming part of his household[268] shall enjoy the privileges and immunities specified in articles 29 to 36 if not nationals of the receiving state. Members of the administrative and technical staff (and their households) if not nationals or permanent residents of the receiving state may similarly benefit from articles 29–35, except that the article 31(1) immunities do not extend beyond acts performed in the course of their duties, while members of the service staff, who are not nationals or permanent residents of the receiving state benefit from immunity regarding acts performed in the course of official duties.[269]

Immunities and privileges start from the moment the person enters the territory of the receiving state on proceeding to take up his post or if already in the territory from the moment of official notification under article 39.[270]

---

88 AJIL, 1994, p. 312. Note that the UK has stated that persistent failure by diplomats to respect parking regulations and to pay fixed penalty parking notices 'will call into question their continued acceptability as members of diplomatic mission in London', UKMIL, 63 BYIL, 1992, p. 700.

[264] See *Intpro Properties (UK) Ltd v. Sauvel* [1983] 2 All ER 495; 64 ILR, p. 384. In the *Deputy Registrar* case, 94 ILR, pp. 308, 311, it was held that article 31(1) q was declaratory of customary international law. In *Hildebrend v. Champagne*, 82 ILR, p. 121, it was held this provision did not cover the situation where a claim was made for payment for charges under a lease.

[265] See *Portugal v. Goncalves*, 82 ILR, p. 115. Note that once a person ceases to be a diplomat, his immunity from jurisdiction is lost, see e.g. *Empson v. Smith* [1965] 2 All ER 881; 41 ILR, p. 407 and *Shaw v. Shaw* [1979] 3 All ER 1; 78 ILR, p. 483. See also Y. Dinstein, 'Diplomatic Immunity from Jurisdiction *Ratione Materiae*', 15 ICLQ, 1966, p. 76.

[266] See UKMIL, 58 BYIL, 1987, p. 549.

[267] Annex F, reproducing a memorandum dated February 1985, *ibid.*, p. 558. See Annex F of the 1992 Memorandum, UKMIL, 63 BYIL, 1992, p. 698.

[268] See Brown, 'Diplomatic Immunity', pp. 63–6.

[269] Customary law prior to the Vienna Convention was most unclear on immunities of such junior diplomatic personnel and it was recognised that these provisions in article 37 constituted a development in such rules, see e.g. Denza, *Diplomatic Law*, pp. 226–33 and *Yearbook of the ILC*, 1958, vol. II, pp. 101–2. See also *S. v. India*, 82 ILR, p. 13.

[270] See also article 10.

In *R* v. *Governor of Pentonville Prison, ex parte Teja*,[271] Lord Parker noted that it was fundamental to the claiming of diplomatic immunity that the diplomatic agent 'should have been in some form accepted or received by this country'.[272] This view was carefully interpreted by the Court of Appeal in *R* v. *Secretary of State for the Home Department, ex parte Bagga*[273] in the light of the facts of the former case so that as Parker LJ held if a person already in the country is employed as a secretary, for example, at an embassy, nothing more than notification is required before that person would be entitled to immunities. While it had been held in *R* v. *Lambeth Justices, ex parte Yusufu*[274] that article 39 in the words of Watkins LJ provided 'at most some temporary immunity between entry and notification to a person who is without a diplomat', the court in *Bagga* disagreed strongly.[275] Immunity clearly did not depend upon notification and acceptance,[276] but under article 39 commenced upon entry. Article 40 provides for immunity where the person is in the territory in transit between his home state and a third state to which he has been posted.[277] Where, however, a diplomat is in a state which is neither the receiving state nor a state of transit between his state and the receiving state, there will be no immunity.[278] Immunities and privileges normally cease when the person leaves the country or on expiry of a reasonable period in which to do so.[279] However, by article 39(2) there would be continuing immunity with regard to those acts that were performed in the exercise of his functions as a member of the mission. It follows from this formulation that immunity would not continue for a person leaving the receiving state for any act which was performed outside of the exercise of his functions as a member of a diplomatic mission even though he was immune from prosecution at the time. This was the view taken by the US Department of State with regard to an incident where the ambassador of Papua New Guinea was responsible for a serious automobile accident involving damage to five cars and injuries to two persons.[280] The ambassador was withdrawn from the US and assurances sought by Papua New Guinea that any criminal investigation of the incident or indictment of the former ambassador under US domestic law would be quashed were rejected. The US refused to

---

[271] [1971] 2 QB 274; 52 ILR, p. 368. [272] *Ibid.*, p. 282; 52 ILR, p. 373.
[273] [1991] 1 QB 485; 88 ILR, p. . 404. [274] [1985] Crim. LR 510; 88 ILR, p. 323.
[275] [1991] 1 QB 485, 498; 88 ILR, pp. 404, 412.
[276] *Ibid.*, 499; 88 ILR, p. 413, 'save possibly in the case of a head of mission or other person of diplomatic rank', *ibid.*
[277] See Brown, 'Diplomatic Immunity', p. 59 and *Bergman* v. *de Sieyès*, 170 F.2d 360 (1948). See also *R* v. *Governor of Pentonville Prison, ex parte Teja* [1971] 2 QB 274; 52 ILR, p. 368. Note that such immunity only applies to members of his family if they were accompanying him or travelling separately to join him or return to their country, *Vafadar*, 82 ILR, p. 97.
[278] See e.g. *Public Prosecutor* v. *JBC*, 94 ILR, p. 339.
[279] Article 39, and see *Shaw* v. *Shaw* [1979] 3 All ER 1; 78 ILR, p. 483.
[280] See 81 AJIL, 1987, p. 937.

accept the view that international law precluded the prosecution of the former diplomat for non-official acts committed during his period of accreditation.[281] Although a state under section 4 of the State Immunity Act of 1978 is subject to the local jurisdiction with respect to contracts of employment made or wholly or partly to be performed in the UK, section 16(1)a provides that this is not to apply to proceedings concerning the employment of the members of a mission within the meaning of the Vienna Convention[282] and this was reaffirmed in *Sengupta* v. *Republic of India*,[283] a case concerning a clerk employed at the Indian High Commission in London.[284]

Waiver of immunity

By article 32, the sending state[285] may waive the immunity from jurisdiction of diplomatic agents and others possessing immunity under the Convention. Such waiver must be express.[286] Where a person with immunity initiates proceedings, he cannot claim immunity in respect of any counterclaim directly connected with the principal claim.[287] Waiver of immunity from jurisdiction in respect of civil or administrative proceedings is not to be taken to imply waiver from immunity in respect of the execution of the judgment, for which a separate waiver is necessary.

In general, waiver of immunity is unusual, especially in criminal cases.[288] In a memorandum entitled *Department of State Guidance for Law Enforcement Officers With Regard to Personal Rights and Immunities of Foreign Diplomatic and Consular Personnel*[289] the point is made that waiver of immunity does not 'belong' to the individual concerned, but is for the benefit of the sending state. While waiver of immunity in the face of criminal charges is not common, 'it is routinely sought and occasionally granted'. However,

---

[281] See also the *Tabatabai* case, 80 ILR, p. 388; *US* v. *Guinand*, 688 F Supp 774 (1988); 99 ILR, p. 117 and *Empson* v. *Smith* [1965] 2 All ER 881; 41 ILR, p. 407.

[282] Or to members of a consular post within the meaning of the 1963 Consular Relations Conventions enacted by the Consular Relations Act of 1968.   [283] 64 ILR, p. 352.

[284] Diplomatic agents are also granted exemptions from certain taxes and customs duties. However this does not apply to indirect taxes normally incorporated in the price paid; taxes on private immovable property in the receiving state unless held on behalf of the sending state for purposes of the mission; various estate, succession or inheritance duties; taxes on private income having its source in the receiving state; charges for specific services, and various registration, court and record fees with regard to immovable property other than mission premises, see article 34 of the Vienna Convention. See also *UK Memorandum*, p. 693.   [285] See Denza, *Diplomatic Law*, p. 184.

[286] See e.g. *Public Prosecutor* v. *Orhan Olmez*, 87 ILR, p. 212.

[287] See e.g. *High Commissioner for India* v. *Ghosh* [1960] 1 QB 134; 28 ILR, p. 150.

[288] See McClanahan, *Diplomatic Immunity*, p. 137, citing in addition an incident where the husband of an official of the US embassy in London was suspected of gross indecency with a minor, where immunity was not waived, but the person concerned was returned to the US.   [289] Reproduced in 27 ILM, 1988, pp. 1617, 1633.

Zambia speedily waived the immunity of an official at its London embassy
suspected of drugs offences in 1985.[290]

In *Fayed* v. *Al-Tajir*,[291] the Court of Appeal referred to an apparent
waiver of immunity by an ambassador made in pleadings by way of
defence. Kerr LJ correctly noted that both under international and
English law, immunity was the right of the sending state and that therefore 'only the sovereign can waive the immunity of its diplomatic representatives. They cannot do so themselves.'[292] It was also pointed out that
the defendant's defence filed in the proceedings brought against him was
not an appropriate vehicle for waiver of immunity by a state.[293] In *A
Company* v. *Republic of X*,[294] Saville J noted that whether or not there was
a power to waive article 22 immunities (and he was unconvinced that
there existed such a power), no mere *inter partes* agreement could bind the
state to such a waiver, but only an undertaking or consent given to the
Court itself at the time when the Court is asked to exercise jurisdiction
over or in respect of the subject matter of the immunities. In view of
the principle that immunities adhere to the state and not the individual
concerned, such waiver must be express and performed clearly by the
state as such.

The Vienna Convention on Consular Relations 1963[295]

Consuls represent their state in many administrative ways, for instance, by
issuing visas and passports and generally promoting the commercial interests of their state. They are based not only in the capitals of receiving states,
but also in the more important provincial cities. However, their political
functions are few and they are accordingly not permitted the same degree
of immunity from jurisdiction as diplomatic agents. Consuls must possess a
commission from the sending state and the authorisation *(exequatur)* of a
receiving state.[296] They are entitled to the same exemption from taxes and
customs duties as diplomats.

Article 31 emphasises that consular premises are inviolable and may
not be entered by the authorities of the receiving state without consent.
Like diplomatic premises, they must be protected against intrusion or

[290] McClanahan, *Diplomatic Immunity*, pp. 156–7.   [291] [1987] 2 All ER 396.
[292] *Ibid.*, p. 411.   [293] *Ibid.*, pp. 408 (Mustill LJ) and 411–12 (Kerr LJ).
[294] [1990] 2 Lloyd's Rep 520, 524; 87 ILR, pp. 412, 416, citing *Kahan* v. *Pakistan Federation*
[1951] 2 KB 1003; 18 ILR, p. 210.
[295] See e.g. L. T. Lee, *Consular Law and Practice*, 2nd edn, Durham, 1991; Lee, *Vienna
Convention on Consular Relations*, Durham, 1966, and *Satow's Guide*, Book III. See also
Oppenheim's International Law, pp. 1142 *et seq.* and *Third US Restatement of Foreign Relations
Law*, pp. 474 *et seq.* The International Court in the *Iran* case stated that this Convention
codified the law on consular relations, ICJ Reports, 1980, pp. 3, 24; 61 ILR, pp. 504, 550.
See also the Consular Relations Act 1968.   [296] Articles 10, 11 and 12.

impairment of dignity, and similar immunities exist with regard to archives and documents[297] and exemptions from taxes.[298]

Article 41 provides that consular officers may not be arrested or detained except in the case of a grave crime and following a decision by the competent judicial authority. If, however, criminal proceedings are instituted against a consul, he must appear before the competent authorities. The proceedings are to be conducted in a manner that respects his official position and minimises the inconvenience to the exercise of consular functions. Under article 43 their immunity from jurisdiction is restricted in both criminal and civil matters to acts done in the official exercise of consular functions.[299] In *Koeppel and Koeppel* v. *Federal Republic of Nigeria*,[300] for example, it was held that the provision of refuge by the Nigerian Consul-General to a Nigerian national was an act performed in the exercise of a consular function within the meaning of article 43 and thus attracted consular immunity.

The Convention on Special Missions 1969[301]

In many cases, states will send out special or *ad hoc* missions to particular countries to deal with some defined issue in addition to relying upon the permanent staffs of the diplomatic and consular missions. In such circumstances, these missions, whether purely technical or politically important, may rely on certain immunities which are basically derived from the Vienna Conventions by analogy with appropriate modifications. By article 8, the sending state must let the host state know of the size and composition of the mission, while according to article 17 the mission must be sited in a place agreed by the states concerned or in the Foreign Ministry of the receiving state.

By article 31 members of special missions have no immunity with respect to claims arising from an accident caused by a vehicle, used outside the official functions of the person involved and by article 27 only such freedom of movement and travel as is necessary for the performance of the functions of the special mission is permitted.

The question of special missions was discussed in the *Tabatabai* case before a series of German courts.[302] The Federal Supreme Court noted that

---

[297] Article 33.   [298] Article 32.
[299] See e.g. *Princess Zizianoff* v. *Kahn and Bigelow*, 4 ILR, p. 384. See generally as to consular functions, DUSPIL, 1979, pp. 655 *et seq*. Note that waiver of consular immunities under article 45, in addition to being express, must also be in writing.
[300] 704 F Supp 521 (1989); 99 ILR, p. 121.
[301] See e.g. Hardy, *Modern Diplomatic Law*, p. 89 and *Oppenheim's International Law*, pp. 1125 *et seq*. The Convention came into force in June 1985.
[302] See 80 ILR, p. 388. See also Böckslaff and Koch, 'The Tabatabai Case: The Immunity of Special Envoys and the Limits of Judicial Review', 25 *German Yearbook of International Law*, 1982, p. 539.

the Convention had not yet come into force and that there were conflicting views as to the extent to which it reflected existing customary law. However, it was clear that there was a customary rule of international law which provided that an *ad hoc* envoy, charged with a special political mission by the sending state, may be granted immunity by individual agreement with the host state for that mission and its associated status and that therefore such envoys could be placed on a par with members of the permanent missions of states.[303] The concept of immunity protected not the diplomat as a person, but rather the mission to be carried out by that person on behalf of the sending state. The question thus turned on whether there had been a sufficiently specific special mission agreed upon by the states concerned, which the court found in the circumstances.[304]

The Vienna Convention on the Representation of States in their Relations with International Organisations of a Universal Character 1975[305]

This treaty applies with respect to the representation of states in any international organisation of a universal character, irrespective of whether or not there are diplomatic relations between the sending and the host states.

There are many similarities between this Convention and the 1961 Vienna Convention. By article 30, for example, diplomatic staff enjoy complete immunity from criminal jurisdiction, and immunity from civil and administrative jurisdiction in all cases, save for the same exceptions noted in article 31 of the 1961 Convention. Administrative, technical and service staff are in the same position as under the latter treaty (article 36).

The mission premises are inviolable and exempt from taxation by the host state, while its archives, documents and correspondence are equally inviolable.

The Convention has received an unenthusiastic welcome, primarily because of the high level of immunities it provides for on the basis of a controversial analogy with diplomatic agents of missions.[306] The range of immunities contrasts with the general situation under existing conventions such as the Convention on the Privileges and Immunities of the United Nations 1946.[307]

---

[303] 80 ILR, pp. 388, 419.   [304] *Ibid.*, p. 420.
[305] See e.g. Fennessy, 'The 1975 Vienna Convention on the Representation of States in their Relations with International Organisations of a Universal Character', 70 AJIL, 1976, p. 62.
[306] It should be noted that among those states abstaining in the vote adopting the Convention were France, the US, Switzerland, Austria, Canada and the UK, all states that host the headquarters of important international organisations, see Fennessy, '1975 Vienna Convention', p. 62.
[307] See in particular article IV. See also for a similar approach in the Convention on the Privileges and Immunities of the Specialised Agencies 1947, article V.

The immunities of international organisations

As far as customary rules are concerned the position is far from clear and the position is usually dealt with by means of a treaty, providing such immunities to the international institution sited on the territory of the host state as are regarded as functionally necessary for the fulfilment of its objectives.

Probably the most important example is the General Convention on the Privileges and Immunities of the United Nations of 1946, which sets out the immunities of the United Nations and its personnel and emphasises the inviolability of its premises, archives and documents.[308]

Internationally protected persons

The 1973 Convention on the Prevention and Punishment of Crimes against Internationally Protected Persons, including Diplomatic Agents came into force in 1977. It seeks to protect heads of state or government, foreign ministers abroad, state representatives and officials of international organisations from the offences of murder, kidnapping or other attack upon their person or liberty.[309]

---

[308] See further, *infra*, Chapter 21, p. 923. See as to the privileges and immunities of foreign armed forces, including the NATO Status of Forces Agreement, 1951, which provides for a system of concurrent jurisdiction, S. Lazareff, *Status of Military Forces under Current International Law*, 1971; I. Brownlie, *Principles of Public International Law*, 4th edn, Oxford, 1990, pp. 369 *et seq.* and J. Woodliffe, *The Peacetime Use of Foreign Military Installations under Modern International Law*, Dordrecht, 1992.

[309] See further *supra* p. 474. It is also the case that immunities akin or analogous to diplomatic immunities will be granted in particular circumstances as for example, UN General Assembly resolutions 22 C(I) and 90(I), 1946, on the Privileges and Immunities of the International Court of Justice and the immunities granted to members of the European Commission and the European Court of Human Rights, see the Second and Fourth Protocols (1956 and 1961 respectively) to the General Agreement on Privileges and Immunities of the Council of Europe, 1950. See also the Memorandum of Understanding on the European Union Administration of Mostar, 1994, which provides, for example, in article 19 for the EU Administrator and EU members of the administration to be granted by the receiving party (i.e. Bosnia and Herzegovina), 'during their mission, mutatis mutandis, the privileges and immunities of diplomatic agents provided for in the Vienna Convention on Diplomatic Relations'.

CHAPTER 14

STATE RESPONSIBILITY

State responsibility is a fundamental principle of international law, arising out of the nature of the international legal system and the doctrines of state sovereignty and equality of states. It provides that whenever one state commits an internationally unlawful act against another state, international responsibility is established between the two. A breach of an international obligation gives rise to a requirement for reparation.[1] Accordingly, one is in the main dealing with a set of principles concerned with second-order issues, in other words the procedural and other consequences flowing from a breach of a substantive rule of international law.[2] In addition to the wide range of state practice in this area, the International Law Commission has been working extensively on this topic. In 1975 it took a decision for the draft articles on state responsibility to be divided into three parts: Part I to deal with the origin of international responsibility, Part II to deal with the content, forms and degrees of international responsibility and Part III to deal with the settlement of disputes and the implementation of international responsibility.[3] Part I of the Draft Articles was provisionally adopted by the Commission in 1980 and work commenced on Part II.[4] Several articles have been provisionally

---

[1] See generally, C. Eagleton, *The Responsibility of States in International Law*, New York, 1928; *International Law of State Responsibility for Injuries to Aliens* (ed. R. B. Lillich), Charlottesville, 1983; R. B. Lillich, 'Duties of States Regarding the Civil Rights of Aliens', 161 HR, p. 329 and Lillich, *The Human Rights of Aliens in Contemporary International Law*, Charlottesville, 1984; I. Brownlie, *System of the Law of Nations: State Responsibility*, Part I, Oxford, 1983; B. Cheng, *General Principles of Law as Applied by International Courts and Tribunals*, London, 1953; *United Nations Codification of State Responsibility* (eds. M. Spinedi and B. Simma), New York, 1987; Société Français de Droit International, *La Responsibilité dans le Système International*, Paris, 1991; S. Rosenne, *The ILC's Draft Articles on State Responsibility*, Dordrecht, 1991 and B. Stern, 'La Responsibilité Internationale Aujourd'hui ... Demain...' in *Mélanges Apollis*, Paris, 1992. See also Nguyen Quoc Dinh, P. Daillier and A. Pellet, *Droit International Public*, 5th edn, Paris, 1994, p. 729 and *Oppenheim's International Law* (eds. R. Y. Jennings and A. D. Watts), 9th edn, London, 1992, Chapter 4.

[2] The issue of state responsibility for injuries caused by lawful activities will be noted in Chapter 15.

[3] *Yearbook of the ILC*, 1975, vol. II, pp. 55–9. See also P. Allott, 'State Responsibility and the Unmaking of International Law', 29 *Harvard International Law Journal*, 1988, p. 1.

[4] *Yearbook of the ILC*, 1980, vol. II, part 2, pp. 30 *et seq.*

adopted.[5] Work has also started on Part III concerning peaceful settlement of disputes.[6]

The nature of state responsibility

The essential characteristics of responsibility hinge upon certain basic factors. First, the existence of an international legal obligation in force as between two particular states; secondly, that there has occurred an act or omission which violates that obligation and which is imputable to the state responsible, and finally that loss or damage has resulted from the unlawful act or omission.[7]

These requirements have been made clear in a number of leading cases. In the *Spanish Zone of Morocco* claims,[8] Judge Huber emphasised that:

> responsibility is the necessary corollary of a right. All rights of an international character involve international responsibility. Responsibility results in the duty to make reparation if the obligation in question is not met.[9]

and in the *Chorzów Factory* case,[10] the Permanent Court of International Justice said that:

> it is a principle of international law, and even a greater conception of law, that any breach of an engagement involves an obligation to make reparation.

Article 1 of the International Law Commission's Draft Articles on State Responsibility reiterates the general rule that every internationally wrongful act of a state entails responsibility, while article 2 emphasises that every state is subject to the possibility of being held to have committed an internationally wrongful act entailing its international responsibility. These basic reaffirmations on the foundation of state responsibility are reinforced by two further articles. Article 3 provides that there is an internationally wrongful act of a state when

> (a) conduct consisting of an action or omission is attributable to the state under international law; and
> (b) that conduct constitutes a breach of an international obligation of the state.[11]

---

[5] See e.g. *Yearbook of the ILC*, 1985, vol. II, Part 2, pp. 35 *et seq.*; Report of the International Law Commission, 1993, A/48/10, pp. 132 *et seq.* and *ibid.*, 1995, A/50/10, pp. 91 *et seq.* See also the various reports by the Special Rapporteurs as detailed *ibid.*

[6] *Ibid.*, pp. 173 *et seq.*

[7] See e.g. H. Mosler, *The International Society as a Legal Community*, Dordrecht, 1980, p. 157, and E. Jiménez de Aréchaga, 'International Responsibility', in *Manual of Public International Law* (ed. M. Sørensen), London, 1968, pp. 531, 534.

[8] 2 RIAA, p. 615 (1923); 2 ILR, p. 157.   [9] *Ibid.*, p. 641.

[10] PCIJ, Series A, no. 17, 1928, p. 29; 4 ILR, p. 258. See also the *Corfu Channel* case, ICJ Reports, pp. 4, 23; 16 ILR, p. 155.

[11] See *Yearbook of the ILC*, 1976, vol. II, pp. 75 *et seq.*

It is, of course, international law that determines what constitutes an internationally unlawful act, irrespective of any provisions of municipal law.[12] The general rules relating to responsibility are, as noted, second-level rules in that, while they seek to determine the consequences of a breach of those rules of international law stipulating standards of behaviour, they do not in themselves concern the content of the latter principle.[13]

The issue of the relationship between the rules of state responsibility and those relating to the law of treaties arose in the *Rainbow Warrior* Arbitration between France and New Zealand in 1990.[14] The arbitration followed the incident in 1985 in which French agents destroyed the vessel *Rainbow Warrior* in harbour in New Zealand. The UN Secretary-General was asked to mediate and his ruling in 1986[15] provided *inter alia* for French payment to New Zealand and for the transfer of two French agents to a French base in the Pacific, where they were to stay for three years and not to leave without the mutual consent of both states.[16] However, both the agents were repatriated to France before the expiry of the three years for various reasons, without the consent of New Zealand. The 1986 Agreement contained an arbitration clause and this was invoked by New Zealand. The argument put forward by New Zealand centred upon the breach of a treaty obligation by France, whereas that state argued that only the law of state responsibility was relevant and that concepts of *force majeure* and distress exonerated it from liability.

The arbitral tribunal decided that the law relating to treaties was relevant, but that:

> the legal consequences of a breach of a treaty, including the determination of the circumstances that may exclude wrongfulness (and render the breach only apparent) and the appropriate remedies for breach, are subjects that belong to the customary law of state responsibility.[17]

It was noted that international law did not distinguish between contractual and tortious responsibility, so that any violation by a state of any obligation of whatever origin gives rise to state responsibility and consequently to the duty of reparation.[18]

The Arbitration Commission on Yugoslavia also addressed the issue of the relationship between state responsibility and other branches of international law in Opinion No. 13, when asked a question as to whether any amounts due in respect of war damage might affect the distribution of assets

[12] Article 4. See generally *Yearbook of the ILC*, 1979, vol. II, pp. 90 *et seq.* and *ibid.*, 1980, vol. II, pp. 14 *et seq.* [13] See *Yearbook of the ILC*, 1973, vol. II, pp. 169–70. [14] 82 ILR, p. 499. [15] See 81 AJIL, 1987, p. 325 and 74 ILR, p. 256. [16] See also the Agreement between France and New Zealand of 9 July 1986, 74 ILR, p. 274. [17] *Ibid.*, p. 551. [18] *Ibid.* See further *infra* p. 554.

and debts in the succession process affecting the successor states of the Former Yugoslavia. The Commission, in producing a negative answer, emphasised that the question of war damage was one that fell within the sphere of state responsibility, while the rules relating to state succession fell into a separate area of international law. Accordingly, the two issues had to be separately decided.[19]

A distinction has been drawn between international crimes and international delicts within the context of internationally unlawful acts. Article 19 of the ILC Draft provides that all breaches of international obligations are internationally wrongful acts.

However, an internationally wrongful act which results from the breach by a state of:

> an international obligation so essential for the protection of fundamental interests of the international community that its breach is recognised as a crime by that community as a whole

constitutes an international crime. All other internationally wrongful acts are international delicts, according to the Draft.[20] Article 19 gives some examples of situations that may give rise to international crimes. These include aggression, the establishment or maintenance by force of colonial domination, slavery, genocide, apartheid and massive pollution of the atmosphere or of the seas. The question as to whether states can be criminally responsible is highly controversial. Brownlie, for example, argues that the concept is of no legal value and cannot be justified in principle. Although of use in the political and moral spheres, it is futile in the legal sphere. State responsibility was limited to the obligation to compensate. The problem of exacting penal sanctions from states, while in principle possible, could only be creative of instability.[21] However, others have argued that particularly since 1945, the attitude towards certain crimes by states has altered so as to bring it within the realm of international law.[22] The Rapporteur in his commentary to article 19 pointed to three specific changes since 1945 in this context; first, the development of the concept of *jus cogens* as a set of principles from which no derogation is permitted;[23] secondly, the rise of individ-

---

[19] 96 ILR, pp. 726, 728.

[20] See E. Mohr, 'The ILC's Distinction between "International Crimes" and "International Delicts" and Its Implications' in *UN Codification*, p. 115 and K. Marek, 'Criminalising State Responsibility', 14 *Revue Belge de Droit International*, 1978–9, p. 460.

[21] *International Law and the Use of Force by States*, Oxford, 1963, pp. 150–4. But cf. *Oppenheim's International Law*, pp. 533 *et seq*. See also G. Gilbert, 'The Criminal Responsibility of States', 39 ICLQ, 1990, p. 345. As far as individual criminal responsibility is concerned, see *supra*, Chapter 5, p. 184 and Chapter 12, p. 471.

[22] See e.g. E. Jiménez de Aréchaga, 'International Law in the Past Third of the Century', 159 HR, p. 1.

[23] See article 53 of the Vienna Convention on the Law of Treaties 1969, *supra*, Chapter 3, p. 97 and *infra*, Chapter 16, p. 665.

ual criminal responsibility directly under international law; and thirdly, the UN Charter and its provision for enforcement action[24] against a state in the event of threats to or breaches of the peace or acts of aggression.[25] However, there are serious problems with regard to state criminal responsibility and the issue is unlikely to be easily resolved.[26]

A rather different distinction in the area of responsibility was drawn in the *Barcelona Traction* case,[27] where the Court referred to the obligations of a state towards the international community as a whole as distinct from those *vis-à-vis* another state in the field of diplomatic protection. In the former case, obligations *erga omnes* are involved and aggression and human rights violations were instanced. Although the two distinctions to some extent overlap, the latter case was not concerned with the criminal liability of states as such but rather with the question of the requisite legal interest and standing of states in the particular situation.[28]

The question of fault[29]

There are contending theories as to whether responsibility of the state for unlawful acts or omissions is strict or whether it is necessary to show some fault or intention on the part of the officials concerned. The principle of objective responsibility (the so-called 'risk' theory) maintains that the liability of the state is strict. Once an unlawful act has taken place, which has caused injury and which has been committed by an agent of the state, that state will be responsible in international law to the state suffering the damage irrespective of good or bad faith. To be contrasted with this

---

[24] See *infra*, Chapter 20, p. 865.   [25] *Yearbook of the ILC*, 1976, vol. II, pp. 102–5.
[26] See also A/C.6/SR. 17, 14 October 1976. Note that the Special Rapporteur has proposed dealing with the consequences of international delicts and international crimes separately, see S. McCaffrey, 'The Forty-first Session of the International Law Commission', 83 AJIL, 1989, pp. 937, 943. See also *infra*, p. 553. Note also the Report of the International Law Commission, 1994, A/49/10, pp. 329 *et seq.* and *ibid.*, 1995, A/50/10, pp. 93 *et seq.*
[27] ICJ Reports, 1970, pp. 3, 32; 46 ILR, p. 178, 206.
[28] Note also the point made by the International Court of Justice in the *Namibia* case, ICJ Reports, 1971, pp. 17, 54; 42 ILR, pp. 2, 44, that 'Physical control of a territory and not sovereignty or legitimacy of title, is the basis of state liability for acts affecting other states.' In *Loizidou* v. *Turkey*, Preliminary Objections, European Court of Human Rights, Series A, No. 310, 1995, p. 20, the Court noted that bearing in mind the object and purpose of the European Convention on Human Rights, 'the responsibility of a contracting party may also arise when as a consequence of military action – whether lawful or unlawful – it exercises effective control of an area outside its national territory. The obligation to secure, in such an area, the rights and freedoms set out in the Convention, derives from the fact of such control whether it be exercised directly, through its armed forces, or through a subordinate local administration.'
[29] See e.g. H. Lauterpacht, *Private Law Sources and Analogies of International Law*, Cambridge, 1927, pp. 135–43; I. Brownlie, *Principles of Public International Law*, 4th edn, Oxford, 1990, pp. 433–41 and *System*, pp. 38–46 and Aréchaga, 'International', pp. 534–40. See also J. G. Starke, 'Imputability in International Delinquencies', 19 BYIL, 1938, p. 104, and Cheng, *General Principles*, pp. 218–32.

approach is the subjective responsibility concept (the 'fault' theory) and this emphasises that an element of intentional (*dolus*) or negligent (*culpa*) conduct on the part of the person concerned is necessary before his state can be rendered liable for any injury caused.

The relevant cases and academic opinions are divided on this question, although the majority tend towards the strict liability, objective theory of responsibility.

In the *Neer* claim[30] in 1926, an American superintendent of a Mexican mine was shot. The USA, on behalf of his widow and daughter, claimed damages because of the lackadaisical manner in which the Mexican authorities pursued their investigations. The General Claims Commission dealing with the matter disallowed the claim, in applying the objective test.

In the *Caire* claim,[31] the French–Mexican Claims Commission had to consider the case of a French citizen shot by Mexican soldiers for failing to supply them with 5, 000 Mexican dollars. Verzijl, the presiding commissioner, held that Mexico was responsible for the injury caused in accordance with the objective responsibility doctrine, that is 'the responsibility for the acts of the officials or organs of a state, which may devolve upon it even in the absence of any "fault" of its own'.[32]

A leading case adopting the subjective approach is the *Home Missionary Society* claim[33] in 1920 between Britain and the United States. In this case, the imposition of a 'hut tax' in the protectorate of Sierra Leone triggered off a local uprising in which Society property was damaged and missionaries killed. The tribunal dismissed the claim of the Society (presented by the US) and noted that it was established in international law that no government was responsible for the acts of rebels where it itself was guilty of no breach of good faith or of no negligence in suppressing the revolt.

It should, therefore, be noted that the view expressed in this case is concerned with a specific area of the law, viz. the question of state responsibility for the acts of rebels. Whether one can analogise from this generally is open to doubt.

In the *Corfu Channel* case,[34] the International Court appeared to tend towards the fault theory[35] by saying that:

it cannot be concluded from the mere fact of the control exercised by a state over its territory and waters that that state necessarily knew, or ought to have known, of any unlawful act perpetrated therein, nor yet that it necessarily

[30] 4 RIAA, p. 60 (1926); 3 ILR, p. 213.   [31] 5 RIAA, p. 516 (1929); 5 ILR, p. 146.
[32] *Ibid.*, pp. 529–31. See also *The Jessie*, 6 RIAA, p. 57 (1921); 1 ILR, p. 175.
[33] 6 RIAA, p. 42 (1920); 1 ILR, p. 173.   [34] ICJ Reports, 1949, p. 4; 16 ILR, p. 155.
[35] See e.g. *Oppenheim's International Law*, p. 509.

knew, or should have known, the authors. This fact, by itself and apart from other circumstances, neither involves *prima facie* responsibility nor shifts the burden of proof.[36]

On the other hand, the Court emphasised that the fact of exclusive territorial control had a bearing upon the methods of proof available to establish the knowledge of that state as to the events in question. Because of the difficulties of presenting direct proof of facts giving rise to responsibility, the victim state should be allowed a more liberal recourse to inferences of fact and circumstantial evidence.[37]

However, it must be pointed out that the Court was concerned with Albania's knowledge of the laying of mines[38] and the question of *prima facie* responsibility for *any* unlawful act committed within the territory of the state concerned, irrespective of attribution, raises different issues. It cannot be taken as proof of the acceptance of the fault theory.

It is suggested that doctrine and practice support the objective theory and that this is right, particularly in view of the proliferation of state organs and agencies.[39]

Imputability[40]

Imposing upon the state absolute liability wherever an official is involved encourages that state to exercise greater control over its various departments and representatives. It also stimulates moves towards complying with objective standards of conduct in international relations.

State responsibility covers many fields. It includes unlawful acts or omissions directly committed by the state and directly affecting other states, for instance, the breach of a treaty, the violation of the territory of another state, or damage to state property. An example of the latter heading is provided by the incident in 1955 when Bulgarian fighter planes shot down an Israeli civil aircraft of its state airline, El Al.[41] Another example of state responsibility is illustrated by the *Nicaragua* case,[42] where the International Court of Justice

---

[36] ICJ Reports, 1949, pp. 4, 18; 16 ILR, p. 157. Cf. Judges Krylov and Ecer, *ibid.*, pp. 71–2 and 127–8. See also Judge Azevedo, *ibid.*, p. 85. [37] *Ibid.*
[38] See Brownlie, *Principles*, pp. 442–4.
[39] The question of intention is to be distinguished from the problem of causality, i.e. whether the act or omission in question actually caused the particular loss or damage, see e.g. the *Lighthouses* case, 23 ILR, p. 352.
[40] See e.g. *Yearbook of the ILC*, 1973, vol. II, p. 189. See also Brownlie, *Principles*, p. 435, and *System*, pp. 36–7 and Chapter 7.
[41] See *supra*, Chapter 10, p. 377. See also the incident where a Soviet fighter plane crashed in Belgium. The USSR accepted responsibility for the loss of life and damage that resulted and compensation was paid, see 91 ILR, p. 287 and J. Salmon, 'Chute sur le Territoire Belge d'un Avion Militaire Sovietique de 4 Juillet 1989, Problèmes de Responsabilité', *RBDI*, 1990, p. 510.
[42] *Nicaragua* v. *United States*, ICJ Reports, 1986, p. 14; 76 ILR, p. 349.

548 INTERNATIONAL LAW

found that acts imputable to the US included the laying of mines in Nicaraguan internal or territorial waters and certain attacks on Nicaraguan ports, oil installations and a naval base by its agents.[43] In the *Corfu Channel* case,[44] Albania was held responsible for the consequences of mine-laying in its territorial waters on the basis of knowledge possessed by that state as to the presence of such mines, even though there was no finding as to who had actually laid the mines. In the *Rainbow Warrior* incident,[45] the UN Secretary-General mediated a settlement in which New Zealand received *inter alia* a sum of $7 million for the violation of its sovereignty which occurred when that vessel was destroyed by French agents in New Zealand.[46] The state may also incur responsibility with regard to the activity of its officials in injuring a national of another state, and this activity need not be one authorised by the authorities of the state.

The doctrine depends on the link that exists between the state and the person or persons actually committing the unlawful act or omission. The state as an abstract legal entity cannot, of course, in reality 'act' itself. It can only do so through authorised officials and representatives. The state is not responsible under international law for all acts performed by its nationals. If an Englishman were to attack and injure a Frenchman on holiday in London, the UK would not be held liable for the injury caused, unless the offender were, for example, a policeman or a soldier.

Since the state is responsible only for acts of its servants that are imputable or attributable to it, it becomes necessary to examine the concept of imputability.

Imputability is the legal fiction which assimilates the actions or omissions of state officials to the state itself and which renders the state liable for damage resulting to the property or person of an alien.

Article 5 of the ILC Draft Articles on State Responsibility provides that the conduct of any state organ having that status under internal law shall be considered as an act of the state concerned under international law where the organ was acting in that capacity and the precise position of that organ in the constitutional structure and hierarchy of the state is irrelevant.[47] Similarly, organs of a 'territorial governmental entity' within a state are

---

[43] Ibid., pp. 48–51 and 146–9; 76 ILR, pp. 382, 480.
[44] ICJ Reports, 1949, p. 4; 16 ILR, p. 155.
[45] See 81 AJIL, 1987, p. 325 and 74 ILR, pp. 241 *et seq.* See also *supra* p. 543.
[46] Note also the *USS Stark* incident, in which a US guided missile frigate on station in the Persian Gulf was attacked by Iraqi aircraft in May 1987. The Iraqi government agreed to pay compensation of $27 million, see 83 AJIL, 1989, pp. 561–4.
[47] Article 6. This reflects customary law, see e.g. the *Massey* case, 4 RIAA, p. 155 (1927); 4 ILR, p. 250. See also the *Salvador Commercial Company* case, 15 RIAA, p. 477 (1902). Note that the state organ concerned may be from any branch of the state, including the judiciary, see e.g. the *Sunday Times* case, European Court of Human Rights, Series A, vol. 30, 1979; 58 ILR, p. 491, and the legislature, see e.g. the *Young, James and Webster* case, *ibid.*, vol. 44, 1981; 62 ILR, p. 359.

assimilated to acts of the state, where acting in that capacity in the case in question.[48]

Article 7(2), in reaction to the proliferation of government organs and entities, notes that the conduct of an organ or of an entity not part of the formal structure of the state or a territorial governmental entity may still constitute acts of the state where internal law empowers them to exercise elements of governmental authority and they were so acting in the case in question. It is a little unclear how far this provision might extend, but the commentary to the article gives as an example the conduct of a railway company to which certain police powers have been granted.[49]

Article 9 provides that the conduct of an organ placed at the disposal of a state by another state or by an international organisation shall be considered as an act of the former state, if that organ was acting in the exercise of elements of the governmental authority of the former state. This would, for example, cover the UK Privy Council acting as the highest judicial body for certain Commonwealth countries.[50]

Ultra vires acts

An unlawful act may be imputed to the state even where it was beyond the legal capacity of the official involved, providing as Verzijl noted in the *Caire* case[51] that the officials 'have acted at least to all appearances as competent officials or organs or they must have used powers or methods appropriate to their official capacity'.

This was reaffirmed in the *Mossé* case,[52] where it was noted that:

> Even if it were admitted that . . . officials . . . had acted . . . outside the statutory limits of the competence of their service, it should not be deduced, without further ado, that the claim is not well founded. It would still be necessary to consider a question of law . . . namely whether in the international order the state should be acknowledged responsible for acts performed by officials within the apparent limits of their functions, in accordance with a line of conduct which was not entirely contrary to the instructions received.

In *Youman's* claim,[53] militia ordered to protect threatened American citizens in a Mexican town, instead joined the riot, during which the Americans

---

[48] Article 7(1). Thus, not only would communes, provinces and regions of a unitary state be concerned, see e.g. the *Heirs of the Duc de Guise* case, 13 RIAA, p. 161 (1951); 18 ILR, p. 423, but also the component states of a federal state, see e.g. the *Davy* case, 9 RIAA, p. 468 (1903), the *Janes* case, 4 RIAA, p. 86 (1925); 3 ILR, p. 218 and the *Pellat* case, 5 RIAA, p. 536 (1929); 5 ILR, p. 145. See also *Yearbook of the ILC*, 1971, vol. II, Part I, pp. 257 *et seq.*

[49] *Yearbook of the ILC*, 1974, vol. II, pp. 281–2.

[50] *Ibid.*, p. 288. See also articles 12 and 13, which in such circumstances deny the responsibility of the dispatching state or international organisation.

[51] 5 RIAA, pp. 516, 530 (1929); 5 ILR, pp. 146, 148.

[52] 13 RIAA, p. 494 (1953); 20 ILR, p. 217.   [53] 4 RIAA, p. 110 (1926); 3 ILR, p. 223.

were killed. These unlawful acts by the militia were imputed to the state of Mexico, which was found responsible by the General Claims Commission. In the *Union Bridge Company* case,[54] a British official of the Cape Government Railway mistakenly appropriated neutral property during the Boer War. It was held that there was still liability despite the honest mistake and the lack of intention on the part of the authorities to appropriate the material in question. The key was that the action was within the general scope of duty of the official.

Article 10 of the ILC Draft provides that the conduct of an organ having the capacity to exercise elements of governmental authority and having so acted is still to be considered an act of the state under international law even if, in the case in question, the organ exceeded its competence or contravened instructions.[55] This article appears to lay down an absolute rule of liability, one not limited by reference to the apparent exercise of authority and, in the context of the general acceptance of the objective theory of responsibility, is probably the correct approach.[56]

Although private individuals are not regarded as state officials so that the state is not liable for their acts, the state may be responsible for failing to exercise the control necessary to prevent such acts. This was emphasised in the *Zafiro* case[57] between Britain and America in 1925. The tribunal held the latter responsible for the damage caused by the civilian crew of a naval ship in the Philippines, since the naval officers had not adopted effective preventative measures.

Individuals

Article 8 of the ILC Draft provides that the conduct of a person or a group of persons shall also be considered as an act of the state if

(a) it is established that such person or group was in fact acting on behalf of that state; or

(b) such person or group was in fact exercising elements of the governmental authority in the absence of the official authorities and in circumstances which justified the exercise of those elements of authority.

The commentary to the article gives as examples of part (a) the crew of the *Zafiro* claim[58] and the Eichmann situation where Israelis kidnapped the war criminal in Argentina.[59]

---

[54] 6 RIAA, p. 138 (1924); 2 ILR, p. 170.   [55] See also *Yearbook of the ILC*, 1975, vol. II, p. 67.

[56] See *ibid.*, p. 69 and the *Caire* case, 5 RIAA, p. 516 (1929); 5 ILR, p. 146. See also T. Meron, 'International Responsibility of States for Unauthorised Acts of Their Officials', 33 BYIL, 1957, p. 851.

[57] 6 RIAA, p. 160 (1925); 3 ILR, p. 221. See also *re Gill*, 5 RIAA, p. 157 (1931); 6 ILR, p. 203.   [58] 6 RIAA, p. 160 (1925); 3 ILR, p. 221.

[59] See *supra*, Chapter 12, p. 472. See also the *Argoud* case, 45 ILR, p. 90 where the accused had been kidnapped in Germany and brought to France for trial.

In the *Iran* case, the International Court noted that the initial attack on the US Embassy by militants could not be imputable to Iran since they were clearly not agents or organs of the state. However, the subsequent approval of the Ayatollah Khomeini and other organs of Iran to the attack and the decision to maintain the occupation of the Embassy translated that action into a state act. The militants thus became agents of the Iranian state for whose acts the state bore international responsibility.[60] Apart from such situations, 'the conduct of a person or a group of persons not acting on behalf of the state shall not be considered as an act of the state under international law'.[61]

Mob violence, insurrections and civil wars

Where the governmental authorities have acted in good faith and without negligence, the general principle is one of non-liability for the actions of rioters or rebels causing loss or damage.[62] The state, however, is under a duty to show due diligence. Quite what is meant by this is difficult to quantify and more easily defined in the negative.[63] It should also be noted that special provisions apply to diplomatic and consular personnel.[64]

Where an insurrectional movement is successful, it will be held responsible for its activities prior to its assumption of authority. Article 15 of the ILC Draft reemphasises the rule and provides that the acts of such a movement which becomes the new government of a state shall be considered as acts of that state.[65]

The issue of the responsibility of the authorities of a state for activities that occurred prior to its coming to power was raised before the Iran–US Claims Tribunal. In *Short* v. *The Islamic Republic of Iran*,[66] the Tribunal noted that the international responsibility of a state can be engaged where the circumstances or events causing the departure of an alien are attributable to it, but that not all departures of aliens from a country in a period of political turmoil would as such be attributable to that state.[67] In the instant case, it was emphasised that at the relevant time the revolutionary movement had not yet been able to establish control over any part of Iranian territory and

---

[60] ICJ Reports, 1980, pp. 3, 34–5; 61 ILR, pp. 530, 560. See also *supra*, Chapter 13, p. 524.
[61] Article 11.
[62] See e.g. the *Home Missionary Society* case, 6 RIAA, pp. 42, 44 (1920); 1 ILR, p. 173; the *Youmans* case, 4 RIAA, p. 110 (1926); 3 ILR, p. 223 and the *Herd* case, 4 RIAA, p. 653 (1930). See also article 14 of the ILC Draft Articles on State Responsibility.
[63] E.g. Judge Huber, the *Spanish Zone of Morocco* claims, 2 RIAA, pp. 617, 642 (1925); 2 ILR, p. 157. See Brownlie, *Principles*, pp. 452–4 and the *Sambaggio* case, 10 RIAA, p. 499 (1903). See also *Yearbook of the ILC*, 1957, vol. II, pp. 121–3, and G. Schwarzenberger, *International Law*, 3rd edn, London, 1957, pp. 653 *et seq.*   [64] *Supra*, Chapter 13, p. 525.
[65] See E. M. Borchard, *The Diplomatic Protection of Citizens Abroad*, 1927, p. 241 and the *Bolivian Railway Company* case, 9 RIAA, p. 445 (1903).
[66] 16 Iran–US CTR, p. 76; 82 ILR, p. 148.   [67] *Ibid.*, p. 83; 82 ILR, pp. 159–60.

the government had demonstrated its loss of control. Additionally, the acts of supporters of a revolution cannot be attributed to the government following the success of the revolution, just as acts of supporters of an existing government are not attributable to the government. Accordingly, and since the claimant was unable to identify any agent of the revolutionary movement the actions of whom forced him to leave Iran, the claim for compensation failed.[68]

In *Yeager* v. *The Islamic Republic of Iran*,[69] the Tribunal awarded compensation for expulsion, but in this case it was held that the expulsion was carried out by the Revolutionary Guards after the success of the revolution. Although the Revolutionary Guards were not at the time an official organ of the Iranian state, it was determined that they were exercising governmental authority with the knowledge and acquiescence of the revolutionary state, making Iran liable for their acts.[70] Falling somewhat between these two cases is *Rankin* v. *The Islamic Republic of Iran*,[71] where the Tribunal held that the claimant had not proved that he had left Iran after the revolution as a result of action by the Iranian government and the Revolutionary Guards as distinct from leaving because of the general difficulties of life in that state during the revolutionary period. Thus Iranian responsibility was not engaged.

The concept of the injured state[72]

Having noted the nature of imputability and thus the identity of the responsible party in the context of an internationally wrongful act, the identity of the state that has suffered in consequence needs to be looked at. Article 5(1) of Part II of the ILC Draft provides that the 'injured state' is any state a right of which is infringed by the act of another state if such act constitutes an internationally wrongful act of that state in accordance with Part I of the Draft. Only an injured state may invoke the responsibility of the 'author' state and thus obtain compensation. Article 5(2) provides that:

> In particular 'injured state' means:
> (a) if the right infringed by the act of a state arises from a bilateral treaty, the other state party to the treaty;
> (b) if the right infringed by the act of a state arises from a judgment or other binding dispute-settlement decision of an international court or tribunal, the other state or states parties to the dispute and entitled to the benefit of that right;[73]

---

[68] *Ibid.*, p. 85; 82 ILR, p. 161.   [69] 17 Iran–US CTR, p. 92; 82 ILR, p. 178.
[70] *Ibid.*, p. 104; 82 ILR, p. 194.   [71] 17 Iran–US CTR, p. 135; 82 ILR, p. 204.
[72] See e.g. C. Annacker, 'Part Two of the International Law Commission's Draft Articles on State Responsibility', 37 German YIL, 1994, pp. 206, 214 *et seq.*
[73] Note that, e.g., article 59 of the Statute of the International Court of Justice provides that the decision of the Court 'has no binding legal force except between the parties and in respect of that particular case'.

(c) if the right infringed by the act of a state arises from a binding decision of an international organ other than an international court or tribunal, the state or states which, in accordance with the constituent instrument of the international organisation concerned, are entitled to the benefit of that right;[74]

(d) if the right infringed by the act of a state arises from a treaty provision for a third state, that third state;[75]

(e) if the right infringed by the act of a state arises from a multilateral treaty or from a rule of customary international law, any other state party to the multilateral treaty or bound by the relevant rule of customary international law, if it is established that:

(i) the right has been created or is established in its favour,

(ii) the infringement of the right by the act of a state necessarily affects the enjoyment of the rights or the performance of the obligations of the other states parties to the multilateral treaty or bound by the rule of customary law, or

(iii) the right has been created or is established for the protection of human rights and fundamental freedoms;

(f) if the right infringed by the act of a state arises from a multilateral treaty, any other state party to the multilateral treaty, if it is established that the right has been expressly stipulated in that treaty for the protection of the collective interests of the states parties thereto.[76]

It should, of course, be noted that the provisions contained in draft article 5 form a sort of safety net, in that in many cases the legal consequences of a breach of a substantive rule of international law will be laid down by that rule itself. Of especial interest in article 5(2) is the reference to multilateral treaties and to customary international law, so that in certain circumstances all states parties to the treaty or bound by the relevant rule of international customary law may be regarded as injured states, thus enabling them to claim compensation or in particular situations to take countermeasures. In the case of human rights treaties, this would occur with no further requirement. The Commentary to the Draft specifically refers to the principle of self-determination in this context.[77]

Draft article 5(3) goes furthest of all in the direction of collective responsibility. It is also probably the most controversial. It provides that if the internationally wrongful act constitutes an international crime, then the term 'injured state' means all other states. The Commentary, recognising some of the consequences that could be drawn from this, notes that the question arises as to whether all other states individually are entitled to respond to an international crime in the same manner as if their individual

---

[74] See e.g. with respect to the United Nations Security Council, *infra* Chapter 19.
[75] See also article 36 of the Vienna Convention on the Law of Treaties 1969, *infra* Chapter 16, p. 652.
[76] See *Yearbook of the ILC*, 1985, vol. II, Part 2, pp. 25–7. Draft article 5 was adopted at this session, but none of the succeeding draft articles, *ibid*. See also B. Simma, 'Bilateralism and Community Interest in the Law of State Responsibility' in *International Law at a Time of Perplexity* (ed. Y. Dinstein), Dordrecht, 1989, pp. 821, 829.   [77] *Ibid.*, p. 27.

rights were infringed by the commission of the international crime. It is emphasised that article 5(3) does not and cannot prejudice the extent of the legal consequences otherwise to be attached to the commission of an international crime. These issues are to be addressed in some of the remaining articles of Part II.[78] However, the complexity and controversy of the issue is apparent. Some of these consequential issues will doubtless underline the difficulties inherent in the notion of state criminal responsibility.[79] Many, if not all, of the relevant situations likely to arise in the context of article 5(3) would fit into the provisions of article 5(2)e.[80]

Reparation[81]

The basic principle with regard to reparation, or the remedying of a breach of an international obligation for which the state concerned is responsible was laid down in the *Chorzów Factory* case,[82] where the Court emphasised that:

> reparation must, as far as possible, wipe out all the consequences of the illegal act and re-establish the situation which would, in all probability, have existed if that act had not been committed.[83]

Restitution in kind is the obvious method of performing the reparation, since it aims to re-establish the situation which ought to exist.[84] While restitution has occurred in the past,[85] it is more rare today, if only because

[78] *Ibid.*   [79] *Supra* p. 544.
[80] It should be emphasised that draft article 5(3) makes a reference in square brackets (indicating its provisional nature) to draft articles 14 and 15, which provide that an international crime entails an obligation for all states not to recognise the legality of that situation, not to assist the 'criminal' state and to join together to carry out the above. Reference is also made to the United Nations and its regime for the maintenance of international peace and security. Note that these draft articles have not been approved by the International Law Commission.
[81] See e.g. M. Whiteman, *Damages in International Law*, 3 vols., Washington, 1937–43; F. A. Mann, 'The Consequences of an International Wrong in International and National Law', 48 BYIL, 1978, p. 1; Aréchaga, 'International Responsibility', pp. 564 *et seq.* and 'International Law' pp. 285–7. See also Cheng, *General Principles*, pp. 233 *et seq.*, Brownlie, *System*, Part VIII and C. Gray, *Judicial Remedies in International Law*, Oxford, 1987.
[82] PCIJ, Series A, No. 17, 1928, pp. 47–8. See also the *Iran* case, ICJ Reports, 1980, pp. 3, 45; 61 ILR, pp. 530, 571, where the Court held that Iran was under a duty to make reparation to the US.
[83] Note, of course, the point made in article 6 of Part II of the ILC Draft Articles, that a state whose conduct constitutes an internationally unlawful act having a continuing character is under the obligation to cease such conduct, without prejudice to the responsibility it has already incurred. See e.g. C. Derman, 'La Cessation de l'Acte Illicite', *Revue Belge de Droit International Public*, 1990 I, p. 477; C. Dominicé, 'Observations sur les Droits de l'Etat Victime d'un Fiat Internationalement Illicite' in *Droit International* (ed. P. Weil), Paris, 1982, vol. I, p. 25 and B. Graefrath, 'Responsibility and Damage Caused: Relationship between Responsibility and Damage', HR, 1984 II, pp. 19, 73 *et seq.*
[84] See e.g. Annacker, 'Part Two', pp. 221 *et seq.*
[85] See e.g. the post-1945 Peace Treaties with Hungary, Romania and Italy. See also the *Spanish Zone of Morocco* case, 2 RIAA, p. 617 (1925); 2 ILR, p. 157; the *Martini* case, 2 RIAA, p. 977 (1930); 5 ILR, p. 153; the *Palmagero Gold Fields* case, 5 RIAA, p. 298 (1931) and the

the nature of such disputes has changed. A large number of cases now involve expropriation disputes, where it is politically difficult for the state concerned to return to multinational companies expropriated property. Recognising some of these problems, article 7 of Part II of the ILC Draft Articles allows for restitution in kind, provided and to the extent that it is not materially impossible, would not involve a breach of *jus cogens*, would not involve a burden disproportionate to the benefit which the injured state would gain from restitution instead of compensation, and would not seriously jeopardise the political independence or economic stability of the injuring state whereas the injured state would not be similarly affected if it did not obtain restitution.[86] Monetary compensation is clearly of importance in reparation. It is intended to replace the value of the asset confiscated and would probably include loss of expected profits, but not more remote prospective gains.[87] Punitive damages are not usual in this context and go beyond the concept of reparation as such.[88] Monetary compensation may also be paid for non-material damage. In the *I'm Alone*[89] case, for example, a sum of $25,000 was suggested as recompense for the indignity suffered by Canada, in having a ship registered in Montreal unlawfully sunk. A further example of this is provided by the France–New Zealand Agreement of 9 July 1986, concerning the sinking of the vessel *Rainbow Warrior* by French agents in New Zealand, the second paragraph of which provided for France to pay the sum of $7 million as compensation to New Zealand for 'all the damage which it has suffered'.[90] It is clear from the context that it covered more than material damage.[91] In the subsequent arbitration in 1990, the Tribunal declared that:

> an order for the payment of monetary compensation can be made in respect of the breach of international obligations involving . . . serious moral and legal damage, even though there is no material damage.[92]

Russian Indemnity case, 11 RIAA, p. 431 (1912). Brownlie notes that in certain cases, such as the illegal possession of territory or acquisition of objects of special cultural, historical or religious significance, restitution may be the only legal remedy, *System*, p. 210 and the *Temple* case, ICJ Reports, 1962, pp. 6, 36–7; 33 ILR, pp. 48, 73.

[86] Note that articles 6 (cessation of unlawful activities); 6 bis (the forms of reparation); 7 (restitution in kind); 8 (compensation); 10 (satisfaction) and 10 bis (assurances of non-repetition) were adopted in 1993, see Report of the International Law Commission, 1993, pp. 130 *et seq.*

[87] Draft article 8(2) provides that compensation 'may include interest' and simply talks of compensation for loss of profits 'where appropriate'. See Report of the International Law Commission on the Work of its Forty-Fifth Session, A/48/10, p. 185.

[88] See generally Whiteman, *Damages,* and Aréchaga, 'International Responsibility', p. 571. See also *Yearbook of the ILC*, 1956, vol. II, pp. 211–12 and Annacker, 'Part Two', pp. 225 *et seq.*

[89] 3 RIAA, p. 1609 (1935); 7 ILR, p. 203.   [90] 74 ILR, pp. 241, 274.

[91] See the Arbitral Tribunal in the *Rainbow Warrior* case, 82 ILR, pp. 499, 574.

[92] 82 ILR, pp. 499, 575.

However, the Tribunal declined to make an order for monetary compensation, primarily since New Zealand was seeking alternative remedies.[93]

A third form of reparation is termed satisfaction. This relates to non-monetary compensation and would include official apologies, the punishment of guilty minor officials or the formal acknowledgement of the unlawful character of an act.[94] In the *Rainbow Warrior* arbitration,[95] New Zealand sought *inter alia* an Order to the French government to return its agents from France to their previous place of confinement in the Pacific as required by the original agreement of 9 July 1986. New Zealand termed this request '*restitutio in integrum*'. France argued that 'cessation' of the denounced behaviour was the appropriate terminology and remedy, although in the circumstances barred by time.[96] The Tribunal pointed to the debate in the International Law Commission on the differences between the two concepts[97] and held that the French approach was correct.[98] The obligation to end an illegal situation was not reparation but a return to the original obligation, that is cessation of the illegal conduct. However, it was held that since the primary obligation was no longer in force (in the sense that the obligation to keep the agents in the Pacific island concerned expired under the initial agreement on 22 July 1989), an order for cessation of the illegal conduct could serve no purpose.[99]

The Tribunal also pointed to the long established practice of states and international courts of using satisfaction as a remedy for the breach of an international obligation, particularly where moral or legal damage had been done directly to the state. In the circumstances of the case, it concluded that the public condemnation of France for its breaches of treaty obligations to New Zealand made by the Tribunal constituted 'appropriate satisfaction'.[100] The Tribunal also made an interesting 'Recommendation' that the two states concerned establish a fund to promote close relations between their respective citizens and additionally recommended that the French government 'make an initial contribution equivalent to $2 million to that fund'.[101] This suggestion, of course, does not constitute an order to France to pay damages, but it is a fascinating approach.

---

[93] *Ibid.* Note that article 8 of Part II of the ILC Draft, provides for compensation for any economically assessable damage sustained, which may include interest and, where appropriate, loss of profits.

[94] See Annacker, 'Part Two', pp. 230 *et seq.*; Aréchaga, 'International Responsibility', p. 572; D. W. Bowett, 'Treaties and State Responsibility' in *Mélanges Virally*, Paris, 1991, pp. 137, 144; and Schwarzenberger, *International Law*, p. 653. See also the *I'm Alone* case, 3 RIAA, pp. 1609, 1618 (1935); 7 ILR, p. 206 and the *Corfu Channel* case, ICJ Reports, 1949, pp. 4, 35; 16 ILR, pp. 155, 167. Note that article 10 of Part II of the ILC Draft includes within satisfaction nominal damages.   [95] 82 ILR, p. 499.   [96] *Ibid.*, p. 571.

[97] See e.g. *Yearbook of the ILC*, 1981, vol. II, Part 1, pp. 79 *et seq.*   [98] 82 ILR, p. 572.

[99] *Ibid.*, p. 573. Note that article 10 bis of Part II of the ILC Draft Articles provides that the injured state is entitled, where appropriate, to obtain assurances or guarantees of non-repetition of the wrongful act.   [100] 82 ILR, p. 577.   [101] *Ibid.*, p. 578.

In some cases, a party to a dispute will simply seek a declaration that the activity complained of is illegal.[102] In territorial disputes, for example, such declarations may be of particular significance. The International Court, however, adopted a narrow view of the Australian submissions in the *Nuclear Tests* case,[103] an approach that was the subject of a vigorous dissenting opinion.[104] Article 10 (2) of Part II of the ILC Draft provides four ways of ensuring satisfaction. These are apologies; nominal damages; punitive damages in cases of gross infringement of the rights of the injured state; and disciplinary action against or punishment of persons responsible where the internationally wrongful act arose from the serious misconduct of officials or from criminal conduct of officials or private parties.

The question of the appropriate reparation for expropriation was discussed in several recent cases. In the *BP* case,[105] the tribunal emphasised that there was:

> no explicit support for the proposition that specific performance, and even less so *restitutio in integrum* are remedies of public international law available at the option of a party suffering a wrongful breach by a co-contracting party . . . the responsibility incurred by the defaulting party for breach of an obligation to perform a contractual undertaking is a duty to pay damages . . . the concept of *restitutio in integrum* has been employed merely as a vehicle for establishing the amount of damages.[106]

However, in the *Texaco* case,[107] which similarly involved Libyan nationalisation of oil concessions, the arbitrator held that restitution in kind under international law (and indeed under Libyan law) constituted:

> the normal sanction for non-performance of contractual obligations and that it is inapplicable only to the extent that restoration of the *status quo ante* is impossible.[108]

This is an approach that in political terms, particularly in international contract cases, is unlikely to prove acceptable to states since it appears a

---

[102] See e.g. S. Rosenne, *The Law and Practice of the International Court*, Leiden, 1965, vol. I, and *Certain German Interests in Polish Upper Silesia*, PCIJ, Series A, No. 7, p. 18 (1926). Note also that under article 50 of the European Convention on Human Rights 1950, the European Court of Human Rights may award 'just satisfaction', which often takes the form of a declaration by the Court that a violation of the Convention has taken place, see e.g. the *Neumeister* case, European Court of Human Rights, Series A, No. 17 (1974); 41 ILR, p. 316. See also the *Pauwels* case, *ibid.*, No. 135 (1989); the *Lamy* case, *ibid.*, No. 151 (1989) and the *Huber* case, *ibid.*, No. 188 (1990).
[103] ICJ Reports, 1974, p. 253; 57 ILR, p. 398.   [104] *Ibid.*, pp. 312–19; 57 ILR, p. 457.
[105] 53 ILR, p. 297. This concerned the expropriation by Libya of BP oil concessions.
[106] 53 ILR, pp. 297, 347.   [107] 17 ILM, 1978, p. 1; 53 ILR, p. 389.
[108] *Ibid.*, p. 36; 53 ILR, pp. 507–8. In fact the parties settled the dispute by Libya supplying $152 million worth of crude oil, *ibid.*, p. 2.

violation of sovereignty. The problems, indeed, of enforcing such restitution awards against a recalcitrant state may be imagined.[109]

Circumstances precluding wrongfulness[110]

In certain situations, a breach of an international obligation attributable to a state may not give rise to responsibility. Generally the consent of the injured state, the legitimate application of a sanction, *force majeure*, self-defence and state of necessity are the circumstances which may preclude the inference of responsibility, or rather wrongfulness giving rise to responsibility.

Where a state consents to an act by another state which would otherwise constitute an unlawful act, wrongfulness is precluded unless a rule of *jus cogens* is involved from which no derogation is permitted.[111] The most common example of this kind of situation is where troops from one state are sent to another at the request of the latter.[112] Similarly, under article 30 of Part I of the ILC Draft the international wrongfulness of an act is precluded where it is committed as a measure legitimate under international law, in consequence of an internationally wrongful act committed by the target state.

The institution of reprisals, certainly the pre-1945 use of force, provides an example of this situation, since an otherwise unlawful act is rendered legitimate by the prior application of unlawful force.[113] The term 'counter-measures' is now the preferred term for reprisals not involving the use of force[114] and is the subject of continuing consideration by the International Law Commission.[115] Counter-measures may be related to the provisions laid down in article 60 of the Vienna Convention on the Law of Treaties 1969, which deals with the consequences of a material breach of a treaty in

---

[109] These points were explained by the arbitrator in the *Liamco* case, 20 ILM, 1981, pp. 1, 63–4; 62 ILR, pp. 141, 198. See also the *Aminoil* case, 21 ILM, 1982, p. 976; 66 ILR, p. 519. See further e.g. A. Fatouros, 'International Law and the International Contract', 74 AJIL, 1980, p. 134. The issue of compensation for expropriated property is discussed further, *infra*, p. 577.

[110] See e.g. Whiteman, *Digest of International Law*, 1967, vol. VIII, pp. 837 *et seq.*: *Yearbook of the ILC*, 1979, vol. II, part 1, pp. 21 *et seq.* and *ibid.*, 1980, vol. II, pp. 26 *et seq.*

[111] See article 29 of Part I of the ILC Draft Articles. As to *jus cogens*, see *supra*, Chapter 3, p. 97.

[112] See e.g. the dispatch of UK troops to Muscat and Oman in 1957, 574 HC Deb., col. 872, 29 July 1957, and to Jordan in 1958, SCOR, 13th Sess., 831st meeting, para. 28.

[113] See e.g. the *Naulilaa* case, 2 RIAA, p. 1025 (1928); 4 ILR, p. 466 and the *Cysne* case *ibid.*, p. 1056; 5 ILR, p. 150.

[114] See e.g. the *US–France Air Services Agreement* case, 54 ILR, pp. 306, 337.

[115] See e.g. Report of the International Law Commission, 1989, A/44/10 and *ibid.*, 1992, A/47/10, pp. 39 *et seq.* See also Annacker, 'Part Two', pp. 234 *et seq.*; E. Zoller, *Peacetime Unilateral Remedies: An Analysis of Countermeasures*, New York, 1984 and O. Y. Elagab, *The Legality of Non-Forcible Counter-Measures in International Law*, Oxford, 1988.

terms of the competence of the other parties to the treaty to terminate or suspend it.[116] However, while counter-measures do not as such affect the legal validity of the obligation which has been breached by way of reprisal for a prior breach, termination of a treaty under article 60 would under article 70 free the other parties to it from any further obligations under that treaty. Article 11 of Part II of the ILC Draft provides that an injured state whose demands for reparation have not been met is entitled not to comply 'with one or more of its obligations' towards the state committing the wrongful act.[117] Article 14 of Part II of the Draft makes it clear that counter-measures may not include the threat or use of force as prohibited by the UN Charter; extreme economic or political coercion designed to endanger the territorial integrity or political independence of the state which has committed the wrongful act; any conduct which infringes the inviolability of diplomatic or consular agents, premises, archives and documents; any conduct which derogates from basic human rights; or any other conduct in contravention of a peremptory norm of general international law.

The importance of proportionality in assessing the legality of counter-measures has been emphasised,[118] while a particular concern currently is to establish an appropriate dispute settlement regime in this context.[119]

Force majeure has long been accepted as precluding wrongfulness,[120] although the standard of proof is high. In the *Serbian Loans* case,[121] for example, the Court declined to accept the claim that the First World War had made it impossible for Serbia to repay a loan. In 1946, following a number of unauthorised flights of US aircraft over Yugoslavia, both states agreed that only in cases of emergency could such entry be justified in the absence of consent.[122]

Article 31 of Part I of the ILC Draft provides for the preclusion of wrongfulness where the act was due to an irresistible force or to an unforeseen

---

[116] See further *infra*, Chapter 16, p. 668.
[117] This draft article, together with draft articles 13 and 14, was provisionally accepted by the ILC in 1994, see Report of the International Law Commission on the Work of its Forty-Seventh Session, A/50/10, p. 92, 1995. Action on draft article 12 relating to the conditions under which an injured state may have recourse to counter-measures was deferred. The Commission has decided not to submit articles on counter-measures to the General Assembly pending action on article 12 and the submission of the relevant commentaries, *ibid.*
[118] See the *US–France Air Services Agreement Arbitration*, 54 ILR, pp. 303, 337 and Report of the International Law Commission, 1992, A/47/10, p. 70. Article 13 of Part II of the ILC Draft provides that 'any counter-measure taken by the injured state shall not be out of proportion to the degree of gravity of the internationally wrongful act and the effects thereof on the injured state'.
[119] See e.g. Symposium on Counter-Measures and Dispute Settlement, 5 EJIL, 1994, p. 20 and Report of the International Law Commission, 1995, A/50/10, pp. 173 *et seq.* See also Annacker, 'Part Two', pp. 242 *et seq.* [120] See e.g. *Yearbook of the ILC*, 1961, vol. II, p. 46.
[121] PCIJ, Series A, No. 20, 1929, p. 39. See also the *Brazilian Loans* case, PCIJ, Series A, No. 20, 1929, p. 120; 5 ILR, p. 466. [122] *Yearbook of the ILC*, 1979, vol. II, p. 60.

external event beyond the control of the state which made it materially impossible for the state concerned to conform with the international obligation in question. An example of the situation envisaged here is provided by the *Gill* case,[123] where a British national residing in Mexico had his house destroyed as a result of sudden and unforeseen action by opponents of the Mexican government. The Commission held that failure to prevent the act was due not to negligence but to genuine inability to take action in the face of a sudden situation.

In its Commentary on this provision, the ILC emphasised that the event in question had to be an act which occurs and takes place without the state being able to do anything to rectify the event or avert its consequences. There had to be a constraint which the state was unable to avoid or to oppose by its own power.[124]

The issue of *force majeure* was raised by France in the *Rainbow Warrior* arbitration in 1990.[125] It was argued that one of the French agents repatriated to France without the consent of New Zealand had to be so moved as a result of medical factors which amounted to *force majeure*. The Tribunal, however, stressed that the test of applicability of this doctrine was one of 'absolute and material impossibility' and a circumstance rendering performance of an obligation more difficult or burdensome did not constitute a case of *force majeure*.[126]

Article 32 of the Draft deals with situations of distress and provides that wrongfulness is precluded in the case of a state not acting in conformity with an international obligation binding upon it if the author of the conduct concerned had no other means 'in a situation of extreme distress' of saving his life or that of persons entrusted to his care. This would cover, for example, emergency unauthorised entry into foreign airspace of the kind envisaged by the 1946 US–Yugoslav correspondence, or the seeking of refuge in a foreign port without authorisation by a ship's captain in storm conditions.[127]

The difference between distress and *force majeure* is that in the former case there is an element of choice. This, as the ILC points out, is illusory only, because this choice is one between observance of an obligation, which would lead to inevitable loss, since distress in this context is to be equated with extreme peril, and breach of that obligation.[128] The Tribunal in the *Rainbow Warrior* arbitration[129] noted that three conditions were required to be satisfied in order for this defence to be applicable to the French action in repatriating its two agents. First, the existence of very exceptional circumstances of extreme urgency involving medical and other considerations of an elementary nature, provided always that a prompt recognition of the existence

---

[123] 5 RIAA, p. 159 (1931); 6 ILR, p. 203.   [124] *Yearbook of the ILC*, 1979, vol. II, p. 133.
[125] 82 ILR, pp. 499, 551.   [126] *Ibid.*, p. 553.   [127] *Yearbook of the ILC*, 1979, vol. II, p. 134.
[128] *Ibid.*, pp. 133–5.   [129] 82 ILR, pp. 499, 555.

of those exceptional circumstances is subsequently obtained from the other interested party or is clearly demonstrated. Secondly, the re-establishment of the original situation as soon as the reasons of emergency invoked to justify the breach of the obligation (i.e. the repatriation) had disappeared. Thirdly, the existence of a good faith effort to try to obtain the consent of New Zealand according to the terms of the 1986 Agreement.[130] It was concluded that France had failed to observe these conditions (except as far as the removal of one of the agents on medical grounds was concerned).

Article 33 of the Draft deals with the related issue of a state of necessity, where the act concerned was the 'only means of safeguarding an essential interest of the state against a grave and imminent peril', provided that an essential interest of the second state is not seriously impaired by the act. An example of this kind of situation is provided by the *Torrey Canyon*,[131] where a Liberian oil tanker went aground off the UK coast but outside territorial waters, spilling large quantities of oil. After salvage attempts, the UK bombed the ship. The ILC took the view that this action was legitimate in the circumstances because of a state of necessity.[132] It was only after the incident that international agreements were concluded dealing with this kind of situation.[133]

The wrongfulness of an act of state would also be precluded if that act constitutes a lawful measure of self-defence taken in conformity with the UN Charter.[134]

The treatment of aliens[135]

The question of the protection of foreign nationals is one of those issues in international law most closely connected with the different approaches adopted to international relations by the Western and Third World nations. Developing countries, as well as communist countries formerly, have long been eager to reduce what they regard as the privileges accorded to capitalist states by international law. They lay great emphasis upon the sovereignty and independence of states and resent the economic influence of the West. The latter, on the other hand, have wished to protect their

---

[130] *Supra* p. 543. [131] Cmnd. 3246, 1967. See also *infra*, Chapter 15, p. 630.
[132] *Yearbook of the ILC*, 1980, vol. II, p. 39. See also the *Company General of the Orinoco* case, 10 RIAA, p. 280.
[133] The defence of state necessity, however, has been characterised as 'controversial': see the *Rainbow Warrior* arbitration, 82 ILR, pp. 499, 554–5.
[134] See further *infra*, Chapter 19, p. 787.
[135] See references in footnote 1. See also S. N. Guha Roy, 'Is the Law of Responsibility of States for Injury to Aliens a Part of Universal International Law?', 55 AJIL, 1961, p. 863; A. Fatouros, 'International Law and the Third World', 50 *Virginia Law Review*, 1964, p. 783; I. Shihata, *Legal Treatment of Foreign Investment*, 1993; *Oppenheim's International Law*, p. 903 and *Third US Restatement of Foreign Relations Law*, Washington, 1987, vol. II, p. 184.

investments and nationals abroad and provide for the security of their property.

The diplomatic protection of nationals abroad arose after the decline of the grant of special letters of reprisal, by which individuals were authorised to engage in self-help activities.[136] Such diplomatic methods of assisting nationals abroad developed as the number of nationals overseas grew as a consequence of increasing trading activities and thus the relevant state practice multiplied. In addition, since the US–UK Jay Treaty of 1794 numerous mixed claims commissions were established to resolve problems of injury to aliens,[137] while a variety of national claims commissions were created to distribute lump sums received from foreign states in settlement of claims.[138] Such international and national claims procedures together with diplomatic protection therefore enabled nationals abroad to be aided in cases of loss or injury in state responsibility situations.[139]

Nationality of claims[140]

The doctrine of state responsibility rests upon twin pillars, the attribution to one state of the unlawful acts and omissions of its officials and its organs (legislative, judicial and executive) and the capacity of the other state to adopt the claim of the injured party. The first part of this equation has been looked at above, the second will now be considered.

Nationality is the link between the individual and his state as regards particular benefits and obligations. It is also the vital link between the individual and the benefits of international law. Although international law is now moving to a stage whereby individuals may acquire rights free from the interposition of the state, the basic proposition remains that in a state-oriented world system, it is only through the medium of the state that the individual may obtain the full range of benefits available under international law, and nationality is the key.

A state is under a duty to protect its nationals and it may take up their claims against other states. However, there is under international law no

---

[136] See generally Lillich, HR, pp. 344 *et seq.* See also the *Mavrommatis Palestine Concessions* case, PCIJ, Series A, No. 2, 1924; 2 ILR, p. 398.

[137] See e.g. A. M. Stuyt, *Survey of International Arbitrations, 1794–1889*, 3rd edn, Dordrecht, 1990.

[138] See e.g. *International Claims* (eds. R. B. Lillich and B. Weston), Charlottesville, 1982 and R. B. Lillich and B. Weston, *International Claims: Their Settlements by Lump-Sum Agreements*, Charlottesville, 1975, 2 vols. See also the US–People's Republic of China Claims Settlement Agreement of 1979, DUSPIL, 1979, pp. 1213–15, and Whiteman, *Digest*, vol. VIII, pp. 933–69.

[139] Note the establishment of the UN Compensation Commission following the ending of the Gulf War in 1991 to enable the settlement of claims arising out of that conflict, see *infra*, Chapter 20, p. 000.

[140] See e.g. *Oppenheim's International Law*, p. 511 and Brownlie, *Principles*, pp. 480–94.

obligation for states to provide diplomatic protection for their nationals abroad.[141] In addition, once a state does this the claim then becomes that of the state. This is a result of the historical reluctance to permit individuals the right in international law to prosecute claims against foreign countries, for reasons relating to state sovereignty and non-interference in internal affairs.

This basic principle was elaborated in the *Mavrommatis Palestine Concessions* case.[142] The Permanent Court of International Justice pointed out that:

> by taking up the case of one of its subjects and by resorting to diplomatic action or international judicial proceedings on his behalf, a state is in reality asserting its own rights, its right to ensure, in the person of its subjects, respect for the rules of international law . . .

Indeed, diplomatic protection was an elementary principle of international law. Once a state has taken up a case on behalf of one of its subjects before an international tribunal, in the eyes of the latter the state is sole claimant.

The corollary of this is that the right of a state to take over claims is limited to intervention on behalf of its own nationals. Diplomatic protection may not extend to the adoption of claims of foreign subjects.[143] Such diplomatic protection is not a right, but merely a discretion exercised or not by the state as an extra-legal remedy.[144] On the other hand, its exercise cannot be regarded as intervention contrary to international law by the state concerned.

The scope of a state to extend its nationality to whomsoever it wishes is unlimited, except in so far as it affects other states. In the *Nottebohm* case,[145]

---

141 See e.g. *HMHK v. Netherlands*, 94 ILR, p. 342 and *Comercial F SA v. Council of Ministers*, 88 ILR, p. 691.
142 PCIJ, Series A, no. 2, 1924, p. 12. See the *Panevezys–Saldutiskis* case, PCIJ, Series A/B, No. 76; 9 ILR, p. 308. See also E. de Vattel, who noted that 'whoever ill-treats a citizen indirectly injures the state, which must protect that citizen', *The Law of Nations*, 1916 trans., p. 136.
143 However, note article 8c of the Treaty on European Union 1992, under which every person holding the nationality of a member state (and thus a citizen of the European Union under article 8(1)) is entitled to receive diplomatic protection by the diplomatic or consular authority of any member state on the same conditions as nationals of that state where in the territory of a third state where the country of his or her nationality is not represented.
144 See *Administrative Decision No. V*, 7 RIAA, p. 119; 2 ILR, pp. 185, 191. See also DUSPIL, 1973, pp. 332–4 and *US v. Dulles*, 222 F.2d 390.
145 ICJ Reports, 1955, p. 4; 22 ILR, p. 349. The Court emphasised that to exercise protection, e.g. by applying to the Court, was to place oneself on the plane of international law, *ibid.*, p. 16. See the *Nationality Decrees in Tunis and Morocco* case, PCIJ, Series B, No. 4, 1923, pp. 7, 21; 2 ILR, p. 349, where it was noted that while questions of nationality were in principle within the domestic jurisdiction of states, the right of a state to use its discretion was limited by obligations undertaken towards other states. See also the *Flegenheimer* case, 14 RIAA, p. 327 (1958); 25 ILR, p. 91, and article 1 of the 1930 Hague Convention on Nationality. See further on nationality and international law, *supra*, Chapter 12, p. 462.

the International Court of Justice decided that only where there existed a genuine link between the claimant state and its national could the right of diplomatic protection arise.

The Government of Liechtenstein instituted proceedings before the International Court of Justice, claiming restitution and compensation for Nottebohm against Guatemala for acts of the latter which were alleged to be contrary to international law. Guatemala replied that Nottebohm's right to Liechtenstein nationality and thus its diplomatic protection was questionable. The person in question was born in Germany in 1881 and, still a German national, applied for naturalisation in Liechtenstein in 1939. The point was, however, that since 1905 (and until 1943 when he was deported as a result of war measures) Nottebohm had been permanently resident in Guatemala and had carried on his business from there. The Court noted that Liechtenstein was entirely free, as was every state, to establish the rules necessary for the acquisition of its nationality, but the crux of the matter was whether Guatemala was obliged to recognise the grant of Liechtenstein nationality. The exercise of diplomatic protection by a state regarding one of its nationals brought the whole issue of nationality out of the sphere of domestic jurisdiction and onto the plane of international law.[146]

The Court emphasised that according to state practice, nationality was a legal manifestation of the link between the person and the state granting nationality and the recognition that the person was more closely connected with that state than with any other.[147]

Having brought out these concepts, the Court emphasised the tenuous nature of Nottebohm's links with Liechtenstein and the strength of his connection with Guatemala. Nottebohm had spent only a very short period of time in Liechtenstein and one of his brothers lived in Vaduz. Beyond that and the formal naturalisation process, there were no other links with that state. On the other hand, he had lived in Guatemala for some thirty years and had returned there upon obtaining his papers from Vaduz. Since the Liechtenstein nationality 'was granted without regard to the concept . . . adopted in international relations' in the absence of any genuine connection, the Court held that Liechtenstein was not able to extend its diplomatic protection to Nottebohm as regards Guatemala.[148] The case has been subject to some criticism relating to the use of the doctrine of 'genuine connection' by the Court. The doctrine had until then been utilised with regard to the problems of dual nationality, so as to enable a decision to be made on whether one national state may sue the other on behalf of the particular

[146] ICJ Reports, 1955, pp. 20–1; 22 ILR, p. 357.   [147] *Ibid.*, p. 23; 22 ILR, p. 359.
[148] *Ibid.*, pp. 25–6; 22 ILR, p. 362. See also the Advisory Opinion of the Inter-American Court of Human Rights in the *Proposed Amendments to the Naturalisation Provisions of the Constitution of Costa Rica* case, Series A, No. 4, 1984.

national. Its extension to the issue of diplomatic protection appeared to be a new move altogether.[149]

The nationality must exist at the date of the injury, and should continue until at least the date of the award settling the claim, although this latter point may depend upon a variety of other facts, for example any agreement between the contending states as regards the claim.[150]

Where an individual possesses dual nationality, either state of which he is a national may adopt a claim of his against a third state, and it may be that the state with which he has the more effective connection may be able to espouse his claim as against the other state. In the *Mergé* case,[151] it was emphasised that the principle based on the sovereign equality of states, which excludes diplomatic protection in the case of dual nationality, must yield before the principle of effective nationality whenever such nationality is that of the claimant state. However, where such predominance is not proved, there would be no such yielding. In other words, the test for permitting protection by a state of a national against another state of which he is also a national is the test of effectiveness. This approach was reaffirmed by the Iran–US Claims Tribunal, where the Full Tribunal held that it had jurisdiction over claims against Iran by a dual national when the 'dominant and effective nationality' at the relevant time was American.[152]

As far as a corporation is concerned, it appears that there must be some tangible link between it and the state seeking to espouse its claim. Different cases have pointed to various factors, ranging from incorporation of the company in the particular state to the maintenance of the administrative centre of the company in the state and the existence of substantial holdings by nationals in the company.[153]

[149] See generally, Brownlie, *Principles*, Chapter 18 and R. Y. Jennings, 'General Course on Principles of International Law', 121 HR, pp. 323, 459.
[150] See e.g. Borchard, *Diplomatic Protection*, pp. 660 *et seq.*; Whiteman, *Digest*, vol. VIII, 1967, pp. 1243–7 and the *Nottebohm* case, ICJ Reports, 1955, p. 4; 22 ILR, p. 349. See also the view of the US State Department that it has consistently declined to espouse claims which have not been continuously owned by US nationals, see 76 AJIL, 1982, pp. 836–9, and the Rules regarding International Claims issued by the UK Foreign and Commonwealth Office, 1971, to the same effect, cited in D. Harris, *Cases and Materials in International Law*, 3rd edn, London, 1983, p. 448 and revised in 1983, see UKMIL, 54 BYIL, p. 520 and in 1985, see 37 ICLQ, 1988, p. 1006. See also I. Sinclair, 'Nationality of Claims: British Practice', 27 BYIL, 1950, p. 125.
[151] 14 RIAA, p. 236 (1955); 22 ILR, p. 443. See also the *Canevaro* case, 11 RIAA, p. 397 (1912). Cf. the *Salem* case, 2 RIAA, p. 1161 (1932); 6 ILR, p. 188.
[152] *Islamic Republic of Iran* v. *USA*, Case No. A/18, 5 Iran–US CTR, p. 251; 75 ILR, p. 176; *Esphahanian* v. *Bank Tejarat*, 2 Iran–US CTR, p. 157; 72 ILR, p. 478, and *Malek* v. *Islamic Republic of Iran*, 19 Iran–US CTR, p. 48. See also *Saghi* v. *Islamic Republic of Iran*, 87 AJIL, 1993, p. 447 and the decision of the Canadian Supreme Court in *Schavernock* v. *Foreign Claims Commission*, 1 SCR 1092 (1982); 90 ILR, p. 220.
[153] See e.g. Brownlie, *Principles*, pp. 485–8 and Schwarzenberger, pp. 387–412. See also *Sola Tiles Inc.* v. *Islamic Republic of Iran*, 83 ILR, p. 460.

The Court in the *Barcelona Traction* case[154] remarked that the traditional rule gave the right of diplomatic protection of a corporation to the state under the laws of which it is incorporated and in whose territory it has its registered office. Any application of the *Nottebohm* doctrine of the 'genuine connection' was rejected as having no general acceptance. Nevertheless, it remains true that some meaningful link must bind the state to the company which seeks its protection. Just how far the traditionalist, rather restrictive approach adopted here by the International Court of Justice will be maintained has yet to be seen.

The position as regards the shareholders in a company was discussed in that case. It concerned a dispute between Belgium and Spain relating to a company established in 1911 in Canada, which was involved in the production of electricity in Spain and the majority of whose shares was owned by Belgian nationals. After the Second World War, the Spanish authorities took a number of financial measures which resulted in harm to the company and in 1948 it was declared bankrupt. The case concerned a Belgian claim in respect of injury to the shareholders, who were Belgian nationals, because of the steps that Spain had adopted. Spain replied by denying that Belgium had any standing in the case since the injury had been suffered by the company and not the shareholders.

The Court rejected the Belgian claim on the grounds that it did not have a legal interest in the matter. Although shareholders may suffer if wrong is done to a company, it is only the rights of the latter that have been infringed and thus entitle it to institute action. If, on the other hand (as did not happen here), the direct rights of the shareholders were affected, for example as regards dividends, then they would have an independent right of action; but otherwise, only if the company legally ceased to exist.

The Court emphasised that the general rule of international law stated that where an unlawful act was committed against a company representing foreign capital, only the national state of the company could sue. In this case Canada had chosen not to intervene in the dispute. To accept the idea of the diplomatic protection of shareholders would, in the opinion of the International Court of Justice, result in the creation of an atmosphere of confusion and insecurity in economic relations especially since the shares of international companies are 'widely scattered and frequently change hands'.[155]

It is interesting to note that the United Kingdom, according to the set of rules regarding the taking up of International Claims produced by the

---

[154] ICJ Reports, 1970, pp. 3, 42; 46 ILR, pp. 178, 216.

[155] *Ibid.*, p. 49; 46 ILR, p. 223. See also the separate opinion of Judge Oda, the *Elettronica Sicula* case, *US* v. *Italy*, ICJ Reports, 1989, pp. 15, 84; 84 ILR, pp. 311, 390.

Foreign Office, most recently in 1985,[156] may intervene in *Barcelona Traction* situations where a national has an interest as a shareholder or otherwise, and the company is defunct, although this is regarded as an exceptional instance. The United Kingdom may also intervene where it is the national state of the company that actively wrongs the company in which a United Kingdom national has an interest as a shareholder or in some other respect; otherwise the UK would normally take up such a claim only in concert with the government of the state of incorporation of the company.

The exhaustion of local remedies[157]

It is a well established rule of customary international law that before international proceedings are instituted, the various remedies provided by the local state should have been exhausted. This is both to enable the particular state to have an opportunity to redress the wrong that has occurred there within its own legal order and to reduce the number of international claims that might be brought. If claims could be brought on behalf of individuals or companies after the alleged violation and before the state responsible had a chance to rectify it, it could tax the international system as well as proving vexatious. Another factor, of course, is the respect that is to be accorded to the sovereignty and jurisdiction of foreign states by not pre-empting the operation of their legal systems.

The rule was well illustrated in the *Ambatielos* arbitration,[158] between Greece and Britain. The former brought proceedings arising out of a contract signed by Ambatielos, which were rejected by the tribunal since the remedies available under English law had not been fully utilised. In particular, he had failed to call a vital witness and he had not appealed to the House of Lords from the decision of the Court of Appeal.

The term local remedies applies only to available effective remedies. It will not be sufficient to dismiss a claim merely because the person claiming had not taken the matter to appeal, where the appeal would not have affected the basic outcome of the case. This was stressed in the *Finnish Ships* arbitration[159] where shipowners brought a claim before the Admiralty Transport

---

[156] *Supra*, footnote 150. The increase in the number of bilateral investment treaties in the 1970s may be partly explained as the response to the post-*Barcelona Traction* need to protect shareholders. See e.g. Sornarajah, 'State Responsibility and Bilateral Investment Treaties', 20 *Journal of World Trade Law*, 1986, pp. 79, 87.

[157] See further, *supra*, Chapter 6, p. 202. See also article 22 of Part II of the ILC Draft, *Yearbook of the ILC*, 1980, vol. II, p. 32. See also the *Panevezys Railway* case, PCIJ, Series A/B, No. 76 (1939); 9 ILR, p. 308; Whiteman, *Digest*, vol. III, p. 1558; E. Borchard, *Diplomatic Protection*, pp. 817–18; A. A. Cançado Trindade, *The Application of the Rule of Exhaustion of Local Remedies in International Law*, Cambridge, 1983 and C. F. Amerasinghe, *Local Remedies in International Law*, Cambridge, 1990.

[158] 12 RIAA, p. 83 (1956); 23 ILR, p. 306.   [159] 2 RIAA, p. 1479 (1934); 7 ILR, p. 231.

Arbitration Board, but did not appeal against the unfavourable decision. It was held that since the appeal could only be on points of law, which could not overturn the vital finding of fact that there had been a British requisition of ships involved, any appeal would have been ineffective. Accordingly the claims of the shipowners would not be dismissed for non-exhaustion of local remedies.

In the *Interhandel* case,[160] the United States seized the American assets of a company owned by the Swiss firm Interhandel, in 1942, which was suspected of being under the control of a German enterprise. In 1958, after nine years of litigation in the US courts regarding the unblocking of the Swiss assets in America, Switzerland took the matter to the International Court of Justice. However, before a decision was reached, the US Supreme Court readmitted Interhandel into the legal proceedings, thus disposing of Switzerland's argument that the company's suit had been finally rejected. The Court dismissed the Swiss government's claim since the local remedies available had not been exhausted. Criticism has been levelled against this judgment on the ground that litigation extending over practically ten years could hardly be described as constituting an 'effective' remedy. However, the fact remains that the legal system operating in the United States had still something to offer the Swiss company even after that time.

The local remedies rule does not apply where one state has been guilty of a direct breach of international law causing immediate injury to another state, as for instance where its diplomatic agents are assaulted. But it does apply where the state is complaining of injury to its nationals.[161] The local remedies rule may be waived by treaty stipulation, as for example in Article V of the US–Mexico General Claims Convention of 1923 and Article XI of the Convention on International Liability for Damage caused by Space Objects 1972.

The issue of local remedies was clarified in the *Elettronica Sicula S.p. A. (ELSI)* case,[162] which concerned an action brought by the US against Italy alleging injuries to the Italian interests of two US corporations. Italy claimed that local remedies had not been exhausted, while the US argued that the doctrine did not apply since the case was brought under the Treaty of Friendship, Commerce and Navigation 1948 between the two states which provided for the submission of disputes relating to the treaty to the

---

[160] ICJ Reports, 1959, p. 6; 27 ILR, p. 475. The Court declared that the 'rule that local remedies must be exhausted before international proceedings may be instituted is a well-established principle of customary international law', *ibid.*, p. 27; 27 ILR, p. 490. See also Rules VII and VIII of the International Claims Rules of the FCO, *supra*, footnote 132; Pleadings, *Israel v. Bulgaria*, ICJ Reports, 1959, pp. 531–2 and T. Meron, 'The Incidence of the Rule of Exhaustion of Local Remedies', 25 BYIL, 1959, p. 95. Note in addition, the *North American Dredging Co.* claim, 4 RIAA, p. 26 (1926); 3 ILR, p. 4.

[161] See e.g. the *Heathrow Airport User Charges Arbitration*, 102 ILR, pp. 215, 277 *et seq.*

[162] ICJ Reports, 1989, p. 15; 84 ILR, p. 311.

International Court, with no mention of local remedies. The Court,[163] however, firmly held that while the parties to an agreement could if they so chose dispense with the local remedies requirement in express terms, it 'finds itself unable to accept that an important principle of customary international law should be held to have been tacitly dispensed with'.[164] In other words, the presumption that local remedies need to be exhausted can only be rebutted by express provision to the contrary.

The Court also dealt with a claim by the US that the doctrine did not apply to a request for a declaratory judgment finding that the treaty in question had been violated. This claim in effect was based on the view that the doctrine would not apply in cases of direct injury to a state. The Court felt unable to find in the case a dispute over alleged violation of the treaty resulting in direct injury to the US that was both distinct from and independent of the dispute with regard to the two US corporations.[165] The Court stressed that the matter 'which colours and pervades the US claim as a whole' was the alleged damage to the two US corporations.[166] In the light of this stringent test, it therefore seems that in such mixed claims involving the interests both of nationals and of the state itself one must assume that the local remedies rule applies.

The Court also rejected the Italian claim that local remedies had not in fact been exhausted in the case because the two US corporations had not raised the treaty issue before the Italian courts. It was held that it was sufficient if the essence of the claim has been brought before the competent tribunals. Accordingly, identity of claims as distinct from identity of issues is not required. The Court was not convinced that there clearly remained some remedy which the corporations, independently of their Italian subsidiary (ELSI) ought to have pursued and exhausted.[167]

The relevant standard of treatment

The developed states of the West have argued historically that there exists an 'international minimum standard' for the protection of foreign nationals that must be upheld irrespective of how the state treats its own nationals, whereas other states maintained that all the state need do is treat the alien as it does its own nationals (the 'national treatment standard').

The reason for the evolution of the latter approach is to be found in the

---

[163] The case was in fact decided by a Chamber of the Court, see further *infra* Chapter 18, p. 748.   [164] ICJ Reports, 1989, pp. 15, 42; 84 ILR, pp. 311, 348.
[165] *Ibid.*, pp. 42–4; 84 ILR, pp. 348–50.   [166] *Ibid.*, p. 43; 84 ILR, p. 349.
[167] *Ibid.*, pp. 46–8; 84 ILR, pp. 352–4. See also Adler, 'The Exhaustion of the Local Remedies Rule After the International Court of Justice's Decision in *ELSI*', 39 ICLQ, 1990, p. 641 and F. A. Mann, 'Foreign Investment in the International Court of Justice: The *ELSI* Case', 86 AJIL, 1992, pp. 92, 101–2.

increasing resentment of Western economic domination rather than in the necessary neglect of basic standards of justice. The Latin American states felt, in particular, that the international minimum standard concept had been used as a means of interference in internal affairs.[168] Accordingly, the Calvo doctrine was formulated. This involved a reaffirmation of the principle of non-intervention coupled with the assertion that aliens were entitled only to such rights as were accorded nationals and thus had to seek redress for grievances exclusively in the domestic arena.[169] It was intended as a shield against external interference.

The international standard concept itself developed during the nineteenth century and received extensive support in case law.

In the *Neer* case,[170] for example, where the American superintendent of a mine in Mexico had been killed, the Commission held 'that the propriety of governmental acts should be put to the test of international standards', while in the *Certain German Interests in Polish Upper Silesia* case,[171] the Court recognised the existence of a common or generally accepted international law respecting the treatment of aliens, which is applicable to them despite municipal legislation. In the *Garcia* case,[172] the US–Mexican Claims Commission emphasised that there existed an international standard concerning the taking of human life and in the *Roberts* claim,[173] reference was made to the test as to whether aliens were treated in accordance with ordinary standards of civilisation.

If the principle is clear, the contents or definition of that principle are far from clear. In the *Neer* claim,[174] the Commission stated that the treatment of an alien, in order to constitute an international delinquency:

> should amount to an outrage, to bad faith, to wilful neglect of duty, or to an insufficiency of governmental action so far short of international standards that every reasonable and impartial man would readily recognise its insufficiency.

In other words, a fairly high threshold is specified before the minimum standard applies. Some indeed have argued that the concept never involved a definite standard with a fixed content, but rather a 'process of decision',[175] a process which would involve an examination of the responsibility of the state for the injury to the alien in the light of all the circumstances of the

---

[168] See e.g. Guha Roy, 'Law of Responsibility'; J. Castañeda, 'The Underdeveloped Nations and the Development of International Law', 15 *International Organisation*, 1961, p. 38 and R. P. Anand, *New States and International Law*, Delhi, 1972.

[169] See e.g. Lillich, HR, p. 349.   [170] 4 RIAA, p. 60 (1926); 3 ILR, p. 213.

[171] PCIJ, Series A, No. 7, 1926; 3 ILR, p. 429.

[172] 4 RIAA, p. 119 (1926). See also the *Chattin* case, 4 RIAA, p. 282 (1927); 4 ILR, p. 248.

[173] 4 RIAA, p. 77 (1926); 3 ILR, p. 227.

[174] 4 RIAA, pp. 60, 61–2 (1926); 3 ILR, p. 213. See similarly, the *Chattin* case, 4 RIAA, p. 282 (1927); 4 ILR, p. 248.

[175] M. S. McDougal *et al.*, *Studies in World Public Order*, New Haven, 1960, p. 869.

particular case.[176] The issue of the content of such a standard has often been described in terms of the concept of denial of justice.[177] In effect, that concept refers to the improper administration of civil and criminal justice as regards an alien.[178] It would include the failure to apprehend and prosecute those wrongfully causing injury to an alien, as in the *Janes* claim,[179] where an American citizen was killed in Mexico. The identity of the murderer was known, but no action had been taken for eight years. The widow was awarded $12,000 in compensation for the non-apprehension and non-punishment of the murderer. It would also include unreasonably long detention and harsh and unlawful treatment in prison.[180]

A progressive attempt to resolve the divide between the national and international standard proponents was put forward by Garcia-Amador in a report on international responsibility to the International Law Commission in 1956. He argued that the two approaches were now synthesised in the concept of the international recognition of the essential rights of man.[181] He formulated two principles. First, that aliens had to enjoy the same rights and guarantees as enjoyed by nationals, which should not in any case be less than the fundamental human rights recognised and defined in international instruments. Secondly, international responsibility would only be engaged if internationally recognised fundamental human rights were affected.[182]

This approach did not prove attractive to the ILC at that time in the light of a number of problems. However, human rights law has developed considerably in recent years[183] and can now be regarded as establishing certain minimum standards of state behaviour with regard to civil and political rights. It is noticeable, for example, that the relevant instruments do not refer to nationals and aliens specifically, but to all individuals within the territory and subject to the jurisdiction of the state without discrimination.[184] One should also note the special efforts being made to deal with non-nationals, in particular the UN Declaration on the Human Rights of Individuals who are not Nationals of the Country in which they Live,[185] and the continuing concern with regard to migrant workers.[186]

It is, of course, recognised that there must be some differences as regards

---

[176] See Lillich, HR, p. 350.
[177] See e.g. A. V. Freeman, *The International Responsibility of States for Denial of Justice*, 1938.
[178] See *AMCO* v. *Indonesia (Merits)*, 89 ILR, pp. 405, 451.
[179] 4 RIAA, p. 82 (1926); 3 ILR, p. 218.
[180] See e.g. the *Roberts* claim, 4 RIAA, p. 77 (1926); 3 ILR, p. 227 and the *Quintanilla* claim, 4 RIAA, p. 101 (1926); 3 ILR, p. 224.
[181] *Yearbook of the ILC*, 1956, vol. II, pp. 173, 199–203.
[182] *Yearbook of the ILC*, 1957, vol. II, pp. 104, 112–13.   [183] *Supra*, Chapters 6 and 7.
[184] See e.g. Article 2 of the International Covenant on Civil and Political Rights, 1966.
[185] General Assembly resolution 40/144. See also E/CN.4/Sub.2/392 (1977) and R. B. Lillich and S. Neff, 'The Treatment of Aliens and International Human Rights Norms', 21 *German Yearbook of International Law*, 1978, p. 97.
[186] See further *supra* Chapter 6, p. 246.

the relative rights and obligations of nationals and aliens. Non-nationals do not have political rights and may be banned from employment in certain areas (e.g. the diplomatic corps), although they remain subject to the local law.

It is also unquestioned that a state may legitimately refuse to admit aliens, or may accept them subject to certain conditions being fulfilled. Whether a state may expel aliens with equal facility is more open to doubt.

A number of cases assert that states must give convincing reasons for expelling an alien. In, for example, the *Boffolo* case,[187] which concerned an Italian expelled from Venezuela, it was held that states possess a general right of expulsion, but it could only be resorted to in extreme circumstances and accomplished in a manner least injurious to the person affected. In addition, the reasons for the expulsion must be stated before an international tribunal when the occasion demanded. Many municipal systems provide that the authorities of a country may deport aliens without reasons having to be stated. The position under customary international law is therefore somewhat confused. As far as treaty law is concerned article 13 of the International Covenant on Civil and Political Rights stipulates that an alien lawfully in the territory of a state party to the Convention:

> may be expelled therefrom only in pursuance of a decision reached in accordance with law and shall, except where compelling reasons of national security otherwise require, be allowed to submit the reasons against his expulsion and to have his case reviewed by and be represented for the purpose before, the competent authority.

Article 3 of the European Convention on Establishment, 1956, provides that nationals of other contracting states lawfully residing in the territory may be expelled only if they endanger national security or offend against public order or morality, and article 4 of the Fourth Protocol (1963) of the European Convention of Human Rights declares that 'collective expulsion of aliens is prohibited'.[188]

The burden of proving the wrongfulness of the expelling state's action falls upon the claimant alleging expulsion and the relevant rules would also apply where even though there is no direct law or regulation forcing the alien to leave, his continued presence in that state is made impossible because of conditions generated by wrongful acts of the state or attributable to it.[189]

---

[187] 10 RIAA, p. 528 (1903). See also *Dr. Breger's* case, Whiteman, *Digest*, vol. VIII, p. 861; R. Plender, *International Migration Law*, 2nd edn, Dordrecht, 1988 and G. Goodwin-Gill, *International Law and the Movement of Persons Between States*, Oxford, 1978.

[188] Note also article 1 of Protocol 7 (1984) of the European Convention on Human Rights to the same general effect as article 13. See as regards refugees, the 1951 Convention Relating to the Status of Refugees and the 1967 Protocol and G. Goodwin-Gill, *The Refugee in International Law*, Oxford, 1983.

[189] See *Rankin v. The Islamic Republic of Iran*, 17 Iran–US CTR, pp. 135, 142; 82 ILR, pp. 204, 214. See also Goodwin-Gill, *International Law*; Brownlie, *Principles*, pp. 76–7 and M. Pellonpaa, *Expulsion in International Law*, 1984.

Where states have expelled aliens, international law requires their national state to admit them.[190]

The expropriation of foreign property[191]

The expansion of the Western economies since the nineteenth century in particular stimulated an outflow of capital and consequent heavy investment in the developing areas of the world. This resulted in substantial areas of local economies falling within the ownership and control of Western corporations. However, with the granting of independence to the various Third World countries and in view of the nationalisation measures taken by the Soviet Union after the success of the communist revolution, such properties and influence began to come under pressure.

In assessing the state of international law with regard to the expropriation of the property of aliens, one is immediately confronted with two opposing objectives, although they need not be irreconcilable in all cases. On the one hand, the capital-exporting countries require some measure of protection and security before they will invest abroad and on the other hand the capital-importing countries are wary of the power of foreign investments and the drain of currency that occurs, and are often stimulated to take over such enterprises.

Nationalisation for one reason or another is now a common feature not only in communist and Afro-Asian states, but also in Western Europe. The need to acquire control of some key privately owned property is felt by many states to be an essential requirement in the interests of economic and social reform. Indeed it is true to say that extensive sectors of the economies of most West European states were at some stages under national control after having been taken into public ownership.

Since it can hardly be denied that nationalisation is a perfectly legitimate measure for a state to adopt and clearly not illegal as such under

---

[190] This is a general principle, but cf. Lord Denning in the *Thakrar* case [1974] QB 684; 59 ILR, p. 450. Note that the Lord Chancellor in dealing with the expulsion of British aliens from East Africa accepted that in international law a state was under a duty as between other states to accept expelled nationals, see 335 HL Deb., col. 497, 14 September 1972. See also *Van Duyn* v. *Home Office*, [1974] ECR 1337; 60 ILR, p. 247.

[191] See e.g. G. White, *Nationalisation of Foreign Property*, London, 1961; B. Wortley, *Expropriation of Public International Law*, 1959; I. Brownlie, 'Legal Status of Natural Resources', 162 HR, p. 245; R. Higgins, 'The Taking of Property by the State: Recent Developments in International Law', 176 HR, p. 267, and *The Valuation of Nationalised Property in International Law* (ed. R. B. Lillich), 3 vols., 1972–5. See also *Oppenheim's International Law*, pp. 911 *et seq.*; P. Muchlinski, *Multinational Enterprises and the Law*, Oxford, 1995, pp. 501 *et seq.*; Mouri, *The International Law of Expropriation as Reflected in the Work of the Iran–US Claims Tribunal*, 1994 and P. M. Norton, 'A Law of the Future or a Law of the Past ? Modern Tribunals and the International Law of Expropriation', 85 AJIL, 1991, p. 474.

international law,[192] the problem arises where foreign property is involved. Not to expropriate such property in a general policy of nationalisation might be seen as equivalent to proposing a privileged status within the country for foreign property, as well as limiting the power of the state within its own jurisdiction.

There is no doubt that under international law, expropriation of alien property is legitimate.[193] This is not disputed. However, certain conditions must be fulfilled.[194]

The question, of course, arises as to the stage at which international law in fact becomes involved in such a situation. Apart from the relevance of the general rules relating to the treatment of aliens noted in the preceding section, the issue will usually arise out of a contract between a state and a foreign private enterprise. In such a situation, several possibilities exist. It could be argued that the contract itself by its very nature becomes 'internationalised' and thus subject to international law rather than (or possibly in addition to) the law of the contracting state. The consequences of this would include the operation of the principle of international law that agreements are to be honoured (*pacta sunt servanda*) which would constrain the otherwise wide competence of a state party to alter unilaterally the terms of a relevant agreement. This proposition was adopted by the Arbitrator in the *Texaco* v. *Libya* case in 1977,[195] where it was noted that this may be achieved in various ways, for example, by stating that the law governing the contract referred to 'general principles of law', which was taken to incorporate international law; by including an international arbitration clause for the settlement of disputes and by including a stabilisation clause in an international development agreement, preventing unilateral variation of the terms of the agreement.[196] However, this approach is controversial and case law is by no means consistent.[197]

International law will clearly be engaged where the expropriation is unlawful, either because of, for example, the discriminatory manner in which it is carried out or the offering of inadequate or no compensation.[198]

---

[192] See e.g. *De Sanchez* v. *Banco Central de Nicaragua and Others*, 770 F 2d 1385, 1397; 88 ILR, pp. 75, 89.   [193] See e.g. *AMCO* v. *Indonesia (Merits)*, 89 ILR, pp. 405, 466.
[194] See e.g. the World Bank Guidelines on the Treatment of Foreign Direct Investment, 31 ILM, 1992, p. 1363.   [195] 53 ILR, p. 389.
[196] See e.g. C. Greenwood, 'State Contracts in International Law – The Libyan Oil Arbitrations', 53 BYIL, 1982, pp. 27, 41 *et seq*. See also A. Fatouros, 'International Law and the Internationalised Contract', 74 AJIL, 1980, p. 134.
[197] See e.g. J. Paulsson, 'The ICSID *Klöckner* v. *Cameroon* Award: The Duties of Partners in North-South Economic Development Agreements', 1 *Journal of International Arbitration*, 1984, p. 145; The *Aminoil* case, 21 ILM, 1982, p. 976; 66 ILR, p. 519 and D. W. Bowett, 'State Contracts with Aliens: Contemporary Developments on Compensation for Termination or Breach', 59 BYIL, 1988, p. 49.
[198] See in particular article 1 of Protocol I of the European Convention on Human Rights 1950 as regards the protection of the right to property and the prohibition of deprivation of possessions 'except in the public interest and subject to the conditions provided for by law

The property question

Higgins has pointed to 'the almost total absence of any analysis of conceptual aspects of property'.[199] Property would clearly include physical objects
and certain abstract entities, for example, shares in companies, debts and
intellectual property. The 1961 Harvard Draft Convention on the
International Responsibility of States for Injuries to Aliens[200] discusses the
concept of property in the light of 'all movable and immovable property,
whether tangible or intangible, including industrial, literary and artistic
property as well as rights and interests in property'. In the *Liamco* case the
arbitration specifically mentioned concession rights as forming part of
incorporeal property,[201] a crucial matter as many expropriation cases in fact
involve a wide variety of contractual rights.[202]

The nature of expropriation

Expropriation involves taking property, but actions short of direct possession of the assets in question may also fall within the category. The 1961
Harvard Draft would include, for example, 'any such unreasonable interference with the use, enjoyment or disposal of property as to justify an inference that the owner thereof will not be able to use, enjoy or dispose of the
property within a reasonable period of time after the inception of such interference'.[203] In 1965, for example, after a series of Indonesian decrees, the
UK government stated that:

> in view of the complete inability of British enterprises and plantations to exer-
> cise and enjoy any of their rights of ownership in relation to their properties in
> Indonesia, Her Majesty's Government has concluded that the Indonesian
> Government has expropriated this property.[204]

and by the general principles of international law'. See e.g. the following cases, *Marckx*,
European Court of Human Rights, Series A, No. 31; 58 ILR, p. 561 and *Sporrong and
Lönnroth, ibid.*, No. 52; 68 ILR, p. 86. However, it has been held that the reference to inter-
national law did not apply to the taking by a state of the property of its own nationals; see
Lithgow, European Court of Human Rights, Series A, No. 102; 75 ILR, p. 438; *James, ibid.*,
No. 98; 75 ILR, p. 397 and *Mellacher, ibid.*, No. 169. See also Brock, 'The Protection of
Property Rights Under the European Convention on Human Rights', *Legal Issues of
European Integration*, 1986, p. 52.   [199] *Op. cit.*, p. 268.

[200] 55 AJIL, 1961, p. 548 (article 10(7)).

[201] 20 ILM, 1981, pp. 1, 53; 62 ILR, pp. 141, 189. See also the *Shufeldt* case, 2 RIAA, pp.
1083, 1097 (1930); 5 ILR, p. 179.

[202] See also *infra* p. 580 concerning the definition of 'investments' in bilateral investment
treaties. See also article 1(6) of the European Energy Charter Treaty 1994.

[203] 55 AJIL, 1961, pp. 553–4 (article 10(3)a).

[204] BPIL, 1964, p. 200. See also 4 ILM, 1965, pp. 440–7. Note also *Shanghai Power Co. v. US*,
4 Cl. Ct. 237 (1983), where it was held that the settlement of the plaintiff's claim by the
US government in an agreement with China for less than its worth did not constitute a
taking for which compensation was required in the context of the Fifth Amendment.

In *Starrett Housing Corporation* v. *Government of the Islamic Republic of Iran* before the Iran–US Claims Tribunal,[205] it was emphasised by the Tribunal that:

> measures taken by a state can interfere with property rights to such an extent that these rights are rendered so useless that they must be deemed to have been expropriated, even though the state does not purport to have expropriated them and the legal title to the property formally remains with the original owner.

In that case, it was held that a taking had occurred by the end of January 1980 upon the appointment by the Iranian Housing Ministry of a temporary manager of the enterprise concerned, thus depriving the claimants of the right to manage and of effective control and use.[206] However, a series of events prior to that date, including armed incursions and detention of personnel, intimidation and interference with supplies and needed facilities, did not amount to a taking of the property, since investors in foreign countries assume certain risks with regard to disturbances and even revolution. The fact that the risks materialise, held the Tribunal, did not mean that property rights affected by the events could be deemed to have been taken.[207] There is clearly an important, but indistinct, dividing line here. It has also been held that the seizure of a controlling stock interest in a foreign corporation is a taking of control of the assets and profits of the enterprise in question.[208] The expropriation of a given property may also include a taking of closely connected ancillary rights, such as patents and contracts, which had not been directly nationalised.[209]

Public purposes

The expropriation must be for 'reasons of public utility, judicial liquidation and similar measures' as noted in the *Certain German Interests in Polish Upper*

---

[205] Interlocutory Award, 4 Iran–US CTR, p. 122; 85 ILR, p. 349.

[206] 4 Iran–US CTR, p. 154; 85 ILR, p. 390. See also *Harza Engineering Co.* v. *The Islamic Republic of Iran*, 1 Iran–US CTR, p. 499; 70 ILR, p. 117, and *AIG* v. *The Islamic Republic of Iran*, 4 Iran–US CTR, p. 96. See also *Sedco* v. *NIOC*, 84 ILR, p. 483.

[207] 4 Iran–US CTR, p. 156; 85 ILR, p. 392. Cf. the concurring opinion by Judge Holtzmann on this issue, 4 Iran–US CTR, pp. 159, 178; 85 ILR, p. 414.

[208] *Kalamazoo Spice Extraction Company* v. *The Provisional Military Government of Socialist Ethiopia*, 86 ILR, p. 45 and 90 ILR, p. 596. See also *Agip SpA* v. *The Government of the Popular Republic of the Congo*, 67 ILR, p. 319 and *Benvenuti and Bonfant* v. *The Government of the Popular Republic of the Congo*, ibid., p. 345.

[209] PCIJ, Series A, No. 7, 1926. See also the *Norwegian Shipowners' Claims* case, 1 RIAA, p. 307 (1922) and the *Sporrong and Lönnroth* case before the European Court of Human Rights, Series A, No. 52 (1982); 68 ILR, p. 86. See also *Papamichalopoulos* v. *Greece*, European Court of Human Rights, Series A, No. 260 (1993), p. 15. Note in addition *Revere Copper* v. *Opic*, 56 ILR, p. 258. See Christie, 'What Constitutes a Taking of Property under International Law?', 38 BYIL, 1962, p. 307; DUSPIL, 1976, p. 444; Brownlie, *System*, pp. 24–5; Whiteman, *Digest*, vol. VIII, pp. 1006 *et seq.* and *Third US Restatement on Foreign Relations Law*, vol. II, pp. 200–1.

Silesia case.[210] But how far this extends is open to dispute, although it will cover wartime measures.

The issue was raised in the *BP* case,[211] where the reason for the expropriation of the BP property was the Libyan belief that the UK had encouraged Iran to occupy certain Persian Gulf Islands. The arbitrator explained that the taking violated international law 'as it was made for purely extraneous political reasons and was arbitrary and discriminatory in character'.[212] This is ambiguous as to the public purpose issue, and in the *Liamco* case[213] it was held that 'the public utility principle is not a necessary requisite for the legality of a nationalisation'.[214] It is to be noted, however, that the 1962 General Assembly Resolution on Permanent Sovereignty over Natural Resources mentions this requirement,[215] although the 1974 Charter of Economic Rights and Duties of States does not.[216] The question is thus still an open one.[217]

Compensation

The requirement often stipulated by Western authorities is for prompt, adequate and effective compensation, the formula used by US Secretary of State Hull on the occasion of Mexican expropriations.[218] It is the standard maintained in particular by the United States[219] and found in a number of bilateral investment treaties.[220] However, case law is less clear. Early cases

---

[210] PCIJ, Series A, No. 7, 1926, p. 22.   [211] 53 ILR, p. 297.   [212] *Ibid.*, p. 329.
[213] 20 ILM, 1981, p. 1; 62 ILR, p. 141.   [214] *Ibid.*, pp. 58–9; 62 ILR, p. 194.
[215] Paragraph 4 of the 1962 Resolution provides that '[n]ationalization, expropriation or requisitioning shall be based on grounds or reasons of public utility, security or the national interest which are recognized as overriding purely individual or private interests, both domestic and foreign. In such cases the owner shall be paid appropriate compensation in accordance with the rules in force in the state taking such measures in the exercise of its sovereignty and in accordance with international law. In any case where the question of compensation gives rise to a controversy, the national jurisdiction of the state taking such measures shall be exhausted. However, upon agreement by sovereign states and other parties concerned, settlement of the dispute should be made through arbitration or international adjudication.'
[216] Article 2(2)c of the 1974 Charter provides that every state has the right to 'nationalise, expropriate or transfer ownership of foreign property in which case appropriate compensation should be paid by the state adopting such measures, taking into account its relevant laws and regulations and all circumstances that the state considers pertinent. In any case where the question of compensation gives rise to a controversy, it shall be settled under the domestic law of the nationalising state and by its tribunals, unless it is freely and mutually agreed by all states concerned that other peaceful means be sought on the basis of the sovereign equality of states and in accordance with the principle of free choice of means.'
[217] See also *Agip SpA* v. *The Government of the Popular Republic of the Congo*, 67 ILR, pp. 319, 336–9.
[218] Hackworth, *Digest*, vol. III, 1940–4, p. 662. See also Muchlinski, *Multinational Enterprises*, pp. 506 *et seq.* and E. Lauterpacht, 'Issues of Compensation and Nationality in the Taking of Energy Investments', 8 *Journal of Energy and Natural Resources Law*, 1990, p. 241.
[219] See e.g. DUSPIL, 1976, p. 444 and D. Robinson, 'Expropriation in the Restatement (Revised)', 78 AJIL, 1984, p. 176.   [220] *Ibid.*, p. 178. See further *infra* p. 580.

did not use the Hull formulation[221] and the 1962 Permanent Sovereignty Resolution referred to 'appropriate compensation'. This phrase, in fact, was cited with approval by the arbitrator in the *Texaco* case[222] as a rule of customary law in view of the support it achieved. This was reinforced in the *Aminoil* case[223] where the tribunal said that the standard of 'appropriate compensation' in the 1962 resolution 'codifies positive principles'.[224] It was stated that the determination of 'appropriate compensation' was better accomplished by an inquiry into all the circumstances relevant to the particular concrete case than through abstract theoretical discussion.[225] This practical and acceptable formulation is likely to prove influential. It should, however, be noted that while the 'appropriate compensation' formula of the 1962 resolution is linked to both national and international law, the 1974 Charter of Economic Rights and Duties of States links the formula to domestic law and considerations only. While the former instrument is accepted, as noted above, as a reflection of custom, the latter is not.[226] But in any event, it is unclear whether in practice there would be a substantial difference in result.[227]

It should also be noted that section IV(1) of the World Bank Guidelines on the Treatment of Foreign Direct Investment provides that a state may not expropriate foreign private investment except where this is done in accordance with applicable legal procedures, in pursuance in good faith of a public purpose, without discrimination on the basis of nationality and against the payment of appropriate compensation. Section IV(2) notes that compensation will be deemed to be appropriate where it is adequate, prompt and effective.[228] Article 13 of the European Energy Charter Treaty

---

[221] See e.g. the *Chorzow Factory* case, PCIJ, Series A, No. 17, 1928, p. 46; 4 ILR, p. 268 and the *Norwegian Shipowners' Claims* case, 1 RIAA, pp. 307, 339–41 (1922). See also O. Schachter, 'Compensation for Expropriation', 78 AJIL, 1984, p. 121.
[222] 17 ILM, 1978, pp. 3, 29; 53 ILR, pp. 389, 489. See also *Banco Nacional de Cuba* v. *Chase Manhattan Bank*, 658 F.2d 875 (1981); 66 ILR, p. 421.
[223] 21 ILM, 1982, p. 976; 66 ILR, p. 519.   [224] *Ibid.*, p. 1032; 66 ILR, p. 601.
[225] *Ibid.*, p. 1033.
[226] See e.g. the *Texaco* case, 17 ILM, 1978, pp. 1, 29–31; 53 ILR, p. 489. Note that the *Third US Restatement of Foreign Relations Law*, p. 196 (para. 712) refers to the requirement of 'just compensation' and not the Hull formula. This is defined as 'an amount equivalent to the value of the property taken and to be paid at the time of taking or within a reasonable time thereafter with interest from the date of taking and in a form economically usable by the foreign national', *ibid.*, p. 197. See also Schachter, 'Compensation', p. 121.
[227] See generally also R. Dolzer, 'New Foundation of the Law of Expropriation of Alien Property', 75 AJIL, 1981, p. 533 and Sornarajah, 'Compensation for Expropriation', 13 *Journal of World Trade Law*, 1979, p. 108 and Sornarajah, *The International Law on Foreign Investment*, 1994.
[228] 31 ILM, 1992, p. 1382. Note also that article 1110 of NAFTA (North American Free Trade Agreement) 1992 provides that no party shall directly or indirectly nationalise or expropriate an investment of an investor of another party in its territory or take a measure tantamount to nationalisation or expropriation except where it is for a public purpose, on a non-discriminatory basis, in accordance with due process of law and upon payment of compensation. The payment of compensation is to be the fair market value of the expropri-

STATE RESPONSIBILITY 579

1994 provides that expropriation must be for a purpose which is in the public interest, not discriminatory, carried out under due process of law and accompanied by the payment of prompt, adequate and effective compensation.[229]

In the sensitive and controversial process of assessing the extent of compensation, several distinct categories should be noted. There is generally little dispute about according compensation for the physical assets and other assets of the enterprise such as debts or monies due,[230] although there are differing methods as to how to value such assets in particular cases.[231] Interest on the value of such assets will also be normally paid.[232] There is, however, disagreement with regard to the award of compensation for the loss of future profits. In *AMCO v Indonesia*,[233] the Arbitral Tribunal held that:

> the full compensation of prejudice, by awarding to the injured party, the *damnum emergens* [loss suffered] and the *lucrum cessans* [expected profits] is a principle common to the main systems of municipal law, and therefore, a general principle of law which may be considered as a source of international law,

although the compensation that could be awarded would cover only direct and foreseeable prejudice and not more remote damage.[234]

However, this approach needs to be carefully considered. In particular one may need to take into account whether the expropriation itself was lawful or unlawful. In *INA Corporation v. The Islamic Republic of Iran*,[235] the Tribunal suggested that in the case of a large-scale, lawful nationalisation 'international law has undergone a gradual reappraisal, the effect of which may be to undermine the doctrinal value of any "full" or "adequate" (when used as identical to "full") compensation standard'. However, in a situation involving an investment of a small amount shortly before the nationalisation, international law did allow for compensation in an amount equal to the fair market value

ated investment immediately before the expropriation took place and shall not reflect any change in value occurring because the intended expropriation had become known earlier. Valuation criteria shall include going concern value, asset value (including declared tax value of tangible property) and other criteria, as appropriate to determine fair market value. In addition, compensation shall be paid with interest, without delay and be fully realisable. See 32 ILM, 1993, p. 605.   [229] 34 ILM, 1995, p. 391.
[230] See e.g. the *Liamco* case, 62 ILR, pp. 140, 201. See also Bowett, 'State Contracts with Aliens', p. 61 and Greenwood, 'State Contracts', pp. 77–9.
[231] See e.g. the *Aminoil* case, 21 ILM, 1982, pp. 976, 1038; 66 ILR, pp. 519, 608–9.
[232] See the Memorandum of the Foreign and Commonwealth Office on the Practice of International Tribunals in Awarding Interest, UKMIL, 63 BYIL, 1992, p. 768.
[233] 24 ILM, 1985, pp. 1022, 1036–7; 89 ILR, pp. 405, 504. See also the *Chorzow Factory* case, PCIJ, Series A, No. 17, 1928; 4 ILR, p. 268; the *Sapphire* case, 35 ILR, p. 136; the *Norwegian Shipowners' Claims* case, 1 RIAA, p. 307 (1922); the *Lighthouses Arbitration*, 23 ILR, p. 299, and *Benvenuti and Bonfant* v. *The Government of the Popular Republic of the Congo*, 67 ILR, pp. 345, 375–9.
[234] 24 ILM, 1985, pp. 1022, 1037; 89 ILR, p. 505. See also *Sola Tiles Inc.* v. *Islamic Republic of Iran*, 83 ILR, p. 460.   [235] 8 Iran–US CTR, p. 373; 75 ILR, p. 595.

of the investment.[236] Fair market value meant the amount that a willing buyer would have paid a willing seller for the shares of a going concern, ignoring the expropriation situation completely.[237] However, Judge Lagergren noted that the 'fair market value' standard would normally be discounted in cases of lawful large-scale nationalisations in taking account of 'all circumstances'.[238]

In *Amoco International Finance Corporation* v. *The Islamic Republic of Iran*,[239] Chamber Three of the Iran–US Claims Tribunal held that the property in question had been lawfully expropriated and that 'a clear distinction must be made between lawful and unlawful expropriations, since the rules applicable to the compensation to be paid by the expropriating state differ according to the legal characterisation of the taking'.[240] In the case of an unlawful taking, full restitution in kind or its monetary equivalent was required in order to re-establish the situation which would in all probability have existed if the expropriation had not occurred,[241] while in the case of lawful taking, the standard was the payment of the full value of the undertaking at the moment of dispossession. The difference was interpreted by the Tribunal to mean that compensation for lost profits was only available in cases of wrongful expropriation. As far as the actual method of valuation was concerned, the Tribunal rejected the 'discounted cash flow' method, which would involve the estimation of the likely future earnings of the company at the valuation date and discounting such earnings to take account of reasonably foreseeable risks, since it was likely to amount to restitution as well as being too speculative.[242]

Bilateral investment treaties and lump-sum agreements

In practice many of the situations involving commercial relations between states and private parties fall within the framework of bilateral agreements.[243] These arrangements are intended to encourage investment in a

---

[236] *Ibid.*, p. 378; 75 ILR, p. 602.   [237] *Ibid.*, p. 380; 75 ILR, p. 603.
[238] *Ibid.*, p. 390; 75 ILR, p. 614.   [239] 15 Iran–US CTR, pp. 189, 246–52; 83 ILR, p. 500.
[240] *Ibid.*, p. 246; 83 ILR, p. 565.
[241] See also Judge Lagergren's separate opinion in *INA Corporation* v. *The Islamic Republic of Iran*, 8 Iran–US CTR, p. 385; 75 ILR, p. 609.
[242] But see e.g. *AIG* v. *The Islamic Republic of Iran*, 4 Iran–US CTR, pp. 96, 109–10, where in a case of lawful expropriation lost profits were awarded. See also Brownlie, *Principles*, pp. 537–9; Section IV of the World Bank Guidelines, and article 13 of the European Energy Charter Treaty 1994
[243] See e.g. E. Denza and D. Brooks, 'Investment Protection Treaties: United Kingdom Experience', 36 ICLQ, 1987, p. 908; Akinsanya, 'International Protection of Direct Foreign Investments in the Third World', *ibid.*, p. 58; F. A. Mann, 'British Treaties for the Promotion and Protection of Investments', 52 BYIL, 1981, p. 241; D. Vagts, 'Foreign Investment Risk Reconsidered: The View From the 1980s', 2 *ICSID Review – Foreign Investment Law Journal*, 1987, p. 1; Gann 'The US Bilateral Investment Treaties Program', 21 *Stanford Journal of International Law*, 1986, p. 373 and I. Pogany, 'The Regulation of Foreign Investment in Hungary', 4 *ICSID Review – Foreign Investment Law Journal*, 1989, p. 39.

way that protects the basic interests of both the capital-exporting and capital-importing states. Indeed, the British government has stated that it is its policy to conclude as many bilateral investment promotion and protection agreements as possible in order to stimulate investment flows. It has also been noted that they are designed to set standards applicable in international law.[244] The provisions of such agreements indeed constitute valuable state practice,[245] but great care has to be taken in inferring the existence of a rule of customary international law from a range of bilateral treaties.[246]

Bearing this important proviso in mind, it is interesting to note some of the features of such treaties. First, the concept of an investment is invariably broadly defined. In article 1(a) of the important UK–USSR bilateral investment treaty 1989,[247] for example, it is provided that:

> the term 'investment' means every kind of asset and in particular, though not exclusively, includes:
>
> (i) movable and immovable property and any other related property rights such as mortgages;
>
> (ii) shares in, and stocks, bonds and debentures of, and any other form of participation in, a company or business enterprise;
>
> (iii) claims to money, and claims to performance under contract having a financial value;
>
> (iv) intellectual property rights, technical processes, know-how and any other benefit or advantage attached to a business;
>
> (v) rights conferred by law or under contract to undertake any commercial activity, including the search for, or the cultivation, extraction or exploitation of natural resources.[248]

Secondly, both parties undertake to encourage and create favourable conditions for investment, to accord such investments 'fair and equitable treatment' and to refrain from impairing by unreasonable or discriminatory measures the management, maintenance, use, enjoyment or disposal of investments in its territory.[249] Thirdly, investments by the contracting parties are not to be treated less favourably than those of other states.[250] As

---

[244] See the text of the Foreign Office statement in UKMIL, 58 BYIL, 1987, p. 620. Such agreements are often termed investment promotion and protection agreements (IPPAs).

[245] The total number of bilateral investment treaties worldwide on record as at 15 July 1996 was 1,010, see 35 ILM, 1996, p. 1130. See also Denza and Brooks, 'Investment Protection Treaties', p. 913 and UKMIL, 58 BYIL, 1987, p. 621.

[246] But cf. R. Dolzer, who argues that such agreements constitute state practice supporting the traditional view of compensation for expropriation, 'New Foundations of the Law of Expropriation of Alien Property', 75 AJIL, 1981, pp. 553, 565–6. See also B. Kishoiyian, 'The Utility of Bilateral Investment Treaties in the Formulation of Customary International Law', 14 *Netherlands Journal of International Law and Business*, 1994, p. 327.

[247] Text reproduced in 29 ILM, 1989, p. 366.

[248] See also, for example, the similar provisions in the UK–Philippines Investment Agreement 1981, and the UK–Hungary Investment Agreement 1987. See also article 1(6) of the European Energy Charter Treaty 1994.

[249] See e.g. article 2 of the UK–USSR agreement.

[250] See e.g. article 3 of the UK–USSR agreement.

far as expropriation is concerned, article 5 of the UK–USSR agreement, by way of example, provides that investments of the contracting parties are not to be expropriated:

> except for a purpose which is in the public interest and is not discriminatory and against the payment, without delay, of prompt and effective compensation. Such compensation shall amount to the real value of the investment expropriated immediately before the expropriation or before the impending expropriation became public knowledge, whichever is the earlier, shall be made within two months of the date of expropriation, after which interest at a normal commercial rate shall accrue until the date of payment and shall be effectively realisable and be freely transferable. The investor affected shall have a right under the law of the contracting state making the expropriation, to prompt review, by a judicial or other independent authority of that party, of his or its case and of the valuation of his or its investment in accordance with the principles set out in this paragraph.

In other words, the traditional principles dealing with the conditions of a lawful expropriation and the provision for compensation are reaffirmed, together with an acceptance of the jurisdiction of the expropriating state over the issues of the legality of the expropriation and the valuation of the property expropriated.[251]

Many disputes over expropriation of foreign property have in fact been resolved directly by the states concerned on the basis of lump-sum settlements, usually after protracted negotiations and invariably at valuation below the current value of the assets concerned.[252] For example, the UK–USSR Agreement on the Settlement of Mutual Financial and Property Claims 1986[253] dealt with UK government claims of the order of £500 million in respect of Russian war debt and private claims of British nationals amounting to some £400 million.[254] In the event, a sum in the region of £45 million was made available to satisfy these claims.[255] The Agreement also provided that money held in diplomatic bank accounts in the UK belonging to the prerevolutionary Russian embassy, amounting to some £2.65 million, was released to the Soviet authorities. As is usual in such agreements, each government was solely responsible for settling the claims

---

[251] Note that provisions for compensation for expropriation may also be contained in Treaties of Friendship, Commerce and Navigation as part of a framework arrangement dealing with foreign trade and investment, see e.g. article IV(3) of the Convention of Establishment 1959 between the US and France, 11 UST 2398.

[252] See e.g. R. B. Lillich and B. Weston, *International Claims: Their Settlement by Lump-Sum Agreements*, Charlottesville, 1975 and Lilich and Weston, 'Lump-Sum Agreements: Their Continuing Contribution to the Law of International Claims', 82 AJIL, 1988, p. 69.

[253] Cm. 30. Note that this Agreement dealt with claims arising before 1939.

[254] As against these claims, the USSR had made extensive claims in the region of £2 billion in respect of alleged losses caused by British intervention in the USSR between 1918 and 1921, see UKMIL, 57 BYIL, 1986, p. 606.

[255] The British government waived its entitlement to a share in the settlement in respect of its own claims, *ibid.*, p. 608.

of its nationals.[256] This was accomplished in the UK through the medium of the Foreign Compensation Commission, which acts to distribute settlement sums 'as may seem just and equitable to them having regard to all the circumstances'. A distinction was made as between bond and property claims and principles enunciated with regard to exchange rates at the relevant time.[257]

The question arises thus as to whether such agreements constitute state practice in the context of international customary rules concerning the level of compensation required upon an expropriation of foreign property. A Chamber of the Iran–US Claims Tribunal in *SEDCO* v. *National Iranian Oil Co.*[258] noted that deriving general principles of law from the conduct of states in lump-sum or negotiated settlements in other expropriation cases was difficult because of the 'questionable evidentiary value . . . of much of the practice available'. This was because such settlements were often motivated primarily by non-juridical considerations. The Chamber also held that bilateral investment treaties were also unreliable evidence of international customary standards of compensation. Views differ as to the value to be attributed to such practice,[259] but caution is required before accepting bilateral investment treaties and lump-sum agreements as evidence of customary law. This is particularly so with regard to the latter since they deal with specific situations rather than laying down a framework for future activity.[260] Nevertheless, it would be equally unwise to disregard them entirely. As with all examples of state practice and behaviour careful attention must be paid to all the relevant circumstances both of the practice maintained and the principle under consideration.

Non-discrimination

It has been argued that non-discrimination is a requirement for a valid and lawful expropriation.[261] Although it is not mentioned in the 1962 resolution, the arbitrator in the *Liamco*[262] case strongly argued that a discriminatory nationalisation would be unlawful.[263] Nevertheless, in that case, it was held that Libya's action against certain oil companies was aimed at preserving its

---

[256] See also the UK–China Agreement on the Settlement of Property Claims 1987, see UKMIL, 58 BYIL, 1987, p. 626.
[257] See with respect to the UK–USSR Agreement, the Foreign Compensation (USSR) (Registration and Determination of Claims) Order 1986, SI 1986/2222 and the Foreign Compensation (USSR) (Distribution) Order 1987.
[258] 10 Iran–US CTR, pp. 180, 185; 80 AJIL, 1986, p. 969.
[259] See e.g. Bowett, 'State Contracts with Aliens', pp. 65–6.
[260] Note the view of the International Court in the *Barcelona Traction* case that such settlements were *sui generis* and provided no guide as to general international practice, ICJ Reports, 1969, pp. 4, 40.   [261] See e.g. White, *Nationalisation*, pp. 119 *et seq.*
[262] 20 ILM, 1981, p. 1; 62 ILR, p. 141.   [263] *Ibid.*, pp. 58–9; 62 ILR, p. 194.

ownership of the oil and was non-discriminatory. Indeed, the arbitrator noted that the political motive itself was not the predominant motive for nationalisation and would not *per se* constitute sufficient proof of a purely discriminatory measure.[264] While the discrimination factor would certainly be a relevant factor to be considered, it would in practice often be extremely difficult to prove in concrete cases.

The Multilateral Investment Guarantee Agency[265]

One approach to the question of foreign investment and the balancing of the interests of the states concerned is provided by the Convention Establishing the Multilateral Investment Guarantee Agency 1985, which came into force in 1988.[266] Article 2 provides that the purpose of the Agency, which is an affiliate of the World Bank, is to encourage the flow of investment for productive purposes among member countries and, in particular, to developing countries. This is to be achieved in essence by the provision of insurance cover 'against non-commercial risks', such as restrictions on the transfer of currency, measures of expropriation, breaches of government contracts and losses resulting from war or civil disturbances.[267] It is also intended that the Agency would positively encourage investment by means of research and the dissemination of information on investment opportunities. It may very well be that this initiative could in the long term reduce the sensitive nature of the expropriation mechanism.[268]

---

[264] *Ibid.*, p. 60. See also Section IV of the World Bank Guidelines on the Treatment of Foreign Direct Investment, and article 13 of the European Energy Charter Treaty 1994.

[265] See e.g. S. K. Chatterjee, 'The Convention Establishing the Multilateral Investment Guarantee Agency', 36 ICLQ, 1987, p. 76 and I. Shihata, *The Multilateral Investment Guarantee Agency and Foreign Investment*, 1987. The Convention came into force on 12 April 1988, see 28 ILM, 1989, p. 1233.

[266] See e.g. the UK Multilateral Investment Guarantee Agency Act 1988.   [267] Article 11.

[268] Note that issues relating to the peaceful settlement of such disputes in general will be discussed in Chapter 18.

INTERNATIONAL ENVIRONMENTAL LAW

Recent years have seen an appreciable growth in the level of understanding of the dangers facing the international environment[1] and an extensive range of environmental problems is now the subject of serious international concern.[2] These include atmospheric pollution, marine pollution, global warming and ozone depletion, the dangers of nuclear and other extra-hazardous substances and threatened wildlife species.[3] Such problems have an

---

[1] See generally P. Sands, *Principles of International Environmental Law*, Manchester, 1995; V. P. Nanda, *International Environmental Law and Policy*, New York, 1995; P. Birnie and A. Boyle, *International Law and the Environment*, Oxford, 1992; A. Kiss and D. Shelton, *International Environmental Law*, 1991; *Greening International Law* (ed. P. Sands), London, 1993; *Basic Documents of International Environmental Law* (ed. H. Hohmann, 3 vols., Dordrecht, 1992; A. Kiss, *Le Droit International de l'Environnement*, 1989 and 'The International Protection of the Environment' in *The Structure and Process of International Law* (eds. R. St J. Macdonald and D. Johnston), 1983, p. 1069, and *Survey of Current Developments in International Environmental Law*, 1976; L. Caldwell, *International Environmental Policy*, 2nd edn, 1990; *International Environmental Diplomacy* (ed. G. Carroll), 1988; J. Barros and D. M. Johnston, *The International Law of Pollution*, 1974; *International Environmental Law* (eds. L. Teclaff and A. Utton), 1974; *Trends in Environmental Policy and Law* (ed. M. Bothe), 1980; Hague Academy of International Law Colloque 1973, *The Protection of the Environment and International Law* (ed. A. Kiss); *ibid.*, Colloque 1984, *The Future of the International Law of the Environment* (ed. R. J. Dupuy); J. Schneider, *World Public Order of the Environment*, 1979; A. L. Springer, *The International Law of Pollution: Protecting the Global Environment in a World of Sovereign States*, 1983; *International Environmental Law* (eds. C. D. Gurumatry, G. W. R. Palmer and B. Weston), St Paul, 1994; I. Brownlie, 'International Customary Rules of Environmental Protection', *International Relations*, 1973, p. 240; E. Brown Weiss, *In Fairness to Future Generations: International Law, Common Patrimony and Intergenerational Equity*, 1989; *Chernobyl: Law and Communication* (ed. P. Sands), Cambridge, 1988 and A. Boyle, 'Nuclear Energy and International Law: An Environmental Perspective', 60 BYIL, 1989, p. 257. See also *Selected Multilateral Treaties in the Field of the Environment*, 2 vols., 1991; A. O. Adede, *International Environmental Law Digest*, 1993 and P. Sands, R. Tarasofsky and M. Weiss, *Documents in International Environmental Law*, 2 vols., Manchester, 1994.

[2] This may be measured by the fact that in July 1993, the International Court of Justice established a special Chamber to deal with environmental questions. It has as yet heard no cases. See R. Ranjeva, 'L'Environnement, La Cour Internationale de Justice et sa Chambre Spéciale pour les Questions d'Environnement', AFDI, 1994, p. 433. Note also the Environmental Annex (Annex IV) to the Israel–Jordan Peace Treaty 1994 and article 18 of the Treaty, 34 ILM, 1995, p. 43. See also Annex II on Water Related Matters.

[3] See as to endangered species e.g. M. Carwardine, *The WWF Environment Handbook*, London, 1990 and S. Lyster, *International Wildlife Law*, Cambridge, 1985. See also the Convention on International Trade in Endangered Species 1973 covering animals and plants, and the Convention on Biological Diversity 1992, which *inter alia* calls upon parties

international dimension in two obvious respects. First, pollution generated from within a particular state often has a serious impact upon other countries. The prime example would be acid rain, whereby chemicals emitted from factories rise in the atmosphere and react with water and sunlight to form acids. These are carried in the wind and fall eventually to earth in the rain, often thousands of miles away from the initial polluting event.

Secondly, it is now apparent that environmental problems cannot be resolved by states acting individually. Accordingly, co-operation between the polluting and the polluted state is necessitated. However, the issue becomes more complicated in those cases where it is quite impossible to determine from which country a particular form of environmental pollution has emanated. This would be the case, for example, with ozone depletion. In other words, the international nature of pollution, both with regard to its creation and the damage caused, is now accepted as requiring an international response.

The initial conceptual problem posed for international law lies in the state-oriented nature of the discipline. Traditionally, a state would only be responsible in the international legal sense for damage caused where it could be clearly demonstrated that this resulted from its own unlawful activity.[4] This has proved to be an inadequate framework for dealing with environmental issues for a variety of reasons, ranging from difficulties of proof to liability for lawful activities and the particular question of responsibility of non-state offenders. Accordingly, the international community has slowly been moving away from the classic state responsibility approach to damage caused towards a regime of international cooperation. The way in which this has occurred forms one of the major themes of this chapter.

A broad range of international participants are concerned with developments in this field. States, of course, as the dominant subjects of the international legal system are deeply involved, as are an increasing number of international organisations, whether at the global, regional or bilateral level. The United Nations General Assembly has adopted a number of resolutions concerning the environment,[5] and the UN Environment Programme was established after the Stockholm Conference of 1972. This has proved a particularly important organisation in the evolution of conventions and instruments in the field of environmental protection. It is based in Nairobi and consists of Governing Council of fifty-eight members elected by the General Assembly. UNEP has been responsible for the development of a number of

---

to promote priority access on a fair and equitable basis by all parties, especially developing countries, to the results and benefits arising from biotechnologies based upon genetic resources provided by contracting parties.   [4] See further *supra*, Chapter 14.
[5] See e.g. resolutions 2398(XXII); 2997(XXVII); 34/188; 35/8; 37/137; 37/250; 42/187; 44/244; 44/228; 45/212 and 47/188.

initiatives, including the 1985 Vienna Convention for the Protection of the Ozone Layer and the 1987 Montreal Protocol and the 1992 Convention on Biodiversity. An Inter-Agency Committee on Sustainable Development was set up in 1992 to improve co-operation between the various UN bodies concerned with this topic. In the same year, the UN Commission on Sustainable Development was established by the General Assembly and the Economic and Social Council of the UN (ECOSOC). It consists of fifty-three states elected by ECOSOC and it exists in order to follow up the UN Conference on Environment and Development 1992. The techniques of supervision utilised in international bodies include reporting,[6] inspection[7] and standard-setting through the adoption of conventions, regulations, guidelines and so forth. In 1994 it was agreed to transform the Global Environment Facility from a three-year pilot programme[8] into a permanent financial mechanism to award grants and concessional funds to developing countries for global environmental protection projects.[9] The Facility is intended to focus upon climate change, the destruction of biological diversity, the pollution of international waters and ozone depletion. Issues of land degradation[10] will also be eligible within this framework. In addition, a wide range of non-governmental organisations are also concerned with environmental issues.

It has been argued that there now exists an international human right to a clean environment.[11] There are, of course, a range of general human rights provisions that may have a relevance in the field of environmental protection, such as the right to life, right to an adequate standard of living, right to health, right to food and so forth, but specific references to a human right to a clean environment have tended to be few and ambiguous.

The preamble to the seminal Stockholm Declaration of the UN Conference on the Human Environment 1972 noted that the environment was 'essential to . . . the enjoyment of basic human rights – even the right to

---

[6] As e.g. under the Prevention of Marine Pollution from Land-Based Sources Convention 1974 and the Basle Convention on the Control of Transboundary Movements of Hazardous Wastes 1989.
[7] See e.g. the Antarctic Treaty 1959 and the Protocol on Environmental Protection 1991. See with regard to the International Whaling Commission, P. Birnie, *International Regulation of Whaling*, New York, 1985, p. 199.   [8] See 30 ILM, 1991, p. 1735.
[9] See 33 ILM, 1994, p. 1273.
[10] See also the UN Convention to Combat Desertification 1994, *ibid.*, p. 1328.
[11] See, e.g. M. Pallemaerts, 'International Environmental Law From Stockholm to Rio: Back to the Future ?' in Sands, *Greening International Law*, pp. 1, 8; *Environement et droits de l'homme* (ed. Kromarek), 1987; G. Alfredson and A. Ovsiouk, 'Human Rights and the Environment', 60 *Nordic Journal of International Law*, 1991, p. 19; W. P. Gormley, *Human Rights and Environment*, Leiden, 1976; *Human Rights and Environmental Protection* (ed. A. Cançado Trindade), 1992; and D. Shelton, 'Whatever Happened In Rio to Human Rights?' 3 *Yearbook of International Environmental Law*, 1992, p. 75. See also Birnie and Boyle, *International Law and the Environment*, pp. 190 *et seq.* See also *Human Rights Approaches to Environmental Protection* (eds. M. Anderson and A. E. Boyle), Oxford, 1996.

life itself', while Principle 1 stated that 'Man has the fundamental right to freedom, equality and adequate conditions of life, in an environment of a quality that permits a life of dignity and well-being.' Article 24 of the African Charter of Human and Peoples' Rights 1981 provided that 'all people shall have the right to a general satisfactory environment favourable to their development', while article 11 of the Additional Protocol to the American Convention on Human Rights 1988 declared that 'everyone shall have the right to live in a healthy environment' and that 'the states parties shall promote the protection, preservation and improvement of the environment'. Article 29 of the Convention on the Rights of the Child 1989 explicitly referred to the need for the education of the child to be directed *inter alia* to 'the development of respect for the natural environment'.

The final text of the Conference on Security and Co-operation in Europe (CSCE) meeting on the environment in Sofia in 1989 reaffirmed respect for the right of individuals, groups and organisations concerned with the environment to express freely their views, to associate with others and assemble peacefully, to obtain and distribute relevant information and to participate in public debates on environmental issues.[12] It should also be noted that the Convention on Environmental Impact Assessment In a Transboundary Context 1991 calls for the 'establishment of an environmental impact assessment procedure that permits public participation' in certain circumstances.

However, the references to human rights in the Rio Declaration on Environment and Development adopted at the UN Conference on Environment and Development in 1992[13] are rather sparse. Principle 1 declares that human beings are 'at the centre of concerns for sustainable development. They are entitled to a healthy and productive life in harmony with nature'. Beyond this tangential reference, human rights concerns were not, it is fair to say, at the centre of the documentation produced by the 1992 conference. In fact, it is fair to say that the focus of the conference was rather upon states and their sovereign rights than upon individuals and their rights.

Nevertheless, moves to associate the two areas of international law are moving cautiously forward. In 1994, the final report on Human Rights and the Environment was delivered to the UN Sub-Commission on Prevention of Discrimination and Protection of Minorities.[14] The Report contains a set of Draft Principles on Human Rights and the Environment, which includes the notion that 'human rights, an ecologically sound environment, sustainable development and peace are interdependent and indivisible' and that 'all persons have the right to a secure, healthy and ecologically sound environ-

---

[12] CSCE/SEM.36. See also EC Directive 90/313, 1990.
[13] See generally as to the Rio Conference, S. Johnson, *The Earth Summit*, Dordrecht, 1993.
[14] E/CN.4/Sub.2/1994/9.

ment. This right and other human rights, including civil, cultural, economic, political and social rights are universal, interdependent and indivisible'. It remains to be seen whether this initiative will bear fruit.

The question of the relationship between the protection of the environment and the need for economic development is another factor underpinning the evolution of environmental law. States that are currently attempting to industrialise face the problem that to do so in an environmentally safe way is very expensive and the resources that can be devoted to this are extremely limited. The Stockholm Declaration of the United Nations Conference on the Human Environment 1972 emphasised in Principle 8 that 'economic and social development is essential for ensuring a favourable living and working environment for man and for creating conditions on earth that are necessary for the improvement of the quality of life', while the sovereign right of states to exploit their own resources was also stressed.[15] Principle 2 of the Rio Declaration, adopted at the United Nations Conference on Environment and Development 1992, noted that states have 'the sovereign right to exploit their own resources pursuant to their own environmental and developmental policies', while Principle 3 stated that 'the right to development must be fulfilled so as to equitably meet developmental and environmental needs of present and future generations'. The correct balance between development and environmental protection is now one of the main challenges facing the international community and reflects the competing interests posed by the principle of state sovereignty on the one hand and the need for international co-operation on the other. It also raises the issue as to how far one takes into account the legacy for future generations of activities conducted at the present time or currently planned. Many developmental activities, such as the creation of nuclear power plants for example, may have significant repercussions for many generations to come.[16] The Energy Charter Treaty[17] signed at Lisbon in 1994 by OECD and Eastern European and CIS states refers to environmental issues in the context of energy concerns in a rather less than robust fashion. Article 19 notes that contracting parties 'shall strive to minimise in an economically efficient manner harmful environmental impacts'. In so doing, parties are to act 'in a cost-effective manner'. Parties are to 'strive to take precautionary measures to prevent or minimise environmental degradation' and agree

---

[15] Principle 21.
[16] See e.g. A. D'Amato, 'Do We Owe a Duty to Future Generations to Preserve the Global Environment?', 84 AJIL, 1990, p. 190; Sands, *Principles*, p. 199 and E. B .Weiss, 'Our Rights and Obligations to Future Generations for the Environment', 84 AJIL, 1990, p. 198 and E. B. Weiss, *Intergenerational Equity*. See also *Minors Oposa* v. *Secretary of the Department of Environment and Natural Resources*, Supreme Court of the Philippines, 33 ILM, 1994, pp. 173, 185 and Judge Weeramantry's Dissenting Opinion in the *Request for an Examination of the Situation in Accordance with Paragraph 63 of the Nuclear Tests* case, ICJ Reports, 1995, pp. 288, 341.   [17] 33 ILM, 1995, p. 360.

that the polluter should 'in principle, bear the cost of pollution, including transboundary pollution, with due regard to the public interest and without distorting investment in the energy cycle or international trade'.

One potentially innovative method for linking economic underdevelopment and protection of the environment is the 'debt for nature swops' arrangement, whereby debts owed abroad may be converted into an obligation upon the debtor state to spend the amount of the debt upon local environment projects.[18]

State responsibility and the environment[19]

The basic duty of states

The principles of state responsibility[20] dictate that states are accountable for breaches of international law. Such breaches of treaty or customary international law enable the injured state to maintain a claim against the violating state, whether by way of diplomatic action or by way of recourse to international mechanisms where such are in place with regard to the subject-matter at issue. Recourse to international arbitration or to the International Court of Justice are also possible provided the necessary jurisdictional basis has been established. Customary international law imposes several important fundamental obligations upon states in the area of environmental protection. The view that international law supports an approach predicated upon absolute territorial sovereignty, so that a state could do as it liked irrespective of the consequences upon other states, has long been discredited. The basic duty upon states is not to so act as to injure the rights of other states.[21] This duty has evolved partly out of the regime concerned with international waterways. In the *International Commission on the River Oder* case, [22] for example, the Permanent Court of International Justice noted that 'this community of interest in a navigable river becomes the basis of a common legal right, the essential features of which are the perfect equality of all riparian states in the use of the whole course of the river and the exclusion of any preferential privileges of any riparian state in relation to others'.[23] But the principle is of far wider application. It was noted in the *Island of Palmas*

---

[18] See e.g. F. G. Minujin, 'Debt-for-Nature Swops: A Financial Mechanism to Reduce Debt and Preserve the Environment', 21 *Environmental Policy and Law*, 1991, p. 146 and S. George, *The Debt Boomerang*, London, 1992, pp. 30–1.

[19] See e.g. B. D. Smith, *State Responsibility and the Marine Environment*, Oxford, 1988. See also R. Lefeber, *Transboundary Environmental Interference and the Origin of State Liability*, Dordrecht, 1996.   [20] See further *supra* Chapter 14.

[21] See the doctrine expressed by Judson Harmon, Attorney-General of the United States in 1895, 21 *Op. Att'y. Gen.* 274, 283 (1895), cited in Nanda, *International Environmental Law*, pp. 155–6.   [22] PCIJ, Series A, No. 23 (1929); 5 ILR, p. 83.

[23] *Ibid.*, p. 27; 5 ILR, p. 84.

case[24] that the concept of territorial sovereignty incorporated an obligation to protect within the territory the rights of other states. In the *Trail Smelter* arbitration,[25] the Tribunal was concerned with a dispute between Canada and the United States over sulphur dioxide pollution from a Canadian smelter, built in a valley shared by British Columbia and the state of Washington, which damaged trees and crops on the American side of the border. The Tribunal noted that:

> under principles of international law, as well as the law of the United States, no state has the right to use or permit the use of territory in such a manner as to cause injury by fumes in or to the territory of another or the properties or persons therein, when the case is of serious consequence and the injury is established by clear and convincing evidence.[26]

The International Court reinforced this approach, by emphasising in the *Corfu Channel* case[27] that it was the obligation of every state 'not to allow knowingly its territory to be used for acts contrary to the rights of other states'.[28] The Court also noted in the *Request for an Examination of the Situation in Accordance with Paragraph 63 of the Nuclear Tests Case 1974* case in 1995, that its conclusion with regard to French nuclear testing in the Pacific was 'without prejudice to the obligations of states to respect and protect the environment'.[29] In addition, in its Advisory Opinion to the UN General Assembly on the *Legality of the Threat or Use of Nuclear Weapons*, the Court declared that 'the existence of the general obligation of states to ensure that activities within their jurisdiction and control respect the environment of other states or of areas beyond national control is now part of the corpus of international law relating to the environment'.[30]

This judicial approach has now been widely reaffirmed in international instruments. Article 192 of the Law of the Sea Convention 1982 provides that 'states have the obligation to protect and preserve the marine environment', while article 194 notes that 'states shall take all measures necessary to ensure that activities under their jurisdiction and control are so conducted as not to cause damage by pollution to other states and their

---

[24] 2 RIAA, pp. 829, 839.
[25] See 33 AJIL, 1939, p. 182 and 35 AJIL, 1941, p. 684; 9 ILR, p. 315. See also Read, 'The Trail Smelter Arbitration', 1 *Canadian Yearbook of International Law*, 1963, p. 213; R. Kirgis, 'Technological Challenge of the Shared Environment: US Practice', 66 AJIL, 1974, p. 291 and L. Goldie, 'A General View of International Environmental Law – A Survey of Capabilities, Trends and Limits' in *Hague Colloque 1973*, pp. 26, 66–9.
[26] 35 AJIL, 1941, p. 716; 9 ILR, p. 317. Canada invoked the *Trail Smelter* principle against the United States when an oil spill at Cherry Point, Washington, resulted in contamination of beaches in British Columbia, see 11 Canadian YIL, 1973, p. 333.
[27] ICJ Reports, 1949, pp. 4, 22; 16 ILR, p. 155, 158.
[28] See also the dissenting opinion of Judge de Castro in the *Nuclear Tests* case, ICJ Reports, 1974, pp. 253, 388; 57 ILR, pp. 350, 533 and the *Lac Lanoux* case, 24 ILR, p. 101.
[29] ICJ Reports, 1995, pp. 288, 306.
[30] ICJ Reports, 1996, para. 29; 35 ILM, 1996, pp. 809, 821.

environment'.[31] The shift of focus from the state alone to a wider perspective including the high seas, deep sea-bed and outer space is a noticeable development.[32]

It is, however, Principle 21 of the Stockholm Declaration of 1972 that is of especial significance. It stipulates that in addition to the sovereign right to exploit their own resources pursuant to their own environmental policies, states have 'the responsibility to ensure that activities within their jurisdiction or control do not cause damage to the environment of other states or of areas beyond the limits of national jurisdiction'. Although a relatively modest formulation repeated in Principle 2 of the Rio Declaration 1992, it has been seen as an important turning-point in the development of international environmental law.[33] Several issues of importance are raised in the formulation contained in Principle 21 and to those we now turn.

The appropriate standard

It is sometimes argued that the appropriate standard for the conduct of states in this field is that of strict liability. In other words, states are under an absolute obligation to prevent pollution and are thus liable for its effects irrespective of fault.[34] While the advantage of this is the increased responsibility placed upon the state, it is doubtful whether international law has in fact accepted such a general principle.[35] The leading cases are inconclusive. In the *Trail Smelter* case[36] Canada's responsibility was accepted from the start, the case focusing upon the compensation due and the terms of the future operation of the smelter,[37] while the strict theory was not apparently accepted in the *Corfu Channel* case.[38] In the *Nuclear Tests* case[39] the Court did not discuss the substance of the claims concerning nuclear testing in view of France's decision to end its programme.

[31] See also Principle 3 of the UN Environment Programme Principles of Conduct in the Field of the Environment concerning Resources Shared by Two or More States 1978; the Charter of Economic Rights and Duties of States adopted in General Assembly resolution 1974 3281(XXIX) and General Assembly resolution 34/186 (1979).

[32] See Boyle, 'Nuclear Energy', p. 271.

[33] See e.g. Kiss, *Survey*, p. 25 and 'The International Protection of the Environment', p. 1075. See also the preamble to the Convention on Long-Range Transboundary Air Pollution 1979.

[34] See e.g. Goldie, 'General View', pp. 73–85 and Schneider, *World Public Order*, Chapter 6. See also Handl, 'State Liability for Accidental Transnational Environmental Damage by Private Persons', 74 AJIL, 1980, p. 525; Birnie and Boyle, *International Law and the Environment*, p. 141 and Sands, *Principles*, pp. 637 *et seq.*

[35] See e.g. Boyle, 'Nuclear Energy', pp. 289–97 and Handl, *State Liability*, pp. 535–53.

[36] 33 AJIL, 1939, p. 182 and 35 AJIL, 1941, p. 681; 9 ILR, p. 315.

[37] See Boyle, 'Nuclear Energy', p. 292 and Handl, 'Balancing of Interests and International Liability for the Pollution of International Watercourses: Customary Principles of Law Revisited', 13 *Canadian YIL*, 1975, pp. 156, 167–8.

[38] ICJ Reports, 1949, pp. 4, 22–3: 16 ILR, pp. 155, 158.

[39] ICJ Reports, 1974, p. 253; 57 ILR, p. 350.

It is also worth noting the *Gut Dam* arbitration between the US and Canada.[40] This concerned the construction of a dam by the Canadian authorities, with US approval, straddling the territory of the two states, in order to facilitate navigation in the St. Lawrence River, prior to the existence of the Seaway. The dam affected the flow of water in the river basin and caused an increase in the level of water in the river and in Lake Ontario. This, together with the incidence of severe storms, resulted in heavy flooding on the shores of the river and lake and the US government claimed damages. The tribunal awarded a lump sum payment to the US, without considering whether Canada had been in any way negligent or at fault with regard to the construction of the dam. However, one must be cautious in regarding this case as an example of a strict liability approach, since the US gave its approval to the construction of the dam on the condition that US citizens be indemnified for any damage or detriment incurred as a result of the construction or operation of the dam in question.[41]

Treaty practice is variable. The Convention on International Liability for Damage Caused by Space Objects 1972 provides for absolute liability for damage caused by space objects on the surface of the earth or to aircraft in flight (article II), but for fault liability for damage caused elsewhere or to persons or property on board a space object (article III).[42] Most treaties, however, take the form of requiring the exercise of diligent control of sources of harm, so that responsibility is engaged for breaches of obligations specified in the particular instruments.[43]

The test of due diligence is in fact the standard that is accepted generally as the most appropriate one.[44] Article 194 of the Convention on the Law of the Sea 1982, for example, provides that states are to take 'all measures . . . that are necessary to prevent, reduce and control pollution of the marine environment from any source, using for this purpose the best practicable means at their disposal and in accordance with their capabilities'. Accordingly, states in general are not automatically liable for damage caused irrespective of all other factors. However, it is rather less clear what is

---

[40] 8 ILM, 1969, p. 118.
[41] See Schneider, *World Public Order*, p. 165. Cf. Handl, 'State Liability', pp. 525, 538 *et seq.*
[42] See e.g. the Canadian claim in the Cosmos 954 incident, 18 ILM, 1992, p. 907.
[43] See e.g. article 1 of the London Convention on the Prevention of Marine Pollution by Dumping of Wastes 1972; article 2, the Convention on Long-Range Transboundary Air Pollution 1979; article 2, the Vienna Convention for the Protection of the Ozone Layer 1985 and articles 139, 194 and 235, the Convention on the Law of the Sea 1982; articles 7 and 8 of the Convention for the Regulation of Antarctic Mineral Resources Activities 1988 and article 2 of the Convention on the Protection and Use of Transboundary Watercourses and International Lakes 1992. See also the Commentary by the International Law Commission to article 7 of the Draft Articles on the Law of the Non-Navigational Uses of International Watercourses, Report of the International Law Commission, 46th Session, 1994, pp. 236 *et seq.*
[44] See e.g. Handl, 'State Liability', at pp. 539–40 and Boyle, 'Nuclear Energy', p. 272.

actually meant by due diligence. In specific cases, such as the Convention on the Law of the Sea 1982, for example, particular measures are specified and references made to other relevant treaties. In other cases, the issue remains rather more ambiguous.[45] The test of due diligence undoubtedly imports an element of flexibility into the equation and must be tested in the light of the circumstances of the case in question. States will be required, for example, to take all necessary steps to prevent substantial pollution and to demonstrate the kind of behaviour expected of 'good government',[46] while such behaviour would probably require the establishment of systems of consultation and notification.[47] It is also important to note that elements of remoteness and foreseeability are part of the framework of the liability of states. The damage that occurs must have been caused by the pollution under consideration. The tribunal in the *Trail Smelter* case[48] emphasised the need to establish the injury 'by clear and convincing evidence'.

Damage caused

The first issue is whether indeed any damage must actually have been caused before international responsibility becomes relevant. Can there be liability for risk of damage? It appears that at this stage international law in general does not recognise such a liability,[49] certainly outside of the category of ultra-hazardous activities.[50] This is for reasons both of state reluctance in general and with regard to practical difficulties in particular. It would be difficult, although not impossible, both to assess the risk involved and to determine the compensation that might be due.

However, it should be noted that article 1(4) of the Convention on the Law of the Sea 1982 defines pollution of the marine environment as 'the introduction by man, directly or indirectly, of substances or energy into the marine environment . . . which results or is likely to result in . . . deleterious effects'. In other words, actual damage is not necessary in this context. It is indeed possible that customary international law may develop in this direction, but it is too early to conclude that this has already occurred. Most general definitions of pollution rely upon damage or harm having been caused before liability is engaged.[51]

The next issue is to determine whether a certain threshold of damage

---

[45] See e.g. the Long-Range Transboundary Air Pollution Convention 1979.
[46] I.e. the standard of conduct expected from a government mindful of its international obligations, see R. J. Dupuy, 'International Liability for Transfrontier Pollution', in Bothe, *Trends in Environmental Policy and Law, op. cit.*, pp. 363, 369.
[47] See *Responsibility and Liability of States in Relation to Transfrontier Pollution*, an OECD Report by the Environment Committee, 1984, p. 4.   [48] 35 AJIL, 1941, p. 716; 9 ILR, p. 317.
[49] See e.g. Kiss, 'International Protection', p. 1076.   [50] See *infra* p. 619.
[51] See also the commentary to the Montreal Rules adopted by the ILA in 1982, *Report of the Sixtieth Conference*, p. 159.

must have been caused. In the *Trail Smelter* case[52] the tribunal focused on the need to show that the matter was of 'serious consequence', while article 1 of the Convention on Long-Range Transboundary Air Pollution 1979 provides that the pollution concerned must result 'in deleterious effects of such a nature as to endanger human health, harm living resources and ecosystems and material property and impair or interfere with amenities and other legitimate uses of the environment'.[53] Article 3 of the ILA Montreal Rules 1982 stipulates that states are under an obligation to prevent, abate and control transfrontier pollution to such an extent that no substantial injury is caused in the territory of another state.[54] Such formulations do present definitional problems and the qualification as to the threshold of injury required is by no means present in all relevant instruments.[55] The issue of relativity and the importance of the circumstances of the particular case remain significant factors, but less support can be detected at this stage for linkage to a concept of reasonable and equitable use of its territory by a state occasioning liability for use beyond this.[56]

As far as the range of interests injured by pollution is concerned, the *Trail Smelter* case[57] focused upon loss of property. Later definitions of pollution in international instruments have broadened the range to include harm to living resources or ecosystems, interference with amenities and other legitimate uses of the environment or the sea. Article 1(4) of the Convention on the Law of the Sea 1982, for example, includes impairment of quality for use of sea water and reduction of amenities. Article 1(2) of the Vienna Convention on the Ozone Layer 1985 defines adverse effects upon the ozone layer as changes in the physical environment including climatic changes 'which have significant deleterious effects on human health or on the composition, resilience and productivity of natural and managed ecosystems or on materials useful to mankind',[58] while the Climate Change Convention 1992 defines adverse effects of climate change as 'changes in the physical environment or

---

[52] 35 AJIL, 1941, p. 716; 9 ILR, p. 317.
[53] Note also that General Assembly resolution 2995 (XXVII) refers to 'significant harmful results'.
[54] Note the formulation by L. Oppenheim, *International Law*, 8th edn, London, 1955, vol. I, p. 291, that the interference complained of must be 'unduly injurious to the inhabitants of the neighbouring state'.
[55] See e.g. Principle 21 of the Stockholm Declaration and article 194 of the Convention on the Law of the Sea 1982.
[56] See the views of e.g. R. Quentin-Baxter, *Yearbook of the ILC*, 1981, vol. II, Part 1, pp. 112–19 and S. McCaffrey, *ibid.*, 1986, vol. II, Part 1, pp. 133–4. See also Boyle, 'Nuclear Energy', p. 275 and 'Chernobyl and the Development of International Environmental Law' in W. Butler (ed.), *Perestroika and International Law*, London, 1990, pp. 203, 206.
[57] 35 AJIL, 1941, p. 684; 9 ILR, p. 315. See also A. Rubin, 'Pollution by Analogy: The Trail Smelter Arbitration', 50 *Oregon Law Review*, 1971, p. 259.
[58] See also the OECD Recommendation of Equal Right of Access in Relation to Transfrontier Pollution 1977 and article 1(15) of the Convention on the Regulation of Antarctic Mineral Resource Activities 1988.

biota resulting from climate change which have significant deleterious effects on the composition, resilience or productivity of natural and managed ecosystems or on the operation of socio-economic systems or on human health and welfare'.[59] The Convention on Regulation of Antarctic Mineral Resources 1988[60] defines damage to the environment and ecosystem of that polar region as 'any impact on the living or non-living components of that environment or those ecosystems, including harm to atmospheric, marine or terrestrial life, beyond that which is negligible or which has been assessed and judged to be acceptable pursuant to [the] Convention'.[61] The Convention on the Protection and Use of Transboundary Watercourses and International Lakes 1992 defines 'transboundary impact', which is the subject of provision, in terms of 'any significant adverse effect on the environment resulting from a change in the conditions of transboundary waters caused by a human activity'.[62] The Council of Europe Convention on Civil Liability for Environmental Damage 1993 defines damage to include loss or damage by 'impairment of the environment',[63] while the environment itself is taken to include natural resources both abiotic and biotic, property forming part of the cultural heritage and 'the characteristic aspects of the landscape'.[64] The type of harm that is relevant clearly now extends beyond damage to property,[65] but problems do remain with regard to general environmental injury that cannot be defined in material form.[66]

Liability for damage caused by private persons

A particular problem relates to the situation where the environmental injury is caused not by the state itself but by a private party.[67] A state is, of course,

---

[59] Article 1(1).

[60] See generally on Antarctica, C. Redgewell, 'Environmental Protection in Antarctica: the 1991 Protocol', 43 ICLQ, 1994, p. 599 and *supra* Chapter 9, p. 365. See also with regard to the Arctic, D. R. Rothwell, 'International Law and the Protection of the Arctic Environment', 44 ICLQ, 1995, p. 280.

[61] Article 1(15). See also article 2 of the Convention on Environmental Impact Assessment in a Transboundary Context 1991 and article 1 of the Code of Conduct on Accidental Pollution of Transboundary Inland Waters 1990.   [62] Article 1(2).   [63] Article 2(7) c.

[64] Article 2(10). Note also that the Draft Articles on International Liability for Injurious Consequences Arising Out Of Acts Not Prohibited by International Law so far adopted by the International Law Commission refer to activities 'which involve a risk of causing significant transboundary harm through their physical consequences', see *Report of the International Law Commission*, 46th Session, 1994, p. 384.

[65] Note that the Canadian claim for clean-up costs consequential upon the crash of a Soviet nuclear-powered satellite was settled, see 18 ILM, 1979, p. 902.

[66] Note that Security Council resolution 687 (1991) declared that Iraq was liable under international law *inter alia* 'for any direct loss, damage, including environmental damage and the depletion of natural resources' occurring as a result of the unlawful invasion and occupation of Kuwait.

[67] See e.g. Handl, 'State Liability', and G. Doeker and T. Gehring, 'Private or International Liability for Transnational Environmental Damage – The Precedent of Conventional Liability Regimes', 2 *Journal of Environmental Law*, 1990, p. 1.

responsible for unlawful acts of its officials causing injury to nationals of foreign states[68] and retains a general territorial competence under international law. In general, states must ensure that their international obligations are respected on their territory. Many treaties require states parties to legislate with regard to particular issues, in order to ensure the implementation of specific obligations. Where an international agreement requires, for example, that certain limits be placed upon emissions of a particular substance, the state would be responsible for any activity that exceeded the limit, even if it were carried out by a private party, since the state had undertaken a binding commitment.[69] Similarly where the state has undertaken to impose a prior authorisation procedure upon a particular activity, a failure so to act which resulted in pollution violating international law would occasion the responsibility of the state.

In some cases, an international agreement might specifically provide for the liability of the state for the acts of non-state entities. Article VI of the Outer Space Treaty 1967, for example, stipulates that states parties bear international responsibility for 'national activities in outer space . . . whether such activities are carried out by governmental agencies or by non-governmental agencies'.[70]

International liability for damage caused by lawful acts[71]

The International Law Commission has been considering since 1978 the topic of 'International Liability for the Injurious Consequences of Acts Not Prohibited by International Law'[72] and the main focus of the work of the Commission has been on environmental harm.[73] International liability differs from state responsibility in that the latter is dependent upon a prior breach of international law,[74] while the former constitutes an attempt to

[68] *Supra*, Chapter 14.   [69] See *infra*, p. 609.
[70] See also article 1 of the Convention on International Liability for Damage Caused by Space Objects 1972 and article XIV of the Moon Treaty 1979. See further *infra* p. 624 with regard to civil liability schemes.
[71] See e.g. J. Barboza, 'International Liability for the Injurious Consequences of Acts Not Prohibited by International Law and Protection of the Environment', 247 HR, 1994–III, p. 291; A. Boyle, 'State Responsibility and International Liability for Injurious Consequences of Acts not Prohibited by International Law: A Necessary Distinction?', 39 ICLQ, 1990, p. 1; M. Akehurst, 'International Liability for Injurious Consequences Arising out of Acts not Prohibited by International Law', 16 *Netherlands Yearbook of International Law*, 1985, p. 3; D. B. Magraw, 'Transboundary Harm: The International Law Commission's Study of International Liability', 80 AJIL, 1986, p. 305 and C. Tomuschat, 'International Liability for Injurious Consequences Arising out of Acts not Prohibited by International Law: The Work of the International Law Commission' in *International Responsibility for Environmental Harm* (eds. F. Francioni and T. Scovazzi), London, 1991, p. 37. See also Birnie and Boyle, *International Law and the Environment*, p. 140 and Sands, *Principles*, p. 650.
[72] See *Yearbook of the ILC*, 1978, vol. II, part 2, p. 149.
[73] See e.g. Quentin-Baxter's preliminary report, *Yearbook of the ILC*, 1980, vol. II, part 1, p. 24.   [74] *Supra*, Chapter 14.

develop a branch of law in which a state may be liable internationally with regard to the harmful consequences of an activity which is in itself not contrary to international law.

It is a controversial approach. Its theoretical basis and separation from state responsibility have been questioned[75] and the capacity of this topic to subsume the law relating to environmental issues is open to criticism. In considering this aspect of international environmental law, it must also be remembered that states bear responsibility for activities that constitute violations of the law.

Article 1 of the 1989 Draft provides that the articles are to apply when the physical consequences of a particular activity 'cause, or create the risk of causing, transboundary injury'. Members of the Commission have been divided as to whether the focus of the topic should be upon risk or upon harm.[76] Article 1 was redrafted in the 1994 Draft and now provides that the articles under consideration apply to 'activities not prohibited by international law and carried out in the territory or otherwise under the jurisdiction or control of a state which involve a risk of causing significant transboundary harm through their physical consequences'. Article 2 of the 1994 Draft provides that 'risk of causing significant transboundary harm' is to be defined as including 'a low probability of causing disastrous harm and a high probability of causing other significant harm'.[77] In other words, the relevant threshold is established by a combination of risk and harm and this threshold must reach a level deemed 'significant'.[78] The International Law Commission has taken the view that this term, while factually based, means something more than detectable, but need not reach the level of serious or substantial.[79]

Under the provisions of the 1989 Draft, states are to co-operate in good faith in trying to prevent such activities from causing transboundary injury and in minimising the effects of any such injury,[80] while reparation is to be made for 'appreciable injury'[81] caused by such activities. Such reparation is to be decided by negotiation by the states concerned, bearing in mind in particular that reparation should seek to 'restore the balance of interests affected by the injury'.[82]

---

[75] See e.g. Boyle, 'State Responsibility', p. 3 and I. Brownlie, *System of the Law of Nations: State Responsibility*, Part I, Oxford, 1983, p. 50.

[76] See e.g. S. McCaffrey, 'The Fortieth Session of the International Law Commission', 83 AJIL, 1989, pp. 153, 170 and McCaffrey, 'The Forty-First Session of the International Law Commission', 83 AJIL, 1989, pp. 937, 944.

[77] Report of the International Law Commission, 46th Session, 1994, p. 384.

[78] *Ibid.*, p. 400. See also article 1 of the Code of Conduct on Accidental Pollution of Transboundary Inland Waters adopted by the Economic Commission for Europe in 1990.

[79] *Ibid.*, p. 401.   [80] Draft article 7.

[81] Defined in article 2 as 'the risk which may be identified through a simple examination of the activity and the substances involved, in relation to the place, environment or way in which they are used, and includes both the low probability of very considerable (disastrous) transboundary injury and the high probability of major appreciable injury'.   [82] Draft article 9.

This conception of reparation differs, of course, from that considered in the context of state responsibility,[83] where the aim is to seek to restore the situation to what it was prior to the act in question. In the case of international liability, the purpose is to limit the compensation by the use of a 'balance of interests' criterion and not necessarily to end the harmful activity.[84] This approach would appear to draw heavily upon notions of equitable sharing developed in the context of the use of international watercourses,[85] but whether it could operate successfully in this rather different context is controversial. It is unclear how it might in practice work, or how it relates to the issue of identifying the point at which the harmful activity becomes wrongful.

The Commission in the 1994 Draft laid down a series of provisions with regard to the prevention of transboundary harm in such circumstances. Article 11 notes that activities covered by article 1 should not be carried out without the authorisation of the state, while article 12 provides that before such authorisation is given the state must conduct a risk assessment of the proposed activity. Indeed where an activity involving a risk of causing significant transboundary harm is being carried out prior to the entry into force of the provisions contained in the Draft, such authorisation must still be obtained.[86] Under article 14 of the Draft, states are to take legislative, administrative and other action to ensure that all appropriate measures are adopted in order to prevent or minimise the risk of transboundary harm of activities referred to in article 1. Where the assessment called for under article 12 does indicate a risk of causing significant transboundary harm, the state of origin is obliged to notify without delay other states likely to be affected and provide them with all relevant information,[87] while under article 18, the states concerned are to enter into consultation with a view to achieving acceptable solutions regarding measures to be adopted in order to prevent or minimise the risk of causing significant transboundary harm. Such solutions must be based on an equitable balance of interests. Article 20 of the Draft lays down a series of relevant factors and circumstances in achieving this 'equitable balance of interests'. These comprise the degree of risk of significant transboundary harm and the availability of means of preventing or minimising such risk or of repairing the harm; the importance of the activity, taking into account its overall advantages of a social, economic and technical character for the state of origin in relation to the potential

---

[83] *Supra* p. 496. See also C. Gray, *Judicial Remedies in International Law*, Oxford, 1987, p. 233.
[84] See e.g. *Yearbook of the ILC*, 1986, vol. II, Part 1, p. 147.
[85] See e.g. G. Handl, 'The Principle of "Equitable Use" as Applied to Internationally Shared Natural Resources', 14 *Revue Belge de Droit International*, 1978–9, p. 40. See further *infra* p. 616.   [86] Article 13.
[87] Article 15. Article 16 bis of the Draft also provides that the state should provide information to its own public.

harm for the states likely to be affected; the risk of significant harm to the environment and the availability of means of preventing or minimising such risk or restoring the environment; the economic viability of the activity in relation to the costs of prevention demanded by the states likely to be affected and to the possibility of carrying out the activity elsewhere or by other means or replacing it with an alternative activity; the degree to which the states likely to be affected are prepared to contribute to the costs of prevention; and the standards of protection which the states likely to be affected apply to the same or comparable activities and the standards applied in comparable regional or international practice.

The problems of the state responsibility approach

The application of the classical international law approach, founded upon state responsibility for breaches of international obligations and the requirement to make reparation for such breaches, to environmental problems is particularly problematic. The need to demonstrate that particular damage has been caused to one state by the actions of another state means that this model can only with difficulty be applied to more than a small proportion of environmental problems. In many cases it is simply impossible to prove that particular damage has been caused from one particular source, while this bilateral focus cannot really come to terms with the fact that the protection of the environment of the earth is truly a global problem requiring a global or pan-state response and one that cannot be successfully tackled in such an arbitrary and piece-meal fashion. Accordingly, the approach to dealing with environmental matters has shifted from the bilateral state responsibility paradigm to the establishment and strengthening of international co-operation.

International co-operation

A developing theme of international environmental law, founded upon general principles, relates to the requirement for states to co-operate in dealing with transboundary pollution issues. Principle 24 of the Stockholm Declaration 1972 noted that 'international matters concerning the protection and improvement of the environment should be handled in a co-operative spirit', while Principle 7 of the Rio Declaration 1992 emphasised that 'states shall co-operate in a spirit of global partnership to conserve, protect and restore the health and integrity of the Earth's ecosystem'. Principle 13 of the Rio Declaration refers both to national and international activities in this field by stating that 'states shall develop national law regarding liability and compensation for the victims of pollution and other environmental damage. States shall also co-operate in an expeditious and more determined manner to develop further international law regarding liability and compensation for adverse effects of environmental damage caused by activities within their jurisdiction or control to areas beyond their jurisdiction'.[88]

The *Corfu Channel* case[89] established the principle that states are not knowingly to allow their territory to be used for acts contrary to the rights of other states and from this can be deduced a duty to inform other states of known environmental hazards. A large number of international agreements reflect this proposition. Article 198 of the Convention on the Law of the Sea 1982, for example, provides that 'when a state becomes aware of cases in which the marine environment is in imminent danger of being damaged or has been damaged by pollution, it shall immediately notify other states it deems likely to be affected by such damage, as well as the competent international authorities'.[90] Article 13 of the Basle Convention on the Control of Transboundary Movement of Hazardous Wastes 1989 provides that states parties shall, whenever it comes to their knowledge, ensure that in the case of an accident occurring during the transboundary movement of hazardous wastes which are likely to present risks to human health and the environment in other states, those states are immediately informed.[91]

It is also to be noted that in 1974 the OECD (the Organisation for Economic Co-operation and Development) adopted a Recommendation that prior to the initiation of works or undertakings that might create a risk of significant transfrontier pollution, early information should be provided to states that are or may be affected.[92] In 1988, the OECD adopted a Council Decision in which it is provided that states must provide information for the prevention of and the response to accidents at hazardous installations and transmit to exposed countries the results of their studies on proposed installations. A duty to exchange emergency plans is stipulated, as well as a duty to transmit immediate warning to exposed countries where an accident is an imminent threat.[93] The point is also emphasised in the Rio Declaration of 1992. Principle 18 provides that states shall immediately notify other states of any natural disasters or other emergencies that are likely to produce sudden harmful effects on the environment of those states, while Principle 19 stipulates that states shall provide prior and timely notification and relevant information to potentially affected states on activities

---

[88] See also Principle 27.   [89] ICJ Reports, 1949, pp. 4, 22; 16 ILR, pp. 155, 158.
[90] See also article 211(7).
[91] See also e.g. article 8 of the International Convention for the Prevention of Pollution from Ships 1973; Annex 6 of the Helsinki Convention on the Protection of the Marine Environment of the Baltic Sea 1974 and article 9 of the Barcelona Convention for the Protection of the Mediterranean Sea, Protocol of Co-operation in Case of Emergency 1976.
[92] Title E, para. 6. See also the OECD Recommendation for the Implementation of a Regime of Equal Right of Access and Non-Discrimination in Relation to Transfrontier Pollution 1977, Title C, para. 8.   [93] C(88)84.

that may have a significant adverse transboundary environmental effect and shall consult with those states at an early stage and in good faith.[94] One may also point to a requirement of prior consultation. Article 5 of the ILA Montreal Rules provides that states planning to carry out activities which might entail a significant risk of transfrontier pollution shall give early notice to states likely to be affected. This provision builds upon, for example, the *Lac Lanoux* arbitration between France and Spain,[95] which concerned the proposed diversion of a shared watercourse. The arbitral tribunal noted in particular the obligation to negotiate in such circumstances.[96] Some treaties establish a duty of prior notification, one early example being the Nordic Convention on the Protection of the Environment 1974. Article 5 of the Long-Range Transboundary Air Pollution Convention 1979 provides that consultations shall be held, upon request, at an early stage between the state within whose jurisdiction the activity is to be conducted and states which are actually affected by or exposed to a significant risk of long-range transboundary air pollution.[97] The increasing range of state practice[98] has led the International Law Association to conclude that 'a rule of international customary law has emerged that in principle a state is obliged to render information on new or increasing pollution to a potential victim state'.[99]

The evolution of a duty to inform states that might be affected by the creation of a source of new or increasing pollution has been accompanied by consideration of an obligation to make environmental impact assessments.[100] This requirement is included in several treaties.[101] Article 204 of the Convention on the Law of the Sea 1982 provides that states should 'observe, measure, evaluate and analyse by recognised scientific methods, the risks or effects of pollution on the marine environment' and in particular 'shall keep under surveillance the effects of any activities which they

---

[94] See also article 3 of the Convention on Environmental Impact Assessment in a Transboundary Context 1991.   [95] 24 ILR, p. 101.

[96] *Ibid.*, p. 119. See also the *North Sea Continental Shelf* cases, ICJ Reports, 1969, pp. 3, 46–7; 41 ILR, pp. 29, 76.

[97] Note also that article 8(b) calls for the exchange of information *inter alia* on major changes in national policies and in general industrial development and on their potential impact, which would be likely to cause significant changes in long-range transboundary air pollution.   [98] See ILA, *Report of the Sixtieth Conference*, 1982, pp. 172–3.

[99] *Ibid.*, p. 173. See also Institut de Droit International, Resolution on Transboundary Air Pollution 1987, but cf. Sands, *Principles*, p. 35. Note also e.g. the UNEP Recommendation concerning the Environment Related to Offshore Drilling and Mining within the Limits of National Jurisdiction 1981 and the Canada–Denmark Agreement for Co-operation Relating to the Marine Environment 1983.

[100] See e.g the UNEP Principles of Environmental Impact Assessment 1987. See also Sands, *Principles*, pp. 579 *et seq.*

[101] See e.g. the Kuwait Regional Convention for Co-operation on the Protection of the Marine Environment from Pollution 1978, article 11. See also the Nordic Environmental Protection Convention 1974, article 6 and the Protocol on Environmental Protection to the Antarctica Treaty 1991, article 8.

permit or in which they engage in order to determine whether these activities are likely to pollute the marine environment'. Reports are to be published, while under article 206, when states have reasonable grounds for believing that planned activities under their jurisdiction or control may cause substantial pollution of or significant and harmful changes to the marine environment 'they shall, as far as practicable, assess the potential effects of such activities on the marine environment and shall communicate reports of such assessments'.[102] The EEC Council Directive 85/337 provides that member states shall adopt all necessary measures to ensure that, before consent is given, projects likely to have significant effects on the environment are made subject to an assessment with regard to their effects, while the issue was taken further in the Convention on Environmental Impact Assessment in a Transboundary Context 1991. Under this Convention, states parties are to take the necessary legal, administrative and other measures to ensure that prior to a decision to authorise or undertake a proposed activity listed in Appendix I[103] that is likely to cause a significant adverse transboundary impact, an environmental impact assessment is carried out. The party of origin must notify any party which may be affected of the proposed activity, providing full information. Once the affected party decides to participate in the environmental impact assessment procedure under the provisions of the Convention, it must supply information to the party of origin of the proposed activity at its request relating to the potentially affected environment under its jurisdiction.[104] The documentation to be submitted to the competent authority of the party of origin is detailed in Appendix III and it is comprehensive. Consultations must take place between the party of origin and the affected parties concerning the potential transboundary impact and the measures to reduce or eliminate the impact[105] and in taking the final decision on the proposed activity the parties shall ensure that due account is taken of the outcome of the environmental impact assessment and consultations held.[106] Post-project analyses may also

---

[102] A similar process is underway with regard to the siting of nuclear power installations, see e.g. the agreements between Spain and Portugal 1980; Netherlands and the Federal Republic of Germany 1977; Belgium and France 1966 and Switzerland and the Federal Republic of Germany 1982. See also Boyle, 'Chernobyl', at p. 212.

[103] These activities include crude oil and certain other refineries; thermal power stations and other combustion installations with a certain minimum power output and nuclear installations; nuclear facilities; major cast iron and steel installations; asbestos plants; integrated chemical installations; construction of motorways, long-distance railway lines and long airport runways; pipelines; large trading ports; toxic and dangerous waste installations; large dams and reservoirs; major mining; offshore hydrocarbon production; major oil and chemical storage facilities; deforestation of large areas.

[104] If it decides not to so participate, the environmental impact assessment procedure will continue or not according to the domestic law and practice of the state of origin, article 3(4).

[105] Article 5.

[106] Article 6(1). Account must also be taken of concerns expressed by the public of the affected party in the areas likely to be affected under article 3(8).

be carried out under article 7.[107] Other instruments provide for such environmental impact assessments[108] and some international organisations have developed their own assessment requirements.[109] The question of environmental impact assessments was raised by Judge Weeramantry in his Dissenting Opinion in the *Request for an Examination of the Situation in Accordance with Paragraph 63 of the Court's Judgment in the 1974 Nuclear Tests case*.[110] It was noted that the magnitude of the issue brought by New Zealand before the Court (the underground testing by France in the South Pacific of nuclear devices) was such as to make the principle of environmental impact assessments applicable. The Judge declared that 'when a matter is brought before it which raises serious environmental issues of global importance, and a prima facie case is made out of the possibility of environmental damage, the Court is entitled to take into account the Environmental Impact Assessment principle in determining its preliminary approach'.[111]

Other principles of international co-operation in the field of environmental protection are beginning to emerge and inform the development of legal norms. Principle 15 of the Rio Declaration states that 'in order to protect the environment, the precautionary approach shall be widely applied by states according to their capabilities. Where there are threats of serious or irreversible damage, lack of full scientific certainty shall not be used as a reason for postponing cost-effective measures to prevent environmental degradation'. This marks a step away from the traditional approach, which required states to act on the basis of scientific knowledge and constitutes a recognition that in certain circumstances to await formal scientific proof may prevent urgent action being taken in time. The Vienna Convention for the Protection of the Ozone Layer 1985 and the 1987 Montreal Protocol to that Convention both referred in their respective preambles to 'precautionary measures',[112] while the Bergen Ministerial Declaration on Sustainable Development 1990 noted that in order to achieve sustainable development, policies must be based on the precautionary principle. It was emphasised that 'environmental measures must anticipate, prevent and attack the causes of environmental degradation' and part of Principle 15 of the Rio Declaration was repeated. The Convention on the Protection and Use of Transboundary Watercourses and International Lakes 1992 provides in article 2(5) a that the parties would be guided by 'the precautionary principle, by virtue of which action to avoid the potential transboundary impact

[107] See also Appendix V.   [108] See e.g. the Antarctic Environment Protocol 1991.
[109] See e.g. the World Bank under its Operational Directive 4.00 of 1989.
[110] ICJ Reports, 1995, pp. 288, 344.   [111] *Ibid.*, p. 345.
[112] See also the preamble to the1994 Oslo Protocol to the 1979 Long Range Transboundary Air Pollution Convention.

of the release of hazardous substances shall not be postponed on the ground that scientific research has not fully proved a causal link between these substances, on the one hand and the potential transboundary impact, on the other'. References to the precautionary principle appear also in the Convention on Biodiversity 1992[113] and in the Convention on Climate Change 1992.[114] The principle was described by Judge Weeramantry as one gaining increasing support as part of the international law of the environment.[115]

Recognition has also emerged of the special responsibility of developed states in the process of environmental protection. Principle 7 of the Rio Declaration stipulates that 'states have common but differentiated responsibilities'. In particular, it is emphasised that 'the developed countries acknowledge the responsibility that they bear in the international pursuit of sustainable development in view of the pressures their societies place on the global environment and of the technologies and financial resources they command'. Article 3 (1) of the Convention on Climate Change provides that the parties should act to protect the climate system 'on the basis of equity and in accordance with their common but differentiated responsibilities and respective capabilities' so that the developed countries would take the lead in combating climate change.[116] In addition, the concept of sustainable development has been evolving in a way that circumscribes the competence of states to direct their own development.[117] Principle 3 of the Rio Declaration notes that the right to development must be fulfilled so as to 'equitably meet developmental and environmental needs of present and

[113] Although the reference in the Preamble does not expressly invoke the term. See generally *International Law and the Conservation of Biological Diversity* (eds. M. Bowman and C. Redgewell), Dordrecht, 1995.

[114] Article 3(3). See also article 130r(2) of the EC Treaty as amended by the Treaty on European Union (the Maastricht Treaty) and article 4(3) f of the OAU Bamako Convention on the Ban of the Import into Africa and the Control of Transboundary Movement and Management of Hazardous Wastes within Africa 1991. Note also articles 5 and 6 of the Straddling Fish Stocks and Highly Migratory Fish Stocks Agreement 1995, see *supra* Chapter 11, p. 428.

[115] In his Dissenting Opinion in the *Request for an Examination of the Situation in Accordance with Paragraph 63 of the Court's Judgment in the 1974 Nuclear Tests case*, ICJ Reports, 1995, pp. 288, 342. See also *The Precautionary Principle and International Law* (ed. D. Freestone), Dordrecht, 1995.

[116] See also articles 4 and 12. Note that the 1990 amendment to the 1987 Montreal Protocol on the Ozone Depleting Substances provides that the capacity of developing countries to comply with their substantive obligations will depend upon the implementation by the developed countries of their financial obligations.

[117] See e.g. *Sustainable Development and International Law* (ed. W. Lang), Dordrecht, 1995; *Sustainable Development and International Law* (eds. K. Ginther, E. Denters and P. de Waart), Dordrecht, 1995; Sands, *Principles*, pp. 198 *et seq.*; P. Sands, 'International Law in the Field of Sustainable Development', 65 BYIL, 1994, p. 303; P. S. Elder, 'Sustainability', 36 *McGill Law Journal*, 1991, p. 832 and D. McGoldrick, 'Sustainable Development and Human Rights: An Integrated Conception', 45 ICLQ, 1996, p. 796. See also the Report of the ILA Committee on Legal Aspects of Sustainable Development, ILA, *Report of the Sixty-sixth Conference*, 1994, p. 111.

future generations',[118] while Principle 4 states that in order to achieve sustainable development, environmental protection shall constitute an integral part of the development process.[119] Principle 27 called for co-operation in the further development of international law in the field of sustainable development.[120] The Climate Change Convention declares in article 3 (4) that 'the parties have a right to, and should, promote sustainable development', while the Biodiversity Convention refers on several occasions to the notion of 'sustainable use'.[121] Quite what is meant by sustainable development is somewhat unclear and it may refer to a range of economic, environmental and social factors.[122] Clearly, however, some form of balance between these factors will be necessitated.[123]

Another emerging principle, more widely accepted in some countries and regions than others, is the notion that the costs of pollution should be paid by the polluter.[124] Principle 16 of the Rio Declaration notes that 'the polluter should, in principle, bear the costs of pollution, with due regard to the public interests and without distorting international trade and investment'. The principle has been particularly applied with regard to civil liability for damage resulting from hazardous activities[125] and has particularly been adopted by the Organisation for Economic Co-operation and Development[126] and the European Community.[127] The polluter-pays principle has been referred to both in the International Convention on Oil Pollution Preparedness, Response and Co-operation 1990 and in the

[118] See also Principle 1 of the Stockholm Declaration 1972.
[119] Note that article 2(1)vii of the Agreement Establishing the European Bank for Reconstruction and Development 1990 calls upon the Bank to promote 'environmentally sound and sustainable development'.
[120] See also Agenda 21, adopted at the Rio Conference on Environment and Development 1992, paras. 8 and 39.
[121] See e.g. the Preamble and articles 1, 8, 11, 12, 16, 17 and 18. See also the Statement of Principles for a Global Consensus on the Management, Conservation and Sustainable Development of All Types of Forests, adopted at the Rio Conference 1992
[122] See e.g. M. Redclift, 'Reflections on the "Sustainable Development" Debate', 1 *International Journal of Sustainable Development and World Ecology*, 1994, p. 3. Note that the Report of the GATT Panel on the United States Restrictions on the Import of Tuna declares that the objective of sustainable development, which includes the protection and preservation of the environment, has been widely recognised by the contracting parties to the General Agreement on Tariffs and Trade, 33 ILM, 1994, p. 839.
[123] Note that the General Assembly established the Commission on Sustainable Development in resolution 47/191 in order to ensure an effective follow-up to the 1992 Conference on Environment and Development as well as generally to work for the integration of environment and development issues and to examine the progress of the implementation of Agenda 21 (the programme of action adopted by the Conference) in order to achieve sustainable development.
[124] See e.g. Sands, *Principles*, pp. 213 *et seq.* and A. Boyle, 'Making the Polluter Pay? Alternatives to State Responsibility in the Allocation of Transboundary Environmental Costs' in *International Responsibility for Environmental Harm*, p. 363.
[125] See further *infra* p. 619.
[126] See e.g. the OECD Council Recommendations C(74)223 (1974) and C(89)88 (1989).
[127] See Article 130r(2) of the EC Treaty as amended by the Treaty on European Union.

Convention on the Transboundary Effects of Industrial Accidents 1992 as 'a general principle of international environmental law'.[128] Again, quite how far this principle actually applies is uncertain. It is, in particular, unclear whether all the costs of an environmental clean-up would be covered. State practice appears to demonstrate that such costs should be apportioned between the parties.[129]

Atmospheric pollution[130]

Perhaps the earliest perceived form of pollution relates to the pollution of the air. The burning of fossil fuels releases into the atmosphere sulphur dioxide and nitrogen oxides which change into acids and are carried by natural elements and fall as rain or snow or solid particles. Such acids have the effect of killing living creatures in lakes and streams and of damaging soils and forests.[131] While the airspace above the territorial domain of a state forms part of that state,[132] the imprecise notion of the atmosphere would combine elements of this territorial sovereignty with areas not so defined. The legal characterisation of the atmosphere, therefore, is confused and uncertain, but one attractive possibility is to refer to it as a shared resource.[133]

The question of how one defines the term 'pollution' has been addressed in several international instruments. In a Recommendation adopted in 1974 by the Organisation for Economic Co-operation and Development,[134] pollution is broadly defined as 'the introduction by man, directly or indirectly, of substances or energy into the environment resulting in deleterious effects of such a nature as to endanger human health, harm living resources and ecosystems, and impair or interfere with amenities and other legitimate uses of the environment'.[135] This definition was substantially reproduced in the Geneva Convention on Long-Range Transboundary Air Pollution 1979[136] and in the Montreal Rules of International Law Applicable to Transfrontier Pollution adopted by the International Law Association in 1982.[137] Several points ought to be noted at this stage. First, actual damage

---

128 See also article 2(5)b of the Convention on the Protection and Use of Transboundary Watercourses and International Lakes 1992.
129 See e.g. Boyle, 'Making the Polluter Pay ?', p. 365.
130 See Sands, *Principles*, Chapter 7 and Birnie and Boyle, *International Law and the Environment*, Chapter 10.
131 See *Keesing's Record of World Events*, pp. 36782 *et seq.* (1989).
132 See *supra* Chapter 10, p. 369.
133 See e.g. Birnie and Boyle, *International Law and the Environment*, p. 390.
134 OECD Doc.C(74)224, cited in *Chernobyl: Law and Communication*, p. 150.
135 *Ibid.*, Title A.
136 The major difference being the substitution of 'air' for 'environment' in view of the focus of the Convention.
137 Note that the term 'air' was replaced by 'environment'. See also article 1 of the Paris Convention for the Prevention of Marine Pollution from Land-Based Sources 1974 and

must have been caused. Pollution likely to result as a consequence of certain activities is not included. Secondly, the harm caused must be of a certain level of intensity and thirdly, the question of interference with legitimate uses of the environment requires further investigation.

The core obligation in customary international law with regard to atmospheric pollution was laid down in the *Trail Smelter* case,[138] which provided that no state had the right to use or permit the use of its territory in such a manner as to cause injury by fumes in or to the territory of another state or to persons or property therein, where the case was of serious consequence and the injury established by clear and convincing evidence.[139]

In 1979, on the initiative of the Scandinavian countries and under the auspices of the UN Economic Commission for Europe, the Geneva Convention on Long-Range Transboundary Air Pollution was signed.[140] The definition of pollution is reasonably broad,[141] while article 1(b) defines long-range transboundary air pollution as air pollution whose physical origin is situated wholly or in part within the area under the national jurisdiction of one state and which has adverse effects in the area under the jurisdiction of another state at such a distance that it is not generally possible to distinguish the contribution of individual emission sources or groups of sources.

The obligations undertaken under the Convention, however, are modest. States 'shall endeavour to limit and, as far as possible, gradually reduce and prevent air pollution, including long-range transboundary air pollution'.[142] The question of state liability for damage resulting from such pollution is not addressed. The Convention provides that states are to develop policies and strategies by means of exchanges of information and consultation[143] and to exchange information to combat generally the discharge of air pollutants.[144] Consultations are to be held upon request at an early stage between contracting parties actually affected by or exposed to a significant risk of long-range transboundary air pollution and contracting parties within which

article 2 of the Barcelona Convention for the Protection of the Mediterranean Sea against Pollution 1976. The Institut de Droit International, in a draft resolution accompanying its final report on Air Pollution Across National Frontiers, defines pollution as 'any physical, chemical or biological alteration in the composition or quality of the atmosphere which results directly or indirectly from human action or omission and produces injurious or deleterious effects across national frontiers', 62 I *Annuaire de l'Institut de Droit International*, 1987, p. 266.   [138] 35 AJIL, 1941, p. 716; 9 ILR, p. 317.
[139] Note that in 1963, the Treaty Banning Nuclear Weapon Tests in the Atmosphere, Outer Space and Under Water was adopted.
[140] See e.g. A. Rosencranz, 'The ECE Convention of 1979 on Long-Range Transboundary Air Pollution', 75 AJIL, 1981, p. 975; L. Tollan, 'The Convention on Long-Range Transboundary Air Pollution', 19 *Journal of World Trade Law*, 1985, p. 615 and A. Kiss, 'La Convention sur la Pollution Atmosphérique Transfrontière à Longue Distance', *Revue Juridique de l'Environnement*, 1981, p. 30.   [141] *Supra*, p. 607.   [142] Article 2.
[143] Article 3. Note that under article 6, states undertake to develop the best policies and strategies using the 'best available technology which is economically feasible'.
[144] Article 4. See also article 8.

and subject to whose jurisdiction a significant contribution to such pollution originates or could originate, in connection with activities carried on or contemplated therein.[145]

The parties also undertook to develop the existing 'Co-operative programme for the monitoring and evaluation of the long-range transmission of air pollutants in Europe' (EMEP) and in 1984 a Protocol was adopted dealing with the long-term financing of the project.

Further Protocols to the Convention have been adopted. In 1985, the Helsinki Protocol was signed, dealing with the reduction of sulphur emissions or their transboundary fluxes by at least 30 per cent as soon as possible and at the latest by 1993, using 1980 levels as the basis for the calculation of reductions. This Protocol requires parties to report annually to the Executive Body of the Convention.[146] The Sophia Protocol was adopted in 1988 and concerned the control of emissions of nitrogen oxides or their transboundary fluxes. Under this Protocol the contracting parties undertook to reduce their national annual emissions of nitrogen oxides or their transboundary fluxes so that by the end of 1994 these do not exceed those of 1987. Negotiations for further reductions in national annual emissions were provided for, as was the exchange of technology in relevant areas and of information. In 1991, the Protocol concerning the control of emissions of volatile organic compounds and their transboundary fluxes was adopted. Specific targets and timetables are established. However, the Protocol provides for a choice of at least three ways to meet the requirements, to be determined by the parties upon signature and dependant upon the level of volatile organic compounds emissions. In 1994, the Oslo Protocol on Further Reduction of Sulphur Emissions was adopted,[147] specifying sulphur emission ceilings for parties for the years 2000, 2005 and 2010, and accompanied by a reporting requirement to the Executive Body on a periodic basis.[148] An Implementation Committee was provided for in order to review the implementation of the Protocol and compliance by the parties with their obligations.[149]

In 1986 a Protocol to the Paris Convention for the Prevention of Marine Pollution from Land-Based Sources[150] extended that agreement to

---

[145] Article 5. See also article 8(b).
[146] Note that for member states of the European Community, this obligation was superseded by the Large Combustion Directive 88/609, 1988. Under this Directive, a distinction is drawn between new and existing large combustion plants. Emission ceilings were set and percentage reductions upon the basis of 1980 emission levels provided for with regard to sulphur dioxide and for nitrogen oxides. The obligations specified are variable, so that, for example, Belgium, Germany, France and the Netherlands are obliged to reduce their sulphur dioxide emissions by 70 per cent by 2003, while Greece, Ireland and Portugal are permitted marginally to increase their emissions over that period. Other Council Directives deal with emissions from vehicle exhausts, see e.g. Council Directives 88/76; 88/436 and 89/458.   [147] See 33 ILM, 1994, p. 1540.   [148] Article 5.   [149] Article 7.
[150] See infra, p. 628.

atmospheric emissions of pollutants.[151] Article 212 of the Law of the Sea Convention 1982 requires states to adopt laws and regulations to prevent, reduce and control atmospheric pollution of the marine environment, although no specific standards are set.[152]

Ozone depletion and global warming[153]

The problem of global warming and the expected increase in the temperature of the earth in the decades to come has focused attention on the issues particularly of the consumption of fossil fuels and deforestation. In addition, the depletion of the stratospheric ozone layer, which has the effect of letting excessive ultraviolet radiation through to the surface of the earth, is a source of considerable concern. The problem of the legal characterisation of the ozone layer is a significant one. Article 1(1) of the Vienna Convention for the Protection of the Ozone Layer 1985 defines this area as 'the layer of atmospheric ozone above the planetary boundary layer'. This area would thus appear particularly in the light of the global challenge posed by ozone depletion and climate change to constitute a distinct unit with an identity of its own irrespective of national sovereignty or shared resources claims. UN General Assembly resolution 43/53, for example, states that global climate change is 'the common concern of mankind'.[154] Whatever the precise legal status of this area, what is important is the growing recognition that the scale of the challenge posed can only really be tackled upon a truly international or global basis.

In the first serious effort to tackle the problem of ozone depletion, the Vienna Convention for the Protection of the Ozone Layer was adopted in

---

[151] Note also that in 1987 the Second International Conference on the Protection of the North Sea urged states to ratify the Protocol, see 27 ILM, 1988, p. 835, while in 1990 North Sea states agreed to achieve by 1999 a reduction of 50 per cent or more in atmospheric and river-borne emissions of hazardous substances, provided that best available technology permitted this, see IMO Doc. MEPC 29/INF.26.

[152] Note that the Canada–United States Air Quality Agreement 1991 requires the reduction of sulphur dioxide and nitrogen oxide emissions from the two states to agreed levels by the year 2000. Compliance monitoring by continuous emission monitoring systems is provided for.

[153] See e.g. *International Law and Global Climate Change* (eds. R. Churchill and D. Freestone), Dordrecht, 1991; Lawrence, 'International Legal Regulation for Protection of the Ozone Layer: Some Problems of Implementation', 2 *Journal of Environmental Law*, 1990, p. 17; Stoel, 'Fluorocarbon: Mobilising Concern and Action' in *Environmental Protection, The International Dimension* (eds. D. A. Kay and H. K. Jacobson), 1983, p. 45; Engelmann, 'A Look at Some Issues Before an Ozone Convention', 8 *Environmental Policy and Law*, 1982, p. 49 and Heimsoeth, 'The Protection of the Ozone Layer', 10 *Environmental Policy and Law*, 1983, p. 34.

[154] See also the Noordwijk Declaration of the Conference on Atmospheric Pollution and Climate Change 1989. See e.g. Fleischer, 'The International Concern for the Environment: The Concept of Common Heritage' in *Trends in Environmental Law and Policy*, p. 321.

1985, entering into force three years later. This Convention is a framework agreement, providing the institutional structure for the elaboration of Protocols laying down specific standards concerning the production of chlorofluorocarbons (CFCs), the agents which cause the destruction of the ozone layer. Under the Convention, contracting parties agree to take appropriate measures to protect human health and the environment against adverse effects resulting or likely to result from human activities which modify or are likely to modify the ozone layer.[155] The parties also agree to co-operate in the collection of relevant material and in the formulation of agreed measures, and to take appropriate legislative or administrative action to control, limit, reduce or prevent human activities under their jurisdiction or control 'should it be found that these activities have or are likely to have adverse effects resulting from modification or likely modification of the ozone layer'.[156] A secretariat and disputes settlement mechanism were established.[157] However, overall the Convention is little more than a framework within which further action could be taken.

In 1987 the Montreal Protocol on Substances that Deplete the Ozone Layer was adopted and this called for a phased reduction of CFCs and a freeze on the use of halons.[158] The control measures of the Protocol are based on the regulation of the production of 'controlled substances'[159] by the freezing of their consumption[160] at 1986 levels followed by a progressive reduction, so that by mid-1998 consumption is to be reduced by 20 per cent in comparison with the 1986 figure. From mid-1998 onwards consumption is to be reduced to 50 per cent of the 1986 level.[161] However, this was subsequently felt to have been insufficient and in 1989, the parties to the Convention and Protocol adopted the Helsinki Declaration on the Protection of the Ozone Layer in which the parties agreed to phase out the production and consumption of CFCs controlled by the Protocol as soon as possible, but not later than the year 2000, and to phase out halons and control and reduce other substances which contribute significantly to ozone depletion as soon as feasible. An Implementation Committee was

---

[155] Article 2(1). 'Adverse effects' is defined in article 1(2) to mean 'changes in the physical environment or biota, including changes in climate, which have significant deleterious effects on human health or on the composition, resilience and productivity of natural and managed ecosystems or on materials useful to mankind'.   [156] Article 2.

[157] Articles 7 and 11.
[158] See 26 ILM, 1987, p. 1541 and 28 ILM, 1989, p. 1301. See also R. Benedick, *Ozone Diplomacy*, Cambridge, MA, 1991 and A. C. Aman, 'The Montreal Protocol on Substances that Deplete the Ozone Layer: Providing Prospective Remedial Relief for Potential Damage to the Environmental Commons' in *International Responsibility for Environmental Harm*, p. 185.   [159] I.e. ozone depleting substances listed in Annex A.

[160] This is defined to constitute production plus imports minus exports of controlled substances, see articles 1(5) and (6) and 3.

[161] There are two exceptions, however, first for the purposes of 'industrial rationalisation between parties' and secondly with regard to certain developing countries, see article 5.

established under the Montreal Protocol together with a non-compliance procedure, whereby a party querying the carrying out of obligations by another party can submit its concerns in writing to the secretariat. The secretariat with the party complained against will examine the complaint and the matter will then be passed to the Implementation Committee, which will try and secure a friendly settlement and make a report to the meeting of the parties which can take further measures to ensure compliance with the Protocol.

The parties to the Protocol made a series of Adjustments and Amendments to the Protocol in June 1990,[162] the main ones being that 1992 consumption and production levels were not to exceed 1986 levels, while 1995 levels are not to exceed 50 per cent with 10 per cent exception to satisfy basic domestic needs; 1997 levels are not to exceed 15 per cent, with 10 per cent exception permitted, and 2000 levels are not to exceed 0 per cent with 15 per cent exception permitted. Broadly similar consumption and production targets have also been laid down with regard to halons. The 1990 Amendments made specific reference to the requirement to take into account the developmental needs of developing countries and the need for the transfer of alternative technologies, and a Multilateral Fund was established. Further Adjustments were made in Copenhagen in 1992,[163] introducing changes to the timetable for the phasing out of various substances, listing new controlled substances and adopting new reporting requirements. The Implementation Committee was enlarged and the Multilateral Fund adopted on a permanent basis.

It should also be noted that European Community Council Regulation 91/594 of 4 March 1991 provides that after 30 June 1997 there shall be no production of CFCs unless the European Commission has determined that such production is essential.

Action with regard to the phenomenon of global warming has been a lot slower. General Assembly resolutions 43/53 (1988) and 44/207 (1989) recognised that climate change was a common concern of mankind and determined that necessary and timely action should be taken to deal with this issue. It also called for the convening of a conference on world climate change, as did the UNEP Governing Council Decision on Global Climate Change of 25 May 1989. In addition, the Hague Declaration on the Environment 1989, signed by twenty-four states, called for the establishment of new institutional authority under the auspices of the UN to combat any further global warming and for the negotiation of the necessary legal instruments. The UN Framework Convention on Climate Change was adopted in 1992.[164]

[162] See 30 ILM, 1991, p. 537.   [163] See 32 ILM, 1993, p. 874.
[164] 31 ILM, 1992, p. 849.

The objective of the Convention is to achieve stabilisation of greenhouse gases in the atmosphere at a level that would prevent dangerous anthropogenic interference with the climate system and such level should be achieved within a time-frame sufficient to allow ecosystems to adapt naturally to climate change, to ensure food production is not threatened and to enable economic development to proceed in a sustainable manner.[165] The states parties undertake *inter alia* to develop, update and publish national inventories of anthropogenic emissions by sources and removals by sinks[166] of all greenhouse gases not covered by the Montreal Protocol; to formulate, implement and update national and, where appropriate, regional programmes containing measures to mitigate climate changes; to promote and co-operate in the development, application and transfer of technologies and processes to control, reduce or prevent such anthropogenic emissions; to promote sustainable management and conservation of sinks and reservoirs of all greenhouse gases not controlled by the Montreal Protocol; to take climate change considerations into account to the extent feasible in their relevant social, economic and environmental policies; to promote and co-operate in research, exchange of information and education in the field of climate change.[167] Developed country parties, and certain other parties listed in Annex I,[168] commit themselves to take the lead in modifying longer-term trends in anthropogenic emissions and particularly to adopt national policies and take corresponding measures on the mitigation of climate change by limiting anthropogenic emissions of greenhouse gases and protecting and enhancing greenhouse gas sinks and reservoirs.[169] Developed country and other Annex I parties must submit within six months of the Convention coming into force and periodically thereafter, detailed information on such matters with the aim of returning anthropogenic emissions to their 1990 levels. This information provided is to be reviewed by the Conference of the parties on a periodic basis.[170] In addition, developed country parties and other developed parties included in Annex II[171] are to provide the financial resources to enable the developing country parties to meet their obligations under the Convention and generally to assist them in coping with the adverse effects of climate change. The parties agree to give full consideration to actions necessary to assist developing country parties that may be, for example, small island countries, countries with low-lying coastal areas, countries prone to natural disasters, drought and desertification and land-locked and transit states.[172]

---

[165] Article 2.
[166] Defined as any process, activity or mechanism which removes a greenhouse gas, an aerosol or a precursor of a greenhouse gas from the atmosphere, article 1 (8).   [167] Article 4(1).
[168] For example, former European Soviet Republics such as Belarus, the Ukraine and the Baltic states.   [169] Article 4(2)a.   [170] Article 4(2)b.
[171] Essentially European Union countries, the US, Australia, Canada, New Zealand, Iceland, Japan, Switzerland and Turkey.   [172] Article 4(8).

The Conference of the parties is established as the supreme body of the Convention and has the function *inter alia* to review the implementation of the Convention, periodically examine the obligations of the parties and the institutional arrangements established, promote the exchange of information, facilitate at the request of two or more parties the co-ordination of measures taken to address climate change, promote and guide the development of comparable methodologies for the preparation of inventories, assess the implementation of the Convention by the parties, consider and adopt regular reports on implementation and make recommendations on any matters necessary for the implementation of the Convention.[173] In addition, the Convention provides for a secretariat to be established, together with a subsidiary body for scientific and technological advice and a subsidiary body for implementation.[174] The Convention as a whole is a complex document and the range of commitments entered into, particularly by developed country parties, is not wholly clear.

The Convention entered into force in 1994 and the following year the first session of the Conference was held in Berlin.[175] It was agreed that the pledges by the developed country parties to reduce emissions by 2000 to 1990 levels was not adequate and preparations were commenced to draft a further legal instrument by 1997. It was also agreed not to establish new commitments for developing country parties, but rather to assist the implementation of existing commitments. The parties decided to initiate a pilot phase for joint implementation projects, providing for investment from one party in greenhouse gas emissions reduction opportunities in another party. In addition, it was decided to establish a permanent secretariat in Bonn and two subsidiary advisory bodies.

Outer space[176]

The Outer Space Treaty 1967 provides that the exploration and use of outer space is to be carried out for the benefit and in the interests of all states.[177] The harmful contamination of space or celestial bodies is to be avoided as are adverse changes in the environment of the earth resulting from the introduction of extraterrestrial matter.[178] Nuclear weapons and other weapons of mass destruction are not to be placed in orbit around the earth, installed on celestial bodies or stationed in outer space and the moon and other celestial bodies are to be used exclusively for peaceful

[173] Article 7.   [174] Articles 8–10.   [175] See 34 ILM, 1995, p. 1671.
[176] See further *infra* Chapter 10, p. 381.   [177] Article 1.   [178] Article 9.

purposes.[179] The Agreement Governing the Activities of States on the Moon and Other Celestial Bodies 1979 provides that the moon and its natural resources are the 'common heritage of mankind' and are to be used exclusively for peaceful purposes.[180] Article 7 stipulates that in exploring and using the moon, states parties are to take measures to prevent the disruption of the existing balance of its environment whether by introducing adverse changes in that environment or by its harmful contamination through the introduction of extra-environmental matter or otherwise.

There is, in particular, a growing problem with regard to debris located in outer space. Such debris, consisting of millions of objects of varying size in space,[181] constitutes a major hazard to spacecraft. While liability for damage caused by objects launched into space is absolute,[182] the specific problem of space debris has been addressed in the Buenos Aires International Instrument on the Protection of the Environment from Damage Caused by Space Debris, adopted by the International Law Association at its 1994 Conference.[183] The draft emphasises the obligations to co-operate in the prevention of damage to the environment, in promoting the development and exchange of technology to prevent, reduce and control space debris and in the flow and exchange of information and to hold consultations when there is reason to believe that activities may produce space debris likely to cause damage to the environment or to persons or objects or significant risks thereto. The principle proclaimed by the draft is that each state or international organisation party to the instrument that launches or procures the launching of a space object is internationally liable for damage arising therefrom to another party to the instrument as a consequence of space debris produced by any such object.[184]

---

[179] Article 4. See also the Principles Relevant to the Use of Nuclear Power Sources in Outer Space, adopted by the UN General Assembly in resolution 47/68 (1992). Goals for radioactive protection and safety are stipulated.

[180] See articles 3 and 11.

[181] Such debris may result from pollution from spacecraft, abandoned satellites, orbital explosions and satellite break-ups or hardware released during space launches and other normal manoeuvres. See e.g. L. Roberts, 'Addressing the Problem of Orbital Space Debris: Combining International Regulatory and Liability Regimes', 15 *Boston College International and Comparative Law Review*, 1992, p. 53. See also S. Gorove, 'Towards a Clarification of the Term "Space Objects" – An International Legal and Policy Imperative?', 21 *Journal of Space Law*, 1993, p. 10.

[182] See e.g. B. Hurwitz, *Space Liability for Outer Space Activities*, Dordrecht, 1992, and see further *supra* Chapter 10, p. 382.

[183] *Report of the Sixty-Sixth Conference*, Buenos Aires, 1994, pp. 317 *et seq.* This, of course, is not a binding treaty, but a suggested draft from an influential private organisation.

[184] Article 8 of the draft.

International watercourses[185]

International watercourses are systems of surface waters and groundwaters which are situated in more than one state.[186] Such watercourses form a unitary whole and normally flow into a common terminus. While historically there has been some disagreement as to the extent of the watercourse system covered, particularly whether it includes the complete river basin with all associated tributaries and groundwater systems, a broader definition is the approach adopted in recent years. Customary law developed rules with regard to equal riparian rights to international rivers,[187] but these were not extensive.[188] The International Law Association, a private organisation of international lawyers, proposed the Helsinki Rules on the Uses of the Waters of International Rivers in 1966,[189] in which it was noted that each basin state was entitled to a reasonable and equitable share in the beneficial use of the waters and that all states were obliged to prevent new forms of water pollution that would cause substantial injury in the territory of other basin states.[190]

In 1992, the Convention on the Protection and Use of Transboundary Watercourses and International Lakes was adopted in Helsinki within the framework of the Economic Commission for Europe of the United Nations.

---

[185] See e.g. Sands, *Principles*, Chapter 9 and Birnie and Boyle, *International Law and the Environment*, Chapter 6. See also R. Baxter, *The Law of International Waterways*, Cambridge, MA, 1964; C. Bourne, 'International Law and Pollution of International Rivers and Lakes', 21 *University of Toronto Law Journal*, 1971, p. 193; F. Florio, 'Water Pollution and Related Principles of International Law', 17 Canadian YIL, 1979, p. 134; J. Lammers, *Pollution of International Watercourses: A Search for Substantive Rules and Principles*, The Hague, 1984; S. McCaffrey, 'The Law of International Watercourses: Some Recent Developments and Unanswered Questions', 17 *Denver Journal of International Law and Policy*, 1989, p. 505; J. G. Polakiewicz, 'La Responsabilité de l'Etat en Matière de Pollution des Eaux Fluviales ou Souterraines Internationales', *Journal de Droit International*, 1991, p. 283; H. Ruiz Fabri, 'Règles Coutumières Générales et Droit International Fluvial', AFDI, 1990, p. 818 and J. Sette-Camara, 'Pollution of International Rivers', 186 HR, 1984, p. 117.

[186] See e.g. article 1(1) of the UN Convention on the Protection and Use of Transboundary Watercourses and International Lakes 1992 and article 2 of the Draft Articles on the Law of the Non-Navigational Uses of International Watercourses adopted by the International Law Commission in 1994, *Report of the International Law Commission*, 46th Session, 1994, p. 197.

[187] See the *Territorial Jurisdiction of the International Commission of the Oder* case, PCIJ, Series A, No. 23, p. 27: 5 ILR, p. 83.

[188] See the *Lac Lannoux* case, 24 ILR, p. 101. The tribunal noted, for example, that while the interests of riparian states had to be taken into account by a riparian state proposing changes to the river system, there was no rule precluding the use of hydraulic power of international watercourses without a prior agreement between the interested states, *ibid.*, p. 130.

[189] *Report of the Fifty-second Conference*, 1966, p. 484.

[190] See also the Rules on Water Pollution in an International Drainage Basin adopted by the ILA in 1982, *Report of the Sixtieth Conference*, 1982, p. 535 and the Rules on International Groundwaters adopted in 1986, *Report of the Sixty-second Conference*, 1986. See also the work of the Institut de Droit International, *Annuaire de l'Institut de Droit International*, 1979, p. 193.

Under this Convention, all parties must take all appropriate measures to prevent, control and reduce any significant adverse effect on the environment resulting from a change in the conditions of transboundary waters caused by a human activity. Such effects on the environment include effects on human health and safety, flora, fauna, soil, air, water, climate, landscape and also effects on the cultural heritage.[191] In taking such measures, states parties are to be guided by the precautionary principle[192] and by the polluter-pays principle, by which the costs of pollution, prevention, control and reduction measures are to be borne by the polluter. Each party undertakes to set emission limits for discharges from point sources into surface waters based on best available technology[193] and to define, where appropriate, water-quality objectives and adopt water-quality criteria[194] for the purpose of preventing, controlling and reducing transboundary impact. The measures to be taken must ensure, for example, the application of low- and non-waste technology; the prior licensing of waste-water discharge; the application of biological or equivalent processes to municipal waste water; the use of environmental impact assessments and sustainable water-resources management.[195]

The Convention also calls for the parties to establish monitoring programmes, to co-operate in research and development projects and to exchange relevant information as early as possible.[196] Riparian parties are to enter into bilateral or multilateral agreements or arrangements in order to co-ordinate their activities and to consult together at the request of any one riparian party.[197] Article 7 provides that the parties 'shall support appropriate international efforts to elaborate rules, criteria and procedures in the field of responsibility and liability'.

The Draft Articles on the Law of the Non-Navigational Uses of International Watercourses adopted by the International Law Commission in 1994 provides that watercourse states shall in their respective territories utilise an international watercourse in an 'equitable and reasonable manner'. In particular, optimal utilisation must be consistent with adequate protection of the watercourse.[198] Factors relevant to equitable and reasonable utilisation include in addition to physical factors of a natural character and the social and economic needs of the watercourse states concerned, the 'conservation, protection, development and economy of use of the water resources of the watercourse and the costs of measures taken to that

---

[191] Articles 1(2) and 2(1). [192] See *supra* p. 604. [193] This is defined in Annex I.
[194] See Annex III. [195] Article 3.
[196] Articles 4–6, and 11–13. Provisions regarding notification about critical situations and mutual assistance appear in articles 14 and 15. [197] Articles 9 and 10.
[198] Article 5. The Draft emphasises indeed in article 8 that watercourse states shall co-operate in order to attain optimal utilisation and adequate protection of an international watercourse.

effect'.[199] Article 7 of the Draft, in a reflection of customary law, provides that watercourse states shall exercise due diligence to utilise an international watercourse in such a way as not to cause significant harm to other watercourse states. Where such harm is caused, consultations are to take place in order to eliminate or mitigate such harm and with regard to compensation where appropriate. The Draft provides for regular exchanges of data and information, while watercourse states are to exchange information and consult in particular on the possible effects of planned measures on the condition of an international watercourse.[200] Before a watercourse state implements or permits the implementation of planned measures which may have a significant adverse effect upon other watercourse states, it is to provide such states with timely notification and sufficient technical data and information for the evaluation of the possible effects of the planned measures.[201] Unless otherwise agreed, the notified states have a period of six months for such evaluation during which exchanges of data and information are to take place and the planned measures are not to be implemented without the consent of the notified states. If no reply to the notification is received, the notifying state may proceed to implement the planned measures. If a reply is received, the states are to consult and negotiate with a view to arriving at an equitable resolution of the situation.[202] Where a watercourse state has serious reasons to believe that measures that may have a significant adverse impact are being planned, it may itself set in motion the above procedures.[203]

Article 20 of the Draft stipulates that watercourse states shall protect and preserve the ecosystems of international watercourses[204] and shall act to prevent, reduce and control pollution[205] of an international watercourse that may cause significant harm to other watercourse states or to their environment. Watercourse states are to take all necessary measures to prevent the introduction of species, alien or new, into an international watercourse which may have effects detrimental to the ecosystem of the watercourse resulting in significant harm to other watercourse states.[206]

While the 1992 Convention is not yet in force and the 1994 Draft Articles have not as yet been translated into a treaty, it is clear that the international community is coming to terms with the need to protect the environment of

---

[199] Article 6.   [200] Articles 9 and 11.   [201] Article 12.   [202] Articles 11–17.
[203] Article 18. Article 19 provides for an expedited procedure where there is the utmost urgency in the implementation of planned measures.
[204] See also article 23 with regard to measures necessary to protect and preserve the marine environment.
[205] Pollution is here defined as 'any detrimental alteration in the composition or quality of the waters of an international watercourse which results directly or indirectly from human conduct', article 21(1).   [206] Article 22.

international watercourses.[207] How evolving international environmental rules relate to the more traditional principles of international law is one of the issues currently before the International Court in the *Gabcikovo-Nagymaros Dam* case.[208] Hungary and Czechoslovakia entered into a treaty in 1977 by which there would be created on the Danube between the two states a barrage system, a dam, a reservoir, hydro-electric power stations and a 25 kilometre canal for diverting the Danube from its original course through a system of locks. A dispute developed in the light of Hungary's growing environmental concerns. Hungary suspended work on the project in 1989, while Czechoslovakia (now the Czech and Slovak Federal Republic) proceeded with a 'provisional solution' as from 1991, which involved damming the Danube at a point on Czechoslovakian territory. In 1992, Hungary announced the termination of the treaty of 1977 and related instruments. The case came before the International Court ultimately by way of a Special Agreement in 1993 between Hungary and Slovakia (the successor to the former Czech and Slovak Federal Republic in so far as the project was concerned). The case essentially revolves around the relationship between the treaty and subsequent environmental concerns. The Court will need to consider whether such concerns justify, for example, suspension and/or termination of a binding treaty and to what extent environmental concerns (as expressed by Hungary) over the 'provisional solution' diversion works on Slovak territory impact upon Hungary's international legal rights.

Ultra-hazardous activities[209]

It has been argued that ultra-hazardous activities form a distinct category in the field of international environmental law and one in which the principle of strict or absolute liability operates. The definition of what constitutes such activity, of course, is somewhat uncertain, but the characterisation can be taken to revolve around the serious consequences that are likely to flow from any damage that results, rather than upon the likelihood of pollution

---

[207] Note that a variety of regional and bilateral agreements and arrangements exist with regard to international watercourses, see e.g. the agreements concerning the International Commission of the Rhine, the US–Canadian International Joint Commission and provisions concerning the Zambezi River System and the Niger Basin, see Sands, *Principles*, pp. 354 *et seq.* and Birnie and Boyle, *International Law and the Environment*, pp. 241 *et seq.*

[208] See 32 ILM, 1993, pp. 1247 *et seq.*

[209] See e.g. Sands, *Principles*, Chapter 11 and Birnie and Boyle, *International Law and the Environment*, Chapters 8 and 9. See also D. A. Bagwell, 'Hazardous and Noxious Substances', 62 *Tulane Law Review*, 1988, p. 433; L. F. Goldie, 'Concepts of Strict and Absolute Liability and the Ranking of Liability in Terms of Relative Exposure to Risk' 16 Netherlands YIL, 1985, p. 247; Barboza, 'International Liability', pp. 331 *et seq.*; W. Jenks, 'The Scope and Nature of Ultra-Hazardous Liability in International Law', 117 HR, 1966, p. 99; Handl, 'State Liability', pp. 553 *et seq.* and R. J. Dupuy, *La Responsabilité des Etats pour les Dommages d'Origine Technologique et Industrielle*, Paris, 1976, pp. 206–9.

occurring from the activity in question. The focus therefore is upon the significant or exceptional risk of severe transnational damage.[210] The effect of categorising a particular activity as ultra-hazardous would, it appears, be to accept the strict liability principle rather than the due diligence standard commonly regarded as the general rule in pollution situations.[211] In other words, the state under whose territory or jurisdiction the activity took place would be liable irrespective of fault.

This exception to the general principle can be justified as a method of moving the burden of proof and shifting the loss clearly from the victim to the state. It would also operate as a further incentive to states to take action in areas of exceptional potential harm.

In determining what areas of activity could be characterised as ultra-hazardous, some caution needs to be exercised. There can be little doubt that nuclear activities fall within this category as a general rule, but beyond this there appears to be no agreement. The Convention on International Liability for Damage caused by Space Objects 1972 specifically provides that a launching state shall be absolutely liable to pay compensation for damage caused by its space objects on the surface of the earth,[212] but this is the only clear example of its kind.

Nuclear activities[213]

The use of nuclear technology brings with it risks as well as benefits and the accident at the Chernobyl nuclear reactor in 1986[214] brought home to international opinion just how devastating the consequences of a nuclear mishap could be. Concern in this area had hitherto focused upon the issue of nuclear weapons. In 1963 the Treaty Banning Nuclear Weapons Testing in the Atmosphere, Outer Space and Under Water was signed.[215] However, France and China did not become parties to this treaty and continued atmospheric nuclear testing. Australia and New Zealand sought a declaration from the International Court that French atmospheric nuclear testing was contrary to international law, but the Court decided the case on the basis that a subsequent French decision to end such testing was binding and

---

[210] Handl, 'State Liability', p. 554.   [211] *Supra*, p. 592.   [212] See *supra*, p. 593.

[213] See e.g. *Chernobyl;* Boyle, 'Nuclear Energy', and 'Chernobyl'; J. C. Woodliffe, 'Tackling Transboundary Environmental Hazards in Cases of Emergency: The Emerging Legal Framework' in *Current Issues in European and International Law* (eds. R. White and B. Smythe), London, 1990 and Woodliffe, 'Chernobyl: Four Years On', 39 ICLQ, 1990, p. 461.

[214] See *Chernobyl*, pp. 1–2. See also IAEA, *Summary Report on the Post Accident Review Meeting on the Chernobyl Accident*, Vienna, 1986.

[215] See also the Treaty on the Prohibition of the Emplacement of Nuclear Weapons and other Weapons of Mass Destruction on the Sea-Bed 1971; the Treaty for the Prohibition of Nuclear Weapons in Latin America 1967; and the South Pacific Nuclear Free Zone Treaty 1985.

thus the issue was moot.[216] In response to renewed French nuclear testing in the South Pacific in 1995, albeit underground rather than atmospheric, New Zealand asked the International Court to review the situation pursuant to the 1974 judgment and declare that France was acting illegally as being likely to cause the introduction into the marine environment of radioactive material and in failing to conduct an environmental impact assessment. While the Court referred to 'the obligations of states to respect and protect the natural environment', it declared that the request had to be dismissed as not falling within the relevant paragraph of the 1974 judgment permitting a re-examination of the situation since the latter judgment had concerned atmospheric tests alone.[217]

Measures to prevent the spread of nuclear weapons were adopted in the Nuclear Non-Proliferation Treaty of 1968, although the possession itself of nuclear weapons does not contravene international law.[218]

A variety of international organisations are now involved to some extent in the process of developing rules and principles concerning nuclear activities and environmental protection. The International Atomic Energy Agency, to take the prime example, was established in 1956 in order to encourage the development of nuclear power, but particularly since the Chernobyl accident its nuclear safety role has been emphasised. The Convention on Assistance in Cases of Nuclear Emergency 1986, for example, gave it a co-ordinating function and an obligation to provide appropriate resources where so requested.[219] The IAEA has established a series of standards and guidelines including, for example, in the context of the design, construction and operation of nuclear power plants, although such standards do not have the force of law.[220] Other international organisations also have a role to play in the sphere of nuclear activities.[221]

The provision of information

There appears to be a general principle requiring that information be provided in certain situations[222] and several bilateral agreements have expressed

---

[216] See the *Nuclear Tests* cases, ICJ Reports, 1974, p. 253: 57 ILR, p. 398.

[217] *Request for an Examination of the Situation in Accordance with Paragraph 63 of the Court's Judgment of 1974 in the Nuclear Tests case*, ICJ Reports, 1995, pp. 288, 305–6.

[218] See e.g. M. N. Shaw, 'Nuclear Weapons and International Law' in *Nuclear Weapons and International Law* (ed. I. Pogany), London, 1987, p. 1. See also the Advisory Opinions of the International Court, *infra* Chapter 19, pp. 812 *et seq.*   [219] See further *infra*, p. 623.

[220] Note, however, that under the Geneva Convention on the High Seas 1958, states are to take account of IAEA standards in preventing pollution of the seas from the dumping of nuclear waste.

[221] E.g. EURATOM (established in 1957), the Nuclear Energy Agency of the OECD (established in 1957) and the ILO (International Labour Organisation). See Boyle, 'Nuclear Energy', pp. 266–8.

[222] See *supra*, p. 602. See also Principle 20 of the Stockholm Declaration and Principle 9 of the Rio Declaration.

this in the context of nuclear accidents.[223] In general, such agreements provide that each state is to inform the other without delay of any emergency resulting from civil nuclear activities and any other incident that could have radiological consequences for the second state. Reciprocal information systems are set up and warning notification centres established. Such agreements, however, do not cover exchange of military information.[224]

Following the Chernobyl accident and the failure of the USSR to provide immediate information, the Vienna Convention on Early Notification of a Nuclear Accident 1986 was rapidly adopted, under the auspices of the IAEA. This provides that in the event of a nuclear accident, the relevant state shall 'forthwith notify, directly or through the International Atomic Energy Agency . . . those states which are or may be physically affected . . . of the nuclear accident, its nature, the time of its occurrence and its exact location'. Additionally, such states must be promptly provided with information relevant to minimising the radiological consequences.[225] States are to respond promptly to a request for further information or consultations sought by an affected state.[226]

It is also to be noted that although the Convention does not apply to military nuclear accidents, the five nuclear weapons states made Statements of Voluntary Application indicating that they would apply the Convention to all nuclear accidents, including those not specified in that agreement.[227]

Since this Convention was adopted, a variety of bilateral agreements have been signed which have been more wide-ranging than those signed beforehand and which in some cases have gone beyond the provisions specified in the Notification Convention. The agreements signed by the UK with Norway, the Netherlands and Denmark during 1988–9, for example, specify that there is an obligation to notify the other parties if there is an accident or activity in the territory of the notifying state from which a transboundary effect of radiological safety significance is likely and additionally where abnormal levels of radiation are registered that are not caused by release from facilities or activities in the notifying state's territory. Extensive provisions are also included dealing with exchanges of information.[228]

[223] The first was concluded between France and Belgium in 1966 concerning the Ardennes Nuclear Power Station. Other examples include Switzerland–Federal Republic of Germany 1978 and France–UK 1983. The latter agreement was supplemented by a formal arrangement between the UK Nuclear Installations Inspectorate and the French equivalent for the continuous exchange of information on safety issues.

[224] See Woodliffe, 'Tackling Transboundary Environmental Hazards', at pp. 117–20.

[225] Article 2; see also article 5.   [226] Article 6.   [227] See text in 25 ILM, 1986, p. 1394.

[228] See e.g. Woodliffe, 'Chernobyl', p. 464. See the European Community Council Directive 87/600 of December 1987, which provides for the early exchange of information in the event of a radiological emergency. See also the EC Environmental Information Directive 1990 providing for a right of access to environmental information; article 9 of the Convention for the Protection of the Marine Environment of the North-East Atlantic 1992 and Chapter 3 of the Convention on Civil Liability for Damage Resulting from Activities Dangerous to the Environment 1993.

The provision of assistance[229]

The earliest treaty providing for assistance in the event of radiation accidents was the Nordic Mutual Assistance Agreement 1963. This dealt with the general terms of assistance, the advisory and co-ordinating role of the IAEA, financing, liability and privileges and immunities. The United Nations established the UN Disaster Relief Office (UNDRO) in 1972[230] and this provides assistance in pre-disaster planning. In 1977 the IAEA concluded an agreement with UNDRO with the purpose of co-ordinating their assistance activities in the nuclear accident field and in 1984 published a series of guidelines[231] setting out the mechanics of co-operation between states, including references to the problems of costs, liability, privileges and immunities.

In 1986, following the Chernobyl accident and at the same time as the Notification Convention, the Vienna Convention on Assistance in the Case of a Nuclear Accident or Radiological Emergency was adopted. This provides that a state in need of assistance in the event of a nuclear accident or radiological emergency may call for such assistance from any other state party either directly or through the IAEA.[232] This applies whether or not such accident or emergency originated within its territory, jurisdiction or control. States requesting assistance (which may include medical assistance and help with regard to the temporary relocation of displaced persons[233]) must provide details of the type of assistance required and other necessary information.[234] The IAEA must respond to a request for assistance by making available appropriate resources allocated for this purpose and by transmitting promptly the request to other states and international organisations possessing the necessary resources. In addition, if requested by the state seeking assistance, the IAEA will co-ordinate the assistance at the international level. The IAEA is also required to collect and disseminate to the states parties information concerning the availability of experts, equipment and materials and with regard to methodologies, techniques and available research data relating to the response to such situations.[235]The general range of assistance that can be provided by the Agency is laid down in some detail.[236]

In general terms, the Assistance Convention seeks to balance considerations relating to the sovereignty of the requesting state,[237] the legitimate

---

[229] See e.g. A. O. Adede, *The IAEA Notification and Assistance Conventions in Case of a Nuclear Accident: Landmarks in the History of Multilateral Treaty-Making*, London, 1987.

[230] A Disaster Relief Co-ordinator was provided for in General Assembly resolution 2816(XXVI). See *Chernobyl*, p. 45.

[231] Guidelines for Mutual Emergency Assistance Arrangements in Connection with a Nuclear Accident or Radiological Emergency, *Chernobyl: Law and Communication*, p. 199.

[232] Article 2(1).   [233] Article 2(5).   [234] Article 2(2).   [235] Article 5.   [236] *Ibid.*

[237] Under article 3(a), and unless otherwise agreed, the requesting state has the overall direction, control, co-ordination and supervision of the assistance within its territory.

rights of the assisting state or states[238] and the interests of the international community in rendering rapid assistance to affected states. Whether the balance achieved is a fair one is open to discussion.[239]

Nuclear safety

The Convention on Nuclear Safety was adopted by the IAEA in 1994. This emphasises that responsibility for nuclear safety rests with the state having jurisdiction over a nuclear installation[240] and obliges states parties to take legislative and administrative measures to implement Convention obligations[241] via a regulatory body[242] and to submit reports to periodic review meetings of all parties.[243] The Convention provides that operators of nuclear installations must be licensed[244] and it is the operators that remain primarily responsible for the safety of the installations.[245] The Convention specifies a number of safety considerations, but these are not in the form of binding obligations upon the parties.[246] Despite this, a general system of accountability has been created which has the potential to generate binding rules in the future.

Civil liability[247]

In addition to the issue of the responsibility or liability of the state for the activity under consideration, the question of the proceedings that may be taken by the individual victims is also raised. One possible approach is to permit the victim to have access to the legal system of the foreign polluter and thus to all remedies available on a non-discriminatory basis. This would have the effect of transforming the transboundary pollution into a national matter.[248] This approach is evident in some treaties.[249] The problem is that while placing the foreign victim on a par with nationals within the domestic

[238] Under article 7, the assisting state is entitled, unless it offers its assistance without costs, to be reimbursed for all the costs incurred by it, which are to be provided promptly, and under article 10(2), unless otherwise agreed, a requesting state is liable to compensate the assisting state for all loss of or damage to equipment or materials and for the death of or injury to personnel of the assisting party or persons acting on its behalf. There is no provision dealing with liability for damage caused by the assisting state. See also article 8 dealing with privileges and immunities.

[239] See e.g. *Chernobyl: Law and Communication*, p. 47 and Woodliffe, 'Tackling Transboundary Environmental Hazards', p. 127.

[240] Defined as 'a land-based civil nuclear power plant', article 2(1).   [241] Articles 4 and 7.

[242] Article 8.

[243] Articles 5 and 20–25. The IAEA is to provide the secretariat for the meetings of the parties, article 28.   [244] Article 7(2)ii.   [245] Article 9.   [246] Articles 10–19.

[247] See e.g. Birnie and Boyle, *International Law and the Environment*, pp. 371 *et seq.* and Sands, *Principles*, pp. 653 *et seq.*   [248] See e.g. Boyle, 'Nuclear Energy', pp. 297–8.

[249] See e.g. the Nordic Convention on the Protection of the Environment 1974. See also OECD Recommendations C(74)224; C(76)55 and C(77)28.

legal system of the offender, it depends for its value upon the legal system possessing internal legislation of appropriate substantive content. This is not always the case.

There are, however, several international agreements dealing specifically with the question of civil liability in the sphere of nuclear activities. The OECD Paris Convention on Third Party Liability in the Field of Nuclear Energy 1960, together with the Brussels Supplementary Convention 1963, provides that the operator of a nuclear installation shall be liable for damage to or loss of life of any person and damage to or loss of any property (other than the nuclear installation and associated property or means of transport). The IAEA Vienna Convention on Civil Liability for Nuclear Damage 1963 has similar provisions, but is aimed at global participation. However, the Paris Convention has only fourteen parties, all European states, including the nuclear states of the UK and France, and the Vienna Convention has just eleven parties, with only Argentina and Yugoslavia possessing nuclear facilities.

Additionally, the Brussels Convention on the Liability of Operators of Nuclear Ships 1962 provides that the operator of a nuclear ship shall be absolutely liable for any nuclear damage upon proof that such damage has been caused by a nuclear incident involving the nuclear fuel of, or radio-active products or waste produced in such ship.[250]

These conventions operate upon similar principles. It is the actual operator of the nuclear installation that is to bear the loss[251] and this is done upon the basis of absolute or strict liability. Accordingly, no proof of fault or negligence is required. The conventions require operators to possess appropriate liability insurance or other financial security under the conditions laid down by the competent public authorities, unless the operator is itself a state[252] and the relevant states are to ensure that claims up to the liability limits are met.[253] This recognition of the residual responsibility of the state is unique.[254] The amount of liability of the operator is, however, limited by the Paris Convention (as amended by the Brussels Supplementary Convention) to 120 million Units of Account (i.e. US dollars[255]).[256] In the

---

[250] This Convention has six parties and is not yet in force. None of the states which licenses nuclear ships is a party. Note that the Convention Relating to Civil Liability in the Field of Maritime Carriage of Nuclear Material 1971 provides that a person held liable for damage caused by a nuclear incident shall be exonerated from such liability if the operator of a nuclear installation is liable for such damage under either the Paris or Vienna Conventions.

[251] A carrier or handler of nuclear material may be regarded as such an operator where the latter consents and the necessary legislative framework so provides, see e.g. article 4(d) of the Paris Convention.

[252] See e.g. article 10 of the Paris Convention; article VII of the Vienna Convention and article III of the Brussels Convention on Nuclear Ships.   [253] *Ibid.*

[254] Cf. the Convention on Civil Liability for Oil Pollution Damage 1969.

[255] Protocols signed in 1982 have changed this to Special Drawing Rights and increased the limit, but the Protocols are not yet in force.   [256] Article 7.

case of the Vienna Convention regime, the installation state is permitted to limit the liability of the operator to a stated amount,[257] provided a minimum of liability is maintained.[258] Under the Brussels Convention on Nuclear Ships the liability of the operator as regards one nuclear ship is limited to 1,500 million gold francs in respect of any one nuclear accident.[259]

The relevant conventions also determine which state has jurisdiction over claims against operators or their insurers. In general, jurisdiction lies with the state where the nuclear incident occurred, although where a nuclear incident takes place outside the territory of a contracting party or where the place of the nuclear incident cannot be determined with certainty, jurisdiction will lie with the courts of the contracting party in whose territory the nuclear installations of the operator liable is situated.[260] Judgments given by the competent courts are enforceable in the territory of any contracting party.

The main problem with the system of the nuclear conventions is the fact that only a very few states are parties to them. Accordingly, a Joint Protocol was adopted in 1988 linking the Paris and Vienna Convention regimes, so that parties under each of these conventions may benefit from both of them. This is, however, only a partial solution and it is to be hoped that major nuclear states such as the US, Russia and Japan, that are not parties to either convention, may reconsider their position.[261]

The issue of inter-state claims is more difficult as was demonstrated by the aftermath of the Chernobyl accident. Many states have paid compensation to persons affected within their jurisdiction by the fallout from that accident, but while positions have been reserved with regard to claims directly against the former USSR, it seems that problems relating to the obligations actually owed by states and the doubt over the requisite standard of care have prevented such claims from having been actually made.[262]

Hazardous wastes[263]

The increasing problem of the disposal of toxic and hazardous wastes and the practice of dumping in the Third World, with its attendant severe health risks, has prompted international action.[264] The Oslo Convention for the Prevention of Marine Pollution by Dumping from Ships and Aircraft

---

[257] Article V.   [258] Article V fixes this at $5 million at 1963 values.   [259] Article III.
[260] Article 13 of the Paris Convention and article XI of the Vienna Convention.
[261] Note also that the Paris and Vienna Conventions do not provide for the costs of environmental clean-up. The IAEA established a Standing Committee on Nuclear Liability to revise the Vienna Convention 1963 in 1989.
[262] See e.g. *Chernobyl: Law and Communication*, pp. 26–8.
[263] See e.g. Sands, *Principles*, Chapter 11 and Birnie and Boyle, *International Law and the Environment*, Chapter 8.
[264] See *Keesing's Record of World Events*, pp. 36788–9 (1989). See also Principle 6 of the Stockholm Declaration 1972 and Principle 14 of the Rio Declaration 1992.

1972[265] provides for a ban on the dumping of certain substances[266] and for controls to be placed on the dumping of others.[267] The London Convention on the Prevention of Marine Pollution by Dumping of Wastes and Other Matter 1972[268] prohibits the dumping of wastes except as provided in the Convention itself, and this is strictly controlled.

In 1988, the Organisation of African Unity adopted a resolution proclaiming the dumping of nuclear and industrial wastes in Africa to be a crime against Africa and its people. In 1991 the OAU adopted the Bamako Convention on the Ban of the Import into Africa and the Control of Transboundary Movement and Management of Hazardous Wastes within Africa,[269] under which parties are to prohibit the import of all hazardous wastes for any reason into Africa by non-parties and to prohibit the dumping at sea of such wastes. The OECD has adopted a number of Decisions and Recommendations concerning the transfrontier movements and exports of hazardous wastes.[270] In 1989 the OECD adopted a Recommendation[271] noting that the 'polluter pays' principle should apply to accidents involving hazardous substances. The Basle Convention on the Control of Transboundary Movements of Hazardous Wastes and Their Disposal 1989 provides that parties shall prohibit the export of hazardous and other wastes to parties which have prohibited the import of such wastes and have so informed the other parties. In the absence of prohibition by the importing state, export to that state of such wastes is only permissible where consent in writing to the specific import is obtained.[272] The Convention also provides that any proposed transboundary movement of hazardous wastes must be notified to the competent authorities of the states concerned by the state of export. The latter shall not allow the generator or exporter of hazardous wastes to commence the transboundary movement without the written consent of the state of import and any state of transit.[273]

In 1990, the IAEA adopted a Code of Practice on the International Transboundary Movement of Radioactive Waste,[274] emphasising that every state should ensure that such movements take place only with the prior notification and consent of the sending, receiving and transit states in accordance with their respective laws and regulations. Appropriate regulatory authorities are called for, as well as the necessary administrative and technical capacity to manage and dispose of such waste in a manner consistent with international safety standards.

The Convention on the Transboundary Effects of Industrial Accidents adopted in 1992 applies to industrial accidents in an installation or during

---

[265] This is limited essentially to the north-east Atlantic area.   [266] Listed in Annex I.
[267] Listed in Annex II.   [268] This is a global instrument.   [269] 30 ILM, 1991, p. 773.
[270] See e.g. 23 ILM, 1984, p. 214; 25 ILM, 1986, p. 1010 and 28 ILM, 1989, pp. 277 and 259.   [271] C(89)88.   [272] Article 4.   [273] Article 6.   [274] 30 ILM, 1991, p. 556.

transportation resulting from activities involving hazardous substances (identified in Annex I). It does not apply to nuclear accidents, accidents at military installations, dam failures, land-based transport accidents, accidental release of genetically modified organisms, accidents caused by activities in the marine environment or spills of oil or other harmful substances at sea.[275] The Convention provides that parties of origin[276] should identify hazardous activities within the jurisdiction and ensure that affected parties are notified of any such proposed or existing activity. Consultations are to take place on the identification of those hazardous activities that may have transboundary effects.[277] A variety of preventive measures are posited.[278] In particular, the party of origin shall require the operator in charge of such hazardous activity to demonstrate the safe performance of that activity by the provision of information.[279] Parties are to develop policies on the siting of new hazardous activities and on significant modifications to existing hazardous activities, while adequate emergency preparedness to respond to industrial accidents is to be established and maintained.[280] An industrial accident notification system is established, [281] while by article 13 the parties 'shall support appropriate international efforts to elaborate rules, criteria and procedures in the field of responsibility and liability'.[282]

Marine pollution[283]

Marine pollution can arise from a variety of sources, including the operation of shipping, dumping at sea,[284] activities on the sea-bed[285] and the

---

[275] Article 2(2).

[276] I.e. parties under whose jurisdiction an industrial accident occurs or is capable of occurring, article 1(g).   [277] Article 4. See also Annexes II and III.

[278] See article 6 and Annex IV.   [279] Article 6(2) and Annex V.

[280] Articles 7 and 8 and Annex V.   [281] Article 10 and Annex IX.

[282] See also the Memorandum of Understanding Concerning Establishment of the Inter-Organisation Programme for the Sound Management of Chemicals 1995 signed by the Food and Agriculture Organisation, the International Labour Organisation, the Organisation for Economic Co-operation and Development, the UN Industrial Development Programme, the UN Environment Programme and the World Health Organisation. The areas for co-ordination include the international assessment of chemical risks, information exchange and the prevention of illegal international traffic in toxic and dangerous products, see 34 ILM, 1995, p. 1311.

[283] See e.g. Sands, *Principles*, Chapter 8; Birnie and Boyle, *International Law and the Environment*, pp. 304 *et seq.*; R. Churchill and A. V. Lowe, *The Law of the Sea*, 2nd edn, Manchester, 1988, Chapter 15; A. E. Boyle, 'Marine Pollution under the Law of the Sea Convention', 79 AJIL, 1985, p. 347; L. Caflisch, 'International Law and Ocean Pollution: The Present and the Future', 8 *Revue Belge de Droit International*, 1972, p. 7 and O. Schachter, 'The Value of the 1982 UN Convention on the Law of the Sea: Preserving our Freedoms and Protecting the Environment', 23 *Ocean Development and International Law*, 1992, p. 55.

[284] See *supra* p. 426, and Churchill and Lowe, *The Law of the Sea*, pp. 268–72. See also D. Bodansky, 'Protecting the Marine Environment from Vessel-Source Pollution: UNCLOS III and Beyond', 18 *Ecology Law Quarterly*, 1991, p. 719 and Y. Sasamura, 'Prevention and Control of Marine Pollution from Ships', 25 *Law Sea Institute Proceedings*, 1993, p. 306.

[285] See Churchill and Lowe, *The Law of the Sea*, pp. 272–7.

effects of pollution originating on the land and entering the seas.[286] There are a large number of treaties, bilateral, regional and multilateral, dealing with such issues and some of the more significant of them in the field of pollution from ships will be briefly noted.

Pollution from ships

The International Convention for the Prevention of Pollution of the Sea by Oil 1954[287] basically prohibits the discharge of oil within 50 miles of land. The International Convention for the Prevention of Pollution from Ships 1973[288] is concerned with all forms of non-accidental pollution from ships apart from dumping and supersedes the 1954 Convention as between parties to it. In five Annexes to the Convention,[289] detailed standards are laid down covering oil, noxious liquid substances in bulk, harmful substances carried by sea in packaged form, sewage and garbage. The Convention covers ships flying the flag of or operated under the authority of a state party, but does not apply to warships or state-owned ships used only on governmental non-commercial service.

Article 211(2) of the Convention on the Law of the Sea 1982 provides that states are to legislate for the prevention, reduction and control of pollution of the marine environment from vessels flying their flag or of their registry. Such rules are to have the same effect at least as that of generally accepted international rules and standards established through the competent international organisation[290] or general diplomatic conference. States

---

[286] Articles 194 and 207 of the Convention on the Law of the Sea 1982 provide in general terms for states to reduce marine pollution from land-based sources. Note that the Montreal Guidelines on the Protection of the Environment Against Pollution from Land-Based Sources 1985 built upon article 207. A number of regional conventions (many of them UN Environment Programme Regional Seas Conventions) lay down specific rules dealing with the control of particular substances, see Churchill and Lowe, *The Law of the Sea*, pp. 277–81. See e.g. the Barcelona Convention for the Protection of the Mediterranean Sea Against Pollution 1976 and its two Protocols of 1980 and 1982; the Kuwait Regional Convention for Co-operation on Protection of the Marine Environment from Pollution 1978 and Protocols of 1978, 1989 and 1990; the Abidjan Convention for Co-operation in the Protection and Development of the Marine and Coastal Environment of the West and Central Africa Region 1981 and Protocol of 1981; the Lima Convention for the Protection of the Marine Environment and Coastal Areas of the South-East Pacific 1981 and Protocols; the Cartagena Convention for the Protection and Development of the Marine Environment of the Wider Caribbean Region 1983 and two Protocols of 1983 and 1990; the Convention on the Protection of the Black Sea Against Pollution 1992; the Convention for the Protection of the Marine Environment of the North East Atlantic 1992 and the Convention on the Protection of the Marine Environment of the Baltic Sea Area 1992.   [287] As amended, see Churchill and Lowe, *The Law of the Sea*, pp. 248–9.
[288] Known as the MARPOL Convention. This was modified by the 1978 Protocol and has been further developed by resolutions adopted by the International Maritime Organisation's Marine Environment Protection Committee.
[289] Note that Annexes I and II are fully binding, while Annexes III, IV and V are options which a state may declare it does not accept when first becoming a party to the Convention, article 14.   [290] The International Maritime Organisation.

are also to ensure that the ships of their nationality or of their registry comply with 'applicable international rules and standards' and with domestic rules governing the prevention, reduction and control of pollution.[291] In addition, coastal states have jurisdiction physically to inspect, and, where the evidence so warrants, commence proceedings against ships in their territorial waters, where there are clear grounds for believing that the ship concerned has violated domestic or international pollution regulations.[292] It should also be noted that a state in whose port a vessel is may take legal proceedings against that vessel not only where it is alleged to have violated that state's pollution laws or applicable international rules in its territorial sea or economic zone,[293] but also in respect of any discharge outside its internal waters, territorial sea or exclusive economic zone in violation of applicable international rules and standards.[294]

Where an accident takes place, the Convention Relating to Intervention on the High Seas in Cases of Oil Pollution Casualties 1969[295] permits states parties to take such measures on the high seas as may be necessary to prevent, mitigate or eliminate grave and imminent danger to their coastline or related interests from pollution or threat of pollution of the sea by oil.[296]

An International Convention on Oil Pollution Preparedness, Response and Co-operation was signed in London in November 1990, with the purpose of ensuring prompt and effective action in the event of a pollution incident. It requires ships to carry detailed plans for dealing with pollution emergencies. Pollution incidents must be reported without delay and in the event of a serious incident, other states likely to be affected must be informed and details given to the International Maritime Organisation. National and regional systems for dealing with such incidents are encouraged and the contracting parties agree to co-operate and provide advisory services, technical support and equipment at the request of other parties.[297]

As far as liability is concerned, the Convention on Civil Liability for Oil Pollution Damage 1969 provides that where oil escaping from a ship causes damage on the territory or territorial sea of a contracting party, the ship-

[291] Article 217.   [292] Article 220(2).   [293] Article 220(1).
[294] Article 218. A provision characterised as 'truly innovatory' by Churchill and Lowe, *The Law of the Sea*, p. 259.
[295] The adoption of this Convention followed upon the *Torrey Canyon* incident in 1967 in which a ship aground, although on the high seas, was bombed in order to reduce the risk of oil pollution; see Churchill and Lowe, *The Law of the Sea*, p. 241. See also the Report of the Home Office, Cmnd. 3246 (1967).
[296] This was extended by a Protocol of 1973 to cover pollution from substances other than oil. Note that the International Convention on Salvage 1989 seeks to integrate environmental factors into the salvage rewards system.
[297] See e.g. the Bonn Agreement for Co-operation in Dealing with Pollution of the North Sea by Oil 1969 and the Agreement for Co-operation in Dealing with Pollution of the North Sea by Oil and Other Harmful Substances 1983. Many of the UN Environment Programme Regional Seas Conventions have Protocols dealing with emergency situations, see *supra* note 286 and Sands, *Principles*, p. 337.

owner is strictly liable for such damage, which includes the costs of both preventive measures and further loss or damage caused by such measures.[298] This liability is limited, however, unless the pollution is the result of the fault of the shipowner.[299] The shipowner must maintain insurance or other financial security to cover its liability. Claims may be brought in the courts of the party in which loss or damage has occurred or preventive measures taken and the judgments of such courts are generally recognisable and enforceable in the courts of all parties. The 1969 Convention was amended by the Protocol on Liability 1992,[300] which includes in the definition of damage compensation for impairment of the environment provided that this is limited to costs of reasonable measures of reinstatement actually undertaken or to be undertaken.[301] The Convention on the Establishment of an International Fund for Compensation for Oil Pollution Damage was adopted in 1971 and enables compensation to be paid in certain cases not covered by the Civil Liability Convention. It is supplemented by three Protocols.[302] The Convention on Civil Liability for Oil Pollution Damage Resulting from Exploration and Exploitation of Seabed Mineral Resources 1977 establishes the liability of the operator of an installation under the jurisdiction of a party for pollution damage resulting from incidents taking place beyond the coastal low-water line.[303]

---

[298] Except where the damage results from war or acts of God; is wholly caused by an act or omission done by a third party with intent to cause damage; or where the damage is wholly caused by the negligent or other wrongful act of any government or other authority responsible for the maintenance of navigational aids, see articles II and III.   [299] Article V.

[300] When this enters into force, the 1969 Convention will become known as the International Convention on Civil Liability for Oil Pollution Damage 1992.   [301] Article 2(3).

[302] When the Fund Protocol 1992 comes into force, the 1971 Convention will become known as the International Convention on the Establishment of an International Fund for Oil Pollution Damage 1992. Up to the end of 1991, the Fund has been involved in the settlement of claims arising out of sixty incidents, and the total compensation paid has amounted to £46 million, see Sands, *Principles*, p. 660. See also the *Patmos* case, *ibid.*, pp. 661–2.

[303] See also *infra* Chapter 19, p. 815 with regard to the environment and armed conflicts.

CHAPTER 16

THE LAW OF TREATIES

Unlike municipal law, the various methods by which rights and duties may be created in international law are relatively unsophisticated.[1] Within a state, legal interests may be established by contracts between two or more persons, or by agreements under seal, or under the developed system for transferring property, or indeed by virtue of legislation or judicial decisions. International law is more limited as far as the mechanisms for the creation of new rules are concerned. Custom relies upon a measure of state practice supported by *opinio juris* and is usually, although not invariably, an evolving and timely process. Treaties, on the other hand, are a more direct and formal method of international law creation.

States transact a vast amount of work by using the device of the treaty, in circumstances which underline the paucity of international law procedures when compared with the many ways in which a person within a state's internal order may set up binding rights and obligations. For instance, wars will be terminated, disputes settled, territory acquired, special interests determined, alliances established and international organisations created all by means of treaties. No simpler method of reflecting the agreed objectives of states really exists and the international convention has to suffice both for straightforward bilateral agreements and complicated multilateral expressions of opinions. Thus, the concept of the treaty and how it operates becomes of paramount importance to the evolution of international law.

A treaty is basically an agreement between parties on the international scene. Although treaties may be concluded, or made, between states and

[1] See generally A. D. McNair, *The Law of Treaties*, Oxford, 1961; J. Klabbers, *The Concept of Treaty in International Law*, Dordrecht, 1996; I. Detter, *Essays on the Law of Treaties*, 1967; T. O. Elias, *The Modern Law of Treaties*, London, 1974; D. P. O'Connell, *International Law*, 2nd edn, London, 1970, vol. I, pp. 195 *et seq.*; I. Sinclair, *The Vienna Convention on the Law of Treaties*, 2nd edn, Manchester, 1984; P. Reuter, *Introduction to the Law of Treaties*, 2nd edn, Geneva, 1995; S. Bastid, *Les Traités Dans La Vie Internationale*, Paris, 1985 and S. Rosenne, *Developments in the Law of Treaties 1945–1986*, Cambridge, 1989. See also *Oppenheim's International Law* (eds. R. Y. Jennings and A. D. Watts), 9th edn, London, 1992, p. 1197; Nguyen Quoc Dinh, P. Daillier and A. Pellet, *Droit International Public*, Paris and I. Brownlie, *Principles of Public International Law*, 4th edn, Oxford, 1990, Chapter 25; 5th edn, 1994, p. 117.

international organisations, they are in essence concerned with relations between states.

An International Convention on the Law of Treaties was signed in 1969 and came into force in 1980, while a Convention on Treaties between States and International Organisations was signed in 1986.[2] The emphasis, however, will be on the appropriate rules which have emerged as between states.

The 1969 Vienna Convention on the Law of Treaties partly reflects customary law[3] and constitutes the basic framework for any discussion of the nature and characteristics of treaties. Certain provisions of the Convention may be regarded as reflective of customary international law, such as the rules on interpretation,[4] material breach[5] and fundamental change of circumstances.[6] Others may not be so regarded, and constitute principles binding only upon state parties.

The fundamental principle of treaty law is undoubtedly the proposition that treaties are binding upon the parties to them and must be performed in good faith.[7] This rule is known in legal terms as *pacta sunt servanda* and is arguably the oldest principle of international law. It was reaffirmed in article 26 of the 1969 Convention, and underlies every international agreement. It is not hard to see why this is so. In the absence of a certain minimum belief that states will perform their treaty obligations in good faith, there is no reason for countries to enter into such obligations with each other.

The term 'treaty' itself is the one most used in the context of international agreements but there are a variety of names which can be, and sometimes

---

[2] This was based upon the International Law Commission's Draft Articles on the Law of Treaties between States and International Organisations or between International Organisations, *Yearbook of the ILC*, 1982, vol. II, Pt.2, pp. 9 *et seq.* These articles were approved by the General Assembly and governmental views solicited and received. A plenipotentiary conference was held between 18 February and 21 March 1986 to produce a Convention based on those draft articles. See Assembly resolutions 37/112, 38/139 and 39/86.

[3] See e.g. the *Namibia* case, ICJ Reports, 1971, pp. 16, 47; 49 ILR, pp. 2, 37 and the *Fisheries Jurisdiction* case, ICJ Reports, 1973, pp. 3, 18; 55 ILR, pp. 183, 198. See also Rosenne, *Developments*, p. 121.

[4] See e.g. the *Beagle Channel* case, HMSO, 1977, p. 7; 52 ILR, p. 93; the *La Bretagne* case, 82 ILR, pp. 590, 612; the *Golder* case, European Court of Human Rights, Series A, No. 18, p. 14; 57 ILR, pp. 201, 213–14 and the *Lithgow* case, European Court of Human Rights, Series A, No. 102, para. 114; 75 ILR, pp. 438, 482–83.

[5] See e.g. the *Namibia* case, ICJ Reports, 1971, pp. 16, 47; 49 ILR, pp. 2, 37.

[6] See e.g. the *Fisheries Jurisdiction* cases (jurisdictional phase), ICJ Reports, 1973, pp. 3, 21; 55 ILR, pp. 183, 201.

[7] Note also the references to good faith in articles 31, 46 and 69 of the 1969 Convention. See the *Nuclear Tests* cases, ICJ Reports, 1974, pp. 253, 268; 57 ILR, pp. 398, 413; the *Nicaragua* case, ICJ Reports, 1986, pp. 392, 418; 76 ILR, p. 104, 129 and the *Legality of the Threat or Use of Nuclear Weapons*, ICJ Reports, 1996, para. 102; 35 ILM, 1996, pp. 809, 830. See also J. F. O'Connor, *Good Faith in International Law*, Aldershot, 1991; E. Zoller, *La Bonne Foi en Droit International Public*, Paris,1977 and H. Thirlway, 'The Law and Procedure of the International Court of Justice, 1960–89, Part One', 60 BYIL, 1989, pp. 4, 7.

are, used to express the same concept, such as protocol, act, charter, covenant, pact and concordat. They each refer to the same basic activity and the use of one term rather than another often signifies little more than a desire for variety of expression.

A treaty is defined, for the purposes of the Convention, in article 2 as:

> an international agreement concluded between states in written form and governed by international law, whether embodied in a single instrument or in two or more related instruments and whatever its particular designation.[8]

In other words, in addition to excluding agreements involving international organisations, the Convention does not cover agreements between states which are to be governed by municipal law, such as a large number of commercial accords. This does not mean that such arrangements cannot be characterised as international agreements, or that they are invalid, merely that they are not within the purview of the 1969 Convention. Indeed, article 3 stresses that international agreements between states and other subjects of international law or between two or more subjects of international law, or oral agreements do not lose their validity by being excluded from the framework of the Convention. One important requirement is that the parties to the treaty intend to create legal relations as between themselves by means of their agreement.[9] This is logical since many agreements between states are merely statements of commonly held principles or objectives and are not intended to establish binding obligations.

For instance, a declaration by a number of states in support of a particular political aim is in many cases bereft of legal (though not political) significance, as the states may regard it as a policy manoeuvre and not as setting up juridical relations between themselves. To see whether a particular agreement is intended to create legal relations, one has to examine carefully all the facts of the situation.[10] Examples of non-binding international agreements would include the Final Act of the Conference on Security and Co-operation in Europe 1975.[11]

It should be noted that the International Court regarded a mandate agreement as having the character of a treaty,[12] while in the *Anglo-Iranian Oil Co.* case[13] doubts were expressed about whether a concession agreement

---

[8] In the 1986 Convention on Treaties between States and International Organisations, the same definition is given, substituting states and international organisations for states alone, *supra*, footnote 2.

[9] See e.g. *Third US Restatement of Foreign Relations Law*, Washington, 1987, vol. I, p. 149.

[10] Registration of the agreement with the United Nations under article 102 of the UN Charter is one useful indication. However, as the International Court pointed out in the *Qatar* v. *Bahrain* case, non-registration does not affect the actual validity of an international agreement nor its binding quality, ICJ Reports, 1994, pp. 115, 121; 102 ILR, pp. 1, 18.

[11] See further *supra*, Chapter 7, p. 281.

[12] *South-West Africa* cases, ICJ Reports, 1962, pp. 319, 330; 37 ILR, pp. 3, 12.

[13] ICJ Reports, 1952, pp. 93, 112; 19 ILR, pp. 507, 517.

between a private company and a state constituted an international agreement in the sense of a treaty.[14] Optional declarations with regard to the compulsory jurisdiction of the International Court itself under article 36(2) of the Statute of the Court, have been regarded as treaty provisions,[15] while declarations made by way of unilateral acts concerning legal or factual situations may have the effect of creating legal obligations.[16] In the latter instance, of course, a treaty as such is not involved.

Where the parties to an agreement do not intend to create legal relations or binding obligations or rights thereby, the agreement will not be a treaty, although, of course, its political effect may still be considerable.[17] In fact a large role is played in the normal course of inter-state dealings by informal non-treaty instruments precisely because they are intended to be non-binding and are thus flexible, confidential and relatively speedy in comparison with treaties.[18] They may be amended with ease and without delay and may be terminated by reasonable notice (subject to provision to the contrary). It is this intention not to create a binding arrangement which marks the difference between treaties and informal international instruments. The International Court addressed this issue in the *Qatar v. Bahrain* case,[19] with regard to Minutes dated 25 December 1990 signed by the parties and Saudi Arabia. The Court emphasised that whether an agreement constituted a binding agreement would depend upon 'all its actual terms' and the circumstances in which it had been drawn up[20] and in the situation involved in the case, the Minutes were to be construed as an international agreement

---

[14] But see *Texaco v. Libya*, 53 ILR, p. 389 and *supra* p. 574.

[15] The *Fisheries Jurisdiction* cases, ICJ Reports, 1973, pp. 3, 16; 55 ILR, pp. 183, 196.

[16] The *Nuclear Tests* case, ICJ Reports, 1974, pp. 253, 267; 57 ILR, pp. 398, 412. See also the Ihlen Declaration, held to constitute a binding statement, in the *Eastern Greenland* case, PCIJ, Series A/B, No. 53, 1933; 6 ILR, p. 95 and *Burkina Faso v. Mali*, ICJ Reports, 1986, pp. 554, 573–74; 80 ILR, pp. 459, 477. See further *supra* p. 95.

[17] The test will focus upon the intent of the parties as seen in the language and context of the document concerned, the circumstances of its conclusion and the explanations given by the parties, see the view of the US Assistant Legal Adviser for Treaty Affairs, 88 AJIL, 1994, p. 515. See also O. Schachter, 'The Twilight Existence of Nonbinding International Agreements', 71 AJIL, 1977, p. 296 and Rosenne, *Developments*, p. 91. See e.g. the Helsinki Final Act of 1975, which was understood to be non-binding and thus not a treaty by the parties involved, DUSPIL, 1975, pp. 326–27. See also the dispute between the USA and the UK as to the legal status of a memorandum of understanding relating to the US–UK Air Services Agreement 1977 (Bermuda 2) in the context of Heathrow Airport User Charges Arbitration, UKMIL, 63 BYIL, 1992, pp. 712 *et seq.* and 88 AJIL, 1994, pp. 738 *et seq.* The Tribunal noted that the memorandum of understanding was not a source of independent legal rights and duties but 'consensual subsequent practice of the parties' and an aid to the interpretation of the Bermuda 2 Agreement, 102 ILR, pp. 215, 353.

[18] See e.g. Rosenne, *Developments*, pp. 107 *et seq.*; A. Aust, 'The Theory and Practice of Informal International Instruments', 35 ICLQ, 1986, p. 787; R. Baxter, 'International Law in "Her Infinite Variety"', 29 ICLQ, 1980, p. 549 and D. Roessler, 'Law, *De Facto* Agreements and Declarations of Principles in International Economic Relations', 21 German YIL, 1978, p. 41.   [19] ICJ Reports, 1994, p. 112; 102 ILR, p. 1.

[20] *Ibid.*, p. 121; 102 ILR, p. 18, citing the *Aegean Sea Continental Shelf* case, ICJ Reports, 1978, p. 39; 60 ILR, p. 511.

creating rights and obligations for the parties since on the facts they enumerated the commitments to which the parties had consented.[21] The 1969 Convention also covers treaties which are the constituent instruments of international organisations, such as the United Nations Charter, and internal treaties adopted within international organisations.[22]

The making of treaties[23]

Formalities

Treaties may be made or concluded by the parties in virtually any manner they wish. There is no prescribed form or procedure, and how a treaty is formulated and by whom it is actually signed will depend upon the intention and agreement of the states concerned.

Treaties may be drafted as between states, or governments, or heads of states, or governmental departments, whichever appears the most expedient. For instance, many of the most important treaties are concluded as between heads of state, and many of the more mundane agreements are expressed to be as between government departments, such as minor trading arrangements.

Where precisely in the domestic constitutional establishment the power to make treaties is to be found depends upon each country's municipal regulations and varies from state to state. In the United Kingdom, the treaty making power is within the prerogative of the Crown,[24] whereas in the United States it resides with the President 'with the advice and consent of the Senate' and the concurrence of two-thirds of the Senators.[25]

Nevertheless, there are certain rules that apply in the formation of international conventions. In international law, states have the capacity to make agreements, but since states are not identifiable human persons, particular principles have evolved to ensure that persons representing states have indeed the power so to do for the purpose of concluding the treaty in ques-

---

[21] *Ibid.*, pp. 121–2; 102 ILR, pp. 18–19. See also K. Widdows, 'What is an International Agreement in International Law ?', BYIL, 1979, p. 117 and J. A. Barberis, 'Le Concept de "Traité International" et ses Limites', AFDI, 1984, p. 239.

[22] Article 5. See further Rosenne, *Developments*, Chapter 4.

[23] See e.g. H. Blix, *Treaty-Making Power*, New York, 1960 and E. W. Vierdag, 'The Time of the Conclusion of a Multilateral Treaty: Article 30 of the Vienna Convention on the Law of Treaties and Related Provisions', 59 BYIL, 1988, p. 75. See also *Oppenheim's International Law*, p. 1222 and Nguyen Quoc Dinh, Daillier and Pellet, *Droit International Public*, p. 125.

[24] See e.g. S. de Smith and R. Brazier, *Constitutional and Administrative Law*, 6th edn, London, 1989, p. 140.

[25] See e.g. *Third Restatement of US Foreign Relations Law*, p. 159. See with regard to the presidential power to terminate a treaty, DUSPIL 1979, pp. 724 *et seq.* and *Goldwater v. Carter*, 617 F.2d 697 and 100 S. Ct. 533 (1979). See also L. Henkin, 'Restatement of the Foreign Relations Law of the United States (Revised)', 74 AJIL, 1980, p. 954.

tion. Such persons must produce what is termed 'full powers' according to article 7 of the Convention, before being accepted as capable of representing their countries.[26] 'Full powers' refers to documents certifying status from the competent authorities of the state in question. This provision provides security to the other parties to the treaty that they are making agreements with persons competent to do so.[27] However, certain persons do not need to produce such full powers, by virtue of their position and functions. This exception refers to heads of state and government, and foreign ministers for the purpose of performing all acts relating to the conclusion of the treaty; heads of diplomatic missions for the purpose of adopting the text of the treaty between their country and the country to which they are accredited; and representatives accredited to international conferences or organisations for the purpose of adopting the text of the treaty in that particular conference or organisation.

Sinclair notes that UK practice distinguishes between 'general full powers' held by the Secretary of State for Foreign and Commonwealth Affairs, Ministers of State and Parliamentary Under-Secretaries in the Foreign and Commonwealth Office and UK Permanent Representatives to the UN, European Communities and General Agreement on Tariffs and Trade, which enable any treaty to be negotiated and signed, and 'special full powers' granted to a particular person to negotiate and sign a specific treaty.[28]

Any act relating to the making of a treaty by a person not authorised as required will be without any legal effect, unless the state involved afterwards confirms the act.[29] One example of this kind of situation arose in 1951 with regard to a convention relating to the naming of cheeses. It was signed by a delegate of both Sweden and Norway, but it appeared that he had authority only from Norway. However, the agreement was subsequently ratified by both parties and entered into effect.[30]

Consent

Once a treaty has been drafted and agreed by authorised representatives, a number of stages are then necessary before it becomes a binding legal obligation upon the parties involved. The text of the agreement drawn up by the negotiators of the parties has to be adopted and article 9 provides that adoption in international conferences takes place by the vote of two-thirds of the states present and voting, unless by the same majority it is decided to apply a different rule. This procedure follows basically the practices

---

[26] See Sinclair, *Vienna Convention*, pp. 29 *et seq.* and M. Jones, *Full Powers and Ratification*, 1946.   [27] See *Yearbook of the ILC*, 1966, vol. II, p. 193.
[28] Sinclair, *Vienna Convention*, p. 32. See also *Satow's Guide to Diplomatic Practice*, 5th edn, 1979, p. 62.   [29] Article 8.   [30] See *Yearbook of the ILC*, 1966, vol. II, p. 195.

recognised in the United Nations General Assembly[31] and carried out in the majority of contemporary conferences.

An increasing number of conventions are now adopted and opened for signature by means of UN General Assembly resolutions, such as the 1966 International Covenants on Human Rights and the 1984 Convention against Torture, using normal Assembly voting procedures.

Another significant point is the tendency in recent conferences to operate by way of consensus so that there would be no voting until all efforts to reach agreement by consensus have been exhausted.[32]

In cases other than international conferences, adoption will take place by the consent of all the states involved in drawing up the text of the agreement.[33]

The consent of the states parties to the treaty in question is obviously a vital factor, since states may (in the absence of a rule being also one of customary law) be bound only by their consent. Treaties are in this sense contracts between states and if they do not receive the consent of the various states, their provisions will not be binding upon them.

There are, however, a number of ways in which a state may express its consent to an international agreement. It may be signalled, according to article 11, by signature, exchange of instruments constituting a treaty, ratification, acceptance, approval or accession. In addition, it may be accomplished by any other means, if so agreed.

An example of a rather unusual arrangement is provided by the General Framework Agreement for Peace in Bosnia and Herzegovina (complete with 12 Annexes) which was initialled on 21 November 1995 at Dayton, Ohio, and signed in Paris on 14 December 1995. An 'Agreement on Initialling' the Framework Agreement, associated with the later document, provided that initialling the Agreement not only committed the parties later to sign the respective texts of the Agreement, but also expressed their consent to be bound by these. Article XI of the Framework Agreement and the annexed Agreements all provided for automatic entry into force upon signature.

Consent by signature[34]

A state may regard itself as having given its consent to the text of the treaty by signature in defined circumstances noted by article 12, that is, where the

---

[31] See article 18 of the UN Charter.
[32] See e.g. the Third UN Conference on the Law of the Sea, see Sinclair, *Vienna Convention*, pp. 37–9. See also the UN *Juridical Yearbook*, 1974, pp. 163–4, where the Director of the General Legal Division, Office of Legal Affairs declared that the term 'consensus' in UN organs, 'was used to describe a practice under which every effort is made to achieve unanimous agreement; and if that could not be done, those dissenting from the general trend were prepared simply to make their position and reservations known and placed on the record'.
[33] Article 9(1). This reflects the classic rule, Sinclair, *Vienna Convention*, p. 33. See also articles 237 and 247 of the EEC Treaty.   [34] See *Yearbook of the ILC*, 1966, vol. II, p. 196.

treaty provides that signature shall have that effect, or where it is otherwise established that the negotiating states were agreed that signature should have that effect, or where the intention of the state to give that effect to the signature appears from the full powers of its representative or was expressed during the negotiations.

Although consent by ratification is probably the most popular of the methods adopted in practice, consent by signature does retain some significance, especially in light of the fact that to insist upon ratification in each case before a treaty becomes binding is likely to burden the administrative machinery of government and result in long delays. Accordingly, provision is made for consent to be expressed by signature. This would be appropriate for the more routine and less politicised of treaties.

The act of signature is usually a very formal affair. Often in the more important treaties, the head of state will formally add his signature in an elaborate ceremony. In multilateral conventions, a special closing session will be held at which authorised representatives will sign the treaty.

However, where the convention is subject to acceptance, approval or ratification, signature will become a mere formality and will mean no more than that state representatives have agreed upon an acceptable text, which will be forwarded to their particular governments for the necessary decision as to acceptance or rejection. In such cases and pending ratification, acceptance or approval, a state must refrain from acts which would defeat the object and purpose of the treaty until such time as its intentions with regard to the treaty have been made clear.[35]

Consent by exchange of instruments

Article 13 provides that the consent of states to be bound by a treaty constituted by instruments exchanged between them may be expressed by that exchange when the instruments declare that their exchange shall have that effect or it is otherwise established that those states had agreed that the exchange of instruments should have that effect.

Consent by ratification[36]

The device of ratification by the competent authorities of the state is historically well established and was originally devised to ensure that the

---

[35] Article 18. See Sinclair, *Vienna Convention*, pp. 42–4 and *Certain German Interests in Polish Upper Silesia*, PCIJ, Series A, No. 7, 1926, p. 30. See also H. Thirlway, 'The Law and Procedure of the International Court of Justice 1960–1989, Part Four', 63 BYIL, 1992, pp. 1, 48 *et seq.*

[36] Defined in article 2(1)b as 'the international act . . . whereby a state establishes on the international plane its consent to be bound by a treaty'. It is thus to be distinguished as a concept

representative did not exceed his powers or instructions with regard to the making of a particular agreement. Although ratification (or approval) was in years past a function of the sovereign, it has in modern times been made subject to constitutional control.

The advantages of waiting until a state ratifies a treaty before it becomes a binding document are basically twofold, internal and external. In the latter case, the delay between signature and ratification may often be advantageous in allowing extra time for consideration, once the negotiating process has been completed. But it is the internal aspects that are the most important, for they reflect the change in political atmosphere that has occurred in the last 150 years and has led to a much greater participation by a state's population in public affairs. By providing for ratification, the feelings of public opinion have an opportunity to be expressed with the possibility that a strong negative reaction may result in the state deciding not to ratify the treaty under consideration.

The rules relating to ratification vary from country to country. In the United Kingdom, although the power of ratification comes within the prerogative of the Crown, it has become accepted that treaties involving any change in municipal law, or adding to the financial burdens of the government or having an impact upon the private rights of British subjects will be first submitted to Parliament and subsequently ratified. There is, in fact, a procedure known as the Ponsonby Rule which provides that all treaties subject to ratification are laid before Parliament at least twenty-one days before the actual ratification takes place.[37] Different considerations apply in the case of the United States.[38] However, the question of how a state effects ratification is a matter for internal law alone and outside international law.

Article 14 of the 1969 Vienna Convention notes that ratification will express a state's consent to be bound by a treaty where the treaty so provides; it is otherwise established that the negotiating states were agreed that ratification should be required; the representative of the state has signed the treaty subject to ratification or the intention of the state to sign the treaty subject to ratification appears from the full powers of its representative or was expressed during negotiations.

Within this framework, there is a controversy as to which treaties need to be ratified. Some writers maintain that ratification is only necessary if it is clearly contemplated by the parties to the treaty,[39] and this approach has

---

from ratification in the internal constitutional sense, although clearly there is an important link, see *Yearbook of the ILC*, 1966, vol. II, pp. 197–8. See also Brownlie, *Principles*, p. 607.
[37] See *supra*, Chapter 4, p. 112.   [38] *Ibid.*, p. 117.
[39] See e.g. G. Fitzmaurice, 'Do Treaties Need Ratification?', 15 BYIL, 1934, p. 129, and O'Connell, *International Law*, p. 222. See also H. Blix, 'The Requirement of Ratification', 30 BYIL, 1953, p. 380.

been adopted by the United Kingdom.[40] On the other hand, it has been suggested that ratification should be required unless the treaty clearly reveals a contrary intention.[41] The United States, in general, will dispense with ratification only in the case of executive agreements.[42]

Ratification in the case of bilateral treaties is usually accomplished by exchanging the requisite instruments, but in the case of multilateral treaties the usual procedure is for one party to collect the ratifications of all states, keeping all parties informed of the situation. It is becoming more accepted that in such instances, the Secretary-General of the United Nations will act as the depositary for ratifications.

In some cases, signatures to treaties may be declared subject to 'acceptance' or 'approval'. The terms, as noted in articles 11 and 14(2), are very similar to ratification and similar provisions apply. Such variation in terminology is not of any real significance and only refers to a somewhat simpler form of ratification.

Consent by accession[43]

This is the normal method by which a state becomes a party to a treaty it has not signed. Article 15 notes that consent by accession is possible where the treaty so provides, or the negotiating states were agreed or subsequently agree that consent by accession could occur in the case of the state in question.

Important multilateral treaties often declare that specific entities may accede to the treaty at a later date. For instance, the 1958 Geneva Conventions on the Sea provided for accession by any member states of the United Nations or any of the Specialised Agencies of the United Nations.[44]

Reservations to treaties[45]

A reservation is defined in article 2 of the Convention as:

a unilateral statement, however phrased or named, made by a state, when signing, ratifying, accepting, approving or acceding to a treaty, whereby it

---

[40] See e.g. Sinclair, *Vienna Convention*, p. 40 and O'Connell, *International Law*, p. 222.

[41] See e.g. McNair, *Law of Treaties*, p. 133.

[42] O'Connell, *International Law*, p. 222. See also DUSPIL 1974, pp. 216–17 and *ibid.*, 1979, pp. 678 *et seq.*   [43] See *Yearbook of the ILC*, 1966, vol. II, p. 199.

[44] See e.g. articles 26 and 28 of the Convention on the Territorial Sea and the Contiguous Zone.

[45] See e.g. C. Redgewell, 'Universality or Integrity ? Some Reflections on Reservations to General Multilateral Treaties', 64 BYIL, 1993, p. 245; G. Gaja, 'Unruly Treaty Reservations', *Le Droit International à l'Heure de sa Codification*, Milan, 1987, p. 313; J. K. Gamble, 'Reservations to Multilateral Treaties: A Macroscopic View of State Practice', 74 AJIL, 1980, p. 372; G. Fitzmaurice, 'Reservations to Multilateral Treaties', 2 ICLQ, 1953,

purports to exclude or to modify the legal effect of certain provisions of the treaty in their application to that state.[46]

This means generally that where a state is satisfied with most of a treaty, but is unhappy about one or two particular provisions, it may, in certain circumstances, wish to refuse to accept or be bound by such provisions, while consenting to the rest of the agreement. By this device of excluding certain provisions, states may agree to be bound by a treaty which otherwise they might reject entirely. This, obviously, may have very beneficial results in the cases of multilateral conventions, by inducing as many states as possible to adhere to the proposed treaty. To some extent it is a means of encouraging harmony amongst states of widely differing social, economic and political systems, by concentrating upon agreed, basic issues and accepting disagreement on certain other matters.

The capacity of a state to make reservations to an international treaty illustrates the principle of sovereignty of states, whereby a state may refuse its consent to particular provisions so that they do not become binding upon it. On the other hand, of course, to permit a treaty to become honeycombed with reservations by a series of countries could well jeopardise the whole exercise. It could seriously dislocate the whole purpose of the agreement and lead to some complicated inter-relationships amongst states.

This problem does not really arise in the case of bilateral treaties, since a reservation by one party to a proposed term of the agreement would necessitate a renegotiation. An agreement between two parties cannot exist where one party refuses to accept some of the provisions of the treaty.[47] This is not the case with respect to multilateral treaties, and here it is possible for individual states to dissent from particular provisions, by announcing their intention either to exclude them altogether, or understand them in a certain way.

Reservations must be distinguished from other statements made with regard to a treaty that are not intended to have the legal effect of a reservation, such as understandings, political statements or interpretative declarations. In the latter

p. 1; D. W. Bowett, 'Reservations to Non-restricted Multilateral Treaties', 48 BYIL, 1976–7, p. 67; P. H. Imbert, *Les Réserves Aux Traités Multilatéraux*, Paris, 1979; Sinclair, *Vienna Convention*, Chapter 3; D. W. Greig, 'Reservations: Equity as a Balancing Force ?', 16 Australian YIL, 1995, p. 21; O'Connell, *International Law*, pp. 229 *et seq.*; J. M. Ruda, 'Reservations to Treaties', 146 HR, p. 95; G. Horn, *Reservations and Interpretative Declarations to Multilateral Treaties*, Leiden, 1988 and *Oppenheim's International Law*, p. 1241. See also A. Pellet, First Report on the Law and Practice Relating to Reservations to Treaties, 1995, A/CN.4/470 and *Report of the International Law Commission*, 1995, A/50/10, pp. 240 *et seq.*

[46] Article 2(1)d of the Vienna Convention on the Law of Treaties between States and International Organisations 1986 provides that a reservation means 'a unilateral statement, however phrased or named, made by a state or by an international organisation when signing, ratifying, formally confirming, accepting, approving or acceding to a treaty, whereby it purports to exclude or to modify the legal effect of certain provisions of the treaty in their application to that state or to that organisation'.

[47] See *Yearbook of the ILC*, 1966, vol. II, p. 203.

instance, no binding consequence is intended with regard to the treaty in question. What is involved is a political manifestation for primarily internal effect.[48] A distinction has been drawn between 'mere' interpretative declarations and 'qualified' interpretative declarations,[49] with the latter category capable in certain circumstances of constituting reservations.[50] In the *Anglo-French Continental Shelf* case,[51] the Arbitral Tribunal emphasised that French reservations to article 6 of the Geneva Convention on the Continental Shelf 1958, challenged by the UK, had to be construed in accordance with the natural meaning of their terms.[52] The UK contended that the third French reservation to article 6 (which concerned the non-applicability of the principle of equidistance in areas of 'special circumstances' as defined by the French government, naming specifically *inter alia* the Bay of Granville) was in reality only an interpretative declaration. The Tribunal, however, held that although this reservation contained elements of interpretation, it also constituted a specific condition imposed by France on its acceptance of the article 6 delimitation regime. This went beyond mere interpretation as it made the application of that regime dependent upon acceptance by other states of France's designation of the named areas as involving 'special circumstances'. It therefore had the purpose of seeking to exclude or modify the legal effect of certain treaty provisions with regard to their application by the reserving state and thus constituted a reservation.[53] In the *Belilos* case[54] in 1988, the European Court of Human Rights considered the effect of one particular interpretative declaration made by Switzerland upon ratification.[55] The Court held that one had to look behind the title given to the

---

[48] See e.g. the *Temeltasch* case, 5 *European Human Rights Reports*, 1983, p. 417 on the difference between reservations and interpretative declarations generally and in the context of the European Human Rights Convention. Cf. the *Ette* case, European Court of Human Rights, Series A, No. 117. See also P. H. Imbert, 'Reservations to the European Convention on Human Rights before the Strasbourg Commission', 33 ICLQ, 1984, p. 558 and *UN Juridical Yearbook*, 1976, pp. 220–1.

[49] See D. McRae, 'The Legal Effect of Interpretative Declarations', 49 BYIL, 1978, p. 155. See also the *Temeltasch* case, pp. 432–3 and the Pellet Report, pp. 58 *et seq.*.

[50] Quite what the effect might be of the former is unclear, see e.g. the Pellet Report, p. 60.

[51] Cmnd. 7438 (1979); 54 ILR, p. 6.

[52] *Ibid.*, pp. 41–2; 54 ILR, pp. 48–9. It was also stressed that reservations have to be appreciated in the light of the law in force at the time that the reservations (and any objections to them) are made, *ibid.*, p. 35; 54 ILR, p. 42.   [53] *Ibid.*, p. 43; 54 ILR, p. 50.

[54] European Court of Human Rights, Series A, No. 132. See also S. Marks, 'Reservations Unhinged: The *Belilos* Case Before the European Court of Human Rights', 39 ICLQ, 1990, p. 300.

[55] Switzerland made in total two interpretative declarations and two reservations upon ratification of the European Convention on Human Rights. The declaration in question concerned article 6, paragraph 1 of the Convention dealing with the right to fair trial and provided that Switzerland considered that that right was intended solely to ensure ultimate control by the judiciary over the acts or decisions of the public authorities. The issue concerned the right of appeal from the Lausanne Police Board to the Criminal Cassation Division of the Vaud Cantonal Court, which could not in fact hear fresh argument, receive witnesses or give a new ruling on the merits and whether the declaration prevented the applicant from relying on article 6 in the circumstances.

declaration in question and to seek to determine its substantive content. It was necessary to ascertain the original intention of those drafting the declaration and thus recourse to the *travaux préparatoires* was required. In the light of these, the Court felt that Switzerland had indeed intended to 'avoid the consequences which a broad view of the right of access to the courts . . . would have for the system of public administration and of justice in the cantons and consequently . . . put forward the declaration as qualifying [its] consent to be bound by the Convention'.[56] Having so decided, the Court held that the declaration in question, taking effect as a reservation, did not in fact comply with article 64 of the Convention, which prohibited reservations of a general character[57] and required a brief statement of the law in force necessitating the reservation.[58] Accordingly, the declaration was invalid. It is hard to escape the conclusion that the Court has accepted a test favourable to states as to the situations under which a declaration may be regarded as a reservation, only to emphasise the requirements of article 64 concerning the validity of reservations to the European Convention. One should therefore be rather cautious before applying the easier test regarding interpretative declarations generally.

The problem is particularly acute, of course, since to constitute a reservation that word itself need not be used. What is clearly required is the intention to modify the legal effect of a particular provision and this should not be too generously interpreted.

The general rule that became established historically was that reservations could only be made with the consent of all the other states involved in the process. This was to preserve as much as possible unity of approach to ensure the success of an international agreement and to minimise deviations from the text of the treaty. This reflected the contractual view of the nature of a treaty,[59] and the League of Nations supported this concept.[60] The effect of this was that a state wishing to make a reservation had to obtain the consent of all the other parties to the treaty. If this was not possible, that state could either become a party to the original treaty (minus the reservation, of course) or not become a party at all. However, this restrictive approach to reservations was not accepted by the International Court of Justice in the *Reservations to the Genocide Convention* case.[61] This was an advisory opinion by the Court, requested by the General Assembly after some states had made reservations to the 1948 Genocide Convention, which contained no clause permitting such reservations, and a number of objections were made.

[56] *Op. cit.*, pp. 18–19. [57] *Ibid.*, pp. 20–1. [58] *Ibid.*, pp. 21–2.
[59] See Sinclair, *Vienna Convention*, pp. 54–5 and Ruda, 'Reservations', p. 112. See also Redgewell, 'Universality or Integrity', p. 246.
[60] Report of the Committee of Experts for the Progressive Codification of International Law, 8 LNOJ, pp. 880–1 (1927). [61] ICJ Reports, 1951, p. 15; 18 ILR, p. 364.

The Court held that:

> a state which has made and maintained a reservation which has been objected to by one or more parties to the Convention but not by others, can be regarded as being a party to the Convention if the reservation is compatible with the object and purpose of the Convention.

Compatibility in the Court's opinion could be decided by states individually since it was noted that:

> if a party to the Convention objects to a reservation which it considers incompatible with the object and purpose of the Convention, it can . . . "consider that the reserving state is not a party to the Convention.[62]"

The Court did emphasise the principle of the integrity of a convention, but pointed to a variety of special circumstances with regard to the Genocide Convention in question, which called for a more flexible interpretation of the principle. These circumstances included the universal character of the UN under whose auspices the Convention had been concluded; the extensive participation envisaged under the Convention; the fact that the Convention had been the product of a series of majority votes; the fact that the principles underlying the Convention were general principles already binding upon states; that the Convention was clearly intended by the UN and the parties to be definitely universal in scope and that it had been adopted for a purely humanitarian purpose so that state parties did not have interests of their own but a common interest. All these factors militated for a flexible approach in this case.

The Court's approach, although having some potential disadvantages,[63] was in keeping with the move to increase the acceptability and scope of treaties and with the trend in international organisations away from the unanimity rule in decision-making and towards majority voting.[64] The 1969 Convention on the Law of Treaties accepted the Court's views.[65]

By article 19, reservations may be made when signing, ratifying, accepting, approving or acceding to a treaty, but they cannot be made where the reservation is prohibited by the treaty, or where the treaty provides that only specified reservations may be made and these do not include the reservation in question, or where the reservation is not compatible with the object and purpose of the treaty.

In the instances where a reservation is possible, the traditional rule

---

[62] *Ibid.*, pp. 29–30.   [63] See e.g. Fitzmaurice, 'Reservations'.
[64] Although the International Law Commission was initially critical, it later changed its mind, see *Yearbook of the ILC*, 1951, vol. II, pp. 130–1, cf. *ibid.*, 1962, vol. II, pp. 62–5 and 178–9. Note also that the UN General Assembly in 1959 resolved that the Secretary-General as a depositary was to apply the Court's approach to all conventions concluded under UN auspices unless they contained provisions to the contrary.
[65] See Redgewell, 'Universality or Integrity', pp. 253 *et seq.*

requiring acceptance by all parties will apply where, by article 20(2), 'it appears from the limited number of the negotiating states and the object and purpose of a treaty that the application of the treaty in its entirety between all the parties is an essential condition of the consent of each one to be bound by the treaty'.

Article 20(4) then outlines the general rules to be followed with regard to treaties not within article 20(2) and not constituent instruments of international organisations. These are that:

(a) acceptance by another contracting state of a reservation constitutes the reserving state a party to the treaty in relation to that other state if or when the treaty is in force for those states;

(b) an objection by another contracting state to a reservation does not preclude the entry into force of the treaty as between the objecting and reserving states unless a contrary intention is definitely expressed by the objecting state;

(c) an act expressing a state's consent to be bound by the treaty and containing a reservation is effective as soon as at least one other contracting state has accepted the reservation.

The effect of reservations is outlined in article 21. This declares that a reservation established with regard to another party modifies, for the reserving state in its relations with the other party, the provisions of the treaty to which the reservation relates, to the extent of the reservation. The other party is similarly affected in its relations with the reserving state. An example of this was provided by the Libyan reservation to the 1961 Vienna Convention on Diplomatic Relations with regard to the diplomatic bag, permitting Libya to search the bag with the consent of the state whose bag it was, and insist that it be returned to its state of origin. Since the UK did not object to the reservation, it could have acted similarly with regard to Libya's diplomatic bags.[66] However, the reservation does not modify the provisions of the treaty for the other parties to the treaty as between themselves.

Article 21(3) provides that where a state objects to a reservation, but not to the entry into force of the treaty between itself and the reserving state, then, 'the provisions to which the reservation relates do not apply as between the two states to the extent of the reservation'. This provision was applied by the arbitration tribunal in the *Anglo-French Continental Shelf* case, where it was noted that:

the combined effect of the French reservations and their rejection by the United Kingdom is neither to render article 6 [of the Geneva Convention on the Continental Shelf, 1958] inapplicable *in toto*, as the French Republic contends, nor to render it applicable *in toto*, as the United Kingdom primar-

[66] See Foreign Affairs Committee, *Report on the Abuse of Diplomatic Immunities and Privileges*, London, 1984, pp. 23–4, and *supra*, Chapter 13, p. 530.

ily contends. It is to render the article inapplicable as between the two countries to the extent of the reservations.[67]

A number of important issues, however, remain unresolved. In particular, it is unclear what effect an impermissible reservation has.[68] One school of thought takes the view that such reservations are invalid,[69] another that the validity of any reservation is dependent upon acceptance by other states.[70] While there is a presumption in favour of the permissibility of reservations, this may be displaced if the reservation is prohibited explicitly or implicitly by the treaty or it is contrary to the object and purpose of the treaty.[71] A further problem is to determine when these conditions under which reservations may be deemed to be impermissible have been met. This is especially difficult where it is contended that the object and purpose of a treaty have been offended. The question is also raised as to the authority able to make such a determination. At the moment, unless the particular treaty otherwise provides,[72] whether a reservation is impermissible is a determination to be made by states parties to the treaty themselves. In other words, it is a subjective application of objective criteria.[73] Once the impermissibility of a reservation has been demonstrated, there are two fundamental possibilities. Either the treaty provision to which the reservation has been attached applies in full to the state that made the impermissible reservation or the consent of the state to the treaty as a whole is vitiated so that the state is no longer a party to the treaty. A further question is whether the other parties to the treaty may accept and thus legitimate an impermissible reservation or whether a determination of impermissibility is conclusive. All that can be said is that state practice on the whole is inconclusive.

However, there is a trend with regard to human rights treaties to regard impermissible reservations as severing that reservation so that the provision

---

[67] Cmnd. 7438 (1979), p. 45; 54 ILR, p. 52. See also E. A. Boyle, 'The Law of Treaties and the Anglo-French Continental Shelf Arbitration', 29 ICLQ, 1980, p. 498 and Sinclair, 'Vienna Convention', pp. 70–6

[68] See e.g. J. K. Koh, 'Reservations to Multilateral Treaties: How International Legal Doctrine Reflects World Vision', *Harvard International Law Journal*, 1982, p. 71 and Redgewell, 'Universality or Integrity', p. 263.

[69] See e.g. Bowett, 'Reservations', pp. 77 and 84. Impermissible reservations are divided into those that may be severed from ratification of or accession to the convention in question and those that are contrary to the object and purpose of the treaty. In the latter case, both the reservation and the whole acceptance of the treaty by the reserving state are to be regarded as nullities. This question of permissibility is the preliminary issue, the question of opposability, or the reaction of other states, is a secondary issue, presupposing the permissibility of the reservation, *ibid.*, p. 88. See also *Oppenheim's International Law*, p. 1247, note 1.

[70] See e.g. Ruda, 'Reservations', p. 190.   [71] See the Pellet Report, p. 50.

[72] Note e.g. that article 20(2) of the International Convention on the Elimination of All Forms of Racial Discrimination 1965 provides that a reservation will be regarded as contrary to the object and purpose of the treaty if at least two-thirds of the states parties to the convention object to the reservation.   [73] See e.g. Ago, *Yearbook of the ILC*, 1965, vol. I, p. 161.

in question applies in full to the reserving state. In the *Belilos* case,[74] the European Court of Human Rights laid particular emphasis upon Switzerland's commitment to the European Convention on Human Rights,[75] so that the effect of defining the Swiss declaration as a reservation which was then held to be invalid was that Switzerland was bound by the provision (article 6) in full. This view was reaffirmed in the *Loizidou (preliminary objections)* case.[76] The Court analysed the validity of the territorial restrictions attached to Turkey's declarations under articles 25 and 46 recognising the competence of the Commission and the Court[77] and held that they were impermissible under the terms of the Convention. The Court then concluded that the effect of this in the light of the special nature of the Convention as a human rights treaty was that the reservations were severable so that Turkey's acceptance of the jurisdiction of the Commission and the Court remained in place, unrestricted by the terms of the invalid limitations attached to the declarations.[78] The UN Human Rights Committee in General Comment 24/52 of 2 November 1994[79] emphasised the special nature of human rights treaties and expressed its belief that the provisions of the Vienna Convention on the Law of Treaties were 'inappropriate to address the problems of reservations to human rights treaties'. The Committee took the view that provisions contained in the International Covenant on Civil and Political Rights 1966 which represented customary international law could not be the subject of reservations, while in the case of reservations to non-derogable provisions not falling into this category, states had 'a heavy onus' to justify such reservations. The Committee also emphasised that the effect of an unacceptable reservation would normally be that the provision operated in full with regard to the party making such a reservation and not that the Covenant would not be in force at all for such a state party.[80] Whether

---

[74] European Court of Human Rights, Series A, No. 132. See also *supra*, p. 643.
[75] The Court noted that 'it is beyond doubt that Switzerland is, and regards itself as, bound by the Convention irrespective of the validity of the declaration', *ibid.*, p. 22.
[76] European Court of Human Rights, Series A, No. 310 (1995).
[77] These were held to constitute 'a disguised reservation', *ibid.*, p. 22.   [78] *Ibid.*, pp. 22–9.
[79] CCPR/C/21/Rev.1/Add.6. See also 15 *Human Rights Law Journal*, 1994, p. 464 and M. Nowak, 'The Activities of the UN Human Rights Committee: Developments from 1 August 1992 to 31 July 1995', 16 HRLJ, 1995, pp. 377, 380.
[80] The Committee also regarded itself as the only body able to determine whether a specific reservation was or was not compatible with the object and purpose of the Covenant. See also the critical observations made by the governments of the US and the UK with regard to this General Comment, 16 HRLJ, 1995, pp. 422 *et seq.* Note in particular the US view that 'reservations contained in the United States instruments of ratification are integral parts of its consent to be bound by the Covenant and are not severable. If it were to be determined that any one or more of them were ineffective, the ratification as a whole could thereby be nullified', *ibid.*, p. 423. The UK government took the view that while 'severability of a kind may well offer a solution in appropriate cases', severability would involve excising both the reservation and the parts of the treaty to which it related, *ibid.*, p. 426. It was noted that a state which sought to ratify a human rights treaty subject to a reservation 'which is fundamentally incompatible with participation in the treaty regime' could not be regarded as a party to that treaty, *ibid.*

practice with regard to human rights treaties, which is in any event far from settled, can be transposed to treaties in general is very doubtful.[81]

In general, reservations are deemed to have been accepted by states that have raised no objections to them at the end of a period of twelve months after notification of the reservation, or by the date on which consent to be bound by the treaty was expressed, whichever is the later.[82]

Reservations must be in writing and communicated to the contracting states and other states entitled to become parties to the treaty, as must acceptances of, and objections to, reservations.

Most multilateral conventions today will in fact specifically declare their position as regards reservations. Some, however, for example the Geneva Convention on the High Seas, 1958, make no mention at all of reservations, while others may specify that reservations are possible with regard to certain provisions only.[83] Still others may prohibit altogether any reservations.[84] Each of these solutions to the problem of reservations is equally valid.

Entry into force of treaties

Basically treaties will become operative when and how the negotiating states decide, but in the absence of any provision or agreement regarding this, a treaty will enter into force as soon as consent to be bound by the treaty has been established for all the negotiating states.[85]

In many cases, treaties will specify that they will come into effect upon a certain date or after a determined period following the last ratification. It is usual where multilateral conventions are involved to provide for entry into force upon ratification by a fixed number of states. To expect every state to ratify when there may have been over a hundred states participating in the negotiations and signature of a treaty could well consign such a treaty to

[81] See also with regard to the Convention on the Elimination of Discrimination Against Women 1979, General Recommendations No. 4 (1987), No. 20 (1992) and No. 21 (1994) of the Committee on the Elimination of Discrimination Against Women. See generally B. Clark, 'The Vienna Conventions Reservations Regime and the Convention on Discrimination against Women', 85 AJIL, 1991, p. 281 and R. J. Cook, 'Reservations to the Convention on the Elimination of All Forms of Discrimination against Women', 30 VJIL, 1990, p. 643. See also Council of Europe Parliamentary Assembly Recommendation 1223 (1993) on Reservations Made by Member States to Council of Europe Conventions and W. A. Schabas, 'Reservations to Human Rights Treaties: Time for Innovation and Reform', 32 Canadian YIL, 1994, p. 39.
[82] Article 20(5) of the Vienna Convention on the Law of Treaties. See the Inter-American Court of Human Rights, Advisory Opinion on *The Effect of Reservations on the Entry into Force of the American Convention on Human Rights*, 22 ILM, 1983, p. 37; 67 ILR, p. 559.
[83] E.g. the 1958 Geneva Convention on the Continental Shelf, article 12(1). See also *supra*, p. 644, regarding article 64 of the European Convention on Human Rights, 1950.
[84] See e.g. article 37 of the Convention on Damage Caused by Foreign Aircraft to Third Parties on the Surface, 1952
[85] Article 24. See Sinclair, 'Vienna Convention', pp. 44–7. See also Thirlway, 1992, 'Law and Procedure', pp. 32 *et seq.*

oblivion since one country alone, by withholding ratification for any reason, could disrupt the whole process.

The Geneva Convention on the High Seas 1958, for example, provides for entry into force on the thirtieth day following the deposit of the twenty-second instrument of ratification with the United Nations Secretary-General, while the Convention on the Law of Treaties itself came into effect thirty days after the deposit of the thirty-fifth ratification.

It should be remembered at this point that even though the necessary number of ratifications has been received for the treaty to come into operation, only those states that have actually ratified the treaty will be bound. It will not bind those that have merely signed it, unless of course, signature is in the particular circumstances regarded as sufficient to express the consent of the state to be bound.

Article 80 of the 1969 Convention (following article 102 of the United Nations Charter) provides that after their entry into force, treaties should be transmitted to the United Nations Secretariat for registration and publication. These provisions are intended to end the practice of secret treaties, which was regarded as contributing to the outbreak of the First World War, as well as enabling the United Nations Treaty Series, which contains all registered treaties, to be as comprehensive as possible.[86]

The application of treaties[87]

Once treaties enter into force, a number of questions can arise as to the way in which they apply in particular situations. In the absence of contrary intention, the treaty will not operate retroactively so that its provisions will not bind a party as regards any facts, acts or situations prior to that state's acceptance of the treaty.[88]

Unless a different intention appears from the treaty or is otherwise established, article 29 provides that a treaty is binding upon each party in respect of its entire territory. This is the general rule, but it is possible for a state to stipulate that an international agreement will apply only to part of its territory. In the past, so-called 'colonial application clauses' were included in some treaties by the European colonial powers, which declared whether or

---

[86] Article 102 of the UN Charter also provides that states may not invoke an unregistered treaty before any UN organ. See also *supra* p. 634.

[87] See e.g. Nguyen Quoc Dinh *et al.*, *Droit International Public*, p. 215 and *Oppenheim's International Law*, p. 1248.

[88] Article 28. See *Yearbook of the ILC*, 1966, vol. II, pp. 212–13 and the *Mavrommatis Palestine Concessions* case, PCIJ, Series A, No. 2, 1924. Note article 4 of the Convention, which provides that, without prejudice to the application of customary law, the Convention will apply only to treaties concluded by states after the entry into force of the Convention with regard to such states.

not the terms of the particular agreement would extend to the various colonies.[89]

With regard to the problem of successive treaties on the same subject-matter, article 30 provides that:

1. Subject to article 103 of the Charter of the United Nations,[90] the rights and obligations of states parties to successive treaties relating to the same subject-matter shall be determined in accordance with the following paragraphs.

2. When a treaty specifies that it is subject to, or that it is not to be considered as incompatible with, an earlier or later treaty, the provisions of that other treaty prevail.

3. When all the parties to the earlier treaty are parties also to the later treaty but the earlier treaty is not terminated or suspended in operation under article 59,[91] the earlier treaty applies only to the extent that its provisions are compatible with those of the later treaty.

4. When the parties to the later treaty do not include all the parties to the earlier one:

(a) as between states parties to both treaties the same rule applies as in paragraph 3;

(b) as between a state party to both treaties and a state party to only one of the treaties, the treaty to which both states are parties governs their mutual rights and obligations.

5. Paragraph 4 is without prejudice to article 41,[92] or to any question of the termination or suspension of the operation of a treaty under article 60[93] or to any question of responsibility which may arise for a state from the conclusion or application of a treaty, the provisions of which are incompatible with its obligations towards another state under another treaty.

The problem raised by successive treaties is becoming a serious one with the growth in the number of states and the increasing numbers of treaties entered into, and the added complication of enhanced activity at the regional level.[94] The rules laid down in article 30 provide a general guide and in many cases the problem will be resolved by the parties themselves expressly.

---

[89] See Sinclair, 'Vienna Convention', pp. 87–92. See also e.g. article 63 of the European Convention on Human Rights, 1950. Practice would appear to suggest that in the absence of evidence to the contrary, a treaty would under customary law apply to all the territory of a party, including colonies, see e.g. McNair, *Law of Treaties*, pp. 116–17.

[90] This stipulates that in the event of a conflict between the obligations of a member state of the UN under the Charter and their obligations under any other international agreement, the former shall prevail. See also the *Lockerbie (Libya v. UK; Libya v. US)* case, ICJ Reports, 1992, pp. 3, 15; 94 ILR, pp. 478, 498.

[91] This deals with termination or suspension of a treaty by a later treaty, see further *infra*, p. 667.

[92] This deals with agreements to modify multilateral treaties between certain of the parties only, see further *infra*, p. 655.

[93] This deals with material breach of a treaty, see further *infra*, p. 667.

[94] See Sinclair, 'Vienna Convention', pp. 93–8. See also McNair, *Law of Treaties*, pp. 219 *et seq.*

Third states

A point of considerable interest with regard to the creation of binding rules of law for the international community centres on the application and effects of treaties upon third states, i.e. states which are not parties to the treaty in question.[95]

The general rule is that international agreements bind only the parties to them. The reasons for this rule can be found in the fundamental principles of the sovereignty and independence of states, which posit that states must consent to rules before they can be bound by them. This, of course, is a general proposition and is not necessarily true in all cases. However, it does remain as a basic line of approach in international law. Article 34 of the Convention echoes the general rule in specifying that 'a treaty does not create either obligations or rights for a third state without its consent'.[96]

It is quite clear that a treaty cannot impose obligations upon third states and this was emphasised by the International Law Commission during its deliberations prior to the Vienna Conferences and Convention.[97] There is, however, one major exception to this and that is where the provisions of the treaty in question have entered into customary law.[98] In such a case, all states would be bound, regardless of whether they had been parties to the original treaty or not. One example of this would be the laws relating to warfare adopted by the Hague Conventions earlier this century and now regarded as part of customary international law.[99]

This point arises with regard to article 2(6) of the United Nations Charter which states that:

> the organisation shall ensure that states which are not members of the United Nations act in accordance with these principles so far as may be necessary for the maintenance of international peace and security.

It is sometimes maintained that this provision creates binding obligations rather than being merely a statement of attitude with regard to non-members of the United Nations.[100] This may be the correct approach since the principles enumerated in article 2 of the Charter can be regarded as part of customary international law, and in view of the fact that an agreement

---

[95] See e.g. Sinclair, 'Vienna Convention', pp. 98–106 and *Oppenheim's International Law*, p. 1260. The rule is sometimes referred to by the maxim *pacta tertiis nec nocent nec prosunt*. See also Thirlway, 1989, 'Law and Procedure', p. 63.
[96] See also *infra*, Chapter 16, p. 682 on succession of states in respect of treaties.
[97] *Yearbook of the ILC*, 1966, vol. II, p. 227.
[98] Article 38. See *supra*, Chapter 3, p. 75, and the *North Sea Continental Shelf* cases, ICJ Reports, 1969, p. 3; 41 ILR, p. 29. See also *Yearbook of the ILC*, 1966, vol. II, p. 230.
[99] See *infra*, Chapter 19, p. 807.
[100] See e.g. H. Kelsen, *The Law of the United Nations*, London, 1950, pp. 106–10. See also McNair, *Law of Treaties*, pp. 216–18.

may legitimately provide for enforcement sanctions to be implemented against a state guilty of aggression. Article 75 of the Convention provides:

> the provisions of the Convention are without prejudice to any obligation in relation to a treaty which may arise for an aggressor state in consequence of measures taken in conformity with the Charter of the United Nations with reference to that state's aggression.

Article 35 notes that an obligation may arise for a third state from a term of a treaty if the parties to the treaty so intend and if the third state expressly accepts that obligation in writing.[101]

As far as rights allocated to third states by a treaty are concerned, the matter is a little different. The Permanent Court of International Justice declared in the *Free Zones* case[102] that:

> the question of the existence of a right acquired under an instrument drawn between other states is . . . one to be decided in each particular case: it must be ascertained whether the states which have stipulated in favour of a third state meant to create for that state an actual right which the latter has accepted as such.

Article 36 of the Vienna Convention provides that:

> a right arises for a third state from a provision of a treaty if the parties to the treaty intend the provision to accord that right either to the third state, or to a group of states to which it belongs, or to all states, and the third state assents thereto. Its assent shall be presumed so long as the contrary is not indicated, unless the treaty otherwise provides.

Instances of treaties providing benefits for third states would include those establishing the legal regimes over the Suez and Kiel canals.[103] In the *Wimbledon* case,[104] the Permanent Court noted that 'an international waterway . . . for the benefit of all nations of the world' had been established. In other words, for an obligation to be imposed by a treaty upon a third state, the express agreement of that state in writing is required, whereas in the case of benefits granted to third states, their assent is presumed in the absence of contrary intention. This is because the general tenor of customary international law has leaned in favour of the validity of rights granted to third states, but against that of obligations imposed upon them, in the light of basic principles relating to state sovereignty, equality and non-interference.

---

[101] See as to the creation here of a collateral agreement forming the basis of the obligation, *Yearbook of the ILC*, 1966, vol. II, p. 227.

[102] PCIJ, Series A/B, No. 46, 1932, pp. 147–8; 6 ILR, pp. 362, 364.

[103] See further *supra*, Chapter 9, p. 367.

[104] PCIJ, Series A, No. 1, 1923, p. 22; 2 ILR, p. 99. See also *Yearbook of the ILC*, 1966, vol. II, pp. 228–9 and J. de Aréchaga, 'International Law in the Past Third of a Century', 159 HR, pp. 1, 54 and de Aréchaga, 'Treaty Stipulations in favour of Third States', 50 AJIL, 1956, pp. 338, 355–6.

The amendment and modification of treaties

Although the two processes of amending and modifying international agreements share a common aim in that they both involve the revision of treaties, they are separate activities and may be accomplished in different manners.

Amendments refer to the formal alteration of treaty provisions, affecting all the parties to the particular agreement, while modifications relate to variations of certain treaty terms as between particular parties only.

Where it is deemed desirable, a treaty may be amended by agreement between the parties, but in such a case all the formalities as to the conclusion and coming into effect of treaties as described so far in this chapter will have to be observed except in so far as the treaty may otherwise provide.[105] It is understandable that as time passes and conditions change, the need may arise to alter some of the provisions stipulated in the international agreement in question. There is nothing unusual in this and it is a normal facet of international relations. The fact that such alterations must be effected with the same formalities that attended the original formation of the treaty is only logical since legal rights and obligations may be involved and any variation of them involves considerations of state sovereignty and consent which necessitate careful interpretation and attention. It is possible, however, for oral or tacit agreement to amend, providing it is unambiguous and clearly evidenced.

Many multilateral treaties lay down specific conditions as regards amendment. For example, the United Nations Charter in article 108 provides that amendments will come into force for all member states upon adoption and ratification by two-thirds of the members of the organisation, including all the permanent members of the Security Council.

Problems can occur where, in the absence of specific amendment processes, some of the parties oppose the amendments proposed by others. Article 40 of the Vienna Convention specifies the procedure to be adopted in amending multilateral treaties, in the absence of contrary provisions in the treaty itself. Any proposed amendment has to be notified to all contracting states, each one of which is entitled to participate in the decision as to action to be taken and in the negotiation and conclusion of any agreements. Every state which has the right to be a party to the treaty possesses also the right to become a party to the amendment, but such amendments will not bind any state which is a party to the original agreement and which does not become a party to the amended agreement,[106] subject to any provisions to the contrary in the treaty itself.

---

[105] Article 39. See also Sinclair, 'Vienna Convention', pp. 106–9; and *Yearbook of the ILC*, 1966, vol. II, p. 232.   [106] See article 30(4)b.

The situation can become a little more complex where a state becomes a party to the treaty after the amendments have come into effect. That state will be a party to the amended agreement, except as regards parties to the treaty that are not bound by the amendments. In this case the state will be considered as a party to the unamended treaty in relation to those states.

Two or more parties to a multilateral treaty may decide to change that agreement as between themselves in certain ways, quite irrespective of any amendment by all the parties. This technique, known as modification, is possible provided it has not been prohibited by the treaty in question and provided it does not affect the rights or obligations of the other parties. Modification, however, is not possible where the provision it is intended to alter is one 'derogation from which is incompatible with the effective execution of the object and purpose of the treaty as a whole'.[107] A treaty may also be modified by the terms of another later agreement[108] or by the establishment subsequently of a rule of *jus cogens*.[109]

Treaty interpretation[110]

One of the enduring problems facing courts and tribunals and lawyers, both in the municipal and international law spheres, relates to the question of interpretation.[111] Accordingly, rules and techniques have been put forward to aid judicial bodies in resolving such problems.[112] As far as international law is concerned, there are three basic approaches to treaty interpretation.[113] The first centres on the actual text of the agreement and emphasises the analysis of the words used.[114] The second looks to the intention of the parties adopting

---

[107] Article 41.   [108] See article 30, and *supra*, p. 651.

[109] See *supra*, Chapter 3, p. 97 and *infra*, p. 665.

[110] See e.g. Sinclair, 'Vienna Convention', Chapter 5; G. Fitzmaurice, 'The Law and Procedure of the International Court of Justice, 1951–4', 33 BYIL, 1957, p. 203 and 28 BYIL, 1951, p. 1; H. Lauterpacht, 'Restrictive Interpretation and the Principle of Effectiveness in the Interpretation of Treaties', 26 BYIL, 1949, p. 48; M. S. McDougal, H. Lasswell and J. C. Miller, *The Interpretation of Agreements and World Public Order*, Yale, 1967 and Dordrecht, 1993; E. Gordon, 'The World Court and the Interpretation of Constitutive Treaties', 59 AJIL, 1965, p. 794; O'Connell, *International Law*, pp. 251 *et seq.* and Brownlie, *Principles*, pp. 626 *et seq.* See also S. Sur, *L'Interprétation en Droit International Public*, Paris, 1974; M. K. Yasseen, 'L'Interprétation des Traités d'après la Convention de Vienne', 151 HR, 1976 III, p. 1; H. Thirlway, 'The Law and Practice of the International Court of Justice 1960–1989', 62 BYIL, 1991, pp. 2, 16 *et seq.* and *ibid.*, 62 BYIL, 1992, p. 3; Nguyen Quoc Dinh *et al.*, *Droit International Public*, p. 248 and *Oppenheim's International Law*, p. 1266.

[111] Note that a unilateral interpretation of a treaty by the organs of one state would not be binding upon the other parties, see McNair, *Law of Treaties*, pp. 345–50 and the *David J. Adams* claim, 6 RIAA, p. 85 (1921); 1 ILR, p. 331.

[112] But see J. Stone, 'Fictional Elements in Treaty Interpretation', 1 *Sydney Law Review*, 1955, p. 344.

[113] See Sinclair, 'Vienna Convention', pp. 114–15 and Fitzmaurice, 1951, 'Reservations'.

[114] See Fitzmaurice, 1957, 'Law and Procedure', pp. 204–7.

the agreement as the solution to ambiguous provisions and can be termed the subjective approach in contradistinction to the objective approach of the previous school.[115] The third approach adopts a wider perspective than the other two and emphasises the object and purpose of the treaty as the most important backcloth against which the meaning of any particular treaty provision should be measured.[116] This teleological school of thought has the effect of underlining the role of the judge or arbitrator, since he will be called upon to define the object and purpose of the treaty and it has been criticised for encouraging judicial lawmaking.

Nevertheless, any true interpretation of a treaty in international law will have to take into account all aspects of the agreement, from the words employed to the intention of the parties and the aims of the particular document. It is not possible to exclude completely any one of these components.

Articles 31 to 33 of the Vienna Convention comprise in some measure aspects of all three doctrines. Article 31 lays down the fundamental rules of interpretation and can be taken as reflecting customary international law.[117] Article 31(1) declares that a treaty shall be interpreted 'in good faith in accordance with the ordinary meaning to be given to the terms of the treaty in their context and in the light of its object and purpose'.[118] The International Court noted in the *Competence of the General Assembly for the Admission of a State to the United Nations* case[119] that 'the first duty of a tribunal which is called upon to interpret and apply the provisions of a treaty is to endeavour to give effect to them in their natural and ordinary meaning in the context in which they occur'.[120] On the basis of this provision, for example, the European Court of Human Rights held in the *Lithgow* case[121] that the use of the phrase 'subject to the conditions provided for . . . by the general principles of international law' in article 1 of Protocol I of the European Convention in the context of compensation for interference with property rights, could not be interpreted as extending the general principles of international law in this field to establish standards of compensation for

[115] See e.g. H. Lauterpacht, 'De l'Interprétation des Traités: Rapport et Projet de Résolutions', 43 *Annuaire de l'Institut de Droit International*, 1950, p. 366.
[116] See e.g. Fitzmaurice, 'Reservations', pp. 7–8 and 13–14 and 'Law and Procedure', pp. 207–9.
[117] The International Court has reaffirmed that article 31 of the Vienna Convention reflected customary law, see the *Libya/Chad* case, ICJ Reports, 1994, pp. 6, 21–2; 100 ILR, pp. 1, 20–1, and the *Qatar v. Bahrain* case, ICJ Reports, 1995, pp. 6, 18: 102 ILR, pp. 47, 59. In the GATT Dispute Settlement Panel Report on United States Restrictions on Imports of Tuna in 1994, it was emphasised that the Vienna Convention expressed the basic rules with regard to treaty interpretation, 33 ILM, 1994, pp. 839, 892. See also *Oppenheim's International Law*, p. 1271.
[118] See e.g. the *German External Debts* arbitration, 19 ILM, 1980, pp. 1357, 1377. See also Judge Ajibola's Separate Opinion in the *Libya/Chad* case, ICJ Reports, 1994, pp. 6, 71; 100 ILR, pp. 1, 69.   [119] ICJ Reports, 1950, pp. 4, 8; 17 ILR, pp. 326, 328.
[120] See also the *La Bretagne* arbitration (*Canada v. France*), 82 ILR, pp. 590, 620.
[121] European Court of Human Rights, Series A, No. 102, para. 114; 75 ILR, pp. 438, 482.

THE LAW OF TREATIES

the nationalisation of property of nationals (as distinct from aliens).[122] The word 'context' is held to include the preamble and annexes of the treaty as well as any agreement or instrument made by the parties in connection with the conclusion of the treaty.[123] In addition, any subsequent agreement or practice relating to the treaty together with any relevant rules of international law must be considered together with the context.[124]

The latter provision, whereby any relevant rules of international law applicable in the relations between the parties shall be taken into account in interpreting a treaty, was applied in *Iran* v. *United States*,[125] which was concerned with the question of whether a dual Iran–US national could bring a claim against Iran before the Iran-US Claims Tribunal where the Claims Settlement Agreement 1981 simply defined a US national as a 'natural person who is a citizen of . . . the United States'.[126] The Full Tribunal held that jurisdiction existed over claims against Iran by dual Iran–US nationals when the dominant and effective nationality of the claimant at the relevant period was that of the US. In reaching this decision, the Tribunal cited article 31(3)c of the 1969 Vienna Convention as the mechanism whereby the considerable body of law and legal literature in the area could be analysed in the context of interpreting the 1981 agreement and which led it to its conclusion.

Where the interpretation according to the provisions of article 31 needs confirmation, or determination since the meaning is ambiguous or obscure, or leads to a manifestly absurd or unreasonable result, recourse may be had to supplementary means of interpretation under article 32. These means include the preparatory works (*travaux préparatoires*) of the treaty and the circumstances of its conclusion and may be employed in the above circumstances to aid the process of interpreting the treaty in question.[127]

---

[122] See also the *James* case, European Court of Human Rights, Series A, No. 98, para. 61; 75 ILR, pp. 397, 423 and the Advisory Opinions of the Inter-American Court of Human Rights in the *Enforceability of the Right to Reply* case, 79 ILR, pp. 335, 343, and the *Meaning of the Word 'Laws'* case, *ibid.*, pp. 325, 329.

[123] Article 31(2). See also the *US Nationals in Morocco* case, ICJ Reports, 1952, pp. 176, 196; 19 ILR, pp. 255, 272; the *Beagle Channel* case, HMSO, 1977, p. 12; 52 ILR, p. 93 and the *Young Loan* arbitration, 59 ILR, pp. 495, 530.

[124] Article 31(3) a-c. See also *Loizidou* v. *Turkey (preliminary objections)*, European Court of Human Rights, Series A, No. 310, p. 25.

[125] Case No. A/18, 5 Iran–US CTR, p. 251; 75 ILR, pp. 175, 188.   [126] Article VII(1)a.

[127] See *Yearbook of the ILC*, 1966, vol. II, p. 223, doubting the rule in the *River Oder* case, PCIJ, Series A, No. 23, 1929; 5 ILR, pp. 381, 383, that the *travaux préparatoires* of certain provisions of the Treaty of Versailles could not be taken into account since three of the states before the Court had not participated in the preparatory conference. See also the *Young Loan* case, 59 ILR, pp. 495, 544–5 and Sinclair, 'Vienna Convention', pp. 141–7, and the *Lithgow* case, European Court of Human Rights, Series A, No. 102, para. 117; 75 ILR, pp. 438, 484. In the *Libya/Chad* case, ICJ Reports, 1994, pp. 6. 27; 100 ILR, pp. 1, 26, the International Court noted that while it was not necessary to have recourse to the *travaux préparatoires* to elucidate the content of the 1955 Treaty at the heart of the dispute, it found it possible to confirm its reading of the text by such recourse. Similarly in the *Qatar* v.

Nevertheless, the International Court has underlined that 'interpretation must be based above all upon the text of the treaty'.[128]

Case law provides some interesting guidelines to the above stated rules. In the *Interpretation of Peace Treaties* case,[129] the Court was asked whether the UN Secretary-General could appoint the third member of a Treaty Commission upon the request of one side to the dispute where the other side (Bulgaria, Hungary and Romania) refused to appoint its own representative. It was emphasised that the natural and ordinary meaning of the terms of the Peace Treaties with the three states concerned envisaged the appointment of the third member after the other two had been nominated. The breach of a treaty obligation could not be remedied by creating a Commission which was not the kind of Commission envisaged by the Treaties. The principle of effectiveness could not be used by the Court to attribute to the provisions for the settlement of disputes in the Peace Treaties a meaning which would be contrary to their letter and spirit. The Court also stressed the nature of the disputes clause as being one that had to be strictly construed. Thus, the character of the provisions to be interpreted is significant in the context of utilising the relevant rules of interpretation.

The principle of effectiveness will be used, however, in order to give effect to provisions in accordance with the intentions of the parties.[130]

In two areas, it should be noted, the principle of effectiveness allied with the broader purposes approach has been used in an especially dynamic manner. In the case of treaties that also operate as the constitutional documents of an international organisation, a more flexible method of interpretation would seem to be justified, since one is dealing with an instrument that is being used in order to accomplish the stated aims of that organisation. In

Bahrain case, ICJ Reports, 1995, pp. 6, 21; 102 ILR, pp. 47, 62, the International Court did not feel it necessary to turn to the *travaux préparatoires* in order to determine the meaning of the instrument in dispute, but noted that 'it can have recourse to supplementary means in order to seek a possible confirmation of its interpretation of the text'.

[128] The *Libya/Chad* case, ICJ Reports, 1994, pp. 6, 22; 100 ILR, pp. 1, 21. The Court also noted in its decision in the Preliminary Objection phase of the *Oil Platforms* case, ICJ Reports, 1996, paras. 27, 28, 31 and 52, that a broad introductory provision in a treaty might be taken in the circumstances as fixing an objective in accordance with the object and purpose of the treaty in question, in the light of which other treaty provisions are to be interpreted and applied. In this case, the Court took the view that article 1 of the Treaty of Amity, Economic relations and Consular Rights, 1955, between the US and Iran, which provided that 'there shall be firm and enduring peace and sincere friendship' between the two states, did not provide of itself a basis for the jurisdiction of the Court. Nevertheless, it was not without legal significance and was able to throw light on the interpretation of the other treaty provisions. The Court found jurisdiction on the basis of article X(1) of the treaty taken with the compromissory clause in article XXI(2).

[129] ICJ Reports, 1950, pp. 221, 226–30; 17 ILR, pp. 318, 320–2. See also *Yearbook of the ILC*, 1966, vol. II, p. 220.

[130] See e.g. the *Ambatielos* case, ICJ Reports, 1952, p. 28; 19 ILR, p. 416. See also the *Corfu Channel* case, ICJ Reports, 1949, pp. 4, 24; 16 ILR, pp. 155, 169 and *Yearbook of the ILC*, 1966, vol. II, p. 219.

addition, of course, the concept and nature of subsequent practice possesses in such cases an added relevance.[131] This approach has been used as a way of inferring powers, not expressly provided for in the relevant instruments, which are deemed necessary in the context of the purposes of the organisation.[132] This programmatic interpretation doctrine in such cases is now well established and especially relevant to the United Nations, where forty years of practice related to the principles of the organisation by nearly 160 states is manifest.

The more dynamic approach to interpretation is also evident in the context of human rights treaties, such as the European Convention on Human Rights which created a system of implementation.[133] It has been held that a particular legal order was thereby established involving objective obligations to protect human rights rather than subjective, reciprocal rights.[134] Accordingly, a more flexible and programmatic or purpose-oriented method of interpretation was adopted, emphasising that the Convention constituted a living instrument that had to be interpreted 'in the light of present-day conditions'.[135] In addition, the object and purpose of

[131] Note that by article 5, the Vienna Convention is deemed to apply to any treaty which is the constituent instrument of an international organisation. See also C. F. Amerasinghe, *Principles of the Institutional Law of International Organisations*, Cambridge, 1996, Chapter 2 and Amerasinghe, 'Interpretation of Texts in Open International Organisations', 65 BYIL, 1994, p. 175; M. N. Shaw, *Title to Territory in Africa: International Legal Issues*, Oxford, 1986, pp. 64–73; S. Rosenne, 'Is the Constitution of an International Organisation an International Treaty?', 12 *Communicazioni e Studi*, 1966, p. 21 and G. Distefano, 'La Pratique Subséquente des Etats Parties à un Traité', AFDI, 1994, p. 41.

[132] See e.g. the *Reparation* case, ICJ Reports 1949, p. 174; 16 ILR, p. 318; the *Certain Expenses of the UN* case, ICJ Reports, 1962, p. 151; 34 ILR, p. 281; the *Competence of the General Assembly for the Admission of a State* case, ICJ Reports, 1950, p. 4; 17 ILR, p. 326 and the *Namibia* case, ICJ Reports, 1971, p. 16; 49 ILR, p. 2. See also Shaw, *Title to Territory*; R. Higgins, 'The Development of International Law by the Political Organs of the United Nations', *PASIL*, 1965, p. 119 and H. G. Schermers and N. M. Blokker, *International Institutional Law*, 3rd edn, The Hague, 1995, Chapter 9. See further *infra*, Chapter 21, p. 915.

[133] See further, *supra*, Chapter 7, p. 257. See also J. G. Merrills, *The Development of International Law by the European Court of Human Rights*, 2nd edn, Manchester, 1993, Chapter 4. Note that the European Court of Human Rights in *Loizidou v. Turkey (preliminary objections)*, Series A, No. 310, p. 26 (1995) emphasised the fundamental differences as between the role and purposes of the International Court of Justice and the European Court.

[134] See e.g. *Austria v. Italy*, 4 *European Yearbook of Human Rights*, 1960, pp. 116, 140 and *Ireland v. UK*, Series A, No. 25, p. 90 (1978). See also the Advisory Opinion of the Inter-American Court of Human Rights on the *Effect of Reservations on the Entry into Force of the American Convention on Human Rights*, 22 ILM, 1983, pp. 37, 47; 67 ILR, pp. 559, 568, which adopted a similar approach.

[135] See e.g. the *Tyrer* case, European Court of Human Rights, Series A, no. 26, at p. 15 (1978); 58 ILR, pp. 339, 553; the *Marckx* case, *ibid.*, no. 32, at p. 14 (1979); 58 ILR, pp. 561, 583; the *Wemhoff* case, *ibid.*, No. 7 (1968); 41 ILR, p. 281 and the *Loizidou* case, European Court of Human Rights, Series A, No. 310, p. 23. See also H. Waldock, 'The Evolution of Human Rights Concepts and the Application of the European Convention on Human Rights' in *Mélanges Offerts à Paul Reuter*, Paris, 1981, p. 535. Note also the approach taken by the UN Human Rights Committee in its General Comment 24/52 of 2 November 1994 on Reservations, see 15 HRLJ, 1994, p. 464.

the Convention requires that its provisions be interpreted so as to make its safeguards practical and effective.[136] Indeed, in this context, it was noted in the *Licensing of Journalists* case[137] that while it was useful to compare the Inter-American Convention on Human Rights with other relevant international instruments, this approach could not be utilised to read into the Convention restrictions existing in other treaties. In this situation, 'the rule most favourable to the individual must prevail'.

Article 31(4) provides that a special meaning shall be given to a term if it is established that the parties so intended. It would appear that the standard of proof is fairly high, since a derogation from the ordinary meaning of the term is involved. It is not enough that one party only uses the particular term in a particular way.[138]

Where a treaty is authenticated in more than one language, as often happens with multilateral agreements, article 33 provides that, in the absence of agreement, in the event of a difference of meaning that the normal processes of interpretation cannot resolve, the meaning which best reconciles the texts, having regard to the object and purpose of the treaty, shall be adopted.[139]

Invalidity, termination and suspension of the operation of treaties[140]

General provisions

Article 42 states that the validity and continuance in force of a treaty may only be questioned on the basis of the provisions in the Vienna Convention.

---

[136] See e.g. *Soering* v. *UK*, European Court of Human Rights, Series A, No. 161, p. 34 (1989); 98 ILR, p. 270; *Artico* v. *Italy, ibid.*, No. 37 (1980) and *Loizidou* v. *Turkey, ibid.*, No. 310, p. 23 (1995). Note that the European Court of Human Rights has pointed out in the *Loizidou (Merits)* decision of 18 December 1996 (paragraph 43) that the European Convention must be interpreted in the light of the Vienna Convention on the Law of Treaties, including the provision that account must be taken of any relevant rules of international law applicable as between the parties. The Court emphasised that while it was mindful of the Convention's special character as a human rights treaty, it had also to take into account any relevant rules of international law when deciding on disputes concerning its jurisdiction.
[137] Advisory Opinion of the Inter-American Court of Human Rights, 1985, 75 ILR, pp. 30, 47–8.
[138] See the *Eastern Greenland* case, PCIJ, Series A/B, No. 53, 1933, p. 49; 6 ILR, p. 95 and the *Anglo-French Continental Shelf* case, Cmnd. 7438, p. 50; 54 ILR, p. 6.
[139] See the *Mavrommatis Palestine Concessions* case, PCIJ, Series A, No. 2, p. 19, which called for the more restrictive interpretation in such cases and the *Young Loan* case, 59 ILR, p. 495.
[140] Nguyen Quoc Dinh *et al.*, *Droit International Public*, p. 294 and *Oppenheim's International Law*, p. 1284. See also N. Kontou, *The Termination and Revision of Treaties in the Light of New Customary International Law*, Oxford, 1995.

Article 44 provides that a state may only withdraw from or suspend the operation of a treaty in respect of the treaty as a whole and not particular parts of it, unless the treaty otherwise stipulates or the parties otherwise agree. If the appropriate ground for invalidating, terminating, withdrawing from or suspending the operation of a treaty relates solely to particular clauses, it may only be invoked in relation to those clauses where:

(a) the said clauses are separable from the remainder of the treaty with regard to their application;

(b) it appears from the treaty or is otherwise established that acceptance of those clauses was not an essential basis of consent of the other party or parties to be bound by the treaty as a whole; and

(c) continued performance of the remainder of the treaty would not be unjust.

Thus the Convention adopts a cautious approach to the general issue of separability of treaty provisions in this context.[141]

Article 45 in essence provides that a ground for invalidity, termination, withdrawal or suspension may no longer be invoked by the state where after becoming aware of the facts, it expressly agreed that the treaty is valid or remains in force or by reason of its conduct may be deemed to have acquiesced in the validity of the treaty or its continuance in force.[142]

Invalidity of treaties

Municipal law

A state cannot plead a breach of its constitutional provisions as to the making of treaties as a valid excuse for condemning an agreement. There has been for some years disagreement amongst international lawyers as to whether the failure to abide by a domestic legal limitation by, for example, a head of state in entering into a treaty, will result in rendering the agreement invalid or not.[143] The Convention took the view that in general it would not, but that it could in certain circumstances.

Article 46 provides that:

[a] state may not invoke the fact that its consent to be bound by a treaty has been expressed in violation of a provision of its internal law regarding competence to conclude treaties as invalidating its consent unless that violation was manifest and concerned a rule of its internal law of fundamental importance.

[141] See Judge Lauterpacht, the *Norwegian Loans* case, ICJ Reports, 1957, pp. 9, 55–9; 24 ILR, pp. 782, 809 and Sinclair, 'Vienna Convention', pp. 165–7.
[142] See e.g. the *Arbitral Award by the King of Spain* case, ICJ Reports, 1960, pp. 192, 213–14; 30 ILR, pp. 457, 473 and the *Temple* case, ICJ Reports, 1962, pp. 6, 23–32; 33 ILR, pp. 48, 62. See also the *Argentina–Chile* case, 38 ILR, p. 10 and *supra*, Chapter 9, p. 350.
[143] See Sinclair, 'Vienna Convention', pp. 169–171, distinguishing between the constitutionalist and internationalist schools, and K. Holloway, *Modern Trends in Treaty Law*, London, 1967, pp. 123–33. See also *Yearbook of the ILC*, 1966, vol. II, pp. 240–1.

Violation will be regarded as manifest if it would be 'objectively evident' to any state conducting itself in the matter in accordance with normal practice, and in good faith.

For example, where the representative of the state has had his authority to consent on behalf of the state made subject to a specific restriction which is ignored, the state will still be bound by that consent save where the other negotiating states were aware of the restriction placed upon his authority to consent prior to the expression of that consent.[144]

This particular provision applies as regards a person authorised to represent a state and such persons are defined in article 7 to include heads of state and government and foreign ministers in addition to persons possessing full powers.[145]

It should, of course, also be noted that a state may not invoke a provision of its internal law as a justification for its failure to carry out an international obligation. This is a general principle of international law[146] and finds its application in the law of treaties by virtue of article 27 of the 1969 Vienna Convention.

Error

Unlike the role of mistake in municipal laws of contract, the scope in international law of error as invalidating a state's consent is rather limited. In view of the character of states and the multiplicity of persons actually dealing with the negotiation and conclusion of treaties, errors are not very likely to happen, whether they be unilateral or mutual.

Article 48 declares that a state may only invoke an error in a treaty as invalidating its consent to be bound by the treaty, if the error relates to a fact or situation which was assumed by that state to exist at the time when the treaty was concluded and formed an essential basis of its consent to be bound by the treaty. But if the state knew or ought to have known of the error, or if it contributed to that error, then it cannot afterwards free itself from the obligation of observing the treaty by pointing to that error.

This restrictive approach is in harmony with the comments made in a number of cases, including the *Temple* case,[147] where the International Court of Justice rejected Thailand's argument that a particular map contained a

[144] Article 47. See e.g. the *Eastern Greenland* case, PCIJ, Series A/B, No. 53, 1933; 6 ILR, p. 95 and *Qatar* v. *Bahrain* ICJ Reports, 1994, pp. 112, 121–2; 102 ILR, pp. 1, 18–19.
[145] *Supra*, p. 637.
[146] See e.g. the *Alabama Claims* arbitration, J. B. Moore, *International Arbitrations*, New York, 1898, vol. I, p. 495 and the *Greco-Bulgarian Communities* case, PCIJ, Series B, No. 17, p. 32; 5 ILR, p. 4. This has been recently reaffirmed in the *Applicability of the Obligation to Arbitrate under Section 21 of the United Nations Headquarters Agreement* case, ICJ Reports, 1988, pp. 12, 34–5; 82 ILR, pp. 225, 252.   [147] ICJ Reports, 1960, p. 6; 33 ILR, p. 48.

basic error and therefore it was not bound to observe it, since 'the plea of error cannot be allowed as an element vitiating consent if the party advancing it contributed by its own conduct to the error, or could have avoided it, or if the circumstances were such as to put that party on notice of a possible error'.[148] The Court felt that in view of the character and qualifications of the persons who were involved on the Thai side in examining the map, Thailand could not put forward a claim of error.

Fraud and corruption

Where a state consents to be bound by a treaty as a result of the fraudulent conduct of another negotiating state, that state may under article 49 invoke the fraud as invalidating its consent to be bound. Where a negotiating state directly or indirectly corrupts the representative of another state in order to obtain the consent of the latter to the treaty, that corruption may under article 50 be invoked as invalidating the consent to be bound.[149]

Coercion

Of more importance than error, fraud or corruption in the law of treaties is the issue of coercion as invalidating consent. Where consent has been obtained by coercing the representative of a state, whether by acts or threats directed against him, it shall, according to article 51 of the Convention, be without any legal effect.[150]

The problem of consent obtained by the application of coercion against the state itself is a slightly different one. Prior to the League of Nations, it was clear that international law did not provide for the invalidation of treaties on the grounds of the use or threat of force by one party against the other and this was a consequence of the lack of rules in customary law prohibiting recourse to war. With the signing of the Covenant of the League in 1919, and the Kellogg-Briand Pact in 1928 forbidding the resort to war to resolve international disputes, a new approach began to be taken with regard to the illegality of the use of force in international relations.

With the elucidation of the Nuremberg principles and the coming into effect of the Charter of the United Nations after the Second World War, it became clear that international law condemned coercive activities by states. Article 2(4) of the United Nations Charter provides that:

[148] Ibid., p. 26; 33 ILR, p. 65.
[149] Such instances are very rare in practice, see Yearbook of the ILC, 1966, vol. II, pp. 244–5 and Sinclair, 'Vienna Convention', pp. 173–6
[150] See e.g. First Fidelity Bank NA v. Government of Antigua and Barbuda Permanent Mission, 877 F 2d 189, 192 (1989); 99 ILR, pp. 126, 130.

[a]ll members shall refrain in their international relations from the threat or use of force against the territorial integrity or political independence of any state, or in any other measure inconsistent with the purposes of the United Nations.

It followed that treaties based on coercion of a state should be regarded as invalid.[151]

Accordingly, article 52 of the Convention provides that '[a] treaty is void if its conclusion has been procured by the threat or use of force in violation of the principles of international law embodied in the Charter of the United Nations'. This article was the subject of much debate in the Vienna Conference preceding the adoption of the Convention. Communist and certain Third World countries argued that coercion comprised not only the threat or use of force but also economic and political pressures.[152] The International Law Commission did not take a firm stand on the issue, but noted that the precise scope of the acts covered by the definition should be left to be determined in practice by interpretation of the relevant Charter provisions.[153]

The Vienna Conference came some way to accepting the approach of the communist and Third World states by issuing a Declaration on the Prohibition of Military, Political or Economic Coercion in the Conclusion of Treaties, which condemned the exercise of such coercion to procure the formation of a treaty. These points were not included in the Convention itself, which leaves one to conclude that the application of political or economic pressure to secure the consent of a state to a treaty may not be contrary to international law, but clearly a lot will depend upon the relevant circumstances.

In international relations, the variety of influences which may be brought to bear by a powerful state against a weaker one to induce it to adopt a particular line of policy is wide-ranging and may cover not only coercive threats but also subtle expressions of displeasure. The precise nuances of any particular situation will depend on a number of factors, and it will be misleading to suggest that all forms of pressure are as such violations of international law.

The problem was noted by Judge Padilla Nervo in the International Court in the *Fisheries Jurisdiction* case[154] when he stated that:

there are moral and political pressures which cannot be proved by the so-called documentary evidence, but which are in fact indisputably real and which have, in history, given rise to treaties and conventions claimed to be freely concluded and subjected to the principle of *pacta sunt servanda*.[155]

[151] See *Yearbook of the ILC*, 1966, vol. II, pp. 246–7. See also the *Fisheries Jurisdiction* case, ICJ Reports, 1973, pp. 3, 14; 55 ILR, pp. 183, 194.
[152] See Sinclair, 'Vienna Convention', pp. 177–9.
[153] *Yearbook of the ILC*, 1966, vol. II, pp. 246–7.
[154] ICJ Reports, 1973, p. 3; 55 ILR, p. 183.   [155] *Ibid.*, p. 47; 55 ILR, p. 227.

It should also be noted that the phrase 'in violation of the principles of international law embodied in the Charter' was used so that article 52 should by no means be construed as applying solely to members of the United Nations but should be treated as a universal rule.

Jus cogens[156]

Article 53 of the Convention provides that:

[a] treaty is void if, at the time of its conclusion, it conflicts with a peremptory norm of general international law. For the purposes of the present Convention, a peremptory norm of general international law is a norm accepted and recognised by the international community of states as a whole as a norm from which no derogation is permitted, and which can be modified only by a subsequent norm of general international law having the same character.

Article 64 declares that '(i)f a new peremptory norm of general international law emerges, any existing treaty which is in conflict with that norm becomes void and terminates'.[157]

As noted in Chapter 3,[158] the concept of *jus cogens*, of fundamental and entrenched rules of international law, is well established in doctrine now, but controversial as to content and method of creation. The insertion of articles dealing with *jus cogens* in the 1969 Convention underlines the basic principles with regard to treaties.

Consequences of invalidity

Article 69 provides that an invalid treaty is void and without legal force. If acts have nevertheless been performed in reliance on such a treaty, each party may require any other party to establish as far as possible in their mutual relations the position that would have existed if the acts had not been performed. Acts performed in good faith before the invalidity was invoked are not rendered unlawful by reason only of the invalidity of the treaty.

Where a treaty is void under article 53, article 71 provides that the parties are to eliminate as far as possible the consequences of any act performed in reliance on any provision which conflicts with *jus cogens* and bring their mutual relations into conformity with the peremptory norm. Where a treaty

---

[156] See e.g. J. Sztucki, *Jus Cogens and the Vienna Convention on the Law of Treaties*, 1974; C. Rozakis, *The Concept of Jus Cogens in the Law of Treaties*, Leiden, 1976; L. Hannikainen, *Peremptory Norms (Jus Cogens) in International Law*, Helsinki, 1988; A. Gomez Robledo, 'Le *Jus Cogens* International: Sa Genèse, Sa Nature, Ses Fonctions', 172 HR, p. 9; L. Alexidze, 'Legal Nature of *Jus Cogens* in Contemporary International Law", *ibid.*, p. 219; G. Gaja, '*Jus Cogens* Beyond the Vienna Convention', *ibid.*, p. 271; Nguyen Quoc Dinh *et al.*, *Droit International Public*, p. 199 and *Oppenheim's International Law*, p. 1292. See also *Yearbook of the ILC*, 1966, vol. II, pp. 247–8 and Sinclair, 'Vienna Convention', Chapter 7.
[157] See also article 71 and *infra*, p. 666. [158] *Supra*, Chapter 3, p. 97.

terminates under article 64, the parties are released from any obligation further to perform the treaty, but this does not affect any right, obligation or legal situation of the parties created through the execution of the treaty prior to its termination, provided that the rights, obligations or situations may be maintained thereafter in conformity with the new peremptory norm.

The termination of treaties [159]

There are a number of methods available by which treaties may be terminated or suspended.

Termination by treaty provision or consent

A treaty may be terminated or suspended in accordance with a specific provision in that treaty, or otherwise at any time by consent of all the parties after consultation.[160]

Where, however, a treaty contains no provision regarding termination and does not provide for denunciation or withdrawal specifically, a state may only denounce or withdraw from that treaty where the parties intended to admit such a possibility or where the right may be implied by the nature of the treaty.[161]

A treaty may, of course, come to an end if its purposes and objects have been fulfilled or if it is clear from its provisions that it is limited in time and the requisite period has elapsed. The Tribunal in the *Rainbow Warrior* case[162] held that the breach of the New Zealand–France Agreement 1986, concerning the two captured French agents who had sunk the vessel in question,[163] had commenced on 22 July 1986 and had run continuously for the three years period of confinement of the agents stipulated in the agreement. Accordingly, the period concerned had expired on 22 July 1989, so that France could not be said to be in breach of its international obligations after that date. However, this did not exempt France from responsibility for its previous breaches of its obligations, committed while these obligations were in force. Claims arising out of a previous infringement of a treaty which has since expired acquire an existence independent of that treaty.[164] The

---

[159] See e.g. David, *The Strategy of Treaty Termination*, 1975; A. Vamvoukis, *Termination of Treaties in International Law*, Oxford, 1985, and R. Plender, 'The Role of Consent in the Termination of Treaties', 57 BYIL, 1986, p. 133. See also Thirlway, 1992, 'Law and Practice', pp. 63 *et seq.*   [160] Articles 54 and 57.

[161] Article 56. Examples given by J. Brierly, *The Law of Nations*, 6th edn, Oxford, 1963, p. 331, include treaties of alliance and commerce. See also *Nicaragua* v. *US*, ICJ Reports, 1984, pp. 392, 420; 76 ILR, pp. 1, 131.   [162] 82 ILR, pp. 499, 567–8.

[163] See *supra* p. 543.

[164] See the dissenting opinion of Judge McNair in the *Ambatielos* case, ICJ Reports, 1952, pp. 28, 63; 19 ILR, pp. 416, 433.

termination of a treaty does not affect any right, obligation or legal situation of the parties created through the execution of the treaty prior to its termination.[165]

Just as two or more parties to a multilateral treaty may modify as between themselves particular provisions of the agreement,[166] so they may under article 58 agree to suspend the operation of treaty provisions temporarily and as between themselves alone if such a possibility is provided for by the treaty. Such suspension may also be possible under that article, where not prohibited by the treaty in question, provided it does not affect the rights or obligations of the other parties under the particular agreement and provided it is not incompatible with the object and purpose of the treaty.

Where all the parties to a treaty later conclude another agreement relating to the same subject-matter, the earlier treaty will be regarded as terminated where it appears that the matter is to be governed by the later agreement or where the provisions of the later treaty are so incompatible with those of the earlier one that the two treaties are not capable of being applied at the same time.[167]

Material breach[168]

There are two viewpoints here to be considered. First, if one state violates an important provision in an agreement, it is not unnatural for the other states concerned to regard that agreement as ended by it. It is in effect a reprisal or counter-measure,[169] a rather unsubtle but effective means of ensuring the enforcement of a treaty. The fact that an agreement may be terminated where it is breached by one party may act as a discouragement to any party that might contemplate a breach of one provision but would be unwilling to forgo the benefits prescribed in others. On the other hand, there is the second point to consider, that to render treaties revocable because one party has acted contrary to what might very well be only a minor provision in the agreement taken as a whole, would be to place the states participating in a treaty in rather a vulnerable position. There is a need for flexibility as well as certainty in such situations.

Customary law supports the view that something more than a mere breach itself of a term in an agreement would be necessary to give the other party or parties the right to abrogate that agreement. In the *Tacna–Arica* arbitration,[170] between Chile and Peru, the arbitrator noted, in referring to

---

[165] Article 70(1)b of the 1969 Vienna Convention. See *infra* p. 671.
[166] Article 41 and *supra*, p. 654.   [167] Article 59.
[168] See e.g. S. Rosenne, *Breach of Treaty*, Cambridge, 1985. See also D. N. Hutchinson, 'Solidarity and Breaches of Multilateral Treaties', 59 BYIL, 1988, p. 151 and M. M. Gomaa, *Suspension or Termination of Treaties on Grounds of Breach*, The Hague, 1996.
[169] See *supra* Chapter 14, p. 558.   [170] 2 RIAA, p. 921 (1925).

an agreement about a plebiscite in former Peruvian territory occupied by Chile, that:

> [i]t is manifest that if abuses of administration could have the effect of termi-
> nating such an agreement, it would be necessary to establish such serious
> conditions as the consequence of administrative wrongs as would operate to
> frustrate the purpose of the agreement.[171]

Article 60(3) of the Vienna Convention declares that a material breach of a treaty consists in either a repudiation of the treaty not permitted by the Vienna Convention or the violation of a provision essential to the accomplishment of the object or purpose of the treaty.[172]

The second part of article 60(3) was applied in the *Rainbow Warrior* case,[173] where the obligation to confine the two French agents in question on a Pacific Island for a minimum period of three years was held to have constituted the object or purpose of the New Zealand–France Agreement 1986 so that France committed a material breach of this treaty by permitting the agents to leave the island before the expiry of the three-year period.

Where such a breach occurs in a bilateral treaty, then under article 60(1) the innocent party may invoke that breach as a ground for terminating the treaty or suspending its operation in whole or in part. On the other hand, in the case of a multilateral treaty, a rather different situation obtains since a number of innocent parties are involved that might not wish the treaty to be denounced by one of them because of a breach by another state. To cover such situations, article 60(2) prescribes that a material breach of a multilateral treaty by one of the parties entitles:

(a) the other parties by unanimous agreement to suspend the operation of the treaty in whole or in part or to terminate it either:
 (i) in the relations between themselves and the defaulting state, or
 (ii) as between all the parties;
(b) a party specially affected by the breach to invoke it as a ground for suspending the operation of the treaty in whole or in part in the relations between itself and the defaulting state;
(c) any party other than the defaulting state to invoke the breach as a ground for suspending the operation of the treaty in whole or in part with respect to itself if the treaty is of such a character that a material breach of its provisions by one party radically changes the position of every party with respect to the further performance of its obligations under the treaty.[174]

---

[171] *Ibid.*, pp. 943–4.
[172] See the *Namibia* case, ICJ Reports, 1971, pp. 16, 46–7; 49 ILR, pp. 2, 37.
[173] 82 ILR, pp. 499, 564–6.
[174] See *Yearbook of the ILC*, 1966, vol. II, pp. 253–5. See also the *Namibia* case, ICJ Reports, 1971, pp. 16, 47; 49 ILR, p. 37 and the *US–France Air Services Agreement* case, 54 ILR, pp. 304, 331.

It is interesting to note that the provisions of article 60 regarding the definition and consequences of a material breach do not apply, by article 60(5), to provisions relating to the 'protection of the human person contained in treaties of a humanitarian character, in particular to provisions prohibiting any form of reprisals against persons protected by such treaties'. This is because objective and absolute principles are involved and not just reciprocal rights and duties.[175]

Supervening impossibility of performance[176]

Article 61 of the Convention is intended to cover such situations as the submergence of an island, or the drying up of a river where the consequence of such events is to render the performance of the treaty impossible. Where the carrying out of the terms of the agreement becomes impossible because of the permanent destruction or disappearance of an object indispensable for the execution of the treaty, a party may validly terminate or withdraw from it. However, where the impossibility is only temporary, it may be invoked solely to suspend the operation of the treaty.

Impossibility cannot be used in this way where it arises from the breach by the party attempting to terminate or suspend the agreement of a treaty or other international obligation owed to any other party to the treaty.[177]

Fundamental change of circumstances[178]

There is a principle in customary international law that where there has been a fundamental change of circumstances since an agreement was concluded, a party to that agreement may withdraw from or terminate it. This is the doctrine of *rebus sic stantibus*. It is justified by the fact that some treaties may remain in force for long periods of time, during which fundamental changes might have occurred. Such changes might encourage one of the parties to adopt drastic measures in the face of a general refusal to accept an alteration in the terms of the treaty.

However, this doctrine has been criticised on the grounds that,

---

[175] See e.g. G. Fitzmaurice, 'General Principles of International Law Considered from the Standpoint of the Rule of Law', 92 HR, pp. 1, 125–6 and *supra*, Chapter 7, p. 258.
[176] See e.g. McNair, *Law of Treaties*, pp. 685–8 and Sinclair, 'Vienna Convention', pp. 190–2.
[177] See *Yearbook of the ILC*, 1966, vol. II, p. 256.
[178] See e.g. C. Hill, *The Doctrine of Rebus Sic Stantibus in International Law*, Leiden, 1934; O. Lissitzyn, 'Treaties and Changed Circumstances (*Rebus Sic Stantibus*)', 61 AJIL, 1967, p. 895 ; P. Cahier, 'Le Changement Fondamental de Circonstances et la Convention de Vienne de 1969 sur le Droit des Traités', *Mélanges Ago*, I, p. 163 and Vamvoukis, *Termination*, Part 1. See also *Yearbook of the ILC*, 1966, vol. II, pp. 257 *et seq.* Note the decision in *TWA Inc.* v. *Franklin Mint Corporation*, 23 ILM, 1984, pp. 814, 820, that a private person could not plead the *rebus* rule.

having regard to the absence of any system for compulsory jurisdiction in the international order, it could operate as a disrupting influence upon the binding force of obligations undertaken by states. It might be used to justify withdrawal from treaties on rather tenuous grounds.[179]

The modern approach is to admit the existence of the doctrine, but severely restrict its scope.[180] The International Court in the *Fisheries Jurisdiction* case[181] declared that:

> [i]nternational law admits that a fundamental change in the circumstances which determined the parties to accept a treaty, if it has resulted in a radical transformation of the extent of the obligations imposed by it, may, under certain conditions, afford the party affected a ground for invoking the termination or suspension of the treaty.[182]

Before the doctrine may be applied, the Court continued, it is necessary that such changes 'must have increased the burden of the obligations to be executed to the extent of rendering the performance something essentially different from that originally undertaken'.[183]

Article 62 of the Vienna Convention, which the International Court of Justice regarded in many respects as a codification of existing customary law,[184] declares that:

> 1. A fundamental change of circumstances which has occurred with regard to those existing at the time of the conclusion of a treaty, and which was not foreseen by the parties, may not be invoked as a ground for terminating or withdrawing from the treaty unless:
> (a) the existence of those circumstances constituted an essential basis of the consent of the parties to be bound by the treaty; and
> (b) the effect of the change is radically to transform the extent of obligations still to be performed under the treaty.
> 2. A fundamental change of circumstances may not be invoked as a ground for terminating or withdrawing from a treaty:
> (a) if the treaty establishes a boundary; or
> (b) if the fundamental change is the result of a breach by the party invoking it either of an obligation under the treaty or of any other international obligation owed to any other party to the treaty.

The article also notes that instead of terminating or withdrawing from a treaty in the above circumstances, a party might suspend the operation of the treaty.

---

[179] This was apparently occurring in the immediate pre-1914 period, see J. Garner, 'The Doctrine of *Rebus Sic Stantibus* and the Termination of Treaties', 21 AJIL, 1927, p. 409 and Sinclair, 'Vienna Convention', p. 193. See also G. Harastzi, 'Treaties and the Fundamental Change of Circumstances', 146 HR, p. 1.
[180] See e.g. the *Free Zones* case, PCIJ, Series A/B, No. 46, pp. 156–58; 3 ILR, pp. 362, 365.
[181] ICJ Reports, 1973, p. 3; 55 ILR, p. 183.   [182] *Ibid.*, pp. 20–1; 55 ILR, p. 200.
[183] *Ibid.*   [184] *Ibid.*

Consequences of the termination or suspension of a treaty

Article 70 provides that:

> 1. Unless the treaty otherwise provides or the parties otherwise agree, the termination of a treaty under its provisions or in accordance with the present Convention:
> (a) releases the parties from any obligation further to perform the treaty;
> (b) does not affect any right, obligation or legal situation of the parties created through the execution of the treaty prior to its termination.
> 2. If a state denounces or withdraws from a multilateral treaty, paragraph 1 applies in the relations between that state and each of the other parties to the treaty from the date when such denunciation or withdrawal takes effect.

Article 72 provides that:

> 1. Unless the treaty otherwise provides or the parties otherwise agree, the suspension of the operation of a treaty under its provisions or in accordance with the present Convention:
> (a) releases the parties between which the operation of the treaty is suspended from the obligation to perform the treaty in their mutual relations during the period of the suspension;
> (b) does not otherwise affect the legal relations between the parties established by the treaty.
> 2. During the period of the suspension the parties shall refrain from acts tending to obstruct the resumption of the operation of the treaty.[185]

Dispute settlement

Article 66 provides that if a dispute has not been resolved within twelve months by the means specified in article 33 of the UN Charter[186] then further procedures will be followed. If the dispute concerns article 53 or 64 (*jus cogens*), any one of the parties may by a written application submit it to the International Court of Justice for a decision unless the parties by common consent agree to submit the dispute to arbitration. If the dispute concerns other issues in the Convention, any one of the parties may by request to the UN Secretary-General set in motion the conciliation procedure laid down in the Annex to the Convention.

Treaties between states and international organisations[187]

The International Law Commission completed Draft Articles on the Law of Treaties between States and International Organisations or between

---

[185] See also article 65 with regard to the relevant procedures to be followed.
[186] See *infra*, Chapter 18, p. 720.
[187] See e.g. G. Gaja, 'A "New" Vienna Convention on Treaties Between States and International Organisations or Between International Organisations: A Critical

International Organisations in 1982 and the Vienna Convention on the Law of Treaties between States and International Organisations was adopted in 1986.[188] Its provisions closely follow the provisions of the 1969 Vienna Convention *mutatis mutandis*. However, article 73 of the 1986 Convention notes that 'as between states parties to the Vienna Convention on the Law of Treaties of 1969, the relations of those states under a treaty between two or more states and one or more international organisations shall be governed by that Convention'. Whether this provision affirming the superiority of the 1969 Convention for states will in practice prejudice the interests of international organisations is an open question. In any event, there is no doubt that the strong wish of the Conference adopting the 1986 Convention was for uniformity, despite arguments that the position of international organisations in certain areas of treaty law was difficult to assimilate to that of states.[189]

Special concern in the International Law Commission focused on the effects that a treaty concluded by an international organisation has upon the member states of the organisation. Article 36 *bis* of the ILC Draft[190] provided that:

> Obligations and rights arise for states members of an international organization from the provisions of a treaty to which that organization is a party when the parties to the treaty intend those provisions to be the means of establishing such obligations and according such rights and have defined their conditions and effects in the treaty or have otherwise agreed theron, and if:
> (a) the states members of the organization, by virtue of the constituent instrument of that organization or otherwise, have unanimously agreed to be bound by the said provisions of the treaty; and
> (b) the assent of the states members of the organization to be bound by the relevant provisions of the treaty has been duly brought to the knowledge of the negotiating states and negotiating organizations.

Such a situation would arise for example in the case of a customs union, which was an international organisation, normally concluding tariff agreements to which its members are not parties. Such agreements would be of little value if they were not to be immediately binding on member states.[191]

However, despite the fact that the European Community was particularly interested in the adoption of this draft article, it was rejected at the Conference.[192] It was replaced by article 74(3) of the Convention, which provides:

Commentary', 58 BYIL, 1987, p. 253 and F. Morgenstern, 'The Convention on the Law of Treaties Between States and International Organisations or Between International Organisations'; *International Law at a Time of Perplexity* (ed. Y. Dinstein), Dordrecht, 1989, p. 435.   [188] *Supra*, footnote 2.   [189] See Morgenstern, 'Convention', pp. 438–41.   [190] Described in the ILC Commentary as the article arousing the most controversy, *Yearbook of the ILC*, 1982, vol. II, Part 2, p. 43.   [191] *Ibid.*, pp. 43–4.   [192] See e.g. Gaja, '"New" Vienna Convention', p. 264.

The provisions of the present Convention shall not prejudge any question that may arise in regard to the establishment of obligations and rights for states members of an international organisation under a treaty to which that organisation is a party.

Accordingly, the situation in question would fall to be resolved on the basis of the consent of the states concerned in the specific circumstances and on a case by case basis.

The other area of difference between the 1986 and 1969 Conventions concerns the provisions for dispute settlement. Since international organisations cannot be parties to contentious proceedings before the International Court, draft article 66 provided for the compulsory arbitration of disputes concerning issues relating to the principles of *jus cogens*, with the details of the proposed arbitral tribunal contained in the Annex. The provisions of the 1969 Convention relating to the compulsory conciliation of disputes relating to the other articles were incorporated in the draft with little change. The 1986 Convention itself, however, adopted a different approach. Under article 66(2), where an international organisation authorised under article 96 of the UN Charter to request advisory opinions is a party to a dispute concerning *jus cogens*, it may apply for an advisory opinion to the International Court, which 'shall be accepted as decisive by all the parties to the dispute concerned'. If the organisation is not so authorised under article 96, it may follow the same procedure acting through a member state. If no advisory opinion is requested or the Court itself does not comply with the request, then compulsory arbitration is provided for.[193]

---

[193] Note also *supra* Chapter 14, p. 543 regarding the relationship between treaties and state responsibility. The issue of state succession to treaties is covered *infra* Chapter 17, p. 682.

STATE SUCCESSION

Political entities are not immutable. They are subject to change. New states appear and old states disappear.[1] Federations, mergers, dissolutions and secessions take place. International law has to incorporate such events into its general framework with the minimum of disruption and instability. Such changes have come to the fore since the end of the Second World War and the establishment of well over 100 new, independent countries. Difficulties may result from the change in the political sovereignty over a particular territorial entity for the purposes of international law and the world community. For instance, how far is a new state bound by the treaties and contracts entered into by the previous sovereign of the territory? Does nationality automatically devolve upon the inhabitants to replace that of the predecessor? What happens to the public property of the previous sovereign, and to what extent is the new authority liable for the debts of the old? State succession in international law cannot be confused with succession in municipal law and the transmission of property and so forth to the relevant heir. Other interests and concerns are involved and the principles of state sovereignty, equality of states and non-interference prevent a universal succession principle similar to domestic law from being adopted. Despite

---

[1] See generally, D. P. O'Connell, *State Succession in Municipal Law and International Law*, Cambridge, 2 vols., 1967; O'Connell, 'Recent Problems of State Succession in Relation to New States', 130 HR, p. 95; K. Zemanek, 'State Succession after Decolonisation', 116 HR, p. 180; O. Udokang, *Succession of New States to International Treaties*, New York, 1972; J. H. W. Verzijl, *International Law in Historical Perspective*, 1974, vol. VII: I. Brownlie, *Principles of Public International Law*, 4th edn, Oxford, 1990, Chapter 28; UN *Materials on Succession of States*, 1967 and supplement A/CN.4/263, 1972, and UN *Materials on Succession of States in Matters Other than Treaties*, 1978; International Law Association, *The Effect of Independence on Treaties*, London, 1965; Mériboute, *La Codification de la Succession d'Etats aux Traités*, 1984; S. Torres Bernardez, 'Succession of States' in *International Law: Achievements and Prospects* (ed. M. Bedjaoui), 1991, p. 381;. D. Bardonnet, *La Succession d'Etats à Madagascar*, Paris, 1970; R. Müllerson, 'The Continuity and Succession of States by Reference to the Former USSR and Yugoslavia', ICLQ, 1993, p. 473; M. Koskenniemi and M. Lehto, 'La Succession d'Etats dans l'ex-URSS', AFDI, 1992, p. 179; M. Bedjaoui, 'Problèmes récents de succession d'Etats dans les Etats nouveaux', 130 HR, 1970, p. 455; *Oppenheim's International Law*, 9th edn, (eds. R. Y. Jennings and A. D. Watts), London, vol. I, p. 208; Nguyen Quoc Dinh, P. Dailler and A. Pellet, *Droit International Public*, 5th edn, Paris, 1994, p. 512 and M. N. Shaw, 'State Succession Revisited', 5 Finnish YIL, 1994, p. 34 (upon which this revised Chapter substantially draws).

attempts to assimilate Roman law views regarding the continuity of the legal personality in the estate which falls by inheritance,[2] this approach could not be sustained in the light of state interests and practice. The opposing doctrine, which basically denied any transmission of rights, obligations and property interests between the predecessor and successor sovereigns, arose in the heyday of positivism in the nineteenth century. It manifested itself again with the rise of the decolonisation process in the form of the 'clean slate' principle, under which new states acquired sovereignty free from incumbrances created by the predecessor sovereign.

The issue of state succession can arise in a number of defined circumstances, which mirror the ways in which political sovereignty may be acquired by, for example, decolonisation of all or part of an existing territorial unit, dismemberment of an existing state, secession, annexation and merger. In each of these cases a once recognised entity disappears in whole or in part to be succeeded by some other authority, thus precipitating problems of transmission of rights and obligations. However, the question of state succession does not infringe upon the normal rights and duties of states under international law. These exist by virtue of the fundamental principles of international law and as a consequence of sovereignty and not as a result of transference from the previous sovereign. The issue of state succession should also be distinguished from questions of succession of governments, particularly revolutionary succession, and consequential patterns of recognition and responsibility.[3]

In many cases, such problems will be dealt with by treaties, whether multilateral treaties dealing with primarily territorial dispositions as for example the Treaty of St Germain, 1919, which resolved some succession questions relating to the dissolution of the Austro-Hungarian Empire,[4] or bilateral agreements as between, for instance, colonial power and new state, which, however, would not bind third states. The system of devolution agreements signed by the colonial power with the successor, newly decolonised state, was used by, for example, the UK, France and the Netherlands. Such agreements provided in general that all the rights and benefits, obligations and responsibilities devolving upon the colonial power in respect of the territory in question arising from valid international instruments, would therefore devolve upon the new state.[5] This system, however, was not seen

---

[2] See O'Connell, *State Succession*, vol. I, pp. 9 *et seq.*   [3] *Supra*, Chapters 8 and 14.
[4] See O'Connell, *State Succession*, vol. II, pp. 178–82. This treaty provided for the responsibility of the successor states of the Austro-Hungarian empire for the latter's public debts. See also the Italian Peace Treaty 1947.
[5] See e.g. the UK–Burma Agreement of 1947. See also N. Mugerwa, 'Subjects of International Law' in *Manual of Public International Law* (ed. M. Sørensen), London, 1968, pp. 247, 300–1, and *Yearbook of the ILC*, 1974, vol. II, p. 186. See also O'Connell, *State Succession*, vol. II, pp. 352–73, and Brownlie, *Principles*, p. 656.

as satisfactory by many new states and several of them resorted to unilateral declarations, providing for a transitional period during which treaties entered into by the predecessor state would continue in force and be subject to review as to which should be accepted and which rejected.[6] In the case of bilateral treaties, those not surviving under customary law would be regarded as having terminated at the end of the period.

However, the issue of state succession in international law is particularly complex. Many of the rules have developed in specific response to particular political changes and such changes have not always been treated in a consistent manner by the international community.[7] The Arbitration Commission established by the Conference on Yugoslavia, for instance, emphasised that 'there are few well-established principles of international law that apply to state succession. Application of these principles is largely to be determined case by case, though the 1978 and 1983 Vienna Conventions do offer some guidance',[8] while the German Federal Supreme Court noted in the *Espionage Prosecution* case that 'the problem of state succession is one of the most disputed areas of international law'.[9] The international aspects of succession are governed through the rules of customary international law. There are two relevant Conventions, the Vienna Convention on Succession of States in Respect of Treaties 1978 and the Vienna Convention on Succession of States in Respect of State Property, Archives and Debts 1983, but neither of them is as yet in force.[10] However, many of the provisions contained in these Conventions reflect existing international law.

State succession itself may be briefly defined as the replacement of one state by another in the responsibility for the international relations of territory.[11] However, this formulation conceals a host of problems since there is a complex range of situations that stretches from continuity of statehood through succession to non-succession. State succession is essentially an umbrella term for a phenomenon occurring upon a factual change in sovereign authority over a particular territory. In many circumstances it is

---

[6] See e.g. the Tanganyika statement of December 1961, quoted in Mugerwa, 'Subjects', p. 302, subsequently followed by similar declarations by, for example, Uganda, Kenya and Burundi. See also *Yearbook of the ILC*, 1974, vol. II, p. 192. In Zambia's case, it was stated that the question would be governed by customary international law, see O'Connell, *State Succession*, vol. II, p. 115.   [7] See Shaw 'State Succession Revisited'.

[8] Opinion No. 13, 96 ILR, pp. 726, 728. See also *Oppenheim's International Law*, p. 236 and *Third Restatement of US Foreign Relations Law*, Washington, 1987, p. 100.

[9] Case No. 2 BGz 38/91, 94 ILR, pp. 68, 77–8.

[10] As of June 1996, the 1978 Convention had twenty signatories and fourteen parties, under article 49, the Convention will come into force on the thirtieth day following the date of deposit of the fifteenth instrument of ratification or accession. The 1983 Convention had six signatories and four parties, ST/LEG/SER.E.

[11] See article 2 of both the Vienna Conventions of 1978 and 1983 and Opinion No. 1 of the Yugoslav Arbitration Commission, 92 ILR, pp. 162, 165. See also *Guinea-Bissau v. Senegal*, 83 ILR, pp. 1, 22 and the *El Salvador/Honduras* case, ICJ Reports, 1992, pp. 351, 598; 97 ILR, pp. 266, 514.

unclear as to which rights and duties will flow from one authority to the other and upon which precise basis. Much will depend upon the circumstances of the particular case, for example whether what has occurred is a merger of two states to form a new state; the absorption of one state into another, continuing state; a cession of territory from one state to another; secession of part of a state to form a new state; the dissolution or dismemberment of a state to form two or more states, or the establishment of a new state as a result of decolonisation. The role of recognition and acquiescence in this process is especially important.

Continuity and succession

Questions relating to continuity and succession may be particularly difficult. Where a new entity emerges, one has to decide whether it is a totally separate creature from its predecessor, or whether it is a continuation of it in a slightly different form. For example, it seems to be accepted that India is the same legal entity as British India and Pakistan a totally new state.[12] Yugoslavia was generally regarded as the successor state to Serbia,[13] and Israel as a completely different being from British mandated Palestine.[14] Cession or secession of territory from an existing state will not affect the continuity of the latter state, even though its territorial dimensions and population have been diminished. Pakistan after the independence of Bangladesh is a good example of this. In such a case, the existing state remains in being, complete with the rights and duties incumbent upon it, save for those specifically tied to the ceded or seceded territory. Where, however, a state is dismembered so that all of its territory falls within the territory of two or more states, these rights and duties will be allocated as between the successor states. In deciding whether continuity or succession has occurred with regard to one of the parties to the process, one has to consider the classical criteria of the creation of statehood,[15] together with assertions as to status made by the parties directly concerned and the attitudes adopted by third states and international organisations.

This issue has arisen recently with regard to events concerning the Soviet Union and Yugoslavia. In the former case, upon the demise of the USSR, the Russian Federation took the position that it was the continuation of that state.[16] This was asserted particularly with regard to membership of the

---

[12] See e.g. *Yearbook of the ILC*, 1962, vol. II, pp. 101–3.
[13] See e.g. O'Connell, *State Succession*, vol. II, pp. 378–9. See also *Artukovic* v. *Rison*, 784 F.2d 1354 (1986).   [14] O'Connell, *State Succession*, vol. II, pp. 155–7.
[15] See *supra*, Chapter 5, p. 139.
[16] See e.g. R. Müllerson, *International Law, Rights and Politics*, London, 1994, pp. 140–5 and Y. Blum, 'Russia Takes over the Soviet Union's Seat at the United Nations', 3 EJIL, 1992, p. 354.

678 INTERNATIONAL LAW

UN.[17] Of great importance was the Decision of the Council of Heads of State of the Commonwealth of Independent States on 21 December 1991 supporting Russia's continuance of the membership of the USSR in the UN, including permanent membership of the Security Council, and other international organisations.[18] Although not all of the instruments produced by the Commonwealth of Independent States at the end of 1991 were strictly consistent with the continuity principle,[19] it is clear that Russia's claim to be the continuation of the USSR (albeit within different borders of course) was supported by the other former Republics and was accepted by international practice.[20] A rather special situation arose with respect to the Baltic states (Estonia, Latvia and Lithuania), which became independent after the First World War, but which were annexed by the Soviet Union in 1940. This annexation had been refused recognition by some states[21] and accepted *de facto* but not *de jure* by some others.[22] The Baltic states declared their independence in August 1991.[23] The European Community adopted a Declaration on 27 August 1991 welcoming 'the restoration of the sovereignty and independence of the Baltic states which they lost in 1941'.[24] The United States recognised the restoration of the independence of the Baltic states on 4 September 1991.[25] The implication of this internationally accepted restoration of independence would appear to be that these states do not constitute successor states to the former USSR and would therefore be free of such rights and obligations as would be consequential upon such succession.[26]

In contrast to this situation, the issue of Yugoslavia has been more complicated and tragic. The collapse of the Socialist Federal Republic

---

[17] See 31 ILM, 1992, p. 138.   [18] *Ibid.*, p. 151.
[19] For example, the Minsk Agreement signed by Russia, Belarus and Ukraine stated that the USSR 'as a subject of international law no longer existed', while the Alma Ata Declaration, signed by all of the former Soviet Republics except for Georgia (which acceded in 1993) and the Baltic states, stated that 'with the establishment of the Commonwealth of Independent States, the Union of Soviet Socialist Republics ceases to exist', *ibid.*, pp. 147–9.
[20] See e.g. the views expressed by the Secretary of State for Foreign and Commonwealth Affairs, UKMIL, 63 BYIL, 1992, pp. 639 and 652–5 and the comments by an official of the FCO submitted to the Outer House of the Court of Session in Scotland in *Coreck Maritime GmbH* v. *Sevrybokholodflot*, UKMIL, 64 BYIL, 1993, p. 636. As to French practice recognising Russia as the continuation of the USSR, see AFDI, 1993, p. 1038. See also L. Henkin, R. C. Pugh, O. Schachter and H. Smit, *International Law Cases and Materials*, 3rd edn, St Paul, 1993, p. 539. Note that there is a distinction between the issue of continuity or succession to membership of international organisations and continuity or succession generally. However, the nature and importance of the UN is such that the question of membership of that organisation is strong evidence of continuity generally.
[21] For example the USA, see *Oppenheim's International Law*, p. 193. As to French practice, see AFDI, 1993, p. 1038 and *Gerbaud* v. *Meden*, 18 ILR, p, 288.
[22] See for example, the UK, see *A/C Tallina Laevauhisus* v. *Tallina Shipping Co.*, (1946) 79 LLR 245 and the statement of the Secretary of State for the Foreign and Commonwealth Office on 16 January 1991, HC Debs., vol. 183, col. 853.
[23] See Müllerson, *International Law*, pp. 119–20.   [24] See UKMIL, 62 BYIL, 1991, p. 558.
[25] See Müllerson, *International Law*, p. 121.   [26] See Shaw, pp. 56 *et seq.*

of Yugoslavia (the SFRY) took place over several months[27] as the various
constituent republics proclaimed independence.[28] The process was
regarded as having been completed in the view of the Arbitration
Commission on Yugoslavia[29] by the time of its Opinion No. 8 issued
on 4 July 1992.[30] The Commission noted that a referendum had been
held in Bosnia and Herzegovina in February and March 1992 producing a majority in favour of independence, while Serbia and
Montenegro had established 'a new state, the "Federal Republic of
Yugoslavia"' on 27 April 1992. The Commission noted that the common
federal bodies of the SFRY had ceased to function, while Slovenia,
Croatia and Bosnia had been recognised by the member states of the
European Community and other states and had been admitted to
membership of the UN.[31] The conclusion was that the former SFRY had
ceased to exist.[32] This was particularly reaffirmed in Opinion No. 10.[33]
Nevertheless, the Federal Republic of Yugoslavia (Serbia and
Montenegro) continued to maintain that it constituted not a new state,
but the continuation of the former SFRY. This claim was opposed by the
other former republics of the SFRY[34] and by the international community.[35] The Security Council, for example, in resolution 777 (1992)
declared that 'the state formerly known as the Socialist Federal Republic
of Yugoslavia has ceased to exist' and that 'the Federal Republic of
Yugoslavia (Serbia and Montenegro) cannot continue automatically the
membership of the former Socialist Federal Republic of Yugoslavia in the
United Nations'.[36] Thus, contrary to the experience of the demise of the
USSR, it would seem that the claim by the Federal Republic of

27 See generally M. Weller, 'The International Response to the Dissolution of the Socialist
    Federal Republic of Yugoslavia', 86 AJIL, 1992, p. 569; Y. Blum, 'UN Membership of the
    "New" Yugoslavia: Continuity or Break?', ibid., p. 830 and Müllerson, International Law,
    pp. 125 et seq.
28 Slovenia and Croatia on 25 June 1991 (postponed for three months) and Macedonia on 17
    September 1991. Bosnia and Herzegovina adopted a resolution on sovereignty on 14
    October 1991. The view taken at this point by Opinion No. 1 issued by the Arbitration
    Commission, established by the Conference on Yugoslavia convened by the European
    Community on 17 August 1991, was that 'the Socialist Federal Republic of Yugoslavia was
    in process of dissolution', 92 ILR, p. 166. See also M. Craven, 'The EC Arbitration
    Commission on Yugoslavia', 66 BYIL, 1995, p. 333.
29 Which consisted of five of the Presidents of Constitutional Courts in EC countries, chaired
    by M. Badinter.   30 92 ILR, p. 199.
31 On 22 May 1992, see General Assembly resolutions 46/236; 46/237 and 46/238. Note that
    the 'Former Yugoslav Republic of Macedonia' was admitted to the UN on 8 April 1993, see
    Security Council resolution 817 (1993).
32 92 ILR, p. 202. See also Opinion No. 9, ibid., p. 203.   33 Ibid., p. 206.
34 See e.g. E/CN.4/1995/121 and E/CN.4/1995/122.
35 Note, for example, that both the International Monetary Fund (on 15 December 1992) and
    the World Bank (on 25 February 1993) found that the former Yugoslavia had ceased to exist,
    see P. R. Williams, 'State Succession and the International Financial Institutions', 43 ICLQ,
    1994, pp. 776, 802–3.
36 See also Security Council resolution 757 (1992) and General Assembly resolution 47/1. See
    also the Genocide Convention case, ICJ Reports, 1993, pp. 3, 13–14; 95 ILR, pp. 1, 28–9.

Yugoslavia (Serbia and Montenegro)[37] to constitute the continuation of the SFRY is not sustainable.

State succession also covers the situation of unification. One method of unification is by the creation of a totally new state, such as the case of the merger of the Yemen Arab Republic and the People's Democratic Republic of Yemen. Under the agreement between the two states of 22 April 1990 the establishment of the Republic of Yemen was accomplished by way of a merger of the two existing states into a new entity with a new name.[38] Unification may also be achieved by the absorption of one state by another in circumstances where the former simply disappears and the latter continues, albeit with increased territory and population. Such was the case with Germany.

Following the conclusion of the Second World War, Germany was divided into the US, USSR, UK and French zones of occupation and a special Berlin area not forming part of any zone.[39] Supreme authority was exercised initially by the Commanders-in-Chief of the Armed Forces of the Four Allied Powers[40] and subsequently by the three Allied High Commissioners in Bonn, with parallel developments occurring in the Soviet zone. The Convention on Relations between the Three Powers and the Federal Republic of Germany (FRG), which came into force in 1955, terminated the occupation regime and abolished the Allied High Commission. The Three Allied Powers retained, however, their rights and obligations with regard to Berlin[41] and relating to 'Germany as a whole, including the reunification of Germany and a peace settlement'.[42] Recognition of the German Democratic Republic (GDR) was on the same basis, i.e. as a sovereign state having full authority over internal and external affairs subject to the rights and responsibilities of the Four Powers in respect of Berlin and Germany as a whole.[43] Accordingly, it was accepted that in some sense Germany as a whole continued to exist as a state in international law.[44] The question of the

---

[37] Now simply termed the Federal Republic of Yugoslavia, see for example the Dayton Peace Agreement of 21 November 1995.

[38] Article 1 of the Agreement declared that 'there shall be established between the State of the Yemen Arab Republic and the State of the People's Democratic Republic of Yemen ... a full and complete union, based on a merger, in which the international personality of each of them shall be integrated in a single international person called "the Republic of Yemen"', see 30 ILM, 1991, p. 820.

[39] See e.g. the *Fourth Report of the Foreign Affairs Committee, Session 1989–90*, June 1990. Note that part of the Soviet Zone was placed under Soviet administration (the city of Königsberg, now Kaliningrad and the surrounding area) and the territory of Germany east of the Oder-Neisse line was placed under Polish administration.

[40] Article 2 of the Agreement on Control Machinery in Germany of 14 November 1944, as amended by the Agreement of 1 May 1945.

[41] See in particular I. Hendry and M. Wood, *The Legal Status of Berlin*, Cambridge, 1987. See also Cmd. 8571, 1952 and the Quadripartite Agreement on Berlin, Cmnd. 5135, 1971.

[42] Article 2 of the Relations Convention. Parallel developments took place in the Soviet zone. Note the USSR–German Democratic Republic Treaty of 1955.

[43] See the Fourth Report, p. 2.   [44] *Ibid.*, p. 3.

relationship of the two German states to each other and with respect to the pre-1945 German state has occasioned considerable interest and generated no little complexity, not least because the Federal German Republic always claimed to be the successor of pre-1945 Germany.[45] On 18 May 1990 a treaty between the two German states was signed establishing a Monetary, Economic and Social Union. In essence this integrated the GDR into the FRG economic system, with the Deutsche Mark becoming legal tender in the GDR and with the Bundesbank becoming the central bank for the GDR as well as for the FRG.[46] On 31 August 1990, a second treaty was signed between the two German states which provided for unification on 3 October 1990 by the accession of the GDR under article 23 of the Basic Law of the Federal Republic. On 12 September 1990 the Treaty on the Final Settlement With Respect to Germany was signed by the two German states and the Four Allied Powers.[47] This latter agreement settled definitively matters arising out of the Second World War. It confirmed the borders of unified Germany as those of the FRG and the GDR (i.e. the post-war Oder-Neisse frontier with Poland), provided for a reduction in the armed forces of Germany and for the withdrawal of Soviet forces from the territory of the GDR. The Four Allied Powers terminated their rights and responsibilities regarding Berlin and Germany as a whole so that the united Germany has full sovereignty over its internal and external affairs.[48]

The Treaty Between the Federal Republic of Germany and the German Democratic Republic of 31 August 1990 clearly provided that the latter was simply assimilated into the former. Article 1 of the Treaty stipulated that 'upon the accession of the German Democratic Republic to the Federal Republic of Germany in accordance with article 23 of the Basic Law[49] taking effect on 3 October 1990, the Länder of Brandenburg, Mecklenburg-Western Pomerania, Saxony, Saxony-Anhalt and Thuringia[50] shall become Länder of the Federal Republic of Germany'. This approach, whereby

---

[45] See e.g. Brownlie, *Principles*, pp. 81, 84–5; M. Whiteman, *Digest of International Law*, Washington, vol. I, pp. 332–8 and F. A. Mann, 'Germany's Present Legal State Revisited', 16 ICLQ, 1967, p. 760. See also the decision of the Federal Constitutional Court of the Federal Republic of Germany in *Re Treaty on the Basis of Relations Between the Federal Republic of Germany and the German Democratic Republic 1972*, 78 ILR, p. 149.
[46] See 29 ILM, 1990, p. 1108.   [47] See 29 ILM, 1990, p. 1186.
[48] Note that by the Declaration of 1 October 1990, the Allied Powers suspended all rights and responsibilities relating to Berlin and to Germany as a whole upon the unification of Germany, pending the entry into force of the Treaty on the Final Settlement, see Annex 2 of the Observations by the Government to the Fourth Report, October 1990, Cm. 1246.
[49] This provided that the Basic Law was to apply in Greater Berlin and specified *Länder* (forming the Federal Republic of Germany), while 'in other parts of Germany it shall be put into force on their accession'. This method had been used to achieve the accession of the Saarland in 1956.
[50] I.e. the constituent provinces of the German Democratic Republic.

unified Germany came about by a process of absorption of the constituent provinces of the former German Democratic Republic into the existing Federal Republic of Germany by way of the extension of the constitution of the latter is reinforced by other provisions in the Unification Treaty. Article 7, for example, provided that the financial system of the FRG 'shall be extended to the territory specified in article 3' (i.e. the Länder of the former GDR), while article 8 declares that 'upon the accession taking effect, federal law shall enter into force in the territory specified in article 3'.[51] International practice also demonstrates acceptance of this approach.[52] No state objected to this characterisation of the process.[53] In other words, the view taken by the parties directly concerned and accepted by the international community demonstrates acceptance of the unification as one of the continuity of the Federal Republic of Germany and the disappearance or extinction of the German Democratic Republic.

Succession to treaties[54]

The importance of treaties within the international legal system requires no repetition.[55] They constitute the means by which a variety of legal obligations are imposed or rights conferred upon states in a wide range of matters from the significant to the mundane. Treaties are founded upon the pre-existing and indispensable norm of *pacta sunt servanda* or the acceptance of treaty commitments as binding. Treaties may fall within the following categories: multilateral treaties, including the specific category of treaties concerning international human rights; treaties concerned with territorial definition and regimes; bilateral treaties and treaties that are treated as 'political' in the circumstances.

The rules concerning succession to treaties are those of customary international law, but one needs also to consider the provisions of the Vienna Convention on Succession of States in Respect of Treaties 1978, which is at

[51] Note also that under article 11, treaties entered into by the Federal Republic of Germany would continue and extend to the *Länder* of the former German Democratic Republic, while under article 12, the question of the continuation, amendment or expiry of treaties entered into by the former German Democratic Republic was to be discussed individually with contracting parties, see *infra*, p. 687.

[52] Such as the European Community. See for example, GATT document L/6759 of 31 October 1990 in which the Commission of the European Community stated that Germany had become united by way of the accession of the GDR to the FRG. See also T. Oeter, 'German Unification and State Succession', 51 *ZaöRV*, 1991, p. 349 and J. Frowein, 'Germany Reunited', *ibid.*, p. 333. [53] See also *Oppenheim's International Law*, p. 210.

[54] Note particularly the work of the International Law Commission on this topic, see *Yearbook of the International Law Commission*, 1974, vol. II, part 1, pp. 157 *et seq.* and the five Reports of Sir Humphrey Waldock (*ibid.*, 1968, vol. II, p. 88; 1969 vol. II, p. 45; 1970, vol. II, p. 25; 1971, vol. II, part 1, p. 143 and 1972, vol. II, p. 1) and the Report of Sir Francis Vallat (*ibid.*, 1974 vol. II, part 1, p. 1). See also the International Law Association, *The Effect of Independence on Treaties*, London, 1965. [55] See *supra*, Chapter 16.

the date of writing not yet in force. Although this Convention would apply only with regard to a succession taking place after the coming into effect of the Convention (article 7), consideration of some of its provisions is warranted, not least because such provisions contained in it as reflect either customary law or treaty law in force for the particular state in question would be independently binding.[56]

As far as devolution agreements are concerned, article 8 of the Convention provides that such agreements of themselves cannot affect third states and this reaffirms accepted principle, while article 9, dealing with unilateral declarations, emphasises that such a declaration by the successor state alone cannot of itself affect the rights and obligations of the state and third states. In other words, it would appear, the consent of the other parties to the treaties in question or an agreement with the predecessor state with regard to bilateral issues is required.

Categories of treaties: territorial, political and other treaties

Treaties may for succession purposes be generally divided into three categories. The first relates to territorially grounded treaties, under which rights or obligations are imposed directly upon identifiable territorial units. The prime example of these are agreements relating to territorial definition. Waldock in his first Report on Succession of States and Governments in Respect of Treaties in 1968 declared that 'the weight both of opinion and practice seems clearly to be in favour of the view that boundaries established by treaties remain untouched by the mere fact of a succession. The opinion of jurists seems, indeed, to be unanimous on the point . . . [and] State practice in favour of the continuance in force of boundaries established by treaty appears to be such as to justify the conclusion that a general rule of international law exists to that effect',[57] while Bedjaoui has noted that 'in principle the territory devolves upon the successor State on the basis of the pre-existing boundaries'.[58]

For reasons relating to the maintenance of international stability, this approach has been clearly supported by state practice. The Latin American concept of *uti possidetis juris*, whereby the administrative divisions of the former Spanish Empire were to constitute the boundaries of the newly independent states in South America in the first third of the last century was the first internationally accepted expression of this approach.[59] It was echoed in

---

[56] See articles 3 and 5.
[57] *Yearbook of the International Law Commission*, 1968, vol. II, pp. 92–3. [58] *Ibid.*, p. 112.
[59] See for example the *Colombia–Venezuela* arbitral award, 1 RIAA, pp. 223, 228 and the *Beagle Channel* award, 52 ILR, p. 93. See also A. O. Cukwurah, *The Settlement of Boundary Disputes in International Law*, Manchester, 1967, p. 114; O'Connell, *State Succession*, vol. II, pp. 273 *et seq.* and P. De La Pradelle, *La Frontière*, Paris, 1928, pp. 86–7.

US practice[60] and explicitly laid down in resolution 16 of the meeting of
Heads of State and Government of the Organisation of African Unity 1964,
by which all member states pledged themselves to respect colonial borders.[61]
The principle of succession to colonial borders was underlined by the
International Court in the *Burkina Faso/Mali* case, where it was noted that
the principle of *uti possidetis* had developed into a general concept of contemporary customary international law.[62] This is reinforced in slightly
different circumstances by the Arbitration Commission on Yugoslavia,
which noted in Opinion No. 3 with respect to the status of the former internal boundaries between Serbia on the one hand and Croatia and Bosnia-
Herzegovina on the other, that 'except where otherwise agreed, the former
boundaries become frontiers protected by international law. This conclusion follows from the principle of respect for the territorial status quo and
in particular, from the principle of *uti possidetis*. *Uti possidetis* . . . is today
recognised as a general principle.'[63] The extension of the principle of *uti possidetis* from decolonisation to the creation of new states out of existing independent states is significant and supported by international practice. It
therefore takes effect as the transformation of administrative boundaries
into international boundaries generally.[64] Of course, much will depend
upon the particular situation, including the claims of the states concerned
and the attitude adopted by third states and international organisations, particularly the United Nations. This principle regarding the continuity of
borders in the absence of consent to the contrary is reinforced by other principles of international law, such as the provision enshrined in article 62 (2)
of the Vienna Convention on the Law of Treaties, which stipulates that a
fundamental change in circumstances may not be invoked as a ground for
terminating or withdrawing from a treaty that establishes a boundary.[65] In
addition, article 11 of the Vienna Convention on Succession to Treaties,
although in terminology which is cautious and negative, specifies that 'A
succession of States does not as such affect: (a) a boundary established by

[60] See the view of the US Secretary of State in 1856 that the US regarded it 'as an established
principle of the public law and of international right that when a European colony in
America becomes independent it succeeds to the territorial limits of the colony as it stood
in the hands of the present country', Manning's *Diplomatic Correspondence*, vol. III (Great
Britain), doc. 2767, cited in Cukwurah, *Settlement*, p. 106.
[61] See for example M. N. Shaw, *Title to Territory in Africa: International Legal Issues*, Oxford,
1986, pp. 185–7.   [62] ICJ Reports, 1986, pp. 554, 565; 80 ILR, pp. 440, 469–70.
[63] 92 ILR, pp. 170, 171. The Opinion refers specifically to the *Burkina Faso/Mali* case here.
[64] See also article 5 of the Minsk Agreement establishing the Commonwealth of Independent
States of 8 December 1991 and the Alma Ata Declaration of 21 December 1991, which
reaffirmed the territorial integrity of the former Republics of the USSR. Note also that
under the Treaty on the General Delimitation of the Common State Frontiers of 29 October
1992, the boundary between the two new states of the Czech Republic and Slovakia, emerging out of Czechoslovakia on 1 January 1993, was to be that of the administrative border
existing between the Czech and Slovak parts of the former state. See further *supra* Chapter
9, p. 356.   [65] See *supra*, Chapter 16, p. 670.

treaty; or (b) obligations and rights established by a treaty and relating to the regime of a boundary.'

The International Court dealt with succession to boundary treaties generally in the *Libya/Chad* case, where it was declared that 'once agreed, the boundary stands, for any other approach would vitiate the fundamental principle of the stability of boundaries, the importance of which has been repeatedly emphasised by the Court'.[66] More particularly, the Court emphasised that 'a boundary established by treaty thus achieves a permanence which the treaty itself does not necessarily enjoy. The treaty can cease to be in force without in any way affecting the continuance of the boundary . . . when a boundary has been the subject of agreement, the continued existence of that boundary is not dependent upon the continuing life of the treaty under which the boundary is agreed.'[67] It is particularly important to underline that the succession takes place, therefore, not as such to the boundary treaty but rather to the boundary as established by the treaty.

Territorially grounded treaties extend somewhat beyond the establishment of boundaries into the more controversial area of agreements creating other territorial regimes, such agreements being termed 'localised' or 'real' or 'dispositive'.[68] Examples of such arrangements might include demilitarised zones, rights of transit, port facilities and other servitudes generally.[69] Despite some reservations by members of the International Law Commission[70] and governments,[71] article 12 of the Vienna Convention provides that a succession of states does not as such affect obligations or rights relating to the use of any territory or to restrictions upon its use established by a treaty for the benefit of any foreign state, group of states or all states and considered as attaching to the territory in question.

Political or 'personal' treaties establish rights or obligations deemed to be particularly linked to the regime in power in the territory in question and to its political orientation. Examples of such treaties would include treaties of alliance or friendship or neutrality.[72] Such treaties do not bind successor states for they are seen as exceptionally closely tied to the nature of the state

---

[66] ICJ Reports, 1994, pp. 6, 37: 100 ILR, pp. 1, 36.   [67] *Ibid.*
[68] See O'Connell, *State Succession,* vol. II, pp. 231 *et seq.* See also Udokang, *Succession,* pp. 327 *et seq.*
[69] See Shaw, *Title to Territory,* pp. 244–8. See also the *Free Zones* case, PCIJ, Series A/B, No. 46, 1932, p. 145; 6 ILR, pp. 362, 364 and the *Aaland Islands* case, LNOJ, Sp. Suppl. No. 3, 1920, p. 18. See *supra,* Chapter 9, p. 366 and *Yearbook of the ILC,* 1974, vol. II, pp. 157 and 196 *et seq.* Note, that by article 12(3), the provisions of article 12 do not apply to treaties providing for the establishment of foreign military bases on the territory concerned. See further Brownlie, *Principles,* p. 669 and O'Connell, *State Succession,* vol. II, pp. 12–23 and pp. 231 *et seq.*
[70] See for example *Yearbook of the International Law Commission,* 1974, vol. I, pp. 206–7.
[71] See for example *UN Conference on Succession of States in Respect of Treaties,* 1977, Comments of Governments (A/Conf.80/5) pp. 145, 153, 161, 167, 170, 171 and 173.
[72] See for example, O'Connell, *State Succession,* vol. II, pp. 2, 80 and 136 and *Oppenheim's International Law,* p. 211.

which has ceased to exist. However, it is not at all clear what the outer limits are to the concept of political treaties and difficulties over definitional problems do exist. Apart from the categories of territorial and political treaties, where succession rules in general are clear, other treaties can not be so easily defined or categorised for succession purposes and must be analysed separately.

Succession to treaties generally

Practice seems to suggest 'a tendency'[73] or 'a general inclination'[74] to succession to 'some categories of multilateral treaties'[75] or to 'certain multilateral conventions'.[76] However, this 'modern-classical' approach is difficult to sustain as a general rule of comprehensive applicability.[77] One simply has to examine particular factual situations, take note of the claims made by the relevant states and mark the reactions of third states. In the case of bilateral treaties, the starting-point is from a rather different perspective. In such cases, the importance of the individual contractual party is more evident, since only two states are involved and the treaty is thus more clearly reciprocal in nature. Accordingly, the presumption is one of non-succession, depending upon all the particular circumstances of the case. Practice with regard to the US, Panama, Belgium and Finland supports the 'clean slate' approach.[78]

(a) Absorption and merger

Where one state is absorbed by another and no new state is created (such as the 1990 accession to the Federal Republic of Germany of the *Länder* of the German Democratic Republic), the former becomes extinct whereas the latter simply continues albeit in an enlarged form. The basic situation is that the treaties of the former certainly in so far as they may be deemed 'political'[79] die with the state concerned,[80] although territorial treaties defining the boundaries of the entity absorbed will continue to define such boundaries. Other treaties are also likely to be regarded as at an end.[81] However, treaties of the absorbing state continue and will extend to the territory of the extinguished state. These principles are, of course, subject to contrary intention

[73] O'Connell, *State Succession*, vol. II, p. 212.   [74] Udokang, p. 225.
[75] O'Connell, *State Succession*, vol. II, p. 213.   [76] Udokang, *Succession*, p. 225.
[77] But see Jenks' view that multilateral law-making treaties devolve upon successor states, 'State Succession in Respect of Law-making Treaties', 29 BYIL, 1952, pp. 105, 108–10.
[78] See for example Udokang, *Succession*, pp. 412–15.
[79] See here for example *Oppenheim's International Law*, p. 211; Oeter, 'German Unification', p. 363 and Koskenniemi and Lehto, 'La Succession', p. 203.
[80] *Oppenheim's International Law*, p. 211.   [81] *Ibid.*, pp. 212–13.

expressed by the parties in question. For example, in the case of German unification, article 11 coupled with Annex I of the Unification Treaty 1990 excluded from the extension of treaties of the Federal Republic of Germany to the territory of the former German Democratic Republic a series of treaties dealing primarily with NATO matters.

Article 31(1) of the Vienna Convention on Succession to Treaties provides that where two or more states unite and form one successor state, treaties continue in force unless the successor state and the other state party or states parties otherwise agree or it appears that this would be incompatible with the object and purpose of the treaty or would radically change the conditions for its operation. Article 31(2) provides that such treaties would apply only in respect of the part of the territory of the successor state in respect of which the treaty was in force at the date of the succession of states. This is so unless the successor state makes a notification that the multilateral treaty in question shall apply in respect of its entire territory[82] or, if the multilateral treaty in question is one in which by virtue either of its terms or by reason of the limited number of participants and its object and purpose the participation of any other state must be considered as requiring the consent of all the parties,[83] the successor state and the other states parties otherwise agree. This general principle would apply also in the case of a bilateral treaty, unless the successor state and the other state party otherwise agree.[84]

While these provisions bear some logic with regard to the situation where two states unite to form a new third state,[85] they do not really take into account the special circumstances of unification where one state simply takes over another state in circumstances where the latter is extinguished. In these situations, the model provided by German unification appears to be fully consistent with international law and of value as a precedent. Article 11 of the Unification Treaty of 31 August provided that all international treaties and agreements to which the FRG was a contracting party were to retain their validity and that the rights and obligations arising therefrom would apply also to the territory of the GDR.[86] Article 12 provided that

---

[82] Unless it appears from the treaty or is otherwise established that the application of the treaty in respect of the entire territory of the successor state would be incompatible with the object and purpose of the treaty or would radically change the conditions for its operation (article 31(3)).   [83] Article 17(3).

[84] See the examples of the union of Egypt and Syria to form the United Arab Republic between 1958 and 1961 and the union of Tanganyika and Zanzibar in 1964, where the treaties of the component territories continued in force within those territorial limits, see O'Connell, *State Succession*, vol. II, pp. 71–8. The article 31 situation has to be distinguished from the situation involving a 'newly independent state', see article 29 and *infra* p. 692, and from the article 15 situation, where part of the territory of one state is transferred to another state, *infra* p. 688.

[85] But see *supra* p. 683 with regard to boundary treaties and *infra* p. 695 regarding human rights treaties.

[86] However, as noted, Annex I to the Treaty provided that certain listed treaties are not to apply to the territory of the former GDR. These treaties relate in essence to NATO activities.

international treaties of the GDR were to be discussed with the parties concerned with a view to regulating or confirming their continued application, adjustment or expiry, taking into account protection of confidence, the interests of the state concerned, the treaty obligations of the FRG as well as the principles of a free, democratic order governed by the rule of law, and respecting the competence of the European Communities. The united Germany would then determine its position after such consultations. It was also stipulated that should the united Germany intend to accede to international organisations or other multilateral treaties of which the GDR, but not the FRG, was a member, agreement was to be reached with the respective contracting parties and the European Communities, where the competence of the latter was affected. The situation thus differs from the scenario envisaged in article 31 of the 1978 treaty.[87]

In the case of mergers to form a new third state, the formulation in article 31 is more relevant and acceptable. Practice appears to support that approach. For example, in the cases of both the Egypt–Syria merger to form the United Arab Republic in 1958[88] and the union of Tanganyika and Zanzibar to form Tanzania in 1964,[89] the continuation of treaties in the territories to which they had applied before the respective mergers was stipulated.

(b) Cession of territory from one state to another

When part of the territory of one state becomes part of the territory of another state, the general rule is that the treaties of the former cease to apply to the territory while the treaties of the latter extend to the territory. Article 15 of the Vienna Convention on Succession of States to Treaties, dealing with this 'moving-frontiers' rule,[90] provides for this, with the proviso that where it appears from the treaty concerned or is otherwise established that the application of the treaty to the territory would be incompatible with the object and purpose of the treaty or would radically change the condition for its operation, this extension should not happen. This is basically consistent with state practice. When, for example, the US annexed Hawaii in 1898, its treaties were extended to the islands and Belgium was informed that US–Belgium commercial agreements were thenceforth to be applied to Hawaii also,[91] similarly it was held that after 1919, German treaties would

---

[87] It should also be noted that the *Third Restatement of US Foreign Relations Law*, Washington, 1987, p. 108, provides that 'when a state is absorbed by another state, the international agreements of the absorbed state are terminated and the international agreements of the absorbing state become applicable to the territory of the absorbed state'
[88] See O'Connell, *State Succession*, vol. II, pp. 71 et seq and D. Cottran, 'Some Legal Aspects of the Formation of the United Arab Republic and the United Arab States', 8 ICLQ, 1959, p. 346.   [89] See O'Connell, *State Succession*, vol. II, pp. 77 *et seq.*
[90] *Yearbook of the ILC*, 1974, vol. II, p. 208.
[91] See e.g. O'Connell, *State Succession*, vol. II, pp. 377–8.

not apply to Alsace-Lorraine, while French treaties would thereafter be extended to that territory.[92] Article 15 would therefore seem to reiterate existing custom,[93] although there have been indications to the contrary in the past.[94]

(c) Secession from an existing state to form a new state or states

The factual situations out of which a separation or dismemberment takes place are many and varied. They range from a break-up of a previously created entity into its previous constituent elements, as in the 1961 dissolution of the United Arab Republic into the pre-1958 states of Egypt and Syria or the dissolution of the Federation of Mali, to the complete fragmenting of a state into a variety of successors not being co-terminous with previous territorial units, such as the demise of Austria-Hungary in 1919.[95] Where there is a separation or secession from an independent state which continues, in order to create a new state, the former continues as a state, albeit territorially reduced, with its international rights and obligations intact.[96] With regard to the seceding territory itself, the leading view appears to be that the newly created state will commence international life free from the treaty rights and obligations applicable to its former sovereign.[97] Reasons for this include the important point that it is difficult to maintain as a rule of general application that states that have not signed particular treaties are bound by them.

State practice has essentially reinforced the basic proposition. When Belgium seceded from the Netherlands in 1830, it was deemed to start international life with 'a clean slate' and the same approach was adopted with regard to the secession of Cuba from Spain in 1898 and that of Panama from Colombia in 1903. Similarly, when Finland seceded from the Russian Empire after the First World War, the view taken by the UK and the US was that Finland was not bound by the existing Russian treaties dealing with the territory.[98]

---

[92] *Ibid.*, p. 379.
[93] The exception to the 'moving treaty-frontiers' rule reflects the concept that 'political treaties' would not pass, *ibid.*, p. 25. See further *supra*, p. 680 with regard to the reunification of Germany 1990. See also article IX of Annex 1 of the Anglo-Chinese Agreement 1984 on Hong Kong, *infra*, p. 715.
[94] See for example O'Connell, *State Succession*, vol. II, pp. 374 *et seq.*
[95] See O'Connell, *State Succession*, vol. II, Chapter 10.
[96] Save, of course, with regard to those that relate solely to the seceding territory.
[97] See O'Connell, *State Succession*, vol. II, pp. 88 *et seq* and *Oppenheim's International Law*, p. 222. See also the *Third Restatement of US Foreign Relations Law*, p. 108, which provides that 'When part of a state becomes a new state, the new state does not succeed to the international agreements to which the predecessor state was party, unless, expressly or by implication, it accepts such agreements and the other party or parties thereto agree or acquiesce.'
[98] *Yearbook of the International Law Commission*, 1974, vol. II, part 1, p. 263. See also O'Connell, *State Succession*, vol. II, pp. 96–100 and *Oppenheim's International Law*, at p. 222. See also *Yearbook of the International Law Commission*, 1974, vol. II, Part 1, pp. 265–6 and Brownlie, *Principles*, p. 668.

While essentially this is the position taken by the Vienna Convention on Succession to Treaties with regard to decolonised territories (discussed in the following subsection), article 34 provides that 'any treaty in force at the date of the succession of states in respect of the entire territory of the predecessor state continues in force in respect of each successor state so formed'. Any treaty which applied only to part of the territory of the predecessor state which has become a successor state will continue in force in respect of the latter only. These provisions will not apply if the states concerned otherwise agree or if it appears from the treaty or is otherwise established that the application of the treaty in respect of the successor state would be incompatible with the object and purpose of the treaty or would radically change the conditions for its operation.[99] The general principle in article 34 of succession to treaties of the predecessor state is by no means supported universally by state practice and it will be interesting to note how future dissolutions will be treated. As far as the predecessor state is concerned in such a situation (assuming the predecessor state remains in existence), article 35 provides that existing treaties remain in force after the succession in respect of the remaining territory, unless the parties otherwise agree or it is established that the treaty related only to the territory which has separated from the predecessor state or it appears from the treaty or is otherwise established that the application of the treaty in respect of the predecessor state would be incompatible with the object and purpose of the treaty or would radically change the conditions for its operation.

The approach in the Vienna Convention was adopted on the basis of the International Law Commission draft which had taken the position that 'in modern international law having regard to the need for the maintenance of the system of multilateral treaties and of the stability of treaty relationships, as a general rule the principle of *de jure* continuity should apply'.[100] This may have been an attempt to distinguish decolonised territories (termed 'newly independent States' in the Convention) from other examples of independence, but it constitutes a rather different approach than the traditional one and the formulation in article 34 cannot be taken as reflective of customary law.

What can be said is that the requirements of international stability in certain areas in particular will stimulate states generally to encourage an approach of succession to multilateral obligations by the newly independent secessionist states. The Guidelines on Recognition of New States in Eastern Europe and the Soviet Union adopted by the European Community on 16 December 1991 certainly noted that the common position of EC member states on recognition required *inter alia* 'acceptance of all relevant commit-

---

[99] See *Yearbook of the ILC*, 1974, vol. II, pp. 260 *et seq.*
[100] *Yearbook of the International Law Commission*, 1974, vol. II, Part 1, p. 169.

ments with regard to disarmament and nuclear non-proliferation as well as to security and regional stability'.[101] But, of course, conditions attached to the essentially political process of recognition are not the same as accepting consequences arising out of succession itself. However, there were certainly indications that the United States was taking the position that Russia and the non-Baltic successor states to the USSR should be regarded as bound by some at least of the Soviet treaties.[102] This approach was clearly developed in view of the political need to ensure continuity with regard to arms control agreements and mechanisms.[103] Of course, the impact of Russia constituting the continuance of the Soviet Union is to maintain in force for the former the obligations of the latter, but there was concern about the control of the nuclear and other weapons subject to treaty regulation which were now situated in the successor states to the USSR. The signing of agreements with the major successor states appears to have mitigated the strength of this particular approach. Indeed, it should be noted that separate agreements with the nuclear successor states of Ukraine, Belarus and Kazakhstan were apparently required in order to ensure the compliance of those states with regard to the arms control treaties binding upon the Soviet Union,[104] although these states had agreed generally to be bound by international obligations deriving from treaties signed by the USSR.[105] The US and Ukraine agreed by an exchange of notes on 10 May 1995 that in so far as bilateral treaties between them were concerned, article 34 of the Convention would be taken as 'a point of departure'. A treaty-by-treaty review by the two states was conducted as a result of which it was decided that some treaties had become obsolete, others would not be applied, and others, specifically listed in the Annex to the note were to be regarded as still in force.[106]

Whether in view of the greatly increased network of multilateral treaties, and the vastly enhanced interdependence of states founded and manifested upon such agreement, it is possible to say that the international community is moving towards a position of a presumption of continuity is in reality

---

[101] See 92 ILR, pp. 173–4.
[102] See for example T. Love, 'International Agreement Obligations after the Soviet Union's Break-up: Current United States Practice and its Consistency with International Law', 26 *Vanderbilt Journal of Transnational Law*, 1993, pp. 373, 396. The author notes that the US practice of arguing that treaties are binding upon the republics (apart from the special case of Russia) is inconsistent with the views expressed in the US Restatement, *ibid.*, p. 410. The views of the US Restatement are referred to *supra* p. 689.   [103] *Ibid.*, at pp. 398–401.
[104] See 'US–CIS Protocol to START Treaty', 86 AJIL, 1992, p. 799. See also the Agreement on Joint Measures with Respect to Nuclear Weapons, 31 ILM, 1992, p. 152 and Müllerson, *International Law*, pp. 150–2.
[105] Alma Ata Declaration, 21 December 1991, 21 ILM, 1992, pp. 148, 149.
[106] See 89 AJIL, 1995, p. 761. The note specifically excluded matters concerning succession to USA–USSR bilateral arms limitation and related agreements, with regard to which special mechanisms had been established.

difficult to establish. Certainly the potentially disruptive effect of the creation of new states needs to be minimised, but it is far too early to be able to
declare that continuity or a presumption of continuity is now the established
norm.

(d) 'Newly independent states'

The post-Second World War period saw the dismantling of the overseas
European empires. Based in international legal terms by the principle of
self-determination, which was founded upon a distinction between such territories and the metropolitan authority, decolonisation produced a number
of changes in the international legal system.[107]

The Vienna Convention on Succession to Treaties sought to establish a
special category relating to decolonised territories. These were termed
'newly independent States' and defined in article 2(1) f as successor states
'the territory of which immediately before the date of the succession of states
was a dependent territory for the international relations of which the predecessor state was responsible'.[108] Article 16 laid down the general rule that
such states were not bound to maintain in force or to become a party to any
treaty by reason only of the fact that the treaty had been in force regarding
the territory in question at the date of succession. This approach was
deemed to build upon the traditional 'clean slate' principle applying to new
states created out of existing states, such as the United States and the
Spanish American Republics when they had obtained independence.[109]
This was also consistent with the view taken by the UN Secretariat in 1947
when discussing Pakistan's position in relation to the organisation, where it
was noted that 'the territory which breaks off, Pakistan, will be a new state;
it will not have the treaty rights and obligations of the old state'.[110]

It should be noted that the provision dealing with bilateral treaties was
more vigorously worded, no doubt because the personal and reciprocal
nature of such treaties is that more obvious, or in the words of the
International Law Commission 'dominant' and also because unlike the case
of multilateral treaties, there is no question of the treaty coming into force
between the new state and the predecessor state.[111] While state practice
demonstrates some continuity in areas such as air services agreements and
trade agreements, the Commission felt that this did not reflect a customary
rule, as distinct from the will of the states concerned, and that the funda-

---

[107] See *supra*, Chapter 5, p. 177.
[108] See also the Vienna Convention on Succession to State Property, Archives and Debt 1983,
article 2(1)e.
[109] See *Yearbook of the International Law Commission*, 1974, vol. II, part 1, p. 211.   [110] *Ibid.*
[111] *Yearbook of the International Law Commission*, 1974, vol. II, part 1 , p. 237.

mental rule with regard to bilateral treaties was that their continuance in force after independence was a matter for agreement, express or tacit, between the newly independent state and the other state party which had contracted with the predecessor state.[112] Article 24 notes that a bilateral treaty in force for the territory in question is considered to be in force for the newly independent state and the other state party where they expressly so agree or by reason of their conduct they are to be considered as having so agreed.[113]

There is, of course, a distinction between a new state being obliged to become a party to a treaty binding the predecessor state and having the facility or perhaps even the right to become a party to that treaty. Practice shows that new states may benefit from a 'fast track' method of participating in treaties. For example, new states are not required to adhere to the formal mechanism of accession as if they were existing non-party states[114] and article 17 of the Vienna Convention provides that a 'newly independent state' may by a notification of succession establish its status as a party to a multilateral treaty which at the date of succession was in force in respect of the territory to which the succession relates, unless it appears from the treaty or is otherwise established that the application of the treaty in respect of the newly independent state would be incompatible with the object and purpose of the treaty or would radically change the conditions of its operation. In addition, where it appears from the nature of the treaty itself that the participation of any other state would require the consent of all the parties, such consent must be forthcoming for the new state to participate.[115]

The 'clean slate' principle has also in practice been mitigated by the terms of the process by which many colonies achieved independence. A number of colonial powers, particularly the United Kingdom, adopted the practice of concluding devolution agreements by which certain treaties signed on behalf of the territory becoming independent continued to apply to the newly independent state.[116] While such agreements would be considered *res inter alios* with regard to third states, they were of value in establishing the appropriate framework for relations between the former colonial power and the new state. Other newly independent states adopted the practice of making unilateral declarations by which they made known their views as to

<hr>

[112] *Ibid.*, pp. 237–9.
[113] The above rules also apply to newly independent states (as defined in the Convention) formed from two or more territories, see article 30 (referring to articles 16–29). Where a treaty affects one or more but not all of the territories in question, there is a presumption that on succession it will apply to the newly independent state, *ibid.* See also *Re Bottali*, 78 ILR, p. 105 and *M v. Federal Department of Justice and Police*, 75 ILR, p. 107.
[114] See *Oppenheim's International Law*, p. 229.   [115] Article 17(3). See also article 27(2).
[116] See for example O'Connell, *State Succession*, vol. II, pp. 352 *et seq.* and *Yearbook of the International Law Commission*, 1974, vol. II, part 1, pp. 182–7. See also article 8 of the Vienna Convention.

treaty succession. Such unilateral declarations often took the form of specifying that treaties would continue in force for an interim period during
which time they would be reviewed,[117] but they could not in themselves, of
course, alter treaty relationships with third states.[118] Devices such as devolution agreements and unilateral declarations were of value, however, in mitigating the effects that an absolute 'clean slate' approach might otherwise
have had.

(e) Dissolution of states

Where an existing state comes to an end as an international person and is
replaced by two or more other states, it is accepted that political treaties will
not continue but that territorially grounded treaties will continue to attach
to the territories in question now subject to new sovereign arrangements.
The situation with regard to other treaties is more uncertain.[119]

State practice concerning dissolution has centred to all intents and purposes upon the dismemberment of 'unions of state', that is the ending of
what had originally been a union of two international persons. Examples
would include Colombia in 1829–31; Norway/Sweden in 1905; the United
Arab Republic 1960; the Mali Federation in 1960; the Federation of
Rhodesia and Nyasaland 1963[120] and the Czech and Slovak Federal
Republic 1992.[121] It is difficult to deduce clear rules of state succession from
these episodes since much depended upon the expressed intentions of the
states concerned. Perhaps a presumption in favour of continuity of treaties
with regard to each component part may be suggested, but this is subject to
expressed intention to the contrary.[122]

Article 34 of the Vienna Convention provides for treaties in force for all

---

[117] See for a survey of practice, *Yearbook of the International Law Commission*, 1974, vol. II, part
1, pp. 187–93.   [118] See article 9 of the Vienna Convention.

[119] See for example O'Connell, *State Succession*, vol. II, pp. 219–20.

[120] See *Yearbook of the International Law Commission*, 1974, vol. II, part 1, pp. 260–3 and
O'Connell, *State Succession*, vol. II, pp. 164 *et seq.*

[121] This state consisted of two distinct units, the Czech Republic and the Slovak Republic each
with their own parliament. The Constitutional Law on the Dissolution of the Czech and
Slovak Republic of 25 November 1992 provided for the dissolution of that state and for the
establishment of the successor states of the Czech Republic and Slovakia. At the same time,
the two republics issued a joint declaration informing the international community that the
two successor states would succeed to all international treaties to which the predecessor
state had been a party and that where necessary negotiations would take place particularly
where the impact upon the two republics differed, see J. Malenovsky, 'Problèmes Juridiques
Liées à la Partition de la Tchécoslovaquie, y compris Tracé de la Frontière', AFDI, 1993,
p. 305.

[122] The case of the dissolution of the Austro-Hungarian Empire in 1918 was a special case,
since it could be regarded as a dissolution of the union of Austria and Hungary (where the
latter unlike the former asserted continuity) coupled with the secession of territories that
either joined other states, such as Romania, or were merged into new states, such as Poland
or Czechoslovakia.

or part of the predecessor state to continue in force with regard to the specific territory unless the states concerned otherwise agree or it appears from the treaty or is otherwise established that the application of the treaty would be imcompatible with the object and purpose of the treaty or would radically change the conditions of its operation. This is acceptable in the particular circumstances, but the vast majority of such situations are likely to be regulated by specific agreements. Upon the dissolution of Czech and Slovak Federal Republic, for example, on 1 January 1993, the UK took the position that, as appropriate, treaties and agreements in force to which the UK and that state were parties remained in force as between the UK and the successor states.[123]

Problems, however, will arise particularly where the nature of the change in sovereignty is disputed by the relevant parties. The case of Yugoslavia as noted above[124] constitutes such an example. For the Federal Republic of Yugoslavia the political changes in effect were simply the secession of the other republics from the Socialist Federal Republic of Yugoslavia, which continued in the form of the Federal Republic of Yugoslavia. For the other former Yugoslav republics, the SFRY itself had been dissolved and all subsequent emerging states including the Federal Republic of Yugoslavia were equal successors to that former state. It may be asked whether there is any essential difference in practice between the two approaches with regard to the law of succession to treaties and the Vienna Convention appears not to envisage any great difference since both the continuing state (where there is one) and all successor states are (with respect to their territories) bound by treaties to which the predecessor state is a party unless the states concerned otherwise agree or this would be incompatible with the object and purpose of the treaty.

International human rights treaties

A territorial treaty binds successor states by virtue of attaching to the territory itself and establishing a particular regime that transcends the treaty. Can it be maintained that international human rights treaties are analogous and thus 'attach' to the inhabitants concerned within the territory of the predecessor state and thus continue to bind successor states? There is no doubt that human rights treaties constitute a rather specific category of treaties. They establish that obligations are owed directly to individuals and often provide for direct access for individuals to international mechanisms.[125] The very nature of international human rights treaties varies somewhat from that

[123] See the letters sent by the UK Prime Minister to the Prime Ministers of the Czech Republic and Slovakia on 1 January 1993, UKMIL, 65 BYIL, 1994, pp. 586 et seq.
[124] *Supra*, p. 678.   [125] See R. Higgins, *Problems and Process*, Oxford, 1994, p. 95.

of traditional international agreements. The International Court in the *Reservations to the Genocide Convention* case emphasised that 'in such a Convention the contracting states do not have any interests of their own; they merely have, one and all, a common interest, namely, the accomplishment of those high purposes which are the *raison d'être* of the Convention'.[126] In the *Barcelona Traction* case,[127] the Court differentiated between obligations of a state towards the international community as a whole and those arising *vis-à-vis* another state. The former are obligations that derive 'from the outlawing of aggression and of genocide, as also from the principles and rules concerning the basic rights of the human person, including protection from slavery and racial discrimination'. In view of the importance of such rights 'all States can be held to have a legal interest in their protection; they are obligations *erga omnes*'. It is also the case that the process of interpretation of international human rights treaties is more dynamic than is the case with regard to other international agreements. Human rights treaties create not merely subjective, reciprocal rights but rather particular legal orders involving objective obligations to protect human rights.[128]

Where a state party to human rights treaties either disintegrates completely or from which another state or states are created, and the classical rules of succession were followed, there is a danger that this might result in a situation where people formerly protected by such treaties are deprived of such protection as a consequence or by-product of state succession.[129] The practice of the UN Human Rights Committee[130] with regard to the Yugoslav tragedy is particularly interesting here. After the conclusion of its 45th session, the UN Human Rights Committee requested special reports with regard to specific issues (for example the policy of 'ethnic cleansing', arbitrary detention, torture and advocacy of hatred) from Bosnia and Herzegovina, Croatia and the Federal Republic of Yugoslavia (Serbia and Montenegro) noting 'that all the peoples within the territory of the former Yugoslavia are entitled to the guarantees of the Covenant'.[131] Representatives of all three states appeared before the Committee to discuss the relevant issues, no objection being made to the competence of the Committee, even

---

[126] ICJ Reports, 1951, pp. 15, 23; 18 ILR, p. 364.
[127] ICJ Reports, 1970, pp. 4, 32; 46 ILR, pp. 178, 206.
[128] See for example *Austria* v. *Italy*, 4 European Yearbook of Human Rights, 1960, pp. 116, 140; *Ireland* v. *UK*, European Court of Human Rights, Series A, vol. 20, 1978, pp. 90–1 and *Effect of Reservations on the Entry into Force of the American Convention on Human Rights*, 67 ILR, pp. 559, 568. See also *supra*, Chapter 16, p. 647.
[129] Note that the editors of *Oppenheim's International Law* take the view that in cases of the separation resulting in the creation of a new state, the latter 'is bound by – or at least entitled to accede to – general treaties of a "law-making" nature, especially those of a humanitarian character, previously binding on it as part of the state from which it has separated', p. 222.   [130] See *supra*, Chapter 6, p. 234.
[131] CCPR/C/SR.1178/Add.1. pp. 2–3.

though only Croatia had actually notified the Secretary-General of its succession to the human rights treaties of the former Yugoslavia.[132] In the formal Comments of the Human Rights Committee upon the initial short reports submitted by the three states,[133] the Committee emphasised clearly and unambiguously that 'all the peoples within the territory of the former Yugoslavia are entitled to the guarantees of the Covenant'.[134]

The Commission on Human Rights adopted resolution 1994/16 on 25 February 1994 in which it 'reiterates its call to successor states which have not yet done so to confirm to appropriate depositories that they continue to be bound by obligations under international human rights treaties' and 'emphasises the special nature of the human rights treaties aimed at the protection of human rights and fundamental freedoms'. In addition, the Commission requested the human rights treaty bodies to continue further the 'continuing applicability of the respective international human rights treaties to successor states' and the Secretary-General 'to encourage successor states to confirm their obligations under the international human rights treaties to which their predecessors were a party as from the date of their independence'.[135] In addition, the fifth meeting of persons chairing the human rights treaty bodies in September 1994 took the view that successor states were automatically bound by obligations under international human rights instruments from the respective date of independence and that observance of the obligations should not depend on a declaration of confirmation made by the government of the successor state.[136]

The issue of succession to the Genocide Convention in the Yugoslav situation was raised before the International Court specifically in the Preliminary Objections phase of the *Application of the Genocide Convention*

---

[132] See Müllerson, *International Law*, p. 157. In the ensuing discussion in the Committee, Müllerson (at the time a member) noted that human rights treaties besides being inter-state instruments also conferred rights upon individuals 'who could not be deprived of those rights in the event of state succession', while Serrano Caldera emphasised that 'state succession should be viewed as a matter of the acquired rights of the population of the state that had ratified the Covenant, which were not diluted when a state was divided'. CCPR/C/SR.1178/Add.1, pp. 2, 4 and 9.

[133] These reports were supplements by Special Reports from each of the three states in April 1993, see that of Croatia, CCPR/C/87; that of the Federal Republic of Yugoslavia (Serbia and Montenegro), CCPR/C/88 and that of Bosnia-Herzegovina, CCPR/C/89.

[134] See CCPR/C/79/Add.14–16, 28 December 1992. Note that at its 49th session, the UN Commission on Human Rights adopted resolution 1993/23 of 5 March 1993 in which it encouraged successor states to confirm to appropriate depositaries that they continued to be bound by obligations under relevant international human rights treaties. See also the Report of the UN Secretary-General, E/CN.4/1994/68. On 25 May 1994, the Committee on the Elimination of Racial Discrimination sent a communication to those successor states of the USSR that had not yet declared their adherence or succession to the Convention inviting them to confirm the applicability of compliance with the Convention's provisions, see E/CN.4/1995/80, p. 3.

[135] See also Commission on Human Rights Resolution 1995/18 adopted on 24 February 1995.

[136] E/CN.4/1995/80, pp. 3–4.

(Bosnia-Herzegovina v. *Yugoslavia)* case.[137] The Court held that it was unnecessary to determine this question in the circumstances since both Bosnia and Yugoslavia were clearly parties to the Convention by one means or another by the date of the filing of the Application.[138] The issue was, however, addressed particularly in two Separate Opinions. Judge Shahabuddeen declared that 'to effectuate its object and purpose, the [Genocide] Convention would fall to be construed as implying the expression of a unilateral undertaking by each party to the Convention to treat successor states as continuing as from independence any status which the predecessor state had as a party to the Convention'. It was suggested that it might be possible to extend this object and purpose argument to human rights treaties generally.[139] Judge Weeramantry in his Separate Opinion undertook a close analysis of the underlying principles and concluded by pointing to 'a principle of contemporary international law that there is automatic state succession to so vital a human rights convention as the Genocide Convention'.[140] One of the main reasons for this was the danger of gaps appearing in the system of human rights protection as between the dissolution of the predecessor state and the acceptance of human rights treaty obligations by the successor state or states.

Accordingly, the question of continued application of human rights treaties within the territory of a predecessor state irrespective of a succession is clearly under active consideration. Whether such a principle has been incontrovertably established is at the present moment a little unclear.

Succession with respect to matters other than treaties

Membership of international organisations[141]

Succession to membership of international organisations will proceed (depending upon the terms of the organisation's constitution) according to whether a new state is formed or an old state continues in a slightly different form. In the case of the partition of British India in 1947, India was considered by the UN General Assembly as a continuation of the previous entity, while Pakistan was regarded as a new state, which had then to apply for admission to the organisation.[142] Upon the merger of Egypt and Syria in

---

[137] ICJ Reports, 1996.   [138] *Ibid.*, para. 23.   [139] *Ibid.*
[140] *Ibid.*, pp. 4–11 of his Separate Opinion.
[141] See O'Connell, *State Succession*, vol. II, pp. 183 *et seq.* and H. G. Schermers and N. M. Blokker, *International Institutional Law*, 3rd edn, The Hague, 1995, pp. 73 *et seq.*
[142] This issue, of a separation of part of an existing state to form a new state, was considered by the UN to be on a par with the separation from the UK of the Irish Free State and from the Netherlands of Belgium, where the remaining portions continued as existing states, see O'Connell, vol. I, pp. 184–7.

1958 to form the United Arab Republic, the latter was treated as a single member of the United Nations, while upon the dissolution of the merger in 1961, Syria simply resumed its separate membership of the organisation.[143] In the case of the merger of North and South Yemen in 1990, the new state simply replaced the predecessor states as a member of the relevant international organisations. Where the predecessor state is dissolved and new states are created, such states will have to apply anew for membership to international organisations. For example, the new states of the Czech Republic and Slovakia were admitted as new members of the UN on 19 January 1993.[144] The sixth (Legal) Committee of the General Assembly considered the situation of new states being formed through division of a member state and the membership problem and produced the following principles:[145]

1 That, as a general rule, it is in conformity with legal principles to presume that a state which is a member of the Organization of the United Nations does not cease to be a member simply because its Constitution or frontier has been subjected to changes, and that the extinction of the state as a legal personality recognised in the international order must be shown before its rights and obligations can be considered thereby to have ceased to exist.

2 That when a new state is created, whatever may be the territory and the populations which it comprises and whether or not they formed part of a state member of the United Nations, it cannot under the system of the Charter claim the status of a member of the United Nations unless it has been formally admitted as such in conformity with the provisions of the Charter.

3 Beyond that, each case must be judged according to its merits.

Succession to assets and debts[146]

As is the case with regard to succession to treaties, the relevant international law is based upon customary law; the Vienna Convention on Succession to

[143] Ibid., pp. 197–8. This situation, which differed from the India-Pakistan precedent of 1947, has been criticised, see e.g. Rousseau, 'Sécession de la Syrie et de la RUA', 66 Revue Générale de Droit International Public, 1962, p. 413. See also E. Cotran, 'Some Legal Aspects of the Formation of the United Arab Republic and the United Arab States', 8 ICLQ, 1959, p. 346.
[144] See Schermers and Blokker, International Law, pp. 73 and 77. See supra p. 677, with regard to the position of the Russian Federation and the Federal Republic of Yugoslavia and membership of the UN.
[145] A/CN.4/149, p. 8, quoted in O'Connell, State Succession, vol. I, p. 187.
[146] See generally, O'Connell, State Succession, vol. I, pp. 199 et seq.; E. H. Feilchenfeld, Public Debts and State Succession, New York, 1931; UN, Materials on Succession of States in Respect of Matters other than Treaties, New York, 1978; C. Rousseau, Droit International Public, Paris, 1977, tome III, p. 374; M. Streinz, 'Succession of States in Assets and Liabilities – A New Regime?', 26 German YIL, 1983, p. 198; P. Monnier, 'La Convention de Vienne sur la succession d'etats en matière de biens, archives et dettes d'etat', AFDI, 1984, p. 221; V. D. Degan, 'State Succession Especially in Respect of State Property and Debts', IV Finnish YIL, 1993, p. 130 and E. Nathan, 'The Vienna Convention on Succession of States In Respect of State Property, Archives and Debts' in International Law at a Time of Perplexity (ed. Y. Dinstein), Dordrecht, 1989, p. 489. See also Yearbook of the International Law Commission, 1981, vol. II, Part 2.

State Property, Archives and Debts 1983 is not in force and is unlikely to come into effect for the foreseeable future. The primary rule with regard to the allocation of assets (including archives) and debts in succession situations is that the relevant parties should settle such issues by agreement. Virtually all of the rules that are formulated for example in the Vienna Convention 1983 are deemed to operate only where such agreement has not taken place.[147] In addition, the Arbitration Commission on Yugoslavia declared in Opinion No. 9 that 'the successor states to the SFRY must together settle all aspects of the succession by agreement'[148] and reinforced this approach in Opinion No. 14, declaring that 'the first principle applicable to state succession is that the successor states should consult with each other and agree a settlement of all questions relating to the succession'.[149]

(i) State property[150]

The classic rule postulates that only the public property of the predecessor state passes automatically to the successor state,[151] but this, of course, raises the question of the definition of public property. The distinction between public and private property is to some extent based upon the conceptual differences between public and private law, a distinction unknown to Common Law countries. Although in many cases there will be a relevant agreement to define what is meant by public property in this context,[152] this does not always occur and recourse to municipal law is often required. This indeed may be necessitated to a large extent also because international law itself simply does not provide many of the required definitions with regard to, for example, public companies or public utility undertakings.[153] The relevant municipal law for such purposes is that of the predecessor state. It is that law which will define the nature of the property in question and thus in essence decide its destination in the event of a succession.[154] Article 8 of the Vienna Convention 1983 provides that state property for the purposes of the Convention means 'property, rights and interests which, at the date of the succession of states, were, according to the internal law of the

---

[147] See e.g. articles 14, 17, 18, 22, 23, 27, 28, 30, 31, 37, 38, 40 and 41.
[148] 92 ILR, p. 205.   [149] 96 ILR, p. 731.
[150] Note that private rights are unaffected as such by a succession, see for example *Oppenheim's International Law*, p. 216.
[151] See e.g. the United Nations Tribunal For Libya, 22 ILR, p. 103.
[152] See e.g. the treaties concerned with the establishment of Cyprus in 1960, 382 *UNTS*, pp. 3 et seq and the Treaty of Peace with Italy 1947, 49 *UNTS*, annex XIV, p. 225.
[153] For an example see the dispute concerning property belonging to the Order of St Mauritz and St Lazarus, AFDI, 1965, p. 323.
[154] See the *Chorzow Factory* case, PCIJ, Series A, No. 7, p. 30 and the *German Settlers in Upper Silesia* case, PCIJ, Series B, No. 6, p. 6 but cf. the *Peter Pazmany University* case, PCIJ, Series A/B, No. 61, p. 236

predecessor state owned by that state'[155] and this can be taken as reflective of customary law. The Arbitration Commission on Yugoslavia reiterated this position by declaring that 'to determine whether the property, debts and archives belonged to the SFRY, reference should be had to the domestic law of the SFRY in operation at the date of succession'.[156] The relevant date for the passing of the property is the date of succession[157] and this is the date of independence, although difficulties may arise in the context of the allocation of assets and debts where different dates of succession occur for different successor states.[158] Such problems would need to be resolved on the basis of agreement between the relevant parties.

The Arbitration Commission was faced with two particular problems. First, the 1974 SFRY Constitution had transferred to the constituent republics ownership of many items of property. This, held the Commission, led to the conclusion that such property could not be held to have belonged to the SFRY whatever their origin or initial financing.[159] Secondly, the Commission was faced with the concept of 'social ownership', a concept regarded as particularly highly developed in the SFRY. In the event, the Commission resolved the dilemma by adopting a mixture of the territorial principle and a functional approach. It was noted that 'social ownership' was 'held for the most part by "associated labour organisations" – bodies with their own legal personality, operating in a single republic and coming within its exclusive jurisdiction. Their property, debts and archives are not to be divided for purposes of state succession: each successor state exercises its sovereign powers in respect of them.'[160] However, where other organisations operated 'social ownership' either at the federal level or in two or more republics, 'their property, debts and archives should be divided between the successor states in question if they exercised public prerogatives on behalf of the SFRY of individual republics'. Where such public prerogatives were not being exercised, the organisations should be regarded as private-sector enterprises to which state succession does not apply.[161]

It is a recognised principle of customary international law that the public property of a predecessor state with respect to the territory in question passes to the successor state.[162] Thus, as a general rule, the test of

---

[155] See also *Yearbook of the International Law Commission*, 1970, vol. II, pp. 136–43 and *ibid.*, 1981, vol. II, p. 23 cf. O'Connell, *State Succession*, vol. I, pp. 202–3.

[156] Opinion No. 14, 96 ILR, p. 732.

[157] Note that article 10 of the Vienna Convention 1983 provides that the date of the passing of state property of the predecessor state is that of the date of succession of states 'unless otherwise agreed by the states concerned or decided by an appropriate international body'. Article 21 repeats this principle in the context of state archives and article 35 with regard to state debts. [158] See e.g. Arbitration Commission Opinion No. 11, 96 ILR, p. 719.

[159] Opinion No. 14, 96 ILR, p. 732. [160] *Ibid.* [161] *Ibid.*

[162] See e.g. the *Third Restatement of US Foreign Relations Law*, pp. 102 *et seq.*; Brownlie, p. 658 and O'Connell, *State Succession*, vol. I, pp. 199–200. See also the *Peter Pazmany University* case, PCIJ, Series A/B, No. 61, 1933, p. 237 and *Haile Selassie* v. *Cable and Wireless Ltd* (no.

succession of public, or state, property as so characterised under the laws of the predecessor state, is a territorial one.

However, one needs to distinguish here between immovable and movable property. State immovable property situated in the territory to which the succession relates, passes to the successor state.[163] This is provided for in the Vienna Convention 1983 in article 14 (with regard to the transfer of part of a state to another state); article 15(i) a (with regard to 'newly independent states'); article 16 (upon a uniting of states to form one successor state); article 17 (with regard to separation of part of a state to form a new state) and article 18 (with regard to the dissolution of a state). It is also evident in state practice,[164] most recently being reaffirmed by the Arbitration Commission on Yugoslavia.[165]

In the case of immovable property situated outside the successor state or states, traditional state practice posits that where the predecessor state continues in existence this property should remain with the predecessor state (subject to agreement to the contrary by the states concerned, of course). Only special circumstances might modify this principle.[166] Where the predecessor state ceases to exist, it would appear that its property abroad should be divided proportionately between the successor states.[167]

Article 15(1)b of the Convention makes out a special, and highly controversial case for 'newly independent states'. This provides that 'immovable property, having belonged to the territory to which the succession of states relates, situated outside it and having become state property of the predecessor state during the period of dependence, shall pass to the successor state', while other immovable state property situated outside the territory 'shall pass to the successor state in proportion to the contribution of the dependent territory'. Neither of these propositions can be regarded as part of customary international law and their force would thus be dependent upon the coming into effect of the Convention, should this happen.[168]

---

2) [1939] Ch. 182; 9 ILR, p. 94. See also *Kunstsammlungen Zu Weimar* v. *Elicofon*, 536 F Supp 829, 855 (1981); 94 ILR, pp. 133, 180. Note that under article 11, which basically reflects practice, no compensation is payable for the passing of state property unless otherwise agreed and article 12 provides that third states' property in the territory of the predecessor state remains unaffected by the succession.

[163] E.g. fixed military installations, prisons, airports, government offices, state hospitals and universities, see *Yearbook of the ILC*, 1981, vol. II, part 2, p. 33.

[164] See for example O'Connell, *State Succession*, vol. I, pp. 220–1. See also *Yearbook of the International Law Commission*, 1981, vol. II, part 2, p. 29.

[165] Opinion No. 14, 96 ILR, p. 731.

[166] See e.g. *Oppenheim's International Law*, p. 223, note 6.

[167] *Ibid.*, at p. 221. Article 18(1)b of the Vienna Convention 1983 provides that 'immovable state property of the predecessor state situated outside its territory shall pass to the successor states in equitable proportions'.

[168] It is to be noted that article 15 does not, unlike other succession situations, refer to agreements between the predecessor and successor states. This was deliberate as the International Law Commission, which drafted the articles upon which the Convention is

As far as movable property connected with the territory in question is concerned,[169] the territorial principle continues to predominate. O'Connell notes that 'such property as is destined specifically for local use is acquired by the successor state',[170] while the formulation in the Vienna Convention 1983 is more flexible. This provides that 'movable state property of the predecessor state connected with the activity of the predecessor state in respect of the territory to which the succession of states applies shall pass to the successor state'.[171] There are, however, likely in specific cases to be difficulties of precision with regard to border-line instances of what may be accepted as either property 'destined specifically for local use' or property 'connected with the activity of the predecessor State in . . . the territory'. The view taken by the Arbitration Commission in Opinion No. 14 appears to be even more flexible for it simply notes that 'public property passes to the successor state on whose territory it is situated',[172] but this is likely to be regarded as too broad.

The situation with regard to movable property outside of the territory in question is more complicated. Article 17(1)c of the Vienna Convention 1983 provides that such property (in the case of separation of part of a state) 'shall pass to the successor state in an equitable proportion'. This must be regarded as a controversial proposition since it appears to modify the dominant territorial approach to the succession of state property.[173] However, in the case of the dissolution of the predecessor state, the argument in favour of an equitable division of movable property not linked to the territory in respect of which the succession occurs is much stronger.[174] The Arbitration Commission on Yugoslavia limited itself to noting the general principle that state property, debts and archives of the SFRY (other than immovable property within each of the successor states) should be divided between the successor states[175] and that while each category of assets and liabilities need not be divided equitably, the overall outcome had to be an equitable division.[176]

based, felt that this was required as a recognition of the special circumstances of decolonisation and the fact that many such agreements are unfavourable to the newly independent state, see Yearbook of the ILC, 1981, vol. II, part 2, p. 38. The article is also unusual in that it provides that immovable state property situated outside the territory and movable state property other than that already covered in the article 'to the creation of which the dependent territory has contributed' shall pass to the successor state in proportion to the contribution of the dependent territory. This was intended to introduce the application of equity to the situation and was designed to preserve inter alia, 'the patrimony and the historical and cultural heritage of the people inhabiting the dependent territory concerned', ibid. It is unclear how far this extends. It may cover contributions to international institutions made where the territory is a dependent territory, but beyond this one can only speculate.
169 E.g. currency and state public funds, Yearbook of the International Law Commission, 1981, vol. II, part 2, pp. 35–6.   170 O'Connell, State Succession, vol. I, p. 204.
171 Article 17. See also articles 14(2)b, 15(1)d and 18(1)c.   172 96 ILR, p. 731.
173 See O'Connell, State Succession, vol. I, p. 204. Cf. Yearbook of the International Law Commission, 1981, vol. II, part 1, pp. 46–7.
174 See article 18(1)d of the Vienna Convention 1983.
175 Opinion No. 14, 96 ILR, pp. 731–2.   176 Opinion No. 13, ibid., . p. 728.

The state succession situation which in general poses the least problem is that of absorption or merger, since the absorbing or newly created state respectively will simply take over the assets and debts of the extinguished state. The issues were, however, discussed in detail in the context of German unification. Article 21 of the Unification Treaty provides that the assets of the German Democratic Republic which served directly specified administrative tasks were to become Federal assets[177] and were to be used to discharge public tasks in the territory of the former GDR. Article 22 dealt with public assets of legal entities in that territory, including the land and assets in the agricultural sectors which did not serve directly specified administrative tasks.[178] Such financial assets were to be administered in trust by the Federal government and be appointed by federal law equally between the Federal government on the one hand and the *Länder* of the former GDR on the other, with the local authorities receiving an appropriate share of the *Länder* allocation. The Federal government was to use its share to discharge public tasks in the territory of the former GDR, while the distribution of the *Länder* share to the individual *Länder* was to take place upon the basis of population ratio. Publicly owned assets used for the housing supply become the property of the local authorities together with the assumption by the latter of a proportionate share of the debts, with the ultimate aim of privatisation.

In fact, state practice demonstrates that with the exception of some clear and basic rules, all will depend upon the particular agreement reached in the particular circumstances. In the case of the former Czech and Slovak Federal Republic, the two successor states agreed to divide the assets and liabilities of the predecessor state[179] in the ratio of two to one (the approximate population ratio of the two new states).[180] In the case of the former Soviet Union, Russia and the successor states signed agreements in 1991 and 1992 apportioning assets and liabilities of the predecessor state with the share of Russia being 61.34 per cent and of the Ukraine being 16.37 per cent.[181]

---

[177] Unless they were earmarked on 1 October 1989 predominantly for administrative tasks which under the Basic Law of the FRG are to be discharged by the *Länder*, local authorities or other public administrative bodies, in which case they will accrue to the appropriate institution of public administration. Administrative assets used predominantly for tasks of the former Ministry of State Security/Office for National Security are to accrue to the Trust Agency established under the Law on the Privatisation and Reorganisation of Publicly Owned Assets (Trust Law) of 17 June 1990 for the purpose of privatising former publicly owned companies.

[178] These were termed 'financial assets' and deliberately exclude social insurance assets.

[179] Apart from immovable property located within each republic which went to the republic concerned in accordance with the territorial principle.

[180] See for example, Degan, *State Succession*, p. 144.

[181] See Müllerson, *International Law*, p. 144. It is unclear at the time of writing whether these arrangements have in fact been put into effect since Ukraine has expressed dissatisfaction with them from time to time, *ibid.*

(ii) State archives

Archives are state property with special characteristics. Many are difficult by their nature to divide up, but they may be relatively easily reproduced and duplicated. Archives are a crucial part of the heritage of a community and may consist of documents, numismatic collections, iconographic documents, photographs and films. The issue has been of great concern to UNESCO, which has called for the restitution of archives as part of the reconstitution and protection of the national cultural heritage and has appealed for the return of an irreplaceable cultural heritage to those that created it.[182] In this general context, one should also note articles 149 and 303 of the 1982 Convention on the Law of the Sea. The former provides that all objects of an archaeological and historical nature found in the International Sea-bed Area are to be preserved or disposed of for the benefit of mankind as a whole, 'particular regard being paid to the preferential rights of the state or country of origin, or the state of historical and archaeological origin', while the latter stipulates that states have the duty to protect objects of an archaeological and historical nature found at sea and shall co-operate for this purpose.

In general, treaties between European states dealing with cessions of territory included archival clauses providing for the treatment of archives, while such clauses are very rare in cases of decolonisation.[183]

Article 20 of the 1983 Vienna Convention provides that state archives in the present context means:

> all documents of whatever date and kind, produced or received by the predecessor state in the exercise of its functions which, at the date of the succession of states, belonged to the predecessor state according to its internal law and were preserved by it directly or under its control as archives for whatever purpose.

Generally, such archives will pass as at the date of succession and without compensation, without as such affecting archives in the territory owned by a third state.[184]

Where part of the territory of a state is transferred by that state to another state, in the absence of agreement, the part of the state archives of the predecessor state which, for normal administration of the territory concerned,

---

[182] UNESCO, Records of the General Conference, 18th Session, Resolutions, 1974, pp. 68 et seq., 20 C/102, 1978, paras. 18–19; and UNESCO Records of the General Conference, 20th Session, Resolutions, 1978, pp. 92–3. See also Yearbook of the ILC, 1979, vol. II, part 1, pp. 78–80. Note in addition the call for a New International Cultural Order, see e.g. M. Bedjaoui, Towards a New International Economic Order, 1979, pp. 75 et seq. and 245 et seq., and General Assembly Resolutions 3026A(XXVII); 3148(XXVIII); 3187(XXVIII); 3391(XXX) and 31/40. [183] Yearbook of the ILC, 1979, vol. II, part 1, p. 93.
[184] Articles 21–24.

should be at the disposal of the state to which the territory is transferred, shall pass to the successor state, as shall any part of the state archives that relates exclusively or principally to the territory.[185] In the case of 'newly independent states', the same general provisions apply,[186] but with some alterations. Archives having belonged to the territory in question and having become state archives of the predecessor state during the period of dependence are to pass to the successor state. The reference here to archives that became state archives is to pre-colonial material, whether kept by central government, local governments or tribes, religious ministers, private enterprises or individuals.[187] One may mention here the Treaty of Peace with Italy of 1947, which provided that Italy was to restore all archives and objects of historical value belonging to Ethiopia or its natives and removed from Ethiopia to Italy since October 1935.[188] In the case of Vietnam, the 1950 Franco-Vietnamese agreement provided for the return as of right of all historical archives,[189] while a dispute between France and Algeria has been in existence since the latter's independence over pre-colonial material removed to France.[190]

Article 28(2) provides that the passing or the appropriate reproduction of parts of the state archives of the predecessor state (other than those already discussed above) of interest to the territory concerned is to be determined by agreement, 'in such a manner that each of these states [i.e. predecessor and successor] can benefit as widely and equitably as possible from those parts of the state archives of the predecessor state'. The reference here is primarily to material relating to colonisation and the colonial period, and in an arrangement of 1975, the French specifically noted the practice of microfilming in the context of France's acquisition of Algeria.[191] Article 28(3) emphasises that the predecessor state is to provide the newly independent state with the best available evidence from its state archives relating to territorial title and boundary issues. This is important as many post-colonial territorial disputes will invariably revolve around the interpretation of colonial treaties delimiting frontiers and colonial administrative practice concerning the area in contention.[192]

Where two or more states unite to form one successor state, the state archives of the former will pass to the latter.[193] Where part of a state secedes to form another state, unless the states otherwise agree the part of the state archives of the predecessor state, which for normal administration of the

---

[185] Article 27.   [186] Article 28(1)b and c.
[187] *Yearbook of the ILC*, 1981, vol. II, part 2, p. 62.   [188] 49 UNTS, p. 142.
[189] See *Yearbook of the ILC*, 1979, vol. II, part 1, p. 113.   [190] *Ibid.*, pp. 113–14.
[191] *Yearbook of the ILC*, 1981, vol. II, part 2, p. 64.
[192] See for example, the Mali–Upper Volta (Burkina Faso) border dispute, Shaw, *Title to Territory*, pp. 257–8 and the *Burkina Faso/Mali* case, ICJ Reports, 1986, p. 554; 80 ILR, p. 459.   [193] Article 29.

territory concerned should be in that territory, will pass, as will those parts of the state archives that relate directly to the territory that is the subject of the succession.[194]

The same provisions apply in the case of a dissolution of a state, which is replaced by two or more successor states, in the absence of agreement, with the addition that other state archives are to pass to the successor states in an equitable manner, taking into account all relevant circumstances.[195]

Articles 28, 30 and 31 also contain a paragraph explaining that the relevant agreements over state archives 'shall not infringe the right of the peoples of those states to development, to information about their history and to their cultural heritage'. Despite the controversy over whether such a right does indeed exist in law as a right and precisely how such a provision might be interpreted in practice in concrete situations, the general concept of encouraging awareness and knowledge of a people's heritage is to be supported. The precise phraseology of the paragraphs, however, would not appear to promote this in the most acceptable manner.

(iii) Public debt[196]

This is an area of particular uncertainty and doubt has been expressed as to whether there is a rule of succession in such circumstances.[197] As in other parts of state succession, political and economic imperatives play a large role and much practice centres upon agreements made between relevant parties.

The public debt (or national debt) is that debt assumed by the central government in the interests of the state as a whole. It constitutes a particularly sensitive issue since third parties are involved who are often reluctant to accept a change in the identity of the debtor. This encourages an approach based on the continuing liability for the debt in question and in situations where a division of debt has taken place for that situation to continue with the successor state being responsible to the predecessor state (where this continues, of course) for its share rather than to the creditor directly. And as article 36 of the Vienna Convention 1983 notes a succession of states does not as such affect the rights and obligations of creditors.[198]

---

[194] Article 30.
[195] Article 31. Note in particular the dispute between Denmark and Iceland, after the dissolution of their Union, over valuable parchments, see Verzijl, *International Law*, vol. VII, 1974, p. 153 and *Yearbook of the ILC*, 1981, vol. II, part 1, pp. 68–9, and the Treaty of St Germain of 1919 with Austria which contained provisions relating to the succession to archives of various new or reconstituted states.
[196] See generally, O'Connell, *State Succession*, vol. I, Chapters 15–17; *Yearbook of the ILC*, 1977, vol. II, part 1, pp. 49 *et seq.* and Zemanek, 'State Succession'.
[197] See for example Brownlie, *Principles*, pp. 658–9.
[198] Note that the Convention does not deal with private creditors, a point which is criticised in the *Third Restatement on US Foreign Relations Law*, p. 106, but article 6 of the Convention constitutes in effect a savings clause here.

Public debts[199] may be divided into national debts, being debts owed by the state as a whole; local debts, being debts contracted by a subgovernmental territorial unit or other form of local authority, and localised debts, being debts incurred by the central government for the purpose of local projects or areas.[200]

Local debts clearly pass under customary international law to the successor state, since they constitute arrangements entered into by subgovernmental territorial authorities now transferred to the jurisdiction of the successor state and a succession does not directly affect them. In effect, they continue to constitute debts borne by the specific territory in question.[201] Similarly, localised debts, being closely attached to the territory to which the succession relates, also pass to the successor state in conformity with the same territorial principle.[202]

In truth, one cannot provide a definitive answer to the question as to the allocation of the national debt as such. In the case of absorption or merger, the expanding or newly created state respectively will simply take over the national debt of the extinguished state.[203] The German unification example is instructive. Article 23 of the Unification Treaty provided that the total national budget debt of the German Democratic Republic was to be assumed by a special Federal fund administered by the Federal Minister of Finance. The Federal government was to be liable for the obligations of the special fund, which was to service the debt and could raise loans *inter alia* to redeem debts and to cover interest and borrowing costs. Until 31 December 1993, the Federal government and the Trust Agency were to each reimburse one half of the interest payments made by the special fund. As from 1 January 1994, the Federal government, the Trust Agency and the *Länder* of the former GDR assumed the total debt accrued at that date by the special fund, which was dissolved.

The sureties, warranties and guarantees assumed by the GDR were taken over by the Federal Republic, while the interests of the GDR in the Berlin State Bank were transferred to the *Länder* of the former GDR. The liabilities arising from the GDR's responsibility for the Berlin State Bank were assumed by the Federal government.

In the case of secession or separation where the predecessor state contin-

---

[199] Note that the Convention is concerned with state debts which are defined in article 33 as 'any financial obligation of a predecessor state arising in conformity with international law with another state, an international organisation or any other subject of international law'.

[200] See O'Connell, *State Succession*, vol. I, Chapters 15–17 and *Yearbook of the ILC*, 1981, vol. II, part 1, p. 76. A variety of other distinctions have also been drawn, *ibid.*

[201] See for example O'Connell, *State Succession*, vol. I, pp. 416 *et seq.*

[202] *Ibid.* See also *Yearbook of the ILC*, 1981, vol. II, part 1, p. 90 and the *Ottoman Public Debt* case, 1 RIAA, p. 529 (1925).

[203] Article 39 of the Convention provides that where two or more states unite to form a successor state, the state debts of the former states will pass to the successor state.

ues to exist, it would appear that the presumption is that the responsibility for the general public debt of the predecessor state remains with the predecessor state after the succession.[204] This would certainly appear to be the case where part of a state is transferred to another state.[205] Generally the paucity of practice makes one reluctant to claim that a new rule of international law has been established with regard to such situations, so that the general principle of non-division of the public debt is not displaced. However, successor states may be keen to establish their international credit worthiness by becoming involved in a debt allocation arrangement in circumstances where in strict international law this may not be necessary.[206]

A brief review of some practice may serve to illustrate the complexity of the area. When Texas seceded from Mexico in 1840, for example, it denied any liability for the latter's debts, although an *ex gratia* payment was in the circumstances made. However, no part of Colombia's debt was assumed by Panama upon its independence in 1903. The arrangements made in the peace treaties of 1919 and 1923 were complex, but it can be noted that while no division of the public debt occurred with regard to some territories emerging from the collapsed empires, in most cases there was a negotiated and invariably complicated settlement. The successor states of the Austro-Hungarian Empire, for example, assumed responsibility for such portions of the pre-war bonded debt as were determined by the Reparations Committee, while Turkey took over a share of the Ottoman public debt on a revenue proportionality basis.[207] When in 1921, the Irish Free State separated from the United Kingdom, it was provided that the public debt of the UK would be apportioned 'as may be fair and equitable', having regard to any claims by way of set-off or counter-claim.

The agreement between India (the continuation of British India) and Pakistan (the new state) provided for the responsibility of the former with regard to all the financial obligations, including loans and guarantees, of British India. India thus remained as the sole debtor of the national debt, while Pakistan's share of this, as established upon the basis of proportionality relating to its share of the assets of British India that it received, became a debt to India.[208]

With regard to secured debts, the general view appears to be that debts secured by mortgage of assets located in the territory in question survive the transfer of that territory. The Treaties of St Germain and Trianon in 1919, for example, (articles 203 and 186 respectively) provided that assets thus

[204] See the *Ottoman Public Debt* case, 1 RIAA, p. 529.
[205] See *Yearbook of the International Law Commission*, 1977, vol. II, Part 1, p. 81.
[206] See Williams, 'State Succession', pp. 786 and 802–3.
[207] See for example, O'Connell, *State Succession*, vol. I, pp. 397–401 and Feilchenfeld, pp. 431 *et seq.*   [208] O'Connell, *State Succession*, vol. I, pp. 404–6.

pledged would remain so pledged with regard to that part of the national debt that had been agreed would pass to the particular successor state. Such debts had to be specifically secured and the securities had to be 'railways, salt mines or other property'.[209] However, where debts have been charged to local revenue, the presumption lies the other way.

Much will depend upon the circumstances and it may well be that where the seceding territory constituted a substantial or meaningful part of the predecessor state, considerations of equity would suggest some form of apportionment of the national debt. It was with this in mind, together with the example of the UK–Irish Free State Treaty of 1921, that led the International Law Commission to propose the draft that led to article 40 of the Vienna Convention 1983.

Article 40 provides that where part of a state separates to form another state, unless otherwise agreed, the state debt of the predecessor state passes to the successor state 'in an equitable proportion' taking into account in particular the property, rights and interests which pass to the successor state in relation to that debt.[210] It is doubtful that this proposition constitutes a codification of customary law as such in view of the confused and disparate practice of states to date, but it does reflect a viable approach.

However, in the case of separation where the predecessor state ceases to exist, some form of apportionment of the public debt is required and the provision in article 41 for an equitable division taking into account in particular the property, rights and interests which pass to the successor states in relation to that debt, is reasonable and can be taken to reflect international practice.[211] The basis for any equitable apportionment of debts would clearly depend upon the parties concerned and would have to be regulated by agreement. A variety of possibilities exists, including taxation ratio, extent of territory, population, nationality of creditors, taxable value as distinct from actual revenue contributions, value of assets and contributions of the territory in question to the central administration.[212]

In common with the other parts of the 1983 Convention, a specific article is devoted to the situation of the 'newly independent state'. Article 38 pro-

---

[209] *Ibid.*, p. 411.

[210] The same rule applies in the case of the transfer of part of a state to another state, see article 37.   [211] See for example *Oppenheim's International Law*, p. 221.

[212] In the 1919 peace treaties, the principle of distribution proportional to the future paying capacity of the ceded territories was utilised, measured by reference to revenues contributed in the pre-war years, while in the Treaty of Lausanne, 1923, concerning the consequences of the demise of the Ottoman Empire, the principle considered was that of proportional distribution based solely upon actual past contributions to the amortisation of debts, see O'Connell, *State Succession*, vol. I, pp. 454–6. Cf. *Yearbook of the ILC*, 1981, vol. II, part 2, p. 113. The phrase ultimately adopted in the Vienna Convention was: 'taking into account, in particular, the property, rights and interests which pass to the successor state in relation to that state debt'. In other words, stress was laid upon the factor of proportionality of assets to debts.

vides that 'no state debt of the predecessor state shall pass to the newly independent state' in the absence of an agreement between the parties providing
otherwise, 'in view of the link between the state debt of the predecessor state
connected with its activity in the territory to which the succession of states
relates and the property, rights and interests which pass to the newly independent state'. State practice generally in the decolonisation process dating
back to the independence of the United States appears to show that there
would be no succession to part of the general state debt of the predecessor
state, but that this would differ where the debt related specifically to the territory in question.[213] It is unlikely that this provision reflects customary law.

(iv) Private rights

The question also arises as to how far a succession of states will affect, if at
all, private rights. Principles of state sovereignty and respect for acquired or
subsisting rights are relevant here and often questions of expropriation
provide the context.

As far as those inhabitants who become nationals of the successor state
are concerned, they are fully subject to its laws and regulations, and apart
from the application of international human rights rules, they have little
direct recourse to international law in these circumstances. Accordingly
what does become open to discussion is the protection afforded to aliens by
international provisions relating to the succession of rights and duties upon
a change of sovereignty.

It is within this context that the doctrine of acquired rights[214] has been
formulated. This relates to rights obtained by foreign nationals and has been
held by some to include virtually all types of legal interests. Its import is that
such rights continue after the succession and can be enforced against the
new sovereign.

Some writers declare this proposition to be a fundamental principle of international law,[215] while others describe it merely as a source of confusion.[216]
There is a certain amount of disagreement as to its extent. On the one hand,
it has been held to mean that the passing of sovereignty has no effect upon such
rights, and on the other that it implies no more than that aliens should be, as
far as possible, insulated from the changes consequent upon succession.

---

[213] See *Yearbook of the ILC*, 1981, vol. II, part 1, pp. 91–105 and *ibid.*, 1977, vol. II, part 1, pp.
86–107. Note the varied practice of succession to public debts in the colonisation process,
ibid., pp. 87–8 and with regard to annexations, *ibid.*, pp. 93–4. See also *West Rand Gold
Mining Co.* v. *R* [1905] 2 KB 391, and O'Connell, *State Succession*, vol. I, pp. 373–83.
[214] See in particular, O'Connell, *State Succession*, Chapter 10; *Oppenheim's International Law*,
pp. 215 *et seq.* and Brownlie, *Principles*, pp. 657–8 and 659–60.
[215] See e.g. O'Connell, *State Succession*, vol. I, pp. 239–40.
[216] See e.g. Brownlie, *Principles*, p. 658.

The principle of acquired rights was discussed in a number of cases that came before the Permanent Court of International Justice between the two world wars, dealing with the creation of an independent Poland out of the former German, Russian and Austrian Empires. Problems arose specifically with regard to rights obtained under German rule, which were challenged by the new Polish authorities.

In the *German Settlers'* case,[217] the facts were that Poland had attempted to evict German settlers from its lands, arguing that since many of them had not taken transfer of title before the Armistice they could be legitimately ejected. According to the German system, such settlers could acquire title either by means of leases, or by means of an arrangement whereby they paid parts of the purchase price at regular intervals and upon payment of the final instalment the land would become theirs. The Court held that German law would apply in the circumstances until the final transfer of the territory and that the titles to land acquired in this fashion would be protected under the terms of the 1919 Minorities Treaty. More importantly, the Court declared that even in the absence of such a treaty:

> private rights acquired under existing law do not cease on a change of sovereignty . . . even those who contest the existence in international law of a general principle of state succession do not go so far as to maintain that private rights, including those acquired from the state as the owner of the property, are invalid as against a successor in sovereignty.

The fact that there was a political purpose behind the colonisation scheme would not affect the private rights thus secured, which could be enforced against the new sovereign. It is very doubtful that this would be accepted today.

The principles emerging from such inter-war cases affirming the continuation of acquired rights, have modified the views expressed in the *West Rand Central Gold Mining Company* case[218] to the effect that upon annexation the new sovereign may choose which of the contractual rights and duties adopted by the previous sovereign it wishes to respect.

The inter-war cases mark the high-water mark of the concept of the continuation of private rights upon succession, but they should not be interpreted to mean that the new sovereign cannot alter such rights. The expropriation of alien property is possible under international law subject to certain conditions.[219] What the doctrine does indicate is that there is a presumption of the continuation of foreign acquired rights, though the matter is best regulated by treaty. Only private rights that have become vested or

---

[217] PCIJ, Series B, No. 6, 1923; 2 ILR, p. 71. The proposition was reaffirmed in the *Certain German Interests in Polish Upper Silesia* case, PCIJ, Series A, No. 7, 1926; 3 ILR, p. 429 and the *Chorzów Factory* case, PCIJ, Series A, No. 17, 1928; 4 ILR, p. 268. See also the *Mavrommatis Palestine Concessions* case, PCIJ, Series A, no. 5, 1924 and *US* v. *Percheman*, 7 Pet. 51 (1830).   [218] [1905] 2 KB 391.   [219] *Supra*, Chapter 14, p. 573.

acquired would be covered by the doctrine. Thus, where rights are to come into operation in the future, they will not be binding upon the new sovereign. Similarly, claims to unliquidated damages will not continue beyond the succession.

Claims to unliquidated damages occur where the matter in dispute has not come before the judicial authorities and the issue of compensation has yet to be determined by a competent court or tribunal. In the *Robert E. Brown* claim,[220] an American citizen's prospecting licence had been unjustifiably cancelled by the Boer republic of South Africa in the 1890s and Brown's claim had been dismissed in the Boer courts. In 1900 the United Kingdom annexed the republic and Brown sought (through the US government) to hold it responsible. This contention was rejected by the arbitration tribunal, which said that Brown's claim did not represent an acquired right since the denial of justice that had taken place by the Boer court's wrongful rejection of his case had prevented the claim from becoming liquidated. The tribunal also noted that liability for a wrongful act committed by a state did not pass to the new sovereign after succession.

The fact that the disappearance of the former sovereign automatically ends liability for any wrong it may have committed is recognised as a rule of international law, although where the new state adopts the illegal actions of the predecessor, it may inherit liability since it itself is in effect committing a wrong. This was brought out in the *Lighthouses* arbitration[221] in 1956 between France and Greece, which concerned the latter's liability to respect concessions granted by Turkey to a French company regarding territory subsequently acquired by Greece.

The problem of the survival of foreign nationals' rights upon succession is closely bound up with ideological differences and economic pressures. The Western nations tend to support the doctrine of acquired rights rather more than communist or Third World states, and the issue is linked closely with state responsibility.

State succession and nationality[222]

The issue of state succession and nationality links together not only those two distinct areas, but also the question of human rights. The terms under

[220] 6 RIAA, p. 120 (1923); 2 ILR, p. 66. See also the *Hawaiian Claims* case, 6 RIAA, p. 157 (1925); 3 ILR, p. 80.
[221] 12 RIAA, p. 155 (1956); 23 ILR, p. 659. Cf. the decision of the Namibian Supreme Court in *Minister of Defence, Namibia v. Mwandinghi*, 91 ILR, p. 341, taking into account the provisions of the Namibian Constitution.
[222] See O'Connell, *State Succession*, vol. I, Chapters 20 and 21; P. Weis, *Nationality and Statelessness in International Law*, 1956; *Oppenheim's International Law*, p. 218 and Report of the International Law Commission, A/50/10, 1995, pp. 68 et seq. See also *supra*, Chapters 12, p. 462 and 14, p. 562.

which a state may award nationality are solely within its control[223] but problems may arise in the context of a succession. In principle, the issue of nationality will depend upon the municipal regulations of the predecessor and successor states. The laws of the former will determine the extent to which the inhabitants of an area to be ceded to another authority will retain their nationality after the change in sovereignty, while the laws of the successor state will prescribe the conditions under which the new nationality will be granted.

The general rule would appear to be that nationality will change with sovereignty, although it will be incumbent upon the new sovereign to declare the pertinent rules with regard to people born in the territory or resident there, or born abroad of parents who are nationals of the former regime. Similarly, the ceding state may well provide for its former citizens in the territory in question to retain their nationality, thus creating a situation of dual nationality. This would not arise, of course, where the former state completely disappears.

Some states acquiring territory may provide for the inhabitants to obtain the new nationality automatically while others may give the inhabitants an option to depart and retain their original nationality. Actual practice is varied and much depends on the circumstances, but it should be noted that the 1961 Convention on the Reduction of Statelessness provides that states involved in the cession of territory should ensure that no person becomes stateless as a result of the particular change in sovereignty. There may indeed be a principle in international law to the effect that the successor state should provide for the possibility of nationals of the predecessor state living in or having a substantial connection with the territory taken over by the successor state.[224] It may indeed be, on the other hand, that such nationals have the right to choose their nationality in such situations, although this is unclear. The Arbitration Commission on Yugoslavia referred in this context to the principle of self-determination as proclaimed in article 1 of the two International Covenants on Human Rights 1966. The Commission stated that 'by virtue of that right every individual may chose to belong to whatever ethnic, religious or language community he wishes'. Further, it was noted that:

In the Commission's view one possible consequence of this principle might be for the members of the Serbian population in Bosnia-Hercegovina and Croatia to be recognised under agreements between the Republics as having the nationality of their choice, with all the rights and obligations which that entails with respect to the states concerned.[225]

Hong Kong

Of particular interest in the context of state succession and the decolonisation process is the situation with regard to Hong Kong. While Hong Kong island and the southern tip of the Kowloon peninsula (with Stonecutters island) were ceded to Britain in perpetuity,[226] the New Territories (comprising some 92 per cent of the total land area of the territory) were leased to Britain for 99 years commencing 1 July 1898.[227] Accordingly, the British and Chinese governments opened negotiations and in 1984 reached an agreement. This Agreement took the form of a Joint Declaration and Three Annexes[228] and lays down the system under which Hong Kong will be governed as from 1 July 1997. It is specified that a Hong Kong Special Administrative Region (SAR) will be established, which will enjoy a high degree of autonomy, except in foreign and defence affairs. It will be vested with executive, legislative and independent judicial power, including that of final adjudication. The laws of Hong Kong will remain basically unaffected. The government of the SAR will be composed of local inhabitants and the current social and economic systems are to continue unchanged. The SAR will retain the status of a free port and a separate customs territory and is to remain an international financial centre with a freely convertible currency. Using the name of 'Hong Kong, China', the SAR may on its own maintain and develop economic and cultural relations and conclude relevant agreements with states, regions and relevant international organisations. The existing systems of shipping management are to continue and shipping certificates relating to the shipping register will be issued under the name of 'Hong Kong, China'.

These policies are to be enshrined in a Basic Law of the SAR and will remain unchanged for fifty years. Annex I of the Agreement also provides that public servants in Hong Kong, including members of the police and judiciary, will remain in employment and upon retirement will receive their pension and other benefits due to them on terms no less favourable than before and irrespective of their nationality or place of residence. Airlines

---

[225] Opinion No. 2, 92 ILR, pp. 167, 168-9. The Commission concluded by stating that the Republics 'must afford the members of those minorities and ethnic groups [i.e. the Serbian population in Bosnia-Hercegovina and Croatia] all the human rights and fundamental freedoms recognised in international law, including, where appropriate, the right to choose their nationality', ibid., p. 169.
[226] See the Treaty of Nanking 1842, 30 BFSP, p. 389 and the Convention of Peking 1860, 50 BFSP, p. 10.
[227] 90 BFSP, p. 17. All three treaties were denounced by China as 'unequal treaties'.
[228] See 23 ILM, 1984, p. 1366.

incorporated and having their principal place of business in Hong Kong may continue to operate and the current system of civil aviation management is to continue. The SAR will have extensive authority to conclude agreements in this field. Current rights and freedoms in Hong Kong are to be maintained, including freedoms of the person, of speech, of the press, of assembly, of belief, of movement, to strike and to form and join trade unions. In an important provision, article XIII of Annex I stipulates that the provisions of the International Covenants on Human Rights 1966 are to continue in force. Accordingly, a high level of succession is provided for, but it is as well to recognise that the Hong Kong situation is unusual.

THE SETTLEMENT OF DISPUTES BY PEACEFUL MEANS

It is fair to say that international law has always considered its fundamental purpose to be the maintenance of peace.[1] Although ethical preoccupations stimulated its development and inform its growth, international law has historically been regarded by the international community primarily as a means to ensure the establishment and preservation of world peace and security. This chapter is concerned with the methods and procedures available within the international order for the peaceful resolution of disputes and conflicts.

Basically the techniques of conflict management fall into two categories: diplomatic procedures and adjudication. The former involves an attempt to resolve differences either by the contending parties themselves or with the aid of other entities by the use of the discussion and fact-finding methods. Adjudication procedures involve the determination by a disinterested third party of the legal and factual issues involved, either by arbitration or by the decision of judicial organs.

The political approach to conflict settlement is divided into two sections, with the measures applicable by the United Nations being separately examined in Chapter 20 as they possess a distinctive character. The adjudication processes will be similarly divided so as to differentiate the techniques of arbitration and judicial settlement. Although for the sake of convenience each method of dispute settlement is separately examined, it should be noted that in any given situation a range of mechanisms may well be utilised. A good example of this is afforded by the successful settlement of the

---

[1] See generally, J. G. Merrills, *International Dispute Settlement*, 2nd edn, Cambridge, 1991; United Nations, *Handbook on the Peaceful Settlement of Disputes Between States*, New York, 1992; L. Henkin, R. C. Pugh, O. Schachter and H. Smit, *International Law Cases and Materials*, 3rd edn, St Paul, 1993, Chapter 10; David Davies Memorial Institute, *International Disputes: The Legal Aspects*, London, 1972; K. V. Raman, *Dispute Settlement Through the UN*, Dobbs Ferry, 1977; O. R. Young, *The Intermediaries*, Princeton, 1967; D. W. Bowett, 'Contemporary Developments in Legal Techniques in the Settlement of Disputes', 180 HR, p. 171 and B. S. Murty, 'Settlement of Disputes'in *Manual of Public International Law* (ed. M. Sørensen), London, 1968, p. 673. See also Nguyen Quoc Dinh, P. Daillier and A. Pellet, *Droit International Public*, 5th edn, Paris, 1994, pp. 775 *et seq.*; P. Pazartzis, *Les Engagements Internationaux en Matière de Règlement Pacifique des Différends entre Etats*, Paris, 1992 and *The UN Decade of International Law: Reflections on International Dispute Settlement* (eds. M. Brus, S. Muller and S. Wiemers), Dordrecht, 1991.

Chad–Libya boundary dispute. Following a long period of conflict and armed hostilities since the dispute erupted in 1973, the two states signed a Framework Agreement on the Peaceful Settlement of the Territorial Dispute on 31 August 1989 in which they undertook to seek a peaceful solution within one year. In the absence of a political settlement, the parties undertook to take the matter to the International Court.[2] After inconclusive negotiations, the dispute was submitted to the International Court by notification of the Framework Agreement by the two parties.[3] The decision of the Court was delivered on 3 February 1994. The Court accepted the argument of Chad that the boundary between the two states was defined by the Franco-Libyan Treaty of 10 August 1955.[4] Following this decision, the two states concluded an agreement providing for Libyan withdrawal from the Aouzou Strip by 30 May 1994. The agreement provided for monitoring of this withdrawal by United Nations observers.[5] The two parties also agreed to establish a joint team of experts to undertake the delimitation of the common frontier in accordance with the decision of the International Court.[6] On 4 May 1994, the Security Council adopted resolution 915 (1994) establishing the UN Aouzou Strip Observer Group (UNASOG) and authorising the deployment of observers and support staff for a period up to forty days.[7] On 30 May, Libya and Chad signed a Joint Declaration stating that the withdrawal of the Libyan administration and forces had been effected as of that date to the satisfaction of both parties as monitored by UNASOG.[8] The Security Council terminated the mandate of UNASOG upon the successful conclusion of the mission by resolution 926 (1994) on 13 June that year.[9]

However, states are not obliged to resolve their differences at all, and this applies in the case of serious legal conflicts as well as peripheral political disagreements. All the methods available to settle disputes are operative only upon the consent of the particular states. This, of course, can be contrasted with the situation within municipal systems. It is reflected in the different

---

[2] See e.g. Report of the UN Secretary-General. S/1994/512, 27 April 1994, 33 ILM, 1994, p. 786 and generally M. M. Ricciardi, 'Title to the Aozou Strip: A Legal and Historical Analysis', 17 *Yale Journal of International Law*, 1992, p. 301.

[3] Libya on 31 August 1990 and Chad on 3 September 1990, see the *Libya/Chad* case, ICJ Reports, 1994, pp. 6, 14; 100 ILR, pp. 1, 13.   [4] *Ibid.*, p. 40; 100 ILR, p. 39.

[5] 100 ILR, p. 102, article 1. See also 33 ILM, 1994, p. 619.

[6] 100 ILR, p. 103, article 6. See also the letter of the UN Secretary-General to the Security Council, S/1994/432, 13 April 1994, *ibid.*, pp. 103–4.

[7] Note that on 14 April the Security Council adopted resolution 910 (1994) by which the initial UN reconnaissance team was exempted from sanctions operating against Libya by virtue of resolution 748 (1992). The observer group received a similar exemption by virtue of resolution 915 B.

[8] See Report of the UN Secretary-General, S/1994/672, 6 June 1994, 100 ILR, pp. 111 *et seq.* The Joint Declaration was counter-signed by the Chief Military Observer of UNASOG as a witness.   [9] *Ibid.*, p. 114.

functions performed by the courts in the international and domestic legal orders respectively, and it is one aspect of the absence of a stable, central focus within the world community.

The mechanisms dealing with the peaceful settlement of disputes require in the first instance the existence of a dispute. The definition of a dispute has been the subject of some consideration by the International Court,[10] but the reference by the Permanent Court in the *Mavrommatis Palestine Concessions (Jurisdiction)* case[11] to 'a disagreement over a point of law or fact, a conflict of legal views or of interests between two persons' constitutes an authoritative indication. A distinction is sometimes made between legal and political disputes, or justiciable and non-justiciable disputes.[12] Although maintained in some international treaties, it is to some extent unsound, in view of the fact that any dispute will involve some political considerations and many overtly political disagreements may be resolved by judicial means. Whether any dispute is to be termed legal or political may well hinge upon the particular circumstances of the case, the views adopted by the relevant parties and the way in which they choose to characterise their differences. It is in reality extremely difficult to point to objective general criteria clearly differentiating the two.[13]

This does not, however, imply that there are not significant differences between the legal and political procedures available for resolving problems. For one thing, the strictly legal approach is dependent upon the provisions of the law as they stand at that point, irrespective of any reforming tendencies the particular court may have, while the political techniques of settlement are not so restricted. It is also not unusual for political and legal organs to deal with aspects of the same basic situation.[14]

The role of political influences and considerations in inter-state disputes is obviously a vital one, and many settlements can only be properly understood within the wider international political context. In addition, how a state proceeds in a dispute will be conditioned by political factors. If the dispute is perceived to be one affecting vital interests, for example, the state would be less willing to submit the matter to binding third party settlement than if it were a more technical issue, while the existence of regional mechanisms will often be of political significance.

Article 2(3) of the United Nations Charter provides that:

[a]ll members shall settle their international disputes by peaceful means in such a manner that international peace and security and justice are not endangered.

---

[10] See further *infra*, p. 751.   [11] PCIJ, Series A, No. 2, 1924, p. 11.
[12] See e.g. H. Lauterpacht, *The Function of Law in the International Community*, London, 1933, especially pp. 19–20.   [13] See further, *infra*, p. 751.
[14] See e.g. the *Iran* case, ICJ Reports, 1980, pp. 3, 22–3; 76 ILR, pp. 530, 548–9 and the *Nicaragua* case, ICJ Reports, 1984, pp. 392, 435–6; 76 ILR, pp. 104, 146–7.

The 1970 Declaration on Principles of International Law Concerning Friendly Relations and Co-operation among States[15] develops this principle and notes that:

> states shall accordingly seek early and just settlement of their international disputes by negotiation, inquiry, mediation, conciliation, arbitration, judicial settlement, resort to regional agencies or arrangements or other peaceful means of their choice.

The same methods of dispute settlement are stipulated in article 33(1) of the UN Charter, although in the context of disputes the continuance of which are likely to endanger international peace and security. The 1970 Declaration, which is not so limited, asserts that in seeking an early and just settlement, the parties are to agree upon such peaceful means as they see appropriate to the circumstances and nature of the dispute.

There would appear, therefore, to be no inherent hierarchy with respect to the methods specified and no specific method required in any given situation. States have a free choice as to the mechanisms adopted for settling their disputes.[16] This approach is also taken in a number of regional instruments, including the American Treaty on Pacific Settlement (the Pact of Bogotá) 1948 of the Organisation of American States, the European Convention for the Peaceful Settlement of Disputes 1957 and the Helsinki Final Act of the Conference on Security and Co-operation in Europe 1975. In addition, it is to be noted that the parties to a dispute have the duty to continue to seek a settlement by other peaceful means agreed by them, in the event of the failure of one particular method. Should the means elaborated fail to resolve a dispute, the continuance of which is likely to endanger the maintenance of international peace and security, the parties under article 37(1) of the Charter, '*shall* refer it to the Security Council'.[17]

Diplomatic methods of dispute settlement

Negotiation[18]

Of all the procedures used to resolve differences, the simplest and most utilised form is understandably negotiation. It consists basically of discussions

---

[15] General Assembly resolution 2625(XXV). See also the Manila Declaration on the Peaceful Settlement of International Disputes, General Assembly resolution 37/590; resolutions 2627(XXV); 2734(XXV); 40/9; the Declaration on the Prevention and Removal of Disputes and Situations which may Threaten International Peace and Security, resolution 43/51 and the Declaration on Fact-finding, resolution 46/59.

[16] See article 33(1) of the UN Charter and section I (3) and (10) of the Manila Declaration.

[17] Emphasis added.

[18] See e.g. UN Handbook, Chapter II; Merrills, *Dispute Settlement*, Chapter 1 and H. Lachs, 'The Law and Settlement of International Disputes' in *Dispute Settlement*, pp. 287–9. See also Murty, 'Settlement', pp. 678–9; A. Watson, *Diplomacy*, London, 1982; F. Kirgis, *Prior*

between the interested parties with a view to reconciling divergent opinions, or at least understanding the different positions maintained. It does not involve any third party, at least at that stage, and so differs from the other forms of dispute management. In addition to being an extremely active method of settlement itself, negotiation is normally the precursor to other settlement procedures as the parties decide amongst themselves how best to resolve their differences.[19] It is eminently suited to the clarification, if not always resolution, of complicated disagreements. It is by mutual discussions that the essence of the differences will be revealed and the opposing contentions elucidated. Negotiations are the most satisfactory means to resolve disputes since the parties are so directly engaged. Negotiations, of course, do not always succeed, since they do depend on a certain degree of mutual goodwill, flexibility and sensitivity. Hostile public opinion in one state may prevent the concession of certain points and mutual distrust may fatally complicate the process, while opposing political attitudes may be such as to preclude any acceptable negotiated agreement.[20]

In certain circumstances there may exist a duty to enter into negotiations arising out of particular bilateral or multilateral agreements.[21] In addition, decisions of tribunals may direct the parties to engage in negotiations in good faith and may indicate the factors to be taken into account in the

Consultation in International Law, Charlottesville, 1983; P. J. De Waart, *The Element of Negotiation in the Pacific Settlement of Disputes between States*, The Hague, 1974; G. Geamanu, 'Théorie et Pratique Des Négociations en Droit International', 166 HR, 1980 I, p. 365 and N. E. Ghozali, 'La Négociation Diplomatique dans la Jurisprudence Internationale', *Revue Belge de Droit International*, 1992, p. 323. Note also that operative paragraph 10 of the Manila Declaration emphasises that direct negotiations are a 'flexible and effective means of peaceful settlement'.

[19] See e.g. Judge Nervo, *Fisheries Jurisdiction* case, ICJ Reports, 1973, pp. 3, 45; 55 ILR, pp. 183, 225. See also the *Mavrommatis Palestine Concessions* case, PCIJ, Series A, No. 2, 1924, p. 15, noting that 'Before a dispute can be made the subject of an action at law, its subject matter should have been clearly defined by diplomatic negotiations', and the *Rights of Passage (Preliminary Objections)* case, ICJ Reports, 1957, pp. 105, 148–8; 24 ILR, pp. 840, 848–9. The Court noted in the *Free Zones of Upper Savoy and the District of Gex* case, PCIJ, Series A, No. 22, p. 13; 5 ILR, pp. 461, 463, that the judicial settlement of disputes was 'simply an alternative to the direct and friendly settlement of such disputes between the parties.

[20] Note that certain treaties provide for consultations in certain circumstances, see e.g. article 84 of the Vienna Convention on the Representation of States in their Relations with International Organisations 1975; article 41 of the Convention on Succession of States in Respect of Treaties 1978 and article 42 of the Convention on Succession of States in Respect of Property, Archives and Debts 1983. Article 282(1) of the Convention on the Law of the Sea 1982 provides that when a dispute arises between states parties concerning the interpretation or application of the Convention, 'the parties to the dispute shall proceed expeditiously to an exchange of views regarding its settlement by negotiation or other peaceful means'.

[21] See e.g. the *Fisheries Jurisdiction* case, ICJ Reports, 1974, p. 3; 55 ILR, p. 238. See also article 15 of the Moon Treaty 1979; article 41 of the Vienna Convention on Succession of States in Respect of Treaties, 1978; article 84 of the Vienna Convention on the Representation of States in their Relations with International Organisations 1975 and article 283 of the Convention on the Law of the Sea 1982.

course of negotiations between the parties.[22] Where there is an obligation to negotiate, this would imply also an obligation to pursue such negotiations as far as possible with a view to concluding agreements.[23] The Court held in the *North Sea Continental Shelf* cases[24] that:

> the parties are under an obligation to enter into negotiations with a view to arriving at an agreement, and not merely to go through a formal process of negotiation as a sort of prior condition . . . they are under an obligation so to conduct themselves that the negotiations are meaningful, which will not be the case when either of them insists upon its own position without contemplating any modification of it.

The Court in the *German External Debts* case[25] emphasised that although an agreement to negotiate did not necessarily imply an obligation to reach an agreement, 'it does imply that serious efforts towards that end will be made'. In the *Lac Lannoux* arbitration,[26] it was stated that 'consultations and negotiations between the two states must be genuine, must comply with the rules of good faith and must not be mere formalities'. Examples of infringement of the rules of good faith were held to include the unjustified breaking off of conversations, unusual delays and systematic refusal to give consideration to proposals or adverse interests.[27]

The point was also emphasised by the International Court in the *Legality of the Threat or Use of Nuclear Weapons*,[28] where it noted the reference in article VI of the Treaty on the Non-Proliferation of Nuclear Weapons to 'pursue negotiations in good faith on effective measures relating to cessation of the nuclear arms race at an early date and to nuclear disarmament, and on a treaty on general and complete disarmament under strict and effective international control'. The Court then declared that:

> The legal import of that obligation goes beyond that of a mere obligation of conduct: the obligation involved here is an obligation to achieve a precise result – nuclear disarmament in all its aspects – by adopting a particular course of conduct, namely, the pursuit of negotiations on the matter in good faith.

---

[22] See e.g. the *North Sea Continental Shelf* cases, ICJ Reports, 1969, pp. 3, 53–4; 41 ILR, pp. 29, 83. See also the *Fisheries Jurisdiction* case, ICJ Reports, 1974, pp. 3, 32; 55 ILR, pp. 238, 267. Section I, paragraph 10 of the Manila Declaration declares that when states resort to negotiations, they should 'negotiate meaningfully, in order to arrive at an early settlement acceptable to the parties'.

[23] See the *Railway Traffic between Lithuania and Poland* case, PCIJ, Series A/B. No. 42, p. 116; 6 ILR, pp. 403, 405. Article 4(e) of the International Law Association's draft International Instrument on the Protection of the Environment from Damage Caused by Space Debris provides that 'to negotiate in good faith ... means *inter alia* not only to hold consultations or talks but also to pursue them with a view of reaching a solution', see Report of the Sixty-sixth Conference, Buenos Aires, 1994, p. 319.

[24] ICJ Reports, 1969, pp. 3, 47; 41 ILR, pp. 29, 76.   [25] 47 ILR, pp. 418, 454.

[26] 24 ILR, pp. 101, 119.

[27] *Ibid.*, p. 128. See also the *Tacna-Arica Arbitration*, II RIAA, pp. 921 *et seq.*

[28] ICJ Reports, 1996, paras. 98 *et seq.*; 35 ILM, 1996, pp. 809, 830–1.

Where disputes are by their continuance likely to endanger the maintenance of international peace and security, article 33 of the UN Charter provides that the parties to such disputes shall first of all seek a solution by negotiation, inquiry or mediation, and then resort, if the efforts have not borne fruit, to more complex forms of resolution.[29]

Good offices and mediation[30]

The employment of the procedures of good offices and mediation involves the use of a third party, whether an individual or individuals, a state or group of states or an international organisation, to encourage the contending parties to come to a settlement. Unlike the techniques of arbitration and adjudication, the process aims at persuading the parties to a dispute to reach satisfactory terms for its termination by themselves. Provisions for settling the dispute are not prescribed.

Technically, good offices are involved where a third party attempts to influence the opposing sides to enter into negotiations, whereas mediation implies the active participation in the negotiating process of the third party itself. In fact, the dividing line between the two approaches is often difficult to maintain as they tend to merge into one another, depending upon the circumstances. One example of the good offices method is the role played by the US President in 1906 in concluding the Russian–Japanese War,[31] or the function performed by the USSR in assisting in the peaceful settlement of the Indian–Pakistan dispute in 1965.[32] Another might be the part played by France in encouraging US–North Vietnamese negotiations to begin in Paris in the early 1970s.[33] A mediator, such as the US Secretary of State in the Middle East in 1973–4,[34] has an active and vital function to perform in seeking to cajole the disputing parties into accepting what are often his own proposals. It is his responsibility to reconcile the different claims and

[29] See the *North Sea Continental Shelf* cases, ICJ Reports, 1969, pp. 3, 47; 41 ILR, pp. 29, 77 and the *Fisheries Jurisdiction* cases, ICJ Reports, 1974, pp. 3, 32; 55 ILR, p. 267.
[30] See e.g. UN Handbook, p. 33; Merrills, *Dispute Settlement*, Chapter 2; R. R. Probst, 'Good Offices' In the Light of Swiss International Practice and Experience, Dordrecht, 1989; *New Approaches to International Mediation* (eds. C. R. Mitchell and K. Webb), New York, 1988; J. Brierly, *The Law of Nations*, 6th edn, Oxford, 1963, pp. 373–6 and Murty, 'Settlement', pp. 680–1. See also *International Mediation in Theory and Practice* (eds. S. Touval and I. W. Zartman), Boulder, 1985 and J. Bercovitch and J. Z. Rubin, *Mediation in International Relations*, London, 1992.
[31] Murty, 'Settlement', p. 681. Note also the exercise of US good offices in relation to a territorial dispute between France, in regards to its protectorate of Cambodia, and Thailand, SCOR, First Year, 81st meeting, pp. 505–7.
[32] See GAOR, 21st session, suppl. no. 2, part I, chapter 3.
[33] See AFDI, 1972, pp. 995–6. Note also the role played by Cardinal Samoré, a Papal mediator in the Beagle Channel dispute between Argentina and Chile, between 1978 and 1985, see e.g. Merrills, *Disputes Settlement*, p. 29 and 24 ILM, 1985, pp. 1 *et seq.* See also *infra*, p. 738.   [34] See e.g. DUSPIL 1974, pp. 656–8 and *ibid.*, pp. 759–62.

improve the atmosphere pervading the discussions. The UN Secretary-General can sometimes play an important role by the exercise of his good offices.[35] An example of this was provided in the situation relating to Afghanistan in 1988. The Geneva Agreements of that year specifically noted that a representative of the Secretary-General would lend his good offices to the parties.[36] Good offices may also be undertaken by the Secretary-General jointly with office-holders of regional organisations.[37]

The Hague Conventions of 1899 and 1907 laid down many of the rules governing these two processes. It was stipulated that the signatories to the treaties had a right to offer good offices or mediation, even during hostilities, and that the exercise of the right was never to be regarded by either of the contending sides as an unfriendly act.[38] It was also explained that such procedures were not binding. The Conventions laid a duty upon the parties to a serious dispute or conflict to resort to good offices or mediation as far as circumstances allow, before having recourse to arms.[39] This, of course, has to be seen in the light of the relevant Charter provisions regarding the use of force, but it does point to the part that should be played by these diplomatic procedures.

Inquiry[40]

Where differences of opinion on factual matters underlie a dispute between parties, the logical solution is often to institute a commission of inquiry to be conducted by reputable observers to ascertain precisely the facts in contention.[41] Provisions for such inquiries were first elaborated in the 1899

---

[35] See e.g. Security Council resolution 367 (1975) requesting the UN Secretary-General to undertake a good offices mission to Cyprus. See the statement by the Secretary-General of the functions of good offices cited in UN Handbook, pp. 35–6. See also B. G. Ramcharan, 'The Good Offices of the United Nations Secretary-General in the Field of Human Rights', 76 AJIL, 1982, p. 130. Note also paragraph 12 of the Declaration on the Prevention and Removal of Disputes and Situations Which May Threaten International Peace and Security 1988, General Assembly resolution 43/51. See also *infra*, Chapter 20, p. 854.

[36] S/19835, annex. See also Security Council resolution 622 (1988).

[37] For example with the Chairman of the Organisation of African Unity with regard to the Western Sahara and Mayotte situations, UN Handbook, p. 39, and with the Secretary-General of the Organisation of American States with regard to Central America, *ibid.*

[38] Article 3 of Hague Convention No. I, 1899 and Convention No. I, 1907.

[39] *Ibid.*, article 2.

[40] See e.g. Merrills, *Disputes Settlement*, Chapter 3 and N. Bar-Yaacov, *The Handling of International Disputes by Means of Inquiry*, London, 1974. See also UN Handbook, pp. 24 *et seq.*; T. Bensalah, *L'Enquête Internationale dans le Règlement des Conflits*, Paris, 1976; P. Ruegger, 'Quelques Réflexions sur le Rôle Actuel et Futur des Commissions Internationales d'Enquête' in *Mélanges Bindschedler*, Paris, 1980, p. 427 and Ruegger, 'Nouvelles Réflexions sur le Rôle des Procédures Internationales d'Enquête dans la Solution des Conflits Internationaux' in *Etudes en l'Honneur de Robert Ago*, Milan, 1987, p. 327.

[41] Inquiry as a specific procedure under consideration here is to be distinguished from the general process of fact-finding as part of other mechanisms for dispute settlement, such as through the UN or other institutions. See e.g. *Fact-Finding Before International Tribunals* (ed. R. B. Lillich), Charlottesville, 1992.

Hague Conference as a possible alternative to the use of arbitration.[42] However, the technique is limited in that it can only have relevance in the case of international disputes, involving neither the honour nor the vital interests of the parties where the conflict centres around a genuine disagreement as to particular facts which can be resolved by recourse to an impartial and conscientious investigation.[43]

Inquiry was most successfully used in the Dogger Bank incident of 1904 where Russian naval ships fired on British fishing boats in the belief that they were hostile Japanese torpedo craft.[44] The Hague provisions were put into effect[45] and the report of the international inquiry commission contributed to a peaceful settlement of the issue.[46] This encouraged an elaboration of the technique by the 1907 Hague Conference,[47] and a wave of support for the procedure.[48] The United States, for instance, concluded forty-eight bilateral treaties with provisions in each one of them for the creation of a permanent inquiry commission between 1913 and 1940. These agreements were known as the 'Bryan Treaties'.[49]

However, the use of commissions of inquiry in accordance with the Hague Convention of 1907 proved in practice to be extremely rare. The *Red Crusader* inquiry of 1962[50] followed an interval of some forty years since the previous inquiry. This concerned an incident between a British trawler and a Danish fisheries protection vessel, which subsequently involved a British frigate. Although instituted as a fact-finding exercise, it did

---

[42] See e.g. Bar-Yaacov, *International Disputes*, Chapter 2. The incident of the destruction of the US battleship *Maine* in 1898, which precipitated the American–Spanish War, was particularly noted as an impetus to the evolution of inquiry as an important 'safety valve' mechanism, *ibid.*, pp. 33–4. This was particularly in the light of the rival national inquiries that came to opposing conclusions in that episode, see the inquiry commission in that case, *Annual Register*, 1898, p. 362.

[43] Article 9, 1899 Hague Convention for the Pacific Settlement of International Disputes.

[44] Bar-Yaacov, *International Disputes*, Chapter 3. See also Merrills, *Disputes Settlement*, pp. 44–6 and J. B. Scott, *The Hague Court Reports*, New York, 1916, p. 403.

[45] The Commission of Inquiry consisted of four naval officers of the UK, Russian, French and American fleets, plus a fifth member chosen by the other four (in the event an Austro-Hungarian). It was required to examine all the circumstances, particularly with regard to responsibility and blame.

[46] It was found that there was no justification for the Russian attack. In the event, both sides accepted the report and the sum of £65,000 was paid by Russia to the UK, Bar-Yaacov, *International Disputes*, p. 70.

[47] *Ibid.*, Chapter 4. Note also the *Tavignano* inquiry, J. B. Scott, *The Hague Court Reports*, New York, 1916, p. 413; the *Tiger* inquiry, Bar-Yaacov, *International Disputes*, p. 156 and the *Tubantia* inquiry, J. B. Scott, *The Hague Court Reports*, New York, 1932, p. 135. See also Merrills, *Disputes Settlement*, pp. 46–50 and Bar-Yaacov, *International Disputes*, pp. 141–79.

[48] Bar-Yaacov, *International Disputes*, Chapter 5.

[49] These were prefigured by the Taft or Knox Treaties of 1911 (which did not come into operation), *ibid.*, pp. 113–17. The USSR has also signed a number of treaties which provide for joint inquiries with regard to frontier incidents, *ibid.*, pp. 117–19.

[50] *Ibid.*, pp. 179–95 and Merrills, *Disputes Settlement*, pp. 51–4. See also 35 ILR, p. 485, Cmnd. 776 and E. Lauterpacht, 'The Contemporary Practice of the UK in the Field of International Law', 1962, vol. 1, pp. 50–3.

incorporate judicial aspects. A majority of the Commission were lawyers and the procedures followed a judicial pattern. In addition, aspects of the report reflected legal findings, such as the declaration that the firing on the trawler by the Danish vessel in an attempt to stop it escaping arrest for alleged illegal fishing, 'exceeded legitimate use of armed force'.[51] There have been no similar inquiries since 1962.

The value of inquiry within specified institutional frameworks, nevertheless, has been evident. Its use has increased within the United Nations generally[52] and in the specialised agencies.[53] Inquiry is also part of other processes of dispute settlement in the context of general fact-finding.[54] But inquiry as a separate mechanism in accordance with the Hague Convention of 1907 has fallen out of favour. In many disputes, of course, the determination of the relevant circumstances would simply not aid a settlement, whilst its nature as a third party involvement in a situation would discourage some states.

Conciliation[55]

The process of conciliation involves a third party investigation of the basis of the dispute and the submission of a report embodying suggestions for a settlement. As such it involves elements of both inquiry and mediation, and in fact the process of conciliation emerged from treaties providing for permanent inquiry commissions.[56]

Conciliation reports are only proposals and do not constitute binding decisions.[57] They are thus different from arbitration awards. The period

[51] *Ibid.*, p. 53, Merrills, *Disputes Settlement*, p. 54 and Bar-Yaacov, *International Disputes*, p. 192.
[52] See e.g. the the announcement by the UN Secretary-General of a mission in 1988 to Iran and Iraq to investigate the situation of prisoners of war at the request of those states, S/20147. See also Security Council resolution 384 (1975) concerning East Timor.
[53] See e.g. article 26 of the Constitution of the International Labour Organisation.
[54] Note, for example, article 90 of Protocol I to the Geneva Red Cross Conventions 1949 providing for the establishment of an International Fact-finding Commission and Security Council resolution 780 (1992) establishing a Commission of Experts to investigate violations of international humanitarian law in the Former Yugoslavia, see M. C. Bassiouni, 'The United Nations Commission of Experts Established Pursuant to Security Council Resolution 780 (1992)', 88 AJIL, 1994, p. 784.
[55] See e.g. UN Handbook, pp. 45 *et seq.*; Lauterpacht, *Function of Law*, pp. 260–9; Merrills, *Disputes Settlement*, Chapter 4; Murty, 'Settlement', pp. 682–3; H. Fox, 'Conciliation' in *International Disputes*, p. 93; J. P. Cot, *La Conciliation Internationale*, Paris, 1968 and Bowett, 'Contemporary Developments', Chapter 2.
[56] See e.g. Murty, 'Settlement', Merrills notes that by 1940, nearly 200 conciliation treaties had been concluded, *Disputes Settlement*, p. 61.
[57] See e.g. paragraph 6 of the annex to the Vienna Convention on the Law of Treaties 1969. The Vienna Convention for the Protection of the Ozone Layer 1985 provides that conciliation awards should be considered in good faith, while article 85(7) of the Vienna Convention on the Representation of States in their Relations with International Organisations provides that any party to the dispute may declare unilaterally that it will abide by the recommendations in the report as far as it is concerned. Note that article 14(3) of the Treaty Establishing the Organisation of Eastern Caribbean States 1981 stipulates that member states undertake to accept the conciliation procedure as compulsory.

between the world wars was the heyday for conciliation commissions and many treaties made provision for them as a method for resolving disputes. But the process has not been widely employed and certainly has not justified the faith evinced in it by states between 1920 and 1938.[58]

Nevertheless, it does have a role to play. It is extremely flexible and by clarifying the facts and discussing proposals may stimulate negotiations between the parties. The rules dealing with conciliation were elaborated in the 1928 General Act on the Pacific Settlement of International Disputes (revised in 1949). The function of the commissions was defined to include inquiries and mediation techniques. Such commissions were to be composed of five persons, one appointed by each opposing side and the other three to be appointed by agreement from amongst the citizens of third states. The proceedings were to be concluded within six months and were not to be held in public. The conciliation procedure was intended to deal with mixed legal-factual situations and to operate quickly and informally.[59]

There have of late been a number of proposals to reactivate the conciliation technique, but how far they will succeed in their aim remains to be seen.[60] A number of multilateral treaties do, however, provide for conciliation as a means of resolving disputes. The 1948 American Treaty of Pacific Settlement; the 1957 European Convention for the Peaceful Settlement of Disputes; the 1964 Protocol on the Commission of Mediation, Conciliation and Arbitration to the Charter of the Organisation of African Unity; the 1969 Vienna Convention on the Law of Treaties; the Treaty Establishing the Organisation of Eastern Caribbean States 1981; the 1982 Convention on the Law of the Sea and the 1985 Vienna Convention on the Protection of the Ozone Layer, for example, all contain provisions concerning conciliation. The conciliation procedure was used in the Iceland–Norway dispute over the continental shelf delimitation between Iceland and Jan Mayen island.[61] The agreement establishing the Conciliation Commission stressed that the question was the subject of continuing negotiations and that the Commission report would not be binding, both elements characteristic of

---

[58] But note e.g. the Chaco Commission, 1929, the Franco-Siamese Conciliation Commission, 1947 and the Franco-Swiss Commission, 1955, see Merrills, *Disputes Settlement*, pp. 62–5. See also Bar-Yaacov, *International Disputes*, Chapter 7.

[59] Article 15(1) of the Geneva General Act as amended provides that 'The task of the Conciliation Commission shall be to elucidate the questions in dispute, to collect with that object all necessary information by means of enquiry or otherwise, and to endeavour to bring the parties to an agreement. It may, after the case has been examined, inform the parties of the terms of settlement which seem suitable to it, and lay down the period within which they are to make their decision.'

[60] See e.g. the Regulations on the Procedure of Conciliation adopted by the Institut de Droit International, *Annuaire de l'Institut de Droit International*, 1961, pp. 374 *et seq*. See also the UN Draft Rules for Conciliation of Disputes Between States adopted by the General Assembly on 28 November 1990 for circulation and comment, 30 ILM, 1991, p. 229.

[61] 20 ILM, 1981, p. 797; 62 ILR, p. 108. The Commission Report was accepted by the parties, 21 ILM, 1982, p. 1222.

the conciliation method. The Commission had also to take into account Iceland's strong economic interests in the area as well as other factors. The role of the concept of natural prolongation within continental shelf delimitation was examined as well as the legal status of islands and relevant state practice and court decisions. The solution proposed by the Commission was for a joint development zone, an idea that would have been unlikely to come from a judicial body reaching a decision solely on the basis of the legal rights of the parties. In other words, the flexibility of the conciliation process seen in the context of continued negotiations between the parties was demonstrated.[62] Such commissions have also been established outside the framework of specific treaties, for example by the United Nations. Instances would include the Conciliation Commission for Palestine under General Assembly resolution 194(III), 1948, and the Conciliation Commission for the Congo under resolution 1474(ES-IV) of 1960.

International institutions and dispute settlement[63]

Regional organisations and the United Nations[64]

Article 52(1) of Chapter VIII of the UN Charter provides that nothing in the Charter precludes the existence of regional arrangements or agencies for dealing with such matters relating to the maintenance of international peace and security as are appropriate for regional action, provided that such arrangements or agencies and their activities are consistent with the purposes and principles of the UN.[65] Article 52(2) stipulates that members of the UN entering into such arrangements or agencies are to make every effort to settle local disputes peacefully through such regional arrangements or by such regional agencies before referring them to the Security Council, and that the Security Council encourages the development of the peaceful settlement of local disputes through such regional arrangements. That having

---

[62] See also the 1929 Chaco Conciliation Commission; the 1947 Franco-Siamese Commission; the 1952 Belgian–Danish Commission; the 1954–5 Franco-Swiss Commission and the 1958 Franco-Mexican Commission. See UN Handbook, p. 48 and Nguyen Quoc Dinh et al., Droit International Public, pp. 790–1.

[63] See infra, Chapter 20 for peaceful settlement of disputes through the United Nations and infra, Chapter 21 generally with regard to international institutions.

[64] See e.g. D. W. Bowett, The Law of International Institutions, 4th edn, London, 1982; Merrills, Disputes Settlement, Chapter 10 ; Murty, 'Settlement', pp. 725–8; K. Oellers-Frahm and N. Wühler, Dispute Settlement in Public International Law, New York, 1984, pp. 92 et seq. and Nguyen Quoc Dingh et al., Droit International Public, pp. 806 et seq.

[65] See e.g. The Charter of the United Nations (ed. B. Simma), Oxford, 1995, pp. 679 et seq. See also H. Saba, 'Les Accords Régionaux dans la Charte des Nations Unies', 80 HR, 1952 I, p. 635; D. E. Acevedo, 'Disputes under Consideration by the UN Security Council or Regional Bodies' in The International Court of Justice at a Crossroads (ed. L. F. Damrosch), 1987; B. Andemicael, Regionalism and the United Nations, Dobbs Ferry, 1979; J. M. Yepes, 'Les Accords Régionaux et le Droit International', 71 HR, 1947 II, p. 235.

been said, article 52(4) stresses that the application of articles 34 and 35 of the UN Charter relating to the roles of the Security Council and General Assembly remains unaffected.[66] The supremacy of the Security Council is reinforced by article 53(1) which provides that while the Council may, where appropriate, utilise such regional arrangements or agencies for enforcement action under its authority, 'no enforcement action shall be taken under regional arrangements or by regional agencies without the authorisation of the Security Council'. It should also be noted that by article 24 the Security Council possesses 'primary responsibility for the maintenance of international peace and security', while article 103 of the Charter emphasises that in the event of a conflict between the obligations of a UN member under the Charter and obligations under any other international agreement, the former are to prevail.[67] In addition, under article 36, the Security Council may 'at any stage of a dispute . . . recommend appropriate procedures or methods of adjustment',[68] while article 37 provides that should the parties to a dispute fail to settle it, they 'shall refer it to the Security Council'. Furthermore, should the Council itself deem that the continuance of a dispute is likely to endanger the maintenance of international peace and security, 'it shall decide whether to take action under article 36 or to recommend such terms of settlement as it may consider appropriate'.[69] Thus, although reference where appropriate to regional organisations or arrangements should take place, this does not affect the comprehensive role of the UN through the Security Council or General Assembly in dealing in various ways with disputes between states.[70] While provisions contained in regional instruments may prevent or restrict resort to mechanisms outside those instruments,[71] this does not constrain in any way the authority or competence of the UN.[72] In many cases, a matter may be simultaneously before both the UN and a regional organisation and such concurrent jurisdiction does not constitute a jurisdictional problem for the UN.[73] In practice and in relation to the adoption of active measures, the UN is likely to defer to

[66] See further *infra*, Chapter 20, p. 842.
[67] See the *Nicaragua* case, ICJ Reports, 1984, pp. 392, 440; 76 ILR, pp. 104, 151.
[68] This refers to disputes the continuance of which is likely to endanger the maintenance of international peace and security, article 33.   [69] Article 37(2).
[70] Note that section I, paragraph 6 of the Manila Declaration on the Pacific Settlement of International Disputes adopted in General Assembly resolution 37/10, 1982, provides that states parties to relevant regional arrangements or agencies shall make every effort to settle disputes through such mechanisms, but that this 'does not preclude states from bringing any dispute to the attention of the Security Council or of the General Assembly in accordance with the Charter of the United Nations'.   [71] See *infra*, p. 881.
[72] See e.g. M. Bartos, 'L'ONU et la Co-opération Régionale', 27 RGDIP, 1956, p. 7.
[73] The International Court noted in the *Nicaragua* case, ICJ Reports, 1984, pp. 392, 440; 76 ILR, pp. 104, 151, in the context of contended regional discussions, that 'even the existence of active negotiations in which both parties might be involved should not prevent both the Security Council and the Court from exercising their separate functions under the Charter and the Statute of the Court'.

appropriate regional mechanisms while realistic chances exist for a regional settlement.[74]

Various regional organisations have created machinery for the settlement of disputes.

The Organisation of African Unity[75]

Article XIX of the 1963 Charter of the OAU refers to the principle of 'the peaceful settlement of disputes by negotiation, mediation, conciliation or arbitration' and to assist in achieving this a Commission of Mediation, Conciliation and Arbitration was established by the Protocol of 21 July 1964.[76] The jurisdiction of the Commission is not compulsory and indeed it has never been resorted to. African states were historically unwilling to resort to judicial or arbitral methods of dispute settlement and in general preferred informal third party involvement through the medium of the OAU. In the Algeria–Morocco boundary dispute,[77] for example, the OAU established an *ad hoc* commission consisting of the representatives of seven African states to seek to achieve a settlement of issues arising out of the 1963 clashes.[78] Similarly in the Somali–Ethiopian conflict,[79] a commission was set up by the OAU in an attempt to mediate.[80] This commission failed to resolve the dispute, although it did reaffirm the principle of the inviolability of frontiers of member states as attained at the time of independence.[81] In a third case, the Western Sahara dispute,[82] an OAU committee was established in July 1978, which sought unsuccessfully to reach a settlement in the conflict,[83] while the OAU also established committees to try to mediate in the

---

[74] In such cases, the Security Council is likely to inscribe the dispute on its agenda and, providing the dispute is not one actually endangering international peace and security, refer the matter to the appropriate regional agency under article 52(2) and (3), keeping it under review on the agenda, see UN Handbook, p. 96.

[75] See generally T. Maluwa, 'The Peaceful Settlement of Disputes among African States, 1963–1983: Some Conceptual Issues and Practical Trends', 38 ICLQ, 1989, p. 299; S. G. Amoo and I. W. Zartman, 'Mediation by Regional Organisations: The Organisation of African Unity (OAU) in Chad' in *Mediation in International Relations*, p. 131; B. Boutros Ghali, *L'Organisation de l'Unité Africaine*, Paris, 1968; M. Bedjaoui, 'Le Règlement Pacifique des Différends Africains', AFDI, 1972, p. 85; B. Andemicael, *Le Règlement Pacifique des Différends Survenant entre Etats Africains*, New York, 1973; E. Jouve, *L'Organisation de l'Unité Africain*, Paris, 1984; T. O. Elias, *Africa and the Development of International Law*, Leiden, 1972; Z. Cervenka, *The Organisation of African Unity and its Charter*, London, 1968 and M. N. Shaw, 'Dispute Settlement in Africa', 37 YBWA, 1983, p. 149. See further on the Organisation of African Unity, *infra*, Chapter 21, p. 906.   [76] Elias, *Africa*, Chapter 9.

[77] See I. Brownlie, *African Boundaries*, London, 1979, p. 55 and M. N. Shaw, *Title to Territory in Africa: International Legal Issues*, Oxford, 1986, pp. 196–7.

[78] See *Keesings Contemporary Archives*, pp. 19939–40 and Shaw, 'Dispute Settlement', p. 153.

[79] See Brownlie, *African Boundaries*, p. 826. See also Shaw, *Title to Territory*, pp. 197–201.

[80] *Africa Research Bulletin*, May 1973, p. 2845 and *ibid.*, June 1973, pp. 2883–4 and 2850.

[81] *Ibid.*, August 1980, pp. 5763–64. This is the principle of *uti possidetis*, see further *supra*, Chapter 9, p. 356.   [82] See e.g. Shaw, *Title to Territory*, pp. 123 *et seq.*

[83] *Ibid.*, and Shaw, 'Dispute Settlement', pp. 160–2.

Chad civil war, again with little success.[84] Despite mixed success, it became fairly established practice that in a dispute involving African states, initial recourse will be made to OAU mechanisms, primarily *ad hoc* commissions or committees.

In an attempt to improve the mechanisms available, the OAU approved a Mechanism for Conflict Prevention, Management and Resolution in 1992.[85] The Mechanism will operate through the Bureau of the Summit, with the Secretary-General and the Secretariat as the operational arm, and will function on the basis of the consent and co-operation of the parties to the conflict. The Bureau will be composed of member states elected annually, based on the principles of equitable regional representation and rotation, and the Secretary-General is empowered to resort to eminent African personalities to assist in the peaceful settlement of disputes. On the African continent, one should also note the development of the Economic Community of West African States (ECOWAS) created in 1975. Article 56 of the 1975 Treaty provides that where friendly settlement of disputes is not possible, any party to the dispute may refer the matter to a Tribunal of the Community whose function will be to settle the dispute by a final decision.

The Organisation of American States[86]

Article 23 of the Charter of the OAS, signed at Bogotá in 1948 and as amended by the Protocol of Cartagena de Indias 1985, provides that international disputes between member states must be submitted to the Organisation for peaceful settlement, although this is not to be interpreted as an impairment of the rights and obligations of member states under articles 34 and 35 of the UN Charter.[87] The 1948 American Treaty of Pacific Settlement (the Pact of Bogotá, to be distinguished from the Charter) sets out the procedures in detail, ranging from good offices, mediation and

---

[84] *Ibid.*, pp. 158–60. See also *The Charter of the United Nations*, pp. 720–1.

[85] AHG/Dec. 1 (XXVIII) and see the Report of the OAU Secretary-General, Doc. CM/1747 (LVIII) and AHG/Dec. 3 (XXIX), 1993. See also M. C. Djiena-Wembon, 'A Propos du Nouveau Mécanisme de l'OUA sur les Conflits', *Revue Générale de Droit International Public*, 1994, p. 377 and R. Ranjeva, 'Reflections on the Proposals for the Establishment of a Pan-African Mechanism for the Prevention and Settlement of Conflicts' in *Towards More Effective Supervision by International Organisations* (eds. N. Blokker and S. Muller), Dordrecht, vol. I, 1994, p. 93.

[86] See e.g. Merrills, *Disputes Settlement*, pp. 209–10 and Bowett, 'Contemporary Development', pp. 215 *et seq*. See also E. Jimenez de Arechaga, 'La Co-ordination des Systèmes de l'ONU et de l'Organisation des Etats Américains pour le Règlement Pacifique des Différends et la Sécurité Collective', 111 HR, 1964 I, p. 423 and A. Cançado Trindade, 'Mécanismes de Règlement Pacifiques des Différends en Amérique Centrale: De Contadora à Esquipulas II', AFDI, 1987, p. 798.

[87] Note that as originally drafted in the 1948 Charter, article 20 (as it then was) provided that submission to the OAS procedures had to occur prior to referral to the Security Council of the UN.

conciliation to arbitration and judicial settlement by the International Court of Justice. This treaty, however, has not been successful[88] and in practice the OAS has utilised the Inter-American Peace Committee created in 1940 for peaceful resolution of disputes. This was replaced in 1970 by the Inter-American Committee on Peaceful Settlement, a subsidiary organ of the Council. Since the late 1950s the Permanent Council of the OAS, a plenary body at ambassadorial level, has played an increasingly important role.[89] One example concerned the frontier incidents that took place on the border between Costa Rica and Nicaragua in 1985. The Council set up a fact-finding committee and after hearing its report, adopted a resolution calling for talks to take place within the Contadora negotiating process.[90] The Esquipulas II agreement of 14 November 1987 established an International Verification and Follow-up Commission to be composed of the Foreign Ministers of the Contadora and Support Group States together with the Secretaries-General of the UN and OAS.[91]

The Arab League[92]

The Arab League, established in 1945, aims at increasing co-operation between the Arab states. Its facilities for peaceful settlement of disputes amongst its members are not, however, very well developed, and in practice consist primarily of informal conciliation attempts. One notable exception was the creation in 1961 of an Inter-Arab Force to keep the peace between Iraq and Kuwait.[93]

---

[88] Although note the *Nicaragua* v. *Honduras* case, ICJ Reports, 1988, pp. 69, 88; 84 ILR, pp. 218, 243, where the Court held that it had jurisdiction by virtue of article XXXI of the Pact of Bogotá.

[89] See e.g. Merrills, *Disputes Settlement*, pp. 214–16. See also articles 82–90 of the OAS Charter.

[90] OAS Permanent Council resolutions CP/Res. 427 (618/85); CP/doc. 1592/85 and A/40/737-S/17549, annex IV.

[91] The countries involved in the Contadora negotiating process were Colombia, Mexico, Panama and Venezuela, while the Support Group consisted of Argentina, Brazil, Peru and Uruguay. See A/43/729-S/20234.

[92] See e.g. H. A. Hassouna, *The League of Arab States and Regional Disputes*, Leiden, 1975; Bowett, 'Contemporary Development', p. 229; M. Abdennabi, *La Ligue des Etats Arabes et les Conflits Inter-Arabes (1962–1980)*, 1985; B. Boutros Ghali, 'The Arab League 1945–1970', 25 *Revue Egyptienne de Droit International*, 1969, p. 67; and S. Al-Kadhem, 'The Role of the League of Arab States in Settling Inter-Arab Disputes', 32 *Revue Egyptienne de Droit International*, 1976, p. 1.

[93] Note also the pan-Arab 'peacekeeping force' in the Lebanon between 1976–82, see *Keesings Contemporary Archives*, pp. 28117 *et seq.* See also I. Pogany, *The Arab League and Peacekeeping in Lebanon*, London, 1987. The Council also appointed committees to deal with the 1963 Algerian–Moroccan and Democratic People's Republic of Yemen–Yemen Arab Republic boundary disputes, H. A. Hassouna, 'The League of Arab States and the United Nations: Relations in the Peaceful Settlement of Disputes', New York, 1979, p. 312. See also *The Charter of the United Nations*, p. 701.

Europe[94]

The European Convention for the Peaceful Settlement of Disputes adopted by the Council of Europe in 1957 provides that legal disputes (as defined in article 36(2) of the Statute of the International Court of Justice) are to be sent to the International Court, although conciliation may be tried before this step is taken.[95] Other disputes are to go to arbitration, unless the parties have agreed to accept conciliation.

Within the NATO alliance,[96] there exist good offices facilities, and inquiry, mediation, conciliation and arbitration procedures may be instituted. In fact, the Organisation proved of some use, for instance in the long-standing 'cod war' between Britain and Iceland, two NATO partners.[97]

The Organisation on Security and Co-operation in Europe (OSCE) has gradually been establishing dispute resolution mechanisms.[98] Under the key documents of this organisation,[99] the participating states are to endeavour in good faith to reach a rapid and equitable solution of their disputes by using a variety of means. Under the Valletta Report 1991, as amended by the Stockholm Decision of 1992, any party to a dispute may request the establishment of a Dispute Settlement Mechanism, which once established may offer comments or advice with regard to negotiations between the parties in dispute, or any other appropriate dispute settlement process, and may engage in fact-finding and other conciliation functions. The Convention on Conciliation and Arbitration was signed in 1992 and came into force two years later. Under this Convention, a Court of Conciliation and Arbitration[100] has been established in Geneva. Conciliation may be undertaken by a Conciliation Commission constituted for each dispute and drawn from a list established under the Convention.[101] The Commission will draw up a report containing its proposals for the peaceful settlement of the dispute and the parties will then have a period of thirty days during which to examine the proposals. If the parties do not accept the proposed settlement, the report will be forwarded to the OSCE Council through the Senior Council (formerly the Committee of Senior Officials).[102] The

[94] See e.g. L. Caflisch, 'Vers des Mécanismes Pan-Européenes de Règlement Pacifique des Différends', *Revue Générale de Droit International Public*, 1993, p. 1.
[95] Note that some states have entered reservations to this provision.
[96] See e.g. Bowett, 'Contemporary Development', p. 180 and Merrills, *Disputes Settlement*, p. 208.
[97] *Ibid.*, p. 213. Such procedures were also proposed following the Suez crisis in 1956 and with regard to the Cyprus crisis in 1963, see Nguyen Quoc Dinh *et al.*, *Droit International Public*, p. 808. [98] See generally *supra*, Chapter 7, p. 281 and *infra*, Chapter 21, p. 902.
[99] See e.g. the Helsinki Final Act 1975; the Charter of Paris 1990 and the Valletta Report of the Meeting of Experts on Peaceful Settlement of Disputes 1991.
[100] This consists of the conciliators and arbitrators appointed under articles 3 and 4.
[101] See articles 1, and 2. Each state party is to appoint two conciliators, article 3.
[102] Article 25.

Convention also provided for the establishment of Arbitral Tribunals, similarly constituted for each dispute and drawn from a list.[103] Such a tribunal would be set up by express agreement between the parties in dispute[104] or where the state brought to arbitration has agreed in advance to accept in advance the jurisdiction of the Tribunal.[105] The award of the Tribunal would be final and binding as between the parties.[106]

In addition, the OSCE is able to send Missions to various participating states, with their consent, as part of its early warning, conflict prevention and crisis management responsibilities. Such Missions have been sent to Yugoslavia to promote dialogue between the populations of Kosovo, Sanjak and Vojvodina and the authorities of the state; to the Former Yugoslav Republic of Macedonia; to Georgia; Moldova; Tajikistan; Estonia; Ukraine and Chechnya.[107] Under the General Framework Agreement for Peace in Bosnia and Herzegovina, initialled at Dayton on 21 November 1995 and signed in Paris on 14 December 1995, the OSCE was made responsible for the supervision of elections, [108] for providing the framework for the conduct of discussions between the Bosnian parties on confidence and security building measures and for measures of sub-regional arms control,[109] and for assisting in the creation of a Bosnian Commission on Human Rights.[110]

International organisations of limited competence[111]

The various specialised agencies[112] which encourage international co-operation in functional spheres have their own procedures for settling disputes between their members relating to the interpretation of their constitutional instruments. Such procedures vary from organisation to organisation, although the general pattern involves recourse to one of the main organs of the institution upon the failure of negotiations. If this fails to result in a

[103] Articles 2 and 4. Each state party is to appoint one arbitrator and one alternate.
[104] Either between two or more states parties to the Convention or between one or more states parties to the Convention and one or more OSCE participating states, article 26(1).
[105] Article 26.
[106] Article 31. See also UN Handbook, p. 87 and OSCE Handbook 1996, 2nd edn, Vienna, 1996, pp. 48 et seq.
[107] See OSCE Handbook 1996, pp. 16 et seq. A series of Sanctions Assistance Missions, operating under the guidance of the OSCE/EU Sanctions Co-ordinator, was sent to various countries in order to assist them in maintaining sanctions imposed by the Security Council in the Yugoslav crisis, ibid., p. 36.   [108] See Annex 3 of the Agreement.
[109] Annex 1–B of the Agreement. The sub-regional arms control involves Yugoslavia, Croatia and Bosnia.   [110] Annex 6 of the Agreement.
[111] See e.g. C. A. Colliard, 'Le Règlement des Différends dans les Organisations Inter-gouvernementales de Caractère Non Politique' in Mélanges Basdevant, Paris, 1960, p. 152 and G. Malinverni, Le Règlement des Différends dans les Organisations Internationales Economiques, Leiden, 1974.
[112] See e.g. Murty, 'Settlement', pp. 729–32. See further infra, Chapter 21, p. 835.

settlement, the matter may be referred to the International Court of Justice or to arbitration unless otherwise agreed.[113] In such cases, recourse to the Court is by way of a request for an Advisory Opinion, although by virtue of constitutional provisions, the judgment of the Court would be accepted as binding and not as advisory.[114] In other cases, the opinions to be given by the International Court or by an arbitral tribunal are to be non-binding.[115] A number of organisations provide for other mechanisms of inquiry and dispute settlement.[116]

The dispute settlement procedures established under the General Agreement on Tariffs and Trade[117] commenced with bilateral consultations under article XXII.[118] From this point, article XXIII provided for a party to refer a dispute for conciliation[119] where it was felt that 'any benefit accruing to it directly or indirectly' under GATT was being 'nullified or impaired'. A Panel, composed of experts chosen by the Director-General of GATT, then would seek to ascertain the relevant facts and reach a settlement.[120] The approach was pragmatic and focused on achieving a settlement between the parties. The report of the Panel would be sent to the GATT Council, which would usually adopt it by consensus. Where the disputing parties have not implemented the recommendations within a reasonable time, the complaining party was able to take retaliatory action with the authorisation of the Council. Such instances were in fact very rare.[121] In 1989, a series of improvements was adopted pending the conclusion of the Uruguay Round of negotiations. These improvements included the provisions that the Council would normally accept the report of the Panel within fifteen months

---

[113] See e.g. article 37 of the International Labour Organisation Constitution; article XIV(2) of the UNESCO Constitution; article 75 of the World Health Organisation Constitution; article XVII of the Constitution of the Food and Agriculture Organisation; article XVII of the International Atomic Energy Agency Statute and articles 50 and 82 of the Convention of the International Telecommunications Union.

[114] See e.g. C. F. Amerasinghe, *Principles of the Institutional Law of International Organisations*, Cambridge, 1996, pp. 28 *et seq.*

[115] See e.g. article 22(1) of the UN International Development Organisation (UNIDO) Constitution and article 65 of the International Maritime Organisation Constitution.

[116] See e.g. the 1962 Special Protocol to the UNESCO Convention against Discrimination in Education which provides for a Conciliation and Good Offices Commission and the 1962 Special Protocol to the ILO Convention against Discrimination in Education which provides for a Conciliation and Good Offices Commission, see Murty, 'Settlement', pp. 729–30 and Bowett, 'Contemporary Development', pp. 152–4. See also the World Intellectual Property Organisation Mediation, Arbitration and Expedited Arbitration Rules 1994, 34 ILM, 1995, p. 559.   [117] See further *infra*, Chapter 21, p. 892.

[118] See e.g. *UN Handbook*, pp. 136 *et seq.*; J. H. Jackson, *The World Trading System*, Cambridge, MA., 1989, Chapter 4 and T. Flory, 'Les Accords du Tokyo Round du GATT et la Réforme des Procédures de Règlement des Différends dans la Système Commercial Interétatique', *Revue Générale de Droit International Public*, 1982, p. 235.

[119] Before this stage, a party may seek the good offices of the Director-General of GATT to facilitate a confidential conciliation, see the 1982 GATT Ministerial Declaration.

[120] See in particular the 1979 Understanding on Dispute Settlement.

[121] See e.g. Henkin *et al.*, *International Law Cases and Materials, op. cit.*, p. 1414.

of the complaint and provisions relating to mediation, conciliation and arbitration were added.[122]

The GATT process was absorbed within the World Trade Organisation, which came into being on 1 January 1995. Annex 2 of the Marrakesh Agreement Establishing the World Trade Organisation 1994 is entitled 'Understanding on Rules and Procedures Governing the Settlement of Disputes'. Under the WTO scheme, disputes arising out of the agreements contained in the Final Act of the Uruguay Round are dealt with by the WTO General Council acting as the Dispute Settlement Body. Where bilateral consultations have failed, the parties may agree to bring the dispute to the WTO Director-General, who may offer good offices, conciliation or mediation assistance. Where consultations fail to produce a settlement after sixty days, the complaining state may turn to the Dispute Settlement Body. This Body may establish a three-member panel, whose report should be produced within six months. Detailed procedures are laid down in the Understanding. The panel report is adopted by the Dispute Settlement Body within sixty days, unless there is a consensus against adoption or one of the parties notifies an intention to appeal on grounds of law. The standing Appellate Body established by the Dispute Settlement Body consists of seven experts, three of whom may sit to hear appeals at any one time. Appeal proceedings generally are to last no more than sixty (or at most ninety) days. Unless there is a consensus against adoption, the Dispute Settlement Body will accept the Appellate Body report within thirty days. Within thirty days of the adoption of the report, the parties must agree to comply with the recommendations and if this does not happen within a reasonable period, the party concerned must offer mutually acceptable compensation. If after twenty days no satisfactory compensation is agreed, the complaining state may request authorisation from the Dispute Settlement Body to suspend concessions or obligations against the other party and this should be granted within thirty days of the end of the reasonable period. In any event, the Dispute Settlement Body will monitor the implementation of rulings or recommendations.[123]

It should also be noted that several international treaties expressly provide mechanisms and methods for the peaceful resolution of disputes arising therefrom.[124]

---

[122] See e.g. E. Canal-Forgues and R. Ostrihansky, 'New Developments in GATT Dispute Settlement Procedures', 24 (2) *Journal of World Trade*, 1990, p. 67 and J.-G. Castel, 'The Uruguay Round and the Improvements to the GATT Dispute Settlement Rules and Procedures', 38 ICLQ, 1989, p. 834.

[123] Note also the dispute settlement provisions contained in Chapters 19 and 20 of the North American Free Trade Agreement 1992, 32 ILM, 1993, pp. 682 *et seq.*

[124] See e.g. *supra* p. 450 with regard to the Convention on the Law of the Sea 1982, and *supra* p. 671 with regard to the Conventions on the Law of Treaties 1969 and 1986.

Arbitration[125]

The procedure of arbitration grew to some extent out of the processes of diplomatic settlement and represented an advance towards a developed international legal system. In its modern form, it emerged with the Jay Treaty of 1974 between Britain and America, which provided for the establishment of mixed commissions to solve legal disputes between the parties.[126]

The procedure was successfully used in the *Alabama Claims* arbitration[127] of 1872 between the two countries, which resulted in the UK having to pay compensation for the damage caused by a Confederate warship built in the UK. This success stimulated further arbitrations, for example the *Behring Sea*[128] and *British Guiana and Venezuela Boundary*[129] arbitrations at the close of the nineteenth century.[130]

The 1899 Hague Convention for the Pacific Settlement of Disputes included a number of provisions on international arbitration, the object of which was deemed to be under article XV, 'the settlement of differences between states by judges of their own choice and on the basis of respect for law'. International arbitration was held to be the most effective and equitable manner of dispute settlement, where diplomacy had failed. An agreement to arbitrate under article XVIII implied the legal obligation to accept the terms of the award. In addition, a Permanent Court of Arbitration was established.[131] It is not really a court since it is not composed of a fixed body of judges. It consists of a panel of persons, nominated by the contracting states (each one nominating a maximum of four), comprising individuals 'of known competency in questions of international law, of the highest moral

---

[125] See e.g. J. G. Wetter, *The International Arbitral Process Public and Private*, 5 vols., Dobbs Ferry, 1979; L. Simpson and H. Fox, *International Arbitration*, London, 1959; L. Caflisch, 'L'Avenir de l'Arbitrage Interétatique', AFDI, 1979, p. 9; Murty, 'Settlement', pp. 684 *et seq.*; Merrills, *Disputes Settlement*, Chapter 5; S. Schwebel, *International Arbitration: Three Salient Problems*, Cambridge, 1987; A. M. Stuyt, *Survey of International Arbitrations (1794–1984)*, Dordrecht, 1990; V. Coussirat-Coustère and P. M. Eisemann, *Repertory of International Arbitral Jurisprudence*, 4 vols., Dordrecht, 1989–91; C. Gray and B. Kingsbury, 'Developments in Dispute Settlement: International Arbitration since 1945', 63 BYIL, 1992, p. 97; L. Sohn, 'International Arbitration Today', 108 HR, 1976, p. 1; *International Arbitration* (ed. F. Soons), Dordrecht, 1990, and H. Fox, 'States and the Undertaking to Arbitrate', 37 ICLQ, 1988, p. 1.

[126] See Simpson and Fox, *International Arbitration*, pp. 1–4. Note also the Treaty of Ghent, 1814, which incorporated the concept of a neutral element within the Commission, *ibid.* See also G. Schwarzenberger, 'Present-Day Relevance of the Jay Treaty Arbitrations', 53 *Notre Dame Lawyer*, 1978, p. 715.

[127] Moore, *International Arbitrations*, 1898, New York, vol. I, p. 495.   [128] *Ibid.*, p. 755.

[129] 92 BFSP, p. 970.

[130] See also 'Projet de Règlement pour la Procédure Arbitrale Internationale', *Annuaire de l'Institut de Droit International*, 1877, p. 126.

[131] See the UK–France Agreement of 1903, providing for referral of differences of a legal nature to the Permanent Court of Arbitration, so long as the 'vital interests' of the parties were not involved, Cd. 1837.

reputation and disposed to accept the duties of an arbitrator'.[132] Where contracting states wish to go to arbitration, they are entitled to choose the members of the tribunal from the panel. Thus, it is in essence machinery facilitating the establishment of arbitral tribunals. The PCA also consists of an International Bureau, which acts as the registry of the Court and keeps its records, and a Permanent Administrative Council, exercising administrative control over the Bureau.[133] Administrative support was provided in this context by the Bureau in the *Heathrow Airport User Charges* arbitration.[134]

Between 1900 and 1932 some twenty disputes went through the PCA procedure, but since then the numbers have fallen drastically so that only three cases have been heard since the early 1930s, although there have been suggestions in the last few years to revitalise the PCA arbitration system.[135] Nevertheless, there has been continuing interest in the arbitration process itself. The International Law Commission formulated a set of Model Rules on Arbitral Procedure, which was adopted by the General Assembly in 1958,[136] while in 1992, the Permanent Court of Arbitration itself adopted Optional Rules for Arbitrating Disputes between Two States.[137]

Arbitration tribunals may be composed in different ways.[138] There may be a single arbitrator or a collegiate body. In the latter case, each party will appoint an equal number of arbitrators with the chairman or umpire being appointed by either the parties or the arbitrators already nominated. In many cases, a head of state will be suggested as a single arbitrator and he will then nominate an expert or experts in the field of international law or other relevant disciplines to act for him.[139] Under the PCA system, and in the absence of agreement to the contrary, each party selects two arbitrators from the panel, only one of whom may be a national of the state. These arbitrators then choose an umpire, but if they fail to do so, this task will be left

[132] Article XLIV of the Convention as revised in 1907.
[133] See Murty, 'Settlement', p. 685. See also Hudson, *The Permanent Court of International Justice 1920–1942*, New York, 1943, p. 11.   [134] See 88 AJIL, 1994, p. 739, note 4.
[135] See generally Von Mangoldt, 'Arbitration and Conciliation' in *The International Arbitral Process*, vol. V, pp. 243 *et seq.* and D. Johnson, 'International Arbitration Back in Favour?', 34 YBWA, 1980, p. 305.
[136] Resolution 1262(XI). These are, however, merely optional. See also Report of the ILC, 1958, A/3859. Note also the 1928 General Act, the 1929 General Treaty of Inter-American Arbitration and the 1949 Revised General Act. See also *Yearbook of the ILC*, 1953, vol. II, p. 208.
[137] See 32 ILM, 1993, p. 572. These are based upon the UNCITRAL (United Nations Commission on International Trade Law) Arbitration Rules, adopted by the UN General Assembly on 15 December 1976 in resolution 31/98.
[138] See e.g. Merrills, *Disputes Settlement*, pp. 83–6. It is, of course, an issue for the parties to decide.
[139] E.g. the *Argentina–Chile* case, 38 ILR, p. 10 and the *Beagle Channel* case, HMSO, 1977; 52 ILR, p. 93. Note also the *Interpretation of Peace Treaties* case, ICJ Reports, 1950, p. 221; 17 ILR, p. 318.

to a third party, nominated by agreement. If this also fails to produce a result, a complicated process then ensues culminating in the drawing of lots. States are not obliged to submit a dispute to the procedure of arbitration, in the absence of their consent.[140] This consent may be expressed in arbitration treaties, in which the contracting states agree to submit certain kinds of disputes that may arise between them to arbitration, or in specific provisions of general treaties, which provide for disputes with regard to the treaty itself to be submitted to arbitration,[141] although the number of treaties dealing primarily with the peaceful settlement of disputes has declined since 1945.[142] Consent to the reference of a dispute to arbitration with regard to matters that have already arisen is usually expressed by means of a *compromis*, or special agreement, and the terms in which it is couched are of extreme importance. This is because the jurisdiction of the tribunal is defined in relation to the provisions of the treaty or *compromis*, whichever happens to be the relevant document in the particular case. However, in general, the tribunal may determine its competence in interpreting the *compromis* and other documents concerned in the case.[143]

The law to be applied in arbitration proceedings is international law,[144] but the parties may agree upon certain principles to be taken into account by the tribunal and specify this in the *compromis*. In this case, the tribunal must apply the rules specified. For example, in the *British Guiana and Venezuela Boundary* dispute,[145] it was emphasised that occupation for fifty years should be accepted as constituting a prescriptive title to territory. And in the *Trail Smelter* case,[146] the law to be applied was declared to be US law and practice with regard to such questions as well as international law.[147]

[140] See e.g. the *Eastern Carelia* case, PCIJ, Series B, No. 5, 1923, p. 27; 2 ILR, p. 394 and the *Ambatielos* case, ICJ Reports, 1953, p. 19; 20 ILR, p. 547.
[141] See *Arbitration and Security: The Systematic Survey of the Arbitration Conventions and Treaties of Mutual Security Deposited with the League of Nations*, 1927, and *Systematic Survey of Treaties for the Pacific Settlement of International Disputes 1928–1948*, 1949.
[142] See L. Sohn, 'Report on the Changing Role of Arbitration in the Settlement of International Disputes', International Law Association, 1966, pp. 325, 334.
[143] In the absence of agreement to the contrary. See e.g. the *Nottebohm* case, ICJ Reports, 1953, pp. 111, 119; 20 ILR, pp. 567, 572. See also article 48 of the Hague Convention, 1899, and article 73 of the Hague Convention, 1907.
[144] See e.g. the *Norwegian Shipowners' Claims* case, 1 RIAA, 1921, p. 309 and the *Dubai/Sharjah* case, 91 ILR, pp. 543, 585–8. Note that article 28 of the 1928 General Act for the Pacific Settlement of International Disputes as revised in 1949, provides that where nothing is laid down in the arbitration agreement as to the law applicable to the merits of the case, the tribunal should apply the substantive rules as laid down in article 38 of the Statute of the International Court of Justice (i.e. international treaties, custom and general principles of law). See further *supra*, Chapter 3, p. 55.   [145] 92 BFSP, p. 970.
[146] 3 RIAA, 1938, p. 1908; 9 ILR, p. 315.
[147] Note that in international commercial arbitrations, the reference often incorporates municipal law, see e.g. the *BP* case, 53 ILR, p. 297, where the basic reference was to 'the principles of the Law of Libya common to the principles of international law'. See also the wide reference to the Iran–United States Claims Tribunal to decide all cases 'on the basis of respect for law, applying such choice of law rules and principles of commercial and

Agreements sometimes specify that the decisions should be reached in accordance with 'law and equity' and this means that the general principles of justice common to legal systems should be taken into account as well as the provisions of international law. Such general principles may also be considered where there are no specific rules covering the situation under discussion.[148] The rules of procedure of the tribunal are often specified in the *compromis* and decided by the parties by agreement as the process commences. Hague Convention I of 1899 as revised in 1907 contains agreed procedure principles, which would apply in the absence of express stipulation.

It is characteristic of arbitration that the tribunal is competent to determine its own jurisdiction and therefore interpret the relevant instruments determining that jurisdiction.[149] Once an arbitral award has been made, it is final and binding upon the parties,[150] but in certain circumstances the award itself may be regarded as a nullity.[151] There is disagreement amongst lawyers as to the grounds on which such a decision may be taken. It is, however, fairly generally accepted that where a tribunal exceeds its powers under the *compromis*, its award may be treated as a nullity, although this is not a common occurrence. Such excess of power (*excès de pouvoir*) may be involved where the tribunal decides a question not submitted to it, or applies rules it is not authorised to apply. The main example of the former is the *North-Eastern Boundary* case,[152] between Canada and the United States, where the arbitrator, after being asked to decide which of two lines constituted the frontier, in fact chose a third line.

It is sometimes argued that invalidity of the *compromis* is a ground of

---

international law as the Tribunal determines to be applicable, taking into account relevant usages of the trade, contract provisions and changed circumstances', Article V, Declaration of Algiers concerning the Settlement of Claims by the Government of the USA and the Government of the Islamic Republic of Iran, 1981, 1 Iran–US CTR, pp. 9, 11; 20 ILM, 1981, p. 232.

148 See e.g. *Re Competence of the Conciliation Commission*, 22 ILR, p. 867 and *supra* Chapter 3, p. 81. See also article 28 of the 1928 General Act as revised in 1949, article 10 of the ILC Model Articles and articles 26 and 28 of the European Convention for the Peaceful Settlement of Disputes. Note in addition the *Rann of Kutch* case, 50 ILR, p. 520.

149 See the *Nottebohm (Preliminary Objections)* case, ICJ Reports, 1953, pp. 111, 119; 20 ILR, pp. 567, 571–3. See also Arbitration Commission on Yugoslavia, Interlocutory Decision of 4 July 1992, 92 ILR, pp. 194, 197.

150 Articles 81 and 84, Hague Convention I, 1907. The principle of *res judicata* also applies to arbitration awards, see e.g. the *Trail Smelter* case, 3 RIAA, 1938, p. 1905; 9 ILR, p. 324 and the *Orinoco Steamship Co.* case, 11 RIAA, 1910, p. 227.

151 See e.g. W. M. Reisman, *Nullity and Revision*, New Haven, 1971; E. K. Nantwi, *The Enforcement of International Judicial Decisions and Arbitral Awards in Public International Law*, Leiden, 1967 and O. Schachter, 'The Enforcement of International Judicial and Arbitral Decisions', 54 AJIL, 1960, p. 1.

152 See C. C. Hyde, *International Law*, 2nd edn, 1945, vol. III, p. 1636. See also the *Pelletier* case, in *ibid.*, p. 1640; the *Panama–Costa Rica Boundary* case, 11 RIAA, 1900, p. 519 and *US Foreign Relations*, 1914, p. 994; the *Chamizal* case, 11 RIAA, p. 309, and the *Cerruti* arbitrations, 6 AJIL, 1912, p. 965.

nullity,[153] while the corruption of a member of the tribunal or a serious departure from a fundamental rule of procedure are further possibilities as grounds
of nullity.[154] Article 35 of the Model Rules on Arbitral Procedure drawn up
by the International Law Commission, for example, provides for a successful
plea of nullity in three cases: excess of power, corruption of a tribunal member
or serious departure from a fundamental rule of procedure, including failure
to state the reasons of the award.[155] 'Essential error' has also been suggested
as a ground of nullity, but the definition of this is far from unambiguous.[156]
It would appear not to cover the evaluation of documents and evidence,[157] but
may cover manifest errors[158] such as not taking into account a relevant treaty
or a clear mistake as to the appropriate municipal law.[159] Of course, once a
party recognises the award as valid and binding, it will not be able to challenge the validity of the award at a later stage.[160] In certain circumstances, it
may be open to a party to request a revision or reopening of the award in order
to provide for rectification of an error or consideration of a fact unknown at
the time to the tribunal and the requesting party which is of such a nature as
to have a decisive influence on the award.[161]

Arbitration as a method of settling disputes combines elements of both
diplomatic and judicial procedures. It depends for its success on a certain
amount of goodwill between the parties in drawing up the *compromis* and
constituting the tribunal, as well as actually enforcing the award subsequently made. A large part depends upon negotiating processes. On the
other hand, arbitration is an adjudicative technique in that the award is final
and binding and the arbitrators are required to base their decision on law.[162]
It will be seen in the following section just how close arbitration is to judicial settlement of disputes by the International Court of Justice, and it is no
coincidence that the procedure of arbitration through the PCA began to
decline with the establishment and consolidation of the Permanent Court
of International Justice in the 1920s.

[153] See e.g. Murty, 'Settlement', pp. 693–64 and A. D. McNair, *The Law of Treaties*, Oxford,
1961, pp. 66–77.
[154] See Schachter, 'Enforcement', p. 3. See also as regards corruption, Moore, *International
Arbitrations*, vol. II, pp. 1660–64 and the *Buraimi* arbitration, Wetter, *Arbitral Process*, vol.
III, p. 357 and 545 HC Deb., vol. 199, 1955.
[155] See the *British Guiana and Venezuela Boundary* case, 92 BFSP, p. 160 and Wetter, *Arbitral
Process*, vol. III, pp. 81 *et seq*. See also the *Arbitral Award by the King of Spain* case, ICJ
Reports, 1960, pp. 188, 216; 30 ILR, pp. 457, 476.
[156] See e.g. Murty, 'Settlement', p. 696 and Merrills, *Disputes Settlement*, p. 100.
[157] *Arbitral Award by the King of Spain*, ICJ Reports, 1960, pp. 188, 215–16; 30 ILR, pp. 457,
475. See also as regards the Argentinian claim of nullity of the *Beagle Channel* award, 17
ILM, 1978, p. 738; 52 ILR, pp. 267–85.
[158] See the *Trail Smelter* case, 3 RIAA, 1938, pp. 1905, 1957; 9 ILR, p. 331.
[159] See e.g. the *Schreck* case, Moore, *International Arbitrations*, vol. II, p. 1357.
[160] *Arbitral Award by the King of Spain*, ICJ Reports, 1960, pp. 188, 213; 30 ILR, p. 473.
[161] See e.g. Wetter, *Arbitral Process*, vol. II, pp. 539 *et seq*. See also article 29 of the ILC Model
Rules. [162] See the definition of arbitration in *Yearbook of the ILC*, 1953, vol. II, p. 202.

742   INTERNATIONAL LAW

In recent years, there has been a rise in the number of inter-state arbitrations. The *Rann of Kutch* case,[163] the *Anglo-French Continental Shelf* case,[164] the *Beagle Channel* case[165] and the *Taba* case[166] were all the subject of arbitral awards, usually successfully.[167] It may be that further inter-state boundary issues may be resolved in this fashion, although a lot depends on the evaluation of the parties as to the most satisfactory method of dispute settlement in the light of their own particular interests and requirements.

Arbitration is an extremely useful process where some technical expertise is required, or where greater flexibility than is available before the International Court is desired.[168] Speed may also be a relevant consideration. Arbitration may be the appropriate mechanism to utilise as between states and international institutions, since only states may appear before the ICJ in contentious proceedings. The establishment of arbitral tribunals has often been undertaken in order to deal relatively quietly and cheaply with a series of problems within certain categories, for example, the mixed tribunals established after the First World War to settle territorial questions, or the Mexican Claims commissions which handled various claims against Mexico.

The Iran–United States Claims Tribunal was established in 1981 as an international arbitral body to adjudicate claims of US nationals against Iran and of Iranian nationals against the United States arising out of alleged violations of property rights as a result of the circumstances surrounding the hostage crisis.[169] The Tribunal also has jurisdiction to hear certain official claims between the US and Iran arising out of contractual arrangements for

---

[163] 50 ILR, p. 2. See also J. G. Wetter, 'The Rann of Kutch Arbitration', 65 AJIL, 1971, p. 346.   [164] Cmnd. 7438, 1978; 54 ILR, p. 6. See further *supra* Chapter 11, p. 395.

[165] HMSO, 1977; 52 ILR, p. 93. See M. N. Shaw, 'The Beagle Channel Arbitration Award', 6 *International Relations*, 1978, p. 415.

[166] 80 ILR, p. 244. See also D. W. Bowett, 'The Taba Award of 29 September 1988', 23 *Israel Law Review*, 1989, p. 429; G. Lagergren, 'The Taba Tribunal 1986–89', 1 *African Journal of International and Comparative Law*, 1989, p. 525 and P. Weil, 'Some Observations on the Arbitral Award in the Taba Case', 23 *Israel Law Review*, 1989, p. 1.

[167] Argentina initially rejected the award in the *Beagle Channel* case, but later mediation and negotiations resolved the issue, see 17 ILM, 1978, p. 738 and 24 ILM, 1985, p. 1.

[168] Note for example that in the *Argentina–Chile* case of 1966, the tribunal consisted of a lawyer and two geographical experts, 38 ILR, p. 10.

[169] See 1 Iran–US CTR, pp. 3–56; 20 ILM, 1981, pp. 223 *et seq.* See also *The Jurisprudence of the Iran-United States Claims Tribunal* (ed. G. H. Aldrich), Oxford, 1996; Stewart and Sherman, 'Development at the Iran–United States Claims Tribunal: 1981–1983', 24 Va JIL, 1983, p. 1; D. Lloyd Jones, 'The Iran–United States Claims Tribunal: Private Rights and State Responsibility', 24 Va JIL, 1984, p. 259; *The Iran–US Claims Tribunal 1981–83* (ed. Lillich), Charlottesville, 1984; S. J. Toope, *Mixed International Arbitration*, Cambridge, 1990, Chapter 9; D. D. Caron, 'The Nature of the Iran–United States Claims Tribunal and the Evolving Structure of International Dispute Resolution', 84 AJIL, 1990, p. 104; A. Avamessian, *Iran–United States Claims Tribunal in Action*, 1993; R. Khan, *The Iran–United States Claims Tribunal*, 1990; W. Mapp, *The Iran–United States Claims Tribunal: The First Ten Years 1981–1991*, Manchester, 1993 and the *Iran–United States Claims Tribunal Reports* (23 vols. to date), 1981–.

the purchase and sale of goods and services, and disputes relating to the interpretation and implementation of the Claims Settlement Agreement itself. Tribunal awards are final and binding and are enforceable under the Agreement in domestic courts. In order to ensure payment of awards to US nationals, a Security Account was established with 1 billion dollars capital from Iranian assets frozen in the US as a result of the hostages crisis. Once the sum falls below $500 million, Iran is under an obligation to replenish the Account.[170] Under the terms of the Agreement, all claims had to be filed by 19 January 1982. The Tribunal is based at The Hague. This settlement procedure is highly complex and one of the most sophisticated attempts at resolving international claims attempted.[171]

A variety of important issues have been addressed by the Tribunal, including the treatment of dual nationality in claims[172] and in particular issues relating to expropriation.[173] A discussion of the precise nature of the Tribunal is beyond the confines of this work, but it should be noted that rather than being a typical inter-state arrangement, it constitutes a fusion of state and private party claims in the one procedure and in a way which ensures the security of the award. Although claims of under $250, 000 are to be represented by the government of the national concerned, claims in excess of this are presented by the individual claimants themselves, while the agents of the two states are present during the hearing with the right of audience.[174] Nevertheless, the Tribunal has emphasised on several occasions that the claim remains that of the individual and is not that of the state, as would be normal in classical state responsibility situations.[175]

Whether this model will be used in other similar situations is an open question, particularly since the trend in the post-war era has tended towards the lump-sum settlement of such disputes.[176] But the value of the Tribunal in general terms in resolving the large number of claims in question and in addressing significant issues of international law cannot be denied.

An attempt was made to tackle issues raised by the situation in the Former Yugoslavia by the establishment of an Arbitration Commission.[177] However, the Commission, while issuing a number of Opinions on issues concerning, for example, statehood, recognition, human rights and boundary matters,

[170] As of 28 March 1989, this had taken place on twenty-six occasions, see 83 AJIL, 1989, p. 915.
[171] As of 30 June 1990, the total number of cases filed with the Tribunal Registry stood at 3,948; 486 awards had been made and a total of 3, 662 cases had been finalised. See Annual Report of the Tribunal, 1990, pp. 25–8. [172] See *supra*, Chapter 14, p. 565.
[173] See *supra*, Chapter 14, p. 573. [174] See Fox, 'States', p. 21.
[175] See e.g. *State Party Responsibility for Awards Rendered Against Its Nationals, Case A/21*, 14 Iran–US CTR, pp. 324, 330. [176] See *supra*, Chapter 14, p. 580.
[177] Established pursuant to the Declaration of 27 August 1991 of the European Community, see Bull. EC, 7/8 (1991). See generally, M. Craven, 'The EC Arbitration Commission on Yugoslavia', 66 BYIL, 1995, p. 333.

was not able to act as an arbitration tribunal as between the parties to the conflict.[178]

Other mechanisms

The International Centre for Settlement of Investment Disputes was established under the auspices of the International Bank for Reconstruction and Development by the Convention on the Settlement of Investment Disputes Between States and the Nationals of Other States 1965 and administers *ad hoc* arbitrations.[179] It provides an autonomous system free from municipal law, while states parties to the Convention undertake to recognise awards made by arbitration tribunals acting under the auspices of the Centre as final and binding in their territories and to enforce them as if they were final judgments of national courts.[180] The jurisdiction of the Centre extends to 'any legal dispute arising directly out of an investment, between a contracting state . . . and a national of another contracting state, which the parties to the dispute consent in writing to submit to the Centre'.[181] Disputes are referred to conciliation commissions or arbitral tribunals constituted under ICSID's auspices. Arbitration is more frequent than conciliation in this system. Bilateral investment treaties between states parties to the Convention frequently provide for recourse to arbitration under the auspices of the Centre in the event of an investment dispute.[182] The arbitration procedure afforded by the Centre has now been utilised in several interesting cases.[183]

Another procedure of growing importance is the Court of Arbitration of the International Chamber of Commerce.[184] A number of agreements provide for the settlement of disputes by arbitration under the Rules of the International Chamber of Commerce and several cases have been heard.[185]

---

[178] See also the Court of Conciliation and Arbitration of the OSCE, *supra*, p. 733.
[179] See e.g. A. Broches, 'The Convention on the Settlement of Investment Disputes', 3 *Columbia Journal of Transnational Law*, 1966, p. 263 and Broches, 'The Convention on the Settlement of Investment Disputes Between States and Nationals of Other States', 136 HR, p. 350; D. O'Keefe, 'The International Centre for the Settlement of Investment Disputes', 34 YBWA, 1980, p. 286; Wetter, *Arbitral Process*, vol. II, p. 139 and P. Muchlinski, *Multinational Enterprises and the Law*, Oxford, 1995, pp. 540 *et seq.*
[180] Wetter, *Arbitral Process*, vol. II, p. 139.   [181] Article 25(1) of the Convention.
[182] See e.g. I. Pogany, 'The Regulation of Foreign Investment in Hungary', 4 *ICSID Review – Foreign Investment Law Journal*, 1989, pp. 39, 51.
[183] See e.g. P. Lalive, 'The First "World Bank" Arbitration (*Holiday Inns v. Morocco*) – Some Legal Problems', 51 BYIL, 1980, p. 123. See also *AGIP Spa v. Government of the Popular Republic of the Congo*, 67 ILR, p. 318 and *Benvenuti and Bonfant v. Government of the Popular Republic of the Congo*, ibid., p. 345, dealing with questions of state responsibility and damages, and *LETO v. Government of Liberia*, 89 ILR, p. 313, concerning expropriation.
[184] See e.g. Wetter, *Arbitral Process*, vol. II, p. 145.
[185] See e.g. *Dalmia Cement v. National Bank of Pakistan*, 67 ILR, p. 611 and the *Westland Helicopters* case, 80 ILR, p. 595.

Judicial settlement – the International Court of Justice[186]

Judicial settlement comprises the activities of all international and regional courts deciding disputes between subjects of international law, in accordance with the rules and principles of international law. There are a number of such bodies.[187] However, by far the most important of such bodies, both by prestige and jurisdiction, is the International Court of Justice. The impetus to create a world court for the international community developed as a result of the atmosphere engendered by the Hague Conferences of 1897 and 1907. The establishment of the Permanent Court of Arbitration, although neither permanent nor, in fact, a court, marked an important step forward in the consolidation of an international legal system. However, no lasting concrete steps were taken until after the conclusion of the First World War. The Covenant of the League of Nations called for the formulation of proposals for the creation of a world court and in 1920 the Permanent Court of International Justice (PCIJ) was created. It stimulated efforts to develop international arbitral mechanisms. Together with arbitration, the Permanent Court was intended to provide a reasonably comprehensive system serving the international community. It was intended as a way to prevent outbreaks of violence by enabling easily accessible methods of dispute settlement in the context of a legal and organisational framework to be made available.[188]

The PCIJ was superseded after the Second World War by the International Court of Justice (ICJ), described in article 92 of the Charter

[186] See e.g. S. Rosenne, *The Law and Practice of the International Court*, 2 vols., 2nd edn, Dordrecht, 1985 and *The World Court*, 5th edn, Dordrecht, 1994; *Fifty Years of the International Court of Justice* (eds. A. V. Lowe and M. Fitzmaurice), Cambridge, 1996; G. G. Fitzmaurice, *The Law and Procedure of the International Court of Justice*, 2 vols., Cambridge, 1986; H. Thirlway, 'The Law and Procedure of the International Court of Justice (1960–1989), 60 BYIL, 1989, p. 1, *ibid.*, 61 BYIL, 1990, p. 1, *ibid.*, 62 BYIL, 1991, p. 1, *ibid.*, 63 BYIL, 1992, p. 1, *ibid.*, 64 BYIL, 1993, p. 1, and *ibid.*, 65 BYIL, 1994, p. 1; R. Y. Jennings, 'The International Court of Justice after Fifty Years', 89 AJIL, 1995, p. 493; G. Guyomar, *Commentaire du Règlement de la CIJ*, Paris, 1983; E. McWhinney, *The World Court and the Contemporary Law-Making Process*, Alphen aan den Rijn, 1979; T. O. Elias, *The International Court of Justice and Some Contemporary Problems*, 1983; Merrills, *Disputes Settlement*, Chapters 6 and 7.; *The Future of the International Court of Justice* (ed. L. Gross), Dobbs Ferry, 1976, 2 vols.; *The International Court of Justice at a Crossroads* (ed. L. Damrosch), 1987; E. Lauterpacht, *Aspects of the Administration of International Justice*, Cambridge, 1991; T. M. Franck, 'Fairness in the International Legal and Institutional System', 240 HR, 1993 III, pp. 13, 302; R. Higgins, *Problems and Process*, Oxford, 1994, Chapter 11; *International Courts for the Twenty-first Century* (ed. M. Janis), 1992 and E. McWhinney, *Judicial Settlement of International Disputes*, 1991.
[187] E.g. the EC Court of Justice, see *infra*, Chapter 21, p. 902; the European Court of Human Rights and the Inter-American Court of Human Rights, *supra*, Chapter 7, p. 291; the Benelux Court of Justice created in 1965; the Court of Justice of the Cartagena Agreement created in 1976 for members of the Andean Group; the European Nuclear Energy Tribunal created in 1957; the European Tribunal on State Immunity, created in 1972; and the International Tribunal on the Law of the Sea, *infra*, p. 775.
[188] For an assessment of its work, see e.g. Rosenne, *Law and Practice*, vol. I, p. 10.

as the United Nations' 'principal judicial organ'. In essence, it is a continuation of the Permanent Court, with virtually the same statute and jurisdiction, and with a continuing line of cases, no distinction being made between those decided by the PCIJ and those by the ICJ.[189]

The organisation of the Court[190]

The ICJ is composed of fifteen members:

> elected regardless of their nationality, from among persons of high moral character, who possess the qualifications required in their respective countries for appointment to the highest judicial offices, or are jurisconsults of recognised competence in international law.[191]

The procedure for the appointment of judges is interesting in that it combines both legal and political elements, while seeking to exclude as far as possible the influence of national states over them. The system established by the Root-Phillimore plan in 1920 is in essence followed. This plan played a large part in the actual creation of the PCIJ and succeeded in allaying many suspicions regarding the composition of the proposed Court.[192]

The members of the Court are elected by the General Assembly and Security Council (voting separately) from a list of qualified persons drawn up by the national groups of the Permanent Court of Arbitration, or by specially appointed national groups in the case of UN members that are not represented in the PCA.[193] This provision was inserted to restrict political pressures in the selection of judges. The elections are staggered and take place once every three years, with respect to five judges each time. In this way some element of continuity amongst the Court is maintained.

In practice, there is close co-ordination between the Assembly and Security Council in electing judges and political factors do obtrude, especially in view of the requirement contained in Article 9 of the Statute that the:

> electors should bear in mind not only that the persons to be elected should individually possess the qualifications required, but also that in the body as a whole the representation of the main forms of civilisation and of the principal legal systems of the world should be assured.

This process has attracted much criticism on the grounds of attendant politicisation but in the circumstances it is difficult to see a way to avoid this

[189] See e.g. M. Shahabuddeen, *Precedent in the World Court*, Cambridge, 1996, pp. 22 *et seq.*
[190] See e.g. Rosenne, *Law and Practice*, vol. I, Chapter 5. See also H. Thirlway, 'Procedural Law and the International Court of Justice' in *Fifty Years of the International Court of Justice*, p. 389.   [191] Article 2, Statute of the ICJ.   [192] See e.g. Murty, 'Settlement', p. 700.
[193] Articles 4 and 5 of the ICJ Statute. In practice, governments exercise a major influence upon the nominations process of the national groups, see Merrills, *Disputes Settlement*, p. 124.

completely.[194] The opinions of individual judges can be crucial, particularly in sensitive cases and the alteration in the stance adopted by the Court with regard to the *Namibia* case between 1966[195] and 1971[196] can be attributed in large measure to changes in the composition of the Court that took place in the intervening period. Candidates must obtain an absolute majority of votes in both the Assembly and the Council,[197] and no two successful applicants may be of the same nationality.[198]

The members of the Court are elected for nine years and may be re-elected.[199] They enjoy diplomatic privileges and immunities when on official business,[200] and a judge cannot be dismissed unless it is the unanimous opinion of the other members of the Court that he has ceased to fulfil the required conditions.[201] These include the requirement that no member may exercise any political or administrative function or engage in any other professional occupation. No member may act as agent, advocate, or counsel in any case and no member may participate in the decision of any case in which he has previously taken part as agent, advocate or counsel for one of the parties, or as a member of a national or international court, or of a commission of inquiry, or in any other capacity.[202] The Court elects a president and vice-president for a three year term which can be renewed,[203] and it is situated at The Hague.[204]

Since the aim of the election procedures relating to the composition of the Court is to produce a judicial body of independent members rather than state representatives, the Statute provides in article 31 that judges of the nationality of each of the parties in a case before the Court shall retain their right to sit in that case. However, the effect of this is somewhat reduced by the provision in that article that the parties to a dispute before the ICJ are entitled to choose a person to sit as judge for the duration of that case, where they do not have a judge of their nationality there already.[205] This procedure of appointing *ad hoc* judges may be criticised as possibly adversely affecting the character of the Court as an independent organ of legal experts.[206] The

---

[194] See e.g. Rosenne, *Law and Practice*, vol. I, pp. 184 *et seq.* and Rosenne, 'The Composition of the Court', in *The Future of the International Court of Justice*, pp. 377, 381–6. See also G. Abi-Saab, 'The International Court as a World Court' in *Fifty Years of the International Court of Justice*, p. 3.   [195] ICJ Reports, 1966, p. 6; 37 ILR, p. 243.

[196] ICJ Reports, 1971, p. 16; 49 ILR, p. 2.   [197] Article 10, Statute of the ICJ.

[198] Article 3, Statute of the ICJ.   [199] Article 13, Statute of the ICJ.

[200] Article 19, Statute of the ICJ.   [201] Article 18, Statute of the ICJ.

[202] Articles 16 and 17, Statute of the ICJ. Note the problem raised particularly in the *Namibia* case, ICJ Reports, 1971, pp. 3, 6 and 9, of judges who had previously been involved in the dispute albeit in another capacity. The Court did not accept the need to remove the judges in question. See Rosenne, in *The Future of the International Court of Justice*, vol. I, pp. 388–90.   [203] Article 21, Statute of the ICJ.   [204] Article 22, Statute of the ICJ.

[205] It is possible for states in this position not to appoint *ad hoc* judges, see e.g. the *Temple of Veah Prihear* case, ICJ Reports, 1962, p. 6; 33 ILR, p. 48.

[206] It should also be distinguished from article 43 of the European Convention on Human Rights, which similarly provides for the appointment of an *ad hoc* judge to the Court. In

reason for the establishment and maintenance of the provision may be found within the realm of international politics and can only be understood as such.[207] Nevertheless, it may be argued that the procedure increases the judicial resources available to the Court in enabling the appointing state's arguments to be fully appreciated[208] and in practice it has not resulted in any disruption of the functioning of the ICJ. While it is overwhelmingly the case that *ad hoc* judges support the state that has so nominated them, this is not invariably so.[209] The Court has also permitted the use of the *ad hoc* judges in advisory proceedings.[210]

Article 29 of the Statute of the ICJ provides for the establishment of a Chamber of Summary Procedure for the speedy despatch of business by five judges. It has not as yet been called upon.[211] A seven-member Chamber for Environmental Matters was established in July 1993.[212] Article 26 permits the creation of Chambers composed of three or more members as the Court may determine for dealing with particular categories of cases[213] or to deal with a particular case. This procedure was revised in the 1978 Rules of the Court[214] and used for the first time in the *Gulf of Maine* case.[215] The question of the composition of the Chamber is decided by the Court after the parties have been consulted, and in such cases the identity of the judges to comprise the Chamber is clearly of critical value. In the *Gulf of Maine* case it was alleged that Canada and the US threatened to withdraw the case if their wishes as to composition were not carried out.[216] Judge Oda has underlined that 'in practical terms, therefore, it is inevitable, if a chamber is to be viable, that its composition must result from a consensus between the

this case, the Court deals with the provisions of municipal law of the member states of the Council of Europe and measures their conformity with the Convention. It is thus necessary to retain some expertise as to the domestic system in the case in question.

[207] See e.g. Rosenne, *Law and Practice*, vol. I, pp. 205 *et seq.* and L. V. Prott, *The Latent Power of Culture and the International Judge*, Abingdon, 1979.

[208] See Franck, 'Fairness', p. 312. See also N. Singh, *The Role and Record of the International Court of Justice*, 1989, pp. 193–4. Note also Judge E. Lauterpacht's discussion of the role of the *ad hoc* judge in the *Bosnia* v. *Yugoslavia* case, ICJ Reports, 1993, pp. 325, 408–9; 95 ILR, pp. 43, 126–7.

[209] See e.g. the *Application for Revision and Interpretation of the Judgment* made in the *Tunisia/Libya* case, ICJ Reports, 1985, p. 192; 81 ILR, p. 419, and the *Great Belt (Finland* v. *Denmark)* case, ICJ Reports, 1991, p. 12; 94 ILR, p. 446.

[210] See the *Western Sahara* case, ICJ Reports, 1975, p. 12; 59 ILR, p. 30. Cf. the *Namibia* case, ICJ Reports, 1971, p. 16; 49 ILR, p. 2. See also L. Gross, 'The International Court of Justice: Consideration of Requirements for Enhancing its Roles in the International Legal Order', in *The Future of the International Court of Justice*, vol. I, p. 61.

[211] See International Court of Justice, *Yearbook 1993–1994*, The Hague, 1994, p. 17.

[212] *Ibid.*, p. 18. It has not yet been called upon.

[213] Labour cases and cases relating to transit and communications are specifically mentioned.

[214] See article 15–18 and 90–93 of the Rules of Court.

[215] ICJ Reports, 1982, p. 3 and *ibid.*, 1984, p. 246; 71 ILR, p. 58. The Chamber consisted of Judge Ago (President) and Judges Gros, Mosler and Schwebel and Judge *ad hoc* Cohen.

[216] See e.g. Merrills, *Disputes Settlement*, p. 126 and Brauer, 'International Conflict Resolution: The ICJ Chambers and the Gulf of Maine Dispute', 23 *Va JIL*, 1982–3, p. 463. See also Singh, *Role and Record*, p. 110.

parties and the Court', although the Chamber is a component of the Court and 'the process of election whereby it comes into being should be as judicially impartial as its subsequent functioning.'[217] This trend may well amount to a significant element in the work of the Court. It provides the parties with flexibility in the choice of judges to hear the case and to that extent parallels arbitration.[218] Of the first two matters before Chambers of the Court, perhaps the more interesting from the perspective of the future development of the ICJ was the *Burkina Faso/Mali* case,[219] since African states have hitherto been most reluctant in permitting third party binding settlement of their disputes. Chambers of the Court have also been utilised in the *Elettronica Sicula* case[220] and in the *Land, Island and Maritime Frontier Dispute* between El Salvador and Honduras.[221] In all cases, the request was for five judges with elections by secret ballot except in the case of *ad hoc* judges.

The Rules of the Court, which govern its procedure and operations, were adopted in 1946 and revised in 1972 and 1978.[222]

The jurisdiction of the Court[223]

General

The International Court is a judicial institution that decides cases on the basis of international law as it exists at the date of the decision. It cannot formally create law as it is not a legislative organ,[224] but its views as to what the law is are of the highest authority. However, the matters that come before it are invariably intertwined with political factors. On occasions, such matters are also the subject of consideration before the political organs of the UN or

---

[217] ICJ Reports, 1987, pp. 10, 13; 97 ILR, pp. 139, 142.
[218] Although concern was expressed about the unity of the jurisprudence of the Court by frequent use of *ad hoc* Chambers, see H. Mosler, 'The *Ad Hoc* Chambers of the International Court of Justice' in *International Law at a Time of Perplexity* (ed. Y. Dinstein), Dordrecht, 1989, p. 449. See also S. Schwebel, 'Chambers of the International Court of Justice formed for Particular Cases', in *ibid.*, p. 739; E. Valencia-Ospina, 'The Use of Chambers of the International Court of Justice' in *Fifty Years of the International Court of Justice*, p. 503 and Franck, 'Fairness', pp. 314 *et seq*. As to the precedential value of decisions of Chambers, see Shahabuddeen, *Precedent*, pp. 171 *et seq*.
[219] See 22 ILM, 1983, p. 1252 and Communiqué of the ICJ no. 85/8, 1 May 1985. The Chamber consisted of Judge Bedjaoui (President) and Judges Lachs and Ruda, with Judges *ad hoc* Luchaire and Abi-Saab, see ICJ Reports, 1986, p. 554; 80 ILR, p. 441.
[220] ICJ Reports, 1989, p. 15; 84 ILR, p. 311.
[221] See ICJ Reports, 1987, p. 10; 97 ILR, pp. 112 and 139.
[222] See S. Rosenne, *Procedure in the International Court*, The Hague, 1983.
[223] See e.g. Rosenne, *Law and Practice*, vol. I, Part 3. See also M. N. Shaw, 'The Security Council and the International Court of Justice: Judicial Drift and Judicial Function', in *The International Court of Justice* (eds. A. S. Muller, D. Raič, and J. M. Thuránszky), The Hague, 1997, p. 219.
[224] See the *Fisheries Jurisdiction* case, ICJ Reports, 1974, pp. 3, 19; 55 ILR, pp. 238, 254.

other international organisations or indeed the subject of bilateral negotiations between the parties. This raises issues as to the proper function and
role of the Court. The International Court of Justice is by virtue of article
92 of the Charter the 'principal judicial organ of the United Nations'. It is
also as Judge Lachs put it, 'the guardian of legality for the international community as a whole, both within and without the United Nations'.[225] It has
been emphasised that the 'function of the Court is to state the law'[226] and it
can only decide on the basis of law.[227] Nevertheless, political factors cannot
but be entwined with questions of law. The Court has noted that while political aspects may be present in any legal dispute brought before it, the Court
was only concerned to establish that the dispute in question was a legal
dispute 'in the sense of a dispute capable of being settled by the application
of principles and rules of international law'.[228] The fact that other elements
are present cannot detract from the characterisation of a dispute as a legal
dispute.[229] The Court has also referred to the assessment of the legality of
the possible conduct of states with regard to international legal obligations
as an 'essentially judicial task'.[230]

The fact that the same general political situation may come before
different organs of the UN has raised the problem of concurrent jurisdiction. The Court, however, has been consistently clear that the fact that the
issue before the Court is also the subject of active negotiations between the
parties,[231] or the subject of good offices activity by the UN Secretary-
General[232] or the subject of consideration by the Security Council[233] will not
detract from the competence of the Court or the exercise of its judicial function. The Court has noted that the Security Council has functions of a political nature, while the Court itself has functions of a legal nature and that

---

[225] The *Lockerbie* case, ICJ Reports, 1992, pp. 3, 26; 94 ILR, pp. 478, 509.
[226] The *Northern Cameroons* case, ICJ Reports, 1963, pp. 15, 33; 35 ILR, pp. 353, 369.
[227] See the *Haya de la Torre* case, ICJ Reports, 1951, pp. 71, 79; 18 ILR, p. 349. See also Judge
    Weeramantry's Dissenting Opinion in the *Lockerbie* case, ICJ Reports, 1992, pp. 3, 56; 94
    ILR, pp. 478, 539.
[228] The *Armed Actions (Nicaragua v. Honduras)* case, ICJ Reports, 1988, pp. 16, 91; 84 ILR,
    pp. 218, 246. See also the *Certain Expenses of the United Nations* case, ICJ Reports, 1962,
    pp. 151, 155; 34 ILR, pp. 281, 285, and the *Tadić* case before the Appeals Chamber of the
    Yugoslav War Crimes Tribunal, IT-94-1-AR72, p. 11. See also R. Higgins, 'Policy
    Considerations and the International Judicial Process', 17 ICLQ, 1968, pp. 58, 74.
[229] *Ibid.*, p. 92; 84 ILR, p. 247. See also the *Iran* case, ICJ Reports, 1980, pp. 7, 19–20; 61
    ILR, pp. 530, 545–6. For the view that rather than concentrate upon definitions of legal
    and political questions, one should focus upon the distinctions between political and legal
    methods of dispute settlement, see R. Y. Jennings, 'Gerald Gray Fitzmaurice', 55 BYIL,
    1984, pp. 1, 18, and Higgins, *Policy Considerations*, p. 74.
[230] See the Advisory Opinion on the *Legality of the Use by a State of Nuclear Weapons in Armed
    Conflict*, ICJ Reports, 1996, para. 16. See also e.g. the *Certain Expenses* case, ICJ Reports,
    1962, pp. 151, 155; 34 ILR, pp. 281, 284–5.
[231] See the *Aegean Sea Continental Shelf* case, ICJ Reports, 1976, pp. 3, 12; 60 ILR, pp. 562,
    571.   [232] See the *Iran* case, ICJ Reports, 1980, pp. 7, 21–2; 61 ILR, pp. 530, 547–8.
[233] See the *Nicaragua* case, ICJ Reports, 1984, pp. 392, 431–4; 76 ILR, pp. 104, 142–5.

therefore both organs could perform their separate but complementary functions with respect to the same events.[234] The Court may also indicate provisional measures of protection at the same time as the UN Secretary-General is organising a fact-finding mission to investigate the same events.[235] The Court's essential function is basically to resolve in accordance with international law disputes placed before it.[236] The provision as to international law relates to the sources of law available for application by the Court and is considered subsequently.[237] The obligation to decide was referred to by the Court in the *Libya/Malta (Application for Permission to Intervene)* case,[238] where it was noted that it was the duty of the Court 'to give the fullest decision it may in the circumstances of each case'.[239] However, this obligation is subject, for example, to jurisdictional limitations (for example, with regard to the rights of third states)[240] and questions related to judicial propriety.[241]

The concept of jurisdiction also imports the notion of seisin, which relates to the way in which the Court's jurisdiction is first engaged. The Court noted in the *Qatar* v. *Bahrain* case[242] that 'as an act instituting proceedings, seisin is a procedural step independent of the basis of jurisdiction invoked', although the question as to whether the Court has been validly seized was a question of jurisdiction.

The nature of a legal dispute

Article 36(2) of the Statute of the Court requires that a matter brought before it should be a legal dispute.[243] Although it is not possible to point to a specific definition, the approach adopted by the Permanent Court in the *Mavrommatis Palestine Concessions (Jurisdiction)* case[244] constitutes the appropriate starting point. The Court declared that a dispute could be regarded as 'a disagreement over a point of law or fact, a conflict of legal views or of interests between two persons'. It is to be distinguished from a

---

[234] *Ibid.*, p. 435; 76 ILR, p. 146.   [235] *Cameroons* v. *Nigeria*, ICJ Reports, 1996, pp. 13, 22
[236] See e.g. Judge Weeramantry's Dissenting Opinion in the *Lockerbie* case, ICJ Reports, 1992, pp. 3, 56; 94 ILR, pp. 478, 539.   [237] *Infra*, p. 762.
[238] ICJ Reports, 1984, pp. 3, 25; 70 ILR, pp. 527, 554.
[239] See also Judge Weeramantry's Dissenting Opinion in the *East Timor* case, ICJ Reports, 1995, pp. 90, 158.
[240] See e.g. the *Monetary Gold* case, ICJ Reports, 1954, p. 32; 21 ILR, p. 399, and the *East Timor* case, ICJ Reports, 1995, pp. 90, 105.   [241] See further *infra*, p. 762.
[242] ICJ Reports, 1995, pp. 6, 23–4; 102 ILR, pp. 1, 64–5.
[243] The Court noted in the *Nuclear Tests* case, ICJ Reports, 1974, pp. 253, 270–1; 57 ILR, pp. 398, 415–16, that 'the existence of a dispute is the primary condition for the Court to exercise its judicial function'. It is also a question which is 'essentially preliminary', *ibid.*, p. 260; 57 ILR, p. 405.
[244] PCIJ, Series A, No. 2, 1924, p. 11. See also the *South West Africa* cases, ICJ Reports, 1962, pp. 319, 328; 37 ILR, pp. 3, 10 and the *Nuclear Tests* case, ICJ Reports, 1974, p. 253; 57 ILR, p. 398.

situation which might lead to international friction or give rise to a dispute. This is a subtle but important difference since, for the process of settlement to operate successfully, there has to be a specific issue or issues readily identifiable to be resolved.

In the *Interpretation of Peace Treaties* case[245] the Court noted that 'whether there exists an international dispute is a matter for objective determination' and pointed out that in the instant case 'the two sides hold clearly opposite views concerning the question of the performance or the non-performance of certain treaty obligations' so that 'international disputes have arisen'. A mere assertion is not sufficient; it must be shown that the claim of one party is positively opposed by the other.[246] This approach was reaffirmed in the *Applicability of the Obligation to Arbitrate under Section 21 of the United Nations Headquarters Agreement* case,[247] where the Court in an advisory opinion noted that the consistent challenge by the UN Secretary-General to the decisions contemplated and then taken by the US Congress and Administration with regard to the closing of the PLO offices in the US (which of necessity included the PLO Mission to the United Nations in New York) demonstrated the existence of a dispute between the US and the UN relating to the Headquarters Agreement. In the *East Timor* case[248] the Court again reaffirmed its earlier case law and went on to note that 'Portugal has, rightly or wrongly, formulated complaints of fact and law against Australia, which the latter has denied. By virtue of this denial, there is a legal dispute.' This acceptance of a relatively low threshold was underlined in the *Genocide (Bosnia and Herzegovina v. Yugoslavia)* case,[249] where the Court stated that 'by reason of the rejection by Yugoslavia of the complaints formulated against it by Bosnia-Herzegovina, "there is a legal dispute" between them'. Such denial of the allegations made against Yugoslavia had occurred 'whether at the stage of proceedings relating to the requests for the indication of provisional measures, or at the stage of the present proceedings relating to those objections'.[250] In other words, in order for a matter to constitute a legal dispute, it is sufficient for the respondent to an application before the Court merely to deny the allegations made even if the jurisdiction of the Court is challenged.

[245] ICJ Reports, 1950, pp. 65, 74; 17 ILR, pp. 331, 336.
[246] *South West Africa* cases, ICJ Reports, 1962, pp. 319, 328; 37 ILR, pp. 3, 10 and the *Nicaragua* case, ICJ Reports, 1984, pp. 392, 429–41; 76 ILR, pp. 104, 140 . Note also that Kelsen wrote that 'a dispute is a legal dispute if it is to be settled by the application of legal norms, that is to say, by the application of existing law', *Principles of International Law* (ed. R. W. Tucker), 2nd edn, 1966, p. 526. See also Rosenne, *Law and Practice*, vol. I, pp. 374–6. Higgins has made the point that generally the Court has taken a robust attitude as to what is a 'legal' matter, *Problems and Process*, Oxford, 1994, p. 195. See also V. Gowlland-Debbas, 'The Relationship between the International Court of Justice and the Security Council in the Light of the *Lockerbie* Case', 88 AJIL, 1994, p. 643.
[247] ICJ Reports, 1988, pp. 12, 30; 82 ILR, pp. 225, 248.
[248] ICJ Reports, 1995, pp. 90, 99–100.   [249] ICJ Reports, 1996, para. 29.
[250] *Ibid.*, para. 28.

The existence of a dispute is merely the beginning, for the Court may need to ascertain 'the true subject of the claim' and this will be done by taking into account not only the submission but the Application as a whole, the arguments of the applicant before the Court and other documents referred to, including the public statements of the applicant.[251] Should the Court conclude that the dispute in question has disappeared by the time the Court makes its decision, because, for example, the object of the claim has been achieved by other means, then the 'necessary consequences' will be drawn and no decision may be given.[252]

The International Court has also emphasised that a legal dispute is one capable of being settled by the application of the principles and rules of international law and that it cannot concern itself with the political motivation of a state in seeking judicial settlement of a dispute.[253]

It should also be noted that in dealing with issues of jurisdiction, the Court will not attach as much importance to matters of form as would be the case in domestic law.[254] The Court possesses an inherent jurisdiction to take such action as may be required in order to ensure that the exercise of its jurisdiction over the merits, once established, is not frustrated, and to ensure the orderly settlement of all matters in dispute, to ensure the 'inherent limitations on the exercise of the judicial function' of the Court and to 'maintain its judicial character'.[255]

Contentious jurisdiction[256]

The jurisdiction of the International Court falls into two distinct parts: its capacity to decide disputes between states, and its capacity to give advisory opinions when requested so to do by particular qualified entities. The latter will be noted in the following section.

[251] The *Nuclear Tests* case, ICJ Reports, 1974, pp. 253, 263; 57 ILR, pp. 398, 408.
[252] *Ibid.*, p. 271; 57 ILR, p. 416.
[253] See the *Case Concerning Border and Transborder Armed Actions (Nicaragua v. Honduras)*, ICJ Reports, 1988, pp. 69, 91. See also the Advisory Opinions on the *Legality of the Use by a State of Nuclear Weapons in Armed Conflict*, ICJ Reports, 1996, para. 17, and the *Legality of the Threat or Use of Nuclear Weapons*, ICJ Reports, 1996, para. 13.
[254] See the *Bosnia v. Yugoslavia (Preliminary Objections)* case, ICJ Reports, 1996, para. 24. See also the *Mavrommatis Palestine Concessions* case, PCIJ, Series A, No. 2, p. 34; 2 ILR, p. 27, and the *Northern Cameroons* case, ICJ Reports, 1963, pp. 15, 28; 35 ILR, pp. 353, 363. The Court in *Cameroons v. Nigeria*, ICJ Reports, 1994, p. 105, in fixing relevant time-limits for the parties, noted that Cameroons had submitted an additional application after its original application, by which it sought to extend the object of the dispute. It was intended as an amendment to the first application. There is no provision in the Statute and Rules of the Court for amendment of applications as such, although in this case Nigeria consented to the request and the Court accepted it.
[255] The *Nuclear Tests* case, ICJ Reports, 1974, pp. 253, 259; 57 ILR, pp. 398, 404, citing the *Northern Cameroons* case, ICJ Reports, 1963, pp. 15, 29; 35 ILR, pp. 353, 365.
[256] See e.g. Rosenne, *Law and Practice*, vol. I, part 3 and R. Szafarz, *The Compulsory Jurisdiction of the International Court of Justice*, Dordrecht, 1993.

Article 34 of the Statute of the Court declares that only states may be parties in cases before the Court. This is of far-reaching importance since it prohibits recourse to the Court by private persons and international organisations, save in so far as some of the latter may be able to obtain advisory opinions. The Court is open to all states that are parties to the Statute. Article 93 of the UN Charter provides that all UN members are *ipso facto* parties to the Statute of the ICJ, and that non-members of the UN may become a party to the Statute on conditions determined by the General Assembly upon the recommendation of the Security Council. In the case of Switzerland, for example, the Assembly and Security Council declared that it could become a party to the Statute of the ICJ provided it accepted the provisions of that Statute, accepted all the obligations of a UN member under Article 94 of the Charter (i.e. undertaking to comply with the decision of the Court), and agreed to pay a certain amount towards the expenses of the Court.[257] As far as other states may be concerned, the Court may be open to them upon conditions laid down by the Security Council, which should not place the parties in a position of inequality before the Court.[258]

The Security Council has in fact resolved that access to the ICJ for a state not party to the Statute is possible provided that such state has previously deposited with the registrar of the Court a declaration (either general or particular) accepting the jurisdiction of the Court and undertaking to comply in good faith with the decision or decisions of the Court.[259] West Germany filed a general declaration with the ICJ on this basis before it joined the UN,[260] while Albania[261] and Italy[262] filed particular declarations with respect to cases with which they were involved. Although only states may be parties before the Court, the Court may request information relevant to cases before it from public international organisations and may receive information presented by these organisations on their own initiative.[263]

Article 36(1)

The Court has jurisdiction under article 36(1) of its Statute in all cases referred to it by parties, and regarding all matters specially provided for in the UN Charter or in treaties or conventions in force. As in the case of

[257] General Assembly resolution 91(I). See also Rosenne, *Law and Practice*, vol. I, pp. 271–4. Liechtenstein and San Marino were also in the same position, *ibid.*, and Assembly resolutions 363(IV) and 806(VIII) and also Nauru. Japan was also until it became a UN member state in 1956.
[258] Article 35(2), Statute of the ICJ. See also Rosenne, *Law and Practice*, pp. 278–82.
[259] Security Council resolution 9 (1946).
[260] The *North Sea Continental Shelf* case, ICJ Reports, Pleadings, vol. I, pp. 6, 8.
[261] The *Corfu Channel* case, ICJ Reports, 1949, p. 4; 16 ILR, p. 155.
[262] The *Monetary Gold* case, ICJ Reports, 1954, p. 19; 21 ILR, p. 399.
[263] Article 34(2), Statute of the ICJ. See also Rosenne, *Law and Practice*, vol. I, pp. 284–90. Individuals, groups and corporations have no right of access to the Court, see here also H. Lauterpacht, *International Law and Human Rights*, London, 1950, p. 48.

arbitration, parties may refer a particular dispute to the ICJ by means of a special agreement or *compromis*, which will specify the terms of the dispute and the framework within which the Court is to operate.[264] This method was used in the *Minquiers and Ecrehos* case,[265] and in a number of others.[266] However, the essence of the process is the consent of the parties to the dispute to submit to the jurisdiction of the ICJ.[267] This consent need not be in any particular form and in certain circumstances the Court will infer it from the conduct of the parties. In the *Corfu Channel (Preliminary Objections)* case,[268] the Court inferred consent from the unilateral applica-tion of the plaintiff state (the United Kingdom) coupled with subsequent letters from the other party involved (Albania) intimating acceptance of the Court's jurisdiction.

The idea whereby the consent of a state to the Court's jurisdiction may be established by means of acts subsequent to the initiation of proceedings, is referred to as the doctrine of *forum prorogatum*.[269] It has been applied in other cases before the Court, but it is carefully interpreted to avoid giving the impression of a creeping extension by the Court of its own jurisdiction by means of fictions. Consent has to be clearly present, if inferred, and not merely a technical creation.[270] In the *Corfu Channel* case the UK sought to found the Court's jurisdiction *inter alia* on the recommendation of the Security Council that the dispute be referred to the Court, which it was agreed was a 'decision' binding upon member states of the UN in accor-dance with article 25 of the Charter.[271] Accordingly it was maintained by the UK that Albania was obliged to accept the Court's jurisdiction irre-spective of its consent. The ICJ did not deal with this point, since it actually

[264] See e.g. L. C. Marion, 'La Saisine de la CIJ par Voie de Compromis', *Revue Générale de Droit International Public*, 1995, p. 258.   [265] ICJ Reports, 1953, p. 47; 20 ILR, p. 94.
[266] See e.g. the *Frontier Land* case, ICJ Reports, 1959, p. 209; the *Tunisia/Libya Continental Shelf* case, ICJ Reports, 1982, p. 18; 67 ILR, p. 4 and the *Libya/Chad* case, ICJ Reports, 1974, p. 6; 100 ILR, p. 1.
[267] See the *Nicaragua* case, ICJ Reports, 1986, pp. 3, 32; 76 ILR, pp. 349, 366. The Court noted in the *Application for the Interpretation and Revision of the Judgment in the Tunisia/Libya Case* case, ICJ Reports, 1985, pp. 192, 216; 81 ILR, pp. 419, 449, that it was 'a funda-mental principle' that 'the consent of states parties to a dispute, is the basis of the Court's jurisdiction in contentious cases', citing here the *Interpretation of Peace Treaties* case, ICJ Reports, 1950, p. 71; 17 ILR, pp. 331, 335.
[268] ICJ Reports, 1948, p. 15; 15 ILR, p. 349.
[269] See e.g. Rosenne, *Law and Practice*, vol. I, pp. 344 *et seq.*
[270] See e.g. the *Monetary Gold* case, ICJ Reports, 1954, pp. 19, 31; 21 ILR, pp. 399, 406. But cf. the *Treatment in Hungary of Aircraft of the USA* case, ICJ Reports, 1964, pp. 99, 103; the *Aerial Incident (USA v. USSR)* case, ICJ Reports, 1956, pp. 6, 9, 12, 15 and the two *Antarctic* cases, ICJ Reports, 1958, p. 158 and *ibid.*, 1959, p. 276. Note that article 38(2) of the 1978 Rules of the Court stipulates that the application shall specify as far as possi-ble the legal grounds upon which the jurisdiction of the Court is said to be based.
[271] Although not a member of the UN, Albania had agreed to assume the obligations of a member with regard to the dispute. This application was on the basis of that part of article 36(1) which specifies that the Court's jurisdiction also comprised 'all matters specifically provided for in the Charter' of the UN.

inferred consent, but in a joint separate opinion, seven judges of the Court rejected the argument, which was regarded as an attempt to introduce a new meaning of compulsory jurisdiction.[272]

A particularly difficult case with regard to the question as to whether relevant events demonstrated an agreement between the parties to submit a case to the Court is that of *Qatar* v. *Bahrain*.[273] The issue centred upon minutes of a meeting signed by the Foreign Ministers of both states (the Doha Minutes) in December 1990. The status of such Minutes was controverted,[274] but the Court held that they constituted an agreement under international law.[275] There was also disagreement over the substance of the Minutes and thus the subject-matter of the dispute to be placed before the Court. Bahrain defined the issue as including the question of 'sovereignty' over Zubarah, while Qatar merely accepted that that was how Bahrain characterised the issue.[276] The Court concluded that this was sufficient to lay the whole dispute, including this element, before it.[277] Questions do therefore remain with regard to the extent of the consensual principle after this decision.[278]

It is a well-established principle that the Court will only exercise jurisdiction over a state with its consent.[279] As a consequence of this principle, the Court will not entertain actions between states that in reality implead a third state without its consent. This rule was underlined in the *Monetary Gold* case,[280] where it was noted that where the legal interests of the third party 'would form the very subject-matter of the decision', the Court could not entertain proceedings in the absence of that state. In the *Nicaragua* case, the Court noted that the circumstances of the *Monetary Gold* case 'probably represent the limit of the power of the Court to refuse to exercise its juris-

---

[272] ICJ Reports, 1948, pp. 15, 31–2; 15 ILR, pp. 349, 354.

[273] ICJ Reports, 1994, p. 112 and ICJ Reports, 1995, p. 6; 102 ILR, pp. 1 and 47. See M. Evans, 'Case Concerning Maritime Delimitation and Territorial Questions Between Qatar and Bahrain (*Qatar* v. *Bahrain*), Jurisdiction and Admissibility', 44 ICLQ, 1995, p. 691.

[274] The argument revolving around whether any application to the Court had to be by both parties or whether unilateral application was provided for.

[275] *Ibid.*, 1994, p. 121; 102 ILR, p. 18.   [276] *Ibid.*, 1995, pp. 9–11; 102 ILR, pp. 50–2.

[277] *Ibid.*, 1995, pp. 17 and 25; 102 ILR, pp. 58 and 66. This was disputed by four of the five dissenting judges, who argued that the Zubarah sovereignty issue had not been properly laid before it, *ibid.*, pp. 49, 55 *et seq.*, 72 and 74–5; 102 ILR, pp. 90, 96 *et seq.*, 113 and 115–16.

[278] See also E. Lauterpacht, '"Partial" Judgements and the Inherent Jurisdiction of the International Court of Justice' in *Fifty Years of the International Court of Justice*, p. 465.

[279] See e.g. the *Libya/Malta* case, ICJ Reports, 1984, pp. 3, 24; 70 ILR, pp. 527, 553, the *Nicaragua* case, ICJ Reports, 1984, pp. 392, 431; 76 ILR, pp. 104, 142, the *El Salvador/Honduras* case, ICJ Reports, 1990, pp. 92, 114–16; 97 ILR, pp. 214, 235–7, and the *Nauru* case, ICJ Reports, 1992, pp. 240, 259–62; 97 ILR, pp. 1, 26–9.

[280] ICJ Reports, 1954, pp. 19, 54; 21 ILR, p. 399, 406. In this case, Italy asked that the governments of the UK and France should deliver to it any share of the monetary gold that might be due to Albania under Part III of the Paris Act of 14 January 1946, as satisfaction for alleged damage to Italy by Albania. Albania chose not to intervene in the case.

diction'.²⁸¹ This approach was underlined in the *Nauru* case, where the Court emphasised that the absence of a request from a third party to intervene 'in no way precludes the Court from adjudicating upon claims submitted to it, provided that the legal interests of the third state which may possibly be affected do not form the very subject-matter of the decision that is applied for'.²⁸² The test referred to was whether the determination of the third state's responsibility was a pre-requisite for the claims raised before the Court by one party against the other.²⁸³ In the *East Timor* case,²⁸⁴ the Court held that it could not rule on the lawfulness of the conduct of another state which was not a party to the case, whatever the nature of the obligations in question (i.e. even if they were *erga omnes* obligations as was the case with regard to the right to self-determination).²⁸⁵ It was felt that in view of the situation, the Court would have to rule on the lawfulness of Indonesia's conduct with regard to East Timor as a pre-requisite for deciding upon Portugal's claims against Australia²⁸⁶ and that such a determination would constitute the very subject-matter of the judgment requested and thus infringe the *Monetary Gold* principle.²⁸⁷

Apart from those instances where states specifically refer a dispute to it, the Court may also be granted jurisdiction over disputes arising from international treaties where such treaties contain a 'compromissory clause' providing for this. In fact, quite a large number of international treaties, both bilateral and multilateral do include a clause awarding the ICJ jurisdiction with respect to questions that might arise from the interpretation and application of the agreements.²⁸⁸ Examples of the more important of such conventions include the 1948 Genocide Convention, the 1965 Convention on Investment Disputes, the 1965 International Convention on the Elimination of all forms of Racial Discrimination and the 1970 Hague Convention on Hijacking. In the *Bosnia* v. *Yugoslavia* case,²⁸⁹ the Court founded its jurisdiction upon article IX of the Genocide Convention. In the *US Diplomatic and Consular Staff in Tehran* case (the *Iran* case),²⁹⁰ the Court founded jurisdiction upon article 1 of the Optional Protocols concerning the Compulsory Settlement of Disputes (to which both Iran and the US were parties), which accompany both the Vienna Convention on Diplomatic

²⁸¹ ICJ Reports, 1984, pp. 392, 431; 76 ILR, pp. 104, 142.
²⁸² ICJ Reports, 1992, pp. 240, 261; 97 ILR, p. 28.   ²⁸³ *Ibid.*
²⁸⁴ ICJ Reports, 1995, pp. 90, 101 *et seq.*   ²⁸⁵ *Ibid.*, p. 102.   ²⁸⁶ *Ibid.*, p. 104.
²⁸⁷ *Ibid.*, p. 105.
²⁸⁸ See Rosenne, *Law and Practice*, vol. I, Chapter 10. Approximately 160 bilateral and trilateral treaties and 87 multilateral treaties refer to the Court in such a way, see e.g. 22(1) *UN Chronicle*, 1985, p. 8. See also J. Charney, 'Compromisory Clauses and the Jurisdiction of the International Court of Justice', 81 AJIL, 1989, p. 85.
²⁸⁹ ICJ Reports, 1996, para. 47 (rejecting preliminary objections). See also ICJ Reports, 1993, pp. 3 and 325; 95 ILR, pp. 18 and 43 (the two Orders on Provisional Measures).
²⁹⁰ ICJ Reports, 1980, pp. 3, 24; 61 ILR, pp. 530, 550.

Relations 1961 and the Vienna Convention on Consular Relations 1963. Common article 1 of the Protocol provides that disputes arising out of the interpretation or application of the Conventions lie within the compulsory jurisdiction of the International Court of Justice. The Court also founded jurisdiction in the *Nicaragua*[291] case *inter alia* upon a treaty provision, article XXIV(2) of the 1956 US–Nicaragua Treaty of Friendship, Commerce and Navigation providing for submission of disputes over the interpretation or application of the treaty to the ICJ unless the parties agree to settlement by some other specific means.

In its judgment on jurisdiction and admissibility in the *Case Concerning Border and Transborder Armed Actions (Nicaragua v. Honduras)*,[292] the International Court emphasised that the existence of jurisdiction was a question of law and dependent upon the intention of the parties. The issue of jurisdiction in the case centred, in the view of the Court, upon article 31 of the Pact of Bogotá 1948, which declared that the parties '[i]n conformity with article 36(2) of the Statute of the International Court of Justice . . . recognise, in relation to any other American state, the jurisdiction of the Court as compulsory *ipso facto* . . . in all disputes of a juridical nature that arise among them'. Objections to jurisdiction put forward by Honduras on the grounds that article 31 was not intended to have independent force, and was merely an encouragement to the parties to deposit unilateral declarations of acceptance of the Court's compulsory jurisdiction, and that article 31 would only operate after the exhaustion of conciliation procedures referred to in article 32, were rejected on the basis of interpretation.[293]

Article 31 nowhere envisaged that the undertaking contained therein might be amended subsequently by unilateral declaration and the reference to article 36(2) of the Statute was insufficient to have that effect,[294] while the reference in article 32 of the Pact to a right of recourse to the International

---

[291] ICJ Reports, 1984, pp. 392, 426–9; 76 ILR, pp. 104, 137. See H. W. Briggs, '*Nicaragua v. United States*: Jurisdiction and Admissibility', 79 AJIL, 1985, p. 373. See also the *Oil Platforms* (Preliminary Objections) case, ICJ Reports, 1996, where the Court found jurisdiction upon the basis of article XX(2) of the Treaty of Amity, Economic Relations and Consular Rights, 1955 between the US and Iran. The question of the appropriate test to be applied when the Court is deciding at the jurisdictional phase that it has jurisdiction with regard to compromissory clauses in a treaty concerning matters detailed in that treaty has also been raised. Cases show some variance as to whether such decision should be provisional or definitive, see e.g. the *Nationality decrees in Tunis and Morocco* case, PCIJ, Series B, No. 4; the *Mavromatis Palestine Concessions* case, PCIJ, Series A, No. 2; the *Certain German Interests in Polish Upper Silesia* case, PCIJ, Series A, No. 6; the Ambatielos case, ICJ Reports, 1953, p. 12; the *Interhandel* case, ICJ Reports, 1959, p. 24 and the *Nicaragua* case, ICJ Reports, 1984, pp. 428. The judgment in the *Oil Platforms* case suggests that the test is the higher one of a definitive interpretation of the treaty in question, see at paras. 16 and 52. See also in particular the Separate Opinions of Judges Shahabuddeen and Higgins.
[292] ICJ Reports, 1988, pp. 69, 76; 84 ILR, pp. 218, 231.
[293] *Ibid.*, pp. 78–90. The decision to affirm jurisdiction and admissibility was unanimous.
[294] *Ibid.*, pp. 85–8.

Court upon the failure of conciliation provided a second basis for the jurisdiction of the Court and not a limitation upon the first.[295] In other words, the commitment contained in article 31 of the Pact was sufficient to enable the Court to exercise jurisdiction.

Where a treaty in force provides for reference of a matter to the PCIJ or to a tribunal established by the League of Nations, article 37 of the Statute declares that such matter shall be referred to the ICJ, provided the parties to the dispute are parties to the Statute. It is basically a bridging provision and provides some measure of continuity between the old Permanent Court and the new International Court.[296] Under article 36(6) of the Statute, the Court has the competence to decide its own jurisdiction in the event of a dispute.[297]

Article 36(2)[298]

This article has been of great importance in extending the jurisdiction of the International Court. Article 36(2), the so-called 'optional clause', stipulates that:

> The states parties to the present Statute may at any time declare that they recognise as compulsory *ipso facto* and without special agreement, in relation to any other state accepting the same obligation, the jurisdiction of the Court in all legal disputes concerning:
> (a) the interpretation of a treaty;
> (b) any question of international law;
> (c) the existence of any fact which, if established, would constitute a breach of an international obligation;
> (d) the nature or extent of the reparation to be made for the breach of an international obligation.

This provision was intended to operate as a method of increasing the Court's jurisdiction, by the gradual increase in its acceptance by more and more states. By the end of 1984, forty-seven declarations were in force and deposited with the UN Secretary-General, comprising less than one-third of the parties to the ICJ Statute. By July 1994, this number had risen to

---

[295] *Ibid.*, pp. 88–90.
[296] See e.g. the *Ambatielos* case (Preliminary Objections), ICJ Reports, 1952, p. 28; 19 ILR, p. 416 and the *Barcelona Traction* case (Preliminary Objections), ICJ Reports, 1964, p. 6; 46 ILR, p. 18. Cf. the *Aerial Incident* case, ICJ Reports, 1959, p. 127; 27 ILR, p. 557.
[297] See I. Shihata, *The Power of the International Court to Determine Its Own Jurisdiction*, 1965. This is a characteristic of the judicial function generally, see e.g. the *Effect of Awards* case, ICJ Reports, 1954, pp. 47, 51–2; 21 ILR, pp. 310, 312, and the *Nottebohm* case, ICJ Reports, 1953, pp. 111, 119; 20 ILR, pp. 567, 572. See also the *Tadić* case before the Appeals Chamber of the Yugoslav War Crimes Tribunal, IT-94-1-AR72, pp. 7–9.
[298] See e.g. Rosenne, *Law and Practice*, vol. I, Chapter 11. See also J. G. Merrills, 'The Optional Clause Today', 50 BYIL, 1979, p. 87 and Merrills, 'The Optional Clause Revisited', 64 BYIL, 1993, p. 197; L. Gross, 'Compulsory Jurisdiction under the Optional Protocol: History and Practice' in *The International Court of Justice at a Crossroads*, p. 19 and E. Gordon, '"Legal Disputes" Under Article 36(2) of the Statute', *ibid.*, p. 183.

fifty-eight. Since 1951, twelve other declarations have expired or been terminated without renewal.[299]

These declarations, pursuant to article 36(2), are in the majority of cases conditional and are dependent upon reciprocity for operation. This means that the Court will only have jurisdiction under article 36(2) where the declarations of the two parties in dispute meet. The doctrine of the lowest common denominator thus operates since the acceptance, by means of the optional clause, by one state of the jurisdiction of the Court is in relation to any other state accepting the same obligation. It is not that declarations in identical terms from the parties are necessary, but both declarations must grant jurisdiction to the Court regarding the dispute in question.

In practice, this can lead to the situation where one party may rely on a condition, or reservation, expressed in the declaration of the other party. This occurred in the *Norwegian Loans* case,[300] between France and Norway. The Court noted that:

> since two unilateral declarations are involved, such jurisdiction is conferred upon the Court only to the extent to which the declarations coincide in conferring it. A comparison between the two declarations shows that the French declaration accepts the Court's jurisdiction within narrower limits than the Norwegian declaration; consequently, the common will of the parties, which is the basis of the Court's jurisdiction, exists within these narrower limits indicated by the French reservation.[301]

Accordingly, Norway was entitled to invoke the French reservation to defeat the jurisdiction of the Court. However, much will depend upon the precise terms of the declarations. Declarations made under the optional clause in the Statute of the PCIJ and still in force are deemed to continue with respect to the ICJ,[302] but in the *Aerial Incident* case[303] between Israel and Bulgaria, the Court declared that this in fact only applied to states signing the ICJ Statute in 1945 and did not relate to states, like Bulgaria, which became a party to the Statute many years later as a result of admission to the United Nations.

The issue also arose in the jurisdictional phase of the *Nicaragua* case.[304] Nicaragua had declared that it would accept the compulsory jurisdiction of the Permanent Court in 1929 but had not ratified this. The US argued that accordingly Nicaragua never became a party to the Statute of the Permanent Court and could not therefore rely on article 36(5). The Court in an inter-

---

[299] International Court of Justice, *Yearbook 1993–4*, The Hague, 1994, p. 82.
[300] ICJ Reports, 1957, p. 9; 24 ILR, p. 782.
[301] *Ibid.*, p. 23; 24 ILR, p. 786. But note Judge Lauterpacht's individual opinion, *ibid.*, p. 34; 24 ILR, p. 793. See also the *Right of Passage* case, ICJ Reports, 1957, pp. 125, 145; 24 ILR, pp. 840, 845 and the *Interhandel* case, ICJ Reports, 1959, pp. 6, 23; 27 ILR, pp. 475, 487.
[302] Article 36(5), Statute of the ICJ.   [303] ICJ Reports, 1959, p. 127; 27 ILR, p. 557.
[304] ICJ Reports, 1984, pp. 392, 403–12; 76 ILR, pp. 104, 114.

esting judgment noted that the Nicaraguan declaration, unconditional and unlimited as to time, had 'a certain potential effect' and that the phrase in article 36(5) 'still in force' could be so interpreted as to cover declarations which had only potential and not binding effect. Ratification of the Statute of the ICJ in 1945 by Nicaragua had the effect, argued the Court, of transforming this potential commitment into an effective one.[305] Since this was so, Nicaragua could rely on the US declaration of 1946 accepting the Court's compulsory jurisdiction as the necessary reciprocal element.[306]

The reservations that have been made in declarations by states under the optional clause, restricting the jurisdiction of the ICJ, vary a great deal from state to state, and are usually an attempt to prevent the Court becoming involved in a dispute which is felt to concern vital interests. One condition made by a number of states, particularly the United States of America, stipulates that matters within the domestic jurisdiction 'as determined by' that particular state are automatically excluded from the purview of the Court. The validity of this type of reservation (known as the 'Connally amendment' from the American initiator of the relevant legislation) has been widely questioned,[307] particularly since it appears to contradict the power of the Court under article 36(6) to determine its own jurisdiction, and in reality it withdraws from the Court the jurisdiction conferred under the declaration itself. Indeed, it is a well established principle of international law that the definition of domestic jurisdiction is an issue of international and not domestic law.[308]

Many reservations relate to requirements of time (*ratione temporis*),[309] according to which acceptances of jurisdiction are deemed to expire automatically after a certain period or within a particular time after notice of termination has been given to the UN Secretary-General. Some states exclude the jurisdiction of the ICJ with respect to disputes arising before or

---

[305] The Court also noted that since Court publications had placed Nicaragua on the list of states accepting the compulsory jurisdiction of the ICJ by virtue of article 36(5) and that no states had objected, one could conclude that the above interpretation had been confirmed, *ibid.* The Court also regarded the conduct of the parties as reflecting acquiescence in Nicaragua's obligations when article 36(5) was argued, *ibid.*, pp. 411–15; 76 ILR, p. 122.

[306] But see the Separate Opinions of Judges Mosler, ICJ Reports, 1984, pp. 461–3; Oda, *ibid.*, pp. 473–89; Ago, *ibid.*, pp. 517–27 and Jennings, *ibid.*, pp. 533–45 and the Dissenting Opinion of Judge Schwebel, *ibid.*, pp. 562–600; 76 ILR, pp. 172, 184, 228, 244 and 273.

[307] See e.g. L. Henkin, 'The Connally Reservation Revisited and, hopefully, Contained', 65 AJIL, 1971, pp. 374, and Preuss, 'The International Court of Justice, the Senate and Matters of Domestic Jurisdiction', 40 AJIL, 1946, p. 720. See also Rosenne, *Law and Practice*, vol. I, pp. 395–9; Judge Lauterpacht, *Norwegian Loans* case, ICJ Reports, 1957, pp. 9, 43–66; 24 ILR, pp. 782, 800; the *Interhandel* case, ICJ Reports, 1959, pp. 6, 77–8 and 93; 27 ILR, pp. 475, 524, 534, and A. D'Amato, 'Modifying US Acceptance of the Compulsory Jurisdiction of the World Court', 79 AJIL, 1985, p. 385.

[308] See *supra*, Chapter 12, p. 454.

[309] See Rosenne, *Law and Practice*, vol. I, pp. 399–400 and Merrills, 'Revisited', pp. 213 *et seq.*

after a certain date in their declarations.[310] Reservations *ratione personae* may also be made, for example the UK reservation concerning disputes between member states of the British Commonwealth.[311] Reservations may also be made *ratione materiae*, excluding disputes where other means of dispute settlement have been agreed.[312] Other restrictive grounds exist.[313] However, once the Court is dealing with a dispute, any subsequent expiry or termination of a party's declaration will not modify the jurisdiction of the case.[314]

A state may withdraw or modify its declaration.[315] The US declaration of 1946 provided for termination after a six-month period of notice. What the Court in the jurisdictional phase of the *Nicaragua* case[316] had to decide was whether a modifying notification[317] expressly deemed to apply immediately could have effect over the original declaration. It decided that the six-month notice provision remained valid and could be invoked by Nicaragua against the US, since it was an undertaking that constituted an integral part of the instrument that contained it.

Sources of law, propriety and legal interest

In its deliberations, the Court will apply the rules of international law as laid down in article 38 (treaties, custom, general principles of law).[318] However,

---

[310] Rosenne, *Law and Practice*, vol. I, pp. 400–3. The UK for example, excluded disputes arising out of events occurring between 3 September 1939 and 2 September 1945 in its 1963 declaration, Cmnd. 2248. This was altered in the 1969 declaration, which is expressed to apply only to disputes arising after 24 October 1945, Cmnd. 3872.

[311] See Merrills, 'Revisited', pp. 219 *et seq.*

[312] *Ibid.*, pp. 224 *et seq.* See the *Nauru* case, ICJ Reports, 1992, pp. 240, 245–7; 97 ILR, pp. 1, 12–14. The Court emphasised that declarations made under article 36(2) related only to disputes between states and did not therefore cover disputes arising out of a trusteeship agreement between the Administering Authority and the indigenous population, *ibid.* See also the *Guinea-Bissau/Senegal* case, ICJ Reports, 1990, p. 64 and1991, p. 54; 92 ILR, pp. 1 and 30.

[313] See e.g. reservations relating to territorial matters, see Merrills, 'Revisited', pp. 234 *et seq.*

[314] See e.g. the *Nottebohm* case, ICJ Reports, 1953, p. 111; 20 ILR, p. 567. See also Judge Shahabuddeen's Separate Opinion, the *Request for an Examination of the Situation in the Nuclear Tests Case* case, ICJ Reports, 1995, pp. 288, 315.

[315] See e.g. Rosenne, *Law and Practice*, vol. I, pp. 415–18. A state may waive its jurisdictional reservation, but this must be done unequivocally, *Application for Revision and Interpretation of the Judgment in the Tunisia/Libya Case*, ICJ Reports, 1985, pp. 192, 216; 81 ILR, pp. 419, 449, and the *Nicaragua* case, ICJ Reports, 1986, pp. 33; 76 ILR, pp. 349, 367.

[316] ICJ Reports, 1984, pp. 392, 415–21; 76 ILR, p. 126.

[317] Excluding disputes related to Central America for a two-year period. See e.g. A. Chayes, 'Nicaragua, The United States and the World Court', 85 *Columbia Law Review*, 1985, p. 1445; K. Highet, 'Litigation Implications of the US Withdrawal from the *Nicaragua* case', 79 AJIL, 1985, p. 992 and US Department of State Statement on the US Withdrawal from the Proceedings Initiated by Nicaragua in the International Court of Justice, 22 ILM, 1985, p. 246.

[318] See further *supra* Chapter 3, p. 55. Note that the Court may be specifically requested by the parties to consider particular factors. In the *Tunisia/Libya* case, ICJ Reports, 1982, pp. 18, 21; 67 ILR, pp. 3, 14, the *compromis* specifically asked the Court to take into account 'the recent trends admitted at the Third Conference on the Law of the Sea'.

the Court may decide a case *ex aequo et bono*, i.e. on the basis of justice and equity untrammelled by technical legal rules.[319] This has not yet occurred, although it should not be confused with the ability of the ICJ to apply certain equitable considerations in a case within the framework of international law.[320] The question of gaps in international law in addressing a case arose in the advisory opinion concerning *The Legality of the Threat or Use of Nuclear Weapons*.[321] Although not a contentious case and therefore not as such binding, the fact that the Court was unable to give its view on a crucial issue in international law has potential ramifications. The Court concluded[322] that it could not 'conclude definitively whether the threat or use of nuclear weapons would be lawful or unlawful in an extreme circumstance of self-defence, in which the very survival of a state would be at stake'. This appearance of a *non-liquet* is of some concern as a matter of principle, unconnected with the substance of the legal principle in question.[323]

Quite often before dealing with the merits of a case the Court will have to deal with preliminary objections as to whether in fact it has the jurisdiction to decide the case before it.[324] The Court has emphasised that objections to jurisdiction require decision at the preliminary stage of the proceedings.[325] A decision on preliminary objections to jurisdiction cannot determine merits issues, even where dealt with in connection with preliminary objections. Such reference can only be provisional.[326] Where it has established its right to exercise jurisdiction, the Court may well decline to exercise that right on grounds of propriety. In the *Northern Cameroons* case,[327] the Court declared that:

> it may pronounce judgment only in connection with concrete cases where there exists, at the time of adjudication, an actual controversy involving a conflict of legal interests between the parties. The Court's judgment must have some practical consequence in the sense that it can affect existing legal rights or obligations of the parties, thus removing uncertainty from their legal relations.

In addition, and following the *South West Africa* cases (Second Phase) in 1966,[328] it may be necessary for the Court to establish that the claimant state

[319] *Ibid.* [320] See e.g. *supra*, Chapter 11, p. 436.
[321] ICJ Reports, 1966. See also 35 ILM, 1996, p. 809.
[322] Para. 2 E of the *Dispositif*, 35 ILM, p. 831. See also para. 97; 35 ILM, p. 830. This is the subject of a strong rebuttal by Judge Higgins in her Dissenting Opinion, *ibid.*; 35 ILM, pp. 934 *et seq.* [323] See *supra*, Chapter 3, p. 78.
[324] See Rule 79 of the Rules of the Court 1978.
[325] The *Nicaragua* case, ICJ Reports, 1986, pp. 3, 30–1; 76 ILR, pp. 349, 364–5.
[326] See the *South West Africa* cases, ICJ Reports, 1966, pp. 3, 37; 37 ILR, pp. 243, 270. It is to be noted that admissibility issues may be discussed at the merits stage, see e.g. the *East Timor* case, ICJ Reports, 1995, p. 90. See also C. M. Chinkin, 'East Timor Moves into the World Court', 4 EJIL, 1993, p. 206.
[327] ICJ Reports, 1963, pp. 15, 33–4; 35 ILR, pp. 353, 369.
[328] ICJ Reports, 1966, p. 6; 37 ILR, p. 243.

has a legal interest in the subject matter of the dispute. The fact that political considerations may have motivated the application is not relevant, so long as a legal dispute is in evidence. Similarly, the fact that a particular dispute has other important aspects is not of itself sufficient to render the application inadmissible.[329]

Unlike domestic courts, the International Court is flexible with regard to the introduction of evidence.[330] Strict rules of admissibility common in domestic legal systems do not exist here.[331] In dealing with questions of evidence, the Court proceeds upon the basis that its decision will be based upon the facts occurring up to the close of the oral proceedings on the merits of the case.[332] The kinds of facts that the Court might take into account could include 'matters of public knowledge which have received extensive coverage' in the world's media,[333] provided that caution was shown and that the reports did not emanate from a single source.[334] Consistency and concordance was important in evaluating such reports. The Court is prepared to attach particular probative value to statements from high-ranking official political figures 'when they acknowledge facts or conduct unfavourable to the state represented by the person making them'.[335] The actual standard of proof required will vary with the character of the particular issue of fact.[336] Expert opinion may be requested, although this is rare.[337]

In so far as the scope of the Court's decision is concerned, it was noted in the *Nicaragua* case that the Court 'is bound to confine its decision to those points of law which are essential to the settlement of the dispute before it'.[338] In so doing, the Court will seek to ascertain 'the true subject of the dispute' taking into account the submissions, the applications, oral arguments and other documents placed before it.[339]

[329] See *supra*, p. 719.
[330] See e.g. K. Highet, 'Evidence and Proof of Facts' in *The International Court of Justice at the Crossroads*, pp. 355, 357. See also D. V. Sandifer, *Evidence before International Tribunals*, 1975 and T. M. Franck, *Fairness in International Law and Institutions*, Oxford, 1995, pp. 335 *et seq.*
[331] See e.g. the introduction of illegally obtained evidence in the *Corfu Channel* case, ICJ Reports, 1949, pp. 4, 32–6; 16 ILR, p. 155.
[332] The *Nicaragua* case, ICJ Reports, 1986, pp. 3, 39; 76 ILR, pp. 349, 373. Although note that in the *Lockerbie* case, ICJ Reports, 1992, pp. 3, 13; 95 ILR, pp. 478, 496, the Court referred in detail to Security Council resolution 748 (1992) adopted three days after the close of the oral hearings.
[333] The *Iran* case, ICJ Reports, 1980, pp. 3, 9; 61 ILR, pp. 530, 535. See also F. A. Mann, 'Foreign Investment in the International Court of Justice: The *ELSI* Case', 86 AJIL, 1992, pp. 92, 94–5 and the *El Salvador/Honduras* case, ICJ Reports, 1992, pp. 351, 574; 97 ILR, pp. 112, 490.
[334] The *Nicaragua* case, ICJ Reports, 1986, pp. 3, 41; 76 ILR, pp. 349, 375.
[335] *Ibid.*; the manner in which such statements become public is also a relevant factor.
[336] Judge Shahabuddeen's Dissenting Opinion in the *Qatar* v. *Bahrain* case, ICJ Reports, 1995, pp. 6, 63; 102 ILR, pp. 1, 104.
[337] See the *Corfu Channel* case, ICJ Reports, 1949, pp. 4, 9; 16 ILR, p. 155.
[338] ICJ Reports, 1986, pp. 3, 110; 76 ILR, pp. 349, 444.
[339] The *Nuclear Tests* case, ICJ Reports, 1974, pp. 466–7.

Interim measures[340]

Under article 41 of the Statute, the Court may grant provisional measures of protection in order to preserve the respective rights of the parties. In deciding upon a request for provisional measures, the Court need not finally satisfy itself that it has jurisdiction on the merits of the case, although it has held that it ought not to indicate such measures unless the provisions invoked by the applicant appear *prima facie* to afford a basis upon which the jurisdiction of the Court might be founded.[341] The purpose of exercising the power is to protect 'rights which are the subject of dispute in judicial proceedings'[342] and thus the measures must be such that once the disputes over those rights has been resolved by the Court's judgment on the merits, they would no longer be required.[343] These are awarded to assist the Court to ensure the integrity of the proceedings. Such interim measures were granted by the Court in the *Fisheries Jurisdiction* case,[344] to protect British fishing rights in Icelandic-claimed waters, and in the *Nuclear Tests* case.[345] Interim measures would appear to be advisory only and are not to be regarded as judgments on the merits of the case. In the *Fisheries Jurisdiction* case, it emphasised that article 41 presupposes 'that irreparable prejudice should

---

[340] See e.g. S. Oda, 'Provisional Measures' in *Fifty Years of the International Court of Justice*, p. 541; B. Oxman, 'Jurisdiction and the Power to Indicate Provisional Measures' in *The International Court of Justice at the Crossroads*, p. 323; Elias, *International Court*, Chapter 3; J. G. Merrills, 'Interim Measures of Protection in the recent Jurisprudence of the International Court of Justice', 44 ICLQ, 1995, p. 90; Rosenne, *Law and Practice*, vol. I, pp. 224–8; L. Gross, 'The Case Concerning United States Diplomatic and Consular Staff in Tehran: Phase of Provisional Measures', 74 AJIL, 1980, p. 395, and M. Mendelson, 'Interim Measures of Protection in Cases of Contested Jurisdiction', 46 BYIL, 1972–3, p. 259. See also Rules 73–78 of the Court, 1978. See also C. Gray, *Judicial Remedies in International Law*, Oxford, 1987, pp. 69–74.

[341] See the request by Guinea-Bissau for the indication of provisional measures in the *Arbitral Award of 31 July 1989 (Guinea-Bissau v. Senegal)* case, ICJ Reports, 1990, pp. 64, 68. See also the *Great Belt* case, ICJ Reports, 1991, pp. 12, 15; 94 ILR, pp. 446, 453, where jurisdiction was not at issue and *Cameroons v. Nigeria*, ICJ Reports, 1996, pp. 13, 21, where it was. The Court in *Bosnia v. Yugoslavia*, ICJ Reports, 1993, pp. 3, 12; 95 ILR, pp. 1, 27, noted that jurisdiction included both jurisdiction *rationae personae* and *ratione materiae*. Note that Jiminez de Aréchaga, a former President of the Court, has written that 'interim measures will not be granted unless a majority of judges believes at the time that there will be jurisdiction over the merits', 'International Law in the Past Third of a Century', 159 HR, 1978 I, pp. 1, 161.

[342] The *Aegean Sea Continental Shelf* case, ICJ Reports, 1976, pp. 3, 9; 60 ILR, pp. 524, 530 and the *Iran* case, ICJ Reports, 1979, pp. 7, 19; 61 ILR, pp. 513, 525. See also the *Arbitral Award of 31 July 1989* case, ICJ Reports, 1990, pp. 64, 69; 92 ILR, pp. 9. 14.

[343] *Arbitral Award of 31 July 1989* case, ICJ Reports, 1990, p. 69; 92 ILR, pp. 9. 14.

[344] ICJ Reports, 1972, p. 12; 55 ILR, p. 160. See also the *Anglo-Iranian Oil Co.* case, ICJ Reports, 1951, p. 89; 19 ILR, p. 501.

[345] ICJ Reports, 1973, p. 99; 57 ILR, p. 360. They were also granted in the *Iran* case, ICJ Reports, 1979, pp. 7, 19; 61 ILR, pp. 513, 525 and in the *Nicaragua* case, ICJ Reports, 1980, p. 169; 76 ILR, p. 35. See also the *Great Belt* case, ICJ Reports, 1991, p. 12; 94 ILR, p. 446, *Bosnia v. Yugoslavia*, ICJ Reports, 1993, pp. 3 and 325 and the *Cameroons v. Nigeria* case, ICJ Reports, 1996, p. 13.

not be caused to rights which are the subject of dispute in judicial proceedings'.[346] However, it was noted in the *Lockerbie* case[347] that the measures requested by Libya 'would be likely to impair the rights which appear prima facie to be enjoyed by the United Kingdom by virtue of Security Council resolution 748 (1992)'. The Court has also stated that provisional measures are only justified if there is urgency.[348]

Provisional measures may also be indicated by the Court, independently of requests by the parties, with a view to preventing 'the aggravation or extension of the dispute whenever it considers that circumstances so require'. [349] Unfortunately the record of compliance with provisional measures is not encouraging.

Enforcement

Once given, the judgment of the Court under article 60 is final and without appeal. Although it has no binding force except between the parties and in respect of the particular case under article 59, such decisions are often very influential in the evolution of new rules of international law.[350] The Court itself is not concerned with compliance and takes the view that 'once the Court has found that a state has entered into a commitment concerning its future conduct it is not the Court's function to contemplate that it will not comply with it'.[351]

Under article 94 of the UN Charter, each member state undertakes to comply with the decision of the Court in any case to which it is a party and if this does not occur, the other party may have recourse to the Security Council which may make recommendations or take binding decisions. In the event, the record of compliance with judgments is only marginally satisfactory. Examples of non-compliance would include Albania in the *Corfu Channel* case,[352] Iceland in the *Fisheries Jurisdiction* case[353] and Iran in the *Iran* case concerning the Teheran hostages.[354] Nevertheless, on a political level such judgments have an impact and should not necessarily be exclusively evaluated on the legal plane.

---

[346] ICJ Reports, 1972, pp. 12, 16, 30, 34; 55 ILR, pp. 160, 164; 56 ILR, pp. 76, 80. See also the *Iran* case, ICJ Reports, 1979, pp. 7, 19; 61 ILR, p. 525, *Bosnia* v. *Yugoslavia*, ICJ Reports, 1993, pp. 3, 19; 95 ILR, pp. 1, 34 and *Cameroons* v. *Nigeria*, ICJ Reports, 1996, pp. 13, 21–2.   [347] ICJ Reports, 1992, pp. 3, 15; 95 ILR, pp. 478, 498.
[348] See the *Great Belt* case, ICJ Reports, 1991, pp. 12, 17; 94 ILR, pp. 446, 455, where there was held to be no such urgency, and the *Cameroons* v. *Nigeria*, ICJ Reports, 1996, pp. 13, 22, where there was held to be such urgency.
[349] *Cameroons* v. *Nigeria*, ICJ Reports, 1996, pp. 13, 23. See also the *Burkina Faso/Mali* case, ICJ Reports, 1986, pp. 3, 9; 80 ILR, pp. 440, 456.   [350] See Shahabuddeen, *Precedent*.
[351] The *Nuclear Tests* case, ICJ Reports, 1974, p. 477.
[352] ICJ Reports, 1949, p. 4; 16 ILR, p. 155.   [353] ICJ Reports, 1974, p. 3; 55 ILR, p. 238.
[354] ICJ Reports, 1980, p. 3; 61 ILR, p. 530.

Application for interpretation of a judgment

Under article 60 of the Statute, an application may be made to the Court for interpretation of a judgment, provided that the object of the request is solely to obtain clarification of the meaning and the scope of what the Court has decided with binding force and not to obtain an answer to questions not so decided. In addition, it is necessary that there should exist a dispute as to the meaning or scope of the judgment.[355]

Application for revision of a judgment

Under article 61 of the Statute, an application for revision of a judgment may only be made when based upon the discovery of some fact of such a nature as to be a decisive factor, which fact was, when the judgment was given, unknown to the Court and also to the party claiming revision, provided that such ignorance was not due to negligence. The application must be made within six months of the discovery of the new fact and within ten years of the date of the judgment. In the *Application for Revision and Interpretation of the Judgment of 24 February 1982 in the Case Concerning the Continental Shelf (Tunisia/Libya)*[356] the Court decided that the 'new fact' in question, namely the text of a resolution of the Libyan Council of Ministers of 28 March 1968 setting out the western boundary of the Libyan oil concessions in the first sector of the delimitation, was a fact that could have been discovered through the application of normal diligence. If Tunisia was ignorant of the facts, it was due to its own negligence.[357] In addition, it could not be said that the new facts alleged were of such a nature as to be a decisive factor as required by article 61.[358]

Examination of a situation after the judgment

The Court may have the competence to re-examine a situation dealt with by a previous decision where the terms of that decision so provide. This is likely to be extremely rare for it runs the risk of allowing the parties to relitigate an issue already decided simply because some of the circumstances have changed. In the *Request for an Examination of the Situation in Accordance with Paragraph 63 of the Court's Judgment of 20 December 1974 in the* Nuclear Tests (New Zealand v. France) *Case* case,[359] the Court was asked to act in accordance with

---

[355] See *Request for Interpretation of the Judgment of 20 November 1950 in the Asylum* case, ICJ Reports, 1950, p. 402; 17 ILR, p. 339 and *Application for Revision and Interpretation of the Judgment of 24 February 1982 in the Case Concerning the Continental Shelf (Tunisia/Libya)*, ICJ Reports, 1985, pp. 191, 214–20; 81 ILR, pp. 420, 447.
[356] ICJ Reports, 1985, pp. 191, 198–214; 81 ILR, p. 431.
[357] *Ibid.*, pp. 206–7; 81 ILR, p. 439.   [358] *Ibid.*, pp. 213–14; 81 ILR, p. 446.
[359] ICJ Reports, 1995, p. 288.

paragraph 63 of its 1974 decision in the light of further proposed French nuclear tests in the South Pacific. Paragraph 63 had noted that 'if the basis of this Judgment were to be affected, the Applicant could request an examination of the situation in accordance with the provisions of the Statute'.[360] The 1974 judgment had concluded that there was no need for a decision on New Zealand's claims with regard to French nuclear testing as France had undertaken not to carry out any further atmospheric nuclear testing.

The Court implicitly accepted that 'a special procedure' in the sense of a re-examination of a situation in the light of changed circumstances could be established as a result of the terms of the original decision which did not amount to either an interpretation of the judgment under article 60 nor to a revision of the judgment under article 61.[361] Such a procedure would in fact have the aim not of seeking changes in the original judgment, but rather of preserving it intact faced with an apparent challenge to it by one of the parties at a later date. As Judge Weeramantry noted, '[t]he Court used its undoubted powers of regulating its own procedure to devise a procedure *sui generis*'.[362] However, in the instant case, the Court found that the basis of its 1974 judgment was a French undertaking not to conduct any further atmospheric nuclear tests and that therefore it was only the event of a resumption of nuclear testing in the atmosphere that would affect the basis of that judgment and that had not occurred.[363] Accordingly, New Zealand's request for an examination of the situation was rejected.

Non-appearance[364]

One unfortunate feature of the Court's work during the 1970s and part of the 1980s has been the reluctance of the defendant government to appear before the Court at all. This occurred in the *Fisheries Jurisdiction* case,[365] the *Nuclear Tests* case,[366] the *Aegean Sea Continental Shelf* case[367] and the *Iran* case.[368] Under article 53 of its Statute, the Court in such a situation may be

---

[360] ICJ Reports, 1974, p. 477.
[361] *Ibid.*, pp. 303–4. Judge Weeramantry noted that the request for an examination of the situation was 'probably without precedent in the annals of the Court' and one that did not fit in with any of the standard applications recognised by the Rules of the Court for revision or interpretation of a judgment, *ibid.*, p. 320.   [362] *Ibid.*, p. 320.
[363] *Ibid.*, pp. 305–6. France was proposing to undertake a series of underground nuclear tests. This it eventually did.
[364] See e.g. H. Thirlway, *Non-Appearance before the International Court of Justice*, Cambridge, 1985; Elias, *International Court*, Chapter 2; G. G. Fitzmaurice, 'The Problem of the "Non-appearing" Defendant Government', 51 BYIL, 1980, p. 89; I. Sinclair, 'Some Procedural Aspects of Recent International Litigation', 30 ICLQ, 1981, p. 338 and J. Elkind, *Non-Appearance before the ICJ, Functional and Comparative Analysis*, 1984.
[365] ICJ Reports, 1974, p. 3; 55 ILR, p. 238.   [366] ICJ Reports, 1974, p. 253; 57 ILR, p. 350.
[367] ICJ Reports, 1978, p. 3; 60 ILR, p. 562.
[368] ICJ Reports, 1980, p. 3; 61 ILR, p. 530. See also the *Pakistani Prisoners of War* case, ICJ Reports, 1973, pp. 328, 347; 57 ILR, p. 606.

called upon by the appearing party to decide in favour of its claim. Before doing so, the Court must satisfy itself not only that it has jurisdiction, but also that the claim is well founded in fact and law. This, of course, means that the Court is compelled to act on behalf of the absent defendant government in the sense of providing legal argumentation to support its case. This is controversial, although not to take into account the defendant's possible legal case in deciding would certainly discourage such state from accepting the judgment. It is a fine balance. The United States, after the Court decided it had jurisdiction to hear Nicaragua's claim, stated that it would withdraw from further proceedings in that case before the Court.[369] Fortunately in more recent years the problem of non-appearance has not been evident.

Third party intervention[370]

There is no right of intervention in cases before the Court by third parties as such, nor any procedure for joinder of new parties by the Court itself, nor any power by which the Court can direct that third states be made a party to proceedings.[371] However, under article 62 of the Statute of the ICJ, any state which considers that it has an interest of a legal nature which may be affected by the decision in a case, may submit a request to be permitted to intervene,[372] while under article 63 where the construction of a convention to which states other than those concerned in the case are parties is in question,[373] the registrar of the Court shall notify all such states forthwith. Every state so notified has the right to intervene in the proceedings.[374]

---

[369] See US statement in 24 ILM, 1985, pp. 246 *et seq*. See also e.g. Highet, 'Litigation', and Chayes 'Nicaragua'. On 7 October 1985, the US announced that it was terminating its acceptance of the compulsory jurisdiction of the ICJ, although it would continue to accept the jurisdiction of the Court in 'mutually submitted' legal disputes, *The International Herald Tribune*, 8 October, 1985, p. 1. See also 24 ILM, 1985, pp. 1742 *et seq*.

[370] See e.g. S. Rosenne, *Intervention in the International Court of Justice*, Dordrecht, 1993; J. M. Ruda, 'Intervention Before the International Court of Justice' in *Fifty Years of the International Court of Justice*, p. 487; C. M. Chinkin, 'Third Party Intervention Before the International Court of Justice', 80 AJIL, 1986, p. 495; Elias, *International Court*, Chapter 4, and Rosenne, *Law and Practice*, vol. I, pp. 430–4. See also Rules 81–86 of the Court, 1978, and P. Jessup, 'Intervention in the International Court', 75 AJIL, 1981, p. 903.

[371] See the *Libya/Malta* case, ICJ Reports, 1984, p. 25; 70 ILR, p. 527, and the *Nicaragua* case, ICJ Reports, 1984, p. 431; 76 ILR, p. 104.

[372] See also Rule 81 of the Rules of the Court. It is for the Court itself to decide upon any request for permission to intervene, see the *Tunisia/Libya (Intervention)* case, ICJ Reports, 1981, pp. 3, 12; 62 ILR, pp. 608,

[373] See here the *SS Wimbledon* case, PCIJ, Series A, No. 1 (1923); 2 ILR, p. 4; the *Haya de la Torre* case, ICJ Reports, 1951, pp. 71, 76–7; 18 ILR, pp. 349, 356–7, and the *Nicaragua* case, ICJ Reports, 1984, pp. 215–16; 76 ILR, pp. 74–5.

[374] See the *Wimbledon* case, PCIJ, Series A, No. 1, 1923, pp. 9–13, and the *Haya de la Torre* case, ICJ Reports, 1951, p. 71; 18 ILR, p. 349.

The Court appears to have set a fairly high threshold of permitted intervention. In the *Nuclear Tests* case,[375] Fiji sought to intervene in the dispute between France on the one hand and New Zealand and Australia on the other, but the Court postponed consideration of this and, after its judgment that the issue was moot, it was clearly unnecessary to take any further steps regarding Fiji. Malta sought to intervene in the *Tunisia/Libya Continental Shelf* case[376] in the light of its shelf delimitation dispute with Libya in order to submit its views to the Court. The Court felt that the real purpose of Malta's intervention was unclear and did not relate to any legal interest of its own directly in issue as between Tunisia and Libya in the proceedings or as between itself and either one of those countries.[377] While Malta did have an interest similar to other states in the area in the case in question, the Court said[378] that in order to intervene under article 62 it had to have an interest of a legal nature which may be affected by the Court's decision in the instant case.

However, the Court has recently, for the very first time in the history of both the ICJ and its predecessor, granted permission to a third state to intervene under article 62 of the Statute. Nicaragua was permitted to intervene in the case concerning the *Land, Island and Maritime Frontier Dispute (El Salvador/Honduras)* in certain respects, the Court having held unanimously that Nicaragua had demonstrated that it had an interest of a legal nature which may be affected by part[379] of the judgment of the Chamber on the merits of the case.[380] The Court noted that the burden of proof in such requests for intervention lies upon the applicant who must demonstrate convincingly what it asserts. Such applicant need only show that its interest may be affected, not that it will or must be so affected. It must identify the interest of a legal nature in question and show how that interest may be affected.[381]

The intervening state does not need to demonstrate a basis of jurisdiction, since the competence of the Court is founded here not upon the consent of the parties as such but is rather derived from the consent given by the parties in becoming parties to the Court's exercise of its powers conferred by the

---

[375] ICJ Reports, 1974, p. 253; 57 ILR, p. 398.   [376] ICJ Reports, 1982, p. 18; 67 ILR, p. 4.
[377] ICJ Reports, 1981, pp. 3, 12; 62 ILR, pp. 612, 621.
[378] *Ibid.*, p. 19; 62 ILR, p. 628. The Court also refused Italy permission to intervene under article 62 in the *Libya–Malta* case, see ICJ Reports, 1984, p. 3; 70 ILR, p. 527. The Court also refused permission to El Salvador to intervene in the *Nicaragua* case under article 63, see ICJ Reports, 1984, p. 215; 76 ILR, p. 74, in as much as it related to the current phase of the proceedings. The Court here more controversially also refused to hold a hearing on the issue, *ibid.*, but see separate opinion of five of the judges, *ibid.*, p. 219; 76 ILR, p. 78.
[379] I.e. concerning the legal regime of the waters within the Gulf of Fonseca only and not the other issues in dispute, such as maritime delimitations and delimitation of the land frontier dispute between El Salvador and Honduras.
[380] ICJ Reports, 1990, p. 92; 97 ILR, p. 112.
[381] *Ibid.*, pp. 117–18; 97 ILR, pp. 238–9.

Statute.[382] Thus the Court may permit an intervention by a third party even though it be opposed by one or both of the parties to the case. The purpose of such intervention is carefully circumscribed and closely defined in terms of the protection of a state's interest of a legal nature which may be affected by a decision in an existing case, and accordingly intervention cannot be used as a substitute for contentious proceedings, which are based upon consent. Thus the intervener does not as such become a party to the case.[383]

The Court in the merits stage of the *El Salvador/Honduras* case,[384] noting that Nicaragua as the intervening state could not become a party to the proceedings, concluded that that state could not therefore become bound by the judgment.[385] The intervenor, upon obtaining permission from the Court to intervene, acquires the right to be heard, but not the obligation of being bound by the decision.[386] Since neither of the parties had given any indication of consent to Nicaragua's being recognised to have any status which would enable it to rely on the judgment,[387] it followed that the decision of the Court could not bind Nicaragua and thus was not *res judicata* for it.[388]

The advisory jurisdiction of the court[389]

In addition to having the capacity to decide disputes between states, the ICJ may give advisory opinions. Article 65 of the Statute declares that 'the Court may give an advisory opinion on any legal question at the request of whatever body may be authorised by or in accordance with the Charter of the United Nations to make such a request', while article 96 of the Charter notes that as well as the General Assembly and Security Council, other organs of the UN and specialised agencies where so authorised by the

---

[382] *Ibid.*, p. 133; 97 ILR, p. 254. The Court noted that 'the procedure of intervention is to ensure that a state with possibly affected interests may be permitted to intervene even though there is no jurisdictional link and it therefore cannot become a party', *ibid.*, p. 135, 97 ILR, p. 256. The earlier cases did not feel it necessary to decide this issue, see e.g. the *Tunisia/Libya* case, ICJ Reports, 1981, pp. 3, 20; 62 ILR, pp. 612, 629, and the *Libya/Malta* case, ICJ Reports, 1984, pp. 3, 28; 70 ILR, pp. 527, 557.
[383] *Ibid.*, pp. 134–5; 97 ILR, pp. 255–6. See also Lauterpacht, *Aspects*, pp. 26 *et seq.*
[384] ICJ Reports, 1992, pp. 351, 609; 97 ILR, pp. 266, 525.
[385] This was partly because article 59 of the Statute of the Court refers to the binding effect of a judgment as between the parties only, *ibid.*, p. 609; 97 ILR, p. 525.
[386] *Ibid.*, p. 610; 97 ILR, p. 526.
[387] Since the consent of the existing parties is required for an intervenor to become itself a party to the case, *ibid.* [388] *Ibid.*
[389] See e.g. D. Negulesco, 'L'Evolution de la Procedure des Avis Consultatif de la Cour Permanente de Justice Internationale', 57 HR, 1936, p. 1; K. Keith, *The Extent of the Advisory Jurisdiction of the International Court of Justice*, Leiden, 1971; M. Pomerance, *The Advisory Jurisdiction of the International Court in the League and UN Eras*, 1973; D. Pratap, *The Advisory Jurisdiction of the International Court*, Oxford, 1972; D. Greig, 'The Advisory Jurisdiction of the International Court and the Settlement of Disputes Between States', 15 ICLQ, 1966, p. 325; R. Higgins, 'A Comment on the Current Health of Advisory Opinions' in *Fifty Years of the International Court of Justice*, p. 567 and Rosenne, *Law and Practice*, vol. II, Chapters 19–21.

Assembly may request such opinions on legal questions arising within the scope of their activities.

Unlike contentious cases, the purpose of the Court's advisory jurisdiction is not to settle, at least directly, inter-state disputes, but rather to 'offer legal advice to the organs and institutions requesting the opinion'.[390] Accordingly, the fact that the question put to the Court does not relate to a specific dispute does not affect the competence of the Court, nor does it matter that the question posed is abstract in nature. In addressing the question put to the Court by a political organ of the UN, the Court will not have regard to the origins or the political history of the request nor to the distribution of votes with regard to the relevant resolution. The fact that any answer given by the Court might become a factor in relation to the subject-matter of the request in other fora is also irrelevant in determining the appropriate response of the Court to the request for the Advisory Opinion.[391]

The general rule established by the *Eastern Carelia* case[392] is that the Court would not exercise its advisory jurisdiction in respect of a central issue in a dispute between the parties where one of these parties refused to take part in the proceedings. However, the scope of this principle, which was intended to reflect the sovereignty and independence of states, has been reduced somewhat in a number of subsequent cases before the Court.

In the *Interpretation of Peace Treaties* case,[393] for example, which concerned the interpretation of the 1947 peace agreements with Bulgaria, Hungary and Romania, it was stressed that whereas the basis of the Court's jurisdiction in contentious proceedings rested upon the consent of the parties to the dispute, the same did not apply with respect to advisory opinions. Such opinions were not binding upon anyone and were given not to the particular states but to the organs which requested them. The Court declared that 'the reply of the Court, itself an "organ of the United Nations", represents its participation in the activities of the organisation, and in principle should not be refused'.[394] Similarly, the Court emphasised in the *Reservations to the Genocide Convention* case,[395] that the object of advisory opinions was 'to guide the United Nations in respect of its own action'. Thus, the Court would lean towards exercising its jurisdiction, despite the objections of a concerned party, where it would be providing guidance for an international body with respect to the application of an international treaty.

---

[390] The *Legality of the Threat or Use of Nuclear Weapons* case, ICJ Reports, 1996, para. 15; 35 ILM, 1996, pp. 818–99.   [391] *Ibid.*   [392] PCIJ, Series B, No. 5, 1923; 2 ILR, p. 394.
[393] ICJ Reports, 1950, pp. 65, 71; 17 ILR, pp. 331, 335.
[394] The Court has gone further and noted that only 'compelling reasons' could lead it to refuse to give an advisory opinion in such circumstances, see e.g. the *Legality of the Threat or Use of Nuclear Weapons*, ICJ Reports, 1996, para. 14 and cases therein cited, see 35 ILM, 1996, pp. 809, 818.
[395] ICJ Reports, 1951, pp. 15, 19; 18 ILR, pp. 364, 366. See also the *Namibia* case, ICJ Reports, 1971, pp. 16, 24; 49 ILR, pp. 2, 14.

In the *Western Sahara* case,[396] the ICJ gave an advisory opinion as regards the nature of the territory and the legal ties therewith of Morocco and Mauritania at the time of colonisation, notwithstanding the objections of Spain, the administering power. The Court distinguished the case from the *Eastern Carelia* dispute on a number of grounds. In the latter case, Russia, which had objected to the Court's jurisdiction, was neither a member of the League (at that time) nor a party to the Statute of the PCIJ, whereas in the *Western Sahara* case, Spain was a UN member and thus a party to the Statute of the ICJ. It had therefore given its consent in general to the exercise by the Court of its advisory jurisdiction. It was also to be noted that Spain's objection was to the restriction of the reference to the Court to the historical aspects of the Sahara question.[397] A vital point for the Court was that the dispute in the 1975 case had arisen within the framework of the General Assembly's decolonisation proceedings and the object of the request for the advisory opinion (by the Assembly) was to obtain from the Court an opinion which would aid the Assembly in the decolonisation of the territory.[398] Accordingly, the matter fell within the *Peace Treaties/Reservations* cases category of opinions to guide the UN. The Court emphasised that the central core of the issue was not a dispute between Spain and Morocco, but rather the nature of Moroccan (and Mauritanian) rights at the time of colonisation. Thus, Spanish rights as administering power would be unaffected by the Court's judgment, which was aimed basically at assisting the Assembly to decolonise the territory.[399] The Court noted that it was the fact that inadequate material was available for an opinion that impelled the PCIJ to refuse to consider the *Eastern Carelia* issue, notwithstanding that this arose because of a refusal of one of the parties to participate in the proceedings. In the *Western Sahara* case, an abundance of documentary material was available to the Court.[400] It is therefore evident that the general rule expressed in the *Eastern Carelia* case has been to a very large extent eroded.

Article 96(2) of the Charter provides that:

[o]ther organs of the United Nations and specialised agencies which may at any time be so authorised by the General Assembly, may also request advisory opinions of the Court on legal questions arising within the scope of their activities.

The Court in the request for an advisory opinion by the World Health Organisation on the *Legality of the Use by a State of Nuclear Weapons in Armed Conflict*[401] held that three conditions were required in order to found the

---

[396] ICJ Reports, 1975, p. 12; 59 ILR, p. 14.   [397] *Ibid.*, p. 24; 59 ILR, p. 41.
[398] *Ibid.*, p. 25; 59 ILR, p. 42.
[399] *Ibid.*, p. 27; 59 ILR, p. 44. Note that the Court dealt with the consent of an interested party in the context not of the competence of the Court, but of the propriety of giving an opinion, *ibid.*, p. 25.   [400] *Ibid.*, pp. 28–9; 59 ILR, p. 45.   [401] ICJ Reports, 1996.

jurisdiction of the Court in such circumstances. First, that the specialised agency in question must be duly authorised by the General Assembly to request opinions from the Court; secondly, that the opinion requested was on a legal question, and thirdly, that the question must be one arising within the scope of activities of the requesting agency.[402] The Court examined the functions of the WHO in the light of its Constitution[403] and subsequent practice, and concluded that the organisation was authorised to deal with the effects on health of the use of nuclear weapons and of other hazardous activities and to take preventive measures with the aim of protecting the health of populations in the event of such weapons being used or such activities engaged in. However, the question put to the Court, it was emphasised, concerned not the effects of the use of nuclear weapons on health, but the legality of the use of such weapons in view of their health and environmental effects. Accordingly, the Court held that the question posed in the request for the advisory opinion did not arise within the scope of activities of the organisation as defined in its Constitution.[404] The importance of advisory opinions delivered by the Court is therefore not to be underestimated.[405]

The role of the court

There are a variety of other issues currently facing the Court. As far as access to it is concerned, it has, for example, been suggested that the power to request advisory opinions should be given to the UN Secretary-General[406] and to states and national courts,[407] while the possibility of permitting international organisations to become parties to contentious proceedings has been raised.[408] Perhaps more centrally, the issue of the relationship between

[402] *Ibid.*, para. 10. See also the *Application for Review of Judgment No. 273 (Mortished)* case, ICJ Reports, 1982, pp. 325, 333–4; 69 ILR, pp. 330, 344–5.
[403] See article 2(a) to (v) of the WHO Constitution adopted on 22 July 1946 and amended in 1960, 1975, 1977, 1984 and 1994.   [404] *Ibid.*, para. 20 *et seq.*
[405] Among other influential Advisory Opinions delivered by the Court are the *Reparation* case, ICJ Reports, 1949, p. 174; 16 ILR, p. 318; the *Admissions* case, ICJ Reports, 1948, p. 57; 15 ILR, p. 333, and the *Certain Expenses* case, ICJ Reports, 1962, p. 151; 34 ILR, p. 281. See also the *WHO–Egypt* case, ICJ Reports, 1980, p. 73; 62 ILR, p. 451; the *Administrative Tribunal* cases, ICJ Reports, 1973, p. 166; 54 ILR, p. 381; *ibid.*, 1982, p. 325; 69 ILR, p. 330; *ibid.*, 1987, p. 18; 83 ILR, p. 296; the *Applicability of the Obligation to Arbitrate* case, ICJ Reports, 1988, p. 12; 82 ILR, p. 225; the *Legality of the Use by a State of Nuclear Weapons in Armed Conflict*, ICJ Reports, 1996, and the *Legality of the Threat or Use of Nuclear Weapons*, ICJ Reports, 1996.
[406] See e.g. Higgins, 'Current Health', p. 569 and S. Schwebel, 'Authorising the Secretary-General of the United Nations to Request Advisory Opinions', 78 AJIL, 1984, p. 4. See also UN Secretary-General, *Agenda for Peace*, New York, 1992, A/47/277, para. 38.
[407] See e.g. S. Schwebel, 'Preliminary Rulings by the International Court of Justice at the Instance of National Courts', 28 VaJIL, 1988, p. 495 and S. Rosenne, 'Preliminary Rulings by the International Court of Justice at the Instance of National Courts: A Reply', 29 VaJIL, 1989, p. 40.
[408] See e.g. D. W. Bowett, J. Crawford, I. Sinclair and A. D. Watts, 'The International Court of Justice: Efficiency of Procedures and Working Methods', 45 ICLQ, 1996, Suppl., p. S24.

the Court and the political organs of the UN, particularly the Security Council, has been raised anew as a consequence of the revitalisation of the latter in recent years and its increasing activity.[409] The Court possesses no express power of judicial review of UN activities, although it is the principal judicial organ of the organisation and has in that capacity dealt on a number of occasions with the meaning of UN resolutions and organs.[410] In the *Lockerbie* case,[411] the Court was faced with a new issue, that of examining the relative status of treaty obligations and binding decisions adopted by the Security Council. In its decision on provisional measures, the Court accepted that by virtue of article 103 of the UN Charter obligations under the Charter (including decisions of the Security Council imposing sanctions) prevailed over obligations contained in other international agreements.[412]

One may also point to the proliferation of judicial organs on the international and regional level.[413] The European Court of Justice, the European Court of Human Rights and the Inter-American Court of Human Rights are joined now by the two Tribunals examining war crimes in Bosnia and Rwanda,[414] while the International Tribunal on the Law of the Sea will shortly commence operations.[415] It is unclear how this may impinge upon the work of the International Court. It may lead to some duplication in the evocation of international legal principles, but it is unlikely to lead to a

[409] See e.g. M. Bedjaoui, *The New World Order and the Security Council*, Dordrecht, 1994.
[410] See e.g. the *Reparation* case, ICJ Reports, 1949, p. 174; 16 ILR, p. 318, concerning the legal personality of the UN, the *Certain Expenses* case, ICJ Reports, 1962, p. 151; 34 ILR, p. 281, by virtue of which the UN was able to take action which did not amount to enforcement action outside of the framework of the Security Council, thus enabling the creation of peace-keeping missions, and the *Namibia* case, ICJ Reports, 1971, p. 56; 94 ILR, p. 2, recognising the succession of the UN to the League of Nations with regard to mandated territories and enshrining the principle of self-determination within international law. See also the *East Timor* case, ICJ Reports, 1995, pp. 90, 103–4, and *infra*, p. 876.
[411] ICJ Reports, 1992, p. 3; 94 ILR, p. 478.
[412] *Ibid.*, p. 15; 94 ILR, p. 498. The merits stage of the case is currently pending.
[413] See e.g. J. I. Charney, 'The Implications of Expanding International Dispute Settlement Systems: The 1982 Convention on the Law of the Sea', 90 AJIL, 1996, p. 69. See also S. Oda, 'The International Court of Justice from the Bench', 244 HR, 1993 VII, pp. 9, 139 *et seq*, ; G. Guillaume, 'The Future of International Judicial Institutions'. 44 ICLQ, 1995, p. 848, cf. S. Rosenne, 'Establishing the International Tribunal for the Law of the Sea', 89 AJIL, 1995, p. 806.
[414] Note the possibility of the establishment of an International Criminal Court, see *supra*, Chapter 5, p. 187.
[415] See Part XV and Annex VI of the Convention on the Law of the Sea 1982. It consists of twenty-one members, elected in August 1996, representing the principal legal systems according to an equitable geographical distribution. Its jurisdiction includes disputes concerning the interpretation or application of the Convention and of international agreements relating to the purposes of the Convention submitted to it in accordance with the particular agreement. The Tribunal may sit in plenary or in chambers and includes a Sea-Bed Disputes Chamber for problems concerning that area. Part XI, Section 5 of the Convention provides for the jurisdiction of the Sea-Bed Disputes Chamber. This jurisdiction, unlike that of the Tribunal itself is obligatory and exclusive, see article 287(2) and Part XI, Section 5. See further *supra*, Chapter 11, p. 450.

pattern of inconsistent decisions. Most of the other tribunals concern disputes between individuals and states rather than inter-state disputes, although the International Tribunal on the Law of the Sea is likely to deal with issues that either have been or may be litigated before the Court.

The decisions and advisory opinions of the ICJ (and PCIJ before it) have played a vital part in the evolution of international law. Having said that, the truth cannot be denied that the role of the ICJ within the international legal system is not as central as many would like. The relatively low number of cases and requests for advisory opinions coming before the Court (even though this has increased during the 1990s) and the acceptance by about a third of the parties to the Statute of the Court of the compulsory jurisdiction of the ICJ under article 36(2) is evidence of the often peripheral role of the Court within the world community. As far as the maintenance of international peace and security is concerned, the ICJ has indeed played a very minor part.

There are a number of reasons for this. Foremost amongst these is the character of the system itself, founded as it is upon some two hundred sovereign and independent states, cautious as to the possibility of permitting third party determination of what may be deemed to be vital interests. The difficulties of enforcing a judgment are sometimes cited as evidence of the unworkability of the system where matters litigated are other than peripheral. Many disputes are submitted to the various diplomatic processes for settlement or to arbitration because of the greater flexibility of these methods, particularly in technical matters. The time and expense involved in ICJ settlements are another factor militating against them, as is the growth in regional judicial arrangements.

Nevertheless, there has recently been an encouraging rise in the number of states that have recently turned to the Court.[416] One may note in this context developing states such as Malta, Libya, Tunisia, Nicaragua, Mali, Burkina Faso, El Salvador, Iran, Honduras and Chad, while the demise of the Soviet system has led to an increase in the number of Central and Eastern European states accepting the jurisdiction of the Court. The development of the Chambers system within the Court and the prospect of financial assistance for poorer litigants via a UN Trust Fund[417] are further examples of an important evolution and one may now envisage a steady increase in the workload of the Court. However, caution must be expressed against a belief that a legal decision by a permanent court will automatically resolve major political disputes.

---

[416] See e.g. K. Highet, 'The Peace Palace Hots Up: The World Court in Business Again ?', 85 AJIL, 1991, p. 646.   [417] As to which, see 87 AJIL, 1993, p. 659.

CHAPTER 19

INTERNATIONAL LAW AND THE USE OF FORCE BY STATES[1]

The rules governing resort to force form a central element within international law and, together with other principles such as territorial sovereignty and the independence and equality of states, provide the framework for international order. While domestic systems have, on the whole, managed to prescribe a virtual monopoly on the use of force for the governmental institutions, reinforcing the hierarchical structure of authority and control, international law is in a different situation. It must seek to minimise and regulate the resort to force by states, without itself being able to enforce its will. Reliance has to be placed on consent, consensus, reciprocity and good faith. The role and manifestation of force in the world community is, of course, dependent upon political and other non-legal factors as well as upon the current state of the law, but the law must seek to provide mechanisms to restrain and punish the resort to violence.

Law and force from the 'just war' to the United Nations[2]

The doctrine of the just war arose as a consequence of the Christianisation of the Roman Empire and the ensuing abandonment by Christians of their

---

[1] See e.g. D. W. Bowett, *Self-Defence in International Law*, Manchester, 1958; I. Brownlie, *International Law and the Use of Force by States*, Oxford, 1963; J. Stone, *Aggression and World Order*, Berkeley, 1958 and *Legal Controls of International Conflict*, 2nd edn, Berkeley, 1959 and *Conflict Through Consensus*, Berkeley, 1977; M. S. McDougal and F. Feliciano, *Law and Minimum World Public Order*, 1961, and *ibid.*, *The International Law of War*, 1994; H. Waldock, 'The Regulation of the Use of Force by Individual States in International Law', 81 HR, p. 415; J. Murphy, *The United Nations and the Control of International Violence*, 1982, and R. A. Falk, *Legal Order in a Violent World*, 1968. See also Y. Dinstein, *War, Aggression and Self-Defence*, 2nd edn, Cambridge, 1994; *Law and Force in the New International Order* (eds. L. Damrosch and D. J. Scheffer), Boulder, 1991; Nguyen Quoc Dinh, P. Daillier and A. Pellet, *Droit International Public*, 5th edn, Paris, 1994, pp. 874 *et seq.* and A. Cassese, *Violence and Law in the Modern Age*, Cambridge, 1988.

[2] See e.g. L. C. Green, *The Contemporary Law of Armed Conflict*, Manchester, 1993; G. Best, *War and Law Since 1945*, Oxford, 1994; S. Bailey, *Prohibitions and Restraints in War*, Oxford, 1972; M. Walzer, *Just and Unjust Wars*, 2nd edn, New York, 1977 and T. M. Franck, *Fairness in International Law and Institutions*, Oxford, 1995, Chapter 8. See also Brownlie, *International Law*, pp. 5 *et seq.*; Dinstein, *War*, Chapter 3, and C. Greenwood, 'The Concept of War in Modern International Law', 36 ICLQ, 1987, p. 283.

pacificism. Force could be used provided it complied with the divine will. The concept of the just war embodied elements of Greek and Roman philosophy and was employed as the ultimate sanction for the maintenance of an ordered society. St Augustine (354–430)[3] defined the just war in terms of avenging of injuries suffered where the guilty party has refused to make amends. War was to be embarked upon to punish wrongs and restore the peaceful *status quo* but no further. Aggression was unjust and the recourse to violence had to be strictly controlled. St Thomas Aquinas[4] in the thirteenth century took the definition of the just war a stage further by declaring that it was the subjective guilt of the wrongdoer that had to be punished rather than the objectively wrong activity. He wrote that war could be justified provided it was waged by the sovereign authority, it was accompanied by a just cause (i.e. the punishment of wrongdoers) and it was supported by the right intentions on the part of the belligerents.

With the rise of the European nation-states, the doctrine began to change.[5] It became linked with the sovereignty of states and faced the paradox of wars between Christian states, each side being convinced of the justice of its cause. This situation tended to modify the approach to the just war. The requirement that serious attempts at a peaceful resolution of the dispute were necessary before turning to force began to appear. This reflected the new state of international affairs, since there now existed a series of independent states, uneasily co-existing in Europe in a primitive balance of power system. The use of force against other states, far from strengthening the order, posed serious challenges to it and threatened to undermine it. Thus the emphasis in legal doctrine moved from the application of force to suppress wrongdoers to a concern (if hardly apparent at times) to maintain order by peaceful means. The great Spanish writer of the sixteenth century, Vitoria, [6] emphasised that 'not every kind and degree of wrong can suffice for commencing war', while Suarez[7] noted that states were obliged to call the attention of the opposing side to the existence of a just cause and request reparation before action was taken. The just war was also implied in immunity of innocent persons from direct attack and the proportionate use of force to overcome the opposition.[8]

Gradually it began to be accepted that a certain degree of right might exist

[3] See Eppstein, *The Catholic Tradition of the Law of Nations*, 1935, pp. 65 *et seq.*; Bailey, *Prohibitions*, pp. 6–9 and Brownlie, p. 5.

[4] *Summa Theologica*, II, ii, 40. See Bailey, *Prohibitions*, p. 9. See also Von Elbe, 'The Evolution of the Concept of the Just War in International Law', 33 AJIL, 1939, p. 669, and C. Parry, 'The Function of Law in the International Community' in *Manual of Public International Law* (ed. M. Sørensen), London, 1968, pp. 1, 27.

[5] Brownlie, *International Law*, pp. 7 *et seq.*

[6] *De Indis et de Jure Belli Relectiones*, ss.14, 20–3, 29 and 60, cited in Bailey, *Prohibitions*, p. 11.

[7] See *ibid.*, pp. 11–12. Suarez felt that the only just cause was a grave injustice that could not be avenged or repaired in any other way, *ibid.*   [8] *Ibid.*, pp. 12–15.

on both sides, although the situation was confused by references to subjective and objective justice. Ultimately, the legality of the recourse to war
was seen to depend upon the formal processes of law. This approach pre-
saged the rise of positivism with its concentration upon the sovereign state,
which could only be bound by what it had consented to. Grotius,[9] in his
systematising fashion, tried to exclude ideological considerations as the
basis of a just war, in the light of the destructive seventeenth-century religious conflicts, and attempted to redefine the just war in terms of self-
defence, the protection of property and the punishment for wrongs suffered
by the citizens of the particular state.

But with positivism and the definitive establishment of the European
balance of power system after the Peace of Westphalia, 1648, the concept of
the just war disappeared from international law as such.[10] States were sovereign and equal, and therefore no one state could presume to judge whether
another's cause was just or not. States were bound to honour agreements
and respect the independence and integrity of other countries, and had to
try and resolve differences by peaceful methods.

But where war did occur, it entailed a series of legal consequences. The
laws of neutrality and war began to operate as between the parties and third
states and a variety of legal situations at once arose. The fact that the war
may have been regarded as unjust by any ethical standards did not in any
way affect the legality of force as an instrument of the sovereign state nor
alter in any way the various rules of war and neutrality that sprang into
operation once the war commenced.

Whether the cause was just or not became irrelevant in any legal way to
the international community (though, of course, important in political
terms) and the basic issue revolved around whether in fact a state of war
existed.[11]

The doctrine of the just war arose with the increasing power of
Christianity and declined with the outbreak of the inter-Christian religious
wars and the establishment of an order of secular sovereign states. Although
war became a legal state of affairs which permitted force to be used and in
which a series of regulatory conditions were recognised, there existed
various other methods of employing force that fell short of war with all the
legal consequences as regards neutrals and conduct that that entailed.
Reprisals and pacific blockades[12] were examples of the use of force as
'hostile measures short of war'.

These activities were undertaken in order to assert or enforce rights or to

---

[9] Ibid., Chapter 2 and Brownlie, International Law, p. 13. See De Jure Belli ac Pacis, 1625.
[10] See e.g. Brownlie, International Law, pp. 14 et seq. See also L. Gross, 'The Peace of
Westphalia, 1648–1948', 42 AJIL, 1948, p. 20.
[11] Brownlie, International Law, pp. 26–8.   [12] Ibid.

punish wrongdoers. There were many instances in the nineteenth century in particular of force being used in this manner against the weaker states of Latin America and Asia.[13] There did exist limitations under international law of the right to resort to such measures but they are probably best understood in the context of the balance of power mechanism of international relations that to a large extent did help minimise the resort to force in the nineteenth century, or at least restrict its application.

The First World War marked the end of the balance of power system and raised anew the question of unjust war. It also resulted in efforts to rebuild international affairs upon the basis of a general international institution which would oversee the conduct of the world community to ensure that aggression could not happen again. The creation of the League of Nations reflected a completely different attitude to the problems of force in the international order.[14]

The Covenant of the League declared that members should submit disputes likely to lead to a rupture to arbitration or judicial settlement or inquiry by the Council of the League. In no circumstances were members to resort to war until three months after the arbitral award or judicial decision or report by the Council. This was intended to provide a cooling-off period for passions to subside and reflected the view that such a delay might well have broken the seemingly irreversible chain of tragedy that linked the assassination of the Austrian Archduke in Sarajevo with the outbreak of general war in Europe.

League members agreed not to go to war with members complying with such an arbitral award or judicial decision or unanimous report by the Council.[15]

The League system did not, it should be noted, prohibit war or the use of force, but it did set up a procedure designed to restrict it to tolerable levels. It was a constant challenge of the inter-war years to close the gaps in the Covenant in an effort to achieve the total prohibition of war in international law and this resulted ultimately in the signing in 1928 of the General Treaty for the Renunciation of War (the Kellogg-Briand Pact).[16] The parties to this treaty condemned recourse to war and agreed to renounce it as an instrument of national policy in their relations with one another.[17]

In view of the fact that this treaty has never been terminated and in the

[13] Ibid., pp. 28 et seq.
[14] Ibid., Chapter 3. But note Hague Convention II of 1907, which provided that the parties would not have recourse to armed forces for the recovery of contract debts claimed from the government of one country by the government of another as being due to its nationals.
[15] Brownlie, International Law, Chapter IV. See especially articles 10–16 of the Covenant.
[16] See e.g. Dinstein, War, Chapter 4 A; K. Skubiszewski, 'The Use of Force by States' in Sørensen, ed., Manual of Public International Law, pp. 739, 742–4 and Brownlie, International Law, pp. 74–92.   [17] Article I.

light of its widespread acceptance, [18] it is clear that prohibition of the resort to war is now a valid principle of international law. It is no longer possible to set up the legal relationship of war in international society. However, this does not mean that the use of force in all circumstances is illegal. Reservations to the treaty by some states made it apparent that the right to resort to force in self-defence was still a recognised principle in international law.[19] Whether in fact measures short of war such as reprisals were also prohibited or were left untouched by the treaty's ban on war was unclear and subject to conflicting interpretations.[20]

The UN Charter[21]

Article 2(4) of the Charter declares that:

> [a]ll members shall refrain in their international relations from the threat or use of force against the territorial integrity or political independence of any state, or in any other manner inconsistent with the purposes of the United Nations.

This provision is regarded now as a principle of customary international law and as such is binding upon all states in the world community.[22] The reference to 'force' rather than war is beneficial and thus covers situations in which violence is employed which fall short of the technical requirements of the state of war.

Article 2(4) was elaborated as a principle of international law in the 1970 Declaration on Principles of International Law and analysed systematically. First, wars of aggression constitute a crime against peace for which there is responsibility under international law.[23] Secondly, states must not threaten or use force to violate existing international frontiers (including demarcation or armistice lines) or to solve international disputes. Thirdly, states are under a duty to refrain from acts of reprisal involving the use of force. Fourthly, states must not use force to deprive peoples of their right to self-determination and independence. And fifthly, states must refrain from organising, instigating, assisting or participating in acts of civil strife or

---

[18] As of 1 January 1993, sixty-six states were parties to the Treaty. It came into force on 24 July 1929 and is still in effect. Many inter-war treaties reaffirmed the obligations imposed by the Pact, see Brownlie, *International Law*, pp. 75–6.   [19] See e.g. Cmd. 3153, p. 10.
[20] See Brownlie, *International Law*, p. 87. Cf. Bowett, *Self-Defence*, p. 136.
[21] See *La Charte des Nations Unies* (eds. J. P. Cot and A. Pellet), 2nd edn, Paris, 1991 and *The Charter of the United Nations* (ed. B. Simma), Oxford, 1995.
[22] See e.g. Skubiszewski, 'Use of Force', p. 745, and L. Henkin, R. C. Pugh, O. Schachter and H. Smit, *International Law Cases and Materials*, 3rd edn., St Paul, 1993, p. 893. See also the *Third US Restatement of Foreign Relations Law*, St Paul, 1987, p. 27.
[23] Article 19(3) of the International Law Commission's Draft Articles on State Responsibility provides that a serious breach of an international obligation of essential importance for maintenance of international peace and security may constitute an international crime for which the state may be criminally liable. See *supra*, Chapter 14, p. 544

terrorist acts in another state and must not encourage the formation of armed bands for incursion into another state's territory. Many of these items are crucial, but ambiguous. Although the Declaration is not of itself a binding legal document, it is important as an interpretation of the relevant Charter provisions.[24] Important exceptions to article 2(4) exist in relation to collective measures taken by the United Nations[25] and with regard to the right of self-defence.[26]

Article 2(6) of the Charter provides that the UN 'shall ensure that states which are not members of the United Nations act in accordance with these Principles so far as may be necessary for the maintenance of international peace and security'. In fact, many of the resolutions adopted by the UN are addressed simply to 'all states'. In particular, for example, Security Council resolution 757 (1992), adopted under Chapter VII of the Charter and therefore binding upon all member states, imposed comprehensive sanctions upon the Federal Republic of Yugoslavia (Serbia and Montenegro). However, the invocation in that decision was to 'all states' and not to 'member states'.

'Force'

One point that was considered in the past[27] and is now being reconsidered is whether the term 'force' in article 2(4) includes not only armed force but, for example, economic force. Does the imposition of boycotts or embargoes against particular states or groups of states come within article 2(4), so rendering them illegal?[28] Although that provision is not modified in any way, the preamble to the Charter does refer to the need to ensure that 'armed force' should not be used except in the common interest, while article 51, dealing with the right to self-defence, specifically refers to armed force, although that is not of itself conclusive as to the permissibility of other forms of coercion.

The 1970 Declaration on Principles of International Law recalled the 'duty of states to refrain . . . from military, political, economic or any other form of coercion aimed against the political independence or territorial integrity of any state' and the International Covenants on Human Rights

---

[24] See e.g. G. Arangio-Ruiz, *The UN Declaration on Friendly Relations and the System of Sources of International Law*, 1979 and R. Rosenstock, 'The Declaration on Principles of International Law Concerning Friendly Relations', 65 AJIL, 1971, p. 713.
[25] See *infra*, Chapter 20, p. 865.   [26] *Infra*, p. 787.
[27] An attempt by Brazil to prohibit 'economic measures' in article 2(4) itself was rejected, 6 UNCIO, Documents, p. 335. See also Goodrich, Hambro and Simons, *Charter of the United Nations*, 3rd edn, New York, 1969, p. 49.
[28] See e.g. *Economic Coercion and the New International Economic Order* (ed. R. B. Lillich), Charlottesville, 1976 and *The Arab Oil Weapon* (eds. J. Paust and A. Blaustein), Dobbs Ferry, NY, 1977.

adopted in 1966 emphasised the right of all peoples freely to pursue their economic, social and cultural development. This approach was underlined in the Charter of Economic Rights and Duties of States, approved by the General Assembly in 1974, which particularly specified that 'no state may use or encourage the use of economic, political or any other type of measures to coerce another state in order to obtain from it the subordination of the exercise of its sovereign rights'. The question of the legality of the open use of economic pressures to induce a change of policy by states was examined with renewed interest in the light of the Arab oil weapon used against states deemed favourable to Israel, in 1973–4.[29] It does seem that there is at least a case to be made out in support of the view that such actions are contrary to the United Nations Charter, as interpreted in numerous resolutions and declarations. But the issue is controversial.

It is to be noted that article 2(4) covers threats of force as well as use of force.[30] This issue was addressed by the International Court in its Advisory Opinion to the General Assembly on the *Legality of the Threat or Use of Nuclear Weapons*.[31] The Court stated that a 'signalled intention to use force if certain events occur' could constitute a threat under article 2(4) where the envisaged use of force would itself be unlawful. Examples given included threats to secure territory from another state or causing it to 'follow or not follow certain political or economic paths'. The Court appeared to accept that the mere possession of nuclear weapons did not of itself constitute a threat. However, noting that a policy of nuclear deterrence functioned on the basis of the credibility of the possibility of resorting to those weapons in certain circumstances, it was stated that whether this amounted to a threat would depend upon whether the particular use of force envisaged would be directed against the territorial integrity or political independence of a state or against the purposes of the UN. If the projected use of the weapons was intended as a means of defence and there would be a consequential and necessary breach of the principles of necessity and proportionality, this would suggest that a threat contrary to article 2(4) existed.[32] One key point here would be the definition of proportionality, in particular would it relate to the damage that might be caused or rather to the scope of the threat to which the response in self-defence is proposed? If the latter is the case, and logic suggests this, then the threat to use nuclear weapons in response to the prior use of nuclear or possibly chemical or bacteriological weapons becomes less problematic.

---

[29] *Ibid.*

[30] Brownlie, *International Law*, p. 364, notes that a threat of force consists 'in an express or implied promise by a government of a resort to force conditional on non-acceptance of certain demands of that government'. See also R. Sadurska, 'Threats of Force', 82 AJIL, 1988, p. 239.   [31] ICJ Reports, 1996, paras. 47–8; 35 ILM, 1996, pp. 809, 823.

[32] See here the Dissenting Opinion of Judge Schwebel; 35 ILM, pp. 836 *et seq.*

The provisions governing the resort to force internationally do not affect the right of a state to take measures to maintain order within its jurisdiction. Accordingly, such a state may forcibly quell riots, suppress insurrections and punish rebels without contravening article 2(4). In the event of injury to alien persons or property, the state may be required to make reparation to the state of the alien concerned,[33] but apart from this the prohibition on force in international law is not in general applicable within domestic jurisdictions.[34]

'Against the territorial integrity or political independence of any state'

Article 2(4) of the Charter prohibits the use of force 'against the territorial integrity or political independence of any state, or in any other manner inconsistent with the purposes of the United Nations'. There is a debate as to whether these words should be interpreted restrictively,[35] so as to permit force that would not contravene the clause, or as reinforcing the primary prohibition,[36] but the weight of opinion probably suggests the latter position. The 1965 Declaration on the Inadmissibility of Intervention in the Domestic Affairs of States[37] emphasised that:

> [n]o state has the right to intervene, directly or indirectly, for any reason what-soever, in the internal or external affairs of any other state. Consequently, armed intervention and all other forms of interference or attempted threats against the personality of the state or against its political, economic and cultural elements, are condemned.

This was reaffirmed in the 1970 Declaration on Principles in International Law,[38] with the proviso that not only were such manifestations condemned, but they were held to be in violation of international law. The International Court of Justice in the *Corfu Channel* case[39] declared specifically, in response to a British claim to be acting in accordance with a right of intervention in minesweeping the channel to secure evidence for judicial proceedings, that:

> the alleged right of intervention [was] the manifestation of a policy of force, such as has, in the past, given rise to most serious abuses and such as cannot . . . find a place in international law.

---

[33] *Supra,* Chapter 14, p. 561.
[34] But see *infra,* regarding self-determination, p. 795 and civil wars, p. 798.
[35] See e.g. Bowett, *Self-Defence,* p. 152.
[36] See Brownlie, *International Law,* p. 268. See also Skubiszewski, 'Use of Force', pp. 745–6.
[37] General Assembly resolution 2131(XX).   [38] General Assembly resolution 2625(XXV).
[39] ICJ Reports, 1949, pp. 4, 35; 16 ILR, pp. 155, 167. See also Brownlie, *International Law,* pp. 283–9 and H. Lauterpacht, *The Development of International Law by the International Court,* London, 1958, p. 90.

The Court noted that to allow such a right in the present case as a derogation from Albania's territorial sovereignty would be even less admissible:

> for, from the nature of things it would be reserved for the most powerful states, and might easily lead to perverting the administration of international justice itself.

The essence of international relations, concluded the Court, lay in the respect by independent states of each other's territorial sovereignty.[40]

Categories of force

Various measures of self-help ranging from economic retaliation to the use of violence pursuant to the right of self-defence have historically been used. Since the establishment of the Charter regime there are basically three categories of compulsion open to states under international law. These are retorsion, reprisal and self-defence.[41]

Retorsion[42]

Retorsion is the adoption by one state of an unfriendly and harmful act, which is nevertheless lawful, as a method of retaliation against the injurious legal activities of another state. Examples include the severance of diplomatic relations and the expulsion or restrictive control of aliens, as well as various economic and travel restrictions. Retorsion is a legitimate method of showing displeasure in a way that hurts the other state while remaining within the bounds of legality. The Hickenlooper Amendments to the American Foreign Assistance Act are often quoted as an instance of retorsion since they required the United States President to suspend foreign aid to any country nationalising American property without proper compensation. This procedure was applied only once, as against Ceylon (now Sri Lanka) in 1963, and has now been effectively repealed by the American Foreign Assistance Act of 1973.[43] Retorsion would also appear to cover the instance of a lawful act committed in retaliation to a prior unlawful activity.

---

[40] See the *Nicaragua* case, ICJ Reports, 1986, pp. 14, 109–10; 76 ILR, pp. 349, 443–4, and see further, *infra*, p. 797.

[41] As to the use of force by the UN, see *infra*, Chapter 20, p. 865.

[42] See e.g. Skubiszewski, 'Use of Force', p. 753 and G. von Glahn, *Law Among Nations*, 7th edn, Boston, 1996, pp. 533 *et seq.*

[43] See e.g. R. B. Lillich, 'Requiem for Hickenlooper', 69 AJIL, 1975, p. 97, and C. F. Amerasinghe, 'The Ceylon Oil Expropriations', 58 AJIL, 1964, p. 445.

Reprisals[44]

Reprisals are acts which are in themselves illegal and have been adopted by one state in retaliation for the commission of an earlier illegal act by another state. They are thus distinguishable from acts of retorsion, which are in themselves lawful acts. The classic case dealing with the law of reprisals is the *Naulilaa* dispute[45] between Portugal and Germany in 1928. This concerned a German military raid on the colony of Angola, which destroyed property, in retaliation for the mistaken killing of three Germans lawfully in the Portuguese territory.

The tribunal, in discussing the Portuguese claim for compensation, emphasised that before reprisals could be undertaken, there had to be sufficient justification in the form of a previous act contrary to international law. If that was established, reprisals had to be preceded by an unsatisfied demand for reparation and accompanied by a sense of proportion between the offence and the reprisal. In fact, the German claim that it had acted lawfully was rejected on all three grounds. Those general rules are still applicable but have now to be interpreted in the light of the prohibition on the use of force posited by article 2(4) of the United Nations Charter. Thus, reprisals short of force[46] may still be undertaken legitimately, while reprisals involving armed force may be lawful if resorted to in conformity with the right of self-defence.[47] Reprisals as such undertaken during peace-time are thus unlawful, unless they fall within the framework of the principle of self-defence.[48] Sometimes regarded as an aspect of reprisal is the institution of pacific blockade.[49] This developed during the nineteenth century and was extensively used as a forceful application of pressure against weaker states. In the absence of war or armed hostilities, the vessels of third states were probably exempt from such blockade, although this was disputed by some writers.

---

[44] See e.g. Skubiszewski, 'Use of Force', pp. 753–55; Brownlie, *International Law*, pp. 219–23 and 281–2 ; D. W. Bowett, 'Reprisals Including Recourse to Armed Force', 66 AJIL, 1972, p. 1 and R. W. Tucker, 'Reprisals and Self-Defence: The Customary Law', 66 AJIL, 1972, p. 581.

[45] 2 RIAA, p. 1011 (1928); 4 ILR, p. 526. See also G. Hackworth, *Digest of International Law*, Washington, 1943, vol. VI, p. 154.

[46] See further with regard to counter-measures, *supra*, Chapter 14, p. 558.

[47] But see Bowett, "Reprisals", footnote 44. See also SCOR, 19th Year, 111th meeting, 8 April 1964, in which the Security Council condemned reprisals as contrary to the UN Charter and deplored the UK bombing of Fort Harib, and R. B. Lillich, 'Forcible Self-Help under International Law', 62 *US Naval War College International Law Studies*, 1980, p. 129. As for episodes that appear to be on the borderline between self-defence and reprisals, see e.g. R. A. Falk, 'The Beirut Raid and the International Law of Retaliation', 63 AJIL, 1969, p. 415 and Y. Blum, 'The Beirut Raid and the International Double Standard', 64 AJIL, 1970, p. 73.

[48] See the *Legality of the Threat or Use of Nuclear Weapons*, ICJ Reports, 1996, para. 46; 35 ILM, 1996, p. 823.

[49] See e.g. Skubiszewski, 'Use of Force', pp. 755–7 and Brownlie, *International Law*, pp. 223–4.

Pacific blockades may be instituted by the United Nations Security Council,[50] but cannot now be resorted to by states since the coming into force of the Charter of the United Nations. The legality of the so-called 'quarantine' imposed by the United States upon Cuba in October 1962 to prevent certain weapons reaching the island appears questionable and should not be relied upon as an extension of the doctrine of pacific blockades.[51]

The right of self-defence[52]

The traditional definition of the right of self-defence in customary international law occurs in the *Caroline* case.[53] This dispute revolved around an incident in 1837 in which British subjects seized and destroyed a vessel in an American port. This had taken place because the *Caroline* had been supplying groups of American nationals, who had been conducting raids into Canadian territory. In the correspondence with the British authorities which followed the incident, the American Secretary of State laid down the essentials of self-defence. There had to exist 'a necessity of self-defence, instant, overwhelming, leaving no choice of means, and no moment for deliberation'. Not only were such conditions necessary before self-defence became legitimate, but the action taken in pursuance of it must not be unreasonable or excessive, 'since the act, justified by the necessity of self-defence must be limited by that necessity, and kept clearly within it'. These principles were accepted by the British government at that time and are accepted as part of customary international law.[54]

There is extensive controversy as to the precise extent of the right of self-defence in the light of article 51. Article 51 of the Charter provides that:

---

[50] See *infra*, Chapter 20, p. 858.
[51] See e.g. Q. Wright, 'The Cuban Quarantine', 57 AJIL, 1963, p. 546 and M. S. McDougal, 'The Soviet–Cuban Quarantine and Self-Defence', *ibid.*, p. 597. See also A. Chayes, *The Cuban Missile Crisis*, Oxford, 1974. But note the rather different declaration by the UK of a Total Exclusion Zone during the Falklands conflict, *supra*, Chapter 11, p. 416.
[52] See Bowett, *Self-Defence*, and Brownlie, *International law*, Chapter 13. See also I. Brownlie, 'The Use of Force in Self-Defence', 37 BYIL, 1961, p. 183; Dinstein, *War*, Chapters 7 and 8; J. Delivanis, *La Légitime Défense en Droit International*, Paris, 1971; S. Schwebel, 'Aggression, Intervention and Self-Defence in Modern International Law', 136 HR, 1972, p. 411, and O. Schachter, 'The Right of States to Use Armed Force', 82 *Michigan Law Review*, 1984, p. 1620; Schachter, 'Self-Defence and the Rule of Law', 83 AJIL, 1989, p. 259 and Schachter, *International Law in Theory and Practice*, Dordrecht, 1991, Chapter 8.
[53] 29 BFSP, p. 1137 and 30 BFSP, p. 195. See also R. Y. Jennings, 'The Caroline and McLeod Cases', 32 AJIL, 1938, p. 82.
[54] See e.g. the Legal Adviser to the US Department of State, who noted that 'the exercise of the inherent right of self-defence depends upon a prior delict, an illegal act that presents an immediate, overwhelming danger to an actual and essential right of the state. When these conditions are present, the means used must then be proportionate to the gravity of the threat or danger,' DUSPIL, 1975, p. 17.

Nothing in the present Charter shall impair the inherent right of individual or collective self-defence if an armed attack occurs against a member of the United Nations, until the Security Council has taken the measures necessary to maintain international peace and security. Measures taken by members in the exercise of this right of self-defence shall be immediately reported to the Security Council and shall not in any way affect the authority and responsibility of the Security Council under the present Charter to take at any time such action as it deems necessary in order to maintain or restore international peace and security.

On the one hand, it is argued that article 51 in conjunction with article 2(4) now specifies the scope and limitations of the doctrine. In other words, self-defence can only be resorted to 'if an armed attack occurs', and in no other circumstances.[55] On the other hand, there are writers who maintain that the opening phrase in article 51 specifying that 'nothing in the present Charter shall impair the inherent right of . . . self-defence' means that there does exist in customary international law a right of self-defence over and above the specific provisions of article 51, which refer only to the situation where an armed attack has occurred.[56] This view is somewhat strengthened by an examination of the *travaux préparatoires* of the Charter, which seem to underline the validity of the use of force in legitimate self-defence.[57] A number of academics and some states have regarded article 51 as merely elaborating one kind of self-defence in the context of the primary responsibility of the Security Council for international peace and the enforcement techniques available under the Charter.[58]

The International Court of Justice in the *Nicaragua* case[59] has, however, clearly established that the right of self-defence exists as an inherent right under customary international law as well as under the UN Charter. It was stressed that:

Article 51 of the Charter is only meaningful on the basis that there is a 'natural' or 'inherent' right of self-defence and it is hard to see how this can be other than of a customary nature, even if its present content has been confirmed and influenced by the Charter . . . It cannot, therefore be held that article 51 is a provision which 'subsumes and supervenes' customary international law.

[55] See e.g. Brownlie, *International Law*, pp. 112–13 and 264 *et seq.* and Jiminez de Aréchaga, 'International Law in the Past Third of the Century', 159 HR, pp. 1, 87–98. See also Skubiszewski, 'Use of Force', pp. 765–8 and H. Kelsen, *The Law of the United Nations*, London, 1950, p. 914.

[56] See e.g. Bowett, *Self-Defence*, pp. 185–6; J. Stone, *Aggression and World Order*, pp. 43, 95–6. See also H. Waldock, 'General Course on Public International Law', 166 HR, pp. 6, 231–7; J. Brierly, *The Law of Nations*, 6th edn, Oxford, 1963, pp. 417–18 and D. P. O'Connell, *International Law*, 2nd edn, London, 1970, vol. I, p. 317.

[57] See e.g. 6 UNCIO, Documents, where it is noted that 'the use of arms in legitimate self-defence remains admitted and unimpaired'.

[58] *Supra*, footnote 56. See also *The Charter of the United Nations*, pp. 661 *et seq.*

[59] ICJ Reports, 1986, pp. 14, 94; 76 ILR, pp. 349, 428.

THE USE OF FORCE BY STATES 789

Accordingly, customary law continued to exist alongside treaty law (i.e. the UN Charter) in this field. There was not an exact overlap and the rules did not have the same content. The Court also discussed the notion of an 'armed attack' and noted that this included not only action by regular armed forces across an international border, but additionally the sending by or on behalf of a state of armed bands or groups which carry out acts of armed force of such gravity as to amount to an actual armed attack conducted by regular armed forces or its substantial involvement therein.[60] The Court did not accept that this concept extended to assistance to rebels in the form of the provision of weapons or logistical or other support. This form of assistance, however, could constitute a threat or use of force, or amount to intervention in the internal or external affairs of the state.[61]

The issue that is then raised is whether a right to anticipatory or pre-emptive self-defence exists. This would appear unlikely if one adopted the notion that self-defence is restricted to responses to actual armed attacks. The concept of anticipatory self-defence is of particular relevance in the light of modern weaponry, that can launch an attack with tremendous speed, that may allow the target state little time to react to the armed assault before its successful conclusion, particularly if that state is geographically small.[62] States have employed pre-emptive strikes in self-defence. Israel, in 1967, launched such a strike upon its Arab neighbours, following the blocking of its southern port of Eilat and the conclusion of a military pact between Jordan and Egypt. This completed a chain of events precipitated by the mobilisation of Egyptian forces on Israel's border and the eviction of the United Nations peace-keeping forces from the area by the Egyptian President.[63] It could, of course, also be argued that the Egyptian blockade itself constituted the use of force, thus legitimising Israeli actions without the need for 'anticipatory' conceptions of self-defence. It is noteworthy that the United Nations in its debates in the summer of 1967 apportioned no blame for the outbreak of fighting and did not condemn the exercise of

[60] The Court noted that this provision, contained in article 3(g) of the Definition of Aggression annexed to General Assembly resolution 3314(XXIX) of 1974 reflected customary international law, *ibid.*, p. 103: 76 ILR, p. 437.
[61] ICJ Reports, 1986, pp. 103–4; 76 ILR, pp. 437–8. But see the Dissenting Opinion of Judge Jennings, *ibid.*, p. 543; 76 ILR, p. 877.
[62] Contrast Bowett, *Self-Defence*, pp. 118–92, who emphasises that 'no state can be expected to await an initial attack which, in the present state of armaments, may well destroy the state's capacity for further resistance and so jeopardise its very existence' and Franck, *Fairness*, p. 267, who notes that in such circumstances 'the notion of anticipatory self-defence is both rational and attractive', with Brownlie, *International Law*, p. 275, and L. Henkin, *How Nations Behave*, 2nd edn, New York, 1979, pp. 141–5. See also R. Higgins, *The Development of International Law Through the Political Organs of the United Nations*, Oxford, 1963, pp. 216–21.
[63] See generally, *The Arab-Israeli Conflict* (ed. J. N. Moore), 3 vols., Princeton, 1974.

self-defence by Israel. The International Court in the *Nicaragua* case[64] expressed no view on the issue of the lawfulness of a response to an imminent threat of an armed attack since on the facts of the case that problem was not raised.

The trouble, of course, with the concept of anticipatory self-defence is that it involves fine calculations of the various moves by the other party. A pre-emptive strike embarked upon too early might constitute an aggression. There is a difficult line to be drawn. The problem is that the nature of the international system is such as to leave such determinations to be made by the states themselves, and in the absence of an acceptable, institutional alternative, it is difficult to foresee a modification of this. States generally are not at ease with the concept of anticipatory self-defence, however,[65] and one possibility would be to concentrate upon the notion of 'armed attack' so that this may be interpreted in a relatively flexible manner.[66] One suggestion has been to distinguish anticipatory self-defence, where an armed attack is foreseeable, from interceptive self-defence, where an armed attack is imminent and unavoidable so that the evidential problems and temptations of the former concept are avoided without dooming threatened states to making the choice between violating international law and suffering the actual assault.[67] According to this approach, self-defence is legitimate both under customary law and under article 51 of the Charter where an armed attack is imminent. It would then be a question of evidence as to whether that were an accurate assessment of the situation in the light of the information available at the relevant time. This would be rather easier to demonstrate than the looser concept of anticipatory self-defence and it has the merit of being consistent with the view that the right to self-defence in customary law exists as expounded in the *Caroline* case.[68] In any event, much will depend upon the characterisation of the threat and the nature of the response, for this has to be proportionate.[69]

Indeed, the concepts of necessity and proportionality are at the heart of self-defence in international law. The Court in the *Nicaragua* case[70] stated that there was a 'specific rule whereby self-defence would warrant only

---

[64] ICJ Reports, 1986, pp. 14, 103; 76 ILR, p. 437.
[65] See e.g. the Security Council debate on Israel's bombing of the Iraqi nuclear reactor in 1981, 20 ILM, 1981, pp. 965–7. See also A. Cassese, *International Law in a Divided World*, Oxford, 1986, pp. 230 *et seq.*, who concludes that a consensus is growing to the effect that anticipatory self-defence is allowed but under strict conditions relating to proof of the imminence of an armed attack that would jeopardise the life of the target state and the absence of peaceful means to prevent the attack, *ibid.*, p. 233.
[66] See e.g. the Dissenting Opinion of Judge Schwebel, *Nicaragua* case, ICJ Reports, 1986, pp. 14, 347–8; 76 ILR, pp. 349, 681. But see Dinstein, *War*, pp. 182 *et seq.*
[67] See Dinstein, *War*, p. 190.   [68] *Supra* p. 787.
[69] Note, for example, the US bombing raid on Libya on 15 April 1986 in retaliation for alleged Libyan sponsored terrorist activities, see *infra* p. 793.
[70] ICJ Reports, 1986, pp. 14, 94 and 103; 76 ILR, pp. 349, 428 and 437.

measures which are proportional to the armed attack and necessary to respond to it, a rule well established in customary international law' and in the Advisory Opinion it gave to the General Assembly on the *Legality of the Threat or Use of Nuclear Weapons*[71] it was emphasised that '[t]he submission of the exercise of the right of self-defence to the conditions of necessity and proportionality is a rule of customary international law'.[72] Quite what will be necessary[73] and proportionate[74] will depend on the circumstances of the case. It also appears inevitable that it will be the state contemplating such action that will first have to make that determination,[75] although it will be subject to consideration by the international community as a whole and more specifically by the Security Council under the terms of article 51.[76]

One further point arises out of the *Legality of the Threat or Use of Nuclear Weapons* case and that relates to the relevant applicable law. The Court noted that the rules governing international armed conflicts (*jus in bello*) as well as those governing resort to force (*jus ad bellum*) might be relevant. It was stated that 'a use of force that is proportionate under the law of self-defence, must, in order to be lawful, also meet the requirements of the law applicable in armed conflict which comprise in particular the principles and rules of humanitarian law'.[77]

The protection of nationals abroad[78]

In the last century, it was clearly regarded as lawful to use force to protect nationals and property situated abroad and many incidents occurred to

---

[71] ICJ Reports, 1996, para. 41; 35 ILM, 1996, pp. 809, 822.

[72] The Court affirmed that this 'dual condition' also applied to article 51, whatever the means of force used, *ibid.*

[73] See Judge Ago's Eighth Report on State Responsibility to the International Law Commission, where it was noted that the concept of necessity centred upon the availability of other means to halt the attack so that 'the state attacked . . . must not, in the particular circumstances, have had any means of halting the attack other than recourse to armed force', *Yearbook of the ILC*, 1980, vol. II, part 1, p. 69.

[74] Judge Ago noted that the correct relationship for proportionality was not between the conduct constituting the armed attack and the opposing conduct, but rather between the action taken in self-defence and the purpose of halting and repelling the armed attack, so that '[t]he action needed to halt and repulse the attack may well have to assume dimensions disproportionate to those of the attack suffered', *ibid.*, p. 69. See also J. G. Gardam, 'Proportionality and Force in International Law, 87 AJIL, 1993, p. 391.

[75] See e.g. H. Lauterpacht, *The Function of Law in the International Community*, London, 1933, p. 179.

[76] See e.g. D. Grieg, 'Self-Defence and the Security Council: What Does Article 51 Require?', 40 ICLQ, 1991, p. 366.

[77] *Ibid.*, para. 42; 35 ILM, 1996, p. 822. See further *infra*, p. 806.

[78] See e.g. M. B. Akehurst, 'The Use of Force to Protect Nationals Abroad', 5 *International Relations*, 1977, p. 3 and Akehurst, 'Humanitarian Intervention' in *Intervention in World Politics* (ed. H. Bull), 1984, p. 95; Dinstein, *War*, pp. 226 *et seq.*; Waldock, 'General Course', p. 467; L. C. Green, 'Rescue at Entebbe – Legal Aspects', 6 *Israel Yearbook on Human Rights*, 1976, p. 312 and M. N. Shaw, 'Some Legal Aspects of the Entebbe Incident', 1 *Jewish Law Annual*, 1978, p. 232. See also T. Schweisfurth, 'Operations to Rescue Nationals in Third

demonstrate the acceptance of this position.[79] Since the adoption of the UN
Charter, however, it has become rather more controversial since of necessity the 'territorial integrity and political independence' of the target state is
infringed,[80] while one interpretation of article 51 would deny that 'an armed
attack' could occur against individuals abroad within the meaning of that
provision since it is the state itself that must be under attack, not specific
persons outside the jurisdiction.[81]

The issue has been raised in recent years in several cases. In 1964,
Belgium and the United States sent forces to the Congo to rescue hostages
(including nationals of the states in question) from the hands of rebels, with
the permission of the Congolese government,[82] while in 1975 the US used
force to rescue an American cargo boat and its crew captured by
Cambodia.[83] The most famous incident, however, was the rescue by Israel
of hostages held by Palestinian and other terrorists at Entebbe, following the
hijack of an Air France airliner.[84] The Security Council debate in that case
was inconclusive. Some states supported Israel's view that it was acting lawfully in protecting its nationals abroad, where the local state concerned was
aiding the hijackers,[85] others adopted the approach that Israel had committed aggression against Uganda or used excessive force.[86]

The United States has recently justified armed action in other states on
the grounds partly of the protection of American citizens abroad. It was one
of the three grounds announced for the invasion of Grenada in 1984[87] and
one of the four grounds put forward for the intervention in Panama in
December 1989.[88] However, in both cases the level of threat against the US
citizens was such as to raise serious questions concerning the satisfaction of

States Involving the Use of Force in Relation to the Protection of Human Rights', German
YIL, 1980, p. 159; D'Angelo, 'Resort to Force to Protect Nationals', 21 *Va JIL*, 1981, p.
485; J. Paust, 'The Seizure and Recovery of the *Mayaguez*', 85 *Yale Law Journal*, 1976, p.
774; D. W. Bowett, 'The Use of Force for the Protection of Nationals Abroad' in *The Current
Legal Regulation of the Use of Force* (ed. A. Cassese), Oxford, 1986, p. 39 and N. Ronzitti,
*Rescuing Nationals Abroad Through Military Coercion and Intervention on Grounds of
Humanity*, Oxford, 1985.   [79] See e.g. Brownlie, *International Law*, pp. 289 *et seq.*
[80] There is, of course, a different situation where the state concerned has consented to the
action.   [81] See e.g. Brownlie, *International Law*, pp. 289 *et seq.*
[82] See M. Whiteman, *Digest of International Law*, Washington, 1968, vol. V, p. 475. See also R.
B. Lillich, 'Forcible Self-Help to Protect Human Rights', 53 *Iowa Law Review*, 1967, p. 325.
[83] Paust, 'Seizure and Recovery', See also DUSPIL, 1975, pp. 777–83.
[84] See e.g. Akehurst, 'Use of Force'; Green, 'Rescue at Entebbe', and Shaw, 'Legal Aspects'.
[85] See e.g. S/PV.1939, pp. 51–5; S/PV.1940, p. 48 and S/PV.1941, p. 31.
[86] See e.g. S/PV.1943, pp. 47–50 and S/PV.1941, pp. 4–10, 57–61 and 67–72. Note that Egypt
attempted without success a similar operation in Cyprus in 1978, see *Keesings Contemporary
Archives*, p. 29305. In 1980, the US attempted to rescue its nationals held hostage in Iran
but failed, see S/13908 and the *Iran* case, ICJ Reports, 1980, pp. 3, 43; 61 ILR, pp. 530,
569.
[87] See the statement of Deputy Secretary of State Dam, 78 AJIL, 1984, p. 200. See also W.
Gilmore, *The Grenada Intervention*, London, 1984 and *infra* p. 800.
[88] See the statements by the US President and the Department of State, 84 AJIL, 1990,
p. 545.

the requirement of proportionality.[89] The US conducted a bombing raid on Libya on 15 April 1986 as a consequence of alleged Libyan involvement in an attack on US servicemen in West Berlin. This was justified by the US as an act of self-defence.[90] On 26 June 1993, the US launched missiles at the headquarters of the Iraqi military intelligence in Baghdad as a consequence of an alleged Iraqi plot to assassinate former US President Bush in Kuwait. It was argued that the resort to force was justified as a means of protecting US nationals in the future.[91] It is difficult to extract from the contradictory views expressed in these incidents the apposite legal principles. While some states affirm the existence of a rule permitting the use of force in self-defence to protect nationals abroad, others deny that such a principle operates in international law. There are states whose views are not fully formed or coherent on this issue. The UK Foreign Minister concluded on 28 June 1993 that:[92]

Force may be used in self-defence against threats to one's nationals if: (a) there is good evidence that the target attacked would otherwise continue to be used by the other state in support of terrorist attacks against one's nationals; (b) there is, effectively, no other way to forestall imminent further attacks on one's nationals; (c) the force employed is proportionate to the threat.

On balance and considering the opposing principles of saving the threatened lives of nationals and the preservation of the territorial integrity of states, it would seem preferable to accept the validity of the rule in carefully restricted situations consistent with the conditions laid down in the *Caroline* case.[93]

Whether force may be used to protect property abroad is less controversial. It is universally accepted today that it is not lawful to have resort to force merely to save material possessions abroad.

Conclusions

Despite controversy and disagreement over the scope of the right of self-defence, there is an indisputable core and that is the competence of states

[89] In the case of Grenada, it was alleged that some American students were under threat, see Gilmore, *Grenada*, pp. 55–64. In the Panama episode one American had been killed and several harassed, see V. Nanda, 'The Validity of United States Intervention in Panama Under International Law', 84 AJIL, 1990, pp. 494, 497.
[90] See President Reagan's statement, *The Times*, 16 April 1986, p. 6. The UK government supported this, see *The Times*, 17 April 1986, p. 4. However, there are problems with regard to proportionality in view of the injuries and damage apparently caused in the air raid. One US serviceman was killed in the West Berlin action. The role of the UK in consenting to the use of British bases for the purposes of the raid is also raised. See also UKMIL, 57 BYIL, 1986, pp. 639–42 and 80 AJIL, 1986, pp. 632–6.
[91] See Security Council Debates S/PV. 3245, 1993, and UKMIL, 64 BYIL, 1993, pp. 731 *et seq*. See also D. Kritsiotis, 'The Legality of the 1993 US Missile Strike on Iraq and the Right of Self-Defence in International Law', 45 ICLQ, 1996, p. 162.
[92] HC Debs., vol. 227, col. 658: 64 BYIL, 1993, p. 732.   [93] *Supra*, p. 787.

to resort to force in order to repel an attack. A clear example of this was provided in the Falklands conflict. Whatever doubts may be entertained about the precise roots of British title to the islands, it is very clear that after the Argentinian invasion of the territory, the UK possessed in law the right to act to restore the *status quo ante* and remove the Argentinian troops.[94] Security Council resolution 502 (1982), in calling for an immediate withdrawal of Argentinian forces and determining that a breach of the peace existed, reinforced this. It should also be noted that it is accepted that a state is entitled to rely upon the right of self-defence even while its possession of the territory in question is the subject of controversy.[95]

Collective self-defence[96]

Historically the right of states to take up arms to defend themselves from external force is well established as a rule of customary international law. Article 51, however, also refers to 'the inherent right of . . . collective self-defence' and the question therefore arises as to how far one state may resort to force in the defence of another. The idea of collective self-defence, however, is rather ambiguous. It may be regarded merely as a pooling of a number of individual rights of self-defence within the framework of a particular treaty or institution, as some writers have suggested,[97] or it may form the basis of comprehensive regional security systems. If the former were the case, it might lead to legal difficulties should Iceland resort to force in defence of Turkish interests, since actions against Turkey would in no way justify an armed reaction by Iceland pursuant to its individual right of self-defence.

In fact, state practice has adopted the second approach. Organisations such as NATO and the Warsaw Pact have been set up since the Second World War, specifically based upon the right of collective self-defence under article 51. By such agreements, an attack upon one party is treated as an attack upon all,[98] thus necessitating the conclusion that collective self-defence is something more than a collection of individual rights of self-defence, but another creature altogether.[99]

This approach finds support in the *Nicaragua* case.[100] The Court stressed

---

[94] See *supra*, Chapter 9, p. 360.   [95] See e.g. Brownlie, *International Law*, pp. 382–3.
[96] See e.g. Dinstein, *War*, Chapter 9.
[97] See e.g. Bowett, *Self-Defence*, p. 245, cf. Goodrich *et al.*, *Charter of the United Nations*, p. 348. See also Brownlie, *International Law*, pp. 328–3
[98] See e.g. article 5 of the NATO Treaty, 1949. See further *infra*, Chapter 21, p. 894.
[99] Note article 52 of the UN Charter, which recognises the existence of regional arrangements and agencies, dealing with such matters relating to international peace and security as are appropriate for regional action, provided they are consistent with the purposes and principles of the UN; see further *infra*, Chapter 20, p. 881.
[100] ICJ Reports, 1986, pp. 14, 103–5; 76 ILR, pp. 349, 437.

that the right to collective self-defence was established in customary law but added that the exercise of that right depended both upon a prior declaration by the state concerned that it was the victim of an armed attack and a request by the victim state for assistance. In addition, the Court emphasised that 'for one state to use force against another, on the ground that that state has committed a wrongful act of force against a third state, is regarded as lawful, by way of exception, only when the wrongful act provoking the response was an armed attack'.[101]

The invasion of Kuwait by Iraq on 2 August 1990 raised the issue of collective self-defence in the context of the response of the states allied in the coalition to end that conquest and occupation. The Kuwaiti government in exile appealed for assistance from other states.[102] Although the armed action taken as from 16 January 1991 was taken pursuant to UN Security Council resolutions,[103] it is indeed arguable that the right to collective self-defence is also relevant in this context.[104]

Force and self-determination[105]

Article 2(4) of the UN Charter calls upon states to refrain in their international relations from the threat or use of force against another state. It does not cover as such the self-determination situation where a people resorts to force against the colonial power. Until comparatively recently such situations were regarded as purely internal matters. The colonial authority could use such force as it deemed necessary to suppress a riot or rising without the issue impinging upon article 2(4). With the growing acceptance of self-determination as a legal right,[106] the question as to the legitimacy of the use of force was raised. It was argued indecisively in the Security Council upon the occasion of India's invasion of Goa[107] and discussed at great length in the debates of the Special Committee leading to the adoption of the Declaration on Principles of International Law in 1970.[108] In the event, the Declaration emphasised that all states were under a duty to refrain from any forcible

---

[101] Ibid., p. 110; see also ibid., p. 127; 76 ILR, pp. 444, 461.

[102] See Keesing's Record of World Events, pp. 37631 et seq. (1990).

[103] Infra, Chapter 20, p. 867.

[104] Note that Security Council resolution 661 (1990) specifically referred in its preamble to 'the inherent right of individual or collective self-defence, in response to the armed attack by Iraq against Kuwait'. See also the Barcelona Traction case, ICJ Reports, 1970, pp. 3, 32; 46 ILR, pp. 178, 206.

[105] See H. Wilson, International Law and the Use of Force by National Liberation Movements, Oxford, 1988. As to the principle of self-determination, see supra, Chapter 5, p. 177.

[106] See e.g. resolution 1514(XV), the Colonial Declaration, 1960 and supra, Chapter 5, p. 177.

[107] SCOR, 16th Year, 897th meeting, pp. 9–11. See also S/5032 and S/5033 and Q. Wright, 'The Goa Incident', 56 AJIL, 1962, p. 617.

[108] See e.g. A/5746, pp. 20, 23, 42–5 and A/7326, paras. 103, 105, 109, 175 and 177. See also A/7619, paras. 167 and 168.

action which deprives people of their right to self-determination.[109] This can now be regarded as accepted by the international community. The Declaration also noted that 'in their actions against, and resistance to, such forcible action' such peoples could receive support in accordance with the purpose and principles of the UN Charter. This modest and ambiguous formulation could not be taken as recognition of a right of self-defence inherent in peoples entitled to self-determination. The UN Charter neither confirms nor denies a right of rebellion. It is neutral. International law does not forbid rebellion, it leaves it within the purview of domestic law. The General Assembly, however, began adopting resolutions in the 1970s reaffirming the legitimacy of the struggle of peoples for liberation from colonial domination and alien subjugation, 'by all available means including armed struggle'.[110] This approach was intensively debated in the process leading to the adoption by the Assembly of the Consensus Definition of Aggression in 1974.[111] In particular the issue centred upon whether the use of force by peoples entitled to self-determination was legitimate as self-defence against the very existence of colonialism itself or whether as a response to force utilised to suppress the right of self-determination. The former view was taken by most Third World states and the latter by many Western states. In the event, a rather cumbersome formulation was presented in article 7 of the Definition which referred *inter alia* and in ambiguous vein to the right of peoples entitled to, but forcibly deprived of, the right to self-determination, 'to struggle to that end and to seek and receive support, in accordance with the principles of the Charter and in conformity' with the 1970 Declaration.[112]

The argument as to whether self-determination (or national liberation) wars could be regarded as international armed conflicts was also raised in the Diplomatic Conference on International Humanitarian Law,[113] which led to the adoption in 1977 of two Additional Protocols to the Geneva 'Red Cross' Conventions of 1949. Ultimately, article 1(4) of Protocol I was approved. It provides that international armed conflict situations 'include armed conflicts in which peoples are fighting against colonial domination and alien occupation and against racist regimes in the exercise of their right to self-determination' as enshrined in the Charter of the UN and the 1970 Declaration. The

[109] See also para. 4 of the 1960 Colonial Declaration and S. Schwebel, 'Wars of Liberation as Fought in UN Organs' in *Law and Civil War in the Modern World* (ed. J. N. Moore), Princeton, 1974, p. 446.
[110] See e.g. resolutions 3070(XXVIII), 3103(XXVIII), 3246(XXIX), 3328(XXIX), 3481(XXX), 31/91, 31/92, 32/42 and 32/154.
[111] See e.g. A/7185/Rev.1, para. 60 and A/7402, paras. 16 and 61. See also A/8019, para. 47 and A/8929, paras. 34, 73, 74, 142 and 143.
[112] Comments made following the adoption of the Definition clearly revealed the varying interpretations made by states of this provision, see e.g. A/C.6/SR.1472, paras. 5, 27 and 48 and A/C.6/SR.1480, paras. 8, 17, 25 and 73. See also Stone, *Conflict Through Consensus*, pp. 66–86.   [113] See e.g. CDDH/SR.2 paras. 8–11 and 44–5.

effect of this (within the clear self-determination context as defined in the Charter and the 1970 Declaration) is that the argument that valid self-determination conflicts are now to be accepted as within the international sphere of the activity of states has been greatly strengthened. The view that articles 2(4) and 51 of the Charter now apply to self-determination conflicts so that the peoples in question have a valid right to use force in self-defence is controversial and difficult to maintain. It is more likely that the principle of self-determination itself provides that where forcible action has been taken to suppress the right, force may be used in order to counter this and achieve self-determination. The use of force to suppress self-determination is now clearly unacceptable, as is help by third parties given to that end.

The question of third party assistance to peoples struggling to attain self-determination is highly controversial, and has been the subject of disagreement between Western and some Third World states. A number of the UN General Assembly resolutions have called on states to provide all forms of moral and material assistance to such peoples,[114] but the legal situation is still far from clear and the provision of armed help would appear to be unlawful.[115]

Intervention[116]

The principle of non-intervention is part of customary international law and founded upon the concept of respect for the territorial sovereignty of states.[117] Intervention is prohibited where it bears upon matters in which each state is permitted to decide freely by virtue of the principle of state sovereignty. This includes, as the International Court of Justice noted in the *Nicaragua* case,[118] the choice of political, economic, social and cultural

---

[114] See e.g. resolutions 2105(XX), 2160(XX), 2465(XXIII), 2649(XXV), 2734(XXV), 2787(XXVI), 3070(XXVII), 3163(XXVIII), 2328(XXIX), 3421(XXX), 31/29, 31/33, 32/10 and 32/154.

[115] See e.g. 17/8018, paras. 234 and 235, and *supra*, p. 796 with regard to the phrase in the 1970 Declaration. See also Stone, *Conflict Through Consensus*, pp. 66–86 and B. Ferencz, *Defining International Aggression*, Dobbs Ferry, vol. II, 1975, p. 48, with regard to the ambiguous formulation in the 1974 Definition of Aggression.

[116] See e.g. T. Komarknicki, 'L'Intervention en Droit International Moderne', *Revue Générale de Droit International Public*, 1956, p. 521; T. Farer, 'The Regulation of Foreign Armed Intervention in Civil Armed Conflict', 142 HR, 1974 II, p. 291 and J. E. S. Fawcett, 'Intervention in International Law', 103 HR, 1961 II, p. 347.

[117] See the *Corfu Channel* case, ICJ Reports, 1949, pp. 4, 35; 16 ILR, pp. 155, 167 and the *Nicaragua* case, ICJ Reports, 1986, pp. 14, 106; 76 ILR, pp. 349, 440. See also the Declaration on the Inadmissibility of Intervention in the Domestic Affairs of States 1965 and the Declaration on the Principles of International Law 1970, *supra* p. 784.

[118] ICJ Reports, 1986, pp. 14, 108; 76 ILR, p. 442. See also article 17 of the Draft Code of Crimes Against the Peace and Security of Mankind currently being formulated by the International Law Commission, see Report of the International Law Commission on the Work of its Forty-Seventh Session, 1995, A/50/10, pp. 40–1. Note particularly the suggestion of the Special Rapporteur to delete this article. See also S. McCaffrey, 'The Forty-First Session of the International Law Commission', 83 AJIL, 1989, p. 937.

systems and the formulation of foreign policy. Intervention becomes wrongful when it uses methods of coercion in regard to such choices, which must be free ones.[119] There was 'no general right of intervention in support of an opposition within another state' in international law. In addition, acts constituting a breach of the customary principle of non-intervention will also, if they directly or indirectly involve the use of force, constitute a breach of the principle of the non-use of force in international relations.[120] The principle of respect for the sovereignty of states was another principle closely allied to the principles of the prohibition of the use of force and of non-intervention.[121]

Civil wars[122]

International law treats civil wars as purely internal matters, with the possible exception of self-determination conflicts. Article 2(4) of the UN Charter prohibits the threat or use of force in international relations, not in domestic situations. There is no rule against rebellion in international law. It is within the domestic jurisdiction of states and is left to be dealt with by internal law. Should the rebellion succeed, the resulting situation would be dealt with primarily in the context of recognition. As far as third parties are concerned, traditional international law developed the categories of rebellion, insurgency and belligerency.

Once a state has defined its attitude and characterised the situation, different international legal provisions would apply. If the rebels are regarded as criminals, the matter is purely within the hands of the authorities of the country concerned and no other state may legitimately interfere. If the rebels are treated as insurgents, then other states may or may not agree to grant them certain rights. It is at the discretion of the other states concerned, since an intermediate status is involved. The rebels are not mere criminals, but they are not recognised belligerents. Accordingly, the other states are at liberty to define their legal relationship with them. Insurgency is a purely provisional classification and would arise for example where a state needed to protect nationals or property in an area under the *de facto*

---

[119] ICJ Reports, 1986, p. 108.   [120] *Ibid.*, pp. 109–10; 76 ILR, p. 443.
[121] ICJ Reports, 1986, p. 111; 76 ILR, p. 445.
[122] See e.g. *Law and Civil War in the Modern World* (ed. J. N. Moore), Princeton, 1974; *The International Regulation of Civil Wars* (ed. E. Luard), Oxford, 1972; *The International Law of Civil Wars* (ed. R. A. Falk), Princeton, 1971; T. Fraser, 'The Regulation of Foreign Intervention in Civil Armed Conflict', 142 HR, p. 291 and W. Friedmann, 'Intervention, Civil War and the Rule of International Law', PASIL, 1965, p. 67. See also R. Higgins, 'Intervention and International Law' in *Intervention in World Politics* (ed. H. Bull), 1984, p. 29; C. C. Joyner and B. Grimaldi, 'The United States and Nicaragua: Reflections on the Lawfulness of Contemporary Intervention', 25 Va JIL, 1985, p. 621 and Schachter, *International Law*, pp. 158 *et seq.*

control of the rebels.[123] On the other hand, belligerency is a formal status involving rights and duties. In the eyes of classical international law, other states may accord recognition of belligerency to rebels when certain conditions have been fulfilled. These were defined as the existence of an armed conflict of a general nature within a state, the occupation by the rebels of a substantial portion of the national territory, the conduct of hostilities in accordance with the rules of war and by organised groups operating under a responsible authority and the existence of circumstances rendering it necessary for the states contemplating recognition to define their attitude to the situation.[124] This would arise, for example, where the parties to the conflict are exercising belligerent rights on the high seas. Other maritime countries would feel compelled to decide upon the respective status of the warring sides, since the recognition of belligerency entails certain international legal consequences. Once the rebels have been accepted by other states as belligerents they become subjects of international law and responsible in international law for all their acts. In addition the rules governing the conduct of hostilities become applicable to both sides, so that, for example, the recognising states must then adopt a position of neutrality.

However, these concepts of insurgency and belligerency are lacking in clarity and are extremely subjective. The absence of clear criteria, particularly with regard to the concept of insurgency, has led to a great deal of confusion. The issue is of importance since the majority of conflicts in the years since the conclusion of the Second World War have been in essence civil wars. The reasons for this are many and complex and ideological rivalry and decolonisation within colonially imposed boundaries are amongst them.[125] Intervention may be justified on a number of grounds, including response to earlier involvement by a third party. For instance, the USSR and Cuba justified their activities in the Angolan civil war of 1975–76 by reference to the prior South African intervention,[126] while the United States argued that its aid to South Vietnam grew in proportion to the involvement of North Vietnamese forces in the conflict.[127]

The international law rules dealing with civil wars depend upon the categorisation by third states of the relative status of the two sides to the conflict. In traditional terms, an insurgency means that the recognising state may, if it wishes, create legal rights and duties as between itself and the

[123] See e.g. H. Lauterpacht, *Recognition in International Law*, Cambridge, 1947, pp. 275 *et seq.*
[124] See e.g. N. Mugerwa, 'Subjects of International Law' in *Manual of Public International Law* (ed. M. Sørensen), London, 1968, pp. 247, 286–8. See also R. Higgins, 'International Law and Civil Conflict' in *International Regulation of Civil Wars*, pp. 169, 170–1.
[125] See e.g. M. N. Shaw, *Title to Territory in Africa: International Legal Issues*, Oxford, 1986.
[126] See e.g. C. Legum and T. Hodges, *After Angola*, London, 1976.
[127] See e.g. *Law and the Indo-China War* (ed. J. N. Moore), Charlottesville, 1972. See also *The Vietnam War and International Law* (ed. R. A. Falk), 4 vols., Princeton, 1968–76.

insurgents, while recognition of belligerency involves an acceptance of a position of neutrality (although there are some exceptions to this rule) by the recognising states. But in practice, states very rarely make an express acknowledgement as to the status of the parties to the conflict, precisely in order to retain as wide a room for manoeuvre as possible. This means that the relevant legal rules cannot really operate as intended in classical law and that it becomes extremely difficult to decide whether a particular intervention is justified or not.[128]

Aid to the authorities of a state[129]

It would appear that in general outside aid to the government authorities to repress a revolt[130] is perfectly legitimate,[131] provided, of course, it was requested by the government. The problem of defining the governmental authority entitled to request assistance was raised in the Grenada episode. In that situation, the appeal for the US intervention was allegedly made by the Governor-General of the island,[132] but controversy exists as to whether this in fact did take place prior to the invasion and whether the Governor-General was the requisite authority to issue such an appeal.[133] The issue resurfaced in a rather different form regarding the Panama invasion of December 1989. One of the legal principles identified by the US Department of State as the basis for the US action was that of assistance to the 'lawful and democratically elected government in Panama'.[134] The problem with this was that this particular government had been prevented by General Noriega from actually taking office and the issue raised was therefore whether an elected head of state who is prevented from ever acting as such may be regarded as a governmental authority capable of requesting assistance including armed force from another state. This in fact runs counter to the test of acceptance in international law of governmental authority, which is firmly based upon effective control rather than upon the nature of the regime, whether democratic, socialist or otherwise.[135]

---

[128] But see *infra*, Chapter 20, p. 868, with regard to the increasing involvement of the UN in internal conflicts and the increasing tendency to classify such conflicts as possessing an international dimension.

[129] See e.g. L. Doswald-Beck, 'The Legal Validity of Military Intervention by Invitation of the Government', 56 BYIL, 1985, p. 189.

[130] Except where the recipient state is forcibly suppressing the right to self-determination of a people entitled to such rights, *supra*, p. 795.

[131] Until a recognition of belligerency, of course, although this has been unknown in modern times, see e.g. Lauterpacht, *Recognition*, pp. 230–3.

[132] See the statement by Deputy Secretary of State Dam, 78 AJIL, 1984, p. 200.

[133] See e.g. J. N. Moore, *Law and the Grenada Mission*, Charlottesville, 1984 and Gilmore, *Grenada*, See also Higgins, *Development of International Law*, note 55, pp. 162–4 regarding the Congo crisis of 1960, where that state's President and Prime Minister sought to dismiss each other.   [134] 84 AJIL, 1990, p. 547.   [135] See *supra*, Chapter 8, p. 301.

The general proposition, however, that aid to recognised governmental authorities is legitimate would be further reinforced where it could be shown that other states were encouraging or directing the subversive operations of the rebels. In such cases, it appears that the doctrine of collective self-defence would allow other states to intervene openly and lawfully on the side of the government authorities.[136] Some writers have suggested that the traditional rule of permitting third party assistance to governments would not extend to aid where the outcome of the struggle has become uncertain or where the rebellion has become widespread and seriously aimed at overthrowing the government.[137] While this may be politically desirable for the third state, it may put at serious risk entirely deserving governments. Practice, however, does suggest that many forms of aid, such as economic, technical and arms provision arrangements, to existing governments faced with civil strife, is acceptable.[138] There is an argument, on the other hand, for suggesting that substantial assistance to a government clearly in the throes of collapse might be questionable as intervention in a domestic situation that is on the point of resolution, but there are considerable definitional problems here.

Aid to rebels

The reverse side of the proposition is that aid to rebels is contrary to international law. The 1970 Declaration on Principles of International Law emphasised that:

[n]o state shall organise, assist, foment, finance, incite or tolerate subversive, terrorist or armed activities directed towards the violent overthrow of the regime of another state, or interfere in civil strife in another state.[139]

The Declaration also provided that:

---

[136] But in the light of the principles propounded in the *Nicaragua* case, ICJ Reports, 1986, pp. 104, 120–3; 76 ILR, pp. 349, 438, 454–7.

[137] See e.g. Q. Wright, 'US Intervention in the Lebanon', 53 AJIL, 1959, pp. 112, 122. See also R. A. Falk, *Legal Order in a Violent World*, Princeton, 1968, pp. 227–8 and 273 and Doswald-Beck, 'Legal Validity', p. 251.

[138] See with regard to the UK continuance of arms sales to Nigeria during its civil war, Higgins, 'International Law and Civil Conflict', p. 173. Note also the US policy of distinguishing between traditional supplier of arms and non-traditional supplier of arms in such circumstances. It would support aid provided by the former (as the UK in Nigeria), but not the latter, see DUSPIL, 1976, p. 7.

[139] See also in similar terms the Declaration on the Inadmissibility of Intervention in the Domestic Affairs of States, 1965, *supra*, p. 784. Article 3(g) of the General Assembly's Consensus Definition of Aggression, 1974, characterises as an act of aggression 'the sending by or on behalf of a state of armed bands, groups, irregulars or mercenaries, which carry out acts of armed force against another state'. See also with regard to US aid to the Nicaraguan 'contras', Chayes, *Cuban Missile Crisis*, and the *Nicaragua* case, ICJ Reports, 1986, p. 14; 76 ILR, p. 349.

[e]very state shall refrain from any action aimed at the partial or total disruption of the national unity and territorial integrity of any other state or country.

This would seem fairly conclusive, but in fact state practice is far from unanimous on this point.[140] Where a prior, illegal intervention on the government side has occurred, it may be argued that aid to the rebels is acceptable. This was argued by a number of states with regard to the Afghanistan situation, where it was felt that the Soviet move into that state amounted to an invasion.[141]

Humanitarian intervention

It has sometimes been argued that intervention in order to protect the lives of persons situated within a particular state and not necessarily nationals of the intervening state is permissible in strictly defined situations.[142] This has some support in pre-Charter law and it may very well have been the case that in the last century such intervention was accepted under international law.[143] However, it is difficult to reconcile today with article 2(4) of the Charter[144] unless one adopts a rather artificial definition of the 'territorial integrity' criterion in order to permit temporary violations. Practice is also in general unfavourable to the concept, primarily because it might be used to justify interventions by more forceful states into the territories of weaker states.[145] Nevertheless, it is not inconceivable that in some situations the international community might refrain from adopting a condemnatory

---

[140] See e.g. Syrian intervention in the Jordanian civil war of 1970 and in the Lebanon in 1976.

[141] See e.g. *Keesings Contemporary Archives*, pp. 30339, 30364 and 30385. See also General Assembly resolutions ES-62; 35/37; 36/34; 37/37 and 38/29 condemning the USSR for its armed intervention in Afghanistan. See also Doswald-Beck, 'Legal Validity', pp. 230 *et seq.*

[142] See e.g. *Humanitarian Intervention and the United Nations* (ed. R. B. Lillich), Charlottesville, 1973; R. B. Lillich, 'Forcible Self-Help by States to Protect Human Rights', 53 *Iowa Law Review*, 1967, p. 325 and Lillich, 'Intervention to Protect Human Rights', 15 *McGill Law Journal*, 1969, p. 205; J. P. Fonteyne, 'The Customary International Law Doctrine of Humanitarian Intervention', 4 *California Western International Law Journal*, 1974, p. 203; Chilstrom, 'Humanitarian Intervention under Contemporary International Law', 1 *Yale Studies in World Public Order*, 1974, p. 93; N. D. Arnison, 'The Law of Humanitarian Intervention' in *Refugees in the 1990s: New Strategies for a Restless World* (ed. H. Cleveland), 1993, p. 37; D. J. Scheffer, 'Towards a Modern Doctrine of Humanitarian Intervention', 23 *University of Toledo Law Review*, 1992, p. 253 and F. Tesón, *Humanitarian Intervention: An Enquiry into Law and Morality*, 1987. See also C. Palley, 'Implications of Humanitarian Activities for the Enjoyment of Human Rights', E/CN.4/Sub.2/1994/39, 1994 and R. B. Lillich, 'Humanitarian Intervention Through the United Nations: Towards the Development of Criteria', 53 *ZaöRV*, 1993, p. 557 and *infra*, Chapter 20, p. 868.

[143] See e.g. H. Ganji, *International Protection of Human Rights*, New York, 1962, Chapter 1 and references cited in previous footnote.

[144] See in particular, Brownlie, 'Humanitarian Intervention' in *Law and Civil War in the Modern World*, p. 217.

[145] See e.g. M. B. Akehurst, 'Humanitarian Intervention' in *Intervention in World Politics*, p. 95. Note that the absence of the nationality link between the state intervening and the persons concerned makes an important difference, see *supra* p. 562.

stand where large numbers of lives have been saved in circumstances of gross oppression by a state of its citizens due to an outside intervention. In addition, it is possible that such a right might evolve in cases of extreme humanitarian need. One argument used to justify the use of Western troops to secure a safe haven in northern Iraq after the Gulf War was that it was taken in pursuance of the customary international law principle of humanitarian intervention in an extreme situation.[146]

One variant of the principle of humanitarian intervention is the contention that intervention in order to restore democracy is permitted as such under international law. One of the grounds given for the US intervention in Panama in December 1989 was the restoration of democracy,[147] but apart from the problems of defining democracy, such a proposition is not acceptable in international law today in view of the clear provisions of the UN Charter. Nor is there anything to suggest that even if the principle of self-determination could be interpreted as applying beyond the strict colonial context[148] to cover 'democracy', it could constitute a norm superior to that of non-intervention.[149]

Terrorism and international law[150]

The use of terror as a means to achieve political ends is not a new phenomenon, but it has recently acquired a new intensity. In many cases, terrorists deliberately choose targets in uninvolved third states as a means of pressurising the government of the state against which it is in conflict or its real or potential or assumed allies.[151] As far as international law is concerned, there are a number of problems that can be identified. The first major concern is that of definition.[152] Whether one terms a particular group of activists terrorists or freedom fighters depends upon one's political standpoint. Similarly difficult is the question of the width of definition one should accept with respect to acts undertaken. For example, should attacks against

---

[146] See the views expressed by a Foreign Office legal advisor to the House of Commons Foreign Affairs Committee, UKMIL, 63 BYIL, 1992, pp. 827–8. See also *infra*, Chapter 20, p. 874.
[147] See e.g. *Keesing's Record of World Events*, p. 37112 (1989). See also Nanda, 'Validity', p. 498.
[148] *Supra*, p. 215.
[149] See e.g. O. Schachter, 'The Legality of Pro-Democratic Invasion', 78 AJIL, 1984, p. 645.
[150] See e.g. *Legal Aspects of International Terrorism* (eds. A. E. Evans and J. Murphy), Lexington, KY, 1978; R. Friedlander, *Terrorism*, Dobbs Ferry, 1979 and R. B. Lillich and T. Paxman, 'State Responsibility for Injuries to Aliens Caused by Terrorist Activity', 26 *American Law Review*, 1977, p. 217. See also *International Terrorism and Political Crimes* (ed. M. C. Bassiouni), 1975; E. McWhinney, *Aerial Piracy and International Terrorism*, 2nd edn, Dordrecht, 1987, and A. Cassese, *Terrorism, Politics and Law*, Cambridge, 1989. See also *supra*, Chapter 12, p. 474.
[151] The hijack of TWA Flight 847 on 14 June 1985 by Lebanese Shi'ites is one example of this phenomenon, see e.g. *The Economist*, 22 June, 1985, p. 34.
[152] See e.g. GAOR, 28th session, Suppl. No. 28, 1973, pp. 7–8.

property as well as attacks upon persons be covered? The extent to which one should take into account the motives and intentions of the perpetrators is raised, as is the question as to whether one should distinguish purely criminal from politically inspired attacks.

There are, of course, also difficulties associated with the enforcement of such international law rules as may be agreed upon, since some states have supported terrorist activities. However, some progress has been made to establish rules of international law applicable to particular manifestations of terrorism. The approach that has in practice been adopted by the international community in recent years can best be described as functional, or pragmatic, rather than comprehensive. This contrasts with the all-embracing view taken by the League of Nations in the 1937 Convention for the Prevention and Punishment of Terrorism, which in the event, and only partly because of the onset of the Second World War, never entered into force.[153]

The spread of aircraft hijacking in the 1950s and the 1960s stimulated a series of three international conventions in 1963, 1970 and 1971, to deal with this particular terrorist activity.[154] These can be regarded as partial successes, although efforts by the International Civil Aviation Organisation to reinforce these measures against hijackers and states harbouring them have so far failed.[155] It is enforcement rather than definition that constitutes the main bar to progress in this field. In December 1972, the General Assembly set up an *ad hoc* committee on terrorism,[156] but this failed to arrive at any agreed recommendations and the matter passed to the Assembly itself, where the whole issue became further entangled with various political disputes, as Third World states concentrated their attention on state terror and in particular the use of force to deprive peoples of the right to self-determination.[157] However, in 1973 the General Assembly adopted a Convention on the Prevention and Punishment of Crimes

[153] Terrorism was here defined as criminal acts directed against a state and intended to create a state of terror in the minds of particular persons, or a group of persons or the general public, see Murphy, *United Nations*, p. 179. See also T. M. Franck and B. Lockwood, 'Preliminary Thoughts Towards an International Convention on Terrorism', 68 AJIL, 1974, p. 69.

[154] See the Tokyo Convention of 1963, which requires parties to return hijacked aircraft and passengers; the Hague Convention of 1970 which declares that states should either extradite or prosecute hijackers and the Montreal Convention of 1971 which extends this requirement to those employed in aircraft sabotage activities, see further *supra*, Chapter 12, p. 474. Note also the 1978 Bonn Declaration under which European Community states resolved that if a country failed to fulfil its obligations under the 1970 Convention, immediate action should be taken to cease flights to that country. See also the Convention for the Suppression of Unlawful Acts against the Safety of Maritime Navigation 1988.

[155] See e.g. Murphy, *United Nations*, p. 181.

[156] See General Assembly resolution 3034(XXVII).

[157] See now the Declaration on Measures to Eliminate International Terrorism, adopted in General Assembly resolution 49/60, 1995.

against Internationally Protected Persons Including Diplomatic Agents. This was an attempt to stop the kidnapping and assaults upon diplomats that had spread throughout South America and parts of Europe and the Middle East. The treaty stipulates that alleged offenders should either be prosecuted or extradited and provides for an improved degree of international co-operation.[158]

In 1979, the General Assembly also adopted the International Convention against the Taking of Hostages.[159] Its aim is to ensure that persons taking hostages are either prosecuted or extradited where found within the jurisdiction of a state party. State parties are also obliged to co-operate in the prevention of such acts. However, one ambiguous provision is found in article 12 which declares that the Convention is not to apply where the Geneva Conventions of 1949 and its Additional Protocols of 1977[160] are relevant so that hostage-taking committed in the course of armed conflicts as defined in the 1949 and 1977 instruments (including self-determination wars) would fall outside the 1979 Hostage Convention.[161] The Assembly has also adopted a number of resolutions calling for ratification of the various conventions and for improvement in co-operation between states in this area.[162] In resolution 40/61, for example, the Assembly condemned as criminal all acts, methods and practices of terrorism wherever and by whomever committed, while in resolution 579 (1985) the Security Council condemned unequivocally all acts of hostage-taking and abduction. The UN has, in asserting an increasing role for itself in the post-cold war world, commented upon the relationship between terrorism and international peace and security. In resolution 731 (1992), the Security Council referred to 'acts of international terrorism that constitute threats to international peace and security'. This resolution was adopted in the context of criticism of Libya for not complying with requests for extradition of suspected bombers of an airplane, but it clearly demonstrates the acceptance of the view that terrorism could impel the Security Council to act under Chapter VII by the

---

[158] This was modelled upon a similar Organisation of American States Convention in 1971, see 65 AJIL, 1971, p. 898. See also the 1977 European Convention on the Suppression of Terrorism.

[159] See J. J. Lambert, *Terrorism and Hostages in International Law*, Cambridge, 1990.

[160] See e.g. article 34 of the Geneva Convention on the Protection of Civilians in Time of War, 1949, which provides that the taking of hostages is prohibited, and see also article 75 of the Protocol I, 1977. See also *infra*, p. 808.

[161] States in such situations would be liable to prosecute or hand over hostage-takers under the 1949 and 1977 instruments.

[162] See e.g. resolutions 34/145, 35/168 and 36/33. See also *supra*, p. 526 with regard to the Iran hostages crisis. See also the statement made by the President of the Security Council on behalf of members condemning the hijacking of the *Achille Lauro* and generally 'terrorism in all its forms, whenever and by whomever committed', 9 October 1985, S/17554, 24 ILM, 1985, p. 1656. See also *supra*, pp. 477 and 781.

imposition of binding sanctions upon states engaging or possibly supporting such activities.[163]

States may also adopt forceful measures in response to terrorist activities, and in certain situations actions against states sponsoring terrorism may be justifiable in the context of self-defence. However, the relevant international norms hardly envisage this kind of situation, but rather concentrate upon the dangers of large-scale state use of force. Since states generally are under an obligation not to sponsor terrorist activity or assist it in any way, the question of how to deal with a violator is posed. A major terrorist incident mounted or supported by one state against another will justify measures under the rubric of self-defence, provided that the necessary requirements as to, for example, proportionality are observed. A series of smaller-scale incidents may have the same effect, but it is unlikely that isolated, relatively minor terrorist activities would justify the use of force by the target state against the state supporting the activity in question.

The laws relating to armed conflicts – international humanitarian law[164]

In addition to prescribing laws governing resort to force, international law also seeks to regulate the conduct of hostilities. Relevant principles cover, for example, prisoners of war, civilians, sick and wounded personnel, prohibited methods of warfare and human rights in such situations.

Development

The law in this area developed from the middle of the last century. In 1864, as a result of the pioneering work of Henry Dunant, who had been appalled by the brutality of the battle of Solferino five years earlier, the Geneva Convention for the Amelioration of the Condition of the Wounded in Armies in the Field was adopted. This brief instrument was revised in 1906.

---

[163] See also Security Council resolution 1070 (1996) adopted with regard to Sudan which reaffirmed that 'the suppression of acts of international terrorism, including those in which states are involved is essential for the maintenance of international peace and security'.

[164] See e.g. Green, *Contemporary Law*; G. Best, *Humanity in Warfare*, London, 1980 and Best, *War and Law Since 1945*; *Studies and Essays on International Humanitarian Law and Red Cross Principles* (ed. C. Swinarski), Dordrecht, 1984; *The New Humanitarian Law of Armed Conflict* (ed. A. Cassese), Naples, 1979; G. Draper, 'The Geneva Convention of 1949', 114 HR, p. 59 and Draper, 'Implementation and Enforcement of the Geneva Conventions and of the two Additional Protocols', 164 HR, p. 1; F. Karlshoven, *The Law of Warfare*, Leiden, 1973; M. Bothe, K. Partsch and W. Solf, *New Rules for Victims of Armed Conflict*, The Hague, 1982 and J. Pictet, *Humanitarian Law and the Protection of War Victims*, Dordrecht, 1982. See also *Documents on the Laws of War* (ed. A. Roberts and R. Guelff), 2nd edn, Oxford, 1989; I. De Lupis, *The Law of War*, Cambridge, 1987 and C. Rousseau, *Le Droit des Conflits Armés*, Paris, 1983.

In 1868 the Declaration of St Petersburg prohibited the use of small explosive or incendiary projectiles. The laws of war were codified at the Hague Conferences of 1899 and 1907.[165] A series of conventions were adopted at these conferences concerning land and naval warfare, which still form the basis of the existing rules. It was emphasised that belligerents remained subject to the law of nations and forbade the use of force against undefended villages and towns. It defined those entitled to belligerent status and dealt with the measures to be taken as regards occupied territory. There were also provisions concerning the rights and duties of neutral states and persons in case of war, and an emphatic prohibition on the employment of 'arms, projectiles or material calculated to cause unnecessary suffering'. However, there were inadequate means to implement and enforce such rules with the result that much appeared to depend on reciprocal behaviour, public opinion and the exigencies of morale.[166] Apart from the 1954 Hague Convention for the Protection of Cultural Property in Time of Armed Conflict, the rules of war remained as they had been formulated and codified in 1907.

A number of conventions in the inter-war period dealt with rules concerning the wounded and sick in armies in the field and prisoners of war.[167] Such agreements were replaced by the Four Geneva 'Red Cross' Conventions of 1949 which dealt respectively with the amelioration of the condition of the wounded and sick in armed forces in the field, the amelioration of the condition of wounded, sick and ship-wrecked members of the armed forces at sea, the treatment of prisoners of war and the protection of civilian persons in time of war. The Fourth Convention was an innovation and a significant attempt to protect civilians who, as a result of armed hostilities or occupation, were in the power of a state of which they were not nationals.

The essence of these Geneva Conventions is the principle that persons not actively engaged in warfare should be treated humanely. A number of practices ranging from the taking of hostages to torture, illegal executions and reprisals against persons protected by the Conventions are prohibited, while a series of provisions relate to more detailed points, such as the standard of care of prisoners of war and the prohibition of deportations and indiscriminate destruction of property in occupied territory. In 1977, two

---

[165] See e.g. Green, *Contemporary Law*, Chapter 2.
[166] Note, however, the Martens' Clause in the Preamble to the Hague Convention concerning the Laws and Customs of War on Land, which provided that 'in cases not included in the Regulations . . . the inhabitants and the belligerents remain under the protection and the rule of the principles of the law of nations, as they result from the usages established among civilised peoples from the laws of humanity and the dictates of the public conscience'.
[167] See e.g. the 1929 Conventions, one revising the 1864 and 1906 instruments on wounded and sick soldiers, the other on the treatment of prisoners of war.

Additional Protocols to the 1949 Conventions were adopted.[168] These built upon and developed the earlier Conventions. The 'Law of the Hague', dealing primarily with interstate rules governing the use of force, and the 'Law of Geneva' concerning the protection of persons from the effects of armed conflicts are to some extent merged,[169] while certain other issues such as wars of liberation, mercenaries and apartheid, were also dealt with.

The scope of protection

The rules seek to extend protection to a wide range of persons. The basic distinction drawn has been between combatants and those who are not involved in actual hostilities. The Geneva Conventions of 1949 for the protection of war victims, as noted, cover the wounded and sick in land warfare; the wounded, sick and shipwrecked in warfare at sea; prisoners of war; and civilians. The first two of these Conventions are fairly self-explanatory and deal with the respect and protection due to medical personnel and establishments, the wounded and sick and the dead. The second instrument, on warfare at sea, also deals with hospital ships.[170] The provisions in these Conventions were supplemented by Protocol I, 1977, Parts I and II.

The Third Geneva Convention of 1949 is concerned with prisoners of war, and consists of a comprehensive code centred upon the requirement of humane treatment in all circumstances.[171] The definition of prisoners of war in article 4, however, is of particular importance since it has been regarded as the elaboration of combatant status. It covers members of the armed forces of a party to the conflict (as well as members of militias and other volunteer corps forming part of such armed force) and members of other militias and volunteer corps, including those of organised resistance movements, belonging to a party to the conflict providing the following conditions are fulfilled: (a) being commanded by a person responsible for his subordinates; (b) having a fixed distinctive sign recognisable at a distance; (c) carrying arms openly; (d) conducting operations in accordance

[168] See e.g. *Studies and Essays*, Part B, and Draper, 'Implementation and Enforcement'. See also B. Wortley, 'Observations on the Revision of the 1949 Geneva "Red Cross" Conventions', 54 BYIL, 1983, p. 143 and G. Aldrich, 'Prospects for US Ratification of Additional Protocol I to the 1949 Geneva Conventions', 85 AJIL, 1991, p. 1.

[169] To form what the International Court of Justice in its Advisory Opinion on the *Legality of the Threat or Use of Nuclear Weapons*, ICJ Reports, 1996, para. 75; 36 ILM, 1996, pp. 809, 827, has recently termed 'one single complex system, known today as international humanitarian law'. The Court also noted that '[t]he provisions of the Additional Protocols of 1977 give expression and attest to the unity and complexity of that law', *ibid.*

[170] See with regard to the use of hospital ships in the Falklands conflict, H. Levie, 'The Falklands Crisis and the Laws of the War' in *The Falklands War* (eds. Coll and Arend), 1985, pp. 64, 67–8.

[171] It applies to all cases of declared war or any other armed conflict and to all cases of partial or total occupation of the territory of a party to the Convention (article 2).

with the laws and customs of war. This article reflected the experience of the Second World War, although the extent to which resistance personnel were covered was constrained by the need to comply with the four conditions. Since 1949, the use of guerrillas spread to the Third World and the decolonisation experience. Accordingly, pressures grew to expand the definition of combatants entitled to prisoner of war status to such persons, who as practice demonstrated rarely complied with the four conditions. States facing guerrilla action, whether the colonial powers or others such as Israel, naturally objected. Articles 43 and 44 of Protocol I, 1977, provide that combatants are members of the armed forces of a party to an international armed conflict.[172] Such armed forces consist of all organised armed units under an effective command structure which enforces compliance with the rules of international law applicable in armed conflict. Article 44(3) further notes that combatants are obliged to distinguish themselves from the civilian population while they are engaged in an attack or in a military operation preparatory to an attack. When an armed combatant cannot so distinguish himself, the status of combatant may be retained provided that arms are carried openly during each military engagement and during such time as the combatant is visible to the adversary while engaged in a military deployment preceding the launching of an attack. This formulation is clearly controversial and was the subject of many declarations in the vote at the conference producing the draft.[173]

The framework of obligations covering prisoners of war is founded upon the following provisions. Article 13 provides that prisoners of war must at all times be humanely treated and must at all times be protected, particularly against acts of violence or intimidation and against 'insults and public curiosity'. This means that displaying prisoners of war on television confessing to 'crimes' or criticising their own government must be regarded as a breach of the Convention.[174] While prisoners of war are bound to divulge their name, date of birth, rank and serial number, article 17 provides that 'no physical or mental torture, nor any other form of coercion, may be inflicted . . . to secure from them information of any kind whatever.

[172] *Infra*, p. 815.
[173] See e.g. H. Verthy, *Guérrilla et droit Humanitaire*, 2nd edn, Geneva, 1983 and P. Nahlik, 'L'Extension du Statut de Combattant à la Lumière de Protocol I de Genève de 1977', 164 HR, p. 171. Note that by article 45 any person taking part in hostilities and falling into the hands of an adverse party shall be presumed to be a prisoner of war and thus protected by the Third Geneva Convention of 1949. Where there are any doubts, such status shall be retained until conclusively determined by a competent tribunal. Where a person is a mercenary, there is no right to combatant or prisoner of war status under article 47. See also the International Convention against the Recruitment, Use, Financing and Training of Mercenaries 1989, see Green, *Contemporary Law*, pp. 111 *et seq.*
[174] See e.g. the treatment of allied prisoners of war by Iraq, *The Economist*, 26 January 1991, p. 24.

Prisoners of war who refuse to answer may not be threatened, insulted, or exposed to unpleasant or disadvantageous treatment of any kind.' Once captured, prisoners of war are to be evacuated as soon as possible to camps situated in an area far enough from the combat zone for them to be out of danger,[175] while article 23 stipulates that 'no prisoner of war may at any time be sent to, or detained in areas where he may be exposed to the fire of the combat zone, nor may his presence be used to render certain points or areas immune from military operations'.[176] Prisoners of war are subject to the laws and orders of the state holding them. They may be punished for disciplinary offences and tried for offences committed before capture, for example for war crimes. They may also be tried for offences committed before capture against the law of the state holding them.[177]

The fourth of the Four Geneva Conventions of 1949 is concerned with the protection of civilians in time of war.[178] This marked an extension to the pre-1949 rules, although limited under article 4 to those persons, 'who, at a given moment and in any manner whatsoever, find themselves, in case of a conflict or occupation, in the hands of a party to the conflict or occupying power of which they are not nationals'. Under article 50(1) of Protocol I, 1977, a civilian is defined as any person not a combatant,[179] and in cases of doubt a person is to be considered a civilian. The Fourth Convention provides a highly developed set of rules for the protection of such civilians, including the right to respect for person, honour, convictions and religious practices and the prohibition of torture and other cruel, inhuman or degrading treatment, hostage-taking and reprisals.[180] There are also various judicial guarantees as to due process.[181] The protection of civilians in occupied territories is covered in section III of the Fourth Geneva Convention, but what precisely occupied territory is may be open to dispute.[182] The situation with regard to the West Bank of Jordan (sometimes known as Judaea and Samari), for example, demonstrates the problems that may arise. By article 2, this Convention is to apply to all cases of partial or total occupation 'of the territory of a high contracting party'. Israel has argued that since the West Bank has never been recognised internationally as Jordanian terri-

---

[175] Article 19.
[176] Thus the reported Iraqi practice during the 1991 Gulf War of sending allied prisoners of war to strategic sites in order to create a 'human shield' to deter allied attacks was clearly a violation of the Convention, see e.g. *The Economist*, 26 January 1991, p. 24. See also UKMIL, 62 BYIL, 1991, pp. 678 *et seq*,
[177] Articles 82 and 85. See Green, *Contemporary Law*, p. 202. See also *US v. Noriega*, 746 F Supp 1506, 1529 (1990); 99 ILR, pp. 143, 171.
[178] See e.g. Green, *Contemporary Law*, Chapters 12 and 15.
[179] As defined in article 4 of the Third Geneva Convention, 1949 and article 43, Protocol I, 1977, *supra*, p. 809.   [180] See articles 27–34.
[181] See articles 71–76. See also article 75 of Protocol I, 1977.
[182] Iraqi-occupied Kuwait was, of course, a prime example of the situation covered by this Convention.

tory,[183] it cannot therefore be regarded as its territory to which the Convention would apply. In other words, to recognise that the Convention applies would be tantamount to a recognition of Jordanian sovereignty over the disputed land.[184] Amongst the provisions in Section III is a prohibition on 'individual or mass forcible transfers' under article 49.[185]

As far as the civilian population is concerned during hostilities,[186] the basic rule formulated in article 48 of Protocol I is that the parties to the conflict must at all times distinguish between such population and combatants and between civilian and military objectives and must direct their operations only against military objectives. Article 51 provides that the civilian population as such, as well as individual civilians, 'shall not be the object of attack. Acts or threats of violence the primary purpose of which is to spread terror among the civilian population are prohibited.' Additionally, indiscriminate attacks[187] are prohibited.[188] In addition, article 52 provides that civilian objects are not to be the object of attack or of reprisals. Civilian objects are all objects which are not military objectives as defined in article 52(2).[189]

Cultural objects and places of worship are also protected,[190] as are objects deemed indispensable to the survival of the civilian population such as

---

[183] It was annexed by the Kingdom of Transjordan, as it then was, in 1949 at the conclusion of the Israeli War of Independence, but this annexation was recognised only by the UK and Pakistan. See e.g. A. Gerson, *Israel, the West Bank and International Law*, London, 1978.

[184] Note that Israel does observe the Convention *de facto*, see e.g. M. Shamgar, 'The Observation of International Law in the Administered Territories', *Israel Yearbook on Human Rights*, 1977, p. 262 and T. Meron, 'West Bank and Gaza', *ibid.*, 1979, p. 108. See also F. Fleiner-Gerster and H. Meyer, 'New Developments in Humanitarian Law', 34 ICLQ, 1985, p. 267 and E. Cohen, *Human Rights in the Israeli-Occupied Territories*, Manchester, 1985.

[185] Israel's policy of building settlements on the West Bank has been criticised on this basis, see e.g. UKMIL, 54 BYIL, 1983, pp. 538–9.

[186] Apart from the inhabitants of occupied territories protected under the Fourth Geneva Convention 1949.

[187] These are defined in article 51(4) as: (a) those which are not directed at a specific military objective; (b) those which employ a method or means of combat which cannot be directed at a specific military objective; or (c) those which employ a method or means of combat the effects of which cannot be limited as required by Protocol I; and consequently in each such case are of a nature to strike military objectives and civilians or civilian objects without distinction.

[188] See 21(5) UN Chronicle, 1984, p. 3 with regard to an appeal by the UN Secretary-General to Iran and Iraq to refrain from attacks on civilian targets. See also Security Council resolution 540 (1983). The above provisions apply to the use by Iraq in the 1991 Gulf War of missiles deliberately fired at civilian targets. The firing of missiles at Israeli cities in early 1991 constituted, of course, an act of aggression against a state not a party to that conflict, see e.g. *The Economist*, 26 January 1991, p. 21.

[189] This provides that military objectives are limited to those objects which in their nature, location, purpose or use make an effective contribution to military action and whose total or partial destruction, capture or neutralisation in the circumstances ruling at the time offers a definite military advantage.

[190] See article 53 and the Hague Convention for the Protection of Cultural Property in the Event of Armed Conflict 1954.

foodstuffs, agricultural areas for the production of foodstuffs, crops, live-
stock, drinking water installations and supplies, and irrigation works so long
as they are not used as sustenance solely for the armed forces or in direct
support of military action.[191] Attacks are also prohibited against works or
installations containing dangerous forces, namely dams, dykes and nuclear
generating stations.[192]

Methods of warfare[193]

International law, in addition to seeking to protect victims of armed conflicts, also tries to constrain the conduct of military operations in a
humanitarian fashion. In analysing the rules contained in the 'Law of the
Hague', it is important to bear in mind the delicate balance to be maintained between military necessity and humanitarian considerations. A principle of long standing, if not always honoured in practice, is the requirement
to protect civilians against the effects of hostilities. The preamble of the St
Petersburg Declaration of 1868, banning explosives or inflammatory projectiles below 400 grammes in weight, emphasises that the 'only legitimate
object which states should endeavour to accomplish during war is to
weaken the military forces of the enemy', while article 48 of Protocol I provides that a distinction must at all times be drawn between civilians and
combatants. The right of the parties to an armed conflict to choose
methods of warfare is not unconstrained. Article 22 of the Regulations
annexed to the Hague Convention IV of 1907 points out that the 'right of
belligerents to adopt means of injuring the enemy is not unlimited',[194] while
article 23(e)[195] stipulates that it is especially prohibited to 'employ arms,
projectiles or material calculated to cause unnecessary suffering'.[196] Quite

---

[191] Article 54.   [192] Article 56.
[193] See e.g. Green, *Contemporary Law*, Chapters 7, 8 and 9, and Best, *War and Law*, pp. 253
et seq. See also M. N. Shaw, 'The United Nations Convention on Prohibitions or
Restrictions on the Use of Certain Conventional Weapons, 1981', 9 *Review of International
Studies*, 1983, p. 109.
[194] This is repeated in virtually identical terms in article 35, Protocol I.
[195] It is generally recognised that the Regulations now form part of customary law, see e.g. the
Nuremberg Tribunal, 41 AJIL, 1947, pp. 248–9 and Roberts and Guelff, *Documents*, p. 54.
See also the Report of the UN Secretary-General on the Statute for the Yugoslav War Crimes
Tribunal, Security Council resolutions 808 (1993) and 823 (1993), and the *Legality of the
Threat or Use of Nuclear Weapons*, ICJ Reports, 1996, para. 80; 35 ILM, 1996, pp. 809, 827–8.
[196] See article 35(2) of Protocol I and the Preamble to the 1980 Convention on Conventional
Weapons; see Shaw, 'Conventional Weapons', p. 113. Note that 'employment of poisonous
weapons or other weapons calculated to cause unnecessary suffering' is stated to be a viola-
tion of the laws and customs of war by article 3(a) of the Statute of the International
Tribunal on War Crimes in Former Yugoslavia, see Report of the UN Secretary-General,
S/25704 and Security Council resolution 827(1993) and see also proposed article 22(2) a
of the Draft Code of Crimes against the Peace and Security of Mankind, Report of the
International Law Commission on the Work of its Forty-seventh Session, 1995, A/50/10,
pp. 52–3.

how one may define such weapons is rather controversial and can only be determined in the light of actual state practice.[197] The balance between military necessity and humanitarian considerations is relevant here. The International Court in its Advisory Opinion on the *Legality of the Threat or Use of Nuclear Weapons*[198] summarised the situation in the following authoritative way:

The cardinal principles contained in the texts constituting the fabric of humanitarian law are the following. The first is aimed at the protection of the civilian population and civilian objects and establishes the distinction between combatants and non-combatants; states must never make civilians the object of attack and must consequently never use weapons that are incapable of distinguishing between civilian and military targets. According to the second principle, it is prohibited to cause unnecessary suffering to combatants; it is accordingly prohibited to use weapons causing them such harm or uselessly aggravating their suffering. In application of that second principle, states do not have unlimited freedom of choice of means in the weapons they use.

The Court emphasised that the fundamental rules flowing from these principles bound all states whether or not they had ratified the Hague and Geneva Conventions since they constituted 'intransgressible principles of international customary law'.[199] At the heart of such rules and principles, lie the 'overriding consideration of humanity'.[200]

Whether the actual possession or threat or use of nuclear weapons would be regarded as illegal in international law has been a highly controversial question,[201] although there is no doubt that such weapons fall within the general application of international humanitarian law.[202] The International Court has emphasised that in examining the legality of any particular situation the principles regulating the resort to force, including the right to self-defence, need to be coupled with the requirement to consider also the norms governing the means and methods of warfare itself. Accordingly, the types of weapons used and the way in which they are used are also part of the legal

---

[197] See e.g. the United States Department of the Army, *Field Manual, The Law of Land Warfare*, FM 27–10, 1956, p. 18 and regarding the UK, *The Law of War on Land*, Part III of the *Manual of Military Law*, 1958, p. 41.

[198] ICJ Reports, 1996, para. 78 ;35 ILM, 1996, p. 827.

[199] *Ibid.*, para. 79; 35 ILM, 1996, p. 827.

[200] *Ibid.* and para. 95; 35 ILM, 1996, p. 829. See also the *Corfu Channel* case, ICJ Reports, 1949, pp. 4, 22; 16 ILR, p. 155. [201] See e.g. *Shimoda v. Japan*, 32 ILR, p. 626.

[202] *Ibid.*, paras. 85–8; 35 ILM, 1996, p. 828. See also e.g. *Nuclear Weapons and International Law* (ed. Pogany), Aldershot, 1987; Green, *Contemporary Law*, pp. 124 *et seq.* and Green, 'Nuclear Weapons and the Law of Armed Conflict', 17 *Denver Journal of International Law and Policy*, 1988, p. 1; N. Singh and E. McWhinney, *Nuclear Weapons and Contemporary International Law*, Dordrecht, 1988; G. Schwarzenberger, *Legality of Nuclear Weapons*, London, 1957 and H. Meyrowitz, 'Les Armes Nucléaires et le Droit de la Guerre' in *Humanitarian Law of Armed Conflict: Challenges* (eds. A. J. M. Delissen and G. J. Tanja), Dordrecht, 1991.

equation in analysing the legitimacy of any use of force in international law.[203]

The Court analysed state practice and concluded that nuclear weapons were not prohibited specifically by express provision.[204] Nor were they prohibited by analogy with poisoned gases prohibited under the Second Hague Declaration of 1899, article 23(a) of the Hague Regulations of 1907 and the Geneva Protocol of 1925.[205] Nor were they prohibited by the series of treaties[206] concerning the acquisition, manufacture, deployment and testing of nuclear weapons and the treaties concerning the ban on such weapons in certain areas of the world.[207] Nor were nuclear weapons prohibited as a consequence of a series of General Assembly resolutions, which taken together fell short of establishing the necessary *opinio juris* for the creation of a new rule to that effect.[208] Insofar as the principles of international humanitarian law were concerned, the Court, beyond noting their applicability, could reach no conclusion. The Court felt unable to determine whether the principle of neutrality or the principles of international humanitarian law or indeed the norm of self-defence prohibited the threat or use of nuclear weapons.[209] This rather weak conclusion, however, should be seen in the context of continuing efforts to ban all nuclear weapons testing, the increasing number of treaties prohibiting such weapons in specific geographical areas and the commitment given in 1995 by the five declared nuclear weapons states not to use such weapons against non-nuclear weapons states that are parties to the Nuclear Non Proliferation Treaty.[210] Nevertheless, it does seem clear that the possession of nuclear weapons and their use *in extremis* and in strict accordance with the criteria

[203] The Court emphasised, for example, that 'a use of force that is proportionate under the law of self-defence, must, in order to be lawful, also meet the requirements of the law applicable in armed conflict', *ibid.*, para. 42; 35 ILM, 1996, p. 822. The Court also pointed to the applicability of the principle of neutrality to all international armed conflicts, irrespective of the type of weaponry used, *ibid.*, para. 89; 35 ILM, 1996, p. 829. See also the *Nicaragua* case, ICJ Reports, pp. 3, 112; 76 ILR, pp. 349, 446.
[204] *Ibid.*, para. 52; 35 ILM, 1996, p. 823.
[205] *Ibid.*, paras. 53–5; 35 ILM, 1996, pp. 823–4. Nor by treaties concerning other weapons of mass destruction such as the Bacteriological Weapons Treaty 1972 and the Chemical Weapons Treaty 1993, *ibid.*, para. 57; 35 ILM, 1996, p. 824.
[206] E.g. the Peace Treaties of 10 February 1947; the Austrian State Treaty 1955; the Nuclear Test Ban Treaty 1963; the Outer Space Treaty 1967; the Treaty of Tlatelolco of 14 February 1967 on the Prohibition of Nuclear Weapons in Latin America; the Nuclear Non-Proliferation Treaty 1968 (extended indefinitely in 1995); the Treaty on the Prohibition of the Emplacement of Nuclear Weapons on the the Ocean Floor and Sub-soil 1971; Treaty of Rarotonga of 6 August 1985 on the Nuclear Weapons-Free Zone of the South Pacific; the Treaty of Final Settlement with Respect to Germany 1990; the Treaty on the South East Asia Nuclear Weapons-Free Zone 1995 and the Treaty on an African Nuclear Weapons-Free Zone 1996.
[207] ICJ Reports, 1996, paras. 58–63; 36 ILM, 1996, pp. 824–6.
[208] *Ibid.*, paras. 70–1; 35 ILM, 1996, p. 826.
[209] *Ibid.*, paras. 94–7 and 105(2) E; 35 ILM, 1996, pp. 829–31.
[210] See Security Council resolution 984 (1995).

governing the right to self-defence are not prohibited under international law.[211]

A number of specific bans on particular weapons has been imposed.[212] Examples would include small projectiles under the St Petersburg formula of 1868, dum-dum bullets under the Hague Declaration of 1899 and asphyxiating and deleterious gases under the Hague Declaration of 1899 and the 1925 Geneva Protocol. [213] Under the 1980 Conventional Weapons Treaty, Protocol I, it is prohibited to use weapons that cannot be detected by X-rays while Protocol II (minimally amended in 1996) prohibits the use of mines and booby-traps against civilians and Protocol III the use of incendiary devices against civilians or against military objectives located within a concentration of civilians where the attack is by air-delivered incendiary weapons.[214]

Article 55 of Protocol I to the 1949 Conventions provides that care is to be taken in warfare to protect the natural environment against widespread, long-term and severe damage. This protection includes a prohibition of the use of methods or means of warfare which are intended or may be expected to cause such damage to the natural environment and thereby to prejudice the health or survival of the population.[215] The Convention on the Prohibition of Military or Any Other Hostile Use of Environmental Modification Techniques 1977 prohibits such activities having widespread, long-lasting or severe effects as the means of destruction, damage or injury to any other state party.

Armed conflicts: international and internal

The rules of international humanitarian law apply to armed conflicts. A distinction has historically been drawn between international and non-international armed conflicts,[216] founded upon the difference between inter-state relations, which was the proper focus for international law, and intra-state matters which traditionally fell within the domestic jurisdiction of states and was thus in principle impervious to international legal regulation. However, this difference has been breaking down in recent decades. In the sphere of humanitarian law, this can be seen in the gradual application of such rules

---

[211] See also the UK *Manual of Military Law*, Part III, section 113 and the US *The Law of Land Warfare*, 1956, s. 35.   [212] See e.g. Green, *Contemporary Law*, pp. 127 *et seq.*
[213] See also e.g. the 1972 Convention on the Prohibition of the Development, Production and Stockpiling of Bacteriological Weapons and the 1993 Convention on the Prohibition of the Development, Production, Stockpiling and Use of Chemical Weapons and Their Destruction. See 21(3) *UN Chronicle*, 1984, p. 3 with regard to the use of chemical weapons in the Iran–Iraq war.   [214] See Shaw, 'Conventional Weapons'.
[215] See, for example, the deliberate spillage of vast quantities of oil into the Persian Gulf by Iraq during the 1991 Gulf War; see *The Economist*, 2 February 1991, p. 20. See also Green, *Contemporary Law*, p. 132.   [216] See e.g. Green, *Contemporary Law*, Chapter 3.

to internal armed conflicts.[217] The notion of an armed conflict itself was raised before the Appeals Chamber of the International Tribunal on War Crimes in Former Yugoslavia in the *Tadić* case.[218] It was claimed that no armed conflict as such existed in the Former Yugoslavia with respect to the circumstances of the instant case since the concept of armed conflict covered only the precise time and place of actual hostilities and the events alleged before the Tribunal did not take place during hostilities. The Appeals Chamber of the Tribunal correctly refused to accept a narrow geographical and temporal definition of armed conflicts, whether international or internal. It was stated that:[219]

> an armed conflict exists whenever there is a resort to armed force between states or protracted armed violence between governmental authorities and organised armed groups or between such groups within a state. International humanitarian law applies from the initiation of such armed conflicts and extends beyond the cessation of hostilities until a general conclusion of peace is reached; or, in the case of internal conflicts, a peaceful settlement is achieved. Until that moment, international humanitarian law continues to apply in the whole territory of the warring states or, in the case of internal conflicts, the whole territory under the control of a party, whether or not actual combat takes place.

This definition arose in the specific context of the Former Yugoslavia, where it was unclear whether an international or a non-international armed conflict or some kind of mixture of the two was involved. This was important to clarify since it would have had an effect upon the relevant applicable law. The Security Council did not as such classify the nature of the conflict, simply condemning widespread violations of international humanitarian law, including mass forcible expulsion and deportation of civilians, imprisonment and abuse of civilians and deliberate attacks upon non-combatants, and calling for the cessation.[220] The Appeals Chamber concluded that 'the conflicts in the former Yugoslavia have both internal and international aspects'.[221] Since such conflicts could be classified differently according to time and place, a particularly complex situation was created. However, many of the difficulties that this would have created were mitigated by an acceptance of the evolving application of humanitarian law to internal armed conflicts.[222] This development has arisen partly because of the increasing frequency of internal conflicts and partly because of the increasing brutality in their conduct. The growing inter-dependence of states in the modern world makes it more and more difficult for third states and international organisations to ignore civil conflicts, especially in view of the scope and insistence of modern communications, while the evolution of international

[217] See further *infra*, p. 817.   [218] Case No. IT-94–1–AR 72, pp. 35 *et seq.*
[219] *Ibid.*, p. 37.   [220] See e.g. Security Council resolution 771 (1992).
[221] Case No. IT-94–1–AR 72, p. 43.   [222] *Ibid.*, pp. 53 *et seq.* and *infra*, p. 817.

human rights law has contributed to the end of the belief and norm that whatever occures within other states is the concern of no other state or person.[223] Accordingly, the international community is now more willing to demand the application of international humanitarian law to internal conflicts.[224]

In the *Tadić* case, the Appeals Chamber concluded that article 3 of its Statute, which gave it jurisdiction over 'violations of the laws or customs of war',[225] provided it with such jurisdiction 'regardless of whether they occurred within an internal or an international armed conflict'.[226]

The United Nations has been concerned to an ever-increasing extent with activities involving its personnel in either an enforcement or peace-keeping capacity within states.[227] The application of international humanitarian law would be appropriate and is UN policy.[228] Nevertheless, there may be some difficulty with the situation where the UN is acting in a purely peace-keeping operation, keeping hostile parties apart, and is thus in a way engaged in an 'armed conflict'.

Non-international armed conflict[229]

Although the 1949 Geneva Conventions were primarily aimed at international armed conflicts, common article 3 did provide in cases of non-international armed conflicts occurring in the territory of one of the parties a series of minimum guarantees for protecting those not taking an active part in hostilities, including the sick and wounded.[230] Precisely where this article

---

[223] See e.g. General Assembly resolutions 2444(XXV) and 2675(XXV), adopted in 1970 unanimously.

[224] See e.g. Security Council resolutions 788 (1992), 972 (1995) and 1001 (1995) with regard to the Liberian civil war; Security Council resolutions 794 (1992) and 814 (1993) with regard to Somalia; and Security Council resolution 993 (1993) with regard to Georgia.

[225] An historic term now subsumed within the concept of international humanitarian law. Article 3 states that such violations shall include, but not be limited to, the employment of poisonous weapons or other weapons calculated to cause unnecessary suffering; wanton destruction of cities, towns or villages or devastation not justified by military necessity; attack or bombardment of undefended towns, villages or buildings; seizure of or destruction or wilful damage done to institutions dedicated to religion, charity and education, the arts and sciences, historic monuments and works of art and science; and plunder of public or private property. [226] Case No. IT-94-1-AR 72, p. 71.

[227] See generally Chapter 20.

[228] See the Model Agreement prepared by the Secretary-General in May 1991 noting that 'United Nations peace-keeping operations shall observe and respect the principles and spirit of the general international conventions applicable to the conduct of military operations.' These conventions would include the 1949 Geneva Conventions and the 1977 Protocols as well as the Convention on the Protection of Cultural Property 1954, see Green, *Contemporary Law*, p. 325.

[229] See e.g. Green, *Contemporary Law*, Chapter 19 and T. Meron, *Human Rights in Internal Strife*, Cambridge, 1987.

[230] Note that the Court in the *Nicaragua* case, ICJ Reports, 1986, pp. 3, 114; 76 ILR, pp. 349, 448, declared that common article 3 also applied to international armed conflicts as a 'minimum yardstick, in addition to the more elaborate rules which are also to apply to international conflicts'.

applied was difficult to define in all cases. Non-international armed conflicts could, it may be argued, range from full-scale civil wars to relatively minor disturbances. This poses problems for the state in question which may not appreciate the political implications of the application of the Geneva Conventions, and the lack of the reciprocity element due to the absence of another state adds to the problems of enforcement. Common article 3 lists the following as the minimum safeguards:

> 1. Persons taking no active part in hostilities to be treated humanely without any adverse distinction based on race, colour, religion or faith, sex, birth or wealth.
> To this end the following are prohibited:
> (a) violence to life and person, in particular murder, cruel treatment and torture;
> (b) hostage-taking;
> (c) outrages upon human dignity, in particular humiliating and degrading treatment;
> (d) the passing of sentences and the carrying out of executions in the absence of due process.
> 2. The wounded and the sick are to be cared for.

Common article 3 was developed by Protocol II, 1977,[231] which applies by virtue of article 1 to all non-international armed conflicts which take place in the territory of a state party between its armed forces and dissident armed forces. The latter have to be under responsible command and exercise such control over a part of its territory as to enable them to carry out sustained and concerted military operations and actually implement Protocol II. It does not apply to situations of internal disturbances and tensions, such as riots, isolated and sporadic acts of violence and other acts of a similar nature, not being armed conflicts. The Protocol lists a series of fundamental guarantees and other provisions calling for the protection of non-combatants. In particular, one may note the prohibitions on violence to the life, health and physical and mental well-being of persons, including torture; collective punishment; hostage-taking; acts of terrorism; outrages upon personal dignity, including rape and enforced prostitution; and pillage.[232] Further provisions cover the protection of children;[233] the protection of civilians, including the prohibition of attacks on works or installations containing dangerous forces that might cause severe losses among civilians;[234] the treatment of civilians, including their displace-

[231] Note, of course, that by article 1(4) of Protocol I, 1977, international armed conflicts are now deemed to include wars against colonial domination, alien occupation and racist regimes. See D. Forsyth, 'Legal Management of International War', 72 AJIL, 1978, p. 272. Note also the UK view that 'a high level of intensity of military operations' is required regarding Protocol I so that the Northern Ireland situation, for example, would not be covered, see 941 HC Deb., col. 237.   [232] See article 4.   [233] Article 6.
[234] Article 15.

ment;[235] and the treatment of prisoners and detainees,[236] and the wounded and sick.[237]

It is also to be noted that there exists an area of civil conflict which is not covered by humanitarian law since it falls below the necessary threshold of common articles 3 and Protocol II.[238] Moves have been underway to bridge the gap between this and the application of international human rights law.[239] The International Committee of the Red Cross has been considering the elaboration of a new declaration on internal strife. In addition, the UN Sub-Commission on the Prevention of Discrimination and the Protection of Minorities has adopted a Declaration of Minimum Humanitarian Standards,[240] which is currently under consideration.[241] This Declaration emphasises the prohibition of violence to the life, health and physical and mental well-being of persons including murder, torture and rape; collective punishment; hostage-taking; practicing, permitting or tolerating the involuntary disappearance of individuals; pillage; deliberate deprivation of access to necessary food, drinking water and medicine, and threats or incitement to commit any of these acts.[242] In addition, the Declaration provides *inter alia* that persons deprived of their liberty should be held in recognised places of detention (article 4); that acts or threats of violence to spread terror are prohibited (article 6); that all human beings have the inherent right to life (article 8); that children are to be protected so that, for example, children under fifteen years of age should not be permitted to join armed groups or forces (article 10); that the wounded and sick should be cared for (article 12) and medical, religious and other humanitarian personnel should be protected and assisted (article 14).[243]

[235] Article 17.   [236] Article 5.   [237] Article 10.
[238] See A. Hay, 'The ICRC and International Humanitarian Issues', *International Review of the Red Cross*, Jan.–Feb. 1984, p. 3. See also T. Meron, 'Towards a Humanitarian Declaration on Internal Strife', 78 AJIL, 1984, p. 859; Meron, *Human Rights in Internal Strife*, and Meron, 'On the Inadequate Reach of Humanitarian and Human Rights Law and the Need for a New Instrument', 77 AJIL, 1983, p. 589, and T. Meron and A. Rosas, 'A Declaration of Minimum Humanitarian Standards', 85 AJIL, 1991, p. 375.
[239] As to international human rights law, see generally Chapter 6. Problems centre upon the situation where humanitarian law does not apply since the threshold criteria for applicability have not been reached; where the state in question is not a party to the relevant instrument; where derogation from the specified standards is involved as a consequence of the declaration of a state of emergency, and where the party concerned is not a government, see A. Eide, A. Rosas and T. Meron, 'Combating Lawlessness in Gray Zone Conflicts Through Minimum Humanitarian Standards', 89 AJIL, 1995, pp. 215, 217.
[240] E/CN.4/Sub.2/1991/55.
[241] See e.g. UN Sub-Commision resolution 1994/26, UN Commission on Human Rights resolution 1995/29 and E/CN.4/1995/81 and 116. See also A. Eide *et al.*, 'Combating Lawlessness'.   [242] Article 3.
[243] See also the Declaration for the Protection of War Victims, 1993, A/48/742, Annex.

Enforcement of humanitarian law [244]

Parties to the 1949 Geneva Conventions and to Protocol I, 1977, undertake to respect and to ensure respect for the instrument in question,[245] and to disseminate knowledge of the principles contained therein.[246] A variety of enforcement methods also exist, although the use of reprisals has been prohibited.[247] One of the means of implementation is the concept of the Protecting Power, appointed to look after the interests of nationals of one party to a conflict under the control of the other, whether as prisoners of war or occupied civilians.[248] Sweden and Switzerland performed this role during the Second World War. Such a Power must ensure that compliance with the relevant provisions has been effected and that the system acts as a form of guarantee for the protected person as well as a channel of communication for him with the state of which he is a national.

The drawback of this system is its dependence upon the consent of the parties involved. Not only must the Protecting Power be prepared to act in that capacity, but both the state of which the protected person is a national and the state holding such persons must give their consent for the system to operate.[249] Since the role is so central to the enforcement and working of humanitarian law, it is a disadvantage for it to be subject to state sovereignty and consent. It only requires the holding state to refuse its co-operation for this structure of implementation to be greatly weakened leaving only reliance upon voluntary operations. This has occurred on a number of occasions, for example the Chinese refusal to consent to the appointment of a Protecting Power with regard to its conflict with India in 1962, and the Indian refusal, of 1971 and subsequently, with regard to Pakistani prisoners of war in its charge.[250] Protocol I also provides for an International Fact-Finding Commission for competence to inquire into grave breaches[251] of the Geneva Conventions and that Protocol or other serious violations, and to facilitate through its good offices the 'restoration of an attitude of respect' for these instruments.[252] The parties to a conflict may themselves, of course, establish an ad hoc inquiry into alleged violations of humanitarian law.[253]

It is, of course, also the case that breaches of international law in this field

[244] See e.g. Best, War and Law, pp. 370 et seq.   [245] Article 1 in all instruments.
[246] See e.g. articles 127 and 144 of the Third and Fourth Geneva Conventions, article 83 of Protocol I and article 19 of Protocol II.   [247] See e.g. articles 20 and 51(6) of Protocol I.
[248] See e.g. Draper, 'Implementation and Enforcement', pp. 13 et seq.
[249] See articles 8, 8, 8 and 9 of the Four Geneva Conventions 1949, respectively.
[250] Note that the system did operate in the Falklands conflict, with Switzerland acting as the Protecting Power of the UK and Brazil as the Protecting Power of Argentina, see e.g. Levie, 'Falklands Crisis', pp. 68–9.
[251] See articles 50, 51, 130 and 147 of the four 1949 Conventions respectively and article 85 of Protocol I, 1977.   [252] Article 90, Protocol I, 1977.
[253] Articles 52, 53, 132 and 149 of the four 1949 Conventions respectively.

may constitute war crimes for which universal jurisdiction is provided.[254] It is to be noted in particular that article 6 of the Charter of the Nuremberg Tribunal 1945 includes as examples of war crimes for which there is to be individual responsibility the murder, ill-treatment or deportation to slave labour of the civilian population of an occupied territory; the ill-treatment of prisoners of war; the killing of hostages and the wanton destruction of cities, towns and villages.[255]

A great deal of valuable work in the sphere of humanitarian law has been accomplished by the International Red Cross.[256] This indispensable organisation consists of the International Committee of the Red Cross (ICRC), over one hundred national Red Cross (or Red Crescent) societies with a League co-ordinating their activities, and conferences of all these elements every four years.

The ICRC is the most active body and has a wide-ranging series of functions to perform, including working for the application of the Geneva Conventions and acting in natural and man-made disasters. It has operated in a large number of states, visiting prisoners of war[257] and otherwise functioning to ensure the implementation of humanitarian law. It operates in both international and internal armed conflict situations. One of the largest operations it has undertaken since 1948 related to the Nigerian Civil war, and in that conflict nearly twenty of its personnel were killed on duty. The ICRC has since been deeply involved in the Yugoslav situation and indeed in 1992, contrary to its usual confidentiality approach, it felt impelled to speak out publicly against the grave breaches of humanitarian law taking place. The organisation has also been involved in Somalia (where its activities including visiting detainees held by the UN forces), Rwanda, Afghanistan and Sri Lanka.[258] Due to circumstances, the ICRC must act with great tact and discretion and in many cases states refuse their co-operation. It performed a valuable function in the exchange of prisoners after the 1967 and 1973 Middle East Wars, although for several years Israel did not accept the ICRC role regarding the Arab territories it occupied.[259]

[254] See e.g. Draper, *Implementation and Enforcement*, pp. 35 *et seq.*
[255] See *supra*, Chapters 5, p. 184 and 12, p. 471, with regard to war crimes, individual criminal responsibility and the establishment of the Yugoslav and Rwanda War Crimes Tribunals, and the proposal for an International Criminal Court.
[256] See e.g. G. Willemin and R. Heacock, *The International Committee of the Red Cross*, The Hague, 1984 and D. Forsythe, 'The Red Cross as Transnational Movement', 30 *International Organisation*, 1967, p. 607. See also Best, *War and Law*, pp. 347 *et seq.*
[257] See e.g. articles 126 and 142 of the Third and Fourth Geneva Conventions respectively.
[258] See e.g. *Challenges of the Nineties: ICRC Special Report on Activities 1990–1995*, 1995, Geneva. Between 1990 and 1994, over half a million prisoners in over sixty countries were visited by ICRC delegates, *ibid.*
[259] See generally *Annual Report of the ICRC*, 1982. See also 'Action by the ICRC in the Event of Breaches of International Humanitarian Law', *International Review of the Red Cross*, March–April 1981, p. 1.

Conclusion

The ICRC recently formulated the following principles as a guide to the relevant legal rules:

1. Persons *hors de combat* and those who do not take a direct part in hostilities are entitled to respect for their lives and physical and moral integrity. They shall in all circumstances be protected and treated humanely without any adverse distinction.
2. It is forbidden to kill or injure an enemy who surrenders or who is *hors de combat*.
3. The wounded and sick shall be collected and cared for by the party to the conflict which has them in its power. Protection also covers medical personnel, establishments, transports and *matériel*. The emblem of the red cross (red crescent, red lion and sun) is the sign of such protection and must be respected.
4. Captured combatants and civilians under the authority of an adverse party are entitled to respect for their lives, dignity, personal rights and convictions. They shall be protected against all acts of violence and reprisals. They shall have the right to correspond with their families and to receive relief.
5. Everyone shall be entitled to benefit from fundamental judicial guarantees. No one shall be held responsible for an act he has not committed. No one shall be subjected to physical or mental torture, corporal punishment or cruel or degrading treatment.
6. Parties to a conflict and members of their armed forces do not have an unlimited choice of methods and means of warfare. It is prohibited to employ weapons or methods of warfare of a nature to cause unnecessary losses or excessive suffering.
7. Parties to a conflict shall at all times distinguish between the civilian population and combatants in order to spare civilian population and property. Neither the civilian populations as such nor civilian persons shall be the object for attack. Attacks shall be directed solely against military objectives.[260]

In addition, the ICRC has published the following statement with regard to non-international armed conflicts:

A. General Rules
1. The obligation to distinguish between combatants and civilians is a general rule applicable in non-international armed conflicts. It prohibits indiscriminate attacks.
2. The prohibition of attacks against the civilian population as such or against individual civilians is a general rule applicable in non-international armed conflicts. Acts of violence intended primarily to spread terror among the civilian population are also prohibited.
3. The prohibition of superfluous injury or unnecessary suffering is a general rule applicable in non-international armed conflicts. It prohibits, in particular, the use of means of warfare which uselessly aggravate the sufferings of disabled men or render their death inevitable.

[260] See *International Review of the Red Cross*, September–October, 1978, p. 247. See also Green, *Contemporary Law*, pp. 335–6.

4. The prohibition to kill, injure or capture an adversary by resort to perfidy is a general rule applicable in non-international armed conflicts; in a non-international armed conflict, acts inviting the confidence of an adversary to lead him to believe that he is entitled to, or obliged to accord protection under the rules of international law applicable in non-international armed conflicts, with intent to betray that confidence, shall constitute perfidy.

5. The obligation to respect and protect medical and religious personnel and medical units and transports in the conduct of military operations is a general rule applicable in non-international armed conflicts.

6. The general rule prohibiting attacks against the civilian population implies, as a corollary, the prohibition of attacks on dwellings and other installations which are used only by the civilian population.

7. The general rule prohibiting attacks against the civilian population implies, as a corollary, the prohibition to attack, destroy, remove or render useless objects indispensable to the survival of the civilian population.

8. The general rule to distinguish between combatants and civilians and the prohibition of attack against the civilian population as such or against individual civilians implies, in order to be effective, that all feasible precautions have to be taken to avoid injury, loss or damage to the civilian population.[261]

[261] See *ibid.*, Sept.–Oct., 1989, p. 404. See also Green, *Contemporary Law*, p. 336. Part B of this Declaration dealing with Prohibitions and Restrictions on the Use of Certain Weapons has been omitted. It may be found at the above references.

CHAPTER 20

THE UNITED NATIONS

The UN system

The United Nations[1] was established following the conclusion of the Second World War and in the light of Allied planning and intentions expressed during that conflict.[2]

The purposes of the UN are set out in article 1 of the Charter as follows:

1. To maintain international peace and security, and to that end, to take effective collective measures for the prevention and removal of threats to the peace, and for the suppression of acts of aggression or other breaches of the peace, and to bring about by peaceful means, and in conformity with the principles of justice and international law, adjustment or settlement of international disputes or situations which might lead to a breach of the peace;

2. To develop friendly relations among nations based on respect for the principle of equal rights and self-determination of peoples, and to take other appropriate measures to strengthen universal peace;

3. To achieve international co-operation in solving international problems of an economic, social, cultural or humanitarian character, and in promoting and encouraging respect for human rights and for fundamental freedoms for all without distinction as to race, sex, language, or religion; and

4. To be a centre for harmonizing the actions of nations in the attainment of these common ends.

While the purposes are clearly wide-ranging, they do provide a useful guide to the comprehensiveness of its concerns. The question of priorities as between the various issues noted is constantly subject to controversy and change, but this only reflects the continuing pressures and altering political

---

[1] See e.g. *United Nations Legal Order* (eds. O. Schachter and C. C. Joyner), Cambridge, 2 vols., 1995; D. W. Bowett, *The Law of International Institutions*, 4th edn, London, 1982, Chapter 3; *The United Nations and a Just World Order* (eds. R. A. Falk, S. S. Kim and S. H. Mendlovitz), Boulder, CO, 1991; B. Broms, *United Nations*, Helsinki, 1990; E. Luard, *A History of the United Nations*, London, 1982, vol. 1; R. Higgins, *The Development of International Law Through the Political Organs of the United Nations*, Oxford, 1963; *United Nations, Divided World* (eds. A. Roberts and B. Kingsbury), 2nd edn, Oxford, 1993; L. M. Goodrich, *The United Nations in a Changing World*, New York, 1974; L. B. Sohn, *Cases on United Nations Law*, 2nd edn, New York, 1967 and the *Bertrand Report*, 1985, A/40/988. See also L. M. Goodrich, E. Hambro and A. P. Simons, *Charter of the United Nations*, 3rd edn, New York, 1969; *The Charter of the United Nations* (ed. B. Simma), Oxford, 1995; and *La Charte des Nations Unies* (eds. J. P. Cot and A. Pellet), Paris, 1991.   [2] See UNCIO, 15 vols., 1945.

balances within the organisation. In particular, the emphasis upon decolonisation, self-determination and apartheid mirrored the growth in UN
membership and the dismantling of the colonial empires, while increasing
concern with economic and developmental issues is now very apparent and
clearly reflects the adverse economic conditions in various parts of the world.
The Charter of the United Nations is not only the multilateral treaty
which created the organisation and outlined the rights and obligations of
those states signing it, it is also the constitution of the UN, laying down its
functions and prescribing its limitations. Foremost amongst these is the
recognition of the sovereignty and independence of the member states.
Under article 2(7) of the Charter, the UN may not intervene in matters
essentially within the domestic jurisdiction of any state (unless enforcement
measures under Chapter VII are to be applied). This provision has inspired
many debates in the UN, and it came to be accepted that colonial issues
were not to be regarded as falling within the article 2(7) restriction. Other
changes have also occurred, demonstrating that the concept of domestic
jurisdiction is not immutable but a principle of international law delineat-
ing international and domestic spheres of operations. As a principle of international law it is susceptible of change through international law and is not
dependent upon the unilateral determination of individual states.[3]

In addition to the domestic jurisdiction provision, article 2 also lays down
a variety of other principles in accordance with which both the UN and the
member states are obliged to act. These include the assertion that the UN
is based upon the sovereign equality of states and the principles of fulfilment
in good faith of the obligations contained in the Charter, the peaceful settlement of disputes and the prohibition on the use of force. It is also provided
that member states must assist the organisation in its activities taken in
accordance with the Charter and must refrain from assisting states against
which the UN is taking preventive or enforcement action.

The UN has six principal organs, these being the Security Council,
General Assembly, Economic and Social Council, Trusteeship Council,
Secretariat and International Court of Justice.

The Security Council[4]

The Council was intended to operate as an efficient executive organ of
limited membership, functioning continuously. It was given primary

---

[3] See *supra*, Chapter 12, p. 454.
[4] See e.g. S. Bailey, *Voting in the Security Council*, Oxford, 1969, and Bailey, *The Procedure of
the Security Council*, 2nd edn, Oxford, 1988; Bowett, *Law*, pp. 26–42 and R. Higgins, 'The
Place of International Law in the Settlement of Disputes by the Security Council', 64 AJIL,
1970, p. 1. See also M. C. Wood, 'Security Council Working Methods and Procedure:
Recent Developments', 45 ICLQ, 1996, p. 150.

responsibility for the maintenance of international peace and security.[5] The Security Council consists of fifteen members, five of them being permanent members (USA, UK, Russia, China and France). These permanent members, chosen on the basis of power politics in 1945, have the veto. Under article 27 of the Charter, on all but procedural matters, decisions of the Council must be made by an affirmative vote of nine members, including the concurring votes of the permanent members.

A negative vote by any of the permanent members is therefore sufficient to veto any resolution of the Council, save with regard to procedural questions, where nine affirmative votes are all that is required. The veto was written into the Charter in view of the exigencies of power. The USSR, in particular, would not have been willing to accept the UN as it was envisaged without the establishment of the veto to protect it from the Western bias of the Council and General Assembly at that time.[6] In practice, the veto was exercised by the Soviet Union on a considerable number of occasions, and by the US less frequently, and by the other members fairly rarely. The question of how one distinguishes between procedural and non-procedural matters has been a highly controversial one. In the statement of the Sponsoring Powers at San Francisco, it was declared that the issue of whether or not a matter was procedural was itself subject to the veto.[7] This 'double-veto' constitutes a formidable barrier, but it is possible under the Rules of Procedure for the President of the Security Council to rule that a matter is procedural and if the ruling is supported by nine members the issue is resolved.[8] Subsequent practice has interpreted the phrase 'concurring votes of the permanent members' in article 27 in such a way as to permit abstentions. Accordingly, permanent members may abstain with regard to a resolution of the Security Council without being deemed to have exercised their veto against it.[9]

It does not, of course, follow that the five supreme powers of 1945 will continue to hold that rank. However, the complicated mechanisms for amendment of the Charter,[10] coupled with the existence of the veto, make

---

[5] Articles 23, 24, 25 and 28 of the UN Charter.
[6] See e.g. H. G. Nicholas, *The United Nations as a Political Institution*, Oxford, 1975, pp. 10–13.
[7] *Repertory of Practice of UN Organs*, vol. II, 1955, p. 104. See also Bowett, *Law*, p. 30.
[8] *Ibid.*, p. 31.
[9] See e.g. A. Stavropoulos, 'The Practice of Voluntary Abstentions by Permanent Members of the Security Council under article 27(3) of the Charter', 61 AJIL, 1967, p. 737. See also the *Namibia* case, ICJ Reports, 1971, pp. 16, 22; 49 ILR, pp. 2, 12, recognising this practice as lawful.
[10] See articles 108 and 109 of the Charter, which require *inter alia* the consent of all the permanent members to any amendment to or alteration of the Charter. It may indeed be suggested that the speed with which Russia was accepted as the continuance of the former USSR with regard to the permanent seat on the Security Council partly arose out of a desire by the Council to avoid opening up the question of membership for general debate, see F. Kirgis, *International Organisations in their Legal Setting*, 2nd edn, St Paul, 1993. pp. 188 *et seq.* See also *supra*, Chapter 17, p. 677.

any change unlikely.[11] Of the ten non-permanent seats, it is accepted that five should be allocated to Afro-Asian states, one to Eastern Europe, two to Latin America, and two to Western European and other powers.[12]

The Security Council acts on behalf of the members of the organisation as a whole in performing its functions, and its decisions (but not its recommendations)[13] are binding upon all member states.[14] Its powers are concentrated in two particular categories, the peaceful settlement of disputes and the adoption of enforcement measures. By these means, the Council conducts its primary task, the maintenance of international peace and security. However, the Council also has a variety of other functions. In the case of trusteeship territories, for example, designated strategic areas fall within the authority of the Security Council rather than the General Assembly,[15] while the admission, suspension and expulsion of member states is carried out by the General Assembly upon the recommendation of the Council.[16] Amendments to the UN Charter require the ratification of all the permanent members of the Council (as well as adoption by a two-thirds vote of the Assembly and ratification by two-thirds of UN members).[17] The judges of the International Court are elected by the Assembly and Council.[18]

The Council has not fulfilled the expectations held of it in the years following the inception of the organisation. This has basically been because of the superpower rivalry which prevented the Council from taking action on any matter regarded as of importance by any of the five members, and the veto was the means by which this was achieved. However, this does tend to mean that initiatives taken by the Council are fairly highly regarded since they inevitably reflect a consensus of opinion amongst its members, and more particularly amongst its permanent members. For example, Security Council resolution 242 (1967)[19] laid down the basis for negotiations for a Middle East peace settlement and is regarded as the most authoritative expression of the principles to be taken into account.[20] Hopes for the

---

[11] Note, however, that the General Assembly has been considering the question of the 'equitable representation on and increase in the membership of the Security Council' and an open-ended working group was established to consider the matter further, see e.g. General Assembly resolution 48/26. See also the Report of the Secretary-General, A/48/264.

[12] General Assembly resolution 1991(XVIII).

[13] Compare, for example, article 36 of the Charter (peaceful settlement) with articles 41, 42 and 44 (enforcement actions). [14] Article 25 of the Charter.

[15] See articles 82 and 83 of the Charter.

[16] See articles 4, 5 and 6 of the Charter. The restoration of the rights and privileges of a suspended member is by the Council, article 5.

[17] Article 108. A similar requirement operates with regard to alteration of the Charter by a General Conference of Members, see article 109.

[18] Article 4 of the Statute of the International Court of Justice.

[19] This resolution was reaffirmed in resolution 338 (1973).

[20] See generally, I. Pogany, *The Security Council and the Arab-Israeli Conflict*, Aldershot, 1984, Chapter 5 and A. Shapira, 'The Security Council Resolution of November 22, 1967 – Its Legal Nature and Implications', 4 *Israel Law Review*, 1969, p. 229.

transformation of the Security Council into the body it was intended to be rose with the development of the *glasnost* and *perestroika* policies in the Soviet Union in the late 1980s. Increasing co-operation with the US ensued and this reached its highest point as the Kuwait crisis evolved and the Council adopted a series of twelve crucial and binding resolutions, culminating in resolution 678 (1990), which authorised the use of all necessary means in order to bring about an Iraqi withdrawal from Kuwait and the restoration of international peace and security in that region.[21] It remains to be seen whether such a transformation on a long-term basis will continue.

The failure of the Council in its primary responsibility to preserve world peace stimulated a number of other developments. It encouraged the General Assembly to assume a residual responsibility for maintaining international peace and security, it encouraged the Secretary-General to take upon himself a more active role and it hastened the development of peace-keeping operations. It also encouraged in some measure the establishment of the military alliances, such as NATO and the Warsaw Pact, which arose as a consequence of the onset of the Cold War and constituted, in effect, regional enforcement systems by-passing the Security Council.

The General Assembly[22]

The General Assembly is the parliamentary body of the UN organisation and consists of representatives of all the member states, of which there are now 185. Membership, as provided by article 4 of the Charter, is open to:

> all other peace-loving states which accept the obligations contained in the present Charter and, in the judgment of the organisation, are able and willing to carry out these obligations,

and is effected by a decision of the General Assembly upon the recommendation of the Security Council.

However, in practice, the process of admitting states to membership became enmeshed in the rivalries of the Cold War and objections were raised as regards states of different ideological persuasions. Despite an advisory opinion by the International Court of Justice that only the conditions enumerated in article 4 were to be taken into account in considering a

---

[21] *Infra*, p. 860. See also *The Kuwait Crisis: Basic Documents* (eds. E. Lauterpacht, C. Greenwood, M. Weller, D. Bethlehem), Cambridge, 1991.
[22] See e.g. Bowett, *Law*, pp. 42 *et seq.*; Nicholas, *United Nations*, Chapter 5; B. Finley, *The Structure of the United Nations General Assembly*, 3 vols., Dobbs Ferry, 1977 and S. Bailey, *The General Assembly of the United Nations*, London, 1964.

request for membership,[23] the practice continued until 1955, when a package deal was concluded and a group of sixteen new members was admitted.[24] On occasions, applications for membership to the UN have been the subject of veto in the Security Council.[25] Other changes do take place. For example in 1991, Byelorussia informed the UN that it had changed its name to Belarus, while the Czech and Slovak Federal Republic ceased to exist on 31 December 1992 to be replaced by two new states (the Czech Republic and Slovakia), who were accepted as UN members on 19 January 1993. The former German Democratic Republic ceased to exist and its territory was absorbed into the Federal Republic of Germany as from 3 October 1990, while 'The Former Yugoslav Republic of Macedonia' was admitted to the UN on 8 April 1993 under that unusual appellation.

Membership of the UN may be suspended under article 5 of the Charter by the General Assembly, upon the recommendation of the Security Council, where the member state concerned is the object of preventive or enforcement action by the Security Council. Article 6 allows for expulsion of a member by the General Assembly, upon the recommendation of the Security Council, where the member state has persistently violated the Principles contained in the Charter.[26] A rather different situation has arisen with regard to Yugoslavia. In 1992, the General Assembly decided upon a Security Council recommendation that the Federal Republic of Yugoslavia (Serbia and Montenegro) could not simply take over the UN membership of the Former Yugoslavia, but would have to apply anew for membership.[27] The issue of membership is here tangential to that of statehood and the view to be taken by the international community as to whether the Federal Republic of Yugoslavia is a new state, in which case it would have to apply for membership of the UN, or a continuation of the Former Yugoslavia, in which case its membership simply continues.

Certain situations may fall below suspension or expulsion and controversies have arisen. The question of refusal of credentials to General Assembly delegations has occasionally arisen in a context beyond mere examination

[23] The *Conditions of Admission of a State to Membership of the United Nations* case, ICJ Reports, 1948, p. 57; 15 ILR, p. 333. See also the *Competence of the General Assembly for the Admission of a State to the United Nations* case, ICJ Reports, 1950, p. 4; 17 ILR, p. 326, where the Court held that the General Assembly alone could not effect membership in the absence of a recommendation by the Security Council.

[24] See e.g. Bowett, *Law*, p. 43 and Luard, *History*, Chapter 19. See also *Charter of the United Nations* (ed. Simma), p. 161 and L. Gross, 'Progress Towards the Universality of Membership in the UN', 50 AJIL, 1956, p. 808.

[25] For example the vetoes cast by China against Bangladesh in 1972 and by the US against Angola and Vietnam in 1976, see Kirgis, *International Organisations*, pp. 144 *et seq.* These vetoes were not renewed, so that Bangladesh, Angola and Vietnam became members of the UN in 1974, 1976 and 1977 respectively.   [26] See article 2.

[27] See General Assembly resolution 47/1 and Security Council resolution 777 (1992). See also *supra*, Chapter 17, p. 678.

of formalities as envisaged by article 9 of the Charter and Rule 27 of the Rules of Procedure of the General Assembly[28] and problems caused by disputed governments.[29] In 1974, the credentials of the South African representative were not accepted[30] and this was interpreted by the President of the General Assembly as meaning that South Africa could not participate in the work of the Assembly. This approach, which differed from that adopted in previous years, was approved by the General Assembly.[31]

Voting in the Assembly is governed by article 18, which stipulates that each member has one vote only and that decisions on 'important questions', including the admission of new members and recommendations relating to international peace and security, are to be made by a two-thirds majority of members present and voting. Other decisions may be taken by a simple majority. This system of one state one vote, although logical in view of the sovereign equality of states, has given rise to considerable criticism, especially when it is realised that in many cases the combined populations of two-thirds of member states may be far less than that of the remaining one-third. Many members of the UN have populations of under 2 million, whereas China has a population well over 1 billion; India has a population approaching that figure and the US has a population in the region of 250 million. This has led to complaints at the apparent inequity of having hostile Assembly resolutions adopted by what amounts to a minority of the world's population, even though something over 90 states may be involved.[32] The position has been underlined by the emergence of bloc voting, whereby, for example, the Afro-Asian states agree to adopt a common stance on particular issues. This means that on a number of occasions resolutions have been passed against the wishes of those states that alone have the actual resources to carry out the terms of such resolutions.

Accordingly, a degree of unreality has pervaded the General Assembly on occasions, as resounding majorities have been accumulated by states that are, in essence, weak in both population and means. On the other hand, this is

[28] See e.g. *The Charter of the United Nations*, pp. 221 *et seq.*; D. Ciobanu, 'Credentials of Delegations and Representation of Member States at the United Nations', 25 ICLQ, 1976, p. 351 and M. Halberstam, 'Excluding Israel from the General Assembly by a Rejection of Its Credentials', 78 AJIL, 1984, p. 179.
[29] Where e.g. the General Assembly has been accepted as having the right to chose between rival claimants seeking accreditation as representatives of a particular member state, see Ciobanu, 'Credentials', p. 368.   [30] *Ibid.*
[31] See e.g. *The Charter of the United Nations*, p. 225. The legality of this has been challenged, *ibid.* Note also the view of the UN Legal Counsel in 1970 that 'participation in the meetings of the General Assembly is quite clearly one of the important rights and privileges of membership. Suspension of this right through the rejection of credentials would not satisfy the foregoing requirements [i.e. of article 5 of the Charter] and would therefore be contrary to the Charter', *United Nations Juridical Yearbook*, 1970, New York, pp. 169–70.
[32] See e.g. Bowett, *Law*, p. 44. See also G. Clarke and L. Sohn, *World Peace Through World Law*, Cambridge, MA, 1958, pp. 19–30; *The Strategy of World Order* (eds. R. A. Falk and S. H. Mendlovitz), New York, 1966, vol. III, pp. 272 *et seq.* and Sohn, *Cases*, pp. 248 *et seq.*

probably the most effective way in which the developing nations of the Third World can assert their views. In any event, no acceptable alternative has been proposed and the interests of the five permanent members of the Security Council, at least, are safeguarded by the existence of the veto in the Council.

Except for certain internal matters, such as the budget,[33] the Assembly cannot bind its members. It is not a legislature in that sense, and its resolutions are purely recommendatory. Such resolutions, of course, may be binding if they reflect rules of customary international law and they are significant as instances of state practice that may lead to the formation of a new customary rule, but Assembly resolutions in themselves cannot establish binding legal obligations for member states.[34] The Assembly is essentially a debating chamber, a forum for the exchange of ideas and the discussion of a wide-ranging category of problems. It meets in annual sessions, but special sessions may be called by the Secretary-General at the request of the Security Council or a majority of UN members.[35] Such special sessions have been held, for example, to discuss the issues of Palestine in 1947–8, Namibia (South West Africa) in 1967, 1978 and 1986 and to debate the world economic order in 1974, 1975 and 1990. Other issues covered include financing the UN Interim Force in Lebanon in 1978, apartheid in 1989, disarmament in 1978, 1982 and 1988, and drug abuse in 1990. Emergency sessions may also be called by virtue of the Uniting for Peace machinery.[36] Nine such sessions have been convened, covering situations ranging from various aspects of the Middle East situation in 1956, 1958, 1967, 1980 and 1982 to Afghanistan in 1980 and Namibia in 1981.

The role of the Assembly has increased since its inception, due not only to the failure of the Security Council to function effectively in the light of East–West hostility, but also to the enormous growth in membership since the advent of decolonisation. These states are jealous of their independence and eager to play a significant part in world affairs, and the General Assembly is the ideal stage. In the sphere of peace-keeping, the influence and activity of the Assembly have proved vital in the creation and consolidation of a new method of maintaining international peace.[37]

To aid it in its work, the Assembly has established a variety of organs covering a wide range of topics and activities. It has six main committees that cover respectively disarmament and international security; economic and financial; social, humanitarian and cultural; special political and decolonisation; administrative and budgetary; and legal matters.[38] In addition, there

---

[33] Article 17 of the Charter. [34] See further *supra*, Chapter 3, p. 90.
[35] Article 20 of the Charter. [36] *Infra*, p. 879.
[37] *Infra*, p. 846.
[38] See e.g. Broms, *United Nations*, pp. 198 *et seq*. Note that in 1993, the Special Political Committee was merged with the Fourth Committee on Decolonisation, see General Assembly resolution 47/233.

is a procedural General Committee dealing with agenda issues and a Credentials Committee. There are also two Standing Committees dealing with inter-sessional administrative and budgetary questions and contributions, and a number of subsidiary, *ad hoc* and other bodies dealing with relevant topics including an Investments Committee and a Board of Auditors. The better known of such bodies include the International Law Commission, the UN Commission on International Trade Law, the UN Institute for Training and Research, the Council for Namibia and the UN Relief and Works Agency.[39]

The Economic and Social Council[40]

Much of the work of the United Nations in the economic and social spheres of activity is performed by the Economic and Social Council, which is a principal organ of the UN. It has the capacity to discuss a wide range of matters, but its powers are restricted and its recommendations are not binding upon UN member states. It consists of fifty-four members elected by the Assembly for 3 year terms with staggered elections and each member has one vote.[41] The Council may, by article 62, initiate or make studies upon a range of issues and make recommendations to the General Assembly, the members of the UN and to the relevant specialised agencies. It may prepare draft conventions for submission to the Assembly and call international conferences. The Council has created a variety of subsidiary organs ranging from nine functional commissions (including the Statistical Commission, the Commission on Human Rights, the Commission on the Status of Women and the Commission on Sustainable Development) to five regional commissions (on Africa, Asia and the Pacific, Europe, Latin America and the Caribbean, and Western Asia) and a number of standing committees and expert bodies (including the Commission on Transnational Corporations; the Commission on Human Settlements; the Committee on Natural Resources; the Committee on Economic, Social and Cultural Rights and the Committee on New and Renewable Sources of Energy and on Energy for Development). The Council also runs a variety of programmes including the Environment Programme and the Drug Control Programme, and has established a number of other bodies such as the Office of the UN High Commissioner for Refugees and the UN Conference on Trade and Development. Its most prominent function has

[39] See e.g. *1993 United Nations Handbook*, Wellington, 1993, pp. 24 *et seq.*
[40] See e.g. *ibid.*, pp. 77 *et seq.*, and Broms, *United Nations*, Chapter 11. See also W. R. Sharp, *The UN Economic and Social Council*, New York, 1969 and *supra*, Chapter 6, p. 225.
[41] Article 61 of the Charter. Note that under article 69, any member of the UN may be invited to participate in its deliberations without a vote.

been in establishing a wide range of economic, social and human rights bodies.

The Trusteeship Council[42]

The Trusteeship Council was established in order to supervise the trust territories created after the end of the Second World War.[43] Such territories were to consist of mandated territories, areas detached from enemy states as a result of the Second World War and other territories voluntarily placed under the trusteeship system by the administering authority (of which there have been none).[44] The only former mandated territory which was not placed under the new system or granted independence was South West Africa.[45] With the independence of Palau on 1 October 1994, the last remaining trust territory, the Council suspended operation on 1 November that year.[46]

The Secretariat[47]

The Secretariat of the UN consists of the Secretary-General and his staff, and constitutes virtually an international civil service. The staff are appointed by article 101 upon the basis of efficiency, competence and integrity, 'due regard' being paid 'to the importance of recruiting the staff on as wide a geographical basis as possible'. All member states have undertaken, under article 100, to respect the exclusively international character of

---

[42] See e.g. Broms, *United Nations*, Chapter 12, Bowett, *Law*, pp. 72–87 and Toussaint, *The Trusteeship System of the United Nations*, 1956.

[43] By article 83 of the Charter, the functions of the UN relating to strategic areas were to be exercised by the Security Council (where each permanent member has a veto) rather than, as normal for trust territories, under article 85 by the General Assembly with the assistance of the Trusteeship Council. The last trust territory was the strategic trust territory of the Pacific Islands, administered by the US.   [44] Article 77 of the Charter.

[45] *Supra*, Chapter 5, p. 160.

[46] See e.g. *Basic Facts About the United Nations*, E.95.I.3.1 and Press Release ORG/1211/Rev.1. Note that the UN Secretary-General has called for its formal termination, but this would require an amendment of the Charter, see A/49/1. See also C. L. Willson, 'Changing the Charter: The United Nations Prepares for the Twenty-First Century', 90 AJIL, 1996, pp. 115, 121–2.

[47] See e.g. S. Bailey, 'The United Nations Secretariat' in *The Evolution of International Organisations* (ed.E. Luard), London, 1966, p. 92 and Bailey, *The Secretariat of the UN*, London, 1962; T. Meron, *The UN Secretariat*, Lexington, KY, 1977; S. Schwebel, *The Secretary-General of the United Nations*, Cambridge MA, 1952 and Schwebel, 'The International Character of the Secretariat of the United Nations' and 'Secretary-General and Secretariat' in *Justice in International Law*, Cambridge, 1994, pp. 248 and 297 respectively; A. W. Rovine, *The First Fifty Years: The Secretary General in World Politics, 1920–1970*, Leiden, 1970; Bowett, *Law*, pp. 87–104 and generally *Public Papers of the Secretaries-General of the United Nations* (eds. A. W. Cordier and W. Foote, and A. W. Cordier and M. Harrelson), New York, 8 vols., 1969–77. See also *Charter of the United Nations* (ed. Simma), pp. 1019 *et seq.* and *infra*, p. 845.

the responsibilities of the Secretary-General and his staff, who are neither
to seek nor receive instructions from any other authority but the UN organisation itself. This provision has not always been respected.

Under article 97, the Secretary-General is appointed by the General
Assembly upon the unanimous recommendation of the Security Council
and constitutes the chief administrative officer of the UN. He (or she) must
accordingly be a personage acceptable to all the permanent members and
this, in the light of effectiveness, is vital. Much depends upon the actual personality and outlook of the particular office holder, and the role played by
the Secretary-General in international affairs has tended to vary according
to the character of the person concerned. An especially energetic part was
performed by Dr Hammerskjöld in the late 1950s and very early 1960s until
his untimely death in the Congo,[48] but since that time a rather lower profile
has been maintained by the occupants of that position. The current holder
of the office is Kofi Annan of Ghana who in January 1997 succeeded Dr
Boutros-Ghali of Egypt.

Apart from various administrative functions,[49] the essence of the
Secretary-General's authority is contained in article 99 of the Charter,
which empowers him to bring to the attention of the Security Council any
matter which he feels may strengthen the maintenance of international
peace and security, although this power has not often been used.[50] In practice, the role of Secretary-General has extended beyond the various provisions of the Charter. In particular, the Secretary-General has an important
role in exercising good offices in order to resolve or contain international
crises.[51] Additionally, the Secretary-General is in an important position to
mark or possibly to influence developments. The publication of *An Agenda
for Peace*[52] by Dr Boutros-Ghali, for instance, constituted a significant point
in the evolution of the organisation, with its optimistic and challenging ideas
for the future.

In many disputes, the functions assigned to the Secretary-General by the
other organs of the United Nations have enabled him to increase the influ-

---

[48] See e.g. Bailey, 'The United Nations Secretariat'.
[49] These include servicing a variety of organs, committees and conferences; co-ordinating the
activities of the secretariat, the specialised agencies and other inter-governmental organisations; the preparation of studies and reports and responsibility for the preparation of the
annual budget of the UN. Note that the Secretary-General also acts as depositary for a wide
range of multinational treaties, and under article 98, submits an annual report on the work
of the organisation.
[50] Article 99 was invoked, for example, in 1950 in the Korean war crisis, in 1960 in the Congo
crisis and in 1979 with regard to the Iranian hostage issue, see Bowett, *Law*, p. 92 and
Yearbook of the UN, 1979, pp. 307–12. See also S/13646 and S. Schwebel, 'The Origins and
Development of Article 99 of the Charter' in *Justice in International Law*, p. 233.
[51] See further *infra*, p. 845.
[52] The Report of the Secretary-General Pursuant to the Statement Adopted by the Summit
Meeting of the Security Council on 31 January 1992, New York, 1992.

THE UNITED NATIONS 835

ence of the organisation.[53] One remarkable example of this occurred in the Congo crisis of 1960 and the subsequent Council resolution authorising the Secretary-General in very wide-ranging terms to take action.[54] Another instance of the capacity of the Secretary-General to take action was the decision of 1967 to withdraw the UN peace-keeping force in the Middle East, thus removing an important psychological barrier to war, and provoking a certain amount of criticism.[55]

The sixth principal organ of the UN is the International Court of Justice, established in 1946 as the successor to the Permanent Court of International Justice.[56]

The specialised agencies[57]

This is the term used to define those organisations established by inter-governmental agreement and having wide international responsibilities in economic, social, cultural and other fields that have been brought into relationship with the United Nations.[58] This task is performed by the Economic and Social Council which also co-ordinates their activities with the approval of the General Assembly, and the agreements made usually specify the sending of regular reports by the agencies to the Economic and Social Council and provide for exchange of information in general.[59]

Specialised agencies are founded upon an international treaty between states that establishes the basic parameters of the organisation and deals inter alia with membership, purposes and structure.[60] Upon signing an agreement with the UN under articles 57 and 63 of the Charter, such an organisation will become a specialised agency. Most constituent instruments distinguish between original and subsequent members, while several agencies provide for associate membership[61] for non-self-governing territories, as for instance Namibia prior to its independence in 1990. Voting powers are variable, although most of the organisations operate on the basis of equal votes for all member states. However, the financial organisations have

[53] Article 98. See also J. Pérez de Cuéllar, 'The Role of the UN Secretary-General' in *United Nations, Divided World*, p. 125. [54] See *infra*, p. 848.
[55] See e.g. Bowett, *Law*, p. 93 and *infra*, p. 849. [56] *Supra*, Chapter 18, p. 745.
[57] See e.g. Broms, *United Nations*, Chapter 14; *Charter of the United Nations* (ed. Simma), pp. 796 *et seq.*; Bowett, *Law*, Chapter 4; C. W. Alexandrowicz, *The Law-Making Functions of the Specialised Agencies of the United Nations*, 1973 and E. Luard, *International Agencies: The Emerging Framework of Interdependence*, London, 1977. [58] Article 57 of the Charter.
[59] See articles 62–66 of the Charter.
[60] See e.g. Bowett, *Law*, pp. 118 *et seq.*; Harrod, 'Problems of the United Nations Specialised Agencies at the Quarter Century', 28 YBWA, 1974, p. 187 and Klein, *Encyclopedia of Public International Law* (ed. R. Bernhardt), Amsterdam, vol. V, 1983, pp. 349–69. See also A. El Erian, 'The Legal Organisation of International Society', in *Manual of Public International Law* (ed. M. Sørensen), London, 1968, pp. 55, 96–106.
[61] See e.g. the UN Educational, Scientific and Cultural Organisation (UNESCO) and the World Health Organisation.

weighted voting systems linked to different contribution quotas. Withdrawal is possible, as for example the United States withdrawal from the International Labour Organisation between 1977 and 1980 and from UNESCO in 1984. The usual structure of a specialised agency is based upon the plenary body, in which all members are represented. This organ elects a smaller executive council in which membership may be determined not only by geographical distribution but also functional conditions.

For instance, of the twenty-four members of the Council of the International Maritime Organisation, six must be governments of states with the largest interest in providing international shipping services, six must be governments of other states with the largest interest in international seaborne trade, while the remaining twelve have to be governments of states (not already elected) with special interests in maritime transport or navigation whose election will ensure an equitable geographical representation.[62] Similarly, the composition of the Council of the International Civil Aviation Organisation is weighted in favour of those states most active in the fields of air transport and the provision of facilities for international air navigation,[63] while the unique structure of the ILO has already been noted.[64]

Most of the specialised agencies have devised means whereby the decisions of the particular organisation can be rendered virtually binding upon members. This is especially so with regard to the International Labour Organisation, UNESCO and the World Health Organisation. Although such institutions are not able to legislate in the usual sense, they are able to apply pressures quite effectively to discourage non-compliance with recommendations or conventions. In the case of the ILO, treaties are submitted to member governments for ratification and within twelve or eighteen months must be laid before the state's legislative organs. The governments, in putting the convention before their parliaments, are required to outline their proposed line of action. Although no obligations are imposed, considerable pressures often build up in favour of ratifying the ILO convention and this is reinforced by the comprehensive system of reporting back to the organisation that exists. Similarly, sanctions and enforcement procedures in the specialised agencies show much subtlety and sophistication and operate, on the whole, beyond the normal confines of strict legal obligations.[65]

---

[62] See e.g. *The International Maritime Organisation* (ed. S. Mankabady), London, 1984.
[63] See e.g. Shenkmann, *International Civil Aviation Organisation*, 1955; Fitzgerald, 'The International Civil Aviation Organisation' in *The Effectiveness of International Decisions* (ed. S. Schwebel), Leiden, 1971, p. 156 and Binaghi, 'The Role of ICAO', in *The Freedom of the Air* (ed. E. McWhinney), 1968, p. 17.   [64] *Supra*, Chapter 6, p. 249.
[65] See e.g. Bowett, *Law*, pp. 140 *et seq.* See also Alexandrowicz, *Law-Making Functions*, and I. Detter, *Law Making by International Organisations*, Norstedt, 1965.

The International Labour Organisation[66]

The International Labour Organisation was set up in 1919 with the aim of protecting and extending the rights of workers throughout the world. It has adopted well over a hundred conventions in pursuance of this, the vast majority of which are in force, which cover such topics as the general conditions of employment, rights to protect the interests of women and children, social security, industrial relations, safety regulations and provisions protecting the right to organise.

The World Health Organisation[67]

The World Health Organisation was established in 1946 with the aim of unifying the standards of health care and it performs a variety of useful functions dedicated to this purpose. These range from the exchange of information to proposals for international treaties and the promotion of research and study in relevant areas. The plenary organ is the World Health Assembly, with equal voting for member states. This body elects representatives to the Executive Board. There is a secretariate and a director-general and it is based in Geneva.

The United Nations Educational, Scientific and Cultural Organisation[68]

The UN Educational, Scientific and Cultural Organisation (UNESCO) exists to further the increase and diffusion of knowledge by various activities including technical assistance and co-operative ventures with national governments. It also operates as a central bank of information. In the mid-1970s, however, the entrance of political considerations (mainly related to the Middle East, but also concerning suggestions for 'a new world information and communication order') somewhat weakened the authority of UNESCO, which was never intended as a political arena, and brought intellectual and financial pressures to bear.[69] The plenary organ is the General Conference, which elects representatives to the Executive Board. There is a secretariat and director-general and it is based in Paris.

The Food and Agriculture Organisation[70]

The Food and Agriculture Organisation was created in 1943 and it works to collect and distribute information related to agricultural and nutritional

---

[66] See *supra*, Chapter 6, p. 249.
[67] See e.g. *Charter of the United Nations* (ed. B. Simma), p. 812 and C. O. Pannenborg, *A New International Health Order*, Alphen aan den Rijn, 1979. [68] See *supra*, Chapter 6, p. 252.
[69] Note that at the end of 1984, the United States withdrew from UNESCO, see 34 ILM, 1985, pp. 489 *et seq*. The UK withdrew as from December 1985.
[70] See e.g. R. W. Phillips, *FAO, Its Origins, Formation and Evolution 1945–1981*, Rome, 1981.

matters. A World Food Programme was established in 1963 and in 1974 a World Food Conference was held in Rome. This called for the establishment of a World Food Council as an organ within the UN system to co-ordinate policies concerning food production, nutrition and other connected topics. It also suggested the creation of an international fund for agricultural development and urged support for the FAO's international fertilizer supply scheme. The increased attention devoted to agricultural issues is due to a growing awareness of the danger of world hunger and starvation, as well as a realisation of the extent to which rural development has been neglected in attempts to industrialise and urbanise in the Third World. The plenary organ is the Conference, which elects the Council. There is a secretariat and director-general and it is based in Rome.[71]

Economic and financial specialised agencies[72]

There are a number of international organisations concerned with economic and financial affairs. The International Bank for Reconstruction and Development (the World Bank) emerged from the Bretton Woods Conference of 1944 to encourage financial investment, and it works in close liaison with the International Monetary Fund, which aims to assist monetary co-operation and increase world trade. A state can only become a member of the World Bank if it is an IMF member. The plenary organ of these agencies is the Board of Governors and the executive organs are the Executive Directors. These agencies, based in Washington DC, are assisted by the International Development Association and the International Finance Corporation, which are affiliated to the World Bank and encourage financial investment and the obtaining of loans on easy terms. These financial organisations differ from the rest of the specialised agencies in that authority lies with the Board of Governors, and voting is determined on a weighted basis according to the level of subscriptions made. Very important decisions require the consent of 70 to 85 per cent of the votes.[73]

---

[71] The following specialised agencies should also be noted in passing: the International Civil Aviation Organisation (as to which see *supra*, Chapter 10, p. 372); the Universal Postal Union; the International Telecommunication Union; the World Meteorological Organisation; the International Maritime Organisation; the World Intellectual Property Organisation; the International Fund for Agricultural Development; the UN Industrial Development Organisation and the International Fund for Agricultural Development. The International Atomic Energy Agency exists as an autonomous organisation within the UN. See e.g. *International Law Cases and Materials* (eds. L. Henkin, R. C. Pugh, O. Schachter and H. Smit), 3rd edn, St Paul, 1993, Chapter 18.

[72] *Ibid.*, Chapter 17 and S. A. Voitovich, *International Economic Organisations in the International Legal Process*, Dordrecht, 1994.

[73] See e.g. Bowett, *Law*, pp. 109–12. See also W. M. Scammell, 'The International Monetary Fund' in the *Evolution of International Organisation*, Chapter 9; A. Shonfield, 'The World Bank', in *ibid.*, Chapter 10 and R. Townley, 'The Economic Organs of the United Nations', in *ibid.*, Chapter 11; and Alexandrowicz, *Law-Making Functions*, Chapter 9.

The peaceful settlement of disputes[74]

The League of Nations[75]

The provisions set out in the UN Charter are to a large degree based upon the terms of the Covenant of the League of Nations as amended in the light of experience. Accordingly, in order to be able better to understand the background of the UN system a brief summary of the procedures provided for within the League for solving disputes is necessary.

Article 12 of the Covenant declared that any dispute likely to lead to a conflict between members was to be dealt with in one of three ways: by arbitration, by judicial settlement or by inquiry by the Council of the League. Article 15 noted that the Council was to try to effect a settlement of the dispute in question, but if that failed, it was to publish a report containing the facts of the case and 'the recommendations which are deemed just and proper in regard thereto'. This report was not, however, binding upon the parties, but if it was a unanimous one the League members were not to go to war 'with any party to the dispute which complies with the recommendations of the report'. If the report was merely a majority one, League members reserved to themselves 'the right to take such action as they shall consider necessary for the maintenance of right and justice'. In other words, in the latter case the Covenant did not absolutely prohibit the resort to war by members. Where a member resorted to war in disregard of the Covenant, then the various sanctions prescribed in article 16 might apply, although whether the circumstances in which sanctions might be enforced had actually arisen was a point to be decided by the individual members and not by the League itself. Sanctions were in fact used against Italy in 1935–6, but in a half-hearted manner due to political considerations by the leading states at the time.[76]

The United Nations system

The UN system is founded in constitutional terms upon a relatively clear theoretical distinction between the functions of the principal organs of the

[74] See e.g. M. Raman, *Dispute Settlement through the United Nations*, Oxford, 1977; J. G. Merrills, *International Dispute Settlement*, 2nd edn, Cambridge, 1991, Chapter 9; Bar-Yaacov, Chapter 8; B. S. Murty, 'Settlement of Disputes', in *Manual of Public International Law* (ed. M. Sørensen), London, 1968, pp. 717 *et seq*; Goodrich and Simons, *Charter; The Evolving United Nations – A Prospect for Peace?* (ed. K. Twitchett), London, 1971; E. Luard, *A History of the United Nations*, London, 1982, vol. I; *The Strategy of World Order*, vol. III; *The United Nations* (ed. R. A. Falk and S. Mendlovitz), New York, 1966; N. D. White, *Keeping the Peace*, Manchester, 1993.
[75] See generally, e.g. G. Scott, *The Rise and Fall of the League of Nations*, London, 1973, and *Strategy of World Order*, Chapter 1. [76] See e.g. Scott, *Rise and Fall*, Chapter 15.

organisation. However, due to political conditions in the international order, the system failed to operate as outlined in the Charter and adjustments had to be made as opportunities presented themselves. The Security Council was intended to function as the executive of the UN, with the General Assembly as the parliamentary forum. Both organs could contribute to the peaceful settlement of disputes through relatively traditional mechanisms of discussion, good offices and mediation. Only the Security Council could adopt binding decisions and that through the means of Chapter VII, while acting to restore international peace and security. But the pattern of development has proved rather less conducive to clear categorisation. An influential attempt to detail the methods and mechanisms available to the UN in seeking to resolve disputes was made by the UN Secretary-General in the immediate aftermath of the demise of the Soviet Union and the unmistakable ending of the Cold War.

In *An Agenda for Peace*,[77] the Secretary-General, while emphasising that respect for the fundamental sovereignty and integrity of states constituted the foundation stone of the organisation,[78] noted the rapid changes affecting both states individually and the international community as a whole and emphasised the role of the UN in securing peace. The Report sought to categorise the types of actions that the organisation was undertaking or could undertake. *Preventive Diplomacy* was action to prevent disputes from arising between states, to prevent existing disputes from escalating into conflicts and to limit the spread of the latter when they occur. This included efforts such as fact-finding, good offices and goodwill missions.[79] *Peacemaking* involves action to bring the hostile parties to agreement, utilising the peaceful means elaborated in Chapter VI of the Charter.[80] *Peacekeeping* is the deployment of a UN presence in the field.[81] *Peace-building* is action to identify and support structures that will assist peace.[82] *Peace Enforcement* is peace-keeping not involving the consent of the parties, which would rest upon the enforcement provisions of Chapter VII of the Charter.[83] It is helpful to keep in mind this thematic classification, which crosses the functional boundaries of the various UN organs concerned in looking at the work of those organs. It is one of the characteristics of the recent period for multiple activities to occur with regard to any particular situation, so that a variety of dispute settlement procedures is resorted to by a number of UN organs.

---

[77] *Op. cit.* This was welcomed by the General Assembly in resolution 47/120. See also the Report of the Secretary-General on the Implementation of the Recommendations in the 1992 Report, A/47/965.   [78] *Ibid.*, p. 9.   [79] *Ibid.*, pp. 13 *et seq.*
[80] *Ibid.*, pp. 20 *et seq.*   [81] *Ibid.*, pp. 28 *et seq.*   [82] *Ibid.*, pp. 32 *et seq.*
[83] See Report of the Secretary-General on the Work of the Organisation, New York, 1993, p. 96.

The Security Council

The primary objective of the United Nations as stipulated in article 1 of the Charter is the maintenance of international peace and security and disputes likely to endanger this are required under article 33 to be solved 'by negotiation, inquiry, mediation, conciliation, arbitration, judicial settlement, resort to regional agencies or arrangements or other peaceful means'. Indeed, the Charter declares as one of its purposes in article 1, 'to bring about by peaceful means and in conformity with the principles of justice and international law, adjustment or settlement of international disputes or situations which might lead to a breach of the peace'. By article 24,[84] the members of the UN conferred on the Security Council primary responsibility for the maintenance of international peace and security, and by article 25[85] agreed to accept and carry out the decisions of the Security Council. The International Court in the *Namibia* case[86] drew attention to the fact that the provision in article 25 was not limited to enforcement actions under Chapter VII of the Charter but applied to '"decisions of the Security Council" adopted in accordance with the Charter'. Accordingly a declaration of the Council taken under article 24 in the exercise of its primary responsibility for the maintenance of international peace and security could constitute a decision under article 25 so that member states 'would be expected to act in consequence of the declaration made on their behalf'.[87] Whether a particular resolution adopted under article 24 actually constituted a decision binding all member states (and outside the collective security framework of Chapter VII)[88] was a matter for analysis in each particular case, 'having regard to the terms of the resolution to be interpreted, the discussions leading to it, the Charter provisions invoked and, in general, all circumstances that might assist in determining the legal consequences of the resolution of the Security Council'.[89]

Under the Charter, the role of the Security Council when dealing with the pacific settlement of disputes specifically under Chapter VI differs from when the Council is contemplating action relating to threats to or breaches of the peace, or acts of aggression under Chapter VII. In the former instance

[84] See e.g. *The Charter of the United Nations*, pp. 397 et seq.   [85] *Ibid.*, pp. 407 et seq.
[86] ICJ Reports, 1971, pp. 16, 52–3; 49 ILR, pp. 1, 42–3.
[87] This approach is controversial and has not, for example, been accepted by western states, see e.g. White, pp. 63 et seq. See also R. Higgins, 'The Advisory Opinion on Namibia. Which UN Resolutions are Binding under Article 25 of the Charter ?', 21 ICLQ, 1972, p. 270.
[88] *Infra*, p. 865.
[89] ICJ Reports, 1971, pp. 16, 53; 49 ILR, p. 43. The question as to whether relevant Security Council resolutions on East Timor could be regarded as binding was raised in the *East Timor* case, ICJ Reports, 1995, pp. 90, 103, but the Court concluded that the resolutions cited did not go so far as to impose obligations. But cf. the Dissenting Opinion by Judge Weeramantry, *ibid.*, pp. 205–8.

there is no power to make binding decisions with regard to member states. It may only make recommendations.

In pursuance of its primary responsibility, the Security Council may, by article 34, 'investigate any dispute, or any situation which might lead to international friction or give rise to dispute, in order to determine whether the continuance of the dispute or situation is likely to endanger the maintenance of international peace and security'. In addition to this power of investigation, the Security Council can, where it deems necessary, call upon the parties to settle their dispute by the means elaborated in article 33.[90] The Council may intervene if it wishes at any stage of a dispute or situation, the continuance of which is likely to endanger international peace and security and under article 36(1) recommend appropriate procedures or methods of adjustment. But in making such recommendations, which are not binding, it must take into consideration the general principle that legal disputes should be referred by the parties to the International Court of Justice. This process was involved when the Security Council recommended that the UK and Albania should take their case regarding the *Corfu Channel* incident to the International Court.[91] Nevertheless, this example proved to be exceptional.[92] Where the parties to a dispute cannot resolve it by the various methods under article 33, they should refer it to the Security Council by article 37. The Council, where it is convinced that the continuance of the dispute is likely to endanger international peace and security, may recommend not only procedures and adjustment methods, but also such terms of settlement as it may consider appropriate.

Once the Council, however, has determined the existence of a threat to, or a breach of, the peace or act of aggression, it may make decisions which are binding upon member states of the UN under Chapter VII, but until that point it can under Chapter VI issue recommendations only.[93] Under article 35(1) any UN member state may bring a dispute or a situation which might lead to international friction or give rise to a dispute before the Council, while a non-member state may bring to the attention of the Council any dispute under article 35(2) provided it is a party to the dispute in question and 'accepts in advance, for the purposes of the

[90] Note that under article 38, the Security Council may make recommendations to the parties with regard to the peaceful settlement of disputes generally if all the parties to the dispute so request.

[91] Security Council resolution 22 (1947). See SCOR, 2nd yr., 127th meeting, 9 April 1947, p. 727. See also Luard, *History*, pp. 209–12.

[92] See also Security Council resolution 395 (1976) calling for negotiations between Turkey and Greece over the Aegean Sea continental shelf dispute and inviting the parties to refer the question to the International Court.

[93] However, note that under article 37(2) if the Council deems that a continuance of a dispute is likely to endanger international peace and security, it 'shall decide whether to take action under article 36 [i.e. recommend appropriate procedures or methods of adjustment] or to recommend such terms of settlement as it may consider appropriate'.

dispute, the obligations of pacific settlement provided in the present Charter'. It is also possible for third parties to bring disputes to the attention of the Council. The General Assembly may make recommendations to the Council regarding any questions or issues within the scope of the Charter or relating to the maintenance of international peace, so long as the Council itself is not already exercising its functions with regard to the same question. The Assembly has the power, under article 11, to call the attention of the Council to situations likely to endanger international peace and security.

Similarly, the Secretary-General of the UN may, by article 99, bring to the Council's attention any matter which in his opinion may threaten the preservation of international peace and security.

In practice, the Security Council has applied all the diplomatic techniques available in various international disputes. This is in addition to open debates and the behind-the-scenes discussions and lobbying that take place. On numerous occasions it has called upon the parties to a dispute to negotiate a settlement and has requested that it be kept informed. The Council offered its good offices in the late 1940s with regard to the Dutch-Indonesian dispute[94] and has had recourse to mediation attempts in many other conflicts, for example with regard to the Kashmir[95] and Cyprus[96] questions.[97] However, the cases where the Council has recommended procedures or methods of adjustment under article 36 have been comparatively rare. Only in the *Corfu Channel* and *Aegean Sea* disputes did the Council recommend the parties to turn to the International Court.

Probably the most famous Security Council resolution recommending a set of principles to be taken into account in resolving a particular dispute is resolution 242 (1967) dealing with the Middle East. This resolution pointed to two basic principles to be applied in establishing a just and lasting peace in the Middle East: first, Israeli withdrawal 'from territories occupied in the recent conflict' (i.e. the Six Day War) and secondly the termination of all claims of belligerency and acknowledgment of the right of every state in the area to live in peace within secure and recognised frontiers. Various other points were referred to in resolution 242, including the need to guarantee freedom of navigation through international waterways in the area, achieve a just settlement of the refugee problem and reinforce the territorial inviolability of every state in the area through measures such

---

[94] See e.g. Luard, *History*, Chapter 9, and S/1156. See also S/514 and S/1234 and Murty, p. 721.   [95] *Ibid.* See also Luard, *History*, Chapter 14.

[96] See e.g. Murty, 'Settlement', p. 721. See also T. Ehrlich, *Cyprus 1958–1967*, Oxford, 1974.

[97] Note also the appointment of Count Bernadotte and Dr Jarring as UN mediators in the Middle East in 1948 and 1967 respectively. See Luard, *History*, Chapters 10 and 11, and *The Arab–Israeli Conflict* (ed. J. N. Moore), 3 vols., Princeton, 1974.

as the use of demilitarised zones. As well as listing these factors, deemed important in any Middle East settlement by the Security Council, the Secretary-General of the UN was asked to designate a special representative to mediate in the dispute and keep the Council informed on the progress of his efforts. Thus, in this instance the Security Council proposed that a dispute be tackled by a combination of prescribed proposals reinforced by mediation.[98]

The General Assembly[99]

Although the primary responsibility with regard to the maintenance of international peace and security lies with the Security Council, this should not be taken as meaning that the General Assembly, comprising all member states of the UN organisation, is denied a role altogether. It may discuss any question or matter within the scope of the Charter, including the maintenance of international peace and security, and may make recommendations to the members of the UN or the Security Council, provided the Council is not itself dealing with the same matter.[100] Under similar conditions, the Assembly may under article 14 'recommend measures for the peaceful adjustment of any situation regardless of origin, which it deems likely to impair the general welfare or friendly relations among nations'.[101] In practice, the resolutions and declarations of the General Assembly (which are not binding) have covered a very wide field, from colonial disputes to alleged violations of human rights and the need for justice in international economic affairs. The Assembly has also asserted its right to deal with a threat to or breach of the peace or act of aggression if the Security Council fails to act because of the exercise of the veto by a permanent member.[102]

The role of the General Assembly increased since 1945 due to two factors. First, the existence of the veto in the Security Council rendered that organ powerless in many important disputes since the permanent members (USA, UK, USSR, France and China) rarely agreed with respect to any particular conflict, and secondly the vast increase in the membership of the UN, which has had the effect of radicalising the Assembly and its deliberations.

---

[98] Resolution 242 (1967) was reaffirmed in Security Council resolution 338 (1973).
[99] See e.g. White, *Keeping the Peace*, part 2 and M. J. Peterson, *The General Assembly in World Politics*, Boston, 1986. [100] Articles 10, 11 and 12 of the UN Charter.
[101] Note e.g. the General Assembly resolution 181(II) of 1947, recommending the partition of Palestine into Jewish and Arab states and an international area around Jerusalem. Since the territory was a mandated territory, there is room for argument that this resolution was more that recommendatory only.
[102] Resolution 377(V), the 'Uniting for Peace' resolution. See further *infra*, p. 879.

The Secretary-General[103]

Just as the impotence of the Security Council stimulated a growing awareness of the potentialities of the General Assembly, it similarly underlined the
role to be played by the United Nations Secretary-General. By article 99 of
the Charter, he is entitled to bring to the attention of the Security Council
any matter which he thinks may threaten the maintenance of international
peace and security and this power is in addition to his function as the chief
administrative officer of the United Nations organisation under article 79.[104]
In effect, the Secretary-General has considerable discretion and much has
depended upon the views and outlook of the person filling the post at any
given time, as well as the general political situation.

The good offices role of the Secretary-General has rapidly expanded.[105]
In exercising such a role, Secretaries-General have sought to act independently of the Security Council and General Assembly, in the former
case, in so far as they have not been constrained by binding resolutions (as
for example in the Kuwait situation of 1990–1). The assumption of good
offices and mediation activity may arise either because of independent
action by the Secretary-General as part of the exercise of his inherent
powers[106] or as a consequence of a request made by the Security Council[107]
or General Assembly.[108] In some cases, the Secretary-General has acted
upon the invitation of the parties themselves[109] and on other occasions, the
Secretary-General has acted in concert with the relevant regional organisation.[110]

[103] See e.g. Rovine, *The First Fifty Years*; Murphy, *The United Nations and the Code of
International Treaties*, 1982, Chapter 5 and Cordier *et al.*,*Public Papers*, 8 vols., New York,
1969–77.
[104] Under article 98, the Secretary-General also performs such other functions as are entrusted
to him by the General Assembly, Security Council, Economic and Social Council and the
Trusteeship Council.
[105] See e.g. T. M. Franck, *Fairness in International Law of Institutions*, Oxford, 1995, Chapter
6; Pérez de Cuéllar, 'Role of the UN Secretary-General' in *United Nations, Divided World*,
p. 125 and T. M. Franck and G. Nolte, 'The Good Offices Function of the UN Secretary-
General', in *ibid.*, p. 143.
[106] See e.g. with regard to Abkhazia, Franck, *Fairness*, p. 207, and Central America, *ibid.*
[107] See e.g. Security Council resolutions 242 (1967) regarding the Middle East; 367 (1975)
regarding Cyprus; 384 (1975) regarding East Timor; 435 (1978) regarding Namibia and
713 (1991) regarding Yugoslavia.
[108] See e.g. with regard to Afghanistan, see General Assembly resolution ES-6/2, 1980, and
The Geneva Accords published by the United Nations, 1988, DPI/935–40420. As to
Cambodia, see Franck, *Fairness*, p. 184.
[109] See e.g. the General Peace Agreement of Rome between the Mozambique government and
RENAMO rebels in 1992, which called upon the UN to monitor its implementation. The
President of Mozambique called upon the Secretary-General to chair the key implementa-
tion commissions and assist in other ways including the despatch of monitors, see Report
of the Secretary-General, S/24635, 1992, and Franck, *Fairness*, p. 188.
[110] See e.g. with the Secretary-General of the Organisation of American States concerning the
Central American peace process from the mid-1980s, the Report of the UN Secretary-
General, A/42/127 – S/18688. 1987.

The development of good offices and mediation activities first arose as a consequence of the severe restrictions imposed upon UN operations by the Cold War. The cessation of the Cold War led to greatly increased activity by the UN and as a consequence the work of the Secretary-General expanded as he sought to bring to fruition the wide range of initiatives undertaken by the organisation. With the experience of Somalia and Bosnia in mind particularly, the middle years of the 1990s decade have witnessed a precipitate decline in dramatic UN activism and this has led to a diminished role for the Secretary-General. The failure to match resources and will to the challenges posed has now led to a lower profile of the organisation than in the immediate post-1989 era.

Peace-keeping and observer missions[111]

There is no explicit legal basis for peace-keeping activities in the UN Charter. They arose in the absence of the contribution of armed forces and facilities to the UN as detailed in article 43. Accordingly, a series of arrangements and operations have evolved since the inception of the organisation, which taken together have established a clear pattern of acceptable reaction by the UN in particular crisis situations. The broad bases for such activities lie in the general provisions in the Charter governing the powers of the Security Council and General Assembly. The Security Council, for example, may establish such subsidiary organs as it deems necessary for the performance of its functions (article 29) and those functions are laid down in articles 34 (powers of investigation); 36, 37 and 38 (powers to recommend appropriate procedures or methods of dispute settlement); and 39 (powers of recommendation or decision in order to maintain or restore international peace and security). The Security Council may, in particular under article 42 take such action by land, sea or air forces as may be necessary to maintain or restore international peace and security. This is the basis for action explicitly taken under Chapter VII of the Charter.[112] However, the majority of peace-keeping activities have not been so authorised and it is unlikely that article 42 can be seen as the legal basis for all such activities. The Security Council can entrust functions to the Secretary-General under article 98 and this mechanism has

[111] See e.g. D. W. Bowett, *UN Forces*, London, 1964; United Nations, *The Blue Helmets: A Review of United Nations Peacekeeping*, 2nd edn, New York, 1990; *The Evolution of UN Peacekeeping* (ed. W. J. Durch), London, 1994; White, *Keeping the Peace*, part 3; R. Higgins, *United Nations Peacekeeping*, 4 vols., Oxford, 1969–81; S. Morphet, 'UN Peacekeeping and Election Monitoring' in *United Nations, Divided World*, p. 183; A. James, *Peacekeeping in International Politics*, London, 1990 and *The Charter of the United Nations*, pp. 565 *et seq.*

[112] The power of the Security Council to resort to force under article 42 is dealt with *infra*, p. 865.

proved significant in practice. The General Assembly has wide powers under articles 10 and 11 to discuss and make recommendations on matters within the scope of the UN Charter, including recommendations concerning the maintenance of international peace and security.[113] Under article 14, the Assembly may recommend measures for the peaceful adjustment of any situation regardless of origin which it deems likely to impair the general welfare or friendly relations among nations. It can, however, take no binding decision in such matters.[114] The Assembly may also establish such subsidiary organs as it deems necessary for the performance of its functions (article 22) and entrust functions to the Secretary-General (article 98).

Peace-keeping and observer missions operate upon a continuum of UN activities and it is helpful to consider these operations together.

The origin of peace-keeping by the UN may be traced to truce supervision activities. The first such activity occurred in Greece, where the UN Special Committee on the Balkans (UNSCOB) was created in 1947.[115] The UN Truce Supervision Organisation (UNTSO) was established in 1948 to supervise the truce in the 1948 Middle East War.[116] Peace-keeping[117] as such arose as a direct consequence of the problems facing the Security Council during the Cold War. The first peace-keeping activity took place in 1956 as a result of the Suez crisis. The UN Emergency Force (UNEF) was established by the General Assembly[118] to position itself between the hostile forces and to supervise the withdrawal of British and French forces from the

---

[113] However under article 11(2), where action is necessary on any question relating to the maintenance of international peace and security, the matter must be referred to the Security Council. [114] See further *infra*, p. 879.

[115] See General Assembly resolution 109. The operation lasted until 1954. See also K. Birgisson, 'United Nations Special Committee on the Balkans' in *The Evolution of UN Peacekeeping*, Chapter 5.

[116] See Security Council resolution 50 (1948) and M. Ghali, 'The United Nations Truce Supervision Organisation' in *The Evolution of UN Peacekeeping*, Chapter 6. It has expanded to supervise the armistice agreements of 1949 and cease-fire arrangements of June 1967. See also the UN Military Observer Group in India and Pakistan (UNMOGIP) established by Security Council resolution 47 (1948) to supervise the cease-fire in Jammu and Kashmir, K. Birgisson, 'United Nations Military Observer Group in India and Pakistan' in *The Evolution of UN Peacekeeping*, Chapter 16.

[117] This has been defined by the Secretary-General as 'the deployment of a United Nations presence in the field, hitherto with the consent of all the parties concerned, normally involving United Nations military and/or police personnel and frequently civilians as well', *An Agenda for Peace*, p. 11. Another definition was put forward by a former UN Legal Counsel, who noted that peace-keeping operations were 'actions involving the use of military personnel in international conflict situations on the basis of the consent of all parties concerned and without resorting to armed force except in cases of self-defence', E. Suy, 'Peace-Keeping Operations' in *A Handbook on International Organisations* (ed. R. J. Dupuy), Dordrecht, 1988, p. 379.

[118] See General Assembly resolutions 997, 998 and 1000(ES-1). The Security Council was unable to act as two permanent members (the UK and France) were directly involved in the crisis and had vetoed draft resolutions. See e.g. M. Ghali, 'United Nations Emergency Force I' in *The Evolution of UN Peacekeeping*, Chapter 7.

Suez Canal and Israeli forces from the Sinai peninsula. It was then deployed along the armistice line until May 1967.

The second crucial peace-keeping operation took place in the Congo crisis of 1960, which erupted soon after Belgium granted independence to the colony, and resulted in mutinies, insurrections and much confused fighting. The Security Council adopted a resolution permitting the Secretary-General to provide military assistance to the Congo government.[119] This was interpreted by Dr Hammarskjöld, the Secretary-General, as a mandate to set up a peace-keeping force on an analogy with UNEF. The exercise of the veto in the Council left the Secretary-General with little guidance as to how to proceed in the situation. Accordingly, he performed many of the tasks that had in 1956 been undertaken by the General Assembly with respect to the Middle East.[120] The development of the Congo crisis from mutiny to civil war faced the United Nations force (known as ONUC from the French initials) with many difficult decisions and these had in the main to be taken by the Secretary-General. The role that could be played by the Secretary-General was emphasised in the succeeding crises in Cyprus (1964)[121] and the Middle East (1973)[122] and in the consequent establishment of United Nations peace-keeping forces for these areas under the general guidance of the Secretary-General.

The creation of traditional peace-keeping forces, whether in the Middle East in 1967 and again in 1973, in the Congo in 1960 or in Cyprus in 1964, was important in that such forces tended to stabilise particular situations for a certain time. Such United Nations forces are not intended to take enforcement action, but to act as an influence for calm by physically separ-

---

[119] S/4387, 14 July 1960. By resolution S/4405, 22 July 1960, the Council requested all states to refrain from action which might impede the restoration of law and order or undermine the territorial integrity and political independence of the Congo. By resolution S/4426, 9 August 1960, the Council confirmed the authority given to the Secretary-General by earlier resolutions and called on member states to carry out the decisions of the Security Council. See e.g. G. Abi-Saab, *The United Nations Operation in the Congo 1960–1964*, Oxford, 1978; C. Hoskyns, *The Congo Since Independence*, Oxford, 1965; L. Miller 'Legal Aspects of UN Action in the Congo', 55 AJIL, 1961, p. 1 and W. J. Durch, 'The UN Operation in the Congo' in *The Evolution of UN Peacekeeping*, Chapter 19.

[120] See Abi-Saab, *Congo*, pp. 15 *et seq.*

[121] See Security Council resolution 186 (1964). See also Ehrlich, *Cyprus 1958–1967*, and Murphy, pp. 46 *et seq.*; Stranger, *The United Nations Force in Cyprus*, 1968 and K. Birgisson, 'United Nations Peacekeeping Forces in Cyprus' in *The Evolution of UN Peacekeeping*, Chapter 13. The force is known as the UN Force in Cyprus (UNFICYP).

[122] The Security Council established the UN Emergency Force (UNEF II) to monitor the Israel–Egypt disengagement process in 1973, see resolution 340 (1973) and a Disengagement Observer Force with respect to the Israel–Syria disengagement process, see resolution 350 (1974). See generally I. Pogany, *The Security Council and the Arab-Israeli Conflict*, Aldershot, 1984, and M. Ghali, 'United Nations Emergency Force II' in *The Evolution of UN Peacekeeping*, Chapter 8. Note also the creation of the UN Interim Force in the Lebanon (UNIFIL) established by the Council in resolution 425 (1978) after Israel's incursion into the Lebanon in 1978, see e.g. M. Ghali, 'United Nations Interim Force in Lebanon' in *The Evolution of UN Peacekeeping*, Chapter 10.

ating warring factions. They are dependent upon the consent of the state upon whose territory they are stationed and can in no way prevent a determined aggression. The various United Nations peace-keeping operations have met with some limited success in temporarily preventing major disturbances, but they failed to prevent the 1967 Arab–Israeli war[123] and the 1974 Turkish invasion of Cyprus.[124] One has to be careful not to overestimate their significance in difficult political situations. In addition to the consent of the host state, such forces also require the continuing support of the Security Council and if that is lost or not provided such forces cannot operate.[125] Just as crucial as these factors is the provision of sufficient resources by the UN and its member states in order to fulfil the agreed mandate. Recent events in Bosnia, for example, have demonstrated that the absence of adequate resources impact severely upon the prospects of such operations.

Nevertheless, peace-keeping and observer operations do have a role to play, particularly as a way of ensuring that conflict situations in the process of being resolved do not flare up as a result of misunderstandings or miscalculations. Some recent UN operations in this area demonstrate this.[126] The UN Good Offices Mission in Afghanistan and Pakistan was established in the context of the Geneva Accords of 14 April 1988 dealing with the withdrawal of Soviet forces from Afghanistan,[127] while the UN Iran–Iraq Military Observer Group was created the same year following the acceptance by the belligerent states of Security Council resolution 598 (1987) calling for a cease-fire.[128] In 1989, in the context of the resolution of the Namibian problem, the UN Angola Verification Mission (UNAVEM I) commenced operation in order to verify the withdrawal of Cuban forces

---

[123] In fact the hasty withdrawal of the UNEF in May 1967 by the Secretary-General following an Egyptian request did much to precipitate the conflict. See generally Special Report of the Secretary-General on Removal of UNEF from Egyptian territory, A/6669, 1967 and T. M. Franck, *Nation Against Nation*, Oxford, 1985.

[124] See e.g. Security Council resolution 359 (1974) criticising the Turkish invasion.

[125] The Israel–Egypt Peace Treaty of 1979 envisaged the deployment of a UN force such as UNEF to supervise the limited forces zones established by the parties but due to Soviet action the mandate of UNEF II expired in July 1979, see e.g. M. Akehurst, 'The Peace Treaty Between Egypt and Israel', 7 *International Relations*, 1981, pp. 1035, 1046 and M. N. Shaw, 'The Egyptian–Israeli Peace Treaty, 1979', 2 *Jewish Law Annual*, 1980, pp. 180, 185. As a result, a special Multinational Force and Observers unit was established by the parties and the United States, independently of the UN, see 20 ILM, 1981, p. 1190 *et seq.* See also M. Tabory, *The Multinational Force and Observers in the Sinai*, Boulder, CO, 1986, and James, *Peacekeeping*, pp. 122 *et seq.*

[126] See generally White, *Keeping the Peace*, Chapter 9.

[127] See S/19836 and Security Council resolution 622 (1988). This activity continued until 1990, see Morphet, 'UN Peacekeeping', p. 213. See also K. Birgisson, 'United Nations Good Offices Mission in Afghanistan and Pakistan' in *The Evolution of UN Peacekeeping*, Chapter 18.

[128] This was to monitor the cease-fire and lasted until February 1991, see e.g. Morphet, 'UN Peacekeeping', p. 213 and B. Smith, 'United Nations Iran–Iraq Military Observer Group' in *The Evolution of UN Peacekeeping*, Chapter 14.

from Angola,[129] while the UN Transition Assistance Group, although originally established in 1978 in Security Council resolution 435 (1978), in fact commenced operations with the Namibian independence process on 1 April 1989.[130]

In 1992, the UN Operation in Mozambique (ONUMOZ) was established in order to monitor the peace agreement between the government and RENAMO rebels,[131] while a UN Observer Group for the Verification of Elections in Nicaragua (ONUVEN) was sent to monitor elections in that country following the 1987 Esquipulas Agreement. This mission is of some interest in being the first electoral observer mission to monitor elections in an independent state. It was also established by virtue of an agreement between Nicaragua and the Secretary-General, which was noted by the Security Council and endorsed by the General Assembly.[132] A UN Observer Group in Central America (ONUCA) was also established in November 1989 in order to observe and verify regional peace-making arrangements.[133] In 1990, the UN set up a mission to supervise elections in Haiti (ONUVEH).[134] Efforts to hold a referendum in Western Sahara are being assisted by the UN Mission for the Referendum in Western Sahara (MINURSO),[135] while the UN Observer Mission in El Salvador was established to verify that the government and rebels in the El Salvador civil war complied with the 1990 peace accord, including human rights provisions.[136] In addition, the UN Iraq–Kuwait Observer Mission (UNIKOM) was set up to monitor the demilitarised zone between these two states following upon the Gulf War.[137] The UN Advance Mission in Cambodia

[129] Security Council resolution 626 (1988). This was completed in 1991. The Security Council then established UNAVEM II to monitor the implementation of the peace accords between the Angolan Government and the UNITA rebels, see Security Council resolution 696 (1991) and V. P. Fortna, 'United Nations Angola Verification Mission I' in *The Evolution of UN Peacekeeping*, Chapter 21 and *ibid.*, 'United Nations Angola Verification Mission II' in *The Evolution of UN Peacekeeping*, Chapter 22. This ended in February 1995.

[130] Security Council resolution 632 (1989). UNTAG monitored the withdrawal of South African troops, confined SWAPO forces to their bases in Angola and Zaire and assisted in the election process. The operation ended in March 1990. See V. P. Fortna, 'United Nations Transition Assistance Group in Namibia' in *The Evolution of UN Peacekeeping*, Chapter 20.

[131] See Security Council resolution 797 (1992) and *supra*, p. 845. The mission ended in December 1994.

[132] See Security Council 637 (1989). See also Morphet,'UN Peacekeeping', pp. 216 *et seq.* and Franck, *Nation Against Nation*, pp. 105 *et seq.*

[133] See Security Council resolution 644 (1989), which endorsed the Secretary-General's efforts to create ONUCA. The mission ended in January 1992. See B. Smith and W. J. Durch, 'UN Observer Group in Central America' in *The Evolution of UN Peacekeeping*, Chapter 24.

[134] See A/44/965 and General Assembly resolution 45/2. See also Franck, *Nation Against Nation*, pp. 106 *et seq.*

[135] See e.g. Security Council resolution 690 (1991). See also W. J. Durch, 'United Nations Mission for the Referendum in Western Sahara' in *The Evolution of UN Peacekeeping*, Chapter 23.

[136] See Security Council resolution 693 (1991). This mission ended in April 1995.

[137] See Security Council resolution 689 (1991).

(UNAMIC)[138] was established pursuant to peace efforts in the civil war in that country and was followed by the UN Transitional Authority in Cambodia (UNTAC).[139] This body was unlike other peace-keeping operations since it was intended to exercise governmental functions pending elections in the country. Until it ended in September 1993, UNTAC not only exercised important administrative functions, it also organised the whole election process and played a part in securing human rights and repatriation.

Further examples of crucial and complex peace-keeping and/or observer activities include observing Eritrea's plebiscite on secession from Ethiopia[140] and South Africa's elections in 1994,[141] supervising the demilitarisation of Eastern Slavonia, Baranja and Western Sirmium (Croatia) and *inter alia* overseeing the return of refugees, training a police force, organising elections and facilitating the removal of mines from the area;[142] monitoring the demilitarisation of the Prevlaka Peninsula in Croatia,[143] assisting the Haitian government in the professionalisation of the police and maintaining a secure environment.[144]

The legal framework for the actual conduct of peace-keeping and observer activities centres upon their status as UN organs, so that they are subject to the law governing the UN organisations as a whole. This would cover, for example, questions of privileges and immunities of UN personnel[145] and responsibility. The UN would be liable for breaches of law committed by members of peace-keeping and observer forces and groups and would, on the other hand, be able to claim compensation for damage

[138] Security Council resolution 717 (1991). This lasted until March 1992.
[139] Security Council resolution 745 (1992). See also Morphet, 'UN Peacekeeping', p. 223. This was the first peace-keeping body to be voted for by Russia, upon the demise of the USSR, and also the first to include Japanese personnel, *ibid.*, p. 224.
[140] See General Assembly resolution 47/114, 1992, and A/47/544.
[141] See Security Council resolution 894 (1994). Over 1, 800 electoral observers were sent, see Franck, *Nation Against Nation*, p. 107.
[142] The UN Transitional Administration for Eastern Slavonia, Baranja and Western Sirmium (UNTAES), see Security Council resolution 1037 (1996). This mission has both a military and a civilian component.
[143] The UN Mission of Observers in Prevlaka (UNMOP), Security Council resolution 1038 (1996).
[144] The UN Support Mission in Haiti (UNSMIH), see Security Council resolution 1063 (1996). In June 1996, this mission succeeded the UN Mission in Haiti (UNMIH) created by resolution 867 (1993) to assist the military and police forces in that state. However, it was prevented from deploying. In resolution 940 (1994) the Security Council authorised the creation of a Multi-National Force (MNF), see *infra*, p. 856, and extended the mandate and scope of UNMIH. After the restoration of the ousted President and the subsequent holding of elections, UNMIH took over responsibility from the MNF (March 1995). See also e.g. the UN Observer Mission in Georgia, Security Council resolution 858 (1993); the UN Aouzou Strip Observer Group, Security Council resolution 915 (1994) and the UN Mission of Observers in Tajikistan, Security Council resolution 968 (1994). See further *infra*, p. 868, for the Yugoslav missions.
[145] See in particular the General Convention on the Privileges and Immunities of the United Nations 1946.

and injuries caused to its personnel. Where forces are stationed on the territory of a state, the usual practice is for formal agreements to be entered into between that state and the UN concerning, for example, facilities, logistics, privileges and immunities of persons and property, and dispute settlement procedures. In 1990, the Secretary-General produced a Model Status of Forces Agreement for Peace-Keeping Operations,[146] which covers such matters. It notes, for instance, that the peace-keeping operation and its members are to respect all local laws and regulations, while the government in question undertakes to respect the exclusively international nature of the operation. Jurisdictional and military discipline issues are also dealt with. The UN has also adopted the Convention on the Safety of United Nations and Associated Personnel 1995 in order to deal with the situation where the UN operation is not an enforcement operation authorised under Chapter VII of the Charter, in combat with local forces and thus operating under the laws of armed conflict. The Convention lays down that the UN and the host state should conclude as soon as possible an agreement on the status of the UN operation and all personnel engaged in the operation, including privileges and immunities issues (article 4) and stipulates that the UN and its personnel shall respect local laws and regulations and refrain from any action or activity incompatible with the impartial and international nature of their duties (article 6). The Convention provides that the intentional commission of activities such as the murder or kidnapping of UN or associated personnel, attacks on official premises or private accommodation or means of transportation, are to be made criminal offences under national law (article 9), while states parties must take such measures as are necessary to establish jurisdiction in such cases when the crime is committed within their territory (or on board a ship or aircraft registered in that state) or when the alleged offender is a national (article 10). In addition, states parties may establish jurisdiction when the crime has been committed by a stateless person whose habitual residence is in the state concerned or with regard to a national of that state or in an attempt to compel that state to do or abstain from doing any act (article 10).[147]

The question as to whether UN forces are subject to the laws of armed conflict[148] has proved controversial. Since the UN is bound by general international law, it is also bound by the customary rules concerning armed conflict, although not the rules contained only in treaties to which the UN is not a party. Nevertheless, many of the agreements state that the UN force would act in accordance with principles of the general international conventions applicable to the conduct of military personnel. Whether the laws of armed

[146] A/45/594.
[147] The Convention also deals with extradition (articles 13–15) and the fair treatment of alleged offenders (article 17). [148] See *supra*, Chapter 19, p. 806.

conflict are actually applicable in the particular situation is another question and in most cases of peace-keeping and observer operations the answer is likely to be in the negative since the UN would not be acting in opposition to any local element but would be separating hostile forces or implementing particular agreements or generally monitoring situations.[149] Where actual conflict arises between the UN forces and local forces, then the laws of armed conflict would clearly be applicable.

Conclusion

The functioning of the United Nations system for the preservation and restoration of world peace has not been a tremendous success in the broadest strategic sense. It constitutes merely one additional factor in international disputes management and one often particularly subject to political pressures. The United Nations has played a minimal part in some of the major conflicts and disputes since its inception, whether it be the Cuban missiles crisis of 1962 or the Vietnam war, the Soviet intervention in Czechoslovakia and Afghanistan or the Nigerian and Angolan civil wars.

Nevertheless, the position of the United Nations improved with the ending of the Cold War and the substantial changes in the approach of the USSR, soon to be Russia, in particular.[150] More emphasis has been laid upon the importance of the UN in the context of an increased co-operation with the US. This began to have a significant impact upon the work and achievements of the UN. The new co-operative approach led to the agreements leading to the independence of Namibia, while substantial progress was made by the five permanent members of the Security Council in working out a solution to the Cambodian problem.

The range and extent of activities now engaged in by the UN is startling by past experience. UN missions may not only be used now to stabilise a tense situation in the traditional exposition of the peace-keeping approach, they may also be utilised in order to carry out key administrative functions; verify peace agreements both international and internal; monitor the implementation of human rights accords; supervise and monitor elections; train and oversee police forces; oversee withdrawal and demilitarisation arrangements, and assist in demining operations.

The Secretary-General has recently emphasised that there are three particularly important principles of peace-keeping.[151] These are the consent of

[149] See e.g. *The Charter of the United Nations*, p. 600 and A. J. T. Dörenberg, 'Legal Aspects of Peace-Keeping Operations', 28 *The Military Law and Law of War Review*, 1989, p. 113.
[150] See e.g. A. Roberts and B. Kingsbury, 'The UN's Role in International Society since 1945' in *United Nations, Divided World*, p. 1.
[151] *Supplement to an Agenda for Peace*, A/50/60, 1995, para. 33.

the parties, impartiality and the non-use of force. While these three may characterise traditional peace-keeping and observer missions, even as these have extended during the 1990s, they do not apply necessarily to a new form of peace-keeping that is mandated under Chapter VII of the Charter, concerning binding decisions of the Security Council and which overlays enforcement activities.

The collective security system[152]

The system established by the United Nations for the maintenance of international peace and security was intended to be comprehensive in its provisions and universal in its application. It has often been termed a collective security system, since a wronged state was to be protected by all, and a wrongdoer punished by all.

The Security Council

The original scheme by which this was achieved laid great stress upon the role of the Security Council, although this has been modified to some extent in practice. By article 24 of the United Nations Charter, the Council was granted primary responsibility for the maintenance of international peace and security, and its decisions are under article 25 binding upon all member states. It was thus intended to fulfil a dynamic, executive function.

While actions adopted by the Security Council in pursuance of Chapter VI of the Charter, dealing with the pacific settlement of disputes, are purely recommendatory, matters concerning threats to, or breaches of, the peace or acts of aggression, under Chapter VII give rise to decision-making powers on the part of the Council. This is an important distinction and emphasises the priority accorded within the system to the preservation of peace and the degree of authority awarded to the Security Council to achieve this. The system is completed by article 103 which declares that obligations under the Charter prevail over obligations contained in other international agreements.[153]

---

[152] See e.g. Franck, *Nation Against Nation*, Chapter 9; R. Higgins, *Problems and Process*, Oxford, 1994, Chapter 15; White, *Keeping the Peace*, Chapter 2; P. M. Dupuy, 'Sécurité Collective et Organisation de la Paix', *Revue Générale de Droit International Public*, 1993, p. 617; G. Gaja, 'Réflexions sur le Rôle du Conseil de Sécurité dans le Nouvel Ordre Mondial', in *ibid.*, p. 297; T. M. Franck and F. Patel, 'UN Police Action in Lieu of War: "The Older Order Changeth"', 85 AJIL, 1991, p. 63 and *The Charter of the United Nations*, pp. 605 *et seq.*

[153] See the *Lockerbie* case, ICJ Reports, 1992, p. 3; 94 ILR, p. 478. But see the discussion of article 103 by Judge Lauterpacht in the second provisional measures order in the *Genocide (Bosnia and Herzegovina* v. *Yugoslavia (Serbia and Montenegro))* case, ICJ Reports, 1993, pp. 325, 440; 95 ILR, pp. 43, 158, and by Judge Bedjaoui in the *Lockerbie* case, ICJ Reports, 1992, pp. 3, 47; 94 ILR, pp. 478, 530.

Determination of the situation

Before the Council can adopt measures relating to the enforcement of world peace, it must first 'determine the existence of any threat to the peace, breach of the peace or act of aggression'. This is the key to the collective security system. Once such a determination has been made, in accordance with article 39 of the Charter, the way is clear for the adoption of recommendations or decisions to deal with the situation. In particular, the adoption of Chapter VII enforcement action constitutes an exception to the principle stated in article 2(7) of the Charter according to which the UN is not authorised 'to intervene in matters which are essentially within the domestic jurisdiction of any state'.

The question is thus raised at this juncture as to the definition of a threat to, or breach of the peace or act of aggression. The answer that has emerged in practice is that it depends upon the circumstances of the case.[154] It also depends upon the relationship of the five permanent members of the Council (UK, USA, Russia, China and France) to the issue under consideration, for a negative vote by any of the permanent members is sufficient to block all but procedural resolutions of the Council.[155] This veto has been one of the major causes of the failure of the Council in its appointed task of preserving international peace and security.

Threat to the peace is the broadest category provided for in article 39 and the one least susceptible to precise definition. In a sense it constitutes a safety net for Security Council action where the conditions needed for a breach of the peace or act of aggression do not appear to be present. It is also the category which has marked a rapid evolution as the perception as to what amounts to a threat to international peace and security has broadened. In particular, the concept has been used to cover internal situations that would once have been shielded from UN action by article 2(7) of the Charter.

A threat to the peace was first determined in the 1948 Middle East War, when in resolution 54 (1948), the Security Council found the situation created by the conflict in the former mandated territory of Palestine where neighbouring Arab countries had entered the territory in order to conduct hostilities against the new state of Israel constituted 'a threat to the peace within the meaning of article 39' and demanded a cease-fire. In resolution 221 (1966) the Council determined that the situation of the minority white regime in Rhodesia constituted a threat to the peace.[156]

With the cessation of the Cold War, the Security Council has been able to extend its activities under Chapter VII to a remarkable extent. In resolution

---

[154] See White, *Keeping the Peace*, Chapter 2. [155] Article 27 of the UN Charter.
[156] See also Security Council resolution 217 (1965).

713 (1991) the Council determined that the situation in former Yugoslavia[157] constituted a threat to the peace and in resolution 733 (1992), it was held that the situation in Somalia amounted to a threat to peace. In resolution 794 (1992), the Council underlined that 'the magnitude of the human tragedy caused by the conflict in Somalia, further exacerbated by the obstacles being created to the distribution of humanitarian assistance, constitutes a threat to international peace and security'.[158] In resolution 788 (1992) the Council decided that the deteriorating civil war situation in Liberia constituted a threat to international peace, while in resolution 955 (1994), it was determined that the genocide in Rwanda constituted a threat to international peace and security. The latter three cases were clearly internal civil war situations and it could be said that the situation in Yugoslavia at the time of the adoption of the 1991 resolution was also a civil war situation, although this is more complex. Further resolutions with regard to former Yugoslavia determined that threats to the peace were involved.[159] In another move of considerable importance, the Council has also determined that 'widespread violations of international humanitarian law' constitutes a threat to peace.[160]

A further expansion in the meaning in practice of a threat to international peace and security took place with regard to Libya. In resolution 748 (1992) the Council determined that 'the failure by the Libyan government to demonstrate by concrete actions its renunciation of terrorism and in particular its continued failure to respond fully and effectively to the requests in resolution 731 (1992),[161] constitute a threat to international peace and security'. Again, in resolution 1070 (1996), the Council determined that the failure of Sudan to comply with earlier resolutions demanding that it act to extradite to Ethiopia for prosecution suspects on its territory wanted in connection with an assassination attempt against the President of Egypt,[162] constituted a threat to international peace and security. In both cases references to 'international terrorism' were made in the context of a determination of a threat to the peace. This constitutes an important step in combating such a phenomenon for it paves the way for the adoption of binding sanctions in such circumstances.

The Haiti situation similarly marked a development in the understanding by the Council as to what may amount to a threat to international peace and

---

[157] This situation was characterised by fighting 'causing a heavy loss of human life and material damage, and by the consequences for the countries in the region, in particular in the border areas of neighbouring countries', *ibid.*
[158] See also Security Council resolution 751 (1992).
[159] See e.g. Security Council resolutions 743 (1992); 757 (1992); 787 (1992) and 827 (1993).
[160] See Security Council resolutions 808 (1993), with regard to former Yugoslavia and 955 (1994) with regard to Rwanda.
[161] Which called for the extradition of alleged bombers of an airplane over Lockerbie in 1988 to the US or UK.   [162] Security Council resolutions 1044 (1996) and 1054 (1996).

security. UN observers monitored an election in that country in 1990, but on 30 September 1991 the elected President Aristide was ousted. In a process which demonstrates the growing interaction between UN organs in crisis situations, the Secretary-General appointed a Special Representative for Haiti on 11 December 1991, the General Assembly authorised a joint UN–Organisation of American States civilian mission on human rights (MICIVIH) on 20 April 1993[163] and on 16 June 1993, the Security Council imposed an arms and oil embargo on Haiti with sanctions to enter into force on 23 June unless the Secretary-General and the OAS reported that such measures were no longer warranted.[164] The Security Council referred to the fact that 'the legitimate Government of President Jean-Bernard Aristide' had not been reinstated and noted 'the incidence of humanitarian crises, including mass displacements of population, becoming or aggravating threats to international peace and security'.[165] The Council determined therefore that 'in these unique and exceptional circumstances', the continuation of the situation constituted a threat to international peace and security. Thus, although the Security Council did not go so far as to declare that the removal of a legitimate government constituted of itself a threat to peace, it was clearly the precipitating factor that taken together with other matters could enable a determination to be made under article 39 thus permitting the adoption of binding sanctions. The sanctions were suspended following the Governors Island Agreement of 3 July 1993.[166] However, in resolution 873 (1993), the Council determined that the failure by the military authorities in Haiti to fulfil obligations under that agreement constituted a threat to international peace and security, and sanctions were reimposed.[167]

After several decades of discussion and deliberation, a definition of aggression was finally agreed upon by the United Nations General Assembly in 1974.[168] Article 1 provides that aggression is the use of armed force by a state against the sovereignty, territorial integrity or political independence of another state, or in any other manner inconsistent with the United Nations Charter. A number of examples of aggressive acts are given in article 3 and these include the use of weapons by a state against the territory of another state, the blockade of the ports or coasts of a state by the

---

[163] See General Assembly resolution 47/20 B. [164] Security Council resolution 841 (1993).
[165] Note that in Security Council resolution 688 (1991), it had been determined that the consequences of the Iraqi repression of its civilian population in different parts of the country, including areas populated by Kurds involving considerable refugee flows over the borders of Turkey and Iran threatened international peace and security.
[166] Security Council resolution 861 (1993).
[167] Security Council resolution 873 (1993). Further sanctions were imposed in resolution 917 (1994). Sanctions were finally lifted by resolution 944 (1994), upon the restoration of President Aristide following a US-led operation in Haiti.
[168] General Assembly resolution 3314(XXIX).

armed forces of another state,[169] and attack by the armed forces of a state on the land, sea or air forces of another state and the sending by, or on behalf of, a state of armed bands to carry out acts of armed force against another state.[170] This elucidation of some of the features of the concept of aggression might prove of some use to the Security Council, but the Council does retain the right to examine all the relevant circumstances, including the gravity of any particular incident, before deciding on the determination to make pursuant to article 39.[171]

Findings as to actual breaches of the peace have occurred four times. In 1950, as a result of the invasion of South Korea by North Korea, the Security Council adopted resolutions determining that a breach of the peace had occurred and calling upon member states to assist South Korea,[172] while in resolution 502 (1982) the Council determined that a breach of the peace in the Falkland Islands region had taken place following the Argentine invasion. The third situation which prompted a finding by the Security Council of a breach of the peace was in resolution 598 (1987) dealing with the Iran-Iraq war, while the fourth occasion was in resolution 660 (1990) in which the Council determined that there existed 'a breach of international peace and security as regards the Iraqi invasion of Kuwait'.

Chapter VII measures[173]

Measures not involving the use of force[174]

Once the Security Council has resolved that a particular dispute or situation involves a threat to the peace or act of aggression, the way is open to take further measures. Such further measures may, however, be preceded by provisional action taken to prevent the aggravation of the situation. This action,

[169] As for example the blockade of the Israeli port of Eilat in May 1967, *supra*, Chapter 19, p. 789.
[170] See the *Nicaragua* case, ICJ Reports, 1986, pp. 14, 103–4; 76 ILR, pp. 349, 437. See also draft article 15 of the Draft Code of Crimes against the Peace and Security of Mankind, Report of the International Law Commission on the Work of its Forty-seventh Session, 1995, pp. 33 *et seq.*
[171] The first finding as to aggression by the Security Council was in 1976 with regard to South African action against Angola, Security Council resolution 387 (1976). See also Security Council resolution 667 (1990) condemning aggressive acts by Iraq against diplomatic premises and personnel in Kuwait.   [172] Security Council resolution S/1501.
[173] See e.g. P. Conlon, 'Legal Problems at the Centre of United Nations Sanctions', 65 *Nordic Journal of International Law*, 1996, p. 73.
[174] See e.g. M. Doxey, *Economic Sanctions and International Enforcement*, London, 1980; J. Combacau, *Le Pouvoir de Sanction de l'ONU*, Paris, 1974; N. Schrijver, 'The Use of Economic Sanctions by the UN Security Council: An International Perspective' in *International Economic Law and Armed Conflict* (ed. H. Post), Dordrecht, 1994 and *Economic Sanctions: Panacea or Peace-Building in a Post-Cold War World* (eds. D. Cortright and G. Lopez), Boulder, CO, 1995.

provided for by article 40 of the Charter, is without prejudice to the rights or claims of the parties, and is intended as a provisional measure to stabilise a crisis situation. Usual examples of action taken by the Security Council under this provision include calls for cease-fires (as in the Middle East in 1967 and 1973),[175] and calls for the withdrawal of troops from foreign territory.[176] However, the adoption of provisional measures by the Council often has an effect ranging far beyond the confines of a purely temporary action. They may induce a calmer atmosphere leading to negotiations to resolve the difficulties and they may set in train moves to settle the dispute upon the basis laid down in the Security Council resolution, which called for the provisional measures.

The action adopted by the Council, once it has decided that there exists with regard to a situation a threat to the peace, breach of the peace or act of aggression, may fall into either of two categories. It may amount to the application of measures not involving the use of armed force under article 41, such as the disruption of economic relations or the severance of diplomatic relations, or may call for the use of such force as may be necessary to maintain or restore international peace and security under article 42.

The Council has not until recently utilised the powers it possesses under article 41 to any great extent. The first major instance of action not including the use of force occurred with respect to the Rhodesian situation following upon the Unilateral Declaration of Independence by the white minority government of that territory in 1965.[177] In two resolutions in 1965, the Council called upon member states not to recognise or assist the illegal regime and in particular to break all economic and arms relations with it.[178] The next year, the Council went further and imposed selective mandatory economic sanctions upon Rhodesia,[179] which were extended in 1968 and rendered comprehensive,[180] although several states did act in defiance of

---

[175] See Security Council resolutions 234 (1967) and 338 (1973).
[176] See e.g. Security Council resolution 509 (1982), with regard to Israel's invasion of Lebanon.
[177] See e.g. R. Zacklin, *The United Nations and Rhodesia*, 1974; J. E. S. Fawcett, 'Security Council Resolutions on Rhodesia', 41 BYIL, 1965–6, p. 103; M. S. McDougal and W. M. Reisman, 'Rhodesia and the United Nations: The Lawfulness of International Concern', 62 AJIL, 1968, p. 1; Murphy, *United Nations*, pp. 139 *et seq.* and J. Nkala, *The United Nations, International Law and the Rhodesia Independence Crisis*, Oxford, 1985. See also V. Gowlland-Debbas, *Collective Responses to Illegal Acts in International Law*, Dordrecht, 1990 and Gowlland-Debbas, 'Security Council Enforcement Action and Issues of State Responsibility', 43 ICLQ, 1994, p. 55.
[178] Security Council resolutions 216 (1965) and 217 (1965).
[179] Security Council resolution 232 (1966). Note that under Security Council resolution 221 (1966) the Council *inter alia* called upon the UK 'to prevent by the use of force if necessary' the arrival in Mozambique of vessels believed to be carrying oil for Rhodesia.
[180] Security Council resolution 253 (1968). See also Security Council resolution 409 (1977).

these resolutions.[181] Sanctions were terminated in 1979 as a result of the agreement leading to the independence of Zimbabwe.[182]

However, the most comprehensive range of economic sanctions thus far imposed by the Security Council was adopted in the wake of the invasion of Kuwait by Iraq on 2 August 1990.[183] Security Council resolution 661 (1990), noting that Iraq had failed to withdraw immediately and unconditionally from Kuwait[184] and acting specifically under Chapter VII of the Charter, imposed a wide range of economic sanctions upon Iraq, including the prohibition by states of all imports from and exports to Iraq and occupied Kuwait,[185] and the transfer of funds to Iraq and Kuwait for such purposes. Additionally, the Security Council decided that states should not make available to the government of Iraq or to any commercial, industrial or public utility undertaking in Iraq or Kuwait any funds or any other financial or economic resources and should prevent their nationals and persons within their territories from remitting any other funds to persons or bodies within Iraq or Kuwait,[186] notwithstanding any existing contract or licence.

The Security Council also established a Committee consisting of all members of the Council to oversee the implementation of these measures.[187] Under Security Council resolution 666 (1990), the Committee was instructed to keep the situation regarding foodstuffs in Iraq and Kuwait under constant review and to bear in mind that foodstuffs (as permitted under the terms of the previous resolutions) should be provided through the UN in co-operation with the International Committee of the Red Cross or other appropriate humanitarian agencies and distributed by them or under their supervision. The Committee was additionally given the task of examining requests for assistance under article 50 of the Charter[188] and making

---

[181] See N. Polakas, 'Economic Sanctions: An Effective Alternative to Military Coercion?', 6 *Brooklyn Journal of International Law*, 1980, p. 289. Note also the importation by the United States of Rhodesian chrome and other minerals under the Byrd Amendment between 1972 and 1977, see Murphy, *United Nations*, pp. 140–1 and DUSPIL 1977, Washington, pp. 830–4.

[182] Security Council resolution 460 (1979). See also 19 ILM, 1980, p. 287 *et seq.* Note in addition Security Council resolution 418 (1977), which imposed an arms embargo upon South Africa. See also White, *Keeping the Peace*, pp. 94 *et seq.*

[183] See *The Kuwait Crisis: Basic Documents*; *The Kuwait Crisis: Sanctions and their Economic Consequences* (ed. D. Bethlehem), Cambridge, 1991 and White, *Keeping the Peace*, pp. 91 *et seq.*   [184] As required in Security Council resolution 660 (1990).

[185] Apart from supplies intended strictly for medical purposes and 'in humanitarian circumstances' foodstuffs, paragraph 3(c).

[186] Except payments exclusively for strictly medical or humanitarian purposes and in humanitarian circumstances foodstuffs, *ibid.*, paragraph 4.

[187] See e.g. M. Koskenniemi, 'Le Comité des Sanctions Créé par la Résolution 661 (1990) du Conseil de Sécurité', AFDI, 1991, p. 121 and P. Conlon, 'Lessons from Iraq: The Functions of the Iraq Sanctions Committee as a Source of Sanctions Implementation Authority and Practice', 35 Va JIL, 1995.

[188] Article 50 provides that if preventive or enforcement measures against any state are taken by the Security Council, any other state which finds itself confronted with special economic problems arising from the carrying out of those measures shall have the right to consult the Security Council with regard to a solution of those problems. Note also the reference to article 50 in Security Council resolution 748 (1992), imposing sanctions upon Libya.

recommendations to the President of the Security Council for appropriate action.[189] The binding economic sanctions imposed on Iraq because of its invasion and purported annexation of Kuwait were tightened in Security Council resolution 670 (1990), in which the Council decided that all states, irrespective of any international agreements or contracts, licences or permits in existence, were to deny permission to any aircraft to take off from their territory if the aircraft was carrying cargo to or from Iraq or Kuwait.[190] In addition, states were to deny permission to any aircraft destined to land in Iraq or Kuwait to overfly their territory.[191]

The economic sanctions were reinforced under Security Council resolution 665 (1990) which authorised those UN member states deploying maritime forces in the area in co-operation with the legitimate government of Kuwait 'to use such measures commensurate to the specific circumstances as may be necessary under the authority of the Security Council' in order to enforce the naval blockade on Iraq. The states concerned were requested to co-ordinate their actions 'using as appropriate mechanisms of the Military Staffs Committee'[192] and after consultation with the UN Secretary-General to submit reports to the Security Council and the Committee established under resolution 661 (1990). It is unclear whether given a substantial period of operation, this impressive range of sanctions would have sufficed to compel Iraq to withdraw from Kuwait, for on 16 January 1991 force was employed. Having once established a comprehensive set of economic and financial sanctions together with mechanisms of supervision, it has become easier to put in place similar responses to other situations.

On 31 March 1992, the Security Council imposed a relatively restricted range of sanctions upon Libya due to the latter's refusal to renounce terrorism and respond fully and effectively to the call in Security Council resolution 731 (1992) to extradite suspected bombers to the UK or US.[193] These sanctions imposed a mandatory arms and air embargo upon Libya. It also called upon states to reduce significantly the number and the level of staff at Libyan diplomatic missions and diplomatic posts. A Committee was set up to monitor compliance with the sanctions.

On 30 May 1992, the Security Council in resolution 757 (1992) imposed a wide range of economic sanctions upon the Federal Republic of Yugoslavia (Serbia and Montenegro), having imposed an arms embargo upon all states within the territory of the former Yugoslavia in resolution 713 (1991).[194]

---

189 Security Council resolution 669 (1990).
190 Other than food in humanitarian circumstances subject to authorisation by the Council or the Committee or supplies intended strictly for medical purposes.
191 Unless the aircraft lands for inspection or the flight has been approved by the Committee or the flight is certified by the UN as solely for the purposes of the UN Iran–Iraq Military Observer Group (UNIIMOG). 192 See *infra* p. 865.
193 Security Council resolution 748 (1992).
194 A Sanctions Committee was established under Security Council resolution 724 (1991).

The resolution, adopted under Chapter VII, prohibited the importation of goods from the Federal Republic of Yugoslavia (Serbia and Montenegro) and the export or trans-shipment of such goods by states or their nationals and the sale or supply of any commodities or products to any person or body in the Federal Republic of Yugoslavia or to any person or body for the purposes of any business carried on in or operated from it. In addition, paragraph 5 of this resolution prohibited states from making available to the authorities in the Federal Republic of Yugoslavia (Serbia and Montenegro) or to any commercial, industrial or public utility undertaking there, any funds or any other financial or economic resources. States were also to prevent their nationals and any persons within their territories from providing to anyone within the Federal Republic any funds or resources at all, except for payments exclusively for strictly medical or humanitarian purposes and foodstuffs. The sanctions were tightened in resolution 787 (1992), which decided that any vessel in which a majority or a controlling interest was held by a person or undertaking in or operating from the Federal Republic were to be considered for the purpose of the sanctions regime as a Yugoslav vessel, irrespective of the flag flown. Further maritime control measures were also adopted under this resolution.

These sanctions were essentially extended by Security Council resolution 820 (1993) to areas of Croatia and Bosnia controlled by the Bosnian Serb forces. In addition, the Danube River was included within the sanctions control system and the transport of all goods (apart from medical supplies and foodstuffs) across the land borders to or from the ports of the Federal Republic was prohibited. Resolution 820 also decided that states were to impound all vessels, freight vehicles, rolling stock and aircraft in their territories in which a majority or controlling interest was held by a person or undertaking in or operating from the Federal Republic. It was further decided to prohibit the provision of services, both financial and non-financial, to any person or body for purposes of any business carried on in the Federal Republic, except for telecommunications, postal services, legal services consistent with resolution 757, and as approved on a case by case basis by the Sanctions Committee,[195] services whose supply may be necessary for humanitarian or other exceptional purposes. Paragraph 21 of the resolution provided for states to freeze funds of the authorities in the Federal Republic or of commercial, industrial or public utility undertakings there, and of funds controlled directly or indirectly by such authorities or undertakings or by entities, wherever located or organised, owned or controlled by such authorities or undertakings. Resolution 942 (1994) extended sanctions to cover economic activities carried on within states by any entity owned or

[195] See e.g. M. Scharf and J. Dorosin, 'Interpreting UN Sanctions: The Rulings and Role of the Yugoslav Sanctions Committee', 19 *Brooklyn Journal of International Law*, 1993, p. 771.

controlled, directly or indirectly, by any person or entity resident in areas of Bosnia under the control of the Bosnian Serb forces.

As negotiations progressed, the sanctions against the Federal Republic of Yugoslavia were progressively eased.[196] After the Dayton peace agreement was initialled, the arms embargo was lifted[197] and was suspended indefinitely by resolution 1022 (1995) on 22 November 1995, except with regard to Bosnian Serb forces. The resolution also provided for the release of frozen assets, 'provided that any such funds and assets that are subject to any claims, liens, judgements, or encumbrances, or which are the funds of any person, partnership, corporation, or other entity found or deemed insolvent under law or the accounting principles prevailing in such state, shall remain frozen or impounded until released in accordance with applicable law'. Sanctions were fully lifted by resolution 1074 (1996) following the holding of elections in Bosnia as required under the peace agreement and the Sanctions Committee was dissolved.

While measures taken under article 41 have traditionally been economic sanctions, other possibilities exist. The Council may, for example, call for action to be taken to reduce the number and level of diplomatic staff of the target state within other states.[198] More dramatically, the Council has on two occasions established international tribunals to prosecute war criminals by the adoption of binding resolutions under Chapter VII.[199] Further, the Council may adopt a series of determinations concerning legal responsibilities of states that will have considerable consequences.

Security Council Resolution 687 (1991) constitutes the supreme illustration of such a situation. This laid down a series of conditions for the ending of the conflict in the Gulf and a resolution was adopted under Chapter VII of the Charter.[200] The resolution demanded that Iraq and Kuwait respect the inviolability of the international boundary as laid down in the Agreed Minutes signed by Iraq and Kuwait on 4 October 1963.[201] The Council then proceeded to guarantee the inviolability of this international boundary, a development of great significance in the history of the UN. The resolution also provided for the immediate deployment of a UN observer unit to monitor a demilitarised zone to be established extending 10 kilometres into Iraq and 5 kilometres into Kuwait from the international boundary.[202] Iraq was called upon to accept the destruction or removal of all chemical and biological

---

[196] See e.g. Security Council resolutions 943 (1994); 988 (1995); 992 (1995); 1003 (1995) and 1015 (1995).   [197] Security Council resolution 1021 (1995).
[198] See e.g. Security Council resolution 748 (1992), with regard to Libya.
[199] See Security Council resolutions 808 (1992) and 827 (1992) with regard to former Yugoslavia, and 955 (1994) with regard to Rwanda.
[200] It would also appear to mark the acceptance of the notion of a continuing threat to the peace once hostilities have been terminated and the act of aggression precipitating the UN response has been reversed.   [201] See further *supra*, Chapter 8, p. 353.
[202] See further *supra*, p. 850.

weapons and all ballistic missiles with a range greater than 150 kilometres. A special commission was provided for to ensure that this happens.[203] Iraq was to agree unconditionally not to acquire or develop nuclear weapons. The Security Council resolution reaffirmed that Iraq was liable under international law for any direct loss, damage, including environmental damage and the depletion of natural resources, or injury to foreign governments, nationals and corporations, as a result of Iraq's unlawful invasion and occupation of Kuwait. In a further interesting but controversial provision, the resolution 'decides that all Iraqi statements made since 2 August 1990, repudiating its foreign debt, are null and void, and demands that Iraq scrupulously adhere to all of its obligations concerning servicing and repayment of its foreign debt'.

The scope and extent of this binding resolution amounts to a considerable development of the Security Council's efforts to resolve disputes. The demands that Iraq give up certain types of weapons and the requirement that repudiation of foreign debt is invalidated would appear to mark a new departure for the Council. In this category would also fall the guarantee given to the inviolability of an international border which is still the subject of dispute between the two parties concerned.

In addition to the provisions noted above, the Council established a fund to pay compensation for claims.[204] The UN Compensation Commission was created by Security Council resolution 692 (1991) to process claims for compensation for 'any direct loss, damage, including environmental damage and the depletion of natural resources, or injury to foreign Governments, nationals and corporations, as a result of Iraq's unlawful invasion and occupation of Kuwait'.[205] It constitutes a subsidiary organ of the Council and consists of a Governing Council (being the fifteen members at any given time of the Security Council), a secretariat and Commissioners appointed to review and resolve claims.[206] In resolution 705 (1991), the Security

---

[203] See also Security Council resolutions 707 (1991) and 715 (1991) requiring the Secretary-General to report to the Council every six months on the implementation of the Special Commission's plan for ongoing monitoring and verification of Iraq's compliance with its responsibilities in this area. See also the Reports of the Special Commission, e.g. S/23165; S/23268; S/24108 and Corr.1; S/24984; S/25977; S/26910; S/1994/750; S/1994/1138; S/1994/1422 and S/1994/1422/Add.1. Security Council resolution 1051 (1996) approved proposals for an export/import monitoring mechanism based upon a joint unit constituted by the Special Commission and the Director General of the International Atomic Energy Agency.   [204] See paragraph 18 of resolution 687 (1991).   [205] Ibid., paragraph 16.
[206] See Report of the Secretary-General of 2 May 1991, S/22559. This Report in particular emphasised that the Compensation Commission was neither a Court nor an Arbitral Tribunal, but 'a political organ that performs an essentially fact-finding function of examining the claims verifying their validity, evaluating losses, assessing payments and resolving disputed claims'. It was recognised, however, that 'some elements of due process should be built into the procedure', ibid., para. 20. See also the Guidelines adopted by the Governing Council on 2 August 1991, S/22885. Both documents are reproduced in 30 ILM, 1991, pp. 1703 et seq. As of January 1996, the Compensation Commission had received 2.6 million claims with an asserted face value of $190 billion, see 35 ILM, 1996, p. 942.

Council, acting under Chapter VII, decided that compensation to be paid by Iraq shall not exceed 30 per cent of the annual value of the exports of petroleum and petroleum products from Iraq. In resolution 706 (1991), the Council authorised states to import a certain amount of Iraqi petroleum and petroleum products in order to pay for essential food and humanitarian purchases by Iraq and provide payments for the UN Compensation Commission via the Compensation Fund.[207] The Compensation Commission has taken a number of decisions, including creating an urgent claims process consisting of three categories.[208] The first compensation awards were made in Spring 1995 and covered claims made in the urgent claims categories.[209]

Measures involving the use of force

Where the Council feels that the measures short of armed force as prescribed under article 41 have been or would be inadequate, it may take 'such action by air, sea or land forces as may be necessary to maintain or restore international peace and security'. Article 42 also provides that such action may extend to demonstrations, blockades and other armed operations by members of the United Nations. In order to be able to function effectively in this sphere, article 43 provides for member states to conclude agreements with the Security Council to make available armed forces, assistance and facilities, while article 45 provides that member states should hold immediately available national air-force contingents for combined international enforcement action in accordance with article 43 agreements. In this manner it was intended to create a United Nations corps to act as the arm of the Council to suppress threats to, or breaches of, the peace or acts of aggression.

Article 47 provides for the creation of a Military Staffs Committee, composed of the Chiefs of Staff of the five permanent members or their

---

[207] See also the Report of the Secretary-General, S/23006, 1991 and Security Council resolution 712 (1991). Note that Iraq has not yet agreed to sell the petroleum and petroleum products in question so that the Compensation Commission remains without the intended resources. In resolution 778 (1992) the Council called upon states which held frozen assets representing the proceeds of sale of Iraqi petroleum to transfer these to a special escrow account, from which 30 per cent would be transferred to the Compensation Fund.

[208] Category 'A' claims cover claims of individuals arising from their departure from Iraq or Kuwait; category 'B' claims cover individual claims for serious personal injury or death and category 'C' claims cover individual claims for damages up to $100, 000. See Decision 1, S/22885, annex II, paras. 14–16, see also 31 ILM, 1992, pp. 1009 *et seq.* Decision 7 deals with other claims by individuals, claims by corporations and other entities, and claims by governments and international organisations, S/23765, annex. In Decision 11, it was decided that members of the Allied Coalition Forces were not eligible for compensation unless in accordance with the adopted criteria, the claimants were prisoners-of-war and the loss or injury arose from mistreatment in violation of international humanitarian law, S/24363, annex II, *ibid.* See also A/AC.26/1994/2, reproduced in 34 ILM, 1995, p. 307.

[209] S/AC.26/1995/2–5. See also 35 ILM, 1996, p. 956.

representatives, to advise and assist the Security Council on the military requirements relating to the maintenance of international peace and security, the employment and command of troops placed at its disposal, the regulation of armaments and possible disarmament. It was intended that the Military Staffs Committee should be responsible for the strategic direction of any armed force placed at the disposal of the Security Council. Indeed, article 46 provides that plans for the application of armed force 'shall be made by the Security Council with the assistance of the Military Staffs Committee'. However, until the Kuwait crisis of 1990–1, the Military Staffs Committee exercised no practical function. During the unfolding of that crisis, it played an important co-ordinating role as the permanent members of the Security Council sought to co-operate and align their positions, while under Security Council resolution 665 (1990) it was given a more general co-ordination function.

Because of great power disputes and other factors, none of the projected agreements has been signed and article 43 remains ineffective. This has weakened article 42 to the extent that the envisaged procedure for its implementation has had to be abandoned. Of course, there are other ways of carrying out the Council's decisions to employ force in any given situation, but actions under article 42 as originally envisaged are likely to be few and far between.

The first example of enforcement action in practice was the United Nations reaction to the North Korean invasion of the South in 1950,[210] and this only occurred because of a fortuitous combination of circumstances. In June 1950 North Korean forces crossed the 28th Parallel dividing North from South Korea and thus precipitated armed conflict. Almost immediately the Security Council debated the issue and after declaring that a breach of the peace had taken place, called upon member states to assist the United Nations in achieving a North Korean withdrawal. Two days later, another resolution was adopted which recommended that United Nations members should furnish all necessary assistance to the South Korean authorities, while the third in the trio of Security Council resolutions on this issue authorised the United States to designate the commander of the unified forces established for the purpose of aiding the South Koreans and permitted the use of the United Nations flag by such forces.[211]

The only reason that these resolutions were in fact passed by the Council was the absence of the USSR in protest at the seating of the Nationalist Chinese delegation.[212] This prevented the exercise of the veto by the Soviet

[210] See e.g. Bowett, *Law*, Chapter 3; White, *Keeping the Peace*, pp. 108 *et seq.* and Franck, *Nation Against Nation*, p. 223.
[211] Security Council resolutions 82 (1950); 83 (1950) and 84 (1950).
[212] See e.g. L. Sohn, *Cases on United Nations Law*, 2nd edn, New York, 1967, pp. 479 *et seq.*

Union and permitted the creation of an authoritative United Nations umbrella for the US-commanded forces combating the North Korean armies. The USSR returned to the Council at the start of August 1950 and effectively blocked further action by the Council on this issue, but they could not reverse what had been achieved, despite claims that the resolutions were not constitutionally valid in view of the Soviet boycott.[213]

However, although termed United Nations forces, the contingents from the sixteen states which sent troops were under effective United States control, pursuant to a series of agreements concluded by that country with each of the contributing states, and were not in any real sense directed by the United Nations other than operating under a general Security Council authorisation. This improvised operation clearly revealed the deficiencies in the United Nations system of maintaining the peace. The lack of defined and clear procedures and the absence of the requisite organs meant that the formulation and establishment of the force could only be attained under the aegis of the one superpower and the *de facto* abdication of the other. It was a combination of circumstances that was probably unique and it was recognised that the likelihood of its recurrence was minimal.

However, the changing relationship between the two superpowers and the new era of co-operation ushered in by the late 1980s suggested an increasing reliance upon the United Nations. This developing possibility was speedily concretised following the invasion of Kuwait by Iraq on 2 August 1990.[214] Resolution 660 (1990), adopted unanimously the same day by the Security Council, condemned the invasion and called for an immediate and unconditional withdrawal. Resolution 662 (1990) declared that the purported Iraqi annexation of Kuwait had no legal validity and was null and void. States and international organisations were called upon to refrain from any action or dealing that might be interpreted as an indirect recognition of the annexation. The Council, specifically acting under Chapter VII of the UN Charter, demanded in resolution 664 (1990) that Iraq permit the immediate departure of the nationals of third countries[215] and in resolution 667 (1990) condemned Iraqi aggressive acts against diplomatic premises and personnel in Kuwait, including the abduction of foreign nationals present in those premises, and demanded the protection of diplomatic premises and personnel.[216]

Eventually, the Security Council, feeling that the response of Iraq to all the foregoing resolutions and measures adopted had been unsatisfactory,

213 *Ibid.*, pp. 481 *et seq.* See also *ibid.*, pp. 509 *et seq.* with regard to the situation following the Chinese involvement in the conflict.
214 See *The Kuwait Crisis: Basic Documents.* See also O. Schachter, 'United Nations Law in the Gulf Conflict', 85 AJIL, 1991, p. 452.
215 See also Security Council resolution 674 (1990).
216 See generally *Keesing's Record of World Events*, pp. 37631 *et seq.* and pp. 37694 *et seq.* (1990).

adopted resolution 678 (1990) on 29 November 1990. This allowed Iraq a further period of grace within which to comply with earlier resolutions and withdraw from Kuwait. This 'final opportunity' was to end on 15 January 1991. After this date, member states co-operating with the government of Kuwait were authorised to use all necessary means to uphold and implement Security Council resolution 660 (1990) and to restore international peace and security in the area. All states were requested to provide appropriate support for the actions undertaken in pursuance of this resolution. The armed action commenced on 16 January 1991 by a coalition of states[217] under the leadership of the United States can thus be seen as a legitimate use of force authorised by the UN Security Council under its enforcement powers elaborated in Chapter VII of the UN Charter and binding upon all member states of the UN by virtue of article 25. This is to be seen in the context of the purposes laid down by the Council in binding resolutions, that is the immediate and unconditional withdrawal of Iraq from Kuwait and the restoration of international peace and security in the area, and within the framework of the exercise of enforcement action in the light of the absence of article 43 arrangements. It is not thought that the wording in article 42, which provides that the Security Council 'may take such action by air, sea, or land forces as may be necessary to maintain or restore international peace and security', is to be read restrictively to refer only to action taken by forces in accordance with article 43.

The use of force in non-enforcement situations

In some recent situations, essentially peace-keeping mandates established under Chapter VII have led to the application of force by the UN. In both Bosnia and Somalia the temptation to resort to more robust tactics (often for the best of humanitarian reasons) involving the use of force, but without adequate political or military resources or support, has led to severe difficulties.

FORMER YUGOSLAVIA

The outbreak of hostilities in Yugoslavia led the Security Council in resolution 713 (1991), adopted on 25 September 1991, to impose an arms embargo on that country. As the situation deteriorated, the decision was taken to establish a peace-keeping force (the UN Protection Force or

---

[217] The following states supplied armed forces and/or warships or aircraft for the enforcement of the UN resolutions: USA, UK, France, Egypt, Syria, Saudi Arabia, Morocco, the Netherlands, Australia, Italy, Spain, Argentina, Belgium, Canada, Pakistan, Norway, Denmark, USSR, Bangladesh, Senegal, Niger, Czechoslovakia and the Gulf Co-operation Council (Kuwait, Qatar, Bahrain, Oman and the United Arab Emirates), see *The Sunday Times* 'War in the Gulf' Briefing, 27 January 1991, p. 9.

UNPROFOR) in order to ensure the demilitarisation of three protected areas in Croatia (inhabited by Serbs).[218] This resolution did not refer to Chapter VII and did specifically note the request of the government of Yugoslavia for a peace-keeping operation.[219] The full deployment of the force was authorised by resolution 749 (1992). During the following months the mandate of UNPROFOR was gradually extended. By resolution 762 (1992), for example, it was authorised to monitor the situation in areas of Croatia under Yugoslav army control,[220] while by resolution 779 (1992) UNPROFOR assumed responsibility for monitoring the demilitarisation of the Prevlaka peninsula near Dubrovnik.[221] At the same time, the situation in Bosnia and Herzegovina deteriorated. Both Croatia and the Federal Republic of Yugoslavia (Serbia and Montenegro) were criticised for their actions in Bosnia in resolution 757 (1992)[222] and sanctions were imposed upon the latter. In resolution 758 (1992), the Council approved an enlargement of UNPROFOR's mandate and strength and authorised the deployment of military observers and related personnel and equipment to Sarajevo, the capital of Bosnia.[223]

In a further measure responding to the dire situation, the Security Council, acting under Chapter VII, adopted resolution 770 (1992) calling on all states to 'take nationally or through regional agencies or arrangements all measures necessary' to facilitate in co-ordination with the UN, the delivery of humanitarian assistance to and within Bosnia. The phrase 'all necessary measures', it will be recalled, permits in UN terminology the resort to force.[224] The mandate of UNPROFOR was augmented by resolution 776 (1992) to incorporate support for the humanitarian relief activities of the UN High Commissioner for Refugees (UNHCR) and in particular to provide protection where requested. It was noted in the Secretary-General's Report, approved by this resolution, that the normal peace-keeping rules of engagement would be followed, so that force could be used in self-defence, particularly where attempts were made to prevent the carrying out of the

---

[218] Security Council resolution 743 (1992). See also the Report of the Secretary-General, S/23592 and Security Council resolutions 721 (1991) and 724 (1991). See also White, *Keeping the Peace*, pp. 251 et seq.   [219] The resolution, however, did mention article 25.

[220] See also Security Council resolution 769 (1992).

[221] Note also Security Council resolution 802 (1993) criticising Croatia for its attacks within or adjacent to the UN protected areas and upon UNPROFOR personnel.

[222] The Security Council in this resolution was explicitly acting under Chapter VII. See also resolution 752 (1992) also criticising outside interference in Bosnia, which did not refer to Chapter VII.

[223] Additional elements were deployed to ensure the security of the airport by resolution 761 (1992). Note that neither of these resolutions referred to Chapter VII. See also S/1994/300, with regard to UNPROFOR's mandate relating to Sarajevo airport. The airlift of humanitarian supplies into this airport was the longest lasting such airlift in history and well over 150,000 tons were delivered, see S/1995/444, para. 23.

[224] The Secretary-General was, however, careful to state that this resolution created no additional mandate for UNPROFOR, see S/1995/444, para. 25.

mandate.[225] However, resolution 776 (1992) made no mention of either Chapter VII or 'all necessary measures'.

A further stage in the evolution of UNPROFOR's role occurred with the adoption of the 'no-fly' ban imposed on military flights over Bosnia by Security Council resolution 781 (1992). UNPROFOR was given the task of monitoring compliance with this ban.[226] The ban on air activity was expanded in resolution 816 (1993) to cover flights by all fixed-wing and rotary-wing aircraft. The resolution also authorised member states to take 'under the authority of the Security Council and subject to close co-ordination with the Secretary-General and UNPROFOR, all necessary measures' to ensure compliance with it. Both of these resolutions were adopted under Chapter VII. At the request of the Secretary-General, the no-fly zone was enforced by aircraft from NATO.[227] A 'dual key' system was put into operation under which decisions on targeting and execution in the use of NATO airpower were to be taken jointly by UN and NATO commanders and the principle of proportionality of response to violations was affirmed.[228]

In order to protect certain Bosnian Moslem areas under siege from Bosnian Serb forces, the Security Council established a number of 'safe areas'.[229] Although Chapter VII was referred to in these resolutions, it was cited only in the context of resolution 815 (1993), which dealt with the security of UNPROFOR personnel. The enforcement of the 'safe areas' was therefore to be attained by UNPROFOR personnel authorised to use force only to protect themselves.[230] Although the Secretary-General stated that approximately 34,000 extra troops would be necessary, only an additional 7,000 were authorised.[231] At the request of the Secretary-General, NATO established a 3 kilometre 'total exclusion zone' and a 20 kilometre 'military exclusion zone' around Gorazde and a 20 kilometre 'heavy weapons exclusion zone' around Sarajevo. These zones were to be enforced by air strikes if necessary, although no Security Council resolutions referred to such zones nor created any special regime with regard to them.[232] Relations between

---

[225] See S/24540. Note that a number of resolutions extended the application of Chapter VII to UNPROFOR's freedom of movement, e.g. resolutions 807 (1993) and 847 (1993), and force was used on a number of occasions in self-defence, see e.g. S/1995/444, para. 55.
[226] See also Security Council resolution 786 (1992).
[227] See e.g. the Report of the Secretary-General, S/1995/444, para. 30.
[228] See e.g. Joint Press Statement of 29 October 1994, PKO/32.
[229] See resolutions 819 (1993) and 824 (1993). These were Srebrenica, Sarajevo, Tuzla, Zepa, Gorazde and Bihac.   [230] See also Security Council resolution 836 (1993).
[231] Security Council resolution 844 (1993). See also S/25939. Note that the Secretary-General called for the demilitarisation of the 'safe areas', S/1994/1389. At the request of the Secretary UNPROFOR was also given the task of monitoring the cease-fire agreement between the Bosnian and Croatian armies, see Security Council resolution 908 (1994), and given additional responsibilities with regard to Sarajevo, see Security Council resolution 900 (1994).   [232] S/1995/444, paras. 48–9.

UNPROFOR and the Bosnian Serbs led to a series of incidents in the Spring of 1995. The latter breached the Sarajevo no heavy weapons arrangement, and this precipitated NATO airstrikes which provoked the taking hostage of several hundred UNPROFOR soldiers. The 'safe area' of Srebrenica was then captured by Bosnian Serb forces in July 1995, involving major human rights abuses against the population. After incidents involving other 'safe areas' and Sarajevo, NATO with UN approval launched a series of airstrikes.[233] At the same time, Bosnian and Croat forces captured areas held by the Bosnian Serbs. A ceasefire agreement came into force on 12 October 1995.[234]

UN peace-keeping missions in former Yugoslavia were reorganised in March 1995, following the capture by Croatian forces of three of the four protected areas inhabited by Serbs in Croatia. The UN missions therefore comprised UNPROFOR in Bosnia,[235] the UN Confidence Restoration Operation in Croatia (UNCRO)[236] and the UN Preventive Deployment Force (UNPREDEP) in the former Yugoslav Republic of Macedonia.[237] As a consequence of the Dayton peace agreement initialled in November 1995, UNPROFOR was replaced by a multinational implementation force (IFOR)[238] composed primarily of troops from NATO countries. In addition, it was proposed to set up a UN International Police Task Force to carry out a variety of police related training and assistance missions.[239]

The evolution of the UN role in the complex Yugoslav tragedy may be characterised as a series of impromptu actions taken in response to traumatic events. The UN force was a peace-keeping mission that was dragged more and more into a fast-moving and complicated situation well beyond its power to seriously influence never mind resolve. UNPROFOR was never authorised to use force beyond that required in self-defence while performing their rapidly expanding duties. The UN sought to fulfil its fundamental mandated responsibilities with respect to Sarajevo and the transportation of humanitarian aid in co-operation with the warring parties based on the peace-keeping principles of impartiality and consent. But the situation was far from a normal peace-keeping situation of separating hostile forces that consent to such separation. Fighting occurred throughout the country between various parties at various times. The use of air power was subsequently authorised both in order to defend UNPROFOR personnel

---

[233] See also Security Council resolution 998 (1995) regarding the proposal to establish a rapid reaction force.   [234] See S/1995/987.
[235] See also Security Council resolution 1026 (1995).
[236] See also Security Council resolutions 990 (1995) and 994 (1995).
[237] Security Council resolutions 981 (1995), 982 (1995) and 983 (1995). The Security Council had authorised deployment of a preventive force in Macedonia in resolution 795 (1992). See also S/24923, annex.   [238] See Security Council resolution 1031 (1995).
[239] See e.g. S/1995/1031 and Security Council resolution 1026 (1995). The International Police Task Force was established under resolution 1035 (1995).

and to deter attacks upon the 'safe areas', which had been proclaimed as such with little in the way of initial enforcement means. Eventually relatively large-scale air strikes by NATO were resorted to in the face of fears of further Bosnian Serb capture of 'safe areas'. Whether a peace-keeping mission in the traditional sense can ever be really mounted in the conditions then faced in Bosnia must be seriously in doubt, although the humanitarian efforts undertaken were important. Only a meaningful enforcement mandate could have given the UN a chance to put an end to the fighting. But that required a major political commitment and substantial resources that these states are rarely willing to provide unless their own vital national interests are at stake.

SOMALIA[240]

The Somali situation marked a similar effort by the UN to resolve a humanitarian crisis arising out of civil war conditions and one that saw a peace-keeping mission drifting into an enforcement one. Following a prolonged period of civil war, the Security Council urged all parties to agree to a cease-fire and imposed an arms embargo. The Secretary-General was requested to organise humanitarian assistance.[241] A UN technical mission was then established to look at mechanisms to provide such aid and to examine peace-keeping options.[242] The UN Operation in Somalia (UNOSOM) was set up shortly thereafter,[243] but this modest operation (of fifty ceasefire observers and a security force) was deemed insufficient to ensure the delivery of humanitarian assistance and the deployment of additional UN security units in order to protect the distribution centres and humanitarian convoys was authorised.[244] However, the situation continued to deteriorate and few humanitarian supplies arrived where needed due to constant attacks.[245] Accordingly, after the Secretary-General had concluded that Chapter VII action was required,[246] the Security Council determined that the 'magnitude of the human tragedy caused by the conflict in Somalia, further exacerbated by the obstacles being created to the distribution of humanitarian assistance, constitutes a threat to international peace and security'. The use of 'all necessary means to establish as soon as possible a secure environment for humanitarian relief operations' was authorised and the Unified Task Force was created

[240] See e.g. Franck, *Nation Against Nation*, pp. 301 *et seq.* and I. Lewis and J. Mayall, 'Somalia' in *The New Interventionism 1991–1994* (ed. J. Mayall), Cambridge, 1996, p. 94. See also J. M. Sorel, 'La Somalie et les Nations Unies', AFDI, 1992, p. 61.
[241] Security Council resolution 733 (1992). See also S/23829, 1992.
[242] Security Council resolution 746 (1992).
[243] Security Council resolution 751 (1992). This was not originally a Chapter VII operation.
[244] Security Council resolution 775 (1992). See also S/244480, 1992. Under resolution 767 (1992) Somalia was divided into four operational zones for the delivery of food aid and ceasefire purposes.   [245] See S/24859, 1992.   [246] S/24868, 1992.

(UNITAF).[247] This comprised troops from over 20 states, including some 30,000 from the US.[248]

This operation was expanded the following spring and UNOSOM II was established with an enlarged mandate with enforcement powers under Chapter VII.[249] UNOSOM II was given the humanitarian mandate of UNITAF, together with 'responsibility for the consolidation, expansion and maintenance of a secure environment throughout Somalia' and the provision of security to assist the repatriation of refugees and the assisted resettlement of displaced persons. The force was also to complete the disarmament of factions, enforce the Addis Ababa agreement of January 1993[250] and help rebuild the country. The authorisation to take all necessary measures was reiterated in resolution 837 (1993), following an attack upon UNOSOM II forces. This authorisation was stated to include taking action against those responsible for the attacks and to establish the effective authority of UNOSOM II throughout the country. A series of military incidents then took place involving UN forces.[251] Security Council resolution 897 (1994), while condemning continued violence in the country especially against UN personnel, authorised a reduction in UNOSOM II's force levels to 22,000.[252] And in resolution 954 (1994), the Council decided to terminate the mission at the end of March 1995 and authorised UNOSOM II to take actions necessary to protect the mission and the withdrawal of personnel and assets and to that end called upon member states to provide assistance to aid the withdrawal process. The Secretary-General concluded his report of 14 October 1994 noting that the vacuum of civil authority and of governmental authority severely hampered the work of the UN, while 'the presence of UNOSOM II troops has had limited impact on the peace process and limited impact on security in the face of continuing interclan fighting and banditry'.[253]

RWANDA[254]

Following a civil war between government forces and RPF rebels, the Security Council authorised the deployment of the UN Observer Mission Uganda Rwanda (UNOMUR) on the Ugandan side of the border.[255] A

[247] Security Council resolution 794 (1992).
[248] The operation was termed 'Operation Restore Hope' and it arrived in Somalia in December 1992, see S/24976, 1992 and S/25168, 1993.
[249] Security Council resolution 814 (1993). See also S/25354, 1993.
[250] See S/25168, annex III.
[251] See e.g. S/26022, 1993, and Security Council resolutions 865 (1993); 878 (1993); 885 (1993) and 886 (1993).
[252] See also Security Council resolutions 923 (1994) and 946 (1994).
[253] S/1994/1166, Part 2, para. 22.   [254] See e.g. Franck, *Nation Against Nation*, pp. 300 et seq.
[255] See Security Council resolution 846 (1993). See also resolutions 812 (1993) and 891 (1993). This mission was terminated in resolution 928 (1994).

peace agreement was signed between the parties at Arusha and the UN set up the UN Assistance Mission for Rwanda (UNAMIR) with a mandate to ensure the security of the capital, Kigali, monitor the ceasefire agreement and monitor the security situation generally up to the installation of the new government.[256] However, the projected transitional institutions were not set up and the security situation deteriorated. Following the deaths of the Presidents of Rwanda and Burundi in an airplane crash on 5 April 1994, full-scale civil war erupted which led to massacres of Hutu opposition leaders and genocidal actions against members of the Tutsi minority. Faced with this situation, the Security Council rejected the option of strengthening UNAMIR and empowering it under Chapter VII in favour of withdrawing most of the mission from the country.[257]

As the situation continued to deteriorate, the Council imposed an arms embargo on the country, authorised the increase of UNAMIR to 5, 500 and its redeployment in Rwanda and expanded its mandate to include the establishment and maintenance of secure humanitarian areas.[258] However, delays in implementing this led to a proposal from France to establish a French-commanded force to act under Chapter VII of the Charter and subject to Security Council authorisation in order to protect displaced persons and civilians at risk. This was accepted in resolution 929 (1994) in which the Council, acting under Chapter VII, authorised a two-month operation (Operation Turquoise) until UNAMIR was up to strength. Member states were authorised to use all necessary measures to achieve their humanitarian objectives. The force, therefore acting as the Gulf War Coalition had on the basis of Security Council authorisation under Chapter VII, established a humanitarian protected zone in south-western Rwanda. Gradually UNAMIR built up to strength and it began deploying troops in the protected zone on 10 August 1994, taking over responsibility from the French-led force shortly thereafter and deploying in areas throughout the country. UNAMIR's mandate ended on 6 March 1996.[259]

IRAQ

Following the Gulf War, revolts against the central government in Iraq led to widespread repression by Iraqi forces against the Shias in the south and the Kurds in the north of the country. Security Council resolution 688 (1991) condemned such repression 'the consequences of which threaten international peace and security' and insisted that Iraq allow immediate access by international humanitarian organisations to those in need in the

---

[256] Security Council resolution 872 (1993). See also resolutions 893 (1994) and 909 (1994).
[257] Security Council resolution 912 (1994).
[258] Security Council resolution 918 (1994). See also resolutions 925 (1994) and 935 (1994).
[259] See Security Council resolution 1029 (1995).

country. It is to be noted that the resolution did not refer to Chapter VII and indeed specifically mentioned article 2(7) of the Charter. In the light of the repression, the US, UK and France sent troops into northern Iraq to create a safe haven for humanitarian operations. They were speedily withdrawn and replaced by a small number of UN Guards operating with the consent of Iraq.[260] In addition, the western states declared a 'no-fly' zone over southern Iraq in August 1992, having established one over northern Iraq in April 1991. The justification of these zones was argued to be that of supporting resolution 688.[261] Further, it was maintained that the right of self-defence existed with regard to flights over the zones, thus permitting proportionate responses to Iraqi actions.[262] Whether resolution 688 can indeed be so interpreted is unclear. What is clear is that such actions were not explicitly mandated by the UN. However, the relevance of the cease-fire resolution[263] in this context cannot be ignored in view of Iraq's non-compliance, nor can the arguable right of humanitarian intervention in cases of extreme need.[264]

The range of UN actions from humanitarian assistance to enforcement – conclusions

The UN has not been able to operate Chapter VII as originally envisaged. It has, however, been able to develop a variety of mechanisms to fill the gap left by the non-implementation of article 43. First and foremost, the Council may delegate its enforcement powers to member states. This occurred in Korea, the Gulf War and to some extent in Rwanda. The UN has also been able to create peace-keeping forces, whose mandate has traditionally been to separate hostile forces with their consent, such as in the Middle East and in Cyprus. The evolution of peacekeeping activities to include confused civil war situations where fighting has not ended and no lasting ceasefire has been put into operation, although prefigured in the Congo crisis of the 1960s, has really taken place in the last few years. It has brought attendant dangers for, as has been seen, the slippage from

[260] See e.g. White, *Keeping the Peace*, p. 192 and Kirgis, *International Organisations*, pp. 854 *et seq.*
[261] See e.g. the statement of the Minister of State at the Foreign Office on 27 January 1993, UKMIL, 64 BYIL, 1993, p. 739 and of President Bush of the US cited in Kirgis, *International Organisations*, p. 856. Note that on 3 September 1996, in response to the entry of Iraqi troops and tanks into the northern 'no-fly' Kurdish zone in order to aid one of the Kurdish groups against another, US aircraft launched a series of air strikes against Iraq and extended the southern 'no-fly' zone from the 32nd to the 33rd parallel. In so doing the US government cited Security Council resolution 688 (1991), see *The Economist*, 7 September 1996, pp. 55–6.
[262] *Ibid.*, pp. 728 and 740 with regard to Western air raids against Iraqi targets on 13 January 1993.   [263] Security Council resolution 687 (1991).
[264] The actions taken were hardly inconsistent with resolution 688 (1991). See further *supra*, Chapter 19, p. 802.

peace-keeping to self-defence activities more widely defined and thence to *de facto* enforcement action is sometimes hard to avoid and complicated to justify in legal terms. Consent is the basis of traditional peace-keeping and irrelevant in enforcement activities. In the mandate drift that has been evident in some situations elements of both consent and imposition have been present in a way that has confused the role of the UN. Nevertheless, behind the difficulties of the UN has lain a dearth of both political will demonstrated by, and material resources provided by, member states for the completion of complex enforcement actions.

Developments that have been seen in recent years have demonstrated an acceptance of a far broader conception of what constitutes a threat to international peace and security, so that not only external aggression but certain purely internal convulsions may qualify, thus constraining further the scope of article 2(7) and the exclusive jurisdiction of states. Secondly, the range of actions taken by the Security Council under Chapter VII has increased to cover a wide variety of missions and the creation of international criminal tribunals to prosecute alleged war criminals for crimes occurring within particular states arising out of civil wars. Not only that, but with regard to Iraq, the Security Council took a range of binding measures of unprecedented scope from the guaranteeing of a contested boundary to implementing strict controls on certain kinds of armaments and establishing a compensation commission to be funded by a levy on oil exports.

The Security Council, international law and the International Court of Justice

The issue of the relationship between binding decisions of the Council and international law generally has arisen with particular force in recent years in view of the rapidly increased range and nature of activity by the Security Council. The issue has involved particular consideration of the role of the International Court.[265] The Security Council is, of course, constrained by

---

[265] See for example, G. R. Watson, 'Constitutionalism, Judicial Review, and the World Court', 34 *Harvard International Law Journal*, 1993, p. 1; V. Gowlland-Debbas, 'Security Council Enforcement Action and Issues of State Responsibility', 43 ICLQ, 1994, p. 55; and Gowlland-Debbas, 'The Relationship between the International Court of Justice and the Security Council in the Light of the *Lockerbie* Case', 88 AJIL, 1994, p. 643; R. St J. Macdonald, 'Changing Relations between the International Court of Justice and the Security Council of the United Nations', Canadian YIL, 1993, p. 3; R. F. Kennedy, '*Libya v. United States*; The International Court of Justice and the Power of Judicial Review', 33 Va JIL, 1993, p. 899; T. F. Franck, 'The "Powers of Appreciation": Who is the Ultimate Guardian of UN Legality?', 86 AJIL, 1992, p. 519 and Franck, *Fairness*, pp. 242 *et seq*; W. M. Reisman, 'The Constitutional Crisis in the United Nations', 87 AJIL, 1993, p. 83; E. McWhinney, 'The International Court as Emerging Constitutional Court and the Co-ordinate UN Institutions (Especially the Security Council): Implications of the *Aerial Incident at Lockerbie*', Canadian YIL, 1992, p. 261; J. M. Sorel, 'Les Ordonnances de la Cour

the provisions of the Charter itself. It must follow the procedures laid down and act within the confines of its constitutional authority as detailed particularly in Chapters V to VII. Its composition and voting procedures are laid down as are the conditions under which it may adopt binding enforcement measures. As the International Court has emphasised, '[t]he political character of an organ cannot release it from the observance of the treaty provisions established by the Charter when they constitute limitations on its powers or criteria for its judgement'.[266] In particular, the Council must under article 24(2) act in accordance with the Purposes and Principles of the Charter, article 1(1) of which declares that one of the aims of the organisation is to bring about a resolution of international disputes by peaceful means 'and in conformity with the principles of justice and international law'.[267]

The Council has recently not only made determinations as to the existence of a threat to or breach of international peace and security under article 39, but also under Chapter VII binding determinations as to the location of boundaries, supervision of destruction of weaponry, liability under international law for loss or damage, methods of compensation, asserted repudiation of foreign debt,[268] the establishment of tribunals to try individual war criminals,[269] and assertions as to the use of force against those responsible for, and those inciting, attacks against UN personnel, including their arrest, prosecution and punishment.[270] In addition, the Council has asserted that particular acts were null and void, demanding non-recognition.[271]

In view of this increased activity and the impact this has upon member states, the issue has arisen as to whether there is a body capable of ensuring that the Council does act in conformity with the Charter and international law. Since the International Court is the 'principal judicial organ' of the

International de Justice du 14 Avril 1992 Dans l'Affaire Relative a des Questions d'Interpretation et d'Application de la Convention de Montreal de 1971 Resultant de l'Incident Aerien de Lockerbie', *Revue Générale de Droit International Public*, 1993, p. 689 and M. N. Shaw, 'The Security Council and the International Court of Justice: Judicial Drift and Judicial Function', in *The International Court of Justice* (eds. A. S. Muller, D. Raič and J. M. Tharánszky), The Hague, 1997, p. 219.

[266] *Conditions of Admission of a State to Membership in the United Nations*, ICJ Reports, 1948, p. 64; 15 ILR, p. 333. See also Judge Bedjaoui, the *Lockerbie* case, ICJ Reports, 1992, pp. 3, 45; 94 ILR, pp. 478, 528.

[267] See Judge Weeramantry's Dissenting Opinion in the *Lockerbie* case, ICJ Reports, 1992, p. 65 and that of Judge Bedjaoui, *ibid.*, p. 46; 94 ILR, pp. 548 and 529. See also Judge Fitzmaurice in the *Namibia* case, ICJ Reports, 1971, pp. 17, 294; 49 ILR, pp. 2, 284–5.

[268] See Security Council resolution 687 (1991) with regard to Iraq after the Gulf War.

[269] Security Council resolutions 808 (1993) and 827 (1993) regarding former Yugoslavia and resolution 955 (1994) regarding Rwanda. See also the *Tadić* case decided by the Appeals Chamber of the International Tribunal on War Crimes in Former Yugoslavia, Case No. IT-94–1–AR72, pp. 13 *et seq.*

[270] Security Council resolution 837 (1993) concerning Somalia.

[271] Security Council resolutions 662 (1990) regarding the purported annexation by Iraq of

UN,[272] it would seem to be the natural candidate, and indeed the problem has been posed in two cases recently. In the *Genocide Convention (Bosnia and Herzegovina* v. *Yugoslavia (Serbia and Montenegro))* case,[273] it was claimed by Bosnia that the Security Council imposed arms embargo upon the former Yugoslavia had to be construed in a maner that did not deprive Bosnia of its inherent right of self-defence under article 51 of the Charter and under customary international law.[274] In the *Lockerbie* case,[275] Libya claimed that the UK and US were seeking to compel it to surrender alleged bombers contrary to the Montreal Convention 1971 (which required that a state either prosecute or extradite alleged offenders) and that the Council's actions in resolutions 731 (1992) and 748 (1992)[276] were contrary to international law.

While the question of the compatibility of Security Council resolutions with international law was not discussed by the Court in the *Bosnia* case, the issue assumed central position in the *Lockerbie* case. The Court here affirmed that all member states were obliged to accept and carry out the decisions of the Security Council in accordance with article 25 of the Charter and that *prima facie* this obligation extended to resolution 748 (1992), which imposed sanctions upon Libya for failing to extradite the suspects. Thus, in accordance with article 103 of the Charter, under which obligations under the Charter prevail over obligations contained in other international agreements, the resolution prevailed over the Montreal Convention.[277] Judge Shahabuddeen in his Separate Opinion underlined that the issue in the case was whether a decision of the Council could override the legal rights of states and, if so, whether there were any limitations upon its power to characterise a situation as one justifying the making of the decision importing such consequences.[278]

While there is no doubt that under the Charter system the Council's discretion to determine the existence of threats to or breaches of international peace and security is virtually absolute, limited only by inherent notions of good faith and non-abuse of rights[279] and its discretion to impose measures

---

Kuwait and 541 (1983) terming the purported Turkish Cypriot state 'legally invalid'.

[272] Article 92 of the Charter.   [273] ICJ Reports, 1992, pp. 3, 6; 95 ILR, pp. 1, 21.

[274] See also the second provisional measures order, ICJ Reports, 1993, pp. 325, 327–8; 95 ILR, pp. 43, 45–6. The Court confined itself to the Genocide Convention.

[275] ICJ Reports, 1992, pp. 3, 14; 94 ILR, pp. 478, 497.

[276] Calling upon Libya to surrender the suspects and imposing sanctions for failing so to do.

[277] ICJ Reports, 1992, p. 15; 94 ILR, p. 498.

[278] *Ibid.*, p. 32; 94 ILR, p. 515. Judge Lachs noted that the Court was bound 'to respect' the binding decisions of the Security Council as part of international law, *ibid.*, p. 26; 94 ILR, p. 509, see Franck, *Fairness*, p. 243 who emphasised that the verb used, to 'respect' does not mean to 'defer to'. Note that Judge Lachs also pointed to the Court as the 'guardian of legality for the international community as a whole, both within and without the United Nations', ICJ Reports, 1992, p. 26.

[279] See e.g. Gowlland-Debbas, 'Security Council Enforcement', pp. 93–4. See also the *Tadić* case decided by the Appeals Chamber of the International Tribunal on War Crimes in Former Yugoslavia, Case No. IT-94-1-AR72, pp. 13 *et seq.*

consequent upon that determination in order to maintain or restore international peace and security is undoubtedly extensive,[280] the determination of the legality or illegality of particular situations is essentially the Council's view as to the matching of particular facts with existing rules of international law. That view, when adopted under Chapter VII, will bind member states, but where it is clearly wrong in law and remains unrectified by the Council subsequently, a challenge to the system is indubitably posed. While the Court can, and has, examined and analysed UN resolutions in the course of deciding a case or rendering an Advisory Opinion, for it to assert a right of judicial review in the fullest sense enabling it to declare invalid a binding Security Council resolution would equally challenge the system as it operates. Between the striking down of Chapter VII decisions and the acceptance of resolutions clearly embodying propositions contrary to international law, an ambiguous and indeterminate area lies.

The role of the General Assembly[281]

The focus of attention during the 1950s shifted from the Security Council to the General Assembly as the use of the veto by the permanent members led to a perception of the reduced effectiveness of the Council. Since it was never really envisaged that the General Assembly would play a large part in the preservation of international peace and security, its powers as defined in the Charter were vague and imprecise. Articles 10 to 14 provide that the Assembly may discuss any question within the scope of the Charter and may consider the general principles of co-operation in the maintenance of international peace and security. The Assembly may make recommendations with respect to questions relating to international peace to members of the United Nations or the Security Council or both, provided (except in the case of general principles of co-operation, including disarmament) the Council is not dealing with the particular matter. In addition, any question respecting international peace and security on which action is necessary has to be referred to the Security Council.

The Uniting for Peace resolution was adopted by the Assembly in 1950 because it was felt that such provisions had to be reinterpreted more specifically if the Assembly was to strengthen its role in dealing with international peace in the event of a veto in the Security Council. This resolution,

---

[280] Note that under article 1(1) actions to bring about the adjustment or settlement of international disputes or situations which might lead to a breach of the peace must be in conformity with 'the principles of justice and international law', while there is no such qualification with regard to effective collective measures to prevent and remove threats to the peace and the suppression of breaches of the peace or acts of aggression.

[281] See e.g. *The Charter of the United Nations*, pp. 215 *et seq.* and White, *Keeping the Peace*, part 2.

organised by the Western nations whose influence predominated in the Assembly at that time, was founded on the view that as the Security Council had the primary responsibility for the maintenance of peace under article 24, it could therefore be argued that the Assembly possessed a secondary responsibility in such matters, which could be activated in the event of obstruction in the Security Council.

The resolution[282] declared that where the Council failed to exercise its responsibility upon the occurrence of a threat to the peace, breach of the peace or act of aggression because of the exercise of the veto by any of its permanent members, the General Assembly was to consider the matter at once with a view to making appropriate recommendations to members for collective measures. Such measures could include the use of force when necessary in the case of a breach of the peace or act of aggression, and if not already in session, the Assembly would be able to meet within twenty-four hours in emergency special session.[283]

Certain aspects relating to this streamlining of the Assembly's procedures and elucidation of its substantive powers caused problems within a short time. Article 11 of the Charter emphasises that any question dealing with international peace and security on which action was necessary had to be referred to the Security Council and this appeared to cast some doubts upon the validity of the provision in the Uniting for Peace resolution under which the Assembly could call for collective measures involving the use of force. This point was particularly stressed by the Soviet Union and its allies. It became of vital significance with the creation by the Assembly in 1956 of the United Nations Emergency Force which was to supervise the cease-fire in the Middle East, and in 1960 of the United Nations Force in the Congo by the United Nations Secretary-General.

The constitutionality of such forces was questioned by a number of states, who refused to pay their share of the expenses incurred, and the matter was referred to the International Court. In the *Certain Expenses* case,[284] the Court took the term 'action'[285] to refer to 'enforcement action', thus permitting action which did not amount to enforcement action to be called for

---

[282] General Assembly resolution 377(V). See e.g. Murphy, *United Nations*, Chapter 4 and J. Andrassy, 'Uniting for Peace', 50 AJIL, 1956, p. 563. See also M. J. Petersen, 'The Uses of the Uniting for Peace Resolution since 1950', 8 *International Organisation*, 1959, p. 219 and F. Woolsey, 'The Uniting for Peace Resolution of the United Nations', 45 AJIL, 1951, p. 129.

[283] The General Assembly under article 20 of the UN Charter meets only in regular annual sessions and in such special sessions as occasion may require.

[284] ICJ Reports, 1962, p. 151; 34 ILR, p. 281.

[285] Article 11(2) of the Charter provides that the General Assembly may discuss any questions relating to the maintenance of international peace and security, but any such question 'on which action is necessary' must be referred to the Security Council

by the General Assembly and the Secretary-General.[286] This opinion, although leading to some interpretive problems, did permit the creation of United Nations peace-keeping forces in situations where because of superpower rivalry it was not possible for the Security Council to reach a decision, provided such forces were not concerned with enforcement action. The adoption of this kind of action remains firmly within the prerogative of the Security Council.

In practice the hopes raised by the adoption of the Uniting for Peace resolution have not really been fulfilled.[287] The procedure prescribed within the resolution has been used, for example, with regard to the Suez and Hungarian crises of 1956, the Lebanese and Jordanian troubles of 1958, the Congo upheavals of 1960, the Middle East in 1967, the conflict leading to the creation of Bangladesh in 1971, Afghanistan in 1980, Namibia in 1981 and the Palestine question in 1980 and 1982. But it cannot be said that the Uniting for Peace system has in effect exercised any great influence regarding the maintenance of international peace and security. It has provided a method whereby disputes may be aired before the Assembly in a way that might not have otherwise been possible, but as a reserve mechanism for the preservation or restoration of international peace, it has not proved very successful. It arose as a result of the use of the veto in the Security Council in the context of superpower rivalry, but the expansion in the membership of the Assembly and the consequent shift in the balance of power against the West affected the use of the system. Indeed, with the ending of the Cold War, the Security Council was able to function in a way impossible before, and the range of actions and initiatives undertaken by it has been on the whole remarkable. This has had the effect of further side-lining the General Assembly.

The UN and regional arrangements and agencies[288]

Chapter VIII of the UN Charter concerns regional arrangements. Article 52 provides that nothing contained in the Charter precludes the existence of regional arrangements or agencies for dealing with such matters relating to international peace and security as are appropriate for such arrangements or agencies, providing that these are consistent with the Purposes and

---

[286] Accordingly, the UN Emergency Force in the Middle East established in 1956 was not contrary to article 11(2) since it had not been intended to take enforcement action, ICJ Reports, 1962, pp. 151, 165, 171–2. This precipitated a crisis over the arrears of the states refusing to pay their contributions, see Murphy, *United Nations*, pp. 82–4.

[287] See e.g. White, *Keeping the Peace*, pp. 152 *et seq.*

[288] See e.g. *The Charter of the United Nations*, pp. 679 *et seq.* and O. Schachter, 'Authorised Uses of Force by the United Nations and Regional Organisations' in *The New International Order and the Use of Force* (eds. L. Damrosch and D. J. Scheffer), Boulder, CO, 1991, p. 65.

Principles of the UN itself.[289] Article 53 notes that the Security Council where appropriate shall utilise such arrangements or agencies for enforcement action under its authority. Without the authorisation of the Security Council, regional enforcement action is not possible.[290] Article 54 provides that the Security Council is to be kept fully informed at all times of activities undertaken or in contemplation by regional organisations. The definition of 'regional arrangements or agencies' is left open, so that a useful measure of flexibility is provided, enabling the term to cover a wide range of regional organisations going beyond those strictly established for defence co-operation.

Several issues arise. First, when regional action may be deemed to be appropriate, and here recent events have demonstrated a broader measure of flexibility akin to the widening definition of what constitutes a threat to international peace and security. Secondly, to what extent regional action is consistent with UN purposes and principles, and here the provisions of article 103, assigning priority to Charter obligations over obligations contained in other international agreements should be noted. Thirdly, there is the question as to whether a broad or a narrow definition of enforcement action is to be accepted.[291] Fourthly, the important issue is raised as to whether prior approval by the Security Council is required in order for a regional organisation to engage in an activity consistent with Chapter VIII. Practice here recently appears to suggest rather controversially that not only is prior approval not required, but that Security Council authorisation need not occur until substantially after the action has commenced.

It is clear from articles 52(2) and (3) that peaceful settlement of disputes through regional mechanisms before resort is had to the Security Council is the preferred route and this, on the whole, has been the practice of the UN.[292] Enforcement action is a different matter and here priority lies with the Council under the Charter. However, the reference to the inherent right of collective self-defence in article 51 does detract somewhat from the effect of Chapter VIII, and it also seems clear that regional peace-keeping operations, in the traditional sense of being based on consent of the parties and eschewing the use of force save in self-defence, do not need the authorisation of the Security Council.

Several crucial issues concerning regional action and the UN arose in the Grenada episode. There the United States argued that regional peace-

---

[289] Note also the relevance of the right of collective self-defence under both customary international law and article 51 of the Charter, see *supra*, Chapter 19, p. 794.

[290] See e.g. M. Akehurst, 'Enforcement Action by Regional Agencies', 42 BYIL, 1967, p. 175.

[291] That is, whether all actions noted in articles 41 and 42 or just those using military force are covered.

[292] Although article 52(4) provides that 'this article in no way impairs the application of articles 34 and 35'.

keeping (as distinct from enforcement action) had occurred and that it constituted one of the legal grounds for its action there.[293] The issue is also raised in that case of the appropriate regional arrangement or agency. The Charter of the Organisation of American States emphasises the territorial inviolability of states and the prohibition of intervention,[294] but article 22 notes that such provisions would not be violated by measures adopted for the maintenance of peace and security 'in accordance with existing treaties'.[295] The US view was that the 1981 treaty establishing the Organisation of Eastern Caribbean states operated as the necessary 'existing' or 'special' treaty. However, the OECS Defence Committee can only act unanimously and in cases of external aggression and the Grenada episode whereby troops landed to overthrow the Marxist government on the island would not satisfy the requirements, while it is only with difficulty that other articles may be used.[296] It is therefore rather problematic to interpret the OECS treaty as including the necessary regional peace-keeping action in the Grenada situation.

In the post-Cold War world, the ending of the rigidity of superpower blocs entrenched in regional defence systems and the increasingly serious resource problems faced by the United Nations have led to a re-appraisal of the importance of Chapter VIII. The Secretary-General in *An Agenda for Peace* emphasised that regional organisations possessed a potential that could be utilised in the fields of preventive diplomacy, peace-keeping, peace-making and post-conflict peace-building. In addition, 'regional action as a matter of decentralisation, delegation and co-operation with United Nations efforts could not only lighten the burden of the Council but also contribute to a deeper sense of participation, consensus and democratisation in international affairs'.[297]

Practice in the post-Cold War era has amply demonstrated the increasing awareness by the Security Council of the potentialities of regional organisations. References in resolutions of the Council have varied in this regard.

---

[293] See statement of Deputy Secretary of State Dam, 78 AJIL, 1984, p. 200.

[294] Articles 20 and 18.

[295] See also article 28, whereby American states are to apply 'special treaties on the subject' in the case of armed conflict or other act or situation endangering the peace of America.

[296] Article 3 includes among the functions and principles of the OECS 'such other activities calculated to further the progress of the Organisation as the member states may from time to time decide', while article 4 calls on parties to carry out the obligations arising out of the treaty; see J. N. Moore, *Law and the Grenada Mission*, Charlottesville, 1984, pp. 45–50 and W. C. Gilmore, *The Grenada Intervention*, London, 1984. See also American Bar Association Section of International Law and Practice, Report on Grenada, 1984.

[297] *Op. cit.*, p. 37. See also the statement of the President of the Security Council on 28 January 1993 calling for greater co-operation between the Council and regional organisations, S/25184. Specific reference is made in this statement to the Arab League, European Community, the Organisation of the Islamic Conference, the Organisation of American States, the Organisation of African Unity and the Conference on Security and Co-operation in Europe.

Some have specifically mentioned, commended or supported the work of named regional organisations without mentioning Chapter VIII,[298] others have referred explicitly to Chapter VIII,[299] while others have stated that the Council is acting under Chapter VIII.[300] A particularly interesting example of the interaction of regional organisations and the UN occurred with regard to Haiti. The OAS adopted sanctions against Haiti upon the overthrow of the elected President Jean-Bertrand Aristide in 1991.[301] Although the General Assembly welcomed the actions,[302] the Security Council did not react. Eventually in June 1993, the Council, acting under Chapter VII, imposed an arms and oil embargo on Haiti. Resolution 841 (1993) specifically referred to a series of OAS resolutions,[303] commended the work of the OAS Secretary-General and stressed the need 'for effective co-operation between regional organisations and the United Nations'.[304] In resolution 875 (1993), the Council acting under Chapters VII and VIII called upon member states 'acting nationally or through regional agencies or arrangements' in co-operation with the legitimate Government of Haiti to act to ensure the implementation of the arms and oil embargo.

Liberia constitutes another instructive example.[305] A complicated civil war broke out during 1989–90 and in the absence of any moves by the UN or the OAS, the Economic Community of West African States (ECOWAS) decided to act. This organisation, which consists of 16 members including Liberia, is aimed at improving living standards in the region.[306] A Protocol on Non-Aggression was signed in 1978 and came into force three years later.[307] This prohibits aggression among member states and does not specifically mention peace-keeping nor provide for the right of unilateral intervention. In May 1990, ECOWAS established a Standing Mediation

---

[298] See e.g. Security Council resolutions 743 (1992) commending the work of the European Community and the CSCE in former Yugoslavia and 855 (1993) endorsing the activities of the CSCE in former Yugoslavia; and resolution 865 (1993) noting the efforts of the Arab League, the OAU and the Organisation of the Islamic Conference with regard to Somalia.

[299] E.g. Security Council resolutions 727 (1992) in regard to former Yugoslavia; 795 (1992) in regard to Macedonia; 757 (1992) in regard to former Yugoslavia; 816 (1993) extending the 'no-fly' zone over Bosnia, and 820 (1993) in regard to former Yugoslavia and resolution 751 (1992) with regard to Somalia 'cognisant of the importance of co-operation between the United Nations and regional organisations in the context of Chapter VIII of the Charter of the United Nations'.

[300] See e.g. Security Council resolution 787 (1992) with regard to the maritime blockade of former Yugoslavia; resolution 794 (1992) with regard to Somalia

[301] OAS resolutions MRE/RES.1/91, MRE/RES.2/91 and MRE/RES.3/92. See article 19 of the OAS Charter.See also S/23109.   [302] See General Assembly resolution 46/7, 1991.

[303] Including in addition to those already mentioned, resolutions MRE/RES.4/92, MRE/RES.5/93 and CP/RES.594 (923/92), and declarations CP/Dec. 8 (927/93), CP/Dec. 9 (931/93) and CP/Dec. 10 (934/93).

[304] See also Security Council resolutions 917 (1994) and 933 (1994).

[305] See e.g. G. Nolte, 'Restoring Peace by Regional Action: International Legal Aspects of the Liberian Conflict', 53 *ZaöRV*, 1993, p. 603.

[306] See article 2 of the ECOWAS Treaty 1975.

[307] See also the Protocol Relating to Mutual Assistance on Defence, 1981.

Committee and this called for an immediate ceasefire in Liberia and for its implementation to be monitored by an ECOWAS monitoring group (ECOMOG). This group, led by Nigeria, landed in Liberia in August 1990 and became involved in actual fighting. It is somewhat unclear whether ECOWAS provides a sufficient legal basis of itself to justify the actions taken, and UN involvement did not occur until January 1991, when the President of the Security Council issued a statement commending the efforts of ECOWAS to promote peace in Liberia and calling upon the parties to the conflict to co-operate fully with ECOWAS.[308] In April 1992, ECOMOG proceeded to secure a buffer zone on the Liberia-Sierra Leone border envisaged by an October 1991 accord (the Yamoussoukro IV Accord) between the Liberian parties, to secure all entry and exit points in the country and to enforce the disarmament of combatants.[309]

The situation, however, continued to deteriorate and the Security Council adopted resolution 788 (1992) in November of that year. This determined that the deterioration of the situation constituted a threat to international peace and security 'particularly in West Africa as a whole' and recalled Chapter VIII of the Charter. The resolution commended ECOWAS for its 'efforts to restore peace, security and stability in Liberia' and, acting under Chapter VII, imposed an arms embargo upon that country. This support was reaffirmed in resolution 813 (1993), which also noted the endorsement of ECOWAS' efforts by the OAU.[310] With the assistance of the special representative of the UN Secretary-General, a new peace agreement was signed at Cotonou on 25 July 1993, which called upon ECOWAS and the UN to assist in its implementation.[311] The UN Observer Mission in Liberia was established to assist in this process.[312] Security Council resolution 866 (1993) in particular noted that 'this would be the first peace-keeping mission undertaken by the United Nations in co-operation with a peace-keeping mission already set up by another organisation, in this case ECOWAS'. Subsequent resolutions continued to commend ECOWAS for its actions and the UNOMIL mission was extended.[313] Despite further agreements signed at the end of 1994, 1995 and 1996, fighting continued.

The Liberian situation is therefore marked by the following features.

---

[308] S/22110/Add.3, 1991.

[309] S/23863, 1992. This was also supported by a statement from the President of the Security Council, S/23886, 1992. See also S/24815.   [310] See also S/25402, 1993.

[311] The peace agreement provided that ECOMOG would have the primary responsibility of supervising the military provisions of the agreement, with the UN monitoring and verifying the process, S/26200, 1993, and Security Council resolution 866 (1993) preamble.

[312] See Security Council resolutions 856 (1993) and 866 (1993). See also S/26200 and S/26422 and Add. 1, 1993.

[313] See e.g. Security Council resolutions 911 (1994); 950 (1994), which also commended African states sending troops to ECOMOG; 1014 (1995), which also encouraged African states to send troops to join ECOMOG; 1020 (1995) and 1071 (1996).

First, intervention into a civil war in an attempt to secure a ceasefire by a regional organisation whose authority in this area was far from clear constitutionally; secondly, delayed support by the Security Council in the context of Chapter VIII until 1992; thirdly, the first establishment of a dual UN-regional organisation peace-keeping operation; fourthly, the acceptance by the UN of the responsibility of the regional organisation for military issues with the UN mission possessing a rather indeterminate monitoring and peace-encouraging role. It should also be noted that apart from the imposition of the arms embargo in resolution 788 (1992), Security Council resolutions refrained from referring to Chapter VII. The UN, therefore, adopted very much a secondary role. While it is clear that the Security Council ultimately supported the action taken by ECOWAS, it is questionable whether the spirit and terms of Chapter VIII were fully complied with.

As already noted, the UN in the situation in Bosnia turned to NATO[314] in particular in order to enforce the arms embargo against all the states of the former Yugoslavia and to implement sanctions against the Federal Republic of Yugoslavia (Serbia and Montenegro). NATO airplanes in particular enforced the 'no-fly' zone over Bosnia (Operation Deny Flight) as from April 1993 and on 28 February 1994, four warplanes were shot down by NATO aircraft for violating the zone. NATO airplanes also provided close air support for UNPROFOR activities as from June 1993 and as from April 1994, air support to protect UN personnel in the 'safe areas' was instituted. NATO airstrikes took place at UN request during 1994–5 in a variety of situations.[315] Following the Dayton Peace Agreement initialled in November 1995, a 60,000 troop NATO-led implementation force (IFOR) commenced operations in Bosnia. This was authorised by the Security Council, acting under Chapter VII, in resolution 1031 (1995), under which authority was transferred from UNPROFOR to IFOR.[316]

---

[314] With the assistance of the WEU in the maritime activities in the Adriatic under Operation Sharp Guard.   [315] See e.g. S/1995/444, 1995.

[316] Note also with regard to the OSCE, the declaration of the Helsinki summit in 1992 that the organisation constituted a regional organisation in the sense of Chapter VIII of the Charter and the increasing range of contacts between the OSCE and the UN, see *OSCE Handbook 1996*, Vienna, 1996, p. 82 *et seq.* Note also the role of the OSCE in Bosnia under the Dayton peace arrangements, see *supra*, p. 734.

CHAPTER 21

INTERNATIONAL INSTITUTIONS

Historical development

The evolution of the modern nation-state and the consequent development of an international order founded upon a growing number of independent and sovereign territorial units inevitably gave rise to questions of international co-operation.[1] Diplomatic representation became more widespread as the system expanded and political and economic relationships multiplied. It soon became apparent, however, that diplomatic contacts in themselves were unable to cope completely with the complexities of the international system and the concept of the international conference evolved as a form of extended diplomacy. Such gatherings dealt with problems that concerned more than two or three states and in many cases resulted in an international treaty or formal peace. The first major instance of this occurred with the Peace of Westphalia in 1648, which ended the thirty-year-old religious conflict of Central Europe and formally established the modern secular nation-state arrangement of European politics.[2]

The French wars of Louis XIV were similarly brought to an end by an international agreement of interested powers, and a century later the

---

[1] See C. F. Amerasinghe, *Principles of the Institutional Law of International Organisations*, Cambridge, 1996; H. G. Schermers and N. M. Blokker, *International Institutional Law*, 3rd edn, The Hague, 1995; D. W. Bowett, *The Law of International Institutions*, 4th edn, London, 1982; N. White, *The Law of International Organisations*, Manchester, 1996; P. Reuter, *International Institutions*, London, 1958; *Encyclopedia of Public International Law* (ed. R. Bernhardt), Amsterdam, vols. V and VI, 1983; G. Schwarzenberger, *International Law*, London, 1976, vol. III; E. Lauterpacht, 'The Development of the Law of International Organisations by the Decisions of International Tribunals', 152 HR, p. 377; F. Kirgis, *International Organisations in their Legal Settings*, 2nd edn, St Paul, 1993; A. El Erian, 'The Legal Organisation of International Society', in *Manual of Public International Law* (ed. M. Sørensen), London, 1968, p. 55; M. Whiteman, *Digest of International Law*, Washington, 1968, vol. XIII; *A Handbook of International Organisations* (ed. R. J. Dupuy), Dordrecht, 1988; I. Seidl-Hohenveldern, *Corporations In and Under International Law*, Cambridge, 1987; F. Morgenstern, *Legal Problems of International Organisations*, Cambridge, 1986 and Nguyen Quoc Dinh, P. Daillier and A. Pellet, *Droit International Public*, 5th edn, Paris, 1994, p. 551. See also G. Schiavone, *International Organisations: A Dictionary and Directory*, London, 1992, and Union of International Associations, *Yearbook of International Organisations, 1996/7*, Brussels, 1996, 4 vols.

[2] See e.g. L. Gross, 'The Peace of Westphalia, 1648–1948', 42 AJIL, 1948, p. 20.

Napoleonic wars terminated with the Congress of Vienna in 1815. This latter conference can be taken as a significant turning point, for it marked the first systematic attempt to regulate international affairs by means of regular international conferences.[3] The Congress system lasted, in various guises, for practically a century and institutionalised not only the balance of power approach to politics, but also a semi-formal international order.[4]

Until the outbreak of the First World War, world affairs were to a large extent influenced by the periodic conferences that were held in Europe. The Paris conference of 1856 and the Berlin gathering of 1871 dealt with the problems of the Balkans, while the 1884–5 Berlin conferences imposed some order upon the scramble for Africa that had begun to develop.

These, and other such conferences, constituted an important prelude to the establishment of international institutions, but became themselves ever more inadequate to fulfil the job they had been intended to do. A conference could only be called into being upon the initiative of one or more of the states involved, usually following some international crisis, and this *ad hoc* procedure imposed severe delays upon the resolution of the issue. It meant that only states specifically invited could attend and these states made decisions upon the basis of unanimous agreement, a factor which severely restricted the utility of the system.[5]

The nineteenth century also witnessed a considerable growth in international non-governmental associations, such as the International Committee of the Red Cross (founded in 1863) and the International Law Association (founded in 1873). These private international unions, as they have been called,[6] demonstrated a wide-ranging community of interest on specific topics, and an awareness that co-operation had to be international to be effective. Such unions created the machinery for regular meetings and many established permanent secretariats. The work done by these organisations was, and remains, of considerable value in influencing governmental activities and stimulating world action.

This can be seen particularly with reference to the International Committee of the Red Cross and the efforts made by it to bring into being the Geneva Conventions and Additional Protocols[7] dealing with, for example, the treatment of prisoners and the regulation of military occupations. In fact, a number of these private international unions rather belie their name by including within their membership state representatives as well as national bodies and private individuals.[8]

---

[3] See e.g. El Erian, *Legal Organisation*, p. 58.
[4] See e.g. Reuter, *Institutions*, pp. 55–6. See also Bowett, *Law*, pp. 1–2.   [5] *Ibid.*, p. 3.
[6] *Ibid.*, pp. 4–65.   [7] *Supra*, Chapter 19, p. 806.
[8] For example, the International Council of Scientific Unions and the International Statistical Institute, Bowett, *Law*, p. 5.

To some extent impelled by the example of the private international unions, there developed during the course of the last century a series of public international unions. These were functional associations linking together governmental departments or administrations for specific purposes, and were set up by multilateral treaties. They fulfilled an increasingly felt need for more sophisticated methods of international co-operation and regulation in an interdependent world. The first instances of such intergovernmental associations were provided by the international commissions established for the more efficient functioning of such vital arteries of communication as the Rhine and Danube rivers, and later for other rivers of Central and Western Europe.[9]

The powers given to the particular commissions varied from case to case, but most of them performed important administrative and legislative functions. In 1865 the International Telegraphic Union was set up with a permanent bureau or secretariat and nine years later the Universal Postal Union was created. This combined a permanent bureau with periodic conferences, with decisions being taken by majority vote. This marked a step forward, since one of the weaknesses of the political order of *ad hoc* conferences had been the necessity for unanimity.

The latter half of the nineteenth century was especially marked by the proliferation of such public international unions, covering transportation, communications, health and economic co-operation. These unions restricted themselves to dealing with specific areas and were not comprehensive, but they introduced new ideas which paved the way for the universal organisations of the twentieth century. Such concepts as permanent secretariats, periodic conferences, majority voting, weighted voting and proportionate financial contributions, were important in easing administrative co-operation, and they laid the basis for contemporary international institutions.

The innovation of the present century has, of course, been the creation of the global, comprehensive organisations of the League of Nations and the United Nations. These were, in many ways, the logical culmination of the pioneering work of the private and public international unions, the large numbers of which required some form of central co-ordination. This function both the League and the UN attempted to provide. This Chapter is thus concerned with institutions that bind together states or governments in common enterprises and not non-governmental organisations.

Approaches to international institutions

There are a number of different ways in which one can approach the phenomenon of international organisation within the world order.

---

[9] *Ibid.*, pp. 6–9.

The rationalist approach[10] emphasises the notion of a world order of states that is moving towards the more sophisticated types of order found within states. It is progressive in that it believes in the transformation of a society of states into a true world community based upon the application of universally valid moral and legal principles. In other words, the development of the United Nations into a real world authority is seen not only as beneficial but also as, in the long run, inevitable. This is to be accomplished by the gradual increase in the influence and responsibility of the organisation in all fields of international peace and security. Thus international organisations have a profound substantive as well as procedural purpose, and are intended to function above and beyond mere administrative convenience. To put it another way, the rationalists emphasise the role of such institutions[11] as active performers upon the world stage rather than as mechanisms to greater efficiency.

Another general line of approach is the revolutionary one, which regards international institutions in terms of specific policy aims.[12] Here, the primary aim is not the evolution of a world community of states based upon global associations as perceived by the rationalists, but rather the utilisation of such institutions as a means of attaining the final objective, whether it be the victory of the proletariat or the rearrangement of existing states into, for example, continental units.

The third approach which may be noted is exemplified by the doctrine of realism.[13] This centres its attention on the struggle for power and supremacy and eschews any concern for idealistic views. The world stage is seen as a constant and almost chaotic interweaving of contentious state powers, and international institutions are examined within the context of the search for dominance. Both the League and the UN were created to reinforce the *status quo* established after the world wars, it is stressed, although the latter institution is now seen as reflecting the new balance of power achieved with the growth of influence of the states of the Third World. Since what can be described as a world order is merely a reflection of the operation of the principle of the balance of power, realists see the role of world organisations as reinforcing that balance and enabling it to be safely and gradually altered in the light of changing patterns of power; although, to be accurate, their overall attitude to such organisations is

---

[10] See e.g. G. Goodwin, 'World Institutions and World Order', in *The New International Actors* (eds. C. Cosgrove and K. Twitchett), 1970, pp. 55–7. See also *The Concept of International Organisation* (ed. G. Abi-Saab), Paris, 1981 and Feld and R. S. Jordan, *International Organisations*, New York, 1983.
[11] See e.g. Bowett, *Law*, Chapter 2; G. Scott, *The Rise and Fall of the League of Nations*, London, 1973; El Erian, *Legal Organisations*, pp. 60 *et seq.* and F. P. Walters, *A History of the League of Nations*, 2 vols., Oxford, 1952.   [12] Goodwin, 'World Institutions', pp. 57–61.
[13] *Ibid.*, pp. 61–4.

usually characterised by cynicism, as the inherent weaknesses in these organisations have become apparent.

A more hopeful way of looking at the international institutions is to concentrate upon those areas where the interdependence of states has impelled them to create viable organs for co-operation. By this means, by identifying such subjects for international agreement, it is hoped to be able to encourage growing circles of cooperation which may eventually impinge upon the basic political areas of world peace. This functional approach[14] appears as a cross between the nationalist and realist trends and is one much examined in recent years. This approach also emphasises the pattern of institutional behaviour and the operations of the relevant bureaucracies, including the way in which the tasks set for the organisation are identified and completed. Decision-making analysis is another useful tool in this area.

It is also possible to examine international organisations in a variety of other ways, ranging from historical and comparative exposition to analysis of the legal rules underlying the establishment and operations of the particular institution.

Because of the great diversity of international and regional intergovernmental organisations, ranging from the United Nations to the North Atlantic Treaty Organisation and the International Labour Organisation, great difficulty has been experienced in classifying the relevant material. In this Chapter, the simplest method of division into institutions of a universal character, regional institutions and the legal aspects of international institutions will be adopted. Within the relevant categories, the particular functions of different organisations, as well as their varying constitutional framework, will be briefly noted.

Institutions of a universal character

The League of Nations[15]

The League of Nations, created in 1919, sought to promote international co-operation, peace and security upon the basis of disarmament, the peaceful resolution of disputes, a guarantee of the sovereignty and independence of member states and sanctions.[16] In essence, it was left to each member to conclude whether a breach of the Covenant of the League had taken place

[14] See e.g. D. Mitrany, *A Working Peace System*, London, 1966 and 'The Functional Approach to World Organisation' in Cosgrove and Twitchett, *The New International Actors*, *op. cit.*, p. 65.
[15] See e.g. Bowett, *Law*, Chapter 2; Scott, *Rise and Fall*; El Erian, *Legal Organisations*, pp. 60 *et seq.* and Walters, *A History*.
[16] See articles 8 and 10–17 of the Covenant of the League of Nations. See also *supra*, Chapter 20, p. 839.

or not, and in the last resort whether or not to apply sanctions. This system worked with regard to certain relatively minor crises in the Balkans and South America, but failed where European powers or Japan were directly involved. The German, Italian and Japanese aggressions in the 1930s, and the Russian invasion of Finland in the Winter War, evoked little meaningful response from the League.

The League consisted of three principal organs. The Council, a semi-executive body, consisted of the Principal Allied and Associated Powers plus a number of non-permanent members, and reached its decisions unanimously. Such decisions were not binding upon member states. The Assembly consisted of representatives of all members and met annually, while the Secretariat functioned as an international civil service.

Although an international organisation, it never became universal. It stayed to all intents and purposes a European-centred institution. It was formally dissolved in April 1946.

The United Nations

The United Nations arose as an attempt to remedy the defects of the League system. It grew out of a series of war-time declarations and conferences, culminating in the San Francisco conferences of 1945, which finally adopted the UN Charter. The establishment of the UN Organisation has proved to be one of the major innovations of this century in international relations, not only in the fields of the peaceful settlement of disputes and the use of force, but also with regard to wide-ranging economic and social co-operation among states. It has had to date a history marked by periods of intense activity interspersed with periods of relative inactivity. The United Nations Organisation has been discussed in more detail in Chapter 20.

International economic organisations

Reference should be made at this stage to other international economic arrangements. The GATT[17] arose out of an international conference held at Havana in 1947–8 at which it was decided to establish an International Trade Organisation. The organisation did not in fact come into being. However, a General Agreement on Tariffs and Trade (GATT) had been agreed shortly before the conference, involving a series of tariff concessions

---

[17] See e.g. K. W. Dam, *The GATT, Law and International Economic Relations*, Chicago, 1970; *International Law Cases and Materials* (ed. L. Henkin, R. C. Pugh, O. Schachter and H. Smit), 3rd edn, St Paul, 1993, pp. 1396 *et seq.*; J. H. Jackson, *The World Trading System*, Cambridge, MA, 1989 and I. Seidl-Hohenveldern, *International Economic Law*, 2nd edn, Dordrecht, 1992, p. 90.

and trade rules, and this originally temporary instrument continued. The arrangement operated on the basis of bilateral approach to trade negotiations coupled with unconditional acceptance of the most-favoured nation principle (by which the most favourable benefits obtained by one state are passed on to other states), although there were special conditions for developing states in this respect. A series of tariff and trade negotiating rounds were held under the auspices of the GATT, which thus offered a package approach to trade negotiations, and a wide variety of tariff reductions was achieved, as well as agreement reached on mitigating non-tariff barriers. The eighth such round, termed the Uruguay round, commenced in 1986 and concluded with the signing at Marrakesh on 15 April 1994 of a long and complex agreement covering a range of economic issues, such as agriculture, textiles and clothing, rules of origin, import licensing procedures, subsidies, intellectual property rights, and procedures on dispute settlement. In addition, the agreement provided for the establishment of the World Trading Organisation on 1 January 1995 as a permanent institution with its own secretariat. The organisation consists of a Ministerial Conference, consisting of representatives of all members meeting at least once every two years; a General Council composed of representatives of all members meeting as appropriate and exercising the functions of the Conference between sessions;[18] Councils for Trade in Goods, Trade in Services and Trade Related Aspects of Intellectual Property Rights operating under the general guidance of the General Council; a Secretariat and a Director-General.[19] The organisation's main aims are to administer and implement the multilateral and plurilateral trade agreements together making up the WTO, to act as a forum for multilateral trade negotiations, to try and settle trade disputes and to oversee national trade policies. The GATT of 1947 continued until the end of 1995, when it was effectively subsumed, with changes, as GATT 1994 within the WTO system.

Regional institutions

The proliferation of regional institutions, linking together geographically and ideologically related states, since the close of the Second World War, has been impressive. A number of factors can help explain this. The onset of the Cold War and the failure of the Security Council's enforcement procedures stimulated the growth of regional defence alliances and bloc politics. NATO, and its various sister organisations covering the Middle and Far East, confronted the Warsaw Pact. The decolonisation process resulted in

---

[18] The General Council will also meet to discharge the responsibilities of the Dispute Settlement Body and the Trade Policy Review Body, see article IV(3) and (4) of the 1994 Agreement.   [19] See article IV of the Agreement.

the independence of scores of states, most of which were eager to play a non-aligned role between East and West. And to this end, regional organisations developed to reflect common interests (and sometimes common hostilities) in a superpower world. These included the Arab League, the Organisation of American States and the Organisation of African Unity, in particular.

But it was in Europe that regionalism became most constructive and political. The establishment of the European Economic Community, in particular, was intended to lay the basis for a resurgent Western Europe with meaningful economic and political integration.

Europe

The North Atlantic Treaty Organisation[20]

This was created in 1949 to counter possible threats from the East. It associated the United States and Canada with fourteen European powers for the protection, in essence, of Western Europe (although Greece and Turkey are also involved). By the Treaty,[21] the parties agreed to consult where the territorial integrity, political independence or security of any of them has been threatened,[22] and accepted that an armed attack against one or more of them in Europe or North America should be considered an attack against all.[23]

The alliance consists of a Council which is the supreme organ and on which all members are represented,[24] and a series of civil and military committees covering all aspects of security work. However, in 1966 France withdrew from the military side of the alliance while remaining a member of the organisation itself.[25] There also exists a NATO parliamentary conference (the North Atlantic Assembly) which acts as an official consultative body. The ending of the Cold War brought about a variety of changes in the organisation. A North Atlantic Co-operation Council (NACC) was established in 1991 with its membership consisting of NATO states and former members of the Warsaw Pact, including the successor states to the USSR. In 1994, the Partnership for Peace programme was inaugurated within the framework of the NACC. This brings together NACC and other OSCE[26] states into a co-operative framework, which has the potential to provide the mechanism for enlarging the membership of NATO itself. While the Partnership

---

[20] See e.g. *The NATO Handbook*, Brussels, 1995; C. Archer, *Organising Europe*, London, 1994, Chapter 9; Bowett, *Law*, pp. 180 *et seq.*; K. Myers, *NATO, The Next Thirty Years*, Boulder, 1980 and L. S. Kaplan and R. W. Clawson, *NATO After Thirty Years*, Wilmington, 1981.
[21] 43 AJIL, 1949, Suppl. p. 159.   [22] Article IV.   [23] Article V.   [24] Article 9.
[25] See e.g. T. Stein and D. Carreau, 'Law and Peaceful Change in a Subsystem: "Withdrawal" of France from NATO', 62 AJIL, 1968, p. 557.
[26] Organisation for Security and Co-operation in Europe, see *infra*, p. 902.

for Peace[27] focuses upon practical, defence-related and military co-operation, the NACC constitutes the forum for broad consultation on political and security issues. Countries participating in the Partnership for Peace sign a Framework Document, affirming the commitment to the preservation of democratic societies and the maintenance of the principles of international law, to fulfil in good faith the obligations of the UN Charter and the principles contained in the Universal Declaration on Human Rights and to respect existing borders. NATO has, in co-operation with the Western European Union, helped in implementing UN sanctions in the Former Yugoslavia and currently leads the multinational implementation force (IFOR) in Bosnia in enforcement of the Dayton Peace Agreement of 1995.[28]

The Western European Union[29]

The WEU was founded upon the basis of the Brussels Treaty of 1948 signed by five Western European states.[30] The proposed defence arrangements were subsumed within NATO. In 1954, Germany and Italy were invited to accede to the Brussels Treaty, thus forming the WEU. The original intention to a large extent was to exercise some kind of control over the extent of German rearmament. A variety of organs were created including a Council, consisting of a Council of Foreign and Defence Ministers of member states and a Permanent Council of representatives, and a Parliamentary Assembly, consisting of member states' delegations to the Council of Europe. Its social and cultural functions were transferred to the Council of Europe in 1960. From 1954 until the late 1980s, the WEU in fact exercised only a very limited role. In 1988, Spain and Portugal joined the WEU. With the ending of the Cold War and the consequential withdrawal of US forces from Europe and with the evolution of the European Community, a new role for the WEU began to be formulated. Under the Treaty on European Union (the Maastricht Treaty) of 1992, the WEU was described as an integral part of the Union[31] and the WEU Declaration adopted at the Maastricht Summit stated that the WEU would be developed as the defence component of the European Union and as a means for strengthening the European pillar of the Atlantic Alliance.[32] In 1992, the WEU Council of Ministers adopted the Petersberg Declaration, under which military units from WEU member states could be used for military

---

[27] This currently has twenty-six members, excluding NATO members, see *NATO Basic Factsheet, No. 9*, 1996.   [28] See *supra*, Chapter 20, p. 886.
[29] See e.g. Archer, *Organising Europe*, Chapter 10 and T. Taylor, *European Defence Co-operation*, London, 1984.   [30] UK, France, Belgium, Holland and Luxembourg.
[31] See Title V (Provisions on a Common Foreign and Security Policy), Article J.4 (2).
[32] Final Act Declarations, see P. Duffy and J. Y. de Cara, *European Union – The Lawyer's Guide – Sources*, London, 1992, pp. 351 *et seq*.

and other purposes in co-operation with the CSCE (now OSCE) and the UN Security Council and a Forum for Consultation with Central and Eastern European states was also created.[33] The WEU also developed a role in the Yugoslav crisis, both in enforcing the Security Council sanctions in co-operation with NATO[34] and in forming part of the joint European Union/WEU administration of the city of Mostar in Bosnia in July 1994. In 1993, the headquarters of the WEU was moved from London to Brussels in order to enhance co-operation with NATO.[35]

The Council of Europe[36]

The Council of Europe was created in 1949 with wide-ranging co-operative aims. There are currently forty member states.[37] The Council comprises the Committee of Ministers, consisting of governmental representatives, and the Parliamentary Assembly, composed of members representing the Parliaments of the member states. The Committee can conclude conventions or agreements; make recommendations to member states and issue declarations.[38] The Committee can invite states to become full or associated members of the Council of Europe and can suspend states from membership.[39] The Parliamentary Assembly is the deliberative organ of the Council. It may recommend action upon matters referred to it by the Committee of Ministers and may adopt resolutions. Recommendations require a two-thirds majority, while resolutions require a simple majority.[40]

The most important part of the work of the Council of Europe is the preparation and conclusion of conventions and protocols. There are a very large number of these, including pre-eminently the European Convention for the Protection of Human Rights and Fundamental Freedoms (1950), but including also the European Social Charter (1961) and agreements dealing with cultural and educational questions and conventions covering patents, extradition, migration, state immunity, terrorism and others.

---

[33] See Archer, *Organising Europe*, p. 248.   [34] See *supra*, Chapter 20, p. 886.
[35] There are currently ten full members, three associate members (being NATO members but not member states of the European Union), five observers (being member states of the European Union, but not members of NATO, apart from Denmark which has decided not to become a full member of the WEU) and a further nine associate partners (having signed association agreements with the European Union).
[36] See e.g. Archer, *Organising Europe*, Chapter 4; A. H. Robertson, *The Council of Europe*, 2nd edn, London, 1961 and T. Ouchterlony, *The Council of Europe in the New Europe*, Edinburgh, 1991. See also *supra*, Chapter 7, p. 255.   [37] Autumn 1996.
[38] See articles 15 and 16 of the Statute of the Council of Europe.   [39] Article 8.
[40] See articles 22 and 23.

The Organisation for Economic Co-operation and Development [41]

This organisation was established in 1960 and developed out of the European machinery created to administer the American Marshall Plan, which was aimed at reviving the European economies.[42] Its membership includes the USA, Canada and Japan,[43] and it exists to maintain and encourage economic growth world-wide. Article 1 of the Convention on the Organisation for Economic Co-operation and Development 1960 specifically provides that the aims of the organisation are to promote policies designed to achieve the highest sustainable economic growth and employment and a rising standard of living in member countries, while maintaining financial stability; to contribute to sound economic expansion in member and non-member states, and to contribute to the expansion of world trade on a multilateral and non-discriminatory basis. Its main organ is the Council, which includes all the members of the organisation and it proceeds by way of unanimity, except in special cases. It is thus by no means a supranational body, since no state can be bound against its will. It possesses an Executive Committee and other committees and autonomous bodies aimed at encouraging co-ordination and co-operation, as well as a secretariat based in Paris consisting of some twenty directorates and services.

The European Union [44]

This is undoubtedly the most important European organisation, as well as being by far the most sophisticated regional institution so far created. It consists, in fact, of three interlocking communities – the European Coal and Steel Community (the ECSC, created in 1951), the European Economic Community and the European Atomic Energy (Euratom) Community (both created in 1957) and operates to a significant extent as a supranational enterprise. The basis of the Union (formerly the European Community) lies in furthering economic integration and, pos-

---

[41] See e.g. Archer, *Organising Europe*, Chapter 3; Bowett, *Law*, pp. 189 *et seq.* and L. Miller, 'The OECD', YBWA, 1963, p. 80.

[42] This was the Organisation for European Economic Co-operation, created in 1948.

[43] By article 16 of the 1960 Treaty, membership is open to any government by unanimous invitation of the Council. There are twenty founding countries and seven states have joined as of summer 1996, the most recent being the Czech Republic in 1995 and Hungary in 1996.

[44] See e.g. T. Hartley, *The Foundations of European Community Law*, 3rd edn, Oxford, 1994; *Lasok and Bridge's Law and Institutions of the European Communities* (ed. D. Lasok and K. P. E. Lasok), 6th edn, 1994; D. Wyatt and A. Dashwood, *European Community Law*, 3rd edn, Oxford, 1993; Commission of the European Communities, *Thirty Years of Community Law*, Luxembourg, 1983; S. Weatherill and P. Beaumont, *EC Law*, 2nd edn, London, 1995, and J. Steiner, *Textbook on EEC Law*, 4th edn, London, 1994.

sibly in the longer term, political union. The EU aims at establishing a single unified market with common external tariffs and the elimination of internal tariffs and quotas, and it promotes the free movement of capital and labour. There also exists a Common Agricultural Policy[45] and a series of association agreements with Third World countries under the Yaoundé, Arusha and Lomé Conventions.[46] The Single European Act, signed in 1986 with the aim of eliminating the remaining impediments to the creation of a single internal market by the end of 1992, introduced several important changes. It created a new co-operation procedure whereby the Parliament is given a second opportunity to consider draft legislation. Where the Parliament objects to the proposal in question as a result of its second consideration, the Council of Ministers may only adopt it by acting unanimously and within a three-month period. Where the Parliament proposes amendments, the European Commission may re-examine the proposal and if it rejects the amendments, they may only be adopted by the Council acting unanimously. The range of issues upon which the Parliament must be consulted was also greatly increased, so that the majority of measures relating to the establishment of the single internal market are included. The Treaty on European Union signed on 7 February 1992 imported further significant changes. The European Union was established, consisting of the European Community (as the European Economic Community was renamed), the ECSC, Euratom, coupled with two processes entitled respectively the 'Common Foreign and Security Policy' and 'Co-operation in Justice and Home Affairs'. This treaty also aimed at the establishment of a common currency through European Monetary Union[47] and at the evolution of social protection through an associated Agreement on Social Policy (the Social Chapter).[48] The European Parliament obtained increased powers under this treaty,[49] while a new Committee of the Regions was established, consisting of representatives of local and regional bodies, and the Court of Auditors gained institutional status.

The European Union, although based on the ECSC, EEC and Euratom arrangements, has a common set of institutions.[50] It was enlarged following the accession of the UK, Ireland and Denmark on 1 January 1973; of Greece on 1 January 1981; of Spain and Portugal on 1 January 1986 and of Austria,

---

[45] See articles 38–47 of the EEC Treaty. See also M. Melchior, 'The Common Organisation of Agricultural Markets' in *Thirty Years of Community Law*, pp. 439 *et seq.*
[46] See e.g. M. Flory, 'Commercial Policy and Development Policy' in *Thirty Years of Community Law*, pp. 375, 387 *et seq.*
[47] Although the UK and Denmark are not committed to this objective.
[48] Which is not binding upon the UK.   [49] See *infra*, p. 899.
[50] See the Treaty Establishing a Single Council and a Single Commission of the European Communities 1965, which entered into force on 1 July 1967.

Finland and Sweden on 1 January 1995.[51] In 1991 an agreement signed with the states of the European Free Trade Area[52] provided for the creation of a European Economic Area under which Community law in relevant areas[53] would apply to these states. However, the European Court of Justice declared this agreement to be contrary to the EC Treaty.[54] A revised version was accepted by the Court in 1992,[55] and came into force on 1 January 1994 with Sweden, Finland, Austria, Iceland and Norway. However, since the first three of these states joined the Union the following year, the future of the European Economic Area is unclear.[56]

The institutions of the Union comprise primarily the European Parliament, the Council of Ministers, the Commission and the Court of Justice.

The European Parliament was first created under the Treaty of Rome in 1957 and consists of at present 626 members, directly elected since 1979. It holds plenary sessions about one week a month and has a variety of standing committees, studying such topics as political, legal, economic, social, agricultural and regional questions. It meets in Strasbourg for the monthly plenary sessions and in Brussels for the committee meetings and for additional sessions, while the secretariat general is based in Luxembourg. Germany since unification has 99 seats; Britain, Italy and France have 87 seats each; Spain has 64 seats; Netherlands 31; Belgium, Greece and Portugal have 25 seats each; Sweden has 22 seats; Austria has 21 seats; Denmark and Finland have 16 seats each; Ireland has 15 seats and Luxembourg has 6 seats.

The powers of the Parliament are rather limited in practice,[57] and vary considerably depending upon the particular treaty under which a proposal is adopted and on the provision of the applicable treaty. In certain circumstances, for example, the agricultural price review, a consultation procedure is applicable under which the Parliament is required to give an opinion before a legislative proposal from the Commission can be adopted by the Council. In other areas, such as research, the environment and overseas co-operation and development, there is a co-operation procedure allowing Parliament to improve proposed legislation by way of amendment.[58] A

---

[51] A variety of other countries have applied for membership including Turkey, Cyprus, Malta, the Baltic states, the Czech Republic and Slovakia. Norway did not join the Union following a referendum after having signed the treaty of accession in 1972, while Greenland left the Community (as it then was) in 1985 after a referendum.

[52] Norway, Sweden, Finland, Iceland, Switzerland, Liechtenstein (an applicant to join EFTA) and Austria.

[53] Including free movement of goods, persons, services and capital, but not agriculture, see e.g. Hartley, *Foundations*, p. 5.   [54] *First EEA Case*, Opinion 1/91 [1991] ECR 6079.

[55] *Second EEA Case*, Opinion 1/92.

[56] Note that Switzerland did not take part following a referendum rejecting the proposed arrangement.   [57] See e.g. Hartley, *Foundations*, pp. 27 *et seq.*

[58] See articles 6 and 7 of the Single European Act 1986 and article 189c of the EC Treaty, following amendment by the Treaty on European Union 1992.

co-decision procedure exists in certain cases, for example, consumer protection, education, health and trans-European networks, by which decision-making power is shared between the Parliament and the Council equally. A Conciliation Committee, consisting of equal numbers of members of the Parliament and of the Council with the Commission present, seeks to reach a compromise on the text of a particular proposal. If there is no agreement, Parliament may reject the proposal outright.[59] Parliament's approval is required for important international agreements, such as the accession of new member states and association agreements with third states. The EU's budget is agreed each year by the Parliament, which may propose modifications and amendments to the Commission's initial proposals and to the position taken by the member states in the Council. The Council has the final decision in some areas, such as agricultural spending, but Parliament decides in co-operation with the Council in other areas, such as education, regional funds and environmental projects. The Parliament exercises a level of scrutiny over the work of the Commission and may vote to dismiss the whole Commission (which has not happened to date).

The Council of Ministers consists of one representative from each of the member states and is the guardian of national interests.[60] It is also the ultimate political authority in the Union, taking the final decision on most legislation, for example. The question of which governmental ministers will attend the meetings depends upon the issues to be discussed. Since the adoption of the Treaty on European Union, the work of the Union takes place upon the basis of three 'pillars'. The first pillar covers the traditional range of Community activities prior to 1992. In the majority of areas (including agriculture, fisheries, the internal market, environment and transport), the Council will decide by qualified majority voting.[61] In this scheme, Germany, France, Italy and the UK possess 10 votes; Spain has 8 votes; Belgium, Greece, Netherlands and Portugal have 5 votes each; Austria and Sweden have 4 votes each; Ireland, Denmark and Finland have 3 votes each, and Luxembourg has 2 votes. Where a proposal of the Commission is concerned, at least 62 votes are required, otherwise the qualified majority is 62 provided that at least 10 member states are involved. Certain other areas, such as taxation, culture, and regional and social funds require unanimity. As far as the other two pillars are concerned (the Common Foreign and Security Policy, and Co-operation in Justice and Home Affairs) unanimity is required, save where a joint action is being implemented. Since ministers do not meet constantly, a Committee of the

---

[59] See article 189b of the EC Treaty, following amendment by the Treaty on European Union 1992.   [60] See e.g. Hartley, *Foundations*, pp. 17 *et seq.*

[61] Areas where proposals are capable of acceptance by qualified majority voting were increased by the Single European Act 1986.

Permanent Representatives of the member states (COREPER) provides continuity and matters needing Council decision appear first at this committee. At least twice a year the Heads of State and Government, together with the President of the Commission, meet as the European Council at which the most important political decisions tend to be made.[62]

Subordinate to the Council, and subject to parliamentary control, is the European Commission.[63] This currently has twenty members chosen for their individual competence, who act independently of government control.[64] The President is chosen by the European Council after consultations with the Parliament, while the other members of the Commission are nominated by the member states in consultation with the President. The full Commission has to be approved by the Parliament. The Commission, situated in Brussels, operates by majority vote and constitutes the bureaucratic machinery of the Community, having a staff of some 15, 000. It is divided into twenty-six directorates-general and a number of additional specialised services. The Commission originates legislative proposals which are then sent to the Council and the Parliament. In addition, it acts as an enforcing mechanism of Community law. States that breach European law will face Commission action, that may include recourse to the European Court of Justice, while in some cases, the Commission may impose fines upon individuals and organisations for violations of European law. The Commission manages the annual budget of the Union and acts as the trade negotiator of the Union. The Commission has certain decision-making powers, in addition to its ability to issue opinions which are solely persuasive, that are binding upon the citizens and institutions of the member states. The Commission can, and does, make decisions which are legally binding upon the recipients, without the need for national legislation to incorporate them into domestic legal systems. This supranational characteristic is what distinguishes the Union from other regional institutions. It involves a restriction by states upon their legislative exclusivity and permits Union institutions to issue orders directly affecting Union citizens in certain cases, irrespective of national parliamentary activity.

The Court of Justice of the European Communities[65] consists of fifteen judges,[66] appointed for renewable six-year terms each. The Court is assisted by nine advocates-general, whose role is to make reasoned submissions on cases before the Court, without taking part in the judgment. The Court

---

[62] See Title I, article D of the Treaty on European Union.

[63] See e.g. Hartley, *Foundations*, pp. 11 *et seq.*

[64] Two each come from France, Germany, Italy, the UK and Spain and one each from the other member states.

[65] See e.g. L. N. Brown and T. Kennedy, *The Court of Justice of the European Communities*, 4th edn, London, 1994.

[66] I.e. one judge from each of the member states. See also articles 165–67 of the EEC Treaty.

applies Community law, a composition of the relevant treaties, Commission regulations, previous case-law of the Court and general principles of member states' municipal law, and performs various functions connected with the European Communities. The Court has a complicated jurisdiction[67] and has established the principle that EEC law prevails over national law.[68] It has so far dealt primarily with issues connected with farm policy, common tariffs, monopolies, patent rights and social security rights of migrant workers. Its major importance has to all intents and purposes been to act as the most proactive and 'federal' element in the structure of the Union.

The Single European Act provided for the creation of a new Court of First Instance in order to hear cases concerning disputes between the community and its employees, competition law issues and certain other minor matters. This Court commenced operations on 1 September 1989. It is composed of fifteen judges appointed for renewable terms of six years and there are no advocates general.

The Organisation for Security and Co-operation in Europe (OSCE)[69]

The Organisation was originally created in 1975 following the Helsinki Conference of European powers (plus the US and Canada). The Helsinki Final Act laid down a series of basic principles of behaviour among the participating states, including sovereign equality; prohibition of the threat or use of force; inviolability of frontiers; territorial integrity of states; peaceful settlement of disputes; non-intervention in internal affairs and respect for

[67] The Court, for example, can hear disputes between states (article 170, EEC Treaty); and between states and the Commission (article 169). It can act as an administrative tribunal hearing allegations of illegal action or inaction by Community organs (articles 173–76, 178 and 184) and as a constitutional court, deciding on the interpretation of the Treaty and Community legislation at the request of national courts (article 177).

[68] See e.g. *Costa* v. *ENEL* [1964] ECR 858; the *Van Gend en Loos* case [1963] ECR 1 and *Simmenthal* v. *Italian Minister of Finance* [1976] ECR 187 and [1978] ECR 629. Note, in particular, the significant assertion in the *Van Gend en Loos* case that 'the Community constitutes a new legal order of international law for the benefit of which the states have limited their sovereign rights, albeit within limited fields, and the subjects of which comprise not only member states but also their nationals. Independently of the legislation of member states, Community law not only imposes obligations upon individuals but is also intended to confer upon them rights which become part of their legal heritage. These rights arise not only where they are expressly granted by the Treaty, but also by reason of obligations which the Treaty imposes in a clearly defined way upon individuals as well as upon member states and upon institutions of the Community' [1963] ECR 1, 12.

[69] See e.g. *The CSCE* (ed. A. Bloed), Dordrecht, 1993; J. Maresca, *To Helsinki – the CSCE 1973–75*, Durham, 1987; *Essays on Human Rights in the Helsinki Process* (eds. A. Bloed and P. Van Dijk), 1985; A. Bloed and P. Van Dijk, *The Human Dimension of the Helsinki Process*, Dordrecht, 1991 and D. McGoldrick, 'The Development of the Conference on Security and Co-operation in Europe – From Process to Institution' in *Legal Visions of the New Europe* (eds. B. S. Jackson and D. McGoldrick), London, 1993, p. 135. See also *supra* Chapters 7, p. 281 and 18, p. 733.

human rights. The Final Act was not a binding treaty but a political document, concerned with three areas or 'baskets', being security questions in Europe; co-operation in the fields of economics, science and technology, and co-operation in humanitarian fields. The Conference itself (at the time termed the CSCE) was a diplomatic conference with regular follow-up meetings to review the implementation of the Helsinki Final Act, together with expert meetings on a variety of topics ranging from human rights, democratic institutions, the environment and the peaceful settlement of disputes. It was only really after the changes in Eastern Europe in the late 1980s that the CSCE began to assume a coherent structure.

The Charter of Paris for a New Europe signed in 1990 provided for the first standing institutions. These were the Conflict Prevention Centre in Vienna, the Office for Free Elections in Warsaw (now renamed the Office for Democratic Institutions and Human Rights) and the Secretariat based in Prague. The Paris Conference also established a system of consultation and decision-making bodies being regular summit meetings of Heads of State or Government; the Council of Ministers, consisting of the Foreign Ministers of participating states, and the Committee of Senior Officials to deal with day to day business.[70] In December 1992, the post of Secretary General was created, while a strengthened Secretariat was established in Vienna. The Permanent Committee was set up in Vienna in 1993 to assist in regular decision-making.

Further institutional steps were taken at the Budapest Summit in 1994. To complete the transformation of the CSCE, it was renamed the Organisation for Security and Co-operation in Europe as from 1 January 1995. The Council of Ministers (now termed the Ministerial Council) constitutes the central decision-making and governing body of the Organisation, while the Senior Council (formerly the Committee of Senior Officials) has the function of discussing and setting forth policy and broad budgetary guidelines. The Permanent Council (formerly the Permanent Committee) is the regular body for political consultation and decision-making and can also be convened for emergency purposes and is composed of the permanent representatives of the participating states meeting in Vienna. Overall responsibility for executive action is exercised by the Chairman-in-Office, who is assisted by the Troika (i.e. the present, preceding and succeeding Chairmen). The High Commissioner on National Minorities was appointed in 1992[71] and there exist a variety of personal representatives of the Chairman-in-Office and *ad hoc* steering groups in order to help the work of the Organisation.[72] The OSCE has established a

---

[70] See *OSCE Handbook 1996*, 2nd edn, Vienna, 1996, p. 8.
[71] See further *supra*, Chapter 7, p. 284.
[72] See Decisions of the Budapest Summit, 34 ILM, 1995, pp. 773 *et seq.*

variety of Missions to assist in dispute settlement and has been assigned a role in the Bosnia peace arrangements.[73] A Parliamentary Assembly was established in 1991. In March 1995, the Final Conference on the Pact on Stability in Europe adoped a Final Declaration, which together with some 100 bilateral and regional co-operation agreements, constitutes an attempt to mitigate tensions in the region. The Declaration contains a commitment to act against intolerance and discrimination, while the agreements include those dealing with cross-border co-operation, economic, environmental and minority protection issues. The pact is supplemented by measures to be taken by the European Union and is integrated within the OSCE system. It has been agreed that in the event of difficulties over observance of the agreements, the states participating in the Pact would rely on existing OSCE institutions and procedures for settling disputes peacefully, including the Court of Conciliation and Arbitration.[74]

The Commonwealth of Independent States

The Commonwealth of Independent States was established by an Agreement signed by Russia, Belarus and Ukraine in Minsk on 8 December 1991, to which eight other former Republics of the USSR adhered at Alma Ata on 21 December that year. Georgia joined in 1993, so that the organisation now comprises all the former Soviet Republics apart from the three Baltic states. The Organisation is based on respect for the territorial integrity of member states and upon co-operation particularly in safeguarding international peace and security and implementing effective measures for the reduction of armaments. The member states of the CIS agreed to maintain and retain under joint command, a common military and strategic space, including joint control over nuclear weapons. It was also agreed to establish common co-ordinating institutions embracing the co-ordination of foreign policy and economic, transport and communications systems co-operation.[75] The CIS adopted a Charter in Minsk in January 1993.[76] Under this Charter, the Commonwealth is expressed to be based on the sovereign equality of its members, who are independent subjects of international law. It is expressly stated that the CIS is not a state nor does it possess supranational powers.[77] The supreme organ is the Council of Heads of State, which is to 'discuss and solve all questions of principle in connection with member states' activities in the sphere of their common interests'.[78] The Council of Heads of Government is to co-ordinate the operation of member states' executive organs in spheres of common interests.[79] Decisions of both

---

[73] See further *supra*, Chapter 18, p. 734.   [74] See *supra*, Chapter 18, p. 733.
[75] See articles 5, 6 and 7 of the Minsk Agreement, 31 ILM, 1992, pp. 143 *et seq.*
[76] See 4 Finnish YIL, 1993, p. 263.   [77] See article 1.   [78] Article 21.   [79] Article 22.

Councils are to be achieved by common consent.[80] The Council of Ministers of Foreign Affairs is to co-ordinate the foreign policy activities of member states, while the Co-ordinating-Consultative Committee is the permanently operating executive and co-ordinating organ of the CIS.[81] In addition, a Council of Ministers of Defence (with a United Military Forces Headquarters) and a Council of Commanders of Border Troops were provided for,[82] together with an Economic Court and a Commission on Human Rights.[83] In 1993, the leaders of the CIS states, apart from Ukraine and Turkmenistan, signed a treaty to create an Economic Union, while in 1995, seven of the twelve member states signed an agreement for the Defence of the CIS External Borders. A large number of agreements have been signed between member states on a variety of subjects, including prevention of drug smuggling and terrorism, but many of these agreements have not been ratified.[84]

The American Continent[85]

The Organisation of American States emerged after the Second World War and built upon the work already done by the Pan-American Union and the various inter-American Conferences since 1890. It consists of two basic treaties: the 1947 Inter-American Treaty of Reciprocal Assistance (the Rio Treaty), which is a collective self-defence system, and the 1948 Pact of Bogatá, which is the original Charter of the OAS and which was amended in 1967 by the Buenos Aires Protocol, in 1985 by the Cartagena de Indias Protocol and by the 1992 Washington Protocol and the 1993 Managua Protocol.[86] There are currently 35 member states. The OAS is a collective security system, an attack on one being deemed an attack on all. The organisation consists of a General Assembly, the supreme organ, which is a plenary organ with wide terms of reference; meetings of consultation of Ministers of Foreign Affairs, which exercise broad powers; a Permanent Council which performs both secretarial supervision and political functions,[87] subject to the authority of the aforementioned institutions and a number of subsidiary organs. The organisation has adopted a Human

---

[80] Article 23.   [81] Articles 27 and 28.   [82] Articles 30 and 31.   [83] Articles 32 and 33.
[84] See *Prospects for the Commonwealth of Independent States*, a Foreign Office Background Brief, 1995.
[85] See e.g. Bowett, *Law*, Chapter 7; *The Organisation of American States, The Inter-American System*, 1963; A. V. W. Thomas and A. J. Thomas, *The Organisation of American States*, 1963; M. Ball, *The OAS in Transition*, Durham, 1969 and M. Wood, 'The Organisation of American States', 33 YBWA, 1979, p. 148.
[86] All but the Washington Protocol are currently in force.
[87] Since 1967, there have also been the Inter-American Economic and Social Council and a Council for Education, Science and Culture. The new Inter-American Committee on Peaceful Settlement is subordinate to the Permanent Council. There is also a General Secretariat, based in Washington DC, USA.

Rights Convention[88] and is the most developed of the regional organisations outside Europe, but without any of the supranational powers possessed by the European Union.[89]

The Arab League[90]

The Arab League was created in 1944 and has broad aims. It provides a useful forum for the formulation of Arab politics and encourages regional co-operation. The Council of the League is the supreme organ and performs a useful conciliatory role and various subsidiary organs dealing with economic cultural and social issues have been set up. Its headquarters are in Tunisia, having been moved there from Egypt after the Israel–Egypt Peace Treaty of 1979. There is also a permanent secretariat and a Secretary-General. The Council of the League has been involved in the peace-keeping operations, in Kuwait in 1961, where an Inter-Arab Force was established to deter Iraqi threats, and in Lebanon in 1976 as an umbrella for the operations of the Syrian troops.[91]

Africa[92]

The Organisation of African Unity was established in 1963 in Ethiopia. Its supreme organ is the Assembly of Heads of State and Government, which is a plenary body meeting annually or in extraordinary session. It has created a series of specialised commissions dealing with economic, health, defence, educational and scientific matters amongst others. There is also a Liberation Committee based in Dar es Salaam and created to assist the various liberation organisations. The Council of Ministers meets before the Assembly and prepares the way for it, while the secretariat performs the usual tasks.

A Commission of Mediation, Conciliation and Arbitration for the peace-

---

[88] *Supra*, Chapter 7, p. 287.

[89] There exists also a number of other American organisations of limited competence, see e.g. Bowett, *Law*, pp. 225–9. These include, for example, the Inter-American Bank (1959); the Andean Pact (1969); the Caribbean Community and Common Market or CARICOM (1973); the Latin American Integration Association (1980); the Southern Cone Common Market or MERCOSUR (1991) and the Association of Caribbean States (1994).

[90] *Ibid.*, pp. 229–33 and R. W. MacDonald, *The League of Arab States*, Princeton, 1965. See also B. Boutros-Ghali, 'La Ligue des Etats Arabes', 137 HR, p. 1 and H. A. Hassouna, *The League of Arab States*, Dobbs Ferry, 1975. Note also the existence of the Organisation of Petroleum Exporting Countries, founded in 1960, which obtained the power to fix crude oil prices in 1973, see e.g. Seymour, *OPEC, Instrument of Change*, 1980.

[91] See e.g. Bowett, *Law*, p. 230 and Feuer, 'Le Force Arabe de Sécurité au Liban', 22 AFDI, 1976, p. 51. See also *supra*, Chapter 18, p. 732.

[92] See e.g. Bowett, *Law*, pp. 241–4; Z. Cervenka, *The Organisation of African Unity and Its Charter*, London, 1969 and *The Unfinished Quest for Unity*, London, 1977; B. Andemicael, *The OAU and the UN*, London, 1976, and M. Wolfers, *Politics in the Organisation of African Unity*, London, 1976. See also *supra*, Chapter 18, p. 730.

ful settlement of African disputes was set up, but has not been utilised, African states preferring to have resort to *ad hoc* mediation efforts.[93] The OAU has faced considerable problems in reconciling member states' policies. The Western Sahara conflict is the prime example of this. That dispute provoked Morocco's withdrawal from the organisation,[94] while the OAU mediation attempts in the Chad civil war were noticeably unsuccessful.[95]

A variety of African regional economic associations exist, in particular the Economic Community of West African States[96] and the Southern African Development Community.[97]

Eastern Europe

There existed a number of important institutions in Eastern Europe, such as the Warsaw Pact, which mirrored the NATO alliance, and Comecon (the Council for Mutual Economic Aid).[98] The process, however, never went as far as in Western Europe and with the collapse of the Soviet system of Eastern Europe, these institutions disintegrated.[99]

Asia

The Association of South East Asian Nations (ASEAN) was created in 1967.[100] It possesses both economic and political aims and groups together Indonesia, Thailand, Malaysia, Singapore, the Philippines, Brunei (which joined in 1984) and Vietnam (which joined in 1995). It operates on the basis of annual ministerial meetings serviced by a Standing Committee and a series of permanent committees covering areas such as science and technology, shipping and commerce. In 1976 three agreements were signed; a Treaty of Amity and Co-operation, which reaffirmed the parties' commitment to peace and dealt with the peaceful settlement of disputes; the Declaration of ASEAN Concord, which called for increased political and economic co-ordination and co-operation, and the Agreement of Establishment of the Permanent Secretariat to co-ordinate the five national secretariats established under the 1967 ASEAN Declaration. The

[93] *Ibid.* [94] *Ibid.*
[95] See e.g. M. N. Shaw, 'Dispute-Settlement in Africa', 37 YBWA, 1983, pp. 149, 158–60. See further *supra*, Chapter 18, p. 730.
[96] See e.g. L. Henkin, R. C. Pugh, O. Schachter and H. Smit, *International Law Cases and Materials*, 3rd edn, St Paul, 1993, p. 1554.
[97] *Ibid.*, p. 1555.See also Bowett, *Law*, pp. 244–8 and L. Sohn, *Documents of African Regional Organisations*, 4 vols., 1971.
[98] Bowett, *law*, pp. 239–40. See also R. Szawlowski, *The System of International Organisations of the Communist Countries*, Leiden, 1976.
[99] See e.g. *Keesing's Record of World Events*, p. 37979 (1991).
[100] See e.g. Bowett, *Law*, p. 235. See also Allen, *The ASEAN Report*, 2 vols., 1979 and *Understanding ASEAN* (ed. A. Broinowski), London, 1982.

Secretariat was further strengthened in 1992. In 1987, the Protocol amending the Treaty of Amity was signed under which countries outside the ASEAN region could accede to the treaty. A number of economic agreements have also been signed ranging from the Manila Declaration of 1987 to the Framework Agreement on Enhancing ASEAN Economic Co-operation 1992 and the decision to establish an ASEAN Free Trade Area within fifteen years.

The highest authority in ASEAN is the Meeting of Heads of Government, while a variety of Ministerial Meetings also take place, including those of foreign ministers and economic ministers. There is a Secretary-General, responsible to the Heads of Government meetings and to meetings of ASEAN ministers, and a Standing Committee, which acts as the policy arm and organ of co-ordination between Ministerial Meetings of Foreign Ministers.

Some legal aspects of international organisations[101]

There is no doubt that the contribution to international law generally made by the increasing number and variety of international organisations is marked. In many fields, the practice of international organisations has had an important effect and one that is often not sufficiently appreciated. In addition, state practice within such organisations is an increasingly significant element within the general process of customary law formation. This is particularly true with regard to the United Nations, with its universality of membership and extensive field of activity and interest, although not all such practice will be capable of transmission into customary law, and particular care will have to be exercised with regard to the *opinio juris*, or binding criterion.[102]

As well as the impact of the practice of international organisations upon international law, it is worth noting the importance of international legal norms within the operations of such organisations. The norms in question guide the work and development of international institutions and may act to correct illegal acts.[103] Questions dealing with the interpretation of treaties

[101] See e.g. Amerasinghe, *Principles*; Schermers and Blokker, *International*; Bowett, *Law*, Part 4; I. Brownlie, *Principles of Public International Law*, 4th edn, Oxford, 1990, Chapter 30 and Reuter, *International Institutions*, pp. 227–64. See also E. Lauterpacht, 'Development', and 'The Legal Effects of Illegal Acts of International Organisations' in *Cambridge Essays in International Law*, Cambridge, 1965, p. 98; K. Skubiszewski, 'Enactment of Law by International Organisations', 4 BYIL, 1965–6, p. 198; Whiteman, *Digest*, vol. XIII, 1968; R. Higgins, *The Development of International Law Through the Political Organs of the United Nations*, Oxford, 1963 and generally other sources cited in footnote 1 *supra*.

[102] See *supra*, Chapter 3, p. 90.

[103] See e.g. the *Inter-Governmental Maritime Consultative Organisation* case, ICJ Reports, 1960, p. 150: 30 ILR, p. 426; the *Conditions of Admission of a State to the United Nations* case, ICJ Reports, 1948, p. 57; 15 ILR, p. 333; and the *Certain Expenses of the United Nations* case, ICJ Reports, 1962, p. 151: 34 ILR, p. 281. See also E. Lauterpacht, 'Development', footnote 1, pp. 388–95.

are particularly relevant in this context, since international organisations are grounded upon treaties that are also constituent instruments, but issues relating to the scope of powers and especially implied powers are also of crucial importance. Nevertheless, a two-way process of legal development is involved.

Personality[104]

The essence of the role of international organisations in the world order centres on their possession of international legal personality. Once this is established, they become subjects of international law and thus capable of enforcing rights and duties upon the international plane as distinct from operating merely within the confines of separate municipal jurisdictions. Not all arrangements by which two or more states co-operate will necessarily establish separate legal personality. The International Court of Justice in *Nauru* v. *Australia*,[105] noted that the arrangements under which Australia, New Zealand and the UK became the joint 'Administering Authority' for Nauru in the Trusteeship Agreement approved by the UN in 1947 did not establish a separate international legal personality distinct from that of the states.

The question of personality will in the first instance depend upon the terms of the instrument establishing the organisation. If states wish the organisation to be endowed specifically with international personality, this will appear in the constituent treaty and will be determinative of the issue.[106] But this actually occurs in only a minority of cases. However, personality on the international plane may be inferred from the powers or purposes of the organisation and its practice.[107] This is the more usual situation and one authoritatively discussed and settled (at least as far as the UN was concerned directly) by the International Court in the *Reparation for Injuries Suffered in the Service of the United Nations* case.[108]

---

[104] *Supra*, Chapter 5, p. 137. See also Amerasinghe, *Principles*, Chapter 3; Schermers and Blokker, *International*, Chapter 11; C. W. Jenks, 'The Legal Personality of International Organisations', 22 BYIL, 1945, p. 267; M. Rama-Montaldo, 'International Legal Personality and Implied Powers of International Organisations', 44 BYIL, 1970, p. 111; M. Sørensen, 'Principes de Droit International Public', 101 HR, pp. 1, 127 *et seq.*; H. Barberis, 'Nouvelles Questions Concernant La Personalité Juridique Internationale', 179 HR, p. 145; F. Seyersted, 'Objective International Personality of Intergovernmental Organisations', 34 *Nordisk Tidskrift for International Ret*, 1964, p. 1 and C. Ijalaye, *The Extension of Corporate Personality in International Law*, 1978.
[105] ICJ Reports, 1992, pp. 240, 258; 97 ILR, pp. 1, 25.
[106] See e.g. article 6 of the European Coal and Steel Community Treaty, 1951, and article 210 of the EEC Treaty, 1957. See also *Costa (Flaminio)* v. *ENEL*, [1964] ECR 585.
[107] Note also the approach championed by Seyersted that international organisations become *ipso facto* international legal persons where there exists at least one organ with a will distinct from that of the member states, see Seyersted, 'International Personality', and Schermers and Blokker, *International*, p. 978.   [108] ICJ Reports, 1949, p. 174; 16 ILR, p. 318.

The Court held that the UN had international legal personality because this was indispensable in order to achieve the purposes and principles specified in the Charter. In other words, it was a necessary inference from the functions and rights the organisation was exercising and enjoying. The Court emphasised that it had to be:

> acknowledged that its [i.e. UN's] members, by entrusting certain functions to it, with the attendant duties and responsibilities, have clothed it with the competence required to enable those functions to be effectively discharged.[109]

The possession of international personality meant that the organisation was a subject of international law and capable of having international rights and duties and of enforcing them by bringing international claims.

In reaching this conclusion, the Court examined the United Nations Charter and subsequent relevant treaties and practice to determine the constitutional nature of the United Nations and the extent of its powers and duties. It noted the obligations of members towards the organisation, its ability to make international agreements and the provisions of the Charter contained in Articles 104 and 105, whereby the United Nations was to enjoy such legal capacity, privileges and immunities in the territory of each member state as were necessary for the fulfilment of its purposes.

The Court emphasised that:

> fifty states, representing the vast majority of the members of the international community, had the power in conformity with international law, to bring into being an entity possessing objective international personality, and not merely personality recognised by them alone.[110]

Accordingly, the Court derived the objective international legal personality of the UN from the intention of the members, either directly or implicitly. Such personality was objective in the sense that it could be maintained as against non-members as well, of course, as against members. Objective personality is not dependent upon prior recognition by the non-member concerned and would seem to flow rather from the nature and functions of the organisation itself. It may be that the number of states members of the organisation in question is relevant to the issue of objective personality, but it is not determinative.[111]

---

[109] *Ibid.*, p. 179; 16 ILR, p. 322.   [110] *Ibid.*, p. 185; 16 ILR, p. 330.

[111] See the *Third US Restatement of Foreign Relations Law*, p. 141, noting that '[a]n international organisation with a substantial membership is a person in international law even in relation to states not members of the organisation. However, a state does not have to recognise the legal personality of an organisation of which it is not a member, which has few members, or which is regional in scope in a region to which the state does not belong', cf. Amerasinghe, *Principles*, p. 86. It should be noted that the question of objective personality is not essentially linked to recognition by non-member states as such. What will, however, be important will be patterns of dealing with such organisations by non-member states.

The attribution of international legal personality to an international organisation is therefore important in establishing that organisation as an entity operating directly upon the international stage rather than obliging the organisation to function internationally through its member states, who may number in the tens or dozens or more. The latter situation inevitably leads to considerable complication in the reaching of agreements as well as causing problems with regard to enforcing the responsibility or claims of such organisations internationally. The question of the effect of international personality upon the liability of member states for problems affecting the organisation will be referred to later in this Chapter.[112] However, one needs to be careful not to confuse international with domestic legal personality. Many constituent instruments of international organisations expressly or impliedly provide that the organisation in question shall have personality in domestic law so as to enable it, for example, to contract or acquire or dispose of property or to institute legal proceedings in the local courts or to have the legal capacity necessary for the exercise of its functions.[113] Article 104 of the United Nations Charter itself provides that the UN 'shall enjoy in the territory of each of its members such legal capacity as may be necessary for the exercise of its functions and the fulfilment of its purposes'. Where such provisions exist, it follows that member states of the organisation have accepted an obligation to recognise such legal personality within their legal systems. How that may be achieved will vary from state to state and will depend upon the domestic legal system. In the UK, for example, becoming a party to a treaty which is a constituent instrument of an international organisation does not of itself incorporate that treaty into English law, so that the further step of incorporating legislation is required. In other states becoming a party to a treaty is sufficient of itself to incorporate the provisions of the treaty directly into domestic law.[114]

The issue also arises at this point as to whether states that are not parties to the treaty in question and thus not member states of the particular international organisation are obliged to recognise the personality of such organisation. This can be achieved either directly, by entering into an agreement with the organisation and a headquarters agreement permitting the establishment of the organisation within the jurisdiction is the obvious example,[115] or indirectly by virtue of the rules of private international law (or conflict of laws). By virtue of this approach, adopted in most legal

---

[112] See *infra*, p. 921.
[113] See e.g. articles IX(2) and VII(2) respectively of the Articles of Agreement of the International Monetary Fund and the International Bank for Reconstruction and Development. See also article 16 of the constitution of the Food and Agriculture Organisation, article 6h of the constitution of the World Health Organisation and article 12 of the constitution of UNESCO. [114] See further *supra*, Chapter 4.
[115] See e.g. *re Poncet*, 15 ILR, p. 346.

systems, a domestic court will determine the legal status and capacity of a legal person by reference to the applicable or proper law, which will be in the case of international organisations, international law. Thus if the organisation had personality under international law, this would suffice to establish personality under domestic law.[116]

However, in the UK, the approach has been rather different.[117] The International Organisations Act 1968 grants the legal capacity of a body corporate to any organisation declared by Order in Council to be an organisation of which the UK and one or more foreign states are members. The view taken by the House of Lords in the *Tin* case[118] was that the legal effect of the Order in Council of 1972 concerning the International Tin Council (ITC) was to create the ITC as a legal person separate and distinct from its members, since 'as an international legal persona [it] had no status under the laws of the United Kingdom'.[119] In other words, without such legislative action, an international organisation would have no legal existence in the UK. There is an exception to this strict approach and that is where the organisation has been granted legal personality in another country. The case of *Arab Monetary Fund* v. *Hashim (No. 3)*[120] concerned the attempt by the AMF to bring an action before the English courts to recover funds allegedly embezzled. The relevant constituent treaty of 1976 between a number of Arab states gave the AMF 'independent juridical personality' and a decree was adopted in Abu Dhabi giving the organisation independent legal status and the capacity to sue and be sued in United Arab Emirates law. There was, however, no Order in Council under the International Organisations Act 1968 giving the AMF legal personality within the UK. The Court of Appeal took the view that the decision of the House of Lords in the *Tin* case[121] meant that the ordinary conflict of laws rules allowing recognition of an entity created under foreign law could not be applied to an organisation established under international law, since this would apparently circumvent the principle that an international organisation with legal personality created

---

[116] See e.g. *International Tin Council* v. *Amalgamet Inc.*, 524 NYS 2d 971 (1988). See also *UNRAA* v. *Daan*, 16 ILR, p. 337 and *Branno* v. *Ministry of War*, 22 ILR, p. 756.

[117] See e.g. J. W. Bridge, 'The United Nations and English Law', 18 ICLQ, 1969, p. 689; G. Marston, 'The Origin of the Personality of International Organisations in United Kingdom Law', 40 ICLQ, 1991, p. 403 and F. A. Mann, 'International Organisations as National Corporations', 107 LQR, 1991, p. 357. See also R. Higgins, Report on the 'Legal Consequences for Member States of the Non-Fulfilment by International Organisations of their Obligations toward Third States', *Annuaire de l'Institut de Droit International*, 1995 I, p. 249.

[118] *J. H. Rayner (Mincing Lane) Ltd* v. *Department of Trade and Industry* [1989] 3 WLR 969, 982 and 1004 *et seq.*; 81 ILR, pp. 670, 678 and 703 *et seq.*

[119] *Ibid.*, 1008; 81 ILR, p. 708 (per Lord Oliver). But see Lord Templeman in *Arab Monetary Fund* v. *Hashim (No. 3)* [1991] 2 WLR 729, 738; 85 ILR, pp. 1, 11, who noted that no argument based on incorporation by one or more foreign states had been relevant or canvassed in the *Tin* case.   [120] [1991] 2 WLR 729; 85 ILR, p. 1.

[121] [1989] 3 WLR 969; 81 ILR, p. 670.

outside the jurisdiction would not have capacity to sue in England without a relevant authorising Order in Council.[122]

The House of Lords, however, by a majority of four to one, expressed the opinion that the majority of the Court of Appeal had felt inhibited by observations made in the *Tin* cases and that the latter cases had not affected the principles that the recognition of a foreign state was a matter for the Crown and that if a foreign state is recognised by the Crown, the courts of the UK would recognise the corporate bodies created by that state. The House of Lords noted that the UK courts could indeed recognise an international organisation as a separate entity by comity provided that the entity was created by one or more of the member states.[123]

In other words, in the UK, an international organisation can be recognised as having personality by one of several methods. First, where Parliament has by legislation incorporated an international treaty establishing such an organisation.[124] Secondly, where the executive expressly recognises an international organisation.[125] Thirdly, where an Order in Council under the International Organisations Act so provides and fourthly, where the courts by virtue of comity recognise an international organisation that has personality in one or more of the member states.[126] It is an approach that is not without some difficulty, not least because of the implication that an international organisation not the subject of a UK Order in Council and not incorporated in the domestic law of member states may not be recognised as having personality in the UK, even though there exists an international treaty establishing such an international organisation with international personality.

To state that an international organisation has international personality does not dispose of the question of what such personality entails. The attribution of international personality to an organisation endows it with a separate identity, distinct from its constituent elements. Whereas states are recognised as possessing the widest range of rights and duties, those of international organisations are clearly circumscribed in terms of express powers laid down in the constituent instruments or implied powers necessarily derived therefrom or otherwise evolved through practice.[127] The International Court emphasised that the attribution of international personality to the UN, for example, was not the same thing as declaring the UN to be a state nor that its legal personality and rights and duties were the same as those of a state. By

---

[122] [1990] All ER 769, 775 (Donaldson MR); 83 ILR, pp. 259–61 and 778 (Nourse LJ); 83 ILR, p. 264.   [123] *Ibid.*, 738–9; 85 ILR, pp. 12–13.
[124] See *ibid.*, 738; 85 ILR, p. 12, giving the example of the Bretton Woods Agreements Act 1945.   [125] *Ibid.*   [126] *Ibid.*
[127] The Court in the *Reparation* case took particular care to emphasise that possession of international personality was far from an ascription of statehood or recognition of equal rights and duties, ICJ Reports, 1949, p. 185; 16 ILR, p. 330.

914 INTERNATIONAL LAW

the same token it did not mean that the UN was a 'super-state'.[128] The Court declared that UN personality involved the competence to possess and maintain rights and the capacity to enforce them on the international stage.[129] Precisely which powers and capacities are involved will in reality depend upon an analysis of the organisation itself and the relationship of such powers and capacities to the stated purposes and duties of that organisation.

The constituent instruments[130]

International organisations are expressly created by states by formal decision as laid down in constituent instruments. The very nature, status and authority of such organisations will therefore depend primarily upon the terms of the constituent instruments or constitutions under which they are established. Such instruments have a dual provenance. They constitute multilateral treaties, since they are binding agreements entered into by states parties, and as such fall within the framework of the international law of treaties.[131] But such agreements are multilateral treaties possessing a special character since they are also methods of creation of new subjects of international law. This dual nature has an impact most clearly in the realm of interpretation of the basic documents of the organisation.[132] This was clearly brought out in the Advisory Opinion of the International Court of Justice (requested by the World Health Organisation) in the *Legality of the Use by a State of Nuclear Weapons in Armed Conflict* case.[133] The Court declared that:

> [t]he constituent instruments of international organisations are also treaties of a particular type; their object is to create new subjects of law endowed with a certain autonomy, to which the parties entrust the task of realising common goals. Such treaties can raise specific problems of interpretation owing, *inter alia*, to their character which is conventional and at the same time institutional; the very nature of the organisation created, the objectives which have been assigned to it by its founder, the imperatives associated with the effective performance of its functions, as well as its own practice, are all elements which may deserve special attention when the time comes to interpret these constituent treaties.

Accordingly, one needs to consider the special nature of the constituent instruments as forming not only multilateral agreements but also constitu-

---

[128] *Ibid.*, p. 179; 16 ILR, p. 322. See also the *WHO* case, ICJ Reports, 1980, pp. 73, 89; 62 ILR, pp. 450, 473. [129] *Ibid.*
[130] See e.g. Amerasinghe, *Principles*, Chapter 2; Schermers and Blokker, *International*, pp. 710 *et seq.* and E. P. Hexner, 'Interpretation by International Organisations of their Basic Instruments', 53 AJIL, 1959, p. 341. [131] As to which see *supra* Chapter 16.
[132] See C. F. Amerasinghe, 'Interpretation of Texts in Open International Organisations', 65 BYIL, 1994, p. 175; M. N. Shaw, *Title to Territory in Africa: International Legal Issues*, Oxford, 1986, pp. 64–73; S. Rosenne, 'Is the Constitution of an International Organisation an International Treaty?', 12 *Communicazioni e Studi*, 1966, p. 21 and G. Distefano, 'La Pratique Subséquente des Etats Parties à un Traité', AFDI, 1994, p. 41. See also H. Lauterpacht, *The Development of International Law by the International Court*, London, 1958, pp. 267–81 and E. Lauterpacht, 'Development', pp. 414 *et seq.*
[133] ICJ Reports, 1996, para. 19.

tional documents subject to constant practice, and thus interpretation, both of the institution itself and of member states and others in relation to it. This of necessity argues for a more flexible or purpose-orientated method of interpretation. It is in fact the element of constant practice occurring in an institutional context that really differentiates the interpretation of constitutions from that of ordinary multilateral treaties, although this may be a matter more of degree than of essence depending upon the identity of the particular agreement.[134] Subsequent practice is to be taken into account in interpreting a treaty by virtue of article 31(3)b of the Vienna Convention on the Law of Treaties 1969,[135] and this has sometimes proved crucial in interpreting constituent instruments.[136] In addition, the provision in article 31(1) of the Convention that a treaty is to be interpreted in the light of its object and purpose has permitted the application of the principle of effectiveness. This is of particular importance in the case of international organisations since such organisations, being in a state of constant and varying activity, need to be able to operate effectively, and this therefore militates towards a more flexible approach to interpretation.[137]

However, one must be careful not to take this too far and ascribe far-reaching powers to international organisations upon the basis of an exaggerated application of the principle of effectiveness, since this will inevitably lead to conflict with member states and third parties, as well as undermining the internationally recognised nature and scope of international organisations.

The powers of international institutions[138]

International organisations are unlike states that possess a general competence as subjects of international law.[139] They are governed by the principle of speciality, so that, as the International Court has noted, 'they are invested

---

[134] Thus, for example, one would expect the comprehensive 1982 Convention on the Law of the Sea to generate substantial practice, including institutional practice via the International Seabed Authority, now that it is in force, see further *supra*, Chapter 11.

[135] Note that by virtue of article 5 of the Vienna Convention on the Law of Treaties 1969, this Convention applies to any treaty which is the constituent instrument of an international organisation and to any treaty adopted within an international organisation, without prejudice to any relevant rules of the organisation.

[136] See e.g. the *Competence of the General Assembly for the Admission of a State to the United Nations* case, ICJ Reports, 1950, pp. 4, 9; 17 ILR, pp. 326, 329; the *Namibia* case, ICJ Reports, 1971, pp. 17, 22; 49 ILR, pp. 2, 12 and the *IMCO* case, ICJ Reports, 1960, pp. 150, 167–8; 30 ILR, pp. 426, 439–41.

[137] See Lauterpacht, 'Development', pp. 420 *et seq.*

[138] See e.g. Lauterpacht, 'Development', pp. 423–74; Amerasinghe, *Principles*, pp. 100 *et seq.*; Rama-Montaldo, 'Legal Personality'; Campbell, 'The Limits of Powers of International Organisations', 32 ICLQ, 1983, p. 523; K. Skubiszewski, 'Implied Powers of International Organisations' in *International Law at a Time of Perplexity* (ed. Y. Dinstein), Dordrecht, 1989, p. 855 and Kirgis, *International Organisations*, Chapter 3.

[139] See the Advisory Opinion of the International Court on the *Legality of the Use by a State of Nuclear Weapons in Armed Conflict* brought by the World Health Organisation, ICJ Reports, 1996, para. 25.

by the states which create them with powers, the limits of which are a function of the common interests whose promotion those states entrust to them'.[140] Such powers may be expressly laid down in the constituent instruments or may arise subsidiarily as implied powers,[141] being those deemed necessary for fulfilment of the functions of the particular organisation. The test of validity for such powers has been variously expressed. The International Court noted in the *Reparation* case that:[142]

> [u]nder international law the organisation must be deemed to have those powers which, though not expressly provided in the charter, are conferred upon it by necessary implication as being essential to the performance of its duties.[143]

In the *Effect of Awards of Compensation Made by the UN Administrative Tribunal* case,[144] the Court held that the General Assembly could validly establish an administrative tribunal in the absence of an express power since the capacity to do this arose 'by necessary intendment' out of the Charter, while in the *Certain Expenses of the UN* case,[145] the Court declared that 'when the organisation takes action which warrants the assertion that it was appropriate for the fulfilment of one of the stated purposes of the United Nations, the presumption is that such action is not *ultra vires* the organisation'. The tests posited therefore have ranged from powers arising by 'necessary implication as being essential to the performance' of constitutionally laid down duties, to those arising 'by necessary intendment' out of the constituent instrument, to those deemed 'appropriate for the fulfilment' of constitutionally authorised purposes of the organisation. There are clearly variations of emphasis in such formulations.[146] Nevertheless, although the functional test is determinative, it operates within the framework of those powers expressly conferred by the constitution of the organisation. Thus any attempt to infer a power that was inconsistent with an express power would fail, although there is clearly an area

---

[140] *Ibid.* The Court here cited the Permanent Court's Advisory Opinion in the *Jurisdiction of the European Commission of the Danube*, PCIJ, Series B, NO. 14, p. 64, which noted that 'As the European Commission is not a state, but an international institution with a special purpose, it only has the functions bestowed upon it by the Definitive Statute with a view to the fulfilment of that purpose, but it has power to exercise those functions to their full extent, in so far as the Statute does not impose restrictions upon it.'

[141] See Schermers and Blokker, *International*, pp. 158 *et seq.*

[142] ICJ Reports, 1949, pp. 174, 182; 16 ILR, pp. 318, 326.

[143] This passage was cited in the *Legality of the Use by a State of Nuclear Weapons* case, ICJ Reports, 1996, para. 25. Compare also the approach adopted by the International Court in the *Reparation* case with that adopted by Judge Hackworth in his dissenting opinion in that case, ICJ Reports, 1949, pp. 196–8; 16 ILR, pp. 318, 328. See also G. G. Fitzmaurice, 'The Law and Procedure of the International Court of Justice: International Organisations and Tribunals', 29 BYIL, 1952, p. 1.

[144] ICJ Reports, 1954, pp. 47, 56–7; 21 ILR, pp. 310, 317–18.

[145] ICJ Reports, 1962, p. 151, 168; 34 ILR, pp. 281, 297.

[146] See also the *Fédéchar* case, Case 8/55, European Court Reports, 1954–6, p. 299.

of ambiguity here.[147] In the *Legality of the Use by a State of Nuclear Weapons* case,[148] the Court noted that the World Health Organisation had under article 2 of its Constitution adopted in 1946 the competence 'to deal with the effects on health of the use of nuclear weapons, or any other hazardous activity, and to take preventive measures aimed at protecting the health of populations in the event of such weapons being used or such activities engaged in'.[149] However, the Court concluded that the question asked of it related not to the effects of the use of nuclear weapons on health, but to the legality of the use of such weapons in view of their health and environmental effects. Whatever those effects might be, the competence of the WHO to deal with them was not dependent upon the legality of the acts that caused them. Accordingly, the Court concluded that in the light of the constitution of the WHO as properly interpreted, the organisation had not been granted the competence to address the legality of the use of nuclear weapons and that therefore the competence to request an advisory opinion did not exist since the question posed was not one that could be considered as arising 'within the scope of . . . activities' of the WHO as required by article 96(2) of the UN Charter.[150]

Of great importance is the question of the capacity of international organisations to conclude international treaties.[151] This will primarily depend upon the constituent instrument, since the existence of legal personality is on its own probably insufficient to ground the competence to enter into international agreements.[152] Article 6 of the Vienna Convention on the Law of Treaties between States and International Organisations 1986 provides that '[t]he capacity of an international organisation to conclude treaties is governed by the rules of that organisation'. This is a wider formulation than reliance solely upon the constituent instrument and permits recourse to

---

[147] See also e.g. The *International Status of South West Africa* case, ICJ Reports, 1950, pp. 128, 136–8; 17 ILR, pp. 47, 53; the *Expenses* case, ICJ Reports, 1962, pp. 151, 167–8; 34 ILR, pp. 281, 296 and the *Namibia* case, ICJ Reports, 1971, pp. 16, 47–9; 49 ILR, pp. 2, 37.

[148] ICJ Reports, 1996, para. 25.   [149] ICJ Reports, 1996, para. 21.

[150] Article 96(2) of the UN Charter provides that organs of the UN (apart from the Security Council and General Assembly) and specialised agencies which may at any time be so authorised by the General Assembly may request advisory opinions of the International Court on 'legal questions arising within the scope of their activities'.

[151] See e.g. Schermers and Blokker, *International*, pp. 1096 *et seq.*; Schneider, *Treaty-Making Power of International Organisations*, 1959 and C. Parry 'The Treaty-Making Power of the UN', 26 BYIL, 1949, p. 147. See also *supra*, Chapter 16, p. 671, with regard to the Convention on the Law of Treaties between States and International Organisations. See also *Yearbook of the ILC*, 1982, vol. II, Part 2, pp. 9 *et seq.*

[152] See e.g. Hungdah Chiu, *The Capacity of International Organisations to Conclude Treaties and the Special Legal Aspects of the Treaties So Concluded*, The Hague, 1966; *Agreements of International Organisations and the Vienna Convention on the Law of Treaties* (ed. K. Zemanek), 1971; G. Nascimento e Silva, 'The 1986 Vienna Convention and the Treaty-Making Power of International Organisations', 29 German YIL, 1986, p. 68 and 'The 1969 and 1986 Conventions on the Law of Treaties: A Comparison' in *International Law at a Time of Perplexity* (ed. Y. Dinstein), Dordrecht, 1989, p. 461.

issues of implied powers, interpretation and subsequent practice. It was noted in the commentary of the International Law Commission that the phrase 'the rules of the organisation' meant in addition to the constituent instruments,[153] relevant decisions and resolutions and the established practice of the organisation.[154] Accordingly, demonstration of treaty-making capacity will revolve around the competences of the organisation as demonstrated in each particular case by reference to the constituent instruments, evidenced implied powers and subsequent practice.

The applicable law[155]

International institutions are established by states by international treaties. Such instruments fall to be interpreted and applied within the framework of international law. Accordingly, as a general rule, the applicable or 'proper' or 'personal' law of international organisations is international law.[156] In addition, the organisation in question may well have entered into treaty relationships with particular states, for example, in the case of an headquarters agreement, and these relationships will also be governed by international law. Those matters that will necessarily (in the absence of express provision to the contrary) be governed by international law will include questions as to the existence, constitution, status, membership and representation of the organisation.[157]

However, the applicable law in particular circumstances may be domestic law. Thus, where the organisation is purchasing or leasing land or entering into contracts for equipment or services, such activities will normally be subject to the appropriate national law. Tortious liability as between the organisation and a private individual will generally be subject to domestic law, but tortious activity may be governed by international law depending upon the circumstances, for example, where there has been damage to the property of an international organisation by the police or armed forces of a state.[158] The internal law of the organisation will cover matters such as

---

[153] See e.g. articles 43 and articles 75, 77, 79, 83 and 85 of the UN Charter concerning military assistance arrangements with the Security Council and Trusteeship Agreements respectively.   [154] *Yearbook of the ILC*, 1982, vol. II, part 2, p. 41.

[155] See e.g. Amerasinghe, *Principles*, pp. 226 *et seq.*; F. A. Mann, 'International Corporations and National Law', 42 BYIL, 1967, p. 145; F. Seyersted, 'Applicable Law in Relations Between Intergovernmental Organisations and Private Parties', 122 HR, 1976 III, p. 427 and C. W. Jenks, *The Proper Law of International Organisations*, London, 1961.

[156] Jenks, *Proper Law*, p. 3, wrote that 'if a body has the character of an international body corporate the law governing its corporate life must necessarily be international in character'. See also the *Third US Restatement of Foreign Relations Law*, St Paul, 1987, vol. I, pp. 133 *et seq.*

[157] See also Colman J. in *Westland Ltd* v. *AOI* [1995] 2 WLR 126, 144 *et seq.* and Millett J. in *In re International Tin Council* [1987] Ch. 419, 452, upheld by the Court of Appeal, [1989] Ch. 309, 330.   [158] See e.g. Amerasinghe, *Principles*, pp. 226 *et seq.*

employment relations, the establishment and functioning of subsidiary organs and the management of administrative services.[159] The internal law of an organisation, which includes the constituent instruments and subsidiary regulations and norms and any relevant contractual arrangements, may in reality be seen as a specialised and particularised part of international law, since it is founded upon agreements that draw their validity and applicability from the principles of international law.

The responsibility of international institutions[160]

The establishment of an international organisation with international personality results in the formation of a new legal person, separate and distinct from that of the states creating it. This separate and distinct personality necessarily imports consequences as to international responsibility, both to and by the organisation. The International Court noted in the *Reparation* case, for example, that[161] 'when an infringement occurs, the organisation should be able to call upon the responsible state to remedy its default, and, in particular, to obtain from the state reparation for the damage that the default may have caused' and emphasised that there existed an 'undeniable right of the organisation to demand that its members shall fulfil the obligations entered into by them in the interest of the good working of the organisation'.[162] Responsibility is a necessary consequence of international personality and the resulting possession of international rights and duties. Such rights and duties may flow from treaties, such as headquarters agreements,[163] or from the principles of customary international law.[164] The precise nature of responsibility will depend upon the circumstances of the case and, no doubt, analogies drawn from the law of state responsibility with regard to the conditions under which responsibility will be imposed.[165] In brief, one can note the following. The basis of international responsibility will be the breach of an international obligation[166] and such obligations will depend upon the situation. The

---

[159] *Ibid.*, pp. 324 *et seq.* See also P. Cahier, 'Le Droit Interne des Organisations Internationales', RGDIP, 1963, p. 563 and G. Balldore-Pallieri, 'Le Droit Interne des Organisations Internationales', 127 HR, 1969 II, p. 1.

[160] See e.g. Amerasinghe, *Principles*, Chapter 8; Schermers and Blokker, *International*, pp. 1166 *et seq.*; Bowett, *Law*, pp. 362 *et seq.*; C. Eagleton, 'International Organisation and the Law of Responsibility', 76 HR, 1950 I, p. 319; Garcia Amador, 'State Responsibility: Some New Problems', 94 HR, p. 410 and Perez Gonzalez, 'Les Organisations Internationales et le Droit de la Responsibilité', 92 RGDIP, 1988, p. 63. See also *supra*, Chapter 14.

[161] ICJ Reports, 1949, pp. 174, 183; 16 ILR, pp. 318, 327.

[162] *Ibid.*, p. 184; 16 ILR, p. 328.

[163] See e.g. the *WHO Regional Office* case, ICJ Reports, 1980, p. 73; 62 ILR, p. 450 and the *Case Concerning the Obligation to Arbitrate*, ICJ Reports, 1988, p. 12; 82 ILR, p. 225.

[164] See the *WHO Regional Office* case, ICJ Reports, 1980, pp. 73, 90; 62 ILR, pp. 450, 474, referring to 'general rules of international law'.   [165] See *supra*, Chapter 14.

[166] See e.g. the *Reparation* case, ICJ Reports, 1949, p. 180; 16 ILR, p. 323.

Court noted in the *Reparation* case[167] that the obligations entered into by member states to enable the agents of the UN to perform their duties were obligations owed to the organisation. Thus, the organisation has, in the case of a breach of such obligations, 'the capacity to claim adequate reparation, and that in assessing this reparation it is authorised to include the damage suffered by the victim or by persons entitled through him'. Whereas the right of a state to assert a claim on behalf of a victim is predicated upon the link of nationality, in the case of an international organisation, the necessary link relates to the requirements of the organisation and therefore the fact that the victim was acting on behalf of the organisation in exercising one of the functions of that organisation. As the Court noted, 'the organisation . . . possesses a right of functional protection in respect of its agents'.[168]

Just as a state can be held responsible for injury to an organisation, so can the organisation be held responsible for injury to a state, where the injury arises out of a breach by the organisation of an international obligation deriving from a treaty provision or principle of customary international law.[169] Again, analogies will be drawn from the general rules relating to state responsibility with regard to the condition under which responsibility is imposed.

The issue of responsibility has particularly arisen in the context of UN peace-keeping operations and liability for the activities of the members of such forces. In such circumstances, the UN has accepted responsibility and offered compensation for wrongful acts.[170] The crucial issue will be whether the wrongful acts in question are imputable to the UN and this has not been accepted where the offenders were under the jurisdiction of the national state, rather than under that of the UN. Much will depend upon the circumstances of the operation in question and the nature of the link between the offenders and the UN. It appears, for example, to have been accepted that in the Korean (1950) and Kuwait (1990) operations the relationship between the national forces and the UN was such as to preclude the latter's responsibility.[171]

---

[167] *Ibid.*, p. 184; 16 ILR, p. 328.
[168] *Ibid.*, p. 184; 16 ILR, p. 329. Note that the Court held that there was no rule of law which assigned priority either to the national state of the victim or the international organisation with regard to the bringing of an international claim, *ibid.*, p. 185; 16 ILR, p. 330.
[169] See e.g. the *WHO Regional Office* case, ICJ Reports, 1980, p. 73; 62 ILR, p. 450. Note that under articles VI and XIII of the Outer Space Treaty 1967, international organisations may be subject to the obligations of the treaty without being parties to it.
[170] See e.g. B. Amrallah, 'The International Responsibility of the United Nations for Activities Carried Out by UN Peace-Keeping Forces', 23 *Revue Egyptienne de Droit International*, 1976, p. 57; D. W. Bowett, *UN Forces*, London, 1964, pp. 149 *et seq*; F. Seyersted, 'United Nations Forces: Some Legal Problems', 37 BYIL, 1961, p. 351. See also Amerasinghe, *Principles*, pp. 242 *et seq.* and *M v. Organisation des Nations Unies et l'État Belge*, 45 ILR, p. 446. [171] See Amerasinghe, *Principles*, p. 244.

Liability of member states[172]

The relationship between the member states of an organisation and the organisation itself is often complex. The situation is further complicated upon a consideration of the position of third states (or organisations) prejudiced by the activities of the organisation. The starting point for any analysis is the issue of legal personality. An international organisation created by states that does not itself possess legal personality cannot be the bearer of rights or obligations separate and distinct from those of the member states. It therefore follows that such organisations cannot be interposed as between the injured third parties and the member states of that organisation. In such cases any liability for the debts or delicts attributable to the organisation causing harm to third parties would fall upon the member states.[173] Where, however, the organisation does possess legal personality, the situation is different. Separate personality implies liability for activities entered into. The question of the liability of member states to third parties may arise subsidiarily and poses some difficulty. Such a question falls to be decided by the rules of international law not least since it is consequential upon a determination of personality which is in the case of international organisations governed by international law.[174] The problem is also to be addressed in the context of the general principle of international law that treaties do not create obligations for third states without their consent (*pacta tertiis nec nocent nec prosunt*).[175] By virtue of this rule, member states would not be responsible for breaches of agreements between organisations and other parties.

The problems faced by the International Tin Council during 1985–6 are instructive in this context.[176] The ITC, created in 1956, conducted its

---

[172] See e.g. Amerasinghe, *Principles*, Chapter 9; Schermers and Blokker, *International*, pp. 990 *et seq.*; Higgins, 'Legal Consequences'; H. Schermers, 'Liability of International Organisations', 1 *Leiden Journal of International Law*, 1988, p. 14; C. F. Amerasinghe, 'Liability to Third Parties of Member States of International Organisations: Practice, Principle and Judicial Precedent', 85 AJIL, 1991,

[173] See e.g. Higgins, 'Legal Consequences' p. 378 and Amerasinghe, *Principles*, p. 254.

[174] It is possible for states to create an international organisation under domestic law, for example, the Bank for International Settlements, but this is very rare, see e.g. M. Giovanoli, 'The Role of the Bank for International Settlements in International Monetary Co-operation and Its Tasks Relating to the European Currency Unit, 23 *The International Lawyer*, 1989, p. 841.

[175] See article 34 of the Vienna Convention on the Law of Treaties 1969, see also *supra*, Chapter 16, p. 652.

[176] See e.g. The Second Report from the Trade and Industry Committee, 1985–6, HC 305–I, 1986 and *The Times*, 13 March 1986, p. 21 and *ibid.*, 14 March 1986, p. 17. See also G. Wassermann, 'Tin and Other Commodities in Crisis', 20 *Journal of World Trade Law*, 1986, p. 232; Lauterpacht, *Principles*, p. 412; I. Cheyne, 'The International Tin Council', 36 ICLQ, 1987, p. 931; *ibid.*, 38 ICLQ, 1989, p. 417 and *ibid.*, 39 ICLQ, 1990, p. 945, and R. Sadurska and C. M. Chinkin, 'The Collapse of the International Tin Council: A Case of State Responsibility ?', 30 Va JIL, 1990, p. 845.

activities in accordance with successive international tin agreements, which aimed to regulate the tin market by virtue of export controls and the establishment of buffer stocks of tin financed by member states. The Sixth International Tin Agreement of 1982 brought together twenty-three producer and consumer states and the EEC. In October 1985, the ITC announced that it had run out of funds and credit and the London Metal Exchange suspended trading in tin. The situation had arisen basically as a result of overproduction of the metal and purchasing of tin by the ITC at prices above the market level.

Since the ITC member states refused to guarantee the debts of the organisation and since proposals to create a successor organisation to the ITC collapsed, serious questions were posed as to legal liabilities. The ITC was a corporate entity enjoying a measure of legal immunity in the UK as a result of the International Tin Council (Immunities and Privileges) Order 1972. It had immunity from the jurisdiction of the courts except in cases of enforcement of an arbitral award. The ITC Headquarters Agreement provided that contracts entered into with a person or company resident in the UK were to contain an arbitration clause. It was also the case that where a specific agreement provided for a waiver of immunity by the organisation, the courts would have jurisdiction.[177] Accordingly, the immunity from suit of the ITC was by no means unlimited.

A variety of actions were commenced by the creditors, of which the most important was the direct action. Here, a number of banks and brokers proceeded directly against the Department of Trade and Industry of the British government and other members of the ITC on the argument that they were liable on contracts concluded by the ITC.[178] The issues were argued at length in the Court of Appeal and in the House of Lords.[179] The main submission[180] for present purposes was that the members of the ITC and the organisation

[177] See e.g. *Standard Chartered Bank* v. *ITC* [1986] 3 All ER 257; 77 ILR, p. 8.
[178] See also the attempt to have the ITC wound up under Part XXI of the Companies Act 1985, *Re International Tin Council* [1988] 3 All ER 257, 361; 80 ILR, p. 181, and the attempt to appoint a receiver by way of equitable execution over the assets of the ITC following an arbitration award against the ITC (converted into a judgment) which it was argued would enable contributions or an indemnity to be claimed from the members, *Maclaine Watson* v. *International Tin Council* [1988] 3 WLR 1169; 80 ILR, p. 191.
[179] *Maclaine Watson* v. *Department of Trade and Industry* [1988] 3 WLR 1033 (Court of Appeal); 80 ILR, p. 49 and [1989] 3 All ER 523 (House of Lords) sub. nom. *J. H. Rayner Ltd* v. *Department of Trade and Industry*; 81 ILR, p. 671.
[180] One submission was that the relevant International Tin Council (Immunities and Privileges) Order 1972 did not incorporate the ITC under English law but conferred upon it the capacities of a body corporate and thus the ITC did not have legal personality. This was rejected by the House of Lords [1989] 3 All ER 523, 527–8 and 548–9; 81 ILR, pp. 677, 703. Another submission was that the ITC was only authorised to enter into contracts as an agent for the members under the terms of the Sixth International Tin Agreement 1982. This was also dismissed, on the basis that the terms of the Order clearly authorised the ITC to enter into contracts as a principal, *ibid.*, 530 and 556–7; 81 ILR, pp. 681, 715.

were liable concurrently for the debts under both English and international law. It was argued that under international law members of an international organisation bear joint and several liability for its debts unless the constituent treaty expressly excludes such liability. Although there have been hints of such an approach earlier[181] and treaty practice has been far from consistent, Lord Templeman noted that 'no plausible evidence was produced of the existence of such a rule of international law'[182] and this, it is believed, correctly represents the current state of international law.[183] The liability of a member state could arise, of course, either through an express provision[184] in the constituent instruments of the organisation providing for the liability of member states or where the organisation was in fact under the direct control of the state concerned or acted as its agent in law and in fact, or by virtue of unilateral undertakings or guarantee by the state in the particular circumstances.[185]

Privileges and immunities[186]

In order to carry out their functions more effectively, states and their representatives benefit from a variety of privileges and immunities. International organisations will also be entitled to the grant of privileges and immunities

---

[181] See e.g. *Westland Helicopters v. Arab Organisation for Industrialisation*, 23 ILM, 1984, 1071; 80 ILR, p. 600. See H. T. Adam, *Les Organismes Internationaux Specialisés*, Paris, 1965, vol. I, pp. 129–30 and Seidl-Hohenveldern, *Corporations*, pp. 119–20.

[182] [1989] 3 All ER 523, 529; 81 ILR, p. 680. This was the view adopted by a majority of the Court of Appeal, see Ralph Gibson LJ [1988] 3 WLR 1033, 1149 and Kerr LJ, *ibid.*, 1088–9 (but cf. Nourse LJ, *ibid.*, 1129–31); 80 ILR, pp. 49, 170; 101–2; 147–9. It is fair to emphasise that the approach of the Court, in effect, was primarily focused upon domestic law and founded upon the perception that without the relevant Order in Council the ITC had no legal existence in the law of the UK. An international organisation had legal personality in the sphere of international law and it did not thereby automatically acquire legal personality within domestic legal systems. For that, at least in the case of the UK, specific legislation was required.

[183] See e.g. the 1991 Partial Award on Liability of the ICC Tribunal in the *Westland Helicopters* case, see Higgins, 'Legal Consequences', p. 393. See also I. F. I. Shihata, 'Role of Law in Economic Development: The Legal Problems of International Public Ventures', 25 *Revue Egyptienne de Droit International*, 1969, pp. 119, 125; Schermers and Blokker, *International*, p. 992 and Amerasinghe, *Principles*, p. 289.

[184] Or indeed a provision demonstrating such an intention.

[185] See articles 7 and 8 of the Draft Resolution of the Institut de Droit International, *Annuaire de l'Institut de Droit International*, 1995 I, pp. 465, 467.

[186] See e.g. Amerasinghe, *Principles*, Chapter 12; M. Singer, 'Jurisdictional Immunity of International Organisations: Human Rights and Functional Necessity Concerns', 36 Va JIL, 1995, p. 53; Bowett, *Law*, pp. 345–62; C. W. Jenks, *International Immunities*, London, 1961; J. F. Lalive, 'L'Immunité de Juridiction et d'Éxecution des Organisations Internationales', 84 HR, 1953 III, p. 205; C. Dominicé, 'Le Nature et l'Étendue de l'Immunité des Organisations' in *Festschrift Ignaz Seidl-Hohenveldern* (ed. K. H. Bocksteigel), 1988, p. 11; Nguyen Quoc Dinh, 'Les Privilèges et Immunités des Organisations Internationales d'après les Jurisprudences Nationales Depuis 1945', AFDI, 1957, p. 55; D. B. Michaels, *International Privileges and Immunities*, The Hague, 1971; Kirgis, *Organisations*, pp. 26 *et seq.*; *Yearbook of the ILC*, 1967, vol. II, pp. 154 *et seq.*; DUSPIL, 1978, pp. 90 *et seq.* and *ibid.*, 1979, pp. 189 *et seq.* and Morgenstern, *Legal Problems*, pp. 5–10.

for their assets, properties and representatives. The two situations are not, of course, analogous in practice, since, for example, the basis of state immunities may be seen in terms of the sovereign equality of states and reciprocity, while this is not realistic with regard to organisations, both because they are not in a position of 'sovereign equality'[187] and because they are unable to grant immunities as a reciprocal gesture. It is also the case that the immunities of states have been restricted in the light of the distinction between transactions *jure imperii* and *jure gestionis*,[188] while any such distinction in the case of international organisations would be inappropriate.[189] The true basis for the immunities accorded to international organisation is that they are necessitated by the effective exercise of their functions. This, of course, will raise the question as to how one is to measure the level of immunities in the light of such functional necessity.

As far as the UN itself is concerned, article 105 of the Charter notes that:

(1) The Organisation shall enjoy in the territory of each of its members such privileges and immunities as are necessary for the fulfilment of its purposes

(2) Representatives of the members of the United Nations and officials of the Organisation shall similarly enjoy such privileges and immunities as are necessary for the independent exercise of their functions in connection with the Organisation.[190]

These general provisions have been supplemented by the General Convention on the Privileges and Immunities of the United Nations 1946, and by the Convention on Privileges and Immunities of the Specialised Agencies 1947.[191] These general conventions, building upon provisions in the relevant constituent instruments, have themselves been supplemented by bilateral agreements, particularly the growing number of headquarters and host agreements. The UN, for example, has concluded headquarters agreements with the United States for the UN Headquarters in New York and with Switzerland for the UN Office in Geneva in 1947.[192] Such agree-

---

[187] The reference, for example, in *Branno* v. *Ministry of War*, 22 ILR, p. 756, to the 'sovereignty of NATO' is misleading.   [188] See *supra*, Chapter 13, p. 500.

[189] See R. Higgins, *Problems and Process*, Oxford, 1994, p. 93.

[190] Note that the provisions dealing with privileges and immunities of international financial institutions tend to be considerably more detailed, see e.g. article VII of the Articles of Agreement of the International Bank for Reconstruction and Development; article IX of the Articles of Agreement of the International Monetary Fund and articles 46 to 55 of the Constitution of the European Bank for Reconstruction and Development.

[191] This also contains separate draft annexes relating to each specialised agency. See also the Agreement on the Privileges and Immunities of the Organisation of American States 1949; the General Agreement on the Privileges and Immunities of the Council of Europe 1949 and the Protocol Concerning the Privileges and Immunities of the European Communities 1965.

[192] See also the agreements with Austria, 1979, regarding the UN Vienna Centre; with Japan, 1976, regarding the UN University and with Kenya, 1975, regarding the UN Environment Programme. Note also the various Status of Forces Agreements concluded by the UN with, for example, Egypt in 1957, the Congo in 1961 and Cyprus in 1964, dealing with matters such as the legal status, facilities, privileges and immunities of the UN peace-keeping forces.

ments, for example, provide for the application of local laws within the head-quarters area subject to the application of relevant staff administrative regulations; the immunity of the premises and property of the organisation from search, requisition and confiscation and other forms of interference by the host state; exemption from local taxes except for utility charges and freedom of communication.[193]

The International Court noted in the *Applicability of the Obligation to Arbitrate* case,[194] which concerned US anti-terrorism legislation necessitating the closure of the PLO Observer Mission to the UN in New York, that the US was obliged to respect the obligation contained in section 21 of the UN Headquarters Agreement to enter into arbitration where a dispute had arisen concerning the interpretation and application of the Agreement. This was despite the US view that it was not certain a dispute had arisen, since the existence of an international dispute was a matter for objective determination.[195] The Court emphasised in particular that the provisions of a treaty prevail over the domestic law of a state party to that treaty.[196]

It is clearly the functional approach rather than any representational perception that forms the theoretical basis for the recognition of privileges and immunities with respect to international organisations. This point has been made in cases before domestic courts, but it is important to note that this concept includes the need for the preservation of the independence of the institution as against the state in whose territory it is operating. In *Mendaro v. World Bank*,[197] for example, the US Court of Appeals held that the reason for the granting of immunities to international organisations was to enable them to more effectively pursue their functions and in particular to permit organisations to operate free from unilateral control by a member state over their activities within its territory. In *Iran–US Claims Tribunal v. AS*,[198] the Dutch Supreme Court pointed to the 'interest of the international organisation in having a guarantee that it will be able to perform its tasks independently and free from interferences under all circumstances' and noted that 'an international organisation is in principle not subject to the jurisdiction of the courts of the host state in respect of all disputes which are immediately connected with the performance of the tasks entrusted to the organisation in question'. The Italian Court of Cassation in *FAO* v.

---

[193] Similar agreements may cover regional offices of international organisations, see e.g. the Agreement between the World Health Organisation and Egypt 1951 concerning a regional office of the organisation in that state. [194] ICJ Reports, 1988, p. 12; 82 ILR, p. 225.
[195] *Ibid.*, pp. 27–30; 82 ILR, p. 245. [196] *Ibid.*, pp. 33–4; 82 ILR, p. 251.
[197] 717 F.2d 610, 615–17 (1983); 92 ILR, pp. 92, 97–9.
[198] 94 ILR, pp. 321, 329. See also *Eckhardt* v. *Eurocontrol (No. 2), ibid.*, pp. 331, 337–8, where the District Court of Maastricht held that since an international organisation had been created by treaty by states, such organisation was entitled to immunity from jurisdiction on the grounds of customary international law to the extent necessary for the operation of its public service.

INPDAI[199] held that activities closely affecting the institutional purposes of the international organisation qualified for immunity, while the Employment Appeal Tribunal in *Mukuro* v. *European Bank for Reconstruction and Development*[200] stated that immunity from suit and legal process was justified on the ground that it was necessary for the fulfilment of the purposes of the bank in question, for the preservation of its independence and neutrality from control by or interference from the host state and for the effective and uninterrupted exercise of its multinational functions through its representatives.

As far as the position of representatives of states to international organisations is concerned, article IV, section 11, of the UN General Convention 1946 provides for the following privileges and immunities:

(a) immunity from personal arrest or detention and from seizure of their personal baggage, and in respect of words spoken or written and all acts done by them in their capacity as representatives, immunity from legal process of every kind;
(b) inviolability for all papers and documents;
(c) the right to use codes and to receive papers or correspondence by courier or in sealed bags;
(d) exemption in respect of themselves and their spouses from immigration restrictions, alien registration or national service obligations in the state they are visiting or though which they are passing in the exercise of their functions;
(e) the same facilities in respect of currency or exchange restrictions as are accorded to representatives of foreign governments on temporary official missions;
(f) the same immunities and facilities in respect of their personal baggage as are accorded to diplomatic envoys; and also
(g) such other privileges, immunities and facilities not inconsistent with the foregoing as diplomatic envoys enjoy, except that they shall have no right to claim exemption from customs duties on goods imported (otherwise than as part of their personal baggage) or from excise duties or sales taxes.

Article IV, section 14 provides that such privileges and immunities are accorded:

in order to safeguard the independent exercise of their functions in connection with the United Nations. Consequently a Member not only has the right but is under a duty to waive the immunity of its representative in any case where in the opinion of the Member the immunity would impede the course of justice, and it can be waived without prejudice to the purpose for which the immunity is accorded.[201]

---

[199] 87 ILR, pp. 1, 6–7. See also *Mininni* v. *Bari Institute, ibid.*, p. 28 and *Sindacato UIL* v. *Bari Institute, ibid.*, p. 37.   [200] [1994] ICR 897, 903.
[201] The question of the representation of states to international organisations is also dealt with in the 1975 Vienna Convention on the Representation of States in their Relations with International Organisations of a Universal Character, which is closely modelled on the 1961 Vienna Convention on Diplomatic Relations, although it has been criticised by a number of host states for permitting more extensive privileges and immunities than is required in the light of functional necessity. See DUSPIL, 1975, pp. 38 *et seq.* Article 30 of

The question of the privileges and immunities of representatives is invariably also addressed in headquarters agreements between international organisations and host states. Article V, section 15 of the UN Headquarters Agreement 1947, for example, states that representatives[202] are entitled in the territory of the US 'to the same privileges and immunities, subject to corresponding conditions and obligations, as it accords to diplomatic envoys accredited to it'.[203]

The International Court has recently delivered an Advisory Opinion[204] concerning the applicability of provisions in the General Convention to Special Rapporteurs appointed by the Sub-Commission on the Prevention of Discrimination and the Protection of Minorities. Article VI, section 22, of the Convention provides that experts performing missions for the United Nations are to be accorded such privileges and immunities as are necessary for the independent exercise of their functions during the periods of their missions. The International Court noted that such privileges and immunities could indeed be invoked against the state of nationality or of residence[205] and that Special Rapporteurs for the Sub-Commission were to be regarded as experts on missions within the meaning of section 22.[206] The privileges and immunities that would apply would be those that were necessary for the exercise of their functions, and in particular for the establishment of any contacts which may be useful for the preparation, the drafting and the presentation of their reports to the Sub-Commission.[207] As far as other international organisations are concerned, the relevant agreements have to be consulted, since there are no generalised rules but rather particular treaties.

International agreements concerning privileges and immunities have been implemented into domestic law by specific legislation in a number of states, examples being the UK International Organisations Act 1968[208] and the US

---

the Convention, in particular, provides that the head of mission and the members of the diplomatic staff of the mission shall enjoy immunity from the criminal jurisdiction of the host state and immunity from its civil and administrative jurisdiction, except in cases of real action relating to private immovable property situated in the host states (unless held on behalf of the sending state for the purposes of the mission); actions relating to succession and actions relating to any professional or commercial activity exercised by the person in question in the host state outside his official functions. See also *supra*, Chapter 13, p. 539.

[202] These are defined in article V, section 15 (1)–(4).

[203] See also *Third US Restatement of Foreign Relations Law*, pp. 518 *et seq*.

[204] The *Applicability of Article VI, Section 22, of the Convention on the Privileges and Immunities of the United Nations*, ICJ Reports, 1989, p. 177; 85 ILR, p. 300. This opinion was requested by the Economic and Social Council, its first request for an Advisory Opinion under article 96(2) of the UN Charter.

[205] In the absence of a reservation by the state concerned, *ibid.*, pp. 195–6; 85 ILR, pp. 323–3.

[206] This applied even though the Rapporteur concerned was not, or was no longer, a member of the Sub-Commission, since such a person is entrusted by the Sub-Commission with a research mission, *ibid.*, pp. 196–7; 85 ILR, pp. 323–4.   [207] *Ibid.*

[208] Replacing the International Organisations (Immunities and Privileges) Act 1950. The International Organisations Act 1981 *inter alia* extended the 1968 Act to commonwealth

International Organisations Immunities Act of 1945.[209] The usual pattern under such legislation is for the general empowering provisions contained in those Acts to be applied to named international organisations by specific secondary acts. In the case of the International Organisations Act 1968, for example, a wide variety of organisations have had privileges and immunities conferred upon them by Order in Council.[210] In the case of the US Act, the same process is normally conducted by means of Executive Orders.[211]

The range of privileges and immunities usually extended includes immunity from jurisdiction; inviolability of premises and archives;[212] currency and fiscal privileges and freedom of communications.[213] In the case of immunity from jurisdiction, section 2 of the UN General Convention 1946 provides that:

> The United Nations, its property and assets wherever located and by whomsoever held, shall enjoy immunity from every form of legal process except in so far as in any particular case it has expressly waived its immunity. It is, however, understood that no waiver of immunity shall extend to any measure of execution.[214]

---

organisations and to international commodity organisations and permitted the extension of privileges and immunities to states' representatives attending conferences in the UK.

[209] See also *Legislative Texts and Treaty Provisions Concerning the Legal Status, Privileges and Immunities of International Organisations*, ST/LEG/SER.B/10 and 11.

[210] See e.g. the African Development Bank, SI 1983/142; Council of Europe, SI 1960/442; European Patent Organisation, SI 1978/179 and SI 1980/1096; International Maritime and Satellite Organisation, SI 1980/187; NATO, SI 1974/1257 and SI 1975/1209 and the UN, SI 1974/1261 and SI 1975/1209.

[211] See e.g. the Executive Order 12359 of 22 April 1980 designating the Multi-National Force and Observers as a public international organisation under s. 1 of the 1945 Act entitled to enjoy the privileges, exemptions and immunities conferred by that Act. See also Executive Order 12403 of 8 February 1983 with regard to the African Development Bank; Executive Order 12467 of 2 March 1984 with regard to the International Boundary and Water Commission, US and Mexico; Executive Order 12628 of 8 March 1988 with regard to the UN Industrial Development Organisation, and Executive Order 12647 of 2 August 1988 with regard to the Multilateral Investment Guarantee Agency. See further *Cumulative DUSPIL 1981–8*, Washington, 1993, vol. I, pp. 330 *et seq.*

[212] The inviolability of premises and archives is particularly important for the effective operation of international organisations. See e.g. articles 4 and 5 of the UN General Convention 1946 and article 5 of the Specialised Agencies Convention 1947. See also Bowett, *Law*, p. 350 *et seq.* and Amerasinghe, *Principles*, pp. 383 *et seq.* Note that in *Shearson Lehman* v. *Maclaine Watson* (No. 2), [1988] 1 WLR 16; 77 ILR, p. 145, the House of Lords held that the inviolability of official documents could be lost as a result of communication to third parties.

[213] Amerasinghe, *Principles*, p. 374. An examination of Orders in Council would demonstrate the following privileges and immunities: immunity from suit and legal process; inviolability of official archives and premises; exemption or relief from taxes and rates, but not import taxes except where the goods or publications are imported or exported for official use; various reliefs with regard to car tax and VAT (value added tax) with regard to cars or goods destined for official use, and priority to be given to telecommunications to and from the UN Secretary-General, the heads of principal organs of the UN and the President of the International Court, see also the International Organisations Act 1968, Schedule I. See also sections 2–7 of the US International Organisations Immunities Act 1945.

[214] See also article 4 of the Specialised Agencies Convention 1947

Other international institutions do not possess such a wide immunity. In many cases, actions brought against the particular organisations in domestic courts are specifically permitted.[215] Waiver of immunity from process is permitted, but must be express.[216]

Dissolution[217]

The Constitutions of some international organisations contain express provisions with regard to dissolution. Article VI(5) of the Articles of Agreement of the International Bank for Reconstruction and Development, for example, provides for dissolution by a vote of the majority of Governors exercising a majority of total voting, and detailed provisions are made for consequential matters. Payment of creditors and claims, for instance, will have precedence over asset distribution, while the distribution of assets will take place on a proportional basis to shareholding. Different organisations with such express provisions take different positions with regard to the type of majority required for dissolution. In the case of the European Bank for Reconstruction and Development, for example, a majority of two-thirds of the members and three-quarters of the total voting power is required, and a simple majority vote is sufficient in the case of the International Monetary Fund. Where an organisation has been established for a limited period, the constitution will invariably provide for dissolution upon the expiry of that period.[218]

Where there are no specific provisions concerning dissolution, it is likely that an organisation may be dissolved by the decision of its highest representative body.[219] The League of Nations, for example, was dissolved by a decision taken by the Assembly without the need for individual assent by each member[220] and a similar process was adopted with regard to other

---

[215] See e.g. article VII of the Constitution of the International Bank for Reconstruction and Development and *Lutcher SA* v. *Inter-American Development Bank*, 382 F. 2d 454 (1967) and *Mendaro* v. *World Bank*, 717 F.2d 610 (1983); 92 ILR, p. 92. See also article 6 of the Headquarters Agreement between the UK and the International Maritime Satellite Organisation 1980. [216] See e.g. Singer, 'Jurisdictional Immunity', pp. 72 *et seq.*

[217] See e.g. Amerasinghe, *Principles*, Chapter 15 and Schermers and Blokker, *International*, pp. 1015 *et seq.* See also C. W. Jenks, 'Some Constitutional Problems of International Organisations', 22 BYIL, 1945, p. 11 and Bowett, *Law*, pp. 377 *et seq.*

[218] This applies particularly to commodity organisations, see e.g. the International Tin Agreement 1981; the Natural Rubber Agreement 1987 and the International Sugar Agreement 1992.

[219] See Amerasinghe, *Principles*, p. 471 and Schermers and Blokker, *International*, p. 1024.

[220] In fact the decision was taken unanimously by the thirty-five members present, ten members being absent, see e.g. Mackinnon Wood, 'Dissolution of the League of Nations', 13 BYIL, 1946, p. 317.

organisations.[221] It is unclear whether unanimity is needed or whether the degree of majority required under the constitution of the particular organisation for the determination of important questions[222] would suffice.[223] The actual process of liquidating the assets and dealing with the liabilities of dissolved organisations is invariably laid down by the organisation itself, either in the constitutional documents or by special measures adopted on dissolution.

Succession[224]

Succession between international organisations takes place when the functions and (usually) the rights and obligations are transferred from one organisation to another. This may occur by way of straightforward replacement,[225] or by absorption[226] or by merger or by effective secession of part of an organisation or by simple transfer of certain functions from one organisation to another.[227] This is achieved by agreement and is dependent upon the constitutional competence of the successor organisation to perform the functions thus transferred of the former organisation. In certain circumstances, succession may proceed by way of implication in the absence of express provision.[228] The precise consequences of such

---

[221] See e.g. the dissolutions of the International Meteorological Organisation; the UN Relief and Rehabilitation Administration; the International Refugee Organisations; the International Commission for Air Navigation; the South East Asian Treaty Organisation and the Latin American Free Trade Association, see Schermers and Blokker, *International*, pp. 1024–5.

[222] E.g. the two-thirds majority required under article 18 of the UN Charter for the General Assembly's determination of important questions.

[223] Organisations may be dissolved where the same parties to the treaty establishing the organisations enter a new agreement or possibly by disuse or more controversially as a result of changed circumstances (*rebus sic stantibus*), see Schermers and Blokker, *International*, pp. 1021–8.

[224] See Amerasinghe, *Principles*, p. 476; Schermers and Blokker, *International*, pp. 1015 *et seq.*; H. Chiu, 'Succession in International Organisations', 14 ICLQ, 1965, p. 83 and P. R. Myers, *Succession between International Organisations*, 1993.

[225] Such as the replacement of the League of Nations by the United Nations.

[226] E.g. the absorption of the International Bureau of Education by UNESCO.

[227] See Amerasinghe, *Principles*, p. 476.

[228] The International Court in the *Status of South West Africa* case, ICJ Reports, 1950, pp. 128, 134–7; 17 ILR, pp. 47, 51–5, held that the supervisory responsibilities of South Africa under the mandate to administer the territory of South West Africa/ Namibia continued beyond the dissolution of the League of Nations and were in essence succeeded to by the UN. This was in the context of the fact that the mandate itself constituted an international status for the territory which therefore continued irrespective of the existence of the League and partly because the resolution of the Assembly of the League dissolving the League of Nations had declared that the supervisory functions of the League were ending, not the mandates themselves. It was emphasised that the obligation to submit to supervision did not disappear merely because the supervisory organ had ceased to exist as the UN performed similar, though not identical, supervisory functions. The Court concluded that the UN General Assembly was legally qualified to exercise these supervisory functions, in the light *inter alia* of articles 10 and 80 of the UN Charter. This was reaffirmed by the Court in the *Namibia* case, ICJ Reports, 1971, pp. 16, 37; 49 ILR, pp. 2, 26–34.

succession will depend upon the agreement concerned between the parties in question.[229]

---

[229] See Schermers and Blokker, *International*, p. 1017 with regard to the relationship between the new World Trade Organisation and the General Agreement on Tariffs and Trade (GATT) arrangements.

INDEX